Nineteenth-Century
Literature Criticism

Guide to Gale Literary Criticism Series

For criticism on	Consult these Gale series
Authors now living or who died after December 31, 1999	*CONTEMPORARY LITERARY CRITICISM (CLC)*
Authors who died between 1900 and 1999	*TWENTIETH-CENTURY LITERARY CRITICISM (TCLC)*
Authors who died between 1800 and 1899	*NINETEENTH-CENTURY LITERATURE CRITICISM (NCLC)*
Authors who died between 1400 and 1799	*LITERATURE CRITICISM FROM 1400 TO 1800 (LC)* *SHAKESPEAREAN CRITICISM (SC)*
Authors who died before 1400	*CLASSICAL AND MEDIEVAL LITERATURE CRITICISM (CMLC)*
Authors of books for children and young adults	*CHILDREN'S LITERATURE REVIEW (CLR)*
Dramatists	*DRAMA CRITICISM (DC)*
Poets	*POETRY CRITICISM (PC)*
Short story writers	*SHORT STORY CRITICISM (SSC)*
Literary topics and movements	*HARLEM RENAISSANCE: A GALE CRITICAL COMPANION (HR)* *THE BEAT GENERATION: A GALE CRITICAL COMPANION (BG)*
Asian American writers of the last two hundred years	*ASIAN AMERICAN LITERATURE (AAL)*
Black writers of the past two hundred years	*BLACK LITERATURE CRITICISM (BLC)* *BLACK LITERATURE CRITICISM SUPPLEMENT (BLCS)*
Hispanic writers of the late nineteenth and twentieth centuries	*HISPANIC LITERATURE CRITICISM (HLC)* *HISPANIC LITERATURE CRITICISM SUPPLEMENT (HLCS)*
Native North American writers and orators of the eighteenth, nineteenth, and twentieth centuries	*NATIVE NORTH AMERICAN LITERATURE (NNAL)*
Major authors from the Renaissance to the present	*WORLD LITERATURE CRITICISM, 1500 TO THE PRESENT (WLC)* *WORLD LITERATURE CRITICISM SUPPLEMENT (WLCS)*

ISSN 0732-1864

Volume 131

Nineteenth-Century Literature Criticism

Criticism of the
Works of Novelists, Philosophers, and Other
Creative Writers Who Died between 1800
and 1899, from the First Published Critical
Appraisals to Current Evaluations

Lynn M. Zott
Project Editor

GALE®

THOMSON
GALE

Detroit • New York • San Diego • San Francisco • Cleveland • New Haven, Conn. • Waterville, Maine • London • Munich

Nineteenth-Century Literature Criticism, Vol. 131

Project Editor
Lynn M. Zott

Editorial
Jessica Bomarito, Jenny Cromie, Kathy D. Darrow, Elisabeth Gellert, Jelena O. Krstović, Michelle Lee, Thomas J. Schoenberg, Lawrence J. Trudeau, Maikue Vang, Russel Whitaker

Research
Nicodemus Ford, Sarah Genik, Tamara C. Nott, Tracie A. Richardson

Permissions
Shalice Shah-Caldwell

Imaging and Multimedia
Robert Duncan, Lezlie Light, Kelly A. Quin

Composition and Electronic Capture
Kathy Sauer

Manufacturing
Stacy L. Melson

LIBRARY OF CONGRESS CATALOG CARD NUMBER 84-643008

ISBN 0-7876-6919-9
ISSN 0732-1864

Printed in the United States of America
10 9 8 7 6 5 4 3 2 1

Contents

Preface vii

Acknowledgments xi

Literary Criticism Series Advisory Board xiii

Preface

Since its inception in 1981, *Nineteeth-Century Literature Criticism* (*NCLC*) has been a valuable resource for students and librarians seeking critical commentary on writers of this transitional period in world history. Designated an "Outstanding Reference Source" by the American Library Association with the publication of is first volume, *NCLC* has since been purchased by over 6,000 school, public, and university libraries. The series has covered more than 450 authors representing 33 nationalities and over 17,000 titles. No other reference source has surveyed the critical reaction to nineteenth-century authors and literature as thoroughly as *NCLC*.

Scope of the Series

NCLC is designed to introduce students and advanced readers to the authors of the nineteenth century and to the most significant interpretations of these authors' works. The great poets, novelists, short story writers, playwrights, and philosophers of this period are frequently studied in high school and college literature courses. By organizing and reprinting commentary written on these authors, *NCLC* helps students develop valuable insight into literary history, promotes a better understanding of the texts, and sparks ideas for papers and assignments. Each entry in *NCLC* presents a comprehensive survey of an author's career or an individual work of literature and provides the user with a multiplicity of interpretations and assessments. Such variety allows students to pursue their own interests; furthermore, it fosters an awareness that literature is dynamic and responsive to many different opinions.

Every fourth volume of *NCLC* is devoted to literary topics that cannot be covered under the author approach used in the rest of the series. Such topics include literary movements, prominent themes in nineteenth-century literature, literary reaction to political and historical events, significant eras in literary history, prominent literary anniversaries, and the literatures of cultures that are often overlooked by English-speaking readers.

NCLC continues the survey of criticism of world literature begun by Gale's *Contemporary Literary Criticism* (*CLC*) and *Twentieth-Century Literary Criticism* (*TCLC*).

Organization of the Book

An *NCLC* entry consists of the following elements:

- The **Author Heading** cites the name under which the author most commonly wrote, followed by birth and death dates. Also located here are any name variations under which an author wrote, including transliterated forms for authors whose native languages use nonroman alphabets. If the author wrote consistently under a pseudonym, the pseudonym will be listed in the author heading and the author's actual name given in parenthesis on the first line of the biographical and critical information. Uncertain birth or death dates are indicated by question marks. Single-work entries are preceded by a heading that consists of the most common form of the title in English translation (if applicable) and the original date of composition.

- The **Introduction** contains background information that introduces the reader to the author, work, or topic that is the subject of the entry.

- A **Portrait of the Author** is included when available.

- The list of **Principal Works** is ordered chronologically by date of first publication and lists the most important works by the author. The genre and publication date of each work is given. In the case of foreign authors whose works have been translated into English, the list will focus primarily on twentieth-century translations, selecting those works most commonly considered the best by critics. Unless otherwise indicated, dramas are dated by first performance, not first publication. Lists of **Representative Works** by different authors appear with topic entries.

- Reprinted **Criticism** is arranged chronologically in each entry to provide a useful perspective on changes in critical evaluation over time. The critic's name and the date of composition or publication of the critical work are given at the beginning of each piece of criticism. Unsigned criticism is preceded by the title of the source in which it appeared. All titles by the author featured in the text are printed in boldface type. Footnotes are reprinted at the end of each essay or excerpt. In the case of excerpted criticism, only those footnotes that pertain to the excerpted texts are included. Criticism in topic entries is arranged chronologically under a variety of subheadings to facilitate the study of different aspects of the topic.

- A complete **Bibliographical Citation** of the original essay or book precedes each piece of criticism.

- Critical essays are prefaced by brief **Annotations** explicating each piece.

- An annotated bibliography of **Further Reading** appears at the end of each entry and suggests resources for additional study. In some cases, significant essays for which the editors could not obtain reprint rights are included here. Boxed material following the further reading list provides references to other biographical and critical sources on the author in series published by Gale.

Indexes

Each volume of *NCLC* contains a **Cumulative Author Index** listing all authors who have appeared in a wide variety of reference sources published by the Gale Group, including *NCLC*. A complete list of these sources is found facing the first page of the Author Index. The index also includes birth and death dates and cross references between pseudonyms and actual names.

A **Cumulative Nationality Index** lists all authors featured in *NCLC* by nationality, followed by the number of the *NCLC* volume in which their entry appears.

A **Cumulative Topic Index** lists the literary themes and topics treated in the series as well as in *Classical and Medieval Literature Criticism, Literature Criticism from 1400 to 1800, Twentieth-Century Literary Criticism,* and the *Contemporary Literary Criticism* Yearbook, which was discontinued in 1998.

An alphabetical **Title Index** accompanies each volume of *NCLC*, with the exception of the Topics volumes. Listings of titles by authors covered in the given volume are followed by the author's name and the corresponding page numbers where the titles are discussed. English translations of foreign titles and variations of titles are cross-referenced to the title under which a work was originally published. Titles of novels, dramas, nonfiction books, and poetry, short story, or essay collections are printed in italics, while individual poems, short stories, and essays are printed in roman type within quotation marks.

In response to numerous suggestions from librarians, Gale also produces an annual paperbound edition of the *NCLC* cumulative title index. This annual cumulation, which alphabetically lists all titles reviewed in the series, is available to all customers. Additional copies of this index are available upon request. Librarians and patrons will welcome this separate index; it saves shelf space, is easy to use, and is recyclable upon receipt of the next edition.

Citing *Nineteenth-Century Literature Criticism*

When citing criticism reprinted in the Literary Criticism Series, students should provide complete bibliographic information so that the cited essay can be located in the original print or electronic source. Students who quote directly from reprinted criticism may use any accepted bibliographic format, such as University of Chicago Press style or Modern Language Association style.

The examples below follow recommendations for preparing a bibliography set forth in *The Chicago Manual of Style,* 14th ed. (Chicago: The University of Chicago Press, 1993); the first example pertains to material drawn from periodicals, the second to material reprinted from books:

Guerard, Albert J. "On the Composition of Dostoevsky's *The Idiot.*" *Mosaic: A Journal for the Interdisciplinary Study of Literature* 8, no. 1 (fall 1974): 201-15. Reprinted in *Nineteenth-Century Literature Criticism.* Vol. 119, edited by Lynn M. Zott, 81-104. Detroit: Gale, 2003.

Berstein, Carol L. "Subjectivity as Critique and the Critique of Subjectivity in Keats's *Hyperion.*" In *After the Future: Postmodern Times and Places,* edited by Gary Shapiro, 41-52. Albany, N. Y.: State University of New York Press, 1990. Reprinted in *Nineteeth-Century Literature Criticism.* Vol. 121, edited by Lynn M. Zott, 155-60. Detroit: Gale, 2003.

The examples below follow recommendations for preparing a works cited list set forth in the *MLA Handbook for Writers of Research Papers,* 5th ed. (New York: The Modern Language Association of America, 1999); the first example pertains to material drawn from periodicals, the second to material reprinted from books:

Guerard, Albert J. "On the Composition of Dostoevsky's *The Idiot.*" *Mosaic: A Journal for the Interdisciplinary Study of Literature* 8. 1 (fall 1974): 201-15. Reprinted in *Nineteenth-Century Literature Criticism.* Ed. Lynn M. Zott. Vol. 119. Detroit: Gale, 2003. 81-104.

Berstein, Carol L. "Subjectivity as Critique and the Critique of Subjectivity in Keats's *Hyperion.*" *After the Future: Postmodern Times and Places.* Ed. Gary Shapiro. Albany, N. Y.: State University of New York Press, 1990. 41-52. Reprinted in *Nineteeth-Century Literature Criticism.* Ed. Lynn M. Zott. Vol. 121. Detroit: Gale, 2003. 155-60.

Suggestions are Welcome

Readers who wish to suggest new features, topics, or authors to appear in future volumes, or who have other suggestions or comments are cordially invited to call, write, or fax the Project Editor:

Project Editor, Literary Criticism Series
The Gale Group
27500 Drake Road
Farmington Hills, MI 48331-3535
1-800-347-4253 (GALE)
Fax: 248-699-8054

Acknowledgments

The editors wish to thank the copyright holders of the criticism included in this volume and the permissions managers of many book and magazine publishing companies for assisting us in securing reproduction rights. We are also grateful to the staffs of the Detroit Public Library, the Library of Congress, the University of Detroit Mercy Library, Wayne State University Purdy/Kresge Library Complex, and the University of Michigan Libraries for making their resources available to us. Following is a list of the copyright holders who have granted us permission to reproduce material in this volume of *NCLC*. Every effort has been made to trace copyright, but if omissions have been made, please let us know.

COPYRIGHTED MATERIAL IN *NCLC*, VOLUME 131, WAS REPRODUCED FROM THE FOLLOWING PERIODICALS:

AUMLA: Journal of the Australasian Universities Language and Literature Association, May, 1985. Reproduced by permission.—*Cahiers Roumains d'Etudes Litteraires: Revue Trimestrielle de Critique, d'Esthetique et d'Historie,* n. 2, 1989 for "The Sacred Mountain and the Abysmal Phenomenon" by Eugen Todoran. Reproduced by permission of the author.—*Canadian-American Slavic Studies,* v. 29, fall-winter, 1995. Reproduced by permission.—*Cervantes: Bulletin of the Cervantes Society of America,* v. 11, spring, 1991. Reproduced by permission.—*Comparative Literature Studies,* v. 7, December, 1970. Reproduced by permission.—*Harvard Journal of Asiatic Studies,* v. 32, 1972. © 1972 Harvard-Yenching Institute. Reproduced by permission.—*Humanities Association Bulletin,* v. 21, spring, 1970 for "A Comparative Approach to 'Tales of Moonlight and Rain'" by Leon M. Zolbrod. Reproduced by permission of the Literary Estate of Leon M. Zolbrod.—*International Philosophical Quarterly,* v. 23, December, 1983 for "The Political Ideas of Andrés Bello" by O. Carlos Stoetzer. Reproduced by permission of the author.—*Latin American Research Review,* v. 6, 1976. Reproduced by permission.—*Monumenta Nipponica,* v. XXII, 1967; v. XLV, spring, 1990; v. LI, spring, 1996. © 1967, 1990, 1996 Sophia University. All reproduced by permission.—*Revista Hispanica Moderna: Columbia University Hispanic Studies,* v. XXXVII, 1972-73. Reproduced by permission.—*Romanian Civilization,* v. II, spring, 1993; v. VII, spring, 1998. Both reproduced by permission.—*Romanian Review,* v. 26, 1972; v. 33, 1979; v. 40, 1986; v. 41, 1987; v. 42, 1988. All reproduced by permission.—*Slavonic and East European Review,* v. 47, July, 1969 for "Bestuzhev-Marlinsky as a Lyric Poet" by Lauren G. Leighton. Reproduced by permission of the author.—*Southeastern Europe/L'Europ du Sud-Est,* v. 7, 1980. Reproduced by permission.

COPYRIGHTED MATERIAL IN *NCLC*, VOLUME 131, WAS REPRODUCED FROM THE FOLLOWING BOOKS:

Bagby, Lewis. From *Alexander Bestuzhev-Marlinsky and Russian Byronism.* The Pennsylvania State University Press, 1995. Copyright © 1995 The Pennsylvania State University. All rights reserved. Reproduced by permission.—Cussen, Antonio. From *Bello and Bolívar: Poetry and Politics in the Spanish American Revolution.* Cambridge University Press, 1992. © Cambridge University Press, 1992. Reproduced by permission of the publisher and the author.—Frank, Frederick S. From "Ueda Akinari (1734-1809)," in *Gothic Writers: A Critical and Bibliographical Guide.* Douglass H. Thomson, Jack G. Voller, and Frederick S. Frank, eds. Greenwood Press, 2002. Copyright © 2002 by Douglass H. Thomson, Jack G. Voller, and Frederick S. Frank. All rights reserved. Reproduced by permission of Greenwood Publishing Group, Inc., Westport, CT.—Jaksi, Iván. From an Introduction to *Selected Writings of Andrés Bello.* Edited by Iván Jaksi. Translated by Frances M. Lopez-Morillas. Oxford University Press, 1997. Copyright © 1997 by Oxford University Press, Inc. All rights reserved. Reproduced by permission of Oxford University Press, Inc.—Jaksi, Iván. From *Andrés Bello: Scholarship and Nation-Building in Nineteenth-Century Latin America.* Cambridge University Press, 2001. © Iván Jaksi. Reproduced by permission of the publisher and the author.—Keene, Donald. From *World Within Walls: Japanese Literature of the Pre-Modern Era, 1600-1867.* Holt, Rinehart and Winston, 1976. Copyright © 1976 by Donald Keene. All rights reserved. Reproduced by permission of Henry Holt and Company, LLC. In the UK, South Africa, and the Middle East by permission of Georges Borchardt, Inc., for the author.—Kovarsky, N. From "The Early Bestuzhev-Marlinsky," in *Russian Prose.* Translated by Ray Parrott. Edited by B. M. Eikhenbaum and Yuri Tynyanov. Ardis, 1985. Copyright © 1985 by Ardis Publishers. All rights reserved. Reproduced by permission.—Landsman, Neil B. From *Problems of Russian Romanticism.* Edited by Robert Reid. Gower, 1986. © Robert Reid, 1986. All rights reserved. Reproduced by permission of the author.—Leighton, Lauren G. From *Alexander Bestuzhev-Marlinsky.* Twayne Publishers, 1975. Copyright © 1975 by G. K. Hall & Co. All rights reserved. Reproduced by permission.—Méndez, Luis Felipe Clay. From "Julián del Casal and the Cult of Artificiality: Roots and Functions," in *Waiting for Pegasus: Studies of the Presence of Symbolism and Decadence in Hispanic Letters.* Edited by Roland Grass and William R. Risley. Western Illinois University, 1979. Copyright © 1979 by Western Illinois University. Reproduced by permission.—Montero, Oscar. From "Julián del Casal and the Queers of Havana," in *Entiendes?: Queer Readings, Hispanic Writings.* Edited by Emilie L. Bergmann and Paul Julian Smith. Duke University Press, 1995. © 1995 Duke University Press. All rights reserved. Reproduced by permission of the publisher.—Pearsall, Priscilla. From "Julián del Casal's Portraits of Women," in *The Analysis of Literary Texts: Current Trends in Methodology.* Edited by Randolph D. Pope. Bilingual Press/Editorial Bilingue, 1980. © 1980 by Bilingual Press/Editorial Bilingue. All rights reserved. Reproduced by permission.—Pearsall, Priscilla. From *An Art Alienated From Itself: Studies in Spanish American Modernism.* University Mississippi Romance Monographs, Inc., 1984. Copyright © 1984 by Romance monographs, Inc. Reproduced by permission.—Reyfman, Irina. From "Alexander Bestuzhev-Marlinsky: 'Bretteur' and Apologist of the Dead," in *Russian Subjects: Empire, Nation, and the Culture of the Golden Age.* Edited by Monika Greenleaf and Stephen Moeller-Sally. Northwestern University Press, 1998. Copyright © 1998 by Northwestern University Press. All rights reserved. Reproduced by permission.—Young, Blake Morgan. From *Ueda Akinari.* University of British Columbia Press, 1982. © The University of British Columbia 1982. All rights reserved. Reproduced by permission.—Zolbrod, Leon M. From an Introduction to *Ugetsu Monogatari: Tales of Moonlight and Rain.* Edited and translated by Leon M. Zolbrod. George Allen & Unwin Ltd., 1974. © George Allen & Unwin Ltd., 1974. All rights reserved. Reproduced by permission of the Literary Estate of Leon M. Zolbrod.

PHOTOGRAPHS AND ILLUSTRATIONS APPEARING IN *NCLC*, VOLUME 131, WERE RECEIVED FROM THE FOLLOWING SOURCES:

Bello, Andrés, portrait. The Library of Congress.—Title page from *Gramatica de la Lengua Castellana destinada Al Uso De Los Americanos,* written by D. Andrés Bello. Graduate Library, University of Michigan. Reproduced by permission.

Gale Literature Product Advisory Board

The members of the Gale Group Literature Product Advisory Board—reference librarians from public and academic library systems—represent a cross-section of our customer base and offer a variety of informed perspectives on both the presentation and content of our literature products. Advisory board members assess and define such quality issues as the relevance, currency, and usefulness of the author coverage, critical content, and literary topics included in our series; evaluate the layout, presentation, and general quality of our printed volumes; provide feedback on the criteria used for selecting authors and topics covered in our series; provide suggestions for potential enhancements to our series; identify any gaps in our coverage of authors or literary topics, recommending authors or topics for inclusion; analyze the appropriateness of our content and presentation for various user audiences, such as high school students, undergraduates, graduate students, librarians, and educators; and offer feedback on any proposed changes/enhancements to our series. We wish to thank the following advisors for their advice throughout the year.

Ueda Akinari
1734-1809

(Also wrote under the pseudonyms Wayaku Tarō, Senshi Kijin, and Ueda Muchō) Japanese short story writer, prose writer, and poet.

INTRODUCTION

Akinari is best known for his stories of the supernatural collected in *Ugetsu Monogatari* (1776; *Tales of Moonlight and Rain*) and *Harusame Monogatari* (1907; *Tales of the Spring Rain*). Writing at a time when Edo (Tokyo) was replacing Osaka-Kyoto as the center of culture and literary activity, Akinari is considered the last great writer of the Osaka-Kyoto literary circle.

BIOGRAPHICAL INFORMATION

Akinari was born July 25, 1734, in Sonezaki, an area of Osaka devoted to prostitution. His mother, who likely worked as a prostitute, abandoned him shortly after his birth; his father is unknown. However, while Akinari acknowledged this account of his background, it has been challenged by recent scholars who claim he was actually the illegitimate son of a samurai. He was adopted by a prosperous merchant, Ueda Mosuke, in 1737, and the following year contracted smallpox. The disease was nearly fatal and its after-effects included life-long poor health and deformed fingers on each hand. In later life, Akinari, sensitive about his physical appearance, wrote under pseudonyms that referred to his deformities, such as Senshi Kijin ("Pruned Cripple") and Ueda Muchō ("Ueda the Crab"). Although his education began fairly late, Akinari eventually attended the Kaitokudō School in Osaka, where literary historians believe he studied the Japanese classics and began writing *haiku*. In 1760, he married Ueyama Tama, a Kyoto native who worked in the home of his adoptive parents. Akinari and his wife adopted a daughter, Mineko. When his adoptive father died in 1761, Akinari assumed control of the family business, a paper and oil shop. In 1771, the business and residence were destroyed by fire, leaving Akinari's family homeless and without means of support. In 1773, Akinari moved to Kashimamura, where he studied medicine for the next two years. Although he was a successful physician, his practice suffered from his own poor health, and he was continually distressed by his limited ability to alleviate the pain and suffering of those in his care. He left the profession in 1788, apparently because his misdiagnosis caused the death of a young patient, and returned to a life of scholarship and writing. In 1789, both Akinari's stepmother and mother-in-law died, and in 1793 he and his wife moved to Kyoto. In 1797, his wife died and Akinari, whose eyesight was failing, was cared for by Mineko for the next three years. Although he had always been somewhat reclusive and misanthropic, his declining health and the loss of his wife contributed to his generally pessimistic outlook. In 1802, apparently preoccupied with death, he designed his own tombstone and destroyed a number of his manuscripts. Nonetheless, he continued to write, producing several works detailing his scholarly pursuits and offering his opinions on a variety of subjects. At the time of his death, Akinari was working on a collection of historical tales. He died in 1809 at the home of a friend.

MAJOR WORKS

Akinari's first publications belonged to the genre of *katagi-bon* ("character book") and included *Shodō kikimimi sekenzaru* (1766) and *Seken tekake katagi* (1767). In 1776, Akinari published his first effort in the *yomihon* ("books for reading") genre, *Tales of Moonlight and Rain,* which comprised nine individual stories. Scholars disagree on when the work was actually composed. Akinari's preface is dated 1768, but many literary historians believe, based on the profoundly pessimistic tone of the stories, that they were written sometime after the 1771 fire that left the author in a state of bitterness and despair. The stories, most of which are adaptations of well-known Chinese and Japanese fables and tales, which in turn were based on actual events, are full of mystery, suspense, and elements of the supernatural, not unlike the Gothic romances that were flourishing around the same time in European literature. *Tales of Moonlight and Rain* is generally considered Akinari's masterpiece. He then turned to writing and publishing collections of poetry in both the *waka* and *haiku* forms, but these never approached the success he had achieved with *Tales of Moonlight and Rain.* Toward the end of his life he produced *Kinsa* (1804) and *Tandai shōshin roku* (1808), collections of scholarly essays, opinions, and accounts of his experiences. At the time of his death, he was working on what would be his most enduring work after *Tales of Moonlight and Rain. Tales of the Spring Rain* contained both historical and human interest tales, ten in all, and was circulated only in manuscript form until the publication of part of the original manuscript in 1907, by which time some of the ten stories had been lost. The complete version did not appear until 1951.

CRITICAL RECEPTION

Akinari's short stories, particularly those collected in *Tales of Moonlight and Rain,* were highly acclaimed in his own time. Today these works are considered the finest example of the *yomihon* genre produced during the eighteenth and nineteenth centuries. Critics praise Akinari's knowledge of Chinese literary traditions as well as those of his own country, his technical mastery, and his originality as a storyteller. According to Leon M. Zolbrod, Akinari's synthesis of the styles, images, and themes of Chinese and Japanese literature, both classical and popular, resulted in "a highly original style of narrative prose." Zolbrod further credits Akinari with achieving respectability for prose fiction in Japan and helping to establish the genre "as a means of expressing historical criticism and cultural values." Many scholars, including Dennis Washburn, consider *Tales of Moonlight and Rain* a classic of Japanese literature. Washburn observes, however, that despite the work's many praiseworthy features, it poses problems for modern readers who are unfamiliar with its Chinese and Japanese source material, uninterested in supernatural tales, or unable to appreciate Akinari's combination of elegant and everyday language. Some scholars have focused on Akinari's personal history as a means of illuminating his prose writing. Blake Morgan Young, for example, contends that the darkly pessimistic tone of *Tales of the Spring Rain* can be traced to the author's general outlook on life, which became darker as he grew older. During Akinari's last years, according to Young, "he was noted for being a sulking, self-scorning old man, bitterly sarcastic toward the world and its people, and feeling that the masses were full of lies and immorality."

PRINCIPAL WORKS

Shodō kikimimi sekenzaru [as Wayaku Tarō] (sketches) 1766
Seken tekake katagi [as Wayaku Tarō] (sketches) 1767
Ugetsu Monogatari [*Tales of Moonlight and Rain*] (short stories) 1776
Kakizome kigenkai (sketches) 1787
Yasaishō (poetry) 1787
Yasumikoto (nonfiction) 1792
Kinsa (nonfiction) 1804
Tsuzurabumi (poetry, prose) 1806

Fumihōgu (letters) 1808
Tandai shōshin roku (essays) 1808
Kuse monogatari (sketches) 1822
Harusame Monogatari [*Tales of the Spring Rain*] (short stories) 1907; revised and enlarged, 1951
Ueda Akinari zenshū. 2 vols. (essays, short stories, sketches) 1917
Akinari Ibun (essays, short stories, sketches) 1919
Ueda Akinari zenshū. 12 vols. (essays, letters, short stories, sketches) 1990-

CRITICISM

James T. Araki (essay date 1967)

SOURCE: Araki, James T. "A Critical Approach to the *Ugetsu monogatari.*" *Monumenta Nipponica* 22, nos. 1-2 (1967): 49-64.

[*In the following essay, Araki offers an overview of criticism of Akinari's tales and an analysis of the structural techniques the author employed in* Tales of Moonlight and Rain.]

1 A SURVEY OF CRITICAL APPROACHES

Ueda Akinari aspired to distinction as a poet and classical scholar. His reputation in Japanese literary history today, however, rests almost exclusively on his genius as a writer of short stories—particularly of the *Ugetsu monogatari* (*Tales of the Misty Moon*), a collection of nine short mysterious tales which he completed probably in 1768. Those in the West who have read the *Ugetsu monogatari* in translation[1] may have felt that some of the tales are curiously composed, and may have questioned their excellence. Apparent even in translation is a diversity among the nine tales in their structural characteristics and style. The reader of translations may understandably find greater enjoyment in those tales which exhibit traits considered admirable in tales and short stories in the West. Nevertheless, another tale which violates Western dicta on "economy of means," "unity," and so forth may receive greater acclaim among the Japanese for the likely reason of its appeal to tastes that have been fashioned by literary and historical traditions quite different from our own. If the reasons for their choice of tales were known to us, we should be enlightened considerably about Japanese tastes.

An appeal to the judgment of the literary historians of Japan will be of little avail in this instance, however, for a tale that may be estimable in the opinions of some may be the object of dispraise by others. Such disagreements have been due to differences in personal taste, as well as differences on the criteria applied in their evaluations—criteria ranging from those based largely on traditional standards of appreciation to those utilizing canons borrowed from recent Western criticism. Evaluations by Western specialists on Japanese literature have also varied depending on the specialist's area of personal preference on this critical spectrum.[2] Indeed, my own critical reactions to the tales have varied through the years, for my criteria are being constantly modified as I gain in familiarity with traditional modes of storytelling.

The correlating of Akinari's personality with the success of his tales has long been standard fare in studies of the *Ugetsu monogatari.* We have been told that the tales are verbal extensions of the author's psychological activities, or that Akinari's belief in the supernatural or else his melancholy, misanthropic nature enabled him to produce masterful tales of mystery and suspense.[3] We may be reminded of similar associations made between an author's idiosyncrasies and his apparent predilection for morbid themes—in particular, Poe and Akutagawa, both of whom were master literary craftsmen. This critical approach is epitomized in remark by Shigetomo Ki, with reference to the final scene depicted in **"Kibitsu no kama"** (**"The Divining Cauldron of Kibitsu"**):

> How could anyone contrive to depict the mysterious so superbly? Yet Akinari did. Since this cannot be explained solely in terms of technique, where can we find an explanation? In view of the presence of mysterious, phantasmic, and psychic elements in his life—a life affirmed by his belief in the supernatural—would it not be reasonable to consider this a manifestation of his expansive fantasy? Can we not regard it as the revelation of the most fearful scene he was capable of imagining—a scene which, at the instant of imagination, thrilled him with terror? Should we concede this, we would have to admit that only such as he, who lived in fantasy, could have done so.[4]

Had Ueda Akinari not produced the *Ugetsu monogatari,* the seeming darkness of his personality would hardly have attracted the attention of those who later were to study him; and, as a matter of fact, it did not up to the 1920's while researchers were concerned primarily with his poetry and scholarly writings. Fortunately Akinari has left us sufficient autobiographical material[5] to permit some exploration into his personal nature. His essays and studies reveal a mind that is intuitive, imaginative, and poetic, and in some respects more rational (perhaps "modern") and freer from traditions than his contemporaries. His personality did not remain static. During his youth he had lived gregariously and savored copiously the life in the "floating world" of teahouses and brothels. At the time of his writing the *Ugetsu monogatari,* Akinari was a gentleman-scholar of thirty-four, with both the resources and leisure at his disposal

to freely pursue his scholarly and artistic endeavors. He was hardly the shrunken, vituperative misanthrope he appears to have been in his old age. To be sure, he bore minor physical deformities caused by smallpox contracted when he was a child of four; and he was throughout his life a devout patron of the Kashima Inari Shrine, where his adoptive parents had prayed for his deliverance from the often fatal malady.[6] But the expression of gratitude for a miraculous cure can hardly be interpreted as a mark of the inveterately superstitious in a traditional society. Though we might assume that the accident of his illness modified his regard for the supernatural, there is little else in his biography up to the writing of the *Ugetsu monogatari* to suggest any peculiar fascination in the morbid or fantastic.[7]

Asō Isoji has described the excellence of Akinari's tales solely in terms of the author's mastery of the craft of storywriting, but an evaluational summary such as his, based entirely on the knowable, has been the exception.[8] Many who have studied Akinari have suggested that the tales of *Ugetsu* were fashioned by a mind steeped in unhappiness and pessimism. There was no precluding such conjecture so long as the question, "When did Ueda Akinari actually write the *Ugetsu monogatari?*" remained unanswered. The preface to the collection of tales is dated 1768—Akinari was then thirty-four—whereas the anthology was published eight years later, in 1776. The less skeptical among literary historians have accepted the date in the preface, as have some others owing simply to a distaste for speculation. Most others, however, have concluded either that the tales were composed shortly before their publication in 1776 or that the tales, had they been drafted in 1768, were revised considerably during the intervening eight years. Reasons, I might add, other than those based on vague notions of Akinari's psychological state have been proffered. Teruoka Yasutaka, for example, rather summarily dismissed the possibility of Akinari having composed tales in such masterful style only two years after his first introduction to the study of classical literature;[9] Uzuki Hiroshi arrived at a similar assumptive point of view on the basis of a careful examination of scholarly manifestations in the tales.[10] A precise dating remains of crucial concern to those whose interpretations of the *Ugetsu* tales have been influenced by a biographical assumption: that the author did not have the manuscript in its final form until after the seventeenth of the first month in 1771, on which day his home and business were destroyed by fire. Very suddenly shorn of his customary means and leisure, Akinari hovered at the depth of despair and darkness; both his sociological outlook and psychological state registered dramatic changes, and the subsequent melancholy and bitterness worked their way into the contents of the *Ugetsu monogatari*—thus have reasoned those favoring the later dating.

Studies of the creative process in literature can be engaging, but surely they are meaningful only if the biographical data on which they are based are reasonably accurate. We may be reminded that even Leon Edel, among the more meticulous of literary biographers, has on one occasion, at least, correlated "Henry James's own haunted state" with the substance of his ghostly tale but instead, having relied on a slim sheaf of biographical misinformation, demonstrated that such associations, though seemingly natural, need not exist.[11] Students of Akinari were given cause recently at least to reflect on the possible dangers of basing literary interpretations on extraliterary propositions. Their attention was directed to a rather startling discovery—a printed announcement which, in the first month of 1771, heralded the "shortly forthcoming publication" of the *Ugetsu monogatari*; and now there were indications that the manuscript may have been ready for press and, perhaps, already set down in woodblocks in preparation for the printing before Akinari lost his home and source of income.[12] Unfortunately, we remain uninformed as to what occasioned the delay of five years before the tales were eventually published in 1776, and we may continue to be told how the brooding melancholy of the then distraught Akinari became the source of his literary inspiration.

It is gratifying to note, on the other hand, that one previously blackened area in the background of the author of the *Ugetsu monogatari* has been brightened up considerably by new information. Akinari's own remarks concerning his parentage suggested that his was an illegitimate birth. Biographical sketches of Akinari often begin with a statement that his mother was a prostitute; Akinari himself had known that it was so rumored, but in his memoirs he neither confirms nor denies the allegation. By whom he was sired remained anyone's guess until the introduction in 1959 of new documentary evidence that could eliminate much of the stigma attached to his pedigree. A passage pertaining to Akinari in the memoirs of the Confucian scholar Rai Shunsui (1746-1816) revealed that Akinari was fathered by a scion of a prominent samurai family and was born, although out of wedlock, to a woman from a family of some importance in present-day Nara Prefecture and, furthermore, that Akinari had been aware of his distinguished pedigree.[13] Takada Mamoru made use of this new fragment of information in reconstructing the circumstances surrounding Akinari's birth, and all other pieces of the biographical puzzle fell neatly into place. As a result, Takada could state with some assurance that Ueda Akinari was a grandson of the eminent shogun retainer Kobori Masamine (died 1760), who was descended from Kobori Enshū (1579-1647), celebrated in his time as a warrior, designer of gardens, and a master of the tea ceremony.[14] Because the statement pertaining to

Akinari was recorded several years after his death and, furthermore, was possibly sourced in hearsay, its reliability may be challenged.

The tenor of critical remarks has remained relatively unchanged through the years. We do note, however, some shift in emphasis toward the view espousing literature as a vehicle for social criticism. Commenting also on the tale **"Kibitsu no kama,"** Uzuki Hiroshi much more recently attributed the success of the tale to the author's antifeudal and anti-Confucianist convictions, and he concluded, "The *Ugetsu monogatari* stands in golden prominence in the history of mystery fiction because it embodies a literary representation of the entire range of Akinari's thought and spirit."[15] We find similar-sounding evaluative statements incorporated into some editions of the *Ugetsu monogatari* designed as high school texts. Inasmuch as critical comments are practically nonexistent in these texts, the few that do appear will surely impress those who may some day specialize in fiction by Akinari. In one such text that has enjoyed at least a dozen reprintings since its initial publication in 1960, the editor concludes his introduction thus: "An especially noteworthy point [in evaluating the *Ugetsu monogatari*] is that the quality of mystery is not infused merely for the interest of the reader; it is the product of a determination to achieve an ideal—to seek a release for emotions felt by the commoner and yet pent up within the oppressive framework of the feudal system of the Tokugawa government."[16] The relating of the success of Akinari's tales to his intention in producing them can be of biographical interest; furthermore, had there existed a direct relationship of this kind, the fact would tell us something about the author's creative process. But we are not at all certain whether Akinari was so motivated when he wrote the *Ugetsu monogatari.* True, he once commented explicitly on the purpose of fiction writing:

> Writers of fiction occupy their thoughts with grief over their personal misfortune, their resentment of the present age, and their nostalgic yearning for the distant past. They see the country flourishing as do the flowers in full bloom and are reminded that all must eventually fade away. . . . Though they would write in order to enlighten those who would reach for the unobtainable treasure of immortality, they instead, for the sake of appearance, relate their thoughts through innocent tales that cannot be traced in ancient history.[17]

This, however, is a very general statement which he recorded some years after the *Ugetsu monogatari* was published, and we must agree that the causal relationship between his world view and his tales remains assumptive.

In the foregoing, I have focused principally on what seem to be among the negative aspects of native literary scholarship treating the *Ugetsu monogatari*. This was inevitable insofar as specialists treading in speculative areas have been the more outspoken. The native scholars and critics, I might add, have been among the first to recognize the often misty character of observations penned by literary historians who have ventured into criticism of traditional literature.[18] Critical observations on the *Ugetsu monogatari* that are both precise and meaningful are more often found embedded within studies of fiction that are essentially descriptive rather than analytical—as in the instance of Asō's critique to which I referred earlier—and within some of the exegetical studies of Akinari's fiction. Nakamura Yukihiko's explicatory volume on the various writings of Akinari, for example, is very richly studded with evaluative statements derived from analytical processes.[19] The fact that the book is addressed primarily to the nonspecialist may account for Mr. Nakamura's inclusion of illuminating critical observations, ostensibly to assist the general reader. I say this in view of the general reluctance among literary historians of Japan to engage in criticism or to regard criticism as a worthy subject in literary scholarship.

Literary historians of Japan have customarily given importance to detailed textual criticism and the exhaustive investigation of historical and literary sources as a means to achieving a total explication of works of literature; and this is reflected in past studies of Akinari's works. One can only marvel at the thoroughness of investigations which have uncovered the source of almost every conceivable theme and motif discernible in Akinari's tales. The less speculative sections of Shigetomo's study of the *Ugetsu monogatari* are veritable mines of such information.[20] Those who study the *Ugetsu monogatari* today are to be envied indeed, for the available products of research, each having been built upon the cumulative results of earlier endeavors,[21] provide nearly all the basic information needed for a sure and complete understanding of the text. The task of literary analysis has been facilitated far beyond modest measure, and the useful scholar henceforth may conceivably be the one who will, as Helen Gardner advocates, uphold the critical torch in order to illuminate, elucidate, and assist the reader to discover the value which he himself discerns in the work.[22]

May we look forward to evaluations of the *Ugetsu monogatari* that will be founded on the results of a full cycle of analyses? The answer depends much on how soon and how often the critical torch is lit in the study of traditional Japanese literature. The professional literary critic in Japan today practices rather exclusively in the area of journalism and confines himself almost entirely to criticism of modern fiction. University students majoring in literary history but with an interest in literary criticism are most often faced with a stultifying indirection. Some among the younger literary historians, aware of the importance given to criticism in Western

literary scholarship and sensing themselves far removed from what they think ought to be the main current, are understandably restive. Some, in reacting against this predicament, have belittled the meticulous scholarship of their predecessors, and this seems unfortunate. We have heard similar outcries in the West.[23] Mr. Uzuki, incidentally, is now vocal in reproving what he calls the "retrogressive and mediocre nature of research in traditional Japanese literature" and the use of "methods in literary research that were current in the West an era ago."[24] But it is to his credit that he has proceeded to contribute studies of individual tales in the *Ugetsu monogatari* and so evidence his recent preference for an internal frame of reference and an analytical approach to literary criticism.[25] For many in Japan have cast strictures against established modes of literary scholarship with no greater purpose than to advance whatever critical approach they themselves espouse.

Youthful aspirants to the academy may eventually contribute significant studies of the classics—of such works as the *Ugetsu monogatari* which, they contend, require restudy and re-evaluation. We may detect among them now, however, an aversion for proceeding in accordance with any approach that is apt to be labeled "orthodox" (to many, it means "old-fashioned") and a penchant for discovering research objectives and procedures that will bestow on their efforts an aura of modernity. But the aspiration of each individual to achieve his own distinctive style of literary scholarship can lead to chaos. Yoshida Seiichi, the rare practising critic among established literary historians, may have had this in mind when he remarked on how often "research results that pass as articles in scholarly journals or as scholarly monographs are products of casual notions and do not represent results of careful and painstaking procedures."[26] With regard to "modern" studies of the *Ugetsu monogatari,* one doctoral candidate was compelled to remark, "I recognize the presence [of the 'modern' commentators] . . . but the question is whether or not I can apprehend the presence of Ueda Akinari."[27] Commenting on the literary quality of the *Ugetsu monogatari,* Noda Hisao, another scholar of note, sounds a warning about the potential inadequacies of critical judgments that rely excessively on insights gained through any one critical point of view:

> [References to] Chinese tales, historical research, and ancient poetry are simply manifestations of the intellectual quality of the work. This work is clearly not of the order of light-minded contemporary fiction; it is fiction in which the tone of erudition is explicit, and intentionally so. The composing of the tales was, for Akinari, a pastime related to his scholarly endeavors; and he probably would have felt disappointed were this not fully appreciated. It is quite by design that the loftiness [of style] contributes to a heightening of the artistry of the tales. We can say this not only with regard to the tale **"Kikka no chigiri"** but to the *Ugetsu monogatari* as a whole. . . . Furthermore, it is clearly a case of over-

emphasis in analysis to regard the work as a piece of satirical or didactic literature by Akinari. The author's world view and personal nature are, of course, reflected in his literary work. But it seems that if one has taken only these to be the source of value, he has only superficially viewed an artistic work of literature. A work of beauty should stand as a thing of beauty. A thing of beauty evokes a response in people for its beauty. . . . The comprehension of its beauty is the only way this work may be appreciated.[28]

Mr. Noda's emphatic regard for the quality of "beauty" should probably not be construed so much as an indication of a preference for yet another single critical procedure than an insistence that critics be concerned primarily with qualities that are evident within the work of art itself. He may have wished to remind us of the method of approach to the *Ugetsu monogatari* taught by Suzuki Toshiya, the earliest explicator of Akinari's tale who, more than thirty years ago, isolated these seven aspects of his critical subject for separate discussion: the "introduction" in which basic textual and publication data are presented, "sources of influences," "synopses of the nine tales," "plot elements," "narrative structure," "theme," and "tone."[29]

The cumulative results of a recent series of studies on Ueda Akinari by Nakamura Yukihiko may, perhaps, be regarded as an exemplary product of a similarly well ordered approach. His studies are founded on a detailed knowledge of the voluminous writings of Akinari and, also, of sources, both literary and historical, that cast illumination on the *Ugetsu monogatari* and its author. His working with a vast range of literary sources led to his discovery, among others, of a set of *haikai* poems which Akinari composed during his youth; an assessment of Akinari as a *haikai* stylist has facilitated our tracing the development of his prose style.[30] Mr. Nakamura has preferred to limit each investigation to some specific aspect of his critical subject. His biographical description of Akinari, for example, stands as a model of clarity and conciseness in a presentation based on verifiable biographical information.[31] His hypothesis on Akinari's theory on fiction writing is, again, based on a carefully selected set of statements recorded personally by Akinari.[32] The critical comments in his volume, cited earlier, are much the more significant because they rest on a foundation of factual knowledge acquired through the exacting procedures of *bunkengaku* (philological research), a method of which some of his younger colleagues have been frankly contemptuous. He has also contributed a brief, essentially analytical study in which he discusses in very general terms the entire range of Akinari's prose.[33] What we should like to anticipate from Mr. Nakamura is a stylistic analysis of the *Ugetsu monogatari* that will be as full and penetrating as the one he did of a Saikaku novel,[34] or, better yet, a critical volume in which we shall find synthesized all the results of his many previous investigations of Akinari's prose fiction.

2 ANALYSIS OF AKINARI'S COMPOSITIONAL TECHNIQUES

A tale of mystery may be among the least likely in fiction to be accorded the status of a literary classic. The interest in plot is so overwhelming that, once read, it is not apt to inspire a rereading as, say *Pride and Prejudice* might for its appreciable levels of irony, or Ullman's *The White Tower,* for its pervasive atmosphere. The Gothic sense of pleasurable horror in a story can impart artistry to a tale of mystery, but this can wear thin on a second reading, even of a tale so masterfully constructed as Poe's "The Fall of the House of Usher."

Although the *Ugetsu monogatari* was published less than two centuries ago, it seems to be as securely established among the classics in Japanese literature as is the *Tale of Genji,* composed a millennium ago. What to us may seem obvious, and serious, shortcomings in the *Ugetsu monogatari* as we read the tales in translation are mostly matters having to do with the composition of the tales. These apparent shortcomings, however, often are attractive elements insofar as native readers are concerned, and without which the tales would be insipid on rereading. What will remain obvious is that these elements are impediments to our achieving a "native" level of appreciation—which is, after all, an ideal to be sought in reading foreign literature. Many readers of Japanese consider Akinari's classical prose style the most attractive element of the *Ugetsu monogatari.* Although the vocabulary and peculiarities of sentence structure can be approximated in translation, the classical quality of the author's diction and grammatical style cannot be adequately reproduced for readers of the English, to whom this paper is addressed. I have chosen, therefore, not to touch upon those subtleties of style. The discussion following will focus primarily on the compositional techniques employed by Akinari, with particular reference given to the narrative structures of **"Kikka no chigiri"** (**"The Vow of the Chrysanthemum"**) and **"Asaji ga yado"** (**"A Lodging amidst Shallow Reeds"**), which represent partial adaptations from Chinese tales, and of **"Buppōsō"** (**"The Buppōsō Bird"**), generally considered the most original tale in the collection.[35]

One evaluative assumption has already been set forth: structural elements which seem perplexing to us and, hence, require explication are very often the ingredients which, according to some native specialists, contribute effectively to the literary excellence of Akinari's tales. Two of the tales, **"Kibitsu no kama"** (**"The Divining Cauldron of Kibitsu"**) and **"Jasei no in"** (**"The Lust of the Serpent's Spirit"**), differ so little in their manner of composition from the usual Western tale of mystery that they do not seem to require special analysis here. I should like to cite Father Pierre Humbertclaude's evaluative remarks on some of the other *Ugetsu* tales, for they generally agree with appraisals by Japanese critics who have preferred to gauge traditional literature by contemporary standards. They represent a valid point of view and shall serve the purpose here of touching off a discussion of some of the traditional concepts of appreciation. With regard to **"Kikka no chigiri"** and **"Asaji ga yado,"** he wrote:

> In **"Kikka no chigiri,"** the avenging of the death is an "hors d'oeuvre" from the point of view of unity of interest, even if the act is justified by the Japanese concept of friendship in which a death cannot remain unavenged. Where this 'parasitism' exceeds the limit is in **"Asaji ga yado,"** with its episode concerning Mama no Tekona that follows an already overextended dialogue with the old man.[36]

The remark on **"Kikka no chigiri"** suggests that the act of vengeance at the conclusion of the tale is not necessarily a structural hors d'oeuvre to a reader familiar with Japanese traditions. The tale is about a vow made by an itinerant samurai that he would revisit his friend, a scholar, on a specified day a year hence. On the day of the rendezvous, the samurai is being held a political prisoner in distant province, in the custody of his treacherous cousin. Rather than violate the vow to return, he kills himself in the belief that the spirit can travel a thousand miles in a day. The highpoint of the story definitely is the unearthly reunion, when Samon, now waiting "alone in the light cast by the icy lunar ring . . . sees the figure of a man in the dim darkness, drifting hither with the wind." But a denouement is necessary, and the motif of the vendetta provides a fitting conclusion to this tale on the theme of loyalty in friendship. **"Kikka no chigiri"** is an adaptation of the Chinese tale "Fan Chü-ch'ing Is Offered Chicken and Millet at a Meeting of the Dead and the Living."[37] In the Chinese tale, Fan Chü-ch'ing is so preoccupied with his activities as a merchant that he simply lets the promised date slip from his mind. Akinari has improved upon the Chinese story by involving the samurai in a political intrigue, so that there is a cogent reason for his inability to return. In the Chinese tale, the survivor kills himself at the tomb of the dead and is honored as a paragon of the faithful friend. Akinari allows the grieved Samon to act honorably with the situation he has placed him in. In either tale the resolution seems appropriate.

We may note, on the other hand, that Akinari's tale begins in curious fashion, with this—a free translation of the opening passage of the Chinese model. It reads:

> Do not plant in your garden the lustily green weeping willow of spring; and do not form personal ties with the perfidious. Although the river willow and weeping willow tend to luxuriate, will they endure even the early winds of autumn? The perfidious mixes easily with others but is quick [to leave and forget]. The willows become tinged with green on each recurring spring; the perfidious man will never again return.

The rather "Chinese" didactic preamble is a literary convention with which readers in Akinari's time were familiar, for they had already been exposed to a virtual deluge of translations of Chinese fiction. Though perhaps even absurd in the eyes of modern-day readers, the pseudo-didactic prologue is a structural peculiarity that was probably regarded as a tasty literary hors d'oeuvre; it is functional, moreover, as a statement of the anticipated theme or counter theme of the story. We might also note that the popular *ukiyo* tales produced earlier by Ihara Saikaku (1642-93) and Ejima Kiseki (1667-1736) were often introduced with such prologues, although the intent there was usually one of irony or a parody on didactic literature. Finally, Akinari concludes **"Kikka no chigiri"** with the statement, "And so they say that one must never form an association with a perfidious man"—it is a recapitulation of the introductory prologue and functions like a coda that sounds a note of finality in a tale so structured. In the eyes of readers accustomed to similarly structured Chinese stories, the design of this tale by Akinari was probably a harmonious one, and also appropriate to the substance of the story.

Not all literary historians have found the above structural feature attractive. Noda Hisao is disturbed by the prologue, which he considers "overornate and reeking of didacticism," and by the concluding sentence, concerning which he states, "The purpose no doubt is to echo the introductory passage, but the statement suggests that Samon was a faithless man."[38] Nakamura Yukihiko, on the other hand, states, "Being a statement of the theme of faithfulness made at the very outset of the tale, the passage, impressively solemn, is indeed appropriate to the tale."[39] And Shigetomo Ki is lavish in his praise of Akinari's adaptation of the Chinese structural device.[40] It is interesting to note that the modern novelist Satō Haruo (1892-1964) was so fond of **"Kikka no chigiri"** that he claimed to have reread it close to thirty times, and that he found particularly attractive the shape given the tale through the addition of the prologue and the recapitulatory concluding passage, whereas Ishikawa Jun (1899-), another prominent novelist, considers the introductory prologue extraneous, irrelevant, and even misleading.[41] Differences in the literary background and tastes of the two novelists probably account for this divergence in appraisal. We may recall that Mr. Satō had been known for his translations of Chinese fiction, and Mr. Ishikawa, as a product of a foreign language academy and one-time translator of French literature. Thus we find them at opposite ends of the critical spectrum of which I spoke earlier.

The tale **"Asaji ga yado"** may, indeed, seem burdened with an extended epilogue that dilutes the atmosphere of mystery. Having at last returned to his provincial home after seven years of misfortune and wandering in war-torn lands, Katsushirō is surprised to find his house still standing. His wife, Miyagi, is there to greet him with tears of joy. But when he awakens after the night of blissful reunion, Katsushirō finds himself bedded alone amidst the roofless ruins of his house. Closeby he sees Miyagi's tomb and discovers this poem, inscribed in Miyagi's hand on a weathered strip of paper:

> Saritomo to
> omō kokoro ni
> hakararete
> yo ni mo kyō made
> ikeru inochi ka

> Deceived
> By my heart that told me,
> "And yet,"
> Have I continued to live
> Till today in this world.

The narrative continues well beyond this structural high-point: the only person to recognize Katsushirō is a venerable neighbor who had been much too infirm to flee the village with the others; the old man leisurely recounts the tragic fate of Miyagi, and then relates an ancient legend about a virtuous maiden named Mama no Tekona and sighs that even the famed virtue of Tekona pales in comparison with the fidelity shown by Miyagi. Rather than end his tale in a crescendo of dramatic wails, Akinari allows the reader to enjoy an aftertaste of melancholy. The mood of passionate grief gives way slowly to one of subdued but deep-felt sorrow. The closing passages, depicting the grief of the two unaffected, unsophisticated rustic characters, provide some attractive strands of realism in the romantic fabric of the story.

Akinari's tales are often said to manifest influences from the traditional Japanese theater. The conclusion of **"Asaji ga yado"** may, indeed, be savored with some of the enjoyment of a nō drama (in performance) on a supernatural theme—for example, *Sumidagawa* (*Sumida River*), in which a frenzied passion aroused by the appearance of a spirit gives way gradually to an awareness of the illusion and, subsequently, of the reality and profoundness of sorrow. What I admire most about the tale is this shift in tone; the atmosphere of mystery is dispelled after the familiar pattern of the nō drama, and the reader is left in a state of musing, not panting excitation. But, as Father Humbertclaude and others have suggested, the episode concerning Mama no Tekona may not have been wisely chosen. Even though the author has prepared the reader for it by placing the setting in the hamlet of Mama, the tone of the story, while the legend of Mama no Tekona is being related, tends toward flatness rather than mellowness. The over-all tone of this tale, I might add, can in no way be compared to that of "The Legend of the Beloved Wife," the fantastic Chinese yarn to which the basic motifs in Akinari's tale can ultimately be traced.[42]

With regard to the tale **"Buppōsō,"** Father Humbert-claude remarks: "'Buppōsō' ends perfectly, but the lengthy introduction is outside the subject; or, rather, we find a juxtaposition of two stories that are even less closely associated with each other in terms of the locale than in the case of the episode of Tekona [in **'Asaji ga yado'**] cited above."[43] Here we may with profit recall what the Japanese have traditionally considered "elegant" prose fiction: a blend of facts, pseudo-facts, legends, and fiction, with decorative embellishments to impart an aura of elegance and erudition to the basic story.

"Buppōsō" seems to approach the ideal form of "elegant" prose fiction. The tale does not appear to be built around a "single preconceived effort" as Poe would have had it, but neither is it an incongruous combination of two unrelated episodes. It begins with a melodious laud of the land of Japan, and no sense of mystery is suggested until the central character, Muzen, and his young son arrive just before nightfall at Kōyasan, or Mount Kōya, the seat of the esoteric Shingon Sect of Buddhism. Having offered prayers at the various temple edifices, they come to the innermost sanctum of the monastic grounds, resolved to spend the night there in prayer. The preceding can be viewed as an extended prologue to the story proper. To note again a parallel with the nō drama, this prologue is similar structurally and in tone to the *michiyuki* (lyrical description of travel) that is recited by the *waki,* or "supporting player," upon his entering the nō stage—with the difference, of course, that in Akinari's tale the journey has taken place in story time. Just as the *waki* typically seats himself at the left-front of the nō stage, awaiting the appearance of the protagonist, Muzen and his son sit quietly in the dark of night, intoning the sutra and conversing. The experienced Japanese reader is well prepared for an extraordinary occurrence.

At this point Akinari may seem to dawdle, for in a nō drama the protagonist (very often a spirit in the guise of the living) would make his appearance immediately. In the nō drama, a phantasmal atmosphere at this point is implicit in the stereotyped structural sequencing, but there is no such convention in the written story. Akinari must, instead, allow the effect of time and the increasing gloominess of the setting to be felt by the reader.

Muzen idles away his wakeful hours by relating an anecdote about Kōbō-daishi (774-835), the founder of the monastery. The piercing cry of the *buppōsō* bird resounds in the night air, and Muzen again has reason to recount historical anecdotes, as well as ancient poems—this time concerning the mysterious bird whose name *buppōsō* (allegedly a stylized onomatopoetic rendering of its cry) consists of verbal elements representing "buddha," "dharma," and "sangha." Subtle sound images effectively heighten the mood of the forlorn. By inserting historical anecdotes and poetry, moreover, Akinari has introduced conventions employed in Chinese tales of the supernatural, thereby furthering the implication of a pending miracle.

In the deep of night, a courtly noble arrives with an entourage of warriors, and an eerie banquet ensues. The mysterious nobleman, it is revealed, is the specter of Toyotomi Hidetsugu (1568-95), known both in history and legend as the archetype of the wicked, sadistic lord. Although Hidetsugu had been adopted by his uncle, Hideyoshi, and made heir apparent to the military suzerainty of the Japanese Empire, his misconduct led to his confinement and eventual execution at Mount Kōya. This supernatural episode is by no means inconsequent. The setting of the story has been closely associated with the memory of Hidetsugu's gory execution, and most readers during the Edo Period—indeed, many today—should have vaguely anticipated the introduction of his ghostly form into the darkened atmosphere. The unspoken presentiment induces in the protagonist a phantasm, or perhaps a dream, in which the dreaded becomes a seeming reality.

Muzen and his son are removed to the far background and become spectators off the scene as the noble and his retainers discuss at considerable length the true meaning of an ancient poem by Kōbō-daishi. Akinari's inclusion of historical anecdotes and comments on ancient poetry contributes little to the plot (here, "plot" as defined by E. M. Forster),[44] but it does contribute to the shape of this piece of "elegant" fiction. This being understood, we need not be particularly concerned whether the presence of such elements signifies a pedantic intent on the part of Akinari the author-scholar. The charm of the author's interpretation of the poem and the above-mentioned aura of erudition redeem the episode from tedium. The remainder, however, is perfection. The apprehension of Muzen turns into alarm as the identity of the men becomes clear, and to terror when the phantoms command him to recite his "poetry of the present era." Although **"Buppōsō"** is related by a narrator (the fictional point of view, however, is that of Muzen), Muzen seemingly becomes the "I" of the story in the climactic moment of fear when he is forced on to the center of the scene. This momentary shift in the narrative point of view is a technique used by Akinari with great effect in other tales as well to intensify the sensation of terror.

The denouement of **"Buppōsō"** is, again, patterned on the nō—on the rapid resolution that characterizes plays belonging to the *mugen,* or "phantasmal," thematic category. The men suddenly revert to their satanic forms and clamor about, threatening the live characters, and then disappear off into the distance. The tale is brought to a close with an epilogue in which Muzen and his son are restored, as dawn breaks, to the world of reality. The concluding passage is entirely conventional: "This, which I have recorded, is exactly as he [Muzen] had related it to the people of the capital."

I should like to add a brief comment on **"Muō no rigyo"** (**"A Carp in a Dream"**), a curious example of a contrast in tone and style in a tale by Akinari. Whereas **"Buppōsō"** is probably the most original story in the *Ugetsu monogatari,* **"Muō no rigyo"** is a close adaptation of a Chinese short story. Akinari in this instance took the "Yü-fu chi" ("Chronicle of the Man in the Suit of a Fish"),[45] placed it in a Japanese setting, and refined it into a tale that is superior in many respects to its model. In the "Yü-fu chi," the utter disregard for an artistic mode of storytelling reduces the tale to a clumsy, though attractive, fable.[46] We find Hsüeh Wei caught in the classic pattern of the confused state of reality, in which he "lives" the experiences of a fish. Any possibility of a sustained suspense is lost when Hsüeh Wei, upon awakening from his death-like state of dream, promptly tells those gathered about him that the fish they had killed was in reality himself. Akinari, on the other hand, tantalizes the reader with only a hint at the direction the plot may take and allows the mystery to unfold gradually amidst mounting amazement and dismay among the listeners. Having selected as his protagonist an obscure painter in Japanese art history by the name of Kōgi, he is able to introduce a number of attractive motifs relating to painting, including the two which allow the tale to end on a note of light drollery. The setting—the great lake Biwako with its many famed scenic views—is well chosen, for it provides Akinari with the opportunity to insert a decorative passage of poetic prose, among the most delightful in the *Ugetsu monogatari.* Being otherwise free of unusual embellishments and structural peculiarities, **"Muō no rigyo"** is a short story that can be read and enjoyed without recourse to burdensome explanatory notes.

Notes

1. All the tales are available in English. For scholarly translations of "Shiramine", "Jasei no in", "Kibitsu no kama", "Himpukuron", and "Asaji ga yado", see Wilfrid Whitehouse, "*Ugetsu monogatari,*" in *Monumenta Nipponica,* I, no. 1 (1938), pp. 242-258, I, no. 2 (1938), pp. 257-275, and IV, no. 1 (1941), pp. 166-191. A faithful rendering of "Muō no rigyo" is contained in *Selections from Japanese Literature,* ed. F. J. Daniels (London: Lund Humphries, 1959); for paraphrased versions of this tale, see "The Carp in a Dream" in *Monogatari: Tales from Old and New Japan,* ed. Don C. Seitz (New York and London: G. P. Putnam's Sons, 1924), and "The Story of Kōgi the Priest" in Lafcadio Hearn, *Shadowings and a Japanese Miscellany,* vol. X of *The Writings of Lafcadio Hearn* (Boston and New York: Houghton Mifflin, 1923). A translation of "Aozukin", I understand, is

available in *The Young East,* II, no. 9 (February 1927), pp. 314-319. As for the ninth tale, "Kikka no chigiri", there is a truncated retelling under the title "Of a Promise Kept" in Lafcadio Hearn's volume cited above. For a complete translation into French, see Ueda Akinari, *Contes de pluie et de lune,* trans. René Sieffert (Paris: Gallimard, 1956). For the translation of "Kikka no chigiri" ("The Chrysanthemum Tryst"), "Buppōsō," and "Aozukin" ("The Blue Hood"), see Dale Saunders, *"Ugetsu monogatari," Monumenta Nipponica,* XXI, nos. 1-2 (1966), pp. 171-202.

2. Wilfrid Whitehouse, for example, states that "Shiramine" is simply a dialogue explaining Akinari's views on "the national spirit" and ideas of sovereignty and is inferior to "Jasei no in" ("The Lust of the Serpent's Spirit"); see *Monumenta Nipponica,* I, no. 1 (January 1938), pp. 244-245. Father Pierre Humbertclaude, on the other hand, holds: "Shiramine l'emporte pour la beauté noble et sévère de la ligne, dans le dépouillement le plus complet de l'action. Il ne se passe absolument rien, et c'est ce minimum de matiére que veut la poésie pure." See his "Essai sur la Vie et l'Oeuvre de Ueda Akinari," *Monumenta Nipponica,* V, no. 1 (January 1942), pp. 83-84.

3. See, for instance, Sasakawa Taneo, *Kinsei bungeishi* (Tokyo, 1931), p. 143; Moriyama Shigeo, "Akinari," in *Nihon bungaku kōza* (Tokyo: Kawade shobō, 1951), IV, 202-206; Aiso Teizō, *Kinsei shōsetsushi,* II (Tokyo, 1956), 249; or Hirosue Tamotsu, *"Ugetsu monogatari* no bungeisei" ("The Literary Quality of the *Ugetsu monogatari"*), *Kokubungaku* (Gakutōsha), IV, no. 7 (June 1959), pp. 21-26.

4. Shigetomo Ki, *Ugetsu monogatari no kenkyū* (Kyoto, 1946), pp. 47-48. His orientation today remains basically the same; see his *Ugetsu monogatari hyōshaku* (enlarged ed., Tokyo, 1957), pp. 31-38, and *Kinsei bungakushi no shomondai* (Tokyo, 1963), pp. 259-261 and 285-298.

5. Details are found throughout the miscellany titled *Tandai shōshin roku* (*A Record of Boldness and Timidity*), which Akinari completed in 1808; the more fleeting emotional impressions are recorded in his *Fumihōgu* (*Literary Scraps*), a collection of his letters, published also in 1808; his social attitudes may be gleaned from the *Kuse monogatari* (*Choleric Tales*), a Juvenalian satire written in his old age and published posthumously in 1822. In the *Kakaika*—some give these characters the reading *Ashikariyoshi*—(*Heckling the Reed-Cutter*), a record compiled in 1790 of his polemics with Motoori Norinaga (1730-1801) over problems of scholarship, we find revealed Akinari's recognition of the sort of tolerance which anthropologists today term "cultural relativism." The above works are contained in the *Ueda Akinari zenshū,* 2 vols. (Tokyo, 1917). For an extended biographical narrative, see Fujii Otoo, *Kinsei shōsetsu kenkyū* (Osaka, 1947), pp. 141-222. Also useful is Tsujimori Shūei, *Ueda Akinari no shōgai* (Tokyo, 1942), a monograph treating most conceivable aspects of Akinari's life and career.

6. Akinari's belief in a divine intervention is stated in his remarks appended to a set of poems of which he made an offering to the Kashima Inari Shrine in 1801, when he was sixty-seven; see *Ueda Akinari zenshū,* I, 155. Because Akinari was adopted as heir into the Ueda family when he was a three-year-old, many specialists contend that the experience resulted in a trauma that left a core of darkness in him; then again, others say that the warm affection of his adoptive parents could have only brightened his personal nature.

7. The following account, recorded in the *Tandai shōshin roku,* has often been cited in this connection. The episode described, however, occurred much later in Akinari's life; moreover, Akinari's statement can be construed to mean two different things "After I had spoken about ghosts (or, after I had told a ghost story), I was greatly humiliated by this comment [made by Takayama Riken]: 'How ignorant can one be! Ghosts and fox-possession simply don't occur. What we call fox-possession is inevitably a malady of the temperament.'" See *Ueda Akinari zenshū.* I, 360.

8. See Asō Isoji, *Edo shōsetsu gairon* (Tokyo, 1956), pp. 174-177.

9. See Teruoka Yasutaka et al., *Koten Nihon bungakushi* (Tokyo, 1962), p. 331. Mr. Teruoka assumes that Akinari was introduced to classical studies for the first time by Katō Umaki (1721-77), whom he met either in 1766 or 1767. There is evidence, however, to suggest that Akinari may have become interested in both classical Japanese literature and Chinese fiction as early as 1759; see Takada Mamoru, *Ueda Akinari nempu kōsetsu* (Tokyo, 1964), pp. 24-27.

10. See Uzuki Hiroshi, "Akinari bungaku no tenkai" ("The Literary Development of Akinari"), *Kokubungaku* (Gakutōsha), IV, no. 7 (June 1959), pp. 10-12.

11. See Earl Roy Miner, "Henry James's Metaphysical Romances," *Nineteenth-Century Fiction,* IX, no. 1 (June 1954), pp. 1-21.

12. Takada Mamoru discusses the significance of this discovery in some detail in his *Ueda Akinari nempu kōsetsu,* pp. 377-384.

13. This passage, from the *Kakan shōroku,* is cited in Takada, p. 351.

14. Takada, pp. 350-360.

15. Uzuki Hiroshi, "Akinari no shisō to bungaku" ("Akinari's Thought and His Literature"), in *Akinari,* ed. Nakamura Yukihiko, vol. XXIV of *Nihon koten kanshō kōza* (Tokyo, 1958), pp. 249-258; the quotation is from p. 258.

16. Ozaki Hideo, *Bumpō shōkai Ugetsu monogatari shinshaku* (13th ed., Tokyo, 1965), p. 12.

17. From *Yoshi ya ashi ya* (*For Better or Worse*), a fascicle of supplementary commentary which Akinari wrote when he edited the commentary by Kamo Mabuchi (1697-1769) on the *Ise monogatari.* See *Ueda Akinari zenshū,* II, 408. According to Nakamura Yukihiko, *Yoshi ya ashi ya* (1793), from which I have quoted, is an abridgement of a longer unpublished commentary that Akinari wrote probably during the 1770's; see his *Akinari,* p. 260. If it were before 1776, my next statement will have to be accordingly modified.

18. I refer the reader to the round-table discussion on the topic "new criticism and Japanese literary studies" transcribed in *Kaishaku to kanshō,* XX, no. 7 (June 1965), pp. 126-142; discussants are Konishi Jin'ichi, Saeki Shōichi, and Shinoda Hajime.

19. Nakamura, *Akinari*; see note 15.

20. *Ugetsu monogatari no kenkyū* (Kyoto, 1946).

21. For example, Mr. Shigetomo, in compiling his list of Akinari's sources, was adding to and refining the store of information brought together in Yamaguchi Takeshi, *Edo bungaku kenkyū* (Tokyo, 1933), pp. 295-337.

22. Helen Gardner, *The Business of Criticism* (London: Oxford University Press, 1959), p. 7. I have taken the liberty, in my paraphrasing, to supply the word "discerns" in the place of "believes" in the clause that in the original reads ". . . the value which he believes the work to have."

23. For a fairly recent example, see Louis D. Rubin, Jr., "What's Wrong with Graduate Literary Study," *The American Scholar,* XXXII, no. 2 (Spring 1963), pp. 213-228. There are probably limitations to all approaches that represent any extreme point of view, and we can appreciate Mr. Rubin's objections to studies that dwell so exclusively on the extraliterary that—to cite an apt comparison stated in Wayne Shumaker's *Elements of Critical Theory* (Berkeley, 1952)—they have no more value than an art-history thesis on Rembrandt's easel.

24. See his review of Matsuda Osamu, *Nihon kinsei bungaku no seiritsu,* in *Bungaku,* XXXII, no. 3 (March 1964), pp. 357-360.

25. His analysis of "Himpukuron," published in 1963, indicates a penchant for precision in defining critical standards, although there are strong manifestations still of the speculative; see *Kinsei shōsetsu kenkyū to shiryō* (Tokyo, 1963), pp. 77-97. His recent evaluative study of "Jasei no in" is more thoroughly analytical in approach, and he is careful to relate his "extrinsic" observations in parenthetical fashion; see "Jasei no in no bungakuteki kachi" ("The Literary Value of 'Jasei no in'"), *Bungaku,* XXXIII, no. 5 (May 1965), pp. 1-15.

26. Yoshida Seiichi, "Kokubungaku no genjō" ("The Present State of Japanese Literary Studies"), *Kokubungaku gengo to bungei,* III, no. 3 (May 1961), pp. 1-7; the quotation is from p. 2.

27. What may be considered representative viewpoints were expressed in a round-table discussion by six doctoral candidates from the University of Tokyo and the Tokyo University of Education on the topic "what is your regard of Japanese literary studies?" reported in *Kokubungaku gengo to bungei,* IV, no. 3 (May 1962), pp. 2-17.

28. See the entry on the *Ugetsu monogatari,* contributed by Noda Hisao, in *Nihon bungaku kanshō jiten koten-hen,* ed. Yoshida Seiichi (Tokyo, 1960), pp. 59-60.

29. Suzuki Toshiya, "*Ugetsu monogatari,*" a fascicle in *Iwanami kōza: Nihon bungaku* (Tokyo, 1932).

30. Mr. Nakamura's study of Akinari's early poetry, originally published in 1955, has been further expanded and included in his *Kinsei sakka kenkyū* (Tokyo, 1961), pp. 201-218.

31. See *Ueda Akinari shū,* vol. LIX (Tokyo, 1959) of *Nihon koten bungaku taikei,* pp. 3-9

32. See his essay, "Monogatarizama—Akinari no shōsetsukan" ("A Mode of Storytelling: Akinari's Theory of Fiction"), in *Akinari,* pp. 259-267.

33. See his *Kinsei sakka kenkyū,* pp. 250-260.

34. His analysis of *Kōshoku ichidai otoko* appears also in *Kinsei sakka kenkyū,* pp. 7-44.

35. Akinari borrowed many of his themes and motifs from earlier works of fiction of both Japan and China. For information regarding their sources, see the convenient reference chart presented in Gotō Tanji, "*Ugetsu monogatari* shutten o saguru" ("Seeking the Literary Sources of Motifs in the *Ugetsu monogatari*"), *Kaishaku to kanshō,* XXIII, no. 6 (June 1958), pp. 52-64.

36. Pierre Humbertclaude, "Essai" (see note 2), p. 78.

37. "Fan Chü-ch'ing chi-shu ssu-sheng chiao" in the *Ku-chin hsiao-shuo.*

38. Noda Hisao, *Hyōchū Ugetsu monogatari zenshaku* (Tokyo, 1963), pp. 57 and 87.

39. Nakamura, *Akinari,* p. 61.

40. Shigetomo, *Ugetsu monogatari no kenkyū,* pp. 72-77.

41. See Satō Haruo, *Ueda Akinari* (Tokyo, 1964), pp. 115-118; this section was originally drafted in 1946. See also Ishikawa Jun, "Akinari shiron" ("A Personal View of Akinari"), in *Edo shōsetsushū,* vol. xxviii (Tokyo 1961,) of *Koten Nihon bungaku zenshū.*

42. "Ai-ch'ing chuan" in the *Chien-teng hsin-hua.* In the Chinese tale, the protagonist Ch'ao returns from a similar journey and learns that his wife is dead. He exhumes the body and finds her as radiant and beautiful as in life. She reappears as a spirit in order to enjoy a momentary earthly reunion with Ch'ao and to bid him farewell. The *Otogibōko* (1666) by Asai Ryōi (d. 1690) contains an earlier adaptation of "Ai-ch'ing chuan," and Akinari was most likely familiar with it.

43. Humbertclaude, "Essai," p. 78.

44. "We have defined a story as a narrative of events arranged in their time-sequence. A plot is also a narrative of events, the emphasis falling on causality." Quoted from *Aspects of a Novel* (New York: Harcourt, Brace and Co., 1954), p. 86.

45. "Yü-fu chi" in the *Ku-chin shuo-hai.*

46. John L. Bishop has cited, among characteristics of Ming Period fiction, ". . . a monotonous preoccupation with 'story' rather than with an individual mode of telling the story." See his article, "Some Limitations of Chinese Fiction," *Far Eastern Quarterly,* xv, no. 2 (February 1956), p. 242.

Leon M. Zolbrod (essay date spring 1970)

SOURCE: Zolbrod, Leon M. "A Comparative Approach to *Tales of Moonlight and Rain.*" *Humanities Association Bulletin* 21, no. 2 (spring 1970): 48-56.

[*In the following essay, Zolbrod explains the complex relationship between* Tales of Moonlight and Rain *and the Chinese and Japanese sources of the collection.*]

Tales of Moonlight and Rain (*Ugetsu monogatari*) is a collection of nine Japanese stories of the supernatural. Although the preface dates from 1768, the book was not published until 1776 in Kyoto and Osaka, and the author, Ueda Akinari (1734-1809), probably completed it shortly before this time. Japanese scholars classify *Moonlight and Rain* under a category of narrative prose known as *yomihon,* or "reading books." These *yomihon,*[1] which were written in the eighteenth and nineteenth centuries, may be thought of as historical novels or tales, remotely reminiscent of the Gothic romances. They were usually based on actual events and typically included supernatural happenings. Ancient Japanese history, medieval literature, Confucian ethics, Buddhist morality, and Chinese scholarship entered into such tales and romances and served to make them a summary and synthesis of traditional Japanese culture. During the period of their ascendancy, between 1750 and 1850, nearly 700 items appeared that scholars now classify as *yomihon.* The best of them, such as *Moonlight and Rain,* represent the culminating development in Japanese narrative prose before the influence of Western fiction after the Meiji Restoration of 1868. Modern scholarly usage of the term *yomihon* specifically denotes collections of short stories and historical romances influenced by Chinese vernacular literature published in Kyoto and Osaka around 1750-1800 or in Edo, 1800-1850. Booksellers issued a typical *yomihon* title in sets of five *kan,* or "sections", of quarto size, with each bound in heavy, soft paper. Sometimes an embossed pattern or design enhanced the covers. On other occasions they displayed shades of beige, amber, peach, blue, or green tinted paper. For customer appeal booksellers wrapped the sets in paper envelopes often illustrated by the best woodblock artists with a design suggestive of the contents.

The complex background of eighteenth century Japan created a fertile setting for the *yomihon.* Famous scholars revived interest in national history, language, and literature. Discontented young samurai experimented with Dutch studies. Edo culture began to flower, and Kyoto and Osaka ceased to be the exclusive centers of culture and society. Chinese vernacular literature came to exert a pervasive influence on educated readers and men of letters. Foreign learning, which before the eighteenth century was restricted to a small elite, by the early nineteenth century became available to any literate man of leisure. Meanwhile, readers found the realistic and risque fiction of the floating world to be vapid and flat. They preferred the exotic *yomihon,* replete with imaginary or legendary heroes, Chinese phrases, classical Japanese stylization, historical events, and allusions to contemporary manners, morals, and even sometimes political events. Japanese society, indeed, seemed to be entering one of those times of radical change of direction in its literary tradition, which especially accompany profound social or political movements or upheavals.

Against such a background as outlined above Ueda Akinari composed nine masterful stories of mystery and suspense entitled *Tales of Moonlight and Rain.* Although they were published less than two hundred years ago, these narratives seem as securely established among classics of Japanese literature as *The Tale of Genji,* which was written by Lady Murasaki nearly a thousand years ago. This is in spite of how *Moonlight and Rain* appears on the surface to be essentially a collection of tales of mystery, ghosts, and supernatural occurrences, a branch of fiction least likely to be accorded the status of a literary classic.[2]

Moonlight and Rain is made up of a brief preface by the author, written in Chinese, and five sections of a single volume each, all but one containing a pair of stories. Also, the original text boasted of twenty woodblock illustrations that form ten *ukiyoe* diptychs. Although these were not signed, to judge from their style Akinari's friend, an Osaka illustrator named Katsura Meisen, probably supplied the drawings.[3] In format *Moonlight and Rain* resembled many representative *yomihon*. At least four distinct woodblock editions of the book appeared during the Tokugawa period. Therefore it gained fairly wide circulation and popularity, at least for a *yomihon*, in spite of its preface in Chinese and the text with its difficult compounds and hodgepodge of archaic and colloquial expressions, which prevented *Moonlight and Rain* from appealing to the common taste. All the tales have been translated into English at least once. But no book version has ever appeared. There exists, however, a French edition published in Paris, and more recently an incomplete Spanish text, which appeared in Mexico.

To characterize Akinari's tales merely as ghost stories is certainly to miss the point, though the casual reader might understandably make such a mistake. After all, each of the nine tales involves the appearance of an apparition. In the first story, **"White Peak"** (**"Shiramine"**), for example, a travelling poet-priest meets the specter of a former emperor. In the second, **"Chrysanthemum Tryst"** (**"Kikuka no chigiri"**), the spirit of a man who has committed suicide keeps a solemn promise that he previously gave to his friend. In the third, **"The House Amidst the Thickets"** (**"Asaji ga yado"**), a husband comes home after long absence and experiences a vision with his dead wife. In the fourth, **"The Carp that Came to My Dream"** (**"Muo no rigyo"**), a man returns as if from the dead and describes how for three days he was transformed into a fish. In the fifth, **"Bird of Paradise"** (**"Bupposo"**), a pilgrim and his son, forced to remain overnight at a Buddhist holy spot, have an eerie audience with a ghostly entourage of court noblemen and warriors. In the sixth, **"The Caldron of Kibitsu"** (**"Kibitsu no kama"**), the ghost of a philandering man's wife rises from the dead to exact her grisly revenge. In the seventh, **"The Lust of the White Serpent"** (**"Jasei no in"**), a young man is haunted by the materialization of a snake in the guise of an attractive and passionate woman. In the eighth, **"The Blue Hood"** (**"Aozukin"**), an itinerant Zen monk in curing an aberrant colleague's cannibalistic behavior witnesses a spiritual transformation. Lastly, in the ninth, **"Wealth and Poverty"** (**"Himpukuron"**), a warrior re-

ceives a visit from the phantom of the gold that he hoards. In every tale, therefore, the supernatural element appears as a dominant motif. To be sure, the pleasurable horror that one gets from a Gothic novel or tale can indicate great artistry, but often it wears thin on second reading. What, then, if the artistic presentation of the spiritual world itself does not suffice, contributes to the importance of *Moonlight and Rain* as a Japanese classic and suggests that it is fully deserving of a wider reputation as part of world literature?

In the following pages I wish to advance the view that Akinari's literary indebtedness to earlier Chinese and Japanese classics conduces to give *Moonlight and Rain* its distinction as one of the memorable works produced in traditional Japan. Much of the high repute accorded *Moonlight and Rain* and a degree of the potential effect of the tales even on the Western reader derives from the author's conscious attempt to synthesize Chinese and Japanese elements with the colloquial language of Akinari's own day. Inspired by Chinese vernacular fiction, Akinari made stylistic innovations in storytelling in Japan. From anecdotes and passages in earlier Chinese and Japanese literature he pieced together a highly original style of narrative prose. Each tale may be found to have its Chinese and Japanese literary prototypes. *Moonlight and Rain,* therefore, may be seen as a specific manifestation of the movement to revive the tradition of National Learning in late eighteenth and early nineteenth century Japan. It exemplifies the neoclassical mode of creativity, though the use of this term must be understood to denote interest not in Greek and Latin classics but in those of China and Japan. Its significance in this respect outweighs the charm of the individual tales as ghost stories. For reasons aside from the aesthetic value of the text that literary analysis can reveal, Akinari's collection numbers among the select masterpieces of world literature that receive a tradition, reinforce it, and pass it on in a stronger form. If *Moonlight and Rain* marks a rare synthesis of traditional Japanese and classical and vernacular Chinese literature, the catalyzing force was Akinari's emotions. Into his tales he poured his own personal outlook and philosophy. In a highly sublimated form he expressed his discontent with contemporary style in life and literature, and the result was conscious art, such as that of the best poets and writers everywhere.

In the third tale, for example, **"The House Amidst the Thickets,"** one can find a juxtaposition of Chinese and Japanese elements. Akinari is chiefly indebted to a chapter in *The Tale of Genji*, to a late-fourteenth or early fifteenth century Chinese tale, "The Story of Ai-ch'ing," ("Ai-ch'ing chuan"), and to a ballad-like verse in the eighth-century Japanese anthology known as the *Man'yoshu*. A full evaluation of **"The House Amidst the Thickets,"** or any other tale in *Moonlight and Rain* can scarcely be attained without examining Akinari's literary sources, just as one can hardly account for certain similarities between *Don Quixote* and the novels of Fielding purely on the basis of biographical research or knowledge of the English literary tradition. Recognition of Akinari's sources is essential to understanding the author's artistic effect. It may sound strange or pedantic to some modern western readers to assert the need for examining the literary sources of *Moonlight and Rain,* but Akinari used them with such vigor that they form as essential a backdrop to the tales as costumes, designs, and stage settings might for a Victorian drama. Just as knowledge of how Shakespeare transmuted material taken from Boccaccio or from Holinshed enhances our appreciation of the works, a full estimate of *Moonlight and Rain* depends on a realization of Akinari's indebtedness to Chinese and Japanese literary sources.

At this point in order to outline a comparative approach to *Moonlight and Rain,* it is appropriate to discuss how a scholar or critic can investigate Akinari's "literary indebtedness" to certain Chinese texts. For convenience's sake, one can analyze Akinari's direct debt to Chinese literature under five headings. These are "translation," "imitation," "stylization," "borrowing," and "source." In addition, one may also discern parallel features between *Moonlight and Rain,* certain Chinese works, and earlier Japanese narrative prose writings. These features, however, do not necessarily indicate a direct relationship.

Translation, the first of the terms, here is defined as expression in one's own language of a work from another tongue, often from a different period in time. All translators more or less adapt and modify the original. Although owing to the degree of freedom that Akinari exercises one can hardly apply this term rigorously to any of the tales in *Moonlight and Rain,* portions of several border on translation. In the fourth story, for example, **"The Carp That Came to My Dream,"** one passage where the protagonist is relating his reverie reads as follows: "Nonetheless, a man swimming in the water can never enjoy it as much as a fish; so when I began to envy how the creatures were gliding about, a large one nearby me said, 'Master, I can easily fulfil your desire. Please wait here for me.' So saying, he disappeared far into the depths. Presently a man wearing a crown and court dress rose up astride the same fish, followed by many other creatures of the deep. He said to me, 'The God of the Sea speaks. You, old priest, by hitherto liberating living creatures, have accrued great merit. Now having entered the water, you wish to live like a fish, and it is our privilege to grant you for a time the garb of a golden carp and to permit you to enjoy the pleasures of our watery domain. But you must take care not to be blinded by the sweetness of bait and get caught on a hook and lose your life. Thereupon he left me and disappeared from sight. With great wonder I

looked around at my own body. Unawares, I had been adorned with fish scales, gleaming like gold, and I had assumed the form of a carp. I flapped my tail, moved my fins, and swam everywhere to my heart's desire, without feeling it the least bit strange."

The Chinese version of this fanciful story, under the title, "The Man who Became a Fish," appears in *Famous Chinese Short Stories, Retold by Lin Yutang.* Although this book is advertised as "fresh and inspired translations," the reader who compares Lin's and Akinari's versions in translation with the original tenth century source will find that in some ways the particular passage quoted above is closer than that of Lin to the Chinese text.

Among other examples of the role of translation in Akinari's tales, the seventh story in *Moonlight and Rain,* **"The Lust of the White Serpent,"** in particular, remains throughout quite close to its Chinese model, "Madame White Is Forever Shut at Thunder-Peak Pagoda" ("Pai Niang-tzu yung chen Lei-feng-ta"), from an early seventeenth century text, one of the so-called *San Yen* collections. To be sure all the Chinese place names have been changed. The scenes are reset in Japan. Akinari's text abounds in stylistic changes and carefully planted allusions to classical Japanese literature. Still, **"Lust"** stays faithful to its foreign model.

Second among the five terms mentioned above is imitation. It figures when the writer in some degree gives up his creative personality to that of another author or work. The term is particularly applicable to *Moonlight and Rain.* Although scholars and critics often condemn the act, imitation can involve, as it does in Akinari's tales, independent aesthetic merit. It need not indicate intellectual poverty but rather may show, in Pushkin's words, "noble trust in one's own strength, the hope of discovering new worlds, following in the footsteps of a genius, or a feeling in its humility even more elevated, the desire to master one's model and give it a second life."[4]

Most often Akinari's imitations were from the Japanese, but he also applied this technique to his Chinese sources. Whenever one decides that Akinari has exceeded the bounds of translation, imitation may be present. Much of Akinari's second tale, **"Chrysanthemum Tryst,"** for instance, involves imitation of another example from the *San yen* collections, "Fan Chü-ch'ing's Eternal Friendship" ("Fan Chü-ch'ing shu ssu sheng chiao"). The opening passage of Akinari's story, which echoes a lofty, didactic tone, is especially close to the original and like it presents a counter-theme to the tale that follows. "Green green grows the spring willow," the tale begins. "But never plant it in your garden. For a friend, never pick a frivolous man. Although the willow may bud early, can it hold up when autumn's first wind blows? A frivolous man make friends easily, but he is fickle. While the willow for many springs takes on new color, a frivolous man will break off with you and never call again." Akinari's subsequent development of the tale is free from the detailed fidelity that one associates with translation. Especially because of its revenge motif, lacking in the Chinese model, **"Chrysanthemum Tryst"** is far more satisfying structurally than "Fan Chü-ch'ing."

Imitation, as Akinari practiced it, may be traced back at least to the twelfth century essays on Japanese poetry and ultimately to Chinese literary criticism of the T'ang Dynasty and earlier. As here defined, it is a technique similar to that elsewhere called—in describing its application to poetry—"allusive variation,"[5] and the basic impulse is akin to what in the West one terms neoclassicism.

By stylization, the third term, is meant the effect that results when an author through a combination of style and material suggests for artistic purposes another author or literary work, or even the style of an entire period. Akinari in *Moonlight and Rain* frequently uses Chinese diction and style. Typically he take Chinese phrase, metaphor, and simile, and reshapes them in accordance with the native literary tradition. These qualities can never be simply lifted intact from another literature.

How then did Akinari handle the stylistic problems that his Chinese literary sources presented? His solution in *Moonlight and Rain* permitted him to retain the best of two worlds by means of a unique system. The method, however, is hard to explain to the reader unfamiliar with the Chinese and Japanese scripts. Simply speaking, Chinese characters have both a semantic and a phonetic value. Therefore, Akinari could keep the Chinese graphs for their semantic meaning, employing them as ideographs, while indicating by the use of the Japanese phonetic gloss how he wanted the symbol to be read. As with other *yomihon* authors, including Takizawa Bakin (1767-1848),[6] Akinari could be as arbitrary as he pleased.

The ninth tale, **"Wealth and Poverty,"** which draws freely on sections of the first century B.C. Chinese historical classic, *Records of the Grand Historian (Shih chi),* and other early Chinese texts, is rich in examples of stylization. Sometimes in a brief statement such as, "To be sure, the Great Sage taught us that the rich need not be haughty" ("Sate mo tomite ogoranu was okihijiri no michi nari") Akinari alludes to a longer passage, in this case one in the *Lün yü (Analects),* which reads in its entirety, "Tse-kung said, 'What do you pronounce concerning the poor man who yet does not flatter, and the rich man who is not proud?' The Master replied, 'They will do; but they are not equal to him,

who, though poor, is yet cheerful, and to him, who, though rich, loves the rules of propriety.'"[7] Here, Akinari's phrase, *"tomite ogoranu"* "the rich need not be haughty," is a close stylization of the Chinese, *"fu erh wu chiao"* "the rich man who is not proud."[8] Owing to the ingenuity of the Japanese script, the reader of the original text can benefit at once from the visual and semantic associations of the Chinese character and the security and immediacy of the Japanese phonetic value. To cite a crude analogy, one might imagine writing English that employs the Greek alphabet for classical roots and our own for function words and inflected endings. Space prohibits presentation of further examples of this technique, but **"Wealth and Poverty"** is a virtual mosaic of such allusive stylizations, and the technique occurs with special frequency throughout *Moonlight and Rain.*

In applying the next expression, "borrowing," to Akinari's work, one refers to the aphorisms, images, figures of speech, motifs, and plot elements that he took from a variety of Chinese texts. It may be thought of as summarizing the three previous terms. Once one perceives such items, or evidence, the critic or scholar may then try to discover how the old material is used in the new work. The various examples quoted above should amply demonstrate that Akinari in *Moonlight and Rain* borrowed considerably from Chinese sources. For the most part the author's purpose seems to have been on the one hand to enlighten his readers by reviving their interest in the earlier literature of China, as well as of his own country, and on the other hand to present his own interpretation of art, life, and literature in an elegant fashion and in what one might term a neoclassical diction. That Akinari borrowed extensively from earlier Chinese and Japanese sources serves to enhance the aesthetic delight of his tales, because through them one can find a guide to numerous previous classics. *Moonlight and Rain,* therefore, at once complements and intensifies one's appreciation of traditional Chinese and Japanese literature. This is a primary reason for the high rank accorded it in Japan, and it explains partly why it is frequently used as a school text.

Lastly, the word "source" denotes the place from which borrowing takes place. Usually the source and the form are quite separate. For example, Pushkin's source for Boris Godunov is Karamzim's *History.* Shakespeare found sources in Holinshed and Boccaccio. But the artistic use of the material came from elsewhere.[9] The same may be said of Akinari. Besides the well-known Chinese classics, including the earliest dynastic histories, Akinari's main foreign sources were as follows: 1) *New Tales for Lamp Light, (Ch'ien teng hsin hua),* a late-fourteenth or early-fifteenth century collection of tales written in the Chinese literary language. This book was first brought to Japan from Korea at the end of the sixteenth century. A Japanese edition was printed in

1648. 2) The three collections of short stories, known together as the *San yen,* which were compiled early in the seventeenth century; Ming printed editions from the 1620's have been preserved in Japan. 3) *Water Margin,* (*Shui hu chuan*), or as Pearl Buck has translated it, *All Men Are Brothers,* which in its earliest form appeared in the fourteenth century. The first annotated Japanese edition dates in manuscript from the year 1727. 4) And lastly *Five Assorted Offerings,* (*Wu tsa tsu*), an encyclopedic compilation published in the early seventeenth century, of which there is an edition printed in Japan in 1666.[10] Although many others can be identified, these four texts from the Ming Dynasty stand out as Akinari's most significant Chinese sources.

Aside from the five terms described above, which indicate direct connections between **Moonlight and Rain** and Chinese literature, one may also discern parallel features. Sometimes a question remains about the actual source of borrowing, because comparable materials are present in several available works. This is often the case with Akinari's tales, especially when classical allusions or conventional metaphors are involved. One can rarely be certain whether Akinari took a phrase from another Japanese work, from a secondary Chinese text, or from an original source. Study of **Moonlight and Rain** also reveals yet another kind of parallel. The fourth tale, **"The Carp that Came to My Dream,"** as stated earlier, derives from a tenth century work, an encyclopedia entitled *Compendious Records from the Era "Great Peace,"* (*T'ai p'ing kuang chi*).[11] But one also finds a later Chinese version in one of the *San yen* collections. Strong evidence, based on similar diction, suggests that Akinari was familiar with both. Thus, it is hard to say merely on textual evidence from which of these sources he derived his initial inspiration.

In its totality the nature of literary indebtedness as discussed above, pertaining to indirect as well as to direct connections between **Moonlight and Rain** and Akinari's Chinese sources, comprises a phenomenon that is frequently termed "influence." The extent of Akinari's indebtedness reveals a great Chinese influence, though to be sure this is not the only one present. In fact, virtually the entire range of Japanese and Chinese literature as it was known and available in Akinari's day is reflected in the style, images, characters, themes, mannerisms, content, thought, ideas, and philosophy of life found in his collection of tales. Still, the Chinese influence is one aspect of the tales that should arouse strong interest among students of comparative literature. Besides the Chinese influence, **Moonlight and Rain** also shows borrowing from a wide range of earlier Japanese sources, including popular tales from Japanese history, Buddhist narratives, collections of supernatural stories, classics of the Heian period, *Man'yoshu* poetry, early

chronicles, the *no* plays, tales of the floating world, *kana* books, philosophical essays, hiakai poetry, linked verse, and military chronicles.

At the beginning of his preface Akinari said, "Lo Kuan-chung wrote *Water Margin,* and for three generations he begot deaf mutes. For writing *The Tale of Genji,* Lady Murasaki was damned to hell. Thus were these authors persecuted for what they had done. But consider their achievement. Each created a rare form, capable of expressing all degrees of truth with infinitely subtle variation and causing a deep note to echo in the reader's sensibility, wherewith one can find mirrored realities of a thousand years ago." Akinari revealed an awareness of both earlier Chinese and Japanese literature, as well as a Confucian attitude toward fiction. These remarks, however, also reflect the low opinion with which serious men of letters regarded popular fiction. Nevertheless, Akinari evinces belief that the suffering previous authors endured for their art was worthwhile, and he goes on to imply that his effort as well is worthy of consideration alongside that of his illustrious predecessors. What stronger self-confidence can any author express?

Most likely Akinari composed his tales not with Lady Murasaki's *Tale of Genji,* Lo Kuan-chung's *Water Margin,* or other old texts in his hand, but rather with the phrases and passages that he had memorized from repeated readings echoing in his head. In eighteenth century Japan rote memory of classical texts of the Confucian tradition, as well as of the national literature, played a pre-eminent role in the learning process. His readers knew many of the texts that Akinari employed. As one aphorism of the time put it, "To read a book and not return to it was as if visiting the marketplace without money to buy." When Akinari's readers, in turn, found echoes of familiar passages in his work, they felt an added pleasure. Akinari's techniques of what one might call shadow-boxing with the old masters, therefore, was not original to him but marked the best of Chinese and Japanese literature from early times. His success in **Moonlight and Rain,** then, was partly owing to his skill in applying traditional techniques and material in a fresh and original combination admirably suited to his age. In fact, Confucius, himself, asserted that he was not an original thinker but merely a transmitter of the best of the ancient wisdom. Although such modesty may be deceptive, it explains much about Akinari's own concept of originality and creative manipulation of the language and thought of the ancients.

With their mixture of bold assertiveness and defensive humility, the views of narrative fiction that Akinari embodied in **Moonlight and Rain** also characterized the best of other authors' *yomihon,* or "reading books." A sense of form, didactic tone, Chinese flavor, and an audacious mixture of colloquial and classical idiom distinguished **Moonlight and Rain** and other *yomihon* from ordinary popular Japanese fiction.[12] As Bakin stated in 1810, in the *yomihon* a moral stance and a well-written story must go together.[13] This required a combination of vast learning and a deep understanding of human feeling, standards which few authors in any age could meet. Prose fiction, as Bakin wrote, must combine penetrating emotion and a successful story. In both of these qualities Akinari excelled.

Notes

1. See my "Yomihon: The Appearance of the Historical Novel in late Eighteenth Century and Early Nineteenth Century Japan," *The Journal of Asian Studies,* XXV, 3 (May 1966), 485-498, for a historical survey of the development of this form. Also available in The University of British Columbia, Department of Asian Studies Reprint Series.

2. James T. Araki, "A Critical Approach to the *Ugestu monogatari*," *Monumenta Nipponica,* XXII, 1-2 (1967), 58.

3. Nakamura Yukihiko, ed., *Nihon koten bungaku taikei,* LVI: *Ueda Akinari-shu* (Tokyo, 1957), p. 9. Surnames precede given names, according to the practice in Japan.

4. Pushkin, writing in 1836, the year before his death, quoted in J. T. Shaw, "Literary Indebtedness and Comparative Literary Studies." in *Comparative Literature Method and Perspective,* ed. Newton P. Stallknecht and Horst Frenz (Carbondale, 1961), p. 63.

5. Robert H. Brower and Earl Miner, *Japanese Court Poetry* (Stanford 1961), pp. 286-287.

6. See my *Takizawa Bakin,* in *Twayne's World Authors Series,* XX (New York, 1967), for a biographical study.

7. James Legge, ed. and trans., *The Chinese Classics* (Hong Kong, 1960), I, 144.

8. Nakamura, ed., *Nihon koten,* LVI, 132.

9. Shaw, "Indebtedness," in *Comparative Literature,* p. 64.

10. See my "Hsieh Chao-che" (with L. C. Goodrich), in "Draft Ming Biographies," No. 10 (Editorial Board of the Ming Biographical History Project, 1968), 8 pp. (internal pagination).

11. Wolfgang Bauer, "The Encyclopaedia in China," *Cahiers D'Histoire Mondiale,* IX, 3 (1966), 664-691, provides a useful study of such compendiums in China, N.B. p. 671.

12. For an essay on this subject, see my "*Kusazoshi:* Chapbooks of Japan," *The Transactions of the Asiatic Society of Japan,* 3rd ser., X (1968), 116-147. Also available in The University of British Columbia, Department of Asian Studies Reprint Series.

13. See "Heiben" ("Horsewhippings"), in *Kyokutei iko* (*Kyokutei's Posthumous Manuscripts*) (Tokyo, 1911), p. 296.

Blake Morgan Young (essay date 1972)

SOURCE: Young, Blake Morgan. "Introduction to 'Hankai': A Tale from the *Harusame Monogatari* by Ueda Akinari (1734-1809)." *Harvard Journal of Asiatic Studies* 32 (1972): 150-68.

[*In the following essay, Young discusses Akinari as a writer who remained outside contemporary literary circles, thus minimizing the influence of other writers on his work.*]

Ueda Akinari (sometimes) has been called a good amateur.[1] He achieved, as a novelist, the distinction to which he had aspired as a *waka* poet and classical scholar, and he is worthy of note as a writer of *haikai* and a devotee of the tea ceremony as well. Possessing a choleric and antisocial disposition, he stayed aloof from the society in which he lived, and that fact is reflected in his writings. Although he acknowledged his debt to certain other men of letters, Akinari maintained a freedom of position which gives his works their own unique flavor.

As nearly as can be determined, Akinari was born on July 25, 1734 in Sonezaki, an Osaka pleasure quarter. According to tradition, he was the son of an unknown father and a courtesan whose surname was Tanaka, but this view has been challenged.[2] The time of Akinari's birth accounts in part for his importance in the history of Japanese literature. He entered the world during the administration of Yoshimune (ruled 1716-1745), the eighth Tokugawa shogun, who had already put forth the reforms which established the Edo government's authority over the Osaka region's commercial power and started Edo on the way to developing an economy and culture of its own. Culture in the Osaka-Kyoto area, which had reached its apex during the Genroku era (1688-1703) when creative writing was epitomized by the works of Bashō, Chikamatsu, and Saikaku was now declining. The next important period of literary production would be the Bunka (1804-1817) and Bunsei (1818-1829) eras, the time of Takizawa Bakin (1767-1848) and Santō Kyōden (1761-1816), when Edo had become the center of culture. Akinari, whose life fell between these two periods of literary activity, was the last major writer of the Kyoto circle and influenced authors of the later period.

In 1737, young Akinari was adopted by Ueda Mosuke, a well-to-do merchant who dealt in oil and paper. His shop, the Shimaya, was situated in Dōjima Era-chō, now the approximate location of the Osaka *Mainichi Shimbun* office. Nothing is known of the circumstances behind the adoption. One can infer that Ueda needed a son to carry on the family name, for his only natural child was a girl, but how he came to choose Akinari is a matter for speculation.

The following year, Senjirō, as Akinari was called during his childhood, contracted a severe case of smallpox that very nearly cut short his life. His father went repeatedly to the Inari Shrine in Kashima-mura on the northern outskirts of Osaka to offer prayers for his recovery, and on one such visit, it is reported, Ueda fell into a doze. While he slept, the god of the shrine appeared in a dream and told him that his son had been granted a life of sixty-eight years. Shortly thereafter the boy's health began to mend. The disease left him with a weakened constitution that would plague him throughout his life, and with his right middle finger and left index finger shortened and deformed. Sensitive about his appearance, Akinari later used such pen names as Senshi Kijin (The Pruned Cripple) and Ueda Muchō (Ueda the Crab[3]) because of it. Nevertheless, his life had been spared, and Akinari shared his father's belief that his recovery had resulted from divine intervention. He remained a faithful patron of the Kashima Inari Shrine all his life, and in 1801, when he entered his sixty-eighth year, he composed sixty-eight *waka* and dedicated them to the shrine in thanks.

Only a few miscellaneous items are known about the next quarter century of Akinari's life. His foster mother died shortly after his recovery from the smallpox, but Ueda remarried shortly, and the new mother was very kind to the children. The childhood name of Senjirō was changed to Tōsaku (also) when he came of age— Akinari was a nickname. His sister, whose name and dates are unknown, left home in 1755, apparently with a lover, and was disinherited by her father, though Akinari seems to have interceded in her behalf. Because of his poor health, Akinari was pampered and allowed considerable freedom during his youth and apparently received little formal education until he was nearly twenty. His friends were often successful in luring him away from his studies and into the gay quarters or some other frivolous activity, but his father was determined to give him a good education and sent him, in his late teens, to the Kaitokudō, an Osaka school for merchant families.[4] It was probably here that he was introduced to classical studies, very likely through contact with Goi Ranshō (1698-1762), who was a Confucian scholar and student of the national literature, and the author of critical works on the Japanese classics. During his late teens and early twenties, Akinari read widely in popular fiction, and like many sons of merchant families,

dabbled in *haikai* writing. Rather than study under a formal teacher, he associated with several of the Kyoto-Osaka *haikai* masters, especially with Takai Kikei (1687-1761) of Kyoto, whom he met around 1756. He also established a relationship with Kikei's son Kitō (1741-1789), which led in turn to a friendship with Kitō's teacher, the *haiku* master Yosa Buson (1716-1783). In 1760, Akinari married Ueyama Tama (1740?-1797), a native of Kyoto who had been adopted into an Osaka family and had worked as a maidservant in the Ueda household. Tama won his respect and devotion, and it proved to be a happy marriage, albeit a childless one.

Akinari's interest in literature grew more serious after his marriage, and in 1766 he published **Shodō kikimimi sekenzaru,** a collection of fifteen stories drawn from his own experiences, which present a witty and satirical picture of society. This success was followed early the next year by **Seken tekake katagi,** twelve tales which deal primarily with the difficulties of keeping a mistress. The stories are droll and satirical in tone, but they consider the feelings of concubines and the men who keep them, probing the dilemma of head versus heart. Both collections were written under the name of Wayaku Tarō. They fall into the class of literature known as *ukiyozōshi* and were strongly influenced by the works of Ejima Kiseki (1667-1738). These collections are historically significant as the last noteworthy *ukiyozōshi,* but it is not for his contributions to a dying genre that Akinari is remembered.

About this same time, Akinari met Katō Umaki (1722-1777), who introduced him to the Mabuchi school of the *kokugaku* movement. *Kokugaku,* though hard to define precisely, was an effort, through study of the Japanese classics, to clarify and understand the ancient language, spirit, and way of life before the advent of continental influences. The field included study of the national language and literature, ancient history, intellectual history, religion, and other areas.[5] Interest in such study had been kindled by Keichū (1640-1701) and continued and expanded by Kamo Mabuchi (1697-1769) and others. Umaki had been a student of Mabuchi and was closer to him in character than was his more famous disciple, Motoori Norinaga (1730-1801). Akinari had been independently studying the works of Keichū and his admirer, Goi Ranshū, but Umaki taught him the spirit of Mabuchi's ideas and thus helped him to shift from popular literature to serious scholarship. Akinari remained on close terms with Umaki until the man's death, either through personal contact or correspondence. After Umaki died, Akinari returned to private study, but having fallen heir to Umaki's teachings, he enlarged upon them, producing some deeply learned writings of his own. Acutely conscious of his position as an indirect disciple of Mabuchi, Akinari all his life paid deep respect to the memory of both Mabuchi and Umaki.

Akinari also studied for a time with the writer Takebe Ayatari (1719-1774), whom he probably met in 1767. They agreed on matters of *kokugaku* at first, but their relationship deteriorated and Akinari came to consider the man a rival. It is commonly believed that Akinari met Umaki through Ayatari, but the record is not clear on this matter.[6]

Nor is the record clear on the matter of his father's death. Until recently it was generally believed that Mosuke died in 1770, and therefore it was assumed that Akinari's early literary studies and published writings were made possible by financial support from his father. However, there is convincing evidence that Mosuke's death occurred as early as 1761.[7] If this is true, it lends support to the commonly held view that Akinari was not diligent in managing his father's business after falling heir to it. He was not a merchant at heart, and whether he took care of the business for only a year or struggled along with it for ten, he was probably somewhat relieved when the establishment was destroyed by fire in 1771, for he made no attempt to salvage anything or make a fresh start. Still, the fire had wiped out his means of livelihood, and he had to find another. He chose medicine, and in 1773 he moved to Kashima-mura and commenced study under the Confucian physician Tsuga Teishō (1718?-1795?). But medicine was not all that he learned.

A new literary genre, the *yomihon,* was emerging. *Yomihon,* as the term implies, were books intended to be read for pleasure rather than instruction, even though a didactic element was often present. Their development was partly an outgrowth of the interest in translation and study of Chinese colloquial novels, which had begun early in the eighteenth century and was now reaching its peak. Early *yomihon* were usually collections of short stories, often based on actual events or classical tales, and influenced by Chinese vernacular literature. Indeed, many of the first *yomihon* were translations or close adaptations of their Chinese sources, but later authors grew more original in their presentation. From 1750 to 1800, most *yomihon* were written in the Kyoto-Osaka region; from about 1800 until the death of Bakin, the last creative author of the genre, in 1848, Edo was the center of productivity. Outstanding among early *yomihon* were Tsuga Teishō's *Hanabusazōshi* (1749) and *Shigeshige yawa* (1766), and Takebe Ayatari's *Nishiyama monogatari* (1768) and *Honchō suikoden* (1773). Teishō's adaptations of Chinese novels were especially influential in generating interest in a new style of literature. Though not a genuine scholar of things Chinese (his translations were aimed at financial profit rather than academic excellence), Teishō was nevertheless a man of wide knowledge and Akinari gained considerable learning from him to supplement what he had obtained from Umaki and study of Mabuchi's writings.

After two years with Teishō, Akinari returned to Osaka and established his own medical practice. The following year, 1776, his masterpiece was published. This was *Ugetsu monogatari,* written under the name of Senshi Kijin. A collection of nine short tales of the supernatural, adapted from Chinese sources and written in an elegant and flowing style, *Ugetsu* is a work of eerie beauty. *Ugetsu,* along with the writings of Ayatari and Teishō, formed the nucleus of the *yomihon* genre and helped provide the transition from early to late Tokugawa styles.

Akinari was a conscientious and successful physician, though it was hardly the ideal occupation for a man of his nervous temperament. He believed that working at one's trade was the proper course; that scholarship and the arts were only means of recreation, so he devoted his energies to his medical practice in spite of the inner turmoil it must have created. His kindness and sincerity enabled him to acquire a large clientele, and by 1781 he was prosperous enough to build a new house. But failure to alleviate suffering was a constant source of pain to him. His own poor health forced many interruptions in his work, and his eyesight began to weaken as well. Nor was he able to suppress permanently his literary inclinations. In 1788, when a young girl in his care died as a result of his mistaken diagnosis, he gave up medicine for a life of study and writing, taking up residence in a house which he called the Uzurai, in Awajishō-mura, not far from Kashima-mura. The period that he spent here determined his own peculiar scholastic position and the views on society that appeared in his writings.

After the publication of *Ugetsu,* which brought him acclaim among men of letters, Akinari seems to have turned away from fiction writing in favor of *waka* and more serious study of phonetics and the classics. His critical essays on old literary works contributed to the revival of interest in the Japanese classics, but the only works of fiction that he produced during this period were *Kakizome kigenkai* (1787) and *Kuse monogatari* (1791, pub. 1822). Both were merely sketches, sarcastic in tone, and quite different from *Ugetsu,* but they reflect his feelings at the time they were written. Akinari never achieved excellence as a *waka* poet. His combination of fresh new expressions with conventional simplicity in subject matter earned him some praise, but his poetry had little popular appeal. He set down some of his views on *haikai* writing in *Yasaishō,* which he wrote under the name of Muchō, though his *haikai* name was Gyoen (also). Written in 1774, this work boasted a preface by Buson, but Akinari withheld publication until 1787, feeling that *haikai* had no value aside from being a source of amusement. Even so, he continued to write *haikai* all his life.

About 1784 or 1785, a long and bitter quarrel broke out between Akinari and Motoori Norinaga. They disagreed on certain aspects of ancient Japanese manners and customs, and with particular sharpness on the subject of phonetics in the old language. Especially famous is Norinaga's contention that the "n" sound was of foreign origin, that "mu" had been the original sound, while Akinari maintained that both sounds had been present in ancient Japanese. Akinari also attacked Norinaga's belief that the "p" sound was not native to Japan. Their dispute appears in such works as *Kashōden* (1785), *Kakaika* (1787), and *Yasumigoto* (1792). Akinari's arguments were considered inadequate at the time, but in later years many scholars came to share his opinions. The depth of Akinari's learning and conviction fell short of Norinaga's, but Akinari displayed a keen wit and a freedom of position. Despite his hot temper and eccentric words and actions, Akinari was a rationalist, and Norinaga took exception to the value which he placed on independence and freedom of emotion. The fastidious Akinari was equally displeased by the passionate faith, fanatically anti-Chinese position, complacent self-satisfaction, and apparent indifference to systematization of Norinaga, whose view of the world was taken from the classics. Nor should jealousy be discounted as a source of Akinari's displeasure.

Akinari's mother-in-law and stepmother both died in 1789, and the following year he himself lost most of the sight in his left eye. In 1793, his wife became a nun, taking the monastic name of Koren'i. Repeated publication had failed to produce any substantial income and his wife was lonely for her old home, so that in the same year Akinari decided to try his fortunes in Kyoto. At first he and his wife took lodgings near the Chion'in, where he is known to have practiced the tea ceremony with a Murase Kōtei who lived in the vicinity. Akinari's liking for the tea ceremony led him to design articles for it, some of which are described in *Seifū sagen* (1794). A year after their arrival in Kyoto, Akinari and Koren'i transferred to quarters near the Nanzenji, and thereafter they continued to move frequently. For a short time they lived at the home of the poet Ozawa Roan (1723-1801), who had often visited them at the Nanzenji. When Koren'i died in 1797, Akinari took the loss hard, and perhaps influenced by his emotional state, his remaining eye began to fail. Even so, he eked out a living by copying manuscripts and continuing to write. Some of his best *kokugaku* writings, including annotated editions of Japanese classics and works of Umaki and Mabuchi, were produced during this period.

Akinari and Koren'i had adopted a girl named Mineko. Very little is known about her, but she took care of him for a few years after Koren'i's death, being assisted by Matsuyama Teikō, a nun from Osaka. But Teikō died three years after Koren'i, and Mineko seems to have left shortly thereafter, possibly to be married. Akinari had always isolated himself and remained cool toward society, being self-conscious about his physical deformity. As he became older, his personality grew darker; in his last years he was noted for being a sulking, self-scorning old man, bitterly sarcastic toward the world and its people, and feeling that the masses were full of lies and immorality. Disenchanted with his own times, he favored the past and felt that the only proper course was to withdraw from the world and live a strict ascetic life. Outwardly he was irritable, foul mouthed, misanthropic, and stubborn, but though his hot temper and free speech bred dislike in many, others realized that he was simply high-strung. Ignoring his temperament, they applauded his wit, recognizing his irritability and keen insight as the sources of his literary talent. Such men watched over him unobtrusively, rather than risk his displeasure by offering direct assistance. Encouraged by them, he wrote *Tsuzurabumi* (1802, pub. 1806), a collection of poetry and prose, including some posthumous works of his wife, and *Kinsa* (1804), his longest work. A miscellany in style, it brings together all his previous studies of the *Man'yōshū*. It was followed the same year by a brief afterword, *Kinsa jōgen*.

Certain actions during his last years suggest that Akinari felt his end approaching. He designed his own tombstone in 1802, and in 1807, it is reported, he dropped a number of his manuscripts down a well. In 1806 he moved back to the Nanzenji, and it was there that he wrote *Tandai shōshin roku* (pub. 1808), a general statement of his ideas. A miscellany of his opinions and experiences, it presents his views as he wanted them to be remembered. He wrote without deference to his superiors or old acquaintances, viciously attacking some while praising others. This work is a good key to his personality and tells us much about his life.

Early in 1809 Akinari moved to the home of Hakura Nobuyoshi, where he died on the eighth day of August, that same year. In accordance with his wishes, his friends interred his remains at the Saifukuji, a temple not far from the Nanzenji, where his gravestone, inscribed with the name "Ueda Muchō," can still be seen.

At the time of his death, Akinari was working on a collection of short tales which he called *Harusame monogatari*. He appears to have begun the stories around 1800, at which time he displayed considerable interest in political and cultural history, but different drafts of the tales reflect the subsequent shift of his concern to social problems. Early manuscripts contain drafts of certain stories, all having historical settings and themes, that were subsequently excluded, and what appears to be the final version of *Harusame* (though Akinari probably was not yet satisfied with the result when he died) is a mixture of historical tales and human interest stories. The ten tales that Akinari seems to have decided to include in the collection are as follows: (1) "**Chikatabira**"; (2) "**Amatsu otome**"; (3) "**Kaizoku**"; (4) "**Nise** no en"; (5) "Me hitotsu no kami"; (6) "Shikubi no egao"; (7) "Suteishimaru"; (8) "Miyagi ga tsuka"; (9) "Uta no homare"; (10) "Hankai."

Harusame monogatari circulated in manuscript form, but was never published until 1907, when all but four complete tales and half of a fifth had been lost. Scholars knew that there had been ten stories in the original, and so it was only natural that when interest in the study of Akinari's works was heightened by the publication of *Ueda Akinari zenshū* in 1918 and *Akinari ibun* in 1919, concerted efforts were made to locate the missing portions.

The first published edition of *Harusame* was edited by Fujioka Sakutarō from the so-called Tomioka hon, a draft of the tales which was then in the possession of a Tomioka Kenzō of Kyoto. This manuscript, now in the Tenri Library, consists of five scrolls in Akinari's own handwriting, and contains the preface to *Harusame* and four and a half tales: **"Chikatabira," "Amatsu otome," "Kaizoku," "Me hitotsu no kami,"** and the first part of **"Hankai."** In order to meet the demands of the average reader, Fujioka freely substituted *kanji* where *kana* had been in the original, and added *okurigana* where he deemed it necessary for clarity. His version was subsequently included in the *Ueda Akinari zenshū* and in the Yūhōdō Bunko collection of Akinari's writings. In order to supply a more scholarly version, Shigetomo Ki, in 1939, published a text that corresponded to the original.

Shortly after the Pacific War, the discovery of another *Harusame* manuscript provided a more complete version. This Urushiyama hon (named for its owner, an Urushiyama Matashirō), a single-volume transcription made in 1833, contains eight tales; the copyist noted that he had decided against including **"Hankai"** and **"Suteishimaru."** Not long after, Maruyama Sueo found a reference to a two-volume transcription of *Harusame* in the catalogue to the Sakurayama Bunko, the collection of Kashima Noribumi who, in the late Tokugawa Period, had been a chief priest at the Ise Shrine. Noribumi's son Noriyuki turned the manuscript over to Maruyama, who published it in 1951. Thus the first complete edition of *Harusame* was offered to the public.

Two other manuscripts, both now in the Tenri Library, deserve mention here. The Seisō Bunko hon, a two-volume transcript copy from the Seisō Bunko, the collection of Ozu Keisō (1804?-1858), contains all ten tales. Ozu Keisō, a bibliographer and collector from Matsuzaka in Ise, was a friend of Takizawa Bakin, and it was through this copy that *Harusame* came to be noted in Bakin's pioneer history of Edo literature, *Edo sakusha burui,* which in turn informed modern scholars that the complete work consisted of ten items. The Tenri Kansubon was preserved by the Matsumuro family, into

which Hakura Nobuyoshi's son Shigemura was adopted by marriage. It consists of three scrolls in Akinari's own handwriting, and contains the tales **"Nise no en," "Shikubi no egao," "Suteishimaru," "Miyagi ga tsuka," "Uta no homare,"** and the second part of **"Hankai,"** but there are many missing portions.

Although other manuscripts exist, modern scholars are primarily concerned with those mentioned above, since they represent the most polished versions of *Harusame.* The Sakurayama, Urushiyama, and Seisō manuscripts were apparently copied from the draft that Akinari wrote in 1808 while in temporary residence at the Nanzenji.[8] The original is probably the manuscript said to be in the possession of a certain Hasegawa of Matsuzaka, but it has never been found. Notwithstanding their common origin, these three manuscripts are not uniform. Even a specialist in old manuscripts finds it a formidable task to decipher Akinari's handwriting, so that there are a number of discrepancies in wording and numerous disagreements in the use of *kanji* and *kana,* one often being substituted for the other. Without the original manuscript it is impossible to say which copy is the most faithful rendition of what Akinari actually wrote.

Research has established that the Tomioka hon and Tenri Kansubon were originally parts of the same manuscript. Comparison of their contents with that of the 1808 version reveals numerous differences in structure, organization, and wording. As the text is, in general, better organized and more polished and refined in the Tomioka hon and Tenri Kansubon, it is commonly assumed that they are a draft of the tales which Akinari wrote in 1809, just before his death. However, since efforts to find the missing portions of the Tenri Kansubon have failed, the complete final draft of *Harusame* remains unavailable. Some hope was provided by the discovery of part of the Tawara hon, a copy made after Akinari's death by a *waka* poet of Kyoto named Tawara Shunsho. This manuscript, now in the Tenri Library, contains the preface and the tales **"Chikatabira," "Amatsu otome,"** and **"Kaizoku,"** and they correspond to the Tomioka version. Discovery of the remainder of the Tawara hon, then, would probably supply Akinari's final rendition.

Although called a *monogatari,* *Harusame* is partly a vehicle for transmitting its author's ideas; it incorporates the knowledge that he gained and the opinions that he formed as the result of his *kokugaku* studies. Most of the stories are based on folk legends or actual events. Unlike *Ugetsu,* Chinese background material is spotty and insignificant. **"Chikatabira"** and **"Amatsu otome"** reflect Akinari's historical views. The former, a tale of treachery and its overthrow, portrays the conflict between the pure Japanese spirit, represented by the Emperor Heizei (reigned 806-809), and corruption, in the guise of Fujiwara conspirators. In the latter, Akinari attempts to show the effects of continental culture on the imperial court during the first half of the ninth century, the period of fascination with things Chinese.

Four of the tales feature criticism of scholarship or religion. **"Kaizoku"** takes for its setting the journey described by Ki no Tsurayuki in *Tosa nikki*. The boat from Tosa is overtaken by a pirate who comes aboard and engages Tsurayuki in a debate on *waka* and politics. In **"Nise no en,"** a priest who had been buried alive long before, seeking the peace of the hereafter, is unearthed and revived. He marries into a poor family, lives by doing hard labor, and is constantly scolded by his wife. Apparently his previous religious actions have gained him nothing. In **"Me hitotsu no kami,"** a man on his way to study at the capital encounters a group of supernatural beings, including a one-eyed deity, who drink with him and talk about *waka* composing and study in general. Stressing the need for self-study rather than instruction, they persuade him to return home. In **"Uta no homare"** Akinari points out striking similarities in the works of certain *Man'yōshū* poets and states that their *waka*, being composed independently, portray the ancient Japanese spirit.

Finally, there are four human interest tales. **"Shikubi no egao"** is the tragic story of a youth torn between his love for a girl and his duty to his father, who opposes the match. Ultimately, the girl is decapitated by her brother when she arrives at her lover's home for the marriage. Akinari based this story on a real event, the same one as that from which Takebe Ayatari's *Nishiyama monogatari* was drawn. **"Suteishimaru"** begins in Northern Honshū, where Suteishimaru, a servant, kills his master and flees. The victim's son traces the murderer to Kyūshū, but finding that he has repented and is constructing a tunnel as a service to the local inhabitants, loses all desire for revenge. The story is based on an old legend which, more recently, Kikuchi Kan (1889-1948) used as the source for his story "Onshū no kanata ni." **"Miyagi ga tsuka"** is the tale of Miyagi, who, forced into prostitution by poverty, finds a lover only to have him killed by a jealous rival. After being consoled by a passing priest, she drowns herself in the sea. Miyagi is patterned after a courtesan of whom Akinari heard while living in Kashima-mura. **"Hankai,"** which is discussed more fully below, is the story of a wild young man who commits all manner of crimes but finally mends his ways and becomes a great priest.

As indicated above, *Harusame* is a motley collection. The tone is generally dark, in keeping with the author's feelings in his later years. All of the tales have subjects worthy of this phase of his life. **"Nise no en"** satirizes the Buddhist doctrine of finding peace in this world and the next. Criticism of scholarship appears in **"Kaizoku,"** **"Me hitotsu no kami,"** and **"Uta no homare."** **"Chikatabira"** and **"Amatsu otome"** are critical of historical figures. **"Miyagi ga tsuka"** portrays the mis-

ery of an innocent victim of evil. Man's better nature is often called into question, although the reformations of Suteishimaru and Hankai are cases of affirmation. The world was not, to the aging Akinari, a place of beauty, and society is portrayed less attractively in *Harusame* than in his earlier works of fiction. Whereas in *Ugetsu* Akinari escaped from reality into a dream world, in *Harusame* he seems to have decided to portray things as he saw them.

Appreciation of *Harusame* is hampered to some extent by a natural tendency to compare it with *Ugetsu*. *Harusame* falls short of *Ugetsu* in eloquence and popular appeal, and its uneven construction (some of the tales are skillfully organized and entertaining, while others are more like discourses) is emphasized by the unity of the earlier work. It also suffers from numerous difficult sentences and crude use of *kanji*. But even so, *Harusame* is a reservoir of its author's ideas and learning; it may even surpass *Ugetsu* in research and classic style. Although not his best work of art, it stands as proof that Akinari, who loved study and research from his young manhood, continued in this spirit to his life's end.

The longest of the *Harusame* tales (and also Akinari's longest single work of fiction) is **"Hankai."** It is the story of a young man who, though guilty of numerous crimes, is led to repentance through Buddhist virtue and ultimately attains enlightenment. For my translation of the tale, I have used the text prepared by Nakamura Yukihiko which is included in *Ueda Akinari shū, Nihon koten bungaku taikei* (hereafter *NKBT*), LVI (Tokyo, 1959), 214-247. Nakamura wanted to provide the most up-to-date version possible, but since only the first part of the 1809 draft of **"Hankai"** was available, he chose the 1809 version for Part I and the 1808 version for Part II. More specifically, he used the Tomioka hon as the standard text for the first part, and the Seisō Bunko hon, with reference to the Tenri Kansubon and Sakurayama hon, for the second. In order to make the text more readily comprehensible, Nakamura supplied punctuation, which is completely lacking in the original, and added some *furigana*. He also made some minor changes and additions, either from reference to the non-standard manuscripts or from the context, but all such items are duly marked and their sources given. I was able to compare Nakamura's text with the Koten Bunko edition, which was published from the Sakurayama manuscript.[9] As one would expect, the second part of **"Hankai"** is almost identical in both editions, but there are numerous differences in the first part, though none sufficient to alter the story.

The name Hankai is the Sino-Japanese reading of Fan K'uai. The real Fan K'uai (d. 189 B.C.) was a faithful retainer of Liu Pang (247-195 B.C.), the founder of the Former Han dynasty. A humble dog butcher by trade, Fan K'uai attached himself to Liu Pang early in that man's career and rose to a high position by virtue of his great strength and military prowess. His most famous exploit was saving Liu Pang from assassination when he met with his rival, Hsiang Yü, in 206 B.C. His name was well known in Tokugawa Japan.[10] It is a fitting nickname for Daizō, the central character of **"Hankai,"** but in creating him Akinari appears to have been inspired not so much by the historical Fan K'uai as by Lu Chih-shen, a key figure in the Chinese novel *Shui hu chuan*. Both Daizō and Lu Chih-shen are coarse and simple in their behavior, lacking in education, but endowed with enough strength and reckless courage to do whatever they please. Both men flee from the law after killing someone, personal descriptions being circulated to facilitate their arrest, and both become priests in order to avoid detection. Likewise, both become thieves, and both at last die peacefully after attaining Buddhist enlightenment.[11]

Daizō is a young man[12] whose home is the traditional environment for producing a delinquent. Being the second son, he is subordinate to his brother, and probably resentful of the fact. His father and brother, who think only of finances and reputation, lack sympathy and understanding, qualities that his mother and sister-in-law have in abundance with a corresponding lack of discretion. Such a home situation bears comparison with the tale in *Ugetsu*, **"Jasei no in,"** in which the younger son is similarly indulged by his mother and even more so by his sister-in-law, while being scorned by his father and brother. In Akinari's own home as well, the father was strict while the mother pampered the children, a point which may have influenced the daughter's flight from home.

"Hankai" begins with the phrase *Mukashi ima wo shirazu*, which indicates an indefinite time in the past, but the society portrayed in the tale appears to be a peaceful feudal establishment such as existed in Japan during the Tokugawa period. This stands to reason, for Akinari was concerned about the corrosion of values in his own day. The society in **"Hankai"** is not a good one. Daizō is raised in a home where utilitarian values replace human feelings. Money is the root of most of his wicked acts. Nearly everyone he meets, seemingly good people included, sacrifice their moral principles for material gain. It is a priest who does not desire money who brings Hankai to his senses. Akinari was impoverished when he wrote **"Hankai,"** and may well have been led to despise monetary greed all the more. But there is not a complete negation of society. True, Hankai is driven to crime by a bad social environment, but it is good social elements that cause him to reform. There is good in the world even though evil may be more conspicuous. This duality, the coexistence of good and evil, is the story's principal theme.

Hankai is first portrayed as a youth who has little for a guide except the world around him. Amoral and unedu-

cated, he possesses the proverbial "might is right" outlook. Life, to him, is something one conquers by his own strength, and as Hankai uses his strength, his belief in it grows. Early in the tale he is punished by a god, but this is defeat at the hands of a supernatural power. He feels no need to change his behavior toward humans, and so the experience, terrifying though it was, has no lasting effect on him. Paradoxically, his first move toward real moral awareness comes when he begins his life of crime. Having committed murder, he has to flee for his life. Even though he remains arrogant and adds to his list of crimes with no apparent reflection, he is now on his own and has to think more seriously than before. In the course of his travels, the good side of his character gradually emerges. He frustrates the scheme of the dishonest merchant. Later he discovers his own musical talent and brings pleasure to others through his performance. On several occasions he displays considerable generosity. But until he meets his match in the old temple, he is fundamentally unchanged. His defeat at the hands of the old warrior, coming at a time when he is most sure of his physical prowess, amounts to shock treatment. And it is the warrior's strength, not his words, that makes the lasting impression. Through this experience, though it neither reforms him nor weakens his courage, Hankai comes to see the limits of his power and is prepared for the experience which does change his heart. When he meets the priest who saves him, Hankai, silhouetted against a blazing fire in a lonely and terrifying place, must present a fearsome spectacle, yet the priest, who is no physical match for him, passes by unmoved. His strength lies in a different realm. It is Hankai, having only physical strength, who is disturbed.

"Hankai" is filled with entertaining episodes and sidelights, but its main purpose is to illustrate the Buddhist concept of *Ten'aku seizen*, "Reform evil and create good." The Buddha nature is present in everyone, no matter how wicked he may be. Evil is not the basic nature of man, but merely the dust which covers his true character. Such a view denies the popular concept of evil as being unchangeable and irreversible. Man longs for virtue and purity, and he who is acquainted with evil will treasure these qualities all the more. In other words, evil serves as a mediator for good and exalts the man who triumphs over it. Man, in **"Hankai,"** is not at the mercy of fate, but responsible for his own actions. There is no employment of Buddhist incantations in order to escape from destiny, nor is there any talk of being reborn in paradise, or much religious talk of any kind, for that matter. Salvation is the peace of mind which can be found here and now through one's own efforts. It is self-discipline, then, or the lack of it, that determines what a person becomes. And so it is with Hankai. When used indiscriminately, his strength and courage are the source of considerable wrongdoing, but when his heart is turned in the right direction, these same qualities help him to attain Buddhahood.

Notes

1. Nakamura Yukihiko, ed., *Akinari, Nihon koten kanshō kōza,* XXIV (Tokyo, 1966), 3. The author wishes to express sincere appreciation to Professor Leon M. Zolbrod and to members of the staff of the University of British Columbia Asian Studies Library for invaluable assistance rendered in preparing this translation.

2. See Takada Mamoru, *Ueda Akinari nempu kōsetsu* (Tokyo, 1964), pp. 1-3, for views on Akinari's parentage. Although the matter presents an interesting puzzle, it was the dark circumstances of his birth rather than the identity of those responsible for it that affected Akinari's future life. His real parents had little time to influence him, but he was very sensitive about his apparently illegitimate origin.

3. Originally this nickname probably referred to his deformed hands, which seem to have born a slight resemblance to a crab's pincers. In his later years, it was used in connection with his vituperative disposition. The name can also be interpreted to mean "gutless," but I have found no evidence that it was ever applied in that sense.

4. This school was established in 1726 by the Confucian scholar Nakai Shūan (1693-1758) under orders from Yoshimune, and continued until 1869 as a center for instruction in Neo-Confucian studies and the national history and literature.

5. One Japanese scholar has summed up his attempt to define *kokugaku* by calling it the study of "something" with the classics as the principal reference works. See Uzuki Hiroshi, "Akinari no shisō to bungaku," Nakamura, ed., *Akinari,* pp. 249-258, N.B. p. 251.

6. See Takada, *Akinari nempu,* pp. 53-55.

7. See *ibid.,* pp. 32, 33.

8. All three manuscripts have the postscript "Bunka, fifth year [1808], third month. Written for pleasure in aged seclusion under Mt. Zuiryū at the age of seventy-five." See Nakamura Yukihiko, "*Harusame monogatari,*" Nakamura, ed., *Akinari,* pp. 196-245, N.B. p. 196.

9. *Harusame monogatari,* ed. Maruyama Sueo (Tokyo, 1951).

10. It appears, for example, in Chikamatsu Monzaemon, *Kokusenya kassen, Chikamatsu jōruri shū ge NKBT,* L (Tokyo, 1959) 227-292, N.B. p. 267.

11. See Sakai Kōichi, "*Harusame monogatari* 'Hankai' to Suikoden to no kankei" *Kokugo Kokubun* 25, no. 12 (December, 1956): 26-33, for a more detailed consideration of these points.

12. The 1808 version gives his age as twenty-one. See *Harusame,* ed. Maruyama, p. 168.

Leon M. Zolbrod (essay date 1974)

SOURCE: Zolbrod, Leon M. Introduction to *Ugetsu Monogatari: Tales of Moonlight and Rain: A Complete English Version of the Eighteenth-Century Japanese Collection of Tales of the Supernatural by Ueda Akinari 1734-1809,* translated and edited by Leon M. Zolbrod, pp. 19-94. London: George Allen & Unwin, 1974.

[*In the following excerpt, Zolbrod provides an overview of Akinari's* Tales of Moonlight and Rain, *discussing the work's style, influences, and historical background.*]

HISTORICAL BACKGROUND

Much of the fascination with travel and the lyric beauty of place names in the tales comes from Akinari's sense of history and the passage of time. For over a thousand years the nation had endured, and as a student of its traditions, Akinari knew what changes had taken place in customs, manners, and institutions. Each of his tales was set in times past, mostly during the middle ages, between the twelfth and the late sixteenth century, as the following list shows:

1 '**White Peak**[1]': late twelfth century.

2 '**Chrysanthemum Tryst**': late fifteenth century.

3 '**The House Amid the Thickets**': mid-fifteenth century.

4 '**The Carp That Came to My Dream**': early tenth century.

5 '**Bird of Paradise**': seventeenth or eighteenth century.

6 '**The Caldron of Kibitsu**': early sixteenth century.

7 '**The Lust of the White Serpent**': unspecified, but apparently the Heian period.

8 '**The Blue Hood**': late fifteenth century.

9 '**Wealth and Poverty**': late sixteenth century.

Although the tales were written in an age of peace, a number of them involve warfare and the conflict between an early system of central government and the new feudal institutions that dominated national life after the middle of the twelfth century. The first story, for instance, is set in the days when rule by code of law was yielding to feudal privilege. The clash between old and new, the role of foreign ideas, and the question of sovereignty figures against a background of cataclysmic change. As a twelfth-century historian wrote, 'When the Emperor Toba died, the Japanese nation was plunged into disorder, and subsequently the age of the warrior began.'[1] Court nobles had never before asked provincial warriors for help to settle by force of arms in the capital itself a dispute over succession to the imperial throne. **'White Peak'** reflects the collapse of an entire society. It describes the end of an epoch in terms that suggest scattering cherry-blossoms, the waning moon, and nostalgia for bygone days.

Before becoming a Buddhist priest, Saigyō, the narrator, had served Toba. Only one year older than Sutoku, Saigyō knew how vexed the emperor felt at being a mere figurehead while his father remained the power behind the throne. He understood how Sutoku had been forced to abdicate in favour of his younger half-brother, Konoe, and how when the latter died, Sutoku wanted his own son, Prince Shigehito, to be emperor, so that in time he himself might hold power as a retired monarch. But Sutoku's wishes were thwarted. His brother, Go-Shirakawa, was placed on the throne, and after the father passed away, the son rebelled. His forces were defeated and he was banished, but according to popular belief he left a curse that led to a series of national calamities, all of which is described in the first tale from Saigyō's point of view.

Along with other early modern scholars and writers, Akinari wondered why disaster struck the imperial house and what form legitimate government should take. In **'White Peak'** he presents this issue as a conflict between the Chinese Confucian point of view and native Japanese ways. Ironically, Sutoku, a descendant of the 'eight hundred myriad gods' supports a foreign institution, while Saigyō, a follower of an alien religion, defends Japanese customs. Political thought and historical fact are combined with fiction in such a manner that Akinari could claim for his tale the respectability long associated with orthodox scholarship. In Japan, as in China, history was thought of as a mirror of truth. The past reflects an image that might help in making decisions for the future. By contrast, fiction was normally scorned as a web of lies. But Akinari's work helped to establish prose fiction as a means of expressing historical criticism and cultural values.

While the background for **'White Peak'** and much of Akinari's interpretation of events may be traced to an early military chronicle, the *Hōgen monogatari (Tales of the Hōgen Era)*,[2] a similar record[3] also figures in **'Chrysanthemum Tryst,'** which is set three centuries later. At this time, during the confused period after the outbreak of the Ōnin Wars, contending forces brought renewed violence and civil discord to the nation, and the ideal of peace and order seemed doomed. Amako Tsunehisa's rise to leadership and his storming of Tomita Castle on the eve of the Japanese New Year typify an age when strong local leaders challenged the authority of distant lords. Just as Tsunehisa went on to become the ruler of many provinces, warriors elsewhere also tried to extend their influence.

Behind Akinari's fascination for this process of change and his nostalgia for what had been lost lies the belief that history has a moral significance and that the past forms a continuous pattern stretching back to antiquity. Men assumed that something had gone wrong, and they believed that by examining certain crucial turning points they might discover why this happened. Then by adjusting national policy one might restore society to normal. Accordingly, the middle ages were thought to be bad, because military authority had been glorified and the strong trampled the weak. Powerful houses had split into rival factions, and it seemed unlikely that a united nation could ever emerge from the chaos. Innocent people, such as Katsushirō and Miyagi, in **'The House Amid the Thickets,'** all too often bore the brunt of the misery and suffering of war.

For this tale, as well as for the previous ones, Akinari turns to the military chronicles.[4] When Uesugi Noritada drove Ashikaga Shigeuji from Kamakura, forcing him to take refuge in Shimōsa, life in eastern Japan was upset, much as described in the tale and in Akinari's historical sources. Similarly, the dispute over succession to the leadership of the Hatakeyama house was an actual occurrence.[5] **'The House Amid the Thickets'** reminds one how simple people were torn from their roots and forced to endure sorrow and bitterness, owing to the evils of a military system that they themselves had in no way created. Around villages that had once prospered weeds grew tall, and in the words of the Chinese poet, Tu Fu, 'New ghosts are wailing there now with the old, / Loudest in the dark sky of a stormy day.'[6]

To some extent the historical significance of the setting for **'The Carp That Came to My Dream,'** around Lake Biwa and the Mii Temple, has already been discussed, but several additional points deserve mention. A priest and painter by the name of Kōgi is said to have lived at the temple in the early ninth century. Also, Shinto places of worship existed here from very early times, associating the place with supernatural powers. The area calls to mind the tragic events of the late seventh century, when the Emperor Tenchi's son was deposed by his uncle, the Emperor Temmu. During the Heian period many court nobles and ladies would visit the famous temples around the southern part of the lake, and according to legend, here Lady Murasaki, inspired by the moon over Ishiyama Temple, wrote *The Tale of Genji*. Awareness of these details adds considerably to the reader's appreciation of Akinari's account of Kōgi's mysterious dream.

Toward the end of the middle ages great barons vied for control of the nation's economic resources, and fierce battles raged between competing leaders. The war cries of massive armies signalled the close of the period. Oda Nobunaga (1534-82) intelligently used new techniques and weapons to bring half of Japan under his rule. Toyotomi Hideyoshi (1536-98), a man of humble birth, skillfully completed the work of unification. After he died, however, his vassals fell to quarrelling, and Tokugawa Ieyasu (1542-1616) emerged as victor. Ieyasu's successors governed Japan peacefully and without serious challenge during the early modern period, and urban centres such as Osaka and Edo prospered and grew. Still, memory of the past lingered on, and the events of the late sixteenth century continued to evoke shock and horror.

These times figure in **'Bird of Paradise,'** which is set when 'the land of Peace and Calm had long been true to its name,' in the seventeenth or eighteenth century. Spending a night on Mt Kōya, Muzen and his son are reminded of earlier days. 'The Mound of Beasts,' in Kyoto, which is mentioned at the end of the tale, stands for the way in which the grotesque conflict between Hideyoshi and his nephew, Hidetsugu, still gripped people's imagination.

Hideyoshi, one of the most remarkable autocrats of the time, like Henry VIII, failed not on the battlefield but in the bedroom. He fathered only two children, both born late in life. The first died in infancy, and because there seemed little chance of his having another, he appointed his nephew, Hidetsugu, as heir. To Hideyoshi's chagrin, the young man led a wanton life and killed men for sport, earning a reputation as 'the murdering regent.' When a second son was born, however, Hideyoshi wished him to be his successor, and relations with his nephew quickly deteriorated. In 1595 Hideyoshi ordered his nephew, together with a small retinue of his followers, to retire to Mt Kōya, and he commanded that they die by ritual suicide. Hidetsugu and his young companions disembowelled themselves, with one of their number beheading the others, and Hideyoshi's emissary performed the same service for the last of the condemned men. The nephew's family was then cruelly slain. His wife, ladies-in-waiting, and small children were dressed in their best clothes and dragged through Kyoto to the common execution ground. Here, on a gibbet, Hidetsugu's head was exposed, and the children were killed in front of their mothers' eyes. All were buried at Sanjō in a common grave marked as 'The Mound of Beasts.'[7] Such were the events that Muzen mulled over following his confrontation on Mt Kōya with Hidetsugu's ghostly entourage. In handling this material, moreover, Akinari had to be very circumspect, because it could be regarded as treasonous to write frivolously about events in which the Tokugawa family or other prominent military houses of that time played a part.

Long before Hideyoshi's rise to power, during the period of the fifth Ashikaga shogun, the Akamatsu family of the province of Kibi became embroiled in one of the many succession disputes of the middle ages. This family was descended from a noble line of warriors who had fought with distinction and found great favour with Ashikaga leaders. When the fifth shogun decided in favour of one claimant, he was assassinated by the other—Akamatsu Mitsusuke—who then fled to his home castle. The deceased shogun's supporters besieged him, and seeing that his cause was hopeless, he committed suicide. Izawa Shōtarō, in **'The Caldron of Kibitsu,'** though a fictional character, is said to have been descended from a samurai who had survived this siege and escaped to a village, where he lived as a peasant. The story itself has little to do with actual events, but significantly enough, Akinari places it against the background of one of the incidents that undermined the authority of the Ashikaga shogun and led to a century of internecine war, thus paving the way eventually for the rise of the Tokugawa family.

Many famous places figure in **'The Lust of the White Serpent,'** making it one of the richest of all the tales in terms of historical geography. The cape of Sano is mentioned in the *Man'yōshū*, as are the mountains of Yoshino. The names of the emperors Jimmu and Nintoku are associated with the Kumano area, to the holy spots of which court nobles and members of the imperial family often made pilgrimage. The Tsuba Market and Hase Temple appear frequently in Heian literature. The Dōjōji Temple, of Komatsubara, is immortalised in the *nō* and on the *kabuki* stage.[8] Although no date is given, internal evidence shows that the tale was set in the Heian period. In spite of the dearth of names of actual persons and events, **'The Lust of the White Serpent'** thus reveals Akinari's sense of history and the passage of time.

Similarly, no specific date is mentioned in **'The Blue Hood.'** But the Zen priest, Kaian, was an actual person who lived in the fifteenth century, and the Daichūji Temple is a real place. The Oyamas were descended from the Fujiwara line and had settled on a manor in the vicinity of Tonda, flourishing as one of the strong local families. Such use of historical detail heightens interest in the priest who is fatally attracted to a beautiful boy, his erotic lust for corpses, and the mysterious change that Kaian witnesses.

Oka Sanai, the principal character of **'Wealth and Poverty,'** is also a historical personage. His master, Gamō Ujisato, served as one of Hideyoshi's comrades in arms. Both men fought with distinction for Nobunaga, and as a reward Ujisato received one of Nobunaga's daughters in marriage; furthermore, he was baptised as a Christian. Later, Hideyoshi assigned him to Aizu, in the east, and it is recorded that he feared Ujisato and eventually had him poisoned. Historical anecdotes tell how Ujisato's famous retainer, Sanai, loved to display his great wealth, how people criticised him for this, and how he rewarded his follower's frugality in a way that suggests Akinari's treatment in the tale.

But more generally speaking, gold is the main subject of the tale. This metal in ancient Japan was valued chiefly for its decorative qualities. During the middle ages it took on a religious meaning, symbolising the Western Paradise to believers of the Pure Land sect of Buddhism or Zen enlightenment to adherents of this school. Not until the Momoyama period and the introduction of new mining techniques from China did it acquire economic significance as a basis for financial transactions. Even then, gold coins such as those minted at the end of the sixteenth and early seventeenth century, which Sanai gave to his follower, were not very practical as currency and were used primarily as rewards or prizes.[9] In the final passage Akinari cautiously touches upon the political situation of the time and mentions the famous generals of the day. Hideyoshi's period of ascendancy, it is said, would be short, and an auspicious prophecy tells that the Tokugawa family would bring both peace and prosperity to the realm, in a passage perhaps designed to mollify would-be censors.

PHILOSOPHY AND RELIGION

Philosophy and religion deal basically with the three questions of where man comes from, where he goes, and how he should spend his life on earth. Traditionally, in Japan Shinto thought and beliefs suggested for the first that the gods gave man life. Buddhism taught regarding the second that when a person died he might attain salvation in paradise. Confucian doctrine, pertaining to the third, urged everyone in moral and ethical terms to live in harmony with his brothers and with the universe. As expressed in a phrase popular in Akinari's day, 'The three teachings are one.' Besides these three main systems of philosophy and religion, the role of Taoism and *Shingaku* deserves mention. Akinari's tales were written for a society in which people felt close to the world of nature and to the gods of the nation. Prayer, music, ritual, and the spiritual life were still valued more highly than the practice of business. Increasingly, however, emphasis on commerce and wealth tended to weaken old traditions, and in a large degree Akinari wished to counteract such developments and strengthen the spiritual quality in national life.

First of all, the vital and emotive side of the tales involved Shinto beliefs. Many able men wished to break away from the constraints of orthodox Confucian teachings. They put renewed faith in native gods, who were chiefly semi-divine and often benevolent local deities and existed in a hierarchy leading up to the imperial family's ancestral spirit. In an unbroken chain, each individual was linked to the rest of society, and time continued from the original creation as if ripples of water from a primordial splash. Life welled and surged without need or plan, in an abundance of forms held together by a throbbing, vital impulse.

The school of national learning served as the scholarly and philosophical arm of Shinto beliefs, and one of the momentous questions of the time involved the matter of sovereignty. Without the crown there would be no England, and without the emperor there would be no Japan. In '**White Peak,**' where Akinari deals with the role of the emperor and state, he reaffirms the Japanese idea of 'one line forever,' and he emphasises the divine right of the imperial family. As noted earlier, Sutoku takes the Confucian point of view that government rests on public opinion, whereas Saigyō argues in favour of national customs and traditions that began in the dawn of history and carry magical significance. The unique character of Japan consists in having a sovereign who traces his lineage to divine origins. According to Akinari's belief, the imperial family must be venerated, Shinto ceremonies observed, and the sacred shrines supported. Indeed, after Akinari's time, partly owing to the influence of '**White Peak,**' Sutoku's spirit was enshrined in Kyoto in an effort to atone for the suffering that he had endured.

Elsewhere, Akinari touches on Shinto shrines and rituals. In '**The Caldron of Kibitsu,**' for instance, he mentions rites involving fire and water. Boiling water was stirred with a wand of dwarf bamboo leaves, and the drops of moisture that rose from the swirling mass were thought to contain the essence of divinity. The singing sound of the caldron was used to prophesy future events. Such caldrons are mentioned in early reports of trial by ordeal, and in shamanistic terms these rituals symbolise a sacred marriage between the god of fire and the goddess of water. Bands of mountain cenobites, known as *yamabushi,* associated the boiling caldron with the mother's womb. To enter it denoted purification by undergoing the pains of hell and achieving rebirth to a higher life. The shrine of the Yamato clan deities figures incidentally in '**The Lust of the White Serpent.**'

In contrast to the Shinto aspect of the tales, the Confucian side deals primarily with morality and ethics. Despite his association with the Shinto movement, which was gaining in power and influence, Akinari shunned the excesses of the school of national learning, thinking of himself as an independent scholar. He upheld the basic virtues of the Confucian classics—loyalty, honour, duty—much in the samurai tradition of his father. He stressed such values as stability and frugality. He respected life and felt deep concern for future generations. He criticised all forms of selfishness and personal indulgence. But his Confucian beliefs were tempered by the conviction that the gods and spirits still flourished and that a man who lacked faith and piety risked madness or death. To him the Confucian calling entailed not sterile didacticism but moral intensity, as exemplified by the ideals that Samon and Soemon share in '**Chrysanthemum Tryst.**' Similarly, the desire to turn over a new leaf, which Katsushirō, Toyoo, and the aberrant monk of **'The Blue Hood'** possess in common, suggest that a person who resists the forces of decline and restores his innate purity and goodness might contribute to the general welfare and help to arrest social decay. This Confucian quality helped bring about the Meiji Restoration and the modernisation of Japan. One might reshape an individual or a civilisation without annihilating it.

Traces of Taoist thought and attitudes also appear in the tales, serving to impart an element of mystery and romance. Oftentimes, however, it is virtually impossible to distinguish Taoist ideas from those of Shinto.[10] Akinari extolled the spontaneous man's innate desire to follow nature and transcend the illusory and unreal distinctions on which all human systems of morality were based. Travelling as a free spirit, living simply, acting naturally, and taking things easy combined with a belief in the irony of life. All living creatures were assumed to be equal. For instance, part of the basic idea in **'The Carp That Came to My Dream'** may be traced to an anecdote in the Chinese Taoist classic, *Lieh tzu,* involving a man who was fond of seagulls and every morning went into the ocean and swam about with them. Another anecdote from the same text, which tells of a man who carved a mulberry leaf out of jade and imitated nature so exquisitely that no one could distinguish his artifice from the real object, resembles Akinari's idea at the end of his carp tale.[11] The 'innocent heart,' a term used to describe Katsushirō, in the third tale, is related to the Taoist ideal of simplicity (as well as that of Shintoism), and conveys a sense of uprightness and scrupulous honesty combined with an easy-going nature. All manner of pretence is equally to be shunned. Akinari's disgust for Shōtarō, the deceitful wretch in the sixth tale, and his ambivalence toward Manago, the serpent spirit of the seventh tale, remind the reader that passion throws out a myriad tentacles. It destroys peace and reduces the mind to a state of turmoil. It has to be quelled in order to maintain one's self-control. Whereas Shōtarō fails to curb his natural appetites, Toyoo succeeds, though only at enormous cost.

Akinari's values and standards were also influenced by *Shingaku,* or 'Heart-learning.' This doctrine began among merchants in Osaka and later spread to other areas, gaining adherents among all classes of people.[12] Although basically Confucian in its emphasis on how man ought to live in the present, it embraced Shinto and Buddhist ideas, as well. Virtues such as hard work, thrift, and ambition were emphasised, though men were enjoined to avoid the extremes of greed and avarice. Warfare, however, held little romantic attraction. As Akinari writes in **'Wealth and Poverty,'** 'Brave men whose business is with bows and arrows have forgotten that wealth forms the cornerstone of the nation, and they have followed a disgusting policy.' His spirit of

gold shows startling resemblance to the God of Wealth, a curious and grotesque folk-deity who holds sheaves of rice, as if to indicate that worldly riches need not be evil. Obviously, then, Akinari's concept of morality, despite its basically Confucian orientation, has little connection with narrowly orthodox views but rather displayed a broad, eclectic spirit.

Buddhist philosophy imparts a universal quality to the tales and contributes much to their subtlety. Akinari's concept of reality shows features of the teachings of the Tendai sect, or T'ien-t'ai, as this distinctively Chinese school that may be related to Taoism was called in the country of its origin. Akinari accepts the Buddhist belief (though to be sure it is shared by the Taoists) that life is but a dream and a shadow. Because people are trapped in the wheel of life and death and endure manifold afflictions, men practice spiritual cultivation—as Priest Kaian in **'The Blue Hood'** forces the aberrant monk to do—in order to gain religious salvation and destroy the illusions that cause suffering. Such meditation was based on the doctrine of 'concentration and insight' (*shikan,* or in Chinese, *chih kuan*), and it required one to silence his active thoughts and to reflect on the true nature of matter and phenomena. Mind was thought to dominate over matter. Man might control his destiny by meditation and monastic discipline, as taught in the Chinese commentaries on the Lotus Sutra.[13]

This philosophy permeates Heian literature,[14] medieval poetry, the *nō* theatre, and *haiku,* as well as Akinari's tales. Indeed, at times the Tendai teachings and those of Christianity seem quite parallel. Milton's lines, 'The Mind is its own place, and in itself / Can make a Heaven of Hell, a Hell of Heaven,' and his idea that 'real and substantial liberty' comes from within rather than from without man's heart,[15] resemble Akinari's assertion that, 'A slothful mind creates a monster, a rigorous one enjoys the fruit of the Buddha.' Akinari believed that without religious discipline, however individualistic a form it might take, man could not survive spiritual crisis, and he accepted the idea that sorrow was inherent in human life, a point of view hardly foreign to the Puritan or Calvinist mind. Although by Akinari's time these ideas were interpreted in Shinto terms and figured prominently in Motoori's writings on classical Japanese literature, they stemmed originally from Buddhist doctrines.

Akinari and other learned men of the eighteenth century agreed that Buddhism as a religion was useless and that the clergy was degenerate. Nevertheless, the underlying themes and imagery of the tales suggest that this faith still dominated the popular imagination. Recurring Buddhist images, such as bells, drums, cymbals, and conch shells, tell of the resonant quality of the universe and indicate auditory and musical harmony. When these reassuring sounds are far away, as in the first, fifth, and eighth tales, one feels an eerie sense of foreboding. The bird of paradise, whose song is Buddha's law, in the fifth tale conveys an apocalyptic sense of miracle. In Akinari's day temples remained powerful landowners and enjoyed political patronage. Those that had been burned at the end of the middle ages, such as the Mii Temple, were rebuilt, and they continued to attract devout pilgrims.

Just as the heavenly bodies revolved, so too might dead souls return to the world of the living, though understandably their form would be altered. The past is never forgotten; the future cannot be ignored. The cosmos itself is constantly changing, and even the soul is subject to metamorphosis. In a Buddhist sense, Miyagi, of **'The House Amid the Thickets,'** is both a reincarnation of the legendary Tegona of old and also a separate individual. Owing to the many changes in Japanese society, faith may have been reduced to a vestige of former days, but Buddhism, together with Shinto, Confucian, and other beliefs, still played a role scarcely less impressive than that of the Church in the Western world. Once having separately discerned the main philosophical and religious elements of the tales, however, the reader must let them commingle and re-emerge in a harmonious union of these beliefs, which the tales represented for an age when myth still had magical power over poets and ordinary people.

THE ART OF FICTION

In the preface to the tales Akinari briefly expresses his views on the art of fiction. Praising *Water Margin* and *The Tale of Genji*—the most widely known works of Chinese and Japanese narrative prose—as monuments of creative imagination, he suggests that they are true to life because they embody deep feeling and evoke an intimate sense of the past. Without being explicit, he compares his own tales to these older masterpieces, inviting readers to enjoy what he has created. He points out that although his tales are somewhat fanciful in subject matter, they show a degree of unity, and he hopes that people will not be misled into thinking that his stories are literally true, so that he need not fear being punished, as Lo Kuan-chung and Lady Murasaki had supposedly been, for deceiving people.

The remarks in his preface reveal an interest in the theory of literature and the uses of fiction, one which lasted for the rest of his life. He first wrote of his views on this subject in the 1770s in an essay that does not survive. Later on, in 1793, when editing Kamo Mabuchi's work on the *Ise monogatari (The Tales of Ise),*[16] he told how the art of fiction had flourished in China and Japan. He explained that the objectives were the same both in Chinese narrative prose and in Japanese tales and romances. Writers wishing to lament their personal unhappiness about the world they lived in showed their feelings in the form of nostalgia for times past. In his own words, 'When an author sees the nation flourishing, he knows that it must eventually decay, like the bloom of a fragrant flower. When he considers what happens in the end to leaders of state, he privately laughs at their folly. He points out to people who might seek longevity what finally became of Urashima Tarō's bejewelled box. He makes foolish men who struggle to collect rare treasures feel ashamed of themselves. He tries to avoid the desire for fame, composing his innocent tales about events of the past for which there are no sources.'[17] Akinari believed that literature is a vehicle by which to express in a highly sublimated form one's discontent with society, and his views remind the Western reader of such works as Shelley's 'Defence of Poetry,' Wordsworth's *Preface to the Lyrical Ballads,* and James's *Art of Fiction.*

Nevertheless, no conflict arose between the demands of art for art's sake and art intended primarily as a means of communicating truth. For Akinari the two were inseparable, and he embraced both, believing that Lady Murasaki and Lo Kuanchung had done likewise. Fiction heightened one's consciousness and carried the soul to a spiritual union with higher reality. In Buddhist terms art was ecstasy, and suggested a mind or heart wonderful and profound beyond human thought. As in Tendai and Zen philosophy, the human heart became its own creator, intuitively forming a mental vision of reality. Accordingly, art did not merely imitate nature; rather, the poet shaped it, as the sculptor did his material or the painter his forms. Artistic excellence depended on the quality of the poet's vision and the level of his spiritual development or awareness. One cut away what was gross, straightened what was crooked, and lightened what was heavy. In the act of literary expression one encompassed truth and knowledge and communicated it concisely and accurately within the limits of one's understanding. Beauty was not subordinate to truth but was an intrinsic part of it. Art was not the handmaiden of religion: the two were as if the wings of a single bird, both of which were needed to fly.

Where did such views come from? On the one hand, Akinari knew of Lady Murasaki's famous passage about the art of fiction, and on the other hand he was familiar with the remarks of the ancient Chinese historian, Ssu-ma Ch'ien. Lady Murasaki herself combined the idea of art for its own sake and art as a medium for conveying truth. While stressing the practical value of literature, she wrote of how fiction might deeply move the reader and how the author himself might be stirred by 'an emotion so passionate that he can no longer keep it shut up in his heart.'[18] Behind Lady Murasaki's views on fiction lay Buddhist and Chinese philosophy, as well as earlier Japanese essays such as the *kana* preface to the *Kokinshū.*[19] Just as the lotus flower grows above the turbid waters, so does purity and truth rise above evil. Fiction might deal with 'lies' or describe evil as well as good, but its ultimate aim is to express truth and help people in their spiritual development.

Actually, as Akinari realised, Lady Murasaki's theory of literature does not contradict Ssu-ma Ch'ien's. According to both views art involves morality, and literature has a social function, though to be sure, in practice Lady Murasaki shows an unsurpassed aesthetic awareness. Utilitarian concerns are as important as strong emotions deeply felt. In Ssu-ma Ch'ien's words, authors of great literary works are aggrieved men who, 'Poured forth their anger and dissatisfaction,' because they feel 'a rankling in their hearts.' Being unable to accomplish what they wished, they write about ancient matters 'in order to pass on their thoughts to future generations.'[20] The reader is immediately reminded of Lady Murasaki's understanding of literature as the outcry of the passionate heart.

In addition to being directly familiar with Ssu-ma Ch'ien and Lady Murasaki's ideas, Akinari admired a famous preface to the *Water Margin,* which was written by a late-Ming Chinese scholar named Li Cho-wu (1527-1602). Like Akinari, he too stressed the importance of profound feeling and asserted that good authors are always motivated by 'anger and dissatisfaction.' 'To write without deep emotion,' he said 'was the equivalent to shivering without suffering from the cold or groaning without feeling sick.'[21] In a flowery passage at the end of his preface, Li explains that a romance should be a serious work, which men must read in order to understand the true significance of life. When vexed and aggrieved, the writer turns to romance and criticises injustice by means of creating an idealised universe. One recalls Dickens's view that the creative faculty must have complete possession of the author or poet and master his whole life.

Deeply influenced by earlier Chinese and Japanese writers, Akinari embodies in almost every tale a typically Confucian moral, a Buddhist concept of fate, and a Shinto belief in the power of the impassioned heart. Virtue must be rewarded and vice punished, in the present as in ages past. If a man is greedy, lustful, or overly ambitious, he might lose what he loves most, suffer great hardship, and experience deep emotional pain. Avarice brings only sorrow and misfortune. Man must also beware of woman's spell, for she might use her charms to destroy him.

Akinari's basic ideas about the art of fiction contrast somewhat with those of Motoori. Whereas Motoori taught that the purpose of the novel, tale, or romance was, 'Not to preach morality but to evoke a certain pattern of emotional sensibility,'[22] Akinari tried to balance artistic and utilitarian ends. He believed that the suffering previous authors endured for their art was worth-while, and he implied that his tales might stand comparison with the best work of his illustrious predecessors. Combining bold assertiveness and defensive humility, Akinari's views on fiction contribute to the moral integrity and the sense of beauty that distinguish his tales from lesser works.

WORLD OF THE SUPERNATURAL

'The music of Heaven. . . . Wordless, it delights the mind,' wrote the Taoist sage, Chuang-tzu.[23] On the one hand Akinari's tales deal with reality and reflect the natural world, but on the other they soar to a loftier realm, where ghosts and spirits freely appear and men encounter inscrutable forces. Out of a precarious balance between the sensory world and the realm of the unknown 'the music of heaven' emerges. To the travelling priest, distraught scholar, wayward husband, artist, pilgrim, or impressionable youth the shadows of the imagination may arise in music and dance. They may be heard and understood, Akinari suggests, by a simple and spontaneous man in a situation highly charged with emotion.

Before all else, the supernatural side of the tales was intended to attract the reader. The original subtitle carried the words *Kinko kaidan,* or 'New and Old Tales of Wonder,' inviting the public to enter a world charged with spectral activity and haunted by gods and spirits. Far from the reassuring notes of bells and trumpets, where Buddhist chants and ringing staves could not be heard, magical sounds fill the air. Matter and energy become fused in a miraculous union of man and shade. Whatever the mind might imagine becomes real, and man gains a sense of mystic vision and illumination, as if the soul suddenly takes light from a supreme being. Like all mystics, Saigyō and the other men in *Ugetsu monogatari* vividly remember their confrontation with spirits that are at once dead and alive. In each tale the climatic action takes place at night, the favourite time for ghosts and apparitions, when the past is turning into the future. The role of the supernatural underscores the belief that Japan was a country rich in gods and spirits.

Although Akinari's ghosts and other worldly creatures show an animal nature that defied control and mastery, they have neither the bleeding skulls nor luminous hands of the spirits of Gothic novels; nor are they headless apparitions clad in armour or eerie forms extending phosphorescent claws toward the victim's throat. Rather, they are at once more primitive and more modern—to curb their power one needs prayer, meditation, and purity of heart. In spite of certain gloomy or even terrifying details, they leave on one an impression not of ugliness but of beauty. Above all, Akinari believed in his spirits and wished to convince his readers that the gods still lived and that the earth was charged with their elemental force. By evoking the gods and spirits he might illumine what was dark within himself and also within the reader.

Stories of ghosts, genies, demons, miracles, and animals that influence human events have always held universal appeal. In China, despite Confucian exhortation that the spiritual world is not a proper topic for human inquiry, tales and anecdotes about supernatural beings are as old as recorded literature. Indeed, the *ch'i lin,* or 'unicorn,' a benevolent spiritual animal, is said to have appeared as an omen to the mother of Confucius before her son's birth. According to legend, a charioteer later wounded a similar beast, foretelling the sage's death. Marvellous creatures appear freely in Taoist writings. Notices of occult beings occur in early dynastic histories. The oldest separate collection of supernatural tales was compiled around the end of the third century AD. In T'ang times the literary tale of the marvellous attained maturity, and from early times Chinese examples inspired Japanese writers.

Myth and legend in Japan expressed belief in the existence of spirits. Fairies and semi-celestial beings were thought to roam about the woods, mountains, seaside, waterfalls, and lakes, appearing in the spring haze or autumn mist. Great deities might journey in search of a loved one's soul or visit palaces under the sea in quest of a lost talisman. Various powers were attributed to the benevolent gods of heaven and earth and also to malicious spirits. Other mysterious forces were felt too vaguely to be personified. One worshipped the forces of good and used various spells to exorcise those of evil. Omens, divination, dreams, and oracles taught people how to live in a world filled with magical power. A verse in *The Tales of Ise,* which suggested several incidents in Akinari's tales, describes how evil spirits had an affinity for abandoned dwellings:

> *Mugura oite*
> *Aretaru yado no*
> *Uretaki wa*
> *Kari ni mo oni no*
> *Sudaku nari keri*

> When the weeds grow tall,
> And a tumble-down house
> Stands awesomely,
> You should beware that demons
> Are swarming there inside.[24]

Wherever shadows were deep, spirits and phantoms were sure to lurk, as indicated in a variety of early and medieval works. Some beliefs and stories were of native origin, and others came from China or even India.

As mentioned earlier, three centuries before Akinari's time new collections of Chinese short stories were brought to Japan, giving fresh impetus to the development of the supernatural tale. After the art of landscape painting was perfected, storytellers tried all the harder to cloak the natural world in a garb of mystery, inviting the reader to exercise his imagination and depicting a universe full of mysterious beings and forces. Consequently, in Akinari's day the Chinese influence in painting and the popularity of the ghostly tale went hand in hand. Japanese collections of supernatural tales were directly inspired by Chinese examples and appeared in several forms of narrative prose, notably the *kana* books, the tales of the floating world, and of course the reading books.

Especially after the appearance of *Otogi bōko* (*The Bedside Storyteller*) in 1666, a number of similar works were issued, leading eventually to Akinari's tales. **Ugetsu monogatari,** however, differs from earlier collections in a number of ways. One finds an emphasis on the human reaction rather than on the sensational appearance of the phantom or apparition, a tendency already found in *Saikaku shokoku-banashi* (*Saikaku's Tales from Various Provinces*). Compared to Akinari's, the earlier works are more anecdotal in nature—like the Buddhist narratives and stories of the middle ages. They typically resemble a sutra turned topsy-turvy: the supernatural event comes first and the moral follows, but the instructional feature of the scriptures nevertheless remains. True enough, in Akinari's tales the moral function has by no means disappeared, but the story stands as an independent work of literary art, similar to a well-wrought ghostly tale by Henry James, or other Western masters. Moreover, Akinari strove to add features that appealed to the scholarly interests of readers who had hitherto scorned popular fiction as unworthy of their attention. Still, at the same time that he paid careful attention to literary craft and scholastic respectability, Akinari (like the Christian mystics and the neo-Platonists) believed in the occult, the supernatural, and the transcendental. To appreciate his viewpoint one must put aside rational criticism and transport himself backward in time to a dimly lit world, where moonlight as the main source of nocturnal illumination was intense and pure. Here, as Saikaku said, 'Everyone is a ghost. Anything in the world is possible.'[25] Or, in Akinari's own words, in the darkness, when the flickering oil lamp dies, 'Demons might appear and consort with men, and humans fear not to mingle with spirits.' Then when the light is restored, 'The gods and devils disappear and hide somewhere, leaving no trace. . . .'[26] Until the end of his life Akinari insisted that the power of the supernatural was real, and he based his argument on personal experience as well as on evidence from earlier literature. As with a Japanese garden, which represents not only nature itself but its idealization, the tales embody not only a view of reality but a vision of its essence. Akinari's reader finds himself ineluctably on the edge of a magic circle, ready to be drawn up by unseen powers in a vortex of light and song.

LITERARY STYLE

By the early middle ages a literary style that mixed both Chinese characters and Japanese phonetic symbols known as *kana* had become the standard form in narrative prose. Akinari's tales were in this style, which until the modern period was used primarily in novels, short stories, and popular histories. Many of the principal words were written with Chinese characters used according to their meaning, while particles, suffixes, and some semantic elements were expressed phonetically. Known descriptively as the *Wakan konkōbun,* or the 'Chinese Japanese mixed style,' it differed from the form of court poetry and Heian romance in three ways. First of all, being more straightforward, it lacked some of the elegant, poetic, and suggestive qualities of classical poetry and romance. Secondly, it permitted additional Chinese constructions, which allowed for more rigour and precision but which also demanded greater learning for its mastery. Lastly, it admitted as much colloquial grammar and vocabulary as the author fancied. In spite of influence from the spoken language, however, the mixed style remained a literary tool, largely divorced from ordinary speech.

For several reasons this style had begun to change by Akinari's time. First of all, popular drama and the rhetoric of the recital hall had a strong influence on narrative prose. Secondly, the revival in learning led by such scholars as Mabuchi and Motoori, who deliberately reverted to the classical mode of literary composition, led to fresh ideas about appropriateness in style. Yet further impetus came with the study of Chinese language and literature. Consequently, Akinari pursued a dualistic ideal. While aiming at a pure and lucid classical style, he wished to convey a sense of plain speech with a Chinese flavour. The result was a variation of the mixed style, known as *gazoku-bun,* 'elegant and plain style,' or *giko-bun,* 'neoclassical style.'

Akinari realised that overly refined expression often fails to convey human sentiment, whereas simple and plain language might communicate such feelings with directness. He tried to combine the good qualities of elegance and simplicity while resisting the weight of blind tradition and refusing to be a prisoner of archaic forms. In the tales everything is expressed as one might wish to talk, but yet more dignified, attractive, and interesting. The result is a powerful and flexible tool able to impart the subtle message of the human heart and reflect the profound wisdom of the ancient sages. Better than anyone of his generation, Akinari mixed the stateliness of the old with the freshness of the new in a uniquely successful style.

By convention in Akinari's day the beginning of a tale or play was usually noble in taste, musical in tone, and composed with an ear for poetry. Ideally, the introductory section gave the reader a telescoped view of the whole. For instance, the opening passage of **'White Peak'** adumbrates not only the theme of the first story but also that of the entire collection—a quest for enlightenment. Likewise, **'Chrysanthemum Tryst'** begins with an imitative and sonorous passage that hints at what was to follow. Then in the body of the tale a plainer tone is employed, and at the end a short summary sentence resumes the earlier style. The rhetorical manner of classical Chinese alternates with the simpler rhythms of Japanese poetry and romance, much as the skylark soaring and diving. Akinari often strove for special effects at the beginning in order to enhance the quality of elegance and attain the desired balance.

Nevertheless, elegance in excess leads to frigidity. By capturing the word or phrase that gives the precise effect he wanted, and by adding an occasional light touch or a deft bit of irony, Akinari avoided this fault. In **'Chrysanthemum Tryst,'** an old warrior grumbles ironically to his youthful companion about how young people are too timid. Throughout **'The Carp That Came to My Dream'** Kōgi is treated with great whimsy. In **'Wealth and Poverty'** Sanai's droll tone creates an atmosphere of lightness, despite the heavy nature of the subject. Akinari tried to convey a full measure of the absurdity and vulnerability of human nature.

For the most part, however, the style remains severe, formal, and erudite, largely owing to the way Akinari used his various literary sources and employed his personal feelings and experiences. Beneath the plain surface of the prose an elaborate beauty lies hidden, reminiscent of that in the *nō* drama or the tea ceremony. The more unwieldy the subject, the more delicately he refined it, as in **'Bird of Paradise.'** Here the material is controlled so strictly that the uninformed reader can scarcely imagine the deeds and events that Hidetsugu's apparition represents. The story overshadows real life, as the moon may eclipse the sun.

Certain mechanical aspects of style also add to the total effect. Most of all, one recalls the cursive, calligraphic script of the original edition, which was carved on wooden blocks and printed on double leaves of soft, hand-made paper. Many abbreviations are used, along with a number of extra *kana* symbols that were not officially considered as part of the syllabary. When the text was printed in movable type, all of this became lost. Punctuation in the original consists simply of a small oval sign that serves as a full stop, comma, semicolon, and question mark. *A waka* verse of five, or a *haiku* of three lines in English takes only a single, slightly indented column in the woodblock text. Because quotation marks are not used, the reader is often free to decide whether a given passage should be dialogue or narrative. To the uninitiated person it is hard to tell where one syllable ends and the next begins or whether a certain symbol is Japanese or Chinese. The hand-printed text represents a work of art, in some ways plain and simple and yet complicated and demanding.

The Western reader deserves to see the calligraphic form, even though he may never learn how the script is deciphered.

Usually Akinari's style was clear and lucid, at least as traditional Japanese literary texts go, but some points remain puzzling. Was the opening tale a first- or a third-person narrative? Was Akinari really telling about Saigyō, or for artistic purposes was he assuming the personage of Saigyō? The tale begins with words attributed to the twelfth-century poet, but later the name is used in a manner that might indicate either a personal narrative or an omniscient narrator. After the ghosts of Hidetsugu and his followers appear in **'Bird of Paradise,'** a similar change in tone occurs. But some degree of vagueness and lack of explicitness is common in traditional Japanese texts. This adds to the appeal of the work and invites the reader's active participation in recreating it in his own mind.

Concerning how Akinari combined Chinese and Japanese stylistic elements, one recalls how the playwright Chikamatsu Monzaemon (1653-1725) wrote that with Chinese hair styles people used Japanese combs, and with the native coiffure they did the reverse, so closely were the two cultures mixed. The same is true of Akinari's diction. Far beyond normal needs, he dotted his text with curious and difficult Chinese characters. These are explained in a Japanese gloss written by the right side of each line. Oftentimes, the diction seems fanciful or even outlandish, with archaic expressions from the *Man'yōshū* and colloquialisms found only in Chinese vernacular novels and tales. But Akinari's mastery of syntax pleased and surprised the reader of his day, though demanding of him the patience and concentration needed to read poetry.

The preface, however, being written entirely in one double leaf of literary Chinese, without any gloss at all, presents stylistic problems of its own. Although it may have been common knowledge in Akinari's day, how many people know nowadays who Lo Kuan-chung is or why his children are supposed to have been deaf? Unless one is familiar with Chinese classics, how could he guess that the phrase 'crying pheasants and quarrelling dragons' is derived from such works as *The Book of Changes*? Few Western readers are familiar with the legend that Lady Murasaki was sent to hell. The Chinese style of the preface and the information it contains was intended to give comfort to scholars and gentlemen who might be tempted to read the tales. The technique of using such a preface that embodies allusions to previous works enhances Akinari's style and marks it as part of the mainstream of early modern Japanese literature. The only recourse for the Western reader is to have copious textual notes and steadfast patience.

Of the two contrasting elements of style—the elegant and stately neoclassicism and plain speech tempered

with a Chinese flavour—the first prevails over the second. A curious mosaic is the result, rich in rhetorical devices from earlier prose and poetry. The formal cadence of Chinese classics, pillow-words from early Japanese poetry, and expressions that echo *The Tale of Genji* all helped Akinari to achieve the desired combination of lyric and narrative qualities. Frequently, decorative elements form images and metaphors. Many of these are quite natural, as when heavy dew is compared to a steady drizzle of rain (a figure found in *The Tale of Genji*). But others are more difficult and arcane. When Sutoku's life in retirement, for instance, is likened to dwelling 'in the Grove of Jewels, or on faraway Kushe Mountain,' knowledge of Chinese classics is needed to understand that the emperor had abdicated and continued to live in dignified circumstances. Ordinary images and obscure literary allusions both serve to intensify the mood, the former by adding intimacy and familiarity, the latter by suggesting depth and profundity. In addition, such devices as the rhythmic progression of numbers near the beginning of **'Bird of Paradise'** and elsewhere are intended as a decorative technique to afford extra pleasure for the attentive reader. Acrostics, logograms, puzzles, riddles, and all manner of play on words have long been popular in Japan.

At times the cadence breaks into song, in a union of poetry and music. To savour the full effect, the tales must be read aloud. Like a *nō* play or a Gregorian chant, the flow of sound rises and falls in a solemn yet lyrical melody, because the texture of the language more nearly resembles that of traditional drama or poetry than that of modern prose fiction. Indeed, musical elements, such as rhythm, harmony, and symmetry, contribute greatly to the stylistic excellence of the tales. But image, metaphor, and music lead one back to myth and allegory. Akinari's style was ideal for spinning parables around an event and for emphasising the frailties of man. To find the ultimate meaning of the tales one must return to the content.

CHINESE INFLUENCE

Just as during the past century the Western influence has been pervasive, so in Akinari's time little remained untouched by the civilisation of China. The Four Books and the Five Classics of the Confucian tradition comprised the basic course of study in the private schools. Such texts were learned by rote and held in respect, much as the family Bible in the West. The wisdom of these classical works went unquestioned, and advanced education was built on its foundation. Quite naturally, Akinari was indebted not only to the basic Confucian texts but also to various other Chinese sources—dynastic histories, T'ang poetry and prose, Ming fiction and essays.

His indebtedness to the Confucian classics shows up in many distinctive expressions scattered throughout the tales. Some of these may have come from his direct knowledge of Chinese sources; yet others were derived indirectly. For instance, 'the crying pheasants and quarrelling dragons' of the preface appear not only in *The Book of Changes* and the *Shu ching,* two pre-Confucian classics, but also in the preface to the Ming collection, *New Tales for Lamplight,* which Akinari admired. Such phrases reflect his broad learning and his taste for classical scholarship, which he shared with other fine minds of the eighteenth century. As one would expect, he was familiar with the *Analects* and *The Book of Mencius,* a pair of texts that until the twentieth century guided men on a path of upright behaviour and taught that human beings are part of a natural order that pervades the entire universe. The laconic words and provocative ideas of Confucius and Mencius helped Akinari to convey a tone of moral urgency, a flavour of folk wisdom, and a touch of popular appeal, aiding him to achieve ready communication with his readers.

After mastering the basic books of the Confucian tradition, students in Akinari's day moved on to refined literature and instructive history. One is therefore hardly surprised to discover in his tales a number of passages indebted to Ssu-ma Ch'ien's *Shih chi* (*Records of the Grand Historian of China*), as well as other titles of the period of the warring states and the early imperial age. In particular, the scepticism and mysticism of the classical Taoist philosophers met with new popularity around Akinari's time, as previously mentioned. Bashō and other *haiku* poets emulated the unrestrained fancy of the Taoist masters, and the scholars of the national learning also accepted such influence in the formulation of their ideas and the development of their style. Wherever Akinari extols the beauty of nature or describes mystery and surprise, the *Tao-te-ching, Chuang-tzu,* and *Lieh-tzu* are never far removed. A measure of Akinari's wry sense of humour comes from Taoist sources.

The influence of T'ang prose and poetry and that of Ming and Ch'ing painting are also obvious, though they come partly through intermediate sources. In Akinari's day the most widely read anthology of T'ang poets was periodically reprinted and extravagantly admired. The Japanese painters who called themselves *bunjin,* or 'literary men,' some of whom were Akinari's close friends and associates, exemplified the ideals and objectives of Li Po and Tu Fu. Like the artists of his day, Akinari practiced calligraphy, poetry, and antiquarian studies. The same transcendental philosophy that these artists conveyed in purely visual terms may be found in the tales. Love of the simple life away from the noise and tension of the city, pleasant conversation with congenial friends, and a sense of the futility of worldly ambitions characterised Po Chü-i's poetry, Buson's painting, and of course Akinari's tales. Ultimately, the account of Saigyō's ascent of Mt Chigogadake owes as much to

poems and paintings of the Yangtze gorges or the mountains of Shensi and Szechuan as to actual descriptions in contemporary guidebooks or earlier literature. The same may be said of Muzen and his son's climb to Mt Kōya and of Kaian's visit to the Daichūji Temple. Largely, the inspiration of T'ang poetry and prose was transmitted through the amateur painters and authors of the Ming dynasty, who worked not to fulfill a patron's wishes but rather to cultivate human character and find personal pleasure.

No doubt the most powerful and direct literary influence, however, remains that of Ming fiction and essays. Every tale shows traces of the language, style, or plots of *New Tales for Lamplight* and the three anthologies of colloquial short stories known as the *San yen.* The long picaresque romance, *Water Margin,* served Akinari not only in his preface but also in his description of the dilapidated temple in **'The Blue Hood.'** One particularly unusual Ming source is an early sixteenth-century encyclopedic compilation entitled *Wu tsa tsu* (*Five Assorted Offerings*), by Hsieh Chao-che, a poet, scholar, official, traveller, and collector of old books and objects of art. Banned in eighteenth-century China, *Wu tsa tsu* was preserved in Japan, where owing to its breadth and scope and highly personal tone, it found special favour among artists and men of letters. Akinari consulted the work frequently in later years, as well as when he was writing the tales.

But how may one analyse the total effect of the Chinese influence on the tales? Above all, Akinari's readers expected a serious author to display his knowledge of recondite classics. They welcomed the Chinese flavour, especially that of relatively fresh and unfamiliar works, such as *Water Margin* and the *San yen.* Therefore, the student of literary history will find one sort of significance. But for the general reader several other points of view come to mind. The first of these is translation. Although one cannot apply this term rigorously to any complete story, owing to the freedom that Akinari takes, some parts of certain tales come very close to being translations. Four of these, **'Chrysanthemum Tryst,' 'The House Amid the Thickets,' 'The Carp That Came to My Dream,'** and **'The Lust of the White Serpent,'** retain much of the spirit of their Chinese models. Names are changed, scenes reset, and stylistic conventions, imagery, and allusions from classical Japanese literature are added, but these tales remain faithful to the Chinese and give somewhat the impression of a free and poetic translation or adaptation.

All of the four tales mentioned above, and especially **'The Lust of the White Serpent,'** nevertheless reveal enough Japanese elements that an uninformed reader might think of them as purely a product of native inspiration. Although the immediate source for **'The Lust of**

the White Serpent' is a Chinese story about a white snake who appears in the form of a beautiful woman and bewitches a young man, Japanese legends about serpents in human guise also existed from early times. While nearly every situation in the Chinese model has its parallel in Akinari's tale, the setting, characters, and diction are all Japanese. Furthermore, the Chinese version is more loosely constructed and designed to appeal to the ordinary city-dweller. Akinari's treatment reminds the reader of a *nō* play. The spirit, whether really that of woman or serpent, must be firmly exorcised. Although the sacrifice is great, man achieves maturity and learns to purify his heart.

Akinari's use of Chinese material (as well as that of his Japanese sources), suggests an attitude toward originality that may seem strange to a modern Western audience. Novelty for its own sake carried a low premium. Readers accepted a story more readily if they thought it was old or had come from China. Consequently, imitation was encouraged. For Akinari this act did not mean intellectual poverty or failure of the imagination; rather, it indicated a noble trust in his own strength. Far from abandoning one's creative personality and yielding himself to another author or work, one practiced imitation in order to gain aesthetic merit. By following in the footsteps of the men of old, one hoped to find new worlds. By mastering his sources, one infused them with fresh life. Imitation as an accepted mode of creativity dated back to the practice of early Chinese and Japanese poets. Far better to copy with skill, it was generally held, than to make something that was new but inane.

By understanding how Akinari uses his Chinese sources one may learn to appreciate passages that suggest another author, literary work, or even the manner of an entire period or culture. One discovers how Chinese phrases or metaphors are skillfully adapted to enrich the Japanese language and how Akinari handles the stylistic problems of his Chinese literary sources. In their visual form Chinese characters and phrases might preserve their original meaning. By adding a phonetic gloss, Akinari could suggest a Japanese interpretation and denote specific literary associations. The possibilities were virtually limitless, as if one were to mix French and English poetry with quotations from Latin and Greek classics. Owing to Akinari's ingenuity, a reader could enjoy the visual and semantic associations of the Chinese character with the security and immediacy of the Japanese phonetic script, keeping the best of both worlds. Accordingly, nearly every tale in some degree makes free use of aphorisms, images, metaphors, motifs, and ideas from Chinese texts. The discovery of how this old material is used adds to one's pleasure and enlarges one's understanding, as if a door has opened, leading into an uncharted realm of the human imagination.

INFLUENCE OF JAPANESE CLASSICS

Two streams of narrative prose flourished in Akinari's day. The first was mainly fed by earlier literature and history—Chinese as well as Japanese. The second was inspired by actual life and experience in the everyday world. More often than not, the former was serious and noble in tone and was meant to enlighten or instruct the reader. The latter was intended to be popular, amusing, and primarily for entertainment. Although a tendency to combine the two streams persisted, on the one hand Saikaku's tales of the floating world and the character sketches published by the Hachimonjiya, or 'Figure Eight Shop,' usually belonged to the second category, and, on the other, *Ugetsu monogatari* and the 'reading books' are properly classified with the first. Quite understandably, Akinari's indebtedness to earlier Japanese works extended to nearly every literary form and period.

No doubt the reader has already realised that the lyric impulse of the *Man'yōshū* and court poetry was preeminent among the Japanese influences. Indeed, poetry pervades the entire Japanese tradition. The poet, hot with the blood of life, seized experience and turned it into song, gracing whatever he touched with a startling awareness of human feelings. Concise and melodious, the poetry that resulted was rooted in everyday life, and its basic aim was to free men and women from the restraint of mundane affairs. Whenever a person was possessed by deep emotions about life and love or overcome with sadness and sorrow, whenever he felt a smothering sense of constraint, he might try through poetry to share his feelings with others and thereby find relief from his frustrations. The simplicity of Japanese poetic forms served to further this ideal. Almost anyone might combine words to form a musical pattern with a reasonably clear meaning, though the best poets in addition achieved intimacy, allusiveness, depth of feeling, and a maximum of content within a minimum of form. Certainly the attentive reader of the tales will recognise the voice of Japanese poetry, even without the aid of detailed notes, though their inclusion may lead one to still fuller appreciation.

Above all, the earliest and greatest anthology, the *Man'yōshū,* exerted a conspicuous influence on the tales. Study of this collection was one of the favourite activities of the scholars of the national learning. Indeed, Akinari contributed his share to its explication and to its revival in late eighteenth-century Japan. In his choice of diction and geographic names and also in the content of the stories themselves, Akinari showed fondness for this fountainhead of Japanese poetry. A few points relating to the influence of the *Man'yōshū* on the tales have already been discussed, but for a full understanding of its inspiration the Western reader should consult Japanese commentaries and studies. Yet other early collections of verse, including the best-known imperial anthologies, also left their mark. *The Tales of Ise,* however, deserves special mention. To an early collection of *waka* verses it is supposed that unknown authors added brief snatches of narrative prose which told about the circumstances behind the poems. The resulting work became a classic of Japanese literature and served as a handbook for young lovers and a guide for mature men and women who wished to convey their feelings for one another in poetry. Besides the specific influence of this work on *Ugetsu monogatari,* in later years Akinari wrote a preface and commentary for *The Tales of Ise,* and the title as well as the style of his light and amusing sketches on contemporary life and manners—*Kuse monogatari* (*Ise,* a place name, becoming *Kuse,* meaning 'Faults')—were derived from this Heian classic.

Traditionally, in Japan, poetry was combined with prose. The two forms harmonised, as a man and a woman well matched. The classical romances that Akinari knew and to which he devoted great energy owe much to both the poet and the storyteller. Although works such as *The Tale of Genji* deal with everyday life, they suggest in lyrical prose interspersed with *waka* verse an unreal world, which one might wind into a painted scroll, each colourful scene merging with the next.

Without suggesting that Akinari's tales in any way rival *The Tale of Genji,* which breaks away in volcanic fashion from the surrounding terrain to form a magnificent peak of its own, both works suggest a quest, that simplest of all romantic structures. Neither Lady Murasaki's novel nor Akinari's collection of tales, however, shows an insatiable craving after absolute knowledge at whatever cost. Rather, each reveals a Buddhist search for wisdom—that most pragmatic and adjustable of virtues. The authors told not of adventure or high romance, but more simply the search of the soul for understanding and the struggle of man to achieve a degree of enlightenment in a human world where people often repeat their old accustomed mistakes. The wisdom found in Akinari's tales, therefore, teaches one to find happiness in this life by casting off worldly desire and by curbing ambition. It represents a Buddhist sense of resignation (though tempered by Chinese thought and native attitudes toward life), as found in the poem,

> *Iro wa nioedo*
> *chiri nuru wo*
> *waga yo tare so*
> *tsune naran*
>
> *Ui no okuyama*
> *kyō koete*
> *asaki yume mi shi*
> *ei mo sezu*

> Though the blossoms may be fragrant,
> They are doomed to fall,
> Just as in this world of ours
> No one lives forever.
>
> Today I'll cross the mountains
> Of this mortal world
> And cast off dreams of vanity
> And forget all futile pleasures.

Indeed, these simple stanzas, which use each phonetic symbol of the Japanese language one time only, have served for a thousand years as a sort of alphabet song, and they very nearly epitomise Akinari's theme.

The literature of the Yamato and Heian periods not only influenced the tone of Akinari's tales, but it also afforded him techniques for integrating poetry with prose and furnished him with his underlying motifs. In another way of expressing the search for wisdom that *Ugetsu monogatari* shares with the best-known works of Japanese literature, Akinari's contemporary, Motoori, wrote of *mono no aware,* or 'the awareness of things,' though he was referring specifically to ancient literary classics. Akinari's tales also evince this quality. Like *The Tale of Genji,* they may help make young people aware of the pain of growing old and recall to old people what it was to be young.

Still another kind of earlier literature that left its mark on the tales was the personal narrative, a form that emerged in the Heian period, developed during the middle ages, and maintained its popularity until the present day. Although in the West few such works figure as memorable classics, some of the most highly regarded books in the Japanese tradition consist of diaries, travel sketches, and personal essays. As with the court novel, these works often combined prose and poetry, showing the Japanese preference for mixed forms and demonstrating what a narrow and shifting boundary separate fact from fiction and art from reality. Moreover, these texts had a special impact on the development of taste. When art springs directly from life, then the personal diary, travel sketch, and random notes might furnish not only pleasure for the original writer but also enjoyment for the casual reader. Examples such as Lady Sei's *Makura no sōshi* (*The Pillow Book*)[27] and Yoshida Kenkō's *Tsurezuregusa* (*Essays in Idleness*) in a general way influenced Akinari's style and helped to form his attitudes toward life. Kenkō's motto, 'The one thing you can be certain of is the truth that all is uncertainty,' indeed applies to Akinari's tales. Beauty was linked to its perishability, and the most precious thing about life was its constant surprise, a point of view that Lafcadio Hearn called 'the genius of Japanese civilization.'[28]

Besides the forms already discussed, collections of medieval Japanese stories known as *setsuwa* figured prominently in the tales. Oftentimes literary versions of legends handed down by word of mouth and compiled by Buddhist priests, these short narratives, that abound in miracles, contributed greatly to the development of the mixed style during the middle ages. Inspired by Buddhist sermons and scriptures, they reveal an intermingling of oral and written tradition, and because they are often allegorical and instructive, many of them resemble fables. Akinari's diction, metaphor, and handling of the supernatural especially benefited from the example of these medieval short stories. In particular, Akinari learned the storyteller's conventional formulas and transitional phrases from the medieval *setsuwa,* which partly helps to explain why he concludes several of his tales with passages that call to mind the raconteur's matter-of-fact ending.

Certain of the war tales, or military chronicles (the best examples of which set the standard for the mixed style from the middle ages until Akinari's day) left their mark as well. Not only did he reflect a familiarity with widely-known titles, such as the *Heike monogatari* (*The Tales of the Heike*) and the *Taiheiki,*[29] but Akinari also reveals indebtedness to lesser-known works. Rather than epic descriptions of massed combat or great warriors equal to a thousand men, however, Akinari found in these texts first of all an interpretation of national history, as discussed earlier. But he also derived from the memorable episodes of the medieval chronicles techniques for treating sad and poignant episodes in a touching manner. The war tales abound in examples of religious enlightenment and supernatural incidents. Among the remote precursors of the medieval chronicles, the *Kojiki*[30] and the *Nihon shoki,*[31] which tell of the lineage of the gods, the conquest of unruly deities, and the exploits of the early emperors, similarly figure in both the style and content of *Ugetsu monogatari.* Behind these sources, no matter how indirectly, lay the inspiration of the oral tales of the mountain and forest peoples of Northern and Central Asia and the ancient prototypes of Eastern European and Siberian mythical songs, heroic folk poetry, and fully developed epics.

One more branch of medieval literature that deserves mention is the *nō* drama. This remarkable form of theatre combines the complex literary devices of Japanese poetry, the epic material from the war tales, the philosophical outlook of Buddhism, and new elements such as the conventional *michiyuki,* or 'travel scene.' The *nō* conveys its lyric beauty in both representational and poetic terms. Many of Akinari's ghosts and spirits, for instance, remind the reader of similar creatures in the *nō*—at once beautiful and gentle, in a world impossible to define and yet ultimately real. During Akinari's day the *nō* ranked high among fashionable amusements, and the ethereal quality of its texts influenced much of the popular literature and drama of the time. Both in the *nō* and in Akinari's tales, art and life mingle independently of time and space in a manner that demonstrates the es-

sential oneness of existence, stirring the imagination by means of music and the dance and using travel as a symbolic motif. The structure of the individual tales reveals striking similarities to that of the *nō* plays, with an introductory portion (equivalent to the *jo,* or 'preface,' of the *nō*), a period of development (the *ha*), and a climax (*kyū,* where music, dance, and poetry merge in flowery splendour). But even more intriguing than that of any individual drama was the influence of the *nō* performance on the overall structure of *Ugetsu monogatari.* This matter deserves separate treatment.

By Akinari's time commercial publishing was widespread. Printed books had become ordinary items for purchase, and the practice of copying manuscripts declined. Authors might expect gain or profit from their occupation, rather than chiefly pleasure and self-satisfaction. New forms of imaginative literature matured, including *haiku* poetry, the short story, and the popular novel. Japanese scholars have come to refer to works of narrative prose by a number of special terms, such as *kanazōshi* (books written in the Japanese mixed style, rather than in pure Chinese), *ukiyo-zōshi* (the fiction of the floating world), *yomihon* (reading books), and *kusazōshi* (chapbooks). Nevertheless, the short stories and novels of the time displayed several features in common. They were written primarily in the mixed style, as previously mentioned. They were intended not for a small literary circle but for anyone who had the money to buy or borrow a book and leisure time to read. Each year new titles vied for success, and many authors relied on light wit, satire, and realism to win acceptance. On the one hand, numerous works catered to a perennial interest in the pleasure quarter and the entertainment world, but on the other hand some popular books inculcated a taste for contemplative pursuits, such as the study of national history, classical learning, and the scholarly branches of literature. Yet others fostered the practical virtues of loyalty and filial piety. A few authors, including Akinari, wrote both kinds of books—those for entertainment and also those for enlightenment. Frequently both purposes were combined in a single work, making it hard for the modern reader to set up clearly defined boundaries between what is frivolous and what is not. Nevertheless, Akinari's tales, like the best of the reading books, reflect not so much the lighter strain but rather the serious tendency in the popular literature of the day. As described above, they were part of the mainstream of Japanese literature.

STRUCTURE

The masterpieces of traditional Japanese literature include unusually long works such as *The Tale of Genji* and exceptionally brief forms like *haiku*. Sometimes small units were linked to make larger pieces that reveal an artistic unity of their own. Akinari's tales exemplify this point. It will be remembered that a tale about a former emperor who in a remote time had predicted an age of war and turmoil begins the collection. An announcement that the leadership of the Tokugawa shogun would bring peace to the realm marks the end. Although the significance of the arrangement of the nine tales and the overall structure might not be obvious at first, a total form emerges, indistinctly as a mystic scene in a Chinese landscape and hauntingly as the supernatural content of the tales.

To some extent certain familiar technical devices impart a unity of tone. One of these is the repetition of similar themes and patterns. For example, in **'White Peak,'** **'Bird of Paradise,'** and **'Blue Hood,'** a holy man on his travels has a supernatural experience. In **'The House Amid the Thickets,' 'The Caldron of Kibitsu,'** and **'The Lust of the White Serpent,'** a man is involved with a woman who later takes the form of a ghost or spirit. Conflict between father and son is mentioned in four of the tales. Warfare figures in five of them. In six of them the main character experiences a physical collapse (reflecting the possibility that Akinari was a sufferer of epilepsy). Various stylistic devices also help to impart a sense of harmony to the collection. Careful use of the well-turned phrase, an occasional ironic or whimsical touch, and numerous scholarly allusions to Chinese and Japanese literary sources all serve this purpose. Intriguing though these qualities are, certain additional elements reinforce the feeling of psychological unity that marks the tales. The idea of the continuity of existence—the cycle of growth, illness, death—is stressed throughout the collection, conveying a sense of man's journey from the cradle to the grave and describing a series of acts and events leading from innocence to experience. Along the way one meets with a fleeting vision of the archetypal female goddess. All of this may be represented by the image of rain and moon.

Each story forms a unit, with a meaning of its own, but taken together the tales suggest an organic whole greater than the sum of its parts, like an imperial anthology of court poetry, a sequence of linked verse, or a full programme of *nō* (with plays about gods, warriors, women, ghosts, and a congratulatory prayer of thanksgiving at the end). Underlying the structural integrity of *Ugetsu monogatari* are Chinese aesthetic values that the Japanese had early adopted. During the T'ang and Sung dynasties poets had begun to write sequences of verse, some of which, for instance, represented the changes of nature throughout the four seasons. Similarly, painters made landscape scrolls that unfolded from one scene to the next in a progress from the fresh new buds of spring to the withering of life in winter, implying a self-renewing cycle of birth, growth, decay, and death. Inspired by magical Buddhist figures and diagrams that symbolise the power and the form of the cosmos, poet and painter learned to depict an entire universe in visual or verbal terms. The contemplative man spending a summer night observing the image of the moon reflected in his garden pool saw in microcosm the vastness of time and space and the relative insignificance of the individual.

Landscape painting and the ghostly tale both lead to mystical experience. After viewing hills and valleys clad in mist and clouds, the painter, whose every brushstroke is charged with life, discovers hidden forms that exist only in the mind's eye. When the poet elaborates on such a vision, he creates the ghostly tale. **'The Carp That Came to My Dream,'** with a powerful touch of irony suggests how such a poetic vision might take on the dimensions of reality. A painted fish could leap into a real lake. Herein lies one of the links between the world of Akinari's tales and that which his contemporaries who called themselves *bunjin*, or 'literary men,' depicted in their landscapes, portraits, or flower and bird studies. Perhaps partly owing to the deformity of his right hand and his consequent inability to master the art of painting, Akinari was able to create an imaginary world by pouring heart and soul into his ghostly tales.

Most of all, however, the organisation of the tales is reminiscent of the arrangement of pieces in a full programme for the *nō* theatre. First came a play about the gods, because they stood for creation and guarded the nation down through the ages. Secondly came a drama about battle, which conveyed the struggle to protect and sustain life and the desire to commemorate the men who pacified the country with bows and arrows. After warfare came peace and a mysterious calm, which woman by means of love helped to perpetuate. But ghosts and spiritual creatures emerged to challenge man and reprove him, showing that his glory might vanish and that life was like a dream. The weaknesses and shortcomings of mankind, as well as human achievements, were thereby represented to the onlookers, but in the end the vital forces auspiciously prevailed. Man was reminded of his moral duties and of the promise that even after spring had passed, again it shall return.

From the middle ages on, sometimes there might be a different number of pieces in a *nō* performance, but the general principles for arranging the programme were usually followed. Akinari prepared his tales similarly (indeed one recalls that his title was derived from the *nō*). **'White Peak'** stands as the equivalent of a play about gods. **'Chrysanthemum Tryst'** brings to mind dramas in which the ghost of a warrior appears. **'The House Amid the Thickets'** suggests a 'wig' play, where the principle character is a woman, and it reminds one that love is usually associated with sorrow. **'The Carp That Came to My Dream'** and **'Bird of Paradise'** show certain characteristics related to the deep and mysterious quality of life in the everyday world. **'The Caldron of Kibitsu,' 'The Lust of the White Serpent,'** and **'The Blue Hood'** all contain scenes that cautioned the reader what disaster might befall the man who failed to show prudence and circumspection in daily conduct. Last of all, **'Wealth and Poverty,'** complementing the opening piece, serves a purpose similar to that of a 'congratulatory' play. In the tales, as in the *nō,* decline is followed by restoration. Peace and prosperity succeed toil and suffering. The tales, therefore, describe a paradigm of life.

Besides calling to mind a full programme of the *nō* theatre, most of the tales, as mentioned earlier, show traces of being organised around the theme of the archetypal quest. Saigyō, searching for enlightenment, meets Sutoku, the rebellious and unrepentant ghost of a former emperor. Samon, a youthful scholar, whose adventures were previously limited to the world of books, takes inspiration from Sōemon's ghost. As a result of confronting the world of real experience, he avenges his friend's murder. Katsushirō leaves home and wife to seek worldly wealth, but in the end what he really achieves is understanding and wisdom. Kōgi's view of the depths of Lake Biwa through the eyes of a fish afford him true knowledge of the impermanence of earthly pleasures and realisation of the fragile quality of life. The experience of Muzen and his son on Mt Kōya has a similar effect on the pair. Katsushirō seeks personal happiness, but he is unprepared to accommodate himself to the demands of home and family. Toyoo at first gives in to temptation, endangering his life, but later he finds maturity, though only at an extreme price. The fatherly mendicant, Kaian, saves a lost soul and in the process discovers a new facet of the human spirit. Lastly, Sanai's ghostly interview with the spirit of gold yields him a vision of a future era of peace.

As with many *nō* dramas, much of the significant action in the tales involves relations among men. In contrast to the earlier court romances, woman plays a secondary role, reminding one of her subordinate position in a Confucian society. According to Buddhist beliefs, as well, she suffers from various hindrances that make it difficult for her to attain enlightenment without first being reborn as a man. Compared to the men in the tales, the women are less firmly in control of their destiny. Nevertheless, Western readers will likely find the three stories in which women play a central role to be the most memorable of all. Despite her subordinate position, woman in the tales suggests the charm and grace of the archetypal female goddess or the mysterious calm of the natural environment, which man never wholly subdues. In her other guise she shows the demonic quality of the witch or shamaness. In **'The House Amid the Thickets'** woman appears in her passive form as a loving but forsaken wife, but in **'The Caldron of Kibitsu'** and **'The Lust of the White Serpent'** she takes on the more active role of the lamia, the witch, and the vampire. The strength of love might transcend the grave. Overwrought feelings transform a jealous woman into a deadly fury. An excess of fervour creates a beautiful woman from a snake—or perhaps it is the other way around. In general, however, Akinari describes a man's world, where woman is either devoted or dangerous. Ironically enough, an excess of devotion leads to danger, which in Buddhist terms means clinging to desire. Akinari suggests that woman must devote herself to man but that too much of this quality might cause pain and anguish.

During the years while he was working on his tales and trying to find a suitable occupation, Akinari possibly felt that his own wife and his step-mother were painfully devoted to him, and that he was undeserving of their love. As did his hero, Samon, he dabbled in scholarship. Like Katsushirō, he had abandoned his father's business, essentially for selfish reasons, to enter a new line of work that offered no assurance of success. Like Shōtarō, he had philandered in the gay quarter and neglected his family's occupation. He felt himself to be weak, like Toyoo, undeserving of his adoptive father's patronage, and remote from the family trade. Thus the tales reflect phases of his own psychological development.

At the beginning of the tales the Buddhist view finds espousal as the quickest way to wisdom, but in the end an attempt is made to transcend this outlook for a more pragmatic approach, in keeping with a new age. Meantime, throughout the collection Akinari sustains his meditative and detached tone. The lonely hermits and the youths who search for fulfilment and enlightenment emerge as his heroes. Mainly he tends to avoid direct confrontation with tragedy, bloodshed, or suffering. Nevertheless, enough gruesome material finds its way into the tales to reveal an ample glimpse of a demonic vision, with symbols of the prison, the madhouse, and death by torture. Shock and horror, one recalls, must figure in any journey from innocence to experience.

But despite certain unusual features in the overall structure and the influence of early Chinese and Japanese works, Akinari in each tale emphasised a single moment of insight, as have good modern short story writers. As a totality of related parts all of the tales combine to form an integral and unified work of art.

AKINARI'S LEGACY

After the first appearance of the tales in Osaka and Kyoto in 1776, they steadily rose in popularity, and the text passed through several editions. Like other books of the time, *Ugetsu monogatari* circulated mainly through lending libraries in the large urban centres and smaller provincial cities. Relatively few people could afford to buy their own private copy, and some readers even transcribed the text that they borrowed. Scholars as well as casual readers took note of the tales, and

Akinari's fame and reputation rose. Motoori Norinaga, doyen of the school of national learning, exchanged views with him on a variety of matters, including Japan's proper role in the world community.[32] By the end of the century Ōta Nampo visited Akinari and called him the outstanding writer of the day.[33] Another Edo author, Takizawa Bakin (1767-1848), tried without success to meet him, but he praised Akinari as a great man of letters and regretted only that he shunned social intercourse and was so retiring by nature.[34]

Meanwhile, the tales began to exert an influence on the literary scene. Itami Chin'en (1751?-81?) in a reading book entitled *Kinko kaidan miyamagusa* (*Deep Mountain Grass: New and Old Tales of Wonder*), which came out in Osaka in 1782, used situations from **'The Caldron of Kibitsu'** and **'The Lust of the White Serpent.'**[35] Other authors, particularly in Edo, the most rapidly growing urban centre in Japan at the time, tried to emulate Akinari's successful combination of a neoclassical style and a popular mode of storytelling. Even authors of chapbooks, such as Tōrai Sanna (1749-1810),[36] borrowed passages from Akinari's tales. Santō Kyōden (1761-1816),[37] realised the significance of Akinari's work and used the same techniques and materials in his historical romances. But above all, Bakin himself perfected the idea of using real or imaginary characters out of the past to create historical novels that appealed to serious readers who were interested in art, scholarship, society, and politics.[38] Bakin several times employed the idea of an interview with the ghost of a famous man, as had Akinari in **'White Peak'** and **'Bird of Paradise.'**[39]

Many of the same names of people, places, events, and even the classical Chinese metaphors of Akinari's tales appeared in Bakin's novels.[40] The idea of a worthless man who for the sake of another woman neglects his wife and eventually meets a violent death at the hands of her rancorous ghost not only found expression in **'The Caldron of Kibitsu'** but also in Bakin's reading book, *Kanzen Tsuneyo no monogatari* (*The Story of Tsuneyo*).[41] The situation described at the beginning of **'The Lust of the White Serpent'** was also imitated by Bakin in *Kinsesetsu bishōnenroku* (*Handsome Youths*),[42] where a young man similarly meets a woman at a temple during a sudden rain shower and lends her his umbrella. Later in the same episode a mysterious serpent appears. But aside from specific influence on Kyōden and Bakin's plots, Akinari's greatest contribution to later authors was his skilful use of classical metaphor and his treatment of the supernatural world. Without his work Japanese literature of the nineteenth and twentieth century would have been much the poorer.

Men such as Nampo, Bakin, and Kyōden helped to preserve the memory of Akinari's work. The former pair correctly identified two earlier titles that Akinari refused to admit having written.[43] Bakin was instrumental in transmitting the posthumous work, *Harusame monogatari* (*Tales of Spring Rain*). During Akinari's own lifetime he and his tales became objects of study. Then not long after his death, a certain Obayashi Kajō (1782?-1862), a retainer in the Ōban, or 'Guard,' the military branch of the government service, who was conversant with Confucian doctrines, as well as the tenets of the school of national learning, in 1823 edited Akinari's *Kuse monogatari,* adding a variety of notes and comments[44] and attesting to the growing recognition of his genius.

With the surge of Western influence after 1868, for a time interest in Akinari and his tales diminished. But by 1890 the climate had changed, and people began paying more attention to things Japanese. The tales were mentioned in an early history of prose fiction.[45] Movable-type editions became available,[46] and hereafter *Ugetsu monogatari* was often reprinted. Writers and poets of the Meiji Era—especially those involved with the Japanese romantic movement—turned to them for inspiration and found the same enduring qualities that had attracted an earlier generation. The novelist Kōda Rohan described Saigyō's journey to the emperor Sutoku's grave in terms that showed **'White Peak'** to have been the model. A poet named Takeshima Hagoromo was influenced by the tales. A poetic version and a dramatisation of **'The House Amid the Thickets'** appeared.[47] During these years Lafcadio Hearn introduced **'Chrysanthemum Tryst'** and **'The Carp That Came to My Dream'** to English-speaking readers, marking the beginning of their recognition in world literature.[48]

In the twentieth century Akinari's literary reputation has continued to flourish, and his tales have been acknowledged as a central work in the Japanese tradition. Suzuki Toshinari's annotated edition in 1916[49] included a lengthy introductory essay on such topics as Akinari's views on literature, how the tales came to be written and published, their literary background, the influence of medieval narrative prose, the role of the supernatural, and the impact on later authors. A revised version of Suzuki's work in 1929 boasted of four illustrations by Kaburagi Kiyokata, in which Akinari's themes were represented in pictorial terms.[50] Suzuki's careful and innovative study influenced later scholars, and Kaburagi's drawings demonstrated the hold that the tales exerted on artists as well as poets.

Literary men continued to respond to Akinari's classical style and emotional power. The novelist Tanizaki Jun'ichirō in 1920 prepared a scenario for a motion picture based on **'The Lust of the White Serpent.'**[51] In 1924 Satō Haruo (who, incidentally, was born in Shingu, the home of Akinari's fictional hero, Toyoo) published the first of many items he was to write about the tales and their author.[52] Akutagawa Ryūnosuke was an ardent student of the tales. One of Dazai Osamu's first stories, 'Gyofukuki,' which appeared in 1933, was inspired by **'The Carp That Came to My Dream,'** and the author wrote that when he first read Akinari's tale as a child, it made him want to become a fish.[53] In the mid-1930s Okamoto Kanoko published an essay on Akinari.[54] As mentioned in the Translator's Foreword, two film versions were produced in the 1950s. Meanwhile, Mishima Yukio in 1949 wrote an appreciative essay that showed the powerful influence Akinari's work had on him during his formative years. To him, Akinari represented 'a marriage of moralist and aesthete,' and Mishima praised the poetry, beauty, irony, and detachment found in the tales. **'White Peak'** was his favourite, followed by **'The Carp'** and **'Chrysanthemum Tryst.'** The romantic quality of Mishima's own writings owes a good deal to Akinari, whom he called 'the Japanese Villiers de L'Isle-Adam.'[55] Literary critics have similarly shared a high opinion of the tales.[56]

Among early twentieth-century scholars, a number of men have helped to make *Ugetsu monogatari* one of the most familiar titles in Japanese literature. Fujii Otoo, for instance, played a special role in Akinari studies. He assisted in editing a collection of the authors representative works; he prepared a separate volume of posthumous writings; he wrote scholarly and critical essays, and he produced a valuable biographical study.[57] Other men in the meantime concentrated on understanding Akinari's indebtedness to earlier literature. Two of the most prominent of these, Yamaguchi Takeshi and Gotō Tanji,[58] have demonstrated the complexity of the Chinese and Japanese literary sources. Tsujimori Shūei published a biographical study.[59] In 1946 an independent monograph on the tales, by Shigetomo Ki, appeared. Maruyama Sueo presented a detailed bibliography of secondary sources, and in 1951 he introduced newly discovered work by Akinari, which enabled readers to grasp more fully the degree of his talent and genius.[60] By the middle of the twentieth century Akinari's tales were sometimes compared in extravagant terms with such works as *The Tale of Genji,* the most remarkable achievement in all of Japanese literature.

More recently, intensive research and analysis has led to new knowledge and understanding. Nakamura Yukihiko, a widely respected scholar of early modern literature, has contributed to a realisation of Akinari's breadth as a literary man.[61] Others, such as Moriyama Shigeo, Sakai Kōichi, Ōba Shunsuke, and Morita Kirō, have published appreciative studies.[62] Takada Mamoru has pieced together all the available details of Akinari's life, and he has also published a well received critical monograph.[63] Until his untimely death, Uzuki Hiroshi was working on an exhaustively thorough annotated text of *Ugetsu monogatari,* which his co-worker, Nakamura Hiroyasu, completed—a monumental effort that all future students of the tales will surely consult. Asano

Sampei has prepared a collection of Akinari's *waka* verse with essays and notes on the sources and criticism and discussion of the author's ideas on poetry. More recently he has edited a text of *Tales of Spring Rain.*[64] Yet other well known scholars and critics have written about the tales, reaffirming their value. General anthologies of Japanese literature normally include selections from them, and a person can hardly claim to be well read unless he is conversant with *Ugetsu monogatari.*

Since Lafcadio Hearn's introduction of two of the tales in English, other translators have tried to convey the elusive beauty of the work to the rest of the world. In the 1920s a version of **'The Blue Hood'** appeared in an English language periodical in Japan.[65] In the 1930s Wilfred Whitehouse published translations of five of the tales with notes and commentary in *Monumenta Nipponica,*[66] an important journal for Japanese studies. Pierre Humbertclaude in the same journal began an ambitious critical study on Akinari including his early popular works.[67] By the early 1940s all of the tales had been translated at least once. In the 1950s René Seiffert, in Paris, published a complete French translation with notes and commentaries on the individual tales.[68] Meanwhile, other Western scholars of Japanese literature were also attracted to Akinari's work. Carmen Blacker and W. E. Skillend translated **'The Carp That Came to My Dream.'**[69] Dale Saunders published new translations of several tales,[70] and Lewis Allen one of **'Chrysanthemum Tryst.'**[71] James Araki wrote an essay introducing scholars to recent Japanese studies.[72] Also, during the 1960s a Hungarian translation appeared in Budapest, a Polish one in Warsaw. Kazuya Sakai, of Mexico City, published eight of the nine tales in a Spanish version.[73] An analysis of the tales may be found in a Czechoslovakian doctoral dissertation available in Prague. The author, Libuse Bohackova, has also published a complete translation.[74] Most recently, several young English-speaking scholars have turned their attention to *Tales of Spring Rain,*[75] and Kengi Hamada has published a translation of *Ugetsu monogatari* in book form.[76]

Notes

1. *Gukanshō,* comp. the priest Jien, in 1220, in *NKBT* [*Nihon koten bungaku taikei,* 99 vols. (Tokyo: Iwanami, 1957-66)], vol. 86, p. 206. See also H. Paul Varley, *Imperial Restoration in Medieval Japan,* Studies of the East Asia Institute (New York: Columbia University Press, 1971), pp. 15-21.

2. The edition that commonly circulated in early modern times was the *Kokatsujibon Hōgen monogatari,* in *NKBT,* vol. 22, pp. 335-99 (hereafter *Hōgen monogatari*). See also William R. Wilson, trans., *Hōgen monogatari: Tale of the Disorder in Hōgen,* A Monumenta Nipponica Monograph (Tokyo: Sophia University, 1971).

3. *Intoku taiheiki,* comp. Kagawa Masanori and Kagetsugu, in the 17th century, in Tsūzoku Nihon zenshi, vols 13-14 (Tokyo: Waseda Daigaku Shuppanbu, 1913).

4. Especially the *Kamakura ōzōshi,* in Gunsho ruijū, vol. 13 (Tokyo: Keizai Zasshi-sha, 1900), pp. 650-714. This work treats events of the 14th-15th century, beginning with an account of the ambitions of Ashikaga Ujimitsu (1357-98) and ending with a description of the rise to power of Ōta Dōkan (1432-86). Unlike the other titles mentioned so far, the *Kamakura ōzōshi* apparently was not printed and circulated only in manuscript.

5. See Varley, *The Ōnin War: History of Its Origins and Background,* Studies of the East Asia Institute (New York: Columbia University Press, 1967), pp. 88-95.

6. In Witter Bynner, trans., *The Jade Mountain: A Chinese Anthology, Being Three Hundred Poems of the T'ang Dynasty* (1928; rpt. New York: Alfred A. Knopf, 1945), p. 170.

7. Akinari's main source was the *Taikōki,* comp. Kose Hoan, in 1625. See Shiseki shūran, vol. 5 (Tokyo: Kondō Kappansho, 1900). Western readers may wish to consult accounts such those by Sir George Sansom, *A History of Japan, vol. 2: 1334-1615* (London: The Cresset Press, 1961), pp. 364-7, 370; and James Murdoch and Yamagata Isoh, *A History of Japan During the Century of Early Foreign Intercourse (1542-1651)* (Kobe: The Chronicle Office, 1903), pp. 380-4.

8. See Donald Keene, ed., *Twenty Plays of the Nō Theatre* (New York: Columbia University Press, 1971), pp. 237-52. Also see text, note 490.

9. See Hayashiya Tatsusaburō, 'Nihon bunka no higashi to nishi,' *Sekai* (Jan. 1971), p. 339.

10. For the relations between the school of national learning and the Taoist teachings and for Akinari's indebtedness to this branch of Chinese philosophy, see Sakai Kōichi, *Ueda Akinari* (Kyoto: San'ichi Shobō, 1959), pp. 138-49; for the similar interest of one of Akinari's contemporaries, see Keene, *The Japanese Discovery of Europe, 1720-1830,* rev. ed. (Stanford: Stanford University Press, 1969), p. 82.

11. Lionel Giles, trans., *Taoist Teachings from the Book of Lieh-Tzu . . . ,* Wisdom of the East Series (1912; rpt. London: John Murray, 1947), pp. 49, 108.

12. See Robert N. Bellah, *Tokugawa Religion* (Glencoe: Free Press, 1957); and Ronald Philip Dore, *Education in Tokugawa Japan* (Berkeley: University of California Press, 1965), pp. 230-43.

13. See Wm. Theodore de Bary, ed., *The Buddhist Tradition in India, China, and Japan,* The Modern Library (New York: Random House, 1969), pp. 155-66; and Morris, *The World of the Shining Prince* (London: Oxford University Press, 1964), p. 103, who refers to the same doctrine as 'calm contemplation.'

14. Morris, ibid., p. 98.

15. 'Paradise Lost,' *The Complete Poetical Works of John Milton . . . ,* ed., William Vaughn Moody (1899; rpt. Boston: Houghton Mifflin, 1924), p. 105; and 'The Second Defence of The English People,' *Milton's Prose Writings,* ed. K. M. Burton, Everyman's Library, No. 795 (1927; rpt. London: Dent, 1958), p. 345.

16. *Ise monogatari ko-i;* for Akinari's preface to it, see *Akinari ibun,* pp. 544-6; for complete English translations of this Heian classic, see Helen Craig McCullough, *Tales of Ise: Lyric Episodes from Tenth-Century Japan* (Stanford: Stanford University Press, 1968); and H. Jay Harris, *The Tales of Ise: Translated from the Classical Japanese* (Tokyo: Chas. E. Tuttle Co., 1972).

17. See 'Yoshiya ashiya,' in *Ueda Akinari zenshū,* II, 408.

18. *The Tale of Genji,* p. 501; *NKBT,* vol. 15, p. 432.

19. An important milestone in the history of Japanese literary criticism, by Ki no Tsurayuki (868?-945?), co-editor of the *Kokinshū,* comp. in AD 905, the first imperial anthology of *waka* poetry. See *NKBT,* vol. 8, pp. 93-104. See also Makoto Ueda, *Literary and Art Theories in Japan* (Cleveland: The Press of Western Reserve University, 1967).

20. Letter to Jen Shao-ch'ing, trans., Burton Watson, *Ssu-ma Ch'ien: The Grand Historian of China* (New York: Columbia University Press, 1958), pp. 65-6; found also in the early Chinese anthology, *Wen hsüan,* a text well known to educated people in Lady Murasaki's day and in Akinari's time. See the Japanese edition, *Monzen bōkun taizen* (Osaka: Ōta Gon'uemon, 1699), 11, 29a-34b.

21. 'Tu Chung-i shui hu chuan chü' (Japanese, 'Doku chūgi suikoden jo'), in *Ritakugo sensei hiten chūgi suikoden,* 1, 1a-3b. See also, Chūgoku koten bungaku taikei, vol. 55 (Tokyo: Heibonsha, 1971).

22. Quoted in Ryūsaku Tsunoda, de Bary, Keene, et al., *Sources of Japanese Tradition* (New York: Columbia University Press, 1959), p. 534.

23. Watson, trans., *The Complete Works of Chuang Tzu* (New York: Columbia University Press, 1968), p. 158.

24. *NKBT,* vol. 9, p. 143.

25. *Hito wa bakemono yo ni nai mono wa nashi.* Preface, *Saikaku shokoku-banashi, Saikaku-bon fukusei,* in Koten bunko, vol. 17 (Tokyo: Koten Bunko, 1953). IV, 4.

26. *Oni mo idete hito ni majiwari, hito mata oni ni majiwarite osorezu;* and *kami mo oni mo izuchi ni hai-kakururu, ato nashi.* 'Me hitotsu no kami,' *Harusame monogatari (Tales of Spring Rain),* Sakurayama Bunko text, ed. Maruyama Sueo, *Ueda Akinari-shū,* in Koten bunko, vols 47-8 (Tokyo: Koten Bunko, 1951), I, 108.

27. For a complete translation, see Morris, *The Pillow Book of Sei Shōnagon,* 2 vols (New York: Columbia University Press, 1967).

28. See Keene, trans., *Essays in Idleness: The Tsurezuregusa of Kenkō* (New York: Columbia University Press, 1967), pp. xviii, 163.

29. For a complete translation of the former, see Arthur Lindsay Sadler, 'The Heike Monogatari,' *Transactions of the Asiatic Society of Japan,* 1st ser., 46, part 2 (1918), i-xiv, 1-278; 49, part 1 (1921), 1-354, 1-11 (rpt. Tokyo: Yushodo, 1965). For a partial translation of the latter, see McCullough, *Taiheiki* (New York: Columbia University Press, 1958).

30. For a recent translation, see Donald Philippi, *Kojiki* (Princeton: University of Princeton Press, 1968).

31. Also called the *Nihongi.*

32. See '*Kakaika,*' *Ueda Akinari zenshū,* I, 423-64.

33. Recorded in 'Tandai shōshin-roku,' *NKBT,* vol. 56, p. 316. Ōta Nampo was also known by his pen name, Shokusanjin.

34. See 'Kiryo manroku,' *Nikki kikō-shū* in Yūhōdō bunko (Tokyo: Yūhōdō Shoten, 1913-15), p. 597.

35. I am indebted to Professor Hamada Keisuke of Kyoto University, for calling this to my attention.

36. Mentioned in my 'Kusazōshi: Chapbooks of Japan,' *Transactions of the Asiatic Society of Japan,* 3rd ser., 10 (1968), 126-7; and James T. Araki, 'Sharebon: Books for Men of Mode,' *Monumenta Nipponica,* 24 (1969), 39, 41-2.

37. For a summary of Kyōden's literary activities, see my *Takizawa Bakin,* Twayne's World Authors Series, 20 (New York: Twayne, 1967), N.B., pp. 56-99; and Araki, 'Sharebon,' *passim.*

38. See Chapter 3 of my *Takizawa Bakin.*

39. Most notably with Sutoku, in *Chinsetsu yumiharizuki;* see *NKBT,* vol. 60, pp. 215-25.

40. As pointed out in Asō Isoji, *Edo bungaku to Chūgoku bungaku* (1946; rpt. Tokyo: Sanseidō, 1957), pp. 661-2.

41. *Kanzen Tsuneyo no monogatari* (Osaka: Kawachiya Tōbei, 1806).

42. See *Kinsesetsu bishōnenroku,* in Teikoku bunko, 2nd ser. (Tokyo: Hakubunkan, 1928-30), vol. 6, pp. 38-9.

43. See Nakamura, ed., *Akinari,* in Nihon koten kanshō kōza, vol. 24 (Tokyo: Kadokawa, 1956), p. 31.

44. First reprinted in Kinko bungei onchi sōsho, vol. 4 (Tokyo: Hakubunkan, 1891), pp. 165-233; more recently, a different text of *Kuse monogatari* has appeared in Maruyama, ed., *Ueda Akinari-shū,* II, 79-197.

45. Sekine Masanao, *Shōsetsu shikō* (Tokyo: Kinkōdō, 1890), N.B., part 2, pp. 29-31.

46. Matsumura Shintarō, ed., *Ugetsu monogatari* (Tokyo, 1893); and the popular series, Teikoku bunko, 50 vols (Tokyo: Hakubunkan, 1893-97), vol. 32.

47. All mentioned in Suzuki Toshinari, *Shinchū ugetsu monogatari hyōshaku,* 2nd ed. (Tokyo: Seibunkan, 1929), pp. 132-4.

48. See 'A Promise Kept,' and 'The Story of Kogi,' *A Japanese Miscellany* (1901), in *The Writings of Lafcadio Hearn* (Boston: Houghton Mifflin, 1922), X, 193-8, 230-7. In addition, readers may find similarities between 'The Caldron of Kibitsu' and Hearn's 'Of a Promise Broken,' pp. 199-207.

49. When the 1st ed. of his *Ugetsu* appeared.

50. *Ibid.,* frontispiece, and facing pp. 290, 300, 310.

51. Mentioned in Joseph L. Anderson and Donald Richie, *The Japanese Film: Art and Industry* (Tokyo: Tuttle, 1959), pp. 39-40.

52. Collected in his posthumous *Ueda Akinari* (Tokyo: Tōgensha, 1964).

53. In *Dazai Osamu zenshū,* I (Tokyo: Chikuma Shobō, 1967), 61-70, XII (1968), 383. See also Keene, *Landscapes and Portraits: Appreciations of Japanese Culture* (Tokyo: Kodansha International, 1971), p. 188. Thomas J. Harper, trans., 'Metamorphosis,' *Japan Quarterly,* 17 (1970), 285-8.

54. Okamoto Kanoko, 'Ueda Akinari no bannen,' *Bungakkai* (Oct. 1935), pp. 351-369. This has been reprinted in Kuwabara Shigeo, ed., *Ueda Akinari: Kaii yūkei no bungaku arui wa monogatari no hokkyoku* (Tokyo: Shichōsha, 1972), pp. 300-11.

55. Mishima Yukio, '*Ugetsu monogatari* ni tsuite,' *Bungei ōrai* (Sept. 1949), pp. 48-51.

56. See Takada Mamoru, *Ueda Akinari kenkyū josetsu* (Tokyo: Nara Shobō, 1968), p. 8.

57. His essays and other work may be found most notably in *Edo bungaku kenkyū* (Kyoto: Naigai Shuppan, 1922); *Edo bungaku sōsetsu* (Tokyo: Iwanami, 1931); and *Kinsei shōsetsu kenkyū* (Osaka: Akitaya, 1947).

58. For Yamaguchi's efforts, see *Edo bungaku kenkyū* (Tokyo: Tōkyōdō, 1933); and 'Kaisetsu,' *Kaidan meisaku-shū,* in Nihon meicho zenshū, vol. 10 (Tokyo: Nihon Meicho Kankōkai, 1927), pp. 1-100; Gotō Tanji's work, more than thirty essays in all, beginning in 1934 appeared in various scholarly journals and collections; these are cited in the detailed bibliography in Uzuki, *Ugetsu,* pp. 713-27, mentioned above.

59. *Ueda Akinari no shōgai* (Tokyo: Yūkōsha, 1942).

60. 'Ueda Akinari kankei shomoku gainen,' *Koten kenkyū,* 4, no. 2 (1939), 76-86; no. 3, 95-104; no. 4, 180-93; and 'Kaisetsu,' in *Ueda Akinari-shū,* I, 5-51; II, 3-7.

61. In addition to editing *Ueda Akinari-shū* and *Akinari* (see notes 4, 57) and other works, he has published numerous essays, all of which are held in high regard.

62. See Moriyama's interpretive essays in various journals and collections; for Sakai, see note 24; for Ōba, see *Akinari no tenkanshō to dēmon* (Tokyo: Ashi Shobō, 1969); for Morita, see *Ueda Akinari,* Kinokuniya shinsho (Tokyo: Kinokuniya, 1970).

63. *Ueda Akinari nempu kōsetsu* (Tokyo: Meizendō, 1964).

64. See . . . his *Kōchū harusame monogatari* (Tokyo: Ōfūsha, 1971).

65. Alf. Hansey, trans., 'The Blue Hood,' *The Young East,* 2 (1927), 314-9.

66. '*Ugetsu Monogatari*: Tales of a Clouded Moon,' *Monumenta Nipponica,* 1, no. 1 (1938), 242-51; no. 2, 257-75; 4, no. 1 (1941), 166-91.

67. 'Essai sur la vie et l'oeuvre de Ueda Akinari,' ibid., 3, no. 2 (1940), 98-119; 4, no. 1 (1941), 102-23; no. 2, 128-38; 5, no. 1 (1942), 52-85.

68. *Contes de pluie et de lune (Ugetsu-Monogatari): Traduction et commentaires* (Paris: Gallimard, 1956).

69. 'The Dream Carp,' in *Selections from Japanese Literature (12th to 19th Centuries),* ed. F. J. Daniels (London: Lund Humphries, 1959), pp. 91-103, 164-71.

70. '*Ugetsu Monogatari, or Tales of Moonlight and Rain,*' *Monumenta Nipponica,* 21 (1966), 171-95.

71. '"The Chrysanthemum Vow," from the *Ugetsu Monogatari* (1776) by Ueda Akinari,' *Durham University Journal* (1967?), pp. 108-16. Mr Allen mentions having received a copy of the tales from a Japanese naval officer in Saigon in 1946.

72. 'A Critical Approach to the *Ugetsu Monogatari,*' *Monumenta Nipponica,* 22 (1967), 49-64.

73. Hani Kjoko and Maria Holti, trans., *Esō ēs hold nesei* (Budapest: Kulture Kiado, 1964) (not seen); Kazuya Sakai, *Cuentos de lluvia y de luna,* Enciclopedia Era, 7 (Mexico City: Ediciones Era, 1969); and a translation by Wieslaw Kotanski, mentioned in Kyrystyna Okazaki, 'Japanese Studies in Poland,' *Bulletin, International House of Japan,* no. 27 (April 1971), p. 12

74. Libuse Bohavkova, 'Ueda Akinari *Ugecu monogatari*: Rozbor sbírky a jednotlivých povídek a jejich motivických prvků' (The *Ugetsu monogatari* of Ueda Akinari: An Analysis of the Collection, of the Individual Stories, and of Their Motifs), Diss. Charles University, Prague, 1966-67, mentioned in Frank J. Shulman, *Japan and Korea: An Annotated Bibliography of Doctoral Dissertations in Western Languages, 1877-1969* (Chicago: The American Library Association, 1970), p. 190. Her translation is entitled *Vyprávění za měcíce a děstě* (Prague: Odeon, 1971), 204 pp.

75. See Anthony Chambers, 'Hankai: A Translation from *Harusame monogatari,* by Ueda Akinari,' *Monumenta Nipponica,* 25 (1970), 371-406; Blake Morgan Young, *The Harvard Journal of Asiatic Studies,* 32 (1972), 150-207.

76. Complete except for the author's preface, *Tales of Moonlight and Rain: Japanese Gothic Tales by Ueda Akinari* (Tokyo: University of Tokyo Press, 1971). Takada Mamoru contributed an essay to this volume, '*Ugetsu Monogatari*: A Critical Interpretation.' See pp. xxi-xxix.

Donald Keene (essay date 1976)

SOURCE: Keene, Donald. "Fiction: Ueda Akinari (1734-1809)." In *World Within Walls: Japanese Literature of the Pre-Modern Era, 1600-1867,* pp. 371-95. New York: Holt, Rinehart and Winston, 1976.

[*In the following excerpt, Keene praises Akinari's talent as a fiction writer and maintains that his stories are still widely read today, unlike the works of most of his contemporaries.*]

During the hundred years after Saikaku's death only one writer of fiction appeared whose works are still widely read today, Ueda Akinari. He is a difficult writer to classify because his literary production extends into many genres and styles. For most people he is known only as the author of *Ugetsu Monogatari* (*Tales of Rain and the Moon*), a brilliant collection of stories, mainly dealing with ghosts and other supernatural phenomena. Akinari undoubtedly considered this work to be of small consequence; his commentaries on the Japanese classics and studies of antiquity, the product of his long association with kokugaku scholars, occupied him during most of his mature years, and only at the end of his life did he turn again to fiction, when he wrote *Harusame Monogatari* (*Tales of the Spring Rain*). Despite the fewness of his stories, there is no mistaking his extraordinary talent, and his life has intrigued many students of eighteenth-century Japan.

Akinari was born in Osaka, apparently the illegitimate child of a prostitute. His mother died when he was three, but soon afterward he was adopted by a prosperous merchant, only to be struck by another misfortune: in 1738, when he was four, he contracted such a severe case of smallpox that one finger on each hand was twisted and shortened out of shape. This affliction did not prevent him from writing voluminously in later years, but he remained sensitive about his misshapen fingers, using a penname for *Tales of Rain and the Moon* that refers obliquely to them.[1] Despite his early misfortunes, he seems to have led a cheerful and even rather wild life as a young man, protected by foster parents who were deeply devoted to him; but he was also interested in his studies, and obtained a better than average education.[2] At the age of twenty-one he first published some haikai, and he continued from then on to associate with leading poets. In 1774 he wrote the essay *Yasaishō*, a discussion of the kireji (cutting words) of haikai; it is graced by a preface by Buson, whom Akinari met in the following year. Seven haikai by Akinari were also included in Buson's collection *Zoku Akegarasu* (1775), to which he contributed a preface. Akinari seemed well on the way to establishing himself as a poet, but he was convinced that writing haikai was no more than a diversion, and refused to allow *Yasaishō* to be published for thirteen years, until he finally succumbed to the pleading of friends.[3]

It was through haikai that Akinari formed some valuable friendships, notably with Fujitani Nariakira and Hattori Seigyo, about 1758, when he was twenty-four. Nariakira, the younger brother of the well-known Confucian literatus (bunjin) Minagawa Kien, was precociously gifted, and from childhood enjoyed reading novels written in colloquial Chinese. Later in life he founded a school of Japanese philology. It was he who stimulated Akinari's interest in kokugaku. Seigyo was not only familiar with colloquial Chinese fiction, but had learned to read it in Chinese pronunciations; he introduced Akinari to these works that so greatly influenced his later fiction.[4]

In 1766, at the age of thirty-two, Akinari published a ukiyo zōshi called *Shodō Kikimimi Sekenzaru* (*Worldly Monkeys with Ears for the Arts*), and in the following year a similar work, *Seken Tekake Katagi* (*Characters of Worldly Mistresses*), both in the vein of the Hachimonji-ya books. He signed these works Wayaku Tarō; this name suggested to some critics that the stories were Japanese translations (*wayaku*) of Chinese works, but there is no evidence of borrowing; *wayaku* was a dialectal word meaning "peculiar" and the name was probably an example of Akinari's drollery.[5] These two books are popular fiction in the tradition of ukiyo zōshi: most of the stories are humorous in conception, and it is hard to detect any deeper purpose than entertainment. Nevertheless, Akinari was so much superior to his predecessors in the genre that critics have found deeper significance in his stories than in similar works. But the modernity, antifeudalism, or cynicism they have read into these two unpretentious collections of stories owes more to their own literary persuasions than to anything Akinari wrote.[6]

Worldly Monkeys and *Worldly Mistresses* are in the tradition of Ejima Kiseki and Tada Nanrei. The sixth story in *Worldly Monkeys,* for example, tells about Yozaemon, the debt-ridden customer of a teahouse run by the fierce Kisuke, known as the Devil. Kisuke goes one day to collect his debts, only to discover that Yozaemon's house has been stripped bare, even to the mats on the floor. He searches the neighborhood until he at last finds his man in another house sitting stark naked in the cold. Kisuke the Devil is so shocked at the sight that he throws down some money and runs off in dismay.[7] The kernel of the story is amusing, and the description of exactly what Kisuke sees when he penetrates Yozaemon's house—"everything had been sold down to the *tatami* and rats had built nests in the bamboo flooring. There was one scrap of paper and a single wooden clog; the only remaining object in sight was a spider's web"[8]—suggests the enumerative skill of the ukiyo zōshi writer. The rest of the story, however, is marked by the typical digressiveness of the genre: it opens with a rather amusing but irrelevant passage describing the varieties of tattooing preferred by dashing young men of Edo, and concludes with Yozaemon, having become a Buddhist priest out of despair at the world, taking part as a drummer in a performance of Nō plays. He wears a wig, to hide his shaven head; but drums so energetically the wig falls off, to his great embarrassment. Nothing in the artistic conception and very little in the style suggests Akinari's superiority to other Hachimonji-ya writers.

His next work, *Worldly Mistresses,* though ostensibly a series of portraits of different varieties of mistresses, deals more with wives than with mistresses. Akinari's preface discloses that he wrote the book not as a keepsake for eternity but in order to raise money to repair his dilapidated house; he also states that his ten stories are sad or funny, depending on how kindly the mistresses were treated. The best story in the collection is definitely sad. It tells of Saitarō, the son of a rich farmer, who loses his fortune gambling on the rice exchange in Osaka. His mistress, a former prostitute named Fujino, is determined to set Saitarō on his feet, and in order to raise money sells herself to a brothel once again. Saitarō gratefully accepts the money and goes to Edo, resolved to win a fortune. He hears of a promising deal in silks and goes to an island to purchase them. On the way back to Edo, however, his ship is intercepted by pirates, and Saitarō is robbed of all his possessions. In despair and humiliation, he commits suicide. When the news reaches Osaka, the master of the brothel where Fujino works shows her the greatest consideration—quite unlike most brothel-keepers of Japanese fiction! He says it is entirely up to Fujino whether she continues to serve as a prostitute or follows Saitarō in death. Fujino, after a suitable period of mourning, bravely decides to show her appreciation to the master by entertaining customers with no suggestion of her personal grief. When her contract expires she becomes a hairdresser in the licensed quarter and, never marrying, spends the rest of her life praying for Saitarō's repose.[9]

Obviously this story is not only markedly superior in every way to the silly tale of Kisuke the Devil, but its tone threatens to break the confines of the ukiyo zōshi. The story opens in the flippant, allusive manner of the Hachimonji-ya books, but once we have entered the main story, it approaches tragedy. The self-sacrificing devotion of Fujino and the decency of Eigorō, the brothel-keeper, belong to a different world from the usual stories about the licensed quarter. At the beginning of the work Saitarō is portrayed as a typical spendthrift, destined to lose the fortune he inherited, but the suicide note he writes to Eigorō, asking him to persuade Fujino to live on without him, is so moving that he seems transformed into an altogether different and superior person. Akinari, evidently much impressed by his heroine, Fujino, remarks at the end that her devotion to Saitarō's memory was "without parallel even in the *Accounts of Virtuous Women (Lieh Nü Chuan)* of those damned Chinese." This last foolish jest, referring to the Chinese by the uncomplimentary expression *ketōjin,* in no way alters the serious, almost tragic nature of the tale. Fujino is the first of Akinari's paragons of Japanese womanly virtues. Even if her portrait is incompletely drawn, it has much more depth than anything we would expect of a "character" in a collection of mistresses. It suggests that Akinari already had in mind a different kind of fiction.

The preface to *Tales of Rain and the Moon* bears the date 1768, the year after the publication of *Worldly Mistresses,* but the book was not published until 1776. The style and content are so unlike Akinari's previous writings that most critics find it impossible to believe that *Rain and the Moon* was in fact completed in 1768; perhaps the preface itself was written in 1768 for an earlier draft of the stories, but they were reworked many times before publication eight years later.[10]

Various changes in Akinari's personal affairs had affected his future writings. In 1771 his house was destroyed in a fire, and Akinari lost all his possessions. When it proved impossible to restore the business Akinari had been left by his foster father, he decided in 1773 to begin the study of medicine. He also took up kokugaku, combining these two disciplines like Motoori Norinaga before him. Akinari himself had a very modest opinion of his abilities as a doctor but he prospered in his new profession, apparently because of the unusual conscientiousness he displayed toward patients, even if not fully equipped to deal with their illnesses. In 1788, however, he made a faulty diagnosis that resulted in the death of a small girl; this so upset him that he gave up his practice. Henceforth he devoted himself mainly to kokugaku.

Akinari's studies of kokugaku undoubtedly account for some stories in *Rain and the Moon,* notably the first, **"Shiramine,"** a dialogue between the priest Saigyō and the retired emperor Sutoku, set in the year 1168. But even more conspicuous than the influence of kokugaku were those from Chinese colloquial fiction. Akinari was the first major writer to benefit by an acquaintance with this body of literature.

The knowledge of colloquial Chinese in Japan had been greatly promoted by the activities of Okajima Kanzan (d. 1727), originally a Nagasaki interpreter, who moved to Edo in 1705. The philosopher Ogyū Sorai, believing that colloquial Chinese was of use in understanding the original meanings of the Chinese Confucian texts, organized a study group around Okajima Kanzan, initiating the first serious study of spoken Chinese among the intellectuals. Kanzan himself undertook to punctuate for reading in Japanese the great Chinese novel *Shui Hu Chuan (All Men Are Brothers).* He published the first ten of the hundred chapters of the book in 1727, the year of his death, and another ten chapters appeared posthumously in 1759. Other men pushed on with the Japanese version of this classic of colloquial fiction, and these translations, together with versions of Ming collections of short stories enjoyed popularity among the intellectuals, as a welcome relief from the tedium of the Hachimonji-ya books.

Ogyū Sorai's disciples used various collections of Chinese ghost stories as texts when learning the colloquial language, but they were not expected to show much interest in the subject matter. The disciples of Itō Tōgai (1670-1736), on the other hand, often became devout admirers of Chinese colloquial fiction. Those with literary talent were not satisfied merely with punctuating texts; instead, they made full translations or even Japanese parallel versions to the Chinese stories. In earlier times such men as Asai Ryōi had included Japanese versions of Chinese ghost tales in his collection *Otogi-bōko* (*Hand Puppets,* 1666), but the originals were in classical Chinese, not the colloquial. The new wave of translation and adaptation drew on both classical and colloquial materials.

The success of these works was so great that in 1754 a new category appeared in booksellers' catalogues—*shōsetsu,* at first a term designating works translated from the Chinese, but later used for all varieties of fiction.[11] These early shōsetsu were popular mainly because of their well-constructed and ingenious plots.

The first author to earn a reputation for his adaptations of Chinese colloquial fiction was an Osaka physician named Tsuga Teishō (1718-*c.* 1794), who had become familiar with these writings as a disciple of the Ogyū Sorai school of Confucianism. In 1749 he published *Hanabusa Sōshi* (*A Garland of Heroes*), a collection of nine stories, all but one derived from the three most famous Ming collections of ghost stories. Teishō's adaptations did not consist merely of rendering Chinese stories in literary Japanese; he recast them completely into tales of the Kamakura and Muromachi periods, adding numerous historical details to lend them a Japanese character. It was, of course, common practice to evade the censorship by shifting contemporary events into the past; *Chūshingura* (*The Treasury of Loyal Retainers*), to cite one example, was set in the fourteenth century and some characters were given the names of historical personages. Teishō's intent, however, was not to circumvent the edict of 1722 prohibiting the discussion in print of contemporary affairs,[12] but to give greater immediacy to his versions of Chinese stories by associating their events with familiar Japanese landscapes and people. This was essentially the same attitude of the author of *Nihon Reiiki* (*Account of Miracles in Japan*), compiled almost a thousand years earlier: by specifying the particular places in Japan where the miracles had occurred he persuaded readers that such extraordinary events were actually much closer to their own lives than they had supposed. This was particularly important in the case of ghost stories. If an author says, "Once upon a time in a distant country a terrible ghost was seen," he certainly does not have the same effect as if he says, "In the village of Saga, not far from the capital, a terrible ghost was seen by—."

Later men sometimes referred to *A Garland of Heroes* as "the ancestor of the *yomihon.*"[13] The *yomihon,* a serious form of fiction intended for "reading" (as opposed to picture books, which were meant to be looked at), developed early in the nineteenth century in reaction to the prevailing frivolous works of fiction. In their stylis-

tic mixture of Chinese and Japanese elements these books did indeed follow the traditions established by Tsuga Teishō. The moral purpose of the yomihon was also foreshadowed by Teishō's concern, announced in the preface to *A Garland of Heroes,* "to describe the importance of a spirit of righteousness."[14]

Teishō published two other collections in the same vein, *Shigeshige Yawa* (1766) and *Hitsujigusa* (1786). There is virtually no stylistic difference, despite the long period that elapsed between his first collection and the last—thirty-seven years. It is now believed that Teishō wrote all twenty-seven stories about the same time, when still a young man.[15]

Some evidence suggests that Ueda Akinari studied medicine with Tsuga Teishō during the years immediately preceding the publication of **Rain and the Moon.**[16] This influence might explain Akinari's use of a similar technique in writing—"naturalizing" Chinese popular fiction by setting the stories in ancient or medieval Japan. But Akinari was at even greater pains to conceal his sources, giving his characters such unmistakably Japanese attitudes and backgrounds that it would never have occurred to the ordinary reader that Chinese models had been followed. Unlike the yomihon writers, moreover, Akinari had no Confucian philosophy to expound; indeed, his attitude was anti-Confucian, as we might expect of a kokugaku scholar. His style is also conspicuously less Chinese in vocabulary and construction than Teishō's. Akinari, for all his eminence, was not considered by Bakin and the other yomihon writers as an "ancestor."

Bakin chose, instead, a writer he much admired, Takebe Ayatari (1719-74), as his candidate for "ancestor of the Edo yomihon."[17] Ayatari, a rival of Akinari, was a samurai from the north of Japan who turned to literature as a young man after a scandalous love affair with his brother's wife had resulted in expulsion from his native fief. He studied haikai poetry with Bashō's disciple Yaha, and painting with the bunjinga artist Sakaki Hyakusen, as well as with a Chinese painter in Nagasaki. In 1763 Ayatari formally became a member of the Kokugaku school of Kamo no Mabuchi. In his desperate eagerness to make a name for himself, he attempted to revive the archaic poetic form called *katauta,* a "half poem" consisting of five, seven, and five syllables, the first three lines of a waka, or else five, seven, and seven syllables, the first three lines of the ancient poetic form called *sedōka.* These efforts met with scant success, so he turned next to writing a monogatari in the pseudo-Heian style, following the example of such kokugaku scholars as Kada no Azumamaro. His first work in this form was *Nishiyama Monogatari* (*Tale of the Western Hills*) published in three volumes in 1768. The story is permeated by the ideals of *bushidō* (the way of the samurai), not surprisingly when we realize that Ayatari was a great-grandson of the foremost exponent of this code, Yamaga Sokō; the manly ideal known as *masuraoburi* was equally appropriate for a disciple of Kamo no Mabuchi. At the same time, Ayatari was trying to inculcate in the samurai of his day a love of the elegant literature of the past. He used archaisms deliberately, explaining them with notes inserted into the body of the text that give both the meaning and the source. This scholarship makes the book rather ponderous, but the style and ideals, if not the literary value, qualify *Tale of the Western Hills* as an ancestor of the yomihon.

The rivalry between Ayatari and Akinari may have led Akinari to date the preface to **Rain and the Moon** 1768, though the book was not published for another eight years. Ayatari published *Tale of the Western Hills* in 1768 and Akinari did not wish to appear to have lagged behind him.[18] There is reason to believe, nevertheless, that Ayatari's archaistic style and themes influenced the writing of **Tales of Rain and the Moon** and Akinari's later works.[19]

Tales of Rain and the Moon consists of nine stories divided into five books. Although Akinari's name nowhere appears in the text, he was identified as the author by Bakin in 1833, and the attribution now seems certain. The collection is generally assigned to the category of ghost stories (*kaidan*). Ghost stories go back very far in Japan, to *Account of Miracles in Japan*, *Konjaku Monogatari* (*Tales of Now and Long Ago*), and other collections. The prominent attention given to ghosts in the Nō plays and even in such works as *The Tale of Genji* hardly needs mentioning. But ghost stories emerged as a distinct genre only during the Tokugawa period. The first collections seem to have been written under Buddhist inspiration, but the emphasis soon shifted from a pious intent to control devils by revealing their nefarious ways, to an artistic effort to narrate an interesting story. The large number of ghost stories that appeared at this time should not be interpreted as signifying that Japanese of the seventeenth or eighteenth century were especially troubled by the fear of ghosts.[20] The stories were almost always set in the past and in distant parts of the country, unlike the ukiyo zōshi, the product of contemporary urban life.

Three early collections of ghost stories established the characteristic varieties of the genre: *Tonoigusa* (1660) by Ogita Ansei (d. 1669), a haikai poet; *Inga Monogatari* (*Tales of Cause and Effect*, 1661) by Suzuki Shōsan (1579-1655), a Zen priest; and *Otogibōko* (*Hand Puppets*, 1666) by Asai Ryōi, a professional writer. *Tonoigusa*, the prototype of the folk-tale ghost story, consists of sixty-eight stories, mainly about the strange doings perpetrated by animals—rats, foxes, spiders, and so on. *Tales of Cause and Effect*, the prototype of the Buddhist ghost story, was written with the intent of bringing about an awakening to the faith by describing prodigies

that had occurred as the result of the inexorable workings of the principle of cause and effect. *Hand Puppets* consists of ghost stories derived from Chinese collections written in the classical language.[21]

Elements from all three varieties of ghost stories are found in **Tales of Rain and the Moon**: in **"Shiramine,"** a tengu, a fabulous beast associated with the folk-tale, appears at the climax; **"The Dream Carp"** and **"The Blue Hood"** are Buddhist tales. **"The Chrysanthemum Tryst"** and **"The Kibitsu Cauldron"** are adaptations from the Chinese. Akinari's work, however, is most strongly marked by the influence of colloquial Chinese fiction.

The antecedents of each of the nine stories in **Rain and the Moon** have been most carefully investigated by Japanese scholars, yet they have not felt it necessary to explain why Akinari is considered the finest Japanese writer of stories about the supernatural. **"Shiramine,"** the first piece in **Rain and the Moon,** for example, hardly qualifies as a ghost story in the usual sense. It relates how the spirit of the retired emperor Sutoku appears before the poet-priest Saigyō and announces his intention of wreaking harm on the imperial household. Saigyō remonstrates with him at length, urging the emperor to renounce his old hatred and turn his thoughts toward salvation. The intractable emperor predicts the imminent destruction of his old enemies, the Taira family, his rage mounting until his face turns scarlet and he breathes fire. He summons a tengu, a winged demon, and orders it to torture and kill his enemies. Saigyō begs the emperor to remember the inevitable sequence of cause and effect. His words and prayers have effect: the emperor's face calms. He and the tengu disappear, leaving Saigyō alone. The story concludes with an account of the disasters that struck the Taira family thirteen years later, in 1179, when the retired emperor Sutoku's curses came to fruition.

Most of **"Shiramine"** is taken up with totally unnovelistic argumentation. A Western reader not familiar with Japanese history has difficulty following the story, which has little intrinsic interest. Even a Japanese reader would probably find **"Shiramine"** insufficiently engrossing if he read it in a modern-language translation; but read in the original, **"Shiramine"** impresses by its overpowering beauty of style, the essence of Akinari's elegant prose. The first paragraphs describe in language that echoes the poetry of the past the travels of an unidentified person in the autumn of 1168 to the island of Shikoku, where he visits the tomb of the retired emperor Sutoku in the village of Shiramine. The description has the cadences of a michiyuki, and the story as a whole takes its structure from the Nō plays. We only gradually learn the traveler's identity: an unknown man is praying before a tomb that Sutoku will be forgiven his sins, when a voice calls to him, "En'i! En'i!" The learned reader would realize that the unidentified person must be Saigyō, known as En'i when a young man; and the ghost who presently appears before Saigyō, much as in a Nō play, proves to be the former emperor Sutoku.

The Japanese reader with the necessary knowledge of the historical background will be intrigued by the plot and enchanted by the style. But it probably would not occur to anyone reading **"Shiramine"** in translation that Akinari was a writer of the first quality, considered by the Japanese to be worthy of a lifetime's research. The main theme of **"Shiramine"** was borrowed from *A Garland of Heroes,* describing the dispute between the emperor Godaigo and his councilor Fujifusa. Other elements were borrowed from a wide variety of sources. Indeed, Japanese scholars have shown that every story in the *Rain and the Moon* can be traced to one or more works of Japanese and Chinese literature. Few elements were invented by Akinari,[22] but thanks to his style, and to an awareness that detected superior literary possibilities in some familiar tale, he produced a work esteemed as a classic.

Probably the most affecting part of *Rain and the Moon* is **"Asaji ga Yado" ("The House in the Reeds")**, based directly on a story in the Chinese collection *Chien Têng Hsin Hua (New Stories after Snuffing the Lamp,* 1378) by Ch'ü Yu (1341-1427), called "The Tale of Ai-Ching."[23] A young man named Chao has fallen in love with a courtesan named Ai-ching. He marries her, and they live happily together in the same house with his mother, a widow. One day a letter arrives from an official in Peking, a relative of his father's, offering to prepare the young man for an important position. Chao is reluctant to leave his mother and wife, but they urge him to go, reminding him that it is a man's duty to seize every opportunity to establish himself in the world and bring credit to his family. He is at length persuaded, but when he arrives in the capital he discovers that his patron is out of favor. Chao bides his time, hoping for some improvement in his fortunes, but in the meantime his mother, worried by his absence, falls seriously ill. Ai-ching tends her with great solicitude, but the mother dies. The grief-stricken Ai-ching spends her days and nights weeping by the mother's grave.

In 1356 warfare erupts, and spreads to the village where Ai-ching lives. Her house is occupied by soldiers, and their leader, attracted by her beauty, decides to ravish her. She runs from him and hangs herself with a silken scarf. The soldier, unable to revive Ai-ching, buries her in the garden. Soon afterward peace is restored, and Chao returns home. Everything has changed: the house is in ruins, rats run over the rafters, and owls nest in the trees. Accidentally learning what has happened from an old man, Chao digs under the garden tree and finds Ai-ching's body. She looks alive, and as beautiful as ever.

He washes her body, clothes it splendidly, and buries Ai-ching beside his mother.

Ten days later Chao is sitting in his room late at night when he hears weeping. He realizes it must be Ai-ching's ghost, and asks that she show herself. She does, and he sees she is quite unchanged, except for an unfamiliar scarf twisted around her neck. Chao thanks her for having served his mother so faithfully, and for having preserved her chastity, even at the cost of her life. Ai-ching in turn expresses her gratitude for having been rescued from the life of a prostitute. She tells Chao that his mother has already been reborn, but that she herself wanted so badly to see her husband again that she postponed her rebirth until the following day. She reveals that she is to be reborn as a boy in a certain city. They spend the night in each other's arms, but at cockcrow she tearfully says goodbye and disappears. Chao later goes to the house Ai-ching described, and sees a baby boy who, he is informed, was twenty months in his mother's womb. The baby has been weeping ever since he was born, but at sight of Chao he smiles. From then on Chao and the baby's family never fail to keep in touch.

The same story was adapted by Asai Ryōi in *Hand Puppets.*[24] Almost every detail in the plot exactly follows the Chinese original, though Ai-ching is given the Japanese name Miyagino, and Chao is known as Fujii Seiroku. Here and there Ryōi also added characteristically Japanese details: Seiroku's mother, hearing that her son has ransomed Miyagino from a brothel and made her his wife, is most distressed, because the Fujii family is of great consequence, and she had intended her son to marry a girl of equal distinction. But she relents when she sees how lovely and gentle Miyagino is, and decides that no girl, no matter of what lineage, could make a better wife. From this point on the story follows the Chinese original closely, though details are drawn from the warfare in Japan of the sixteenth century. Only the end is different: unlike Ai-ching, Miyagino's ghost does not sleep with her husband; she vanishes, instead, like the mist after revealing that she is to be reborn imminently. Seiroku goes to Kamakura and finds a baby boy who smiles at him.

Asai Ryōi added extremely little to the plot, but his adaptation is so skillful it reads quite naturally as a Japanese story, and some details are superior to the original. Ueda Akinari's version, on the other hand, transforms the Chinese tale into an infinitely more artistic story.

"The House in the Reeds" opens about 1455 in the province of Shimōsa. In the village of Mama, there lives a man named Katsushirō. Although born into a prosperous family of farmers, he is of a happy-go-lucky disposition, and allows his house to go to rack and ruin, rather than work in the fields. The very fact that one can describe Katsushirō's character places him in an altogether different category from Chao or Seiroku, neither of whom displays any distinctive traits. Katsushirō is eventually obliged to consider seriously how he can earn a living. He asks a silk merchant to take him along to the capital, and the merchant agrees. Katsushirō sells his remaining property to buy silk to sell in the capital.

Katsushirō's wife, Miyagi, is worried about her husband's new plan, knowing his disposition, but it is useless to argue with him. Soon after his departure warfare breaks out in the region. Miyagi considers taking refuge, like others in her village, but she remembers her husband's command that she wait for his return in the autumn. Ever obedient, she braves the danger. Soldiers come and try to seduce her, but she resolutely repulses their advances and bars the door.

In the meanwhile Katsushirō, having successfully sold his wares in Kyoto, attempts to return to Shimōsa, only to find the roads blocked. Robbers steal his money, leaving him nothing, and he has no means of making his way home. In the province of Ōmi he is suddenly stricken with a fever and must give up all thought of travel. As he recuperates he becomes friendly with the people of the village and before he knows it "seven years have passed like a dream." Akinari's decision to make Katsushirō remain away from home for seven years, instead of the one year of the two earlier versions, may have been in the interests of making more plausible such enormous changes in his village that Katsushirō does not recognize it when he returns; seven years seems an excessively prolonged absence, even for someone who has been described as happy-go-lucky, but it serves to emphasize the contrast between Katsushirō and his wife.

Finally, in 1461, Katsushirō at last begins "to think seriously" about his absence, and feels ashamed he has abandoned his wife for so long. He supposes Miyagi is dead, but decides he must return, if only to erect a funeral monument to her memory. He arrives in Shimōsa some ten days later.

It is the rainy season and the atmosphere evoked perfectly fits a collection called *Tales of Rain and the Moon*. The day is drawing to a close as Katsushirō approaches his village, but he is sure he cannot go astray; after all, he has lived there most of his life. But everything has changed completely. Here and there he sees what appears to be an inhabited house, but it is unfamiliar. As he is wondering what to do, he suddenly notices the lightning-struck pine that had stood before his house. He approaches it, and only then notices the house itself, not in the least altered. To his great surprise he finds Miyagi, alive but much changed: her eyes are hollow, and her complexion looks dark and dusty. They exchange recollections of how each has spent the past

seven years. Miyagi concludes by saying, "But the night is short. . . ." The two lie together.

The next morning Katsushirō is awakened by rain falling on him. He sees now that the house is in ruins and the roof is gone. He searches for Miyagi but she has disappeared. He realizes that she was a ghost, and the only trace he can find of her is a scrap of paper with a poem she wrote just before she died. Katsushirō asks in the village what happened, and finally encounters an old man who witnessed the ravages of the warfare and the death of Miyagi. The old man concludes by describing how, many many years ago, there lived in the same village a girl named Tekona who had died of love, and Katsushirō is moved to tears by a tragedy that parallels his own.

In comparing the different versions of the same story we cannot but be struck by Akinari's genius. Not only did he create characters in Katsushirō and Miyagi, in place of the stock figures of an anecdote, but he reorganized the story in an infinitely more effective manner. The crucial change was in not revealing to the reader that Miyagi is a ghost until Katsushirō discovers it. The description of Miyagi, which suggests that the passage of seven years and the hardships she endured have aged her, makes us suppose that she is alive, even though Katsushirō had assumed she must be dead. Her momentary expression of indignation at Katsushirō's long absence not only confirms this impression but suggests a real woman, rather than the effigy of a virtuous wife in the Chinese story. The surprise of Katsushirō's awakening is our own, no less than his; even without any explanations we realize how strong Miyagi's love must have been for her to return as a ghost to spend one more night with her husband.

Miyagi, unlike her predecessors, is not a former courtesan turned wife (perhaps because the virtuous courtesan was all too familiar a figure from the ukiyo-zōshi); she is an ordinary woman who nonetheless embodies the virtues of Japanese womanhood. Katsushirō, on the other hand, is implicitly condemned; his absence is so described as to suggest it was occasioned by his indolent disposition, rather than by internal warfare he was powerless to circumvent. Akinari also made the structure of the story much neater by deleting the unnecessary character of the mother and by giving the narration of what happened in the village during Katsushirō's absence only once, instead of three times. The story is marred only by the ending, the recitation of the *Manyōshū* account of the girl Tekona who came from the village where Miyagi died. Perhaps it was intended to give additional depth to the events, by drawing a parallel with the distant past; in context, however, it is an unnecessary embellishment and seems like a heavyhanded display of scholarship. The inartistic ending of the original story, the rebirth of the wife as a baby boy, was naturally omitted by Akinari.

Akinari in **Rain and the Moon** raised the ghost story to a remarkably high literary level. Some scholars have suggested that this was possible only because he actually believed in ghosts and spirits.[25] Certainly his book of random jottings **Tandai Shōshin Roku** (**Courage and Caution**), written in 1808, when he was seventy-four, again and again reveals his belief in spirits, foxes, badgers, and the like, and he declared his contempt for Confucian scholars who, in their insistence on rationalism, refused to believe in irrefutable evidence of the supernatural.[26] Perhaps a belief in the supernatural helped to make the stories more effective, but the style, depiction of character, and mastery of construction surely were the principal factors in Akinari's transformation of stories of small intrinsic merit into moving works of art.

It might have been expected that Akinari, having perfected the ghost story, a genre with a long history in both China and Japan, would have continued to explore the vein, like the Hachimonji-ya authors turning out book after book of character sketches after the success of the first, but Akinari never again wrote any ghost stories. Akinari did not explain his reasons for abandoning the genre, but perhaps he found such satisfaction in his kokugaku studies that he had little time for other writing.[27] During the forty years between the preface to **Tales of Rain and the Moon** (1768) and the writing of **Tales of the Spring Rain** (1808), Akinari composed only two minor works of fiction (**Kakizome Kigen Kai** and **Kuse monogatari**),[28] but he wrote many books of kokugaku scholarship, including commentaries on the old classics, discussions of Japanese philology, and descriptions of Shinto theology.

Akinari's interest in kokugaku apparently originated in his middle twenties when he met a kokugaku scholar named Kojima Shigeie (d. 1760), who urged him to read the works of Keichū. Kojima was a neighbor of the poet Ozawa Roan, and introduced the young Akinari to him, thus beginning a long friendship. Akinari later attended lectures given in Kyoto by Takebe Ayatari, a member of Mabuchi's school; Akinari was disillusioned when he discovered Ayatari's knowledge of Chinese characters was faulty, and his competence in kokugaku so shaky he could only stammer when someone asked him a question.[29] However, it was through Ayatari that Akinari met Katō Umaki (1721-77), about 1765. Akinari was extremely critical of almost every other scholar, but he always showed great respect for Umaki, whom he considered his only teacher.

Akinari's kokugaku writings are no longer widely read, but they are of interest especially because of Akinari's polemics against Motoori Norinaga. In 1785 Motoori published a work expressing his belief in the literal truth of the *Kojiki*. An essay written by Akinari in the following year rejected this view, insisting that the

Kojiki account of the Age of the Gods applied only to Japan, not to the rest of the world. In the same year Akinari also challenged Motoori on whether or not a final -*n* had occurred in ancient Japanese. Motoori claimed that because there was no symbol for this sound it could not have existed, but Akinari insisted that even if the sound was written as *mu* it must have been pronounced as -*n*.[30] Akinari also took issue with Motoori on his claim that Japan must be superior to all other countries because the sun goddess was born in Japan. Akinari, observing from a Dutch map of the world how small Japan was, saw no likelihood it could have been the first country created or the source of all civilization.[31] In **Courage and Caution** Akinari abused Motoori for making money out of his *Kojiki* studies from his disciples. He even wrote this waka:

> *higagoto wo*
> *iute nari to mo*
> *deshi hoshi ya*
> *Kojiki Dembei to*
> *hito wa iu to mo*

> Even though he says
> The most utter nonsense
> He still wants pupils—
> Even though people call him
> Dembei the Kojiki beggar.

The point of this verse is the pun on *Kojiki* and *kojiki,* a beggar; Norinaga's great study *Kojiki-Den* is made into the comic name Kojiki Dembei.[32]

Akinari's opposition to Motoori was otherwise expressed in **Yasumikoto** (1792), the most important of his kokugaku studies. This work denied the authenticity of the *Kojiki,* and suggested that it had been drastically edited by later men.[33] Akinari's arguments were intuitive rather than logical, and he was certainly no match for Motoori in scholarly debate, but he was right in his contention that the final -*n* occurred in old Japanese,[34] and his reluctance to accept the *Kojiki* literally was proof of his good sense.

Akinari's devotion to kokugaku, despite his quarrels with Motoori, seems to have originated in his dislike of Confucian philosophy. The rigid, constricting Confucianism favored by the government seemed to him a denial of the wonder of life. His bitterest attacks were directed against such Confucian scholars as Nakai Riken (1732-1817) who rejected, in the name of reason, the evidence that foxes bewitch people and similar prodigies.[35] Akinari repeatedly insisted that the Japanese gods were unlike either Confucius or Buddha because they had never been human beings; they were gods through and through, unknowable to man and not to be measured by his standards.[36] Men sometimes performed completely irrational acts when possessed by a god; Akinari related a horrendous story about a family of woodcutters—a mother, two sons, and a daughter. The children were always well behaved, but one day the eldest son, after cutting down some trees in the forest, suddenly went mad and killed his mother with his ax. The younger son joyfully leaped into the act, hacking his mother's body into pieces, and the daughter chopped up the flesh on a cutting-board. The three of them died in prison, but no stigma was ever attached to their name because it was recognized that they had been possessed when they performed their murderous actions.[37] Akinari does not explain the anecdote, but clearly the horror here, as in the more frightening of the stories in *Rain and the Moon,* is inexplicable in rational terms. Only kokugaku, with its insistence on wonder and its belief in mysteries that cannot be explained, could satisfy Akinari. But he did not find it necessary to accept the nationalistic implications of the *Kojiki.*

Akinari's final work of fiction, *Harusame Monogatari (Tales of the Spring Rain)* was not published in entirety until 1951, after a series of discoveries of missing parts had at last brought to light the entire manuscript. It has since been widely acclaimed; some critics believe *Spring Rain* is even superior to *Rain and the Moon.* Yet surely it is a far less appealing work. A distinguished Akinari scholar wrote, "*Tales of the Spring Rain* is the kind of work whose importance we can first appreciate imprecisely after someone else has logically explained it to us."[38] Perhaps the surprise of the discovery of an important work excited certain critics so much their discrimination was blurred; or perhaps the fact that *Spring Rain* was composed so close to the end of Akinari's life suggested it must contain maturer wisdom and philosophy than in the early *Rain and the Moon.* Judged in purely literary terms, *Spring Rain* lacks the vitality of *Rain and the Moon*; there is such a tired, etiolated quality to many of the stories that one critic wrote, "*Spring Rain,* or at any rate the story '**The Bloodstained Smock,**' was the dying gasp of Akinari's wisdom and art."[39]

Akinari did not use Chinese materials in writing *Spring Rain,* nor is the work prevailingly about the supernatural, despite the occasional mention of the wrath of a god or similar themes. Akinari derived inspiration chiefly from works of classical Japanese literature and history, but one story was based on an actual event of 1767, and another may ultimately have been inspired by Saikaku. The stories vary in length from the page or so of **"In Praise of Poetry,"** hardly more than a discussion of some *Manyōshū* poems, to the forty pages of **"Hankai."** Everywhere there are traces of hasty revisions or of unfinished ideas; an earlier draft of part of the manuscript reveals the kinds of changes Akinari made, and they are not always felicitous. The story **"The Pirate,"** for example, expands and dramatizes the passage in the *Tosa Diary* where Ki no Tsurayuki's ship is pursued by pirates. In this version the pirate boards

Tsurayuki's ship, to everyone's dismay, but he proceeds to engage Tsurayuki in a long discussion about poetry and the compilation of anthologies! The pirate criticizes Tsurayuki for the excessive number of love poems in *Kokinshū,* expresses sympathy for Sugawara no Michizane, who was exiled, and finally informs Tsurayuki that his name should really be pronounced Tsuranuki. If the intent had been comic—the fierce pirate spouting the classics and telling the great poet how to pronounce his own name—there might be something to praise in the story, but Akinari seems instead to be parading his knowledge of the classics in peculiarly inappropriate guise.

The most engrossing of the stories is probably **"Nise no en"** (**"A Bond of Two Generations"**). A certain rich farmer, hearing a bell ringing in a corner of his garden, decides to dig up the place. His men uncover a stone coffin, and find inside the shriveled mummy of a priest. The farmer supposes the mummy must have been there for at least ten generations, but detects signs of life, and the mummy is given water for fifty days. The color gradually returns to the mummy's face, and finally the eyes open. The farmer naturally expects that this resurrected priest will be some extraordinary, holy being, but to his dismay he discovers the ex-mummy is quite ordinary, or even below average. At first the farmer does not give the man any fish, supposing a priest will not want animal food, but the man's looks reveal all too plainly his eagerness for fish, and when he gets it he devours it bones and all. In place of the words of wisdom the farmer had hoped to receive from a priest who had returned from the dead, he learns nothing at all; the man does not even remember his name. Finally the ex-mummy is put to menial labor, the only work he is capable of. As a result of this experience the farmer's old mother loses her faith in Buddhism, and the people of the neighborhood, also disillusioned, avoid the temples.

"A Bond of Two Generations" has strong anti-Buddhist overtones, but it succeeds not because of the sharpness of its attacks, but because of the amusing central theme: we, like the farmer, are disappointed to discover that even a man returned from the dead may be no wiser than anybody else!

Tales of the Spring Rain stands or falls as a collection on **"Hankai"**; it is not only by far the longest story, but has generally been treated as the single masterpiece. Daizō, a powerfully built young man, goes on a dare to a mountaintop temple known for the ferocious god who emerges every night. He reaches the temple without incident, and decides to take back a heavy chest as proof he was actually there. To his astonishment, the chest lifts him into the air and carries him many miles away to an island. He makes his way back home much chastened. For a time Daizō leads a virtuous life, but his passion for gambling gets the better of him. In order to pay his gambling debts he compels his mother to hand over the family fortune, then shoves the mother into the money chest. His father and brother run after him, but he pushes them off a cliff into the sea. He goes then to Kyushu and has an affair with a woman in Nagasaki, but she is so terrified of Daizō that she takes refuge in a Maruyama brothel. He pursues her, charging into a room where a Chinese merchant is disporting himself. The Chinese cries out in alarm that Daizō is another Hankai (Fan K'uai, a heroic Chinese general) and Daizō proudly takes this as his nickname.

Adventure after adventure follows. Though occasionally he shows a more amiable side, it is hard to speak of any character development; the most one can say is that, despite Hankai's violence and brutality, he is fairly generous with his money. One day he and his companions are walking along the road when they see a Buddhist priest. Hankai demands his money and is given one coin. Shortly afterward the priest returns and confesses that he had actually had two coins; he is ashamed of this sin of attachment to worldly goods, and insists on giving Hankai the other coin. A wave of awe passes over Hankai as he contemplates a man of such pure, selfless character. He contrasts the priest's ways with his own life and decides to become the priest's disciple. At the end of the story we learn that Hankai subsequently led a life of great holiness and died blessed.

Tales of the Spring Rain has frequently been cited to prove what strong anti-Buddhist and anti-Confucian beliefs Akinari held. Certainly **"A Bond of Two Generations"** is anti-Buddhist, and **"The Bloodstained Smock"** has a pronounced anti-Confucian bias, describing (like **"Shiramine"**) the evils that afflicted Japan as the result of the adoption of Confucian political thought. However, the conclusion of **"Hankai"** is exactly in the manner of a typical Buddhist story and there is no suggestion of cynicism. Perhaps Akinari, remembering the Buddhist fiction of the Muromachi period, decided that a miraculous reform in Hankai's character was the only possible ending for a story of almost unmitigated cruelty and perversion. Nothing has prepared us for the instant conversion of a man who not only killed without a qualm his parents (and many others) but pretended for years to be a priest without noticeable effect; the ending can be accepted only as a miracle, not as a logical development in Hankai's character.

"Hankai," unlike the best stories in *Rain and the Moon,* is long-winded and crammed with useless details. There is no apparent structure and the plot consists merely of a series of incidents. Perhaps Akinari intended it as an elaborate parable demonstrating that even the most evil of men may have some redeeming quality that will gain him salvation, but more convincing Buddhist stories had been written on this theme.

Spring Rain is, nevertheless, far more interesting than most works of ukiyo-zōshi literature.[40] The style, if inferior to that of *Rain and the Moon,* is still that of a master, concise and evocative. It has been said about *Spring Rain* that its characters sometimes display a striking "human" quality anticipatory of modern literature; when we contrast it with other examples of novelistic production in Japan at this time, devoted to trivial incidents of the licensed quarters or to the implausible doings of paper-thin heroes, we can see that despite its relative failure it possesses a literary integrity found nowhere else. The stories were not intended merely to divert readers but to express in some sense the author's view of the world. Akinari was a lonely figure at the end of his life, and something of his bitterness and cynicism comes to the surface in *Spring Rain.* Though it failed to repeat the brilliant success of *Rain and the Moon,* it has qualities of depth and craftsmanship found nowhere else in the popular fiction of the time.

Notes

1. Teruoka Yasutaka and Gunji Masakatsu. *Edo Shimin Bungaku no Kaika,* p. 110.

2. Morita Kirō. *Ueda Akinari,* p. 15.

3. Teruoka and Gunji, p. 112.

4. Nakamura Yukihiko (ed.), *Ueda Akinari Shū* (henceforth abbreviated *UAS*), p. 3.

5. Teruoka and Gunji, p. 118. The theory that *way-aku* meant "Japanese translation" was proposed by Takada Mamoru in *Ueda Akinari Kenkyū Josetsu,* p. 38, but was devastatingly refuted by Morita, pp. 67-71.

6. See Morita, pp. 61-71, for a discussion of various theories.

7. Nagai Kazutaka (ed.), *Ueda Akinari Shū,* pp. 40-45.

8. *Ibid.,* p. 42.

9. *Ibid.,* pp. 172-88.

10. Morita, p. 75.

11. Nakano Mitoshi, "Atarashii Shōsetsu no Hassei," p. 82.

12. Teruoka and Gunji, p. 102.

13. Ōta Nampo in *Ichiwa Ichigen,* quoted by Aiso Teizō in *Kinsei Shōsetsu Shi: Edo-hen,* p. 239.

14. Matsuyama Eitarō (ed.), *Gabun Shōsetsu Shū,* p. 1.

15. Teruoka and Gunji, pp. 108-109.

16. Nakamura Yukihiko, *Kinsei Sakka Kenkyū,* p. 161.

17. Quoted in Nakano, p. 84.

18. Shigetomo Ki, *Ugetsu Monogatari no Kenkyū,* p. 137.

19. See Nakamura, *UAS,* p. 4.

20. Noda Hisao, "Kaii Shōsetsu no Keifu to Akinari," p. 37.

21. *Ibid.,* pp. 38-40.

22. See Morita, pp. 78-85, 104.

23. See Japanese translation by Iizuka Akira in *Sentō Shinwa,* pp. 151-66.

24. Aeba Kōson (ed.), *Kinsei Bungei Sōsho,* III, pp. 62-66.

25. Nakamura Hiroyasu, "Ueda Akinari no Shimpi Shisō," p. 96.

26. See Nakamura Yukihiko, *UAS,* pp. 258, 268, 276, etc., for examples of fox magic; pp. 258, 268, 270, etc., for condemnations of materialistic Confucianists.

27. Sakai Kōichi, *Ueda Akinari,* pp. 56, 63.

28. For a good discussion of the latter work, see Shigetomo Ki (ed.), *Ueda Akinari Shū,* pp. 30-35.

29. Sakai, p. 60.

30. Morita, p. 20.

31. Takada Mamoru, *Ueda Akinari Kenkyū Josetsu,* pp. 362-81. The original texts are found in Iwahashi Koyata (ed.), *Ueda Akinari Zenshū,* I, pp. 423-64.

32. Nakamura Yukihiko, *UAS,* p. 254. The fact that Motoori Norinaga came from the region of Ise is alluded to: the inhabitants of Ise depended so much on the income provided by visitors to the shrines that they were known as "Ise beggars."

33. Text in Iwahashi, I, pp. 466-89.

34. See Roy Andrew Miller, *The Japanese Language,* pp. 207-208.

35. Nakamura Yukihiko, *UAS,* p. 270.

36. *Ibid.,* p. 272.

37. *Ibid.,* pp. 274-75.

38. Uzuki Hiroshi, "Akinari no Shisō to Bungaku," p. 254.

39. Matsuda Osamu, "Chi Katabira no Ron," p. 39.

40. See the complete translation by Barry Jackman, *Tales of the Spring Rain* (Tokyo: Tokyo University Press, 1975).

Bibliography

Aeba Kōson (ed.). *Kinsei Bungei Sōsho,* III. Tokyo: Kokusho Kankōkai, 1910.

Aiso Teizō. *Kinsei Shōsetsu Shi: Edo-hen.* Tokyo: Asahi Shuppan Sha, 1956.

Araki, James T. "A Critical Approach to the *Ugetsu Monogatari,*" in *Monumental Nipponica,* XXII, 1-2, 1967.

Iizuka Akira (trans.). *Sentō Shinwa,* by Ku Yü, in *Tōyō Bunko* series, Tokyo: Heibonsha, 1965.

Matsuda Osamu. "Chi Katabira no Ron," in *Bungaku,* XXXII (February 1964).

Matsuyama Eitarō (ed.). *Gabun Shōsetsu Shū,* in *Yūhōdō Bunko* series. Tokyo: Yūhōdō Shoten, 1926.

Miller, Roy Andrew. *The Japanese Language.* Chicago: University of Chicago Press, 1967.

Morita Kirō. *Ueda Akinari.* Tokyo: Kinokuniya Shoten, 1970.

Moriyama Shigeo. *Ueda Akinari,* in Iwanami Kōza Nihon Bungaku Shi series. Tokyo: Iwanami Shoten, 1958.

Nagai Kazutaka (ed.). *Ueda Akinari Shū,* in *Yūhōdō Bunko* series. Tokyo: Yūhōdō Shoten, 1926.

Nakamura Hiroyasu. "Ueda Akinari no Shimpi Shisō," in *Kokubungaku Kenkyū,* 26, (1962).

Nakamura Yukihiko. *Akinari,* in Nihon Koten Kanshō Kōza series. Tokyo: Kadokawa Shoten, 1958.

———. "Chi Katabira no Setsu," in *Gobun Kenkyū,* XVII (1967).

———. *Kinsei Sakka Kenkyū.* Tokyo: San'ichi Shobō, 1961.

——— (ed.). *Ueda Akinari Shū,* in Nihon Koten Bungaku Taikei series. Tokyo: Iwanami Shoten, 1959.

Nakano Mitoshi. "Atarashii Shōsetsu no Hassei," in Nakamura Yukihiko and Nishiyama Matsunosuke (eds.), *Bunka Ryōran.* Tokyo: Kadokawa Shoten, 1967.

Noda Hisao. "Kaii Shōsetsu no Keifu to Akinari," in Kōza Nihon Bungaku series, VIII. Tokyo: Sanseidō, 1969.

Sakai Kōichi. *Ueda Akinari.* Kyoto: San'ichi Shobō, 1959.

Shigetomo Ki. *Kinsei Bungakushi no Shomondai.* Tokyo: Meiji Shoin, 1963.

———. *Ueda Akinari Shū,* in Nihon Koten Zensho series. Tokyo: Asahi Shimbun Sha, 1957.

———. *Ugetsu Monogatari Hyōshaku.* Tokyo: Meiji Shoin, 1954.

———. *Ugetsu Monogatari no Kenkyū.* Kyoto: Ōyashima Shuppan, 1946.

Shimizu Masao. "Akinari no Haikai," in *Geibun Kō,* 1 and 2 (1967-68).

Takada Mamoru. *Ueda Akinari Kenkyū Josetsu.* Tokyo: Nara Shobō, 1968.

Teruoka Yasutaka and Gunji Masakatsu. *Edo Shimin Bungaku no Kaika,* in Nihon no Bungaku series. Tokyo: Shibundō, 1967.

Uzuki Hiroshi. "Akinari no Shisō to Bungaku," in Nakamura Yukihiko, *Akinari.*

Zolbrod, Leon (trans.). *Ugetsu Monogatari.* London: George Allen & Unwin, Ltd., 1974.

Blake Morgan Young (essay date 1982)

SOURCE: Young, Blake Morgan. "The Final Years." In *Ueda Akinari,* pp. 115-40. Vancouver: University of British Columbia Press, 1982.

[*In the following excerpt, Young provides an overview of the composition and contents of* Tales of the Spring Rain, *while also discussing Akinari's literary reputation during and after his life.*]

During the last years of his life—perhaps as much as the last decade—Akinari was working sporadically on his second major work of fiction, *Harusame monogatari* (*Tales of the Spring Rain*). He probably never finished it to his own satisfaction. It was read as a manuscript by a small number of admirers, but it was not published until 1907, and then only in fragmentary form. Not until after World War II did the complete text become available in print.[1] Akinari may never have intended the work for publication, for its contents are not aimed at the general reader. A work of deep meaning, it is pervaded by a philosophical element and covers a wide range of subjects, including historical events, literature and literary conventions, religion, ethics, and social problems, with Akinari's personal views on them. Its lack of form is an outstanding feature. The ten tales have no uniformity of length, the longest one being about twenty times the length of the shortest. Some of the stories are scarcely worthy of the name, being little more than collections of random thoughts or disjointed narrations of events, while even those which do qualify as tales suffer from imperfect organization and roughness of narrative. The uneven quality may be no more than evidence that Akinari was still revising *Harusame* when he died, but in any case the reader will appreciate the collection more if he examines its component parts, rather than the work as a whole.

The two stories that begin the collection may be considered together, since the second is a continuation of the first. **"Chi katabira"** (**"The Bloodstained Robe"**), is set during the reign of the emperor Heizei (774-824; r. 806-9), who is the central character and whose gentle and upright nature is the focal point of the story. Heizei is the embodiment of *naoki kokoro,* that legendary quality of the ancients that encompassed the virtues of purity and sincerity and total lack of deceit, leading them to do as a matter of course that which was right and proper. The tranquility of the realm is idyllically portrayed, but it soon becomes apparent that this is a façade. Heizei is a vanishing species, for the native Japanese virtues are being assailed by corrupting influences from China. In contrast to the simple and guileless Heizei stands his brother, the Crown Prince Kamino. Well-versed in Buddhist and Confucian teachings and in continental manners and culture, he is talented and sagacious and, above all, ambitious. Although supernatural manifestations portend disaster, Heizei proceeds with his plans to abdicate and so retires to the former capital of Nara, where scheming courtiers, led by Fujiwara no Nakanari and his sister Kusuriko, conspire to persuade him to rescind his abdication, rally support to his side, and declare Nara to be the imperial capital once again. Prince Kamino, now reigning as the emperor Saga (r. 809-23), hears of the plot and has Nakanari put to death. Kusuriko is placed in confinement, but she stabs herself to death, unrepentant. The depth of her corruption and resentment are made clear when the blood that has stained her clothing refuses to dry. Arrows cannot cause her robe to move, and swords shatter against it. Recognizing his own negligence in having been unaware of the conspiracy, Heizei takes monastic vows.

"Amatsu otome" (**"The Celestial Maidens"**), continues the action of **"Chi katabira."** The efforts of Saga and his successors, the emperors Junna (r. 823-33) and Nimmyō (r. 833-50), to reproduce in Japan the splendour of China, are portrayed together with the further rise of the continental influences, the increasing luxury and frivolty of the court, further plots against the throne, Buddhist influence on domestic politics, and the concomitant decline of the Japanese spirit. But the material is not clearly represented. The sentence structure lacks polish, and the events are isolated from one another, not following smoothly in logical sequence. In sum, the tale emerges as little more than a collection of brief episodes and does not succeed as a story.

The didactic element overshadows the story in **"Chi katabira,"** and overwhelms it in **"Amatsu otome."** In these two tales Akinari used literature as a podium from which to propound his view of history as a process of decay, rather than of progress. Like many other scholars of his time, he saw the early Heian period as an era of upheaval in Japanese thought which had led to corruption of the native spirit. Confucian and Buddhist teachings, with their promise of limitless rewards had, he believed, stimulated human desires, causing men to forget the simple virtues of the past and provoking power struggles even among members of the imperial family, who ought to have been above such things. Thus in **"Chi katabira"** it is continental learning that has corrupted Prince Kamino and made him eager for authority. Heizei is portrayed as a man who is good, but not in step with the times. His nature is better suited to the past, when ruler and subject alike possessed upright hearts and the Japanese emperor could rule like the Taoist sage-king, through non-action. In his own day, Heizei's extreme simplicity appears not so much a virtue as an unfortunate naivete, but Akinari's tone is not condemnatory. Rather he is lamenting for a bygone era. Retaining his own virtue while others are losing theirs, Heizei transcends the corruption around him with a kind of greatness. But though he transcends, he lacks the power to overcome, and therein lies the tragedy.

Akinari saw the decay that had begun in the Heian period as extending to his own time. His later writings, especially *Tandai shōshin roku,* are filled with passages lamenting that things are no longer as they were in his youth. Everything had changed, and for the worse. Scholars had become lax, no longer rigorous in their pursuit of truth. Artists were no longer striving for excellence, but thinking only of money. In former times, courtesans had been good-hearted, wearing simple costumes with few adornments, and they had been besieged by wealthy patrons; now they had become scheming women with petty thieves for customers. Even the sumō champions of his old age were inferior to those of his youth, he felt, succeeding only through lack of competition. "In Shikoku," he once said, "it is badgers that take possession of people; in Kyushu, water imps. In Kyoto and Osaka it is courtesans, teachers, and tea masters who possess you and cause you grief. You cannot be at ease anywhere in this world."[2]

The third tale, **"Kaizoku"** ("The Pirate"), takes as its setting the poet Ki no Tsurayuki's voyage back to the Capital in 935 after completing his term as governor of the province of Tosa. In his *Tosa Diary,* Tsurayuki spoke repeatedly of the danger of pirates, though none were actually encountered, but in Akinari's version a pirate does overtake the ship and comes aboard. His objective, however, is not to plunder, but to criticize Tsurayuki and expound his own views on poetry, scholarship and society. At this point, what has been an interesting narrative gives way to an undisguised polemic that touches on such topics as the correct interpretation of the *Man'yōshū* title, whether the varieties of poetry can be classified or whether they are as numberless as the human emotions they express, the doubtful propriety of including poetry about illicit love in the imperial anthologies, and other matters. No doubt most readers will find **"Kaizoku"** the least satisfying of *Harusame monogatari*'s ten items. It begins quite well as a tale, but it fails to fulfil its promise. The story stops in midstream to end in a welter of disconnected scholarly arguments, most of them hair-splitting and pedantic and

not clearly presented. The story and the polemic stand apart from each other; there is no fusion of the two, and neither is really successful.

After these first three attempts, however, Akinari managed to settle into the role of storyteller and yet retain that of moral apologist. The next two tales, while quietly didactic, remain stories from beginning to end. **"Nise no en" ("The Destiny that Spanned Two Lifetimes")**, is a satirical tale with a religious theme. A young farmer, sitting up late one night reading, becomes aware of the sound of a bell. Mystified, he searches for its source, finally determining that it comes from beneath a stone in a corner of his garden. Next morning, when his servants excavate the site, they unearth a coffin in which lies a man, old and shrivelled, his hair grown down past his knees, but alive. They realize that he is a priest in a state of *zenjō,* a trancelike condition of suspended animation said to be achieved by certain devout followers of religious disciplines. At length they succeed in reviving him, but the words of inspiration they expect to hear are not forthcoming. The priest cannot even remember his own name, let alone his former life or the paradise he sought. As his condition improves, he exhibits an ordinary man's desire for food, including forbidden things such as fish. When he has fully recovered, he makes his living at the lowest sort of menial labour. He takes a wife and proves to have a normal sexual appetite. He displays anger. His wife nags and henpecks him. Such is the man who had aspired to spiritual greatness. He seems, if anything, even lower than the average man, as though his religious austerities have had a negative effect. With this example of the fruits of piety before their eyes, the villagers lose their faith and turn away from religious activity, disregarding their priests' efforts to explain the situation.

Observers laughingly suggest that the priest has remained in the world in order to fulfil the saying, *Fūfu wa nise,* which refers to the teaching that a married couple's relationship extends from this life into the next. The implication is that the man's new wife is a reincarnation of his former mate, and this is the reason for the title, **"Nise no en."** Phonetically, however, the same words may be interpreted to mean "fake destiny," and the pun was probably intentional, since the Buddhist teachings on the relationship of cause and effect are made to appear false. Still, Akinari had not simply become anti-Buddhist, for it becomes clear in subsequent tales that this was not the case. It was not religion as such, but the hypocritical practice of religion for ostentatious display or personal gain that he was opposed to. He recognized that there were many among both clergy and laity who were motivated by selfish concerns, and he abhorred that kind of false piety, but true religious devotion, which led to personal peace of mind and rectitude of heart, remained his ideal.

"Me hitotsu no kami" ("The One-Eyed God"), may remind readers of *Ugetsu monogatari,* for it has the strongest supernatural element of all the *Harusame* tales, but it is a light-hearted and amusing supernatural, the world of "Muō no rigyo" or of "Himpukuron." Aspiring to become an accomplished *waka* poet, a youth from Sagami, in the uncultured eastern part of the country, sets out for Kyoto to take instruction from the masters there. On the last night of his journey, he lies down to sleep in front of a small shrine in the midst of a forest. He is awakened by the arrival of a Shinto priest, an itinerant Buddhist mendicant, and two women who are actually foxes in disguise. A weird-looking deity with only one eye emerges from the shrine to join them. Terrified, the lad pretends to be still asleep. A cask of wine is carried in by a monkey and a hare, and the group begins to drink. At length they call on the youth to join them. The situation is reminiscent of that on Mt. Kōya in "Buppōsō," though these supernatural beings are a good-humoured, harmless lot, and the sinister and terrifying atmosphere of that tale is totally missing. As the boy consumes wine with the group, the one-eyed god counsels him against going to study under the so-called masters of poetry in the Capital. Such men are all imposters with no real ability, he says, and in any case, it is better to develop one's talents by oneself. He concedes that a teacher may be necessary to get started, but he maintains that true poetry comes only from the heart and cannot be learned. The story concludes with the youth agreeing to accept this advice and being whisked back to his home in Sagami by supernatural power. In this tale, the polemic element does not intrude into the story. It fits in smoothly and is kept short enough to prevent it from overshadowing the action. The mood is light and entertaining throughout. Akinari was particularly successful in this attempt to tell a story and at the same time restate his oft-repeated views on poetic talent. It should not be overlooked that he himself was a one-eyed person when he wrote the tale.

In four of the last five stories, overt didacticism virtually disappears, and the emphasis shifts from scholarship to human interest, with stress on what Akinari considered virtues to be cultivated and vices to be avoided. "Shikubi no egao" ("The Smiling Death's-Head"), a tragic tale of romantic love, is based upon the same incident that Takebe Ayatari had used as his source for *Nishiyama monogatari.* There are varying reports of the actual event, but the basic facts are that in 1767, in a village on the northern outskirts of Kyoto, a youth named Watanabe Unai, the son of the village headman, fell in love with Watanabe Yae, who lived in the neighbouring house with her mother and two brothers. The families, though related by blood, were on bad terms, and the affair was carried on secretly until it became a matter for village gossip. The girl's mother had her elder son, Genta, try to arrange a marriage, but Unai's father refused the overtures and sent his son away to the home of a relative. At last, in a final attempt to allow the young people to marry, the mother sent her daughter to her lover's home once again, escorted by Genta. When the father ordered them away, Genta abruptly drew his sword and decapitated his sister on the spot.[3] In 1806 Akinari, who had long been interested in the incident, had chanced to meet the now elderly Watanabe Genta in person and had heard his version of the affair. Following this encounter, he had written *Masurao monogatari* (*A Tale of a Man of Valour*), in which he related the facts as Genta had presented them, and condemned Ayatari (for whom, it will be remembered, he had little regard) for the way he had distorted the truth in *Nishiyama.*[4]

Nevertheless, having set the record straight, as he supposed, with *Masurao monogatari,* Akinari went on to adapt the events to suit his own purpose in "Shikubi no egao." Gosōji, as the father is called in this tale, is a very prosperous *sake* brewer, but the epitome of miserliness, while his son, Gozō, is quite a different person, accomplished in the arts, refined in his behaviour, and considerate of others. Nearby lives Mune, the daughter of a once-wealthy family now forced to rely upon the meagre wages of the son, Motosuke, to maintain a state of genteel poverty. Gozō and Mune pledge themselves to each other, but Gosōji violently opposes a marriage with a girl from such a family and forbids his son to visit her home. His wife is more sympathetic but begs Gozō to obey, even so. Mune becomes genuinely ill with grief and longing, and her mother summons Gozō in desperation. Gozō affirms his vow to Mune, whose condition thereupon shows a marked improvement, but then he must return home to face his father's wrath and his mother's pleas. He begs their forgiveness and thereafter spends each day diligently working in the brewery, obeying his father's every command and neglecting his pledge to Mune, who once again starts to pine away. When she seems to be at the point of death, word is sent to Gozō. Going to her home, he tells her mother to send her to his house the next day as his bride, and together they celebrate the betrothal before he has to return home. But next morning, when Motosuke and his sister, dressed for her wedding, appear at his door, Gosōji is taken completely by surprise and orders them away. Gozō, it would appear, has not spoken to his father. Now he attempts to leave his home and family, taking Mune with him, but Motosuke forestalls such action by drawing his sword and striking off his sister's head. Throughout the story, to this point, Motosuke has presented an air of indifference, as though he did not care what happened to his sister, but at last this seeming insensitivity is revealed as stolid self-control. He has felt deeply and acted in accordance with those feelings, killing his sister with no outward display of emotion in order to spare her the disgrace of going through life as the wife of a disinherited son and to save his own family name from Gosōji's insult. Although his crime is a capital offence, the judge recognizes the purity of his motives and lets him off with banishment. Motosuke continues as the filial son he has been, working to support his mother, who accompanies him into exile. Gosōji's wealth and property are confiscated, and he and Gozō are likewise banished from the province. Unrepentant and greedy to the end, Gosōji disinherits his son and goes into exile vowing to become rich once more. Gozō himself becomes a monk.

Akinari left no doubt as to where his sympathies lay in this conflict between romantic love and filial duty, but Gozō's behaviour is subject to differing interpretation. On the surface, he appears to be vacillating, led first by love to pledge himself to Mune, then by duty to obey his parents, and lacking the determination to adhere strictly to either course. The tragedy may be seen to result from his indecision, and thus his entering the priesthood becomes an act of penance. But this is probably not what Akinari had in mind. More likely, considering his praise of Gozō's character, he wanted to portray him as striving to win his parents' approval for his love through his exemplary conduct as a son, but this is nowhere clearly stated, and the resulting ambiguity is the story's fundamental weakness. There is no such uncertainty as to Akinari's view of the other characters, however. Mune, who dies a martyr to her love, and Motosuke, who saves her from shame, both display the courage and uprightness of heart that Akinari so much admired. Unable to wed the man of her choice, Mune seals her love for him with her death, and the smile that remains on her lifeless face symbolizes the victory of this pure love over the squalid world she has left. But, Akinari would appear to be saying, such purity has little place in the present day. One must leave the contemporary world if one is to be unsullied by it. The gap between the ideal and the reality cannot be bridged in any other way.

"Suteishimaru" also has its roots in fact, though much more loosely than **"Shikubi no egao."** It was suggested by the actions of the priest Zenkai, who devoted thirty years of his life in the mid-eighteenth century to digging the Ao no Dōmon tunnel in what is now Shimoge-gun, Ōita-ken, in order to bypass a precipitous mountain route over which many travellers had lost their lives.[5] Akinari's story, however, begins in the far northeastern part of Honshu, where Suteishimaru, the protagonist, is in the service of a wealthy landowner. He is a natural man, exceedingly strong, unrefined, naive and simple, uneducated, and relatively untouched by philosophies or religion. The master, an inveterate tippler, often invites Suteishimaru to join him in his cups. During one such spree Suteishimaru, befuddled by drink, begins to struggle with his master, and thinking that he has killed him, he takes flight. When the master actually does die during the night, Suteishimaru is branded a murderer. The master's son, Kodenji, is ordered by the local magistrate and the provincial governor to go and bring back the supposed killer's head or have the property to which he is heir confiscated. Kodenji is neither physically strong nor skilled in the use of weapons, but he spends the next two years assiduously training under a master of the martial arts, and then sets off on his mission of revenge.

Meanwhile, Suteishimaru makes his way to Edo where, after making his living as a *sumō* wrestler for a time, he enters the service of a daimyo and goes to the domain in Kyushu. At length his habit of drinking to excess produces abscesses in his legs which render him a cripple. Now he begins to reflect on his past life and is struck with remorse at having killed his former master. To atone for his supposed crime he vows to spend the remainder of his life digging a tunnel through the nearby mountain, making the hazardous route safe for travellers. Thus when Kodenji, after three years of searching, at last tracks him down, it is to find him engaged in this labour. Touched by his virtue, Kodenji loses all desire for revenge and stays to help dig the tunnel. Together they work on, completing the task just before Suteishimaru dies. Akinari was not the only person to write a fictionalized account of Zenkai's labour,[6] but while others concentrated on the avenger's change of heart, he placed the emphasis on Suteishimaru's spiritual growth, which changes him from a natural man to a saint. He saw the simple, unsophisticated Suteishimaru as the clay from which a Buddha may be fashioned; it is the same theme that he developed more fully in **"Hankai,"** the final story in the collection.

Miyagi, the heroine of **"Miyagi ga tsuka"** (**"The Grave of Miyagi"**), evokes memories of the Miyagi of **"Asaji ga yado"** and of Fujino of *Seken tekake katagi*—the gentle, pure, self-sacrificing, and above all, faithful woman whose virtue transcends the worldly corruption around her. Miyagi is the daughter of an imperial councillor who dies, leaving her, her mother, and a servant of the family in desperate poverty. Through the machinations of the servant, the mother is deceived into selling her daughter to a brothel. Though hating the life she now leads, Miyagi dutifully accepts her fate for her mother's sake. Soon she becomes a celebrated beauty, beloved of Jūtabei, a wealthy and refined young man who determines to ransom her and make her his own. But Miyagi is also coveted by Fujidayū, a man of considerable authority. Fujidayū arranges for Jūtabei to be murdered and then courts Miyagi himself. She, unaware of his responsibility for her lover's death, finally yields to him, and only later, to her dismay, learns the truth. Just at that time, it happens, the priest Hōnen, known as the founder of the Pure Land sect of Buddhism, is about to depart from the Capital on his way into exile in Shikoku. Hearing that his boat is to pass her way, Miyagi has herself taken out into the middle of the river to meet him. As the priest's boat draws near she calls out to him, asking what a person like herself must do to obtain salvation. Then and there Hōnen teaches the efficacy of the *nembutsu,* whereupon Miyagi, chanting this invocation to the Buddha Amida, casts herself into the river and drowns.

Akinari's tale of Miyagi was based on a purportedly factual incident. The grave of the real Miyagi was located at Kanzaki, just across the river from Akinari's dwelling at Kashima-mura, where he had first heard her story more than thirty years before. The tale closes with an account of his visit to her grave and with the long poem he had composed in her memory. His lingering affection for the area is apparent in this postscript, but more important is his view of Miyagi herself, as a strong, intelligent, faithful, and pure woman whose spirit remains unsullied by what her body is compelled to do. She was only the latest manifestation of this kind of woman in his writings, indicating that he retained her as his ideal woman nearly all his life.

The polemic element revives briefly in **"Uta no homare"** (**"The Glory of Poetry"**). This item is no more than a short discourse; Akinari did not even attempt to tell a story. Rather he presented four *waka* from the *Man'yōshū,* each of which describes cranes crying out as they fly over the sea. The wording in all four poems is similar, which fact, says Akinari, is not the result of plagiarism, for the upright men of old would never have stooped to pirate the work of another. In former times, he maintains, since people were not burdened with restraining conventions, they simply expressed in poetry what they perceived with their senses. The result was a brand of verse independent of theory and rules, which came directly from the heart of man. Since two upright hearts would see the same thing in the same way, it was only to be expected that they would describe it in similar terms. Thus, he argues, the four poems were composed independently of one another, and their common expressions are a reflection of the spirit of ancient times.

Finally, there is **"Hankai."** It is the story of a rough, untutored, wild and impulsive young man who fears neither gods nor men and makes no distinction between good and evil, relying on his own near-superhuman strength to surmount all difficulties—much like Suteishimaru. His character becomes apparent right at the beginning of the tale when, challenged to pay a nocturnal visit to the shrine of a reputedly ferocious deity, he goes with no hesitation and with some bravado. He is punished for his sacrilege and returns home chastened and subdued, but the lesson does not last. Greed leads him to steal from his family. He murders his father and brother in the process and must flee. Akinari uses this flight to take his hero on a journey to enlightenment—an odyssey whereby he comes to recognize the limits of physical strength, to distinguish right from wrong, and at last to change from a scoundrel to a saint.

As Hankai begins his journey he is much the same as he has always been, living by his own means, removing obstacles by brute force. In Hakata and Nagasaki he makes his way by gambling; in Shikoku he joins a band of robbers. Gradually, however, it becomes apparent that his character is not all bad. He saves a family from being deceived by a dishonest merchant. During the winter he cultivates his own musical talent. After robbing the treasury of a wealthy man, he handsomely rewards his friend who had once saved his life. And in Edo he risks his own life out of genuine concern for the welfare of his two comrades. The action moves rapidly from one place to the next, and Akinari manipulates his character, not always logically, in order to give him the experience prerequisite to his conversion. The tale is episodic, but the grand tour of Japan on which the reader is taken is engrossing in itself.

There are two key episodes in Hankai's transformation. The first takes place in a dilapidated temple where, for the first time in his life, he is soundly beaten in a fight—and by a most unlikely opponent—and comes to realize that he is not invincible. The second occurs on the Moor of Nasuno where, impressed by the virtue of a priest he has robbed, he experiences an abrupt but lasting change of heart. No details of his subsequent life are given, but the final glimpse of him is as the abbot of a Zen temple in northeastern Honshu, at the point of death and entry into enlightenment.

Akinari's final comment on the action: "All who rule their passions have the Buddha nature; all who set them free are monsters,"[7] sums up the theme of **"Hankai."** It is well to note that Hankai, like Suteishimaru, reforms not through the preaching of others, but through himself. His salvation is not something acquired, but simply the result of his own innate goodness coming to the fore; it comes not so much through religious or philosophical teachings as through cultivation of qualities that he already possesses. This is not to say that Akinari rejected such teachings. He recognized their value, and they do prove helpful to Hankai in his quest for salvation. Akinari himself was affiliated with religious institutions throughout his life. As before, it was the misuse of religion, not religion as such, that he was against. He had no sympathy for those who self-consciously strove for salvation as personal gain or who sought for magical formulas which would produce salvation without effort on their own part. In sum, he believed that in ancient times people had been good by nature. By his own day, human nature had become corrupt. It was not possible to go back to the past, but one could, nevertheless, incorporate the spirit of former times into oneself. The virtues of old Japan had not vanished; they had merely become tarnished. A man could still discover this ideal nature within himself and nourish it to fruition. But there were no shortcuts; to rely on them was to shirk responsibility. It was only through simple living, shunning worldly matters, upright conduct, and strict self-mastery that one could obtain peace within his own mind and in the world. Such was Akinari's conviction, and if one looks for a common theme running through the diversities of *Harusame monogatari,* this must be it. Indeed, it runs through much of his other writing as well.

It is not always the work into which a writer puts his greatest effort that wins the most favour with the critics. *Harusame* is a good example. Though recognized as an important work, it has suffered from the natural tendency to compare it with *Ugetsu.* The style of *Harusame* is relatively straightforward with little artistic embellishment, and its structure and organization are lacking in polish. Reading it does not provide the aesthetic experience of *Ugetsu.* In part, this may be just a reflection of the fact that Akinari was in poor health and nearly blind when he wrote it, and that he died before he considered it finished, but his basic intentions when he wrote the two works were not the same. *Ugetsu* was conceived and executed as a work of pure literature; *Harusame,* more as a summary of what Akinari considered truth to be. When writing the latter, he saw his role to be more one of informing his readers than of pleasing them. This was relative, of course. Some of the *Harusame* tales are first-rate examples of the storyteller's craft, and Akinari's opinions are propounded to some degree in all of the *Ugetsu* pieces. But even in the openly didactic *Ugetsu* tales, Akinari paid such attention to the artistic element that they remain primarily literature, and only secondarily intellectual discourses. The essential difference between *Ugetsu* and *Harusame* is that in the former work the scholarly and literary qualities are fused and digested, while in the latter they tend to be separate. *Harusame* is clearly unequal to *Ugetsu* as a work of literature, but such a comparison is neither fair nor, in the end, possible, for they are not really specimens of the same kind of writing.

In 1808, the same year that *Harusame monogatari* and *Tandai shōshin roku* were completed, Akinari declared that he had cast his writing brush away.[8] In 1809 he did revise some of his entries in *Tandai* and compile his favorite haiku compositions, and he apparently wrote a new draft of *Harusame* as well, but his statement was probably an accurate reflection of his state of mind, nevertheless. *Tandai* and *Harusame* together amounted to a summation of what he wanted to leave behind. Thus, "All who rule their passions have the Buddha nature; all who set them free are monsters," may be seen not only as his final comment on "Hankai," but as his final comment on life. He now felt that his work was finished. There was little more to say, he was almost totally blind, and his general health was failing rapidly.

He was well enough to make the journey to Osaka toward the end of 1808 to observe the fiftieth anniversary of his father's death,[9] but he had little time remaining.

Sometime in 1809, probably sensing that the end was truly near, he left his Nanzenji dwelling to live once again at the home of Hakura Nobuyoshi. It was there that, 8 August 1809 (Bunka Era, sixth year, sixth month, twenty-seventh day), the death he had so long awaited, and had at times longed for, claimed him at last. His grave may still be seen today, standing by itself in honoured isolation in the garden of the Saifukuji Temple, marked by the simple stone monument that his surviving friends erected on the thirteenth anniversary of his death.[10]

Akinari's reputation as an author was already secure long before he died. Both Ōta Nampo and Takizawa Bakin had given him high praise, and the continuing popularity of *Ugetsu monogatari* and *Shodō kikimimi sekenzaru,* and the posthumous publication of some of his other works attest to the regard in which he was held. His popularity suffered for a time in the general preoccupation with things Western and the corresponding indifference to traditional Japanese culture that followed in the wake of the Meiji Restoration, but by the last decade of the nineteenth century the pendulum was starting to swing back. Akinari again became a subject for appreciation and, for the first time, academic research. Beginning in the 1880's and 90's, a solid base of scholarship was gradually built up over the next few decades and after a brief hiatus during World War II, study of Akinari truly began to flourish. Some of the stimulus, both in Japan and elsewhere, may be credited to Mizoguchi Kenji's film, *Ugetsu monogatari,* based primarily on the tales, **"Asaji ga yado"** and **"Jasei no in,"** which won the grand prize at the Venice Film Festival in 1953 and remains an international classic. The discovery of the complete text of *Harusame monogatari* (purchased during the war in a secondhand bookshop for a mere twenty sen[11]) and its publication in 1950 made possible more extensive scholarship on that work and led to a more complete appreciation of Akinari's talents. It may in part be the emphasis on scholarship and *waka* verse in *Harusame* that has sent some researchers delving into Akinari's role as a *kokugakusha* and poet. Much remains to be done, especially in these latter areas, but the trend shows every sign of continuing and is gradually rounding out the general view of the man who once was known almost exclusively as a writer of supernatural fiction.

In the West, Akinari has attracted attention ever since Lafcadio Hearn retold the *Ugetsu* tales, **"Kikuka no chigiri"** and **"Muō no rigyo"** in his *A Japanese Miscellany* in 1905. English translations of individual *Ugetsu* stories have been appearing since 1927, and two complete versions came out during the 1970's. *Ugetsu* has also recently appeared in French, German, Hungarian, Polish, Spanish, and Czech translations, and a complete English rendition of *Harusame* has come off the press as well.

Study of Akinari's works is rewarding both for its own sake and for the debt owed him by other Japanese writers. Tanizaki Jun'ichirō, Ishikawa Jun, Mishima Yukio, Satō Haruo, Kawabata Yasunari, Kōda Rohan, Izumi Kyōka, Akutagawa Ryūnosuke, Dazai Osamu, Ibuse Masuji, and Enchi Fumiko have all acknowledged his influence on their own writings. Today Akinari's place in the literature of Japan is secure and interest in him is, if anything, growing. A recent report from Japan indicated that university students are turning from modern to classical Japanese literature, and suggested that studies of Akinari may rank closely after *The Tale of Genji* in popularity as topics for graduation theses.[12] It is as though there is something in an age of rational scepticism and scientific technology that sends people back to the haunting imagery, absorbing fantasy, and pursuit of traditional beauty to be found in his works. Likewise, in a world of confusion with the breakdown of long cherished social and moral attitudes, the study of Akinari's life reveals a man who did not seek to ingratiate himself with the world, but strove, sometimes unsuccessfully, but without ceasing, to live according to his own principles and beliefs.

Notes

1. For a discussion of the various *Harusame* manuscripts, and their discovery and publication, see *Tales of the Spring Rain,* trans. Barry Jackman (Tokyo: University of Tokyo Press, 1975), pp. xix-xxiii.

2. *Tandai,* no. 35, NKBT [*Nihon Koten Bungaku Taikei*], 56: 276. See also nos. 54, 55, 70, 138, pp. 287, 295, 341-43.

3. Readers who are interested in the actual incident should consult Asano Sampei, "Genta sōdō to Ayatari, Akinari," (1962) in *Akinari,* ed. Nihon Bungaku Kenkyū Shiryō Kankōkai, pp. 231-46; Noma Kōshin, "Iwayuru Genta sōdō wo megutte: Ayatari to Akinari," *Bungaku* 37 (June 1969): 46-55; (July 1969): 39-50. See also my "A Tale of the Western Hills: Takebe Ayatari's *Nishiyama Monogatari,*" in *MN* [*Monumenta Nipponcia*] 37 (1982) 77-121.

4. *Masurao monogatari* was, in fact, the name given to this work by Fujii Otoo when compiling *Akinari ibun.* Akinari's own manuscript was untitled.

5. See *Dai Nihon hyakka jiten,* 1: 69.

6. "Onshū no kanata ni" by Kikuchi Kan is the best-known work of fiction based on this episode, but Akinari's "Suteishimaru" was unknown at the time it was written and so could not have had any influence. For comparative notes on the two tales, see Morita Kirō, *Ueda Akinari* (Tokyo: Kinokuniya Shoten, 1970), pp. 189, 190; *Spring Rain,* trans. Jackman, pp. 117-19.

7. *NKBT* 56: 247.

8. *Jiden, Ibun,* p. 256.

9. Letter to a Mr. Kin'ya, quoted in Takada, *Akinari nempu,* p. 344.

10. See Takada, *Akinari nempu,* p. 348.

11. Reported in *Nihon Dokusho Shimbun,* 30 August, 1950, p. 4. Although the copyist had purposely omitted "Suteishimaru" and "Hankai," this was the most complete version of *Harusame* to be discovered up to that time. Edited by the finder, Urushiyama Matashiro, it was published as *Urushiyama bon Harusame monogatari* by Iwanami Bunko in 1950.

12. *The Japan Foundation Newsletter* 7 (Feb.-Mar. 1980); 20.

Selected Bibliography

A. COLLECTIONS OF AKINARI'S WORKS

Akinari ibun. Ed. Fujii Otoo. Tokyo: Shūbunkan, 1919.

B. TRANSLATIONS OF AKINARI'S WORKS IN WESTERN LANGUAGES

Jackman, Barry. *Tales of the Spring Rain.* Tokyo: University of Tokyo Press, 1975.

C. BOOKS AND ARTICLES IN JAPANESE

Akinari. Ed. Nihon Bungaku Kenkyū Shiryō Kankōkai. Tokyo: Yūseidō, 1972.

Takada Mamoru. *Ueda Akinari nempu kōsetsu.* Tokyo: Meizendō Shoten, 1964.

Dennis Washburn (essay date spring 1990)

SOURCE: Washburn, Dennis. "Ghostwriters and Literary Haunts: Subordinating Ethics to Art in *Ugetsu Monogatari.*" *Monumenta Nipponica* 45, no. 1 (spring 1990): 39-74.

[*In the following essay, Washburn contends that in* Tales of Moonlight and Rain *Akinari achieves a delicate balance between artistic considerations and elements of the supernatural.*]

The collection of tales **Ugetsu Monogatari (Tales of Rain and Moon)**, written by Ueda Akinari, 1734-1809, has been an acknowledged classic of Japanese literature almost from the time of its publication in 1776. The work has been praised for the beauty of its prose style, the careful way in which ethical or aesthetic arguments are woven into the stories, and the sophistication of the narrative perspectives. There is throughout a pleasing tension between the apparent controlling artistic consciousness and the supernatural subject matter. Indeed, the achievement of *Ugetsu Monogatari* rests not on any single aspect of the work, but rather on that tension— the strangely beautiful, precarious balance created by the synthesis of diverse elements in the stories. That balance, moreover, is not merely fortuitous, but is the result of certain ideological assumptions that led Akinari to adapt earlier Chinese and Japanese tales of the supernatural to his own purposes.

In spite of its secure position in the canon, many elements essential to the success of *Ugetsu Monogatari* pose problems for the modern reader. To begin with, the skeptical nature of modern rationalism puts any type of narrative dealing with the supernatural (with the possible exception of horror stories that have a 'psychological' basis) at some remove from contemporary tastes. Second, the method of composition makes the work less accessible now. Each of the stories is literally a pastiche, with Akinari borrowing not simply the plot outlines from Chinese and Japanese sources, but even minute details of characterization or description, sometimes lifting whole lines from the original texts.[1] This method of composition may perhaps call into question the originality of the author, although it is more likely that even with an annotated text the modern reader (especially the Western reader) will not be able to sense the extent or quality of Akinari's borrowing. More troublesome than the potential misunderstanding of Akinari's creativity is the possibility that the modern reader will not see the debt, and consequently will not read the work within the context of the literary tradition that it is consciously and continuously invoking.

Third, the style of the work is problematic. This is not a question of language only, although the passage of time and the intentional archaism have certainly rendered the text more difficult. The greater problem lies in the mixture of vernacular usages with an elegant style that intentionally echoes the literary language of the Heian classics. Apart from the difficulty of recognizing these different styles and their narrative functions, there is the possibility that certain stories or passages where the language seems less opaque will be given undue emphasis.

The present article addresses those aspects of *Ugetsu Monogatari* that seem alien to modern readers. Why did Akinari choose to write about the supernatural? Why did he develop a style that combined elements of both elegant and vulgar language? Why did he compose his stories in the manner of an adaptation? These questions cannot be answered separately, but must be considered together as part of a larger set of critical assumptions that guided Akinari's conceptions about fiction. He wrote *Ugetsu Monogatari* at a period in his life when he was preoccupied with various interests. Through his contact with *kokugaku,* or national learning, he came to share the assumption of the importance

of language as a means to understand and, to a certain extent, recover an idealized past. Through his practice of *haikai* poetry he came to view the *bunjin* (literati), or artist, as an interpreter of the tradition whose aesthetic values transcended the mundane. And through his study of *pai hua* fiction he found models of narrative structure and perspective that not only shaped his own work, but also contributed to the development of the *yomihon,* a major narrative mode of Edo fiction.

The importance of these various pursuits is apparent in the narrative form, the ghost story, that Akinari chose for the composition of his masterwork. That choice represents his concern with achieving a synthesis of his ideas about art and ethics. Stories of the supernatural are a kind of narrative that, by virtue of their fantastic elements, may be used to call attention to their own rhetorical qualities, suggesting a concern with the practice of literature for its own sake. At the same time, the adaptation of this type of narrative, which often involved a mixture of literary styles and modes, invokes the authority of the ethical traditions of the past. Examining *Ugetsu Monogatari* within the larger ideological framework that guided Akinari and shaped the development of narrative in the mid-Edo period will counterbalance the interjection of modern tastes into the judgment of his work, and thus will bring us closer to that literary sensibility that was so attracted to stories of the supernatural.

KOKUGAKU AND THE SUBORDINATION OF ETHICS TO ART

Akinari's work as a *kokugaku* scholar put him in contact with one of the major intellectual movements of the Edo period. Although *kokugaku* arose in avowed opposition to Neo-Confucianism and to all other 'foreign' systems of thought, it was nevertheless greatly indebted in its methodology and in the structure of its ideology to Neo-Confucian developments, especially *kogaku,* or ancient learning.[2] *Kogaku* scholars brought together the rationalism implicit in their empirical methodology for linguistic research and the anti-rational, intuitionist acceptance of the authority of the ancient past in all areas of intellectual and ethical inquiry. By stressing research into the past, they encouraged the growth of nativist movements that adapted *kogaku* to an examination of Japan's ancient history and literature.

The primary aim of *kokugaku* research was to recover the linguistic origins of Japanese. This research was empirical insofar as it was based on the observation of linguistic changes over time. Yet underlying the *kokugaku* project was the assumption that there was once a linguistic 'golden age', a mythic, pre-Babel epoch that was characterized by absolute unity or correspondence between words and the objects, thoughts, and actions they signified. In that mythic world irreconcilable linguistic polarities such as art and nature, the intuited and the rational, the rustic and the sophisticated, the human and the superhuman were not recognized. This unity was destroyed with the passage of time as the original meanings of words were forgotten, or as new systems of thought were introduced. *Kokugaku* research sought to move between and reconcile the intellectual poles created by what was perceived to be the corruption of the language.

The relativism implicit in this historical awareness of linguistic change was part of the trend in fiction toward a particularization of form and content that resembles in broad outline similar developments that gave rise to the modern European novel.[3] Ian Watt has tied the appearance of the novel in Europe to what he identifies as a tendency from the Renaissance onward for 'individual experience to replace collective tradition as the ultimate arbiter of reality.'[4] In the Edo period the autonomy of literary practice was recognized, but that did not necessarily free the individual writer from the authority of tradition. Because it was assumed that literary and cultural renewal depended upon recovering an ideal past, the writer was, paradoxically, ever more tightly bound to the tradition as the arbiter of reality.[5]

This paradox is reflected, for example, in the clear setting out of the historical context of the tales in **Ugetsu Monogatari.** On the one hand it indicates a concern with establishing a connection to the past, and on the other it reveals a historical consciousness that subsumes ethical judgments beneath a relativistic understanding of all human activities, including the practice of literature, according to the particular laws appropriate to them.

Akinari's research on Japan's early literature, his investigations of the *kireji* words *ya* and *kana,* and of *makurakotoba,* suggests that he concurred with this approach to literary practice. The impact of *kokugaku* on his critical conceptions is apparent in the short study of *Genji Monogatari* titled **Nubatama no Maki (Black-Jewel Scroll)** that he wrote under the pseudonym Muchō. The preface dates this work 1779, and it explains that the study is a reworking into modern language of a treatise written by a man named Sōchin, who lived in the late years of the Muromachi period. Sōchin is devoted to the study of *Genji Monogatari,* and tells us that he has copied the work in its entirety twenty-four times. One night, while working on yet another copy, he falls asleep over his manuscript and dreams that he is walking along the strand at Akashi. There he meets Kakinomoto no Hitomaro, the great *Man'yōshū* poet, with whom he discusses *Genji Monogatari.* Sōchin wonders whether, considering the way the novel succeeds in capturing the scene, Murasaki Shikibu had not once strolled along the same beach. Hitomaro replies:

> *Genji Monogatari* has always delighted the people of the world because it recreates so completely and inter-

estingly the world as it was then. Yet it is nothing more than empty words that have trifling value. The courtiers in the capital thought of this sort of writing as nothing more than playing with beautiful phrases; indeed, setting down things as they were came quite naturally to them. It is extremely foolish to take these idle pastimes for the teachings of the world.[6]

Hitomaro admits the resemblance between fiction and reality, but he emphasizes the rhetorical, fictional nature of *Genji Monogatari,* which is meant for enjoyment, not moral instruction. Sōchin acknowledges that in China fiction is treated as 'empty words', but argues that the ideas of an author may at times be expressed in a vague manner that disguises present reality, and thereby contains a measure of truth. He then cites the so-called *monogatariron* of the 'Hotaru' chapter in which Genji argues that fiction performs a moral function by instructing in the manner of the Buddhist *hōben,* or expedient teachings, and by providing important details of the past not contained in historical chronicles.

Hitomaro replies that Sōchin's view is the product of a heart that looks at fiction too narrowly, that mistakes empty words for reality, and he insists there is now a divided conception of fiction as either a diversion that gives vent to an expression of human emotions, or a representation of the real world that serves as a means for moral instruction. Hitomaro asserts that this divided conception did not exist in Japan in the ancient days. Instead, 'there was no theoretical distinction between fiction and reality. There was but one tradition that was recorded in their writings.'[7] That tradition was lost because with the passage of time 'the meanings of ancient words became obscure. Confucian and Buddhist teachings, as well as the doctrine of *yin* and *yang,* were taken up, and there were only shallow things.'[8] Hitomaro adds that as later interpretations appeared the original customs and outlook of Japan gradually became confused, and ancient waka and fiction were thus misread.

In **Nubatama no Maki** Akinari argues that there was a spirit in ancient Japan that was pure, honest, and emotional. That spirit was reflected in its language, which made no distinctions between fiction and reality, or between aesthetic and moral purpose. It represented the ideal toward which political, scholarly, or literary activities should strive. While Akinari did not believe it possible to recover the past, he did try to regain something of the ancient spirit of Japan through the study of its language and writings. As a *kokugakusha* his approach combined a rationalistic methodology for the study of language with a fundamentalist belief in the authority of the past.

Although the authority of the past must be filtered through and distorted by the language of the present, Muchō's text, which is presented as a translation of an earlier manuscript, more nearly achieves a conflation of the past and present through *kokugaku* discourse. Moreover, there is a supernatural element, the dream sequence, that allows the narrator to overcome the distortions of time and present a supposedly accurate account of the nature of fiction.

The impact of *kokugaku* on **Ugetsu Monogatari** is not to be found in the specific arguments about language or ethics presented in the tales. The impulse to seek out and recover the original unity between language and the world is instead reflected in the effort to subordinate ethical concerns to the demands of art. That effort situates **Ugetsu Monogatari** within the general trend of critical ideas about fiction in the middle of the Edo period. Throughout the collection ethical matters are related closely to concerns about language and literary convention; and the most common ethical theme deals with the effects either of a lack of moral discipline, or of maintaining an unusual degree of moral discipline. Often the loss of control over (or the transcendence of) the course of human affairs leads to some form of haunting, the main element of a supernatural narrative. The ethical theme serves a narrative function, and thus the structure of the supernatural tale mirrors the ideological structure of *kokugaku*.

The language of *kokugaku* is often used as a medium that both expresses and creates a junction between the human and the supernatural worlds. The opening tale of **Ugetsu Monogatari** is **Shiramine, 'White Peak',** the name of a mountain in Shikoku. The story is a retelling of the historical events of twelfth-century Japan from the perspective of the ghost of Emperor Sutoku, and reveals that the upheavals of the time were the result of that exiled sovereign's curse. **Shiramine** owes a great deal to the *jo-ha-kyū* structure of noh drama, specifically the play *Matsuyama Tengu*.[9] The opening travelogue, which makes extensive use of *utamakura*, tells of a journey taken by the poet Saigyō, and is much like the prologue that introduces the *waki*, the secondary character in a noh play. This is followed by the appearance of the ghost of Sutoku, whose role is like that of the *shite*, the main figure in a noh drama. We discover the true identity or purpose of the *shite* during his/her exposition in which a story that is well known to the audience is retold. Once the true identity or purpose of the *shite* has been learned, the true form of the *shite* is also revealed. **Shiramine** follows this pattern, for after Sutoku explains his discontent, he shows himself to be a demon king. The fury of the ghost of Sutoku near the end of the story corresponds to the final, frenzied dance that is part of a noh finale in which the *shite* departs, leaving the *waki* to pray for his salvation.

A number of variations are introduced in Akinari's version that stress the position and power of the poet, Saigyō. First, the story is told by the ghost, but it is the poetry of Saigyō that brings forth the spirit and makes the narration possible. Poetry is used as a narrative frame, and its function is to bring the supernatural into the human realm, and to make the past comprehensible to the present.

A second element introduced into the noh structure is the way in which Saigyō engages the ghost in debate. It is not unusual for a *waki* to question or banter with the *shite*, but Saigyō's questions do not so much draw the ghost out as to challenge Sutoku's rationale for the Hōgen Disturbance, 1156. The story moves into the realm of political philosophy, and Saigyō becomes a mouthpiece for nativist ideology. He suggests that Sutoku was going against the teachings of the native gods of Japan when he rebelled.[10] The ghost defends his actions on Confucianist grounds, claiming that he had been a filial son while his father, Toba, was alive. He then cites Mencius's claim that rebellion is justified if it represents the mandate of Heaven.[11]

Saigyō at once challenges this rationale by arguing that it is not necessary to look to China for examples of proper action, and points to Ōsasagi and Uji, the sons of Emperor Ōjin, who are portrayed in *Nihon Shoki*. The ancient kings of Japan did not need Confucius to comprehend ethical behavior for it was immanent in them. Saigyō remarks that the work of Mencius has never reached Japan because the native gods will not permit the importation of such a dangerous foreign doctrine and will wreck all ships that try to bring the book. Having descended from the gods, the imperial line is inviolable, and thus the doctrine of rebellion is not applicable to Japan.[12]

The language of this part of the story differs from that of the travelogue and of Saigyō's poetry. The vocabulary and style of the debate are anachronistic since they reflect *kokugaku* methods and terminology, but that anachronism places *kokugaku* discourse within the context and authority of the poetic tradition. Saigyō's arguments, after the ghost admits rebellion is wrong, exert a strong influence on the way the story of Sutoku is read. Not only are Confucianist and Buddhist interpretations of events discredited, but also *kokugaku* assumptions shift the emphasis onto Sutoku's personal responsibility for allowing a foreign doctrine to obscure his native ethical qualities and set in motion the disaster that overtakes the court and the Taira family. Throughout **Shiramine** the process of history takes a secondary place to the process of language, of reinterpretation. Saigyō's narrative function as the observer-poet is transformed by the interjection of a new type of discourse, that of the *kokugakusha*, into the narrative.

A similar type of narrative transformation occurs in the collection's second story, **Kikuka no Chigiri, The Chrysanthemum Oath.** Its main source is the story *Fan Chu-ch'ing chi-shu ssu-sheng-chiao, Fan Chu-ch'ing: A*

Meal of Chicken and Millet, A Friendship of Life and Death, contained in the anthology *Yü-shih ming-yen, Clear Words to Illuminate the World,* compiled by Feng Meng-lung, 1574-1646. The Chinese story tells of an exemplary friendship between Fan Chu-ch'ing and Chang Shao. Akinari elaborated on this tale of loyalty by introducing a revenge plot that is justified and facilitated by *kokugaku* argumentation.

Akana Sōemon, the Fan character, served as a teacher of military strategy to En'ya Kamonnosuke, d. 1486, who served Sasaki Ujitsuna as lord of Tomita Castle in Izumo. Sōemon was sent on a secret mission to Ujitsuna in Ōmi province, and during his absence, Amako Tsunehisa, 1458-1541, attacked Tomita Castle and killed En'ya. When Ujitsuna did nothing, Sōemon tried to return to Izumo. On the way he fell ill and was nursed back to health by Hasebe Samon, the Chang character, a poor but honest scholar-physician.

Sōemon was alone in the world, and his friendship with Samon grew so strong that he agreed to become Samon's adoptive older brother. Soon after, he set out for Izumo, promising to return on the 9th day of the Ninth Month, the day of the Chrysanthemum Festival. When he arrived in Izumo, he found that no one remembered his duty to En'ya; even Sōemon's cousin, Akana Tanji, had switched allegiance to Tsunehisa. Sōemon considered Tsunehisa a paranoid man who inspired scant loyalty, and using his promise to meet Samon as an excuse, he asked for permission to leave. This was denied and he was placed under arrest by Tanji. Whereupon Sōemon killed himself so that his spirit could make the journey and keep the promise to return.

The day after Sōemon's ghost visits him, Samon leaves for Izumo to gather his brother's remains. He goes directly to Tanji's house and lectures him about loyalty. He tells the story of Kung-shu Tso, chief adviser to Liang, the ruler of the state of Wei during the Warring States period. Tso was ill and Liang, worried that he would soon be without a trusted adviser, asked who should take his place. Tso recommends the youthful Shang Yang, but warns Liang that if he chooses not to make use of the young man, then he should kill him. For if Shang Yang were to go to another state he would pose a threat to Wei. When it is clear to Tso that his recommendation will not be heeded, he secretly calls in Shang Yang and urges him to escape. Samon tells Tanji that he should have treated Sōemon in this manner, and at the very end of the narrative, Samon's purpose is revealed.[13]

Samon's argument is not important for its moral content, which is rather ordinary, but for its function as a plot device that lulls the reader (as well as the onlookers in the story, Tanji and his retainers) into a sense of complacency that is shattered by an act of revenge. Fin-ishing his lecture, he suddenly draws his sword, cuts down Tanji, and makes his escape. When considering Samon's revenge, its ethical motivation is not so clearcut. After all, should not Tsunehisa, or even Sasaki Ujitsuna, have been the object of his hatred? The structure of the work, in which the act that makes Samon the hero occurs so suddenly and so near the end, forces the reader to focus on that act, not on the moral reasoning behind it. The language that precedes the climactic moment is that of the *kokugakusha,* and this particular idiom moves the reading of Samon's actions away from ethical interpretations and toward an intuitive admiration for the beauty of the act of revenge. In reworking the model story, Akinari transforms the original moral implications into an emotional, aesthetic experience.

The fifth story in the collection, ***Buppōsō, The Bird of the Three Treasures,*** clearly reveals its debt to *kokugaku* in the philological argument that comprises the central scene of the narrative. Muzen, a *haikai* poet, and his son have come to Mt Kōya to worship, and decide to spend the night there in prayer and meditation. During the night Muzen explains the significance of the sacred mountain, and recounts the miracles performed by the temple's founder, Kūkai. When he finishes his account they hear the call of a *buppōsō,* a bird whose cry, 'Buppan' or 'Buppōsō', was identified with the Three Treasures of Buddhism.[14] Muzen takes this as an auspicious sign, and recites two poems for his son's benefit: a *kanshi* by Kūkai,[15] and a waka by Fujiwara Mitsutoshi, 1210-1276.[16] He is then inspired to produce his own verse, which he composes in the seventeen-syllable *haikai* form that he favors.[17]

This series of poems sets the stage for the encounter of the two men with the ghosts of Toyotomi Hidetsugu, 1568-1595, and his retinue. Like the ghost of Emperor Sutoku, the spirit of Hidetsugu is an angry one. The period of his rule as *kampaku,* or chancellor, was a reign of terror that ended in 1595 when his uncle, Hideyoshi, forced him to commit suicide. The ghost of Hidetsugu calls for Satomura Jōha, 1524-1602, a renowned master of *renga,* and he questions the poet about the things of antiquity. Jōha's learned answers win praise and reward from the nobleman. The activities of the ghostly retinue are carried out in the language of philological scholarship. As in ***Shiramine*** and ***Kikuka no Chigiri,*** there is a strong connection between this language and the appearance of the supernatural.

As the discussions continue, one of the warrior-ghosts cites the following waka by Kūkai:

> *Wasurete mo*
> *kumiyashitsuran*
> *tabibito no*
> *takano no oku no*
> *Tamagawa no mizu*

> Lest you forget,
> traveler, you should not drink
>   the poisonous waters
> of Tamagawa
> in the recesses of Takano.[18]

The warrior points out that Kūkai, whose virtue gave him extraordinary powers, could easily have purified the stream, and asks Jōha why he did not. The poet explains that the poem, from *Fūgashū,* the seventeenth imperial anthology, is prefaced by the following *koto-bagaki*:

> On the road to the shrine in the recesses of Takano is a river called the Tamagawa. Because many poisonous insects cover the surface of the water, the following poem was composed to keep those who read it from drinking from this stream.[19]

Jōha maintains that because of the great priest's powers the *kotobagaki* cannot be correct. The word *tama* in Tamagawa, for example, means 'jewel', and was used to praise the purity of the stream. He concludes that the *kotobagaki* was a later, mistaken addition to the poem, and should be read:

> Even though pilgrims to the shrine in the recesses of Takano may have forgotten this stream, they will be struck by its purity and instinctively scoop up the water and drink.[20]

Hidetsugu is delighted and calls for a poem by the *renga* master. Jōha declines, and urges Muzen to recite the poem he composed earlier that evening. Identifying each of the ghosts, Jōha tells Muzen, 'You and your son have been granted a wonderful audience.'[21]

The design of the story of the ghostly encounter, initiated by the earthly attachments of Hidetsugu, reflects a historical awareness of the order and language of the poems recited earlier by Muzen to his son. The sequence moves from the seriousness of Kūkai's *kanshi* to a classical waka, and then to Muzen's modern stanza that seeks to echo its ancient models. Within that poetic context Jōha's arguments are not an empty pedantic exercise, but constitute an important element that draws together the various parts of the narrative—the poetry, the setting, the allusions to Kūkai and to Hidetsugu—and connects them with the *haikai* world of Muzen. The fact that Muzen has been granted 'a wonderful audience' indicates the power of his art to invoke the past in its own way and time. Yet this power, while it brings the poetic past alive in the present, also helps to create an aesthetic effect appropriate to the narrative, the sense of horror that accompanies the ghostly encounter.[22]

Himpukuron, the final story of the collection, is, as the title suggests, 'a dialogue about poverty and wealth'. With its prophecy of peace and prosperity to come un-der the wise rule of the Tokugawa regime, it provides a sense of closure for the collection in both a chronological and an ideological sense. Disputation plays an important role in many of the stories, but usually the dialogues take place within a larger context. In ***Himpukuron,*** Akinari moves most completely to the language of *kokugaku* as his literary medium in an attempt to elevate the rhetoric of argument to the level of art. From the standpoint of modern expectations his concept of a literary language in this story is an alien one, and his effort may not seem satisfactory. Thus, the tale must be read within the context of *kokugaku* language and method of argumentation.

Akinari's hero is based on a real-life warrior, known as Okano Sanai, who fought for Gamō Ujisato, 1556-1595, and for the Uesugi clan. He appears in a number of books that served as sources for ***Himpukuron.***[23] The story opens with a discussion of Sanai's character. He is a good warrior, but the pleasure he derives by counting out his pieces of gold repels people. His miserly reputation is changed one day when he finds out that one of his servants has secretly managed to set aside a *koban,* a small ingot of gold. He summons the man and tells him that because the power of wealth far exceeds that of weapons, a warrior must never waste gold. Extremely pleased that the servant has saved more than was expected of him, Sanai rewards him with ten *ryō* of gold and a sword. From that day on people stopped thinking of Sanai as a miser, but as 'merely eccentric'.[24]

On the night of the incident with his servant, Sanai is awakened by a tiny old man who is the spirit of the gold that Sanai has managed to accumulate. Pleased with the treatment accorded the servant, the spirit has come to share his thoughts. Their dialogue consists of three sections. In the first part the spirit praises wealth. In the second, Sanai offers his defense of poverty. In the final section the spirit presents his main argument that the accumulation of wealth, or the failure to do so, has nothing to do with moral behavior. The spirit of wealth has to be respected because it is different from the spirit of man.

> Even though it is often said that the accumulation of wealth is related to morals, in fact neither the wealth of an immoral man nor the wealth of a gentleman has anything to do with morality. The person who acts according to his opportunities will live frugally, save, and work hard, and his house will flourish of its own accord. I know nothing of the Buddhist teaching about previous lives, nor do my ideas have any connection with the Confucian idea of the will of Heaven. I travel in a different realm.[25]

The way to wealth is a practical art that requires experience and learning to master, and the empty theorizing of Buddhists and Confucians does not explain its nature. And how is this practical art learned? By looking to the way of the ancient sages who made no distinction between moral and immoral wealth. Each activity of human life has its own reasons and its own proper place. Wealth and poverty must be understood on their own terms. This argument forms the heart of the story, and it is structurally similar to *kokugaku* views of literary practice in that it strongly suggests that the act of narration also stands independent of the interpretations of narrow ethical systems.

NOTIONS OF THE ARTIST: THE BUNJIN IDEAL

The ideas about art and the artist presented in **Ugetsu Monogatari** play a significant role in shaping both the structure and language of the tales. Two notions are especially important. The first is the idea of the literary artist as an interpreter of tradition who, like a musician interpreting a composition, plays out variations on established themes. Since his material was already known, the interest of any new story lay in the degree and quality of its variation. Thus the idea of the artist as an interpreter of his tradition not only justified the rewriting of earlier ghost stories, but also provided the narrative mechanism by which to achieve these variations. The second is the notion of the artist as having some connection with the supernatural. Often supernatural encounters in the stories are the result of an act of artistic creativity, so that the notion of a deep connection between art and the supernatural is embedded in the text. The primary sources for these ideas were the Chinese ideal of the literatus, and the naturalization of that ideal by the practitioners of *haikai* poetry.

Although the ideal of the *bunjin* was to a large extent an adaptation of Chinese conceptions by Edo-period writers, some general differences should be noted. First, the educational and social background of the Chinese *wenjen* (J. *bunjin*) was more uniform than that of their Japanese counterparts. This was the product of the stronger institutional support provided *wenjen* culture by the bureaucracy's examination system. Because Neo-Confucian and *kokugaku* aesthetic ideals were so influential, the literary ideas of most *bunjin* shared certain structural and methodological similarities. Thus it would be misleading to portray the *bunjin* as a much more varied class than the *wenjen*. All the same, Robert Hegel points to certain social constraints, especially 'the Confucian legacy of attention to social roles, models, and responsibilities', that tended to make the *wenjen* relatively more uniform in outlook.

> Despite the avowed emphasis on the pursuit of individual self-expression among late Ming literati, their lives followed common patterns, life styles determined to a greater extent by externals such as economic and social considerations than by individual will. . . . The discernible limits of individualism among the elite as a consequence of this [Confucian] tradition likewise tended to curb the extent to which eccentric behavior could go.[26]

I do not suggest that the *wenjen* ideal was a fixed, universal concept. Rather, there was an ambivalence between the particularism of methodology and the absolutism of belief in certain values such that the outlook of the literati moved across a range defined by the tension between individualism and traditionalism. Within that range several concerns dominated *bunjin* thought.

First, there was a commitment to orthodox morality. This commitment was an ideological expression of the values of a particular class that shared a common background and transmitted a conservative cultural tradition. Neo-Confucian developments in Ming China contributed to this conservatism by seeking to recover linguistic origins. Consequently, the literature of the period often attacked the shortcomings of the present age, and sought for proper models to define the correct way of writing.[27]

Balancing this traditionalism was an emphasis on self-cultivation. This did not imply unbridled freedom, but within the restraints imposed by traditionalism some leeway was permitted through eclectic style and personal interpretation. Operating strictly within the canons of taste that defined the literati class, it was possible for the individual to give expression to his personal understanding of these canons. As Joseph Levenson has observed about literati painters in China:

> By late Ming times, the end of the approved painter was the demonstration of his mastery of means. Style became a counter in an artist's game of self-display, while gentry-literati-officials and their set were the self-appreciative few who recognized the rules and knew the esoterica.[28]

Expression of the self was tied to a knowledge of the tradition, to a concern with style and structure, but it did not depend on technical proficiency alone. Technical proficiency was the concern of the craftsman; for the literati, connoisseurship and amateurism were far more important. Connoisseurship was the bridge between personal preference and established canons. It defined the individual in relation to the tradition.

Akinari consciously invoked his relationship with his tradition throughout his work. That he believed he was following accepted practice in borrowing or adapting other works is apparent in his willingness to acknowledge his debts to both the Chinese and Japanese literary traditions in comments he made in the preface to **Seken Tekake Katagi,** his second *ukiyo-zōshi,* written shortly before he began composing **Ugetsu Monogatari.**

> Looking among the many *hachimonjiyabon* and the playful works of Kiseki and Jishō, you will find the manners of the present-day world described as they really are. The calculating spirit of the merchant, or the stinginess of the old man, are played out for us in imitation of notes first plucked by Saikaku. When you

read about the endless self-indulgence of a son who gambles away the wealth of his parents, or loses his home and fortune one evening in a disreputable place, ignoring the admonitions of a faithful servant and the love of his mother, you feel that it really happened.[29]

One of the appealing aspects of the *hachimonjiyabon*, Akinari writes, is its way of portraying the world exactly as it is. Kiseki and Jishō are likened to musicians who interpret the work of a composer; and the verisimilitude of their own writings stems not just from the details of their stories, but from the degree to which the stories remain true to literary types and conventions familiar to the reader. Originality becomes a matter not just of 'newness', but of the degree of variation on narrative types.

Akinari elaborates on his notion of the arts in the preface of *Ugetsu Monogatari.*

> Lo Kuan-chung wrote *Shui hu chuan,* and subsequently monstrous children were born to three generations of his descendants. Murasaki Shikibu wrote *Genji Monogatari* and subsequently she descended into hell. It is thought that the reason for their suffering was punishment for having led people astray with their fiction. Yet when we look at their works we see in them an abundance of strange and wondrous things. The force of their words draws near the truth; the rhythm of their sentences is mellifluous and lovely, touching the heart of the reader like the reverberations of a koto. They make us see the reality of the distant past.
>
> As for myself, I have a few stories that are nothing more than the products of idleness in an age of peace and prosperity. But when the words come tumbling from my lips, they sound as strange and inauspicious as the raucous crying of pheasants, or the roar of dragons. My tales are slipshod and full of errors. Accordingly, those who thumb through this volume are not expected to mistake my jottings for the truth. On the other hand, I shall avoid the retribution of descendants with three lips or noseless faces.[30]

Although the tone here is light, it is in keeping with the contrast that Akinari wants to make between his approach, which claims to understand the pleasures of literature, and that of the overly serious moralists. The achievement of writers such as Lo and Murasaki is that their works have the power to elicit strong emotional responses that bring the reader near the truth, or that reveal the reality of a different time or place. But Akinari is not putting forth a purely realistic view of fiction. The interest of the stories of Lo and Murasaki lies in the telling of 'strange and wondrous things', and is not limited to the merely plausible. Fictional narrative is not equated with reality, and in his choice of the phrase *shin ni semari,* 'drawing near the truth', Akinari emphasizes that a distance remains between literary language and the real world. The verisimilitude of great literature instead rests on the truth of language and rhetorical convention.[31]

This approach seeks to understand literature according to its particular laws and methods, not according to a predetermined reading based on an inflexible set of values. Akinari's argument clearly shows his debt to *kokugaku* notions of the autonomy of literary practice, and it follows naturally from that point that he looks to the literary language of the past to find his models. He praises Lo and Murasaki for their skilled use of language, repeating the musical image he drew in his earlier homage to Saikaku. He emphasizes that the affective quality of literary language is the mechanism by which truth is revealed. This suggests that the emotional response elicited by fiction is somewhat entwined with the real world.[32] His assessment that the work of Lo and Murasaki 'make us see the reality of the distant past' foreshadows the idea he later put forth in *Nubatama no Maki* that long ago fiction and reality were not divided; and his emphasis on the correctness of ancient models leads him to humbly state that his own work is defective.

Akinari then ridicules Confucianist and Buddhist interpretations that, in reading only a narrow realism in *Shui hu chuan* and *Genji Monogatari,* conclude that these works threatened to lead people astray by presenting fictional experience as true. Out of the tradition of this type of moralistic reading legends arose about how both Lo and Murasaki were punished for writing so well.[33] That Akinari took an ironic view of these legends is suggested by the name he used for the preface—Senshi Kijin, 'the eccentric with clipped fingers'.[34] When Akinari was five years old he contracted smallpox, and an infection caused two of his fingers, one on each hand, to atrophy, leaving him noticeably deformed. Like another of his pseudonyms, Muchō ('the crab'), Senshi Kijin is a self-mocking reference to his crippled hands. In all his surviving works, 'Senshi Kijin' is used only once.[35] This choice of names was a sly way for Akinari to reject the moralists and proclaim the value of literature and of his own position as one of the deformed descendants of Lo.

Writers such as Akinari did not simply adopt the concerns of the *wenjen*, but adapted them to their own particular situations. This tendency arose mainly because of the difference, mentioned above, between the *bunjin* and their Chinese counterparts, that is, the greater uniformity among the gentry-officials who made up the literary class in China. There was a greater degree of diversity in Japan, with members of the literati class drawn from administrators, professionals, and merchants. The elitism inherent to such a class was there, but it was a class defined by its occupation with literature, not by its uniform social background. Differences from the Chinese conception of the literati ideal also arose because of the greater commercialization of *bunjin* culture, partly attributable to the growth of the publishing industry. But it was not merely the tangible products of literary practice that were merchandised, for many poets set themselves up as masters of their own schools and lived off the proceeds of their teaching. Akinari, who made very little from his own writing, deplored such activities.[36] Regardless of his low opinion of the state of the arts, it was perhaps inevitable that the *bunjin* turned to their art to make a living, since they lacked official status and support. Mark Morris notes that the Chinese 'who considered themselves *wenjen* had the education and income to make artistic amateurism a viable stance.'[37] He also points out that for an artist such as Yosa Buson, a *haikai* poet and painter, life was a different matter.

> Like other eighteenth-century *bunjin* 'literati' artists, he was in theory as a much a poet as a painter. In practice, he was a painter who enjoyed *haikai* as a vocation. However much a Japanese *bunjin* might admire his Chinese *wenjen* predecessors' ideal of multitalented amateurship, a *bunjin* like Buson had to put one or another of his talents to work in the cultural marketplace.[38]

The greater lack of uniformity among the *bunjin* is manifested in the proliferation of schools of literature or art that grew up around master artists. This feature is most apparent in *haikai* poetry, which Akinari avidly practiced. Although he treated waka with more scholarly seriousness, much of his literary activity centered on his connections with poetry circles. His most famous relationship in the world of *haikai* was with Buson. Theirs was not a close personal friendship, but they appear to have felt a sense of mutual admiration.[39] In the preface to a collection of verse titled *Shundei Kushū*, 1777, Buson sets forth his ideas about *haikai* and literature. The preface is in a question-and-answer format, with a disciple interrogating Buson. The first question, 'What is *haikai*?' receives the following reply:

> *Haikai* is that which values detachment from the vulgar while using vulgar language. Using the vulgar to be free of the vulgar, the rule of detachment is very difficult. *Haikai* is like the rule of detachment in Zen, when Priest So-and-So asks about the sound of one hand clapping.

Because detachment from the vulgar, which is likened to a form of enlightenment, is so difficult to attain, the disciple next wants to know whether there is a quick way to achieve it.

> Yes, there is. You must study Chinese poetry. You must, from the beginning, always study Chinese poetry. Do not follow any other way.

On a later occasion, we are told, Buson urges his pupil 'to become friends with', that is, to study closely, four great *haikai* masters of the past. He also recommends him to become well acquainted with nature.

> Enjoying the calm spirit of natural scenery, making elegance your state of mind—these are like the beginning of things. Close your eyes and struggle to write a poem; when you have the verse, open your eyes. Soon you will leave the poets of the past behind, and without knowing how, you will be transformed into an immortal. Spellbound, you will tarry by yourself a while. In time the fragrance of the flowers will waft on the breeze; the moonlight will float on the water. You are in the realm of *haikai*.[40]

One of the most interesting propositions here is Buson's appropriation of vulgar language for the purpose of literature. The notion that vulgar language has value only when it is used within a context created by a literary consciousness is a reworking of earlier ideas about composition that governed the efforts of Chinese literati, especially compilers such as Feng, and that affect the methods of adaptation in Edo fiction. A second idea that is notable concerns the way to achieve detachment. The artist must study the classical models of the past. Study is crucial to determine what is vulgar, for it provides the *bunjin* with a sense of discrimination. The model here is the ideal of connoiseurship, in which the *bunjin* strives for self-cultivation through an understanding of the canons of taste.

A third idea expressed by Buson is significant for Akinari's work. *Haikai* is achieved not only by looking to models of the past, but also by observing the natural world. By virtue of observation the poet is able to discriminate, to understand an elegant state of mind, and thereby transform himself into an immortal. The artist is connected to the supernatural, and the image of the artist as an immortal reveals the shared values of Buson and Akinari. Implicit in this notion is an affective theory of poetry that places value upon the intuited and natural over the artificial. The power of intuition is nonetheless cultivated, or learned, and in this respect Buson owes much to the *wenjen* ideal. Moreover, his conception of *haikai* fits comfortably into the larger complex of aesthetic and philosophical ideas outlined above. It moves between the opposite poles of intellectualism and intuitionism that formed the defining boundaries of the literati ideal of mid-Edo Japan; and it was an integral part of the literary trend toward a subordination of ethics to art.

The power of art and literature is closely associated throughout ***Ugetsu Monogatari*** with the supernatural, with the artist acting as a mediator between the supernatural and mundane. For example, in ***Shiramine*** and ***Kikuka no Chigiri*** the ghostly encounters are initiated by the actions of characters who are associated with art or with scholarship. The third story in the collection, ***Asajigayado,*** presents a similar synthesis by stressing the beauty of the moral ideal depicted, the loving devotion and feminine piety of the heroine, Miyagi. Miyagi is left behind by her young husband, Katsushirō, when he travels to the capital to rebuild his fortune. War and other circumstances prevent him from returning for seven years. When he finally goes home he is surprised to find his wife still alive. He spends the night with her, only to discover on the following day that he has slept with her ghost.

Perhaps the most interesting aspect of the narrative in this story is its heavy reliance on poetic allusion to an archetypal motif in Japanese literature, the longing of an abandoned woman.[41] In particular, the two poems Akinari creates for the story, Miyagi's death poem and Katsushirō's lament, stress the theme of longing. Her poem is discovered on her grave.

> *Saritomo to*
> *omou kokoro ni*
>   *hakararete*
> *yo ni mo kyō made*
> *ikeru inochi ka*
>
>   Deceived by my longing heart,
> which thought he would return,
>   how have I continued
> even to this day
> to live in the world?[42]

When Katsushirō later learns the details of his wife's death, how she fought off suitors and preserved her devotion to the end of her life, he is moved to compose the following poem of farewell in what is described as the faltering, clumsy manner of an uncouth rustic:

> *Inishie no*
> *Mama no Tegona o*
>   *kaku bakari*
> *koite shi aran*
> *Mama no Tegona*
>
>   Did they yearn
> in olden days
>   for Tegona from Mama
> the way I yearn for you?
> Ah, Tegona from Mama.[43]

Katsushirō's poem compares the story of his beloved wife with the tale related in *Man'yōshū* about a woman named Mama no Tegona who killed herself when she could not have the man she loved. About Katsushirō's poem, the narrator remarks,

> He was not able to scratch even the surface of his emotions, and yet it could be said that his work had more true feeling [*masarite aware nari*] than the poems of people who are much more skilled at versifying.[44]

It is strange that the tale should end with a verse that is acknowledged as pedestrian. It is possible that Akinari wanted to write a poor poem in order to maintain the consistency of his portrait of Katsushirō as unsophisticated, but I do not believe that he was so concerned with that aspect of the story. Instead, the flatness of the language seems to serve the purpose of invoking the poetic tradition represented by *Man'yōshū*. The comparison calls forth the emotional response that produced

the poem, a response that is sincere and heartfelt, emulating at least the poetic spirit that produced great works in the past. Katsushirō's verse cannot compete with those works, but by recapturing at least the spirit of the past, if not its elegant language, the poem, and, by implication, the story of Miyagi's longing and devotion, is worthy of the tradition.

The literary conventions of the ghost story and the motif of the longing, devoted woman are joined in a nearly perfect match in Akinari's variation. There were two main sources for his plot. The first is a tale from *Konjaku Monogatari* that tells of a man who, tired of living in poverty in the capital, leaves his wife and takes a position and a new wife in the provinces.[45] Returning to the capital years later he finds his house in ruins, but his first wife is there waiting for him. She forgets her resentment at once (an action repeated by Miyagi), and he spends the night with her only to make the shocking discovery on the following morning that he is embracing a corpse. The second model is a Chinese story titled *Ai-ch'ing chuan* that appears in *Chienteng hsin-hua*, c. 1378, a collection of ghost stories compiled by Ch'u Yu. Ai-ch'ing is a beautiful, educated courtesan who is skilled at poetry. Like Miyagi, she is an extremely pious wife who is left behind when her husband goes to the capital, and she commits suicide rather than submit to the advances of another man. When Chao, her husband, finally returns, he buries Ai-ch'ing next to his mother, and after ten days of prayer her ghost appears to him. She thanks him for making her his wife and saving her from the life of a courtesan, and he thanks her for her devoted love. She is later reborn as a baby boy.[46]

Akinari borrows two noteworthy elements. First, he retains the element of surprise found in the *Konjaku* story. **Asajigayado** is structured so that Miyagi's fate is left unresolved. Katsushirō then acts as our eyes and ears to complete her story. His discovery is also the reader's discovery, although the allusive nature of the text creates the suspicion that Miyagi is a ghost by constantly situating the text within a tradition of love-yearning/haunting tales. The second element is the similarity between Ai-ch'ing and Miyagi as poets. They are both archetypes of uxorial love and devotion, and that quality manifest itself in their literary abilities. The borrowing and allusion in the story create a context in which the mysterious, lyrical beauty of Miyagi, which is both an ethical and an artistic ideal, can be expressed.

Another example in **Ugetsu Monogatari** where the connection between the artist and the supernatural plays a prominent role is provided by the story **Muō no Rigyō**. There is no other story in the collection that reproduces so faithfully the details of the materials it adapts,[47] but Akinari varied the account through the portrait of his hero, Kōgi. The tale is set in the Enchō period, 923-

931, when Kōgi is a priest at Miidera, and also a painter whose skill is widely acclaimed. He paints only fish, and often goes out onto Lake Biwa to observe and sketch, paying fishermen to free the fish they have caught. Filling in Kōgi's background, Akinari prefaces his main story with the following anecdote:

> One time, as he was putting all his skill and heart into a painting, he fell asleep; in his dream he entered the river and played with the various kinds of fish. When he awoke he at once painted the fish exactly as he had seen them. Hanging the painting on the wall he titled it himself, calling it *Muō no Rigyo* [*Carp inspired by a dream*].

Kōgi's artistic method is ostensibly realistic—he paints things as he sees them—but it is realism of a different order, inspired by his vision, not by the real world. His moral actions are transformed into art, which takes on its own life. Kōgi's vision of art is apparent in his attitude toward his painting of carp, the fish he loves the best, which he is reluctant to give up. His reason, he jokes, is, 'I couldn't possibly give away fish raised by a priest to Philistines who would take their lives and eat them.'[48]

One year Kōgi falls seriously ill, and his spirit wanders from his body. Because of the great merit he has accured by saving living creatures, the god of the sea grants his wish to become a carp. His adventure ends when he is caught and eaten by friends. Upon the death of the fish his spirit returns to his body and he recovers. He proves the truthfulness of his story by pointing out details about his friends that he witnessed as a carp. *Muō no Rigyo* then concludes as follows:

> Kōgi recovered after this and lived to a ripe old age. When he was approaching death, he took his many paintings of carp and scattered them on the lake. Whereupon the carp that had been painted leapt off the silk scrolls and sported in the water. For this reason his paintings were never handed down. His disciple, Narimitsu, inherited his master's art and gained renown. Once he painted a rooster on a sliding door in the Kan'in Palace, and a live rooster, seeing the painting, scratched at it. So it is written in old tales.[49]

Narimitsu's skill is said to have been great enough to fool a rooster, but his skill never attains the standard set by his master. Kōgi managed to break down the distinction between art and reality, so that painted fish were capable of swimming off the silk and into nature. The miraculous transformation portrayed in the story is the one achieved by the artist. By shifting the emphasis from the concern with narrative credibility, reflected in the model stories by the use of circumstantial detail to prove the truth of the extraordinary experience, to the artistic spirit that brings life to the story, Akinari has, in his own 'carp inspired by a dream', created a metaphor for the process of art.

Yet another striking portrait of the artist is presented in *Aozukin.* This story resembles the short religious tales found in *setsuwa* collections such as *Nihon Ryōiki* and *Konjaku Monogatari,* and borrows elements from two common types of Buddhist *setsuwa*: the miraculous deeds performed by a priest, and the explanation of the founding of a particular temple.[50] The narrative of *Aozukin* is also fairly straightforward, and its simplicity calls to mind the *setsuwa* form. Like *Muō no Rigyo,* it presents a supernatural transformation. However, the transformation in this case is not the result of saintliness, but of a fall from grace into a demonic state.

The hero of the tale, the priest Kaian Zenji, visits the village of Tomita on a pilgrimage. There he hears the story of a local priest who was once an enlightened man but who fell in love with a young boy. The priest's obsession was so great that when the boy died he would not give him up. Not able to bear watching the body decay, the priest went insane and devoured the corpse. He turned into a flesh-eating demon who terrorized the province.

Upon hearing this story Kaian resolves to intervene, in a sense to rewrite the story, in order to save the man. He goes up to a desolate mountain where he encounters a sinister-looking priest who warns him to return before dark. Despite the eerie setting, Kaian remains. Around midnight, under a beautiful moon, the demon-priest re-emerges, ready to devour Kaian. But Kaian's virtue renders him invisible to the demon-priest, who, after searching here and there in a frantic, crazy dance, collapses in the garden.[51] On the following morning he recognizes that Kaian is a living Buddha, and asks to be taught the way to salvation. Kaian gives him a koan in the form of two verses.[52] He places a blue hood, or *aozukin,* a symbol of Sōtō priesthood, on the demon-priest's head, and he tells him to sit there and meditate on the meaning of the verses.

A year passes and there is no more trouble around Tomita. When Kaian returns he finds the priest still here, chanting in a voice so muffled that it is like the murmuring of a mosquito. He recognizes the koan and demands an answer, striking the demon-priest on the head. At once the body of the priest and his demonic possession disappear, leaving only a skeleton and a blue hood. Kaian's fame spreads, and he turns the temple into a Sōtō establishment.[53]

The main elaboration is on the structure of the *setsuwa* form. Kaian's visit to Tomita and his miraculous act of salvation are the frame that contains the primary story of the demon-priest. Like tales in *Nihon Ryōiki,* for example, the story of the priest could be interpreted as a simple moral fable illustrating the evil effects of lust and the workings of karmic retribution. But in *Aozukin* this *setsuwa*-like kernel story is left incomplete, and the hero, Kaian, enters into and interacts with the world created by that story. His intervention goes the original story one better, not in an ethical sense, since the moral of *Aozukin* is not really different from the moral of the *setsuwa*-like story, but in a literary sense.

This shift to literary or artistic concerns is further indicated by the priest's miraculous transformation, which is determined by the nature of his human desires. Here *Aozukin* bears a marked resemblance to *Muō no Rigyo*. Kōgi's vision and the priest's tenacity transport them to realms beyond normal human existence, not only as a fish or a demon, but as men who achieve salvation. The mundane language represented by the circumstantial detail of *Muō no Rigyo* and by the simplicity of the *setsuwa* form sets off the elevated language associated with the supernatural. The realms that Kōgi and the demon-priest enter overlap the realm of art. Kaian first hears the tale and then enters into the world of that tale; a poem provides both the instrument of salvation and the narrative frame marking the beginning and end of the progress to enlightenment. Thus the structure of *Aozukin* suggests a close connection between salvation and art.

CHINESE VERNACULAR FICTION AND THE DEVELOPMENT OF THE YOMIHON

Kokugaku ideology stressed the autonomy of literary practice, while the notion of the artist prevalent in Akinari's time defined that practice as one involving an adaptation of the tradition. Under these influences the processes of language—the creation of new modes of narrative and the variation of style—became his primary concern. Given the diversity of materials he borrowed, it is hardly surprising that the language and narrative techniques in *Ugetsu Monogatari* are of a hybrid nature. It was, however, Chinese vernacular fiction that provided the primary models for the narrative form to convey his aesthetic ideology.

Because of his extensive use of models, the stories in *Ugetsu Monogatari* are referred to as *hon'an shōsetsu,* or adapted novels. The use of foreign materials seems strange in light of the nativist tendencies of *kokugaku,* but since matters of literary practice or rhetorical convention were considered separate from larger ethical concerns, it is likely that Akinari did not sense any contradiction in adapting Chinese vernacular fiction. In any case his view of the arts as an interpreter of the tradition meant that he was free to use Chinese models for his own purposes.[54]

For the most part the Ming novels and anthologies that were adapted by Japanese writers were not the products of a popular tradition but of a literati one. The popular tradition in China was certainly vibrant, nurtured by an urban culture and by expanding social and economic circumstances similar to those that helped shape the *chōnin,* or townsman, culture in Japan. The growth of the Chinese population, increased foreign contacts, shifts to new types of manufacture and marketing, and a general rise in the level of education had an 'undeniable effect on the broadening of the audience for printed fiction.'

> But it is still the scholar-official class, with its own sense of identity and mission, along with its special aesthetic pretensions, that forms the social basis for the emergence of the sophisticated novel genre in the sixteenth century.[55]

As in Edo Japan, the reading audience in sixteenth- and seventeenth-century China increased, and distinctions that might be likened to classes of readership subsequently appeared, with the levels and types of reading material growing more diversified. The authors and readership of the sophisticated works of Ming fiction, which were by and large the works that served as models for writers such as Akinari, constituted a literary elite.[56] One of the characteristics of this group was a tendency to use colloquial language or popular literary conventions within a framework provided by the classical idiom of their education.[57]

The most important influence on Japanese fiction was not so much the specific linguistic features of the classical and vernacular idioms, but the general critical distinction between a classical, elegant style and a vernacular, vulgar one. This distinction became widespread in Japan in the early eighteenth century when it was used by students of Chinese fiction, *kogaku* scholars such as Sorai, to refer to the classical and vernacular components of Ming fiction; and it was later employed by nativist Japanese critics to distinguish between the classical idiom of the Heian period and the colloquial language of their own day.[58] The use of colloquial language within the context of a classical idiom, or in contrast to that idiom, suggests a consciously literary approach to fiction by those Chinese literati emulated in Japan. For example, Feng made his material, by and large popular tales, more literary not simply by rewriting them, but by collecting them in an anthology, an act that places the stories within a context created by an editorial sensibility.

The presence of the compiler-editor pervades a number of important mid-Edo works. In 1749 Tsuga Teishō, 1718-?1795, published *Kokon Kidan Hanabusa Sōshi,* a collection of nine stories in five volumes, eight of which were based on tales from Feng's collection. Teishō reworked the stories, setting them in the Kamakura and Muromachi periods, but perhaps the most significant aspect of the work is its style. Teishō remarks in his preface that he has tried to echo the stylistic qualities of his Chinese models, with their mix of vernacular and classical elements, and to separate his work from other *sōshi*, which he considers entertaining but vulgar. He has therefore chosen to rewrite using what he terms an 'elegant' style of language.[59] Teishō's experiments were emulated by other writers. Takebe Ayatari, 1719-1774, for example, recast *Shui hu chuan* into a native form, publishing *Honchō Suikoden* in 1773; and Akinari even copied the format of *Hanabusa Sōshi* by dividing his nine stories into five volumes.[60] Chinese fiction thus had a direct impact on Edo fiction in general, and on *Ugetsu Monogatari* in particular.

The influence of Chinese literature on Akinari's narrative choices is found not only in the specific elements he borrowed, but also in the general outlook he brought to fiction. His method of adaptation was not a blind adherence to models, but was shaped by both a strong awareness of his literary tradition and a sense of the need to vary that tradition. The critical distinction between classical and vernacular styles lies at the heart of his work. The classical idiom provided a way (although certainly not the only way) to invoke the authority of the past and to place the colloquial within a traditional context; and the vernacular idiom provided a means to create variations on the classical idiom and place the old within a new context.

A broad correspondence with the aims and methods of *kokugaku* is apparent here in the sense that, as a literary approach, this method of adaptation seeks justification for itself in a kind of neo-classical invocation of an ideal past. The transmission of the ideology of Ming Neo-Confucianism, and thus of *kokugaku,* was greatly facilitated by similarities in the social realities and cultural assumptions of China and Japan, and by the importation of literary models that bore the stamp of that ideology. The choice of the supernatural narrative for *Ugetsu Monogatari* thus reflects both the literary prestige of Chinese fiction and its ideological function; and that choice in turn helped to pave the way for the development of one of the important narrative forms of the latter half of the Edo period, the *yomihon.*

Although some scholars, notably Nakamura Yukihiko, have classified *Ugetsu Monogatari* as an early *yomihon,* that classification requires some refinement.[61] The *yomihon* was not fully developed and recognized as a separate form until around the beginning of the nineteenth century; as its name indicates, it was a book intended for reading, for most other forms of fiction relied as much upon pictures as upon text for appeal. As it did not utilize the picture-text format, the *yomihon* presupposed a higher degree of literacy among its readership than, for example, the *sharebon* or *kokkeibon,* two forms of popular, humorous fiction.[62] Moreover, the *yomihon* was often published in printings of no more than 1,000 or 2,000 copies, and was usually more expensive than other types of books; this put it beyond

the reach of most readers.[63] Although it is difficult to give an accurate estimate of the numbers of *yomihon* readers, the figures cited above and the specialization of fictional forms are evidence that both writers and printers produced their books with specific audience in mind. It thus seems reasonable to view the *yomihon* as an exclusive type of book that was aimed at a relatively more sophisticated readership.[64]

Strictly speaking, **Ugetsu Monogatari** is not a *yomihon.* The exhaustive classification of fictional types that distinguished the *yomihon* as a special form developed after **Ugetsu Monogatari** was published. Nonetheless, even though late contemporaries of Akinari did not refer to his work as a *yomihon,* it seems likely that they read and understood it within a group of works that constituted the origins of the form. Ōta Nampo, 1749-1823, for example, looked upon Teishō's *Hanabusa Sōshi* as the ancestor of *yomihon;*[65] and Kyokutei Bakin, 1767-1848, made a claim for *Honchō Suikoden* as the first true *yomihon.*[66] Of course, Bakin and Nampo were reinterpreting the tradition to fit their own literary goals, but in general they shared the same intellectual background and literary concerns as Teishō, Ayatari, and Akinari, and their critical interpretations shared similar tendencies. Thus, while **Ugetsu Monogatari** is perhaps not a true *yomihon,* it does not greatly distort the reading of the work to speak of it within that particular tradition. At the least, **Ugetsu Monogatari** shares two characteristics with the works of Teishō and Ayatari: an emphasis on matters of style, as seen in the mixture of elegant and vernacular elements, and the adaptation of Chinese fiction.

Asō Isoji has noted some other important aspects of the form, especially its dual narrative aims. The world view expressed is essentially a moralistic one, suggesting that the work performs primarily a social or public function as a tool of moral instruction. Yet Asō stresses the essentially artistic characteristic of the form by noting its preoccupation with language and rhetorical convention. His description suggests that the practice of literature is essentially an ethical act.

Asō's view of the *yomihon* is sympathetic, but his observations do not resolve the ambivalent aims of the form. Further, he clearly indicates his belief that the *yomihon* is first and foremost a work of literature, and that it 'is not intrinsically religious or moral writing.'[67] Indeed, in its preoccupation with language it is, compared with other types of books, self-consciously literary.

This synthesis of a moralistic outlook and an aesthetic approach goes beyond the simple formula embodied in the notion of *kanzen chōaku,* the promotion of virtue and the chastisement of evil, and points to a more complex system of values shared by the writers of *yomihon* and their readership. This is perhaps obscured at times by the narrative convention that consciously draws the reader's attention to the 'moral' of the story, even when that 'moral' holds a tenuous relationship with the rest of the text. But whereas later *yomihon* show increasing didactic tendencies, *Ugetsu Monogatari* generally maintains a balance.

As noted above, ethical problems are central to the nine tales, for the breaking of a moral code, or in some cases the strict adherence to a code of behavior, creates the possibility in the narrative for a supernatural encounter. However, Akinari uses his ethical arguments to serve narrative functions. In some cases he uses them to help create suspense or surprise, and in other cases the moral element of the story provides the means by which Akinari can present his variation. In all the stories the moral concerns are transformed into elements that produce not a didactic statement, but an aesthetic effect.

An example of how the process of adaptation shifts the emphasis toward narrative function and away from ethical arguments is provided by *Kikuka no Chigiri*. The model story profoundly shapes the language and structure of the tale. The tale of *Fan Chu-ch'ing* begins with the following poem:

> When you plant a tree, do not plant the weeping willow.
> When making friendships, do not choose fickle companions.
> The purple willow cannot withstand the autumn wind blowing.
> A fickle friend is easily made, and just as easily lost.
> You do not see, but yesterday a letter arrived saying that he is thinking of you.
> Today you meet, but he does not recognize you.
> A fickle friend is not so good as a willow, which lasts longer.
> For every time the spring breezes blow,
> The branches of the willow will at least sway again.[68]

Akinari uses this as a narrative frame for his opening lines:

> Do not plant the verdant willow of spring in your garden. Do not form friendships with fickle people. The willow easily grows thick, but it cannot withstand the first blasts of autumn. A fickle person easily makes friends, but just as quickly will cut you off. And even though the willow will always blossom again in the spring, a fickle friend, once he has cut you off, will never call a second time.[69]

The story closes with a reprise of this sentiment in a single line, 'Ah! one must not make friends with a fickle person!'[70]

The fact that Akinari made such prominent use of his Chinese source as a framing device would suggest that he was interested primarily in dealing with the ideal of friendship; and except for the addition of historical detail to naturalize the account, *Kikuka no Chigiri* does not significantly elaborate on the main story. Nonetheless, it does elaborate on the narrative structure. Akinari's version creates greater tension and surprise, and thus has more dramatic impact. It accomplishes this by its use of language, and by the interjection of the revenge plot at the last moment.

Akinari both borrows and expands the details of the story. In particular, the scene on the day when Samon is waiting for his friend's return is considerably longer than Feng's version, and the sense of impatience is more palpable. Samon makes his preparations and assures his mother that Sōemon will keep his word. The repetition and tedium of his actions are given further emphasis by the scenes he observes on the street outside his door.

> This day the weather was clear, the cloudless sky seemed to stretch out forever, and groups of travelers passed by, talking about this and that.
>
> 'Today's the day that so-and-so is going to the capital. It's fortunate that he has this kind of weather. This is a sign that he'll make a good profit.'
>
> A warrior, who was past fifty, turned to his companion, a man of about twenty dressed in the same fashion, and said, 'The seas would be calm on a day like this. If we had taken a boat to Akashi, leaving in the early morning, we would have been at Ushimado by now. Young men are so timid, and they squander their money.'
>
> The young samurai replied, 'When our lord went to the capital he crossed from Azukijima to Murotsu by boat. But I heard from a friend that they ran into trouble, and when you think about that, anyone would be hesitant to cross there. So don't be angry. When we get to Uogobashi, I'll treat you to some soba.' They passed by while he was pacifying the old man.
>
> Then a packhorse driver lost his temper, and angrily rearranging the saddle he shouted, 'You goddam nag! Can't you keep your eyes open?'[71]

This detailed description draws the story out, delaying the resolution of the plot. The language is the colloquial idiom of the *ukiyo-zōshi*, a form Akinari understood well. It serves to provide a familiar, ordinary context for the narrative, and to establish a kind of ground that highlights the crucial moment of the story, the ghostly encounter, which is then described in a different language. In Feng's story, Chang is depicted waiting by the gate for his friend's arrival.

> The wind blew, sounding in the grasses and trees, but Fan did not come. It was all naturally wondrous and awesome. When he looked up, the Milky Way was dazzling, the heavens, like a jeweled palace, were clear and bright. As the time approached the third watch, the moonlight quickly faded. It grew dark, and as he peered into the black shadows a person arrived there carried by the wind. When he looked more closely, it was Fan.[72]

Akinari remains faithful to his model in the depiction of Samon waiting for Sōemon, but he expands the scene, adding details that create an even more suspenseful atmosphere.

> Samon believed that Sōemon might yet come and so went out the door to take a look. The stars of the Milky Way twinkled coldly. He felt a sense of sadness, as if the moon were shining on him alone. He could hear the howling of a watchdog somewhere. The sound of the waves seemed to draw near to where he stood. When the moon disappeared behind the rim of the mountains and it was completely dark, Samon thought, 'He won't be coming now.' He closed the door and was about to go inside when suddenly something caught his eye. There among the misty shadows was a man who seemed to have come drifting on the wind. Thinking it strange, Samon took a closer look and found that it was Akana Sōemon.[73]

The sounds of the dog howling and of the waves, and the light of the moon, all act to heighten in Samon's mind the sense of his own loneliness. This type of detail also draws the story out, but the language that conveys the descriptive details is different. It has less of the colloquial familiarity and vulgarity of the earlier daytime scene, and is more allusive. This allusiveness is achieved by the close borrowing of the language of the model tale, and by the nature of the imagery used. The image of the moon that conveys Samon's loneliness is a well-worn poetic conceit, and the mention of the sound of the waves is a reference to the Suma chapter in *Genji Monogatari*.[74] The contrast in the language heightens the mood of the story and serves as a prelude to the moment when Samon finally gives up. His disappointment seems to confirm for us that Sōemon is one of those fickle friends we were warned about at the beginning.

Just when Samon's sense of isolation and disappointment is confirmed, however, Sōemon appears; and just when he feels joy that his original faith in his friend is justified, Samon learns the truth. This constant undercutting reveals Samon's impatience and suspense, and produces a sense of uncertainty. He does not really know (nor does the reader) whether Sōemon is a true friend until the ghost appears. The warning against fickle people presented at the outset of the tale creates the suspicion that perhaps Sōemon will not keep his promise. The moral lesson that frames the story does not lose its validity, but is transformed by the tension of the contrasting styles of language into a narrative element that adds significantly to the mood. This transformation is carried even further in the last section of the story when the language of *kokugaku* is introduced.

Another example of how the mixture of techniques characteristic of the *yomihon* shapes the narrative, in particular the narrative perspective, is found in **Kibitsu no Kama**, the most ghastly of the nine tales. This influence is revealed by comparing the story to its original model, *Mu-tan teng-chi*, from *Chien-teng hsin-hua*. The story, set in the year 1360, concerns a man named Ch'iao whose wife has just died and whose life is becoming tedious. One night a beautiful woman, Li Ch'ing, passes by his gate; she is accompanied by a maid, Chin Lien, who carries a pair of peony lanterns. He follows Li Ch'ing as if possessed, and she tells him that their meeting is not accidental. They exchange vows, and she visits him every evening for a fortnight.

One night an old man who lives nextdoor glimpses the two lovers and sees Ch'iao talking to a skeleton. On the following day he warns Ch'iao, who then seeks out Li Ch'ing. Unable to find her at home, he stops to rest at a nearby temple. To his horror he finds a coffin with her name on it. At its head are a pair of peony lanterns and the doll of a maid with the characters 'Chin Lien' on its back. He flees and seeks the advice of the old man, who sends him to a diviner. This man gives him a charm and tells him that he must avoid the temple at all costs. Ch'iao heeds this advice and a month passes.

One night, however, he gets drunk and, forgetting the warning, passes in front of the temple, where he meets Chin Lien, who takes him inside. Li is sitting there waiting for him. She rebukes him for his coldness and takes him by the hand. The coffin opens by itself and she pulls him into it. On the following morning the old man goes to search for Ch'iao and finds his corpse. After that the three spirits wander about on moonless nights until a priest exorcises them.[75]

Akinari's version of this tale introduces the pattern of the love triangle—a dissolute husband, a devoted wife, a beautiful courtesan—that figured so prominently in Edo fiction and drama. Like **Kikuka no Chigiri**, he makes use of a framing device, an aphorism from *Wu tsa tsu*: 'A jealous wife is difficult to control, but when you grow old then you will understand her value.' In this case the narrator contradicts this aphorism in order to introduce his own ideas about manly virtue.[76] In addition he makes use of an element found in *Asaji-gayado*, the lingering spirit of an abandoned woman.

Kibitsu no Kama tells the story of Shōtarō, a young man given to drinking and sexual indulgence. His parents try to correct his behavior by arranging a match with Isora, a lovely and devoted woman. Although the oracle at Kibitsu Shrine, a 'singing' caldron, warns against the union, the marriage takes place. The prophecy comes true when Shōtarō becomes friendly with a prostitute named Sode. This dalliance angers Shōtarō's father, who confines his son at home, but Shōtarō escapes and runs off with Sode. Sode is possessed and killed by Isora's living jealous spirit, and Isora herself dies soon after.

Both Shōtarō and Ch'iao incur the vengeance of female ghosts by breaking their vows. Shōtarō, however, is responsible for creating Isora's ghost, and his initial role is less passive. This variation sets the stage for the development of the narrative. With the death of Sode the power to control the action is taken from Shōtarō. Because he does not die with his lover, in the manner of a love-suicide, he loses the potential to become a hero, and is eventually reduced to the role of the haunted man. The imaginative variation in *Kibitsu no Kama* is that it focuses on the narrative process of Shōtarō's transformation, which is revealed by the changing perspectives of the text. Up to Shōtarō's desertion of Isora the story is narrated from an impersonal perspective. After that crucial event, the narrative shifts somewhat to the perspective of Shōtarō. This shift is similar to that in *Asajigayado,* where the story of Miyagi is left suspended in order to follow the story of Katsushiro, who then completes his wife's story.

When Sode dies, Shōtarō suspects that Isora is the cause. He visits Sode's grave every evening until one night he notices a new grave. A woman mourner comes to say a prayer, and tells him that the new grave is that of her lord, whose beautiful widow continues to live in a hut nearby. Shōtarō is roused to curiosity by this, and he goes to visit the woman.

> Standing by a moss-covered well, Shōtarō peeked inside the house through the slightly open door covered in Chinese paper, and saw the light of a lamp flickering in the breeze, and a black lacquered shelf. He wanted to see more.[77]

The setting, and the stolen glimpse, or *kaimami,* are reminiscent of the beginning of many literary love affairs. Indeed, Shōtarō is anticipating a romantic encounter as he is shown into the room where the woman is waiting. Instead he confronts the ghost of Isora, whose pale face, sunken eyes, and bluish, emaciated hands are so terrifying that he falls into a faint.[78]

On the following morning Shōtarō seeks the help of a famous diviner, who calculates that, because spirits wander the earth for forty-nine days after death, the danger will last for another forty-two days. He writes ancient Chinese characters on Shōtarō's body and gives him slips of vermilion paper on which are written special charms. That night the ghost of Isora appears, but is warded off by the charms. This continues for forty-one days. On the final evening Shōtarō takes special care and after hours of waiting the night sky seems to lighten. In his joy he tells his friend Hikoroku, who has endured the ordeal with him in an adjacent room, to meet him outside. When Hikoroku goes to the door, he hears a scream so shocking that it knocks him over. He grabs an axe and rushes out, but cannot find his friend. A late moonrise has deceived him.

> He wondered what could have happened; trembling in awe and fear, he picked up a lantern and looked around. There, on the wall beside the door, was warm blood flowing, trickling down into the earth. Yet neither corpse nor bones were to be seen. Then, by the moonlight, he caught sight of something underneath the eaves. Raising his light, he saw a man's topknot dangling. There was nothing else. No pen can ever do justice to the feeling of amazement and horror.[79]

The description of the climax is vivid, but at the same time the narrative is also oddly oblique. Words are no substitute for what they purport to describe, and we are not presented with an explicit account of the final scene. The perspective constantly deflects the reader and creates suspense. We share with Shōtarō the dread of a ghostly presence that remains unseen in its demonic manifestation. Then, through Hikoroku, we indirectly witness the ending and are left with the grisly traces that suggest the fury behind Shōtarō's destruction. Disembodied voices and topknots hint at something even more horrific that we are unable to know, and the structure of the tale enhances the power of suggestion.

The shifting of perspectives is the crucial element in *Kibitsu no Kama.* Initially the sympathy of the story lies with Isora, but once she has lost her human qualities that sympathy shifts to her husband. This is not to say that he is somehow redeemed as a character, but by presenting things through his perspective we naturally share his horror and anxiety, and the question of his moral guilt gives way before the techniques of the supernatural tale. The structure of the tale and its shift in perspective, with Shōtarō alone and quite literally confined by the circumstances he helped create, provide a narrative metaphor for his psychic as well as physical destruction. As the story draws to a close we gain a kind of double perspective on events through Hikoroku. Through the thin wall he vicariously shares the horrors his friend is enduring, and his perspective, in which words alone connect us with the supernatural, is equivalent to the act of reading the text.

The technique of shifting perspectives as a means of connecting the mundane with the supernatural is nowhere given more emphasis in *Ugetsu Monogatari* than in *Jasei no In.* This is the longest and most complex tale because in utilizing different perspectives it also raises important questions not only about the credibility of the narrative, but also the control that man exerts over his life. Akinari tries to make the supernatural world credible and comprehensible by seeking for a rational explanation of the supernatural encounter in ordinary terms. The effect is a story complicated by the act of the text denying itself. This development is not entirely original with Akinari, as the length and complexity of the work have as much to do with the qualities of his main sources, the story *Pai Niang-tzu yung chen Lei-feng-ta,* from Feng's *Ching-shih heng-yen,* and the noh play *Dōjōji,* as with any special design.

Like *Asajigayado* and *Kibitsu no Kama, Jasei no In* depicts a variation on the motif of a woman's longing, emphasizing the obsessive nature of the desire that the serpent-women, Manago, has for the hero, Toyoo.

Toyoo is a young man who, although kind and cultivated, has no practical skills to make a living. Takesuke, his father, does not think highly of his youngest child, but decides to let things run their course in the hope that he will become a scholar or a priest. He 'does not try to forcibly discipline' Toyoo, and so neglects his ethical responsibilities.[80] This not only sets the stage for what is to follow, but also suggests that the cause of events lies as much with the internal qualities of the human characters as with the external desire of Manago.

Toyoo's affair with Manago begins because he lacks moral discipline, a flaw suggested by his disturbing dreams in which he acts out his sexual desire for her. This weakness leads to a loss of control over his life that threatens to destroy him. The narrative reveals that loss of control by a repetition of the basic plot. Toyoo is twice beguiled, and nearly destroyed, by Manago's beauty. The first time she tempts him, he agrees to exchange vows. In gratitude she makes a present of a valuable sword, which turns out to have been stolen. Toyoo comes close to losing his life when he is arrested as a thief, and only the act of exposing Manago as a supernatural being saves him from punishment.

Ashamed of his conduct, Toyoo moves away to his sister's home. There he again meets with Manago and her servant, Maroya. What follows is a remarkable scene, heavily indebted to *Pai Niang-tzu,* in which Manago turns the narrative on its head. She first convinces Toyoo that she is really human, and, when Toyoo lists the evidence against her, including her supernatural escape from the magistrates, she explains it as a trick suggested by Maroya, and blames her former husband for the theft of the treasures. Manago is so convincing, and her behavior seems so proper, that Toyoo again comes to love her, and at the urging of his relatives promises to marry her. He is saved only by the intervention of a venerable priest, who recognizes the true serpent forms of Manago and Maroya.

After this second misadventure Toyoo's parents try to help him by arranging a desirable marriage with a woman named Tomiko. Just when Toyoo feels that he is finally safe, Manago appears a third time as a vengeful, jealous spirit who possesses his human bride. At each important point in the story, Toyoo is tricked into accepting things as they appear, not as they really are. The mechanism of denying what has been previously presented as the truth results in an extremely complex narrative structure. Toyoo's initial erotic fantasy is shown to be an allusion when Manago is exposed. She then reinterprets what happened, and gives an entirely new reading to events, turning what Toyoo believed was true into fiction. This story is in turn denied when we learn that she is really a serpent.

In order to break the pattern of repetition Toyoo marries Tomiko, but this shattering of the plot proves to be a false ending to the story when Manago possesses the bride. The continuous use of false leads and false climaxes is a reflection of the state of the hero's mind within the structure of the narrative. Because Toyoo is concerned with finding his true self, and with learning the question of narrative truth, *Jasei no In* is designed to create the sense of both Manago's obsessiveness and of Toyoo's helplessness.

Like Spencer's Duessa, who, although outwardly beautiful, is in reality a hideous serpent, Manago is a temptress whose dual nature threatens to destroy the hero. The only way to escape the peril she represents is through an inner strength and moral uprightness that permit the individual to see things for what they are. The structure of Akinari's story suggest this allegorical reading through its depiction of the progress of Toyoo toward the moral ideal of manliness, of control over himself and his environment. There is an ambivalence in the narrative as it moves between archetypal literary figures and individuated ones. This ambivalence is a result of the tension between the poles of traditionalism and individualism that shaped Akinari's literary ideas.

The range of variations in the supernatural encounters, and the attempt to make them comprehensible, not only in *Jasei no In* but throughout *Ugetsu Monogatari,* suggest that the experience of the supernatural moves across a continuum, ranging from the demonic through the human to the divine; and within that continuum the realm of art and language intersects experience at all levels.

The intermingling of realms of experience in the story precludes an interpretation of events from a single vantage point, denies the kind of absolute interpretation that a reading based on a rigid ethical system would provide, and emphasizes the literary elements of the narrative. In nearly all important aspects, then, *Jasei no In* adheres to the qualities of the *yomihon* identified above. The aim of writers such as Akinari was to find a narrative language and form that would subordinate ethics to art, and would give expression to the authority of the past, of history and the literary tradition, in terms that were comprehensible to the present. Insofar as the *yomihon* developed in response to that aim, and insofar as many *yomihon* contained elements of the supernatural tale, it is useful to read *Ugetsu Monogatari* as an important example of that type of fictional narrative. Although his reasons for choosing to adapt tales of the supernatural can never be determined absolutely, it is reasonable to believe that Akinari shared an apparently widespread preference to use such stories as a formal, rhetorical means to convey the specific aims of his literary ideology.

Notes

1. For a list of Akinari's sources, both Japanese and Chinese, see Uzuki Hiroshi, *Ugetsu Monogatari Hyōshaku,* Kadokawa, 1969, pp. 707-12.

2. This is the conclusion of Maruyama Masao in his well-known study of the philosophies of Ogyū Sorai and Motoori Norinaga, *Studies in the Intellectual History of Tokugawa Japan,* Princeton U.P. & Tokyo U.P., 1974.

3. Ian Watt, *The Rise of the Novel,* University of California Press, 1957, pp. 17-18.

4. Watt, p. 14.

5. Wm Theodore deBary, 'Sagehood as a Secular and Spiritual Ideal in Tokugawa Neo-Confucianism', in Wm Theodore deBary & Irene Bloom, ed., *Principle and Practicality: Essays in Neo-Confucianism and Practical Learning,* Columbia U.P., 1979, p. 130.

6. Ueda Akinari, *Akinari Ibun* [=*Ibun*], Fujii Otoo, ed., Kokusho Kankōkai, 1974, pp. 101-02. For a discussion of the critical terminology in *Nubatama no Maki,* see Tanaka Toshikazu, *Ueda Akinari Bungei no Sekai,* Ōfūsha, 1979, pp. 7-18.

7. *Ibun,* pp. 104-05 & 108.

   I have rendered *tsutae* as 'tradition'. An interlinear note in the text explains that *fumi,* or 'writings', refers to *Nihon Shoki.* This is in accordance with Akinari's belief that *Kojiki* was a faulty text.

8. *Ibun,* p. 109.

9. Uzuki, pp. 102-04.

   The entire collection shows the influence of noh, not only as a source but also in its ordering of auspicious and inauspicious stories.

   The first four stories are auspicious by virtue of either their subject matter, or the ideal behavior they depict. The next three tales deal with the inauspicious subject of the unappeased spirit. The last two stories create an upward movement, ending on a prophecy of peace and prosperity under the Tokugawa regime.

   For a more complete description of the organization of a program of noh plays, and of the importance of auspicious and inauspicious subjects as a structural element, see C. Andrew Gerstle, *Circles of Fantasy: Convention in the Plays of Chikamatsu,* Harvard U.P., 1986, pp. 4-7.

10. That is, Sutoku is alleged to have flouted *ame no kami no oshie,* the traditional account of imperial descent from the sun goddess, Amaterasu.

11. Nakamura Yukihiko, ed., *Ueda Akinari Shū* [=UAS], NKBT [*Nihon Koten Bungaku Taikei*] 56, Iwanami, 1968, p. 40.

12. UAS, pp. 41-42.

13. UAS, pp. 57-58. Shang Yang does escape and goes to Ch'in. He later assists in the conquest of Wei.

14. Uzuki, p. 327. The Three Treasures are the Buddha, the Law, and the Priesthood.

    In *Tandai Shōshinroku,* Akinari claims that on a trip to Mt Kōya he heard the bird himself, although he did not actually catch sight of it. UAS, p. 281.

15. UAS, p. 79. The poem appears in *Seireishū,* a ninth-century collection of Kūkai's verse.

16. UAS, p. 80. The poem appears in *Shinsenrokujō,* 6, under the topic 'Birds'.

    Matsunoo no / mine shizukanaru / akebono ni / aogite kikeba / buppōsō naku.

    Looking upward / at the quiet dawn / on the peak of Matsunoo, / when I listen, / I hear the cry, '*Buppōsō*'.

17. UAS, p. 80.

    Tori no ne mo / himitsu no yama no / shigemi kana.

    A bird chants the Three Treasures. / The silence of the thick undergrowth / on the sacred mountain of mysteries.

18. UAS, p. 82.

19. UAS, p. 82. The poem appears in Book 16, 'Miscellaneous Poems'.

20. UAS, p. 83. The same argument appears in *Tandai.* See UAS, pp. 281-82.

21. UAS, p. 84.

22. UAS, p. 86. Later, in the capital, when Muzen passes by the mass grave of Hidetsugu and his family, called the *Chikushōzuka,* or the Mound of Beasts, he recalls his experience and thinks, 'Even in the daytime it is a fearful thing.'

23. The most important source is *Okinagusa,* a miscellany compiled by Kamisawa Sadamoto, 1710-1795. Sanai also briefly figures in Akinari's *ukiyozōshi, Seken Tekake Katagi,* 1767. Apart from his courage, Sanai was best known for his love of money. Uzuki, pp. 635-36.

24. UAS, p. 132.

25. UAS, pp. 138-39.

26. See Robert E. Hegel, *The Novel in Seventeenth-century China,* Columbia U.P., 1981, pp. 56-57.

27. Hegel, p. 58. Hegel notes that the seventeenth-century fashion for editing and anthologizing was 'most likely the product of the contradictory Neo-Confucian injunction to seek truth in the writings of the past and to express one's own perceptions of universal laws.'

28. Joseph Levenson, 'The Amateur Ideal in Ming and Early Ch'ing Society: Evidence from Painting', in John K. Fairbank, ed., *Chinese Thought and Institutions,* University of Chicago Press, 1957, p. 338.

29. Ueda Akinari, *Seken Tekake Katagi,* in Moriyama Shigeo, *Ueda Akinari Shoki Ukiyo-zōshi Hyōshaku,* Kokusho Kankōkai, 1977, p. 181.

    Hachimonjiya was the name of a publishing company operated by Jishō, d. 1745. The *ukiyo-zōshi* published by that firm were so successful that *hachimonjiyabon* came to be used as an alterative term for the form.

30. UAS, p. 36.

31. The phrase in the preface that points to what I am referring to as 'verisimilitude' or 'realism' is *shin ni semari.* This is glossed in the notes as *hakushinryoku,* or 'verisimilitude', by the editors of both UAS and the Shōgakukan edition.

    Akinari's concept of verisimilitude indicates both a consistency of the text with reality (the truth of what is said), and the ability to convince the reader that the text is consistent with reality (the credibility of its way of saying).

    These two senses of verisimilitude resemble Western notions of realism: realism in its original meaning, which is now defined as idealism; and realism in its modern sense, marked by the use of circumstantial detail as a major narrative convention.

32. Ōwa Yasuhiro, *Ueda Akinari Bungaku no Kenkyū,* Kasama, 1976, p. 31.

33. For a list of works containing legendary material about Lo and Murasaki, see Uzuki, pp. 11-12.

34. This name has a number of possible meanings. Senshi could mean 'pruning' or 'cut finger', while Kijin could mean 'eccentric' or 'cripple'. It should also be noted that the character *sen* is the first character in the title of the Chinese collection *Chien-teng hsin-hua* (cited on p. 59, below).

35. Ōwa, pp. 27-28.

36. Blake Morgan Young, *Ueda Akinari,* University of British Columbia Press, 1982, p. 128.

37. Mark Morris, 'Buson and Shiki', in HJAS [*Harvard Journal of Asiatic Studies*] 44:2 (December 1984), p. 389.

38. Morris, p. 385.

39. Their professional relationship was close enough that each provided material for use in works by the other. Buson wrote a preface for *Yakanashō,* Akinari's study of *kireji,* in 1773. Two years later Akinari contributed an epilogue and several poems to Buson's *haikai* collection, *Zoku Akegarasu.*

40. Kawashima Tsuyu & Teruoka Yasutaka, *Busonshū, Issa-shū,* NKBT 58, Iwanami, 1959, pp. 290-91.

41. There are numerous examples of allusion in the story. The title comes from a poem in the 'Kiritsubo' chapter of *Genji Monogatari.* Yamagishi Tokuhei, ed., *Genji Monogatari,* NKBT 14, Iwanami, 1958, p. 41.

    Kumo no ue mo / namida ni kururu / aki no tsuki / ikade sumuran / asajifu no yado.

    Clouded over by my tears / here at the palace, / how could the autumn moon / appear clearly to you / in a hut amid the tangle grasses.

    Other examples are provided on the eve of Katsushirō's departure. Miyagi quotes lines from *Kokin Wakashū,* nos. 947 & 387, to express her sorrow, and Katsushirō seals his promise to return by autumn by citing a verse from the 'Matsukaze' chapter of *Genji Monogatari.*

    Near the end of the story, when he discovers that Miyagi is really dead, Katsushirō expresses his grief by quoting the last line of a famous poem by Ariwara no Narihira, in *Kokin Wakashū,* 747. See UAS, pp. 60-61 & 66.

42. UAS, p. 66. This poem is a variation on one by Fujiwara Atsutada, in *Goshūishū,* 11:1086.

43. UAS, p. 70. The story of Tegona and references to Mama appear in *Man'yōshū,* nos. 431-33, 1807-08, & 3386-87.

44. UAS, p. 70. The reference to Katsushirō as an *inakamono* is not meant to be a serious criticism of him. The characters in *Asajigayado* are best regarded as types rather than analyzed as fully developed psychological studies.

    In this respect my reading of the story differs from that of Donald Keene in his *World Within Walls,* Holt, Rinehart & Winston, New York, 1976, pp. 384-86. In my opinion the beauty of Miyagi's story, not its plausability, is what Akinari was after. Katsushirō and Miyagi are simply not the rounded portraits that Keene claims, and his argument that the introduction of the story of Tegona mars the work makes sense only if one ignores the heavy reliance of poetic allusion that creates the context and meaning of the tale.

45. Yamada Takao *et al., Konjaku Monogatari-shū,* NKBT 25, Iwanami, 1968, pp. 510-12. The story, 27:24, is *Hito no Tsuma, Shinite nochi, Moto no Otto ni Aeru Koto,* 'A Wife Meets Her Former Husband After She Dies'.

46. Uzuki, pp. 269-74.

47. The most immediate source for Akinari was probably a story titled *Hsüeh lu-shih yu fu cheng hsien,* 'Hsüeh the Archivist Takes the Form of a Fish and Proves the Miraculous', found in Feng's anthology, *Hsiung-shih heng-yen.*

    This is in turn based on a tale from a T'ang collection, *T'ai-p'ing kuang-chi,* titled *Hsüeh Wei* after the name of the hero.

48. UAS, p. 71.

49. UAS, p. 76.

50. Uzuki, pp. 628-31.

51. UAS, p. 128. The word *odorikurui* calls to mind the final, passionate dance often presented in a noh play.

52. UAS, p. 129. These poems are drawn from *Cheng tao ko,* 103 & 104, a T'ang collection by the Sōtō monk Hsüan Chüeh, 665-714. They also appear in the noh play *Yoroboshi.*

53. UAS, p. 131. The temple is Daichūji on Taiheisan.

54. For a fuller discussion of Akinari's debt to *pai hua* fiction, see Shigetomo Ki, *Kinsei Bungakushi no Shomondai,* Meiji Shoin, 1963, pp. 226ff.

55. Andrew H. Plaks, *The Four Masterworks of the Ming Novel,* Princeton U.P., 1987, p. 15.

    For a more complete analysis of urban culture and popular literature, see Jaroslev Prusek, 'Urban Centers: The Cradle of Popular Fiction', in Cyril Birch, ed., *Studies in Chinese Literary Genres,* University of California Press, 1974, pp. 260ff.

56. Plaks, p. 45.

57. C. T. Hsia, *The Classic Chinese Novel: A Critical Introduction,* Columbia U.P., 1968, pp. 12-13.

58. For a discussion of the development of critical distinction between elegant (*ga*) and vulgar (*zoku*) styles in Japanese literature, see Nakamura Yukihiko, *Kinsei Shōsetsushi no Kenkyū,* Ōfūsha, 1961, pp. 285-89.

59. Tsuga Teishō, *Kokon Kidan Hanabusa Sōshi,* NKBT 48, Shogakukan, 1973, p. 74. For a brief discussion of the influence of Chinese models on Teishō's style, see Ōwa, pp. 207-08.

60. It is possible that Akinari studied medicine under Teishō in the early 1770s. There is little documentation about their relationship, so it is difficult to assess the extent of Teishō's influence on Akinari. For a brief discussion of this problem, see Nakamura, p. 161.

61. Nakamura, pp. 245-98.

62. Asō Isoji has studied the relative difficulty of reading *yomihon* compared to the *ninjōbon, sharebon,* and *kokkeibon.* Using representative works for each type of book, his analysis reveals that on average the *yomihon* contains more than twice the number of Chinese characters.

    He also found that the average length of a *yomihon* sentence is greater than that of the *sharebon* and *kokkeibon,* but less by far than the *ninjōbon*—differences that surely reflect narrative functions.

    Asō Isoji, *Edo Bungaku to Chūgoku Bungaku,* Sanseidō, 1957, pp. 375ff.

63. Robert Leutner, *Shikitei Sanba and the Comic Tradition in Edo Fiction,* Harvard U.P., 1985, p. 6.

    Leutner points out that accurate figures for the readership of *yomihon* are impossible to determine because the huge nationwide network of lending libraries would have greatly increased the circulation of these books.

64. Nakamura, pp. 323-30.

    The emphasis here must be on the relative differences among classes of readership. Nakamura concurs with other scholars that such classes existed, but points out that there were wide variations among *yomihon* that arose primarily because *yomihon* authors tried to tailor their works to specific sectors of the market.

65. Cited in Keene, p. 377.

66. Cited in Young, p. 48.

67. Asō, p. 538.

68. Uzuki, p. 175.

69. UAS, pp. 47-48.

70. UAS, p. 58.

71. UAS, pp. 52-53.

72. Uzuki, p. 178.

73. UAS, 53-54.

74. Uzuki, p. 147.

75. Uzuki, pp. 458-62.

76. UAS, p. 86.

    Wu tsa tsu, compiled by Hsieh Chaoche in the early sixteenth century, is a miscellany containing excerpts from and commentary on classical texts.

It was widely read by Japanese intellectuals, and from the Kambun era, 1661-1673, it was available in editions printed in Japan. The work survives because of these editions.

The work's influence on Akinari is apparent in the notion of *masurao,* or manly virtue, that is an important part of the argument of *Kibitsu no Kama.* The narrator quotes *Wu tsa tsu* again: 'To tame a bird requires spirit; to control a wife requires the husband to be manly.' This idea, he claims, is certainly true.

77. UAS, p. 93.

78. UAS, p. 94.

79. UAS, pp. 96-97.

80. UAS, p. 98.

Susanna Fessler (essay date spring 1996)

SOURCE: Fessler, Susanna. "The Nature of the Kami: Ueda Akinari and *Tandai Shoshin Roku.*" *Monumenta Nipponica* 51, no. 1 (spring 1996): 1-15.

[*In the following excerpt, Fessler explains Akinari's philosophy on the nature of deities.*]

Ueda Akinari, renowned for his fiction writing, was also a serious scholar of *kokugaku,* or National Learning. Of particular concern for him was the nature of the *kami*—their ethics (if any) and how those ethics reflected the cognitive nature of the beings themselves. In an age when the nature of the kami was being discussed by a number of kokugaku scholars, including the great Motoori Norinaga, 1730-1801, Akinari was but one voice in a crowd, yet his ideas on this issue differ distinctly from those of his peers. He agreed with them that Confucian and Buddhist scholars were wrong to impose their philosophical ethical framework upon the realm of the kami, for, he declared, the kami did not conform to such a normative structure. Akinari related the kami to what may be called 'animal spirits'—foxes, badgers, and the like, animals that are attributed in Japanese folklore with supernatural powers. He held that the kami and animal spirits were behaviorally the same; both were characterized by an inability to conceive of a moral right and wrong.

Akinari kept a notebook of random thoughts and jottings on varied topics, titled *Tandai Shōshin Roku,* '**A Record of Courage and Cowardice**', 1808. A supplementary text of further jottings, plus re-edited sections of *Tandai,* followed in 1809. Written in a mixture of literary and colloquial language, the entries present Akinari's ideas about philosophy, history, and literature, as well as his frank opinions of his contemporaries. The views expressed in the work are strong and at times biting. By the time *Tandai* was published, its author was seventy-six years old, blind in one eye and visually impaired in the other. He knew that he was at the end of his life and believed that it was time to make public his thoughts, regardless of the consequences.[1]

THE NATURE OF THE KAMI

One of the recurring topics in *Tandai,* and the primary subject of the present article, is the nature of the kami. Akinari combines his commentary on the kami with criticism of Buddhism and Confucianism, for, like other kokugaku scholars, he felt that Buddhism and Confucianism were misguided philosophies. In *Tandai,* he both discusses the nature of the kami as he understood them and criticizes his Buddhist and Confucian contemporaries.[2]

Akinari was concerned with two issues regarding the kami: first, their cognitive nature, and second, how that nature helped shape their ethics and behavior. Here I shall refer to animal spirits and the kami together ('kami/animal spirits'), because Akinari equated the two. The central idea is introduced in *Tandai,* 13:

> By nature, such [fox] spirits do not distinguish between good and bad, or right and wrong. They protect what is good for them and curse what is bad. . . . The kami are believed to be the same. . . . They bless their faithful with happiness and curse the unfaithful.[3]

Here the concept of 'good and bad, right and wrong' is expressed by the term *zen'akujasei*.[4] The same word is used later in Section 30:

> According to *I Ching,* 'That aspect of it which cannot be fathomed in terms of the light and dark is called spirit.'[5] This shows that the Chinese, too, understood that man cannot judge the nature of the kami. It is precisely because of this that we have no disputes about the good and evil natures [*zen'akujasei*] of the kami, as we do about mankind.

> The kami love well the man who serves them well. If someone scorns them, they punish him. Foxes and badgers seem to be the same as the kami.[6]

We can surmise from this passage that the kami recognize when someone does well or poorly by them, but that they have no overriding moral sense of right and wrong. It may be helpful to think of this in the following way: kami/animal spirits are perceptual beings, whereas humans are conceptual. The kami perceive good or ill will at a specific point in time, but do not conceive of a greater system of moral right and wrong. The kami neither recognize a way by which humans can store virtue for a future time, nor do they punish humans repeatedly for past evil deeds that have already been punished once.

Blake Morgan Young sums up Akinari's view as follows:

> Akinari contended that foxes, badgers, and other animals, unlike people, have no moral sense of right and wrong, but merely reward what is good for them and punish what is bad. The deities of Japan were of the same nature, he believed, blessing those who serve them and cursing those who neglect them, unlike Buddhas and sages, who have human bodies and feelings. In animals and supernatural beings Akinari saw a quality that rose above considerations of good and evil—a simple, pure, amoral instinct, beyond normal logic, to protect one's self and one's personal interest.[7]

According to Young, Akinari believed that the kami acted only to 'protect one's self and one's personal interest', in other words, they behaved only selfishly. But in *Tandai,* 31, he illustrated how some kami behavior could be altruistic:

> During the Jōgan period, Mt Fuji erupted; mountain peaks crumbled and buried the valleys, and the land tumbled into the sea. People were injured, and the damage was so severe that it affected the neighboring regions. The ruler of Kai later declared, 'This has happened because the priests have neglected to perform rituals for the kami of Asama Shrine on top of Mt Fuji.' And so an imperial decree was issued and the priests were duly warned. When we think about this, we wish that the kami would have punished only the priests who neglected the rituals. Why were the kami willing to inflict this disaster upon the world?
>
> There were two stone kami and one pond kami on Mt Aso in Higo. One day, the kami set fire and dried up all the water in the pond; the water itself seemed to become fire and remained like that for days. Provincial officials summoned a diviner to interpret the situation. He said, 'This is an omen that there will be fires of war.' Soldiers were mustered to protect Kyushu.
>
> The kami of Asama Shrine on Mt Fuji harmed the country for its own sake. The stone kami produced an omen for the sake of the country. How is it that the kami can behave so differently?[8]

According to Akinari, therefore, the kami could at times act altruistically, but did not necessarily do so. He also showed that kami behavior was puzzling to humans, and suggested that it could not be judged on the basis of human moral constructs. The passage recording the eruption of Mt Fuji offers a good example of this: although on the one hand it appears that the kami understood 'good and evil' because they punished people for failing to worship them, it is important to keep in mind that such people did not fail to pay obeisance out of malice. Their unfaithfulness was caused by a slackening of devotion, true, but it did not involve animosity toward the kami. If the kami, like an animal, could only perceive the actions of humans, and not conceive of the intentions behind them, then it follows that their behavior might well be as Akinari declared.

Moriyama Shigeo also addresses Akinari's view of the kami, interpreting his philosophy as follows. Logical standards are a human phenomenon that cannot be applied to other animals; sense of harm also differs between humans and animals. Humans lead a life based on societal relationships, but fox and badger spirits exist in a world that lacks such norms. Theirs is a primal existence.[9] The societal relationships that Akinari attributed to humans were the five basic Confucian relationships and the Buddhist teacher/disciple relationship. For Akinari, Buddhism and Confucianism were part of the human world, as distinguished from the realm of the kami, precisely because there was a direct relationship between humans and the deities of those two teachings. He states in *Tandai,* 30:

> Buddhists say, 'The kami and the buddhas share the same body.' My thoughts on this are as follows. Like the Confucian sages, the buddhas send out leafy branches and roots of good deeds throughout the world; they spread their teaching far and wide. But the master who said that he would clothe everyone in dark robes and lead them on the Buddhist path[10] was too narrow-minded.[11] The kami are divine entities; humans cannot follow religious practices and someday become a kami.[12]

This differentiates Shinto from Confucianism and Buddhism, for followers of the latter two religions can aspire to become 'deities': a Buddhist can attain enlightenment and a Confucian can become a sage. But no matter how devout, a follower of Shinto cannot possibly become a kami. By their nature the kami are distinct from humans.

But here a question may be posed—what of humans who are in fact considered kami, such as Tenjin or Hachiman?[13] Akinari made no mention of this problem, but he could have presented three arguments to explain their existence: (1) they were never really kami, but were viewed as such in folklore; (2) they were never really human, but kami in human form; and (3) they were possessed by a kami or perhaps a fox spirit, and this empowered them to exhibit supernatural behavior. The last explanation is perhaps the most probable.

ANIMAL SPIRITS

In *Tandai,* 27 & 28, Akinari used an animal parable and an account of fox possession to illustrate the bestial lack of a sense of 'good and evil'. In 27, a dog steals a fish from a basket, only to be chased with a long pole by the fishmonger. After the man retrieves the fish, the dog continues to try to steal it. The dog neither learns a lesson, feels guilt, nor applies its experience to realize that the fish does not belong to it. It merely perceives the existence of the fish and consequently desires to possess it. Akinari remarks:

> After observing the dog's behavior, I got to thinking that if a man steals something, he won't do it again, so

this happening proved that a dog's nature is not the same as a man's. Its nature is just as I saw it.[14]

Because Akinari has already told us that the kami have the same nature as animals, we can apply the above conclusion about a dog's nature to the kami as well. Section 28 tells the story of an innocent girl possessed by an angry fox; it believes that she purposely poured dirty water on it while it was asleep, but in fact she did this quite unintentionally. A monk comes to exorcise the girl, and in the monk's words to the fox, Akinari explains the difference between human and animal (and kami) morals:

> 'The place where you were sleeping was not your den. It's not as if the girl knew you were there and poured water on you deliberately. It's wrong to blame her for making a mistake out of ignorance. Mistakes people make out of ignorance are not really mistakes.'[15]

The priest sees right and wrong in the situation, but vainly tries to explain this distinction to the fox, who cannot distinguish between malicious and unintentional error. It can perceive only the result of the girl's action and take retaliation. A human would both perceive the result and conceive of the reason (here, an unintended accident) behind it. In essence, Akinari understood kami/animal spirits as simple beings, unhindered by the contemplation and conceptualization that humans employ in their attempt to understand the world.

In *Tandai,* 13 & 26, Akinari argues that Confucian scholars, specifically Nakai Riken, 1732-1817, were wrong in their contention that supernatural entities do not exist. Akinari had at one point been a member of the Kaitokudō, the Merchant Academy of Osaka, the same academy with which Riken was associated, but in his later years he became alienated from its Confucian philosophies. Riken and his contemporaries at the Kaitokudō focused on a rational epistemology, one that did not allow for supernatural events. But what were inadmissible superstitions to the Kaitokudō scholars were valid beliefs to Akinari.[16]

Akinari quotes Riken as saying, 'There are no such things as ghosts,' and 'I question whether people can really be possessed by spirits.'[17] To this Akinari replied that fox possession was indeed a reality: 'There have been plenty of cases of fox and badger possession.'[18] In 29, he tells of presumed cases of fox possession not only of his friend and Confucian scholar Hosoai Hansai, 1717-1803, but also of himself. He concludes that scholars such as Riken deny fox possession because they spend too much time confined within the walls of their academy, isolated from the real world.

NORINAGA

Along with the kokugaku scholar Motoori Norinaga, Akinari criticized Buddhism and Confucianism because of their normative structure. Both men also rejected any normative analysis of Shinto, spurning the Chinese concept of an ordered universe with clear distinctions between good and evil. But Akinari did not agree with Norinaga on all kokugaku issues. He had a distinct distaste for philosophical constructs, so not only did he dismiss Buddhism and Confucianism, but he also rejected some of the popular views at the time about Shinto and kokugaku. For example, whereas Norinaga regarded the two earliest Japanese national histories, *Kojiki,* 712, and *Nihon Shoki,* 720, as accurate accounts, Akinari believed that the former was contrived to glorify the imperial line, and that only *Nihon Shoki* was a valid historical text.[19]

Akinari is also critical of the kokugaku notion that the *Kojiki* creation myth was the only true creation myth. In *Tamakushige,* Norinaga held:

> The True Way is one and the same, in every country and throughout heaven and earth. This Way, however, has been correctly transmitted only in our Imperial Land. Its transmission in all foreign countries was lost long ago in early antiquity . . . [t]he ways of foreign countries are no more the original Right Way than end-branches of a tree are the same as its root.[20]

But Akinari saw Japan and its kami as merely one country and its myths among many. He explained:

> Each [of the other myths] has a separate account of the creation of the universe for each country . . . and even if one transfers them to other countries they would not be accepted, being self-regarding accounts.[21]

Yet another point on which Akinari disagreed with Norinaga concerned the morals of the kami. As discussed above, the statements in *Tandai* imply that the kami operate on a perceptual level, judging events as they occur, rewarding the immediate good and punishing the immediate bad. For Akinari, the behavior of the kami was comprehensible, albeit quixotic. But Norinaga did not share this view. For him, the Japanese kami were august entities whose behavior could not be understood by human beings. He wrote, 'It was an act of insolence for humans to impose their impertinent logic on the kami.'[22]

Like Akinari, Norinaga felt that the kami were operating according to a set of principles, but unlike Akinari, he believed those principles to be so sophisticated that they were beyond human comprehension. According to Norinaga:

> Given that the kami are not of the same sort as the Confucian sages or buddhas associated with foreign countries, we cannot judge them by using common worldly logic. It is difficult to inquire into the goodness or evil of a kami's nature from the standpoint of human nature. All things in heaven and earth come from that kami nature. And because what the kami do is different from what humans may think, there are bound to

be many small differences between kami behavior and the reason recorded in these Chinese Confucian and Buddhist texts.[23]

This accounted for irrational kami behavior and did not differ significantly from Akinari's views on the subject. Both men noted that the kami could not be equated with buddhas or Confucian sages, and that the kami used a rationale different from that employed by humans. Some years later, however, Norinaga expressed resignation about his hope of truly understanding the actions of the kami:

> The kami differ from buddhas and the like. There are good kami and bad kami, and they perform their deeds in accordance with their nature. Although we may think that good people are necessarily good and bad people are necessarily bad, in many cases bad people are good and good people are bad. All of their actions are deeds of the kami, so it must be that the kami do not act simply according to what is good and bad. There is nothing for humans to do but fear the kami's wrath, and take comfort in prayer.[24]

Norinaga recognized that the kami did not behave like humans, but he avoided any discussion aimed at understanding their motives. For him, it was enough to say that the kami were different and therefore incomprehensible. He placed the kami's morality on a superior, unreachable level because any closer examination would threaten their status in his writings.[25] He dismissed the entire question of humans imposing a normative structure on the kami, asserting, 'We must understand that the kami are simply superior to the common man.'[26] In other words, humans should accept that fact and not examine kami behavior any further. Norinaga's hesitation to judge the kami led him eventually to hesitate to judge human behavior as well:

> Even extremely good people become angry at times, and it is not necessarily bad for persons to lose their temper. Moreover, on rare occasions bad people will do a good deed. It seems difficult to set any certain rules about human behavior.[27]

Akinari, on the other hand, believed that human behavior clearly followed the dictates of zen'akujasei. Humans conceived of 'good and bad, right and wrong', and regulated their behavior accordingly. Akinari did not see people as inherently good or bad by nature, but as beings who, unlike the kami, were able to conceive of both good and bad, and who had free will to choose one or the other.

Notes

1. See the 'Ueda Akinari' chapter in Shūichi Katō, *A History of Japanese Literature,* Kodansha International, 1983, 2, for specific citations of Akinari's social criticism. The annotated text of *Tandai Shōshin Roku,* 1809, is found in Nakamura Yuki-hiko, ed., *Ueda Akinari Shū* [UAS], NKBT [*Nihon Koten Bungaku Taikei*] 56, Iwanami, 1959, pp. 251-381.

2. Among the translations of *Tandai,* pp. 8-15, below, sections 13, 26 & 30 are direct commentaries on the mistaken conceptions of Buddhists and Confucianists regarding the kami, while 27, 28, 29 & 31 are short parables illustrating the nature of both kami and other spirits, in accordance with the ideas expressed in 13, 26 & 30.

3. UAS, p. 258; pp. 8-9, below.

4. This is a standard term used in Neo-Confucian writings, such as Motoori Norinaga's *Genji Monogatari Tama no Ogushi,* 1793-1796. Akinari uses it here with emphasis on the last two characters, which imply moral rights and wrongs, as opposed to the qualitative good and bad aspects of material objects.

5. Richard Wilhelm, tr., *The I Ching or Book of Changes,* Princeton U.P. 1967 edition, p. 301. The word here in Chinese is *shen,* which can be translated as 'spirit' or 'spiritual'. Although the same character is used to write the Japanese word *kami,* it here clearly refers to a broader concept than Japanese deities. Akinari uses this line specifically to support his argument about kami. This may seem to be quoting *I Ching* slightly out of context, but given that he felt that deities in any country had the same nature as those in Japan, the use of *I Ching* here does not invalidate his argument.

6. UAS, p. 272; pp. 12-13, below.

7. Blake Morgan Young, *Ueda Akinari,* University of British Columbia Press, 1982, p. 61.

8. UAS, pp. 273-74; p. 14, below.

9. Moriyama Shigeo, *Gen'yō no Bungaku: Ueda Akinari,* San'ichi, 1982, p. 316.

10. This refers to poem #1134 in *Senzai Wakashū,* 1183, compiled by Fujiwara Shunzei:

> ōke naku
> ukiyo no tami ni
> ōu kama
> waga tatsu some ni
> sumizome no sode

>   How unfitting
> for the people of this world
>   to don
> darkly dyed robes
> here for the first time.

The poem refers to leading all living beings, dressed in dyed robes, along the Buddhist path.

The term *ukiyo no tami* refers to lay people who for the first time are participating in this religious practice.

11. Here Akinari uses the Buddhist term *shōjō*, the 'lesser vehicle', or Hinayana Buddhism, to indicate that the view expressed is overly simple.

12. UAS, p. 272; p. 12, below.

13. Tenjin is the name given to Sugawara Michizane, 845-903, a scholar and court figure in the early Heian period. After his death in exile, a series of natural disasters were attributed to his angry spirit. A major shrine in the capital was dedicated to him, and he is posthumously referred to as the kami Tenjin. Since the Heian period, the kami Hachiman has been identified as the deified spirit of Emperor Ōjin, r. 270-310.

14. UAS, p. 269; p. 5, below.

15. UAS, p. 270; p. 11, below.

16. For the Kaitokudō, see Tetsuo Najita, *Visions of Virtue in Tokugawa Japan: The Kaitokudō, Merchant Academy of Osaka,* University of Chicago Press, 1987.

17. UAS, pp. 258 & 268; p. 8, below.

18. UAS, p. 258; p. 8, below.

19. In *Tandai,* 30, Akinari mentions the importance of *Nihon Shoki,* emphasizing that it did not embellish facts in order to legitimize the imperial reign. He also expressed his distrust of *Kojiki* in *Yasumigoto,* 1792. UAS, n. 30, pp. 399-400.

20. Ryusaku Tsunoda et al., ed., *Sources of Japanese Tradition,* Columbia U.P., 1958, pp. 520-21.

21. As quoted in Katō, p. 193.

22. Hino Tatsuo, *Norinaga to Akinari,* Chikuma, 1984, p. 175.

23. Hino Tatsuo, ed., *Motoori Norinaga Shū,* Shinchōsha, 1983, pp. 462-63.

24. Quoted in Hino, *Norinaga to Akinari,* p. 175. It is interesting to note that Norinaga implied that human actions were at least sometimes controlled by kami. It is not clear whether he meant that humans were occasionally possessed by kami or whether kami could actually be humans simultaneously.

25. For example, if the kami were not superior to humans, how would it be possible to justify the importance accorded them in the creation of Japan? Kokugaku was founded on the concept that Japan was central in the world; any belittling of the kami threatened to weaken the nationalist arguments of the kokugaku scholars.

26. From Norinaga's *Suzunoya Tōmon Roku,* 'A Compilation of Norinaga's Answers', published posthumously by his students in 1835. In *Zōho Motoori Norinaga Zenshū,* Yoshikawa, 1928, 6, p. 115.

27. *Suzunoya Tōmon Roku,* in *Zōho Motoori Norinaga Zenshū,* p. 115. For a detailed discussion of Norinaga's views on Shinto, see Maruyama Masao, *Studies in the Intellectual History of Tokugawa Japan,* Princeton U.P., 1974.

Frederick S. Frank (essay date 2002)

SOURCE: Frank, Frederick S. "Ueda Akinari." In *Gothic Writers: A Critical and Bibliographical Guide,* edited by Douglass H. Thomson, Jack G. Voller, and Frederick S. Frank, pp. 12-19. Westport, Conn.: Greenwood Press, 2002.

[*In the following excerpt, Frank discusses Akinari's work as part of the Western Gothic tradition.*]

The writings of the eighteenth-century Japanese Gothicist Ueda Akinari confirm the presence of the Gothic spirit in oriental literature. All of the traditional features of the genre are firmly embedded in Akinari's tales of terror, with a special place given to the psychological monstrosities of the dream life and the intrusion of the malicious supernatural into human lives at their most vulnerable moments. The residue of feudalism and bushido codes of Japanese culture in the eighteenth century provide that sense of enclosure and entrapment crucial to the evocation of Gothic fear. The superiority of evil to goodness in Akinari's Gothic work links him with Western Gothicism at its most pessimistic extremes. According to Akinari's modern translator Leon Zolbrod, "The form that Akinari helped to perfect led to a species of historical romance similar to the Gothic novel in the West. Although Akinari's ghosts and otherworldly creatures show an animal nature that defied control and mastery, they have neither the bleeding skulls nor luminous hands of the spirits of Gothic novels; nor are they headless apparitions clad in armour or eerie forms extending phosphorescent claws toward the victim's throat. Rather, they are at once more primitive and more modern" (*Tales of Moonlight and Rain* 53-54). While his characters are often menaced by supernatural forces, it is their psychological and spiritual peril that links Akinari's Gothicism to primitive and modern monstrosity.

Early in the twentieth century, Akinari's place in the Gothic tradition was recognized by the orientalist Lafcadio Hearn (Koizumi Yakumo, 1850-1904), who included two Akinari tales in *A Japanese Miscellany* (1901). More recently, his Gothic virtuosity has been admired and praised by Yukio Mishima (1925-1970), whose sensational ritual suicide in 1970 might have been borrowed from one of Akinari's lurid plots. Currently gaining in popularity with general readers as well as students of Gothic fiction, his works remained almost unknown and untranslated in the West until the appearance of a monographic assessment by Pierre Humbertclaude in 1940.

Akinari's life was filled with mystery, misery, rejection, and physical affliction. He was born in Osaka in 1734, possibly in a bordello, to a woman who may have been a prostitute. The stigma of illegitimacy would mar him for life. Rejected by his mother, he was adopted by Ueda Masuke, a former samurai who had become a paper dealer. He contracted smallpox, which left him marked for life by a crippling deformity of the middle finger of the right hand. The digital deformity accounts for Akinari's occasional use of the pen name "Senshi Kijin" (Mr. Oddfinger). Never having known his real father, Akinari thought of himself as a pariah stigmatized by disease and doomed to misfortune. Such a stance accounts for the pathological tone of many of the narrators as well as the recurrence of mutilation and youthful failure in the tales. As a young man, he developed an interest in *haiku* poetry, signing his own compositions with the pseudonym "Mucho." The muted quality of the three-line *haiku* verse form was later reflected in the style of the Gothic pieces, particularly in the understated horror of the climaxes. In 1760, he married Ueyama Tama and in 1766 published his first book, a collection of "naughty" character profiles, *Shodo kikimimi sekenzaru* [*Worldly Apes with a Smattering of Various Arts*]. This was followed in 1768 by the first Gothic work, nine stories collected under the title *Ugetsu monogatari* [*Tales of Moonlight and Rain*]. An elegant volume complete with woodcuts was later published in 1776. After his home and paper business in Osaka were destroyed by fire, Akinari moved to Kashima, where he began the study of medicine under the tutelage of Tsuga Teisho, a physician and writer of sophisticated, belletristic literature called *yomihon*. He returned to Osaka, practiced medicine, and there became preoccupied with classical literary study and serious writing in his determination to transcend his marked life by achieving artistic success. By 1788, he had abandoned his medical practice to devote himself wholly to literature, most especially *tanka* poetry (a thirty-one-syllable verse form also called *waka*). Total loss of sight in his left eye and visual problems hampered his work but deepened his Gothic vision of self and society. Impoverished and facing permanent blindness, he moved to Kyoto, where he contemplated suicide after the death of his wife in 1797. Possibly to forestall suicidal desires, Akinari began writing another Gothic short-story set, *Harusame monogatari* [*Tales of the Spring Rain*], finishing the manuscript in 1802. After a period of physical distress and intellectual inertia, he attempted to destroy all of his writings in 1807. He died two years later in Kyoto at the age of seventy-five, unaware of the fact that *Tales of Moonlight and Rain* would soon be regarded in Japan as one of the most important prose works of the eighteenth century.

Each of the nine tales in *Tales of Moonlight and Rain* displays immediately identifiable Gothic occurrences, situations, conflicts, and characterization. Their settings are historical, with action placed in tenth- to seventeenth-century Japan, a medieval period of samurai warfare, social disorder, and imperial intrigue. Akinari's management of malign supernatural forces etched against the blood-stained canvas of feudal history was influenced to some extent by the Chinese supernatural tales in *Ch'ien tang hsin hua* [*New Tales for Lamplight*], in which the cultural and historical horrors of violent social transition figure prominently. The severe and simple style of the tales also demonstrates the influence of the *setsuwa,* a Japanese story form rooted in fable, parable, and supernatural incident. Akinari was also familiar with the *kusazoshi,* the Japanese literary equivalent of the Gothic chapbook or rapid tale of terror.

Functioning as a symbol of the desire for permanence, peace, and stability, rain signifies throughout the tales that form of innocence that precedes any deep contact with evil, while moonlight signifies the sinister illumination of experience, a knowledge often accompanied by death, madness, or psychic torment. In many of the tales, the precarious balance of good and evil is often tipped in evil's favor as Akinari depicts moments of dark enlightenment when rain yields to moonlight. Within this general symbolic context, three characteristic Gothic motifs empower the stories and link them to one another in a chain of supernatural cause and effect. The perilous or fatal journey during which the characters undergo an unexplainable supernatural experience is a story pattern found in several of the nine tales. A pestilential or pathological atmosphere fraught with spectral depictions of disease is common to many of the pieces. Confining spaces charged with phantasmic energy "where demons might appear and consort with men, and humans fear not to mingle with spirits" (114) are deployed throughout Akinari's closed Gothic world. Within the framework of the dark journey, the terrible place, and palsied universe are to be found most of the horrific objects and conditions of mainstream Western Gothicism, including cadaverous confrontation, psychotic retrospection, imminent mutilation by architectural forces, torture, ghostly assaults, gruesome prophecies, peripatetic corpses, haunted abodes presided over by restless spirits, madness, murder, erotic sadism, satanic transformation, demonic dominance and possession, necrophagia or corpse eating, and psychotic pleasure in pain. Several of the nocturnal climaxes in Akinari's tales have close psychological and stylistic parallels with the night scenes in Poe's homicidal and suicidal fantasies.

"White Peak," the opening story in *Tales of Moonlight and Rain,* is a tale of demonic encounter, dark prophecy, and an awakening to the power of evil. Out of a kind of Faustian curiosity and desire for contact with the demonic world, the poet-narrator conjures up the phantom of the emperor Sutoku (reigned 1123-1141) by chanting a cabalistic verse. The imperial ghost delivers a hideous account of his potency, informing the narrator that it is "I who have recently caused all of the trouble in the world" (100) and accusing him of a selfish ignorance of the ways of the world. Centuries ago, the emperor had written an oath in blood, thrown the sutras or scriptural precepts into the sea, and denounced humankind to become "a king of Evil." "I finally became a great king of Evil, head of the more than 300 kinds of demons. Every time my band sees happiness, they turn it into misery. Whenever they see the country at peace, they cause war" (100). His satanic revelation climaxes in his gruesome metamorphosis into a hawk-like being. Now realizing his peril of soul, the narrator dispels the king of evil with another charm, but recollecting the bloody history of the realm, the narrator has to admit the power of the demon emperor and, by extension, his own and every man's involvement with the evil of the world. Now wiser, the poet-narrator knows and will build on the knowledge that "what he related was as terrifying as it was mysterious" (108).

"The Cauldron of Kibitsu" is a story of appalling spectral revenge taken by a dead wife upon her unfaithful husband. Akinari uses the familiar Gothic situation of the ghost vigil along with some precisely installed Gothic acoustics in the form of a single "scream of bloodcurdling intensity" (159) to dramatize a dark truth about the human heart. The dissolute and unfaithful Shotaro has a posthumous rendezvous with Isora, whose spirit has been lurking about his house for forty-one nights. The dire consequences of his adultery and the supernatural power of the phantom spouse have been ominously foreshadowed by the silent boiling of the cauldron at the shrine of Kibitsu. On the forty-second night of his vigil, his friend Hikoroku hears Shotaro shout in agony (the tale's single scream), then vanish. As a grisly memento of her return and revenge, Isora has left on display atop the house eaves "nothing else than a bleeding head torn and mangled. This was the only trace of Shotaro that remained" (160). Like the formalized violence of a *No* theater scene, the bloody head illuminated by Hikoroku's raised torch highlights the tale's moral by showing "the power of the supernatural. Thus, the story has been handed down" (160). Such abrupt, unrelieved horror has led some commentators to point out the closeness in method between Akinari's horror tableaux and the formalized violence of the *No* drama.

The longest tale in the set, **"The Lust of the White Serpent,"** should remind Western readers of the legend of the snake that inhabits a human body, a "bosom serpent" as in Hawthorne's gruesome fantasy "Egotism; or, The Bosom Serpent." Akinari gives another snake figure shared by many folklores, the Lamia or serpent lady, an especially grotesque vitality in his descriptions of the tale's fatal woman, Manago. Encountering her in a storm and giving her his umbrella, the naïve young man, Toyoo, finds himself entangled in her guileful coils. Giving him an antique sword, Manago proposes to the young man, pledging "a thousand years of love with you" (166). Invading Toyoo's life in a ghostly manner, she works her will upon him until he is tormented to the point of obsession by the beautiful demon and begs for release from an old Buddhist priest. He marries Tomiko, thinking that taking a natural mate might expel the evil spirit of the snake-woman, but the effect is the opposite when Tomiko's voice and appearance change to "unmistakably that of Manago" (179). When a priest tries to seize and destroy her, she asserts her power over men by transforming herself into an enormous serpent.

> No sooner did he open the door of the sleeping chamber, than a demon thrust its head out at the priest. The projecting extremity was so huge that it filled the doorway, gleaming even whiter than newly fallen snow, with eyes like mirrors and horns like the bare bows of a tree. The creature opened its mouth more than three feet wide; its crimson tongue darted, as if to swallow the priest in a single gulp.
>
> (180)

In a final effort to free himself from his snake-bride, Toyoo throws a monk's robe over Manago to smother her, but upon removing the robe "there lay Tomiko, unconscious, with a white serpent more than three feet in length coiled motionlessly on her breast" (183). The Lamia's victory over human love is complete. Like the "Horla" in Maupassant's tale of demonic possession by a deadly creature or like the invasion of the Lady Rowena's body by Ligeia, the strength of the vampiric woman or "conqueror worm" in beautiful disguise is reaffirmed by the remorseless climax.

The story in the set that most resembles the monastic horrors of many eighteenth-century Gothic novels is **"The Blue Hood,"** a parable of dark enlightenment. When the Zen Buddhist priest Kaian Zenji pauses at the mountain hamlet of Tomita, he is mistaken by the frightened residents for the mountain demon, a mad Buddhist abbot who fell in love with a boy, then devoured his corpse after the boy's death. Akinari's description of the abbot's corpse feast is a loathsome horror photograph. "Then, refusing to allow the body to rot and decay, he sucked the flesh and licked the bones until he utterly devoured it. 'The abbot has turned into a devil,' the people in the temple said, and they all fled" (188).

After his bestialization by the taste of human flesh, the abbot becomes a ghoul who raids and cannibalizes the villagers. Like Matthew Gregory Lewis's Ambrosio in *The Monk,* he is changed by sexual lust into a monster. "Once he descended into the sinful path of lust and covetousness, he was changed into a demon, and he fell victim to the flames of the fires in the hell of delusion. This probably came to pass because of his self-righteous and arrogant nature" (192). Deciding to rid the mountain of the monster, Kaian Zenji goes alone to the ruined temple where the abbot lurks in mad solitude. Giving him his blue-dyed hood, Kaian Zenji recites a gnostic verse for the reclamation of the abbot's soul. After a year, Kaian revisits the ruined temple, there to encounter the abbot's wraith, now a living ghost that continually chants the salvational stanzas. When Kaian strikes him with his Zen rod, the figure vanishes, "leaving only the blue hood and a skeleton lying in the weeds. At this instant the monk probably overcame his stubborn attachment to evil. Surely a divine principle was in operation" (193). Allegorically, the tale deals with the salvational power of art over the savagery of human nature and is rare among Akinari's stories in its moralized depiction of the triumph of goodness over evil and the human over the inhuman.

Two stories in the collection *Tales of the Spring Rain,* **"The Smiling Death's-Head"** and **"The Grave of Miyagi,"** are tales of passion with strong Gothic overtones in atmosphere and characterization. In contrast to the gruesome supernatural content of most of the pieces in *Tales of Moonlight and Rain,* these tales achieve their effect by a concentration on the morbid beauty of death. In fact, several of the tales may be read as extended epitaphs with minimal supernatural action but a great deal of supernatural reverie. The narrator of **"The Grave of Miyagi,"** a poet, has come to Kanzaki near Osaka to trace the legend and locate the grave of the prostitute Miyagi. Her lover, Jutabei, had been poisoned, and she had been made the sexual slave of his murderer, Fujidayu. She ended her tragic life with a prayer to Buddha and a leap into the sea. Now her soul is elegized by the poet, whose quest after her memory finally brings him to a "stone monument scarcely the width of an outspread fan. Thus I wrote, paying homage to the soul of Miyagi. I have heard that now not a trace remains of her grave, for it was thirty years ago that I wrote the poem" (*Tales of the Spring Rain* 154). As may be seen, Akinari's Gothicism in this tale is lyric and not episodic, its mood celebrating the joy that resides in sorrow itself.

In the almost naturalistic story **"The Smiling Death's-Head,"** a father's avarice destroys his son's happiness, and a brother murders his sister to prevent his family honor from being tainted. The saki brewer Gosoji is determined to block the love match between his son, Gozo, and the beautiful Mune simply because "she hasn't any money" (102). Complicating the conflict between father and son is Motosuke, Mune's honor-driven brother. When Gozo brings Mune into Gosoji's house as his bride, the stage is set for the tale's Gothic resolution. Abruptly and without warning, Motosuke intervenes. "'She is your wife. She must die in your house.' With these words, he drew his sword and struck off his sister's head. Gozo lifted up Mune's severed head and wrapped it in his kimono sleeve. Not letting fall a single tear, he started to walk out of the gate" (109). Following a trial for murder, the three men are banished and dispossessed of all wealth, while the legend of the severed head of Mune, a head that "retains even in death its brave smile and courageous expression" (112), is absorbed into the legends of the district. Although Akinari's use of the living head lacks the horrific impact of the screaming skull of a Western Gothic writer like F. Marion Crawford, he nevertheless succeeds in inspiring the fear, awe, and wonder that lie at the heart of Gothic beauty.

The dramatic and episodic Gothicism of *Tales of Moonlight and Rain* is counterpointed by the lyric and reflective Gothicism of *Tales of the Spring Rain.* Both sets of stories establish Ueda Akinari as a Gothic innovator worthy of the attention of all modern readers who are interested in the persistence of the Gothic in non-Western cultures. Akinari's influence on the development of a Japanese Gothic tradition is registered in the work of Izumi Kyoka (1873-1939), whose masterful short stories of the Meiji period (1868-1912) have been compared with Poe's tales. Four recently translated Kyoka stories, "The Surgery Room," "The Holy Man of Mount Koya," "One Day in Spring," and "Osen and Sokichi," clearly show the influence of Ueda Akinari on his Gothic successors as an inspirational model.

In the two prefaces to the first Gothic novel, *The Castle of Otranto,* Horace Walpole advised his readers to expect to find the characters in "extraordinary positions" and further indicated that his Gothic tale would provide "a constant vicissitude of interesting passions." Walpole's criteria for Gothic liminality are repeatedly applied with astonishing force in the demonized universe of Japan's Ueda Akinari.

FURTHER READING

Biography

Saunders, Dale. "Introduction to a Translation of *Ugetsu Monogatari*." *Monumenta Nipponica* 21, nos. 1-2 (1966): 171-202.

  Discusses Akinari's life and times.

Takamasa, Sasaki. Introduction to *Ueda Akinari's Tales of a Rain'd Moon,* translated by Sasaki Takamasa. Tokyo: The Hokuseido Press, 1980, 182 p.

Comments on Akinari's life and the sources of *Tales of Moonlight and Rain.*

Criticism

Chambers, Anthony. "'Hankai': A Translation from *Harusame monogatari.*" *Monumenta Nipponica* 25, nos. 3-4 (1970): 371-406.

Provides a brief overview of Akinari's life and writings while introducing a translation of the most famous story from the *Tales of the Spring Rain.*

Jackman, Barry. Introduction to *Tales of the Spring Rain: Harusame Monogatari by Ueda Akinari,* translated by Barry Jackman. Tokyo: The Japan Foundation, 1975, 249 p.

Suggests that the stories collected in *Tales of the Spring Rain.* should be studied individually rather than as a whole.

Kato, Shuichi. "Ueda Akinari." In *A History of Japanese Literature, Volume 2: The Years of Isolation,* translated by Don Sanderson, pp. 191-99. London: Macmillan Press, 1983.

Contrasts Akinari's career with that of his contemporary Motoori Norinaga.

Whitehouse, Wilfrid. "Introduction to Shiramine: Ueda Akinari and His *Ugetsu Monogatari.*" *Monumenta Nipponica* 1, no. 1 (January 1938): 242-58.

Provides a brief discussion of Akinari's writing career and commentary on the story "Shiramine."

Zolbrod, Leon. "Yomihon: The Appearance of the Historical Novel in Late Eighteenth Century and Early Nineteenth Century Japan." *Journal of Asian Studies* 25, no. 3 (May 1966): 485-98.

Discusses the Japanese literary genre known as *yomihon,* citing Akinari as the best practitioner of this literary form.

Andrés Bello
1781-1865

(Full name Andrés Bartolomé Bello) Venezuelan poet, translator, essayist, and editor.

INTRODUCTION

One of the foremost intellectual figures during the Spanish-American wars of independence and the subsequent formation of Latin American nations, Bello produced works in a variety of genres, including literature, philosophy, political writings, and civil law. An editor, teacher, politician, and formulator of a Latin American grammar, Bello is credited with giving life to the "americanismo" movement and inspiring Latin Americans to celebrate their independence and freedom in the wake of Spanish colonialism. A leading advocate of Spanish language and culture, Bello helped to empower Latin Americans both intellectually and politically and played an important role in the development of postcolonial Latin America.

BIOGRAPHICAL INFORMATION

Bello was born November 29, 1781, in Caracas, Venezuela, which only four years earlier had been declared the capital of Venezuela. The eldest of eight children, he descended from a prestigious line of artists, painters, and musicians. Bello's mother, Ana Antonia López, was the daughter of Venezuela's leading sculptor, painter, and artist of the eighteenth century, Juan Pedro López. Bello's father, Bartolomé Bello y Bello, was a notable musician with a degree in civil law. As a youth Bello studied Latin and immersed himself in classicism, translating into Castilian the fifth book of Virgil's *Aeneid* at the age of 15. He went on to pursue a bachelor's degree in the arts, graduating from the Real y Pontificia Universidad de Caracas in 1800. While at the university, Bello taught Simón Bolívar, the future revolutionary leader and statesman. After graduation Bello studied literature, French, and English, which helped prepare him for his many years in London. He also wrote literary works which brought him recognition and prestige. In 1802 Bello was awarded the political position of second official of the Captaincy General of Venezuela, and from this time forward Bello was an active civic, diplomatic, and cultural figure. When in 1808 the first printing press was brought to Caracas, the Captaincy General selected Bello as the editor of the first official newspaper, *La*

Gaceta de Caracas. During this time Bello continued to produce poetry based on the classical traditions he studied and enjoyed as a boy.

In 1810 Bello travelled to England with Bolívar, who was sent as a political envoy from Venezuela. While the stay was a brief one for Bolívar, who soon returned to Venezuela to continue the fight for independence, Bello remained in London. Political instability in Venezuela made the next ten years difficult for Bello, who was left without the financial support of his country and had to provide for himself. While in London he married Mary Ann Boyland in 1814, who died seven years later. In 1824 he married Isabel Antonia Dunn. During this time he served in various capacities as a political representative for South American countries, including Venezuela, Colombia, and Chile. He also continued his literary pursuits, editing and contributing to several Spanish language literary journals. Along with Juan Garcia del Rio, Bello published *Biblioteca Americana* in 1823 and *El Repertorio Americano* in 1826, two influential journals that also featured Bello's work, which included poetry, scientific investigations, philosophy, translations, and literary criticism. Throughout his time in London, which was characterized by his study, writing, and diplomatic duties, Bello longed to return to South America. In 1829, he and his family left London for Chile, where he was named the undersecretary of the Ministry of the Interior. His skill and experience as an editor was again put to work in the publication of the newspaper *El Araucano* for which he was principal editor from 1830 to 1853. He continued to be very active in government, serving as a senator of the Republic from 1837 to 1855. He was instrumental in founding the University of Chile in 1842. Two of his most significant works during this time were his 1847 *Gramática de la lengua castellana destinada al uso de los americanos,* a formal grammar of Castilian for use by Latin Americans, and his 1852 *Código civil chileno,* or *The Chilean Civil Code,* which was ratified by the Chilean Congress in 1855. His diplomatic skills were again called upon in 1865, when he served as an arbiter between Ecuador and the United States. His long and esteemed political and literary career came to a close October 15, 1865, when he died at the age of 84 in Santiago, Chile, after a prolonged illness.

MAJOR WORKS

Bello's work has been compiled into two large collections and between his poetry, essays, philosophy, grammar, legislation, and criticism, there is much for Bello scholars to consider. Among the unifying themes in all of his work are his philosophy of *americanismo,* or celebrating and enlightening Latin American peoples, his concern for a unified grammar, his belief in the regulation of social life to ward against the dissolution of city life amid unchecked vice, and his literary interest in combining both Classic and Romantic schools of thought. His poem "Alocución a la Poesía, en que se introducen las albanzas de los pueblos é individuos americanos, que más se han distinguido en la Guerra de la independencia. (Fragmento de un poema inédito, titulado 'América')" ("Discourse to Poetry, which presents the glories of the peoples and individuals of America who have most distinguished themselves in the war of independence. [Fragment of an unpublished poem entitled 'America']") is a strong example of his concern with validating and celebrating the Latin American, or *americanismo* experience. He published the first 447 lines of the poem in the first issue of the journal *Biblioteca Americana* in July 1823, and the remaining 387 lines in the second (and final) volume of that same journal. This poem can be considered in two sections divided by style; a Georgic section and an Epic section. In the Georgic lines, the poet invites the Goddess of Poetry to the new world, enticing her with descriptions of its lush natural beauty and vast potential. The Goddess is then asked if she would rather hear of the heroics of those who valiantly died in the wars for independence from Colonial Spain. The Epic section remains focused on the experience of war and those who fought for an end to colonial tyranny. The poem, often called simply "América," has been considered a declaration of the spiritual and intellectual independence of Latin America, while at the same time relying upon the classical and European conventions of poetry.

Another of Bello's most significant poetic works is his "Agricultura," which again uses Georgic conventions in both theme and tone to represent the transformations in Latin America brought on by the wars for independence. Following the natural and political history of Latin America, it first portrays rich images of the fertility of the torrid zone's climate. The abundance and easy way of life are celebrated, and the land is represented as providing everything the indigenous people need to live healthy lives. Then the Spaniards arrive, and place the indigenous people into servitude, which while restrictive was nevertheless idyllic, because the land still provided for simple and easy living. The poem then demonstrates how European consumption soon overtaxed both the land and the people, and the relationship became one of master and slave. The Church's role in this increasingly oppressive colonial rule is strongly criticized, and the Church is portrayed as instigating tensions between the peasants and the Spanish for its own financial gain. Bello blames the Church for fanning the flames of civil war, and for driving the peasants from their land into vice-ridden cities. The poem exhibits how revolution has destroyed the simple way of life that was presented in the early sections, and shows that Latin Americans can regain control over their lands and their self-determination through agriculture. Although agriculture is a harder life than what existed before the Spanish colonization, the poem argues, it is the only way for Latin Americans to claim freedom for themselves.

CRITICAL RECEPTION

The body of critical inquiry in English into Bello's life and work remains scarce, primarily due to a lack of translations; however, his literary, philosophical, and political accomplishments are thoroughly studied in Spanish-language criticism. There exists several trends in the available English-language scholarship. In separate studies, critics Iván Jaksić and O. Carlos Stoetzer focus on the correlation between Bello's political and social experiences and his literary work. The importance of revolutionary figures and his central part in the definition of independent Latin American culture, especially his influence on the formal grammar of Latin America, are also of great interest to critics. Antonio

Cussen discusses the significance of *Bioblioteca Americana* as a Spanish-language journal and explains its importance to Bello's philosophy of *americanismo*. Jaksić examines Bello's experience in London, which is characterized by his personal study, diplomatic appointments, and editorial endeavors. The critic finds Bello's commitment to the championing of Latin American culture in all facets of his life abroad.

PRINCIPAL WORKS

Análisis ideológico de los tiempos de la conjugación castellana (nonfiction) 1809

El Calendario manual y guía universal de forasteros en Venezuela para el año 1810 (history) 1810

Poem of the Cid [translator] (poetry) 1816

Biblioteca Americana [editor; with Juan García de Río] (journal) 1823

Repertorio Americano [editor; with Juan García de Río] (journal) 1826-27

Principios del derecho de gentes (nonfiction) 1832

Principios de ortología y méterica de la lengua castellana (nonfiction) 1835

El incendio de la Compañia. Canto elegiaco (poetry) 1841

Discurso pronunciado . . . en la instalación de la Universidad de Chile el día 17 de septiembre de 1843 (speech) 1843

Instituciones de derecho romano (philosophy) 1843

Proyecto de Código civil (1841-1845) (philosophy) 1846

Teresa [translator] (drama) 1846

Gramática de la lengua castellana destinada al uso de los americanos (nonfiction) 1847

Cosmografia, o descripción del universo conforme a los últimos descubrimientos (history) 1848

Compaendio de historia de la literatura (criticism) 1850

Colección de poesías originales por Andrés Bello (poetry) 1870

Filosofía del entendimiento (essays and criticism) 1881

Obras completas. 15 vols. (poetry, essays, criticism, philosophy, and nonfiction) 1881-93

Obras completas. 26 vols. (poetry, essays, criticism, philosophy, and nonfiction) 1981-86

CRITICISM

Elijah Clarence Hills (essay date 1920)

SOURCE: Hills, Elijah Clarence. Introduction to *The Odes of Bello, Olmedo, and Heredia*, pp. 3-9. New York: G. P. Putnam's Sons, 1920.

[*In the following excerpt, Hills briefly outlines Bello's life and major works, noting their general reception by critics.*]

The three pre-eminent classic poets of Spanish America are Bello of Venezuela, Olmedo of Ecuador, and the Cuban Heredia.

Of these, Don Andrés Bello (1781-1865) was the most consummate master of poetic diction, although he lacked the brilliancy of Olmedo and the spontaneity of Heredia.

Born in Caracas and educated in the schools of his native city, Bello was sent to England in the year 1810 to further the cause of the revolution, and he remained in that country till 1829, when he was called to Chile to take service in the Department of Foreign Affairs. His life may, therefore, be divided into three distinct periods. In Caracas he studied chiefly the Latin and Spanish classics and the elements of international law, and he made metrical translations of Virgil and Horace. Upon arriving in England at the age of twenty-nine years, he gave himself with enthusiasm to the study of Greek, Italian, and French, as well as English.

These nineteen years in England were still a part of the formative period of Bello's life, for, unlike Heredia and many other Spanish-American poets, his development was slow. He read and wrote incessantly when not engaged in giving private lessons in order to earn his livelihood,—for he received little support from America. He came to know many scholars, and he was especially intimate with James Mill, whom he is said to have helped to decipher an enigmatic document of Bentham, and with Blanco-White and other Spanish men of letters who were living there in exile on account of their liberal views. Bello joined with the Spanish and Hispano-American scholars in London in the publication of several literary reviews, notably the *Censor Americano* (1820), the **Biblioteca Americana** (1823), and the **Repertorio Americano** (1826-27), and in these he published many of his most important works. Here appeared his studies of Old French and of the **"Song of My Cid,"** his excellent translation of fourteen cantos of Boiardo's **"Orlando Innamorato,"** several important articles on Spanish syntax and prosody, and the best of all his poems, the **Silvas Americanas.**

In 1829, when already forty-eight years of age, Bello removed to Chile, and there entered upon the happiest period of his life. Besides serving as editor of the *Araucano* and, for a time, as secretary to the Minister of Foreign Affairs, he gave private lessons until 1831 when he was made rector of the College of Santiago. In the year 1843 the University of Chile was established at Santiago, and Bello became its first rector. He held this important post till his death twenty-two years later at the ripe age of eighty-four. In 1864 the government of the United States submitted to Bello the arbitration of a dispute with Ecuador, and again a year later he was chosen to settle a dispute between Peru and Colombia.

During this third and last period of his life Bello completed and published his *Spanish Grammar* and his *Principles of International Law,* works which, with occasional slight revisions, have been used as standard text-books in Spanish America, and to some extent in Spain, to the present day. The *Grammar,* especially, has been extraordinarily successful, and the edition with notes by José Rufino Cuervo is still the best text-book of Spanish grammar we have. In the *Grammar,* Bello sought to free Castilian from Latin terminology; but he desired, most of all, to correct the abuses so common to writers of the period, and to establish linguistic unity in Spanish America.

Bello wrote little original verse during these last years of his life. At one time he became very fond of Victor Hugo and even tried to imitate him; but his classical training and methodical habits made success difficult. Nevertheless, his best poetic work during his residence in Chile are translations of Victor Hugo, and his free metrical rendering of **"La Prière pour Tous"** (from the *Feuilles d'Automne*) is amongst his finest and most popular verses.

It is interesting that Don Andrés Bello, a distinguished scholar in linguistics and in international law, should also have been a pre-eminent poet. All critics, except possibly a few of the present-day *"modernistas,"* place his **American Silvas** amongst the best poetic compositions of all Spanish America. The *Silvas* are two in number: the **"Allocution to Poetry"** (**"Alocución a la Poesía"**), and the **"Silva to the Agriculture of the Torrid Zone"** (**"Silva a la Agricultura de la Zona Tórrida"**). The first is fragmentary: apparently the poet despaired of completing it, and he embodied in the second poem an elaboration of those passages in the first work which describe nature in the tropics. The **Silvas** are in some degree imitations of Virgil's *Georgics,* and they are the best of Spanish imitations. The great literary critic, Menéndez y Pelayo, was willing to admit (*Antología de Poetas Hispano-americanos,* II, p. cxlii) that Bello, is, "in descriptive and georgic verse, the most Virgilian of our [Spanish] poets." Caro, in his splendid biography of Bello, classifies the **Silvas** as "scientific poetry," which is quite true if this sort of poetry gives an esthetic conception of nature, expressed in beautiful terms and adorned with descriptions of natural objects. It is less true of the **"Allocution,"** which is largely historical, in that it introduces and sings the praises of towns and persons that won fame in the revolutionary wars.

The **"Silva to Agriculture,"** which is both descriptive and moral, may be best described in the words of Caro. It is, says this distinguished critic, "an account of the beauty and wealth of nature in the tropics, and an exhortation to those who live in the equator that, instead of wasting their strength in political and domestic dissensions, they should devote themselves to agricultural pursuits." Bello's interest in nature had doubtless been stimulated by the coming of Humboldt to Caracas in the first decade of the nineteenth century. In the attempt to express his feeling for nature in poetic terms, he probably felt the influence not only of Virgil, but also of Arriaza's *Emilia or the Arts* and of the several poems descriptive of nature written in Latin by Jesuit priests, such as the once famous *Rusticatio Mexicana* by Father Landívar of Guatemala. And yet there is very little in the *Silvas* that is directly imitative. The **"Silva to the Agriculture of the Torrid Zone,"** especially, is an extraordinarily successful attempt to give expression in Virgilian terms to the exotic life of the tropics, and in this it is unique in Spanish literature. The beautiful descriptive passages in this poem, the noble ethical precepts, and the severely pure diction, combine to make it a classic that will long hold an honored place in Spanish letters.

O. Carlos Stoetzer (essay date December 1983)

SOURCE: Stoetzer, O. Carlos. "The Political Ideas of Andrés Bello." *International Philosophical Quarterly,* 23, no. 4 (December 1983): 395-406.

[*In the following essay, Stoetzer examines Bello's political views and how personal and environmental influences manifest themselves in his logic, opinions, and literature.*]

I

Andrés Bello (1781-1865), the eminent Venezuelan philosopher and statesman who later chose Chile as his homeland and whose bicentennial was just celebrated in 1981, remains Spanish America's greatest humanist. The extraordinary work of this true scholar still echoes in our own times and radiates his beneficial influence.

Three distinct phases span his life: his formative years in Venezuela, from his birth in 1781 to the establishment of the Caracas junta in 1810; the second and maturing phase, his English exile in London from 1810 to 1829, full of hardships but also intellectually rewarding; and finally, his third and last phase in Chile from 1829 to his death in 1865, where he was always the great teacher, but also worked as a Senator, a government advisor, and as director of his host country's international policies. It was here in Santiago de Chile that his fertile mind produced his most significant works and where his presence and activities had the most profound impact on all social spheres.

His works, published in Chile in the years 1881-1893 in 15 volumes, and in Caracas during 1960-1969 in 23 volumes, cover an extraordinary variety of subjects.

They include his most famous works: the *Filosofía del entendimiento,* in philosophy; his **"Silva a la agricultura, de la zona tórrida"** in poetry; his *Gramática de la lengua castellana,* in philology, still the best Spanish grammar to this day; his Chilean civil code, in law, which was taken as a model in Colombia, Ecuador, Nicaragua, and Uruguay, and his *Principios del derecho de gentes,* in international law, which turned him into the founder of Latin American international law.

Several factors influenced the political thought of Andrés Bello. First and foremost were his personality and temperament, characterized by his virtues of modesty, harmony, and balance; his sense of responsibility and duty; his wisdom, his respect for life and for human rights. Bello was deeply rooted in tradition, but at the same time this was not in a negative, sterile, or even reactionary manner, but instead represented more an evolutionary concept, thus adjusting to changing times. Bello was a realist; he was also aristocratic, with an outgoing nature. His entire character emphasized generosity in the best tradition of the rising liberal creed. Thus, the most striking element of his personality was one of avoiding extremes and approaching life and political realities with wisdom and tolerance. His character thus mirrored in an extraordinary way several of the main philosophic currents based on common sense or on eclecticism.

In the second place, Bello was much influenced by the European thought of the age. Already as a student in Caracas he felt the impact of the personality and the ideas of Alexander von Humboldt, and later this influence of European thought was further strengthened when he arrived in England as one of the three members of the famous diplomatic mission which the recently established government of Caracas had entrusted to Simón Bolívar (1810-1812). Bello, who had been one of the three teachers of Bolívar, was the official secretary of the mission, and his arrival in London was eventually to lead to almost two decades of uninterrupted residence and work in Great Britain (1810-1829). In the words of his biographer Rafael Caldera, "Bello was the life and soul of the Captaincy General of Caracas from 1801 to 1810,"[1] and by the time he joined the diplomatic mission he ". . . was already a trained humanist, but in London he was able to acquire wide learning and gain the scholarly refinement which made possible his later work."[2] London at that time was not only the headquarters of the resistance to Napoleon, but the homeland of constitutional government, of responsible ministers, neutrality of the crown, religious tolerance, freedom of the press and assembly. It was also the center of Spanish and Spanish American exiles,[3] such as the Venezuelan Francisco de Miranda, the Ecuadorean José Joaquin Olmedo, the Colombians García del Río and José Fernández Madrid, and the Spaniard José María Blanco. It was also in London that Bello negotiated with personalities like the Duke of Wellington and became personally acquainted with influential thinkers like Jeremy Bentham and James Mill. Here in England he was profoundly influenced by the British political and constitutional environment and by the several currents of thought, mainly the Scottish School, Kant's philosophy, and Cousin's Eclecticism.

This English influence, further enhanced by his two English marriages (1815-1821; 1824),[4] coupled to his own strong and serious personality, resulted in a very successful and happy attempt to find reasonable and wise solutions to all problems. However, despite his long stay in England, Bello never became a European or British thinker; he remained faithful to his South American roots and his English connection produced a rather rare and extraordinary harmonious blending that resulted in great benefits to the various countries he served.

Besides becoming the great journalist and poet, educator and philologist, Bello also delved into philosophy, law, and political science. With his *Filosofía del entendimiento* he became a philosopher in his own right, and both his scholarly work and his diplomatic performance, first in London and later in Chile, earned him a great reputation as an authority in the law of nations and as an able South American statesman. During his long stay in England, Bello continued to serve the Venezuelan junta after 1812, and in the 1820s he was Secretary of the Chilean Legation under the Guatemalan Antonio José de Irisarri (1823-1824), and later from 1825 to 1829 Secretary of the Colombian Legation with Manuel José Hurtado and Fernández Madrid; in 1827 he headed the Colombian Mission in London.

II

Bello's political thought is, first of all, contained by analogy in his *Filosofía del entendimiento.* Furthermore, much of his political philosophy is found in his *Principios de derecho de gentes,* in his official and personal correspondence, signed or not, when he served the governments of Caracas, Chile and Colombia, and, of course, in the writings, official or otherwise, in Chile (1829-1865); the latter cover not only the official documents as a member of the Chilean Chancery but also articles which he published in *El Araucano.* Finally, the single most important document of the period from which we can further deduce his political philosophy is the famous Chilean Constitution of 1833, and although he was not directly responsible for its elaboration, it is known that Bello was very much involved in the matter.[5] His name did not officially appear as a matter of tact and delicacy, since he was not a born Chilean and had arrived only a few years before the constitution saw the light of day.

To understand Bello's political thought it is also necessary to take into account his basic belief in God and in the law of nature, since everything else flows logically from this essential intellectual premise. Bello's firm belief in a Supreme Being represents, thus, the religious and philosophic basis which in turn furnishes us the key to his political ideas. In his *Filosofía del entendimiento*—Chapter IX dealing with the relation of cause and effect—Bello stated that

> From effects we infer causes, as from causes effects, through the linking of phenomena we call laws of nature. If we see a movement in a different direction from that of a free-falling object, we infer that it was produced by a push. If we see a fruit, we cannot doubt that it was developed and formed in a plant by the ordinary procedure of vegetation. If we see order, agreement of parts, means directed toward the attainment of an end, we deduce from that the existence of a will that planned the means, and of a power that put them in action. In this manner we were led to knowledge of the adored Author of nature. The marvellous harmony of the universe where each part seems to have been made to accord with the others, and all agree in the conservation and propagation of animate beings; . . . this marvellous harmony, these correlations, this order, forces us to recognize an intelligent cause, endowed with superior power and wisdom, beyond all comparison and measure to those that man employs in his works.[6]

Following logically this argument, Bello pointed out that this harmony compelled him to recognize

> . . . an all powerful Author and legislator whose will has established the connection of phenomena of which the general order is the result. The power of lesser causes is finite and desired, and that of the primary cause is infinite and original . . . *God willed that there be light,* and there was light, is a concrete but complete expression of the original causal relation.[7]

For Bello, then, the existence of a creative will, of an Eternal Being, of God, was, as he repeats it, "of an irrefutable evidence."[8] The principle of causality was the work of God, was "one of the laws established by God."[9] From this discussion Bello turned to the question of free will and continued:

> The freedom of the first cause is original and unlimited; the freedom of the human spirit is derived and finite; it is a faculty impressed on man just like all the other faculties which his soul and body enjoy. A voluntary action of man has consequently its immediate cause in the same human spirit which respectively has its own in the creative spirit. Thus the freedom or free will of man, when it exists, not less than the power or action of each one of the created things acknowledges divine essence, sovereignly free as sovereignly powerful, as its only source. Thus, on the first cause depend universally all the causes that constitute the phenomenal connections.[10]

Bello argued that there did not exist any people or race which did not have some notion of a Supreme Being, and in this respect quoted the famous saying of Voltaire, with whom otherwise he would have little in common, that ". . . si Dieu n'existait pas, il faudrait l'inventer,"[11] and looking further, he stated:

> . . . in order that man be truly virtuous, in order that in the most obscure place, and in complete solitude he be willing, if necessary, to sacrifice his very life to duty, it is necessary that he view it as a law emanating from God; it is necessary that he firmly believe that his actions, even if the world ignore them, are known and appreciated by an infallible judge; by a judge that permeates the most profound depths of the soul and is witness to our most intimate thoughts.[12]

Applying this conviction to the world in which we live, Bello then pointed out:

> Supreme Intelligence is not only the principle of order, but the type of the perfection of order; and since justice, truth, beneficence constitute the very essence of moral order whose laws the Creator has marked in the conscience and the heart of man, it is necessary that the Principle of order be absolutely just, true and beneficent.[13]

God, the Supreme Being, was thus the dispenser of life and happiness; He profoundly disburses life in the air, on earth, in water, and this profusion of life extends not only to the incalculable number of living beings but also to the millions and millions of the microscopic world, and without doubt, also to all planets of our solar system.[14]

Bello realized that not everything was happiness. He affirmed that it was true that the happiness of the living beings was interrupted by sorrow and often by the most painful experience. Was it not true, asked Bello that sorrow sharpened pleasure and that ". . . , pleasure could be less pleasing, would become dull, would make us totally insipid, without the alternatives which from time to time interrupt it in order to make its enjoyment more desirable and intense."[15] However, Bello continued, without this mixture of pleasure and pain, the most beautiful of God's works, virtue, could not exist, and virtue supposed temptation, struggles, painful privations, sacrifices. Virtue was one of the main elements that composed the moral order, the world of free agencies.[16] The sufferings of man were, then, on one side, a means of improvement, and on the other, a pledge of immortality. "Thus, even in them glitters divine beneficence,"[17] and he ended with the question:

> . . . If reason takes us up to the edge of an infinite settlement of mysteries and enigmas, don't we know at least enough to fill us with confidence in the goodness of that Being who did not judge it unworthy of his greatness to provide for the wants of his most humble and brutish creatures?[18]

In Bello's part on logic, and more specifically, in his Chapter I on knowledge, he made it clear that in his reasoning he proceeded from the *principle of the stabil-*

ity of the laws of nature, that his observations were based on the stability of certain connections, that given a cause, a certain effect necessarily followed, that is, that given the preceding phenomenon, the second phenomenon necessarily followed.[19] The principle of stability of natural laws was *a priori* knowledge in the Kantian sense; phenomena did not follow one another accidentally.[20] Bello who so often discussed and adhered to the Scottish School dealt in this context with the concept of common sense pointing out that:

> The primary elements of reason, axioms, truths that have a complete certainty and which are found within reach of all, are the peculiar objects of common sense, a denomination to which some give a more extensive meaning than others and which has been much abused in modern times because the limits have not been drawn within which the jurisdiction of this unimpeachable tribunal must be circumscribed.[21]

This quotation from Bello's *Filosofía del entendimiento* tells us a great deal and by analogy shows us the general tendency of his political thought. Also, in his study of logic another topic is interesting for our discussion. In his Chapter VIII dealing with the causes of error, Bello argued that in the realm of facts general principles would give us only approximate truths: each one of them would express an isolated phenomenal connection; and in nature phenomenal connections are mixed up and continuously disturb each other. Hence, general principles were inapplicable to real facts, and this was the reason why the mere theorist frequently exposed himself in practical applications to the ridicule of those he scorned for the inferiority of learning. As an example Bello mentioned mechanics and stated that here yardstick and weight were disregarded. The level was considered as an inflexible mathematical line; strings as mathematical lines of perfect flexibility; the subject matter in this science thus entered the domain of geometric demonstrations, but its theorems represented natural phenomena in an inaccurate way. A machine adjusted to them would produce movements very different from those calculated.[22] Bello then applied this same principle to the reality of political life:

> . . . In the same way, politics reduces the various forms of governments to certain general classes to which we attribute certain characteristic tendencies; and notwithstanding that every government is more or less mixed, if not in its legal theory at least in its way of operating and in its real effects, we discuss the advantages and disadvantages of monarchy, aristocracy and democracy as if there were political institutions that corresponded exactly to our definitions. There is more. Assuming a perfectly pure form of government, its effects would be modified largely by the concurrence of an endless number of causes: the antecedents of the people ruled by it, the climate, the religion, the industrial condition, the intellectual culture, and various others; all things that operating jointly produce complex results that are very difficult to evaluate. From this follows the stormy and

brief duration of some improvised institutions whose articles are so many more demonstrative deductions of abstract principles but only calculated for a people in abstract, or for a people that lacked special firmness that would contradict or modify them, a supposition that is morally impossible.[23]

It is easy, in the above discussion, to see in Bello a distant echo of Aristotle and St. Thomas Aquinas' mixed regime as well as somewhat closer the echo of Bodin and Montesquieu. However, demonstrating further his wisdom and justice, harmony and common sense, Bello stated that, on the other hand, if mere practical men were endowed with a certain insight in their views and plans, it was only within the restricted circle of their daily experience; they could not go a step beyond. They were incapable of applying their knowledge to new combinations of circumstances; they were incapable of filling the important posts that extensive ideas require; incapable even of enriching the very acts that they exercise with original inventions.[24] Thus, showing again his middle-of-the-road approach, his *via media,* he concluded that there were, therefore,

> . . . two opposite habits equally rich in error: that of the mind which disparages specialties and is occupied with abstractions and generalizations, and that of those men who, paying exclusive attention to the aspects and forms that are within reach of daily experience, do not lift themselves up to general principles and extensive views.[25]

III

Bello's *Principios de derecho de gentes* (1832) includes much of his political thought. Written between 1831 and 1832, it was actually based on a lifelong interest in both international law and international relations, but it was in Chile that he was able to put into practice his extraordinary knowledge and expertise.

His belief in God and in the traditional law of nature is here repeated: God is the author of international law and reason only interprets it. The law of nations was, thus, for Bello the natural law applied to the different peoples of the globe, spread over the earth as one great family and in which all had the same obligations as the individuals of the human species among themselves.[26] Every law presumed a sanction through which, as he said, the common good becomes the specific condition of the individual good, but as to the various sanctions which confer on natural law all its dignity, one was that of human conscience, and the other was religious.[27] Bello was, thus, in perfect agreement with the traditional natural law of Antiquity and of the Christian Middle Ages, in which natural law was the echo of Divine Law, and positive law, to be just, had to be in keeping with this norm. After all, natural law was supposed to be reasonable, generally acceptable, and simple. Everything that was right, according to the nature of things, was part of the natural law. *Do good and avoid evil, Justice must be done, Do unto others as you would like them to do unto you, pacta sunt servanda,* are all principles of natural law.[28]

The influence of natural law on international law was clearly interwoven with Roman law. The early Roman law showed the ability to adjust to the needs of an imperial civilization and this strength was made possible by admitting side by side with the *jus civile* a more liberal and flexible law, the *jus gentium,* regarded as simple and reasonable so that it was easily recognized. In medieval times, natural law operated within a Christian and Scholastic framework. It flowered in Spain's Golden Age with the *magni Hispani* while in northern Europe it was attacked in the fourteenth and fifteenth centuries and later dismissed in Protestant countries. Natural law continued to be the basis, however, for philosophy in Hispanic American colonial times and, as seen in Bello's *Filosofía del entendimiento* and *Principios de derecho de gentes,* still maintained a very strong position in the nineteenth century, clearly demonstrating the correct judgment of Heinrich Rommen about the eternal recurrence of natural law.[29] Moreover, Bello's natural law was not the rationalistic version of the seventeenth and eighteenth centuries which ushered in the justification of Enlightened Despotism on one side, and Constitutionalism on the other. The old Scholastic natural law—to which Bello also adhered—never proclaimed certain definite forms of government but was based on the common good and on the *regimen mixtum* with participation of the people,[30] a concept Bello followed, as we have seen earlier, and as will be exemplified in the Chilean Constitution of 1833.

The same traditional and Scholastic point of view shines clearly when Bello talked about the meaning of law and where within the characteristic formula of *quid pro quo* the rights must be circumscribed by duties.[31] How different from our own times where human rights are always invoked, proclaimed, and defended, and human obligations are seldom mentioned! Bello, though certainly not a Scholastic thinker, and critical in his *Filosofía del entendimiento* of the Scholastic syllogism, took another Scholastic position when he considered sovereignty to be "originally" rooted in the nation.[32] That had also been the point of view of José María Morelos in Art. 5 of the Mexican Constitution of Apatzingan (1814) and did not follow the Spanish Constitution of Cadiz of 1812, which preferred the more modern term "essentially." Also, Bello's discussion of the separation and independence of states was based on the law of nature.

Bello's attachment to the traditional view of natural law also came to the fore in the case of the two Bolivian exiles in Chile about which he wrote in *El Araucano,* and in which he refuted their idea that there was no

universal, immutable law of nature; without such a moral and legal basis utter confusion would arise. He pointed out, on the contrary, that it seemed to him irrefutable that there were rules of international law which without prior consent of the nations must be obeyed.[33] In the same case he referred repeatedly to the existence of natural law and to this law as the foundation of the law of nations. As he said:

> . . . The special and *perfect* obligation to keep an agreement has its foundation in the general and *perfect* obligation to keep agreements which is pure natural law. And thus one more evidence of such a law. In reality it is the foundation of all the others. Without it, none other would exist.[34]

Going a step further in this discussion, Bello argued that the government not only has to obey its own constitution but all laws, and among the latter were also the laws of nations; in case of conflict between the law of nations and the laws of Chile the government would try to harmonize and choose that which protects and strengthens peace and security, not only for itself but for other nations as well. Several times Bello refuted the arguments of the two Bolivian exiles based on a political ideology more in keeping with the French Revolution, the *idéologues* and the Utilitarians, and concerned with liberty, property, security, pointing out that his political views would in reality protect these principles more than theirs—a system which did not acknowledge natural law, and thus no human rights.

Bello's philosophy, based on a Supreme Being and on the existence of a law of nature, determined his political beliefs. It showed not only his classical background but his solid conservative and traditional foundation, which was part and parcel of his life and his personality and which can be seen in all his writings. His traditional philosophy already came to the fore in the **"Reply to the Spanish Regency"**[35] which was written by the younger Bello, as is generally acknowledged, and in which he justified the establishment of the Caracas junta of 1810 on the basis of equality and denied the right of the Peninsular authorities to rule over the overseas areas. This was the Scholastic *pactum translationis* which was the lever for the Spanish American emancipation: power is given by God to the people who in turn transfer this authority to a ruler; when the ruler has no legitimate successor this authority returns whence it came. This situation arose when Napoleon forced the abdication of the legitimate King Ferdinand VII and illegally put his brother Joseph on the Spanish throne. The Spanish people then rose up in arms, setting up a *Junta Suprema Central* and then a Regency on behalf of the deposed king, and arrogating to themselves the same rights as the former monarch. The Spanish Americans denied this right to the Spanish authorities—the Regency was entitled to rule over Spain and defend it against the French but not to demand obedience from Spanish

America, since the overseas areas had exactly the same rights of equality as the Peninsula, rights which in the sixteenth century had been granted by the Spanish kings to the early conquistadors. Caracas was thus justified in establishing a junta, a symbol of deep loyalty to king and empire, and not to be construed as disobedience and rebellion.[36] These legal arguments were very clear and sound, and Bello thus demonstrated his great knowledge based on the traditional teachings of law in colonial colleges and universities. The document expressed its fidelity to the "beloved sovereign King Ferdinand VII" and "its true and cordial sentiments of brotherly love" to the Peninsular Spaniards, but considered their claims to rule the overseas areas illegal,[37] since with the usurpation of the Spanish throne by the French, authority had returned to the various peoples of the Empire. After all, in line with the proprietory character of the Indies, loyalty of the various Spanish American areas was never to Spain but solely to the legitimate monarch. The **"Reply"** ended with the hope that if Spain set up a legitimate authority, then the Caracas junta would give the greatest aid in the pursuit of its "holy struggle"[38] against Joseph Bonaparte.

In a very interesting comment on the Spanish American republics, Bello gives us a clear concept of his political views. The independence of America, he said, excited the enthusiasm of the friends of principles and the fear of the enemies of liberty, and many had hoped that an entire continent based on similar values of history and origin, customs, and religion would rise up to establish a respected community of nations which in time would balance European politics; but few foresaw that this path would be paved with lots of bloodshed in view of political inexperience and the legacy of the colonial past. Others, he continued, believed that Spanish America was incapable of developing free institutions, since they were in opposition to Spanish America's traditions. No doubt, Bello pointed out, the United States was different from the Spanish American republics—in the former social and economic conditions were more equal and equitable, in the latter a few were familiar with the exercise of great political rights, whereas the majority had neither enjoyed them nor held them as important. Thus, in the United States it had been possible to give liberal principles all their latitude while the South American republics, though independent from Spain, were facing a numerous and powerful class with whom liberal principles simply collided. This was for Bello the most important distinction between the two areas,[39] and he drew the following conclusion which parallels precisely his political work in Chile:

> Indeed, to introduce more or less plausible constitutions and to balance the powers ingeniously, to proclaim guarantees and to show liberal principles, are rather easy things given the state of progress which the social sciences have reached in our times. But to know deeply the disposition and the needs of the peoples to-

ward whom the legislation must be applied, to distrust the seductions of brilliant theories, to listen with attention and impartiality to the voice of experience, to sacrifice beloved opinions to the common good, is not the most common in the childhood of nations, and in a crisis where a great political transition such as ours inflames all minds. Institutions which in theory seem worthy of the highest admiration because they are in conformity with the principles established by the most famous writers find for their observance invincible obstacles when applied in practice; perhaps they are the best which the study of politics in general may give, but not, as those which Solon elaborated for Athens, the best which could be given to a certain people. The science of legislation, not much studied among ourselves when we did not play an active part in the government of our countries, could not acquire all the necessary attention from the beginning of our emancipation, so that the Spanish American legislators would make of them meditated, judicious and exact applications—a much surer norm than that which abstract maxims and the general rule can provide.[40]

Surely, there is here an echo of Edmund Burke's hostility to abstract political systems and his predilection for a prescribed constitution. Furthermore, the statement explicitly excludes an extreme democratic solution.

However, Bello was a balanced thinker, a man of the *via media*. Immediately thereafter he argued against an exaggeration of this view which, so he said, would be even worse than all the revolutionary zeal. Such a policy would do great damage to Spanish American patriotism, and obviously, was in contradiction to the spirit which animated the struggle against tyranny. He acknowledged the need to adapt the governmental system to the national localities, customs, and character, but this should by no means be interpreted as if Spanish America could never live under the shadow of free institutions and could never have the healthy guarantees which secure freedom, the patrimony of any human society that merits such a name. In any case, Spanish America was living a period of transition, and the peoples must suffer certain calamities because they represented the first steps of their political career, but this would come to an end and Spanish America would play an important role in world affairs, a role which it was called upon in view of its territorial extension, its resources and other elements of prosperity. Chile, he pointed out, was indeed lucky to be an island of peace and stability due to three elements: its institutions, the spirit of order which characterized the national temperament, and the lessons of past tragedies.[41] These comments appeared in *El Araucano*[42] and demonstrated in a nutshell his entire political philosophy: liberal-conservative or conservative-liberal. These ideas were incorporated in the Constitution of 1833 which gave Chile the stability and greatness for which it was justly renowned. As Bello himself stated: ". . . In Chile, the peoples are armed with the law; but until now these weapons have only been used for the maintenance of order and for the enjoyment of the most precious social goods."[43]

IV

With independence restored in 1817, Chile had experimented with various liberal alternatives: from the extreme of Enlightened Despotism (Constitutions of 1818 and 1822) to the extreme of revolutionary zeal with the very moralistic and Rousseauian Constitution of 1823, the federalism of José Miguel Infante (Constitution of 1826) and finally José Joaquín de Mora's *idéologue* attempt to mediate between both centralism and federalism (Constitution of 1828). The battle of Lircay, 1830, ended the liberal period and opened the conservative republic which lasted until 1861 and which was based on one of the most realistic, and hence, best Hispanic American charters: the Constitution of 1833, which endured until 1925, even though after 1861 it was gradually liberalized and democratized to fit changing times.

Bello had arrived in Chile in the midst of growing anarchy and soon got involved in a polemic with Mora who remained the intellectual leader of the liberal faction. Bello joined the conservative *Colegio de Santiago* while Mora taught at the *Liceo de Chile* which he had founded in 1828. In 1830 *El Araucano,* the official government newspaper, saw the light of day and Bello was charged with its section on foreign news, letters, and science. In 1831 began the constitutional reform to the Charter of 1828, which in many respects had followed the venerable Spanish Constitution of Cádiz of 1812, and the Convention which initiated this study was also the one that conferred Chilean citizenship on Bello (1832). This constitutional reform produced the Constitution of 1833 whose main authors were the conservative Mariano Egaña and the more liberal Manuel José Gandarillas, with Bello acting behind the scenes with much advice. It was for the first time in Chile's independent life a realistic constitution, totally in line with the ideas and ideals of Bello's *via media.*

The Constitution of 1833 was an echo of the July Monarchy and of the conservative movement of the Doctrinaire Liberals of Maine de Biran and Victor Cousin in philosophy, and of Pierre-Paul Royer-Collard in politics. Linked to this group was also the legendary Benjamin Constant, although not strictly speaking a Doctrinaire Liberal. They were aristocratic and elitist but not reactionary, progressive though not radical or *idéologue,* and they produced a very workable and efficient political program. This group had realized that the rising forces of industrialization and capitalism, the middle classes, needed a political system which gave the bourgeoisie both power and security. They opted for constitutional monarchy which seemed to be the middle way

between the abuse and excesses of the Revolution and the extreme of arbitrariness of both the Napoleonic system and the Enlightened Despotism of the eighteenth century. Cousin, the founder of Eclecticism, had provided the philosophic foundation for the Doctrinaire Liberal movement: influenced by German idealism and historicism and fighting sensualism and materialism, he had also absorbed much of the philosophy of the Scottish School and was a disciple of Herder. Cousin's eclectic spiritualism—defending healthy, noble and generous ideas which did not go against religion and the prevailing social order—facilitated the conciliation of the extremes and created an atmosphere in which a settlement along the lines of the *via media* became a tangible possibility.[44]

The man who in Chile had by now assumed dictatorial powers was Diego Portales, the rare exception in Latin American politics since he was a businessman—the Duque de Mauá would later be the Brazilian version—and although he was not a member of the Convention and did not participate in its deliberations, it no doubt reflected his political thought. Portales found in Bello the right man for a strong regime, in line with the Hispanic American temperament and the Chilean reality of the time, based on the former monarchical tradition but within a republican framework and coupled to an evolutionary concept of progress, as it gradually developed later. Bello, of course, by temperament and character, by education and inclination had no use for any abstract general ideas and certainly not for the utopian and messianic message of Bentham's Utilitarianism or Rousseau's totalitarian democracy. Also, Bello understood very early as few did that Spain and the Spanish heritage were not to be blamed for every shortcoming. He was thus opposed to the *tavola rasa* concept of many of his Chilean friends, most *pipiolos,* who advocated a rather naive course in trying to deny the past and to reject the Spanish heritage. On the contrary, he advocated a government based on the realities of the country which would gradually evolve into a modern state, a synthesis of tradition and progress.

The Constitution of 1833, more realistic than those of 1818, 1822, 1823, 1826 and 1828, showed this philosophy and was fundamentally the Chilean version of the Doctrinaire Liberal movement. It manifested the influence of Spanish Liberalism and joined to it the traditional and conservative thought of Spain, England and France. The two-chamber system followed the Anglo-Saxon model and suffrage was restricted. The Senate acted as a fourth power—Constant's *pouvoir neutre*—in the sense that it took the role of a great moderating body. While the executive received ample powers, including extraordinary powers from Congress in case of emergencies, the Constitution also acknowledged individual rights in the sense Constant would have approved.

This elected monarchy within a republican form through a presidential term of five years, but with the possibility of one second term, left the President with the effective management of public affairs, a policy which Minister Portales carried out with great statesmanship. It allowed only the Catholic faith—like the Constitution of Cádiz—maintained the *mayorazgos* (entailed estates), and generally symbolized the vision and the wisdom of an aristocracy which had witnessed the evil of the revolutionary creed to society and state and which was determined to lead Chile toward a better future through the adoption of a sound political organization. The Constitution of 1833, the application of Bello's own eclecticism, and an echo of the Doctrinaire Liberal movement and of Constant's liberalism mixed with traditional thought, was the effective instrument to accomplish this goal.[45] Chile was thus able beginning with the 1830s to avoid the extremes of tyranny and chaos, and to set up a sound, stable, and effective representative government in which political liberty was a fact. That was one of Bello's contributions to Chile and of his interpretation of human rights, which certainly were a reality and not a much touted fanfare with no basis whatsoever.

Summarizing, we will find in the political philosophy of Andrés Bello a belief in freedom within responsibility, "not the abstract rights of the French Revolution and of the modern Liberal, i.e., rights without duties; but what Edmund Burke calls the *real* rights of man."[46] Bello's approach to human rights would be much more in line with the simple old maxim "the more responsibility the more freedom," and thus his entire philosophy of man and the state followed very much traditional principles because it built on evidence in common sense and did not balk at mystery, was free of 'postulates' and admitted of no 'myths', very much the traditional Christian principles which originated in St. Augustine, were carried over by St. Thomas Aquinas, were redefined by the Spanish Golden Age, and found a reaffirmation in Burke.[47]

Notes

1. Rafael Caldera, *Andrés Bello. Philosopher, Poet, Philologist, Educator, Legislator, Statesman* (London: Allen & Unwin, 1977), p. 21.

2. *Ibid.*, p. 23.

3. Cf. Vincente Llorens Castillo, *Liberales y románticos. Una emigración española en Inglaterra (1823-1834)* (Mexico: El Colegio de México, 1954).

4. Caldera, p. 26.

5. Cf. Ricardo Donoso, "Prólogo," in Andrés Bello, *Obras completas* (23 vols.; Caracas: Ministerio de Educación, 1950-1969), XVII: "Labor en el Senado de Chile," pp. xlix-lxi. Cf. Also Simon

Collier, *Ideas and Politics of Chilean Independence, 1808-1833* (Cambridge: Cambridge Univ. Press, 1967), p. 332.

6. Andrés Bello, *Filosofía del entendimiento* (Mexico: Fondo de Cultura Económica, 1946), pp. 115-116.

7. *Ibid.*, p. 117.

8. *Ibid.*, p. 130.

9. *Ibid.*, p. 131.

10. *Ibid.*

11. *Ibid.*, p. 132.

12. *Ibid.*

13. *Ibid.*, p. 137.

14. *Ibid.*

15. *Ibid.*, p. 138.

16. *Ibid.*

17. *Ibid.*, p. 139.

18. *Ibid.*

19. *Ibid.*, pp. 328-29.

20. *Ibid.*, p. 333.

21. *Ibid.*, p. 342.

22. *Ibid.*, p. 459.

23. *Ibid.*, pp. 459-60.

24. *Ibid.*, p. 460.

25. *Ibid.*

26. Bello, *Obras completas*, X: "Derecho Internacional," pp. 13-14.

27. *Ibid.*, pp. 14-15.

28. Cf. Bernice Hamilton, *Political Thought in Sixteenth-Century Spain* (Oxford: Clarendon Press, 1963), pp. 11-29.

29. Cf. Heinrich Rommen, *Die ewige Wiederkehr des Naturrechts* (2d ed.; Munich: Kösel, 1947).

30. *Ibid.*, p. 258.

31. Bello, *Obras completas*, X, 17.

32. *Ibid.*, pp. 32-33. Cf. O. Carlos Stoetzer, *El pensamiento político en la América española durante el período de la emancipación (1789-1825)* (2 vols.; Madrid: Instituto de Estudios Políticos, 1966), II, 193-252, especially p. 232.

33. "La detención de los extranjeros" in *El Araucano* (Santiago de Chile), December 16 and 30, 1842;

January 6, 1843 [643, 645; 647] in Bello, *Obras completas,* X, 477.

34. *Ibid.,* p. 480. Cf. also *ibid.,* p. 488.

35. Caracas, May 3, 1810.

36. Cf. Bello, *Obras completas,* X, 411-18.

37. *Ibid.,* p. 413.

38. *Ibid.,* p. 417.

39. *Ibid.,* pp. 421-22.

40. *Ibid.,* pp. 422-23.

41. *Ibid.,* pp. 423-24.

42. *El Araucano* (Santiago de Chile), July 22, 1836 [#307].

43. Bello, *Obras completas,* X, 424-25.

44. Cf. O. Carlos Stoetzer, "Benjamin Constant and the Doctrinaire Liberal Influence in Hispanic America," *Verfassung und Recht in Übersee* (Hamburg), II (1978), 145-65.

45. *Ibid.,* pp. 158-59.

46. Moorhouse F. X. Millar, S. J., "The Modern State and Catholic Principles," *Thought,* 12 (1937), 54.

47. *Ibid.,* p. 63.

Antonio Cussen (essay date 1992)

SOURCE: Cussen, Antonio. "Poetry Visits America." In *Bello and Bolívar: Poetry and Politics in the Spanish American Revolution,* pp. 96-126. Cambridge: Cambridge University Press, 1992.

[*In the following excerpt, Cussen examines Bello's short-lived but significant Spanish language journal* Biblioteca Americana, *and provides a close reading of his poems "Alocución" and "Agricultura"—two poems singing the praises of Spanish American history and its heroes.*]

> Besides, a fate attends on all I write,
> That when I aim at praise, they say I bite.
>
> Alexander Pope

The first issue of the ***Biblioteca Americana,*** published in July 1823, was a lavish volume of 470 pages with several color plates of scenes of the New World. Opposite the first page is a lithograph showing a woman in classical attire who is visiting an Indian woman with naked breasts and feathers on her head. The Indian woman is surrounded by palm trees and is sitting on a craggy outcropping at the foot of a mountain. In the background one can see a llama. Between the two

women three half-naked children are eagerly playing with gifts that seem to have been presented by the classical woman, who stands with her right arm extended. The gifts include a globe, telescope, lyre, book, bust, palette, and brush. Under the lithograph is the dedication of the journal: "Al Pueblo Americano."

From its very first page, the ***Biblioteca Americana*** insists on its *americanismo,* its Americanness. It announces that it is underwritten by a Society of Americans ("Por una Sociedad de Americanos"), and the prospectus, signed by García del Río, states, "We shall emphasize throughout everything that is related to America." The editors explain that they will not show a preference for this or that country of the New World; they will address all the inhabitants of the American continent: "We shall not give exclusive consideration to the Colombian, the Argentine, the Peruvian, the Chilean, the Mexican; written for all of them, the *Biblioteca* will be preeminently *American.*"

What, we may ask, does the word "América" mean to the editors of the journal? More specifically, what kind of relationship do they envision between Europe and America, between the Old World and the New? The lithograph presents an emblematic answer: Europe, dressed in classical attire, visits America and brings the utensils and objects that mark Western civilization. America's children, in turn, eagerly absorb this culture, as symbolized by their leafing through a printed volume or holding a classical bust. The prospectus of the journal develops this close cultural dependence: the accumulated knowledge of the West must be spread throughout the New World, thus ending three centuries of isolation and ignorance. García del Río, his head filled with the financial transactions that preoccupied him at the time, expresses the relationship between Europe and America as one of creditor and debtor. In the closing paragraph of the prospectus, he elevates the tone of his prose, stating that he foresees a day when rays of truth will shine throughout the New World, when America will traverse with giant steps the roads of the civilized peoples who have advanced before, "until the happy era arrives when America, protected by moderate governments and by enlightened social institutions, rich, flourishing, free, gives back to Europe with interest the wealth of knowledge that she is borrowing today and, fulfilling her lofty destiny, receives the incense of the world."

The *Biblioteca* is divided into three sections: the first is devoted to poetry, literature, and philology; the second, to science and technology; and the third, to politics and history, or—to use the term preferred by the editors—"Ideología," a term borrowed from Destutt de Tracy and the French *idéologues.*[1] Only the first volume of the journal was published in its entirety. Of the second and last volume, only the section devoted to literature was published, in October 1823.

The first piece in the *Biblioteca*'s inaugural issue is a poem by Bello: **"Alocución a la Poesía, en que se introducen las alabanzac de los pueblos e individuos americanos, que más se han distinguido en la guerra de la independencia. (Fragmento de un poema inédito, titulado 'América.')"** (**"Discourse to Poetry, which presents the glories of the peoples and individuals of America who have most distinguished themselves in the war of independence. [Fragment of an unpublished poem entitled 'America.']"**) In the first volume, Bello published the first 447 lines of the poem. The remaining 387 lines opened the second volume of the journal. The manuscripts of the **"Alocución"** reveal that Bello completed a large portion of the poem between 1821 and 1823, that is, during the years in which he worked as Irisarri's assistant. Sheets 9, 12, and 18 through 25 (containing some three hundred lines of the poem) all show watermarks of those years. Other manuscripts that contain lines of the **"Alocución"** have no dates, with the exception of sheet 5, which has a watermark of 1814 (see Appendix).

The poem is divided into two sections, which we may term "georgic" (1-206) and "epic" (207-834). In the georgic section the poet invites the goddess Poetry to visit the New World, and to entice her he describes the continent's luscious vegetation and agricultural potential. But on line 207 the poet interrupts his paean to the peaceful beauty of America and asks Poetry if she prefers to sing instead the deeds of war. The rest of the poem is an evocation of the heroes who have perished in the wars of independence. The **"Alocución"** is thus a reconstruction of the two stages of poetic composition we have noted in Bello's London years. He first focuses on the natural beauty of America, and then—unable to ignore the theme of war—begins to write about the men who gave their lives for independence. The passage that serves as a pivot between these two sections is one that I have dated around 1815 (sheet 5, watermark of 1814), the year that marked a turning point in Bello's reluctant commitment to the patriots. Lines 207-15, in which Bello asks Poetry if she would rather sing about the "impious war" (*la guerra impía*), remind the reader that this poem, which ostensibly celebrates the Revolution, is also a denunciation of those wars.

The poem begins in a mood of rustic serenity, as Bello summons "divine Poetry" to abandon cultivated Europe and to visit the world of Columbus:

> Divina Poesía,
> tú de la soledad habitadora,
> a consultar tus cantos enseñada
> con el silencio de la selva umbría,
> tú a quien la verde gruta fue morada,
> y el eco de los montes compañía;
> tiempo es que dejes ya la culta Europa,
> que tu nativa rustiquez desama,
> y dirijas el vuelo adonde te abre

> el mundo de Colón su grande escena.

([Andrés Bello, *Obras completas,* 2nd ed. (Caracas, 1981), hereafter *OC*] 1: 43, ll. 1-10)

> (Divine Poetry, you who live in solitude and are taught to learn your songs in the silence of the shady forest; you whose dwelling was the green grotto and whose company was the mountains' echo; it is time that you now abandon Europe, that cultivated land that no longer appreciates your native rusticity, and direct your flight to a place where the world of Columbus opens its great stage to you.)

Ever since Pedro Henríquez Ureña described Bello's poem as a declaration of the spiritual and intellectual independence of Spanish America, these lines have become the cornerstone of *americanismo,* a word that expresses the search for cultural autonomy. Henríquez Ureña was not the first to assign this role to Bello; before him, Juan María Gutiérrez had placed Bello's poem as the front piece of the most famous poetry anthology of mid-nineteenth-century Spanish America, *América Poética,* which was devoted entirely to poetic productions since the Revolution.[2]

To understand what *América* means for Bello and the relationship between the New and the Old World in the **"Alocución,"** we may first look to the context of the published poem. The **"Alocución"** opens a journal whose guiding hands were two Spanish Americans, Bello and García del Río, who until the eve of publication had advocated inviting a prince of a European royal house to head a monarchy in the New World. The co-editors had earlier embraced Spanish American emancipation in *El Censor Americano* and *La Biblioteca Columbiana,* a journal edited by García del Río in Lima in 1821. But their ideal was an emancipation with close political ties to the monarchies of the European continent. By the time the **Biblioteca Americana** went to press, the monarchic formula was no longer viable, but one still finds testimony to America's dependence on Europe on every page of the journal. The lithograph shows America receiving Europe's gift of accumulated knowledge and glory and America's children promising a new flourishing of the arts and sciences of the West. García del Río's financial metaphor goes even further in suggesting that America is borrowing European culture today and that over the years the New World will repay this loan.

Then comes Bello's **"Alocución,"** whose *americanismo* closely fits that of the journal. Poetry and America are the two elements that establish the drama of his poem. Bello invites Poetry to abandon Europe because the Old World can no longer offer her the natural setting she needs to thrive. But Bello's Poetry is in every sense a classical construct, a topic of invocation of Greek, Roman, and British poets. Like the classically attired woman in the frontispiece lithograph, Poetry is the personification of the European spirit in search of a new stage on which to extend the march of civilization.

If the opening of the **"Alocución"** is the cry of Spanish America's cultural independence, the cornerstone of its spiritual emancipation, Bello defines that autonomy not as a break with Europe, but as an incorporation of the very essence of European culture. America is to be the newest home for a goddess who has earlier visited the different lands of the European continent and the British Isles. In "The Progress of Poesy," Thomas Gray, a poet praised by Bello in the *Biblioteca,* similarly shows the route followed by the Muses, who abandon Greece and Italy—which have been enchained by pomp, power, and vice—and arrive on the coast of Britain:

> Alike they scorn the pomp of tyrant-Power,
> And coward Vice, that revels in her chains.
> When Latium had her lofty spirit lost,
> They sought, oh Albion! next the sea-encircled
>   coast.[3]

Gray's lines are unmistakably the direct antecedent of the opening of the **"Alocución."** The theme of wandering Poetry, or Poesy, who abandons the tyranny and decadence of the European continent in search of a fresh natural setting, is identical in both poems. The same distance is established between the new setting of the goddess and the previous places she has visited. The opening of the **"Alocución"** may well be the starting point of *americanismo,* but for Bello this term implied something essentially akin to Gray's "Englishness," a kind of rhetorical patriotism, with distinguished classical antecedents, that reasserted the centrality and continuing importance of European civilization.

As in Gray's poem, there is in the **"Alocución"** a break with Europe, but it is a break with the decrepitude of the European continent. At the beginning of his poem, Bello offers to Poetry a setting that Europe itself can no longer offer her. His strategy will be to entice Poetry to abandon the corrupt courts of continental Europe and settle in the fresh lands across the Atlantic that still preserve the original vigor of Creation ("*el vigor guardan genital primero*"). Bello thus adopts a topos used by enemies of the ancient régime since the eighteenth century, according to which Europe is an old and tired land and America a land of freshness and freedom:

> ¿Qué a ti, silvestre ninfa, con las pompas
> de dorados alcázares reales?
> ¿A tributar también irás en ellos,
> en medio de la turba cortesana,
> el torpe incienso de servil lisonja?
>
> (ll. 24-8)[4]

(What does the pomp of golden royal castles have to offer you, sylvan nymph? Will you also go there and offer, amidst a crowd of courtiers, the dishonest incense of servile flattery?)

The poem proper thus begins with a loud condemnation of the very kind of poetry Bello had practiced in the colonial days, when he set Charles IV amidst clouds of incense. No, he now argues, that is not the setting for Poetry. In the youth of humankind she did not attend luxurious palaces, but simply tried to sing the first laws to the people and their kings. In these lines Bello also calls for "natural" poetry, an aesthetic that will shun the excesses of neoclassicism and return to the models of the Spanish Middle Ages and the Golden Age.[5]

Bello then returns to his attack on the European continent but now he is more specific:

> No te detenga, oh diosa,
> esta región de luz y de miseria,
> en donde tu ambiciosa
> rival Filosofía,
> que la virtud a cálculo somete,
> de los mortales te ha usurpado el culto;
> donde la coronada hidra amenaza
> traer de nuevo al pensamiento esclavo
> la antigua noche de barbarie y crimen;
> donde la libertad vano delirio,
> fe la servilidad, grandeza el fasto,
> la corrupción cultura se apellida.
>
> (ll. 33-43)

(O Goddess, do not linger in this region of light and misery where Philosophy, your ambitious rival who subjects virtue to calculation, has usurped from you the worship of mortals; where the crowned hydra threatens to bring to the enslaved mind the ancient night of barbarity and crime; where liberty is called vain delirium; servility, faith; pomp, greatness; and corruption, culture.)

Arturo Ardao has argued convincingly that the first lines of this passage are an attack against Bentham's "moral arithmetic" and his use of "calculation" in ethics.[6] Next, Bello assaults the *coronada hidra,* the tyrannical absolute monarchy, personified by the Holy Alliance, which threatens to restore the old order. Bello also criticizes the conditions of Europe, above all those of Spain and France in 1823; these conditions have distorted the meaning of words and exacerbated domestic tensions. And Bello censures equally the *liberales* for having transformed the meaning of freedom into "vain delirium," and the *serviles* for hiding their political backwardness under the mask of religious faith. Here for the first time Bello uses "*fe*" (faith) to describe the reactionary spirit of the Catholic Church and its backing of the absolutist cause. In Chapter 9 we shall see the significance of this word in the **"Agricultura de la zona tórrida."** This entire passage, in short, is a criticism of the political conditions that have existed in Europe, and specifically in Spain, during at least the preceding decade.

Later in the **"Alocución"** Bello levels a more explicit criticism at both sides of continental politics—the side of the *liberales* and that of the *serviles*. In a passage describing the events in Spain since Ferdinand's reconquest, Bentham's "calculations" again appear:

¿Puebla la inquisición sus calabozos
de americanos; o españolas cortes
dan a la servidumbre formas nuevas?

. . . . .

Columbia vence; libertad los vanos
cálculos de los déspotas engaña.

(ll. 546-48, 551-2)

(Does the Inquisition populate its dungeons with Americans? Do Spanish Cortes give new forms to servitude? Colombia wins; liberty outwits the vain calculations of the despots.)

The two sides of Spanish politics are presented as simply two different versions of despotism. The old version Bello calls the *"inquisición,"* his favorite synecdoche for the alliance of Crown and Church; the new version is the liberal Cortes, whose tyranny over the New World is even more absolute.[7] Poetry, therefore, should leave the regions now dominated by the philosophy of Bentham and servitude to the past.

As an alternative Bello presents to Poetry the attractions of America. She could settle near the clear river of Buenos Aires, where the heroes of Albion were defeated; or in the valleys of Chile, where the innocence and candor of the ancient world are combined with valor and patriotism, or in the city of the Aztec, rich with inexhaustible veins that almost satiated the avarice of Europe; or in Quito, Bogotá, or the valleys of Venezuela. Any of these settings would prove hospitable to Poetry, and the day will come when an American Virgil will sing about the agriculture of the New World:

Tiempo vendrá cuando de ti inspirado
algún Marón americano, ¡oh diosa!
también las mieses, los rebaños cante,
el rico suelo al hombre avasallado,
y las dádivas mil con que la zona
de Febo amada al labrador corona;
donde cándida miel llevan las cañas,
y animado carmín la tuna cría,
donde tremola el algodón su nieve,
y el ananás sazona su ambrosia.

(ll. 189-98)

(A time will come, O Goddess! when some American Maro inspired by you will also sing the fields of grain, the flocks, the rich soil subdued by man, and the thousand gifts with which the zone loved by Phoebus crowns the peasant, where the canes bear white honey and the prickly pear nurtures lively crimson, where cotton waves its snow and the pineapple ripens its ambrosia.)

The "American Maro" is, of course, Bello himself, and these lines are the announcement of his next poem, **"Agricultura de la zona tórrida."** But Bello has already begun to sing America's beauty in the first part of the **"Alocución"**; we have already tasted his georgic passion, his gift for describing nature and human transformation of nature.

Thus far, Bello has defined his *americanismo* as a rejection of a specific version of European culture, of which the Spain of the 1820s offers the best example. In the first fourth of the poem he has drawn on the contemporary topos of European corruption and American youth, a ubiquitous theme in the post-Napoleonic era, and he has shown the New World's luscious and pure vegetation. Now the **"Alocución"** moves from geography to history, and the remaining three-fourths of the poem are devoted to the heroes of the wars of independence.

The names of the greatest heroes—Bolívar, San Martín, O'Higgins—however, do not figure in Bello's catalogue. San Martín is briefly mentioned in a periphrasis. Of O'Higgins, who has just fallen from power, nothing is said. And Bolívar is praised in a roundabout *recusatio* at the end of the poem when Bello says that the deeds of the Libertador will be written by a more skilled pen:

Mas no a mi débil voz la larga suma
de sus victorias numerar compete;
a ingenio más feliz, más docta pluma,
su grata patria encargo tal comete,
pues como aquel samán que siglos cuenta,
de la vecinas gentes venerado,
que vio en torno a su basa corpulenta
el bosque muchas veces renovado,
y vasto espacio cubre con la hojosa
copa, de mil inviernos victoriosa;
así tu gloria al cielo se sublima,
Libertador del pueblo colombiano;
digna de que la lleven dulce rima
y culta historia al tiempo más lejano.

(ll. 821-34)

(But my weak voice is not qualified to enumerate the long account of his victories; his grateful fatherland entrusts such a work to a happier talent, to a more learned pen. For just like that *samán* of centuries, venerated by the neighboring peoples, which saw the forest renewed many times around its massive base, covers a vast space with its leafy top, victorious over a thousand winters, thus your glory is sublimated to the sky, Liberator of the Colombian people, worthy to be carried to the most distant future by sweet rhyme and erudite history.)

In the **"Alocución"** Bolívar's glory is enhanced outside the poem. But we have to go back to the poem in order to realize that the American Virgil declines to praise the new Augustus for reasons that have little to do with the poet's "weak voice." We may then understand why his name is not included in the list of Spanish Americans "who have most distinguished themselves in the wars of independence."

For his list of heroes Bello was inspired, as noted in Chapter 6, by Anchises' catalogue of heroes in book 6 of the *Aeneid*. In a passage devoted to Francisco Javier Ustáriz, Bello names the classical heroes who will accompany the new Spanish American heroes in the Elysian fields:

De mártires que dieron por la patria
la vida, el santo coro te rodea:
Régulo, Trásea, Marco Bruto, Decio,
cuantos inmortaliza Atenas libre,
cuantos Esparta y el romano Tibre.

(ll. 653-7)

(The holy choir of martyrs who gave their lives for
their fatherland surrounds you: Regulus, Thrasea, Marcus Brutus, Decius, all those whom free Athens, Sparta
and the Roman Tiber immortalize.)

Each of these Roman republicans brings to mind Augustus, who, of course, is not named in the poem. The
Decii, for example, were favorite heroes of Virgil
praised in both the *Georgics* and the *Aeneid.* The name
symbolizes self-sacrifice: with a purple-edged toga,
with a veiled head, and invoking the Roman gods, the
first Decius ran to meet his death, causing terror among
Rome's enemies. Years later, the same act was imitated
by the second Decius. The Decii appear in line 169 of
book 2 of the *Georgics,* one line before Caesar, and
again in line 824 of book 6 of the *Aeneid,* shortly after
Anchises has described Augustus to Aeneas (ll. 789-
807).

Regulus, the hero immortalized in Horace's Ode 3.5,
urged the Roman Senate to reject the unfavorable terms
for peace proposed by the Carthaginians, announcing
that he would rather be tortured defending the integrity
of the Roman republic than yield to its perfidious foes.
But Horace praises Regulus in a poem devoted to Augustus—"In honorem Augusti." In his move from mon-
archism to republicanism, Bello thus alludes to a poem
in which the divinely inspired monarch ("divus
Augustus") is set against a background of republican
life. But unlike the Augustan poets, Bello refuses to celebrate any monarchs or would-be monarchs.

If Regulus and Decius suggest positive images of the
princeps, Marcus Brutus and Thrasea are renowned for
their opposition to absolute monarchy. Brutus, along
with Cassius and other leading Roman senators, assassinated Julius Caesar in 44 B.C. He was later defeated by
the forces of Antony and Octavian at Philippi, having
failed to restore the republic of the *optimates.* The arch-
enemy of monarchy, Marcus Brutus is placed by Dante
in the last circle of hell. Thrasea represents the Stoics
who wished to preserve the fortitude of old republican
values during a period of imperial oppression. He refused to flatter Nero or to believe in Poppaea's divinity.
His unjust death, decreed by that mask of legality that
the Senate had become under the Caesars, closes the
extant text of the *Annals* of Tacitus, who was, of course,
Augustus's classical foe.

Thus, Augustus is absent from the **"Alocución"** and his
foes are celebrated. The same is true of Bolívar, for a
large number of the heroes celebrated in the second part

of the poem—Ribas, Castillo, Miranda, Piar—were in
some important way at odds with the Libertador. Ribas
(ll. 490-509) blamed Bolívar for the disaster of Aragua
in 1814 and incarcerated him; Castillo (l. 528) was
Bolívar's enemy in the civil war that contributed to the
fall of Cartagena. Still more incriminating are the long
sections on Miranda (ll. 674-702), in whose fall Bolívar
was implicated, and Piar (ll. 736-50), who was executed
in 1817 for disobeying the Libertador.

Moreover, a veiled but sharp criticism of Bolívar is implied by the overall charge of perfidy that runs throughout the poem. Bello brandishes this charge against the
Church (ll. 605-20), but also against the patriots who
acted disloyally. After singing the praises of Miranda,
Bello defends his capitulation and assails the treachery
of those who handed him over to the Spaniards:

y si, de contratiempos asaltado
que a humanos medios resistir no es dado,
te fue el ceder forzoso, y en cadena
a manos perecer de una perfidia,
tu espíritu no ha muerto, no;

(ll. 694-8)

(and if, assaulted by mishaps that human means are not
able to avoid, you were forced to yield, and died in
chains at the hands of a treacherous act, your spirit has
not died, no;)

Bolívar, as we have seen, played a principal role in the
transactions leading to Miranda's imprisonment, and
Bello had earlier, in the **"Outline,"** used a softer word—
"ingratitude"—to describe Bolívar's conduct in the matter.

Perfidy also marks the conclusion of the long passage
devoted to Morillo (ll. 509-81). The beginning of this
passage is straightforward. As in the **"Outline,"** Morillo is charged with cruelty, particularly in his murderous rampages at Cartagena and Bogotá. The passage
continues with what at first appears to be an address to
Morillo, who is compared, unfavorably, to Spanish conquerors like Cortés and Pizarro and to the duke of Alba.
But the passage ends with accusations that are entirely
inappropriate to Morillo:

Quien te pone con Alba en paralelo,
¡oh cuánto yerra! En sangre bañó el suelo
de Batavia el ministro de Felipe;
pero si fue crüel y sanguinario,
bajo no fue; no acomodando al vario
semblante de los tiempos su semblante,
ya desertor del uno,
ya del otro partido,
sólo el de su interés siguió constante;
no alternativamente
fue soldado feroz, patriota falso;
no dio a la inquisición su espada un día,
y por la libertad lidió el siguiente;
ni traficante infame del cadalso,
hizo de los indultos granjería.

(ll. 567-81)

(He who draws a parallel between you and Alba, oh how greatly he errs! Philip's minister soaked the soil of Batavia with blood, but if he was cruel and bloody, he was not base; he did not adjust his appearance to the changing appearance of the times, a deserter now of this, now of the other party; he only followed with constancy the party of his own interest; he was not, alternatively, a ferocious soldier, a false patriot; he did not give his sword to the Inquisition one day, and fight for freedom the next, nor as a shameless dealer of the gallows, did he profit from pardon.)

The subject of these lines cannot possibly be Morillo, who defended the royalist cause with persistence and intransigence. No one could say that he had ever surrendered his sword to the Inquisition. This would imply that at some point Morillo was the enemy of Spain. Nor had Morillo ever struggled for freedom. Until 1820, the year he left Venezuela after being forced to sign an armistice with the patriots, Morillo was a relentless foe of the patriots' cause.

Who, then, is Bello talking about in this passage? Who is this man who one day surrendered to the Spaniards and the next day fought for the cause of freedom? The details suggest episodes in the life of Bolívar, particularly the events surrounding the fall of Miranda. It would seem that Bello has veiled his acute censure of Bolívar in the guise of an attack on Morillo. As we shall see in Chapter 10, Bello's criticism did not escape the sharp eye of Bolívar, who offered a fascinating reading of the **"Alocución"** in his conversations with Perú de Lacroix.

Bello's feelings toward Bolívar covered the spectrum of human emotion, from admiration to anger. In 1820 Bello still expressed even to close friends his admiration for the Libertador. In one of his letters Irisarri refers to Bello's constant friendship with Bolívar, and Alamiro de Avila has suggested that a very favorable biography of Bolívar, which appeared as an appendix to Irisarri's *Carta al Observador de Londres,* was written by Bello.[8] Other documents, especially a letter of November 1826, bear out similar feelings. But in Bello's poetry one detects an undercurrent of sharp criticism of Bolívar, a kind of verbal sneering. In the **"Alocución"** this criticism is veiled; in other poems—especially the **"Carta"** to Olmedo of 1827—it becomes explicit.

The reasons for Bello's anger are understandable. By October 1823 details about the Guayaquil negotiations had probably reached London, and it became clear that the real enemy of the monarchists' cause was Bolívar. Bello had little choice but again to redefine his political outlook. Bolívar's continued ascendancy dashed Bello's hopes for establishing in America political and cultural systems modeled on eighteenth-century Britain: in politics, a controlled or limited monarchy; in literature, an emulation of the Roman Augustan aesthetic reshaped by the absence of Augustus.[9] Like the British Augustans, Bello and the monarchists hoped to fill the center of power with a figure who would preserve the legacy of monarchic institutions and at the same time revoke the absolutist and tyrannical elements those institutions had acquired since the sixteenth century.

In the eyes of the monarchists, the throne could not be entrusted to a Spanish American. The luster of lineage, the almost immemorial ascent to power, gave the royal houses of Europe a privilege and respect that could not be emulated by any upstart. Iturbide was proof of the dangers of any *"monarquía criolla."* First the pretense of freedom, then tyranny. The one experiment with a Spanish American monarchy had devolved into absolute power or, as Bello put it, the "yoke of Iturbide" (*la coyunda de Iturbide,* **"Alocución,"** l. 286). Now that Bolívar had barred any hope of establishing a European royal house in America, Bello creates a poem that extols Bolívar's enemies and declares that Bolívar will have to look elsewhere for his poet. The closing allusions to the future glory of the Libertador and the closing *recusatio* are an elegant form of political attack.

Though Bello has broken with Augustus, he preserves a certain nostalgia for the Augustan order, for its pomp and solemnity. The Augustan model of power never became completely distasteful to Bello:

> ¿Dó está la torre bulliciosa
> que pregonar solía,
> de antorchas coronadas,
> la pompa augusta del solemne día?
> Entre las rotas cúpulas que oyeron
> sacros ritos ayer, torpes reptiles
> anidan, y en la sala que gozosos
> banquetes vio y amores, hoy sacude
> la grama del erial su infausta espiga.

(ll. 423-31)

(Where is the boisterous tower crowned with torches which used to proclaim the august pomp of the solemn day? Among the shattered domes that only yesterday witnessed sacred rites ugly reptiles make their nests, and in the hall that saw happy banquets and loves, now wild grass shakes its ill-fated spike.)

But the political model of colonial Caracas could no longer survive. Bello was forced, as were the philosophers and poets of the Enlightenment, to find a political model that could replace absolute monarchy. His next choice, a British-style monarchy, was not to be. He then was willing to settle for the model on which limited or constitutional monarchies were often based, that of republican Rome. Like Voltaire, Bello—though probably still believing in the advantages of monarchy—could call himself a republican. Like Montesquieu, he could easily shift his allegiances between British limited monarchy and Roman republicanism. Like Horace and Virgil, he could hail republican heroes.

By 1823 Bello was convinced that the future of Spanish America would be linked to republicanism. His task would be to give shape to this political formula, to adapt it as closely as possible to a model of constitutional monarchy. As for the luster of kingdoms, the glory of empires—these, like Rome, were fallen. To close the literary section of the second volume of the *Biblioteca Americana,* Bello chose Quevedo's famous poem on what remains of Roman glory. Bello's initials follow the poem, as a signature at the end of his journal, to be sure, but almost as though he has taken an oath of allegiance to Quevedo's theme:

> Buscas en Roma a Roma, oh peregrino,
> y en Roma misma a Roma no la hallas;
> Cadáver son las que ostentó murallas,
> Y tumba de sí propio el Aventino.
>
> Yace, donde reinaba, el Palatino,
> Y limadas del tiempo las medallas
> Mas se muestran destrozo a las batallas
> De las edades, que blasón latino.
>
> Sólo el Tibre quedó, cuya corriente
> Si ciudad la regó, ya sepultura
> La llora con funesto son doliente.
>
> ¡Oh Roma! en tu grandeza, en tu hermosura
> Huyó lo que era firme, y solamente
> Lo fugitivo permanece y dura.

(You look for Rome in Rome, O pilgrim! and in Rome itself you do not find Rome. The walls she once flaunted are now a corpse, and the Aventine is its own tomb.

The Palatine lies where it once reigned, and the medals filed down by time resemble more the destruction of the battle of the ages than a Latin coat of arms.

Only the Tiber was left; and if its current irrigated her as a city, as a grave it now mourns her with a sad, aching sound.

O Rome! from your greatness, from your beauty all firmness escaped, and only what is fugitive remains and endures.)

Dans les pays Despotiques, où l'esclave n'ose parler à son maître, la langue prendra un ton allégorique et mystérieux: et c'est là que naîtront les apologues et le style figuré.

Jacques Delille

In 1823 the Revolution was coming to an end, and Spanish Americans were beginning to enjoy peace and international support. While Castlereagh had persisted in a policy of neutrality, Canning was decisively in favor of independence, viewing it as inevitable in the long run and also desirable for British commercial interests. In October Canning obtained from Polignac, the French ambassador to London, a memorandum stating that French troops would not invade Spanish America. The same month Canning sent consuls to Buenos Aires,

Montevideo, Santiago, and Lima, paving the way for full recognition of Spanish American independence. In December President Monroe announced that the United States would oppose any European power that launched an invasion anywhere on the American continent.[10]

Despite these unmistakable signs of support, there was the unresolved problem of Peru. As Bello had said in the **"Alocución"**: "la ciudad que dio a los Incas cuna / Aún gime esclava" (the city that gave birth to the Incas still groans as a slave). The Spaniards still occupied large zones of the Peruvian *altiplano,* and the patriots were resolved to expel them. There was to be no vestige of imperialism in the New World. On August 9, 1824, cavalry troops from Colombia, Peru, Ireland, and England, under Bolívar's command, defeated the Spaniards in the battle of Junín. Not a shot was fired, and the Spaniards fled after an hour. As Bolívar wrote to Peñalver in one of his rare references to this event: "So great is the reputation of our army that the Spaniards have not dared to fight us. We have made marvelous progress in this country without firing a single rifle shot."[11] Sucre sealed the struggle for independence in December when some five thousand patriots, mostly Colombians, defeated the troops of Viceroy La Serna in Ayacucho.

Meanwhile, Bello had lost his position as secretary of the Chilean mission. After O'Higgins's fall, Freire's new government had sent Mariano Egaña to London, primarily to settle the matter of the Irisarri loan. Egaña did not dismiss Bello from the Chilean mission; not knowing any English, he badly needed his help. But since Bello insisted on defending Irisarri, the tensions between the two men rapidly increased. Bello had already written to Pedro Gual, the secretary of foreign affairs, in August 1824, seeking a position in the Colombian mission. It seems that Bello had first considered the possibility of moving to Chile, but soon dismissed the idea: "The idea of moving to the Antarctic pole and abandoning forever my homeland is unbearable to me" ([Andre's Bello, *Obras Completas,* hereafter *OC*], 25: 133).

Bello wrote to Gual again in January 1825 and renewed his petition. He begins the letter by evoking their happy youth as university students and then asks for news of the university: "And how is our ancient and venerable nurse? Has she already discarded the hoop skirt of the Aristotelian-Thomistic doctrine, and agreed to dress herself for the times? I have no doubt that she has, because the impetus given by the Revolution to new opinions cannot have been favorable to the outmoded fashions that fed pabulum to the imagination rather than the understanding of the Americans" (*OC,* 25: 142). Again Bello tells Gual that he does not want to end up at the Antarctic pole, and paraphrasing Virgil's first eclogue, he says that he does not wish to die among the Chileans, who are so distant from the rest of the world: "It is painful for me to abandon the country of my birth, and to face death sooner or later at the Antarctic pole among the *toto divisos orbe chilenos* who will no doubt consider me an intruder." In both letters Bello expresses the hope that he can still count on Bolívar's support.

Late in 1824 Pedro Gual wrote to Bello naming him secretary to Manuel José Hurtado, the Colombian envoy in London. In January of the following year the British government announced to Spain its intention to recognize Buenos Aires, Mexico, and Colombia. Bello, who assumed his new position on February 7, participated in the negotiations that led to Britain's full diplomatic recognition of Colombia.[12] British recognition was the long-awaited sign that marked the end of the wars of independence; but Spanish America's problems were far from over. The Revolution had left the new states bankrupt. Several countries were borrowing heavily from Great Britain, but only a small fraction of the £21 million in loans was invested in the new countries. For one thing, the loans were discounted by huge margins: Buenos Aires, for example, received £600,000 for a loan of £1,000,000. For another, a large portion of the funds received had been used to finance the wars, against Brazil in the case of Buenos Aires, against Spain in the campaigns of Junín and Ayacucho in the case of Colombia. Finally, a large outflow of capital from Spanish America resulted from consumer purchases. Nor were the new countries capitalized with direct foreign investment. The investments that poured into Spanish America in 1824 and 1825 went mainly into speculative mining ventures that soon became insolvent. In 1825 Chile, Colombia, and Peru stopped payments on their debt, causing the bankruptcy of seven financial institutions in England and a crisis that had repercussions throughout Europe.[13]

In addition to the economic crisis, Spanish America was suffering from the sordid manipulations of the defeated Ferdinand, who in 1824 used his influence with Pope Leo XII to stage a last attempt to recover the colonies. The Pope's encyclical, which urged the Spanish American nations to recognize the Spanish monarch as their legitimate leader, contributed to the instability of the new republics, though it met with solid opposition. Servando Teresa de Mier wrote an impassioned *Discurso sobre la encíclica del Papa León XII*. His language was scathing: "It is a mere letter of formality written in mystical gibberish, or more exactly: it is an Italian swindle typical of those the Roman court uses to dismiss the straits and bonds in which the crowned heads place her." He charges the Spaniards with creating divisions among Spanish Americans by means of "a Gothic-ultramontane parchment." He even dares the Holy Alliance to attack the New World. Let the Holy Alliance come to our coasts, he says. And if the Pope wishes to form part of the expedition, as temporal

prince, war will also be waged against him, as in the times of Charles V and Philip II. The friar concludes his diatribe by warning all Mexicans not to be seduced by the maneuvers of Ferdinand VII and Leo XII.[14]

The Vatican soon accepted the fact that Spain had lost the Indies, and diplomatic relations were established. As the threat of a new invasion from Spain became less likely, the new nations started to exhibit a frail domestic political equilibrium. Bolívar had once said that he was more afraid of peace than of war, and events would bear out his premonition.

A large part of the postwar debate in Colombia concerned the role of the Church. Government representatives, on the one hand, wished to preserve the regalist primacy of state over church and to encourage religious toleration. The Constitution of Cúcuta allowed foreigners to settle in Colombia and also allowed Masonic and Protestant organizations to publish material in opposition to the supremacy of Rome. The leading figures of the Colombian government, furthermore, took a personal interest in promoting a new air of tolerance. Santander, the vice-president of Colombia, and Restrepo, the minister of the interior, encouraged Masonic organizations and anti-clericalism. And Pedro Gual became the first president of the Colombia chapter of the British Bible Society, a chapter founded by James Thompson during his extensive travels throughout Spanish America.

The ultramontane clergy, who saw the rise of government-sponsored anticlericalism as a direct threat to the monopoly they had enjoyed, were not ready to yield. It was not, however, in the center of Colombian power, in Bogotá, that the confrontation between the clergy and the state was felt most strongly, but in Caracas. Here the Church opposed the distribution of Spanish Bibles and resorted to the familiar tactics of inciting slaves to rebellion. In 1824 the slaves of Petare, a Caracas suburb, rose in defense of Ferdinand; a priest was accused of promoting the insurrection. Other similar incidents followed, and it was suspected that the Church was coordinating the efforts of rebellion with the forces of Spain and France.[15]

Buoyed by the diplomatic progress with Great Britain, but disheartened by the religious, economic, and political crises, Bello and García del Río decided to resume publishing a journal. This time, however, they would be more realistic and design a shorter and less expensive format. The title of the new journal was **El Repertorio Americano,** of which four volumes appeared in 1826 and 1827. Guillermo Guitarte is probably right to argue that García del Río played the leading role in the *Biblioteca,* but he is incorrect to extend this observation to the **Repertorio.** As a perusal of the index of the facsimile edition of the **Repertorio** reveals, Bello signed twenty-nine poems, translations, and articles. In contrast, García del Río signed only thirteen articles.[16]

In the *Repertorio* Bello finally seems comfortable with the radical breach brought about by the Revolution, but he continues emphasizing the need to preserve links with Europe, including Spain, and with classical culture and the Enlightenment. His *americanismo* is in the tradition of Miranda, marked by a complex weaving of Western tradition and the energy of the emerging nations. In an article on Columbus, Miranda's tutelary figure, Bello tries to settle the issue of the animosity between Spain and Spanish America, which is perhaps the thorniest topic in any discussion of *americanismo*. Bello says: "We do not have the slightest inclination to vituperate the Conquest. Whether it was atrocious or not, we owe the origin of our rights and our existence to it, and through the Conquest our soil received that part of European civilization that could sift through the prejudice and tyranny of Spain" (*OC,* 23: 452).

Religious tolerance is another topic often raised in the *Repertorio.* In the first volume there is a review of Mier's *Discurso* and one of a favorite work among regalists, Tamburini's *Verdadera idea de la Santa Sede,* both of which emphasize the division of church and state and the limited power of the papacy. In the second volume an article by James Thompson informs the British Bible Society of the progress of Lancaster's educational reform in Spanish America despite orthodox resistance. An attack on innate ideas and a reliance on experience, origins, and clear language run throughout the journal, especially in the articles on philosophy, orthographic reform, and education. Bello uses inductive reasoning in all his scientific articles and expounds on this method in some detail in the **"Introducción a los elementos de física del dr. N. Arnott."** This article, a translation of Arnott's *Elements of Physics,* originally published in 1825, is a recapitulation of all the advantages of the British Enlightenment and a declaration of faith in scientific progress, economic growth, and free trade.

Many pages of the journal were written by Spanish liberals exiled in London. Vicente Salvá, a philologist and politician, wrote bibliographical notes on classic Spanish texts; Pablo Mendibil, a Basque recommended to Bello by Blanco White, wrote ten articles for the *Repertorio,* including a review of the British legislative and judiciary bodies, based on a book translated into Spanish by Blanco White. In addition, publications by liberal Spaniards—Mora, Canga Argüelles, and Urcullu—were often reviewed in the journal. The Spanish *liberales,* who had been the object of Bello's attack since the beginning of the Revolution, are now his friends, denoting the first sign of reconciliation between Spaniards and Spanish Americans after the wars of independence.

As had *La Biblioteca Americana, El Repertorio Americano* opens with a poem by Bello. The title lines read:

Silvas Americanas
Silva I. - La Agricultura De La Zona Torrida

In a footnote, Bello writes: "The fragments published in the *Biblioteca Americana* under the title **'América'** belong with these silvas. The author thought of recasting them all in a single poem; convinced that this was impossible, he will publish them in their original form, with certain corrections and additions. In this first part, one will find only two or three lines from those fragments." This explanatory note, the cause of much misunderstanding among Bello scholars, is clarified by an examination of Bello's manuscripts. Shortly before the publication of the **"Agricultura"** in the *Repertorio* in October 1826, Bello attempted to merge this poem with the **"Alocución"** in another text, titled **"El campo americano."**[17]

So as not to confuse readers who were expecting a continuation of the poem **"América,"** Bello announces his new project, a series of *Silvas americanas,* the first one being the **"Agricultura."** The fragments published in the *Biblioteca* now also belong to this collection of silvas. But this new project, like **"América"** and **"El campo americano,"** was never completed. Of the *Silvas americanas* Bello published only the **"Agricultura."** The **"Alocución"** was not republished under the new series title, though Bello's footnote has led most readers to include it with the **"Agricultura"** as one of the *Silvas americanas.*

In the **"Agricultura"** Bello abandons entirely the epic mode and returns to the georgic tone and theme that had been his first inspiration upon arriving in London. After Junín and Ayacucho, the threats of Spanish reconquest had diminished, and thus the focus of the *Repertorio* shifts from war and independence to the future organization of the Spanish American republics. Like Virgil after Actium, like Pope after Utrecht, Bello turns his attention to a plan for peace. But more significantly, in the **"Agricultura"** Bello offers a recapitulation of the transformations that the wars of independence have brought about. It is his most profound meditation on the shift from colonial servitude to freedom.

In the first two sections of the poem (ll. 1-63) Bello invokes the natural fecundity of the torrid zone. The first line—"Salve, fecunda zona"—is drawn, as many critics have observed, from line 173 of book 2 of the *Georgics*—"Salve, magna parens frugum, Saturnia tellus" (Hail, land of Saturn, great giver of fruits)—which immediately follows the three lines devoted to Octavian in book 2 (ll. 170-2). Bello's opening lines are also inspired by the opening lines of Lucretius's *De rerum natura.* The Venezuelan poet recalls nostalgically the fertility of the torrid zone, where jasmine and cotton, wheat and grapes grow in abundance. The second section closes with a description of the banana tree, which Bello associates with *both* slavery and happiness:

> y para ti el banano
> desmaya al peso de su dulce carga;
> el banano, primero
> de cuantos concedió bellos presentes
> Providencia *a las gentes*
> *del ecuador feliz con mano larga.*
> No ya de humanas artes obligado
> el premio rinde opimo;
> no es a la podadera, no al arado
> deudor de su racimo;
> *escasa industria bástale, cual puede*
> *hurtar a sus fatigas mano esclava*;
> crece veloz, y cuando exhausto acaba,
> adulta prole en torno le sucede.

> (*OC*, 1: 66-7, ll. 50-63; my emphasis)

(for you [torrid zone] the banana tree faints under the weight of its sweet burden; the banana tree, the first of all the beautiful gifts offered generously by Providence *to the people of the happy equatorial region*. Unforced by the skill of man, it yields a rich reward; it owes its bunch neither to the pruning knife nor to the plow; *it requires only a small amount of effort, such that an enslaved hand can steal from its labors*; it grows quickly, and when it dies of exhaustion, a grown progeny succeeds it all around.)

Bello also remarks on the relationship between slavery and a carefree, if not happy, existence in one of his footnotes to the poem. He says that from the banana tree, and with minimal effort, the slaves in the haciendas and plantations derive their nourishment and everything that makes their life tolerable.[18]

In Chapter 1 we observed that Bello frequently drew analogies between the colonial period and the golden age. The first two sections of the **"Agricultura"** elaborate on these similarities. As in the golden age, there is here an abundance of fruits; and almost no labor, no special technique, no "agricultura" is needed for the satisfaction of basic human needs. The inhabitants of the torrid zone live in carefree servitude, in a kind of passable but unenlightened existence. Theirs is a prolongation of life, as Humboldt put it, and not a full exploration of its secrets. It is the New World before the Fall.

In the third section of the poem (ll. 64-132), Bello describes the tensions that underlay the wars of independence. Slavery the infancy of colonialism, cannot be prolonged forever. Minimal effort is no longer a blessing for an undeveloped mass of slaves; rather, indolence hinders the Americans from developing a simple, yet rich life, and Bello launches a tirade against the "*indolente labrador*" (indolent peasant), who is no longer identified with the slaves but with the privileged few.

Servitude is sweet and happy—provided that no one challenges it. As soon as prospects for growth and development arise, the equilibrium of dependency is destroyed. Each of the two sides of the struggle is an object of Bello's criticism: the Creole aristocracy has abandoned its fields, and the Church, in representing the Crown, has taken over the fields of the elite and promoted civil disorder:

> ¿Por qué ilusión funesta
> aquellos que fortuna hizo señores
> de tan dichosa tierra y pingüe y varia,
> al cuidado abandonan
> y a la fe mercenaria
> las patrias heredades,
> y en el ciego tumulto se aprisionan
> de míseras ciudades,
> do la ambición proterva
> sopla la llama de civiles bandos,
> o al patriotismo la desidia enerva;
> do el lujo las costumbres atosiga,
> y combaten los vicios
> la incauta edad en poderosa liga?

> (ll. 75-88)

(By what ill-fated illusion those fortunate owners of such a happy, rich, and variegated land abandon their ancestral properties to the mercenary faith, to its care, and trap themselves in the blind tumult of miserable cities, where perverse ambition fans the flame of civil factions, or patriotism is enervated by laziness; where luxury poisons customs, and the vices, assembled in a powerful league, attack those of unwary age.)

"*Fe mercenaria*" (mercenary faith) alludes to the Church's role during both the colonial period and the Revolution. During the colonial period, the Church had a virtual monopoly on official credit in the colonies through the system of *censos,* or mortgage loans. One kind of *censo* could be redeemed after the capital had been paid in full, while a second type—sometimes called *censo perpetuo* (mortgage in perpetuity)—was nonredeemable and served a spiritual rather than a temporal function. Under a *censo perpetuo* the Church would dispense favors (e.g., say a mass on a given date, year after year) in return for interest payments representing 5 percent of the value of the property, which was mortgaged in favor of some parish, chaplaincy, or convent. Established in perpetuity, the *censo* created an obligation that was passed from generation to generation.[19]

A contemporary source illustrates the kind of animosity toward the Church that these mortgages generated during the last years of the war. In a pamphlet published in 1823, José Tomás Sanauria explains that almost all the mortgage loans in Venezuela had been extended by the Church. The holders of these loans, or *censualistas,* Sanauria charges, have seized and liquidated agricultural property at a time when the disasters of the war have prevented normal repayment. The author blames the Church for the pitiful state of postwar Venezuelan agriculture: "The valleys of Tuy, Caucagua, Guatire, Aragüita, Río Chico, Mamporal, Santa Lucía, and others present the most dreary and horrible effects of the arbitrary foreclosures performed upon the request of the chaplains, trustees, and administrators of churches, for the sake of a miserable sum of past-due interest owed to them."[20] Throughout Spanish America during the years of the Revolution, the Church became a mortgage bank that made loans to landowners. Though the rate of interest was low, the clergy gained considerable influence over its clients.[21]

Bello's specific charge in this section of the **"Agricultura"** is that the landowners lost their property to the Church and flocked to the city, where they became slaves to the allure of new luxuries. In the city the Church fanned the fires of civil war—a charge Bello made in the letter to the Pope. Similarly, in the **"Alocución"** Bello accused the clergy of serving as an accomplice of Spanish tyranny. It is possible that in the **"Agricultura"** Bello is defending the Colombian government's strong stance against orthodox intolerance, a debate that reached its peak in Caracas in March 1826, some seven months before the poem's publication.[22]

Bello's criticism of city life continues as he shows the landowners becoming experts in seduction and gambling. His attack on urban life is drawn in part from the closing of book 3 of Virgil's *Georgics* but more significantly from Tibullus and Jovellanos.[23] Against the image of contemporary city life, Bello evokes the strong government of the ancient Roman republic, when citizens were called from the fields to run the state, long before Rome had tasted the luxuries of empire. Bello is now ready to specify the political ideal of the **"Agricultura."** He has had to give up his ideal of a constitutional monarchy, but the powerful executive arm of the first centuries of the Roman republic, the consuls who inherited in part the majesty of kings, is a close substitute. Addressing America's idle urban dwellers, he argues:

> No así trató la triunfadora Roma
> las artes de la paz y de la guerra;
> antes fió las riendas del estado
> a la mano robusta
> que tostó el sol y encalleció el arado;
> y bajo el techo luminoso campesino
> los hijos educó, que el conjurado
> mundo allanaron al valor latino.
>
> (ll. 125-32)

(Triumphant Rome did not handle the skills of war and peace in this way. Instead, she entrusted the reins of the state to the strong hand which the sun tanned and the plow hardened; and under the luminous ceiling of the countryside she educated her children, who subjected the conspiring world to Latin valor.)

In the fourth section of the **"Agricultura"** (ll. 133-201) Bello again recalls republican Rome and the virtues of a simple life. This section is based almost entirely on the famous passage of book 2 of the *Georgics*: "O fortunatos nimium, sua si bona norint / agricolas . . ." (How exceedingly happy are the farmers, if they only knew their blessing). In the preceding section of the **"Agricultura"** Bello associated city life with civil war. He now focuses on a passage in which Virgil associates the countryside with a particular kind of peacefulness. The countryside is distant from civil factions (the *"discordibus armis"* of Virgil's passage), and Bello tells the landowners, the *"afortunados poseedores,"* to return to the countryside; there, freedom can be found. In the countryside, Bello says, they will find pure feelings and honest love, and will be free from the machinations of the *"ajena mano y fe"* (foreign hand and faith) that marries people *"por nombre o plata"* (for renown or for money)—another attack on the Church's financial ambitions.

The countryside in the aftermath of the Revolution is the setting for the beginning of the poem's fifth section (ll. 202-68). The lands have been abandoned by the war. The jungles are again to be laid low, so that coffee and fruit trees can be planted. Now, for the first time, the word *"agricultura"* appears in the poem:

> Ya dócil a tu voz, agricultura,
> nodriza de las gentes, la caterva
> servil armada va de corvas hoces.
>
> (ll. 224-6)

(Agriculture, nurse of the people, the servile throng armed with curved sickles now advances obeying your voice.)

The wars of independence have completely altered the terms of existence described at the beginning of the poem, when colonial servitude was associated with the easy sustenance provided by the banana tree. The natural fecundity is now replaced by the toil of agriculture; the happy slaves are now a servile throng. But the Revolution has also created an opportunity for transforming this situation, which is what Bello does in this extraordinary section of the poem. Each member of the servile throng, as he first destroys the jungle and then cultivates the land, is transformed into a *"fatigado agricultor"* (tired farmer, l. 261).

In the fifth section (ll. 269-350) Bello speaks of "la gente agricultora / del ecuador" (the agricultural people of the equatorial region). This expression concludes the series of transformations from the colonial period to the postwar era, from happy servitude to a new freedom that allows people to change their lives, till their lands, and, as Bello says later in the poem, trade their goods:

> lines 54-5: *"las gentes del ecuador feliz"* (the people of the happy equatorial region)—colonial slavery

lines 224-5: *"agricultura, nodriza de las gentes"* (agriculture, nurse of the people)—the aftermath of war

lines 271-2: *"la gente agricultora del ecuador"* (the agricultural people of the equatorial region)—the future period of freedom

On almost all counts the model of Augustan Caracas is now crumbling and the institutions that shaped that order have also fallen, despite the attempt of the Crown and its ecclesiastical branch to regain power. The golden age of peace and easy sustenance is never to be regained. Instead, the sacrifice and the higher challenge of *"agricultura"* and freedom are the new alternatives.

What is extraordinary about the **"Agricultura"** is that Bello chose to inscribe the fall of the old order within a Virgilian framework, the very framework that had given legitimacy to that order. And Bello organized the ***Repertorio Americano*** in a way that emphasized this framework: immediately after his poem is the article **"Estudio sobre Virgilio, por P. F. Tissot,"** a translation signed by Bello of a review article originally published in 1826 in the *Révue Encyclopédique* of Tissot's Virgil studies. The article begins with a condemnation of the eighteenth century for not having paid close attention to the sacred language of the ancients. But the political turmoil of the last decades, it continues, has opened the eyes and expanded the minds of many authors, who have realized that the best way to surpass the moderns is to be as good as the ancients. Tissot, who had been chosen by Jacques Delille—*"el primer poeta del siglo"*—to take over the chair of classical studies at the Sorbonne, is praised for revealing in this study of Virgil the ancient mysteries of the Muses. After an extensive quotation of Tissot that surveys the whole gallery of Western authors, the article pays tribute to Delille:

> And you, illustrious translator of the Georgics, whose friendship honors me, whose selection [of me] caused me such lively restlessness! If from the day of your death I have not let pass a single day without paying homage to your memory; if faithful to the duties of the heart, I have directed all my work to the one who imposed them on me in an adoption that was so dear to me—condescend to accept these studies as the religious offering of a disciple to his master.

Bello surely chose to publish Tissot's tribute to Delille as a way of making his own tribute. Delille, born in 1738, was a proponent of the seemingly contradictory alliance between neoclassical poetry and antiabsolutist politics that surfaced in eighteenth-century Britain and that seemed to have reached a climax in prerevolutionary France. He was a fairly active member of the intellectual opposition, yet at the same time he was almost entirely dedicated to the revival of the Virgilian tradition, both in his original poems—such as "L'homme des champs"—and in his translations of the *Aeneid* and the *Georgics*. While in London, Bello had translated

two of Delille's long poems under the titles **"La luz"** and **"Los jardines."** But it is in Delille's most famous work, his translation of the *Georgics,* that we find the most fruitful connection between the two poets and an explanation of the secret meaning of *"agricultura."*

In Delille's preface to his translation of the *Georgics* one can see the coexistence of the georgic vogue and the virulent anti-Augustan tradition that had been brooding throughout the eighteenth century. The preface was both a defense of the Roman republic and an attack on Augustus. Written in 1756, it exemplifies the savage feelings against the *princeps* in the years that preceded the French Revolution. This is, for instance, Delille's comment on the proem to the *Georgics*:

> There is nothing more pompous and more base than this invocation to Caesar. Two poets after Virgil degraded themselves with less poetic and more base invocations; Lucan lavished the vilest adulations on Nero, and Statius on Domitian. The latter is the guiltiest of the three. Augustus succeeded at the end of his reign, and Nero at the beginning of his; Domitian was always a monster. At any rate, one should not accuse these poets of deifying human beings—the customs of their country allowed such a practice—but of placing assassins who barely deserved to be called human in the ranks of the gods.[24]

Delille also tells us that one can easily recognize in the *Georgics* the influence of Maecenas, to whom the ideas and intention of the proem can be attributed. The lamentation at the end of book 1, Delille says, is caused by the decay of agriculture (*"la décadence de l'Agriculture"*). At the end of book 2, he adds, in his beautiful praise of country life Virgil seems to have assembled all the power and grace of poetry to excite among Romans their ancient love for agriculture. Delille always capitalizes *agriculture* in the preface, and its figurative meaning becomes clearer in the following sentence: "L'Agriculture a exercé non seulement les plus grand héros, mais encore les plus grands écrivains de l'antiquité" (Agriculture fostered not only the greatest heroes of antiquity but also the greatest writers, p. 4), an echo of the opening of the *Histories,* where Tacitus says that the best Roman minds vanished after Actium. It is not just the tilling of fields Delille is praising. Rather, "Agriculture" is a code word for the Roman republic. Elsewhere in the preface Delille explains that figurative language arises when writers cannot speak freely.

Whereas Delille views Augustus and Agriculture as enemies, Bello instead organizes his **"Agricultura"** so as to describe the transformation from a servile model to an order in which freedom prevails. Although Bello sometimes referred to the colonial period as a time of chains and despotism, more often he thought of the colonial era as a stage of civilization in its infancy, dominated, or, as he said in the **"Alocución,"** "lulled," by superstition. It was not a world of unbearable oppression, but one deprived of freedom. In the last section of the **"Agricultura,"** when Bello compares the two orders, he says, "La libertad más dulce que el imperio" (Liberty, sweeter than empire). The liberal model is justified as a higher good.

In the eighteenth century European culture was torn between two world views—in one, power was centralized, symbolized by the figure of Augustus; in the other, freedom predominated and individuals sought to restore the values of republican Rome and to develop the arts and sciences under freedom. Virgil's *Georgics* became the battleground for these conflicting world views. Depending on which aspects of Virgil one chose or omitted— whether Octavian's apotheosis in book 1 or the simple life in book 2—one was choosing monarchy or republic, obedience to established rules or free inquiry. In his final version of the *Georgics* Bello has suppressed Augustus and tipped the balance on the side of freedom, the higher challenge—*agricultura*.

Notes

1. For the influence of the term *"idéologie"* on Bello, García del Río, and other Spanish Americans see Arturo Ardao, *Andrés Bello, filósofo* (Caracas, 1986), 58-93, 98-109.

2. Juan María Gutiérrez, *América Poética* (Valparaíso, 1846), 11-16; Pedro Henríquez Ureña, "El descontento y la promesa," *Seis ensayos en busca de nuestra expresión* (Buenos Aires, 1928), and idem, *Las corrientes literarias en la América Hispánica* (México: 1978 [1st ed. in English, 1945]), esp. 103. For more recent comments on the "Alocución" as a milestone of *americanismo* see Donald Shaw, "'Americanness' in Spanish American Literature," *Comparative Criticism*, 8 (1986), 213, and Arturo Ardao, "Primera idea del americanismo literario," in his forthcoming *La inteligencia latinoamericana*.

3. Thomas Gray, *The Complete Poems,* ed. H. W. Starr and J. R. Hendrickson (Oxford, 1966), 15.

4. For the significance of this topos in the 1820s see Llorens, *Liberales y románticos*, 330.

5. Bello shared this aesthetic ideal with such Spanish contemporaries as Blanco White, Mora, and Alcalá Galiano. In a review article on Cienfuegos in the *Biblioteca,* he expressed this ideal in a memorable line: "Among the ancients [i.e., in the poets and dramatists of the sixteenth and seventeenth centuries] nature prevails, while art prevails among the moderns. In the former we find ease, grace, fire, fecundity, a frequently irregular and even wild exuberance, which carries nevertheless

a seal of greatness and daring that is impressive even when it goes astray. Generally speaking, the poets who have flourished since Luzán do not show these traits" (*OC* [*Obras Completes*], 9: 199-200). The article on Cienfuegos, incidentally, was the first published writing of Bello's that he signed—but only with his initials, A. B.

6. Arturo Ardao, "La etapa filosófica de Bello en Londres," in *Bello y Londres,* [2 vols. (Caracas, 1980-81,] 2: 158.

7. Cf. "Reflexiones sobre la presente constitucíon de España, *"El censor Americano,* 1 (1820), 33: "If the 1812 Constitution were Permanently ratified (which is, fortunately, very unlikely), the Spanish chains would weigh over us more heavily than ever. A free people has always ruled with an iron hand over its distant possessions. The government of an absolute monarch, surrounded by an opulent nobility and by aging bureaucrats, is naturally less oppressive for the colonies than a popular congress."

8. *OC,* 25: 105; Alamiro de Avila Martel, *Dos elogios chilenos a Bolívar en 1819* (Santiago, 1976).

9. For the criticism of Augustus among the British poets of the eighteenth century, see [Howard D. Weinbrot, *Augustus Caesar in "Augustan" England: The Decline of a Classical Norm* (Princeton, N.J., 1978), 51.]

10. John Lynch, "Great Britain and Latin American Independence, 1810-1830," in *Bello y Londres,* 1: 46-7.

11. *Cartas del Libertador,* 2nd ed., Vicente Lecuna, ed. (Caracas, 1966), 4: 188.

12. [Miguel Luis Amunátegui, *Vida de don Andrés Bello* (Sahtjags, 1882)] 200; [D. A. G.] Waddell, "Las relaciones británicas con Venezuela, [Nueva Granada y la Gran Columbia, 1810-1829. Primera Parte: en Londres," in *Bello y Londres* (Caracas, 1980) 80].

13. [R. A. Humphreys, *Liberation in South America, 1806-1827: The Career of James Paroissien* (London, 1952)] chap. 9; Lynch, "Great Britain and Latin American Independence," 75-81; John Ford, "Rudolph Ackermann: Publisher to Latin America," in *Bello y Londres,* 1: 204-5. For a more detailed description and analysis of the debt crisis see Jaime Rodríguez, "The Politics of Credit," *The Emergence of Spanish America: Vicente Rocafuerte and Spanish Americanism, 1808-1831* (Berkeley, Calif., 1975), 108-28.

14. Servando Teresa de Mier, *Discurso sobre la encíclica del Papa León XII* (México, 1825), 4, 14.

15. This description of the rise of anticlericalism in Colombia closely follows Mary Watters, *A History*

of the Church in Venezuela, 1810-1930 (Chapel Hill, N.C., 1933).

16. [Guillermo L.] Guitarte, "El papel de Juan García del Río en las revistas de Londres," 59-73 [*Bello y Londres,* 2]; *El Repertorio Americano,* facsimile edition with notes and preface by Pedro Grases (Caracas, 1971). For Bello's role in soliciting material for publication in the *Repertorio* see the first volume of his correspondence (*OC,* 25: 203, 213, 261, 270, 279, 310, 341, 343, 345, 350, 364, 377). Bello's leading role in the journal is confirmed by José Joaquín de Mora, who wrote in 1830: "[El] Repertorio Americano, publicado en Londres bajo la dirección de Andrés Bello," in Alamiro de Avila Martel, *Bello y Mora en Chile* (Santiago, 1982), 141.

17. "El campo americano" appears in *OC,* 2: 70-93, ll. 775-1305. The four manuscript sheets (14, 15, 16, 17) of this composite poem have watermarks of 1824 and 1825.

18. For the use of footnotes, especially of a scientific kind, in the poetry of the late Enlightenment see William Powell Jones, *The Rhetoric of Science: A Study of Scientific Ideas and Imagery in Eighteenth-Century English Poetry* (Berkeley, Calif., 1966), 186-7, 191. Many of the poems studied by Jones are descriptions of the nature of the New World.

19. In *Los censos en la Iglesia colonial venezolana,* a three-volume study published in 1982 (Caracas), Emilia Troconis de Veracoechea revealed the extensive use of the Church's mortgage financing not only during the colonial period, but throughout the wars of independence and beyond.

20. José Tomás Sanauria, *Fomento de la agricultura: Discurso canónicolegal sobre la necesidad de una ley que reduzca los censos en Venezuela* (Caracas, 1823), 18-19.

21. See Miguel Luis Amunátegui and Diego Barros Arana, *La Iglesia frente a la emancipación americana* (Havana, 1967), 137.

22. At the center of the turmoil was the publication in Caracas of *La serpiente de Moisés,* an orthodox pamphlet originally published in Bogotá in 1822 in which religious toleration is assailed. The liberal authorities accused the editors of sedition, and a public trial was held on March 13, 1826, in front of the Church of San Francisco. Objections to *La serpiente* were made in a number of pamphlets published in Caracas in 1826. In *Discurso teológico político sobre la tolerancia en que se acusa y reputa el escrito titulado "La serpiente de Moisés,"* José de la Natividad Saldanha charges that without a doubt the work in question promotes rebellion. In *Cartas de un alemán a S.E. el Vicepresidente,* the anonymous author charges that the clergy has placed the "torch of rebellion in the hands of fanaticism." *La serpiente* was defended by its editor, Miguel Santana, in *Día que no se contará entre los de Colombia: El 18 de marzo de 1826, en que se comenzó a hollar en Caracas la libertad de imprenta.*

23. For the influence of Tibullus on the "Agricultura" see Manuel Briceño Jáuregui, "Andrés Bello, humanista latino," in *Bello y la América Latina* (Caracas, 1982), 317-36.

24. Jacques Delille, *Les Géorgiques de Virgile,* 4th ed. (Paris: Bleuet, 1770), note to the poem.

Iván Jaksić (essay date 1997)

SOURCE: Jaksić, Iván. Introduction to *Selected Writings of Andrés Bello,* by Andres Bello, translated by Frances M. Lopez-Morillas, edited by Iván Jaksić, pp. xxvii-lv. New York: Oxford University Press, 1997.

[*In the following essay, Jaksić examines Bello's life and works, arguing that Bello's primary concern in all his writing and political work was creating order.*]

Andrés Bello was a central figure in the construction of a new political order in post-independence Latin America. A quiet, unassuming, self-effacing man, Andrés Bello was nevertheless a person of enormous influence, a mentor to generations, an advisor to powerful political figures, and a builder of institutions. Andrés Bello was also a product of his times, a man whose long life straddled the eighteenth and the nineteenth centuries; who lived long enough to have known and participated as an official in the Spanish imperial bureaucracy; who was an actor in the independence process, a friend and interlocutor of many of the leaders of emancipation; who represented several Latin American nations before England, a country where he also worked with some of the most influential intellectuals of the Spanish and English-speaking worlds; who steered a nascent Latin American republic into a model of stability and prosperity; and who wrote some of the most enduring and influential pieces of scholarship and policy in nineteenth-century Latin America.

Andrés Bello was also a bridge between religious and secular traditions, a scholar who responded to the dissolution of the Spanish empire with a rationale for the construction of a new order which was rooted in a humanistic tradition. Bello bridged the ancient and the modern, the neoclassic and the romantic, the scientific and the humanistic worlds, and brought Europe and Latin America into closer contact. Bello was a person who balanced disparate traditions and interests for the sake of constructing new nations.

As might be expected, Bello has been celebrated to the point of sycophancy, and vilified to the point of slander, by a large contingent of contemporaries and subsequent historians who have struggled to understand his role, often from the standpoint of their own partisan positions. Somehow, the Bello that bears witness to the dramatic creation of new nations in the nineteenth century has been obscured, his record distorted, and his ultimate objectives misunderstood. With significant exceptions, it is only with the research of the last few decades, culminating with the newest edition of Bello's complete works in 1981-86, that the proper assessment of his role in a variety of areas is beginning to emerge. And yet he remains virtually unknown in the English-speaking world, despite his centrality for understanding key nineteenth-century issues in Latin America and beyond.

Part of the difficulty in understanding Bello comes from the variety, complexity, and enormity of his intellectual production. His writings range from poetry to philosophy, from philology to civil law, from education to history, from international relations to literary criticism. Two recent tomes of correspondence complete the twenty-six volumes of Bello's collected works. This astonishing variety has led to much learned, but generally field-specific, commentary, often bearing little relationship to the larger body of his work. The task of the contemporary scholar is to identify the inner dynamics of Bello's work; probe the relationship between his various areas of concern and the larger social, cultural, and political issues of the period; and attempt to analyze his significance vis-à-vis the national and international contexts in which he operated. My own view is that Bello's fundamental, life-long concern was the problem of order, a problem of particular urgency for a region struggling to build durable social and political arrangements in the wake of the collapse of the Spanish empire. Bello advanced a view of order that rested on three interrelated spheres: the ordering of thought via language, literature, and philosophy; the ordering of national affairs via civil law, education, and history; and the participation of the new nations in the world order of the nineteenth century via international law and diplomacy. The persistence of Bello's interest in order reflects, I believe, not only his informed reading of nineteenth-century needs for national development, but also a deep and very personal search that was motivated by the dramatic events that he witnessed and experienced. Certainly the most dramatic of all was the disintegration of the imperial order, which opened some hopeful possibilities, but which in the beginning offered a nightmarish picture of blood, chaos, and confusion.

Bello's contribution to the history of nineteenth-century Latin America, in short, consisted of the elaboration of a rationale for order that looked past the initial chaos of the aftermath of war in order to build the new republics on solid ground. Just as nations struggled, and often failed, to establish order via political experimentation or force, Bello concentrated on the quieter, but deeper and ultimately more successful, development of an agenda for order that emphasized the rule of law—both domestic and international—and sought unity via education and a concept of language that served as the basis for the structuring of nationhood. Although not applied, or even applicable, in every country of Latin America (due to myriad historical factors) Bello's rationale for order remains the most important nineteenth-century contribution to the complex and still relevant issues of nation-building.

THREE BIOGRAPHICAL PERIODS: VENEZUELA, ENGLAND, AND CHILE[1]

Andrés Bello was born in Caracas, Venezuela, on 29 November, 1781. The eldest son of a minor official in the Spanish colonial bureaucracy, Bello grew up during a period of significant economic growth and political importance resulting from the upgrading of the Captaincy General of Venezuela.[2] He received an extraordinary education by the standards of the time, one which he would remember with fondness. He studied Latin and philosophy, receiving a Bachelor's degree from the University of Caracas in 1800, at which time he could translate texts in Latin and impress mentors and classmates with his scholastic abilities.[3] By this time, he had instructed Simón Bolívar on literature and geography, and had assisted Alexander von Humboldt during the latter's research in Venezuela. The anecdote is often told of the time when an enthusiastic, if out of breath, young Bello accompanied Humboldt on his ascent to Mount Avila. Although they did not reach the top together, Bello followed Humboldt's scientific interests. He may well have learned from Humboldt about the linguistic theories of Humboldt's younger brother, Karl Wilhelm. Bello continued, but did not complete, studies in law and medicine. Economic necessity prompted him to go to work for the colonial government in 1802. He launched a successful career in administration without abandoning his literary interests, especially in poetry and linguistics. Bello's colonial position allowed him to participate in projects of national scope, such as smallpox inoculation, a major development that probably contributed to his positive view of the enlightened reforms and scientific emphasis of the late colonial period. In 1808, he was entrusted with the major responsibility for editing the *Gaceta de Caracas,* the first newspaper of Venezuela, and among the first on the South American continent.

It was in that year that the fate of the Spanish empire, and his own, changed forever with the French invasion of the Iberian peninsula. Bello remained with the colonial government, navigating the increasingly difficult waters of international politics as the Spanish Juntas came and went, and as conflicting reports about lines of authority confused the local population. It was probably due to Bello's competence in matters of government, plus his language ability (in English and French, in addition to Latin), that the creole Junta that overthrew the Captain General invited him to join the revolutionary government as first officer in the ministry of foreign relations in April 1810. Soon after, in June 1810, he set sail for England with Colonel Simón Bolívar and government representative Luis López Méndez, to seek the protection of Great Britain in the event of either Spanish retaliation or French invasion.

Andrés Bello was to remain in England for nineteen years, a rich period for his intellectual development, but at times a period of economic hardship, frustration, and personal tragedy.[4] In London, he met and admired Francisco Miranda, his compatriot and early advocate of independence, lived in his house at Grafton Street, and benefited from Miranda's substantial library. By 1812, with the collapse of the revolutionary government, Bello was forced to seek a variety of employments, and even attempted to return to the service of Spain during a desperate moment in 1813. During the 1812-1822 period he worked in various temporary jobs that were always insufficient for sustaining his growing family, and received some temporary assistance from the British government. He tutored English children, he translated or proofread various works, and also worked with James Mill in attempting to decipher Jeremy Bentham's handwriting. This appears to have been a miserable period for Bello; he could not find the means to return to Venezuela, he could not find stable employment, and his first wife and youngest child died in 1821. It was only in 1822 that he achieved some relative security when he returned to the diplomatic service, this time for the government of Chile. Soon thereafter, in collaboration with Juan García de Río, he launched two extremely significant publications, the **Biblioteca Americana** (1823), and the **Repertorio Americano** (1826-27). These two journals addressed to a Spanish American audience reveal, on the one hand, the substantial amount of research work that Bello had carried out at the library of the British Museum, and, on the other, Bello's by now clear and public effort to build a Spanish American culture that would serve as a vehicle for continental unity.

Although he worked in a variety of positions at the legations of Chile and Gran Colombia from 1822 until 1829, this work was not stable, and led to his permanent alienation from Simón Bolívar and other members of the government of Gran Colombia. Bello had been suspected of monarchical leanings, was rumored to have betrayed the revolution, and had shown less than energetic enthusiasm for a Bolívar who in the late 1820s had a few problems of his own. Despite increasingly urgent requests from Bello to improve his situation in England, Bolívar could not or would not give him assistance until it was too late.[5] Bello left England for Chile, and would never return to his homeland. Negative rumors about Bello were only slowly proven false, and may have contributed to his decision not to return to Venezuela, even after Bolívar's death.

Chile proved to be, in most respects, a congenial place for Bello. In Santiago, he quickly became a respected public and intellectual figure. Arriving in 1829 at the age of forty-seven, Bello brought with him enormous experience as government official in Caracas, diplomat, publisher, and scholar-at-large in England, and had matured into a cautious and moderate political thinker who had a unique perspective on both the functioning of government institutions in Europe, and the potential of the new republics for a role in the larger community of nations. Bello was, from the beginning, very close to Chilean government circles. He became Undersecretary of Finance and then Foreign Relations from his arrival until his retirement in 1852. He became the editor of the government newspaper, *El Araucano,* from its inception in 1830 until his retirement in 1853. He was elected senator in 1837 and was reelected in 1846 and 1855, a position he held until his death. He wrote most official Chilean documents concerning foreign relations, and also wrote presidential messages and congressional responses. He contributed to the discussions on the constitution of 1833 and wrote Chile's Civil Code, promulgated into law in 1855. All along, he was a respected voice in government circles in Chile and abroad, and he was frequently asked to chair government commissions and preside over diplomatic negotiations.[6]

Andrés Bello was also a successful educator. His first position in education in Chile was as Director of the Colegio de Santiago, a short-lived school that was nevertheless at the center of some of the first significant intellectual debates of the period. He was part of several commissions reviewing educational developments in Chile beginning in the 1830s. He tutored students privately in his house, including many who would become leading intellectual and political figures, and became the creator and first Rector of the University of Chile in 1843, a position for which he was reelected by the faculty four times (1848, 1853, 1858, and 1863) and that he held until his death. The University of Chile, which became known as *La Casa de Bello,* successfully concentrated the supervision of national education, and served as the center for research activities with a national focus.[7]

Despite his multiple public activities, Bello maintained an astonishing level of intellectual production. Although the origin of his many intellectual concerns goes back to his Caracas and London years, it was in Chile that he wrote all of his major works, including the **Gramática de la Lengua Castellana** (1847), the **Principios de Derecho Internacional** (1832, 1844, and 1864), and the **Código Civil** (1855). He also wrote poetry, reviewed books and theatrical productions, engaged in scholarly debates, and even wrote on astronomy, one among many other scientific interests. The first edition of his posthumous collected works published in Santiago in 1881-86, comprising what was then known about the extent of his intellectual production, included fifteen volumes.

In spite of his multiple public activities and the forceful and authoritative tenor of his writings, Bello was an intensely shy and sensitive man. Reports from his closest friends and the letters to and from his family show him to have been loyal, patient, and caring. He exhibited the sadness of an exile who was never able to return to his native land, never saw his Caracas family again, and mourned the loss of nine of his fifteen children. He was, however, capable of good humor, as shown by several of his poems and some of his letters, and was also a good conversationalist. He lived a long life, but was plagued by headaches, poor eyesight, and was severely impaired in the last eight years of his life. Although almost blind and confined to a wheelchair, he worked on various projects, but most consistently on poetry and the revision of his publications until he was bedridden in September of 1865. He died on October 15 of that year, reportedly struggling to read passages of Latin and Greek poetry.

In view of Bello's personal qualities and intellectual achievements, it is perhaps not surprising that a literature of celebration should have developed, some of it written by his descendants and perpetuated by his admirers. But this should not obscure the magnitude of the criticisms, both fair and unfair, directed against Bello's personality and larger role in the politics of the period. He was accused of betraying the revolutionary movement in Caracas, and was suspected of complicity with writer and diplomat Antonio José de Irisarri in the latter's dubious financial dealings in London. Ventura Marín, a Chilean philosopher in the 1830s, denounced him as a corruptor of youth while José Miguel Infante, the Chilean advocate of federalism, frequently denounced him in the press as a monarchist and a reactionary. Bello's friendship with Diego Portales, the power behind the throne in the Chile of the 1830s, made him anathema to the liberals who had suffered Portales' heavy-handedness. Other contemporaries—including the Chilean writer and politician José Victorino Lastarria and the Argentine educator, journalist, and later president Domingo Faustino Sarmiento—attempted for various reasons to present Bello as an authoritarian, somewhat passé old man. If the all-too-human jealousies are discounted, it appears that Bello's austere and serious demeanor, combined with a clear commitment to the conservative (but liberalizing) side of the Chilean political spectrum, generated genuine opposition to his influence. The challenge for the contemporary scholar is not to defend him—in fact, Bello sometimes needs to be defended from his defenders—but to clearly understand his intellectual and political positions.

To begin an assessment of Bello's thought and his contributions to the process of nation-building in the nineteenth century, one must recall the difficulties of transferring the solid legitimacy of monarchical rule claiming divine origin to the untested and fragile institutions of representative government.[8] In addition, the devastation of the wars of independence and the disappointing economic performance of the new nations provided fertile ground for social and political tensions that often exploded in civil wars in an ever-increasing spiral of violence and instability. Much intellectual energy was devoted to defending various political models, but they often degenerated into partisan bickering that only compounded the difficulties of the new nations. It is in this context that Bello identified the issue of order as central to the consolidation of the new states, and approached it from a variety of perspectives. He posited that without internal order there would be little hope for the trade and exchange that could come from, and contribute to, the external world. In turn, the domestic order could only be achieved if individuals developed the civic virtues essential to the functioning of republican institutions.

Bello's extensive production can be divided in three major clusters of concerns: language and literature; education and history; and government, law, and international relations. They represent Bello's key intellectual interests, but they also represent key vehicles for the establishment and consolidation of nationhood.

Language and Literature

Although Bello became proficient, and indeed an expert, in a wide variety of fields, language was perhaps his most central and sustained concern. Language, in the context of Bello's intellectual interests, translated into at least three major areas of activity: grammatical studies; poetry; and literary history. His most consistent efforts, and probably his most successful, were devoted to the first, although the second and third were also important ingredients in his larger plans for language and national development.

Language, for Bello, was the key vehicle for the construction of a new political order in post-colonial Latin America. The potentialities of language, in this respect, were not immediately apparent to Bello; in fact, it took him years of study and experience before he could make a connection between the two. But once he made it, in the 1820s, he pursued the relationship between language and nationhood with a tenacity that was paralleled only by his work on the Chilean civil code. And even in this latter activity, the connection that Bello established between language and the law is strong.

Just as there are three clearly discernible periods in Bello's life, there are three periods in his approach to language issues. During his years in Caracas he devoted considerable time to the study of Latin, which he pursued at the University of Caracas under the direction of the preeminent scholars of his day. He also devoted considerable energy to the philosophical study of language, particularly through the works of Etienne Bonnot de Condillac. It is widely believed—and indeed Bello himself implied so—that his famous work on the tenses of the Spanish verb, which first saw the light in Santiago in 1841, had originally been prepared in Caracas. Lastly, during the Caracas years he also read and wrote poetry, some of it imitative of Vergil, but some of it original work designed to aesthetically probe into the possibilities of the Spanish language, as well as to celebrate such events as the introduction of the smallpox vaccine in Venezuela and the victory of the Spanish resistance at Bailén.

Through his position in the colonial government, Bello also had two other important contacts with language-related matters: one was his experience with the English language, which he used for reading London newspapers, for communicating with English officials in Curaçao, and for translating various documents. English-language newspapers had become extremely important to Caracas officials, especially as the Napoleonic invasion of the Iberian peninsula unfolded. Bello emerged as the key person in government who could converse in the language, and this was probably one of the major reasons why he was appointed secretary of the first diplomatic mission to England after the creation of the first independent government in Caracas.

The other important experience related to language involves the dissemination of information through the medium of print. Bello became the chief writer for the first paper printed in Caracas, the *Gaceta de Caracas,* founded in 1808.[9] His role in the *Gaceta* is probably among the least studied, but it was substantial enough to provide him with an understanding of, and experience with, the significant possibilities of print. The periodical press was a rarity in Spanish America at the time, a medium that was closely controlled by government. Bello became the chief writer of this first newspaper at a time when political flux in the peninsula provided him with an opportunity to select and present information that was enormously influential in the process of independence. His knowledge of English allowed him to publish information about Spain that was almost contemporary with events in the peninsula. Because England had become an ally of Spain against Napoleon, Bello was in a position to convey relevant British information and to offer several of the first defenses of the Spanish resistance. This experience would serve him well: he became the principal writer and editor of several other periodicals in his career, most notably the

Biblioteca Americana and the *Repertorio Americano*—both published in London—and *El Araucano,* the official newspaper of independent Chile.

It was in London, however, that he devoted concentrated attention to the scholarly study of language. He had an important early exposure to philological studies at the impressive library in Miranda's house.[10] Bello taught himself Greek during his residence there between 1810-12, and there is some speculation that he might have begun his study of medieval literature at Miranda's library as well. But unquestionably, it was at the library of the British Museum, which he began to consult in 1814, that he found the materials and the inspiration for the work that would occupy him the rest of his life. Although he did not publish some of the results of his work at the British Museum until the 1820s, the general direction of his language concerns becomes clear from an examination of the notebooks he kept during the 1810s. He first concentrated on medieval literature, especially the *Cantar de Mío Cid,* but also on such specialized matters as the origins of meter, rhyme, and the use of assonance. In retrospect, it can be said without any doubt that he was actively investigating the origins of vernacular literature after the decline of Latin as the language of educated Europe. He was also looking into the emergence of national languages, their sources and their influences. He was especially interested in chronicles and romances as foundations for national myths.[11]

There is probably a more personal reason for Bello's language concerns. Though he had become conversant in Latin and English prior to his departure for England, extended exposure to the latter language—he lived in England for nineteen years and was twice married to British women—might have made him sensitive to the need of studying and keeping his Spanish. He was also in contact with several peninsular Spanish scholars, including such accomplished linguists as Bartolomé José Gallardo and Antonio Puigblanch, who surely encouraged, even if they were puzzled by, his interests in the origins of romance languages.[12] Some of the extant correspondence indicates that he communicated frequently with these and other scholars on matters of philology. One might also speculate that the vagaries of the early independence period, which had catastrophic implications for his personal situation, may have inspired him to look into the processes of social dissolution and subsequent creation of geographic-linguistic entities in medieval Europe. After all, the emergence of ten new nations out of the ruins of the Spanish empire had few precedents in history, and posed startling questions about their future. Intellectually and personally, the London years are probably the source of Bello's most enduring philological, grammatical, and literary interests.

Four of the pieces included in the language section of this collection were written during Bello's London years. Though on the surface some of them appear to be quite specialized, they are animated by two central concerns, which can only be understood fully in the context of historical developments resulting from the breakdown of the Spanish empire: Bello may have had some doubts about the fate of the independence movements in the 1810s, but by the early 1820s he was convinced that the revolutions had succeeded or were about to succeed in most places in the continent. One of Bello's central objectives was to provide a document, both aesthetic and political, about the meaning of independence, and the tasks that lie ahead. As early as 1823, with his **"Allocution to Poetry,"** he launched perhaps the first overview of independence as a continental phenomenon. From Mexico to Chile, Bello described the various movements as heroic Latin American responses to the desire for independent nationhood. In Bello's poem, political differences, civil war, and the agonizing confusion of the early independence period gave way to a foundational myth that celebrated the deeds of selfless patriots. In his **"Allocution,"** Bello provided the language and the events that served as the basis for the myth and aesthetics of independence. The **"Allocution"** is also a document for considering a less fortunate event in Bello's life. His inclusion of Francisco Miranda in the pantheon of Latin American heroes, and his rather lukewarm celebration of the deeds of Simón Bolívar, may have caused his downfall in the eyes of the Liberator and some of his followers. As indicated above, it may also have influenced Bello's decision not to return to his native Venezuela.[13]

The other central matter to be addressed was the political organization of the new republics. Independence could be a fact, but the biggest challenge in Bello's eyes was the construction of a new political order. In this respect, he was confident that there was something that he could contribute from London, and from his unique perspective concerning matters of language. London, as he presents it in the prospectus of the first *Repertorio* issue, was well positioned to serve as the center for the dissemination of useful information to the new nations. Not only did England provide an example of political freedoms at work, but it was also the center of much needed trade. Bello was clearly proposing a new order for Latin America that would have England as its most important partner, if not model. As for Latin America itself, he envisioned an agricultural society of farmer-citizens who would alternate vigorous physical labor with the tasks of government. As presented in his justly famous **"Ode to Tropical Agriculture,"** Latin America would exploit its natural endowments for the ultimate aim of good government.

From a language perspective, and informed to a large extent by his research in medieval languages and litera-

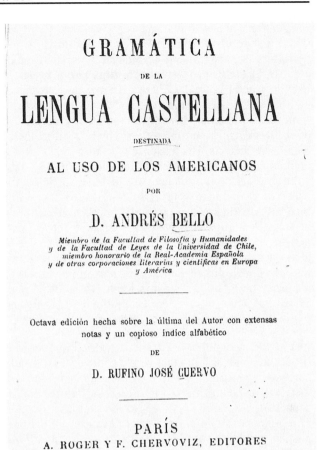

GRAMÁTICA

DE LA

LENGUA CASTELLANA

DESTINADA

AL USO DE LOS AMERICANOS

POR

D. ANDRÉS BELLO

*Miembro de la Facultad de Filosofía y Humanidades
y de la Facultad de Leyes de la Universidad de Chile,
miembro honorario de la Real-Academia Española
y de otras corporaciones literarias y científicas en Europa
y América*

Octava edición hecha sobre la última del Autor con extensas
notas y un copioso índice alfabético

DE

D. RUFINO JOSÉ CUERVO

PARÍS

A. ROGER Y F. CHERVOVIZ, EDITORES

7, RUE DES GRANDS-AUGUSTINS, 7

1903

Propiedad de los editores

tures, Bello also articulated a rationale for the defense of a Spanish language that would be uniquely Latin American, and that would undergird the new political order. Bello understood quite early that such a new arrangement could succeed only to the extent that Spanish America became united in terms of purpose and language. Unity in commercial and political terms was essential to the success of the post-colonial order, and England appeared to be ready to support such a process. But more problematic was the unity of language now that the peninsular Spanish center no longer held. It was essential, in Bello's view, to strengthen unity by producing a language that was more responsive to Spanish American needs. In essence, as illustrated by his first article on orthography published in London in 1823, he sought a simplicity of rules that would make the acquisition of educated Spanish easier for the larger, mostly illiterate or semi-literate, population. Spanish Americans would, in his view, have an easier learning experience if they could establish a closer correspondence between speech and the alphabet. In terms of ultimate objectives, Bello believed that only an educated population, steeped in a common language, could ensure the stability of the new political order.

Long after the new order had been secured, Bello insisted on the necessity of clear rules not only for the writing of Spanish, as can be seen in his second major defense of a Spanish American orthography in 1843, but for general grammar. Even from the most stable of nations—at least by nineteenth-century standards—Bello often expressed his concern about the dissolution of core languages and their fragmentation into incommunicable dialects. His response was a rationale for the predominance of the written word over a primarily oral culture. This predominance would have to be established by a grammar specifically designed for the use of Spanish Americans, and promoted at the highest levels of state. Nothing else—education and the law in particular—could succeed if the fundamental basis of language was not firmly established. This central concern initially developed in London, with the publication of his essay on **"The Origin and Progress of the Art of Writing,"** which was primarily a rationale for viewing the written word as the culmination of civilized order.

Just as the recognition of independence led to questions about the political order that would follow, Bello's early language concerns evolved from foundational myths, in the form of poems, to reform proposals for specific aspects of the Spanish language, to the ultimate adoption of a grammar. Bello did not succeed in each of his proposals, but his *Gramática de la Lengua Castellana destinada al uso de los Americanos* did, providing him not only with the rare recognition—indeed the first for a former subject of the Spanish empire—of the Royal Academy but also with the publication of more than seventy editions of his work in such countries as Chile, Venezuela, Colombia, Peru, Argentina, and Spain itself. This single work continues to be studied and reprinted, undoubtedly because of its inherent qualities, but also because it contained a most practical response to the complexities of establishing a new political order in Spanish America.[14]

What was Bello's blueprint, from the unlikely field of grammatical studies, for addressing the central issues of nation-building in nineteenth-century Latin America? Quite simply, to reform and adjust the institutions of Spain to the new realities of the Spanish American nations; to establish needed continuities between past and present, especially at the level of literature and culture; and to establish a well-regulated language firmly rooted in the ancient traditions of Spain, yet responsive to changing Spanish American realities. When placed in the context of the more radical solutions offered by Domingo Faustino Sarmiento, Francisco Bilbao, José Victorino Lastarria, and many others around the continent who wanted a cleaner break with the Hispanic past, Bello's blueprint appeared hopelessly conservative. But it was successful precisely because it was moderate: it offered a rationale for the reconciliation of tradition and change, past and present, that a war-torn region eager to

achieve stability, prosperity—or both—could understand. And it offered more than a solution to contemporary issues and debates; it offered a long-term plan for the education of the new generations that would make independence, both cultural and political, a reality.

Three of the selections in the language section illustrate Bello's fundamental views on grammar. The earliest is his **"Ideological Analysis of the Tenses of the Spanish Conjugation,"** published in 1841, but probably prepared in Caracas before 1810. In it, he shows an early concern for the need to systematize verb tenses (in disarray on both sides of the Atlantic) without postulating the existence of a universal grammar for all languages, as more optimistic eighteenth-century logicians had proposed. This early statement would serve as the basis for his fuller argumentation in favor of a national grammar. By "national," however, Bello did not mean a grammar for each of the nations of Latin America. That is precisely what he most vehemently tried to avoid. "National" was meant as a geographic-linguistic category, as a grammar of the Spanish language. The title of his grammatical masterwork, however, adds the telling subtitle of "for the use of Spanish Americans." This is on the surface a problematic subtitle, but key to understanding his grammatical position and the reasons for his success. Bello differed sharply from other Spanish Americans who understood the direct relationship between language and nationhood just as he did, but who wanted local usage to be the means for the assertion of independence and national identity. Bello, for his part, did not seek to separate peninsular from Latin American Spanish, but rather to organize the Spanish language as spoken in Latin America on the basis of categories that responded directly to the linguistic practices of the continent. He was not seeking new languages, separate from one another and from their linguistic source. Rather, he insisted on a point that is particularly poignant in both the grammar article of 1832 and the prologue of the *Gramática* in 1847, both included in this section: The Spanish Royal Academy could not serve as a useful model for contemporary Spanish on either side of the Atlantic because of its insistence on basing grammar on the model of the Latin language. Bello demonstrated that Latin grammatical categories not only did not conform to, but in fact obscured, an understanding of the grammatical workings of Spanish. Latin categories constrained the verb, and, as shown by various examples of peninsular orthography, they also imposed etymology as a criterion for spelling, a practice that made the acquisition of literate Spanish difficult for people just making the transition from oral to written language. Bello's grammar was thus an argument for systematization within the parameters of the Spanish language, independent from other languages or from abstract logical categories.[15] This search for uniqueness and balance is, in many ways, a linguistic counterpart to Bello's hopes for the larger process of Latin American nation-building.

Although Bello's key writings on language were published between the 1820s and 1840s, they reflect much longer and more central concerns than this relatively short period would suggest. They speak of Bello's unique contribution to political developments in nineteenth-century Latin America. On the basis of his early education, combined with his London experience, Bello understood that it was in the area of language that he could effect the most profound changes in Latin American society. Language rooted him firmly in ancient tradition and a community of nations. The study of language provided him with a sense of how reform could be accomplished within tradition, and how language could provide the sort of unity that was essential for post-colonial Latin America. In a region divided by numerous cleavages (economic, social, and cultural, among others), language could serve an important integrating role in that it could not only provide a bridge between literate groups and the larger population, but also cement the sense of nationhood so vital for order and stability.

EDUCATION AND HISTORY

An examination of his major activities in Chile, beginning with the creation of an educational system and the development of the field of history, demonstrate that Bello's philosophy of language informed these two key areas of nation-building: his experience with language studies allowed him to develop views of education and history as sources of national unity. In each of these areas, one can see the same principles at work: Bello tried to reconcile tradition and change; use rather than reject the Hispanic past; and build a sense of nationhood that was not separate from the larger community of nations. Both areas, in addition, required the firm establishment of a culture based on the written word. Indeed, his view of a community of nations depended heavily on the extent that they shared a written language that could bring the past into the present, benefit from the same sources of knowledge, and be easily and massively disseminated.

Upon his arrival in Chile in 1829, Bello was soon seen as a major intellectual force who could develop Chile's fledgling educational system. Education had been a long-term concern (sometimes a necessity) of his, as seen in his teaching and tutoring activities in Caracas and London. In the latter city, he studied the teaching techniques of Joseph Lancaster with a view to its possible application in Latin America (he was not convinced). But it was in Chile that he devoted concentrated attention to educational matters. His views on education were usually articulated in the context of spe-

cific reforms or institutional obligations, or sometimes in the heat of debate, but in all cases one can see important connections to the building of a new political order.[16]

The study of the evolution of Bello's thinking on education can be framed in the context of a search for the means to spread literacy in order to make the concept of citizenship—and therefore nationhood—a reality. Once Bello understood that the change in political regime from monarchy to republic called for the authority of the law and the institutions of representative government, he viewed education as the principal means for the introduction of civic values into the larger population. Bello's writing style sometimes makes it difficult to discern what was most important to him: education of the larger population or education of the elite; religious education or secular education; humanities or sciences. But this difficulty can be easily overcome once one understands that at different times he was emphasizing different aspects of the same overall project: there must be a national system of education, closely supervised and supported by the state, in order to bring literacy to the larger population so that citizens could contribute and become loyal to the workings of representative government. That education should also bring in several other elements: religion, which he viewed as indispensable for public and private morality; respect for Hispanic traditions stretching back to Roman origins; and a practical emphasis that would provide the citizenry with the instruments to benefit from the scientific and technological advances of the contemporary world. Bello was very (perhaps overly) confident that all of these disparate elements could be reconciled. Such confidence depended on the ability of the state to provide a space for education to flourish despite increasingly divisive partisan politics. That ability was eroding even during Bello's lifetime. But for as long as he was an actor on the educational stage, he operated as if education could create a sense of citizenship that was at once socially constructive and privately liberating.

One of the selections in this collection speaks directly to the centrality of primary education as the vehicle for the construction of citizenship. Bello's **"The Aims of Education,"** published in 1836, makes a case for the necessity of universal primary education in political, economic, and moral terms. A republic, Bello argued, cannot survive without an educated citizenry aware of its rights and responsibilities. At this early date, he proposed some practical solutions that would guide the successful development of national education in subsequent years: the establishment of a strong tutelary role for the state in education; and the creation of teacher-training schools. As a more subtle, but no less important point in this essay, Bello established a rationale for education as a means to instill civic values strongly informed by religion.

This is, in fact, the thread that ties all of his educational writings, be they of a more philosophical or a more practical hue: there must be an institutional machinery that links individual and society in a series of interlocking mechanisms; and there must be a strong philosophical principle that guides the system by reconciling the religious and secular worlds, and by bringing Chileans close to the spiritual and intellectual accomplishments of humanity.[17] It is in this context that one can understand his eloquent and insistent defense of the need for constantly expanding the moral and intellectual horizons of the population. While government institutions were necessary, it was also important to bring the population to a stage of self-imposed civic virtue.

Perhaps no work of Bello summarizes these views better than his inaugural speech at the University of Chile in 1843. It is a carefully crafted presentation that, in addition to placing the university at the center of national education, establishes a key political and educational principle, one that comes closest to defining his intellectual outlook, and the most important challenge for independent nations in nineteenth-century Latin America: the extent and meaning of the concept of freedom. Freedom may have meant military victory and political emancipation from Spain. To some, it continued to mean the destruction of the Hispanic legacy. But in a context of nation building, freedom must be closely connected with, perhaps even subordinated to, the concept of order. Bello did not think that one concept contradicted the other. Quite to the contrary, it was Bello's conviction that there could be no true freedom without restraints on personal and political passions. Order, therefore, had political and moral connotations. The challenge was to move nations from the external imposition of order to an internalized self-discipline that achieved social and political stability while ensuring civic and personal freedoms.

How to achieve such an aspect of the concept of order? Bello's unequivocal answer was: through the cultivation of reason understood in moral and intellectual terms, and disseminated through appropriate educational institutions. This required a humanistic culture in which religious and secular traditions were reconciled and encouraged. That is the reason he defended the study of Latin and advocated an approach to jurisprudence that transcended legal practice; both could connect Latin Americans to a long humanistic tradition as well as a sense of the historical search for social and political order. It is in this context that one can understand Bello's appeal to the religious community not merely to join in the educational efforts of the government, but to understand the benefits to be accrued by exposure to secular traditions. It is in this context, finally, that Bello's elaborate construction of a national educational machinery can be understood: order would come from widely shared values based on a humanistic tradition that also encouraged participation in the political and economic life of the nation.

Underlying Bello's educational views was his determination to separate all levels of education from the political divisiveness that was all too present as Latin American nations, Chile included, experimented with new political systems. One key area where education was likely to be politicized was history, for its study involved competing interpretations of the past and disparate political proposals for the future. At the same time, it could be a significant instrument for building a sense of nationhood, and thus he encouraged its cultivation at the university. As a result, in the 1840s Bello wrote a series of articles on history that provides significant insights into his views not just on the discipline, but on the task of defining a past that was consistent with his larger vision of order.

The occasion for Bello's reflections on history was provided by José Victorino Lastarria's essay on the colonial legacy of Spain, presented in 1844.[18] In this essay, Lastarria invited the rejection of the Iberian past in order to build a truly free and independent future, and claimed that his conclusions were based on the impartial and objective examination of historical facts. He also claimed that it was his search for objectivity that prevented him from writing about the more recent events of independence, where impartiality was nearly impossible. Bello replied by contesting both the interpretation of the past and Lastarria's historiographical choices and assumptions. In the process, he produced a rationale for an approach to history that could serve both the advancement of the field and the larger process of nation building.[19]

An important element in this discussion was treatment of the delicate issue of how Chile was to view itself vis-à-vis its colonial past. It was at this time, in the 1830s and 1840s, that Chile was negotiating the reestablishment of relations with Spain. All of this called for reflection on matters that went far beyond historical scholarship. Bello's position, as indicated above, was informed by his experience with language studies, which was in turn the product of a search for the rise of national identities and their linkages to previous traditions. The history of Chile included the Spanish imperial past, and both history and the country would be ill-served by summarily rejecting it. Spain was the bridge to a Roman past as well as to legal and literary traditions that Chile could not afford to do without. But more than an argument for utility, in Bello's response there was a statement about the historical development of nations: empires dissolved and new national configurations emerged. Traditions meshed (though some predominated, like Roman traditions in Spain, and Iberian traditions in Latin America), and they called for study and reflection rather than rejection in the name of emancipation and freedom.

Bello could not be comfortable with Lastarria's interpretation of the past, which was more of a call to destroy the persistence of Spanish institutions in independent Chile. This call depended on the assessment of historical events, and therefore questions had to be asked about historical scholarship *the craft itself*. Beginning with his comments on the **"Investigations,"** but especially in the **"Historical Sketch"** and **"The Craft of History,"** Bello rejected, though not as completely as claimed by Jacinto Chacón—a history teacher friendly to Lastarria's views—the vogue of a "philosophical" approach to history that dispensed with the cumbersome establishment and description of historical facts.[20] What was important to the propounders of the "philosophy of history" was to determine the general direction of historical developments, which in the case of Chile called for a radical break with the past. In the essay on historical scholarship **"The Craft of History"** included in Part Two, Bello presented a case for the need to work on original documents and manuscripts, for the need to carefully establish evidence and context before interpretations, philosophical or otherwise, could be produced. Although this was not known in detail until recently, Bello was speaking from actual experience working with medieval manuscripts at the British Museum.[21] His reconstruction of the origins and development of vernacular Spanish had given him a sense of the importance of documentation, and explains the insistence with which he drove home this point. A history that did not carefully and thoughtfully establish its evidence was likely to lead to misinterpretation and political manipulation. Chile could ill afford the prospect of political divisiveness resulting from a misunderstanding of the past.

An interesting aspect of the debate is that many if not most of Bello's references to historical works were of European origin. But it would be mistaken to conclude from this use of illustrations that he advocated a "European" model. On the contrary, it is in his historical reflections that we find the most explicit arguments in favor of a scholarship using Chilean sources, and written with due consideration to the Chilean peculiarities of geography, economics, and social development. As in his grammatical pieces, Bello took into consideration other models (like Latin and some aspects of the "universal" grammar of eighteenth-century thinkers) but was decidedly in favor of a history that emerged from, and developed its own categories to interpret, Chilean events. If there was anything to imitate from European models, it was "independence of thought." A corollary of this emphasis was, in disagreement with Lastarria's protests of objectivity, that no aspect of Chilean history was closed to scrutiny as long as it combined factual accuracy, judgment, and accountability. In particular, Bello advocated research on Chilean events since independence and, in his capacity as Rector of the University of Chile, commissioned several works on the subject that provided the basis for Chilean historiography.

Bello spoke on historical matters on the basis of his own experience with the field, and on the basis of his assessment of how history could either be a divisive element or an important vehicle for the construction of national unity. In both cases, it is the larger project of nation building that informed his historical interests. Language, education, and history were all significant elements in Bello's search for national unity. With different degrees of emphasis, these were his fundamental intellectual concerns. But there is still an important part of his work, and an important ingredient in the construction of a new political order, that needs to be addressed and which is perhaps the most difficult: the establishment of the rule of law in a context of political freedom.

LAW, POLITICS, AND INTERNATIONAL RELATIONS

First, it is important to establish the vicissitudes of Bello's own political development. He was, after all, a faithful servant of the colonial regime who found himself in the midst of the whirlwind of independence, pronounced himself at one point in favor of a limited monarchy, and eventually embraced the republican system with conviction. There is no sharp break or transition from one political advocacy to the other, and in effect there is a clear thread uniting the two. Bello's fundamental concern was social and political order; the form of government, although by no means unimportant, was subordinated to the larger project of achieving functioning institutions that responded to local conditions without being separate, or militantly distinct, from the rest of the world.

Bello's experience of nineteen years in England, where he examined first hand the emergence of a new world order in the post-Waterloo years, but most importantly where he saw the political system of England at work, inclined him in favor of a constitutional monarchy. Perhaps the key distinction—not always understood by Bello's critics—between traditional monarchy (as exemplified by Ferdinand VII in Spain in the 1820s) and constitutional monarchy is the legitimacy of popular sovereignty recognized by the latter. In the post-independence period, Bello defended constitutional monarchy precisely because of its recognition of popular sovereignty, which reflected his own evolving political views. As it is clarified in his letter to the Mexican advocate of independence, Servando Teresa de Mier (included in this collection) Bello's recommendation for a constitutional monarchy was qualified and mild, but brought him both short and long term problems. His letter was intercepted and played a role in his isolation from his country in the 1820s, and perhaps contributed to his decision to serve the Chilean legation in London and to eventually move to Chile. Since Bello never disclaimed his inclination, and even continued to affirm that monarchy was not intrinsically a bad political system, he was continually under attack for his allegedly conservative views.

In practice, Bello did not advocate monarchy as *the* political system for Latin America. He wanted to achieve order at a time when examples of good government could more often come from constitutional monarchies than from fledgling republics. His own arrival in Chile was punctuated by a civil war resulting from political experimentation along republican lines in the 1820s. Order, it appeared to him and others in Chile, could only be ensured by a political system that provided for strong executive powers, limited the number of elected offices, especially at the provincial level, and discouraged popular mobilization. The issue was not finding the most perfect political system, but simply one that would work given the peculiar conditions and challenges of the post-independence period. The result was, in the case of Chile (where Bello had influential supporters) a strong, even authoritarian, centralized government that also contained the potential for subsequent liberalization. Bello's support for the 1833 constitution, which he may have helped craft, is made clear in his **"Reforms of the Constitution"** essay included in this section.[22] This is the constitution that would prove to be one of the most durable in Latin America, lasting until 1925. But more than for its longevity, this constitution is significant for the institutional framework that it provided to establish and consolidate the republic.

Bello's fundamental concern about order had both internal and external aspects. Bello's work in these two areas translated into two masterpieces, the *Principios de Derecho Internacional* and the *Código Civil*. Both were enormously influential works that were repeatedly edited, printed, and even plagiarized. The first guided the external relations of the Spanish American nations and informed the principles that culminated in the creation of the Organization of American States. The second, which is still in use, was adopted by several nations in the region, including Colombia, Ecuador, and Nicaragua. Understandably, both works have invited enormous amounts of commentary, much of it extremely specialized and confined to the fields of international and civil law. But they have a larger significance in the context of the emergence of Latin American nations as independent republics and the construction of a domestic blueprint for order that was not simply a copy of European models (the French civil code most often comes to mind).[23]

Both the **"Principios"** and the *Código Civil* have their own intellectual history, and the contents of both are illustrated in this section by related essays and selections from the volumes themselves. The **"Principios,"** as already indicated, was the product of a search for Latin America's position in the new international order. The literature on international law available in the 1820s and 1830s did not take into consideration the emergence of the new Latin American nations. Its limited focus on non-European areas was insufficient for guiding the international relations of nations that viewed themselves as independent and sovereign. Bello's major concern was, on the one hand, to provide an adaptation of the existing literature to the new phenomenon of independence, and, on the other, to work toward the recognition of nationhood by other countries from his position as a high official in the ministry of foreign relations. One of the fundamental elements of the **"Principios"** is its emphasis on the equality of nations, regardless of their political system or the way in which they originated as countries. In a new world order that included the nations of Latin America, countries were only required to exercise their sovereignty by providing for internal order and by appointing representative officials for the conduct of affairs that concerned relations with other nations.[24]

From the more practical standpoint, Bello was centrally involved in the search for the recognition of independence and nationhood on the part of Spain. This was an extremely delicate political issue that had implications for national unity and identity, as indicated in my previous comments on national language, education, and history. But Bello was able to demonstrate that there was little to lose, and much to gain, from the recognition of independent nationhood by the former empire. For one thing, Latin America was still outside the pale of international law, and other European nations could support Spain, as in fact they did, in its search for what it considered legitimate claims. Achieving the recognition of Spain itself would substantially reduce that threat. There was also the matter of the benefits to be accrued by trade and other exchanges in a context of peace. At any rate, the very rationale for reestablishing relations between Chile and Spain, which materialized in 1844, (Mexico and Spain reestablished relations earlier, in 1836) was part of the larger project of securing the position of the Latin American republics on a firm international legal basis. His thoughts on the desirability of a Latin American congress—although partly dismissed later as experience proved the difficulties of balancing national and supra-national interests—also reveal Bello's emphasis on the search for international arrangements sustained by the rule of law.

The search for this legitimate international position was not unrelated to internal order. Countries would not be able to deal with other nations without a political system that was legitimate and ensured accountability. Bello's view of internal order, however, went beyond the achievement of a strong government able to impose its will on the citizenry. Bello hoped that order would be internalized in the form of civic virtue and practice. Order could not be achieved if the laws were not seen as just and beneficial, and were consequently not observed, or if governments were expected to move the country forward without the understanding and support of the larger society.

Bello's *Código Civil* was prepared with the aim of reducing the areas of conflict most likely to engage the citizenry and therefore threaten both the internal and external components of the larger vision. The very structure of the work, which occupied him for more than twenty years, reveals a search for clear rules and regulations to guide the conduct of complex, yet central, human affairs. The major areas covered in the 2,525 articles of the Civil Code include (1) definitions of personal status (marital, national, residential, juridical, etc.); (2) control, possession, and use of assets; (3) matters of inheritance and donations; and (4) contracts and other obligations. That is, the multiplicity of daily human affairs whose lack of attention had led either to litigation without uniform results, or simply neglect and abuse. Latin American nations up to the promulgation of the civil code only had the old imperial legislation to deal with the changing realities of independent nations that were in addition more complex and more a part of the larger world. Bello's work provided a precedent and a model for other nations to follow.

Bello's *Código Civil* is justly considered a masterpiece because it involved a compilation and elaboration of numerous sources, from modern legislation to traditional Hispanic documents, in order to respond to peculiar national conditions. While the work called for civil legislation covering a number of private issues, it still provided recognition to the Church on matters of marriage. A union that was acceptable to the Church was also legitimate for civil law. Just as in his other intellectual endeavors, Bello made sure that tradition and change would be reconciled, that the guiding elements of the new political order would combine the best civil legislation of the past with the best of the present, and that there would be a role for religion. Bello's civil code was promulgated into law in 1855, and although modified in several parts, it continues to be used today, in Chile and elsewhere, a testimony to the applicability of its central principles.

CONCLUSION

The massive extent and variety of Bello's writings are only superficially difficult to assess. The fundamental motive for Bello's intellectual activity was the achievement of order, which he explored from at least three angles: individual, national, and international. In the process, he invited the reconciliation of ancient and modern traditions, religious and secular thought, and argued in favor of a strong yet liberalizing state that instilled civic virtues through education in the larger population so that representative government could be predictable and self-sustaining.

Bello's position in the history of Latin America is strong and secure, but unfortunately misunderstood. There are numerous examples of esteem for Bello's contributions. There are also deserved tributes to his scholarly stature and his poetic achievements. But there is little reflection, especially in English, about the relationship between Bello's intellectual production and the fundamental issues of that critical period in Latin American history: the creation and consolidation of nationhood. This is certainly a historical concern: we need to better understand Bello, and we need to better understand the intellectual and political history of Latin America. But the issue of how to respond to change and construct appropriate institutions and arrangements goes beyond the field of history; it relates to the resources that intellectuals at all times have mustered, often in very creative ways, to offer solutions to contemporary problems. Bello witnessed the dissolution of the Spanish empire in America, and contemplated with no small concern the available options. That he would go back to the medieval chronicles—and even farther back to Roman law—to construct one of the most enduring blueprints for order and stability in the nineteenth century, reveals a great deal about the ingenuity of Bello and the resources offered to him by a humanistic tradition. The following selection will illustrate both the richness and variety of Bello's thought, as well as the complexity of the issues involving the process of national consolidation in Latin America.

Notes

1. The best comprehensive biographies of Andrés Bello's life and works include Miguel Luis Amunátegui, *Vida de don Andrés Bello* (Santiago: Imprenta Pedro G. Ramírez, 1882); Rafael Caldera, *Andrés Bello* 7th ed. (Caracas: Editorial Dimensiones, 1981). First published in 1935, Caldera's book has been translated into English as *Andrés Bello: Philosopher, Poet, Philologist, Educator, Legislator, Statesman,* trans. by John Street (Caracas: La Casa de Bello, 1994); Emir Rodríguez Monegal, *El Otro Andrés Bello* (Caracas: Monte-Avila Editores, 1969); and Fernando Murillo Rubiera, *Andrés Bello: Historia de una Vida y de una Obra* (Caracas: La Casa de Bello, 1986). Among the most lucid studies of Bello's various intellectual endeavors is Pedro Grases, *Estudios sobre Andrés Bello,* 2 vols. (Barcelona: Editorial Seix Barral, 1981).

2. An important collection of essays on Bello's life in Caracas, where he lived from 1781 to 1810 is La Casa de Bello, *Bello y Caracas* (Caracas: La

Casa de Bello, 1979). See also John V. Lombardi, *Venezuela: The Search for Order, the Dream of Progress* (New York: Oxford University Press, 1982), and Caracciolo Parra-Pérez, *Historia de la Primera República de Venezuela* (Caracas: Biblioteca Ayacucho, 1992).

3. For a description of higher education in Venezuela at the time of Bello's life in Caracas see Caracciolo Parra-León, *Filosofía Universitaria Venezolana*, in *Obras* (Madrid: Editorial J. B., 1954).

4. The England that Bello encountered upon arrival in London, and much of the background to independence as well as British policy to it, has been described by William Spence Robertson, *The Life of Miranda*, 2 vols. (New York: Cooper Square Publishers, 1969). On the various facets of Bello's life in London, see the essays collected in La Casa de Bello, *Bello y Londres*, 2 vols. (Caracas: La Casa de Bello, 1981). See also John Lynch, ed., *Bello: The London Years* (Richmond, Surrey: The Richmond Publishing Co., 1982), and Karen L. Racine, "Imagining Independence: London's Spanish American Community, 1790-1830," (Ph.D. Dissertation, Tulane? University, 1996).

5. Simón Bolívar and Andrés Bello exchanged twelve letters between 1826 and 1828. They have been collected in vol. 25 of Bello's *Obras Completas*, 26 vols. (Caracas: La Casa de Bello, 1981-86). Bolívar's frustration at the imminent departure of Bello can be seen in his letter to José Fernández Madrid dated April 29, 1829, included in Bello, *Obras*, vol. 26, p. 9.

6. A collection of essays on the various activities of Bello in Chile is La Casa de Bello, *Bello y Chile*, 2 vols. (Caracas: La Casa de Bello, 1981). See also Guillermo Feliú Cruz, *Andrés Bello y la Redacción de los Documentos Oficiales Administrativos, Internacionales y Legislativos de Chile* (Caracas: Biblioteca de los Tribunales del Distrito Federal, Fundación Rojas Astudillo, 1957), and Simon Collier, *Ideas and Politics of Chilean Independence, 1808-1833* (Cambridge: Cambridge University Press, 1967).

7. See Sol Serrano, *Universidad y Nación: Chile en el Siglo XIX* (Santiago: Editorial Universitaria, 1994), and Iván Jaksić and Sol Serrano, "In the Service of the Nation: The Establishment and Consolidation of the Universidad de Chile, 1842-1879," *Hispanic American Historical Review* 70, No. 1 (1990): 139-171.

8. The complexities of this transition have been discussed by Tulio Halperín-Donghi, *Reforma y Disolución de los Imperios Ibéricos, 1750-1850* (Madrid: Alianza Editorial, 1985). See also David

Bushnell and Neill Macauley, *The Emergence of Latin America in the Nineteenth Century*, 2nd ed. (New York: Oxford University Press, 1994); and Frank Safford, "Politics, Ideology and Society," in Leslie Bethell, ed., *Spanish America After Independence, c. 1820-c. 1870* (Cambridge: Cambridge University Press), 48-122.

9. Bello carried the primary responsibility for writing the articles of the *Gaceta* between 1808 and 1810; that is, the period from the Napoleonic invasion of the Iberian peninsula to the establishment of local governments in the colonies. There is a facsimile edition of the *Gaceta de Caracas, 1808-1810* (Paris: Établissements H. Dupuy, 1939).

10. A listing of the books in Miranda's library is in Arturo Uslar Pietri, *Los libros de Miranda* (Caracas: La Casa de Bello, 1979).

11. Bello's fourteen London notebooks are deposited in Box 94 of the Archivo Central Andrés Bello at the Biblioteca de la Universidad de Chile in Santiago, Chile. Marcelino Menéndez y Pelayo did not consult these notebooks, but learned about Bello's scholarship on Spanish medieval literature through Miguel Luis Amunátegui. It was Menéndez y Pelayo's impression that Bello had anticipated much of the research that would be conducted later in the Spanish peninsula. See his letters of 25 August 1885 and 26 February 1886 in Domingo Amunátegui Solar, *Archivo Epistolar de Don Miguel Luis Amunátegui*, vol. 2 (Santiago: Ediciones de la Universidad de Chile, 1942), pp. 678-681.

12. An important study of the Spanish exile community in London in the 1820s is by Vicente Lloréns, *Liberales y Románticos: Una Emigración Española en Inglaterra, 1823-1834*, 3d ed. (Madrid: Editorial Castalia, 1979). See also Diego Martínez Torrón, *Los Liberales Románticos Españoles ante la Descolonización Americana* (Madrid: Editorial MAPFRE, 1992).

13. Antonio Cussen, *Bello y Bolívar: Poetry and Politics in the Spanish American Revolution* (Cambridge: Cambridge University Press, 1992). See also the important discussion of Bello's poetry by Marcelino Menéndez y Pelayo in *Historia de la Poesía Hispano-Americana*, 2 vols. (Madrid: Librería General de Victoriano Suárez, 1911), I: 353-416.

14. An important study of the political uses of grammar in nineteenth-century Latin America is by Malcolm Deas, "Miguel Antonio Caro y Amigos: Gramática y Poder en Colombia," in Deas, *Del Poder y la Gramática (y Otros Ensayos sobre His-*

toria, Política y Literatura Colombiana) (Bogotá: Tercer Mundo Editores, 1993), pp. 25-60.

15. See the important study by Amado Alonso, "Introducción a los Estudios Gramaticales de Andrés Bello," in Bello, *Obras Completas,* vol. 4, pp. ix-lxxxvi, and his *Castellano, Español, Idioma Nacional: Historia Espiritual de Tres Nombres* 2nd. ed. (Buenos Aires: Editorial Losada, 1949). See also Lidia Contreras, *Historia de las Ideas Ortográficas en Chile* (Santiago: Centro de Investigaciones Diego Barros Arana, Biblioteca Nacional, 1993), and Barry L. Vellerman, "The *Gramiatica* of Andrés Bello: Source and methods" (Ph.D. Dissertation, University of Wiscousin-Madison, 1974).

16. Volumes 21 and 22 of Bello's *Obras Completas* compile Bello's writings on education. For an interpretation, see Julio César Jobet, *Doctrina y Praxis de los Educadores Representativos Chilenos* (Santiago: Editorial Andrés Bello, 1970), especially chapter 4: "Don Andrés Bello, Orientador de la Enseñanza de su Epoca," pp. 155-279.

17. On Bello's philosophy and its connection to education and politics, see Iván Jaksić, "Racionalismo y Fe: La Filosofía Chilena en la Epoca de Andrés Bello," *Historia,* Vol. 29 (1995-96): 89-123. See also O. Carlos Stoetzer, "The Political Ideas of Andrés Bello," *International Philosophical Quarterly* 23, No. 4 (December 1983): 395-406; and Antonio Scocozza, *Filosofía, Política y Derecho en Andrés Bello* (Caracas: La Casa de Bello, 1989).

18. The "Investigaciones Sobre la Influencia Social de la Conquista i del Sistema Colonial de los Españoles de Chile" by Lastarria first appeared in *Anales de la Universidad de Chile* No. 1 (1843-44): 199-271. It was reprinted in his *Miscelánea Histórica y Literaria,* vol. 1 (Valparaíso: Imprenta de la Patria, 1868), 3-136.

19. The historiographical implications of this debate have been amply covered by Allen L. Woll, *A Functional Past: The Uses of History in Nineteenth-Century Chile* (Baton Rouge and London: Louisiana State University Press, 1982).

20. See Jacinto Chacón's prologue to José Victorino Lastarria, *Bosquejo Histórico de la Constitución del Gobierno de Chile* (Santiago: Imprenta Chilena, 1847), pp. v-xxiv. For an examination of Lastarria's significance in nineteenth-century Chile, see Bernardo Subercaseaux, *Cultura y Sociedad Liberal en el Siglo XIX (Lastarria, Ideología y Literatura)* (Santiago: Editorial Aconcagua, 1981).

21. Pedro Grases points out that in addition to his studies in medieval literature, Bello produced an important historical piece, the *Resumen de la Historia de Venezuela* (1810). See his discussion of this work in his *Estudios sobre Andrés Bello,* vol. 1, pp. 109-277. Bello's historical works have been included in vol. 22 of his *Obras Completas.*

22. Bello's involvement in the writing of the 1833 constitution is suggested by Diego Portales, who was well positioned to know, in a letter to Antonio Garfias dated 3 August 1833. The relevant passage is cited in Feliú Cruz, *Andrés Bello y la Redacción,* pp. 310-311.

23. Bernardino Bravo Lira, "Difusión del Código Civil de Bello en los Países de Derecho Castellano y Portugués," in La Casa de Bello, *Andrés Bello y el Derecho Latinoamericano* (Caracas: La Casa de Bello, 1987), 343-373. See also John Henry Merryman, *The Civil Law Tradition,* 2nd ed. (Stanford: Stanford University Press, 1985), 58.

24. See Frank Griffith Dawson, "The Influence of Andrés Bello on Latin American Perceptions of Non-Intervention and State Responsibility," *The British Yearbook of International Law, 1986* (Oxford: The Clarendon Press, 1987), 253-315.

Iván Jaksić (essay date 2001)

SOURCE: Jaksić, Iván. "The Diplomacy of Independence." In *Andres Bello: Scholarship and Nation-Building in Nineteenth-Century Latin America,* pp. 63-93. Cambridge: Cambridge University Press, 2001.

[In the following excerpt, Jaksić considers Bello's role as a political figure representing the interests of Latin America in England, examining his relationships with other notable Latin American political figures and authors, and his Spanish language journals, Biblioteca Americana *and* El Repertorio Americano.*]*

London in the 1820s became the hub of diplomatic, financial, and cultural transactions between Great Britain and the newly independent countries of Latin America. After the fall of Napoleon, Great Britain was unquestionably the leading power in the world. No longer needing to maintain an alliance with Spain, the British government gradually moved from a steadfast policy of neutrality to a pragmatic policy of limited recognition of those countries of Spanish America that appeared to have made some headway in the consolidation of their states, and which offered beneficial terms of trade. It was a cautious policy, but caution was limited to official circles. Financial circles, and the investing public, rushed to buy Latin American bonds in the first half of the 1820s.

Spanish Americans who had languished in oblivion in London during the previous decade now found themselves the center of attention. They actively sought to accelerate the process of recognition, and aggressively promoted a view of the New World as a continent of boundless riches. They were catapulted into action by the liberal revolution led by Major Rafael Riego in Spain in 1820. This event, known as Riego's *pronunciamiento,* or military coup, curbed Ferdinand VII's absolutist rule by forcing the monarch to govern under the terms of the Constitution of 1812. Turmoil in Spain, combined with patriot victories in Spanish America, all but assured the independence of the continent. Even after the second "restoration" of King Ferdinand in 1823, Spanish American exiles in London could confidently conclude that Spanish imperial rule was finished. Thus, they devoted themselves to promoting recognition of the nation-states in various publication ventures. In the process, they collaborated closely with the wave of Spanish liberals fleeing the reactionary rule of Ferdinand VII. Together, they attempted to build bridges between Europe and the emerging nations of Latin America. Andrés Bello, in London since 1810, was now at the center of diplomatic and cultural activities. He emerged as a leading voice in the interpretation of European foreign policy, as well as in the articulation of a Spanish American response to the new opportunities and challenges of independence. Bello not only closely observed the policies of British Foreign Secretary, and then Prime Minister George Canning (1822-1827), but also had a chance to both exchange diplomatic correspondence with him, and eventually to meet him on the occasion of the treaty celebrated between Great Britain and Gran Colombia in 1825.

George Canning is generally acknowledged as the architect of British recognition of Spanish American independence. He contributed to the enshrining of his role in this history with the now famous dictum pronounced in the House of Commons on December 12, 1826: "I called the New World into existence to redress the balance of the Old." It is well worth remembering, however, that Lord Castlereagh, his predecessor (1812-1822), had already taken the substantial step of recognizing Spanish American flags in British ports in 1822. It is also important to remember that European politics dictated a British response to French—and Holy Alliance—intervention in Spain in 1823, which raised the perennial question of the status of Spanish America under the absolutist rule of Ferdinand VII. There was, in addition, the 1822 recognition by the United States of the independence of the republics to the south, and President James Monroe's warning against European intervention in December 1823. Although the United States was in no position to prevent any such intervention, it challenged European, including Russian interests in the Western Hemisphere.[1]

Finally, it is important to remember that Canning actually delayed recognition of Spanish American independence in the hope that these countries would adopt monarchical institutions once they understood the signals coming from his office. Therefore, until 1824, when Canning could no longer delay recognition of independence, Spanish Americans concluded that there would be no British recognition without serious consideration of a monarchical political model.[2] As seen in Chapter 2, Bello's queries to Blanco White and his statements to Fr. Servando Teresa de Mier on constitutional monarchy represented a sensible reading of the intentions of official British policy. This was the policy that Bello tried to convey both officially and unofficially to various friends and Spanish American states.

Bello's role in Spanish American diplomacy was not a happy one, largely because the expectations of both Great Britain and Spanish America were so quickly and so painfully disappointed in the 1820s. But for a time, such expectations appeared to be realistic, and Bello and others allowed themselves, perhaps naively, to believe that the recognition of independence heralded a new era of world politics and civilization. Travelers went back and forth; books, articles, and reports provided abundant information about the new countries; trade and finance reached unprecedented levels. For a fleeting moment in the 1820s, Great Britain and Spanish America appeared poised to show that a new era had indeed begun. The illusion was soon to be dispelled.

THE CULTURAL OFFENSIVE

Aware that the tide was slowly turning in the direction, or at least the possibility, of a patriot victory, Spanish Americans in London in the early 1820s launched a series of efforts to spread news and information about the prospects and promise of an independent Latin America. As we have seen, Bello had already served as one of the primary sources of news on South American affairs since 1810. He had provided information to Blanco White and James Mill, and his work on the English-language publications *Interesting Official Documents Relating to the United Provinces of Venezuela,* and *Outline of the Revolution in Spanish America* are a clear indication of this side of his activity. The political climate of the 1820s was even more conducive to the placing of news, because the emergence of the new republics generated strong demand for information about the New World.

By inclination as well as a sense of duty, Bello became actively involved in the publication of Spanish-language materials in the 1820s. His purpose was to make information available in London, and also to distribute it to the new countries of Spanish America at a time when they were more likely to learn about one another from London, effectively the capital of the world, than directly from each other. The three journals to which Bello contributed allowed him not only to publish the results of his own research, but also to bring the dimension of culture into the emerging definitions of independence and nationhood. These journals were committed to the spreading of useful information, but they had a political purpose as well.[3]

Such a political purpose was clearest in *El Censor Americano,* a journal published by Antonio José de Irisarri in London in 1820. The journal openly advocated constitutional monarchy, an advocacy that few wanted to maintain, or even remember, by the middle of the decade, but which was very much a reasonable option at the time. Bello did not sign any articles in this periodical, but his participation in it was established by Irisarri himself, who on June 16, 1820, invited Bello to write for the journal: "please join me and take an active part in this endeavor by sending me your interesting writings . . . consider yourself my official collaborator from this moment on."[4] Bello did indeed oblige. Later, Irisarri recalled that "I published a monthly periodical under the title *El Censor Americano,* where my purpose was to point to the accomplishments as well as errors of the governments of America in their new political trajectory. The result was a thick volume that has some value for what I contributed, but mostly because of the articles by the erudite and very kind Mr. Bello."[5]

The subjects of *El Censor Americano* have the imprimatur of Irisarri, but Bello's contributions are also clear, especially on subjects that were of direct interest to him, and about which he would write more in the future. Issues No. 3 (September 1820) and No. 4 (October 1820), for example, contain articles such as **"To-pografía de la Provincia de Cumaná," ["Topography of the Province of Cumaná, Venezuela"]** an area that Bello knew intimately from his visits as a young man to his father; additional extracts from Humboldt's *Personal Narrative of Travels to the Equinoctial Regions of America*; and an article on smallpox vaccination. Even the more political writings were in line with statements that Bello had made to Blanco White and Mier concerning constitutional monarchy. "To the argument that the times are not favorable to kings, because monarchies are everywhere being reformed," asserted the journal, "we answer that the times may not be favorable to despotic kings, but they are certainly favorable to the establishment of moderate monarchies, which are the favorite system of the day."[6] In the climate of the early 1820s, Bello and Irisarri shared similar political ideas. Although such ideas evolved with the events of independence, it is important to note that Bello's emphasis on practical and scientific information became established during his collaboration with *El Censor Americano.*

Bello developed these interests much more fully in the journal *Biblioteca Americana,* published in London in 1823.[7] This publication was founded by a so-called

"Sociedad de Americanos," but the main writers were Bello and the Colombian intellectual and diplomat Juan García del Río, who had arrived in London as an envoy of General José de San Martín the year before.[8] Born in Cartagena, Colombia, García del Río had been active in the periodical press in Lima. Even before he departed for England, he had determined to publish news on developments in the region in London. On his way there in 1822, he wrote to Chilean Foreign Minister Joaquín Echeverría: "please remember what I requested from Mendoza. Alert Don Manuel de Salas about my project, and encourage him to send me articles for publication in Europe, such as interesting manuscripts, statistical information, biographies and portraits of illustrious Chileans, plans of all kinds . . . all of this will serve my purpose."[9] This was Bello's own purpose, and in London the two writers soon initiated one of the most productive Spanish American intellectual collaborations of the early independence period. They had to interrupt publication of the journal after only the second volume because of costs and other demands on their time, but they resumed their collaboration with *El Repertorio Americano,* publishing four volumes between 1826 and 1827.

As described in Chapter 2, these journals became the vehicles for Bello's poetic writings and some of his research on medieval literature. Beginning with the *Biblioteca Americana,* he also published works that were specifically designed to disseminate useful knowledge in the new republics. Foremost among the practical matters that Bello thought needed circulation in Spanish America was knowledge of the geography, products, and species of the region. The *Biblioteca*'s statement of editorial policy indicated that "Spanish [colonial] policy kept the doors of America closed for three centuries to the countries of the world. Not content with depriving the continent of communication with the world, Spain also prevented it from knowing itself."[10] The themes of knowledge and liberation were also prominently highlighted by the journal's choice of a motto, from Petrarch's *Rime*:

> Dunque ora è'l tempo da ritrare il collo
> Dal giogo antico, e da squarciare il velo
> Ch'è stato avolto intorno a gli occhi nostri
>
> [Now is the time to free our neck and brace
> Ourselves after the yoke, and tear the veil
> That has been swaddled all around our eyes]

Bello's role as editor was to translate, extract, and prepare review articles on such subjects as magnetism, chemistry, mountain ranges, as well as the flora and fauna of the region. Many of these articles were translated from English and French publications, and were designed to both convey information as well as illustrate how scientific research was conducted in Europe. Other contributors to the periodical did likewise, but a division of labor existed, as was clearest in the case of García del Río, who concentrated on social and political writings.

One article that was signed jointly by García del Río and Bello was **"Indicaciones sobre la Conveniencia de Simplificar y Uniformar la Ortografía en América"** [**"Notes on the Advisability of Simplifying and Standardizing Orthography in America"**]. This was a piece probably mostly prepared by Bello, and in fact it proved to be the foundation for his subsequent grammatical works. In an emphasis reminiscent of Noah Webster's work on spelling in revolutionary America, Bello was primarily concerned with the potentialities of language for contributing to the development of nationhood.[11] The article argued that the simplification of current Spanish orthography was all the more urgent now that independence created the need for expanded literacy. It was Bello's belief that the acquisition of literacy would be facilitated by removing useless letters from the alphabet, and keeping only those that represented a sound. Just as Webster before him (although there is no indication that Bello was familiar with the American's work), he argued that the Latin model of spelling on which the Spanish language of the Royal Academy was based complicated rather than aided this process of literacy. Bello emphasized the importance of such reforms not only on linguistic grounds, but for moral and political reasons as well: "This is the only way to establish rational freedom, and with it the advantages of civic culture and public prosperity."[12]

In *El Repertorio Americano,* Bello reinforced his dual emphasis on scientific dissemination and cultivation of the Spanish language.[13] There was a larger number of collaborators in this new publication; the contributors included, in addition to Bello and García del Río, the poets José Fernández Madrid (Colombia), José Joaquín Olmedo (Ecuador), and the Spanish scholars Pablo Mendíbil and Vicente Salvá. It is especially significant that the editors decided to reprint, with slight variations, the *Biblioteca* essay on orthography, clearly in an effort to emphasize the timeliness and relevance of grammatical studies for the process of nation building. Bello added an essay on the etymology of Spanish words, and another on **"The Origin and Progress of the Art of Writing,"** which was designed to promote reforms of written Spanish. This last essay resorted to history to show that written language was constantly changing, implying that the progress of civilization required concurrent reforms in the language used to convey it, cultivate it, and expand it. Ultimately, such reforms were expected to bring "incalculable benefits" by "disseminating instruction and making education general among the mass of people."[14] Such statements were in keeping with the larger agenda, as stated in the prospectus of the **Biblioteca Americana,** of spreading the enlightenment that Spain had tried to prevent. Independence,

therefore, acquired a lofty purpose in the spreading of literacy, and hence civilization.

This central focus did not detract from the journal's purpose of disseminating useful information, very much in the format of other British journals, especially the *Edinburgh Review.* The **Biblioteca** contained articles on the teaching of economics, travel narratives, the use of the barometer, cultivation of cotton and cochineal, a cure for mumps, and an assortment of other medical and scientific subjects. Bello educated himself on various scientific subjects through extensive reading and also by attendance at the meetings of the Royal Institution in London, to which he became a subscriber in April 1823, that is, at the time when Sir Humphry Davy was presenting his research on chemistry and electromagnetism.[15] Bello also developed a strong friendship with Dr. Neil Arnott, the author of *The Elements of Physics* (1827), with whom he also frequented the reading room of the British Museum's Library. Bello's interest in, and coverage of, scientific subjects was not isolated or arcane. Instead, he viewed scientific dissemination as a vehicle for the consolidation of republican institutions, now that countries depended on their own enlightenment to organize themselves and educate the new generations under a new political system. Science, in this respect, was part and parcel of a larger process of nation-building, and Bello availed himself of information and resources in England and beyond. The book review section of **El Repertorio Americano** provided various illustrations of how European countries dealt with such issues as the organization of the judiciary, parliamentary procedures, education, and elections. Bello wrote most of the book reviews in the four volumes of the **Repertorio.**

Many of the apparently most recondite subjects provided Bello and others with the opportunity to elaborate on recommendations for the new republics. For instance, while reviewing the activities of a Parisian society for the promotion of elementary education, Bello used the opportunity to give synopses of his emerging agenda for the establishment of new nations: he urged that the inclusion of the Spanish past be retained in the teaching of national history because the subject was "full of valuable lessons." The new states should also avoid "the affectation of philosophical principle and declamation intended to perpetuate national hatreds," meaning the use of French revolutionary rhetoric in elementary instruction. In addition, the new countries should promote the purity of Spanish in primary education, in contrast to "the shameful and lamentable lack of grammatical soundness of the Spanish American press, in addition to the flow of foreign expressions that threatens to turn the language of our elders into a barbaric blabber."[16] Bello's emerging view of independence included the preservation of the Spanish language, renewed cultural linkages with Europe (Spain included), and the avoidance of revolutionary ideology. Such an agenda was very much in step with the Whig reformist ideology that dominated liberal circles in London and which rejected the Jacobinism of the French Revolution. "It was not, as some think, the enthusiasm for ill-understood and exaggerated theories [i.e., French] that produced and sustained our revolution," Bello stated, but rather "the aspiration inherent in any society to administer its own affairs, and not receive laws from another country."[17]

Bello's effort to convey useful information to the new Spanish American states, and his ideologically anti-Jacobin positions, could be seen combined in his proposals for the curriculum of the University of Caracas. Probably at the request of José Rafael Revenga, the Colombian representative in London between 1822 and 1824, Bello prepared a list of key texts to be considered for adoption by the university. This is a highly significant list, for it shows Bello's view of a modern university curriculum, his knowledge of sources acquired in England, and his choices of titles in some key humanistic areas. Bello recommended a total of seventy-eight books distributed in two separate lists ("A" and "B," probably to separate advanced from preparatory higher education). List A included the subjects of Latin, mathematics, physics, chemistry, natural history, and intellectual and moral sciences. List B included Spanish, ancient and modern history, Humanities and intellectual and moral sciences, and political economy.[18]

These varied subjects are significant in themselves: Bello placed great emphasis on the experimental sciences, retained Latin but expanded the sources for the study of Spanish, and introduced the subject of political economy. The authors to be studied in this latter area included Adam Smith, Jean Baptiste Say, and David Ricardo. Bello noted that he did not expect a widespread knowledge of the English language, and therefore emphasized works in French and Spanish. But he still recommended William Paley's *Natural Theology* and *The Principles of Moral and Political Philosophy*; John Locke's *An Essay Concerning Human Understanding*; Thomas Reid's *An Inquiry into the Human Mind* and *Essays on the Powers of the Human Mind*; Dugald Stewart's *Philosophy of the Human Mind,* and George Campbell's *The Philosophy of Rhetoric*. These titles prove that Bello had acquired a significant knowledge of the work of Scottish philosophers while in London. He recommended their study in Spanish America probably because of their moderate political views and their marriage of religion and science.[19] In France, Victor Cousin was also drawn to Scottish philosophy, especially the work of Reid, as he engaged in the reform of higher education. Scottish philosophers were also widely read and discussed in the United States, as scholars on both continents probed into the integrative claims of moral philosophy. Bello, for his part, would explore the themes of Scottish philosophy more fully in his *Filosofía del Entendimiento,* a work that concentrated on logic and the acquisition of ideas.

In the context of recommendations for the university curriculum, Bello made other, perhaps more surprising choices. He included a number of Spanish authors whom few would have expected (even today), given that this was a time when battles for independence from Spain were still being fought. In addition to such classics as Cervantes and Garcilaso de la Vega, Bello included works by Juan Meléndez Valdés (1745-1817), and Manuel José Quintana (1772-1857), who had played a role in the Spanish government just a decade earlier.

Clearly, Bello, who had never been an advocate of sharp breaks with Spain, felt that the education of independent Spanish Americans should not neglect the literature of their former rulers. An important part of this agenda was reinforced by the presence in London of numerous Spaniards fleeing the reactionary rule of Ferdinand VII after 1823. In the opinion of Vicente Llorens, the leading scholar of this exile generation, the period between 1824 and 1828 brought Spaniards and Spanish Americans together in ways that helped temper the animosities of a war that had not yet fully ended.[20] During the previous decade, Bello had cultivated relations with Blanco White and the Spanish literary scholar Bartolomé José Gallardo. The new wave of immigration expanded his network of contacts, including Pablo Mendíbil and Vicente Salvá, who contributed essays to *El Repertorio Americano,* the intellectuals José Joaquín de Mora, Agustín Arguelles, José Canga Arguelles, Antonio Alcalá Galiano and Joaquín Lorenzo Villanueva.[21] There is no evidence that Bello may have met linguist Antonio Puigblanch, but he certainly read his works and those of other Spanish emigrés who contributed essays to journals like *Variedades,* and *Ocios de Españoles Emigrados.*[22] It was not uncommon for these writers to collaborate in one or more periodicals, and comment on each other's work. They also shared the tribulations of exile and some of the joys of café socializing. Thomas Carlyle left the following impression of the Hispanic community in Somers Town, where most of them lived, in 1824:

> In those years a visible section of the London population, and conspicuous out of all proportion to its size or value, was a small knot of Spaniards, who had sought shelter here as Political Refugees. 'Political Refugees': a tragic succession of that class is one of the possessions of England in our time. Six-and-twenty years ago, when I first saw London, I remember those unfortunate Spaniards among the new phenomena. Daily in the cold spring air, under skies so unlike their own you could see a group of fifty or a hundred stately tragic figures, in proud threadbare cloaks; perambulating, mostly with closed lips, the broad pavements of Euston Square and the region about St. Pancras new Church. Their lodging was chiefly in Somers Town as I under-

stood; and those open pavements about St. Pancras Church were the general place of rendez vous. They spoke little or no English; knew nobody, could employ themselves on nothing, in this new scene. Old, steel-gray heads, many of them; the shaggy, thick, blue-black hair of others struck you; their brown complexion, dusky look of suppressed fire, in general their tragic condition as of caged Numidian lions.[23]

This vivid description by the Scottish writer is probably a good example of how Spaniards (and Spanish Americans) were viewed by some uncomprehending hosts in London. These "caged Numidian lions," however, felt that they were in the midst of momentous changes and collaborated accordingly. The balance of the efforts of Bello and his Spanish American as well as Iberian colleagues was a positive one: As a result of their activities, various journals were published that contained essays and proposals which became central to the intellectual and political history of Latin America. Moreover, by virtue of residing in London, a number of Spanish Americans developed a keen sense of the international environment surrounding the events of independence, and acquired an experience in diplomacy that would serve them well when they returned to their home countries. But this positive balance sheet should not obscure the fact that their cultural activities took place in an often difficult personal and diplomatic context.

NEW ANXIETIES

Bello's successful publication record, unfortunately, was not an indication of success in other areas of his life. In a letter to Colombian Foreign Minister Pedro Gual dated January 6, 1825, Bello provided a rare and candid description of his personal situation in London. He explained to Gual how urgently he wanted to return to Gran Colombia, and listed the types of employment he thought he was qualified for. These included, (1) *Oficial Mayor* (First Secretary) positions in any of the ministries, (2) diplomatic assignments in other countries, and (3) leadership positions in educational and cultural establishments.

> But, as I have said, I would accept any position that the government may find appropriate for me and which can provide me with a living. . . . I mastered the principal languages of Europe even before I came here. . . . Of the fourteen years of residence [in London] I have spent six as Legation Secretary. . . . I have, as you know, studied the humanities since I was a child. I can say that I have a command of mathematics. I have the knowledge necessary, although I have lacked the instruments to perform it, for the description of maps and planes. I also have a general knowledge of other scientific subjects. . . . You are well aware of my old habits of study and work, and those who have known me in Europe can attest to both that I conserve them, and that they have become second nature to me.

Both Bello and Gual had attended the University of Caracas in the 1790s, and knew one another well enough

to allow Bello to give full expression to the urgency of his situation. Still, the appeal made Bello uncomfortable and sad, as the following passage suggests:

> Therefore, I request the help of Colombia, and have confidence that the government will recognize the right of this Venezuelan employee to claim protection. It was the cause of liberty that brought me to London. The misfortunes of the fatherland condemned me to a long exile and to a life of difficulties and deprivations. Will the fatherland abandon me now that it has triumphed? . . . The decision is in your hands, my friend, that I might serve it again. Your recommendation to the government can do a great deal to improve my situation, which I assure you is delicate and critical. Although I have never disdained any type of work, I believe that the way in which I have spent my youth, or rather my entire life, makes me capable of something more important than the obscure role of scribe and interpreter to which I have been reduced in my current position.[24]

This last sentence indicates that Bello had reached a point of alienation, believing that his position at the Chilean legation in London had become untenable—an episode to be examined shortly. Furthermore, Bello was in dire financial straits, was anxious about growing old without a secure employment, and feared the worst for the future of his family. After the death of Mary Ann, Bello had married Elizabeth Dunn (1804-1873) on February 24, 1824. In addition to Bello's sons Carlos and Francisco, the new couple had four children of their own in London: Juan, born in 1825; Andrés Ricardo, born in 1826; Ana Margarita, born in 1827; and Miguel, born in 1828. Eight others were born later in Chile.

Little is known about how Bello and Elizabeth met, but Bello's correspondence shows that a "young Dunn," most likely a sibling of Elizabeth, delivered his mail when he lived at Clarendon Square.[25] One of their descendants, Inés Echeverría Bello, implied that Elizabeth was Irish, although this is not apparent from the name.[26] The neighborhood of Somers Town, however, had a strong Irish component, and thus the likelihood is high.[27] The records of the British Museum Library, where Bello regularly renewed his admissions to the Reading Room, show that Bello lived at 39 Clarendon Square until at least November 4, 1822. By early 1823, he had moved to 6 Solls Row, at Hampstead Road, which was not far from Somers Town, most likely in anticipation of his marriage.[28] After the couple married and their second child was born, they moved in early 1826 to a house at 9 Egremont Place, on New Road (today's Euston Road at St. Pancras Station).[29] This is the house where the family lived until they departed for Chile. These frequent address changes, and his rapidly growing family, explain to a great extent Bello's financial anxiety.

Still, the Bellos were eager to stay in close contact with a wide circle of friends. Of these, perhaps the closest was the Ecuadorean poet José Joaquín Olmedo, who had arrived in England in 1825 as the representative of Peru. Diplomatic duties took him to France in November 1826, but he returned to London in July 1827 and stayed through March 1828. During that time, he cultivated an intense friendship with Bello. He became godfather to the young Andrés Ricardo, and sent affectionate letters to the Bello family from Paris. Bello reciprocated heartily, and wrote a celebration of their friendship in the form of a poem titled **"Carta Escrita de Londres a París por un Americano a Otro"** [**"A Letter from London to Paris from one American to Another"**],

> Es fuerza que te diga, caro Olmedo,
> que del dulce solaz destituido
> de tu tierna amistad, vivir no puedo.
> ¡Mal haya ese París tan divertido,
> y todas sus famosas fruslerías,
> que a soledad me tienen reducido!
>
> (I, 93)

[I must tell you, dear Olmedo,
that I cannot live without the sweet comfort
of your tender friendship.
Damned be that entertaining Paris,
and all its famous frivolities
that condemn me to this loneliness!]

Bello then urges Olmedo to return to London, for there

> Me aguarda una alma fiel, veraz, constante,
> que al verme sentirá más alegría
> de la que me descubra en el semblante.
>
> (I, 94)

[A faithful, true and constant friend awaits you
who will experience more joy
than will show in his face when he sees you].

Even in times of difficulty, Bello was capable of offering a warm and thoughtful friendship. Such qualities of character were appreciated by Olmedo, who also had a gift for expressing his own feelings uninhibitedly. As he left for South America on March 7, 1828, he wrote to Bello, perhaps knowing that he would never see him again: "The moment has come. By the time you receive this letter I will be far away from London; yet those who love are never far. I am taking you, dear Andrés, deep inside my soul, and in my heart" (XXV, 384-385).

Bello appears to have been able to confront his darkest moments with the assurance of friendships like this and that of Blanco White. He seemed to open his heart with ease to those who shared his sensitivity, but he could be distant and reserved when he found himself depending on others. He also felt quite helpless and insecure about his overall situation. The fact that he did not receive a response to his direct appeal to Pedro Gual for a position in Gran Colombia reinforced his sense of having been abandoned by his homeland. He had no choice but

to stay in London. His years in the diplomatic crops would be punctuated by these disappointed expectations, and were compounded by the fragility, and at times chaos, of the diplomatic missions of the early republican period.

BELLO'S ROLE IN SPANISH AMERICAN DIPLOMACY

Early Spanish American diplomatic efforts had been limited to securing the protection of Great Britain in the case of a possible French invasion. After Bolívar's convening of the Congress at Angostura (1819), and the military victories of his troops at Boyacá and Carabobo in northern South America, Spanish Americans on both sides of the Atlantic switched to a more ambitious agenda of independent nationhood. At Angostura, deputies were commissioned to renew efforts to secure European recognition, this time not in the form of protection from foreign enemies, but rather in the name of the sovereignty and self-determination of the new nations. Recognition by Great Britain was certainly the main objective, but Article 31 of the instructions to representatives Fernando Peñalver and José María Vergara also included recognition by the Vatican.[30] In light of the magnitude of Catholic Church opposition to the independence movement during the First Republic, the Angostura Congress sought to neutralize Spain's ability to use the Church against the new nations by establishing a direct concordat with the Vatican. In theory, this would give the new governments the ability to appoint ecclesiastical personnel friendly to independence, and defuse a potential source of opposition to the new political order.

Once in London in 1820, envoys Peñalver and Vergara found themselves unable to change the British position of strict neutrality, and thus they concentrated on communications with the Vatican. They commissioned Andrés Bello to prepare a letter to Pope Pius VII to request formal relations with the Vatican. Bello completed the letter in Latin on March 27, 1820.[31]

Much of the missive dwelled on the sorry state of peoples deprived of religious comfort. But it also asserted the fundamental right of self-determination, especially from regions subjected to both foreign threats and the inability of Spain to come to terms with its own internal political disagreements. The letter asserted that there being no chance of a return to the status quo ante, the issue now became how to ensure that the new states could provide for the spiritual needs of the population: *"Inde factum est ut, quamquam tantae rei Status impensa cura consuluerint, maxima sacerdotum inopia laboremus"* [This is why it has come about that although the states try to provide for so important a matter with lavish care, we are suffering from a shortage of priests]. Without priests, the letter added, one could legitimately predict "the total ruin of religion" (VIII, 461). And yet, the argument proceeded, these new states were unequivocally Catholic. Hence efforts ought to be made to reconcile the need to minister to the faithful with the reality of the new republican political arrangements. If Spain still held the monopoly of ecclesiastical appointments, the people of Gran Colombia would be left with the dismal choice of being without clerics entirely, or being unable to be comforted by appointees of the enemies of their government. Priests selected by Spanish authorities would aggravate ills rather than solve them. In short, the letter called for the transfer of royal patronage (long enjoyed by the Spanish crown in colonial days) to the newly installed republics, the emphasis being on the existence of such new republics. Clearly, the letter conveyed not only the dilemmas of the current political situation, but also showed how important Vatican approval was to the new states.

The impact of the letter was not immediate, but the Vatican agreed to name bishops for Gran Colombia in 1827, the first such act of recognition for Spanish America.[32] Bello's letter shows that as early as 1820 he was in a position to elaborate on arguments in favor of independence that were based on national sovereignty, even if much of the argumentation was couched in religious and humanitarian terms. It is important to note, however, that Bello articulated these views without the sanction of an official appointment. It was only when Antonio José de Irisarri asked him to join the Chilean Legation as secretary, that Bello formally represented a Spanish American government after his earlier mission in 1810. This appointment materialized in June 1822. As noted earlier, Bello had asked for a position the year before, when his economic penury seemed to have reached yet another new low.

Antonio José de Irisarri (1786-1868) was born in Guatemala. Business and family connections took him to Chile in 1809, where he married into the prominent Larraín family. He soon immersed himself in the politics of independence, rising, for a brief period in 1814, to the highest position in government, that of Supreme Director. After the royalist military routed patriot forces at Rancagua later in the year, Irisarri fled to Mendoza across the Andes mountains, and then moved to London, where he arrived in 1815 and stayed through 1817. Irisarri was a close ally of independence hero and statesman Bernardo O'Higgins, who asked him to lead his cabinet in 1818 and later that year dispatched him to England as Chilean envoy.[33] It was during this second London visit that Irisarri met Bello, possibly in 1819, but most certainly by 1820, when both collaborated in the publication of *El Censor Americano*. Irisarri was a self-assured, contentious and flamboyant man who could be reckless in the management of diplomatic and financial affairs. But he was also a notable writer, as he had proven in his articles in the Chilean papers *El Semanario Republicano* and *El Duende de Santiago* during

the first decade of independence. He was a learned man who had an appreciation for scholarship and who, despite his usually dismissive character, was completely captivated by Bello. He determined, early on, to attract the Venezuelan to the service of Chile. It is thanks to Irisarri, as with Blanco White before him, that descriptions of Bello's personal character exist during this period.

In a letter to Chilean Foreign Minister Joaquín Echeverría dated October 10, 1820, Irisarri described Bello as "a very capable man who commands a vast literature and an extensive knowledge of the sciences. He also possesses a seriousness and nobility of character that make him all the more estimable. These qualities, my friend, so difficult to find these days, make me strongly attracted to him."[34] To his wife Mercedes he described how he passed the time in London at the British Museum Library "completely devoted to reading and to studying certain literary matters with an excellent friend, Mr. Andrés Bello. He is a true sage on account of his knowledge and character, and also because of the humility with which he endures a lack of means that is similar if not greater than mine."[35] To Supreme Director Bernardo O'Higgins, Irisarri wrote that

> There is a man here of Venezuelan origin whom I consider a friend and in whom I am particularly interested: I met him not long ago, but we see each other frequently because of his experience in diplomatic affairs, a field among many others in which he possesses a vast knowledge. I am persuaded that of all the [Spanish] Americans who have been commissioned to this Court [England], he is the most serious and attentive to his duties, to which qualities he adds a beauty of character and an impressive knowledge.[36]

Irisarri was in a position to judge Bello's abilities because he had asked him to produce a report on the Lancasterian system of education, which Bello duly prepared and submitted on September 11, 1820.[37] Irisarri thus expressed his hope, in the same letter to O'Higgins, that he might employ Bello in some capacity, urging immediate action because "he will probably not be able to stay at this Court much longer due to the extreme conditions in which he and his family find themselves, and that might force them to leave to who knows where." After this letter, Irisarri wrote to Bello on March 21, 1821 to inform him that he was waiting for a response from Chile. There, he took the opportunity to criticize Simón Bolívar: "You can call yourself a friend of General Bolívar, and declare yourself his supporter, but I, who am neither one nor the other, and having no other knowledge of him than his public deeds, cannot consider him such a great man if he is unable to make good use of people like you."[38] This statement suggests that Irisarri, and perhaps others, had asked Bello why Bolívar had not come to his aid. He could only beg the question.

THE CHILEAN LEGATION

Irisarri was determined to hire Bello, and the opportunity presented itself when the current secretary, Francisco Ribas, left the service of the Chilean legation in late 1821. Irisarri contacted Bello from Paris to offer him the job in an acting capacity, until he could obtain confirmation from Chile. The formal offer indicated that Bello was to be hired as Acting Secretary, and that he would retain the Venezuelan rank of Commissioner of War. The offer consisted of an annual salary of $2,000 Chilean pesos (approximately £400), a sum that however modest for Bello's needs was much more than he had ever enjoyed in London on a steady basis. Irisarri accompanied the offer with an explanatory letter, which, however matter-of-fact, could not hide his enthusiasm.[39]

Such enthusiasm was justified, for Irisarri had only a few days earlier (May 18, 1822) made arrangements with the house of Hullett Brothers for a loan of £1 million to the government of Chile.[40] Irisarri needed a competent official to administer the legation while he shuttled between London and Paris to invest, or as some more skeptical observers in Chile and England preferred to term, squander the funds. Irisarri paid himself the handsome commission of £20,000 for contracting the loan, and took another £18,000 which he claimed as back pay. This is the infamous loan that landed Irisarri in a British court of law in 1825 and forever destroyed his credibility, although he was acquitted. It was, moreover, the loan whose negative consequences for Chile made the government send an official, Mariano Egaña, to London on a mission to investigate Irisarri's handling of the proceeds.

By virtue of his position at the Chilean Legation, Bello had signed the contract for the loan, but all evidence suggests that his responsibilities were administrative and political rather than financial. Irisarri wanted, for obvious reasons, to keep close control over the proceeds of the loan. With Irisarri absent in Paris for most of the time, the responsibility fell on Bello to keep the Chilean Foreign Ministry informed and perform the day-to-day tasks of the legation. In two key dispatches dated May 8, 1823, and June 24, 1824, Bello offered the European perspective on the state of Spanish American affairs.[41]

In the first dispatch, he described in stark terms how the restoration of Ferdinand VII with the Holy Alliance and French support made the recognition of independence by continental powers virtually impossible. In fact, one could even expect renewed efforts to recover the former colonies for Spain. The better prospect lay in British recognition, especially in the stated intent of George Canning to prevent French intervention in Spanish American affairs. But much more was needed to prevent the aggression of the continental powers. In order to secure British recognition, Bello suggested, Spanish American countries needed to represent how much British trade stood to suffer should Spain reconquer the region. But more importantly, they needed to be prepared to offer substantial concessions. In the case of Chile, Bello urged guidance on how to respond to predictable questions from Canning, should a meeting to discuss the matter of recognition materialize. In particular, was Chile prepared to consider financial or other concessions to Spain in exchange for British recognition?

Such questions were in line with British pronouncements in the past, for its policy of neutrality urged the contending parties to find an accommodation. The underlying message of Bello's communication was that Spanish America needed to secure British recognition at all costs, for the lack of it rendered the region especially vulnerable to the Holy Alliance designs. Another important dimension of the dispatch was the acknowledgment that Great Britain refrained from extending recognition for lack of certainty about the political stability of government institutions. He strained to be diplomatic in conveying this point: "We are told that we are not believed to be in a position to be recognized." Although this statement was vague, the implication was that Chile should produce a clear indication of what its form of government was, knowing that Canning would continue to affect uncertainty until Chile and other nations embraced constitutional monarchy. This was, of course, Irisarri's and Bello's view as much as Canning's.[42]

Meanwhile, Chile was preoccupied precisely with the same questions concerning political stability, although not exactly because British recognition was at stake. O'Higgins had been forced to resign by a rebellion headed by General Ramón Freire in January 1823, but the resulting change of government did not stop continued factionalism. Political organization was not helped by the Constitution of 1823, a complex document authored by the erudite intellectual Juan Egaña that called Chile a republic, but which provided for confusing and often contradictory functions to the various branches of government.[43] A frustrated Congress suspended the Constitution after Supreme Director Freire resigned in July 1824 claiming that he could not govern under the terms of the constitutional document. Later in the year, the Congress abrogated the Constitution without even producing a replacement. That state of affairs, duly reported to the British government, did not help the Chilean case for recognition. On the basis of information provided by the British Consul in Chile, Christopher Nugent, Canning concluded that "Chile is not yet ripe for recognition."[44]

Communications between the British government and its consuls in various countries were faster and better than those of the Spanish American governments with their own representatives. Unaware of political developments in Chile, Bello produced a second dispatch dated June 24, 1824. There, Bello expanded once again on the dangers presented by the activities of the Holy Alliance, and the bitter hostility of Ferdinand VII's government toward Spanish America. In measured paragraphs, Bello returned to the issue of political organization. He reported that Canning was on the verge of announcing a very limited recognition of a Spanish American state, most likely Gran Colombia. This recognition, however, would involve no promise of alliance in a war against Spain. Bello reported that Canning left the door open for the recognition of other countries, but that this would depend "on the progress that the new states make in the consolidation of their institutions." He also added that the Foreign Secretary had recently represented to Juan García del Río, in his capacity as Peru's envoy, that "the strength of the new states was the pivotal point on which recognition rested," and that "the cabinets of Europe would look more favorably, and predict better results, if the new states adopted constitutional monarchies following European principles." However persuasive the arguments might have been, Chilean leaders had a completely different set of priorities.

By this time, the Chilean state was more concerned about the fate of the proceeds of the 1822 loan, and duly sent Foreign Relations Minister Mariano Egaña (Juan Egaña's son) to London to investigate the actions of Irisarri.[45] Bello's role was not a part of the investigation, but his position was precarious given that he had assisted Irisarri (or most likely, had been used by him) during the financial negotiations. In the event, Bello was soon caught in the acrimonious dispute between the two officials, and as a result he eventually abandoned the service of Chile. A brief review of this affair illustrates both the disastrous consequences of the Chilean loan, as well as the course Bello's life took as a result of Egaña's mission.

Mariano Egaña lacked the finesse, and perhaps even the stomach, to rein in Irisarri and advance Chilean interests in London. The British Consul in Chile bluntly called him "much more a hawker of diplomacy than a substantial character."[46] Knowing not a word of English, Egaña was helpless even to clear through customs when he arrived at Gravesend on August 26, 1824. The cunning Irisarri took full advantage of Egaña's helplessness and managed to trick the envoy into delivering his luggage to one of Irisarri's agents. With advance knowledge of Egaña's plans and instructions, Irisarri determined to obstruct the envoy's mission and in a few days left for Paris carrying the legation's seal and papers, leaving Bello in charge of the office.

In three letters to his father Juan, dated September 1, 22, and 24, 1824, an exasperated Mariano Egaña described in full detail his troubles upon arrival in England, and Irisarri's refusal to cooperate with his mission. He indulged in a free flow of invective against Irisarri, which was probably justified, but he soon became suspicious of anyone who was close to his declared enemy. Bello had the distinct misfortune of meeting Egaña precisely at the moment when the Chilean envoy had lost his bearings upon realizing that his belongings had been taken. In Egaña's own description, when Bello introduced himself and mentioned that Irisarri was in London at the moment, he was seized by the sudden realization that Irisarri had taken his luggage: "I was besides myself and as if possessed I ran into streets I did not know in search of my belongings."[47] From then on, a confused Bello had to endure the suspicion of Egaña, who believed him to be an accomplice in Irisarri's dubious dealings. As Egaña put it, "[Antonio] Gutiérrez [Moreno] and Bello are not to be trusted due to their friendship with Irisarri, and especially the latter, because he seems to me to be too cautious and reserved. He makes me quite uncomfortable."[48] Still, Egaña needed Bello, and resentfully kept him in his employ once he learned that Bello's salary had been paid in advance. It was only slowly that Egaña came to appreciate him, consider him his friend, and even engineer his transfer to Chile later in the decade.

Meanwhile, Bello felt enormous pressure under the nervous gaze of the paranoid Egaña. On January 6, 1825, he issued an anxious call for help from the government of Gran Colombia, stating that "the removal of Mr. Irisarri has made my staying on the job scarcely compatible with the preservation of my integrity as an employee. The government of Chile has not confirmed my continuation, and I have no credit with its present representative, who considers me a protégé and a friend of his predecessor."[49] To Irisarri he wrote on February 3, 1825, that "Mr. Egaña has concluded that the relations between you and me are so detrimental to his commission that he has permitted himself such indiscretions that I can no longer tolerate." Bello added that his explanations and rebuttals to Egaña were of no use and had led to an almost complete breakdown of communication. He proceeded to ask Irisarri for a job, so that "you can free me from the nightmare of Mr. Egaña."[50] Irisarri was in London at the time but the was in no position to help, as his financial affairs were headed toward bankruptcy. He took the opportunity, however, to indulge in a barrage of epithets against Egaña.

Just when he seemed to be at the very end of his tether, Bello learned that as a result of his previous requests to the government of Gran Colombia, Vice-President Francisco de Paula Santander had appointed him First Secretary of the Colombian Legation (November 8, 1824). Santander was in charge of the government of Gran Colombia while Simón Bolívar was occupied with the liberation of Peru, which culminated in the battle of Ayacucho on December 9, 1824. While these events were unfolding, the document of appointment finally reached London on February 5, 1825, and was acknowledged by the Colombian Minister Plenipotentiary in London, Manuel José Hurtado. He must have notified Bello soon afterwards, and Bello himself accepted immediately, for he received the appointment and swore the customary oath of allegiance to the country at Hurtado's residence at 33 Portland Place on February 7, 1825.[51] Bello's instructions were spelled out by Foreign Minister Pedro Gual in two letters dated November 9, 1824. One asked Bello to "work diligently on dispelling the errors that prevail in Europe, especially in the continent, concerning the current state of the Spanish American republics."[52] The other detailed his administrative functions as "organizing and maintaining the archives, conducting correspondence, coding and decoding communications, etc., and handling with exactitude and confidentiality all matters regarding your office."[53] This must have been an exhilarating moment for Bello, as shown by the effusiveness of his response to Pedro Gual on February 10, 1825. After asking Gual to convey his thanks to Santander, Bello pledged that "I will never lose sight of my obligations to a fatherland from whose service I was separated by imperious and until now irresistible circumstances, but which I have always considered mine."[54]

Meanwhile, the chagrined Egaña wrote to his father that "in early February Bello notified me that he had received an appointment at the Colombian Legation and that he was no longer a secretary to that of Chile. Without further ado, he left me. *Quid faciendum,* and who to turn to?"[55] He vented his anger against Bello, always in the context of discussing Irisarri, as for example when he served as witness in Irisarri's libel suit against *The Morning Chronicle* on December 19, 1825.[56] He continued to find opportunities to criticize Bello for yet another year, until he found another target in Vicente Rocafuerte, the Ecuadorean-born representative of Mexico in London who had dared criticize a publication by his father Juan.[57] Egaña eventually mellowed, as the prospects of returning to Chile became imminent by the close of the decade. Not even the comforts of Paris, where he spent most of his time in the late 1820s, reconciled him to a job that by all accounts made him miserable.

Gran Colombia

Freed from Egaña's temperament, Andrés Bello was able to enjoy a brief period of calm and even success when he joined the Colombian legation in 1825. At that time, Gran Colombia was in the midst of establishing a Treaty of Friendship, Navigation, and Commerce with Great Britain. The Treaty had been under discussion since 1824, and by early 1825 George Canning had dispatched envoys to Gran Colombia to discuss terms. The envoys returned to London with a document signed by Colombian authorities on April 18, 1825. After a meeting between George Canning and Manuel José Hurtado on July 2, 1825, the former announced the readiness of Great Britain to recognize Gran Colombia on July 5, 1825. After considerable administrative work, in which Bello was centrally involved, the Treaty was ratified on November 7, 1825. A few days later, on November 11, King George IV formally received Hurtado, who was accompanied by Canning, as the first fully accredited representative of a Spanish American nation. Andrés Bello himself was formally introduced to George Canning on November 12, 1825.[58] The long-desired diplomatic recognition of Spanish American independence, although limited for the time being to Gran Colombia, Mexico, and Buenos Aires, appeared to usher in a most promising entrance into the community of sovereign nations.

Such optimism proved to be painfully short-lived. The seeds of financial trouble had already been planted by the Colombian government's debt to British merchants who had provided capital to support Bolívar's war effort. Colombian envoy Francisco Antonio Zea had compounded the problem with refinancing schemes and further commitment of government income to service the debt in 1820. Then, on March 13, 1822, he contracted a loan of £2 million with the house of Herring, Graham and Powles, much of which went to meet the obligations of 1820, dividend payments, and commissions.[59] Zea acted on the basis of extensive powers granted to him for his representation in London, but slow communications and the dynamics of recently introduced parliamentary procedure in Colombia disavowed his authority and his actions. As a result, Zea was caught between investors who believed him to be in a position to negotiate on behalf of his country, and a home government that exercised its power to ratify international arrangements, which in this case chose not to. British investors' confidence plummeted when it became clear that Zea's signature was not good enough, and in any case he died unexpectedly in November 1822. Just as the British government was contemplating recognition of Gran Colombia, financial circles had begun to panic about the country's solvency. Were Zea's commitments binding for the government of Gran Colombia? Would the country honor commitments made on its behalf? Gran Colombia under Santander had no choice but to take responsibility, even if this involved the acquisition of new loans in 1824.[60]

The sad conclusion of Zea's activities, and Santander's acquisition of new obligations spelled the complete collapse of Gran Colombia's financial creditworthiness. Meanwhile, the London market's crash of 1826 dampened the emerging enthusiasm over the economic potential of the newly liberated regions of Spanish America. Hence, Bello found himself in the contradictory situation of serving a government that had achieved a major diplomatic victory with the 1825 Treaty while at the same time losing financial credibility. As a result, the legation of Gran Colombia was besieged by the claims of disappointed and angry investors, while at the same time it tried to act the part of a sovereign nation recently recognized by the most powerful country on earth.

Although freed from the antics of Egaña, Bello found the legation of Gran Colombia to be no panacea. In addition to the regular duties of the legation, Bello was often immersed in financial affairs, attempting to exercise some damage control over the ill-fated loans. He made strenuous efforts to prevent the government of Gran Colombia from acquiring additional loans to meet its debt obligations. In a frank letter, co-signed by Consul Santos Michelena, Bello stated that "such is the credit of the Republic that, even with enormous efforts, we will not find an investor willing to advance funds." He added that the reputation of Gran Colombia was not only damaged, but that "such is the irritation that exists here, that we frankly do not know how to even begin new financial negotiations."[61] In a private letter to Minister José Rafael Revenga, he had already stated with obvious anxiety that "I want to be a thousand leagues away from London the day that [our country] misses a payment of the debt. I would be ashamed to look at anyone in the eye who knows me to be from Colombia." He added the following statement in English:

> The outcry would be dreadful, and depend upon it, the effects of the shock received at this center of the commercial world would be felt everywhere, and not the least in Colombia. I hope, my dear friend, for our country's sake, that this terrible calamity has been viewed in all its frightful bearings, and that our statesmen have exerted, & will continue to exert themselves to avert it, for there is hardly a sacrifice worth regretting, when the object is to prevent this injury and moral stain of a national bankruptcy.[62]

There was not much that Bello or anyone could do to prevent the deterioration of Gran Colombia's credit; the country was not alone in this situation, as nation after nation in Spanish America defaulted during the course of 1826. In another letter to Revenga, a dispirited Bello exclaimed: "What a sudden and painful fall from the position in which we were just a few months ago! And yet the tempest [i.e., the consequences of financial disaster] has only begun. . . . Dear God! So many sacrifices, bloodshed, and glory, will they all end in dishonor and ruin? I say ruin, because without credit and honor there can be no health for any state, and especially not for an emerging republic."[63]

To make matters worse, Bello also found that his relationship with Manuel José Hurtado was severely strained, as he suspected, because of the Colombian government's decision in July 1826 to transfer fiscal re-

sponsibilities to Bello and Santos Michelena.[64] Bello found himself excluded from a number of diplomatic functions, and treated coldly by his superior. Tensions built up in December of that year, to the point that Bello wrote letters to Santander, to the Finance Minister, and to Bolívar, to ask them to transfer him as soon as possible to another destination. The letter to Bolívar dated December 21 is particularly noteworthy. There he painted in stark terms his inability to support himself and his family, and asked Bolívar for help in ways that reveal the extent of the tensions with Hurtado:

> Let me ask your excellency to exercise your powerful influence in favor of a sincere and faithful servant of the cause of America, so that I can have a better position than I currently do. I am the dean of the legation secretaries in London, and though not the most inefficient, I am the one treated with the least consideration by his own superior.[65]

In early January 1827, Bello informed the Ministry of Foreign Relations that Hurtado had refused to pay the salaries of the staff, and that he had met with him to represent both the personal and political consequences of such an act. Hurtado, according to Bello, refused to reconsider his decision stating that he no longer had responsibility over fiscal affairs.[66] Bello, as a result, was forced to acquire a loan under his own name to pay for his and the staff's salaries. He then confronted Hurtado on January 10, 1827, asking him whether he had done anything to merit Hurtado's slights, and demanding, if such was the case, that he articulated any grievances in writing so that he could respond formally to the government.[67] The letter, however, was not answered. Bello was unaware, but the government of Gran Colombia had already relieved Hurtado from his position by decree of October 19, 1826, which also named Bello as Chargé d'Affaires. Such an action vindicated Bello, but he did not know about it until late January or early February, 1827. In the event, he assumed the position on February 7, and held it until May 4, 1827, when envoy José Fernández Madrid, who was then in Paris, formally assumed Hurtado's post.

This was not, however, the end of Bello's troubles, tied as they were to the destinies, financial and political, of Gran Colombia. Although his difficult situation was compounded by Hurtado, even without him Bello's salary was insufficient to cover the needs of his growing family. Moreover, his requests for a promotion went without a reply. Simón Bolívar had written a letter to Fernández Madrid on February 21, 1827, conveying regards for Bello "with the friendship and affection that I have always had for him," but without mentioning anything about Bello's request and predicament.[68] Furthermore, in the same letter Bolívar commissioned Bello, along with Fernández Madrid and Santos Michelena, to oversee the sale of his copper mines in Aroa, Venezuela, a commission that led to the frustration of all parties concerned.[69] But probably the biggest blow to Bello came when he learned that upon the appointment of Fernández Madrid, he would return to the same position of secretary, which he expected, but with the same previous level of salary, which he did not. In a letter to Bolívar, Bello pointed to the injustice of the measure, for the secretary's salary was pegged to the Minister Plenipotentiary's in a relation of one to three, and he was falling short of that figure ($3,333 instead of $4,000 Colombian pesos). He asked Bolívar to correct the error, but added "I am grieved by this measure, not so much because of the financial loss that it represents (which in my circumstances is very serious), but because of the slight [*desaire*] that it implies." The usually reserved Bello added that "I am on the verge of old age, and I see no other prospect for my children than a legacy of indigence."[70]

Bello was comforted by the arrival of Fernández Madrid in London on April 30, 1827. They shared literary interests and they had liked each other even before they met through the good offices of their common friend, the poet José Joaquín Olmedo. Their collaboration for the next two years was harmonious, and their exchanges show strong ties of friendship. But Bello's financial situation was indeed desperate, and he was convinced that Bolívar held some grudge against him. From his position as Minister of Foreign Relations, José Rafael Revenga did his best to convince Bello that Bolívar was sympathetic and that help would be forthcoming. Bello, however, could not live with the uncertainty.[71] He renewed his appeals to José Manuel Restrepo, another government official and friend, and insisted that he could no longer afford to live in London. He asked Restrepo to intervene on his behalf so that he could be transferred to another location, perhaps in France or Holland, where he could live somewhat better on his meager salary.

Bolívar himself confronted grave problems. He had rushed back to Gran Colombia from Peru in late 1826 to confront the challenge of Venezuela against the central government in Bogotá. Bolívar was convinced that the key to the problem was Santander's doctrinaire legalism and insensitivity to regionalist sentiment in Caracas. Bolívar broke relations with Santander on March 16, 1827. In a letter to Fernández Madrid dated May 26, 1827, he acknowledged the seriousness of his problems. He also admitted that Peru was "lost" and that southern Colombia (soon to become Ecuador) was "compromised" by the treason of a military group inspired, he suspected, by Santander. He also reviewed the long list of conflicts brewing in the territory, and admitted to being overwhelmed. He sent regards to Bello but indicated that he had no time to address his concerns. He asked, incidentally, if there had been any movement on the sale of his mines.[72] When he finally responded to Bello on June 16, 1827, it was to indicate

that he no longer had any influence over Santander, who was in charge of the government and hence, foreign affairs. In a sentence that must have struck the already wounded Bello, Bolívar sharply added "I regret that you have not yet concluded the business of the mines."[73] Clearly, Bolívar did not fully understand the extent of Bello's alienation. The Liberator had other things on his mind, in addition to the mines, and within a year he assumed dictatorial powers in an attempt to salvage the rapidly disintegrating unity of Gran Colombia.[74]

The Decision to Move to Chile

Soon after the disappointing news from Bolívar, in late 1827, Bello contacted Mariano Egaña. The Chilean envoy had by now become a devoted friend, and Bello felt free to tell him of his willingness to leave the service of Colombia. Egaña, in turn, contacted the Chilean government on November 10, and recommended that Bello be appointed to a position in Santiago.[75] Meanwhile, Bello's friends in Bogotá did what they could to find Bello a better post, but all they secured for him was an appointment as Minister Plenipotentiary to Portugal, which in diplomatic terms was more of a demotion than a career advancement. He could, while waiting for the appointment to be approved, serve as Consul General of Gran Colombia in France, but from London and without any mention of salary and expenses. On September 15, 1828, Bello, who had spent most of the year without a salary, finally heard that the government of Chile had authorized his appointment at the rank of *Oficial Mayor* in one of the ministries in Santiago. The Chilean government offered to pay his travel costs and, in case he decided not to stay in Chile, to fund his relocation to another Spanish American country.[76] He did not wait long to make a decision and on September 19, he responded to the Chilean legation's secretary, José Miguel de la Barra: "I of course accept your offer and I am ready to leave as soon as I can put my affairs in order."[77] Thus, it is clear that Bello's motivation to take this step was guided by a combination of factors: his desperate financial situation; his skepticism that Gran Colombia would secure him a better position and fund it; his sense that the country had not only lost financial credibility, but was also falling apart politically; and the fear that Bolívar had some serious grievance against him. On December 2, 1828, he politely, but not without a bitter edge, turned down the honor of a consulship in Paris, and requested that his overdue salary be paid to both his family in Caracas and to his creditors in London. He announced that he would move to Chile, from which country he would be glad to be of help to Gran Colombia.[78]

It was only to Fernández Madrid that he revealed the agitated state of his mind upon leaving London for Chile. "I am writing to you at 4:30 a.m., when I have finally readied all that I need to leave. I impatiently await dawn so that I can depart this city, which is in so many ways hateful to me, and in so many other ways the object of my love, especially now that you, the foremost of Colombia's sons, and the best of all men, inhabits it . . . ¡Adiós!, ¡Adiós!"[79]

Fernández Madrid, who was aware of Bello's plans, was torn between his friendship with Bello and his desire to retain him in the service of Gran Colombia. He thought that something could still be done and wrote to Bolívar on November 6, 1828,

> In my view the loss of Mr. Bello would be a blow to Colombia: we have very few men who combine his integrity, talent, and knowledge. I am very sorry to see him go away, because if anything serious emerges, I will miss his counsel and his knowledge. I need not say that my means and my house have always been at his complete disposal; but you know about [Bello's] extremely reserved character. He has never made use of my sincere and insistent offers.[80]

Bolívar reacted to the news with obvious urgency:

> Three thousand pesos have recently been sent to Bello so that he can [take his assignment] in France. I implore you to not let our enlightened friend go to the land of anarchy [Chile]. Persuade him that Colombia is the least bad among the countries of America, and that if he wants to be employed in this country, he should just say so and he will be appointed to an appropriate position. He should prefer his fatherland above all else, and he is worthy of a very important position in it. I know the superior talents of this Caracas native who is my contemporary: he was my teacher when we were of the same [young] age; and I loved him with respect. His diffidence has kept us apart to a certain extent, and because of that, I want to be reconciled with him, that is to attract him to Colombia.[81]

It was too little, too late. By the time Bolívar sent his letter, Bello and his family were crossing the Atlantic. They had departed in the merchant brigantine *Grecian* from Gravesend on February 14, 1829. Bello eventually received and kept a copy of Bolívar's letter, but never acted upon it. By the end of 1830, Bolívar was dead, and Bello had just entered, not the twilight that he had expected, but the most productive period of his life.

Notes

1. For accounts of U.S. policy and attitudes toward Latin America, see Arthur P. Whitaker, *The United States and the Independence of Latin America, 1800-1830* (New York: W. W. Norton & Co., 1964), and Lars Schoultz, *Beneath the United States: A History of U.S. Policy Toward Latin America* (Cambridge, MA: Harvard University Press, 1998).

2. Harold Temperley, *The Foreign Policy of Canning, 1822-1827: England, the Neo-Holy Alliance, and the New World* (London: Frank Cass & Co., 1966). See also C. K. Webster, ed., *Britain and the Independence of Latin America, 1812-1830. Select Documents from the Foreign Office Archives* (London: Oxford University Press, 1938), and D. A. G. Waddell, "International Politics and Latin American Independence," in Leslie Bethell, ed., *The Cambridge History of Latin America,* 11 vols. (Cambridge: Cambridge University Press, 1985), III, pp. 197-228.

3. On the Spanish-language press in London, see María Teresa Berruezo León, *La Lucha de Hispanoamérica por su Independencia en Inglaterra, 1800-1830* (Madrid: Ediciones de Cultura Hispánica, 1989); Vicente Llorens, *Liberales y Románticos: Una Emigración Española en Inglaterra, 1823-1834,* 2nd ed. (Madrid: Editorial Castalia, 1968), and Karen Racine, "Imagining Independence: London's Spanish American Community, 1790-1829" (Ph.D. Dissertation, Tulane University, 1996). See also John Ford, "Rudolph Ackermann: Publisher to Latin America," in *Bello y Londres,* 2 vols. (Caracas: La Casa de Bello, 1981), I, pp. 197-224, and his "Rudolph Ackermann: Culture and Commerce in Latin America, 1822-1828," in John Lynch, ed., *Andrés Bello: The London Years* (Richmond, Surrey: The Richmond Publishing Co., 1982), pp. 137-152.

4. Irisarri to Bello, June 16, 1820, in Andrés Bello, *Obras Completas* [henceforth *OC*] 26 vols. (Caracas: La Casa de Bello, 1981-1984), XXV, 97-98.

5. Quoted by Ricardo Donoso, *Antonio José de Irisarri, Escritor y Diplomático* (Santiago: Prensas de la Universidad de Chile, 1934, 2nd ed., 1966), p. 34. See also Berruezo, *La Lucha,* pp. 270-279. Guillermo Feliú Cruz dismissed the notion that Bello participated in the journal, but on the basis of an examination of two issues (of four), and on stylistic grounds. See his "Bello, Irisarri y Egaña en Londres," in *Andrés Bello y la Redacción de los Documentos Oficiales Administrativos Internacionales y Legislativos de Chile* (Caracas: Fundación Rojas Astudillo, 1957), p. 14.

6. *El Censor Americano,* No. 4 (October 1820), p. 288. This extremely rare journal can be consulted at the Archivo Central Andrés Bello, Universidad de Chile, Santiago, Chile [henceforth *ACAB*].

7. For an account of Bello's role in the *Biblioteca,* as well as an identification of authors, see Pedro Grases, "La Biblioteca Americana (Londres, 1823)," in *Estudios sobre Andrés Bello* [Henceforth *ESAB*], 2 vols. (Caracas, Barcelona, Mexico: Editorial Seix Barral, 1981), II, pp. 318-328. See also his "Tres Empresas Periodísticas de Andrés Bello" in the same volume, pp. 307-314.

8. San Martín had appointed García del Río Minister of Foreign Relations in August 1821, and sent him to England in November of the same year. See Jaime E. Rodríguez O., *The Independence of Spanish America* (Cambridge: Cambridge University Press, 1998), p. 217. For an account of García del Río's role in the press of the period, see Guillermo Guitarte, "El Papel de Juan García del Río en las Revistas de Londres," in *Bello y Londres,* II, pp. 59-74.

9. García del Río to Echeverría, May 13, 1822, *ACAB,* Bandeja 4, Caja 36, No. 1218. Manuel de Salas (1754-1841) was a respected creole intellectual, educator, and leader of the early Chilean Republic.

10. "Prospecto," *Biblioteca Americana,* No. 1 (April 1823), p. v.

11. Noah Webster, "Introduction to the Blue-Black Speller, 1783," in Richard M. Rollins, *The Autobiographies of Noah Webster* (Columbia: University of South Carolina, 1989), pp. 68-79. Orthographic reforms have accompanied other revolutionary situations, particularly Russia after 1917.

12. Andrés Bello and Juan García del Río, "Indicaciones," *Biblioteca Americana,* No. 1 (April 1823), 50-62. An English translation of this text by Frances M. López-Morillas is in Iván Jaksié, ed., *Selected Writings of Andrés Bello* (New York and Oxford: Oxford University Press, 1997), pp. 60-71. Bello expanded on the difference between Latin and Greek pronunciation, on the one hand, and that of Spanish, on the other, in his "Prosodia Castellana," in *Biblioteca Americana,* No. 2 (1823), 24-40. He advocated the study of prosody in order to eliminate "vices that become incorrigible, corrupt language, and destroy language uniformity in the various provinces and states that speak it." Prosody, it should be noted, was a standard subject in Latin grammars from the Middle Ages through the Renaissance and beyond. Bello maintained a focus on prosody in his grammatical studies.

13. On Bello's role in this journal, see Pedro Grases "El Repertorio Americano (Londres, 1826-1827)," in *ESAB,* II, pp. 329-355, and "Tres Empresas" by the same author.

14. Bello, "Bosquejo del Origen y Progresos del Arte de Escribir," *El Repertorio Americano,* No. 4 (August 1827), 11-25. The translation is in *Selected Writings,* p. 58.

15. Bello's name is recorded in the Managers' Minutes of April 14, 1823, vol. 6, p. 386, Archives of the Royal Institution of Great Britain. For studies of the Royal Institution, see Morris Berman, *Social Change and Scientific Organization: The Royal Institution, 1799-1844* (Ithaca, NY: Cornell University Press, 1978), and Bence Jones, *The Royal Institution: Its Founder and its First Professors* (New York: Arno Press, 1975 [originally published in 1871]).

16. Andrés Bello, "Sociedad Parisiense de Enseñanza Elementar [sic]," in *El Repertorio Americano,* No. 1 (October 1826), p. 68.

17. Andrés Bello, "Colección de los Viajes y Descubrimientos que Hicieron por Mar los Españoles desde Fines del Siglo XV," in *El Repertorio Americano,* No. 3 (April 1827), 194.

18. This hand-written manuscript was found in the Archivo de José Rafael Revenga in Caracas, and first published by the Dirección de Cultura of the Universidad Central de Caracas in 1950. Pedro Grases included it in *ESAB,* II, pp. 249-257 with his own study and notes under the title "Andrés Bello y la Universidad de Caracas: Dictamen sobre la Biblioteca Universitaria."

19. For a good description of the Scottish Enlightenment, see Richard B. Sher, *Church and University in the Scottish Enlightenment: The Moderate Literati of Edinburgh* (Princeton: Princeton University Press, 1985). See also George Elder Davie, *The Democratic Intellect: Scotland and Her Universities in the Nineteenth Century,* 2nd ed. (Edinburgh: Edinburgh University Press, 1964).

20. Llorens, *Liberales y Románticos,* p. 164. See also Antonio Alcalá Galiano, *Recuerdos de un Anciano* (Buenos Aires: Espasa-Calpe, 1951). Alcalá was one of the members of the Spanish community in Somers Town. His book was first published in 1878.

21. Emir Rodríguez Monegal, *El Otro Andrés Bello* (Caracas: Monte Avila Editores, 1969), pp. 80-81.

22. The *Variedades, o Mensagero de Londres* (1823-1825) was edited by Bello's friend Blanco White, who asked for his advice and invited him to collaborate. Bello commented on Puigblanch's philological work from Chile in 1831. See Bello, "Filología," in *OC,* VII, 363-367.

23. Thomas Carlyle, *The Life of John Sterling* (London, New York and Toronto: Oxford University Press, 1907), pp. 66-67.

24. Bello to Gual, January 6, 1825, Latin American Manuscripts. Venezuela. Manuscript Department, Lilly Library, Bloomington, Indiana. An incomplete version of this letter is in *OC,* XXV, 142-144.

25. The words "from young Dunn" are scribbled on the back of letters from Blanco White dated July

8, 1821, September 13, 1821, and October 4, 1822. Colección de Manuscritos Originales, Fundación La Casa de Bello, Caracas, Venezuela [henceforth *CMO*], Box 2, items No. 14, 15, and 17, respectively.

26. Iris [Inés Echeverría Bello], *Nuestra Raza: A la Memoria de Andrés Bello; Su Cuarta Generación* (Santiago: Ediciones de la Universidad de Chile, n.d.), p. 7. Inés was the granddaughter of Juan, the first child of the Bello-Dunn marriage.

27. On Somers Town, see Claire H. G. Gobbi, "The Spanish Quarter of Somers Town: An Immigrant Community, 1820-30," *The Camden History Review,* No. 6 (1978), 6-9. The area initially had a heavy French and Irish presence, and later received the influx of Spanish (and Spanish American) immigration.

28. These addresses are recorded in "Admissions to Reading Room, January 1820-November 1826," Central Archives, British Museum. He used the address at Solls Road on April 14, 1823, when he became a subscriber at the Royal Institution. See note no. 15 in this chapter.

29. Definitive evidence that he was living at this address by February 15, 1827 is in "Admissions to the Reading Room, 1827-1835," p. 4. Central Archives, British Museum.

30. Aurelio Espinosa Pólit, "Bello Latinista," in Bello, *OC,* VIII, lxxvii.

31. Bello, "Informe al Papa Pío VII Redactado en Londres por Don Andrés Bello y Suscrito por Fernando de Peñalver y José María Vergara," in *OC,* VIII, 457-469.

32. David Bushnell, *The Making of Modern Colombia: A Nation in Spite of Itself* (Berkeley, Los Angeles, Oxford: University of California Press, 1993), pp. 57-58. A brief survey of the relations between the Vatican and other Spanish American republics is by Leslie Bethell, "A Note on the Church and the Independence of Latin America," in Leslie Bethell, ed., *The Cambridge History of Latin America,* vol. 3 (Cambridge: Cambridge University Press, 1985), pp. 229-234.

33. In addition to Donoso's biography of Irisarri cited in note 5, see John Browning, *Vida e Ideología de Antonio José de Irisarri* (Guatemala City: Editorial Universitaria de Guatemala) 1986, and Simon Collier, *Ideas and Politics of Chilean Independence, 1808-1833* (Cambridge: Cambridge University Press, 1967), passim.

34. Irisarri to Echeverría, October 10, 1820. Quoted by Feliú Cruz in "Bello, Irisarri y Egaña," p. 11.

35. Irisarri to Mercedes Trucíos, October 10, 1820, quoted in Ibid., 13.

36. Irisarri to O'Higgins, October 22, 1820, in Ibid., 27.

37. Bello to Irisarri, September 11, 1820, in Bello, *OC,* XXII, 613-615.

38. Irisarri to Bello, March 21, 1821, in *OC,* XXV, 104-105.

39. Irisarri to Bello, May 29 and June 1, 1822, *CMO,* Box 2, items No. 26 and 68. Francisco Ribas Galindo was the son of Venezuelan General José Félix Ribas. Although little is known about him, the younger Ribas appears to have been well connected in patriot circles. See J. León Helguera, "Tres Cartas de Nariño," *Boletín de Historia y Antiguedades* 48, No. 555 (January-February 1961), 113-116. See also Berruezo, *La Lucha,* p. 262.

40. The terms of the loan are in *Documentos de la Misión de Don Mariano Egaña en Londres (1824-1829),* comp. by Javier González Echenique (Santiago: Ministerio de Relaciones Exteriores de Chile, 1984), pp. 534-536. See also Frank Griffith Dawson, *The First Latin American Debt Crisis: The City of London and the 1822-25 Loan Bubble* (New Haven and London: Yale University Press, 1990), pp. 32-34.

41. They are printed in Bello, *OC,* X, 429-433, and 437-442, respectively. For an overview of Chilean foreign relations during the period see Ricardo Montaner Bello, *Historia Diplomática de la Independencia de Chile* (Santiago: Editorial Andrés Bello, 1961).

42. In a letter dated November 25, 1820, Irisarri presented the matter of recognition to O'Higgins in even stronger terms: "no one knows what is to be recognized, a democratic or aristocratic republic, a monarchy, or a government without principles." Quoted by Donoso, *Irisarri,* p. 105.

43. The text of the Constitution is in Luis Valencia Avaria, *Anales de la República. Textos Constitucionales de Chile y Registros de los Ciudadanos que han Integrado los Poderes Ejecutivo y Legislativo desde 1810,* 2nd ed. (Santiago: Editorial Andrés Bello, 1986), pp. 115-150. See also Brian Loveman, *The Constitution of Tyranny: Regimes of Exception in Spanish America* (Pittsburgh and London: University of Pittsburgh Press, 1993), pp. 324-325. On Egaña's constitutional ideas and the failure of his project, see Collier, *Ideas and Politics,* pp. 277-286.

44. Webster, *Britain and the Independence of Latin America,* I, pp. 362-365.

45. Egaña's instructions are in *Documentos de la Misión,* pp. 32-34.

46. Christopher Nugent to George Canning, June 4, 1824, in Webster, *Great Britain and the Independence of Latin America,* I, p. 354.

47. Mariano Egaña to Juan Egaña, September 24, 1824, in *Cartas de don Mariano Egaña a su Padre, 1824-1829* (Santiago: Sociedad de Bibliófilos, 1948), p. 31. A more tempered version appears in *Documentos de la Misión,* pp. 48-51.

48. Ibid. I translate from Feliú Cruz's, "Bello, Irisarri y Egaña," p. 55, because his transcription of this letter includes some lines that were omitted in Egaña's *Cartas.*

49. Bello to Pedro Gual, January 6, 1825. Latin American Manuscripts. Manuscripts Department, Lilly Library.

50. Bello to Irisarri, February 3, 1825, in *OC,* XXV, 145-146.

51. "Nombramiento de Bello como Secretario de la Legación de Colombia en Londres," *CMO,* Box 2, item no. 69. Bello's son Juan was born on the same day. Perhaps as a gesture of peace, he asked Mariano Egaña to be godfather to his child. Egaña agreed and attended the ceremony on February 13. That was not, however, the end of the tensions between them.

52. Gual to Bello, in *OC,* XXV, 140.

53. Gual to Bello, November 9, 1824, *CMO,* Box 2, item No. 71.

54. Bello to Gual, February 10, 1825, in *OC,* XXV, 149.

55. Mariano Egaña to Juan Egaña, May 25, 1825, in *Cartas,* p. 77.

56. Mariano Egaña to Juan Egaña, December 21, 1825, in Ibid., pp. 128-129. Irisarri sued the paper for libel, and won, because of its unfavorable coverage of his role in the transaction. The transcript of the trial, in which Bello served as witness, is in "Chilian Loan: A Report of the Trial of Yrisarri v. Clement, in the Court of Common Pleas, 19th December, 1825," (London, 1826).

57. Mariano Egaña to Juan Egaña, November 20, 1826, in *Cartas,* p. 175. In *Cartas de un Americano sobre las Ventajas de los Gobiernos Republicanos Federativos* (London, 1826), Rocafuerte and co-author José Canga Arguelles had rebutted Juan Egaña's *Memorias Políticas sobre las Federaciones y Lejislaturas en Jeneral i con Relación a Chile* (Santiago: Imprenta de la Independencia, 1825). At the insistence of Mariano, Juan Egaña produced an ill-tempered counter-rebuttal that Rocafuerte and Arguelles ignored.

58. José M. de Mier, "Andrés Bello en la Legación de Colombia en Londres," *Bello y Londres,* I, pp. 513-577.

59. Dawson, *Debt Crisis,* pp. 22-31.

60. Dawson, *Debt Crisis,* pp. 74-75; Bushnell, *Colombia,* pp. 59-60, and Antonio Vittorino, *Relaciones Colombo-Británicas de 1823 a 1825 según los Documentos del Foreign Office* (Barranquilla: Ediciones Uninorte, 1990).

61. Bello and Santos Michelena to the Minister of Finance (Colombia), November 15, 1826, in *OC,* XI, 112-115.

62. Bello to Revenga, February 8, 1826, in *OC,* XXV, 167.

63. Bello to Revenga, April 12, 1826, in *OC,* XXV, 182.

64. José María del Castillo y Rada to Andrés Bello and Santos Michelena, July 20, 1826, *OC,* XXV, 190-195. Oscar Sambrano Urdaneta provides a good summary of this affair in his introduction to vol. XXV of *OC,* lv-lxii.

65. Bello to Bolívar, December 21, 1826, in *OC,* XXV, 224-225.

66. Bello to the Minister of Foreign Relations, January 4, 1827, in *OC,* XXV, 231-235.

67. Bello to Manuel José Hurtado, January 10, 1827, in *OC,* XXV, 236-237.

68. Bolívar to Fernández Madrid, February 21, 1827, in *Cartas del Libertador,* V, pp. 387-388.

69. Paul Verna, "Bello y las Minas del Libertador. Andrés Bello Corredor de Minas y Bienes Raíces en Londres," in *Bello y Londres,* I, pp. 469-486.

70. Bello to Bolívar, April 21, 1827, in *OC,* XXV, 296-297.

71. Revenga to Bello, April 30, 1827, *OC,* XXV, 307-308.

72. Bolívar to Fernández Madrid, May 26, 1827, in *Cartas del Libertador,* V, pp. 473-475.

73. Bolívar to Bello, June 16, 1827, in Ibid., pp. 491-492.

74. Bello explained to Bolívar that he was not in a position to complete the sale of the mines because the potential buyers, the Bolívar Mining Association of London, could not agree on terms and, it was Bello's suspicion, they did not have the means to afford it. Bello to Bolívar, January 3, 1828, in *OC,* XXV, 367-368. The mines were eventually sold, but not during Bolívar's lifetime.

75. Egaña to the Minister of Foreign Relations [José Miguel Solar], November 10, 1827, in *Documentos de la Misión,* pp. 447-448. It is difficult to determine why and when the shift in Egaña's atti-

tude toward Bello may have occurred, but a good indicator of their improved relationship was Bello's sponsorship of Egaña as a reader at the British Museum's Library on March 29, 1827. See "Admissions to Reading Room, 1827-1835," p. 7. Central Archives, British Museum.

76. José Miguel de la Barra to Andrés Bello, September 15, 1828, in *Documentos de la Misión,* pp. 609-610. De la Barra indicated that the government of Chile had approved Egaña's request of November 10, 1827, on May 6, 1828.

77. Bello to José Miguel de la Barra, September 19, 1828, in *OC,* XXV, 401.

78. Bello to José Manuel Restrepo, December 2, 1828, in *OC,* XXV, 407-408.

79. Bello to Fernández Madrid, February 13, 1829, in *OC,* XXV, 408-409.

80. Fernández Madrid to Bolívar, November 6, 1828. Quoted by Rodríguez Monegal, *El Otro Andrés Bello,* p. 130.

81. Bolívar to Fernández Madrid, April 27, 1829, in *Cartas del Libertador,* VII, pp. 127-128.

FURTHER READING

Criticism

Caldera, Rafael. "The Sage." In *Andrés Bello: Philosopher, Poet, Philologist, Educator, Legislator, Statesman,* translated by John Street, pp. 47-52, 71-82. London: George Allen & Unwin LTD, 1977.

Considers Bello's accomplishments, with particular focus on his poetic, prose, and aesthetic theories.

Castronovo, Brian J. "The Concept of Mood: Bello's Influence on Ramsey." *Hispanic Linguistics* 3, no 1-2 (fall 1989): 99-121.

Details the linguistic influence of Bello's *Gramática* on Marathon Montrose Ramsey's seminal English language grammar of Spanish, *A Textbook of Modern Spanish.*

Grases, Pedro. "Andrés Bello, Cultural Liberator." *Americas* 15, no. 11 (November 1964): 1-4.

Provides a brief overview of Bello's literary output, praising the author for his humanistic efforts.

———. Introduction to *Anthology of Andrés Bello,"* translated by Barbara D. Huntley and Pilar Liria, p. 1-7. Washington D.C.: General Secretariat Organization of American States, 1981.

Provides a brief introduction to an anthology of some of Bello's poetry and prose, noting significant Bello scholars.

Henkin, Alan Barry. "Joaquín García Monge and his 'Repertorio Americano': A Legacy of Andrés Bello." *Hispania* 54, no. 2 (May 1971): 345-48.

Examines Monge's journal *Repertio Americano* for its significance to Latin American literature and considers the influence of Andrés Bello's groundbreaking journal of the same name, published 100 years earlier.

Kilgore, W. J. "Notes on the Philosophy of Education of Andrés Bello." *Journal of the History of Ideas* 22, no. 4 (October-December 1961): 555-60.

Provides a critical overview of Bello's theories on education.

Rotker, Susan. "Nation and Mockery: The Oppositional Writings of Simón Rodríguez." *Modern Language Quarterly* 57, no. 2 (June 1996): 253-67.

Focuses primarily on the works of Simón Rodríguez, with consideration of Andrés Bello's position on the formulation of a standard, legitimized Latin American grammar.

Velleman, Barry L. "The Dynamics of a Literary Standard: the Bello *Gramática.*" In *LA CHISPA '87: selected proceedings: the Eighth Louisiana Conference on Hispanic Languages and Literatures, Tulane University, New Orleans, 1987,* pp. 305-15. New Orleans, La.: The Conference, 1987.

Provides an overview of Bello's *Gramática,* including a discussion of the revisions made to the work over the course of its numerous editions.

Additional coverage of Bello's life and career is contained in the following sources published by the Gale Group: *Latin American Writers,* Vol. 1; *Literature Resource Center.*

Aleksandr Aleksandrovich Bestuzhev
1797-1837

(Also published under the pseudonyms Cossack Marlinsky, Alexander Marlinsky, and Aleksander Bestuzhev-Marlinsky) Russian novelist, poet, essayist, and literary critic.

INTRODUCTION

Bestuzhev was a well-known literary critic, a minor poet of the Golden Age of Russian verse, and a popular writer of prose fiction. He took part in the Decembrist Revolt in 1825 and was exiled first to Siberia and later to the Caucasus. While in exile, he began a second writing career under the pseudonym Marlinsky and began promoting himself as the quintessential Romantic hero. Bestuzhev's popularity waned after the middle of the nineteenth century; his work was briefly revived in his own country in the middle of the twentieth century but has been largely forgotten elsewhere in the world.

BIOGRAPHICAL INFORMATION

Bestuzhev was born in St. Petersburg on October 23, 1797, to Aleksandr Fedoseevich Bestuzhev and Praskovya Mikhailovna Bestuzheva. He attended school in St. Petersburg and at nineteen joined the military and became an officer a year later. By 1820 he was already gaining a considerable reputation for his literary criticism, his poetry, and his translations, and within the next five years he published a number of popular novellas based on Russian and Baltic history. In 1825 Bestuzhev and his four brothers were part of the Decembrist Revolt, a failed conspiracy designed to force Nicolas I into implementing reforms. Bestuzhev turned himself into the police and appealed to the tsar for forgiveness and was exiled to Siberia from 1827-29; he then received permission to serve in the army in the Caucasus, and he lived there for the rest of his life. In exile he began a second, even more successful, writing career under the pen name Cossack Marlinsky, producing many more novellas and two longer works that some critics classify as novels. Bestuzhev died in battle on June 7, 1837, but since his body was never recovered, rumors circulated for a number of years that he had been rescued and was living with the mountain people of the Caucasus.

MAJOR WORKS

Bestuzhev embarked on his writing career as a translator of political and literary works from English, German, and French sources, and as a literary critic and reviewer. He rejected the classicism associated with the previous generation and embraced the aesthetic of European Romanticism (to an extreme, according to his detractors). From 1818 until the Decembrist Revolt in 1825, Bestuzhev produced numerous works of translations and criticism, establishing himself as an important contributor to the literary debates of the day. He composed several political poems and revolutionary songs, some of which detailed the misery of the peasantry and advocated the overthrow of the tsar. At the same time he began publishing fiction in various journals based on Russian and Livonian historical figures and events, including "Zamok Venden (Otryvok iz dnevnika gvardeiskogo ofitsera)" (1821; "Castle Wenden (A Fragment from a Guard Officer's Diary)"); "Roman i Ol'ga: Starinnaia povest'" (1823; "Roman and Olga: A Tale of Olden Times"); and "Zamok Neigauzen: Rytsarskaia povest'" (1824; "Castle Neihausen: A Tale of Chivalry"). After he was exiled, Bestuzhev published numerous works of fiction under the pseudonym Marlinsky, featuring extreme versions of the Romantic hero—men of action who were dashing, reckless, and skilled in weaponry. Fascinated with the sea, he produced a series of sea stories, the most famous of which is the naval adventure story *Fregat "Nadezhda"* (1832; *The Frigate "Hope"*). His descriptive seascapes figured prominently in a number of his other tales and in some of his essays. He also wrote three horror tales that contain elements of Russian folklore and were influenced by the Gothic works of Walter Scott and Anne Radcliffe. "Latnik: Rasskaz partizanskogo ofitsera" (1831; "The Cuirassier: A Partisan Officer's Story"), is considered the best of the horror tales; it consists of a main narrative and two anecdotes, each with its own narrator and frame story. Bestuzhev's tales of the Caucasus are filled with authentic detail on the history and cultures of the region, including information on the dialects of the area, which he quickly mastered, and on various ethnic customs and modes of warfare. The most famous of the Caucasian tales are the two longest, characterized by some scholars as novels rather than novellas: *Ammalat-bek: Kavkazskaia byl'* (*Ammalat-bek: A Caucasian Legend*) written in 1831, and *Mulla Nur,* written in 1836.

CRITICAL RECEPTION

Bestuzhev's early work, prior to his exile, captured the attention of readers and established his reputation as an important writer. According to some critics, however, Bestuzhev's fame was due largely to his stylistic novelty. N. Kovarsky explains Bestuzhev's success: "His ability to say everything somehow differently, and not just simply, was tremendously appealing; his similes were striking neither for their fidelity to nature nor for their beauty, but rather for their unexpectedness and strangeness." Neil B. Landsman asserts that Bestuzhev was a leading figure in a uniquely Russian subgenre of Romanticism, Decembrism. Landsman describes Bestuzhev's style, both before and after the Decembrist Revolution, as "an amalgam of countless sayings, witticisms and turns of phrase." By the 1830s, Bestuzhev was Russia's most famous writer of prose tales. His sea stories, his historical tales, his horror stories, and most especially his tales of the Caucasus, were enormously popular with the reading public. Ironically, though, it was the latter category that led to Bestuzhev's declining reputation among more sophisticated readers and scholars. Lauren G. Leighton reports that the Caucasian tales, written under the pseudonym Marlinsky, are characterized by "their wild improbability, their extreme exoticism, and their passionate tone of narration," all of which were considered excessive and extravagant in serious literary circles. His name became closely associated with the worst excesses of Romanticism, and mature writers such as Turgenev and Tolstoy quickly outgrew their youthful enthusiasm for "Marlinism," as they termed the aesthetics of the Caucasian tales. By the 1850s, Bestuzhev's work was no longer popular and remained out of print, even in Russia, until the middle of the twentieth century, when it captured the interest of scholars and literary historians. Lewis Bagby, in a book-length study of Bestuzhev's relationship to Russian Byronism, has attempted to restore the author's reputation as "arguably the most advanced writer of prose in the 1820s and demonstrably the most popular writer in Russia in the 1830s."

Although many critics consider Bestuzhev a minor poet of Russia's Golden Age whose verse was inferior to his prose tales, Leighton insists that his lyric poetry deserves further consideration by modern scholars. According to Leighton, "in his technical practice, in his choice of verse genres, and in his Romantic attitudes, Marlinsky strikes a poetic stance which is remarkably apt as an illustration of the verse standards of his day." She acknowledges his initial lack of imagination, but finds merit in the "strikingly unusual metric experiments in his later poetry."

PRINCIPAL WORKS

Poezdka v Revel' [*Journey to Revel*] (novella) 1820-21
Roman v semi pis'makh [*A Romance in Seven Letters*] (novella) 1824

Andrei, kniaz' Pereiaslavskii [published anonymously; *Andrey, Prince of Pereiaslavl*] (poetry) 1827
Ammalat-bek: Kavkazskaia byl' [*Ammalat-bek: A Caucasian Legend*] (novel) 1831
Fregat "Nadezhda" [*The Frigate 'Hope'*] (novella) 1832
Mulla Nur (novel) 1836
Sochineniya v dvukh tomakh. 2 vols. (poetry, literary criticism, novellas, and letters) 1958

CRITICISM

Lauren G. Leighton (essay date July 1969)

SOURCE: Leighton, Lauren G. "Bestuzhev-Marlinsky as a Lyric Poet." *Slavonic and East European Review* 47, no. 109 (July 1969): 308-22.

[*In the following essay, Leighton discusses Bestuzhev's poetry as a representation of the technical and aesthetic standards of Russia's Golden Age.*]

'Marlinsky is out of fashion these days', recalled Turgenev in the 1870s, 'no one reads him and his name is even sneered at; but in the thirties he thundered forth like no one else . . . put his stamp on the entire generation contemporary to him.'[1] A fierce literary critic on behalf of Romanticism in Russia, a glamorous revolutionary of the ill-fated Decembrist movement, the author of a brilliant variety of ultra-Romantic prose tales—these are the things for which Aleksandr Bestuzhev (pseudonym Marlinsky) is remembered today. But if he should be most properly remembered for these other achievements, he is also well worth modern scrutiny as a lyric poet. As one of those poets of Russia's Golden Age whose output D. S. Mirsky considered 'perfect even when it is minor poetry',[2] he is well worth consideration for his own sake. Moreover, in his technical practice, in his choice of verse genres, and in his Romantic attitudes, Marlinsky strikes a poetic stance which is remarkably apt as an illustration of the verse standards of his day. He himself once remarked 'I am a true microcosm',[3] and his poetry stands as an excellent representation of the artistic problems faced by the poets of one of the most critical stages in the development of Russian poetry.

As a soldier, an exile, and a persecuted Decembrist, Marlinsky led a nomadic life, and thus the heritage he left was somewhat chaotic. It was only after over a century of painstaking scholarship that it became possible, in this decade, to publish the carefully compiled and edited *Biblioteka poeta* edition of his poetry.[4] During his career as a poet, from 1816 to 1838, Marlinsky wrote 44 original lyric poems and translated, imitated, or rendered 16 poems from French, German, Persian, Turkish and Yakut (but not, surprisingly, from English, the foreign language he knew best and the literature he loved most). Although five poems of this basic group (three of them translations) were written anonymously, they have been convincingly ascribed to his authorship.[5] To this basic group of sixty lyric poems must be added twenty 'sets' of epigraphs and verse passages in prose contexts. Although it is possible to break this count down to 27 separate verse passages and 22 epigraphs, it is best to consider them as sets, especially since they cannot always be extracted from their contexts without disrupting their unity. A third and final group of poems is composed of five *agitatsionnyye* and seven *podblyudnyye* songs which Marlinsky wrote in collaboration with his closest literary friend, Kondratiy Ryleyev.[6]

Marlinsky's value as a microcosm of his age is particularly evinced in his choice of verse genres. In his early poetry there can be found a number of ventures in traditional neo-classical genres—odes, satires, burlesques, epigrams, and even charades. Coincident with these genres are the poems in the 'sentimental-elegiac' vein of Karamzin—elegies, love poems, and the so-called 'friendly messages' of the *Arzamas* school. In the course of his development Marlinsky was influenced by the 'civic-Decembrist' movement, and the result is not only the revolutionary songs, but also patriotic verses on historical themes, including a quite unusual *duma*.[7] It was not until the period of his Siberian exile (1827-30), however, that Marlinsky began to write mature and Romantic poetry. Among the Romantic genres he cultivated are his excellent love lyrics, especially a series of translations from Goethe, his plaints from exile on the theme of individual isolation, his nature poems, and his poetry of 'Death and the Grave'. The most unusual genres Marlinsky practised—nay, invented—are his folk poems, comprising a beautiful Yakut ballad and, of particular interest, the fierce Caucasian war chants he wrote just before his tragic death.[8] And finally, there are the many epigraphs and sets of verse passages, the latter a variety of ventures ranging from sentimental love elegies and epistolary declarations to patriotic rhetoric.

In terms of linear production Marlinsky's metric practice is also a reflection of the general standards of his day. During his 22 years of poetic creativity he wrote a total of 4529 lines, of which 3624 lines are iambic, 375 trochaic, 283 ternary, and 247 lines are written in folk or musical rhythms, in cadences, or in inter-linear metric mixtures. Of this total count, 1920 lines belong to the Romantic verse tale, ***Andrey, knyaz' Pereyaslavskiy***, and the 1858 iambic lines of this non-lyric genre actually exceed the 1766 iambic lines of his lyric poetry. The preponderance of iambic lines (about 80%), largely

in iambic tetrametre, is a clear adherence to contemporary preferences, and in this he is quite close to Pushkin (84%) and Baratynsky (195 poems in iambic metre of a total of 222 poems).[9] His trochaic lines amount to about 8% of his work, as compared to Pushkin's 10.6% and Denis Davydov's 23%:[10] Pushkin is considered to be typical of the general standard and Davydov well above the norm. His 6.5% ternary usage is again quite typical for his time. Pushkin's ternary usage (1.5%) was exceptionally low.[11]

Like most contemporary poets, Marlinsky began his career with iambic lines, and only later turned to trochees and ternaries. Excluding the revolutionary songs written with Ryleyev, only three of his first 31 lyric poems, written in his first twelve years, are in a metre other than iambic. If anything, he is conservative on this point. The fact that Marlinsky devoted his ternary lines largely to folk poetry indicates that he shared the general belief of his contemporaries that they were best suited to this genre. Lermontov was the first to use ternary metres significantly in other ways, and not until Tyutchev, the Parnassians, and the civic poets of the mid-nineteenth century did they really come into their own. Marlinsky differs from his contemporaries in his metric practice in that no other poet of his time made such a literal and unimaginative use of syllabo-accentual versification techniques in his early poetry or, conversely, made such strikingly unusual metric experiments in his later poetry.

A clear indication of Marlinsky's initially pedestrian understanding of syllabo-accentual versification is the low number of pyrrhic feet in his early poems. It was not until 1823 or 1824 that he seems to have realised that poetry is dependent at least as much upon variety as unity, and really not until 1827 or 1828 that he introduced more variety into his metric patterns by omitting stresses more liberally and with more ingenuity. The rhythmic monotony of his early poems is both perceptible and annoying. In the poem **"Mikhail Tverskoy"** (1824), for example, 148 of the total of 180 iambic feet are determinedly honoured with stress, an astonishingly high rate of honour. Of the poem's 45 four-foot lines, only two have as many as two omissions of stress, only 29 omit one of the four possible stresses, and 14 lines are rigidly honoured with all four stresses. The rhythm of the poem is all the more monotonous in that of the ten pairs of rhymed lines of the first stanza—largely in couplets—seven share identical stress patterns. Added to all these sins is an obvious lack of sense of degree of stress that mars much of the early poetry. Clearly, like Lomonosov, the young Marlinsky understood the rules of syllabo-accentual versification all too literally.[12]

A curious fact: whereas Marlinsky undoubtedly learned his rules of versification from Lomonosov, his early diction is clearly Karamzinian. More than one scholar has noted that Marlinsky came to literature as a disciple of Karamzin, and thus his first poems are exactly what we should expect from a young man of his time and place. The first poem in the *Biblioteka poeta* edition, for example, begins with the line: 'Bliz stana yunosha prekrasnyy', and contains such other affectedly sentimental lines as: 'Yego volnystymi vlasami / Vecherniy veterok igral' and 'Togda vy, veterki, letite / K lyubeznoy serdtsu s vest'yu sey'. The second poem, **"Sebe lyubeznogo ishchu,"** is also noticeably Karamzinian. Such lines as 'S streloy smeyotsya Kupidon' and 'Mog plakat' v nedrakh sladostrast'ya', and such phrases as 'v plamennykh ochakh', 'perly slyoz', and 'na list'yakh roz', as well as the last melodramatic line: 'Ili umru', are well in the sentimental-elegiac tradition of Karamzin and his successors. Moreover, in his ventures in this genre Marlinsky is so transparently imitative of current mode that he has all the faults and none of the charm of Karamzin, Zhukovsky, or V. L. Pushkin.

Diction is not the only weakness in Marlinsky's early poetry. He was often hard put to reconcile his syntax with metric demands, and frequently forced an unnatural stress. In the first of two verse passages from early love letters, **"Iz pis'ma k S. V. Savitskoy"** (1816 or 1817), one line is particularly awkward in the attempt to provide a rhyme for *stopóy* by forcing a shift to an unnatural stress: 'Na vse okréstnosti brosáyete vzor svóy'. A frequent compromise in syntax is also to be found in Marlinsky's resort to short-form adjectives for the sake of metric pattern, as in the line from **"Sebe lyubeznogo ishchu"**: 'Kotory tmyat prelestny vzory'. The attributive use of short-form adjectives was still within the province of poetic licence in the early 19th century, but the practice had been dwindling ever since Lomonosov began avoiding it in the mid-eighteenth century. It is a common feature of the poetry of Derzhavin, but even that grammatically anarchic eccentric subordinated the usage to stylistic effect in his later years. The young Zhukovsky resorted to the practice in his first poems and quickly abandoned it, again except for stylistic effect. More comparable to Marlinsky would be Pushkin or Yazykov, and it can be found that they both used it in very early poems and then quickly abandoned it.[13] Marlinsky, on the other hand, employed it for more than a decade with no other apparent intent than to force agreement between syntax and metre. Moreover, while 'serdechny chuvstva,' 'zvuchny struny,' and 'granitnu tsep' may be accepted as 'poetic' epithets of the early 19th-century, 'russki uzy' must have ground upon the ear.

Marlinsky should not be treated too harshly for his early shortcomings, however. His contemporaries for the most part had ample opportunity to destroy or polish their early poetry. Marlinsky's sudden death denied him this grace. Moreover, there are also indications of talent in his early poems. As a critic and as a person he possessed a sardonic wit, and he expressed it well in his poetry. **"K nekotorym poetam"** (1819), a satire in the neo-classical vein, is a sustained effort directed against the slavish imitation of foreign literature, an attack on the contemporary lack of appreciation for such poets as Derzhavin, Karamzin and Zhukovsky. Of particular promise for its wit is **"Epigramma na Zhukovskogo"** (1824), an expression of Decembrist dissatisfaction with the older poet's court status.[14] Written in six iambic lines of mixed lengths with an ABABBA rhyme scheme (indicative of Marlinsky's decreased dependence on couplets), the epigram accuses Zhukovsky of being a lackey and ends with the strikingly contrastive and effective two-foot line: 'Bédnyy pevéts!', the inversion drawing immediate attention to the line, to its semantic intent, and to its play on the title of one of Zhukovsky's more popular poems of the day.

It was under the influence of Ryleyev that Marlinsky developed as a poet. This is particularly evident in the revolutionary songs, and it also becomes apparent in his poetry of the mid-twenties on civic-Decembrist themes. The poem **"Mikhail Tverskoy,"** actually a *duma* similar to Ryleyev's own *duma* of the same title, is a case in point, despite its metric shortcomings. Based on Karamzin's treatment of the execution of Mikhail Yaroslavovich, Prince of Tver', by the Tatar Khan in 1318 it is an outright glorification of the Russian past, and it has all the over- and undertones of the patriotic nationalism espoused by the early Russian civic poets. Treating as it does of a martyred Russian and an equally martyred *Rus'*, such lines as: 'V stolitse khishchnykh, zlobnykh khanov / Rossii yarostnykh tiranov,' are especially well suited to tone and theme. The use of historical grammatical forms like 'yunyye dni', 'vlasy', 'glavy', and 'mladoy' is much more effective to a theme of Slavic antiquity than to the sentimental-elegiac poems.

A far finer civic poem is Marlinsky's treatment of Aleksandr Nevsky in a verse passage which forms part of an early prose work, **"Listok iz dnevnika gvardeyskogo ofitsera"** (1821). It reveals an increasing appreciation of euphony (e.g. 'Dlya zhazhdushchey dushi moyey'), and in general the more flexible rhythm, skilful use of repetition, smoother syntax and blending of words, and a more sophisticated stanzaic articulation heighten the poem's artistic value. All of these features are well illustrated by this patriotic passage:

И дали рыцари хребет,
И плен, и кровь, и труп их след.
И нет от гибели спасенья
Посереди безбрежных льдов,
И Александр, как ангел мщенья,
Следил, разил, губил врагов . . .[15]

The group of *podblyudnyye* and *agitatsionnyye* songs are an expression of Decembrist civicism and political protest. The form had only recently been introduced to

Russian literature. At the turn of the century Denis Davydov wrote four quite sharp political fables and satires, including *Orlitsa, turukhtan i teterev* (1804) which caused him to be posted to a remote military station. Pushkin's political verses, particularly *'Noël.' Ura!* and *Kinzhal,* are important contributions to this tradition. P. A. Katenin's *Otechestvo nashe stradayet,* of which only a fragment has survived, Prince Vyazemsky's *Ay da tsar',* and Yazykov's *Svobody gordoy vdokhnoven'ye* (still incorrectly ascribed to Ryleyev in *The Oxford Book of Russian Verse*)[16] are only three of the many political-revolutionary poems which, along with the songs of Marlinsky and Ryleyev, laid the foundation of a tradition so important to Russian literature.

The revolutionary songs were all written between 1823 and 1825 (the period in which Marlinsky and Ryleyev collaborated most closely in their Decembrist activities), and they quickly became popular accompaniments to champagne and oyster banquets. The agitation songs were first published by Aleksandr Herzen in 1859; most of the *podblyudnyye* songs, however, were lost until 1950 when copies were found in the Ostaf'yevsky archive of P. A. Vyazemsky.[17] Soviet scholars have done a great deal of excellent work in the reconstruction of the precise form of these songs from a variety of manuscripts and hand-written copies. It has never been satisfactorily established which songs, or passages from the songs, were written by Marlinsky.[18] The most notable feature of the songs is their unusual metric schemes. The Soviet scholar N. I. Mordovchenko has noted that the two authors employed 'available peasant, soldier, and urban folk forms to which they joined their political themes of the day',[19] and most Soviet scholars agree with this. But there is also evidence, both firm and fleeting, of syllabo-accentual mixtures, and thus it is quite important that the two poets were collaborating on an aesthetic, as well as a political experiment. The stanzas of the first two of the five agitation songs, for example, are articulated on the basis of two-foot anapests counterpointed by one-foot trochees. Thus, the first song begins with these stanzas:

> Áх, где тé островá,
> Где растéт трынь-травá,
>   Брáтцы!
>
> Где читáют Pucélle
> И летт под постéль
>   Свтцы.

The second song has an identical stanzaic construction:

> Ты скажи, говори,
> Как в Росси цари
>   Прáвят.
>
> Ты скаж поскорéй,
> Как в России царéй
>   Дáвят.

Both songs maintain their metric pattern until the very last line: 'Khódit v kázhdyy kabák' and 'Bédnym lyúdyam pomóg', respectively. It could be that these deliberate disruptions of harmony are meant to be raucous finales to essentially raucous songs. The first song is a ringing satire on Petersburg and the court, including even *Bestuzhev-dragun,* who at that time was a brilliant young adjutant at the Winter Palace. The second is a jeer at autocratic rule-by-assassination.

The third song, **"Akh, toshno mne,"** is written to the tune of a popular romance of the time, and it is an attack on the banality and brutality of Russian autocracy. The principles which unite each of its eighteen stanzas are quite unique. The first two lines are always rhymed with each other and, occasionally, with the fifth and last line. Lines three and four, both shorter than the others, are also always rhymed, and they almost inevitably have the same metric pattern (— —'—). And finally, while lines one, two, and five do not have consistent metric patterns, they are rough anapestic-trochaic mixtures and usually two, occasionally all three, will agree in metric pattern. Stanzas six and seven are apt illustrations of these articulatory principles:

> А тепéрь господá
> Грáбят нáс без стыдá,
>   И обмáном
>   Их кармáном
> Стáла нáша мошнá.
>
> Они кóжу с нáс дерýт,
> Мы посéем—они жнýт.
>   Они вóры,
>   Живодёры,
> Как пиявки, крóвь сосýт.

The fourth song is again a mixture of metres, each of its fourteen stanzas being comprised of a satiric couplet in trochees and ending with a common refrain in folk rhythm:

> Цáрь наш—нéмец рýсский
> Нóсит мýндир ýзкий.
> Ай да цáрь, ай да цáрь,
> Православный государь![20]

The *podblyudnyye* songs, seven in all, are either composed of a few long lines or many short lines, and they are all in folk rhythm. In contrast to the politically sophisticated agitation songs, their appeal is to soldier and peasant. The term *podblyudnyye*—literally 'under saucer'—stems from a Novgorodian folk custom which Marlinsky describes in his prose tale **"Strashnoye gadan'ye"** (1830): 'A cock, placed in a circle along the outer edge of which were sprinkled little heaps of oats and barley with rings buried in them, proclaimed the destined marriage of the youth or maiden being divined by honouring one or another of the heaps with a peck . . . After placing a saucer over a cup in which were placed pieces of sanctified bread, the maidens' rings, and coals, whose significance I was never able to ascertain, everyone began singing *podblyudnyye* songs, that lottery of fate and its verdicts.'[21] The colloquial appeal of the songs is indicated by their use of such jargon as 'plut', 'topor', 'na knyaz'kov-soplyakov', and 'peki pirogi'. Their raucous tone is reinforced by heavy use of such exclamations as 'akh!', 'ay da tsar'', and 'toshno tak, chto oy, oy, oy!' They deal with subjects having more of a folk appeal—maidens, merchants, soldierly gossip, and even a fable of two rainbows.

It is not until the period of Marlinsky's exile to Siberia following the failure of the Decembrist revolt, during the years from 1827 to 1829, that a totally new artistic level, a mature Romantic creativity, can be found in his poetry. His stay in Siberia was one of intense scholarly and poetic creativity, and one of the finest results of the latter is his series of renderings of love poetry from Goethe's *West-Östlicher Divan*.[22] To this series belong **"Yunost'"** (**"podrazhaniye Gete"**), **"Iz Gafiza, Iz Gete"** (**"s persidskogo"**), **"Iz Gete"** (**"podrazhaniye"**), **"Zyuleyka, S persidskogo,"** **"Vsegda i vezde,"** and **"Magnit"** (all 1828). Usually composed of stanzas of four, six, or eight lines, with none longer than two six-line stanzas, they are written in trochees or iambs, with the exception of the unusual **"Magnit,"** composed of two truncated dactylic couplets ('— —'— —'). Without exception they are remarkable for their clarity and simplicity, each expressing its thought with brevity.

Thus, **"Iz Gete"** (**"podrazhaniye"**) is composed of two four-line stanzas with alternating rhyme scheme, the first expressing the brilliance and gaiety of a ball, the second providing this intimate contrast:

> Но в мраке и в тиши
> Тебя, не видя, нахожу я
> По жару девственной души,
> По сладкой неге поцелуя.

Closely related to these responses to Goethe is the original poem **"Yey"** (also 1828), the first four of its eight iambic lines offering proof:

> Когда моей ланитой внемлю
> Пыланию твоих ланит,
> Мне радость небеса и землю
> И золотит и серебрит . . .

It may be noted here that while the odd lines are almost fully honoured with stress, the even lines, especially line four with its double masculine paeon, are more free. Full cadence is thus alternated with rapid rhythm to lend a quick-shifting pace to the stanza. To this is added the metric, syntactic, and semantic repetition of line four, as well as the entire poem's excellent alliteration.

More in keeping with Marlinsky's fate and his milieu is a new contemplative, even religious, tone in his poetry.

For it is at this stage of his life that we find a post-Zhukovsky treatment of the pre-Romantic theme of death and the grave. The first hint of this new quality appears in 1828 in the poem **"Nadpis' nad mogiloy Mikhalevykh v Yakutskom monastyre."** Indicative of theme and tone are the lines:

> Счастливцы! Здесь и там не знали вы разлуки,
> Не знали пережить родных тяжёлой муки.[23]

Further indication of Marlinsky's contemplative attitude, as well as a religious flavour, is to be found in the brief and sudden consideration of the final line: 'I vse my svidimsya v ob'yatiyakh tvortsa.' ('And we shall all be reunited in the arms of the creator'). Marlinsky's concept of death and the grave is quite different from that of Zhukovsky, who introduced into Russian literature the melancholy tone and pastoral descriptiveness of the German and English Romantics and pre-Romantics, particularly of Gray's *Elegy*. He refuses to be passive before the mystery of death and he actually defies the grave, thus dissociating himself from Zhukovsky's less passionate attitude. Perhaps this, as well as the contemplative tone and metaphysical pondering of Marlinsky's poetry on the theme, is best illustrated by this passage from **"Cherep"** (1828):

> Где ж доблести? Отдай мне гроба дань,
> Познаний светлых тёмный вестник!
> Ты ль бытия таинственная грань?
> Иль дух мой—вечности ровесник?

From the theme of Death and the Grave Marlinsky turned to the enigma of his own fate, first as a recurring motif, then as a theme which came to dominate his poetic creativity. The two themes are closely related—both are contemplative and both have an introspective concern with death and eternity. But where the first is religious, sometimes morbid, even daemonic, the second becomes more and more the plaint of an isolated human being yearning desperately for 'homeland and freedom'. The plaint of exile first appears as a motif in 1829, in the poem **"V den' imenin."** A promise to appear cheerful for the sake of the addressee's name day, it is nevertheless plaintive in tone, as in the opening lines: 'Nevol'nyy gost' v krayu chuzhbiny, / Zabyvshiy svet, zabyvshiy lest' . . .' In the very next poem, **"Lide,"** the motif is extended to encompass the desperation of a young man cut off from the normal needs of life, and the same note of desperation engulfs another poem of the same year, **"E. I. B[ulgarinoy]"**:

> Зачем, зачем же вы желали
> Мне сердце пробудить опять,
> В свои летучие скрижали
> Мою кручину записать?

In this poem, however, there is still a note of optimism, even of good humour:

Но дайте года два терпенья,
И, может быть, как важный гусь,
И я по озеру смиренья
Бесстрастно плавать научусь.

At the point where the motif becomes a fully mature theme, Marlinsky turns to an image which was already of significance in Russian literature, especially in regard to the fate of the Decembrists, and was to have further import through Marlinsky's influence on Lermontov. This occurs in the poem **"Son"** (1829), which begins with the image of horse and rider and then turns to the image of the bark (*chelnok*) already employed by Pushkin in his *Arion* (1827). **"Son"** is comprised of two parts, the first built on the swift, nightmarish pace of horse and rider racing over the Siberian tundra:

И случай, преклоняя темя,
Держал мне золотое стремя,
И, гордо бросив повода,
Я поскакал туда, туда! . . .

Then, with a pause after a nightmarish plunge through space, the poem's second part resumes with the calm, placid pace of the lines introducing the image of the bark:

Очнулся я от страшной грёзы,
Но всё душа тоски полна,
И мнилось, гнут меня желёзы
К веслу убогого челна.

Marlinsky was undoubtedly aware of Pushkin's poem to the Decembrists, *Arion,* for both its vocabulary and its use of the image of the bark is similar:

Нас было много на челне;
Иные парус напрягали,
Другие дружно упирали
Вглубь мощны весла . . . В тишине
На руль склонясь, наш кормщик умный
В молчанье правил грузный челн;

He could not have been aware of *Arion* during the writing of his Romantic verse tale, **Andrey, knyaz' Pereyaslavskiy,** in 1827, yet perhaps the most beautiful lines of the verse tale fragment are similar to Pushkin's lines in their use of the images of bark, sail, and storm:

И гром катится вдалеке.
Но вот ярящимся Дунаем,
То видим, то опять скрываем,
Ловец плывёт на челноке.
Белеет парус одинокий,
Как лебединое крыло,
И грустен путник ясноокий;
У ног колчан, в руке весло.
Но, с беззаботною улыбкой,
Летучей пеной орошён,
Вестрепетно во влаге зыбкой
Порывом бури мчится он.

The images of sail and storm are, of course, the focus of Lermontov's famous *Parus* (1832), and his use of

Marlinsky's line from the verse tale to begin this poem indicates how greatly he admired Marlinsky: 'Beleyet parus odinokiy'. Marlinsky's use of imagery differs from that of Pushkin and Lermontov. In *Parus* and *Arion* 'bark' or 'storm' or 'sail' are used symbolically, in the former to dramatise the rebellious Byronic figure tempting fate, in the latter to allude covertly to its author's role as a passive fellow-traveller of the Decembrists and to the fate of the Decembrists themselves. Marlinsky's images, on the other hand, are concrete and pictorial, direct references to an actual setting in his verse tale.[24]

Before the year 1829 was over Marlinsky's plaint of exile lost its optimism and revealed itself as a theme centering on homeland and freedom. In the poem of that year, **"K oblaku,"** he likens himself and his fate to a cloud, ending with the lines: 'I ya pogibnu vdaleke / Ot rodiny i voli!' ('And I shall perish far away from homeland and freedom'). The theme of personal fate is again evident in the poem **"Shebutuy"** (1829). Drawing a personal analogy to the vivid and sounding waterfall, he addresses Shebutuy:

Тебе подобно, гордый, шумный,
От высоты родимых скал
Влекомый страстию безумной,
Я в бездну гибели упал![25]

In reading Marlinsky's prose works, both fictional and factual, one is struck by the great value he placed on language, ethnography, history, and folklore. In point of fact, he was a serious scholar, and used his talent for languages to saturate his works with authentic linguistic, historic, ethnographic, and folkloristic facts and atmosphere. It is little wonder then, that in that very period of the thirties when he was fascinating Russia with his ultra-Romantic prose tales, he was also writing undeniably excellent folk songs and poems of the Caucasus, such as the Yakut ballad **"Saatyr'"** (1828) which, as Marlinsky noted, was based on a popular Siberian folk legend. Written in alternating four- and three-foot amphibrachic lines, the ballad comprises fourteen ten-line stanzas. Quite reminiscent of Zhukovsky's *Lyudmila* (his 1811 adaptation of Bürger's *Lenore*), the ballad falls not into the purely death-and-the-grave category, but into the realm of the supernatural and the fantastic. **"Saatyr'"**—Marlinsky also noted that the name meant *igrivaya*—is the tale of a young Yakut beauty who, having been a faithful wife, asks on her deathbed that her ring be given to the man she truly loved, Prince Buydukan. Using the ring, Buydukan calls his beloved from the grave to a tryst. For having dared to defy the grave, the lovers are doomed to a terrible death. The supernatural tone of the ballad is well illustrated by this sensual stanza:

И вот поцелуев таинственный звук
Под кровом могильной святыни,

И сладкие речи—Но вдруг и вокруг
  Слетелися духи пустыни.

Two of the finest sets of folk songs and poems are embodied in the Caucasian prose tales, *Ammalat-bek* (1831) and *Mulla-Nur* (1836). The excerpts from the latter are a chorus sung to welcome the rain, approximately iambic, and a folk song in trochees. Both are translated from Azeri. Of better, perhaps because stranger, quality is the set of verses from *Ammalat-bek,* especially the *smertnyye pesni* which D. S. Mirsky has called 'a thing unequalled of its kind in the language'.[26] The first passage of the set is a song of Kabardinian antiquity sung by one of the tale's characters to the accompaniment of a balalaika. Written in trochaic tetrametre, its first stanza is illustrative:

На Казбек слетелись тучи,
Словно горные орлы . . .
Им навстречу, на скалы
Узденей отряд летучий
Выше, выше, круче, круче
Скачет, русскими разбит:
След их кровию кипит.

The *smertnyye pesni* are the more unusual in that they are written for full- and half-choruses, each choral part written in a different metre or even in a metric mixture. The opening and closing refrain, for example, is composed of a couplet, both lines of which are hemi-stiched, each hemi-stich comprised of an amphimachris:

Сла́ва на́м—сме́рть врагу́,
А́лла-га́, А́лла-гу́!

While the first half-chorus sings one choral accompaniment in dactyls and a second in a mixture of iambs and trochees, the second half-chorus sings first in a mixture of trochees and anapests and then in pure iambs. The full chorus then concludes with an arrangement in amphibrachs and the trochaic refrain. The *smertnyye pesni* were to be sung high in the mountains on the eve of battle; perhaps the first arrangement for the second half-chorus exemplifies both content and form:

Де́вы, не пла́чьте; ва́ши сестрцы,
  Гу́рии, све́тлой толпо́й,
К сме́лым склоня со́лнца-зенцы,
  В рай увлеку́т за собо́й.

Бра́тья, вы нас помина́йте за ча́шей:
Бо́льная сме́рть нам бессла́вия кра́ше!

Another strange folk song is **"Adlerskaya pesnya,"** which Marlinsky wrote on the eve of his death in 1838. The song comprises twenty four-line stanzas, the second and fourth lines being a repeat and the third being a refrain common to all stanzas. The song has no metric pattern, and is written to the tune of a Russian song. Each of the stanzas is a curse of the Russians and a challenge to battle:

Плывет по мо́рю стена́ корабле́й,
Сло́вно ста́до лебеде́й, лебеде́й.
А́й, жги, жги, жги, говори,
Сло́вно ста́дно лебеде́й, лебеде́й.

Ей вы, го́й еси кавка́зцы-молодцы!
Уда́льцы, госуда́ревы стрельцы!
А́й, жги, жги, жги, говори,
Уда́льцы, госуда́ревы стрельцы!

Particularly striking is the third line, the jeering refrain with its four consecutive initial stresses, but the entire poem is indicative of the fact that Marlinsky had come a long way, from his first awkward attempts and erring imitations of mode, to some very bizarre and extremely original experiments in metre and rhythm.

'We are like winged fish', Marlinsky once mused, 'we wish to fly to the heavens and we fall back into the sea.'[27] The remark is markedly Romantic, and it is as equally apt to a final evaluation of him as a poet. For he did indeed wish to fly to the heavens, and he did fall back into the sea. But in his attempt he did create a body of lyric poetry which cannot be denied proper appreciation even after all these years. Moreover, as this examination has attempted to show, he was very much a man of his time and ran the gauntlet of the creative areas of his age. His maturing artistic attitudes, his choice of lyric genres, his concept of versification, and his attempts to enlarge the potential of syllabo-accentual versification—all of these make him a lyric microcosm of the Pushkin era.

Notes

1. The statement was made by a character in Turgenev's story *Stuk . . . stuk . . . stuk . . .* Aleksandr Bestuzhev, who took his pseudonym Marlinsky from the pavilion of Marli at Peterhof, was the first Russian writer to enjoy wide public popularity, and Turgenev was one of many 19th-century Russian writers who grew up on Marlinsky's tales. Born in 1797, Marlinsky sacrificed his career in the army and at court by his active role in the preparation and carrying out of the Decembrist revolt of 1825. Thanks largely to his already considerable reputation as a literary critic and theoretician, journalist, writer, and poet, he was able to resume his literary career in 1830. In the next eight years, he published a whole series of exciting adventure tales written in Siberia and the Caucasus. The degree to which these stories influenced Russian literature has not yet been estimated.

2. D. S. Mirsky, *A History of Russian Literature,* New York, 1958, p. 73.

3. 'Pismo k N. A. Polevomu, 13 avgusta 1831 g.' (*Russkiy vestnik,* XXXII, 3, 1861, p. 304).

4. Bestuzhev-Marlinsky, *Polnoye sobraniye stikhotvoreniy* (cited hereafter as *PSS*), Bol'shaya seriya, 2nd ed., Leningrad, 1961.

5. *Izveshcheniye, Zavtra!* and *Bespechnyy* (all 1818 translations from Parny), *K sochinitel'yu poemy 'Ruslan i Lyudmila'* (1822), and *Nadpis' na 'Polyarnoy zvezde'* (1825?) (*ibid.*, pp. 298-300).

6. Excluded from this consideration of purely lyric poetry is Marlinsky's Romantic verse tale, *Andrey, knyaz' Pereyaslavskiy,* which he began while in prison in 1827. Written on a patriotic historical theme, it is composed of two almost complete initial chapters and two fragments of a fifth and final chapter.

7. The Russian *duma* (literally 'thought' or 'council') is based on an Ukrainian oral source, the so-called *narodnaya pesnya* which began to replace the *bylina* in the late seventeenth century. As a literary genre, it was cultivated by Katenin, Yazykov, Vyazemsky, and Pushkin, but it was the acknowledged speciality of Kondratiy Ryleyev who dramatised the historical significance of Dimitriy Donskoy, Yermak, Ivan Susanin, Bogdan Khmel'nitsky, Peter the Great, and many others.

8. Marlinsky was killed in a battle with Circassian mountaineers at Cape Adler on the Caspian Sea on 7 June 1837. Because of his notoriety and the fact that his body was never found, a great many legends grew up concerning his fate. His correspondence of the later thirties leaves no doubt that he was cruelly persecuted by the government, and his letters to his brothers in the months just preceding his death indicate that he may have deliberately sought a 'Byronic' death in battle.

9. Data on Marlinsky are my own. For figures on Pushkin and Baratynsky, see: B. O. Unbegaun, *Russian Versification,* Oxford, 1956, p. 14.

10. The Davydov count is my own; for Pushkin count, see: *ibid.,* p. 27.

11. *Ibid.*

12. *Ibid.,* p. 19.

13. Thus, Zhukovsky: 'Tam mrámorny stolpý stoyát' (*Dobrodetel'*, 1798), or Pushkin: 'Il' mós'ku prestarélu' and 'Il' smótrish' v tyómny dál'' (*K sestre*, 1814), or Yazykov: 'V plenyónnom sérdtse nézhnu strást'' (*Poslaniye k Kulubinu*, 1819). Derzhavin, who is notorious for his willingness to sacrifice grammar to almost any aesthetic effect, used the form until well along in his career, but had abandoned it almost entirely by the advent of the 19th century. Finally, so far as I am aware, no other poet of the period relied so much upon this device as did Marlinsky.

14. *PSS,* pp. 271-72.

15. 'And the knights turn tail, / And captives, and blood, and corpses (mark) their way. / And there is no salvation from death / Amidst the merciless ice, / And Aleksandr, like an angel of vengeance, / Pursued, struck down, destroyed the foes . . .'

16. See: N. M. Yazykov, *Polnoye sobraniye stikhotvoreniy,* Moscow/Leningrad, 1934, pp. 726-27. The poem was sent to Ryleyev for inclusion in *Zvezdochka na 1826 god,* a new almanac he edited with Marlinsky, and was confiscated after the Decembrist revolt.

17. M. A. Briskman, 'Agitatsionnyye pesni Dekabristov', in M. P. Alekseyev and B. S. Meylakh (eds.) *Dekabristy i ikh vremya,* Leningrad, 1951, pp. 20-21.

18. A definitive study is: Yu. Oksman, 'Agitatsionnyye pesni Dekabristov' (*Literaturnoye nasledstvo,* LIX, 1954). See also: *PSS,* pp. 288-98.

19. N. I. Mordovchenko, 'A. A. Bestuzhev-Marlinsky,' in *ibid.,* pp. 19-20.

20. The Russian theorist of versification Georgiy Shengeli would call the first line of the refrain a double amphimachris ('—') and the second a combination anapest and paeon (— —'/— — —'). Shengeli is quite useful in cases like this in that he concentrates on the foot, rather than the line, and defines four two-syllable, eight three-syllable, and sixteen four-syllable feet: *Traktat o russkom stikhe,* 2nd ed., Moscow/Petrograd, 1923, I, p. 136.

21. Bestuzhev-Marlinsky, *Sobraniye sochineniy v dvukh tomakh,* Moscow, 1958, I, p. 318.

22. *PSS,* pp. 280-1.

23. 'Fortunates! here as there you knew no parting, / Knew not the bearing of loved ones' heavy burdens.'

24. A less widely known poem also influenced by Marlinsky is Aleksandr Polezhayev's *Pesn' pogibyushchego plovtsa* (early 1830s): Veter svistit, / Grom gremit / More stonet— / Put' dalyok . . . / Tonet, tonet / Moy chelnok!

25. Quite relevant here is Professor Dmitrij Čiževskij's study of the motif of the waterfall in Slavic Romantic literature (*On Romanticism in Slavic Literatures,* The Hague, 1957, pp. 16, 22), for he has pointed out that not only *Shebutuy,* but also a verse passage from the prose work *Poyezdka v Revel'* (1821), and the poem *Finlyandiya* (1829) are direct descendants from Derzhavin's introduction of the motif in *Vodopad* (1791-94). In his opinion,

Marlinsky exhibits a more mature Romanticism in his new imagery, in his 'psychologisation' of a natural phenomenon, and particularly in his lyric address to a phenomenon of nature.

26. Mirsky, *op. cit.*, p. 120.

27. 'Pis'mo k N. A. Polevomu, 12 fevralya 1831 g.' (*Russkiy vestnik*, XXXII, 3, 1861, p. 294).

Lauren G. Leighton (essay date 1975)

SOURCE: Leighton, Lauren G. "Alexander Marlinsky: The Extravagant Prose—1830-37." In *Alexander Bestuzhev-Marlinsky*, pp. 94-116. Boston: Twayne Publishers, 1975.

[*In the following excerpt, Leighton examines Bestuzhev's prose works produced as Alexander Marlinsky, including the sea stories, the horror stories, and the tales of the Caucasus.*]

The return of Alexander Bestuzhev to an active literary career under the name Alexander Marlinsky was met with heartily if privately expressed relief, and the event was probably interpreted as a harbinger of imminent political change. Far off in Siberia the exiled Decembrist Küchelbecker received a copy of Marlinsky's new tale of men and passions, **"The Test,"** and he noted in his diary: "There is so much life, intellect, action, and feeling in it that it may be reckoned without the least doubt among the finest prose tales in our language. . . . God bless whoever spared this man of talent for our fatherland! *Sapienti sat.*"[1]

As it turned out, the event did not presage any liberalization of the regime of Nicholas I, but it was indeed a boon for Russian literature. It announced a new and relatively high standard of Russian prose writing, and it is apparent that Alexander Marlinsky was a far better writer than his predecessor. His tales of the second period are longer, revealing a confident ability to control form and structure. The mature prose tales are characterized by a wide variety of stylistic manners—exposition, digression, dialogue, descriptive passages, direct and indirect narrative—and they are remarkable for the myriads of stylistic devices that made the style known as Marlinism so powerful in its effect on the reader of the 1830's. Alexander Marlinsky was obviously his own writer, no longer dependent on external models. This is the period of a skilled literary craftsman.

I THE SEA STORIES

Marlinsky wrote two fine tales of men and passions in the 1830's—**"The Test"** and **"The Clock and the Mirror"**—and both tales are closely related to the third ge-

neric category, the sea stories. There are three sea stories—**"Leitenant Belozor"** (**"Lieutenant Belozor,"** 1831), *Fregat* **"Nadezhda"** (*The Frigate* **"Hope,"** 1832), and **"Morekhod Nikitin"** (**"Merchant Sailor Nikitin,"** 1834)—and the first two are tales of impetuous men in conflict with society. It was not by chance that Marlinsky became the first Russian author of naval adventures. He was fascinated by the sea, and his seascapes are a prominent feature of many of his tales and essays. "He was unable to speak tranquilly about the sea," noted Nikolay A. Kotlyarevsky, "and beneath his pen a seascape was involuntarily transformed into a lyric elocution."[2]

In his youth Marlinsky wanted to become a naval officer. His brothers Nikolay and Mikhail were naval officers, and the former was the author of sea stories. During his teens Marlinsky spent summers at sea with Nikolay and gained a proficient technical knowledge of ships. When Nikolay Polevoy expressed surprise at the appearance of a type of tale he had not expected from Marlinsky, the author commented in a letter of 1833: "Do not be surprised that I know naval technology—I am a sailor born and a sailor bred. The sea has been my passion, ships my vice, and although I never served with the fleet, I will not yield place in any way to a genuine sailor, even in the minute details of shipbuilding. There was a time when I hungered for service with the fleet, but for all that I prefer a horse to a ship—at least one can abandon the former."[3]

Marlinsky's three sea stories, all lengthy, are united into a single generic category by their sea setting and their use of richly authentic naval language, including a healthy dose of sailor's jargon. With the exception, perhaps, of *The Frigate* **"Hope"**, they are not the best of Marlinsky's works, but they are well-done tales of exciting adventure and became very popular. Belinsky, for example, declared that "for me [Marlinsky's] best tales are easily **"The Test"** and **"Lieutenant Belozor"**—one can admire his talent without reservation, for he is in his proper element in them."[4]

The authenticity of technical terms and jargon is without doubt the most striking feature of the sea stories. In **"Lieutenant Belozor"** the hero's ship is described in minute detail, with all the regalia of its topmasts and yardarms, storm sails, gutters, rigging, admiral's mainmast, and spars. The ships make such maneuvers as "to come up to the fleet in full sail," and orders are given to "haul into the line and cast anchor to the flagship's portside." Such terms are encountered as reserve pumps, flares, north-north-west, flag, signals, and signal book. Passing ships are called "gentlemen" in sailor's slang, and in one instance it is mentioned that "the commands rigged their sails in what is called *in honor.*" Once a sailor shouts in English: "Don't skid away, my boys! Hard aport and close up to the wind!" The same conscientiously careful and colorfully colloquial naval language is a dominant feature of the other two sea stories.

"Merchant Sailor Nikitin" is saturated with such English terms as "hot-pressed," "man-of-war," "boat-ahoo! strike your colors," "down with your rags!" "put the helm up, damn!" "strike, or I'll run over and sink you!" and "god damn your eyes! you scoundrels, ruffians, and barbed dogs!" English terms are also given in Cyrillic transcription, such as *kutter, shkiper, yanki, blokshif, kapery i kreysery, flagman, boy, puding i grog,* and *angliyskie goddemy.* Betraying his interest in language for its own sake, Marlinsky explains that an East Indies ship is "an 'Indianen' [sic], as the English say." In a footnote to one still fairly new British expression, Marlinsky observes: "The English call the North-Americans Yankee as a means of ridicule." Authentic terms are so profuse in the sea stories, and the device of saturating whole passages with technical terminology and jargon is so pronounced a feature, that it must be concluded once again Marlinsky's first love was for languages. And he succeeded again in making the device an entertaining feature, one that must have fascinated Russian readers of the 1830's.

The best of Marlinsky's sea tales is **The Frigate "Hope",** which illustrates most readily the adventure tale qualities of this generic category. Captain-Lieutenant Ilya Petrovich Pravin is the captain of the finest ship in the Russian fleet, the "Hope." He is adored by his sailors, respected by his officers, and known even to Tsar Nicholas for his devotion to ship, duty, and honor. Beneath his staunch, practical exterior, however, he is an idealist and a dreamer—not very different from Colonel Mechin of the hussar stories—and he is also completely naïve with regard to hypocritical St. Petersburg society. "He knew well the nature of the sea," Marlinsky observes, "but where could he have learned the nature of men?" Chosen by highest authority to command a somehow important but never fully explained voyage to the Mediterranean, Pravin looks forward, in the year 1829, to a fine and honorable career. At just this critical juncture of his life Pravin meets and falls in love with Vera, the wife of an elderly court official, Prince Pyotr***

At first it seems that his sense of duty will vanquish his passion. Led to believe that Vera has been toying with his emotions, he buries himself in the difficult technical preparations for the voyage. He encounters Vera alone one day, however, and upon learning that his suspicions were unfounded, makes an emotional declaration of love. On the eve of departure, the "Hope" is boarded by Prince Pyotr and Vera, who has used her husband's influence to arrange a pleasure trip to England. The inexperienced Pravin neglects his duty and gives himself over to an affair with Vera. And when she departs the ship in Plymouth harbor, he is unable to resist the demands of his passion. Even though a storm is rising, and his second officer begs him to stay with the "Hope", he goes ashore for one last rendezvous with the woman he loves.

The following morning, after a night in Vera's boudoir, the lovers are discovered by Prince Pyotr, and Pravin is numbed by the realization he has compromised his beloved. Worse yet, at this moment Pravin learns his ship has been struck by the storm. Torn between his commitment to Vera and his duty to the "Hope," he is unable to act. Only when it is too late, does he attempt to return to his ship. He is injured in the attempt and, tormented by the knowledge of his failure to both Vera and the ship, dies in disgrace.

***The Frigate* "Hope"** provides a good illustration of the nature of Marlinsky's mature prose tales. Primarily an exciting adventure tale, its action-packed story can be ranked with the best adventure tales of Scott, Cooper, Hugo, and Dumas, père. Within another decade this type of literary endeavor no longer appealed to the sophisticated Russian reader, but tales such as ***The Frigate* "Hope"** are the reason for Marlinsky remaining a popular writer well into the twentieth century. The love story, the exciting events, the glamor of the sea, the tragedy of a brave hero's failure to meet a challenge to his manhood, the fascinatingly technical descriptions of ships—these features have had a lasting and powerful effect on the imagination of young readers.

The tale is also notable for its structural complexity, a consistent quality of the mature tales. The main narrator is still that stylized Byronic narrator, but point of view is varied by a number of devices which enable the characters to conduct parts of the narrative. We learn a great deal about Pravin and are given an insight into Vera's personality by her letters to a friend; Pravin's lofty ideals and passionate character emerge from his letters to his best friend aboard the "Hope." Point of view is varied further by dialogue, and we gain a more objective view of the love situation from the pungent remarks of a sarcastic ship's doctor. The plot is relieved and enhanced by descriptive passages, digressions, and the seascapes. The aftermath of the tragedy at sea is conveyed in an understated postscript to the tale, half of which shows that Vera was able to return unaffected to her position in St. Petersburg society, the other half being a curious news story in *The Northern Bee* about the "Hope's" return to her home port. The tale is marked by *literaturnost'*—the Russian art of literary allusion—and many of these allusions, including the news story, indicate that the tale is a thinly disguised allegory of Marlinsky's own fate in the Decembrist conspiracy.[5] The main narrative, the epistolary interludes, the dialogue, the descriptive and expository passages, and the literary allusions—all reinforced by deftly inserted witticisms—make this tale complex, variegated, and entertaining. Best of all, these diverse elements are blended organically into a single, graceful literary work which is far superior to the awkward experiments of the early period.

II The Tales of Horror: Mrs. Radcliffe

Just as well written are the three tales of horror which make up the fourth generic category: **"Vecher na kavkazskikh vodakh v 1824 godu" ("An Evening at a Caucasian Spa in 1824,"** 1830), including an addendum entitled **"Sledstvie vechera na kavkazskikh vodakh v 1824 godu" ("A Sequel to an Evening at a Caucasian Spa in 1824")**; **"Strashnoe gadanie: Rasskaz" ("The Terrible Divination: A Story,"** 1830); and **"Latnik: Rasskaz partizanskogo ofitsera" ("The Cuirassier: A Partisan Officer's Story,"** 1831). The first and last of these tales are, like the earlier hussar stories, anecdotal in structure. All three tales are ventures into Russian folklore. Marlinsky was always interested in the supernatural as a source of literary themes and as an enticing Romantic tradition. Many of his early tales contain references to Mrs. Radcliffe, and his castle tales were a response to the Gothic novel. By 1825 he had achieved an estimable proficiency in the conveyance of sweet terror, as indicated by **"The Traitor."** Nevertheless, it is apparent that in the 1820's Marlinsky had not yet detected the delicate devices of the Gothic novel, for his early attempts at the creation of horror are direct, and thus ineffective. This bluntness of technique is absent from the mature tales of horror, and it is evident Marlinsky learned a great deal about Gothic methods in the interim.

Curiously, it was not from the models of Mrs. Radcliffe that Marlinsky learned Gothic techniques, but from Walter Scott. In 1824 Scott wrote a "Prefatory Memoir to the Novels of Mrs. Ann Radcliffe" in which he analyzed the methods of a woman and a genre he admired. The memoir was published in Russian in 1826.[6] Marlinsky undoubtedly read at least the Russian version, for he restated some of Scott's ideas in his own comments on the supernatural as a literary subject. The chief assumption of Scott's view of the Gothic novel is that the reader of his time was too sophisticated to be affected by a straightforward treatment of horror and too rational to accept unexplained supernatural events. "The public of the current day," he noted, "deals . . . rigidly in moving for a *quo warranto* to compel an explanation from the story-teller, and the author must either at once represent the knot as worthy of being severed by supernatural aid, and bring on the stage his actual fiend or ghost, or, like Mrs. Radcliffe, explain by natural agency the whole marvels of his means." The Gothic novelist is faced with a dilemma, for his materials are incredible and his reader a skeptic: "In the age of universal credibility, we must own it would require, at the present day, the support of the highest powers, to save the su-

pernatural from slipping into the ludicrous." In short, there is a fine line between credible terror and ridiculous incredibility, and Scott summed up this most crucial esthetic problem of the Gothic novel in Napoleon's observation that "there is but one step betwixt the sublime and the ridiculous."[7]

According to Scott, writers had attempted to deal with this problem in two contrary ways: those who like Horace Walpole "compound betwixt ancient faith and modern incredulity . . . without giving a defined or absolute opinion;" those who like Mrs. Radcliffe imposed the rule that "all circumstances of her narrative, however mysterious, and apparently superhuman, were to be accounted for on natural principles, at the winding up of the story." In Scott's opinion, the first class of writers had merely "eliminated the obstacle without solving the problem," and the second had achieved only partial success in the achievement of credibility. Mrs. Radcliffe, for example, was "more successful in exciting interest and apprehensions than in giving either interest or dignity of explanation to the means she has made use of." That is, her rational explanations of supernatural events "at the winding up of the story" ruined the effect of all that had gone before. The Gothic novelist cannot be direct in manner. In all other respects, however, Mrs. Radcliffe's novels were successful, and Scott especially liked two of the keys she had discovered to the creation of genuine terror: the conveyance of a sense of guilt and the building up of suspense. Her novels are good because "the materials . . . and the means employed in conducting the narrative, are all selected with a view to the author's primary object, of moving the reader by ideas of impending danger, hidden guilt, supernatural visitings—by all that is terrible, in short, combined with much that is wonderful." They are all the better because "to break off the narrative, when it seemed at the point of becoming most interesting—to extinguish a lamp when a parchment ought to have been read, to exhibit shadowy forms and half-heard sounds of woe, were resources which Mrs. Radcliffe has employed with more effect than any other writer of romance."[8]

Marlinsky must have read Scott very carefully, for his best tale of horror, **"The Cuirassier,"** observes each of the methods which Scott praised in Mrs. Radcliffe's novels, and it solves the crucial problem of credibility by providing natural explanations of supernatural events in a convincing way. **"The Cuirassier"** is in fact one of the best of Marlinsky's prose tales and his most sophisticated narrative. Told in a single narrative body, without division into chapters, it consists of two similar anecdotes enlarged into full stories and merged with a main narrative body to form a graceful literary unity. The two frame stories are merged with and interrupted by events of the main narrative and alternate with one another to achieve interruption at a suspenseful moment. This device of alternation facilitates a natural explanation to each story at its "winding up," with the explanations negotiated so naturally and with such an adroit contrast in point of view that they add to, rather than detract from, the feeling of horror.

The main narrator of **"The Cuirassier"** is a hussar commander of a partisan detachment in 1812, and his story begins with an account of a fierce skirmish in which the hussars are rallied to victory by a Russian cuirassier, who plunges into the midst of the enemy and hacks the unit's commander to pieces. The cuirassier then vanishes, leaving the hussars horrified by his atrocity. When they settle down to their evening bivouac in a deserted manor house, their mood prompts the telling of the two frame stories.

The first story, told by an old serf-retainer, is the legend of the Glinsky manor. At one time the household had rung with happiness, but then, in quick succession, word was received that the daughter's—Felicia's—fiancé had died, Felicia was obliged to marry an avaricious neighbor, Ostrolensky the father died, and Felicia was driven to death by her cruel husband. Shortly before her death Felicia had been seen in the garden with a black horseman, and on the eve of her death she had been overheard conversing with an uncanny presence. Now the Glinsky manor is believed to be occupied by terrible dark powers.

The second story, told by the brooding hussar Zarnitsky, is the legend of the manor of Shuran, once dominated by Zarnitsky's grandfather, the cruel tyrant Prince K. When the daughter, Liza, eloped with her tutor, Bayanov, the old man captured and imprisoned them. Eventually Liza went insane, and it was believed that the mysterious screams of a young man locked in a dungeon were connected with Prince K.'s own insanity and death. In his childhood, Zarnitsky was fascinated by the legend of Shuran, and when he grew up, he decided to dispel its mystery. Despite his dread, he explores the manor, finds a secret passage to a tower, and climbs the stairs. There, before his eyes, beyond doubt, stands the martyred Liza, still young and beautiful.

At this moment Zarnitsky's narrative is interrupted by the reappearance of the cuirassier. He gazes at the portrait of Felicia on the wall, proclaims he has avenged her, and falls into a faint. The hussars realize he is the supposedly deceased fiancé, and in the morning he retells the old serf's story from his own point of view, thus resolving the mystery. The news of his death had been falsified by Ostrolensky with a forged letter, and he was the black horseman in the garden, who had come to curse Felicia for betraying him. He soon learned of Ostrolensky's treachery, however, and the voices heard on the eve of Felicia's death had been the lovers' reconciliation. Ostrolensky had run off to Paris and come

back to Russia as a renegade in Napoleon's army: the cuirassier had finally caught up with his enemy that day. It is *à propos* of this revelation that the mystery of Shuran is also explained. For in a now calm and matter-of-fact tone, Zarnitsky reveals that the girl in the tower was the daughter of Liza and Bayanov. Ending his story with a confession of unrequited love for the girl explains his obsession with the legend of Shuran. The tale ends with the death of the cuirassier, and the hussars prepare for another day in battle.

In writing **"The Cuirassier,"** Marlinsky used three of Scott's suggestions on the esthetics of horror tales. It is significant, for example, that his tale is marked by a careful selection of materials and narrative method aimed at "moving the reader by ideas of impending danger, hidden guilt, supernatural visitings." The mysterious black horseman, the voices on the eve of Felicia's death, the uncanny resurrection of the beautiful Liza, and the aura surrounding the legends of the Glinsky manor and Shuran—these ideas do indeed convey a sense of impending danger. Feelings of guilt are also present in the tale: Zarnitsky's brooding character, his obsession with Shuran, and the hint of incest implied by his love for his cousin; the cuirassier's terrible vengeance and his guilt for tormenting Felicia unjustly. Marlinsky treats these aspects of the tale skillfully and he also reveals an expertise at selecting details for their effect on the reader's imagination. When Zarnitsky approaches Shuran, he perceives certain external objects which have a specific effect on his nerves and create a feeling of "impending danger." His way through the yard is hindered by startled frogs in the grass, and the fallen porch reminds him of his childhood dread: ". . . fantastic beings brushed me with familiar wings, and that former feeling of sweet terror clenched my breast. I stood once again a schoolboy before an ancient castle." When he enters the house, his feeling of dread is heightened by the sight of such objects as scattered furniture, a spider web, green bronze door hinges and rusted fastenings, hanging wallpaper, and streams of rain marks down the walls. A simile is drawn between "bats with membranous wings" and "the butterflies of ruined edifices," and this simile is effective in imparting the feeling, as opposed to the embodiment, of dread. The thought that "in every quiver of the wallpaper I seemed to hear the moan of a dying victim" is a well-contrived exhibition of those "shadowy forms and half-heard sounds of woe" which Scott singled out as one of Mrs. Radcliffe's techniques. Above all, the passage shows that Marlinsky had realized one of the most important things about the Gothic technique: that objects—accoutrement—are chosen not for their own sake, but for their power to evoke a feeling of the supernatural.

Scott's recommendation that the narrative be interrupted "when it seemed at the point of becoming most interesting" was also followed carefully in the writing of Marlinsky's tale. The mystery of the Glinsky manor, first represented in the old serf's story, is not resolved until almost the end of the tale, when the cuirassier explains the mysterious and apparently superhuman circumstances of the legend. The interruption of Zarnitsky's story is even more abrupt, and here the problem of suspense is well handled. The effect of the manor house on Zarnitsky's overwrought imagination is culminated in Zarnitsky's digression to explain his obsession with the legend of the beautiful Liza. This is followed by an increase of suspense as Zarnitsky approaches the tower, and then the climax, the discovery of the girl. If Marlinsky had added anything at this point, or attempted to increase a tension that had already hit its peak, he would have destroyed his effect. Once the narrative has been interrupted, however, and attention has been drawn back to the legend of the Glinsky manor, Zarnitsky is able to explain his mystery in a calm tone which contrasts and enhances, rather than destroys, the suspense.

The way in which Marlinsky chose to handle suspense shows also that he devoted thought to Scott's third point—the danger that the accounting of "all circumstances of the narrative . . . at the winding up of the story" would annoy, rather than satisfy. Marlinsky handled his explanations of natural causes for supposedly supernatural events with considerable skill. The explanations clear up the mysteries by natural means but leave an aftermath effect: they preserve the aura of the supernatural and invoke a feeling of lingering dread. This is due in part to the mood of the narrators themselves, for the cuirassier explains the mystery of the Glinsky manor in a state of frenzy, while Zarnitsky's matter-of-fact resolution accentuates his brooding personality. Moreover, the explanations are not only removed from the mysteries by prolonged intervening events, but they are given from a strikingly different point of view. Marlinsky found his solution to the problem of credibility in the very method of narration, exploiting this solution efficiently. The mystery of the Glinsky manor is narrated by a serf, a barely literate and highly superstitious old man who does not comprehend the ways of the nobility, while the explanation is provided by the cuirassier, a normally rational man who has been driven by his quest for revenge beyond the borders of rationality. The point of view is by no means so sharply contrasted in the legend of Shuran; but when Zarnitsky narrates the mystery he is in a disturbed state, and this contrasts effectively with his calmly stated explanation. Both contrasts in point of view lead the reader from the temptation to compare the supernatural story with the natural explanation, and they deceive him into accepting the explanations without analyzing them.

Marlinsky completely ignored a fourth point made by Scott in his memoir. In Scott's opinion, the Gothic Revival was a resumption of the tradition of the medieval

Romance, and tales of horror are best treated in medieval surroundings. Marlinsky, on the other hand, convinced that contemporary life was rich in supernatural themes, believed that no country could compete with Russia when it came to skeletons in family closets. He emphasizes this conviction several times in **"The Cuirassier,"** and his main narrator declares in one instance: "How unfair it is that our writers complain we do not live in a Romantic era! . . . If they would just glance into our villages and towns . . . they would find an inexhaustible source, a key purely Russian, virgin, without admixture." Marlinsky was not interested in the life of the Middle Ages in his tales of horror. Instead, he used his tales to dramatize extraordinary human situations of contemporary Russia. Nor did he have difficulty finding sources for modern tales of the supernatural. The legend of Shuran is true, and the scholar V. G. Bazanov has established that it is based on "the popular oral legend" of an actual landowner on the Kama River.[9] Marlinsky was also convinced that Russian folklore was an excellent source of themes and materials for his tales of horror. M. Vasilev has pointed out that the supernatural stories which make up **"Evening at a Caucasian Spa in 1824"** are common Russian fairy-tale motifs to be found in such compilations of folklore as those of Onchukov and Afanasev.[10]

Russian folklore is important to the horror ales, and folk legends do much to enhance their literary appeal. Perhaps a good illustration of this is **"The Terrible Divination,"** a prose tale containing several elaborate treatments and even detailed descriptions of authentic folk customs and rituals. The most important of these is the terrible divination itself, a demonic ritual which involves calling forth a satanic power from the grave. This ritual is the key mechanism of the tale's action, a device which moves the tale from reality into fantasy.

The skeptical hero-narrator of the tale is challenged to participate in the divination by a sinister stranger, who entices him further with a promise to unite him with the woman he desires. Under the influence of the graveyard scene, and of his own "frenzied" passion for his mistress, the hero experiences a terrifying hallucination in which he is transported to his sweetheart's home, elopes with her, murders her pursuing husband, and is cast as punishment into the abyss of the grave from which he helped call forth the devil.

Less important to the tale, but equally as fascinating, are the marriage divinations which lead up to the terrible divination. The marriage divinations are performed under the guidance of an old peasant by young men and maidens in a hut where the hero-narrator has taken refuge from a snowstorm. The ritual involves the placing of the participants' rings under heaps of grain arranged in a circle. A chicken is placed in the center of the circle and encouraged by a series of incantations to peck at the heaps. In this fashion, the chicken selects and matches rings which are then placed in a cup under a saucer. "Under-the-Saucer Songs" are then sung by the participants to celebrate the chicken's prediction of who will marry whom. (I, 318-19).

Although neither the terrible divination nor the marriage divinations can be identified as strictly local customs, the precise details and techniques, as described in the tale, are variants associated with the Novgorod region. It is important here that the members of the Bestuzhev family took pride in their Novgorodian origins (this is why Marlinsky's tales of Russian history usually take place in the Novgorod region), and Marlinsky's descriptions are known to be authentic. As will be shown in the chapter on Marlinsky's poetry, he and Ryleev wrote a series of "Under-the-Saucer Songs" as part of their Decembrist activities, and the descriptions of the songs in this tale thus take on a political significance. These songs, together with a series known as "Agitational Songs," are prominent in the Russian tradition of political-revolutionary poetry.

Folk language is central to the tales of horror. The narrator's conversation with a sledgedriver is conducted in a peasant colloquial language, and it would be difficult to find such an authentic use of folk language in any other literary work at this stage of Russian literature. Peasant language is also important to the old serf-retainer's story of the Glinsky manor. Marlinsky took pride in his knowledge of authentic peasant dialects, and in a letter of 1832 he ridiculed the inability of other Russian writers to utilize folk speech properly: "Yes, and who is it among us who writes? The frequenters of salons who once a year eavesdrop on the language of the common people at carnivals and are as happy as happy can be when they capture some vulgar expression over which they fuss like a child with a new toy."[11] Folksayings are a prominent feature of the tales of horror and, in fact, in most of Marlinsky's tales. In **"The Cuirassier"** the old serf employs such folksy sayings as "Property and a good name are not bought with bad debts," "To the Lord it is high, to the Tsar it is far," and "To the tiger a man is always guilty." The same narrator is also given to such folkish statements as "The poor countess pined away like a blade of grass on a stone." In each of Marlinsky's tales one encounters such sayings as "In someone else's hands a tom-tit might just as well be a pheasant," "In order to strengthen one's legs, one must pamper one's belly," "It's nice to be a guest, but better at home" and "An idler always has a good time on his mind." A few tales—**"Merchant Sailor Nikitin"** and **"The Terrible Divination,"** for example—are saturated with folk sayings and colloquial language. The latter tale contains a fine scene in which the hero-narrator converses with his peasant sledgedriver about peasant superstitions and the many supernatural creatures which populate Russian folklore: house de-

mons, water sprites, wood imps, witches, werewolves, and those inimitable Russian devils known as *besy*. The sledgedriver's lecture on these creatures borrows heavily from general and localized terms, and these, combined with his expertly localized colloquial speech, fully justify Marlinsky's claim to an expert knowledge of colloquial Russian.

III THE TALES OF THE CAUCASUS

Although it would not be proper to trace all of Marlinsky's literary popularity solely to the tales of the Caucasus, it was especially this fifth and last generic category that enthralled his reading public. For their wild improbability, their extreme exoticism, and their passionate tone of narration, these tales could not but have appealed to admirers of Marlinism. At the same time, precisely the extravagance and extremism of the tales of the Caucasus ensured Marlinsky's decline in the more sophisticated literary circles. Shortly after Marlinsky's death, Stepan Shevyryov noted:

> Here, under the influence of Asiatic taste, which also loves exaggeration, Marlinsky's shortcomings reached their final extreme. For the passion for the variegated and the bizarre had to pass—and so it was, especially when Pushkin's muse shifted from verse to prose, and turned the Russian vernacular to that pure, transparently clear, marvelous simplicity which outdid even Karamzin. Nowadays Marlinsky no longer appeals to anyone except inexperienced youths, who are wont to be carried away by his style and curl their speech in much the same way as they curl their hair.[12]

And this is true. "Do you know," Turgenev once confessed to Tolstoy, "that I used to kiss Marlinsky's name on journal covers?"[13] Tolstoy might have confessed the same thing about his own adolescence, for it was at least partly under the influence of Marlinism that he volunteered for military duty in the Caucasus. But in one of his first literary works he remarked: "I was introduced to one of our young officers 'daredevil-Djigits' educated in the manner of Marlinsky and Lermontov. These men view the Caucasus in no other way than through the prism of heroes of our time, Mulla Nurs, and such like."[14] Marlinsky was outgrown with the adolescence of educated Russians, and it was especially Marlinism that writers like Turgenev and Tolstoy had in mind when they reacted to Romantic literature. They almost always referred to the tales of the Caucasus when professing dislike of all that was represented by Marlinsky's literary standard. The extremism, the exaggeration, the enthusiasm of these tales ensured his lasting popularity with the unsophisticated reader and his swift demise in the opinion of serious *literati*.

The tales of the Caucasus are the most extraordinarily imaginative and incredible of Marlinsky's prose tales, although at the same time they are the most authentic of all Russian literary works on the Caucasus. When

Marlinsky arrived in the Caucasus in late 1829, he plunged himself into study of the area in all of its social, cultural, historical, geographical, and linguistic aspects. Perhaps no other Russian writer had a more sound knowledge of the region, and no other writer did more to educate his countrymen about their most exotic imperial acquisition. His desire to educate as well as to entertain his readers was immense, and no other Russian writer of the Caucasus—Pushkin, Lermontov, Tolstoy—can compete with his erudition.

He swiftly mastered the Persian and Tatar dialects of the region; he became an authority on Caucasian literatures and culture. Just as he had saturated his Russian and Livonian tales with authentic atmosphere, he set about now to endow his Caucasian tales and essays with technically detailed facts and lessons in the nuances of languages. In a study of Marlinsky's works on the Caucasus, the Georgian scholar Vano Shaduri has noted that "he interlaced his tales and essays with numerous historical references and ancient legends, described in minute detail the various rituals, the nature and mode of life of the Caucasus, supplied his works with a multitude of ethnographic, historical, and linguistic comments and elucidations. . . ." In Shaduri's view, "it was through ethnic facts that the writer strove to penetrate into the dynamics of life in the Caucasus."[15]

Marlinsky was upset by Russian ignorance of the Caucasus. In the preface to the Caucasian tale, **"Rasskaz ofitsera, byvshego v plenu u gorcev"** (**"The Story of a Russian Officer in Captivity among the Mountaineers"**), he complained: "We regret that there are no worthwhile testimonies about the peoples of the Caucasus. . . . But who is to blame for this if not ourselves? For thirty years we have girdled the mountains with a belt of steel bayonets; and to this day our officers have brought back from the Caucasus, instead of useful, or at least entertaining news, only swords, robes, and girdles of black silver. The most venturous of them have learned to dance the lezghinka—but beyond this, not so much as a kernel."[16]

The first important feature of the Caucasian works, consequently, is their pedagogical fervor, and it is their multitude of facts that makes them so fascinating as literary works. The amount and variety of information packed into the essays are especially impressive. In **"Put' do goroda Kuby"** (**"The Route to the Town of Kuba,"** 1834) Marlinsky notes: "What I say about the Dagestanians does not apply to the Chechens or the Circassians. Every people in the Caucasus has its own mode of warfare and brigandage, its own mores, its own customs, its own peculiar ways and whimsies." Reporting the looting of Russian churches in **"Pis'ma iz Dagestana"** (**"Letters from Dagestan,"** 1831) he adds in a footnote: "A strange event occurred which

proves the Circassians' respect for St. Nicholas. While looting a Russian church to the bare boards they left only a rich icon of this holy man untouched." In **"Proshchanie s Kaspiem"** (**"Farewell to the Caspian,"** 1834) Marlinsky augments his poetic praise of the sea with such technical observations as: "Humboldt proved the level of the Caspian Sea is below the level of other seas by about three hundred feet; consequently the opinion that there is a subterranean connection with the Indian Ocean falls by the wayside; if this were the case, it would necessarily seek the level of other seas." In **"Doroga ot stantsii Almaly do posta Mugansy"** (**"The Road from Station Almala to the Post at Mugansa,"** 1834) he notes that "the half-slippers of the Lezghins and Georgians not infrequently have a point on the heels about one-quarter length longer than during the time of Charles VII among the French *(poulins)*."

The vast majority of factual observations deal with languages. In **"Letters From Dagestan"** Marlinsky refers to the rebel leader Kazi Mulla as Tazi Mulla and notes that *tazi* means dog. In the same essay he uses the Persian word *Sardar* for the Russian commander-in-chief. He frequently explains the meaning of Tatar words in footnotes, observing in one instance that "a *chapar* is a messenger, a driver, a wagoner; a *chapar-khan* is a relay-station inn." In reading the essays it is possible to learn that *kervan* means "caravan," *shegin-shah* means "master of masters" and a *felakka* is "a board with two holes in which are placed the legs of a criminal—his soles are twisted upwards and beaten with a stick." In one instance Marlinsky explains that "*kar-sirty* is a snow-covered range, but *kara-syrt* and *kara-dag* mean a black range, a black mountain." A typical note is: "Eastern peoples constantly use pleonasms—*gyur, bakh* ("look, see"), *ishliady, kurtardy* ("done, finished") are heard ten times a minute." In **"The Road from Station Almala to the Post at Mugansa"** he notes with tongue in cheek: "I think almost every reader knows that the Turkic, or, if you wish, Tatar exclamation *gaida, gai-da* means 'well, well now, come on there!' Those who know this will recall that they have themselves used it, exclaiming, for example, '*aida, molodets!* (they there, well done!).' From this it follows that they have been speaking and writing in Tatar perfectly, without even realizing it."

The Caucasian tales also provide a rich education in customs and languages. In **Ammalat-bek** it may be learned that Asiatics wear their knives over the abdomen and can sever a man's head with a single slice; the Circassians have been famed as doctors for centuries; mountain women do not wear veils; Circassians do not bare their weapons until the last moment in the charge; Kabardinians do not destroy property in war and are shocked when others do; Tatars give a piece of their own clothing as a gift to the bearers of good news; Moslem Tatars do not eat pork, but they love boar hunts;

Circassians are socially superior to Avarians; Asiatics love puns and their languages are full of them; Avarians use bronze bullets because their guns are bronze; when a Tatar wishes to speak to his Bey he bows to the ground and places his slippers on the floor before him. A typical footnote is apt to impart such information as: "All mountaineers are poor Mussulmans, but they hold to the Sunni sects; on the other hand, the majority of Dagestanians are Shagids, as are the Persians. . . . Both these sects hate each other from the bottom of the heart."

Throughout the tale there is a quick succession of literary treatments of ethnic customs, from a raid on a Cossack settlement to a discussion of the severe upbringing of children, from a contest of martial abilities to a boar hunt, from one colorfully detailed dramatization of the life of the Avarians, Kabardinians, Circassians, Tatars, and Cossacks to another. *Mulla Nur* is characterized by the same kaleidoscopic procession of ethnographic details. Among the imaginative subjects Marlinsky treats in footnotes are beards, vodka, the absence of names on graves, Circassian horses, religious sects, and the ninety-nine names of Mohammed. The tale itself contains literary dramatizations of a rendezvous between young Caucasian lovers, an Asiatic marriage, the Eastern attitude toward women, the character of the people of Dagestan, and the Oriental atmosphere of Derbent in the evening. Marlinsky effortlessly imparts such bits of authenticity as "an Asian is like a child when a gun is placed in his hands," or "only in the midst of his family does the Mussulman dare to be himself, because his wife and children are for him objects to which he is not the least obligated."

Ammalat-bek and *Mulla Nur* are also notable for Marlinsky's preoccupation with languages. In the former tale he notes: "*Ur, ura* means 'kill!' in Tatar. There is no doubt that this call entered into our own usage during the time of the reign of the Mongols, and not at the time of Peter, the notion that it is the 'hurrah' borrowed from the English." He explains that the plural of *bek* is *begliar* and that of *aga* is *agalar,* but Russians say *begi* and *agi.* He teaches his readers to count to ten and recite the days of the week in Tatar, and even mentions that an *agach* is seven versts by horse, but only four on foot. A *kekkhud* is the equivalent of the Russian *starosta* (elder) and an *empdzhek* is a suckling or milk brother (a sort of bosom buddy). *Gakim* is doctor, *aziz* is dear, *aga* is sir and *gadzhi* is a pilgrim to Mecca. *Mulla* is a holy man, *yakhunt* is an elder *mulla,* and *imam* means holy. *Dzheud* has the same connotation as the Russian term *zhid* (Yid), and Russians are always "unwashed Russians." A footnote to the title of *Mulla Nur* explains: "A *Mulla* is not only a holy man, but any literate or learned person; occasionally it is a proper name. *Nur* means 'light' and is encountered very often in combinations of Mussulman names, for example,

Darya-Nur." Marlinsky adds that *Nur-magal* means "Light of the Region, and not Light of the Harem, as Thomas Moore mistakenly named the heroine of his charming poem."

The Caucasian cycle is composed of a handful of brief or incomplete works on Siberia, a long philosophical-scientific-political-literary essay entitled **"Pis'mo k doktoru Ermanu"** (**"Letter to Doctor Erman,"** 1831), ten travel-ethnographic essays remarkable for their Caucasian *paysage,* the four uncompleted chapters of the novel titled **"Vadimov,"** and five prose tales: ***Ammalat-bek*** (1831), **"Krasnoe polryvalo"** (**"The Red Cape,"** 1831 - 32), **"On bly ubit,"** (**"He Was Killed,"** 1835 - 36), **"The Story of an Officer in Captivity among the Mountaineers,"** 1834), and ***Mulla Nur*** (1836). The prose tales mark the crowning point of Marlinsky's career as a writer. There can be no doubt that ***Ammalat-bek*** is the best known of the tales of the Caucasus—in fact, it is the most well-known of all his tales—and it serves as a perfect illustration of the nature of this category.

IV *Ammalat-bek*

Ammalat-bek has been included in all editions of Marlinsky's works and has been a popular seller in individual editions. The tale has been translated into German, Danish, Czech, Polish, French, and English. It was the second Russian literary work published in English in the United States. Translations in French, German, and English were published under the name of Alexandre Dumas, père, and Dumas also published the same translation as his own original work under the title *Sultanetta.*[17] When the final serialized chapter of ***Ammalat-bek*** had been printed in Nikolay Polevoy's *Moscow Telegraph,* Marlinsky added a postscript in which he elaborated on the tale's origin. He admitted that he had made free use of rumors and legends, but insisted that "the event described is not an invention, names and characters are preserved with exactness."

The facts he then gave are these: In 1819 Ammalat, a young and politically important Tatar bey, was captured by the Russians and sentenced to death by the proconsul of the Caucasus and the famous hero of 1812, General A. P. Ermolov. A Colonel Verkhovsky intervened on Ammalat's behalf, however, and became his sponsor, friend, and teacher. In 1823 Ammalat murdered his benefactor and later dug up his body and removed his head. Ammalat's motives for a crime that shocked the entire region were never clearly established, but it was known that he loved an Avarian girl, Seltaneta, and the popular legend was that her father, Sultan Akhmet-khan, had demanded Verkhovsky's head in return for his daughter's hand. Ammalat-bek was killed in 1828 while participating in a suicide charge as an *abrek,* a man who agrees to risk his life in this way for a certain period of time as a way of obtaining his salvation.[18] Seltaneta lived a long life and enjoyed great fame for her role in the legend of Ammalat-bek. Marlinsky knew her personally, and he also interviewed many of the other persons who figure in his tale.

Marlinsky believed—correctly—that he should have written **Ammalat-bek** as a novel. The tale is his most difficult undertaking, and its materials are so complex that it strains the limits of the prose tale as a literary form. He revised the tale several times while it was being published, and it is apparent that the legend of Ammalat-bek is uncomfortable in the form it finally took. Nevertheless, **Ammalat-bek** is a fine Romantic prose tale. Its narrative never sags, its expository, documentary, and descriptive addenda do not detract from the fast-paced plot, and its tendency to grow out of its frame even serves to enhance the kaleidoscopic effect of the variegated materials it offers to the reader.

The tale is divided into fourteen chapters. Its plot structure adheres to actual events, although it compresses the chronology of four years into two. The tale employs a great many devices—letters, diaries, digressions, verbal landscapes, descriptive interludes, monologues, and dialogues—to both advance and expand the narrative. The main narrator is the usual stylized Marlinsky, but the point of view is varied by presentation of Ammalat's diary and the letters of Verkhovsky to his fiancée.

The story centers on the psychological development of Ammalat from a primitive chieftain to a civilized man, but this center shifts to the story of Verkhovsky. There are thus two themes—one central, the other peripheral but integral—that of the civilizing of Ammalat and, in contrast, that of the idealistic and ultimately ineffectual ideas and actions of Verkhovsky. Both characters are Romantic in the extreme—the one a fiery rebel, the other a dreamy escapist—and their mutual tragedy is their inability to reconcile themselves to their alien milieux and to bridge the gap between their diametrically opposed cultural experiences. The theme of civilized society versus the natural man is Roussellian, of course, but the Soviet critic Nikolay Stepanov is correct in his observation that "despite all the conventional coloring and decoration of the Caucasus, as he depicted it, Marlinsky understood perfectly well that this is not Jean-Jacques' utopia come true."[19]

Marlinsky was also correct in his conviction that the character of Ammalat is made clear from the very beginning. When his horse balks at a jump, the willful young Tatar smashes it to the ground with his sabre handle, shocking even his savage retainers with his powerfully impatient will. In long letters to his fiancée, the introspective Verkhovsky analyzes his hot-tempered charge, elaborating on the carelessness of his upbringing and emphasizing that "his intellect is a marvelous mixture of every absurdity, of ideas most absurd and conceptions most sensible." Coupled with constant strife between impulse and good sense is Ammalat's youth and inexperience. His lack of maturity draws him under the power of Sultan Akhmet-khan and, still in the first chapter, the crafty old Avarian succeeds in inciting revolt among Ammalat's own people. Forced to flee into the mountains, and wounded in the pursuit, Ammalat is nursed back to health by Seltaneta, and he falls in love with her.

Skillfully exploiting Ammalat's feelings, Sultan Akhmet washes away the thin veneer of civilization acquired from proximity to the "despicable" Russians, and persuades Ammalat to join a raid on a Cossack settlement. Although the Avarian leader is certain that Ammalat will become the symbol to inspire the entire Caucasus against Russian rule, the young Tatar is captured in the raid. Sentenced to death by Ermolov, Ammalat is saved by Verkhovsky, who guarantees his parole and determines to civilize him. Fascinated by Ammalat's passionate, yet sensitive character, Verkhovsky believes that if he can win his total trust and friendship, he will be able to show the way to reconciliation between Russians and Caucasians.

Verkhovsky is the total antithesis to Ammalat. He is an idealistic dreamer but a hardy soldier—the true partner of Mechin and Pravin. He has a deep sympathy for the peoples of the Caucasus and a painful realization of the antipathy between their lusty, savage cultural milieu and his European civilization. He is a sincere man, a brave and honorable soldier, and a rational thinker who sees the injustice of Russian rule over the Caucasus just as clearly as he believes in its ultimate efficacy. But his constant dreaming and idealization of the Caucasian reality, joined with his prim sentiments, his inability to accept and sympathize with the innocent guile and savage behavior of the Caucasians, make him unfit for the task he has set himself. In his long letters to his fiancée he complains of the "savage and confining" Caucasian milieu. He partly understands Ammalat, and he succeeds in awakening the Tatar's consciousness of a world beyond his own will and instinct. He even discovers the key to Ammalat's trust—his love for Seltaneta—and Verkhovsky determines to wrest the girl away from her father, give her to Ammalat as the final proof of his friendship, and use their bond of perfect trust to tear down the barrier between their mutual misunderstandings. In the final analysis, however, he is himself unable to trust Ammalat, and he disapproves of the Tatar's sometimes savage quests for revenge, to say nothing of the ease with which he employs perfidy to destroy his enemies.

The relationship between Verkhovsky and Ammalat is a skilfully contrived microcosm of the larger relationship between Russians and the peoples they are trying to pacify. Behind Verkhovsky is Ermolov, that giant of a Russian bear whose brutal pacification of the Caucasus contradicts the admiration of the man by the younger generation of the 1820's. Ermolov's policies are summed up in his own words, as reported by Verkhovsky: "One execution will save hundreds of Russians from destruction and thousands of Moslems from treason."

Ermolov's character and policy are treated with sympathy by Marlinsky, but he does not deny that the Russians are hated, as well as respected and feared, by the Caucasians. Sultan Akhmet is especially determined there will be no peace in the region until the Russians are driven out. And as Ermolov is to Verkhovsky, so Sultan Akhmet is to Ammalat. Determined to provoke or force the influential young bey to revolt, he slowly weaves a web of Asiatic intrigues around him. Ammalat's vanity, his resentment of parole, his primitive longing for freedom, his thirst for glory, his duty to his people, his distrust of Verkhovsky and his failure to understand the Russian, and, above all, his hot desire for Seltaneta—all of these forces are craftily exploited by Sultan Akhmet through messengers in the night and meetings in the mountains. Verkhovsky's hopes for peace and reconciliation are thus in contradiction to the irreconcilable interests of larger political powers.

The tragedy of the tale is not to be accounted for in the larger scope of political policies, however. Tragedy, in Marlinsky's Romantic terms, is personal and individual: it stems from the fatal failure of the two principals to understand one another. Verkhovsky admires Ammalat and idealizes their friendship. Despite his resentment of parole, Ammalat is sincerely grateful to Verkhovsky for his life. Although both men desire sincere friendship, they are unable to overcome their respective shortcomings. Verkhovsky distrusts Ammalat's "Asiatic perfidy"; he is too overwhelmed by the idea that "the barbaric despotism of Persia . . . has cultivated in the Caucasian Tatars the most base passions, introduced the most despicable vices into their honor"; but he is too confident that, once he has obtained Seltaneta for his passionate bey, "it will be to me, to me that he will be obligated for the bliss of his life. . . ."

For his part, Ammalat is just as fatally mistaken. He interprets Verkovsky's scrupulous honesty as either a superior form of guile or a weakness. Initially, he is grateful that "Verkhovsky not only is showing me the way to knowledge, but is giving me the means to make use of it." But he is also tortured by the knowledge that "I once considered myself an important person, but now I am convinced of my insignificance." He especially resents feeling that Verkhovsky "stifles me with his irreproachable honor," and he doubts that "such a man, with all his goodness, can understand my passions. . . ." Trapped between his desire for freedom

and his obligation to Verkhovsky, only his agonized conscience tells him that Sultan Akhmet is treachery, Verkhovsky—friendship; Sultan Akhmet—the slavery of ignorance, Verkhovsky—the freedom of knowledge. Unfortunately, Ammalat, unused to heeding his conscience, is guided more often by his instinctive dependence on craftiness.

The end is thus inevitable. While Verkhovsky exults over his successful scheme to obtain Seltaneta for Ammalat, Sultan Akhmet has ensured that "the poison of slander burns inside Ammalat." Verkhovsky's mysterious actions in quest of Seltaneta are mistaken by Ammalat for some insidious intrigue against himself. Torn by doubts and suspicions, on the way to the surprise rendezvous with Seltaneta he concludes he is being tricked into Siberian exile. As the two men ride alone through a wood: "A shot rang out . . . and silently, slowly the Colonel slid from his saddle. . . . Ammalat sprang from his horse, and leaning on his smoking rifle, he gazed intently for several moments into the face of the murdered man, as if wishing to prove to himself that he need not fear that immovable gaze, those dimming eyes, the congealing blood. . . ."

And three days later Ammalat crowns the terrible betrayal: "Twisting the head of the corpse, he began to chop at Verkhovsky's neck, in an oblivion. . . . At the fifth blow the head separated from the shoulders. With great aversion he threw it into a ready sack and hastened to crawl from the grave."

There is great irony in Ammalat's belief he has revenged and liberated himself. When he goes to Sultan Akhmet, he finds the old Avarian on his deathbed. Now as fearful for his soul as he had been fearless for revolt, the dying man reproaches the young bey for his crime. Worse yet, Ammalat finds that the horror of his crime has aroused universal contempt, and even in his beloved Seltaneta's eyes he reads pity and aversion. Years later—still an outcast—he is killed during a suicide charge. The Russian who kills him is Verkhovsky's younger brother.

Ammalat-bek is not the last of Marlinsky's prose tales, but it serves well as a summation of his second period and as an example of the highest level he attained as a prose writer. For the tale exposes all of Marlinsky's shortcomings as a writer, and it demonstrates his finest talents. In its manner of expression the tale is one of Marlinsky's most hyperbolic, filled with torrid passions, exclamatory tones, declamation, and rhetoric.

Despite the tale's basis in fact, the presentation of many events and plot situations strain credulity to the extreme. The tale is, therefore, a perfect example of that definition of ultra-Romanticism as a concentration on "the extreme and the unusual." Little wonder that **Ammalat-bek** became a favorite point of reference for later criticisms of Russian Romantic works.

On the other hand, the tale is Marlinsky's most psychologically credible work. The themes of awakening of the consciousness of a primitive man, confrontation between the man of nature and the man of civilization, individual freedom, and the resentment of one man in the face of another's selfless generosity are unexpectedly sophisticated themes for Russian literature of the 1830's. Nor can Marlinsky be faulted for his handling of these difficult themes. His excessive hyperbole detracts from their seriousness, but he delves deeply into his thematic materials and illuminates nuances of human behavior in a way that shows care and thought. He does not falter once in his adroit handling of the mechanisms by which an author conveys theme through plot situations: Ammalat's resentment of parole, suspicions of Verkhovsky, desire for Seltaneta, and longing for freedom are expressed well in his diary and demonstrated skillfully in his actions. Ammalat stands out clearly as a child of nature whose metaphysical consciousness has been awakened deliberately and irrevocably. And his tragedy—his failure to reconcile his newly-awakened conscience with his savage upbringing—is handled masterfully in plot development, exposition, clever shifts in point of view, and his own tortured psychology. All of the motivations for the final murder are fully exposed and explored in advance, and they are developed inexorably toward the tale's climax. The situations, in fact the entire tale, are ironic, and Marlinsky treats this irony credibly. The tale is Marlinsky's most famous, it is his most extreme, and it stands as the finest illustration of his talents as Russia's first beloved writer of prose tales.

Notes

1. Kiukhel'beker, "Dnevnik (glava VI, 1834 g.)," *Russkaia starina,* VIII (1883), 253.

2. N. A. Kotliarevskii, *Dekabristy: Kniaz' A. I. Odoevskii i A. A. Bestuzhev-Marlinskii* (St. Petersburg, 1907), p. 254.

3. "Pis'ma Aleksandra Aleksandrovicha Bestuzheva k N. A. i K. A. Polevym," ed. K. Polevoi, *Russkii vestnik,* XXXII (1861), 443.

4. V. G. Belinskii, "Literaturnye mechtaniia," *Polnoe sobranie sochinenii* (Moscow, Leningrad, 1954), I, 85.

5. V. G. Bazanov, "Svetskie povesti," *Ocherki dekabristskoi literatury: publitsistika, proza, kritika* (Moscow, 1953), pp. 389-405.

6. "Anna Radkliff (Iz sochineniia Val'tera Skotta)," *Syn otechestva,* CV (1826), 131-60, 368-82; CVI, 81-93, 260-72.

7. Sir Walter Scott, "Mrs. Ann Radcliffe," *Lives of Eminent Novelists and Dramatists* (London, n. d.), pp. 568-69.

8. Ibid., pp. 562, 563, 566, 567.

9. Bazanov, "Povest' o zamke na Kame," *op. cit.,* pp. 421-23. Bazanov has also pointed out connections between *The Cuirassier* and Karamzin's tale *Bornholm Island.*

10. M. Vasil'ev, "Dekabrist A. A. Bestuzhev kak pisatel'-etnograf," *Nauchno-pedagogicheskii sbornik Vostochnogo pedagogicheskogo instituta v Kazani,* I (1926), 72.

11. "Pis'ma Bestuzheva k Polevym," *Russkii vestnik,* XXXII (1861), 318.

12. Stepan Shevyrev, "Vzgliad na sovremennuiu russkuiu literaturu, stat'ia vtoraia: Storona svetlaia (sostoianie russkogo iazyka i sloga)," *Moskvitianin,* II (1842), 167.

13. I. Turgenev, *Polnoe sobranie sochinenii* (Moscow, Leningrad, 1961), III, 62.

14. Leo N. Tolstoi, "Nabeg," *Polnoe sobranie sochinenii* (Moscow, Leningrad, 1928), III, 22.

15. Vano Shaduri, *Dekabristskaia literatura i gruzinskaia obshchestvennost'* (Tbilisi, 1958), p. 315.

16. *The Story of an Officer in Captivity among the Mountaineers* is not available in the 1958 edition and must be consulted in one of the earlier editions.

17. Data relating to translation and publication of Marlinsky's works abroad is available in catalogues of the Library of Congress and the Slavonic Collection of the New York Public Library. It has not yet been sufficiently appreciated that Marlinsky enjoyed a wide vogue in Europe, England, and the United States during the 1840's, 1850's, and 1860's. This topic of comparative literature deserves scholarly attention. Marlinsky's propagandizer abroad was Alexandre Dumas, père, who was notorious as a plagiarizer. Dumas visited the Caucasus in the 1850's, and there paid homage to Seltaneta's grave. There are French, German, and English translations of several of Marlinsky's prose tales under Dumas' name. Although Dumas claimed that his version of *Sultanetta* was his own work, a textual comparison shows that it is a direct translation.

18. See A. A. Bestuzhev-Marlinskii, *Sochineniia v dvukh tomakh* (Moscow, 1958), I, 622-23. For an exhaustive study of the writing of *Ammalat-bek* see M. P. Alekseev, "Istochniki povesti 'Ammalat-bek,'" *Etiudy o Marlinskom* (Irkutsk, 1928).

19. Nikolay L. Stepanov, "Aleksandr Marlinskii," in *Izbrannye povesti Aleksandra Marlinskogo* (Leningrad, 1937), p. 26.

N. Kovarsky (essay date 1985)

SOURCE: Kovarsky, N. "The Early Bestuzhev-Marlinsky." In *Russian Prose,* edited by B. M. Eikhenbaum and Yury Tynyanov, translated and edited by Ray Parrott, pp. 109-26. Ann Arbor: Ardis, 1985.

[In the following essay, Kovarsky studies Bestuzhev's prolific literary output during the 1820s.]

A. A. Bestuzhev begins his literary activity at the onset of the 1820s, indeed even earlier. A project related to this early period is the publication of a journal with the characteristic title *Zimtserl* (compare the attraction for all sorts of ancient Russian mythological names in sentimental-historical tales, such as in Narezhny's *Slovenian Evenings* [*Slovenskie vechera*]). The journal, however, was not approved by the censor and, apparently, even the first number was not prepared.

Bestuzhev publishes a great deal in the 1820s and, moreover, in the most diverse journals: in *The Loyalist* [*Blagonamerennyi*]; *The Champion of Enlightenment and Philanthropy* [*Sorevnovatel' Prosveshcheniia i Blagotvoreniia*]; Bulgarin's *Literary Leaflets* [*Literaturnye Listki*]; *Son of the Fatherland* [*Syn Otechestva*]; and *The Nevsky Spectator* [*Nevskii Zritel'*]. In a single year he placed the following articles and notes in *The Champion,* all, for the most part, translations: **"The Definition of Poetry"** [**"Opredelenie poezii"**], **"A Letter from the Pope to the Bishop of Rochester Prior to his Exile"** [**"Pis'mo Popa k episkopu Rochesterskomu pered ego izgnaniem"**], **"The Orator"** [**"Orator"**], **"A Passion for Questions"** [**"Strast' sprosit'"**], **"A Critique of Walter Scott's New Novel *Kenilworth*"** [**"Kritika na novyi roman Val'ter Skotta—Kenil'vort"**], **"The Teaching and Sayings of Bacon"** [**"Uchenie—aforizmy iz Bekona"**], the beginning of a large work on riding, **"A Gallery of Portraits"** [**"Portretnaia Gallereia"**], and **"A Day in an English Village Tavern"** [**"Den' v traktire Angliiskogo gorodka"**].

The predominance of translations is not accidental. Throughout his life Bestuzhev intently pursues the course of Western European writing, while nourishing an almost complete disregard for his native literature. In letters to his brothers he bursts into long polemical tirades on Hugo and Balzac, yet makes very scant and sparing observations on Veltman, Zagoskin and Dal.

In addition to translations, the early Bestuzhev writes a few long reviews (including a celebrated article on Katenin's translation of Racine's *Esther,* which pro-

voked a storm of criticism at the time) and a considerable number of critiques and counter-critiques responding to attacks on his annual surveys published in *The Polar Star* [*Poliarnaia Zvezda*].

Finally, Bestuzhev's ***Journey to Reval*** [***Poezdka v Revel'***] is published in 1821, first in *The Champion* and subsequently in a separate edition. Since a special article is devoted to the genre of travel literature in the present collection, I will not present a general analysis of the tale and will note only that this "journey" is related to the Karamzin-Dupaty line, i.e., to the line of travel literature seemingly constructed on two parallels: 1) the journey proper (the external plane); 2) the description of "feelings" and events.

Marlinsky's verse epigraph to ***Journey to Reval*** is characteristic in this regard:

> You wished—and I promised,
> My exacting friends,
> That I devote to tales
> The leisure of momentary respites
> And that I describe à la Dupaty
> The adventures of the road.

As T. A. Roboli writes, "the objective and heterogeneous material of anecdotes, dramatic scenes, and so forth interwoven with this memoir-epistolary basis is motivated, in any event, by the sense of an author. A large belletristic form is created with a natural, seemingly self-motivated fusion of parts."

By the beginning of the 1820s, i.e., at the moment of Bestuzhev's departure onto the literary high road, however, the basic character of "travel literature" naturally had to change. It was necessary to differentiate the material of individual prose works from the broadly-developed material of anecdotes, lyrical digressions, historical sketches, and so forth. The role of travel literature no longer comprised so much the gathering as the preservation of accumulated material. Thus, Bestuzhev used one of the episodes in *Journey to Reval* as the plot of the tale **"Tournament at Reval"** [**"Revel'skii turnir"**]; the stylistic material of puns, witticisms and similes was distributed among other stories. Among Bestuzhev's later works **"A Leaf from the Diary of a Guard Officer"** [**"Listok iz dnevnika Gvardeiskogo ofitsera"**] and **"Another Leaf"** [**"Eshche listok"**] from the same diary in essence are little more than fragments, albeit wholly independent, of a "journey." Just as the lyric poem of the 1820s is already beginning to disintegrate into small, independent "excerpts from a poem"[1] in the 1830s, for Bestuzhev the material of travel literature begins to acquire a certain independent character and develops into separate novellas.[2]

The very fact that ***Journey to Reval*** belongs to the Karamzin-Dupaty line is not fortuitous. Karamzin's influence on Marlinsky has already been noted, although not in the official history of literature. Contemporaries either did not notice this fact or passed over it in silence. Only Shevyrev made an attempt to compare Marlinsky with Karamzin: "A writer appeared, gifted with a fervid imagination and, what's more, with the play of wit. He began to embroider and embellish Karamzin's simple and smooth language: after the harmoniously correct and finished forms of Classicism, whose uniformity itself evokes a certain coldness, a diversity of language seemed extremely attractive. This striking brilliance of ornate form was taken for fervor, liveliness and power; a grimace for an expression of the soul. Here is the clue to Marlinsky's initial and rapid success: he was a reaction to the classical school of Karamzin. His *Journey to Reval,* initial stories and literary surveys published in *The Polar Star* strongly attracted the readers' attention. His ability to say everything somehow differently, and not just simply, was tremendously appealing; his similes were striking neither for their fidelity to nature nor for their beauty, but rather for their unexpectedness and strangeness."

In analyzing Karamzin's influence on the Russian literary language, and thereby presenting material for an analogy between Karamzin and Bestuzhev, Shevyrev is hoisting himself on his own petard. Just like every other prose writer at the beginning of the 1820s, Bestuzhev was unable to escape even the temporary influence of Karamzin; not even Narezhny and the lesser known authors of sentimental tales at the turn of the century could avoid this influence; even as a pupil of Grech, Bestuzhev was unable to escape this domination. He himself acknowledged in his letters that he was greatly indebted to Grech [and Bulgarin]: "In a moral sense," he writes in a letter to Andreev, "I am irredeemably indebted to them for their earlier good will and advice," and further: "[Grech], so to speak, nurtured me under his arm like a nestling; he was the first to encourage and the first to appreciate me. I am indebted to him for my *knowledge of the language's grammar*; if I now less often err in the use of the letter 'yat,' he also is to blame for this." Although Marlinsky subsequently wrote to Polevoi that even though he had been close to Grech and Bulgarin he "still had sharp words for them," one may doubt the sincerity of this declaration. In the 1820s both Grech and Bestuzhev seemingly had agreed only to bow and scrape to one another: after Bestuzhev had praised Grech's grammatical studies in *The Polar Star,* Grech placed some highly patronizing reviews of Bestuzhev's essays in *Son of the Fatherland.* It is not accidental that of all the Decembrists of whom Grech writes in "Notes on my Life" ["Zapiski o moei zhizni"], Bestuzhev is the only one to emerge absolved and justified.[3]

Grech himself was a zealous admirer of Karamzin (notwithstanding a certain disapproval of the general "Karamzinolatry," as he puts it in his notes) and, more-over, an admirer of Karamzin as a novelist though not at all as a historian. (Compare his remarks: "His tales, *Letters of a Russian Traveler* [*Pis'ma russkogo puteshestvennika*] and articles in *The Messenger of Europe* [*Vestnik Evropy*] are written in a pleasant, natural style, which, while not spurning embellishment, still does not strive for beautiful effects . . . A certain constraint, an effort to be eloquent, and the forced rounding of periods are evident in the style of his history: everything is artificial, measured, and not at all as it was earlier.")

Marlinsky's opinion of Karamzin in the 1820s is still wholly dependent on Grech's teaching. (Compare his remarks about Karamzin in 1822: "He transformed the bookish Russian language, a rich, powerful, sonorous, but already untamed language in the hands of untalented writers and ignorant translators . . . He set the rusty wheels of its mechanism in motion with apt novelty, discarded an alien motley quality in lexical choices and word-combinations, and gave it a national countenance. Time will judge Karamzin as a historian, but a sense of truth and the gratitude of his contemporaries crown this eloquent writer, who, with his delightful florescent style caused a decisive revolution for the better in the Russian language.")

Marlinsky abruptly changes his attitude toward Karamzin in the second half of his life. And it is characteristic that he begins his attacks on him precisely with *A History* [*Istoriia*], making no reference whatsoever to Karamzin the novelist. It is as if he officially still holds to his former views (the article on Polevoi's "Vow at the Grave of Christ" ["Kliatva pri grobe Gospodnem"]), while the break is absolutely clear in the letters of this period: "I never liked that Grandma Karamzin, a man without any philosophy, who wrote page after page of his *History* neither thinking through the next page nor coming to grips with the preceding one. He was an eloquent, industrious, but small-minded windbag who concealed his own insignificance behind the stir of others' maxims. Not so Polevoi . . . ," etc. (Letter to his mother, January 1831).

And then, quite openly in a letter to Bulgarin in 1834: "I consider *The Telegraph* [*Moskovskii Telegraf*] to be the best journal with respect to conviction; *A History of the Russian People* [*Istoriia Naroda Rossiiskogo*] (Polevoi) is better than *A History of the Russian State* [*Istoriia Gosudarstva Rossiiskogo*]; perhaps I am making a mistake here, but if so, it is sincere. What for ten years seemed beautiful to me now appears quite different."

Thus, during the course of Marlinsky's literary activity we encounter on his part a wholesale acknowledgment of Karamzin the novelist, and a break with Karamzin the historian, who returned to archaic forms of the language in his *History.*

II

"An Ancient Tale—Roman and Olga" ["**Starinnaia povest'—Roman i Ol'ga**"], published in 1823, chronologically was one of Bestuzhev's first stories; it bears traces of the typical cliches of the period's sentimental tales.

"Roman and Olga" still borrows wholesale from Karamzin and the later sentimentalists that smoothness and pleasantness of lexicon, that middle style, and that typically Karamzinian intonation which are so peculiar to sentimental tales at the beginning of the nineteenth century.

I shall cite one instance to illustrate precisely to what degree Karamzin's and Bestuzhev's intonations are related in this story:

> Her heart flew to meet him, but timidity told her "stay." The beauty obeyed this latter voice only by an agonizing force of will and great anguish . . . and though a calm voice from the depths of her heart, as if from a distant cave, asked her: "What are you doing, foolhardy one?" another much stronger voice in that very same heart answered for her "I love you!"
>
> (Karamzin, "Natalya, the Boyar's Daughter")

> Сердце ее летело к нему навстречу, но робость говорила ей „останься". Красавица повиновалась сему последнему голосу только с мучительным принуждением, с великою тоскою . . . и хотя тихий голос из глубины сердца, как будто из отдаленной пещеры, спрашивал ее: „что ты делаешь, безрассудная"? но другой голос, гораздо сильнейший в том же самом сердце отвечал за нее „Люблю!"
>
> (Карамзин, „Натальы, боярская дочь")

> In vain did the beauty tear herself away: reason counseled her "flee," while the heart whispered "stay." "What will good people say?" the mind repeated. "What will become of your beloved when you hide yourself away?" the heart remarked. Her struggle with fear and shyness had not yet ended when Olga reluctantly, without realizing it, found herself seated arm in arm with Roman.
>
> (Bestuzhev, **"Roman and Olga"**)

> Красавица вырывалась напрасно рассудок советывал ей„беги", сердце шептало „останься". „Что скажут добрые люди—повторял разум. „Что станется с милым, когда ты скроешься—замечало сердце". Еще борьба страха и стыдливости не кончилась, а Ольга нехотя, сама не зная, как уже сидела с Романом рука об руку.
>
> Бестужев,„ **"Роман и Ольга"**

Many similar examples could be cited. Bestuzhev wrote in the notes to **"Roman and Olga"**: "The time frame of my tale is set midway through the years 1396 and 1398 . . . All the historical events and personages mentioned are presented with unyielding accuracy, whereas I depicted the mores, prejudices and customs, both imaginatively and from extant language texts. I sought to approximate the simple, genuine Russian tale and can vouch that the vocabulary, which will seem strange to many, is not imagined but drawn from ancient chronicles, songs and fairy tales."

It must be noted, however, that the vocabulary did not strike anyone as strange: the attacks on Bestuzhev's language, on his "barbaric idiom," by no means stemmed from the tales, but rather from his literary surveys; indeed, every attempt to introduce "strange vocabulary" was confined to borrowing from the wholly inoffensive and accepted dialectisms or syntactical phrasings so widespread at the time in the songs of Merzlyakov and Neledinsky.[4]

In this story, however, the comparatively new lexical and syntactic elements are incidental. Marlinsky himself subsequently made a curious reservation (in one of the late stories, **"Cavalry Raids"** [**"Naezdy"**]) concerning the language and psychology of the heroes in his historical tales. After a long sententious statement uttered by one of the story's heroes, Marlinsky observes: ". . . *I cannot vouch that similar thoughts were whirling in the Prince's head—such thoughts did not pertain to his time, and even less so to his social position.*"

This reservation is reminiscent of Karamzin's aside in the story "Natalya, the Boyar's Daughter": "The reader will sense that lovers of old did not at all speak as they do here; nowadays we would not even understand the language of that era. It was necessary only in some fashion to imitate the ancient character of speech."

Notwithstanding this acknowledgment, Bestuzhev continues at an even later date to take credit for introducing the "simple, genuine Russian tale." He writes (in an article on Polevoi): "Karamzin disposed us toward the legends of our antiquity; archeological searches gathered certain elements for the novel. Marlinsky's historical tales, in which he cast off the fetters of the bookish language and began to speak in the living Russian idiom, served as doorways into the mansion of the full-scale novel."

Belinsky responded to this phrase with cruel irony: "The strangest thing of all about Marlinsky is that he recently confessed with amazing modesty to a sin for which he is guilty neither in body nor in spirit: that his stories ostensibly introduced national character into Russian literature. Here's a patent falsehood for you! These stories number among his most unsuccessful efforts; he is no more national in them than Karamzin, because his Old Russia cruelly smacks of his cherished, beloved Livonia". . . . "Marlinsky was the first to begin writing Russian tales. They were to his era precisely what Karamzin's were to his . . ." And again: "Their (Marlinsky's historical tales) national character consisted of employing Russian names, avoiding an obvious breach of fidelity to events and customs, imitating the manner of Russian speech, and using sayings and proverbs, but no more than this."[5]

In one of Bestuzhev's letters to the Polevoi brothers dating from the beginning of the 1830s, we find the following lines: "Indeed, who writes among us? Either drawing-room habitués, who once a year bend an ear to the language of the folk in fair booths and are overjoyed that they've caught some banal expression, making a big deal of it. For them this is a pretentious little birthmark! The rest of the language is just a sour cream mish-mash: some sweet-sour object floating in the whey of mediocrity, and all strewn with the leaden sugar of personality or the licorice of flattery: excellent medicine for a cough, but not for boredom. Or people for whom, of course, it's nothing to clamber after *pot-house* expressions, yet who labor in vain to lend them an engaging quality."

Precisely this disdain for the eavesdroppers on the folk language of the fair-booth compelled Bestuzhev to pay a very caustic compliment directed at Dal: "Lugansky's fairy tales deserve our gratitude, although their merit lies wholly in the mind of the publisher" and "Lugansky's own fabrications are not very apt."

Belinsky's attacks were justified. The lexicon of Bestuzhev's early stories still remains within the limits of the tendencies outlined by Karamzin, the short-story writer. Yet it is clear from the letters cited that even later, in the 1830s, the efforts to renew the literary language which are so characteristic of the creative activity of Veltman, Pogodin and Dal remained alien to Bestuzhev. Hence his scorn for "the eavesdroppers on the folk language of the fair-booth" and for "pot-house expressions."

III

Bestuzhev's basic efforts in organizing "poetic, rather rhetorical" prose (Shevyrev) follow two paths: first, the increased usage of rhetorical intonations (interrogative and exclamatory) and sententious maxims characteristic of the rhetorical style; second, the structuring of narrative and rhetorical phrases in specific rhythmic units.

Among Bestuzhev's early works (almost his earliest ones) we find a curious fragment entitled **"A Word on Fools"** [**"Nechto o gluptsakh"**], published in an 1820 issue of *The Champion*. The note consists entirely of a series of maxims and aphoristic forms, which later will be fused into a narrative as authorial commentary upon a hero's actions, moods and speech.

Given the weak distinction between the storyteller and a tale's hero in stories of the 1820s, these maxims likewise enter into the heroes' speech; this gives rise to the monotonous stylistic background of the rhetorical monologue ("The Russian characters in Marlinsky's stories speak and act like Teutonic knights: their language is rhetorical in the manner of monologues in classical tragedies"—Belinsky). Bestuzhev obviously liked this form since, along with notes consisting entirely of a chain of maxims (as in **"A Word on Fools"**), his work contains several passages where the maxims are presented as separate thoughts whose linking is motivated either by a single source (**"The Teaching and Sayings of Bacon"**) or is completely devoid of motivation (**"Thoughts from Various Authors"** [**"Mysli iz raznykh avtorov"**], *The Champion* for 1821).

There are many analogous examples in Karamzin (this form evidently passes on to him from the eighteenth century. Compare but the maxim inserted directly into the narrative phrase: "for peasant women also know how to love"—**"Poor Liza"** [**"Bednaia Liza"**]).

This style, replete with aphorisms, subsequently provided constant grounds for Bestuzhev's play with it; later he will construct puns on these maxims, preserving the seriousness of the maxim proper while setting it off against a whole series of words and word combinations drawn from a different lexical milieu. Such was the punning application of the maxim. (Compare but the conversation between the physician and the lieutenant in the story *The Frigate* **"Hope"** [*Fregat* **"Nadezhda"**]—the very same chapter which, by Bestuzhev's own admission, was inserted in the story "wholly beyond the specified number"—where the physician is constantly uttering maxim-like phrases with references to famous doctors, while the officer is continually parodying them).

In the 1820s, however, and while still under the direct influence of Karamzin's style, Bestuzhev does not resort to this play between a low lexical context and a high rhetorical maxim. Therefore his style quite naturally still remains exclusively within the bounds of Karamzinian rhetoric: "A girl's love is like ice in the spring: she'll weep a bit, yearn a bit, and then another suitor will wipe away her tears with the beaver-fur cuff of his coat"; "A man's fearlessness instills into a maiden's breast a certain lofty regard for him, sympathy befriends and draws one together with a sufferer, and love steals into the soul like the gentlest of breezes"; "woe to a youth if an empty-headed beauty only thinks that she loves him—woe to a maiden if she does not love falsely."

The maxim is not only a static motif, i.e. does not participate in the forward movement of a story [fabula] and in changing the situation, but is also free, i.e., generally is not used as a motif in a story.[6] Thus, its introduction into the narrative is usually accompanied by a transition from the past tense of the narrative phrase into the present tense of the maxim. This is what we find in Karamzin: "Moreover, the poor widow, almost constantly shedding tears over the death of her husband—for peasant women also *know how* to love, grew weaker day by day and couldn't work at all."

We find the same in Bestuzhev: "But kind thoughts are *ephemeral* in hearts hardened by riotous conduct and pride, in hearts eternally reproachful of fate and not of oneself, and revenge, hatred and jealousy *boiled up* anew and ever more powerfully."

Or: "However, owing to some fatal passion I could in no way live without people with whom I could not get on. Such are the fetters of society; *we do not have the strength to remove them,* nor the resolve to burst them. Godunov *ascended* to the throne . . . ," and the narrative continues in this vein.

Thus, in the course of a narrative the maxim takes the form of an apparent aside and as such is an integral feature of Karamzin's rhetorical style, and, later, of Bestuzhev's as well.

The style of "poetic" prose, however, is not restricted to authorial comments in the form of maxims as asides. In this prose the narrative style attains specific phrasal constructions which appear just as frequently in Bestuzhev's work as do maxims. I have in mind those rhetorical questions and exclamations which transform the novella into something similar to a lyrical poem. As soon as we approach Bestuzhev's prose from this point of view, the following thought, expressed by B. M. Eikhenbaum in his work on the melodics of the verse line in Zhukovsky's poetry, becomes applicable: "Judging wholly a priori, we foresee that we will discover in melodious lyric poetry a preferable selection of certain verbal intonations which serve as material for developing verse melodies. It is natural that the intonations selected inevitably will prove to be characteristic of emotionally-colored language, but not of the business or purely narrative styles which predominate in the language. In other words, these intonations must be interrogative and exclamatory."

In the prose of Bestuzhev as well, judging wholly a priori, we must discover a preferable selection of these intonations, which function to create a specific style of prose language. The following passage is particularly revealing in this regard, since it represents almost a strophic construction framed by identical interrogative phrases: "Kind old woman, why is it that you do not have any charms against the love of an enchantress? With them you would have cured your boyar's daughter of her sorrow, grief, and weariness of heart. Or why has

your heart lost the memory of youth? You should have foreseen dear Olga's passion and stifled it with advice and distractions while it was still in full bloom. But you yourself fanned the flame, you yourself sang her songs of Roman, and praised his manners and figure. Woe to a youth if an empty-headed beauty only thinks that she loves him—woe to a maiden if she does not love falsely! In the stir of martial camp life with its foreign beauties, a young man forgets his former sweetheart, while deadly passions lodge in the stillness of a maiden's chamber and love stings an innocent soul deeply. Ah, why is it, kind nurse, that you do not know any charms against the love of an enchantress? Why has age clouded your eyes?"

Marlinsky, however, is not alone even on this path; even here he obviously proceeds from Karamzin, differing only in that Karamzin's prose still does not present a developed system of lyrical narration, a system which then passes on to Lermontov and manifests itself fully in his *Vadim.*

Karamzin employs these intonations principally in authorial commentary and in remarks about his characters' conversations and actions; they are most frequently encountered as the author's direct lyrical apostrophes to a character: "Reckless youth! don't you know your own heart? Can you always answer for your actions? Is reason always the ruler of your feelings?" "Ah, Liza, Liza! Where is your guardian angel, where is your innocence?" and so on. We find the same in Bestuzhev, only the questions and exclamations are expressed with greater emphatic force. His heroes' speech is systematically accompanied by the author's lyrical apostrophes and alternates with narrative phrases almost with periodic regularity: "For the last time farewell to everything that gladdened me for seventeen years! Farewell dear, kind parents! And Olga burst into bitter tears." "Where will you find peace, disobedient daughter, without the blessing of parents whose hearts you have broken? Deeply moved, Olga prayed with new reverence and grace descended upon her heart like a bright thought."

Rhetorical questions and exclamations function in Bestuzhev's prose, however, not only as lyrical apostrophes from the author; they also occur after descriptive passages at the beginning of the narrative, introducing the reader directly into the flow of action. For example, we read in the story **"Wenden Castle"** [**"Zamok Venden"**] ". . . Whose shadow is fleetingly glimpsed in the mists that betray the river's course in the depths of the savage forest? Is it not an apparition, the treasure-house guard for the princes of Hersica, who perished in the wilds? . . . No, it is not a belated Russian *strelets* . . ." and so on.

It should be noted that interrogative and exclamatory intonations are almost never encountered in Karamzin in this function. Rhetorical phrases, like maxims, bear the character of bound and free motifs in his work, and this is why they so easily develop into digressions. In this instance, then, Marlinsky seemingly proceeds not directly from Karamzin but from the later authors of sentimental tales. Thus, we find in Mamyshev's story "Unfortunate N." ["Neschastnaia N."]: "A dark storm cloud flies along with a roar. A nearby grove moans . . . But who is wandering there amidst the gravestones and crosses?" and so on.

Moreover, a rhetorical system of interrogative and exclamatory intonations is only weakly marked in Karamzin; such intonations occur sporadically in his work. Bestuzhev, on the other hand, proceeding from Karamzin and the sentimental tales, develops this system into wide-ranging rhetorical constructions. His dialogues are especially characteristic in this regard, and at times they are constructed entirely on a system of emphatic intonations: "Knight! In the name of honor and the good repute of your innocent wife, I demand proof of this." "Innocent? Have wolves long been preaching the innocence of foxes? Have Russians long been speaking about honor?"

Belinsky wrote in 1839, i.e., at a time when this entire rhetorical system must have already seemed false and artificial: "Read the 'Speech' that Pravin[7] addressed to his Vera on two whole pages and ask yourself: do people really speak that way, and did the story's hero declame it for himself or for the reader?" . . . "And would all these phrases have been appropriate in a letter, much less in a conversation or in a monologue" . . . "and this is literature, and not rhetoric?"[8]

In Bestuzhev the declamatory character of dialogue to a considerable degree is created by a system of emphatic intonations. It is quite evident that rhetorical trumpery was one of Bestuzhev's chief tendencies. Whether simply in a dialogue, in a "false" dialogue, where the tale is narrated by the hero (Ich-Erzählung), or in a simple tale narrated by the author, Bestuzhev always prefers to the simple narrative phrase the lofty, declamatory, emphatic phrase, which like the maxim will later serve his play with high and low styles and thereby acquire a totally new semantic coloration.

In *Karamzin* the basic devices for setting the period to rhythm (see K. A. Skipina's study) are the tri-membered period and the intensified use of a dactylic ending, which thereafter is adhered to very consistently. These devices are passed on to the writers of sentimental tales, then to Bestuzhev and to Lermontov, where they play a vital role not only in the early *Vadim* but in *A Hero of Our Time* [*Geroi nashego vremeni*] as well. There is even a third factor, namely Karamzin's effort to extend the number of unstressed syllables between two stressed syllables by means of a whole series of inversions (a simple example would be "my heart" ["moe serdtse"]

(—"—) and "heart of mine" ["serdtse moe"] ('— —'), thereby avoiding a concentration of stressed syllables.

The writers of sentimental tales picked up these devices for incorporating rhythm in prose from Karamzin and carried them to the point of monotony and wearisome uniformity. Therefore, Bestuzhev's remark about Narezhny's *Slovenian Evenings* is quite natural: "His prose is too measured and monotonic."[9]

Bestuzhev does not shun the dactylic ending, employing to this end the customary inversion of adjectives and pronouns at the end of a phrase, and while the pronouns preserve minimal stress at the end of phrases, they are nevertheless perceived almost as enclitic particles: "alien sand will bestrew *thine eyes* ["chuzhdyi pesok zasyplet *glaza tvoi*"]; "*his* turbulent *soul*" ["*kipuchaia dusha ego*"], etc. Dactylic endings, on the other hand, are only a secondary factor for creating rhythm in Marlinsky's prose. For Bestuzhev the basic "marking point," to use B. V. Tomashevsky's expression, is an irregular syntactical division, i.e., nonsymmetrically arranged segments with respect to pauses, and a dissimilar number of stresses in contiguous syntactical segments, yet an order in the sentence's part in contiguous phrases. For example:

> I no longer wish to waste words on a man,
> who dreams of overturning the world and yet cannot conquer foolish prejudices,
> who breathes fratricide and yet is fearful of betrayal,
> who desires everything and yet dares nothing.
> Go, bow before those who regard the support of their stirrup as happiness,
> gnaw furtively, like a mouse, at the heels of enemies who hold you in contempt,
> be off to your younger brother for gossip,
> wait for a crumb from the table,
> make friends with a woman to whom you can be a husband
> cordially shower the young with hops, when you would like to crush them with curses,
> count the kisses of others,
> nurse your brother's future children.

> Я не хочу долее терять слов с человеком,
> Который мечтает перевернуть свет и не может переломить
>> вздорные предрассудки,
> который дышит братоубийством и страшится измены,
> который всего хочет и ничего не смеет.
> Поди, кланяйся тем, который за счастье должны бы считать
>> поддержать свое стремя,
> грызи, украдкою, как мышь каблуки презирающих тебя врагов,
> ступай на вести к своему меньшему брату,
> жди подачки со стола,
> добивайся в дружки той, которой ты можешь быть мужем,
> осыпай молодых приветливо хмелем, когда ты бы хотел

задавить их под проклятиями
считай чужие поцелуи,
няньчи будущих детей братниных.

In this example the sentences are not phonetically identical, nor equally broken into segments, and the phrase's rhythm is wholly maintained by the anaphoric, imperative verb. Thus, this entire succession constitutes an incomplete rhythmico-syntactical parallelism, where the rhythm's impulse apparently is provided by the initial verb, and the reader, under the influence of this impulse, senses the entire fragment as a rhythmically constructed whole.

We encounter isolated examples of syntactical parallelism in Karamzin as well, though, again, they are not developed into an entire system:

> Russians count their gnawing misfortunes
> While Novgorodians count gold coins.
> The Russians are in bonds,
> While Novgorodians celebrate their freedom.

> Русские считают язвы свои;
> новгородцы считают золотые монеты.
> Русские в узах,
> новгородцы славят вольность свою.

Bestuzhev especially liked to construct phrases on the principle of the syntactic syllogism wherein we sense an obvious rise in intonation in premises, and then a falling intonation toward the phrase which corresponds to the conclusion:

> The silence lasted a long time.
> Yury, displeased with the matchmaking's scant success, saw that he had insulted his
> brother's vanity.
> Simeon was vexed at him for his opposition, and at himself for bringing up seniority.
> One glanced out the *slanting* window,
> While the other played with the tassel on his *patterned* sash.
> Both sought words for conversation, but did not find them.

> Долго длилось молчание.
> Юрий, недовольный худым успехом сватовства, видел, что
>   он оскорбил самолюбие брата.
> Симеон досадовал на него за противоречие, а на себя за
>   помин о старшинстве.
> Один глядел в косящятое окошко,
> Другой играл кистью своего узорчатого кушака.
> Оба исдаил слов к разговору и не находили.

Bestuzhev's rhythmical system is constructed on the principle of syntactical parallelism. He almost does not recognize periods, substituting for them short sentences constructed in parallel and linked by belonging to a single rhythmical whole. It is characteristic in this regard that the early Marlinsky avoids indirect discourse, which requires a complex system of coordination and inclusion as well as a large number of formless words serving as connections; all these forms came into usage afterwards, by the 1830s. Prior to 1825 Bestuzhev's syntax on the whole is constructed around the simple sentence and the syntactical parallelism of these sentences.

IV

Having established Bestuzhev's tendencies toward the creation of rhetorical prose, we can now engage problems concerning the particulars of genre in the early tales, an area in which Bestuzhev no longer follows Karamzin's lead but seemingly overcomes his influence.

In analyzing the genre features of his tales one above all must touch upon, if only briefly, the question of foreign influences upon the early Bestuzhev, a problem which requires a considerably more detailed examination. Scholars who have studied him to date have even been inclined to supplant Bestuzhev's name with the names of foreign writers, from Hugo to Irving inclusive (N. A. Kotlyarevsky, V. V. Gippius).

It was not Hugo who exerted any real influence on the early Marlinsky (as is evident from his correspondence, Bestuzhev became generally acquainted with Hugo only in the 1830s; consequently, there can be no talk of Hugo's influence upon him prior to 1825), nor Walter Scott, but rather the "horror novels" and the "novels of mystery and terror" (Ann Radcliffe, Walpole, Lewis and others) so popular at the beginning of the nineteenth century [i.e., Gothic]. As Vyazemsky indicates, the influence of French melodrama is also highly possible in this period. Indeed, contemporaries received Betuzhev's initial stories in just this way. In 1825 a reviewer for *The Northern Bee* [*Severnaia Pchela*] wrote concerning the story **"The Traitor"** [**"Izmennik"**]: "In **'The Traitor'** Mr. Bestuzhev painstakingly traces the horrible death of one of Russia's fallen sons. Just before death he experiences the torments of Hell: instead of singing a funeral dirge to the dying man, the people to whom he betrayed his fatherland repeat over and over: the earth will not receive one who has betrayed her" (the story's fearful motifs are deliberately emphasized).

Vyazemsky wrote Bestuzhev concerning the story **"Neihausen Castle"** [**"Zamok Neigauzen"**]: "There are some truly wonderful passages in your story; but I don't like the gardener's German jokes and the German self-advertisement inherent in the crime. One does not encounter such people in the real world, only in German dramas and French melodramas."

Bestuzhev ostensibly begins to parody the "horror novels" as early as in the fragment **"Another Leaf from the Diary of a Guard Officer"**: "Our journey would

171

make a splendid setting for a novel of wonders," I said to my comrade, laughing. "Yes, and the night is truly Radcliffian," he responded, "blacker than the Sixth Squadron's stallions. All that's lacking is . . . a cave and some thieves."

However, even the problem of the influence of the "horror novels" upon Bestuzhev's tales is not so simple. The fact is that by the 1820s a reflection of the "novels of mystery and terror" already existed in literature, and namely in those sentimental tales in which motifs of love are relegated to the background and the villain comes to the fore.

In his early experiments Bestuzhev proceeds just from these tales; the tales **"The Execution Bell"** [**"Kolokol kazni"**], **"Dolefully"** [**"Zaunno"**], and others, are especially characteristic in this regard. Compare but the striking conclusion to the tale *A Novel in Seven Letters* [*Roman v semi pis'makh*], which is close to the "horror novels" both in terms of its motifs and style: "It's night now; all around everything is dozing, yet the worm of my heart cannot sleep. Day passes in the pangs of remorse; night peoples the darkness with fearsome objects and—would you believe, my friend—every knock, every call of the sentry causes me to shudder. If I doze off, weary, apparitions wander around the bed and whisper something in my ear. If I fall asleep terrible dreams agitate my heart, a fateful shot resounds and a death groan rends my ears; then again a whispering calm, suddenly broken by a funeral dirge . . . the thump of a spade above me . . . I am suffocating . . . inhaling the dust of my grave . . . a coffin board crushes my breast . . . a worm crawls across my face . . . ough . . . I leap up and the drops of cold sweat seem like drops of blood."

We encounter in the tales effects of illumination characteristic of the genre (B. M. Eikhenbaum, *Lermontov, on Vadim*). It is not without reason that Bestuzhev later recalls on several occasions Anne Radcliffe's beloved Salvatore Rosa.[10]

Bestuzhev even alters the structure of the tales in accordance with the basic lines of the genre: the central passage in each chapter is devoted to some striking melodramatic features, which Bestuzhev usually concentrates in dialogues.[11] An approximate scheme of the tale looks like this: the customary descriptive beginning (a landscape or the interior of some rooms) coupled with dialogue; the chapter then closes with a descriptive passage. It is precisely here that one finds a narrative concentration upon striking melodramatic settings and situations (which Bestuzhev, by the way, very much likes to emphasize with such remarks as: "The picture was terrible," or "It is horrible!"). This lack of a smoothly flowing narrative line caused Pushkin to write Bestuzhev: "Your **"Tournament"** is reminiscent of Walter Scott's tournaments. Drop these foreigners and turn to us Orthodox Russians; enough of your writing *quick-paced tales with romantic transitions*—that is all right for a Byronic poem. But a novel requires chatter, so say everything plainly."

In 1825, for these very same reasons, a *Moscow Telegraph* reviewer noted that Marlinsky's tales were reminiscent of Byron's poems.

V

In 1825 Bestuzhev publishes the tale **"Tournament at Reval"** in the last number of the *Polar Star*; he extensively employs in it all the comic devices basic to the prose of the 1830s.[12] One can discover the origin of these devices by examining Bestuzhev's early critical articles and reviews.

We find among these articles a very curious letter to the publisher of *The Loyalist* in which Bestuzhev proposes to assemble a chamber of rare literary artifacts. The letter struck a responsive chord: answers from An Inhabitant of Vasilievsky and An Inhabitant of Galley Harbor were placed in *The Loyalist* and *The Nevsky Spectator*. The latter two authors' letters are serious critical articles, however, whereas Bestuzhev obviously is parodying this type of article in his letter: "Well, I've been sitting here a week already working out a system for arranging my future study, searching, comparing, and rearranging everything, but I still haven't found an appropriate classification system in the books, both rhymed and otherwise, on freaks and degenerates in our century, commencing with the worms and proceeding right up to the camels of the Russian language. Advise me, Mr. Publisher, should I prefer Lineev's or Buffon's method, and what order is better to employ in the placing of artificial rarities from overseas, such as, for example: Tatar and Vandal phrases, cleverly-turned endearments, Gordian thoughts, philosophical bubbles, petrified similes, and, in a word, all the prominent cripples of common sense. Oh, if you could see how many jumping spiders I've gathered; snub-nosed jugs; genuflecting grass snakes; pigeons and ducks with teeth, loud-talking corks, and endless peepholes; how many blood-thirsty mushrooms, courteous African lions, perch striding along with cudgels, et cetera, et cetera, you surely would compose an encomium to me."

It is very possible that the later Bestuzhev's comic, punning style in part derives precisely from the parodying of these "literary rarities": "Tatar and Vandal phrases," "petrified similes," "cleverly-turned endearments," and the like. The "snail of conversation," which Zagoskin attacked, is a good example of this. Bestuzhev's system of comic similes and metaphors is based precisely on the comparison of wholly incomparable objects.[13]

One of Bestuzhev's favorite comic devices, the device of the realized metaphor, undoubtedly was conceived as the chief method of his early critical articles. Compare but the critique of Katenin's translation of Racine's *Esther*:

> In reading the translation, one seemingly sees oneself at a masquerade; everything in it is singing and dancing: Israelite women, babbling, praise the Lord, raise a lament and sob constrainedly; all inanimate objects are personified and stroll about, as when Artaxerxes says to Aman:
>
> Come closer, steadfast shield of my throne,
>
> and the shield approaches with a low bow. The word *appui* is used in the original, which the French always understand in a figurative sense. But the translator wanted to embellish Racine, so now in his work they even praise the Most High with their bellies:
>
> My lips, my heart and my entire belly
> Praise the Lord, the bearer of blessings to me.
>
> It is difficult to believe that the Jewish maidens were ventriloquists, and yet it is impossible to understand this in a figurative sense, since the singing Israelite is enumerating the parts of her body in the passage. In the original we read:
>
> Que ma bouche et mon coeur
> et tout ce que je suis.
>
> I leave others to judge whether it should have been translated as it was.

In later years Bestuzhev repeatedly sought to justify the peculiarities of his style almost as features of his psychic makeup; however, the basis of his "Bestuzhevian drops" which he himself provides in a letter to Andreev is more reliable:

> The remark about glitter is wholly justified, but it is in my nature: whoever is acquainted with my everyday conversation will recall that I unwittingly speak in figures and similes, and Nikolai Ivanovich (Grech) did not call my oral pranks Bestuzhevian drops for nothing. However, *the tale is one matter, the novel another. It seems to me that the brevity of the former must seize the mind through wit, since it does not afford space for the development of descriptions, passions and plot complication.* If you smile in reading it, I shall be satisfied; if you laugh, my pleasure will be doubled. One can get along in a novel without curvets and leaps: its characters and situations create a consistent, entertaining quality; God forbid that my Sivka-Burka should start to act up there as well. That, however, is still in the future.

Judging by his letters to his brothers, Polevoi, Bulgarin, and Grech, Bestuzhev repeatedly sought to write a novel; the fragment of a proposed large form has even been preserved. Kostenentsky, who met with him in the Caucasus, relates that Bestuzhev even described in detail for him the outline of a future novel. Yet, he continued until the very end to write "quick-paced tales with romantic transitions" which seized the reader's mind through wit. Bestuzhev did not succeed in creating a novel void of glitter. The "Bestuzhevian drops" and the large form proved to be incompatible.

Notes

1. See V. M. Zhirmunsky, *Byron and Pushkin* [*Bairon i Pushkin*], Academia, 1924.

2. The device of framing likewise lends the tale "Castle Eisen" ["Zamok Eizen"] the character of an episode from a journey. It begins thus: "During the last Guards campaign, while hunting on the outskirts of Narva," etc. We find the same in "Castle Wenden": "They say that the route has been changed, and that our regiment will be stationed in Wenden."

3. N. I. Grech, *Notes on My Life* [*Zapiski o moei zhizni*], St. Petersburg, 1886.

4. Bestuzhev himself, incidentally, indicates the source of these borrowings: three epigraphs in his tale are taken from "folk" songs. Two of them are presented with no indication of their source and reworking and, evidently, belong to Bestuzhev himself; the third epigraph is drawn from Merzlyakov:

   > Why should I listen to all human gossip?
   > The heart loves, without seeking others' permission;
   > The heart loves, without even asking me.

   The whole of "Castle Eisen" comprises a stylistic reworking of proverbs and sayings designed to reproduce the oral quality of the storyteller's language, i.e., the focus is on his narrative and not on declamation.

5. Compare what Belinsky said about Karamzin in this regard: "Karamzin probably attempted to write as one speaks" and "his error in this instance lies in that he held the Russian idioms in contempt, did not pay attention to the language of the simple folk, and generally did not study his native sources."

6. See B. Tomashevsky, *The Theory of Literature* [*Teoriia literatury*], Leningrad, 1925.

7. In Marlinsky's tale "The Frigate *Hope*" ["Fregat Nadezhda"].

8. It is characteristic that Marlinsky does in fact motivate the development of this rhetorical monologue in his early period by means of the epistolary form. Compare "A Novel in Seven Letters" ["Roman v semi pis'makh"].

9. Shevyrev's remarks on the dactylic ending are interesting: "Listen to the harmony of the Russian

language, to the composition of its sounds; the Karamzinian tradition can still be heard here, with a few inevitable changes due to the variety of all human endeavor. In his work the harmony, or rather the cantilena, which Karamzin imparted to Russian prose was a purely national element and resulted from the uncommon consonance which existed between his ability to perceive nuances of sound and the sound composition of the Russian language. Indeed, Karamzin was gifted with an extraordinary ear for Russian; an ear alien to any foreign influence in the realm of sound; an ear which through instinct alone grasped that harmony, that measure of Russian prose with which he replaced Lomonosov's oratorical style (numerous oratorius). In carefully listening to national songs and tales Karamzin observed the Russian language's special fondness for the dactylic ending. His tale 'Ilya Muromets,' an extremely monotonous and boring work, is a very important document in the history of Russian prose with respect to its poetic qualities. It seemingly served as a tuning-fork for Karamzin whence his ear proceeded in forming a new harmony for the Russian language. The influence of this tuning-fork still tells very sharply in the particular fondness for the dactylic ending which we observe in his phrases and sentences, in those adjectives and pronouns which are placed at the end, in the lowering of a voice concluding a speech, with the peculiar aim of somehow attaining his beloved dactyl. This pet dactyl, spoiled by Karamzin's ear, echoed unwittingly even in the title of his favorite work, to which the greater part of his glorious life was devoted: the Karamzinian dactyl resounds quite sharply and significantly in the words of *A History of the Russian State* [*Istoriia gosudarstva Rossiiskogo*]. . . . In prose nowadays all of us sing in Karamzin's voice: due to his legacy, there is a conventionality in cadence which we can no longer violate. We can sing freely and easily, owing to our glorious master; and yet it is we who, in a burst of queer ingratitude, criticize him our teacher, who revealed to us the mystery of harmony in the Russian language, for falling occasionally into the extreme of monotony and for repeating too often those beloved sounds of his without which the music of our contemporary prose could not have been created."

10. It is very possible that Bestuzhev is indebted to the ballad for certain plot and stylistic motifs found in the Horror Tales. For example, the element of an avenger arriving at a church where a wedding is taking place is typical of the ballad. Incidentally, the novella in which we encounter this motif was originally entitled not "Castle Eisen," but even more "fearsomely," "Blood upon

Blood" ["Krov' za krov'"], (*The Star* [*Zvezdochka*] for 1826). However, the problem of the influence of the ballad upon the "horror tale" requires a special study of the genre and for that reason I note it here only as a supposition.

11. The dialogue form was a customary phenomenon in Russian prose of the 1820s and 1830s. Just as in a play, the names of the dialogue's participants were carefully delineated in special type, followed directly by their speeches with almost no authorial comments. We find this already in Karamzin's tale "Natalya, The Boyar's Daughter" and frequently in *Letters of a Russian Traveler.* Later sentimental tales avoid this device, however, and it is primarily cultivated in short journal articles under the sections on "manners and mores." There is a very curious dialogue in Bestuzhev's tale "Cavalry Raids," where an authorial comment truly becomes a stage direction; moreover, the characters' actions are marked in the present tense. Comments enclosed in parentheses can already be found in the earliest editions of Bestuzhev's work.

12. It is interesting that Bestuzhev prefaced "Tournament at Reval" with an epigraph which motivates this departure from the horror tale: "You are accustomed to seeing knights through the colored panes of their castles, through the haze of antiquity and poetry. Now I shall open the door of their dwelling to you and show them up close and faithfully."

13. Bestuzhev himself was reproached time and again for using Vandal phrases. See, for example, Zagoskin's letter:

> I don't understand how Burachek could have called Marlinsky a colossus! The Lord forgive him for this sin in this life and in the hereafter! What was Marlinsky? A talented and imaginative storyteller, nonetheless Marlinsky is at times the most slavish imitator of the French Frenetic School; a wit, who flaunts the most absurd similes and jokes; a clever man, who, while residing in the Caucasus, described the manners of Moscow society à la Balzac, but probably was better acquainted with the life of the Derbent Tatars than that of the Russian peasants; a corrupted, affected writer, spangled with faded French sequins, this Marlinsky says "the snail of conversation switched to a different subject", and thinks he has expressed himself cleverly; an indisputable admirer of the West and all its vileness. It was Marlinsky who, without the slightest mercy, mangled, mutilated, broke and rent the Russian language to pieces . . .

Neil B. Landsman (essay date 1986)

SOURCE: Landsman, Neil B. "Decembrist Romanticism: A. A. Bestuzhev-Marlinsky.'" In *Problems of Russian Romanticism*, edited by Robert Reid, pp. 64-95. Aldershot, Hants, England: Gower, 1986.

[*In the following essay, Landsman discusses Bestuzhev's role as the foremost practitioner of Russian Romanticism in the 1830s.*]

It is refreshing to see the wealth of attention being lavished recently on romanticism by distinguished Soviet scholars. Particularly heartening is the attempt to extend the bounds of romanticism and allot it its rightful place in the development of Russian literature. N. L. Stepanov, for example, in 1968 rejects the previous commonly-held view of romanticism as something inferior and hostile to realism[2] and in 1973 criticises the general failure to appreciate romanticism by those who consider realism the sole progressive literary force.[3] Marlinsky for the large part remains unaffected by all this reassessment; from the 1820s to the present day he has retained his unshaken position as the most faithful and eclectic adherent to the movement. Indeed his name is synonymous with it; N. K. Piksanov in 1967 equates the man and the movement: 'the basic style of *Vadim* is not romanticism or "Marlinism" . . .'[4] In the 1830s he was a cult figure, the representative of the Romantic school. Turgenev's story, *Knock . . . knock . . . knock!* (*Stuk . . . stuk . . . stuk! . . .*) of 1870 illustrates this beautifully:

> [Marlinsky] in the [18]30s thundered like no one else—even Pushkin, according to the youth of that time, could not be compared to him. He not only enjoyed the fame of being the foremost Russian writer, he even—which is much more difficult and is met with rarely—set his seal to some degree on the generation contemporary to him. Heroes *à la* Marlinsky turned up everywhere, particularly in the provinces and especially amongst soldiers and gunners; they spoke with 'a storm in the heart and fire in the blood'. Women's hearts were 'devoured' by them. The nickname 'fatal' was coined about them. This type, as is generally known, was preserved for a long while until the time of Pechorin.[5]

The criticism of the 1960s and 1970s has come up with a wide variety of labels in an attempt to define romanticism once for all.[6] It is interesting to note that whatever the label, Marlinsky fits it remarkably well. If 'liberalism', then the early stories such as **"Roman and Olga"** and **"Wenden Castle"** (**"Zamok Venden"**) can be viewed as efforts to incorporate progressive Decembrist ideals in literature. If 'individualism' or 'subjectivism', we have an entire panoply of Marlinsky heroes who challenge society and assert their individual rights—Mulla-Nur, Pravin in *The Frigate 'Hope'* (*Fregat 'Nadezhda'*) and Gremin in **"The Test"** (**"Ispytaniye"**). If 'the fantastic', there exists a range of

Gothic stories from **"Eisen Castle"** (**"Zamok Eyzen"**) to **"The Cuirassier"** (**"Latnik"**) which show Marlinsky to be a foremost exponent of this trend. If the phrase 'conflict between dream and reality' is used, we can look to a series of heroes who feel disillusioned because their ideals are too bold and lofty for this world—Sitsky in **"The Traitor"** (**"Izmennik"**) and Lidin in **"Evening on a Bivouac"** (**"Vecher na bivuake"**).

Not only did Marlinsky epitomise the general romantic movement, he was also one of the leading figures (then Bestuzhev) in an important branch of romanticism specific to Russia—Decembrism. Decembrist romanticism flourished in Russia between 1812 and 1825, from the time when the French armies were expelled until the Decembrist revolt. It includes the poetry of Ryleyev and Kyukhel'beker, the stories of Bestuzhev, the political tracts of Orlov, Pestel and Muravyov, the agitational songs of Ryleyev and Bestuzhev. Much of the most recent criticism is devoted to this aspect of romanticism. Ye. M. Pulkhritudova analyses the closeness of the Decembrists to the romantic aesthetic;[7] G. A. Gukovsky maintains that Decembrist poetry was linked with Russian romantic poetry as a whole;[8] B. Meylakh contends that it reflected reality more vividly.[9] V. G. Bazanov has contributed several important works to the subject, in which he allots considerable space to discussion of Bestuzhev.[10] Two of the major anthologies of Decembrist literature, one edited by V. A. Arkhipov, Bazanov and Y. L. Levkovich, the other by Vl. Orlov, reveal the significant role played by Bestuzhev in the development of civic romanticism.[11]

Possibly the only serious bone of contention raised in this spate of criticism is the discussion over whether there is any significant development or change in Marlinsky's work from the early, pre-1825 period to the later, post-Decembrist period. I. V. Kartashova argues that his work undergoes an evolution in the 1830s, when, though not a realist in the strict sense, he is concerned with everyday reality, the life and customs of the Caucasian tribes. While still seeking, as in his early work, the mysterious and extraordinary in the humdrum, and while elevating the imagination, he often shuns the exotic and idealistic and prefers to concentrate on the simple life of the mountaineers. Secondly, whereas earlier he had sharply categorised reality into good and evil, beauty and ugliness, and had divided his heroes into the positive and negative, in the 1830s he attempts to show the capricious complexity of life, its transitions and contradictions. In *The Frigate 'Hope'* he describes not just the external conflicts between man and society so prevalent in the 1820s stories but the inner torments of Pravin and Vera; there is none of the former moralising. Thirdly, the romantic hero changes in essence, as doubt and scepticism encroach after the Decembrist *débâcle* and in the bitterness of exile. Though the 'natural' harmonious man still exists in the person of Iskander-Bek, the contradictory, divided hero, exiled, alone and suffering, makes his appearance with Mulla-Nur. Finally philosophical motifs increase, dealing with the external problems of life and death, the enigmatic human heart, and so on.[12]

F. Z. Kanunova likewise attacks the widely-held opinion that Marlinsky remained true in theme and style to the traditions of Decembrism. She says he moves closer to Kant, Fichte and Schelling, that is, towards German idealistic philosophy, and away from the mechanistic eighteenth-century materialism which had dominated his earlier phase. Thus in his Caucasian tales he glorifies the heroic, active and wilful principle in man and tries to reach some understanding of man's conditioning by history and national culture. In the early stories ethnographic material and folklore had a merely decorative function; in the Caucasian tales they are a psychological factor and demonstrate how man's character is formed in conjunction with history and culture.[13]

But R. F. Yusufov, who has written one of the most authoritative works on romanticism and national cultures, puts forward precisely the opposite theory. He claims that while Pushkin, Lermontov and Gogol overcame romanticism, Marlinsky continued to develop Decembrist romanticism into the 1830s. Admittedly new content was involved since he was dealing with a different society, but his understanding of this society and his method of treatment remained identical. Like Piksanov and others, he employs the term 'Marlinism' to describe what he calls 'the accumulation of internal elements, one-sided judgments and evaluations'.[14]

The benefit of the doubt must be given to Yusufov in this dispute. A careful comparison between the work of the two periods shows the static nature of Marlinsky's talent. The style is still an amalgam of countless sayings, witticisms and turns of phrase. He persists in peppering his stories with metaphors, similes and rhetorical speeches. Dialogue and narrative are still burdened with declamation and clever puns. Gothic tendencies are in evidence along with his typical romantic plots, digressions and incidents. His Byronic method of characterisation remains unaltered: his heroes oppose society, for example Pravin and Vera in *The Frigate 'Hope,'* and Gremin and Olga in **"The Test."** They may be endowed with supreme courage and patriotism as is the case with Nikitin and Belozor. They express themselves passionately, as the heroes of **"Raids"** (**"Nayezdy"**) do, or display lofty aspirations like the dreamers of **"The Cuirassier"** and **"Raids."** Moreover he continues to write historical, social and military tales as well as poetry, travelogues and literary criticism. There is no doubt that his adaptation of local colour, his feeling for the nature of Russian society, and his lyrical poetry become more impressive, but they are easily recognisable as the work of Marlinsky. They bear the hallmark of 'Marlinism'.

No efforts seem to have been made in the last two decades, however, to resolve the conflict between pre-revolutionary critics, who consider Bestuzhev's tales devoid of political significance, and Soviet critics who take for granted their patent revolutionary ideology. The former emphasise his lack of serious political activity and a consequent absence of political content in his work. S. A. Vengerov, for example, is of the opinion that Bestuzhev's involvement in politics was mere coincidence, the result of his love of danger and the influence of his friends. He contrasts his participation in the Decembrist plot unfavourably with that of other conspirators to whom political activity was second nature. He therefore denies that Bestuzhev's work ever dealt with social and political themes.[15]

I. I. Zamotin too declares that Bestuzhev was only drawn into the Decembrist movement because his own romantic temperament responded impetuously and joyously to the opportunity afforded him to play a leading role in this phenomenon of the romantic revolutionary epoch.[16] Zamotin likewise pays the minimum of attention to social protest in Bestuzhev's work.

A. N. Pypin also adopts this attitude and refuses to admit that Bestuzhev was a sincere and influential member of the Northern Society. Though active in the uprising of 14 December, his conspiratorial role was negligible and his main concerns were always literature, society life and amorous adventures.[17] Pypin goes on to say that there are few traces of political bias in his work, which is thus markedly different from Ryleyev's, where civic themes occupied a prominent place.

Yet another critic of this time, N. A. Kotlyarevsky, insists that Bestuzhev did not consider political thought a necessity of intellect or political action a necessity of temperament. His liberalism was not a matter of deep conviction but a lightly adopted pose. His stories, articles and correspondence do not contain any hints whatsoever of general liberalism, let alone political liberalism.[18]

On the other hand Soviet critics in a body acclaim Bestuzhev as an eminent Decembrist thinker and activist. M. V. Nechkina writes that he was of unquestionable revolutionary zeal and chose to arouse the Moskovsky regiment on the day of the rebellion as this was the least reliable and would hence require extra effort.[19] A. P. Sharupich numbers him among the most energetic plotters and refers to him as the friend and collaborator of Ryleyev, a member of the supreme Duma of the Northern Society, the organiser and leader of the armed revolt.[20] Nor does N. Maslin have any misgivings about affirming the radical position Bestuzhev occupied in the Northern Society and the active part he played in preparing and carrying out the rebellion.[21] N. L. Stepanov discusses him in the strongest possible political terms and asserts that his publication of the *Polar Star,* his reviews propagandising new political ideas, his agitational songs and his deeds on 14 December all testify to his commitment to revolutionary ideology and his outstanding role in the Decembrist movement.[22] Like the aforementioned, N. Mordovchenko and V. G. Bazanov entirely relate the literary work of Bestuzhev to his participation in the Decembrist secret society and regard the two as inextricably linked and interdependent.[23]

An examination of Bestuzhev's life and literary output before 1825 will go a long way to proving where the truth lies. It is an incontrovertible fact that he sometimes produced an unfavourable impression on his contemporaries. N. I. Grech, while speaking of his intelligence, talent and education, attributes his involvement in the Northern Society to pride, braggadocio and ambition.[24] F. Glinka puts it all down to romantic chivalry and excitable temper.[25] Batenkov asserts that he was a man capable of any extremity[26] and Trubetskoy remarks on his hotheadedness and fiery imagination.[27] Orlov lashes him for his senseless, nonsensical and indecent behaviour in society[28] and Shteyngel' describes Bestuzhev and Kakhovsky as keen terrorists.[29] Bestuzhev himself confessed to the above shortcomings in his character, pointing out that he was boastful, impatient and intemperate, deluded, hasty and over-imaginative.[30]

These comments present a flimsy argument when counterbalanced by the other side of the picture. Indeed there were those among his contemporaries who bore witness to his ardent revolutionary beliefs and his important contribution to the uprising. Kakhovsky states that Bestuzhev's motives were altruistic and disinterested.[31] A. Ye. Rozen wrote that had Ryleyev, the Bestuzhevs, Obolensky and two or three others been arrested, the events of 14 December would never have come about.[32] The statement of the investigatory commission bears eloquent testimony to this fact:

> Junior-captain Alexander Bestuzhev. Plotted regicide and the annihilation of the imperial family; incited others to this; consented also to the deprivation of freedom of the imperial family. Took part in the design of a rebellion through the enticement of comrades and the composition of revolutionary verses and songs; was personally active in the revolt and stirred up lower ranks to take part in it.[33]

It is evident that they clearly comprehended the extent of his implication. This is why they sentenced him to death—later rescinded to twenty years penal servitude.

Statements by Bestuzhev himself over a lengthy period outweigh the faults he had admitted to; like many of his fellow-conspirators he experienced fear and disillusionment when in prison and under the intense pressure of importunate interrogation, and so attributed his crimes to congenital recklessness. His assurances that: 'Ac-

cording to the inclination of the age, I belonged above all to History and Politics',[34] and '. . . in the past I considered literature as a side-line',[35] can be taken as a sign of where his priorities lay. He narrates how he discussed dreams of reform and his willingness to take up arms with Griboyedov,[36] Ryleyev,[37] Batenkov[38] and Obolensky.[39] He directly rebuffs the charges that he was nothing but a scapegrace by saying that he had deliberately contributed to this legend: 'My frivolity was a masquerade for the social carnival . . . Society amused me very rarely, but never captivated me'.[40]

It might well be argued that his whole life had revolved around the revolutionary ferment of the age. His father, Aleksandr Fedoseyevich, was linked with the oppositional groups and radical thought of the previous reign. He belonged to the Radishchevites and together with the most prominent of them, I. P. Pnin, published the short-lived *St Petersburg Journal* in 1798.[41] The young Alexander passed his boyhood in an atmosphere of culture and enlightenment. His father strove to introduce his pedagogical ideas into the education of his own family and after his death the eldest son Nikolay tried to uphold these precepts in the upbringing of his four younger brothers.[42] It follows that they were united by a common bond; they all shared an interest in literature and the pursuit of knowledge, love for their country, and hatred for despotism and serfdom.[43] It is hardly surprising that four of them participated in the Decembrist movement and suffered exile, while the fifth was implicated afterwards.

In his testimony to the Investigatory Commission, Bestuzhev confessed: 'From nineteen years of age I began to read liberal books and this set my head spinning',[44] and 'I adopted a free way of thinking primarily from books, and progressing gradually from one opinion to another, I took to reading the French and English publicists'.[45]

These liberal sympathies, inculcated by education and reading, were manifested in his visit to the Semyonovsky regiment in Kronstadt fortress in the autumn of 1820. The entire regiment had been incarcerated there as a punishment for protesting against the cruelty of Colonel Shvarts, who had restored corporal punishment and had several soldiers flogged.[46] Further evidence as to his growing proclivity towards liberalism can be seen when in 1821 he broke off his literary contributions to *The Loyalist* (*Blagonamerennyy*), the organ of the Society of the Lovers of Literature, Science and Art, because this organisation was becoming progressively more hostile to romantic tendencies and was headed by the reactionary A. Ye. Izmaylov. He joined at the end of 1820 the Free Society of the Lovers of Russian Literature, made up mostly of Decembrist writers, where he could find a *milieu* conducive to his liberal inclinations.[47]

Now he began to mix with all the leading Decembrist figures, until in 1824 he was accepted into the secret society itself. Such was the esteem in which he was held, he was appointed to the leadership along with Ryleyev and Obolensky in April 1825. That he should have enjoyed the friendship and trust of such an avowed champion of freedom as Ryleyev is an additional pointer to his serious intentions at this juncture.[48] Since 1823 he and Ryleyev had co-operated as the joint editors of *Polar Star,* the highly successful Decembrist anthology of contemporary literature.

On 27 November 1825, together with his brother Nikolay and Ryleyev, he spent the night walking round the town impressing upon the soldiers that they had not been informed about the late Tsar Alexander's will promising an end to serfdom and the reduction of military service from twenty-five to fifteen years. Nikolay claims in his memoirs: 'It is impossible to imagine the eagerness with which the soldiers listened to us; it is impossible to explain the speed with which our words were spread among the troops'.[49]

And on the day of the rebellion itself Bestuzhev was one of the major protagonists in the futile but courageous endeavour to overthrow the autocracy. Early in the morning, accompanied by his brother Mikhail and Shchepin-Rostovsky, he hurried to the barracks of the Moskovsky regiment and roused the soldiers with his fiery oratory.[50] They marched to Senate Square, where Bestuzhev remained until the rebels were routed by the Tsar's cannons. Instead of fleeing in a panic like the majority, he and Nikolay halted several dozen men so as to defend the retreat and repulse a possible cavalry charge.[51] Nor while the grim events of that fateful day unfolded had he been without a definite plan of action: 'If the Izmaylovsky regiment had joined us, I would have taken command and decided on an attempt to attack, the plan of which was already whirling in my head'.[52]

Like all the other Decembrist philosophers and poets, Bestuzhev felt the impact of European developments from 1789. All of them at various stages frankly admitted their allegiance to *avant-garde* European thought from the Enlightenment down to the 1820s. The names of Rousseau, Voltaire, Helvétius, Holbach and Condorcet were constantly on their lips; the works of Byron and Schiller were highly popular; the revolutionary disturbances in Spain, Portugal, Piedmont, Naples and Greece served as reminders and examples to the young Russian nobles; the latter chose as their real-life heroes men such as Brutus, Riego, Chénier and Byron who laid down their lives for the liberty of their countries. Their literary heroes were also men who rebelled against tyranny, Byron's Corsair and Schiller's Karl Moor. Bitterness was increased by the failure of Tsar Alexander's unofficial committee (Kochubey, Czartoryski, Novosilt-

sev, Stroganov) and Speransky's reform projects to achieve any positive progress. Moreover the Great Patriotic War of 1812 had brought about no improvement in the lot of the Russian people, who had sacrificed so much in the struggle for the liberation of their country. Affairs of state were hampered by reactionaries: the brutal Count Arakcheyev in the military, the fanatical monk Photius in the church, Prince Golitsyn, aided and abetted by Magnitsky and Runich, in education. A whole series of secret societies sprang up—the Union of Salvation, Union of Welfare, Northern and Southern Societies—to combat the forces of reaction, just as the liberal Carbonari groups in Italy or Hetairea in Greece had done. Bestuzhev, as a central figure in the Decembrist movement, could scarcely have been unaffected by this wave of ideas which swept across Europe and Russia.

Having established Bestuzhev's firm attachment to liberal trends, the way is now open to a study of the political aspects in his early work. This falls into several categories: (1) literary criticism; (2) the travelogue ***Journey to Reval (Poyezdka v Revel')***; (3) the agitational songs; (4) poetry; (5) the historical tales of old Livonia; and (6) the document, **"On the Historical Progress of Free Thought in Russia."**

Bestuzhev's literary criticism, contained in a series of articles he wrote between 1818 and 1825, clearly followed the lines laid down by the civic romanticism of the Decembrists, in particular by their literary society the Republic of Letters. Basically the Decembrists believed that literature had to be harnessed to the politics of the day. It was the Great Patriotic War of 1812 which gave birth to political consciousness. As Bestuzhev explained:

> Napoleon invaded Russia, and then the Russian people for the first time became aware of its strength; then there awoke in all hearts a feeling of independence, at first political, and subsequently national too. This was the beginning of free thought in Russia.[53]

In his article, **"A Look at Russian Literature During 1823,"** he underlined the link between literature and national crises: '. . . the thunder of distant battles inspires the style of the author and arouses the idle attention of readers; . . . and under a political seal literature revolves in society' (***Soch.*** [***Sochineniya v dvukh tomakh***], II, p. 540).

Literature could be used as an educational tool in the battle against prevailing ignorance. If, as Ryleyev asserted, 'The ignorance of peoples is the mother and father of despotism, is the true and chief cause of all the violence and crime which have ever been perpetrated in the world',[54] then it was vital to spread enlightenment. The code of the Union of Welfare assigned it a special category,[55] and Bestuzhev's **"Look at Old and New Literature in Russia"** blames the retarded development of contemporary Russian literature on the low standards of education in schools and universities, the poor taste of the reading public, the contempt felt for the scholar and writer, and the scorn for the Russian language in society. Literature and Enlightenment thus went hand in hand, and the same code spoke of 'the elegant arts . . . strengthening, ennobling and exalting our moral being'.[56]

The main stress of Decembrist literature was on national spirit, the national independence of Russian literature. The aspiration to create a literature which was not a mere carbon copy of foreign models grew into the prime concern of the Decembrists. They demanded a literature that dealt exclusively with Russian history, folklore and contemporary issues. They called for a renewal of pride in the Russian language itself, which had been so neglected and undergone so much foreign influence. The code of the Union of Welfare urged its members 'to expose the totally absurd attachment to the foreign and its ensuing evil consequences'.[57] Bestuzhev was an indefatigable advocate of the ideal of national spirit and constantly railed against imitativeness of any kind. In his **"Look at Russian Literature during 1824 and the Beginning of 1825"** he complained bitterly: 'We imbibed with our milk lack of national spirit and admiration for only the foreign' (**Soch.**, II, p. 547).

In 1831 he reiterated this feeling of abhorrence for the foreign in one of his letters: 'I ardently hated German cosmopolitanism, which killed off every noble sentiment of patriotism and nationalism'.[58]

In **"A Look at Old and New Literature in Russia"** he recommended reliance on national sources and called on writers to study the ancient chronicles such as *The Lay of Igor's Host, The Chronicle of Nestor, Russkaya Pravda* and *The Song of the Battle on the Don,* which offer a faithful reproduction of Russian national characteristics and the roots of the language.[59] Elsewhere he proclaimed: 'I shall not forsake the language of my ancestors, in which they rejoiced and grieved, sang and deliberated'.[60]

In the 1830s he continued to criticise strongly those writers he thought were over-dependent on foreign culture, such as Karamzin[61] and Zhukovsky,[62] just as he had heaped scorn on them in the 1820s:

> There was a time when we sighed irrelevantly in the manner of Sterne, were courteous in the French style, and flew off to the ends of the earth in German fashion. When will we follow our own track? When will we write directly in Russian? God alone knows!
>
> (**Soch.**, II, p. 551)

His highest praise is reserved for those writers who were able to capture national spirit—Fonvizin[63] and

Krylov.[64] He illustrates the necessity for national spirit in his critical maxim, 'characters and incidents pass, but nations and the elements last forever' (**Soch.**, II, p. 549).

The Decembrist ethic preached that the content of literature must be 'lofty feelings which attract one to good'.[65] Ryleyev's article, *Some Thoughts on Poetry,* contains the words: 'We shall employ all our efforts to realise in our writings the ideals of lofty feelings, thoughts and eternal truths'.[66] Kyukhel'beker led the struggle for lofty themes and genres and hailed 'the sacred mysteries of lofty art'.[67] Bestuzhev was not slow to herald this trend and in his literary criticism systematically eulogised works which were full of 'lofty feelings', such as Ryleyev's *Meditations (Dumy)*.[68] He sees in Gnedich 'a fiery soul accessible to all that is lofty' (**Soch.**, II, p. 532). He rebukes Pushkin for wasting time and effort on a fashionable dandy like Onegin and assures him: 'I involuntarily give precedence to that which stirs the soul, exalts it, and touches the Russian heart' (**Soch.**, II, p. 627). In the same vein he is extremely critical of literature which is devoid of noble and lofty thoughts and is hard on Karamzin and his followers, treating them with irony.

The travelogue **Journey to Reval**, 1820-1, has been the subject of some controversy. Ostensibly it is an account of a journey to Estonia in the manner of Sterne's *Sentimental Journey* and Karamzin's *Letters of a Russian Traveller.* It has been looked upon by pre-revolutionary critics as belonging to the Karamzinian tradition, along with the travelogues of Sumarokov, Izmaylov, Nevzorov and Shalikov. However, on closer inspection (duly carried out by thorough Soviet critics) it becomes apparent that Bestuzhev's work is of a very different kind. Instead of lyrical enthusiasm for nature, the unfolding of tender feelings, and the relaying of melancholy or pleasant experiences, which the sentimentalists are so fond of indulging in, we get a serious and painstaking attempt to review the position of the Baltic peoples under their foreign oppressors.

He expresses sympathy for the downtrodden Estonians who rebelled against their German overlords in 1343. He castigates the behaviour of the knights, who were coarse and ignorant, besotted and depraved, extravagant and godless. These so-called standard-bearers of religion and culture robbed the Estonians and 'adorned their own wives with pearls and diamonds and themselves with golden chain-mail'.[69] His compassion becomes stronger as his narrative develops and he describes the torments of the vassals, the hunger, pestilence, wars and pillaging they had to endure.[70]

He displays a profound interest in the traditions and customs, the life and history of the Estonian nation. He made a serious study of the region and his references to

Estonian sources reveal his knowledge of Livonian works and chronicles.[71] He apparently refutes the theories of the German-Baltic chroniclers who had sung the exploits of the German conquerors, intimating that they combated paganism, brought enlightenment and culture, and were men of honour and justice. Bestuzhev portrays them as taskmasters and represents the struggle of the Estonians for national liberation as a just and righteous one in the true spirit of Decembrist civic romanticism. In fact *Journey to Reval* is in the tradition of Radishchev's *Journey from St Petersburg to Moscow,* Glinka's *Letters of a Russian Officer,* and Von Ferelzt's *Journey of Criticism*—travel books which fearlessly pictured Russian reality, the misfortunes of the people, the horrors of serfdom and the arbitrary rule of landowners.

Yet nowhere did Bestuzhev express the anguish of the people with such vehemence as in the agitational or ritual (*podblyudnyye*) songs. He was the co-author with Ryleyev of **'Ah, I feel wretched . . .'** (**'Akh, toshno mnye . . .'**) but was solely responsible for the others.[72] These songs had a great effect on the simple people and spread like wildfire among the troops.[73] Little wonder, since they are written in a straightforward and forceful style. **'Ah, I feel wretched . . .'** surveys the injustices and malpractices suffered by the martyred peasants. It is an outcry against the incredible cruelty of the landowning classes:

> Ah, I feel wretched
> Even in my native land;
> All is in bondage
> Will the Russian people
> Long be the junk of masters
> And will they long be traded
> Like cattle?
>
> Who enslaved us,
> Who conferred nobility on them?
> And freedom
> Among the people
> Is stifled by the power of the lords.
> And now our masters
> Rob us shamelessly
> They flay us alive,
> We sow—and they reap.
> They are thieves,
> Fleecers,
> And they suck our blood, like leeches.

> (*Soch.,* II, pp. 514-15)

The Decembrists were loud in their denunciation of extortion and bribery in high places, especially the courts. Pestel condemned 'the injustice and venality of the courts and other authorities';[74] Lunin claimed that one of the objects of the secret society was the abolition of procrastination, secretiveness and costs in law-suits;[75] and Bestuzhev himself did not spare the shameful bartering with justice in the judiciary, exclaiming: 'Every-

where honest people suffered, whilst rogues and cheats rejoiced'.[76] **'Ah, I feel wretched . . .'** deplores these abuses:

> Peasant,
> Anywhere in court
> . . . . .
> The judges are deaf,
> Though innocent, you are guilty.
> . . . . .
> There every soul
> Is twisted just for a farthing.
> The assessor,
> The chairman,
> At one with the secretary.

> (*Soch.,* II, pp. 515-16)

Even the parish priest joins in the wholesale exploitation of the defenceless peasants. The Tsar has blighted their lives with extortionate taxes and roadwork. The soldiers in the countryside treat them as though they were enemies. They are obliged to pay exorbitant sums even for water. The decrees inspired by Arakcheyev are an added burden. This song is convincing proof that although the Decembrists ignored the people as a concrete factor in the revolutionary struggle against the autocracy, they could reflect their mood and depict their hardships. Ryleyev and Bestuzhev's song is a savage indictment of conditions in Russia and is written with indignation and embitterment.

Military service in Russia was another circumstance the Decembrists found loathsome. They abhorred the system of military colonies established by Arakcheyev, which symbolised the arrant tyranny of the regime and had transformed Russia into a gigantic Prussian barracks. Pestel expressed his horror at 'what he had heard about the military colonies' and at 'the oppression of military service'.[77] Rayevsky devoted a whole treatise entitled *The Soldier* to this problem; he listed rigid disciplinary procedures, tyrannical, mercenary and unreasonable leadership, disproportionately severe corporal punishment, illegality and inequity, lack of rights of defence or channels of complaint, irksome tasks and duties.[78] A heartfelt protest against the soldier's unenviable fate was voiced by Yakubovich, who singled out the wearisome length of service, the forced abandonment of one's family, the fear dominating one's life, the corruption and ignorance rife amongst officers and their inhumane treatment of subordinates.[79] The management of the military colonies was entrusted to Arakcheyev; the choice could not have been a worse one, for from all accounts he was a bigot and petty bureaucrat, undiplomatic and merciless, the object of universal hatred.[80] Bestuzhev subjected this aspect of life in Russia to harsh criticism:

> The colonies paralysed not only the intellects but all
> the trades of the places where they were established

and struck terror in the remainder. . . . The soldiers grumbled at exhausting drills, fatigues and sentry-duty, the officers at meagre wages and excessive severity.[81]

He had occasion himself to witness the military establishment at first hand as member of a dragoon regiment and later as aide-de-camp in turn to Count Komarovsky, General Bétancourt and Duke Wurtembergsky. Indeed the vanguard of the Decembrist movement consisted of high-ranking officers such as Trubetskoy, Obolensky, Pestel and Orlov.

The song **'Our Tsar is a Russian (Prussian) German . . .'**[82] (**'Tsar nash, nemets russkiy . . .'**) satirises Alexander's Prussian-like maniacal obsession with military parades and ostentation:

> Our Tsar is a Russian German
>
> . . . . .
> Where does he reign?
> He spends every day at riding-school.
>
> . . . . .
> Though the enemy of enlightenment,
> He loves drills.
>
> . . . . .
> Only for parades
> Does he dispense rewards.
>
> . . . . .
> And for compliments—
> Blue ribbons.
>
> . . . . .
> And for mother-truth
> He sends you packing to Kamchatka.

The notorious Arakcheyev comes in for his share of parody both here: 'And Count Arakcheyev / Is the worst of villains . . .' (**Soch.,** II, pp. 512-13), and in the previously discussed **'Ah, I feel wretched . . .'**:

> For all these enterprises
> Arakcheyev
> Is the one to blame.
>
> He eggs on the Tsar,
> The Tsar signs a decree.
> To him it's a joke,
> But to us it's terrible.
>
> (**Soch.,** II, pp. 516-17)

"Along the River Fontanka" (**"Vdol' Fontanki-reki"**) sketches the misery of the soldier's lot: 'They are drilled and tortured, / There is no light, no dawn' (**Soch.,** II, p. 514). These songs are an open call for reprisals with the landowners, officials and the Tsar himself. **'Say, Tell Me . . .'** (**'Ty skazhi, govori . . .'**) begins: 'Say, tell me / How in Russia tsars / Are crushed . . .' (**Soch.,** II, p. 511); while **"Along the River Fontanka"** asks:

> Have they really no hands
> To save themselves from torments?

> Have they really no bayonets
> For snivelling princes?

> Have they really no lead
> For the villainous tyrant?
>
> (**Soch.,** II, p. 514)

The peasants in **'Ah, I feel wretched . . .'** threaten: 'And what is taken from us by force / We will restore by force' (**Soch.,** II, p. 515). In the song **'When the Blacksmith Leaves his Forge . . .'** (**'Kak idyot kuznets da iz kuznitsy . . .'**) we read:

> Here is the first knife—for the evil grandees.
> And the second knife—for the priests, those hypocrites.
> And uttering a prayer—the third knife for the Tsar.
>
> (**Soch.,** II, p. 517)

Another song breathes menace and hostility:

> Now you are weaving ropes for the heads of lords,
> You are sharpening knives for eminent princes:
> And in the place of lamps you will hang tsars!
> Then warmth, intellect and light will reign. Glory be![83]

Much of Bestuzhev's pre-revolutionary poetry contains social comment imbued with Decembrist leanings. In 1819 he wrote **"Imitation of Boileau's First Satire"** (**"Podrazhaniye pervoy satire Bualo"**), where he stigmatises the society of St Petersburg for its mercenariness and insincerity. He enumerates the defects which poison it: insidiousness, boastfulness, deceit, slander, flattery, ignorance and arrogance. Judges, clerks and spies are in abundance. Many devote their lives to acquiring wealth which they flaunt instead of knowledge. The servile poor are under the heel of the haughty rich. Fools rise to the highest posts, while the talented are left to starve. The *leitmotif* of the poem is escape:

> I shall flee from you, I shall flee, walls of Petropol,
> I shall hide in the gloom of forests, in remote caverns,
>
> . . . . .
> I shall flee! I have found the golden thread of freedom.
>
> . . . . .
> Let us leave the corrupt town
>
> . . . . .
> I hasten to save myself from corruption.
> Luxurious Babylon! For the last time farewell.
>
> (**Soch.,** II, pp. 465-9)

The whole poem is symptomatic of the typical Decembrist viewpoint and is reminiscent of Chatsky's diatribes in *Woe from Wit* (*Gore ot uma*). It is close in spirit to the first speech in Bestuzhev's extract from **"The Optimist"** (**"Otryvok iz Komedii 'Optimist'"**). Here, after delineating the natural phenomena afflicting man, he excoriates the vices introduced into the world by man himself. The main brunt of his attack is borne by the young generation which leads an aimless dissipated life:

The sources of pleasure are lacklustre from satiety.
We are old at twenty and dissolute at fifty.
. . . All men are spiteful, and foolish, and miserable!

(*Soch.*, II, pp. 469-70)

A comparison with Lermontov's similar poem *Meditation (Duma)* is all too obvious.

At the heart of the Decembrist ethos were the principles of patriotism and heroic self-sacrifice. The Decembrists were fervid patriots, convinced of the greatness of Russia and its noble people's right to freedom and political justice. They loved their land so passionately that everything concerning its countryside and life in their writing, particularly lyric poetry, is imbued with a highly emotional tone. Glinka, Ryleyev and Rayevsky extolled the beauties of their country and the glory of patriotism.[84] Bestuzhev too filled his work with exclamations like Sitsky's in **"The Traitor"**:

Has a Russian suggested to a Russian that he betray his country and become a traitor to his fatherland?

(*Soch.*, I, p. 141)

O my land, my sacred native land! Which heart on earth would not throb on seeing you? Which icy soul would not melt upon breathing your air?

(*Soch.*, I, p. 132)

In his poem **'Near the camp stood a handsome youth . . .'** (**'Bliz stana yunosha prekrasnyy . . .'**) the young warrior professes that he was always true to his country, which inspired him in battle and implanted the spirit of heroism in his breast.[85]

The precept of self-sacrifice accompanied the patriotic ideal. Ryleyev perpetually exhorted his fellow conspirators to be prepared to die valiantly. Nikolay Bestuzhev relates in his memoirs some truly moving scenes with speeches typical of Ryleyev:

I am sure we shall die, but the example will remain. We shall sacrifice ourselves for the future freedom of our country. . . . If I fall in the struggle . . . posterity will render me justice and history will write my name together with the names of great men who have died for mankind.[86]

Ryleyev[87] and Odoyevsky[88] acclaimed self-sacrifice as the pinnacle attained by those supreme in bravery. Bestuzhev's **"Exploit of Ovechkin and Shcherbina in the Caucasus"** (**"Podvig Ovechkina i Shcherbiny za Kavkazom"**)[89] (written shortly before the Decembrist uprising) is a paean to Russian gallantry in the face of death. In the poem **'Near the Camp . . .'** the youth announces his pride at being able to lay down his life: 'Tell her I fell fighting for my country' (*Soch.*, II, p. 475), and in **"Mikhail Tverskoy,"** a poem which reminds one of Ryleyev's *Meditations,* the scene is set in a sombre prison where a young man bids farewell to

his aged father, who remains steadfast at the moment before his execution. In this same poem the motif of revenge on the tyrant is repeated; coming, as it did, only a year before the rebellion it served as a prophetic warning. The young prince observes his father's mutilated corpse, sheds bitter tears and rends his garments. He calls upon the God of vengeance:

He heeded him, this powerful God,
Helped Russians to rebel,
And removed the tyrants from the face of the earth.

(*Soch.*, II, pp. 477-8)

It is on Bestuzhev's four tales of old Livonia that most debate is centred. To regard them simply as Gothic adventure stories, as prerevolutionary critics have done, is to miss the point entirely. The Decembrists were of the considered opinion that to set one's narrative in bygone ages was the most effective guise for concealing its true intentions. The historical tale, poem or drama did not incur the censor's wrath. In addition the past was an excellent school for the present; contemporary lessons could be read into heroic accounts of the struggle against the Tartar invasion, or the Ukraine's battle against the Polish gentry, or the republican exploits of ancient Novgorod and Pskov. Objective understanding was not so important; their view of historical events was entirely subjective. Ryleyev's *Meditations* are the best examples of national antiquity employed as material for civic preaching. He confessed that they were intended 'to remind youth of the exploits of their ancestors and to acquaint them with the brightest epochs of national history'.[90] Bestuzhev was captivated by the idea of historical narrative, as he enthusiastically avers in **Andrey, Prince of Pereyaslavl'** (**Andrey, knyaz' pereyaslavskiy**)[91] and **"Page from the Diary of a Guards Officer"** (**"Listok iz dnevnika gvardeyskogo ofitsera"**)[92] and always treated it subjectively and imaginatively.[93]

The historical tale of Novgorod **"Roman and Olga"** is the clearest illustration of how Bestuzhev utilised history for modern purposes. Among the Decembrists Novgorod occupied a symbolic place as the home of freedom and democracy. Ryleyev once advised Pushkin to write about the Novgorod-Pskov region, 'that true land of inspiration' where 'the last sparks of Russian freedom were stifled'.[94] Pestel shared this cult of ancient Novgorod and declared in his testimony: 'The story of great Novgorod also confirmed me in the republican mode of thought'.[95] Bestuzhev at one time was even preparing to undertake a history of Novgorod.[96]

Roman Yasensky is endowed with all the qualities that go to make up the Novgorodian hero; he is above all a good citizen ready to sacrifice himself for a righteous cause. The democratic assembly is a model of the Decembrist ideal of the people's right to self-determination.

Roman's speech is replete with the rhythmic style of Decembrist rhetoric and culminates in a powerful battle-cry. The Decembrists attached great importance to political eloquence and among them were men of brilliant oratorical gifts, such as Orlov, Pestel, Muravyov, Bestuzhev-Ryumin, Rayevsky and Lunin. They considered oratory an integral part of revolution. Muravyov-Apostol's *Orthodox Catechism*[97] and Bestuzhev-Ryumin's *Speech at a Meeting of the United Slavs* and *Proclamation to the People*[98] are exemplars of the art. Bestuzhev appreciated the value of eloquence and drew a vivid portrait of Demosthenes in action in his article **"The Orator"**[99] He himself stirred the soldiers of the Moskovsky regiment with his speech on the morning of 14 December 1825.

Roman speaks warmly of Church and State self-government, the subtleties of international law, the need for a close union between Russia and the West. He tries to destroy the myth of omnipotent Moscow and implores the people not to concede their rights. He appeals to them to choose freedom even at the cost of their lives.

The subsequent trials of Roman, his encounter with the honourable outlaw Berkut, their participation in the battle against Moscow—all propagate the Decembrist ideal of the perfect hero.

It is when the controversial Livonian tales are studied in context, that is, in conjunction with **"Roman and Olga"** and the foregoing Decembrist philosophy, that their real meaning becomes apparent. Perhaps the worst problem confronting the Decembrists was that of serfdom, an evil which had to be eradicated before any economic or moral progress could be made. Nikolay Turgenev,[100] Pestel[101] and Rayevsky[102] displayed deep concern for the pitiful condition of the peasantry. Bestuzhev's letter to the Tsar[103] and *Journey to Reval* deal with the identical theme—the maltreatment of serfs by their masters. In **"Wenden Castle"** the brutal and overbearing Von Rorbach has no regard for his vassals, on whose behalf Von Serrat takes up cudgels and proclaims, 'I do not consider it a joke when humanity suffers' (*Soch.,* I, p. 39). Serrat protests passionately against Rorbach's callous flouting of the peasants' rights.[104] Bestuzhev sums up the situation thus:

> The knights who conquered Lithuania and subdued the savages invented everything which the Spaniards later repeated in the New World to torment an unarmed race. Death threatened the stubborn and degrading slavery was the reward for submission . . . the blood of the innocent flowed beneath the swords of warriors and the whips of masters. Arming themselves in the name of sacred truth, the knights acted according to the dictates of grasping self-interest or brutal caprice.
>
> (*Soch.,* I, pp. 38-9)

The individual act of violence perpetrated by Serrat in killing Rorbach is in vain, as Bestuzhev points out:

'The magistrate no longer existed, but his power remained'.[105] Though sympathising with the despair seizing Serrat, Bestuzhev cannot fail to condemn his deed; the leaders of the Northern Society had the utmost trouble in restraining Yakubovich and Kakhovsky from assassinating the Tsar. They believed that such action must be consciously intended for the social good and should not be a matter of momentary rage.

The second Livonian tale, **"Neuhausen Castle" ("Za-mok Neygauzen")**[106] affirms Bestuzhev's detestation of feudalism by showing the inner conflicts it produces within a seemingly normal family. The scheming Von Mey, who typifies the unscrupulous feudal lords, is put to death, while again it is the gallant Novgorodians, Vseslav and Andrey, who are portrayed as men of prowess. Furthermore justice is seen as prejudiced and ruthless, administered by a court which operates in secret and favours the mighty and influential.

In the third of the cycle, **"The Reval' Tournament" ("Revel' skiy turnir")**, the knights and nobles are caustically satirised. The knights are perpetually in a drunken stupor. They are supercilious and have no respect for intellectual qualities. They are devoid of consideration for passing travellers and think nothing of seizing land from each other. Baron Burtneck behaves insultingly to his servants and treats them inhumanely. The nobles likewise are empty-headed and foolish. Pestel,[107] Bestuzhev's brother Nikolay,[108] and Muravyov[109] all spoke with scathing disapproval of the aristocracy, as did Bestuzhev who analysed them thoroughly.[110]

This story also covers a favourite topic of the Decembrists, the rise of the middle class. This class, composed of merchants and petty bourgeoisie, they felt would play an increasingly crucial role in the economic stability of Russia. Like his brother Nikolay,[111] Pestel,[112] and Kakhovsky,[113] Bestuzhev mentioned the handicaps suffered by the middle class: 'The middle class is respected and important in all other countries; in our country this class is miserable, poor, burdened with obligations, deprived of means of a livelihood . . .'; and detailed the causes of the dissatisfaction of the merchants.[114]

In line with these views, Edwin, as representative of the merchant class, holds the centre of the stage. He is morally superior to the knights and nobles. He is brave, sincere and loyal:

> He was able to dream and have feelings, but the Livonian knights could only arouse laughter and rarely amuse. . . . He had grown accustomed to social proprieties, and in education and astuteness surpassed with ease the knights of Livonia . . .
>
> (*Soch.,* I, p. 107).

His defeat of Ungern in the tournament leads to open warfare between the merchants and the knights and nobles, a furious battle for supremacy. Bestuzhev refers to the merchants as 'the most active, honourable and useful class' in Livonia (*Soch.*, I, p. 127). They will supersede the knights, who have outlived their age and squandered their wealth, and the nobles, who are now impoverished and lack all progressive inclinations.

The last in this cycle, **"Eisen Castle,"** has the fearsome Baron Bruno Von Eisen as its centrepiece. He gathers round him hardened criminals for his raids and reckless adventures, but he outdoes them all in ferocity. He maltreats his serfs, kills them and his guests wilfully, and has a vicious, uncontrollable temper. When Reginald redresses wrong by murdering his uncle, we get precisely the same assessment of his act as we had in **"Wenden Castle,"** that is, approval because it benefited the people and gave rise to rejoicing, but reserve because its motives were selfish:

> Why did he lack the will to refuse resolutely [to plunder] or to rebel against him openly? . . . But no, he did not stand up for the oppressed until he was personally offended; he only rebelled to save his own skin

> (*Soch.*, I, p. 166).

The final clincher in the argument over the political interests of Bestuzhev must be the letter he wrote to the Tsar when under arrest in the Petropavlovsk fortress, entitled **"On the Historical Progress of Free Thought in Russia."**[115] It is outstanding as one of the best Decembrist treatises on the political situation; it discusses the psychological and economic factors which generated social discontent and revolutionary thought. It analyses all the classes in society and draws a picture of Russia after the Napoleonic invasion in a state of devastation and afflicted by harsh measures and innumerable abuses. It includes the projects of reform harboured by the rebels. It is hardly the work of a person indifferent to politics.

There is a second conflict between pre-revolutionary and Soviet critics about Marlinsky's work. With a few notable exceptions the latter utterly ignore the influence of Western European literature on it and their approach is purely nationalistic. The former however pay full tribute to Western European sources. A. Veselovsky,[116] Zamotin,[117] Kotlyarevsky,[118] M. N. Rozanov,[119] et al, carried out exhaustive surveys of the extent and nature of these influences which must be regarded as indisputable. To deny this overwhelming evidence is also to overlook the numerous memoirs of the period which indicate the enormous interest of the public in the works of Rousseau, Byron, Scott, Radcliffe and so on. Even to admit the potent influence of Karamzin, as Soviet critics do, is to pay homage to the Gallic influence in style and theme. And to imply that Marlinsky isolated himself from the European romantic movement is nothing short of ludicrous, when one thinks that Belinsky called him 'our first story-teller . . . the instigator of the Rus-

sian tale';[120] that he was the leading literary critic of his day, to whom Pushkin wrote: 'I admit that there is no one I like to argue with more than you and Vyazemsky—only you two can excite me',[121] and whom Pushkin named 'the representative of taste and the true guard and patron of our literature';[122] that he had been appointed censor of bibliography in the Republic of Letters, whose secretary had addressed him in highly respectful terms in 1821, appreciating his 'talents, zeal and labours', praising him as 'one of the society's most honoured and worthy members', entreating further endeavours from his pen.[123]

His articles, reviews and correspondence are brimful of references to all the contemporary English, French and German writers. Here we will concentrate on Byron, Scott and Radcliffe, as well as Rousseau, Balzac and Hugo, the first three of whom represent his early phase and the last three his time in exile.

Bestuzhev wrote to Pushkin on 9 March 1825:

> I thirstily gulp in English literature and my soul is grateful to the English language: it taught me to think, it directed me to nature, it is an inexhaustible spring! I am even prepared to say: *il n'y a point de salut hors la littérature anglaise*

> (*Soch.*, II, p. 628).

Perhaps his favourite among the English writers was Byron, whose name first appeared in print in Russia as early as 1815 and by 1819 turned up more and more frequently until it was the main talking-point. Zhukovsky, Kozlov, Vyazemsky and Batyushkov were all delighted with him. In the early 1820s his influence was widely acknowledged; the liberal press spoke of him with veneration, the reactionaries with loathing. Bestuzhev's love for Byron was boundless; his letters are sprinkled with comments such as, 'I still read Byron assiduously. What a fiery soul he has!'[124] He never lost an opportunity to discuss him[125] and his articles contain many encomiums to his work:

> [Alfieri and] the matchless Byron proudly cast off the golden chains of fortune, scorned all the allurements of high society—in return the whole world lies at their feet and an eternal day of glory is their inheritance

> (*Soch.*, II, p. 551).

His enthralment with Byron caused him to misjudge Pushkin and offer him well-meaning advice:

> You grasped St Petersburg society, but did not penetrate it. Read Byron; without knowing our St Petersburg, he described it more exactly where a profound knowledge of people was concerned. . . . I know no one who could sketch characters better or more picturesquely. . . . And how cruel and fresh is his satire!

> (*Soch.*, II, p. 627)

His letter of 17 June 1824 to Vyazemsky mourns the loss of Byron as a fellow-poet and a champion of human rights.[126]

The popular romantic contrast between corrupt life in the city and idyllic life in the country or on a desert island or a nomadic existence came to Bestuzhev via Byron. The latter's Don Juan, Corsair, Giaour and Childe Harold escape the chains of society; so do Bestuzhev's Berkut, who lives in the woods unhampered by social prejudice and restrictions, and Vladimir Sitsky, who contrasts stifling court life with the open-air life of freedom and self-indulgence.[127]

Secondly, one of the recurrent themes in Byron which Bestuzhev borrowed was the cowardice, stupidity and cant of English society life. **"Night on Board Ship"** (**"Noch' na korable"**) relates how Mary Aston is intoxicated with glamorous society life and is eventually ruined. It is this same society which brings about the downfall of Berkut, who is destroyed by its dissipation and luxury. In **"Evening on a Bivouac"** the cynical Major Vladov advises Mechin against the folly of choosing a bride from high society, educated to value only clothes, coiffure, fine carriages, visiting cards, dancing, and the social graces.[128]

Thirdly, Byron's attitude to women was not in the usual romantic mould; for him love was not an exalted, divine expression of the soul. His criticism of women was bitter and mocking, and it is that aspect which Bestuzhev takes up. Roman, in his exasperation, berates Olga:

> 'Women, women!' he pronounced with savage mockery, 'and you boast of your love, constancy, sensibility! Your love is mere whim, garrulous, and fleeting like a swallow; but when you have to prove it by deed and not by word, how profuse are your excuses, how generous your advice, old fables and reproaches!'
>
> (*Soch.*, I, p. 10).

Major Vladov is just as sharp,[129] Dr Lontzius in *The Reval Tournament* just as biting,[130] and Bestuzhev's own asides just as caustic.[131]

Fourthly, Byron's cult of Hellenism is paralleled by Bestuzhev's admiration for Novgorod, Pskov and Pereyaslavl'. These towns symbolise past glories and exploits and evoke rapture and pride. In the manner of Byron, he stands near the ruins of castles and monuments recollecting former triumphs and events.

Next, Byron's major contribution to European romanticism was his brand of the individual hero. Generally there were two types: the active and the passive. Byron's belonged to the former, the group known as Titans, and were not only outsiders, as was usually the case, but were obsessed by the constant need to prove their value and outshine everyone else. They flouted society and its rules and engaged in astounding exhibitions of energy, emotion and fury or bombastic tirades (Cain, Manfred, Lara). Bestuzhev's heroes are modelled on this prototype. Roman and Edwin, when they feel that their love is unrequited, indulge in outbursts of unbounded despair,[132] but are generous in the extreme when they realise their mistake.[133] All display immense courage: Ronald risks his life and scorns death;[134] Roman faces death stoically;[135] Von Nordeck despises death at the hands of the Teutonic knights;[136] Edwin, quite unpractised in the art of jousting, presumes to challenge the redoubtable Ungern; Ovechkin and Shcherbina cannot contemplate surrender even when the odds are impossibly stacked against them; Von Mey has inflexible will-power.[137] They protest against any social coercion, against the spiritual enslavement of the personality by the conventions and morality of hypocritical society. Schreiterfeld accuses Gideon of ruining his life;[138] Reginald revolts against the ill treatment and evil upbringing he has received at the hands of his uncle;[139] Von Serrat arraigns the rapacity of the feudal order.[140] Nevertheless these Byronic heroes feel no pleasure at such manifestations of delight, courage, feeling or will. They are bored and indifferent. Bestuzhev's knights are afflicted with boredom and the faces of his characters wear a habitually sad expression because 'stern sorrow' involuntarily imparts to their 'pallid' faces 'solemnity and an interesting look'.[141] Their melancholy proceeds from an unsuccessful adventure or personal misfortune (Ronald), or from unrequited love (Edwin), or criminal thoughts (Sitsky), or from an overall pessimistic world-view— the common *mal du siècle* (Sitsky, Lidin).

The sixth way in which Byronic influence is visible is in the use of rapid transitions of action. This did not pass unnoticed by contemporaries. Pushkin advised Bestuzhev in 1825 with particular reference to **"The Traitor"**: 'Enough of writing rapid tales with romantic transitions—this is all right for a Byronic poem',[142] and it was said of another story: '**"Night on Board Ship"** can be compared to a poem by Byron'.[143]

If we take **"Neuhausen Castle"** as an example, we can witness quite conspicuous transitions. At one moment we are faced by the castle itself; then we are transported to a forest glade and its strange occupants; next comes the shore of Livonia and Andrey's band of Russians, the castle tower in which Ewald is held prisoner, the sea where the Russians seize the boat in which Emma is captive, and finally we return to Ewald's cell for the denouement. These switches highlight each scene. They occur without forewarning or intermediate pause. They are meant to emphasise the melodrama inherent in the situation, to heighten the tension and to make all incidents seem more striking.

Lastly we have the device of digression, which Bestuzhev admits to having copied from Byron. The epigraph to Chapter 2 of **"The Test"**—'if I have any fault, it is digression'[144]—is taken from Byron. These digressions which allow the author to comment on the action or his characters develop into long and tiresome philosophical paragraphs in the later stories like **Ammalat-Bek** and **Mulla-Nur.**

The influence of Scott is likewise pronounced. Scott was known and loved in all circles and Bestuzhev was likely to have read all the thirteen works published in Russia between 1821 and 1825.[145] Dramatic adaptations from Scott's novels were made by Prince Shakhovskoy.[146] At balls in high society 'they loved to take costumes . . . from the novels of Walter Scott'.[147] Bestuzhev's diary for 1824 mentions *The Abbot, Old Mortality* and other unnamed works.[148] His articles carry numerous references to Scott:

> Walter Scott determined the inclination of the century towards historical details, created the historical novel, which now became required reading . . .
>
> *(Soch.,* II, p. 594)

> The genius of Walter Scott guessed at the domestic life and everyday tenor of the age of chivalry . . . sprinkled them with the vivifying water of his artistic imagination, breathed into their nostrils, said 'live'—and they came alive, with the flush of life on their cheeks, with the beat of reality in their breasts.
>
> *(Soch.,* II, p. 593)

In **"The Test"** he says that Scott's novels could be found in the homes of country squires[149] and in **"The Clock and the Mirror"** (**"Chasy i zerkalo"**) in the boudoirs of society beauties in the capital.[150]

At the beginning of the nineteenth century historical tales derived from chronicles or other sources appeared: Gerakov's *Prince Menshchikov,* 1801, the anonymous *Kseniya, Princess of Galicia,* 1808, the tales of S. Glinka, 1810, and novels based on Ukrainian history by F. Glinka, Somov and Narezhny. But Bestuzhev paid them only desultory attention. His inspiration came directly from Scott, and it was Bestuzhev who laid the foundations for the Russian historical novel. As N. Polevoy said of his tales, 'They were the first attempts at the real historical novel in Russia'.[151] Contemporaries saw plainly the presence of Scott's influence; Pushkin wrote to Bestuzhev at the end of May, 1825: 'Your tournament reminds me of Walter Scott's Tournament'.[152]

Scott's method amounted to the poetisation of national life and national spirit. The first entailed descriptions of the outer trappings of life. Whereas Scott's scenes of town and country were highly impressive, Bestuzhev's were stereotyped and lifeless. Apart from his picture of Reval on the day of the tournament, when he succeeds in capturing the bright revelry, he fails to make his historical scenes seem genuine and satisfying. In spite of taking great pains to refer to ancient armour, clothing, horses, knights, skirmishes, hunting sorties and the like, he appears unable to create the real atmosphere of domestic history. And whilst striving to ratify the historical or ethnographical veracity of his incidents, many of his dates and facts are not authentic. History for him was not archaeological data, but a matter of subjective interpretation, as he explained:

> Let others burrow in manuscripts . . . I am sure, I am convinced that it *was* thus . . . in this my Russian heart, my imagination . . . is a guarantee. What purpose has poetry if not to recreate the past and prophesy the future, if not to create always according to the image and likeness of truth![153]

As for national spirit, Scott became the poet of individual nationality. He put Scotland on the map by instilling his characters and landscapes with a true Scottish spirit. Bestuzhev was totally incapable of this. It was Pushkin who fulfilled this task for Russia and so his advice to Bestuzhev is perfectly fitting: 'Abandon these Germans and turn to us Orthodox Russians . . . The novel requires a conversational style; express everything openly. Your Vladimir speaks the language of German drama, looks at the sun at midnight, etc.'[154]

Indeed Bestuzhev's characters talk and behave like the romantics of Germany, England or France. It is difficult to see them as Russians who have imbibed Russian culture, customs and beliefs. There exists only a superficial treatment—no Russian spirit or soul. The scenery too is not distinctively Russian; his towns, castles and landscapes would serve as well on the pages of any European novel of the period.

After the romantic poem and the historical tale, the most popular genre was the Gothic novel. A host of contemporaries told of their enthusiasm, particularly for Ann Radcliffe. In **"Another Page from the Diary of a Guards Officer"** (**"Yeshcho listok iz dnevnika gvardeyskogo ofitsera"**) Bestuzhev remarks jestingly: 'Our journey makes a fine scene for a horror novel', and his companion retorts, 'Yes, and the night is most Radcliffian' (**Pol. sob.** [**Polnoye sobraniye sochineniy,**], XII, p. 37).

The Gothic novel of Radcliffe, Lewis and Walpole left its traces on almost all writers, including Shelley, Burns and Keats; Bestuzhev was no exception. The setting, characters and dialogues smack of the Gothic, not to mention the deliberate accumulation of horrific situations. The castles loom dark and menacing, and within Wenden Castle the chilling atmosphere presages brooding evil. Neuhausen Castle is surrounded by lurking shadows and is eerie and forbidding. Eisen Castle is a formidable and awesome edifice. The settings forebode ill and dread, none more so than the following:

Four torches, thrust into the ground, cast a sort of greenish glow on the menacing faces of those present, and at each flicker of the flame, the shadows of the trees flitted like spectres across the glade. . . . The sky was black, the sepulchral firs whispered in the wind, and when their noise was stilled, at times the splash of waves could be heard on the stones at the river's edge.

(*Soch.,* I, pp. 76-7)

In characterisation the men are truculent and passionate, the heroines sweet and innocent maidens. The former cannot control themselves, whether experiencing hatred or love. The text is full of descriptions like:

Beside himself, rigid, gnashing his teeth in anger . . . feelings of frenzy poured out in oaths and threats.

(*Soch.,* I, p. 41)

His face burned with rage and his bloodshot eyes darted here and there.

(*Soch.,* I, p. 70)

Love sets me aflame but jealousy gnaws my soul still more.

(*Soch.,* I, p. 69)

The latter, such as Emma and Minna, swoon at any mishap, are ideal soul-mates, harbour dreams of happiness, and yearn for some indeterminate ideal.

The characters relapse occasionally into dialogue of the Gothic type, a mixture of expletives, insults and threats. They launch into bombastic outbursts so exaggerated that they seem absurd.

Finally the situations usually involve revenge and violence. Incident after incident recounts horror and murder, enough to slake the thirst of any reader: 'Romuald, emaciated, pierced by a sharp log, was hanging head down and flowing with blood; his hands were dying with a convulsive jerk and his lips were uttering indistinct curses, (*Soch.,* I, p. 91). The burial of the heroine alive in **"Eisen Castle"** is gruesome: 'Poor Louisa came to herself, a shiver ran through her veins . . . Loud, hellish laughter rang out above her. "Death for death, faithless one!" said someone, and her blood ran cold.' (*Soch.,* I, pp. 167-8).

The later work, composed in exile, bore the name Marlinsky. It underwent added influences from western Europe, particularly French. Undoubtedly the most pervasive and enduring influence on Russian sentimentalism and romanticism was Rousseau. Marlinsky embodies in Ammalat-Bek the traits of the 'noble savage', courageous, good-hearted and endowed with rich intellectual potential. His colourful appearance—black curls, red trousers, yellow boots, gold-encrusted gun, dagger, Circassian saddle, stirrups of black steel—symbolise his princely worth and the poetry of free life. Marlinsky

follows Rousseau in his extolling of the natural man. In Rousseauist fashion the mountaineers are depicted as independent, freedom-loving, brave, and loyal to their religion and community. The theme of escape by outlaw, criminal or renegade is represented by the bandit Mulla-Nur, who becomes the defender of the poor and oppressed. His protest however is tinged with regret and a sense of alienation. Marlinsky's **"Story of an Officer Held Captive by Mountaineers"** (**"Rasskaz ofitsera byvshego v plenu u gortsev"**) shows Marlinsky developing his theories and entering a polemic with Rousseau. Here the Utopian ideal is abandoned in favour of a more realistic and prosaic approach. The poverty and starkness of the mountaineers' lives are underlined, as are their quarrels, reprisals and hard work. The conditions of the natives are primitive and unattractive. Although they are the true children of nature, equal, devoid of vices, passions and ambition, they lack the advantages of civilisation and progress.

Balzac and Hugo are markedly influential in this phase. Marlinsky never tired of re-reading *La Peau de Chagrin* and loved to pit himself against Balzac's talent.[155] He admired Balzac's power of narration, his philosophical gifts, profound emotion, clear, marvellous form, and expressive genius.[156] But as for Hugo, he felt 'humble before him . . . his is not a talent, but a genius in full flower' (*Soch.,* II, p. 650). He called him 'an inimitable, mighty talent . . . a single page of whose work is worth all the Balzacs put together' (*Soch.,* II, p. 660). He had read *Notre Dame de Paris, Marion de Lorme, Le Roi s'amuse, Bug-Jargal, Han d'Islande,* among others. With them, increased depth is attained in the descriptions of society life in stories such as **"The Test"** and *The Frigate 'Hope.'* Marlinsky satirises the society of the day, empty, vain and frivolous. His heroes reject its values in the name of individual honour and integrity. A more painstaking attempt is made to describe society's conventions, foibles and customs. As the inventor of the military, Caucasian, nautical, social and historical tales, the debt of Russian literature to Marlinksy is enormous. Although much of his style was inflated, it paved the way for Pushkin, Lermontov and Gogol to found the Russian sociological novel. Belinsky's sound comment is a just tribute to his contribution:

Just as Sumarokov, Kheraskov, Petrov, Bogdanovich and Knyazhnin tried with all their might to withdraw from reality and naturalness in invention and style, so Marlinksy endeavoured to the fullest extent to draw near to both.[157]

Notes

1. Marlinsky was the pseudonym which A. A. Bestuzhev assumed in exile after the Decembrist revolt of 1825. As a member of a dragoon regiment in 1816, he had been stationed in Marli near Peterhof.

2. N. L. Stepanov, 'Chto takoye romantizm?' (*Voprosy Literatury,* XII, 1968, pp. 176-81).

3. N. L. Stepanov, 'Romanticheskiy mir Gogolya', in *K istorii russkogo romantizma,* ed. Yu. V. Mann, et al., Moscow, 1973, pp. 188-218.

4. N. K. Piksanov, *Krest'yanskoye vosstaniye v 'Vadime' Lermontova,* Saratov, 1967, p. 43.

5. I. S. Turgenev, *Polnoye sobraniye sochineniy i pisem',* Moscow-Leningrad, 1965, X, pp. 266-7.

6. See, for instance, F. Leonidov, 'Romantizm v sovetskom literaturovedenii' (*Voprosy Literatury,* VII, 1971, pp. 199-202); L. Dorofeyeva, 'Silovyye linii romantizma' (*Voprosy Literatury,* IX, 1971, p. 234); I. F. Volkov, 'Osnovnyye problemy izucheniya romantizma', in Mann, op. cit., pp. 5-36; Ye. A. Maymin, *O russkom romantizme,* Moscow, 1975.

7. Ye. M. Pul'khritudova, 'Literaturnaya teoriya dekabristskogo dvizheniya v 30—ye gody XIX v.', in *Problemy romantizma: Sbornik statey,* Moscow, 1967, pp. 232-91.

8. G. A. Gukovsky, *Pushkin i russkiye romantiki,* Moscow, 1965.

9. B. Meylakh, *Poeziya dekabristov,* Leningrad, 1950, p. 35.

10. V. G. Bazanov, *Ocherki dekabristskoy literatury: Proza,* Moscow, 1953; *Ocherki dekabristskoy literatury: Poeziya,* Moscow-Leningrad, 1961; *Uchonaya respublika,* Moscow-Leningrad, 1964.

11. *Polyarnaya zvezda,* ed. V. A. Arkhipov, et al., Moscow-Leningrad, 1960; *Dekabristy,* ed. Vl. Orlov, Moscow-Leningrad, 1951 (hereafter Orlov).

12. I. V. Kartashova, 'A. A. Bestuzhev-Marlinsky', in *Russkiy romantizm,* ed. N. A. Gulyayev, Moscow, 1974, pp. 86-91.

13. F. Z. Kanunova, *Estetika russkoy romanticheskoy povesti,* Tomsk, 1973.

14. R. F. Yusufov, *Russkiy romantizm nachala XIX veka i natsional'nyye kul'tury,* Moscow, 1970.

15. S. A. Vengerov, *Kritiko-biograficheskiy slovar' russkikh pisateley i uchonykh,* St Petersburg, 1892, III, p. 157.

16. I. I. Zamotin, *Romanticheskiy idealizm v russkom obshchestve i literature 20-30-kh godov XIX stoletiya,* St Petersburg, 1907, p. 170.

17. A. N. Pypin, *Istoriya russkoy literatury,* IV, St Petersburg, 1907, p. 430.

18. N. A. Kotlyarevsky, *Dekabristy Knyaz' A. I. Odoyevskiy i A. A. Bestuzhev-Marlinsky,* St Petersburg, 1907, pp. 122-5.

19. M. V. Nechkina, *Dvizheniye dekabristov,* I, Moscow, 1955, p. 131.

20. A. P. Sharupich, *Dekabrist Aleksandr Bestuzhev,* Minsk, 1962, pp. 15-17.

21. N. Maslin, 'A. A. Bestuzhev-Marlinksy', in A. A. Bestuzhev-Marlinsky, *Sochineniya v dvukh tomakh,* Moscow, 1958, I, p. 3 (hereafter *Soch.*).

22. N. L. Stepanov, 'A. A. Bestuzhev-Marlinsky', in A. Marlinsky, *Izbrannyye povesti,* Leningrad, 1937, p. 6.

23. N. Mordovchenko, 'A. A. Bestuzhev-Marlinsky', in Bestuzhev-Marlinsky, *Sobraniye stikhotvoreniy,* Moscow, 1948; V. G. Bazanov, *Ocherki dekabristskoy literatury,* Moscow, 1953.

24. N. I. Grech, *Zapiski o moyey zhizni,* St Petersburg, 1886, p. 393.

25. F. Glinka, *Pokazaniya,* IRLI (Institut Russkoy Literatury), AN SSSR (Akademiya Nauk SSSR); also see Bazanov, *Uchonaya respublika,* Moscow-Leningrad, 1964, pp. 317-34.

26. M. V. Dovnar-Zapolsky, *Memuary dekabristov,* Kiev, 1906, p. 175.

27. Ibid., pp. 316, 88.

28. Ibid., p. 11.

29. P. Ye. Schogolev, *Dekabristy,* Moscow-Leningrad, 1926, p. 190.

30. *Vosstaniye dekabristov: Materialy,* ed. M. N. Pokrovsky, Moscow-Leningrad, 1925-58, I, pp. 431-42.

31. Shchogolev, op. cit., p. 193.

32. A. Ye. Rozen, *Zapiski dekabrista,* St Petersburg, 1907, p. 62.

33. *Dekabristy: Otryvki iz istochnikov,* ed. Yu. G. Oksman, Moscow-Leningrad, 1926, pp. 446-7.

34. Pokrovsky, op. cit., I, p. 430.

35. Letter to N. Polevoy, *Russkiy vestnik,* 4, 1861.

36. Shchogolev, op. cit., p. 90.

37. Pokrovsky, op. cit., I, p. 433.

38. Dovnar-Zapolsky, op. cit., pp. 164-6.

39. Pokrovsky, op. cit., p. 435.

40. Letter to N. Polevoy, *Russkiy vestnik,* 3, 1851.

41. M. K. Azadovsky, 'Memuary Bestuzhevykh kak istoricheskiy i literaturnyy pamyatnik', in *Vospominaniya Bestuzhevykh,* ed. M. K. Azadovsky, Moscow-Leningrad, 1951, pp. 597-8.

42. Mikhail Bestuzhev, 'Destvo i yunost A. A. Bestuzheva-Marlinskogo', in Azadovsky, op. cit., p. 207.

43. Azadovsky, op. cit., p. 600.

44. Pokrovsky, op. cit., p. 433.

45. Ibid., p. 430.

46. Letter to Ye. A. Bestuzheva, *Pamyati dekabristov*, Leningrad, 1926, I, p. 21.

47. Mordovchenko, op. cit., p. 12.

48. Azadovsky, op. cit., pp. 8, 15.

49. Ibid., pp. 30-1.

50. Pokrovsky, op. cit., p. 437.

51. Azadovsky, op. cit., p. 42.

52. Letter to Tsar Nicholas, Orlov, op. cit., p. 513.

53. Orlov, op. cit., p. 510.

54. I. M. Semenko, 'Poeticheskoye naslediye dekabristov', in *Poety-dekabristy*, ed. Semenko, Leningrad, 1960, p. 8.

55. *Izbrannyye sotsial'no—politicheskiye i filosofskiye proizvedeniya dekabristov*, ed. I. Y. Shchipanov, Moscow-Leningrad, 1951, I, p. 266.

56. Ibid., p. 271.

57. Ibid., p. 266.

58. Letter to Polevoy (*Russkiy vestnik*, 3, 1861, p. 296).

59. *Soch.*, II, p. 523.

60. *Syn otechestva*, LXXVII, 20, 1822, pp. 253-69.

61. *Russkiy vestnik*, 6, 1870, p. 507.

62. *Soch.*, II, p. 591.

63. Ibid., p. 526.

64. Ibid., p. 530.

65. Shchipanov, op. cit., p. 270.

66. Orlov, op. cit., p. 559.

67. Ibid., p. 103.

68. *Soch.*, II, p. 554.

69. A. A. Bestuzhev-Marlinsky, *Polnoye sobraniye sochineniy*, St Petersburg, 1838, pp. 70-2 (hereafter *Pol. sob.*).

70. Ibid., pp. 113-14.

71. Ibid., p. 69.

72. Pokrovsky, op. cit., p. 457.

73. Azadovsky, op. cit., pp. 27-8.

74. Orlov, op. cit., p. 503.

75. Ibid., p. 515.

76. Ibid., p. 512.

77. Ibid., p. 503.

78. Ibid., pp. 475-8.

79. A. K. Borozdin, *Iz pisem i pokazaniy dekabristov*, St Petersburg, 1906, p. 78.

80. Orlov, op. cit., p. 3; Azadovsky, op. cit., pp. 11-12.

81. Orlov, op. cit., pp. 511-12.

82. Texts vary.

83. M. P. Alekseyev and B. S. Meylakh, *Dekabristy i ikh vremya*, Moscow-Leningrad, 1951, p. 13.

84. F. Glinka, *Stikhotvoreniya*, Leningrad, 1951, pp. 123-4; Shchipanov, op. cit., p. 519; Orlov, op. cit., p. 475.

85. *Soch.*, II, p. 474.

86. Azadovsky, op. cit., pp. 10, 34.

87. K. F. Ryleyev, *Stikhotvoreniya, stat'i, ocherki, zapiski, pis'ma*, Moscow, 1956, pp. 214-15.

88. A. I. Odoyevsky, *Polnoye sobraniye stikhotvoreniy i pisem*, Moscow-Leningrad, 1934, p. 190.

89. *Soch.*, I, pp. 93-7.

90. Orlov, op. cit., p. 5.

91. Mordovchenko, op. cit., p. 81.

92. Ibid., p. 205.

93. *Syn otechestva*, 4, 1823, pp. 183-4; *Russkiy vestnik*, 3, 1861, p. 328.

94. Shchipanov, op. cit., p. 548.

95. Pokrovsky, op. cit., IV, p. 91.

96. *Russkiy vestnik*, XXXII, 1861, p. 295.

97. Orlov, op. cit., pp. 500-1.

98. Ibid., p. 502.

99. *Sorevnovatel'*, 3, 1824, pp. 302-3.

100. Orlov, op. cit., p. 450.

101. Ibid., p. 503.

102. Ibid., p. 473.

103. Ibid., p. 511.

104. *Soch.*, I, p. 40.

105. Ibid., p. 45.

106. Ibid., pp. 67-92.

107. Shchipanov, op. cit., II, p. 164.

108. Ibid., I, p. 437.

109. Ibid., p. 296.

110. Orlov, op. cit., pp. 511-12.

111. Shchipanov, op. cit., I, p. 435.

112. Ibid., II, p. 164.

113. Borozdin, op. cit., p. 30.

114. Orlov, op. cit., p. 511.

115. Ibid., pp. 510-14.

116. A. Veselovsky, *Zapadnoye vliyaniye v novoy russkoy literature,* Moscow, 1896.

117. I. I. Zamotin, *Ranniye romanticheskiye veyaniya v russkoy literature,* Warsaw, 1900.

118. N. A. Kotlyarevsky, *Literaturnyye napravleniya aleksandrovskoy epokhi,* St Petersburg, 1907; also *Mirovaya skorb' v kontse XVIII i v nachale XIX veka,* St Petersburg, 1910.

119. M. N. Rozanov, *Russo i literaturnoye dvizheniye kontsa XVIII i nachala XIX v.: Ocherki po istorii russoizma na zapade i v Rossii,* I, Moscow, 1910.

120. V. G. Belinsky, *Polnoye sobraniye sochineniy,* Moscow, 1953-6, IV, p. 272.

121. A. S. Pushkin, *Sobraniye sochineniy v desyati tomakh,* Moscow, 1962, IX, p. 67.

122. Ibid., p. 40.

123. IRLI (Institut Russkoy Literatury), AN SSSR (Akademiya Nauk SSSR), *Bumagi Bestuzhevykh,* Arkh., 3 (5572).

124. *Pamyati dekabristov,* p. 69.

125. Ibid., p. 60; see also Azadovsky, op. cit., pp. 524-5.

126. *Soch.,* II, p. 623.

127. Ibid., I, p. 145.

128. Ibid., pp. 49-50.

129. Ibid., p. 65.

130. Ibid., p. 121.

131. Ibid., p. 166.

132. Ibid., pp. 6-7, 116-17.

133. Ibid., pp. 126, 11.

134. *Pol. sob.,* I, p. 178.

135. *Soch.,* I, p. 22.

136. Ibid., p. 78.

137. Ibid., p. 70.

138. *Pol. sob.,* XII, p. 51.

139. *Soch.,* I, pp. 164-5.

140. Ibid., pp. 39-40.

141. *Pol. sob.,* I, p. 171.

142. Pushkin, op. cit., IX, p. 160.

143. *Moskovskiy telegraf,* XLIX, 1833, p. 328.

144. *Soch.,* I, p. 178.

145. *Rospis' rossiyskim knigam dlya chteniya iz biblioteki Aleksandra Smirdina,* St Petersburg, 1828-47.

146. P. Arapov, *Letopis' russkogo teatra,* St Petersburg, 1861.

147. *Zapiski A. O. Smirnovoy,* St Petersburg, 1897, II, p. 49.

148. *Pamyati dekabristov,* I, pp. 60-6.

149. *Soch.,* I, p. 203.

150. *Pol. sob.,* IV, p. 239.

151. N. Polevoy, *Klyatva pri grobe gospodnem,* Moscow, 1832, Part I, Chapters 11-12.

152. Pushkin, op. cit., IX, p. 160.

153. *Russkiy vestnik,* 3, 1861, p. 328.

154. Pushkin, op. cit., IX, p. 160.

155. *Soch.,* II, p. 643.

156. Ibid., p. 650.

157. Belinsky, op. cit., IV, p. 28.

Lewis Bagby (essay date fall-winter 1995)

SOURCE: Bagby, Lewis. "Bestuzhev's Byron: Cross-Cultural Transformation." *Canadian-American Slavic Studies* 29, nos. 3-4 (fall-winter 1995): 271-84.

[*In the following essay, Bagby examines some of Bestuzhev's correspondence which reveal the writer's affinity for Byron's life and work, particularly the poem "Darkness."*]

It is the text, with its universal power of world disclosure, which gives a self to the ego.

Paul Ricoeur, *Interpretation Theory*

This article is an investigation of a reference by Alexander Bestuzhev-Marlinskii to Lord Byron's uncharacteristic poem, "Darkness."[1] Bestuzhev uses the citation to create an illusion of solidity and coherence in his experience.[2] It appears in a letter of 1831 to his publishers, Ksenofont and Nikolai Polevoi, of *The Moscow Telegraph* (1825-34). Bestuzhev's letters of exile are peopled with figures from Western literature, but the greatest affinity he felt was for the person and work of Byron. In his letters to the Polevoi brothers Bestuzhev was wont to discuss literary matters more, say; than with his mother and sisters, and even, for that matter, with his brothers Nikolai and Mikhail. The Polevoi letters are for this reason particularly valuable in understanding Bestuzhev's rendering of a self he conceived in literary terms.

At the time Bestuzhev wrote the letter in question, he was on the verge of becoming the most popular writer of prose fiction in the 1830s (a popularity which extended into the twentieth century for many readers, but ended among literati in the 1840s). I say this with no trepidation even though the 1830s introduced the fiction of Aleksandr Pushkin and Nikolai Gogol', two giants whose work dwarfs Bestuzhev's. In terms of the modest but growing popular culture of early nineteenth-century Russia, Bestuzhev successfully claimed primacy among bourgeois readers who, like the Polevoi brothers, were immersed in the literature of European Romantics. Bestuzhev must be counted among this group for two reasons. First, his family mixed aristocratic and merchant origins (the latter of which instilled a great sense of pride in him). Second, he and his audience were of one aesthetic temperament, not least because he helped create bourgeois taste in the early 1820s.

Bestuzhev had been a publisher in the early 1820s with Kondratii Ryleev, issuing the literary almanac *Polar Star* for the three years prior to the revolt of 14 December 1825, in which they both participated and for which they suffered the consequences. Ryleev was hanged; Bestuzhev exiled to Siberia and the Caucasus. Although permitted after 1830 to publish under the pseudonym Marlinskii, Bestuzhev's real identity remained a fairly well kept secret until his death in 1837 when it became known that the famous writer Marlinskii was the Decembrist Bestuzhev. The richest period in Bestuzhev's fictional output was from 1830 to 1834. At that time he was stationed in Derbent where he had been transferred from Iakutsk, at his own request, to fight Turkish hegemony in the region. Bestuzhev's arrival in the Caucasus had direct parallels in his mind with Byron's Oriental poems, *Childe Harold,* and the British poet's self-imposed exile to the Northern Mediterranean (an area proximate to the Caucasus and for Bestuzhev its topographical equivalent). In this point of similarity emerge the contours of Bestuzhev's transformation of the By-

ronic canon (the one which combines his life and letters),[3] for in *seeing* the parallels as they pertained to his own life, he worked them into a configuration that suited his own subjective experience. This subjective move is recapitulated textually in his appropriation of Byron's "Darkness" in a manner which "removes" the very real distance between them.[4]

The chasm separating Byron and Bestuzhev is apparent when we consider facts which escaped Bestuzhev. For instance, Byron traveled to Greece to support the cause of freedom and national integrity. Bestuzhev was on a converse mission—the subjugation of the peoples of the Caucasus to the Russian empire. He was not a liberator, but an oppressor, or at least a player in the imperialist game. Thus, anything Bestuzhev has to say to the Polevoi brothers about his experience must be understood as his attempt to fashion an image of himself on the basis of literary patterns rather than as a valid discovery of consonance with Byron. In terms of personal substance, aesthetic accomplishment, and rational facility, Byron and Bestuzhev are far apart. But Bestuzhev's insistence on the opposite indicates something about the man and his desires.

Bestuzhev corresponded regularly with the Polevoi brothers from 29 January 1831 to 12 May 1837, that is, up to one month before he died at the hands of Cherkes natives during a military skirmish on Adler Promontory on the Black Sea. In Bestuzhev's eighth extant letter one senses an energy behind every word as he revels in his regained contact with the literary world. He is anxious to learn about the contemporary literary scene, expressing himself in a figure not unusual for him: "At one time even I lived in the world of print; now I am entirely alienated from it. Like Irving's awakened Rip Van Winkle I see the same tavern sign, but new guests with dram in hand."[5] . . . This casual remark is filled with gestures we can associate with Bestuzhev's writing, at once multivalenced and subtle, then clumsy and rather too direct, but most always culturally dense (at least in the sense we say so in the late twentieth century). These qualities inhere in Bestuzhev's fiction as well, where the infelicitous too often vitiates the more refined and consequently points to the inferiority of the imitation in comparison with the original. Be that as it may, Bestuzhev's reference to Rip Van Winkle stands out rather clearly, perhaps too much so, for it overshadows more interesting allusions to Bestuzhev's life prior to the Decembrist Revolt. "At one time even I lived [*i ia zhil*] in the world of print" contains information that summarizes how Bestuzhev perceives himself and his world. First, the particle "i" allows him to suggest a humility that is at once genuine (he has indeed departed the literary scene) and at the same time false (for he *was* a significant figure, with Ryleev, in the world of print). Furthermore, he had already had several poems published from 1829 to 1831 in *Syn otechestva, Moskovskii telegraf,* and *Literaturnaia gazeta,* and had seen his prose tale **"The Test" ("Ispytanie")** appear in *Syn otechestva i Severnyi arkhiv* in 1830).[6] Second, when Bestuzhev says that he lived formerly "in the world of print," metaphoric allusion is made to a cultural dominant of the early nineteenth century, to wit, that lives were lived in accordance with models established in literature.[7] From this perspective, Bestuzhev's "at one time" can be viewed as ironic; in 1831 he had not ceased to conceive of his life in terms of literary models.[8] The point here is that Bestuzhev *peoples* his letters with self-referents that are literary. Although brief, not the least of these is the reference to Byron's "Darkness."

By 1831 the *idea* of Byron had grown large in Russian culture.[9] There were already five separate Russian translations of "Darkness" by then.[10] If only intuitively, Bestuzhev appreciated the degree to which the Russian public's apprehension of the poet came, like his, with a set of suppositions, a mythology connected with Prometheus, Napoleon, revolution and war,[11] all of which Bestuzhev could utilize to project an idea of himself upon his sundry audiences. In the letter of December 1831 to the Polevoi brothers Bestuzhev presents a passage that interweaves physical, social, and emotional contexts as well as his subjective experience of them, and he rises to an emotional pitch that culminates in the line: "My inner world has become miraculous: read *The Darkness* [sic] by Byron and you will understand something of what it is like; it is an ocean, 'beset by a heavy gloom, immobile, dark and silent . . . over which glimmer some unclear forms.'"[12] To appreciate what significance the reference to "Darkness" might have for Bestuzhev, it is necessary to briefly examine the poem itself.

"Darkness" was penned in the period July-August 1816 during a time of personal crisis and concomitant literary activity in Byron's life. He was in some financial difficulties associated with his marriage obligations and his rather profligate way of life. Byron and his wife had recently separated (after only one year of residency together), and, after signing papers formalizing their legal affairs, he left for Switzerland where he spent the summer before moving on to Italy.[13] In Geneva he met the Shelleys who were also traveling under a cloud of scandal. This was Byron's first meeting with Shelley, which came about thanks to the efforts of the latter's sister-in-law, Claire Clairmont, step-sister of Mary Shelley, author of *Frankenstein; or The Modern Prometheus.*[14] The apocalyptic genre, in which "Darkness" is cast, was rarely used by Byron, but on several occasions this small group of literati engaged in Gothic speculations that might have stimulated the verse's imagery. McGann suggests that the brief presence among them of M. G. "Monk" Lewis, with his preference for dark musings, may have impelled Byron in this direc-

tion.[15] The poem is bleak, as one would expect, in its vision of "man's last days in a dying universe."[16] If it is a poem rather uncharacteristic of Byron's creativity, it nevertheless shares a dramatic sense of isolation, death, and longing with other poems of the four months in Switzerland, particularly "The Dream," "Prometheus," and ["A Fragment"].[17]

Since this was the beginning of a period of great productivity coupled with a hope of eventual release,[18] Bestuzhev's reference to "Darkness" might seem a bit puzzling. But, as the letter makes amply clear, Bestuzhev was frustrated by the conditions in which he lived and attempted to write. The fullness of life and its new promises were matched by a contrary feeling of emptiness and misery in which his potentials as a human being were being thwarted and his talents as a writer wasted on trifles. These elements become matters of signification in Bestuzhev's citation of the Byron poem, which begins: "I had a dream, which was not all a dream."[19] This prefatory line encapsulates several facets of Bestuzhev's relationship to the poem. First, through it he likens poetry to experience, or meaning to sense (to cite a distinction Ricoeur makes),[20] and thereby claims the relevance of Byron's verse to his life. Second, Bestuzhev operates within the dialectic embodied in the relationship of dreams and waking advanced by Byron and Romantic aesthetics in general. These factors taken together prompt the reader, the Polevoi brothers and us, to comprehend the text at two levels—as Bestuzhev's experience of life (somehow unreal to him yet concretely experienced) and as our mode of assessing Bestuzhev's discourse (through the metaphor Bestuzhev proffers: "'Darkness' is like my life").

Within this dream world, with equal emphasis on both words, elements pertaining to the end of time take on special signifying value for Bestuzhev:[21]

> The bright sun was extinguish'd, and the stars
> Did wander darkling in the eternal space,
> Rayless, and pathless, and the icy earth
> Swung blind and blackening in the moonless air;
> Morn came and went—and came, and brought no day,
> And men forgot their passions in the dread
> Of this their desolation; and all hearts
> Were chill'd into a selfish prayer for light.

These lines possess double referential value—they signify Byronic themes (which implies an interpretation of Byron's texts) and Bestuzhev's status in exile (which requires another, structurally similar act of interpretation of Bestuzhev's text, i.e., the letter to the Polevoi brothers). At yet another level, each of the interpretative centers of Bestuzhev's rhetoric are "validated" by the presupposition that readers like Bestuzhev equated Byron's poetry with Byron's life. The distance separating Byron and Bestuzhev, as tenor and vehicle in metaphoric utterance, is thus nullified, at least if Bestuzhev's readers do their work of equation in a manner isomorphic to Bestuzhev's reading of Byron.

Bestuzhev's reader familiar with either the original or one of the several translations of "Darkness" is asked to equate poem and life text through the intermediacy of Byron's descriptive language:

> And they did live by watch fires—and the thrones,
> The palaces of crowned kings—the huts,
> The habitations of all things which dwell,
> Were burnt for beacons; cities were consumed,
> And men were gather'd round their blazing homes
> To look once more into each other's face.

The apocalyptic destruction of habitations, cities, and relationships is reminiscent of the war in which Bestuzhev participated. In the letter's post scriptum Bestuzhev's description of his part in the war indicates the degree to which the borrowed poetic text and the self-text Bestuzhev generates for the Polevoi brothers can be viewed by a willing reader as equivalent.[22] The impact of ultimate demise on individuals who, like Bestuzhev, experience personally the waste of war/apocalypse, and others who *read* about it, becomes a point of contact for addressers (Byron and Bestuzhev) and addressees (Bestuzhev and the Polevoi brothers):

> The brows of men by the despairing light
> Wore an unearthly aspect, as by fits
> The flashes fell upon them; some lay down
> And hid their eyes and wept; and some did rest
> Their chins upon their clenched hands, and smiled;
> And others hurried to and fro, and fed
> Their funeral piles with fuel, and look'd up
> With mad disquietude on the dull sky,
> The pall of a past world; and then again
> With curses cast them down upon the dust,
> And gnash'd their teeth and howl'd.

The distance which separates people within the poem reiterates the theme of Bestuzhev's letter. Yet there is a difference. In the poem death separates people in ultimate terms. That is, within the self-referential world of "Darkness" human beings die each apart from the other; there is no reversal possible when "Darkness . . . [is] the Universe." Bestuzhev, however, works two themes at one time, separation and union, distance and communion. In his letter he refers to the inevitability of the soldier's death on the front lines and makes specific reference to himself:

> Your brother asks that I guard my life: that's a bit tough for a soldier. Nature has not bestowed upon me an animal daring which is extolled as bravery; but I am less impulsive in my actions than I used to be. Glory cannot shield me from danger with its azure wings and hope does not gild the smokey dust. I throw myself forward [in battle], but this is more out of duty than from inspiration. Labor and fatigue and the ill weather I bear with patience: no one has heard me mumble in complaint, 'the beard is not bemoaned once the head is severed.'[23]

In the parallels Bestuzhev suggests between the specific content of "Darkness" and his life (as he describes it), he draws down the explicit content of "Darkness" onto the surface description of his own experience. At the same time, he works at nullifying the ultimate separation inhering in "Darkness" and draws his reader into close personal proximity with him:

> And War, which for a moment was no more,
> Did glut himself again;—a meal was bought
> With blood, and each sate sullenly apart
> Gorging himself in gloom. No love was left;
> All earth was but one thought—and that was death,
> Immediate and inglorious; and the pang
> Of famine fed upon all entrails—men
> Died, and their bones were tombless as their flesh;

These stark images function as stimuli which are meant to activate parallel structures in the reader's perception of three texts—Bestuzhev's letter with its citation, the full text of the poem itself, and the life texts of the two authors, Byron and Bestuzhev. The separation across cultures, individuals, languages, codes, genres, and messages is vitiated, but, again, only if the addressee is willing to perform the part scripted for him in Bestuzhev's text. The model for proximity, rather than distance, is supplied in "Darkness" with its famous reference to faithfulness:

> The meagre by the meagre were devour'd,
> Even dogs assail'd their masters, all save one,
> And he was faithful to a corse, and kept
> The birds and beasts and famish'd men at bay,
> Till hunger clung them, or the dropping dead
> Lured their lank jaws. Himself sought out no food,
> But with a piteous and perpetual moan,
> And a quick desolate cry, licking the hand
> Which answer'd not with a caress—he died.

Byron's ironic reference to friendship is not matched by Bestuzhev's rhetoric. Bestuzhev would not have dogs, but humans (the Polevoi brothers, his Decembrist confreres) be friends of the type idealized in the literary and Masonic circles of the late eighteenth and early nineteenth centuries. Reference to his brothers, Nikolai and Mikhail (exiled to Siberia), and to Kondratii Ryleev occur elsewhere in the letter and set up cross-references which reinforce the theme of personal relations (e.g., Byron's man/dog, Bestuzhev's man/man) as distinct from the failed relations catalogued in "Darkness" in its metaphoric depiction of society. From this perspective Bestuzhev utilizes Byron's poem as a negative example, one which his readers were asked covertly to supersede in an act of understanding and sympathy (but not pity).

My claim here is not that there is any ontologically necessary tie between Byron's imagery and Bestuzhev's or, for that matter, between Bestuzhev's argument and its reception. Rather, emphasis is placed on Bestuzhev's utilization of the poem to activate reader associations available to him/her in the symmetry of the texts (poem and letter). To this end Bestuzhev presents the Polevoi brothers with some guidance. Overt parallels, however, are to be drawn by them. It is in this form that Bestuzhev's rhetoric is most effective, for it involves suggestion, not declaration, persuasion, not command. By supplying the reader the opportunity to invest meaning in his reading experience, making connections explicit where merely suggested, Bestuzhev signifies the condition in which the normal and necessary distance which separates authors and readers can be surmounted and emotional proximity established. This was the goal of the word for Bestuzhev in exile.

Within the nexus of associations available to Bestuzhev as a reader of Byron, to Bestuzhev as writer of self-texts, and to the Polevoi brothers as readers of Byron and Bestuzhev, perhaps most compelling is Byron's use of images of water and ships. For the Russian reader they came to symbolize the plight of the Decembrist and of post-Decembrist society:

> The world was void,
> The populous and the powerful was a lump,
> Seasonless, herbless, treeless, manless, lifeless—
> A lump of death—a chaos of hard clay.
> The rivers, lakes, and ocean all stood still,
> And nothing stirr'd within their silent depths;
> Ships sailorless lay rotting on the sea,
> And their masts fell down piecemeal; as they dropp'd
> They slept on the abyss without a surge—
> The waves were dead; and tides were in their grave,
> The Moon, their mistress, had expired before;
> The winds were wither'd in the stagnant air,
> And the clouds perish'd; Darkness had no need
> Of aid from them—She was the Universe.

This imagery of the boat at the conclusion of the poem signals a relationship between the cosmic and the earthly domains, both in ruins, static, and lifeless. As elsewhere in the poem, Byron reinforces the emptiness of the universe in the repetition of the suffix -less. It is this absence which apparently prompts Bestuzhev's interest in referencing the poem, replacing the emptiness to which the poem refers with the substance of verbal encounter. Again distance is overcome as separation yields to proximity through the shared word.

Bestuzhev feels no need to cite the entire poem in his letter to the Polevoi brothers. They would have known the poem in any one of its variants available to the reading public. Bestuzhev chooses to highlight only one part of the poem (interestingly, not its dense third and fourth stanzas[24]). On the basis of the line Bestuzhev recites, it is difficult to ascertain with any precision its relationship to the original. Of the myriad images available to him, Bestuzhev refers only to part of the sixth "stanza": "[an ocean] beset by heavy gloom, motionless, dark and silent." This seems to refer inexactly, but conceptually and imagistically, to Byron's lines: "The

rivers, lakes, and ocean all stood still [*nedvizhnyi*] / And nothing stirr'd within their silent [*nemoi*] depths".

Whether Bestuzhev, at the time of his writing, was recalling from memory the lines he cites, referring to a Russian or French translation of the poem, or simply engaging in poetic license,[25] the changes he makes in comparison to the original are suggestive. First, Bestuzhev excludes the rivers and lakes. Whether conscious or not, the elimination of these images may be the result of a desire to have the poem correspond to his actual circumstances: he was living at the time in Derbent, which is located on the Caspian Sea. The sea, of course, is a romantic convention used to suggest a dualism inherent in personality, a dualism, moreover, which Bestuzhev keenly felt if we can, in some measure, believe his remarks to the Polevoi brothers.[26] Second, Bestuzhev includes the qualifiers "dark/gloomy" (*mrachnyi*) and the epithet "heavy gloom" (*tiazhelaia mgla*), evaluative addenda which suggest Bestuzhev's reading and/or memory of the original, not its specific content. In effect, he offers an interpretation of the poem's mood (which is not too difficult to do)[27] and encapsulates it in his rhythmic rendering of the lines. In sum, Bestuzhev's reference to "Darkness" and his translation of two of its lines indicate both biographical and aesthetic information usually associated with him. He is a remaker of myths in order to create his own.

These two categories—biography and aesthetics—form the center of any rendering of texts by Bestuzhev, whether his own or others': they incline in two directions: (a) beyond the text toward Bestuzhev's life and the persona he develops in society through his writing, and (b) internally toward the dialogical transformation of the text from within (as though from a prior, preutterance code to another that emerges secondarily as a response to the first).[28] These two simultaneous events underscore the cross-cultural transformation Bestuzhev makes for his readers—through verbal art as well as in his letters he attempts to render a literary image of self both as author and hero.[29] It is a self-making not unlike Byron's, at least structurally, if not in terms of the details or the image's complexity. For the Polevoi brothers, and through the reference to Byron, Bestuzhev demonstrates his affinity to literary texts that equate with his life and at the same time provides proof of his sensitivity to the aesthetic word—not a bad act for a writer to perform in his correspondence with his publishers, particularly those in direct contact with the literary milieu from which Bestuzhev was excluded and through whom he could be reintroduced qua hero.

Bestuzhev's brief mention of "Darkness" is significant for what it indicates more or less overtly. But it is perhaps more dramatic for what it leaves out—80 lines of verse, or 98 percent of the entire poem. Bestuzhev's reference to two lines supplies the Polevoi brothers (and anyone they would grant the privilege of reading Bestuzhev's private correspondence) with a manner of interpreting Bestuzhev's relationship to Byron's poem, not the poem itself. In effect, through Bestuzhev's allusion to Byron's text, he instructs his publishers how to read the image of his life he wishes to project (and in which he sincerely believed). The transformation inherent here is significant not for what it does aesthetically with Byron's poem, but for what it imposes on a reader sensitive to Bestuzhev's life circumstances. It asks the reader (the Polevoi brothers, their circle of intimates, and, by extension, you and me) to place Bestuzhev in a mental landscape adjacent to a vast and powerful body of water, the dualism of which can be inferred by poetic canon, and the political nature of which can be read by reference to other post-Decembrist texts, e.g., Pushkin's "Arion" (1827).[30] It asks the reader to understand the qualifiers Bestuzhev uses, particularly those he adds to the original, as they pertain to his life.

Bestuzhev equates his isolation with immobility and stasis ("*nedvizhnyi*"), and he views himself as silenced ("*nemoi*") because of the censorship of his work under the name Bestuzhev. This brings up a crucial issue—Bestuzhev's identity before the public, his self-making, which is the central, albeit unstated (and perhaps even unconscious), concern of his letter to the Polevoi brothers. Its heart is conditioned by the very real distance which separates him from his family, friends, publishers, the literary world, and social scene in the north. It is the source of his desire, the fount of his "dream . . . not all a dream," to remove the distance, to overcome the isolation, and feel (if not be) proximate to a world that is alive and responsive to him, not cold and out for his blood.[31]

Bestuzhev would like to be seen in a tragic and romantic guise. To foster the image of self as martyred hero, for which he had no small claim, he emphasizes literary antecedents. He is not only a Rip Van Winkle (an image which reinforces his isolation from contemporary life and literature in the major Russian cities), but the Byronic "I" of "Darkness" which in "a dream, which was not all a dream" views the microcosm (Petersburg and Moscow) from the macrocosmic vantage point of the end of time. This is at one and the same time a witty condemnation of vacuous society and a longing for its ambiguous and varied pleasures. It is grand society, after all, that has driven him, at least indirectly, into exile, but that same society which once held him in high esteem as a writer, publisher, and promising young officer. These are clear Byronic themes. Interestingly enough, there is sufficient truth to them in Bestuzhev's life to make the rendering relatively accurate. Bestuzhev saw to that.

Bestuzhev projects an image of himself that is "of" the world and "above" it, much like the image of Prometheus the Romantics valorized in their lives and texts, and like the image of Christ Bestuzhev also invokes in his letter. With the aid of these man-god images, Bestuzhev places "Darkness" in the self-mythologizing context he seeks before his audience:

> In place of harmony I find within myself a desert wind whispering in the ruins. Beneath my cross, my burdensome cross (which is more spiritual than material), I fall for a moment, and not just once. My spirit is strong; but this is more a [physical] numbness than firmness [of character]. Only two jewels have I extracted from the flood: the soul's pride and peace before everything that is beautiful. My inner world has become incredible: read Byron's *The Darkness* [sic] and you will get a sense of something of which I speak.

In Bestuzhev's use of Byron's stark poem we observe a felicitous collision of cultures in which the extreme Romantic, Bestuzhev, suggests a manner by which he might best be understood as a cultural monument; condemns the society that supports him even as it exiles him; and mythologizes himself on the order of the cosmic "I" of Byron's poem. Bestuzhev insures these readings by topographical allusion (his location on the Caspian Sea); meaningful subtractions from the original poem; biographically significant additions to the original poem; and reference to Lord Byron as a pan-cultural phenomenon (whose biographical and literary texts lionized the poet for Russian and world culture). Bestuzhev's literal absorption of Byron into his life and literary texts indicates dramatically his desire to achieve a specific form of selfhood. Paraphrasing Ricoeur, it is the Byronic text (life text and aesthetic texts). with its power of world disclosure, which gives a self to Bestuzhev's ego.[32] It is not inappropriate that he should be called Russia's Byron, not because of the accuracy of the description at the surface level, but because of its conformity to Bestuzhev's deepest wish and his brief success at realizing it.

Notes

1. Virtually all commentators on the poem have noted its uniqueness within Byron's body of work. John Clubbe calls the work "the most pessimistic of Byron's poems." See "'The New Prometheus of New Men': Byron's 1816 Poems and *Manfred,*" in *Nineteenth Century Literary Perspectives: Essays in Honor of Lionel Stevenson*. Ed. Clyde de L. Ryals (Durham, NC: Duke Univ. Press, 1974), p. 27. M. Raizis comments, "'Darkness' is an ostensibly strange poem." See "Byron's Promethean Rebellion in 1816: Fictionality and Self-projection," *The Byron Journal,* No. 19 (1991), p. 43.

2. It is something of an irony, inherent in cross-cultural transformations of the type described here, that the "jarring co-existence, so often noted in Byron, of skepticism and belief" is glaringly ab-

sent in Bestuzhev's reading of Byron. See R. J. Dingley, "'I had a Dream': Byron's 'Darkness,'" *The Byron Journal,* No. 9 (1981), p. 30.

3. Contemporary critics labor against the propensity to equate the two. Gleckner mentions "the depths to which biographizing has plunged the general state of Byron criticism from his day to ours" and traces an alternative course in his study. See Robert F. Gleckner, *Byron and the Ruins of Paradise* (Baltimore: Johns Hopkins Univ. Press, 1967), p. xii. Bestuzhev's reading, of course, was in keeping with the fashion which drew proximate the poet's life and his letters. But more, he went to school on this reading.

4. Paul Ricoeur discusses the problem of "distanciation" and "appropriation" in his *Interpretation Theory: Discourse and the Surplus of Meaning* (Fort Worth, TX: Texas Christian Univ. Press, 1976), pp. 43-44, 91-95. This study's theoretical framework, applied in some measure in this article, illuminates how very much Bestuzhev was trying to accomplish in his letter to the Polevoi brothers.

5. "Pis'ma Aleksandra Aleksandrovicha Bestuzheva k N. A. i K. A. Polevym," *Russkii vestnik,* No. 3 (1861), p. 291.

6. See Aleksandr Bestuzhev-Marlinskii, *Sochineniia v dvukh tomakh* (Moscow: Khudlit, 1958), I, 608; II, 708-13.

7. Iurii Lotman has persistently made this point. See "The Theater and Theatricality as Components of Early Nineteenth-Century Culture," in *The Semiotics of Russian Culture.* Ed. Ann Shukman (Ann Arbor: Michigan Slavic Contributions, 1984), pp. 141-64.

8. It should be noted, too, that Bestuzhev's work, under the pen name Marlinskii (or, rarely, as A. B.), had already begun to appear in print in the late 1820s.

9. "Beginning with 1818 the anti-Karamzinist journal *Vestnik Evropy* (published by M. T. Kachenovskii) initiated a continuous publication of papers on Byron's work, derived mainly from French, but also partly from German, magazines." (Diakonova, Nina and Vadim Vacuro, "Byron in Russia," in *Byron's Cultural and Political Influence in Nineteenth-Century Europe.* Ed. Paul Graham Trueblood. [Atlantic Highlands, NJ: Humanities Press] 1981], p. 144.) As early as 1823 Bestuzhev had encouraged Pushkin to take up English so that he might read Byron in the original, for it is only in the language native to the poet, he argued, that Byron might best be appreciated. "Appreciation" in Pushkin's case may be the correct word, but in Bestuzhev's instance something more like "acquired" might better fit, for Bestuzhev used with great consistency his idea of Byron to inform his life and letters.

10. "The eschatological motifs of Byron's "Darkness" became firmly rooted in Russian poetry. In the 1820s alone it was translated at least five times (by O. Somov, F. Glinka, D. Glebov, M. Vronchenko, A. Rotchev); in the years to follow it attracted Lermontov (1830) and Turgenev (1846)" (Diakonova and Vacuro, p. 152). I use the Rotchev translation here; see Dzhordzh Gordon Bairon, *Izbrannaia lirika* (Moscow: Raduga, 1988), pp. 246-50.

11. Byron's poems, letters, and journal entries of 1816 indicate how closely entwined these figures and events were for him. See George M. Ridenour, "Byron in 1816: Four Poems from Diodati," in *George Gordon, Lord Byron.* ed. Harold Bloom (New York: Chelsea House Publishers, 1986), pp. 65-74, but particularly Leslie A. Marchand, *Byron: A Biography,* 3 vols. (New York: Alfred A. Knopf, 1957), II, 563-660.

12. "Pis'ma A. A. Bestuzheva," p. 310. Bestuzhev misnames Byron's poem, which lacks the article.

13. Byron also suffered rumors about incestuous relations with his half-sister Augusta. His 1816 poem "Epistle to Augusta" (Diodati, 1816) could only fuel those rumors.

14. For details concerning Byron's and Shelley's relationship, see John Buxton, *Byron and Shelley: The History of a Friendship* (New York: Harcourt, Brace & World, 1968). Buxton overstates Shelley's influence on "Darkness" and the other poems of 1816 (p. 262). The intellectual and climatological atmosphere which produced "Darkness" may have influenced the creation of *Frankenstein* as well; see John Clubbe, "The Tempest-toss'd Summer of 1816: Mary Shelley's *Frankenstein,*" *The Byron Journal,* No. 19 (1991), pp. 26-40. On the basis of her acquaintance with Byron for the three months she and her husband lived adjacent to him on Lake Geneva, Mary Shelley portrayed Byron in the character Raymond in *The Last Man* (Buxton, p. 267).

15. *Lord Byron: The Complete Poetic Works,* 4 vols., ed. Jerome J. McGann (Oxford: Clarendon Press, 1986), IV, 459n.

16. Marchand, *Byron: A Biography,* II, 637.

17. Clubbe emphasizes the Promethean theme. Note that Bestuzhev mentions Prometheus in his letter. Clubbe's description of the mythological figure's importance to Byron might easily apply to Be-

stuzhev as well: "In [1816] Byron came to understand better the essential character of the myth: that while Prometheus' fate was symbolic of the general human lot, it was still a fate ennobled by suffering and by a tremendous effort to maintain his mind's independence" (p. 17).

18. Bestuzhev apparently hoped that by winning distinction in battle he would be promoted to the rank of officer, a privilege which could technically win him freedom before his twenty years of servitude were to expire in 1846. Unbeknownst to him, Nicholas I had seen to the impossibility of this maneuver already in 1829 when he approved Bestuzhev's transfer to the Caucasus from Iakutsk.

19. I have here used the text in *Lord Byron: The Complete Poetic Works,* IV, pp. 40-43.

20. Ricoeur, *Interpretation Theory,* pp. 19-22.

21. Bestuzhev's argument, in effect, is that his life is a representation of a representation, a blending of verbal discourses which, and this is the key moment in his rhetoric, refer to a substantive reality. The *literariness* of identity and lived experience is highlighted here (as elsewhere) in Bestuzhev's letter.

22. "Communication has been cut off, our mounts starve . . . Kazi-Mulla . . . threatens all the local cities and towns with a new siege. . . . The battle of Agach-Kale cost us four hundred men. . . . Eight of our excellent officers went down. . . ." "Pis'ma A. A. Bestuzheva," p. 316.

23. *Ibid.*

24. The third "stanza" ("The brows of men by the despairing light") is especially marked for unique prosodic elements. It contains a higher frequency of enjambment than the rest of the poem (56 percent versus 44 percent). This gives the verse a particular drive during its initial stark descriptive passages. Furthermore, the third "stanza" contains a fairly regular caesura, which again distinguishes it and reinforces rhythmically the description of man's persistent degradation. The poem's sole truncated foot occurs in the third stanza during a dramatic moment when flame and the heavens are linked in something of an inverted Promethean image. In addition, the same stanza contains a high frequency of trochaic inversion, or spondees, which make highly noticeable and impactful the epithets "dull sky," "past worlds," "wild birds shriek'd." And finally, the stanza contains rhymed elements otherwise missing from the poem and consequently deserving of attention as a coherent lexical series: "brutes/multitude/food." These prosodic features reinforce the poem's focus on a death that is rendered in individual, group, and

cosmic terms. The fourth stanza contains similar features, but not in the density of the third. Bestuzhev is clearly more moved by imagery than prosodic elements, something which distinguished him from the poets of his day and, perhaps, made him a prose writer first, a poet fourth (after literary critic and epistolary writer).

25. This passage also enticed British readers contemporary to Byron, excluding Scott and other literati (Dingley, "I had a Dream," p. 20). Rotchev translated these lines as follows: ". . . *Ozera, reki / I more—vse zatikhlo. Nichego / Ne shevelilos' v bezdne molchalivoi*" (*Izbannaia lirika,* 249). In Bestuzhev's rendering, "*okean*" replaces "*more,*" "*nemoi*" displaces "*zatikhlo,*" "*nedvizhnyi*" supplants "*ne shevelilos',*" and "*mrachnyi*" substitutes for "*molchalivoi.*" This suggests that Bestuzhev was either recomposing the poem from memory or utilizing a different translation (perhaps French). Concordances of Byron, Pushkin, and Shakespeare, with whom Bestuzhev was familiar, do not deliver the images of the ocean he here cites. It seems likely that he recalled the lines and images from memory. Note, too, Bestuzhev incorrectly cites the poem's title: there is no article in Byron's "Darkness," an interesting translinguistic addition on Bestuzhev's part and perhaps an indication of his finely attuned, if here misguided, understanding of English. If Bestuzhev was referring to a French translation, entitled "Le Tenebres," this could have supplied the article he inserted in English in his letter. I am indebted to Professor Khama Basilli Tolo for his comments on the use (or lack thereof) of the article in nineteenth-century French translations from English.

26. The dualism is isomorphic to Bestuzhev's use of Byron's poem.

27. Stevenson argues that the "general idea . . . that people get the sort of apocalypse they deserve," is offset, even balanced, by the "double exception implied" in lines 47-54, where the good, obedient, and faithful dog's qualities can be inferred for the master (who has not made food of his companion). See Warren Stevenson, "Byron and Coleridge: The Eagle and the Dove," *The Byron Journal,* No. 19 (1991), p. 120. His view is contrary to the usual reading of the poem as "immitigable cynicism and despair" (Leslie A. Marchand, *Byron's Poetry: A Critical Introduction* [Boston: Houghton Mifflin, 1965], p. 128) or as a "fatalistic acceptance of man's evil and man's doom" (Carl Woodring, *Politics in English Romantic Poetry* [Cambridge, MA: Harvard Univ. Press, 1970], p. 174).

28. This process is most apparent in translations from one language to another, but less so at the surface

level within the same language. Bakhtin's descriptions of this process are most enlightening: "An element of response and anticipation penetrates deeply inside intensely dialogic discourse. Such discourse draws in, as it were, sucks in to itself the other's replies, intensely reworking them." See Mikhail Bakhtin, "Discourse in Dostoevsky," *Problems of Dostoevsky's Poetics*. ed. and tr. Caryl Emerson (Minneapolis: Univ. of Minnesota Press, 1984), p. 197.

29. Bestuzhev makes a good model of what Mikhail Bakhtin describes at length in "Author and Hero in Aesthetic Activity," *Art and Answerability*. ed. Michael Holquist and Vadim Liapunov, tr. Vadim Liapunov (Austin: Univ. of Texas Press, 1990), pp. 4-256.

30. For a discussion of "Arion" and of the relations between Pushkin and Bestuzhev, both concerned with Decembrist fate, see Lauren G. Leighton, "Puskin and Marlinskij: Decembrist Allusions," *Russian Literature,* No. 14 (1983), pp. 351-82.

31. Pechorin as an authentic social type is prefigured here, rendering Lermontov's editorial claim, in the introduction to *A Hero of Our Time,* valid as a socio-literary event of romantic interpretation. Like Bestuzhev's letter, Lermontov's discourse is poised on the threshold where art and life meet in aestheticized belief, that is, in self-fulfilling prophecy.

32. Ricoeur, *Interpretation Theory,* p. 95.

Lewis Bagby (essay date 1995)

SOURCE: Bagby, Lewis. Introduction to *Alexander Bestuzhev-Marlinsky and Russian Byronism*, pp. 1-18. University Park, Penn.: Pennsylvania State University Press, 1995.

[*In the following essay, Bagby reviews Bestuzhev's accomplishments and contributions to the history of Russian literature.*]

> Literature is a good friend but an evil master.
>
>   —Bestuzhev-Marlinsky

In early-nineteenth-century Russia, the narratives of Alexander Alexandrovich Bestuzhev-Marlinsky (1797-1837) literally moved men to action, catalyzing life choices by literary example. They captured the imagination of not only his generation but the next. In his memoirs Ivan Turgenev (1818-83) insisted that Bestuzhev-Marlinsky's heroes were to be met everywhere in society, young men conversing in "marlinisms," a special metaphoric and flamboyant language

coined from Bestuzhev's pen name Marlinsky to describe the style he innovated in Russian letters. According to Turgenev, these "marlinist" poseurs appeared haughty and insolent, alternately pulling sorrowful and belligerent faces, and lived their short days and long nights, "with storms in their souls and fire in their blood."[1] He himself was moved to youthful excess by Bestuzhev-Marlinsky's fiction and in a letter to Leo Tolstoy (1828-1910) confessed that he would "kiss Marlinsky's name on journal covers."[2] Tolstoy went even further, journeying south from Great Russia to the Caucasus, a land Bestuzhev-Marlinsky had popularized in his stories, in quest of the archetypal romantic hero within.

Bestuzhev-Marlinsky was arguably the most advanced writer of prose in the 1820s and demonstrably the most popular writer in Russia in the 1830s. He was an individual in whom Russian culture was condensed with incredible richness. We need only survey his life, examine his work, and review his mysterious death to see that he represents the challenges and dilemmas of his time and bears dramatic witness to the desires and imperfections of mankind.

It is my purpose to restore him to cultural history in a manner that befits his accomplishments. So frequently is his importance attested in the documents of the great Russian writers and in the life patterns of the forgotten readers of his time that his contribution to that culture deserves an accounting. An assessment of his legacy must also address the reasons for his having been neglected since then, for only when this issue is put in historical perspective is an objective picture of his place in Russian romanticism possible.

In the second decade of the nineteenth century, Bestuzhev-Marlinsky dedicated himself to a new and radical behavioral model only recently acquired from the West, specifically from Lord Byron (1788-1824), whose works were known to the Russian public in French and Russian translations. A repository of ambiguity, social masks, intentional inconsistency, and ironic play with an unsuspecting audience, Byronism in Russia accounts for some of Bestuzhev-Marlinsky's historic inaccessibility. When Bestuzhev-Marlinsky donned a Byronic mask, Russian society was alternately horrified and delighted. There was, however, an important difference between Byron's reception in the West and the Byronic character's apprehension in Russian culture. Byron in his time represented an enigma to his audience; he challenged conventional social and literary norms in a manner that would not submit to simplistic interpretation. Russian Byronism, however, was perceived against the background of the cultural model already supplied from England. Consequently, Bestuzhev-Marlinsky was seen as a comprehensible phenomenon. His many stories and tales of adventure were treated as clues to his substantive identity. His literary heroes were so thoroughly fused with the persona he projected in everyday life, that for the Russian readers from 1820 to 1850 there was no enigmatic self lurking behind a mask; Bestuzhev-Marlinsky's literary identity, social persona, and authentic self were assumed to be one and the same.

Because of his readers' assumptions, Bestuzhev-Marlinsky found it possible to encode more than literary texts; he created stories of himself in daily life to meet the expectations created by those texts. In effect, he wrote both his fiction and his life. In addition to his literary efforts (which won the Grand Dowager's favor in the 1820s), he was a military officer whose exemplary behavior promised to bring him into the service of Tsar Alexander I (1801-25). But after his participation in the first Russian revolution, the Decembrist Revolt of 1825, which challenged the succession of Nicholas I (1825-55) to the throne, Bestuzhev-Marlinsky was stripped of his noble status and exiled first to Siberia and then to the Caucasus. Temporarily forgotten by his public, his fate was kept secret until his death in 1837 when it was announced that the exiled Alexander Alexandrovich Bestuzhev had authored many popular tales of the 1830s under the pseudonym Marlinsky. His works were immediately published in a multivolume set that sold out within weeks of its issue. His political activism became a model for later generations of revolutionaries, and his martyrdom in exile inspired legends about him after he disappeared. Successive generations of readers have assumed that the mask was the man and interpreted Bestuzhev-Marlinsky's persona as an authentic representation of his self.

The memoirist P. S. Shchukin, who visited Bestuzhev-Marlinsky when he was living in exile in the far north of Siberia, confessed, "I gazed upon him with altogether different eyes [than earlier in my life]. I virtually reread his stories [while listening to what he had to say] and I attempted to catch in his character features of the heroes he had introduced on the stage [of his art]."[3] Society and the individual colluded to form an identity by reinforcing the generation and reception of the persona. The authorial projection in life as well as in letters coupled with public response (which confirmed the projection in every detail) to structure the unique nature of aesthetics in early-nineteenth-century Russia.

Nicholas Karamzin (1766-1826) is the acknowledged father of the sentimental tale in Russian letters. His first publications, appearing in print before Bestuzhev-Marlinsky was born, projected a narrator, hero, and authorial persona in confluence with one another. It was Karamzin's prose that most influenced Bestuzhev-Marlinsky's development of a personal voice three decades later. To Karamzin's prose model must be added those of Vasily Zhukovsky (1782-1856) and Konstantin

Batyushkov (1787-1855). Although meager in their production of fiction, together with Karamzin they established the norm for sentimental prose at the turn of the century. Vasily Narezhny (1780-1825), who preceded Bestuzhev-Marlinsky as well, represented an opposite pole. Working from the tradition of the didactic adventure novel of the eighteenth century, Narezhny enlivened his *Gil Blas* imitations with a coarse, vernacular Russian that contrasted with the sensitivity and musicality of the Karamzin school's salon language. By the 1820s, however, the voices of these initiators of a modern prose fiction in Russia had, for the most part, fallen silent. Karamzin turned from belles lettres in order to complete his *History of the Russian State* (*Istoriia Gosudarstva Rossiiskogo,* 1818); Batyushkov was overcome by mental illness, which lasted until his death; Zhukovsky continued to make only a minor contribution to prose fiction.

Bestuzhev-Marlinsky was one of a small group of prose writers in the early 1820s. He is acknowledged to be the prime bearer of the Karamzinian tradition and at the same time to have advanced Russian prose beyond the limitations imposed on it by that tradition. Orest Somov (1783-1833), Fyodor Glinka (1786-1880), Nicholas Grech (1800-1858), and Nicholas Bestuzhev (1791-1855) all made contributions of a disparate kind to the travelogue, which revitalized the cloying sentimentalist prose. Unlike Bestuzhev-Marlinsky's, Somov's prose inclined toward the metonymic rather than the metaphoric. Glinka's military accounts developed the literary language in the direction of a virile and direct form of address, but his historical tales maintained the Karamzinian affective style. Grech entertained a matter-of-fact discourse in his narrator, and his style was metonymic. Bestuzhev-Marlinsky's brother Nicholas opened the literary language to naval vocabulary and used an analytic style more representative of eighteenth-century rationalism than nineteenth-century romanticism.

In romantic excess, Bestuzhev-Marlinsky surpassed all of his contemporaries. His prose is saturated with metaphors, flights of fancy, and the "marlinism" (the peculiar and witty style of his characters' and narrators' speech). It distinguishes itself from that of his peers in the early 1820s by its adherence to the theatricality of the Byronic pose and the techniques of *L'École frenetique* associated with early Victor Hugo. Almost single-handedly Bestuzhev-Marlinsky revived the historical tale, a genre which had lost its efficacy through the sentimentalist restrictions placed upon it. He reinvigorated it through his ultraromantic style, the symmetry of his period, a dashing bravado in relation to the utterance, and a reliance on new models of discourse encountered in French and English literature. Although Wilhelm Küchelbecker's (1797-1846) characters and plots echo many of Bestuzhev-Marlinsky's Livonian tales, his style has an ease and a sense of effortlessness that Bestuzhev-Marlinsky rarely achieved. Bestuzhev-Marlinsky's goals were entirely different. Where his contemporaries used restraint and natural expression to form their discourse, Bestuzhev-Marlinsky inclined toward the extreme, the improbable, and the self-aggrandizing.

The marlinism in Bestuzhev-Marlinsky's prose (as in his criticism and letters) is distinguished by several stylistic features, all of which he activated in art and in life. Many derive from the sentimentalist's stylistic arsenal: sound repetition, alliteration, assonance, symmetry, isocolon, anaphora, epithet inversion, rhythm, and parallel construction. These techniques occur as linear phenomena, elaborated in time as the syntagma moves forward, as any given utterance develops from beginning to end (whether edited or not). The syntagma is not developed out of a dialogic relationship to what has been uttered, by questioning what has been committed to the page. Rather the initial word or words condition what follows, structuring a rhythmic sound repetition based on the initial segment of the utterance. To these sentimentalist techniques Bestuzhev added other linear features: ellipsis, aphoristic sententiousness, unmotivated shifts (for example, from high to low speech), verb strings, and three constantly recurring rhetorical devices—paregmenon, polyptoton, and antithesis.

In exile Bestuzhev-Marlinsky was separated from the literary milieu, which was expanding in every conceivable direction: new authors, genres, and language. The late 1820s brought a variety of new story types, including the supernatural tale (and its parody), the frame tale (à la Washington Irving), the physiological sketch, the society tale, story cycles, the picaresque novel, the tale of merchant life, and the historical novel. Authors developed interests in merchants and peasants and sprinkled (or saturated) their narratives with phrases of the lower classes: proverbs, idioms, folk locutions, as well as the vernacular. The expansion of the literary language brought about by Mikhail Pogodin (1800-1875), Nicholas Polevoy (1796-1846), Faddei Bulgarin (1789-1859), Alexei Perovsky-Pogorelsky (1787-1836), Mikhail Zagoskin (1790-1852), and Orest Somov surely caused Bestuzhev-Marlinsky to consider what future contribution he might make to the development of Russian prose.

When Bestuzhev-Marlinsky entered the prose arena for a second time (under the pseudonym Marlinsky), he quickly established his place among writers, who included people familiar to him from the 1820s like Vladimir Odoyevsky (1803-69) or his friend Alexander Pushkin (1799-1837), but new writers as well: Nikolai Gogol (1809-52), Ivan Lazhechnikov (1792-1869), Nicholas Pavlov (1803-64), Osip Senkovsky (1800-1858), Alexander Veltman (1800-1870). These authors won the interest of a growing readership through a variety of styles peculiar to each. Gogol's innovations hardly require mention here except to say he represented the greatest challenge to Bestuzhev-Marlinsky's preeminence. Lazhechnikov and Zagoskin engaged in a genre that remained beyond Bestuzhev's grasp—the historical novel. For their roughly hewn achievement they were duly rewarded by critical acclaim and wide popularity. Odoyevsky's philosophical prose also remained beyond Bestuzhev-Marlinsky; his bent toward German idealism left Bestuzhev-Marlinsky as cold and uncomprehending as when he read *Faust.* Veltman and Senkovsky, however, afforded Bestuzhev-Marlinsky hours of enjoyment, but he was quick to note their deficiencies, which, interestingly, he shared—a penchant for long periods, effusiveness, and an unabated irony and wittiness that sometimes submerges the substance of the narrative.

As the competition increased, Bestuzhev-Marlinsky persisted in his well-developed style of the 1820s. Although the consistency eventually marked him as an easy target for the next generation of writers, his extreme romantic style, narrators, characters, plots, and exotic settings made him the author of the decade, Gogol notwithstanding. The marlinism is the most salient element that binds his work together, from literary criticism to personal letters, and from anecdote to historical fiction. Early-nineteenth-century Russian poets sought a special stamp by which even their unsigned work could be recognized. Bestuzhev's was the marlinism, his trademark in fiction and in society. He prepared his audience to read his literary texts and his life-text as one and the same, thereby fulfilling the period's expectation that art and life are most meaningful when they coincide. Bestuzhev-Marlinsky's witty narrators were taken for the author himself. The confusion of Bestuzhev's personality with his Marlinsky persona began very early in his career.

Bestuzhev-Marlinsky's writings also became a textbook from which students learned how to view reality. A. L. Zisserman, who participated in the Caucasian wars and distinguished himself there, published his memoirs in the 1870s in which he attests to the deep penetration of the literary model into his personal life. Drawing a direct line between his reading of Bestuzhev-Marlinsky's Caucasian tales and his own life, Zisserman bears witness to the psychological impact of Bestuzhev-Marlinsky's model:

> When I was seventeen and yet living in the provinces I chanced to read some of Marlinsky's stories for the first time. I cannot begin to describe with what enthusiasm I praised his ***Ammalat-bek, Mulla Nur,*** and sundry sketches of the Caucasus. Suffice it to say that this reading gave birth in me to the thought that I should give everything up and fly to the Caucasus, to that enchanted land, with its awesome natural surroundings, its warrior inhabitants, marvelous women, poetic sky,

high mountains eternally covered in snow, and other such charms which entirely entranced the imagination of a seventeen-year-old mind, not to mention of a child who since birth had shown an inclination toward experiences and emotions very much stronger than the usual schoolboy fancies.[4]

Zisserman's remarks depict traditional romantic literary values, particularly self-absorption to the extent of needing to mythologize the self in quasi-hagiographical terms. It took a major turn in Russian culture to extract Russian youth and Russian letters from Bestuzhev-Marlinsky's compelling grip.

By the 1830s Russian criticism had begun to move away from the dynamic and flamboyant conception of self and the world. Since Bestuzhev-Marlinsky was the most popular writer of fiction at the time, it was quite natural that he should come under attack. Vissarion Belinsky (1811-48) represented the first prominent voice advancing a new relationship between literature and reality. He thought literature was meant to serve the public by educating its audience about social, economic, and political life and to serve reality by depicting it adequately. Belinsky opposed the Bestuzhevan tendency to replace reality with fantasy and to advocate personal desire over social good. For him Bestuzhev-Marlinsky's example constituted an outworn and even dangerous phenomenon in Russian cultural history. Aiming his barbs directly, Belinsky challenged Russia's readership in 1834: "We have very few authors who have written as much as Mr. Marlinsky, but this abundance springs not from the largess of talent, not from a surplus of [authentic] creative energy, but from habit, simply from doing the same thing over and over again. . . . He has talent, but not a great talent, for it is weakened by his eternal compulsion to be witty."[5] No one, perhaps, more than Bestuzhev realized his limitations as a writer, but unlike Belinsky, he appreciated his own real accomplishments: "I am far from being an egotist, but just as far from self-abasement. I know my worth in the world of Russian letters, even though I have attained my value by chance, through the lack of prose writers in contemporary literature. Thus, I still feel that I have services to perform for our native language."[6] This balanced view became all the more rare with each passing decade of the nineteenth century.

At this historical juncture, with the rise of the age of realism, both Bestuzhev-Marlinsky's life and fiction began to be measured by criteria that did not belong to his time. What had once elicited enthusiastic responses from young Turgenev and Tolstoy was now seen as excess. Bestuzhev-Marlinsky's fiction was dismissed outright because it did not hold to a new set of values. In the middle of the nineteenth century Tolstoy reflected Belinsky's reorientation when he concluded that romantic fiction clouded the minds of naive readers (as he had

been in his youth) and created expectations in life that could not be fulfilled. To assert his own definition of reality, in his early fiction Tolstoy assailed Bestuzhev-Marlinsky's prose. If Bestuzhev-Marlinsky presumed that art produces as well as reproduces reality, Tolstoy promulgated the contrary notion, that life informs fiction. Tolstoy satirized Bestuzhev-Marlinsky's dual texts—both the fiction that proffered its audience models for daily life and the author himself, whose biography reinforced the fiction.

In "The Raid" ("Nabeg," 1853) Tolstoy's narrator recreates the Bestuzhev-Marlinsky code of behavior only to expose its artificiality:

> A couple of hundred yards ahead of the infantry rode some Tatar horsemen. With them, riding on a large white horse and dressed in Caucasian costume, was a tall, handsome officer. Throughout the regiment he had a reputation for reckless courage and for not hesitating to tell anyone what he thought of him. His soft, black Oriental boots were trimmed with gold braid as was his black tunic under which he wore a yellow silk Circassian shirt. The tall sheepskin hat on his head was pushed back carelessly. A powder flask and a pistol were fastened to silver straps across his chest and back. Another pistol and a silver-mounted dagger hung from his belt next to a saber in a red leather sheath. A rifle in a black holster was slung over his shoulder. From his dress, his style of riding, all his movements, it was obvious that he wanted to look like a Tatar. He was even saying something to the Tatars in a language I couldn't understand. But then, judging by the bewildered, amused looks they exchanged with one another, I guessed they couldn't understand him either.
>
> He was one of those dashing, wild young officers who attempt to model themselves on the heroes of Lermontov and Marlinsky. These officers see the Caucasus only through the prism of romance, and in everything they are guided solely by the instincts and tastes of their models.[7]

Tolstoy's assault on the Bestuzhev-Marlinsky canon reflected a broad cultural movement in the second half of the nineteenth century to reassess romantic art. Both his and Belinsky's renderings of Bestuzhev-Marlinsky, however, represent the mechanism by which cultural systems evolve, not the objectivity of a culture to describe itself.

Since the end of the nineteenth century the rejection of Bestuzhev-Marlinsky's persona and fiction has been balanced by critics seeking to reestablish his contribution. Nevertheless, these critics persist in the notion that the persona was the man. Turn-of-the-century criticism sought the roots of Bestuzhev-Marlinsky's fiction in the European romantic tradition. N. Kozmin's *Sketches on the History of Russian Romanticism* (*Ocherki iz istorii romantizma,* 1903), A. N. Pypin's *History of Russian Literature* (*Istoriia russkoi literatury,* 1903), and I. I. Zamotin's *Romanticism of the 1820s in Russian Litera-*

ture (*Romantizm dvadtsatykh godov XIX stoletiia v russkoi literature,* 1911) made important contributions to our appreciation of the foreign influences on Bestuzhev's work, for example, Irving, Hoffman, Radcliffe, Scott, and Byron. These same critics, however, cite the words of Bestuzhev-Marlinsky's protagonists as representative of the author's own utterances about himself. In their writings it is not unusual to find a passage from a Bestuzhev-Marlinsky story juxtaposed with a passage from one of his personal letters. If there is reason to make such a reading (and there surely is), it does not lie in the simplistic linkage of Bestuzhev's mask with his personality. The two must be differentiated.

In response to this approach, Soviet criticism inclined in two general directions, one reacting strongly to the deficiencies of the earlier tradition and the other honing and reshaping it. Russian Formalist critics disconnected life from letters and proceeded to examine Bestuzhev's art as a discrete system. In an article titled "The Early Marlinsky" ("Rannii Marlinskii," 1920s), N. Kovarsky, a young student of Yury Tynianov and Boris Eikhenbaum, focused on the development of Bestuzhev-Marlinsky's style and on the evolution of the historical genre in his hands. Yet the linkage of literature to life that so dominated the early nineteenth century was viewed as tangential, rather than integral to the text, its generation, and its reception. The Formalist approach could neither account for Bestuzhev-Marlinsky's popularity nor measure his cultural significance save in the narrowest terms.

For historical and political reasons, the Formalist approach to Bestuzhev-Marlinsky's work ceased soon after it was initiated and was replaced by a branch of Soviet criticism that foregrounded Bestuzhev-Marlinsky, rather than his work. The voices of his heroes were again made to speak for the author, but this time with a significant change. These critics focused on the ideological content of the protagonists' and narrators' tirades and monologues. In Soviet criticism of this type we learn of Bestuzhev's attitude toward the people, revolution, and bourgeois society. A. G. Tseitlin's *Russian Literature of the First Half of the Nineteenth Century (Russkaia literatura pervoi poloviny XIX veka,* 1940) and B. S. Meilakh's "The Literary and Aesthetic Program of the Decembrists" ("Literaturnoesteticheskaia programma dekabristov," 1958) are two of a very large group of monographs and essays that used this approach. This form of ideological criticism culminated in S. Golubov's *Bestuzhev-Marlinsky (Bestuzhev-Marlinskii,* 1960), a fictional biography that made no attempt to distinguish the author from his fiction or his literary persona, and A. P. Sharupich's two book-length studies of Bestuzhev-Marlinsky's fiction. The first, *The Decembrist Alexander Bestuzhev: Questions of Worldview and Creativity (Dekabrist Bestuzhev-Marlinskii: Voprosy mirovozzreniia i tvorchestva,* 1962),

attempts to consider Bestuzhev-Marlinsky's prose at a philosophical level, which it hardly contains, and the second, *Alexander Bestuzhev's Romanticism (Romantizm Aleksandra Bestuzheva,* 1964), treats the quintessential aspects of Bestuzhev-Marlinsky's extreme form of romanticism.

S. G. Isakov, writing from Tartu in the 1960s, presented a historical approach to Bestuzhev's art as it addressed Livonia and the Baltic region. His studies focus on the historical veracity of Bestuzhev-Marlinsky's work, its political orientation toward Decembrist themes, and the author's importance to early-nineteenth-century prose development. The central issue of Bestuzhev-Marlinsky as simultaneously literary, political, and social phenomenon is considered tangential, which is surprising given the early theoretical formulations of the Tartu school of semioticians. Nevertheless, Isakov's studies encapsulate concisely Bestuzhev-Marlinsky's contribution to historical prose of the early 1820s. More characteristic of the Tartu school in the 1960s, Kh. D. Leyemets's dissertation on Russian romantic prose of the 1820s and 1830s offers a more thorough examination of the formal attributes of Bestuzhev-Marlinsky's prose. Leyemets's article, "Toward the Question of the Semantic Structure of the Metaphoric Epithet in Russian Prose at the Beginning of the Nineteenth Century (on the basis of Marlinsky's Works)" ("K voprosu o semanticheskoi strukture metaforicheskogo epiteta v russkoi proze nachala XIX v. [na materiale proizvedenii A. Marlinskogo]," 1971), suggests how strongly the Formalist school continued to operate in some corners of the Soviet Union.

More recent Soviet scholarship also turned to a formal examination of Bestuzhev-Marlinsky's texts. E. M. Pulkhritudova in her "Literary Theory in Decembrist Romanticism in the 1830s" ("Literaturnaia teoriia dekabristskogo romantizma v 30-e gody XIX veka," 1968) respects the difference between aesthetic and biographical information and attempts to survey Bestuzhev-Marlinsky's development as a writer from the 1820s to the 1830s. She brings a thematic focus to her work and touches on topics of universal appeal, such as Bestuzhev-Marlinsky's understanding of man. Kanunova's *Aesthetics of the Russian Romantic Tale (A. A. Bestuzhev-Marlinsky and the Romantic Literati of the 1820s and 1830s) (Estetika russkoi romanticheskoi povesti A. A. Bestuzhev-Marlinskii i romantiki-belletristy 20-30-kh godov XIX v.,* 1973) advances Pulkhritudova's work significantly. Her study is psychological and treats the theme of personal identity in Bestuzhev-Marlinsky's fiction. Her scrutiny of his rough drafts allows us to observe Bestuzhev-Marlinsky's writing process and his editing practices.

Bestuzhev-Marlinsky criticism has also brought national questions to the fore, spawning a series of works devoted in part or wholly to Bestuzhev-Marlinsky's presentation of Siberia and the Caucasus in his fiction. A. V. Popov's *The Decembrist Writers in the Caucasus* (*Dekabristy-Literatory na Kavkaze,* 1963), based on an earlier study, *Russian Writers in the Caucasus* (*Russkie pisateli na Kavkaze,* 1949), treats Bestuzhev-Marlinsky's contribution to Russian society's understanding of the Caucasus from an ethnographic perspective. Similarly, V. Shaduri's *Decembrist Literature and Georgian Society* (*Dekabristskaia literatura i gruzinskaia obshchestvennost',* 1958) describes the authenticity with which Bestuzhev-Marlinsky presented Georgian culture to the Russian reading public in the 1830s. R. Yu. Yusufov's *Dagestan and Russian Literature at the End of the Eighteenth and First Half of the Nineteenth Centuries* (*Dagestanskaia i russkaia literatura kontsa XVIII i pervoi poloviny XIX vv.,* 1964) includes a chapter on Bestuzhev-Marlinsky's **"Dagestan Theme."** Yu. S. Postnov's *Siberia in Decembrist Poetry* (*Sibir'v poezii dekabristov,* 1976) picks up on the regional theme, too, but since Bestuzhev-Marlinsky's creativity inclined more toward prose genres, the chapter on his Siberian poetry is necessarily scanty. All of these studies have their beginnings in the brief study of Bestuzhev-Marlinsky in Siberia by G. V. Prokhorov. His "A. A. Bestuzhev in Yakutsk" ("A. A. Bestuzhev v Iakutske," 1926) and V. Vasil'ev's "The Decembrist A. A. Bestuzhev-Marlinsky as a Writer and Ethnographer" ("Dekabrist A. A. Bestuzhev-Marlinskii kak pisatel'-etnograf," 1926) formed the basis for extracting historical and ethnographic information from Bestuzhev-Marlinsky's fiction and letters. Indeed, since that time virtually every decade has produced a study along these lines, including V. Vasil'ev's own *Bestuzhev-Marlinsky in the Caucasus* (*Bestuzhev-Marlinskii na Kavkaze,* 1939). Ismorphic to the reading of Bestuzhev's persona as the man, these critical studies extract what is considered fact from his fiction.

Outside the Soviet Union scholarly interest in Bestuzhev-Marlinsky has been limited. Lauren Leighton's *Alexander Bestuzhev-Marlinsky* is the second complete survey in the West, the only one in English. It was preceded by H. V. Chmielewski's book-length study, *Alexander Bestuzhev-Marlinsky* (*Aleksandr Bestuzhev-Marlinskii,* 1966); Janusz Henzel's comprehensive study of Bestuzhev-Marlinsky's early prose fiction, *The Prose of Alexander Bestuzhev-Marlinsky in the Petersburg Period* (*Proza Aleksandra Biestużewa-Marlinskiego w okresie Petersburgskim,* 1967); and Dominique Barlesi's "The Function and Language of the Dramatis Personae of Bestuzhev-Marlinsky's Historical Fiction" ("Fonction et Langue de Personnages dans les Nouvelles Historiques de Bestuzev-Marlinskij," 1973), which takes a structuralist approach to character types in the fiction. Leighton's concise introduction to Bestuzhev-Marlinsky's life, literary criticism (in which the study excels), tales, and poems presents an overview of Bestuzhev-Marlinsky criticism since 1834 and steers an

objective scholarly course through the myriad problems attending Bestuzhev-Marlinsky research. While thoroughly cataloguing Bestuzhev-Marlinsky's contribution to the early nineteenth century, like Chmielewski and Henzel, Leighton does not penetrate the Byronic guise under which all the author's writings are subsumed.

In effect, Bestuzhev-Marlinsky has slipped through all the critical nets thrown into his waters. Kanunova's attentiveness to the question of personal identity in Bestuzhev-Marlinsky's fiction comes close to broaching the topic from as fresh a perspective as has been written since N. Kotliarevsky's *The Decembrists Prince A. I. Odoyevsky and A. A. Bestuzhev-Marlinsky: Their Life and Literary Activity* (*Dekabristy Kn. A. I. Odoevskii i A. A. Bestuzhev-Marlinskii: ikh zhizn' i literaturnaia deiatel' nost',* 1907). Kotliarevsky's penchant to disbelieve the Bestuzhev-Marlinsky persona is as often comic as it is instructive, but his excessive disdain for romantic speech and gesture creates an imbalance in his study, which militates against an objective understanding of Bestuzhev-Marlinsky's contribution. Kotliarevsky, however, can be credited with suggesting covertly that Bestuzhev is not Marlinsky, an idea that I have taken as the thesis of this book. Kanunova must be given credit, too, for raising the theme of identity in a compelling manner that revisits Kotliarevsky's point, albeit from a different perspective.

A psychological portrait must in some manner accommodate the distinction between the man and the dashing, heroic idea of himself he presented to the public. Since critics, like Bestuzhev-Marlinsky's contemporaries, have read his fiction as a coded diary and have viewed his behavior and speech in everyday life as a guide to his literature, the question is not whether Bestuzhev-Marlinsky resembled his heroes, but how he created this effect. It is quite remarkable that Bestuzhev-Marlinsky has managed to convince his readership for over a century that his art represents his person. But we must now ask ourselves what the equation of biography and literature meant both in his life and in his writing. If we are to address them so that both Bestuzhev-Marlinsky and his art might be viewed clearly, a precise idea of the internal conflicts the author experienced must first be extracted from his texts and developed into a coherent picture of the man who fostered such a compelling persona. Only then may we begin to appreciate why he went about convincing himself and the world that he was a living example of what he wrote.

Guided by contemporary literary theory, we may begin to unravel the texts Bestuzhev-Marlinsky created—those printed onto the page, those encoded into his life, and the critical literature about him, which mixes the two together. From this perspective it is possible to view Bestuzhev's equation of self to art as a form of communication in which each component is assigned a distinct value and a discrete function. Such an approach recommends itself by allowing us to separate Bestuzhev-Marlinsky's personality from his persona.

As we examine Bestuzhev-Marlinsky's many words, both fictional and otherwise, study the accounts memoirists and diarists have left that depict him, peruse government documents of the Decembrist Revolt, scrutinize the record of his interrogation, and survey letters and recollections of members of his family, a dialogue between Bestuzhev's heroic persona and his private personality emerges. We shall refer to the authentic self as "Bestuzhev," and to the heroic persona he projected in daily life and in fiction as "Marlinsky." The separation of Bestuzhev from Marlinsky is of utmost importance to an objective rendering both of his contribution to Russian culture and of his humanity.

For Bestuzhev the pseudonym Marlinsky operated first as a disguise, then as a secret literary code, and finally as a container into which he attempted to pour his whole identity. Bestuzhev originally had taken the name Marlinsky in 1817 when he was stationed near Peterhof, the tsar's summer palace, at Marli. By 1819 he was using the name to mask his well-known identity and biases from his opponents in the literary polemics of the day. He rarely used it, but it attests very early in his career to a recourse to disguise, albeit superficial. Later, in exile, Bestuzhev was allowed to publish only under the condition that he assume a pen name. Again he selected Marlinsky, this time as a code, the import of which was to disclose his identity to, not hide his identity from, a public that had lost contact with him. Throughout his life, the heroic persona, which was so compelling to him for the problems it ostensibly solved, constituted a disguise and a code that allowed him alternately to conceal and reveal himself to the world about him. In exile the romantic persona Bestuzhev projected in his fiction and nonfictional writings took on the exclusive name Marlinsky. "Marlinsky," as heroic self-idea, became the repository of the identity Bestuzhev conceived for himself and propagated at every turn in life and in letters.

Unlike the persona, an authentic personality represents something immanent, it is the whole human being seeking to find him or herself in the process of representing that self in the material world. Its actual representation, deceptive or true, is inevitably a partial presentation of self, for it is virtually impossible to be everything one is at all times in every gesture, word, act, and thought. Human beings are reduced by sheer materiality to personae. Bestuzhev, from this perspective, is no different from anyone else. During Bestuzhev's early adult years, however, the persona took on the distinct forms that create differences between people.

The persona, acquired from the period's confluence of life and art, and with Bestuzhev's psychologically profound dedication toward its heroic manifestations, seemed to be an adequate means for fully expressing his personality. The dynamic changes wrought in the years immediately following the Napoleonic wars forged new ideas of identity that influenced Bestuzhev directly. The epoch's concern with the search for identity appealed to young minds in their quest for a unique sense of self. The heroic persona supplied an aestheticized form of personality as fluid and vital as the times in which Bestuzhev came to maturity. The idea of self in the early 1820s proved adequate to reality.

The Decembrist Revolt, the interrogation, and the years of exile severely challenged the persona's integrity. It had to be either dismissed out of hand or altered to permit a wider range of human characteristics and to suit new circumstances. Introspection and analytic skill were required to render the persona anew, skills that Bestuzhev did not possess, a point he actively argued with his brother Nicholas. Consequently, the next stage in the development of Bestuzhev's persona, for dismissing it was out of the question, represented an imaginative continuation of the basic heroic outline, but with distinct Byronic characteristics affixed to it—weariness of life; impatience with human imperfections; a keen sense of one's superiority and consequent isolation from the herd; a consciousness of life's transience; a combative, confident and assertive grasp of one's right to define reality, and with it a glorification of the ego and its authority in such matters; and the idea of death as the consummate act of the heroic will. Bestuzhev wove these features into his view of himself and the world and encoded them onto the pages of his fiction.

Having reached this stage in the evolution of the romantic persona, Bestuzhev began to interpret the whole of world history and the evolution of art in similar terms—as the product of the romantic spirit. For example, in his defense of his publisher Nicholas Polevoy's novel, *The Oath on the Tomb of the Lord* (*Kliatva pri grobe gospodnem*), Bestuzhev asserted that the history of Western literature beginning with the early Christians is romantic. This is a grandiose claim that has been examined from two distinct perspectives. First, it reproduces arguments made in the West that advanced romanticism as a complete philosophical system. Bestuzhev was hardly a theoretician, for he lacked the essential skills by which discursive logic posits its thesis and argues its validity. Consequently, his turn toward philosophy and history must be explained from another perspective. This raises the second point: Bestuzhev's attempt to comprehend both history and contemporary life and art have been attributed to the Marlinsky persona and its inclination to aggrandize itself through dramatic utterance and bold gestures, in this instance, the positing of extreme propositions. But this interpretation treats Bestuzhev's motivation at the surface level. A third possibility incorporates the utterances of the persona and simultaneously the speaker's motivation for making them. More specifically, in viewing Bestuzhev's self-serving and grandiose claims for romanticism as an expression of personal desire and human need, we obtain a view of the man separate from his persona.

Bestuzhev's humanistic portrait has at its base a most compelling theme. Just as his whole personality has eluded capture in the critical literature, he, too, may have been unaware of his complete self. Studying his words and behavior for inconsistencies, for structural clues into the workings of his mind, and for coherent (but unconsciously encoded) symbolic information, we may extract from the fiction and the biography the outline of a thoroughly human identity that is at once heroic and common, unique and average, daring and fearful. With Bestuzhev's unwitting aid we are guided into the privacy of an authentic personality, into the enigmatic life of an elusive self he apparently could neither admit to nor totally suppress in his creations. From this portrait it is but one step to an understanding of Belinsky's, Tolstoy's, and later generations' apprehension of the man, and then to a rectification of his place in Russian culture.

In this study I begin with a description of Bestuzhev's early life, his family, and his initial endeavors to invent himself à la Byron. I pay particular attention to the quality of his mind and his reading habits. I discuss romanticism, as it stormed Russia in the second decade of the nineteenth century, with a focus on Bestuzhev's earliest attempts at poetry, his more successful literary criticism, and his fiction. I examine these genres to determine the psychological force that motivated him to turn toward an extreme representation of romanticism in letters and in life. I discuss in detail Bestuzhev's part in the Decembrist Revolt and the unconscious recesses of his psyche brought forward by it. His behavior during the interrogation and afterward represents one of the first opportunities by which we may scrutinize the effectiveness with which his social persona ("Marlinsky") operated in reality. I examine Bestuzhev's exile to Yakutsk in northern Siberia, where his self-idea was challenged severely, and then to the Caucasus where he experienced two divergent movements: personal disintegration and simultaneously a deeper projection of his self-idea in society. It was his Caucasus fiction that conditioned generations of readers either to reject his fiction outright or to accept him and his art as manifestations of Byronism. I conclude my analysis by discussing Bestuzhev's theatrical death and the impact it made on his reception.

Bestuzhev-Marlinsky's place in Russian cultural history is advanced in this study, but in the final analysis Bestuzhev's humanity motivates it. In these chapters I attempt to introduce a new Bestuzhev, to describe the world in which he lived, to elucidate the norms by which he wrote and acted, and to illuminate how he influenced the aestheticization of his rise and fall in Russian culture. In the vast web that entangles life and letters, Bestuzhev's biography and art are exemplary if only because they make such wonderful witness to the chance discoveries, revelations, joys, sorrows, triumphs, and utterly dismal failures that, despite our loftiest intentions, make up our lives. He strove with all his talent and enthusiasm to overcome the frailties and imperfections of being human. Bestuzhev's dilemma—the endless search for a unified self and persona—belongs to us all.

Notes

1. "Stuk . . . stuk . . . stuk," in *Polnoe sobranie sochinenii i pisem v 30 tomakh* (Moscow, 1978), 8:228. The line "with storms in their souls" is taken from Bestuzhev's tale, "Lieutenant Belozor" (1831). Turgenev attests that in the 1830s Bestuzhev was more popular than even Pushkin.

2. *Perepiska I. S. Turgeneva,* ed. K. I. Tiun'kin (Moscow, 1980), 2:118.

3. "A. Bestuzhev-Marlinskii v Iakutske," in *Pisateli-dekabristy v vospominaniiakh sovremennikov,* ed. V. Vatsuro et al. (Moscow, 1980), 2:140-47.

4. "Otryvki iz moikh vospominanii," *Russkii vestnik* 5 (1876): 52.

5. *Polnoe sobranie sochinenii* (Moscow, 1953), 1:84-85.

6. "Pis'ma Aleksandra Aleksandrovicha Bestuzheva k N. A. i K. A. Polevym, pisannye v 1831-1837 godakh," *Russkii vestnik* 3 (1861): 323.

7. "The Raid," in *The Cossacks and the Raid,* trans. Andrew MacAndrew (New York, 1961), 190-91.

Irina Reyfman (essay date 1998)

SOURCE: Reyfman, Irina. "Alexander Bestuzhev-Marlinsky: *Bretteur* and Apologist of the Duel." In *Russian Subjects: Empire, Nation, and the Culture of the Golden Age,* edited by Monika Greenleaf and Stephen Moeller-Sally, pp. 243-57. Evanston: Northwestern University Press, 1998.

[*In the following essay, Reyfman discusses Bestuzhev's many representations of dueling within his fiction, maintaining that the author was especially sensitive to the political implications of the practice he so passionately defended.*]

Dueling arrived in Russia later and also stopped later than in other European countries except Germany. Furthermore, it was transplanted at the time when complex social changes that shaped post-Petrine Russia were taking place. Most important, the assimilation of dueling paralleled the incorporation of the Russian nobility as a privileged class striving for autonomy from the central government. This was a two-sided process, the initiative coming both from the nobility itself and from Russian monarchs—the latter needing the incorporated nobility as much as the nobility longed to be independent and privileged. Ideally, the monarchs wanted a noble class that would be loyal to the monarchy and the state, serving them willingly and honestly. For these purposes, they promoted the idea of honor as corporate devotion to service. The unintended by-products, however, were the notions of gentleman's honor, which defined not only the corporate but also the personal integrity of a gentleman, and the duel of honor, which regulated relations between individuals within the privileged class without the state's interference.

The duel was an appropriate vehicle for the formation of the independent Russian noble class, because of its inherent capacity to serve as a weapon in the power play between the monarch and the nobility. As François Billacois points out regarding the French situation, "[s]uch was the political meaning of duels: both a violent challenge to the man in power, a refusal to submit to his orders, and a refusal to take power or to participate in his power. The duel is an injunction to the King to be the King and a warning to the monarch to behave as a gentleman."[1] With amendments, Billacois's observation also applies to Russia. However, while the French duel for the most part played a balancing, stabilizing role in the struggle between the monarch and the nobility, in Russia its function as a statement of the nobility's emancipation from and even opposition to the government was far more prominent. Moreover, in going to a duel, a Russian gentleman claimed not only his independence from the state, but also his right to defend his personal integrity—both against his peers and against central authority. In a state that for centuries had tended to curtail the autonomy of the individual, such behavior not only registered the nobility's protest against the monarch's excessive power, but, most important, served as a powerful means of safeguarding personal rights.

Alexander Bestuzhev-Marlinsky belonged to the generation of the most passionate duelists in the history of the Russian duel—the generation that was particularly sensitive both to the duel's political symbolism and to its ability to define and defend personal space. Accordingly, he was an ardent apologist and a prolific portrayer of dueling: in the years between the early 1820s, his literary debut, and 1833, when his interest in literary duels diminished, he portrayed in detail ten conflicts of honor and mentioned scores more. Moreover, he established the framework of dueling discourse in Russian literature. He was the first to discuss the technicalities of dueling, as well as the philosophical and psychological questions pertaining to dueling behavior. He examined the duel's capacity to protect an individual's private space and pointed out its limitations. He was the first to pay attention to the duel's capacity to deprive a person of free will. He also probed the controversial question—later taken up by Dostoevsky—of how to refuse a duel.

As a Romantic writer, Bestuzhev preached what he lived and lived what he preached. His life was rich in adventures and his talents were remarkably versatile. His extraordinary personality fostered rumors and legends both about his life in the Caucasus and especially about his death. The legends portrayed him as a man who enjoyed exceptional success with women, and as a soldier of uncommon courage who, due to his linguistic facility and exotic appearance, could go live among the enemy either as an intelligence agent or a supporter of their cause. After Bestuzhev's death in action in June 1837, he became one of those figures in Russian cultural memory who, despite clear evidence to the contrary, were presumed to have survived death and continued a posthumous existence full of adventures. Posthumously Bestuzhev was credited with both passionate love affairs and amazing military exploits.[2]

Bestuzhev's death came less than six months after Pushkin's, and in the popular consciousness the two writers' tragic ends intertwined. One contemporary mourned the deaths of "three great Alexanders": Alexander I, Alexander Pushkin, and Alexander Bestuzhev-Marlinsky.[3] Bestuzhev himself interpreted Pushkin's death as a foreboding of his own: "Yes, I sense that my own death will also be violent and unusual, that it is already close; I have too much hot blood, blood that boils in my veins, too much for old age to freeze it. I beg for one thing: not to die on a bed of suffering or in a duel" (2:674). Nonetheless, Bestuzhev considered challenging D'Anthès, Pushkin's killer, in order to avenge the death of Russia's national poet: "Let him know (God is my witness, I am not joking) that after our very first meeting one of us will not return alive" (2:674). Bestuzhev's legendary persona thus naturally incorporated the idea of dueling.

One of the legends about Bestuzhev's death (although by far not the most popular) maintained that he was killed in a duel with a jealous husband.[4] While the legend was false, it seemed fitting for a person who not only frequently depicted duels in his fiction but also participated in several actual duels, either as the principal or as a second. Bestuzhev's first duel occurred in the early years of his military career, while he was serving in the Light Dragoon Regiment of the Guards. In his memoir, Bestuzhev's younger brother, Mikhail, tells that Bestuzhev's first duel was over his caricature portraits of fellow officers: "Everyone laughed as they recognized themselves. Only one officer, who was portrayed as a turkey-cock, took offense at the joke, and they fought."[5] In his addendum to the memoir, Mikhail Bestuzhev mentions two other duels that his brother fought: "His second duel was over dancing. The third was with an engineer staff-officer who was with the duke of Württemberg. [M]y brother and the engineer were among his suite and my brother was challenged for some word that had been considered insulting."[6] Bestuzhev's sister, Elena, reports that Alexander shot into the air all three times.[7] In his memoir of their older brother, Nikolai Bestuzhev, Mikhail also mentions Alexander's near duel with Pavel Katenin, whose translation of Racine's *Esther* he had criticized.[8] Finally, Bestuzhev tried but failed to gain a duel with a certain von Dezin, Nikolai's fellow officer, who, as Mikhail reports "became jealous of my brother Alexander, but, instead of getting even with my brother, spoke rudely to our mother as they left church. My brother challenged him to a duel, but he refused."[9] Kondraty Ryleev helped Bestuzhev to teach the reluctant duelist a lesson: "Ryleev met him by chance and, in response to his impertinent talk, lashed his stupid mug with a whip that he had in his hand."[10]

In fact, Ryleev and Bestuzhev often participated in conflicts of honor together. Bestuzhev was Ryleev's second in his February 1824 duel with Prince Konstantin Shakhovskoi, the lover of Ryleev's unmarried half-sister. The conditions of this duel were extremely harsh: there was no barrier (that is, the minimal distance between the opponents was not determined) and the duelists had to shoot simultaneously, at a second's command. The opponents agreed to shoot as many times as it would take to wound seriously or kill one of them. They exchanged two shots at a distance of three paces. By sheer luck both times the bullets hit the opponents' pistols. One of the bullets ricocheted and wounded Ryleev in the heel. The seconds then ended the duel.[11] Significantly, it was Ryleev who had insisted on these brutal conditions, despite the fact that by this time he was a married man and the father of a young daughter. Initially, Shakhovskoi was reluctant to fight. According to Bestuzhev, "[a]t first, [Shakhovskoi] refused, but after Ryleev had spat in his face, he made up his mind."[12] Ryleev, however, resolved to engage his opponent in a deadly duel neither because of a quarrelsome disposition, nor because of brotherly love for his sister. He did it as a matter of principle. He felt it necessary both to hold the insolent aristocrat responsible for his actions toward a young woman without social prominence and to demonstrate that Prince Shakhovskoi and the insignificant nobleman Ryleev were equals under the honor code.

Bestuzhev shared Ryleev's sentiments concerning all noblemen's equality under the honor code, regardless of their social status, wealth, or rank. Like Ryleev, he believed this cause to be important enough to risk his or his friends' lives. Both Bestuzhev and Ryleev participated in another conflict of honor that had distinct social undertones and that shocked contemporaries as a reckless and cruel affair: the 10 September 1825 duel between a young aristocrat, Vladimir Novosil'tsev, an aide-de-camp of Alexander I, and a petty noble, Lieutenant of the Guards Konstantin Chernov, a member of the Decembrist conspiracy. While Ryleev, who was Chernov's cousin, served as his second, Bestuzhev participated informally: Chernov's deathbed letter, explaining the duel's significance, is in Bestuzhev's handwriting and displays the idiosyncrasies of his style.

The duel was fought over Novosil'tsev's treatment of Chernov's sister: he had proposed to her, but backed out because of his mother's objections to a socially inferior daughter-in-law. As in the Ryleev-Shakhovskoi duel, the conditions were severe: the distance was set at eight paces (at one point, Chernov suggested three), and the opponents were to shoot simultaneously. Furthermore, if Konstantin were to be killed, three of his brothers and, finally, his father planned to challenge Novosil'tsev one by one. Both Novosil'tsev and Chernov were mortally wounded and died soon after. Chernov's funeral attracted a large crowd of supporters, which his friends interpreted as the first political rally in Russian history.[13] In this case also, the Chernovs and their friends perceived the duel as a matter of principle. They wanted Novosil'tsev to recognize the Chernovs as his social peers. After the duel, Ryleev praised Chernov precisely for insisting on his equality with Novosil'tsev under the honor code: "[He] showered Chernov's family with enthusiastic praise, claimed that this duel—between a man of the middle class and an aristocrat and aide-de-camp—was a notable phenomenon, and it demonstrated that there were people among the middle class who highly valued their honor and their good name."[14] Chernov's sentiments, as expressed in the letter written by Bestuzhev in his name about the impending duel, were similar: "Let me die, but let him also die, as a lesson to miserable prideful fellows and in order that neither gold, nor noble origin should sneer at innocence and nobility of the soul."[15] According to a contemporary, Bestuzhev greeted the rally at Chernov's funeral as a "democratic celebration."[16]

Bestuzhev thus viewed the duel as a means to formulate the notions of the individual and his rights. He and his contemporaries often behaved as *bretteurs*—a special type of reckless duelist, ready to fight at any provocation—and this behavior represented the Russian nobility's response to the failure of the Russian legal system to guarantee their individual rights. Together with Ryleev and other like-minded people of his generation, Bestuzhev attempted to shape the honor code into an institution protecting the individual in the absence of legal safeguards. They did so as part of their confrontation with the wealthy and powerful wing of the Russian nobility created by and loyal to the central government. Casting themselves as representatives of the Russian "middle" class and champions of the Russian national tradition, the early nineteenth-century *bretteurs* succeeded in formulating their conflict with the new aristocracy in populist terms. Although they were motivated by class interests in their hostility against the aristocrats, in the long run their egalitarian stance helped establish the general idea of innate individual rights.

Bestuzhev and his comrades were especially anxious about the absence of firm guarantees of physical inviolability. This anxiety reflected the fear of physical violation that arose among the Russian nobility at the turn of the eighteenth century, after their hopes for legal protection offered by the 1785 Charter to the Nobility proved futile. This fear powerfully promoted the duel's popularity in Russia.[17] Corporal punishment is an act of violence by a superior (either the state or an individual acting in the name of the state) against a subordinate. Dueling is an act of violence between equals. The nobility used dueling to signal their refusal to accept the state's authority over their bodies. Their campaign was fairly successful. In the mid-eighteenth century, Mavra Shuvalova held a church service every time her husband, Count Petr Shuvalov, came home from a hunting trip with Elizabeth's favorite, A. G. Razumovsky, without having been flogged by the latter. By the turn of the century, however, a commanding officer could no longer strike a subordinate officer without facing an imminent duel.[18] Nonetheless, rumors about noblemen flogged or tortured persisted into the second half of the nineteenth century, reflecting the abiding need for reliable legal guarantees of physical inviolability.

In trying to secure their rights, the Russian *bretteurs* frequently endowed duels with political significance. In extreme cases, the duel was seen to function as a political assassination or a tyrant's execution. Alexander Iakubovich attempted to frame his planned assassination of Alexander I as a duel. A well-known *bretteur,* Iakubovich was sent to serve in the Caucasus for his role as a second in the 1817 duel between Vasily Sheremetev and Alexander Zavadovsky, in which Sheremetev was killed. In 1825, while in St. Petersburg on a leave of absence, Iakubovich offered to assassinate the tsar for the Decembrist leaders. For him personally the proposed regicide was a means to avenge his "unjust transfer" to the Caucasus, which he interpreted as an insult to his honor.[19] Mikhail Lunin's attempts to challenge Grand Duke Constantine, as well as the group of officers' 1822 demand for "satisfaction" from Grand Duke Nicholas for threatening a fellow officer with physical violence, evidence similar reasoning.[20]

Bestuzhev's stories about dueling reflect this historical context and the view that the duel was a means to affirm an individual's rights as well as to promote a political cause. However, his fiction also shows Bestuzhev's awareness of the duel's deficiencies. His support for the duel is never unequivocal and never without reservations. Significantly, this ambivalence is least evident when the conflict of honor arises over a physical assault. In other cases, Bestuzhev's stories, while teaching the reader how to behave in dueling situations, always point out the duel's shortcomings as a means of resolving personal conflicts.

Bestuzhev's ambivalence about dueling was fed by the European and nascent Russian literary tradition (stories like the anonymous 1802 "A New Sentimental Traveler, or My Excursion to A***," which contains the first full-scale—and very negative—description of a conflict of honor in Russian literature). However, his ambivalence also drew on his and his contemporaries' own dueling experiences. Early nineteenth-century Russian duelists engaged in brutally harsh duels and thus faced a high probability of killing an opponent or of being killed themselves. They witnessed duelists dying and they knew duelists who had killed. Witnesses of the Zavadovsky-Sheremetev duel vividly recalled Sheremetev's agony at the dueling site even decades later.[21] The Decembrist Evgeny Obolensky, who had taken the place of his younger cousin in a duel and killed his opponent, could never forgive himself. One contemporary compared his mental anguish to the sufferings experienced by Orestes: "This unfortunate man fought a duel—and killed. From that time on, like Orestes pursued by Furies, he could not find peace."[22] Early nineteenth-century duelists thus understood the duel's violent nature and knew its power to traumatize a victorious duelist for life. And yet they not only accepted the duel but cultivated its most brutal forms. It was in literature that they allowed themselves to explore the duel's limitations and sometimes to argue eloquently against dueling.

Bestuzhev examined duels in two genres: historical tales and society tales. He wrote two types of historical tales: about ancient Russia (his so-called Russian cycle) and about the medieval Baltic area (his so-called Livonian cycle). Only one of his Russian tales, the 1831 **"The Raids: A Tale of the Year 1613,"** set in Poland, features dueling.[23] In contrast, Bestuzhev's Livonian tales, cast in the Middle Ages and populated with German knights, abound in conflicts of honor. All of these tales condone a person's right to a duel regardless of his social status. I shall focus on two tales that specifically address the question of physical inviolability: the 1821 **"Castle Wenden"** and the 1825 **"Castle Eisen."**[24]

Bestuzhev's very first Livonian tale, **"Castle Wenden,"** features a conflict between two opponents of unequal social standing: the powerful Magister, Winno von Rohrbach, and a knight, Sir Wigbert von Serrat. Rohrbach disregards Serrat's claim to independence and denies his right to protect his vassals. When Serrat protests,

Rohrbach lashes him with a whip. Rohrbach clearly wants to establish his opponent's inferior status: "'A scoundrel!' he exclaimed in fury, 'For your insolence, for your opinions you deserve punishment befitting a slave.' With these words he struck the unarmed Wigbert with a whip" (*1*:41).

To restore his honor, Serrat seeks a duel, but Rohrbach refuses to accept his challenge, citing Serrat's inferior status and alluding to the lashing that he has endured as a proof of his inferiority. Having anticipated Rohrbach's refusal, Serrat warns him in his challenge: "Beware of rejecting an honest fight: the one who offends and does not give satisfaction with his lance deserves to be killed as a thug. In case of rejection—I swear on my knightly honor—the last drop of Rohrbach's blood will dry on my dagger" (*1*:41). Bestuzhev's narrator is not blind to the fact that Serrat's intention is criminal (at one point, he calls Serrat's dagger "murderous"), but he seems to share Serrat's conviction that it is a lesser dishonor to kill and be executed than not to avenge the offense and thus accept inferior status. Serrat then sneaks into Rohrbach's castle at night, kills the offender with a dagger, is caught and executed.

Serrat carefully stages his murder to resemble a duel: he challenges Rohrbach, warns him about his intention to kill him, uses the so-called noble weapon in his assault, and wakes him up before assaulting him, thus giving him a chance to defend himself (*1*:44-45).[25] In presenting Serrat's attack as a surrogate duel, Bestuzhev protects his character's reputation as a man of honor: while some nineteenth-century duelists felt that an opponent who had dishonored himself (as Rohrbach did when he rejected Serrat's challenge) was not worthy of a duel and could be killed "like a dog,"[26] the prevailing view condemned such assaults. When, in 1832, Konstantin Chernov's brother Alexander, instead of challenging Alexander Shishkov over a slap in the face, slew him on the spot, public indignation against him was unanimous.[27] However, contemporaries were more lenient toward Nikolai Pavlov who, in 1836, mortally wounded Alexander Aprelev on the steps of the church, after first challenging him several times over his sister's honor and then staging his assault as a surrogate duel in a fashion very similar to that of Serrat.[28]

Furthermore, Bestuzhev adds the flavor of political execution to this killing by inserting the phrase "Rohrbach's blood irrigated the scaffold" (*1*:45). "Scaffold" (*pomost*) among other things denotes the platform where executions take place. Its appearance in the story is unmotivated, making it a probable transmitter of a political message. The story's political overtone is further enhanced as Serrat dies as a political criminal, an assassin, rather than a common murderer: "The Magister ceased to exist, but his power remained, and the lawless [*samosudnyi*] murderer, mauled by torture, died broken on the wheel" (*1*:45).

A conflict over the right to physical inviolability also occurs in Bestuzhev's last Livonian tale, **"Castle Eisen,"** where the offender is again socially superior. In this work, the evil Baron Bruno von Eisen oppresses everyone around him, including his nephew Reginald. Bruno takes from Reginald his bride, Louise, and marries her himself. Later Bruno orders his nephew to commit an act of cruelty; when Reginald refuses, Bruno threatens his nephew with violence. His threat refers both to a glove, an attribute of a knightly duel, and straps, an instrument of corporal punishment: "Be quiet, you brat, or I shall order this iron glove to be stuffed into your mouth. . . . Go away, or I will flog you with straps, as if you were the lowest among stablemen" (*1*:161). Furious, Reginald prepares to shoot an arrow at Bruno but is restrained and locked up in a dungeon. While Bruno is away, Louise frees Reginald and the two have an affair. Upon his return, Bruno discovers them kissing in the woods and attacks Reginald. Reginald defeats Bruno, ties him up, and slays him, despite Bruno's entreaties and Louise's intercession.

In contrast to the **"Castle Wenden,"** in which Serrat imitates a duel, Reginald kills a defenseless man. This difference is crucial; the narrator censures Reginald's egotistical motives and in his case rejects the idea of punishment without trial (*samosud*). Accordingly, Reginald and Louise are punished for their transgression: when they come to the altar to be married, Bruno's ghost (actually Bruno's long-lost twin brother) arrives in the church on a black horse, tramples Reginald to death, kidnaps Louise, and buries her alive.[29]

Bestuzhev's historical tales, although cast in foreign lands and in past historical epochs, reflected the contemporary Russian situation. The conflicts of honor that Bestuzhev examined were thinly disguised allusions to the early nineteenth-century antagonism between the independent-minded and politically weak lower nobility who tried to assert their personal rights by means of dueling and the powerful high nobility who tended to disregard those rights. Bestuzhev never seriously aspired to reenact history, but used it as a backdrop for the unfolding of what he presented as a timeless human conflict, and what in fact was a contemporary controversy for which he sought historical precedents.[30] The conflict between Winno von Rohrbach and Wigbert von Serrat portrayed in **"Castle Wenden"** bears little resemblance to the story of the quarrel between Magister Wenno and Wickbert von Soest as described in contemporary sources.[31] In **"Castle Eisen,"** Bestuzhev did not even attempt to reconstruct a concrete historical epoch, he merely created a vaguely medieval Livonian setting. In **"Castle Neihausen"** and **"Tournament in Revel,"** plots and characters are pure inventions.

Bestuzhev's tales foreshadowed reality as often as they reflected it. Serrat's plight, in **"Castle Wenden,"** anticipated the plights of Ryleev, Konstantin Chernov, and

Bestuzhev himself, who, in order to be taken seriously by their socially superior opponents, felt it necessary to behave like *bretteurs,* overreacting in response to perceived offenses and, if necessary, using brutal force to persuade their opponents to accept their challenges. Pavlov's and Alexander Chernov's assaults on their offenders resemble, respectively, Serrat's and Reginald's murders of their opponents. In **"Tournament at Revel,"** Bernhard von Burtneck's reluctance to accept Edwin, a commoner, as his son-in-law anticipates Novosil'tsev's unwillingness to marry a social inferior.

Bestuzhev expected his tales to be interpreted in an early nineteenth-century context and signaled his wish to his readers. One effective clue was Bestuzhev's use of a narrator who was not just a contemporary of the story's readers, but also their peer and an expert on the honor code. Bestuzhev's narrator in **"Castle Wenden"** is a Guards officer, a person very much like himself and many of his friends. This narrator not only recounts events, but also passes judgment on the characters' conduct, particularly on their actions in situations involving honor. For example, he instructs readers how to interpret Serrat's behavior: "I hate the villain in Serrat; but how can I totally refuse to empathize with the unfortunate man who was carried away by the spirit of the barbaric time and by the force of despair that possessed him?" (*1*:45) Similarly, in **"Castle Eisen,"** a first-person voice that Bestuzhev's readers recognized as their contemporary's pronounces judgment on the characters' actions, thereby making the ancient story topical.

Bestuzhev's readers picked up his clues and deftly uncovered allusions to contemporary circumstances in his historical tales. The first readers of **"Castle Eisen"** not only interpreted it as a work about tyranicide, but also identified a likely prototype for Reginald—Iakubovich, the famous *bretteur* and self-appointed would-be-assassin of Alexander I. Stepan Nechaev, a Decembrist and minor poet, wrote to Bestuzhev in November 1825: "[Vasily] Davydov correctly guesses that 'Blood for Blood' originated in the Caucasus. Iakubovich was your muse. Shake his heroic hand for me."[32] Interestingly, Bestuzhev's readers approved Reginald's killing of the cruel tyrant more enthusiastically than Bestuzhev himself, who, in the voice of his narrator, questioned his character's (and, by extension, Iakubovich's) selfish motives.

Readers identified the theme of the duel in its medieval guises all the more easily in that the writer also examined dueling in society tales cast in their own time. The earliest society tale dealing with a duel is the 1823 **"Evening at a Bivouac,"** the latest, the 1832 **"The Frigate Hope."** Bestuzhev's society tales provide a far more complex and even contradictory view of the duel. By offering detailed descriptions of the dueling ritual, Bestuzhev teaches his readers how to fight a proper duel. At the same time, he examines the duel's negative aspects and even suggests that there could be—and should be—honorable ways out of dueling situations. I shall concentrate on three of Bestuzhev's society tales, in which the contradictory treatment of the duel is the most evident: *A Novel in Seven Letters* (1824), **"The Test"** (1830), and **"The Terrible Divination"** (1830; published in 1831).

While all of Bestuzhev's society tales are ambivalent about dueling, *A Novel in Seven Letters* judges the duel the most harshly, pointing out its uselessness in mitigating complex psychological conflicts and especially its dangerous capacity to induce a puppetlike state in duelists and make them act against their principles. The hero of the story, who is in love with the beautiful and virtuous Adèle, challenges his fortunate rival, Erast, and kills him, despite his earlier resolve not to shoot at all. He describes the strange inertia that overcame him during the duel:

> We approached each other from twenty paces. I advanced firmly—three bullets had flown past my head [in previous duels]—I advanced firmly, but without any thought, any intention: the feelings buried in my soul completely darkened my mind. At six paces, I do not know why and do not know how, I pulled the fateful trigger—and the shot echoed in my heart![33]

The rest of the tale dwells on the hero's painful memory of his terrible deed, which is likely to haunt him forever and which makes him desire death. The tale also underscores the irony that killing a rival exacerbates the hopelessness of a successful duelist's position, turning him into his beloved's enemy.

The remorseful hero of *A Novel in Seven Letters* cites a "false sense of honor" as the power that drove him to the duel and murder.[34] Bestuzhev's condemnation of the duel echoes Rousseau's argument, in *La nouvelle Héloïse,* that duels spring from a false sense of honor and that truly honorable behavior requires the avoidance of dueling altogether. Julie develops these ideas in her letters to Saint-Preux and Milord Edouard mitigating their conflict over her honor. She supports her criticism of the duel with a vivid description of her father's tormenting memories of the friend he had killed in a duel.[35]

In Rousseau's novel, Julie's intercession works: convinced by her arguments, the rivals reconcile. Common in the European literary tradition, this device was never popular with Russians who, in real life as well as in literature, remained hostile to the idea of backing out of a duel. Rousseau's solution posed special problems for them due to the Russian duel's status as a safeguard against abuses of individual rights. To make the duel protect an individual and his private space, Russian duelists had to be belligerent in their insistence on strict adherence to the honor code.[36] Hence spitting in the face, "lashing [one's] stupid mug with a whip," threatening to kill (and actually killing) were used as "arguments" to force an opponent to accept a challenge. At the same time, Russians agreed that in principle Rousseau was right and that the duel was sustained by social convention and a falsely understood sense of honor.[37] Hence the ambivalence in their treatment of the duel in fiction and, at the very time when dueling was at its peak, their search for honorable ways for their fictitious characters to avoid dueling.

Bestuzhev, in *A Novel in Seven Letters,* implies that it suffices to recognize the duel's evil nature in order to stop it. Pushkin, in *Eugene Onegin,* both develops Bestuzhev's thesis regarding the duel's evil power over a duelist and, at the same time, disagrees with his simplistic solution. Similarities in plot and style between the dueling scenes in **"A Novel"** and *Eugene Onegin* mark this polemic.[38] Notably, Onegin is even more aware of the duel's evil nature than is Bestuzhev's character. He knows that he should not accept Lensky's challenge; he is aware that he is driven by a false sense of honor. Onegin's failure to act on his convictions demonstrates the difficulty, even the impossibility, of extracting oneself from a dueling situation. In Pushkin's view, once initiated, a duel is likely to run its course.[39]

In his turn, Bestuzhev took issue with Pushkin's acceptance of the honor code's tyranny. After having read the novel's sixth chapter, he wrote to his brothers that the duel in *Eugene Onegin* "is described quite perfectly, but one can see everywhere the old school and bad logic."[40] Accordingly, in **"The Test,"** Bestuzhev explores the means of regaining one's free will and escaping a duel without compromising one's honor. He suggests a new way to halt the duel's inertial force: the interference of a person who by virtue of her special status is free from social conventions. In this tale, Prince Gremin, commander of a hussar squadron, asks his friend, Major Strelinsky—who is traveling to St. Petersburg to spend a leave of absence with his younger sister, Olga—to test the feelings of the rich and beautiful young widow, Countess Alina Zvezdich, with whom Gremin had had a brief platonic love affair while her husband was still alive. Since Strelinsky himself had also been attracted to Alina, he is reluctant to accept the commission, but Gremin assures him that he will not mind if Strelinsky and Alina fall in love: he just needs to know whether she still is interested in him.

Strelinsky and Alina indeed fall in love, while Gremin realizes that he has feelings for Alina and hurries to St. Petersburg. Once there, he learns about Strelinsky's and Alina's imminent marriage and decides to challenge Strelinsky. Gremin goes to Strelinsky's house, discovers that he is out, and instead spends some time with Strelinsky's sister, Olga, who has been in love with Gremin since childhood. Gremin is moved by her love, but nonetheless challenges Strelinsky, who accepts. Olga suspects a duel in the making and secretly listens in on the seconds' negotiations. She then arrives at the dueling site in time to stop the duel. Thanks to Olga, the two opponents reconcile, Gremin proposes to her, Strelinsky gets Alina, and a double wedding is planned. The happy ending signifies that the spell of the duel can be broken.

Curiously, **"The Test"** offers its readers two contradictory sets of advice: on the one hand, its lengthy passages on the dueling ritual instruct them how to fight a duel; on the other, it teaches how not to fight one. The instructions on the particulars of the dueling ritual are extensive and detailed: they contain precise descriptions of how bullets are made, dueling sites are prepared, and seconds conduct their negotiations. The seconds and other characters involved in the prearrangements discuss pistols, bullets, gunpowder, and types of wounds. These discussions frequently become technical, offering advice on a duelist's diet on the morning of a duel, indicating the preferred type of carriage, and reminding readers that preparations have to remain secret, lest the police find out and prevent the duel. These discussions neither move the plot, nor add to the personages' characterizations. They serve primarily as an instruction manual and thus promote dueling.

And yet **"The Test"** also contains the opposite message. The story suggests that it is proper to stop an arranged duel and offers advice on how to do so. The author indicates from the outset that the Gremin-Strelinsky duel does not have a serious cause, and thus should not be undertaken. Even the seconds consider the duel frivolous: "How stubborn they are! If they at least would fight over some serious matter, not over a woman's caprice and their own whims" (*1*:222). They nonetheless proceed with the duel. Gremin too knows that he is wrong in challenging his friend because of a woman he does not even love. Furthermore, Gremin now realizes that he likes Olga and that he will lose her, regardless of the duel's outcome. Even so, fear of public opinion pushes him forward:

> But the voice of prejudice sounded like a trumpet and drowned all gentle, all kind sentiments. "Now it is too late to hesitate," [Gremin] said [to himself] with a sigh that tore his heart apart. "What is done cannot be undone and it is shameful to change my decision. I do not want to be the talk of the town and my regiment, if I agree to make peace in front of the pistol's barrel. People more easily believe in cowardice than in noble inspirations. I would still shoot at Strelinsky even if more gratifying hopes and more precious existence were placed in my barrel."
>
> (*1*:226)

Strelinsky, being the challenged party, is not in a position to offer peace. Besides, he wants to die, since he mistakenly believes that Alina has abandoned him. Thus, under the honor code's spell, everyone proceeds with the duel.

Olga, however, breaks this spell. Disregarding all rules of proper behavior, she goes to the tavern where both parties are assembled and pleads with Gremin to make peace with her brother, threatening her own death: "Beware, Prince Gremin! If the word of truth and nature is not accessible to souls who have been brought up in bloody prejudices, you can reach my brother only though this heart. I have not spared my reputation, and I will not spare my life" (*1*:229). Gremin's prejudices and Olga's reputation are mentioned here with a purpose: Olga succeeds precisely because she is bound neither by the conventions of the honor code ("bloody prejudices"), nor by the conventions of social decorum. She escapes the requirements of the dueling ritual by virtue of being a woman; and she can dispense with proper behavior because she is an *institutka,* that is, a graduate of the Smolny Monastery.

Founded by Catherine the Great as the first educational institution for girls in Russia and charged with the task of creating a new kind of noblewoman—well versed in foreign languages and fine arts, yet natural and pure—Smolny Monastery produced an educated female that in the Russian tradition received the names *smolianka* and *monastyrka* (from Smolny Monastery) or *institutka* (from the school's other name, Smolny Institute). A student of Russian cultural history offers a brief description of an *institutka* as a peculiar and paradoxical creature: "Some education and worldly naïveté; strictly ceremonious manners and childish spontaneity in expressing their feelings; thirst for a merry and free life and timidity, fear of life; dreaminess and acceptance of one's fate—such were the main features of this sociopsychological type."[41] *Institutki* markedly differed from other women of their time, and contemporaries' opinions about them varied: some admired them as ideal, pure, and natural creatures, whereas others ridiculed their ignorance of real life and their belated infantilism.[42]

"The Test" portrays Olga as an *institutka* in a decidedly positive light:

> Brought up in Smolny Monastery, she, as her other girlfriends, has paid with ignorance of society life's trifles for the beneficial ignorance of vice's early impressions and of passions' untimely riot. In society, she was charming as a paragon of lofty simplicity and childish frankness. It was delightful to settle one's eyes on her bright face, on which neither the play of passions, nor the hypocrisy of manners had left their prints yet, had cast their shadows. It was delightful to warm one's heart with her gaiety, since gaiety is the bloom of

innocence. In the muddy sea of societal prejudices, gilded depravity, and vain triviality, she towered like a green island, where the tired swimmer could find repose.

> (*1*:200-201)

Olga's naïveté, while sometimes amusing, makes her capable of distinguishing between true values and prejudices fostered by social conventions and permits her to act in a truly noble manner. Because of her special status, she violates decorum with impunity. Moreover, she can help others do the same. When she defies the rules and goes to the dueling site, the dueling convention collapses. Her actions free others to act in accordance with their true beliefs and feelings. Gremin forgets that it is shameful to reconcile under the pistol's barrel and asks Strelinsky's forgiveness. Strelinsky gladly accepts his apology and offers his own. Their seconds also shake free from the ritual's inertia and voice their support, praising the opponents' decision to reconcile. Strelinsky momentarily falters, fearing that Olga's intervention will stain his reputation as a duelist. However, Olga's natural behavior again forces him to change his attitude:

> Valerian entered the other room, hand in hand with the prince, merrily and light-heartedly, but his face darkened [*chelo ego podernulos' kak zarevom*] when he saw his sister there. "What does this mean?!" he exclaimed wrathfully. But when his sister, with the joyful greeting "You will not remain enemies, you will not fight!" fell senseless on his bosom, his voice softened.

> (*1*:230)

Although Strelinsky is still concerned about his sister's reputation, Gremin's marriage proposal dissolves this concern.

Olga is able to interfere successfully with the dueling ritual thanks to her special status as an *institutka*—a person who is different, innocent, and thus free to act on her convictions. No one else is allowed to do so: what for Olga is right and good, for Gremin, Strelinsky, and their comrades would be wrong and dishonorable. Unless someone like Olga helps them, duelists have to follow the honor code. Hence the detailed dueling instructions offered in the story. The story's double message thus reflects a double standard in respect to dueling: while it is far from perfect and often wrong, the honor code is obligatory for the majority of people. Only special people are exempt from its tyranny because they have an intuitive sense of true justice.[43]

Olga is a woman, which makes it easier for her to defy the honor code. Bestuzhev's tale **"The Terrible Divination"** explores the possibility that a man can also come to understand true values, thereby gaining his freedom from the honor code. This can happen, however, only by way of an extraordinary experience, such as contact with the supernatural. An anonymous hero, a young officer, is in love with a married woman, Polina, who returns his love. In order to preserve Polina's virtue and reputation, the lovers decide to part without consummating their affair. The hero struggles to stay away from his beloved, but on New Year's eve he goes to see her. On his way, he gets lost in a snowstorm and finds himself in a peasant's hut, where the local youth have gathered to divine and tell Yuletide stories. There the hero meets a mysterious stranger, in whom the reader, but not the hero, easily recognizes the devil. On a dare, the hero goes to the graveyard to practice divination. After the divination's apparent failure, the stranger shows up and drives the hero to the ball. Once there, the hero, at the stranger's urging, elopes with Polina. Her husband catches up with them and confronts the hero who is ready to give him satisfaction. The husband attempts to slap him in the face instead, and the hero reacts with fury. In retrospect, he describes his response as a reflex reaction, caused by a deeply ingrained sense of personal dignity: "Who among us was not from infancy nourished by notions of a gentleman's inviolability, of a well-born person's honor, of human dignity?" (*1*:338). Like Reginald in **"Castle Eisen,"** the hero kills his defenseless opponent, and the stranger helps him push the body into the ice-covered river. Polina is horrified and, although the lovers continue their flight, the hero realizes that he has ruined their chance for happiness. He also recognizes the duel as an immoral and cruel act of "bloody vengeance" (*1*:342). The narrator has learned the lesson offered to him on this terrible evening through a supernatural experience—which turns out to be a Yuletide dream.[44] He makes good use of this lesson and, upon waking up, decides never to see Polina again.

Significantly, Bestuzhev's ambivalent treatment of the duel, evident in **"The Test,"** can be detected in **"The Terrible Divination"** as well. The hero speaks against dueling, yet retains a reflex reaction to any threat to his physical inviolability: "A lot of time has passed since then in my head; [time] has cooled it, my ardent heart beats slower, but until now, given all my philosophical principles and all my experience, I cannot vouch for myself, and even the touch of a finger would blow up both me and my offender" (*1*:338). Despite its flaws, the honor code helps define and defend a person's private space, and Bestuzhev's character is not ready to forfeit it altogether.

The ultimate lesson about dueling offered in Bestuzhev's tales is that while *point d'honneur* has limitations, it is still indispensable. Bestuzhev's duelists recognize the duel's weak sides: the vanity and egotism that frequently underlay duelists' behavior (especially evident in his society tales), the duel's cruelty as an act of violence against human life, and its uselessness in avenging certain kinds of offenses (such as marital infi-

delity, which the duel cannot undo even if the transgressor is killed). Nonetheless, Bestuzhev's characters feel obliged to answer any perceived threat to their honor with a challenge. This readiness to fight serves a useful purpose: it guards against violations of a person's private space and defends his individual rights, physical inviolability in particular.

While Bestuzhev's treatment of the duel in his fiction was never fully positive, the very attention that he paid to it promoted it as a popular literary topic. His dueling tales profoundly influenced the contemporary and subsequent Russian literary tradition. Bestuzhev formulated many questions concerning the duel, which continued to be discussed and reexamined throughout the nineteenth century. His literary descendants made use of his discoveries not only when his fiction was still popular, but also long after his name had disappeared from the rosters of read and admired Russian writers.

Notes

1. François Billacois, *The Duel: Its Rise and Fall in Early Modern France,* ed. and trans. Trista Selous (New Haven: Yale University Press, 1990), 233.

2. About Bestuzhev's life and his legendary biographies, see Lewis Bagby, *Alexander Bestuzhev-Marlinsky and Russian Byronism* (University Park: Pennsylvania State University Press, 1995), especially chapters 2 and 4 and the conclusion; Lauren G. Leighton, *Alexander Bestuzhev-Marlinsky* (Boston: Twayne, 1975), chap. 1, 13-36; Iu. Levin, "Ob obstoiatel'stvakh smerti A. A. Bestuzheva-Marlinskogo," *Russkaia literatura* 2 (1962): 219-22; M. P. Alekseev, "Legenda o Marlinskom," in his *Etiudy o Marlinskom: Sbornik trudov Irkutskogo universiteta* 25 (1928): 113-41; P. V. Bykov, "Zagadka (Iz legend o Bestuzheve-Marlinskom)," *Niva* 52 (1912): 1039-40; repr. in Bykov, *Siluety dalekogo proshlogo* (Moscow: Zemlia I fabrika, 1930), 28-34.

3. See Iv. Abramov, "K kharakteristike chitatelia Pushkinskogo vremeni," *Pushkin i ego sovremenniki* 16 (1913): 104. It should be noted that a fourth Alexander, Griboedov, was murdered in 1828 in Teheran. Bestuzhev considered this a significant coincidence: the morning after receiving the news about Pushkin's death, he went to Griboedov's grave in the monastery of Saint David, ordered a mass to be served at the site of his burial, and wept through the service. See his 23 February 1837 letter to P. A. Bestuzhev, in *Sochineniia v dvukh tomakh,* 2 vols. (Moscow: Gosudarstvennoe izdatel'stvo khudozhestvennoi literatury, 1958), 2:673-74. Unless otherwise noted, all citations to Bestuzhev's writings are taken from this edition and will appear in parentheses in the body of the article.

4. This version of Bestuzhev's death is mentioned as one of the wild rumors in F. D. K . . . , "Smert' Aleksandra Aleksandrovicha Bestuzheva," in *Pisateli-dekabristy v vospominaniiakh sovremennikov*, 2 vols. (Moscow: Khudozhestvennaia literatura, 1980), 2:176.

5. M. A. Bestuzhev, "Detstvo i iunost' A. A. Bestuzheva," in *Pisateli-dekabristy*, 2:124. See also *Vospominaniia Bestuzhevykh*, ed. M. K. Azadovskii (Moscow: Izdatel'stvo Akademii nauk SSSR, 1951), 210.

6. M. A. Bestuzhev, "Melkie zametki ob A. A. Bestuzheve," in *Pisateli-dekabristy*, 2:135; *Vospominaniia Bestuzhevykh*, 222.

7. "Rasskazy E. A. Bestuzhevoi," in *Vospominaniia Bestuzhevykh*, 413.

8. M. A. Bestuzhev, "Iz 'Vospominanii o N. A. Bestuzheve,'" in *Pisatelidekabristy*, 2:207; *Vospominaniia Bestuzhevykh*, 284.

9. M. A. Bestuzhev, "Moi tiur'my," in *Pisatelidekabristy*, 1:53; *Vospominaniia Bestuzhevykh*, 55.

10. Ibid. Mikhail Bestuzhev also refers to this episode in his "Vospominaniia o N. A. Bestuzheve," in *Vospominaniia Bestuzhevykh*, 269. Mikhail believed that von Dezin was behind Alexander Bestuzhev's 1831 transfer to active duty from Tiflis, a relatively safe and pleasant place to serve. See also Nikolai Bestuzhev's account of the confrontation, in his "Vospominanie o Ryleeve," *Pisatelidekabristy*, 2:75; *Vospominaniia Bestuzhevykh*, 22.

11. For a description of the duel, see Bestuzhev's letter to Iakov Tolstoy, first published in *Russkaia starina* 11 (1889): 375-76; M. A. Bestuzhev, "Melkie zametki ob A. A. Bestuzheve," in *Pisatelidekabristy*, 2:135 and *Vospominaniia Bestuzhevykh*, 222; Dm. Kropotov, "Neskol'ko svedenii o Ryleeve. Po povodu zapisok Grecha," in *Pisateli-dekabristy*, 2:17-18.

12. A. A. Bestuzhev, letter to Tolstoy, in *Pisatelidekabristy*, 2:376.

13. For descriptions of the conflict see "Bumagi o poedinke Novosil'tseva i Chernova," in P. I. Bartenev, ed., *Deviatnadtsatyi vek: Sbornik* 1 (1872): 333-37; *Pisateli-dekabristy*, 1:291 n; 2:18-19, 53, and 321-22; T. I. Ornatskaia, ed., *Rasskazy babushki. Iz vospominanii piati pokolenii. Zapisannye i sobrannye ee vnukom D. Blagovo* (Leningrad: Nauka, 1989), 289, 291. The memory of this duel is still alive in Russia: in 1992, a monument was erected at the site of the encounter.

14. P. P. Karatygin, "P. A. Katenin," in *Pisatelidekabristy*, 1:291 n.

15. "Bumagi o poedinke Novosil'tseva s Chernovym," 334.

16. "Iz bumag Baten'kova," in *Memuary dekabristov*, ed. M. V. Dovnar-Zapol'sky (Kiev: Izdatel'stvo knizhnogo magazina S. I. Ivanova, 1906), 165.

17. On the link between the nobility's anxiety about the absence of firm guarantees of physical inviolability and the growth of the duel in Russia, see my "The Emergence of the Duel of Honor in Russia: Corporal Punishment and the Honor Code," *Russian Review* 54 (1995): 26-43.

18. For a report on Mavra's plight, see "Semeistvo Razumovskogo," in Petr Bartenev, ed., *Os'mnadtsatyi vek. Istoricheskii sbornik*, 2 (1869); quoted in A. Romanovich-Slavatinskii's *Dvorianstvo v Rossii ot nachala XVIII veka do otmeny krepostnogo prava. Svod materialov i prigotovitel'nye etiudy dlia istoricheskogo issledovaniia* (St. Petersburg: Tipografiia ministerstva vnutrennikh del. 1870), 20. The 1803 duel between A. P. Kushelev and N. N. Bakhmet'ev over Bakhmet'ev's having hit Kushelev with a walking stick during military training in 1797 exemplifies the nobility's newly acquired intolerance of physical abuse. I discuss this duel in my "Emergence of the Duel," 41-42.

19. Iakubovich's fellow Decembrists testified that he formulated his proposal to assassinate Alexander I in terms of a duel of honor; see *Vosstanie dekabristov*, vol. 2 (Moscow: Gospolitizdat, 1926), 293-94, 296; "Iz pokazanii Kondratiia Fedorovicha Ryleeva," in *Iz pisem i pokazanii dekabristov: Kritika sovremennogo sostoianiia Rossii i plany budushchego ustroistva*, ed. A. K. Borozdin (St. Petersburg: Izdanie M. V. Pirozhkova, 1906), 182; M. V. Nechkina, *Dvizhenie dekabristov*, 2 vols. (Moscow: Izdanie Akademii nauk SSSR, 1955), 2:108-9.

20. The date and circumstances of this episode vary in different accounts. V. N. Zvegintsov, in *Kavalergardy dekabristy: Dopolnenie k sborniku biografii kavalergardov. 1801-1826* (Paris: [n.p.], 1977), 74, places it in 1808; A. E. Rozen, in *Zapiski dekabrista* (St. Petersburg: Tipografiia tovarishchestva "Obshchestvennaia pol'za," 1907), 30, after 1812. S. Komovskii, in "Zametki" (*Russkii arkhiv* [1868], col. 1034-35) and Natan Eidelman, in his *Lunin* (Moscow: "Molodaia gvardiia," 1970), 29, cite two other versions of the incident. See the discussion of Lunin's actions as a political statement in Iakov Gordin, *Pravo na poedinok* ([Leningrad]: "Sovetskii pisatel'," 1989), 408-10. On the officers' clash with Nicholas, see Gordin, *Pravo na poedinok*, 409-10. Herzen, in *Byloe i dumy*, relates yet another story about an

officer's conflict of honor with Nicholas; see his *Sobranie sochinenii v 30-ti tomakh,* 30 vols. (Moscow: Izdatel'stvo Akademii nauk SSSR, 1954-64), 8:58.

21. See D. A. Smirnov, "Rasskazy o A. S. Griboedove, zapisannye so slov ego druzei," in *A. S. Griboedov v vospominaniiakh sovremennikov* (Moscow: Khudozhestvennaia literatura, 1980), 213, 242. Smirnov recorded S. N. Begichev's and I. G. Ion's accounts in the early 1840s.

22. V. A. Olenina, "Pis'ma k P. I. Bartenevu, 1869," in *Dekabristy: Letopisi gosudarstvennogo literaturnogo muzeia* (1938), 3:488; see also 3:491.

23. I cannot discuss here how the tradition of dueling in Poland, which was very strong, influenced the Russian duel. I point out, however, that Russians consistently mocked Polish duelists as both hotheaded and not serious enough. The beginning of this attitude can be traced at least back to Petr Tolstoy's account of his stay in Warsaw in 1697 (see *Puteshestvie stol'nika P. A. Tolstogo po Evrope. 1697-1699* [Moscow: Nauka, 1992], 25, 28). Bestuzhev's tale contributes to this view.

24. "Castle Wenden (A Fragment from a Guard Officer's Diary)" was first published in 1823. "Castle Eisen" initially was to appear in Ryleev's and Bestuzhev's almanach *The Little Star* under the title "Blood for Blood." After 14 December 1825, the whole edition of the almanac was confiscated and released only in 1861. The tale was published in 1827 as "Castle Eisen." The original version was recently published in *Faksimil'noe vosproizvedenie piati listov (80 stranits) almanakha A. Bestuzheva I K. Ryleeva ZVEZDOCHKA, otpechatannikh v 1825 godu* (Moscow: Kniga, 1981), 1-36. Two other Livonian tales are "Castle Neihausen: a Tale of Chivalry" (1824) and "Tournament at Revel" (1825). In light of Bestuzhev's populist treatment of the duel, it is noteworthy that "Tournament at Revel" upholds a commoner's right to a duel.

25. Serrat's historical prototype used an ax in his assault. See *The Chronicle of Henry of Livonia: A Translation with Introduction and Notes* by James A. Brundage (Madison: University of Wisconsin Press, 1961), 88-89.

26. A. N. Vul'f, *Dnevniki* (Moscow: Izdanie "Federatsiia," 1929), 246.

27. For contemporary reactions, see *Pis'ma P. V. Kireevskogo k N. M. Iazykovu,* ed. M. K. Azadovskii (Moscow: Izdatel'stvo Akademii nauk SSSR, 1935), 26 (published as volume 1, issue 4 of *Trudy Instituta antropologii, etnografii i arkheologii*); V. Vrasskaia, "Pushkin v perepiske rodstvennikov," *Literaturnoe nasledstvo* 16-18 (1934): 781. For a more recent publication of this letter, see *Famil'nye bumagi Pushkinykh-Gannibalov,* vol. 1, *Pis'ma Sergeia L'vovicha i Nadezhdy Osipovny Pushkinykh k ikh docheri Ol'ge Sergeevne Pavlishchevoi. 1828-1835* (St. Petersburg: "Pushkinskii fond," 1993), 122.

28. On Pavlov's case, see the report in a contemporary newspaper *Severnaia pchela,* no. 124 (1836), June 3; A. S. Pushkin, letter to N. N. Pushkina, 18 May 1836, in his *Polnoe sobranie sochinenii v 16-ti tomakh* (Leningrad: Izdanie Akademii nauk SSSR, 1946), 16:117; A. V. Nikitenko, *Dnevnik* (Leningrad: Gosudarstvennoe izdatel'stvo Khudozhestvennaia literatura, 1955), 1:183-84; N. Makarov, *Kaleidoskop v dopolnenie k "Moim semidesiatiletnim vospominaniiam"* (St. Petersburg: Tipografiia V. V. Komarova, 1883), 164-66; *Russkii arkhiv* (1906), cols. 433-34.

29. The narrator justifies her horrible execution with a peculiar reasoning that indirectly endorses the duel: "It seems that Louise was least of all guilty, and she suffered most of all. But God knows what He does. Blood upon man often washes away past stains, but upon woman it is almost always worse than Cain's mark" (1:168).

30. Leighton, in his *Alexander Bestuzhev-Marlinsky* (71-74), argues that Bestuzhev's historical tales were more accurate than most Romantic works about past events. While this might be true, Bestuzhev never seriously intended historical allusions to be more than a disguise for the discussion of contemporary issues. The 1820s censors intuited Bestuzhev's intentions and caused him difficulties in publishing his tales. The publication of "Wenden Castle" was initially banned by Moscow censors; see Sergei Isakov, "O 'livonskikh' povestiakh dekabristov (K voprosu o stanovlenii dekabrskogo istorizma)," *Uchenye zapiski Tartuskogo gosudarstvennogo universiteta* 167 (1965): 37. In his essay, which is devoted to the problem of historical accuracy in the Decembrists' works about the Baltic area, Isakov points out that Bestuzhev's knowledge of Livonian history was superficial and derived not from authentic historical sources or serious scholarly works, but from popular textbooks, which he used uncritically (38-40, 50-51). For example, Bestuzhev picked up a typo from one such source, F. G. de Bray, *Essai critique sur l'histoire de la Livonie,* vol. 1 (Dorpat: 1817), naming the character in his "Castle Wenden" Serrat instead of the historically correct Soest. For an analysis of Bestuzhev's "Livonian tales" as historical fiction see also Mark Altshuller, *Epokha Val'tera Skotta v Rossii (Istoricheskii roman 1830-kh godov)* (St. Petersburg: Gumanitarnoe

agenstvo "Akademicheskii proekt," 1996), 50-53. Both Altshuller and Leighton point out Scott's influence on Bestuzhev.

31. See *The Chronicle of Henry of Livonia,* 88-89.

32. Nechaev's letter is published in *Russkaia starina* 61 (1889): 320.

33. Bestuzhev, "Roman v semi pis'makh," in his *Vtoroe polnoe sobranie sochinenii,* 4th ed. (St. Petersburg: Ministerstvo gosudarstvennogo imushchestva, 1847), vol. 2, part 4, 126-27. Lotman, in his essay "Duel'," published in his *Besedy o russkoi kul'ture: Byt i traditsii russkogo dvorianstva (XVIII—nachalo XIX veka)* (St. Petersburg: Iskusstvo—SPB, 1994), briefly discusses the duel's capacity to deprive a person of free will (175). This aspect of the duel was later examined by Pushkin in *Eugene Onegin* and by Tolstoy in *War and Peace.*

34. Bestuzhev, "Roman v semi pis'makh," 126.

35. Jean-Jacques Rousseau, *La nouvelle Héloïse,* part 1, letters 57 and 60.

36. This is not to say that everyone in Russia shared this attitude and that reluctant duelists did not exist (this essay mentions at least two: Shakhovskoi and von Dezin). I am talking about a small group of like-minded people trying to establish the duel as a deterrent against personal abuses. Their cultural prestige, however—and therefore their influence—were significant.

37. Besides "A Novel in Seven Letters," this idea can be seen in "A New Sentimental Traveler" and in an anonymous 1809 "Ode on Duels" ("Oda na poedinki"). *Eugene Onegin* and, later, Dostoevsky's *Notes from Underground* are examples of polemical responses to Rousseau's argument. "Ode on Duels," which was first published in *Vestnik Evropy,* no. 16 (August 1809): 279-82, and signed G-v, can be found in A. S. Griboedov, *Sochineniia* (Moscow: Khudozhestvennaia literatura, 1988), 377-79, among the works ascribed to him. The influence of Rousseau is suggested in the commentary, 696. S. A. Fomichev argues that the ode was written by the adolescent Griboedov; see Fomichev, "Spornye voprosy griboedovskoi tekstologii," *Russkaia literatura* 2 (1977): 72-74.

38. Onegin's shooting at Lensky while still on his way to the barrier and without intent to kill follows the dueling scenario in Bestuzhev's story. The description of Erast's dying in the snow stylistically reverberates in Onegin's later recollection of Lensky's death.

39. Pushkin also rejects the solution offered by the European literary tradition: unlike Julie and other Sentimental heroines, Tatiana cannot prevent the duel because the male characters, in accordance with the honor code, keep her in the dark about the upcoming duel. William Mills Todd III, in his *Fiction and Society in the Age of Pushkin: Ideology, Institutions, and Narrative* (Cambridge: Harvard University Press, 1986), 128, briefly discusses Pushkin's disagreement with literary convention.

40. Quoted in V. G. Bazanov, "Tvorchestvo Aleksandra Bestuzheva-Marlinskogo," in his *Ocherki dekabristskoi literatury. Publitsistika. Proza. Kritika* (Moscow: Gosudarstvennoe izdatel'stvo khudozhestvennoi literatury, 1953), 408. Bazanov argues (409-18) that "The Test" was written in response to the first six chapters of *Eugene Onegin.*

41. A. F. Belousov, "Institutka: sotsial'no-psikhologicheskii tip i kul'turnyi simvol "peterburgskogo" perioda russkoi istorii," in *Antsiferovskie chteniia: Materialy i tezisy konferentsii (20-22 dekabria 1989 g.)* (Leningrad: Leningradskoe otdelenie Sovetskogo fonda kul'tury, 1989), 181.

42. On the treatment of *institutki* throughout the nineteenth century and on presentations of this type in Russian literary works, see ibid., 181-84.

43. Dostoevsky later developed this idea in *The Idiot:* Prince Myshkin is exempt from the honor code due to his special status.

44. Yelena Dushechkina, in her *Russkii sviatochnyi rasskaz: stanovlenie zhanra* (St. Petersburg: Izdatel'stvo Sankt-Peterburgskogo gosudarstvennogo universiteta, 1995), analyzes traditional and literary Yuletide stories as a genre offering instruction on proper behavior. In chapter 3, 102, she discusses "The Terrible Divination" as a Yuletide story.

FURTHER READING

Criticism

Bagby, Lewis. "Bestužev-Marlinskij's 'Mulla Nur': A Muddled Myth to Rekindle Romance." *Russian Literature* 11, no. 2 (February 15, 1982): 117-28.
    Maintains that in his last fictional work, Bestuzhev fails to bring together its disparate elements in a coherent manner.

———. "Bestužev-Marlinskij: Personality-Persona." *Russian Literature* 22, no. 3 (October 1, 1987): 247-310.

Considers the true identity of Bestuzhev, which is often erroneously considered identical to the public image he projected.

Čiževskij, Dmitrij. "Romantic Prose." In *History of Nineteenth-Century Russian Literature: Volume I. The Romantic Period,* edited by Serge A. Zenkovsky, translated by Richard Noel Porter, pp. 97-134. Nashville: Vanderbilt University Press, 1974.

Contains a brief overview of Bestuzhev's life and prose works.

Karlinsky, Simon. "Bestužev-Marlinskij's *Journey to Revel'* and Puškin." In *Puškin Today,* edited by David M. Bethea, pp. 59-72. Bloomington: Indiana University Press, 1993.

Discusses the influence of Bestuzhev's travelogue *Journey to Revel* on two of the mature works of Pushkin.

Leighton, Lauren G. "Marlinskij's 'Ispytanie': A Romantic Rejoinder to *Evgenij Onegin.*" *Slavic and East European Journal* 13, no. 2 (summer 1969): 200-16.

Discusses Bestuzhev's criticism of Pushkin's *Eugene Onegin* and compares the first six chapters of Pushkin's tale with Bestuzhev's own early prose works, particularly "Ispytanie."

———. "Marlinsky." *Russian Literature Triquarterly* 3 (1972): 249-68.

Provides an overview of Bestuzhev's life and career with an emphasis on his literary criticism and his prose tales.

———. "Bestuzhev-Marlinskii's 'The Frigate *Hope*': A Decembrist Puzzle." *Canadian Slavonic Papers* 22, no. 2 (June 1980): 173-86.

Analyzes *The Frigate "Hope"* as an adventure tale, as an allegory of its author's part in the Decembrist movement, and as a hidden textual message to those readers with an insider knowledge of the Decembrist plot.

Proffer, Carl R. "Washington Irving in Russia: Pushkin, Gogol, Marlinsky," *Comparative Literature* 20, no. 4 (fall 1967): 329-42.

Studies Irving's influence on Marlinsky's use of fictitious narrators and framing devices.

Additional coverage of Bestuzhev's life and career is contained in the following sources published by the Gale Group: *Dictionary of Literary Biography,* **Vol. 198;** *Literature Resource Center.*

Julián del Casal
1863-1893

(Full name José Julián Herculano del Casal y de la Lastra; also wrote under the pseudonym Hernani) Cuban poet and essayist.

INTRODUCTION

Considered one of the earliest and more significant poets of Spanish-American modernism, Casal's poetry is permeated with an awareness of the growing complexities of modern life. His writing reflected his own philosophies, but also serves as a representative example of the developments in the Spanish-American modernist movement at the time. Casal's poetry included sonnets and prose poems, and although his technique was fairly traditional, the subjects he addressed in his writing were very modernist in nature. Today, Casal is studied as one of the foremost poets of the Cuban modernist movement, and his writings provide insight into the historical and political world he inhabited.

BIOGRAPHICAL INFORMATION

José Julián Herculano del Casal y de la Lastra was born in Havana, Cuba, on November 7, 1863 to a Spanish mother and Cuban father. Casal's mother died when he was only five, leaving the young boy grief-stricken. His father did not provide much emotional support, instead rebuking the young Casal for his feelings of abandonment and guilt. As a result, many critics believe that Casal never really recovered from his mother's death, and the feelings of loneliness and fear that permeate his poetry are a result of this early trauma in life. In line with his own somber and traditional thinking, Casal's father sent the young boy to the Real Colegio de Belén, from which he graduated in 1879. A year of law school followed at the University of Havana, after which Casal left his studies to accept a job at the treasury department in Havana. At the same time he began writing articles for *La Habana Elegante,* but comments he made in one of these articles regarding the governor general of Havana led to dismissal and an end to this phase of his journalistic career.

To escape disfavor, Casal left for Spain. Dejected and out of money after only a few weeks, he returned to Cuba and began working for two newspapers. However, anxiety and despair, the feelings that he struggled with all his life, ultimately led him to quit his job and retreat into himself, restricting his social interactions to a few close friends. He did, however, maintain a correspondence with many intellectuals outside Cuba, including Rubén Darío and Gustave Moreau. Although Casal began writing years before, none of his work was published until after his father's death in 1885. Mostly poetry, his work was published in such periodicals as *La Habana Elegante* and *El Figaro*. His first collection of poems, *Hojas al viento,* was published in 1890 and he followed this with two other collections, *Nieve* (1892) and *Bustos y rimas* (1893). In addition to poetry, Casal wrote various prose works and translated the works of such authors as Charles Baudelaire. In the late 1880s he worked for two newspapers, publishing numerous articles under the pseudonym Hernani. Plagued by tuberculosis for many years, Casal died in October, 1893, shortly before *Rimas* was published.

MAJOR WORKS

Casal published only two poetry collections during his lifetime, *Hojas al viento* and *Nieve*. His last collection, *Bustos y rimas,* appeared in 1893, shortly after his death, and was completed with the help of Casal's friend Hernández Miyares. It differs from his earlier works because it contains both prose and poetry. *Hojas* includes forty-nine poems and is considered an example of Casal's early writing style. The poems in this collection are topical in nature and often refer to contemporary events. A few of them were even characterized as "imitations" and show the influence of other writers. The work was well received by his contemporaries as an early offering by a poet with much promise. Casal continued to publish poems in various Cuban periodicals, and in 1892 he collected many of these pieces in his second collection, *Nieve*. Divided into five sections, the poems in this collection are categorized according to theme. The first section, "Bocetos antiguos" includes poems inspired by pagan and Judeo-Christian thought; the second section, "Mi museo ideal," is famous because the poems contained in it were inspired by the art of Gustave Moreau, with whom Casal had an ongoing correspondence. The third section, "Cromos españoles," is a collection of well-known Spanish word pictures; the fourth, "Marfiles viejos," contains sixteen sonnets, all reflecting his fears and concerns about life in general. The fifth section, titled "La gruta del ensueño," completes the collection with seventeen miscellaneous poems. *Nieve* met with some critical success, although most contemporaries in Cuba felt that Casal's themes were too dark and pessimistic.

CRITICAL RECEPTION

During his lifetime, Casal was hailed as a fresh new talent following the publication of his first collection. However, the dark themes and perceived nihilism of his second collection led many contemporaries to label Casal as repetitive and oppressive. His work has since been acknowledged as one of the first examples of Spanish-American modernist writing, reflecting the concerns of writers with respect to the changing times in which they lived. In his discussion of Casal's place in the development of Cuban modernism, Ivan A. Schulman notes that Casal's preoccupation with his fears has led many scholars to characterize him as a "dreamer" and an "escapist." Yet, stresses Schulman, his concerns with respect to art and reality were shared by numerous artists of that era, all of whom were struggling with a social and cultural crisis of advancing technology and urbanization. In his introduction to an edition of Casal's poetry, Robert Jay Glickman notes that unlike other artists and writers, who were mostly able to ignore the ugliness of modernization, Casal was deeply affected by it. His concern for the future of art and literature in the face of modernization is reflected clearly in both his poetry and prose. Many scholars have proposed that Casal used his writing as a means to create distance between himself and society, and as a way of dealing with his anxieties. Priscilla Pearsall notes that Casal's poetry reflects his personal crises and that he used poetry as both a cathartic release and for philosophical articulation. Luis Felipe Clay Méndez also notes that Casal's prose provided him with release. According to Méndez, in order to gain a complete understanding of Casal's ideology, a study of both his prose and poetry is necessary as only an analysis of both provides a balanced view of Casal's writing and philosophy.

PRINCIPAL WORKS

Hojas al viento (poetry) 1890

Nieve (poetry) 1892

Bustos y rimas (poetry, prose) 1893

Poesías completas (poetry) 1945

Prosas. 3 vols. (prose) 1963-64

Julián del Casal: Letters to Gustave Moreau (letters) 1974

The Poetry of Julián del Casal: A Critical Edition. 3 vols. (poetry) 1976-78

CRITICISM

Lee Fontanella (essay date December 1970)

SOURCE: Fontanella, Lee. "Parnassian Precept and a New Way of Seeing Casal's *Museo ideal.*" *Comparative Literature Studies* 7, no. 4 (December 1970): 450-79.

[*In the following essay, Fontanella discusses the form and function of Casal's poetry series "Mi museo ideal," which can be interpreted as an ode to French painter Gustave Moreau. The middle ten sonnets each focus on a separate painting of Moreau, while the first and last pieces act as framing elements that situate the collection as a type of museum or "temple for art."*]

Very few of those critics who have paid due attention to the Cuban poet Julián del Casal (1863-1893) have elaborated on their observations of the media in and from which the poet worked in creating **"Mi museo ideal."**[1] The question is significant, for the French poets of the later nineteenth century, especially the Parnassians whom Casal so admired, determined in great part his use of particular poetic modes and forms.[2] Thus the main body of **"Mi museo ideal"** is a group of ten sonnets, each depicting a work by the French painter Gustave Moreau (1826-1898). That these ten sonnets are preceded by another sonnet, whose subject is a portrait of the painter, and that they are followed by a final poem, of 130 lines, which is not fashioned after a specific painting,[3] is also significant. In the discussion which follows, the framework provided by the first and last poems functions in conjunction with the subjects of these poems to underscore the structural and formal aspects of both the composite collection and the ten sonnets individually.

We must not forget, as we discuss Casal's **"Museo,"** his awareness of having "transposed" his subject from one medium, painting, to another, poetry. Nor may we merely consider the beginning and final poems apart from the ten sonnets, which are, almost invariably, the only poems of **"Mi museo ideal"** to capture the critics' attention.[4] The arrangement in twelve parts—first **"Vestíbulo: Retrato de Gustavo Moreau,"** then the ten sonnets on the paintings, and finally **"Sueño de gloria: Apoteosis de Gustavo Moreau"**—is equivalent to the structuring of a "museum," which houses the ten sonnets by means of the first and twelfth poems of the collection. Furthermore, the idea of opening in the "vestibule" connotes from the start a spatial relationship from one poem to another, by which we are to see that Casal is poetizing painted art as if it were on exhibit.[5]

Pertinent here is E. H. Gombrich's discussion of representation in plastic art forms. For him, the factor of substitution may precede the factor of portrayal; further, that the artist's representation of objects of the external world may be initially a substitution for them implies the idea of function:

> It needed two conditions, then, to turn a stick into our hobby horse: first, that its form made it just possible to ride on it; secondly—and perhaps decisively—that riding mattered. . . . If we keep in mind that representation is originally the creation of substitutes out of given material we may reach safer ground. The greater the wish to ride, the fewer may be the features that will do for a horse. But at a certain stage it must have eyes—for how else could it see? At the most primitive level, then, the conceptual image might be identified with what we have called the minimum image—that minimum, that is, which will make it fit into a psychological lock.[6]

Gombrich's approach, applied to **"Mi museo ideal,"** raises the central question with which we deal in this essay. How did Casal's poems, and the way he presented them, function to satisfy both the demands of his literary tradition and his own needs as a poet? Since the meaning of the new form cannot carry the total meaning of the original from which it is derived, what, in brief, has Casal brought to the Moreau paintings? No matter how accurately the poems may re-present the formal and structural elements of the paintings (this is basic to the aims of Parnassian poetic *ekphrasis* and, therefore, of no little pertinence in this essay), they cannot mean, solely, the paintings. The approximation of the function of **"Mi museo ideal"** to that of the original set of paintings is one of the best means of determining the equivalence of the sonnets and the paintings. Obviously, what Casal brings to the paintings not only indicates what his new medium may afford him; it also makes the paintings his own. Casal's title insists that it is his own ("Mi") museum, which he creates, at least in part, for himself.

In general, whereas the symbolists persisted in making the poem a step-by-step, visible development of thought, the Parnassians usually considered themselves capable of perceiving form prior to idea.[7] For the Parnassians—as for Casal, who was describing pictorial art—the form existed prior to the poem, as an aspect of the transposable object being viewed. When Théophile Gautier was in vogue, "transposition d'art" was a commonplace, and "poets set about writing 'pastels' and artists painting 'sonnets.'"[8] Gautier himself considered traditional forms "containers" into which thoughts might be methodically and concentratedly worked, and he regarded the "sonnet orthodoxe" in this way:

> Il a une forme géométriquement arrêtée: de même que, dans les plafonds, les compartiments polygones ou bizarrement contournés servent plus les peintres qu'ils ne les gênent en déterminant l'espace où il faut encadrer et faire tenir leurs figures. Il n'est pas rare d'arriver, par le raccourci et l'ingénieux agencement des lignes, à

loger un géant dans un de ces caissons étroits, *et l'œuvre y gagne par sa concentration même.* Ainsi une grande pensée peut se mouvoir à l'aise dans ces quatorze vers méthodiquement distribués.[9]

(Italics mine.)

He went on, of course, to say that if one does not intend to submit to the laws of the sonnet ("Il faut donc se soumettre absolument à les lois"), then one ought not to compose sonnets at all. In this regard, Gautier's insistence derived, as Jean Ducros has observed in a treatment of Leconte de Lisle, from the Parnassian preference for impersonal art:

> Cette théorie [of imitation, to which the theory of impersonal art is intimately ("étroitement") linked] suppose que la qualité d'un poème ne vient pas seulement de l'originalité et de la profondeur de l'émotion, ou de l'idée qu'il exprime, mais aussi de l'observation de règles idéales que devine le génie poétique. Ces règles ont, comme les idées platoniciennes, une existence propre et indépendante. Elles s'opposent à la réalité, changeante et confuse. Elles excluent l'émotion personnelle comme l'intention morale, car l'une et l'autre sont inséparables de l'intelligence et de la sensibilité individuelles. C'est dire qu'elles ne s'appliquent pas à la matière de l'œuvre d'art, monde intime ou monde extérieur, mais seulement à sa forme. Il y a des règles formelles en sculpture, qui commandent à la ligne. La poésie doit aussi soumettre ses images et ses rythmes à des lois idéales, et ces lois ont une valeur éternelle: les rapports de longueurs et les principes de proportions sont indépendants des personnes et des temps.[10]

Today it is easy for us to agree with the basis, at least, of the principle that "only *creative* transposition is possible: either intralingual transposition—from one poetic shape into another, or interlingual transposition—from one language into another, or finally intersemiotic transposition—from one system of signs into another, e.g., from verbal art into music, dance, cinema, or painting" (italics mine).[11] But deformation on the part of the Parnassians was, theoretically, an unpurposed consequence of art that re-presented objects of the external world. On the other hand, the aesthetic, moral, and linguistic deformation on the part of the symbolists was a systematic, therefore intentional, effort (stemming largely from Schopenhauer's world view) at personal representation.[12] Nevertheless, the very impracticability of the aesthetic of "transposition," as we shall see, in part accounts for an approximation of the Parnassian to the symbolist: both in effect create a world of "personal representation." Casal's completed **"Museo"** is, indeed, a personalized re-formation, answering only in theory to the phrase "transposition d'art."

Furthermore, the Parnassian group was not always consistent in giving form priority over thought, or in making form independent of idea. The periodical *L'Artiste,* which stood for "l'art pour l'art" and in which Gautier collaborated in 1856, affirmed that "nous n'avons jamais pu comprendre la séparation de l'idée et de la forme. . . . Une belle forme est une belle idée."[13] Nor were the Parnassians unaware of a dichotomy in their aesthetics. Anatole France caused a stir at a meeting of the Parnassians when he read a paper in which he defined the poet as the perceiver of objects in the external world—objects which are transformed by the perceiver's "prisme cérébral," then decomposed and given new substance in another medium. It is, he said, in the redirection of the ideal outward from the poet's mind that the split between form and idea occurs; they meet again in the total poem. The association was immediately made with Hérédia's creative process, as Leconte de Lisle kept hush and as one unknown rose to object: "Oui, si vraiment, ainsi que France vient de nous le faire entendre, la poésie n'est qu'une vibration de l'œil du poète, réfléchie sur le papier; si, pour en tirer les plus beaux effets, il suffit d'avoir dans la cervelle quelques plaques sensibles, alors Hérédia, le plus étonnant réflecteur d'images, serait aussi le plus grand de nos poètes."[14]

What probably upset the gathering was that Anatole France's paper made the act of perception so mechanical that it deprived the poet of the subjective powers which would set him apart from the unimaginative perceiver. But France's way of thinking also implied a refashioning of the ideal image by the poet, and not merely the Parnassian concept of the form's containment of the image. Leconte de Lisle's silence at the meeting may, perhaps, be explained by his agreement with France, for in 1864 Leconte wrote: "La pensée surabonde nécessairement dans l'œuvre d'un vrai poète, maître de sa langue et de son instrument. Il voit du premier coup d'œil plus loin, plus haut, plus profondément que tous, parce qu'il contemple l'idéal à travers la beauté visible, et qu'il le concentre et *l'enchâsse* dans l'expression propre, précise, *unique*" (italics mine).[15]

Despite differences of opinion like these, Parnassians generally agreed upon art's double purpose: to perpetuate and reveal beauty. Only through art was beauty made available to all—although art had no utilitarian aim, even so. As Leconte de Lisle warned, "L'art n'a pas mission de changer en or fin le plomb vil des âmes inférieures. . . . L'art est donc l'unique révélateur du beau, et il le révèle uniquement."[16] The concept of "transposition" thus implied a repositioning to a double end, the re-presentation and perpetuation of the image of beauty—and through a single poetic form of inherently perpetuating qualities.

This form, above all others, was the sonnet. What could the sonnet afford the poet of *ekphrasis,* such as Hérédia or Casal? Hérédia said of the "exquise tapisserie," the sonnet, that "on la termine, tout le cavenas [sic] tient dans la main, et rien ne favorise mieux la constance. De là, vint qu'on n'a jamais fabriqué tant de sonnets

qu'aujourd'hui."[17] The sonnet's extraordinary favor among the Parnassian poets gave rise to its polemical nature at the time, an example of which we have already seen in Gautier's insistence on the poet's obedience to the laws of the sonnet.[18] It was by virtue of submission to the "règles idéales" (which alone could give art its changelessness and which applied only to forms, not to moral intention) that the poet could prevent his art from falling into oblivion. By universalizing his poetic structure in this way—which is what Casal did also when he chose his subject matter from myth and the classics—the poet could remove the destructive temporal factor from his art object.

Hérédia, fighting the use of the lengthy poem, called the sonnet an eternal form: "Une forme a persisté, qui ne pouvait pas périr, car elle est admirablement assortie à la secrète horreur des compositions étendues, c'est le sonnet."[19] The sonnet, like Ducros' "règles idéales" and Gautier's "lois," was not subject to vicissitude. Baudelaire may have been extreme when he said that "le meilleur compte rendu d'un tableau pourra être un sonnet ou une élégie,"[20] but there is something very worth noting in his comment: traditional poetic forms could, it was thought, be put to use for the expression of certain poetic modes; to perpetuate a painting, one could "transpose" it to the sonnet. The sonnet was the place where the image of the ideal would be safe from the harsh realities of the world of non-art. It was not by chance, then, that Pierre Martino employed a metaphorical temple to discuss Hérédia ("un vrai desservant du temple . . . officiant dans la plus sainte des chapelles, celle du sonnet"); here, the sonnet became, figuratively, a composite part of a sanctified place where art is preserved.[21]

The preservation of art, the perpetuation of the image, became an extended analogy that was almost a commonplace in the latter half of the nineteenth century in France. The precept of "l'art pour l'art" was expanded from what was an attitude toward art to what became the artist's active practice of constructing measures of defense for his own work. This implied a whole lifestyle for the artist himself, as we shall see. Catulle Mendès, a Parnassian and Judith Gautier's husband, told how the publisher of the first issue of *Parnasse* intended "Le *Parnasse* sera à la poésie ce que le Salon est à la peinture."[22] Book is to poem as museum is to painting. Gustave Moreau himself conceived of the museum as an elaborate exhibition of the artist's ideal, and it is curious how much the arrangement of his paintings in his own home reminds one of the makeup of a book, each of whose pages is an object of visual study:

> Moreau requested that the state "keep as long as possible [his] collection, conserving its character as an ensemble which shows the sum of work and the effort of the artist during his life." The idea of making an en-

semble of the emblems of his working imagination occurred to Moreau early in his career. It appears that he personally installed the hundreds of oil paintings and thousands of watercolors and drawings in elaborate cabinets opening out like Chinese puzzles; in the walls throughout his house which fold upon themselves like accordions; in the revolving *meuble* occupying the largest of his two studios on the top floor.[23]

The physical suspension of a painting corresponded, we may say, to the suspension of poetic subject, the arresting of image in time and space. One of the most illuminating statements of this analogy is from Gautier's "Le Musée ancien":

> Les tableaux, autrefois, étaient accrochés çà et là à peu près au hasard, ou plutôt d'après les dimensions et les angles de leurs cadres, sans souci de la chronologie; l'œuvre du même maître, éparpillée à de grandes distances, perdait la moitié de son effet. Aucune idée, aucune doctrine n'avait présidé à l'arrangement de ces trésors du génie lentement amassés par les siècles. C'était un magasin rempli de merveilles, non un musée.
>
> Cette idée si simple de réunir les Œuvres de chaque école, les manières de chaque maître, de les faire se suivre chronologiquement de façon que l'on pût lire comme dans un livre ouvert les origines, les progrès et la décadence de l'art de tel pays ou de tel siècle, n'était venue, la routine l'avait repoussée. Aucun conservateur du Musée ne s'était aperçu qu'il avait sous la main tous les matériaux pour écrire la plus magnifique histoire de la peinture sans faire les moindres frais de critique ou de style. Les pages toutes prêtes attendaient, ne demandant qu'à être numérotées.
>
> Maintenant, une promenade au Musée est un cours d'art complet, fait par des professeurs qui, pour être muets, n'en sont pas moins éloquents. La longue muraille vous enseigne, et chaque pas vous donne une connaissance: l'on voit naître, se développer et mourir les grandes écoles d'Italie, de Flandre et de Hollande, auxquelles se substitue, peu à peu, l'école de France, la seule qui vive aujourd'hui. Aucune histoire, aucun traité de peinture, ni Vasari, ni l'abbé Lanzi, ni Decamps, ni Sery d'Agencourt, ne sauraient vous en apprendre autant. Voilà les Byzantins. . . .[24]

All Gautier's curator had to do was to number each painting that lay helter-skelter in the museum and he would effect a metamorphosis of picture into page and museum into book. Moreover, the museum would be an open book; it would serve an aesthetic function, which is to reveal the beautiful. It would not perform the utilitarian task, would not alter beauty, as Leconte de Lisle warned it must not, but, rather, would perpetuate its pictorial images.

Let us look at Gautier's statement even more closely. The museum wall was not merely able to replace the professor of art; it could be more eloquent than he. The museum, not just the painting, would speak out. The arrangement (museum) of paintings, like the paintings themselves, would have an "éloquence"—an eloquence

which, paradoxically, would not be verbally interpretable. It would hold just as much of a radiant truth as the total meaning of the individual painting. Now since, like a painting, a completed poem could have, theoretically, a nonverbal significance, and since Casal's language is often used to daze and charm, not to further conceptual discernment, we may see that it was through language that imitated the iconic quality of the visual image that Casal had his poetry "speak out" (made it an *ekphrasis*). But since no poem can speak only a nonverbal language, Casal's poems can merely attempt, through words, an imitation of visual significance, and it is in this sense that **"Mi museo ideal"** can be thought of as a collection of "transpositions."[25] In the case of **"Mi museo ideal,"** the "transposition" itself and the most significant aspect of the process are, respectively, *ekphrasis* by *ekstasis*. That is, the description in poetic form of pictorial art, the "speaking out" of the pictorial art, is achieved primarily through the poet's exhibiting, his holding forth, the emblematical image. Casal's contemplation of the work of art leads to an exposition of the object that for him has most descriptive and archetypal meaning.

How then did Casal's "museum" of poetic paintings become an eloquent defense for his art and himself? To reiterate briefly, Casal chose the sonnet form so admired by the Parnassians for the first eleven poems of his poetic "museum"; only for the last poem did he lay aside the sonnet and adopt a poetic form whose rhyme scheme is varied and whose length is 130 lines. His sonnets on the paintings we may define as within the category of "the poem of imaginative confrontation, where a close connection between the poet's mood and the imagery is expressed by the personifying of the imagery [This] is the genre of the Keats ode, the Grecian Urn being the nearest to the emblem poem."[26] Casal, like Keats, tried to represent in words original objects d'art, or, more accurately, objets d'art that he had never really seen. His individual sonnets may be considered emblematical, and so too may be the composite **"Museo,"** which progressively acquires functionalism in the course of the composition, but Casal's sonnets, like Keat's poem, are certainly not "pura descripción pictórica," as R. Blanco-Fombona would have them be.[27] Rather, **"Mi museo ideal"** is, in part, a willful projection of Casal's imaginings, a reflection of his private life, and a defense for his art and himself, whereby the poet translated his various moods into the images that he depicted.

Now where the lyric is purposefully focused on visual imagery, we may think of it as overseen as well as overheard: as Frye says, "there are thousands of lyrics so intently focussed on visual imagery that they are, as we may say, set to pictures. In the emblem an actual picture appears."[28] In this respect, the poems of **"Mi museo ideal"** were probably not so purposeful an experiment as Appollinaire's "calligrammes," but they do show a sense of the relation of literary form to the subject treated, that is, to the paintings. Casal may simply have been following tradition—that of Hérédia, let us say—or he may have been consciously aware of what the sonnet afforded him as a medium for *ekphrasis*. But since when dealing with actual works by Moreau, Casal chose the sonnet form in order to represent the *objet d'art*, we may venture to say that the framing of the subject of each individual painting is partly achieved by the visual shape of the corresponding poems.

In fact, "frame" constitutes a primary aesthetic idea in the poems, especially when a "frame" quality, inherent in several of the pictures, comes into play; in these instances, Casal has reproduced such an effect in the poems. In the painting *Salomé,* the femme fatale dances beneath pillared arches which form a cupola above her; nearly the same effect is used in *L'Apparition,* where Moreau depicts the same figures in the same locale but from a different point of view; in *Prometée* the Titan is bound beneath an overhanging rock; in *Galatée* (the painting perhaps most suggestive of the effect of inherent frame), Moreau looks out from within a grotto, through its entrance, past Galatea, and to the face of the Cyclops, even more emphatically, into his eye; the moment of *Hercule et l'Hydre de Lerne* occurs within a labyrinth. Four of the sonnets which correspond to these paintings open with prepositions whose function is to suggest frameworks for the central image. These frameworks are immediately foretold in the statements of preposition, then named by their representational nouns: "En el palacio hebreo" (**"Salomé"**); "Bajo el dosel de gigantesca roca" (**"Prometeo"**); "En el seno radioso de su gruta" (**"Galatea"**); "En el umbral de lóbrega caverna" (**"Hércules ante la Hidra"**). **"La aparición"** is the exception ("Nube fragante y cálida") among these five sonnets. Nevertheless, we should remember that its context is historically and locally an immediate continuation of **"Salomé."** The palace mentioned in the first quatrain of **"La aparición"** has already acquired representational value in the anteceding sonnet, where the palace was three times emphasized in the first quatrain. The poet, rather than renaming, engages the tactile sense in **"La aparición,"** and he builds up the palace by the naming of its elements ("granito, / ónix, pórfido y nácar").

In **"Galatea"** (as in **"Retrato de Gustavo Moreau"**) Casal has invented representative detail to "transpose" the quality of "frame" to his sonnet.[29] The means for achieving this are not reduced to the simplicity of "Bajo el dosel," the opening of the **"Prometeo"** sonnet, where we have nothing to further this end except the localizing preposition and the noun itself, the mere printed sign for an architectural structure which projects and suspends overhead; "en" and "gruta" alone would perform an analogous function in **"Galatea."** In this son-

net, where the concavity of "gruta," for example, receives double emphasis with metaphorical "seno," the descriptive components are indicative of the pervasiveness of enclosure. The carpeted ("alfombrada") grotto becomes a sacrosanct place where beauty and order, personified in the figure of Galatea, can enjoy sleep, static life; and we might venture to say that the grotto is visually suggested by the literary form, the sonnet, especially if we bear in mind that the Parnassians thought of the sonnet itself as a sacrosanct place. As subject of the sonnet, Galatea requires of it that it be her symbolically powerful refuge. As the eternal, changeless image of art itself, she contributes to the **"Museo"'**s substitutional function (as do many of the artistic subjects with which we are concerned) and merits the framing that stresses her emblematic value.

The representative elements which make up the second quatrain of **"Galatea"** sprang from the imagination of Casal; these elements do not show up in Moreau's painting. Their validity, of course, is to be found in the way they interrelate with other elements of the poem, not the painting. When the poet asks himself what occurs outside the limited space of the grotto from which he views the subject of the painting, he imagines it to be in contrast to what occurs within the grotto and in opposition, also, to the whole mood of the "withinness" of beauty's temple. Sound and haphazard movement outside contrast with silence and static motion within:

> Desde la orilla de dorada ruta
> donde baten las ondas cristalinas,
> salpicando de espumas diamantinas
> el pico negro de la roca bruta,
>
> Polifemo. . . .

This contrast—of the elements within and those outside—extends the visual framework. The words "baten," "ondas," "salpicando de espumas," suggest the elements outside of the grotto, and the verbal units of the final line of this second quatrain accomplish the contrast: "pico" is the physical opposite of "gruta" (on a sexual as well as conceptually spatial level), "negro" connotes something ominous, contrary to the neutral quietude of Galatea with her "piel color de rosa." The physical attributes of the grotto outlined in the first quatrain are not those of "roca bruta." The poet thus lends spatiality to his poem by projecting through the rectilinear plane of the visual image, thus persuading the reader to orient himself and better apprehend the "central" image by referring to other imaginary planes, too.

As the reader of a poem begins his perception of the work's significance with the first word, so the viewer of a picture begins his understanding of the meaning of the work with the initial perception of any graphic sign.[30] But it would be proper to keep in mind that a logical syntax is often operative in a poem, especially in lineally descriptive poetry, to a greater degree than it is in a painting. The poet's syntax might arrange sense data in a more direct way than might that of the painter; and the poet better controls the reader's orientation, the more explicit his descriptive language. Granted the particular nature of Casal's and Moreau's works, we may correctly speak in terms of relatively oriented vision when we compare these, for in the case of the latter, the beholder's attention is more random, at least initially. The first word of the poem is, therefore, of particular importance to Casal as poet of *ekphrasis*. In the poems mentioned above, Casal situates the particular subject matter and thus impels the reader to a specific reference point for the emblematic meaning. For example, Casal shocks us immediately upon exit from the grotto with the mention of the Cyclops' name: the ninth line of **"Galatea"** begins "Polifemo"; the two tercets are dedicated to him. The written name "Polifemo" is an economical sign for his visage, which is precisely the subject content of the space framed by the opening of the grotto in the painting. Thus, the written word, syntactically located, could approximate the painted visage.

We can see at work in Casal's act of poetic painting, as Susanne Langer would have it, that the poem becomes not merely "a shape in space, but a shaping *of* space—of all the space that [the beholder] is given."[31] Quantitatively considered, his sonnet gives less importance to Galatea, although she is the titular subject, than it does to Polyphemus, who exists for the dramatic encounter between reader and subject. Casal has emphasized psychological condition ("lujuria") and deemphasized the portrayal of beauty (Galatea) in this "transposition." The quantitative deemphasis of the latter, in fact, allows for the emphasis of the former, and it is tempting to think of Polyphemus and his ambience as occupying more of the poem's visual space.

The poet does not run helter-skelter over the surface of the painting, accumulating visual detail for his poem. No more would Casal portray sky, to take an obvious example, at the "base" of a sonnet than would Gombrich admit the likelihood of the child's placing the eyes on the haunches of the hobby horse. Although both are possible, of course, these artistic applications would diminish the representation's initial substitutional value. (Compare the order of poetic subject in **"Sueño de gloria,"** which more concerns the narration of an apotheosis than the hypostatization of a preexistent image.) Nearly all the sonnets either begin with a portrayal of sky or, at least, go from the diaphanous to the concrete. Further, Casal impels the reader to shape his own painting as he takes him to and through the planes that lend a dimensional aspect to the sonnet. It is by leading *to* that the poet marks the particular images which best define the total meaning of the poem; it is by leading *through* that he creates the illusion of virtual space within the sonnet medium. As with "extasiado" in

the ninth line of **"Galatea,"** for example, Casal suggests a halting point (Polyphemus' visage) for the reader of the poem, who, Frye would say, is also supposed to be seeing a picture appear in the emblematic poem; so it is the Cyclops' eye that is held in *ekstasis*. A similar technique is used to discover Jupiter waiting in ambush for Europa.

It is significant that Casal ended his sonnet with the mention of the Cyclops' eye ("incendia la lujuria su ojo verde"). Polyphemus' dramatic function is to look back into the grotto, on the sleeping Galatea (after the mention of the name "Polifemo" we are again told of a sleeping goddess); his function, in other words, is to look out toward the reader. Galatea is doubly perceived, once by the reader and then by Polyphemus. The repetition of this detail in a poetic form so condensed as the sonnet lends a spatial value to the poetic image, as the reader associates the two allusions to Galatea and simultaneously relates these to her two beholders, himself and the Cyclops. What this achieves for Casal is an impression of momentaneousness. It is a process that contradicts the temporal aspect implicit in the written poem, and it is essential to the concepts of *ekstasis* and exhibit. Placement of "ojo" at the end of the poem urges the reader from a witnessing of representational detail and brings him to a recognition of the meaning of the poem: the state of beauty (Galatea at rest in her grotto) threatened by elements in opposition (Polyphemus and the unruly world outside the grotto). As "transposer," Casal has underscored the dramatic aspect of the painting, and his rendering of the traditional image in new perspectives has made possible the perpetuation of the image. The linear progression of the poem has achieved what the painting could not automatically achieve. The poet has acted as a guide through the syntactical format within which he worked. Like Gautier in his *Guide de l'amateur au musée du Louvre,* Casal could lead in a particular sequence into, through, and out of his "museum," and he could dictate the sequence in which each of its units was to be viewed, too.

In "Hélène sur les remparts de Troie" Moreau shows Helen in a graceful stance upon the ruined walls, holding a lily in her hand and overlooking with nonchalance the dead soldiers and rubble of the recently ended battle. In Casal's sonnet **"Elena,"** the apparently random naming of the effects of the war at Troy is the poet's means of representing the chaos of recent historical past. "What?" is answered before "Where?" As soon as we are informed of the locale, a mysterious figure is presented as apart ("envuelta") from the surroundings, but is not identified for us until the thirteenth line of the sonnet. The emblematical subject thus undergoes a process of *ekstasis* through circumscription before it is held up toward the reader at the end of the poem: "mira Elena hacia el lívido horizonte / irguiendo un lirio en la rosada mano." By the device of circumscription, Casal has lent to his sonnet the quality of riddle, which is broken, finally, by the terminal identification of the poem's principal subject, Helen.[32] That is, Casal has made both circumscription and description operative in this poem especially, and in this way he seems to lean toward the symbolist's (Mallarmé's) propensity for suggesting rather than naming.

The lily, the central symbol of the final line and the main focal point of Moreau's painting, is merely an extension of Helen: a depersonalized Helen takes form in the lily. In terms of meaning, then, they are one and the same image. Both stand erect. Both are incongruous with their surroundings: they have survived what nothing else has survived. They are cold, fresh beauty grown up out of the burning ugliness of death ("homicidas mechas"). They are isolated by their physical position ("desde el monte / de ruinas hacinadas en el llano") and by their position in the sequence in which things are mentioned in the sonnet. In one sense, the spatial identification of the lily with Helen emphasizes Helen's lack of empathy with her surroundings. But as the person becomes the flower by virtue of the verbal succession of the inanimate object after the human figure of Helen, the impersonality of art's image is stressed, and the titular subject acquires its completeness in the final line when its association with the nonhuman lily is established.

The Helen-lily image may be thought of as symbolically representative of Casal's poetic work: the art object is worth all of wasted civilization; it is the object for which civilization has sacrificed itself, and yet, ironically, it denies this sphere of action. There is also a methodological significance to be observed here. A flower may possess a symbolic value similar to that which it has in **"Salomé"**; yet the particularity of its presentation in each poem indicates how the contexts lend it special meaning. The common symbol, in turn, helps to define the meaning of both of these sonnets at once and that of the composite collection as well.

The meeting of methodology and aesthetic in Casal's "transpositions" is clarified by his **"Elena."** In Moreau's paintings, the artistic ideal is symbolized, time and again, by the human figure. His Helen is one example; Galatea and Hercules are others. Prometheus' lofty position is associable with Helen's, and in Casal's sonnet, Prometheus' moan—only a potentially audible moan, there by virtue of Casal's projection of meaning—is correlative with his solitary indifference. Whereas condition (indifference and solitude) is stressed in the figures of Prometheus and Helen, Hercules and Salomé are the human embodiments of physical harmony. Galatea, isolated, sleeping, and protected, encompasses all these qualities. Moreau's paintings and Casal's use of them reflect the "two beliefs—in the Image as a radiant truth out of space and time, and in the necessary

isolation or estrangement of men who can perceive it—[beliefs which] are inextricably associated."[33] "Radiant" seems to be a strategic word for both Moreau and Casal; it was not enough in their attempts to represent the image as truth merely to leave it compromisingly positioned within the picture or the poem. It must be set apart descriptively (sheathed Helen), or it must be held forth to occupy the foremost plane of imaginary space (as in **"Salomé"**). Also, the image must be timeless, without definable past or future, for conscious relation to any other thing implies contemporaneity, thereby breaking the illusion of the image's perfect isolation. The image must be devoid of its own mental process. In Casal's sonnet, Helen of Troy is "indiferente," she reflects non-thought; she actively shows non-concern, choosing to look toward nothingness rather than at the human question so immediately present—indeed, attributable to her. The emphasis on Helen, indifferent and emphatically apart from anything else, is what the word "envuelta" and the structure of her appearance within the spatial and temporal limits of the sonnet achieve for the reader.

"Hércules ante la Hidra" is another complex example of the problem of *ekstasis*. Again, both structure and descriptive usage serve to effect this desired end. An indication that it is, in fact, a process of *ekstasis* at work is to be found in the very title of the sonnet. His alteration of Moreau's title, *Hercule et l'Hydre de Lerne,* shows Casal's more explicit concern for the psychological drama represented in the painting. The poet could rely only partially on the visual effect of his poem to determine the physical relationship of his two primary subjects, so Casal's title set the mood for the theme of dramatic confrontation by clearly positioning Hercules *before* ("ante") the Hydra.[34] In **"Galatea"** the poet achieved psychological drama by ultimately directing the reader's vision toward the eye of the Cyclops. To somewhat the same effect, the Hydra here moves outward from within, threateningly, and is identified by name at the end of the first quatrain: "surge, acechando del viajero el paso, / invencible y mortal, la Hidra de Lerna."

In the description of the Hydra, motive is emphasized; in the description of Hercules, the opposing force to the Hydra, physical attributes are emphasized. Casal has posed Hercules in this manner, plasticized him in agreement with Moreau's having plasticized him in his painting. The tercets show Hercules charged with potential energy, at the moment of confrontation:

> Hércules, coronado de laureles,
> repleto el carcaj en el áureo cinto,
> firme en la diestra la potente maza,
>
> ante las sierpes de viscosas pieles
> detiénese en mitad del laberinto,
> fulminando en sus ojos la amenaza.

This potentiality is a favorite theme for Moreau, and it is the one Casal correspondingly underscores in his literary "transposition." In order to achieve the sense of potentiality, stasis is put to function, and the final line emphasizes Hercules' stare. (The contrary of functional stasis was true of Keats's urn, where a kinetic sense was more apt for the *ekphrasis*.) In **"Hércules ante la Hidra,"** the phrases "umbral de lóbrega caverna" and "mitad del laberinto" describe the frames from which the two opposing images project themselves outward and freeze before the reader. Once Hercules and the Hydra are thus held forth, detained in opposition to each other, the sonnet acquires formal meaning. That "deliberate pause in practical activity"[35] practiced by so many artists in the latter half of the nineteenth century is an idea immediately associable with the subject of the poem. In **"Hércules ante la Hidra,"** where the emphasis is on a potential activity, where a psychological drama is created at the expense of a physical one, the artist's own "overcoming of action in cosmic contemplation" is suggested.

Casal opened his "museum" with a sonnet on Salomé, whose function, according to story, was to charm. This function is imitated in the language of the first quatrain of **"Salomé,"** where Casal creates an illusion of pervasive fragrance:

> el suave
> humo fragante por el sol deshecho,
> sube a perderse en el calado techo
> o se dilata en la anchurosa nave. . . .

What he achieves by this is the most immediate synesthesia and the most efficacious means for sensorial recall of the whole iconology of poems after the reader has passed through it.[36] This phenomenon of total perception of a series of images as one simultaneous whole is treated by Georges Poulet and elaborated upon by Wylie Sypher: it implies a vision of eternity, traceable in all the "imaginative" romantics, a blending of feeling and thought that shows up as a natural achievement in De Quincey and Baudelaire.[37]

"Salomé" and **"La aparición"** are presented as a diptych; the story of the first poem directly precedes that of the second, as the paintings themselves indicate by the repositioning of their subject matter, the omission and transformation of certain subjects, and the introduction and holding forth of new ones. And, especially since the two poems begin the succession of ten, their historical successiveness is an impetus for the "promenade." Given these temporal and spatial considerations, and since in **"La aparición"** there is a breakdown in the harmony of the Salomé figure, as a result of the appearance of the head of John the Baptist before her, we can see the alternation between the images of plasticized harmony and the pathological, traced by Praz in the course of his *The Romantic Agony.* Huysmans, from whose prose descriptions Casal derived the bases for these two sonnets, "correlated the pathological and aesthetic aspects of the Dancer motif."[38] Salomé's paralysis in **"La aparición"** is particularly remarkable in light of the importance of her image as dancer in the sonnet just preceding, where, as the traditional Salomé figure, she appeared as an image of harmonious organic movement, which was hypostatized, at the end of the poem, in the lotus.

As in **"Elena,"** the femme fatale was depersonalized into a flower to emphasize her organic perfection as image and her implicit lack of human concern, since between the moments of **"Salomé"** and **"La aparición,"** Salomé's function as charmer was complete with the decapitation of John the Baptist. Her foremost position in the temporal progression of **"Salomé"** implies the formal completion of this function, while it also gives primacy to the dancer-flower motif.[39] In order to give primacy to this motif, Casal has moved from the vaguest to the least vague, from the most scopic to the most minute visual object, the pistils of the lotus. Within the perceptual vagueness of the quatrains he has located Herod, the orientation point for other symbols; before Herod ("delante de él") is Salomé, who holds up the lotus in her right hand. Casal has chosen the progression from vagueness, to center, forward, then upward, to create a sensation of space in his poem by suggesting the physical planes which, in fact, correspond to the pictorial illusion of Moreau's painting. By the nature of the medium, however, the sequence of planes remains more or less arbitrary for the beholder of the painting; there is no sequential equivocation in the poem, and for the reader, perceptual progression is fixed. The depersonalization of Salomé, or of Helen, into flower does more than reflect the attitude of the traditional figure. The flower is metaphorically the work of art as unconscious organic life and, as such, merits its structural location in the two sonnets as the final detail in *ekstasis.* Moreover, the flower, although requiring continual refashioning and perpetuation, resists literal "transposition," because it is "utterly original" (Kermode) and inimitable.

"Una peri" demonstrates, perhaps most clearly of all the poems, a full process of *ekstasis.* The peri balances herself atop a high promontory (line 1). She moves off into space, where she is portrayed in resplendence ("retratada en la fúlgida marea," line 8). As she descends, in a noiseless spin ("en silencioso giro, / como visión lumínica de plata"), a feeble sigh idles upon her lips ("vaga en sus labios lánguido suspiro"), and finally, weariness is outlined in her violet-colored eyes. Just before her spin begins (line 9), she is held momentarily in space, clasping her lyre (like the flower, a symbol of perfection). She descends so near to us that we can perceive the weariness and the color of her eyes. As in the case of Prometheus' moan, although the peri sighs, she cannot be heard. She is so close that we *see* her sigh; it idles upon her lips. The peri, then, is caught in temporal arrest twice: once in midair, at the end of the quatrains, and again before the beholder of her fall, at the end of the tercets. Moreau's painting(s) *La Péri* shows her as Casal saw her, caught in midair, clasped to her lyre. But her departure from the balancing point on the high promontory and her spin toward the beholder are inventions by Casal. One important critic recently remarked with surprise that Moreau's *La Péri* "n'offre aucune ressemblance avec le sonnet de Casal—à la différence de ce qui se passe pour les neuf autres sonnets, tous reproductions fidèles des tableaux du peintre. Nous avouons ignorer quelle Œuvre de Moreau servit de modèle au poète pour composer son sonnet."[40] But herein lies a mistreatment of the poem: Faurie shows no way to account for a willfully "imperfect" *ekphrasis* and thus neglects to distinguish between stated Parnassian aesthetic and actual practice.

The intention of the poet to make the image stand out for the reader, to "speak" her condition, could scarcely be clearer. Not only is Casal mindful of framing the peri in space, as Moreau did so elaborately, in an "encadrement floral," but he makes her "step forth" a second time, this time stopping closer to the poet. What a closer viewing allows is a sure perception of the peri's condition ("suspiro," "cansancio"). So the peri has gone beyond the simply revelatory nature of herself as visual image. Through the double *ekstasis* Casal chose to bring about, he has better perceived the image by writing into it a mood, and in this sense, he has incorporated himself in Moreau's art.

Casal, like so many of his contemporaries, was so absorbing himself into his own art forms that he was becoming them.[41] The ten sonnets of the **"Museo,"** taken as a series of distinct members, may be said to represent a structuring of the inner life of the poet. The ten sonnets may also be taken as a single mode of art set forth within a poetic structure that symbolizes the poet's mind and private life, and which literally stands for them, emblematically. As a whole, the **"Museo"** becomes correlative with the poet's life, and it is the life in its projected state, the printed poems.

Casal saw himself as the creator in confrontation with adverse destiny, and his empathy with Moreau's self-portrait is definable primarily in these terms. His **"Vestíbulo"** sonnet begins: "Rostro que desafía los crueles / rigores del destino." It is the same image we saw Moreau project into *Hercule et l'Hydre de Lerne* and *Prometée,* and which Casal projected into his corresponding sonnets. It is, in Kermode's words, the "necessary isolation and estrangement of men who can perceive [the Image]." As Casal put it in a letter written to a friend, Esteban Borrero Echevarría, and dated 19 March 1891, that is, shortly before the first publication of the collection **"Mi museo ideal"** in 1892:

Mi ideal consiste hoy en vivir obscurecido, solo, arrinconado e invisible para todos, excepto para usted y dos o tres personas. . . .

Ahora quiero buscar una habitación alta, aislada en una azotea, abierta a los cuatro vientos, porque preciso aprender a pintar y porque creo que mi neurosis, o como se llame mi enfermedad, depende en gran parte de vivir en la ciudad, es decir, rodeado de paredes altas, de calles adoquinadas, oyendo incesantemente estrépito de coches, ómnibus y carretones. Procuraré irme a vivir en un barrio lejano, cerca del mar, para aguardar allí la muerte, que no tardará mucho en venir. Mientras llegue, viviré entre libros y cuadros, trabajando todo lo que pueda literariamente, sin pretender alcanzar nada con mis trabajos, como no sea matar el tiempo. . . .

Múdeme o no, pienso terminar un tomo de versos que tengo ya a más de la mitad y otro de cuentos que está en el mismo estado. Cuando descanse, me entregaré a la pintura. Después quiero escribir algunas impresiones literarias y dos novelas que ya se están convirtiendo para mí en una verdadera obsesión.[42]

Was knowing how to paint going to serve a need ("porque preciso")? Was painting going to be just another way to "kill time," as he had determined that literature would become for himself? Or were paintings simply the things to "live among," as the vogue of the day dictated? Casal's letter continues with a description of what the hero of the novel he plans to write will be like; there are striking similarities between this hero's life, that of Des Esseintes, and that which Casal dreamed for himself, as we are led to believe by autobiographical fragments. Huysmans' hero Des Esseintes, like Casal, built up his own "maison d'un artiste." It is significant that so much of *A rebours* is a lapidary, a "florilegium," bibliothetical description; that Des Esseintes is an olfactologist, a bibliotaph, and so on. Huysmans wrote partly in the tradition of those catalogers like Gautier, Sainte-Beuve, and Edmond de Goncourt; but Ralph Freedman points out an important difference, one which shows the kinship between Casal and his admired Huysmans, as they stand in contrast to the pure catalogers: "The romantic pilgrimage through a world of images is replaced by the inner wanderings of an essentially sedentary self."[43]

While Casal was more than just a guide or a cataloger, he did not relinquish totally his capacity to describe objective reality. He performed as descriptive guide in several curious ways, however, as we have observed already. There is yet another way in which Casal is a special kind of guide. He put into effect the two guiding principles professed by Moreau for the creation of art: "la belle inertie" and "la richesse nécessaire."[44] The former principle has already been discussed; the latter is demonstrated by Casal's dependence on representational detail. For Moreau and for Casal, representational detail was one more means of negating the interpretative process. That is, the more nominal the information, the less possibility there is for projection into the art work and thus the more changeless the work remains. Captivate the senses by dazzling, stupefying, them, would be another way of putting it.[45]

There is, indeed, a functional parallel between "el sacro poder de sus pinceles" and the consecrating powers of the pen of Casal. Both the paintbrush and the pen, the means by which the image is fashioned and refashioned, are the instruments for effectuating the respective artistic media of Moreau and Casal. For the self-sustainment of its fashioner, the image is vital (Casal's "porque preciso"), because it is that which the fashioner opposes to death as a possible escape from the antiaesthetic world. Moreau would time and again treat the same subject. *La Péri, Salomé,* and *Galatée,* for example, are the titles for several of his pieces; all three happen to be titles that Casal used also, and sometimes, in **"Galatea,"** let us say, it is difficult to choose precisely which painting Casal had in mind. What is so significant about this, however, is that Moreau was practicing reexposition after reexposition of his own subjects. His continual refashioning of his own work seems directly related to that practiced by the Parnassian poets with their most cultivated images. Moreau was not merely defending the Parnassian image; he was bit-by-bit building a projection of himself in which he could exist in life and through which he could live on after death: "On the eve of his death he is said to have gone over hundreds of his drawings signing and lightly correcting them. He saw his life as the works it engendered."[46]

Casal's choice to alternatively internalize and artistically externalize this image was a means to attain his own spiritual existence. This was a real-life process poetically displaced in the imagery of **"Sueño de gloria,"** where the poet, by analogy with Moreau, could lead himself out of the sepulcher and raise himself all the way to godhood. Casal, as an example of those "artists and contemplatives in a world built for action," whose possibilities for escape are two, death and the refashioning of the image, made Moreau and his work the means to victorious escape from the rigorous destiny of the artist in an antiaesthetic world.[47] The wish for this escape is implicit early in the collection with a "vestibular" departure from the external world into the **"Museo."** We have in the second quatrain of **"Vestíbulo"**:

> Creador luminoso como Apeles,
> si en la Grecia inmortal nacido hubiera,
> cual dios entre los dioses estuviera
> por el sacro poder de sus pinceles.

The subjunctive verbal mood here is unique in the collection of sonnets, and it expresses Casal's desire for the equation of the artist with the image. This is precisely what Casal does for the artist in the final poem.

But first, the poet passes from **"Vestíbulo"** into the world of the paintings through the eyes of the artist in the portrait. This figurative filtering of perception of the world of the paintings through Moreau's own vision gives substance to the final poem, **"Sueño de gloria,"** where Casal makes a poetized Moreau, as aesthete-creator, the encompassing symbol for the ten images of **"Mi museo ideal"** and for the ideal itself.

"Sueno de gloria" is Casal's own vision. With it, the poet passes from the "poem of imaginative confrontation" to one of "expanded consciousness."[48] The poem is a dream (as we know by its title) that occurs on the day of universal judgment, in a terrestrial atmosphere where acrid-smelling sepulchers open to free the dead. Casal alters Helen's condition from what we have seen in the sonnet by having her fall blushingly and stammeringly in love with Moreau, her Creator, and rise to godhood with him in holy union sanctioned by God. This disruption of the harmonic perfection of the traditional image makes way for Moreau's becoming the encompassing image, whereby he will stand for all the rest. Both Helen and Moreau are positioned apart from their surroundings. Their ascension is described as follows:

> y, cual fragantes lirios enlazados,
> por la región magnífica del viento
> ascienden los eternos desposados. . . .

Moreau, as well as Helen ("lirios enlazados"), is absorbed into one of the traditional forms the image takes, into the autonomous art object symbolized by the flower. He becomes indistinguishable from his own artistic creation by virtue of his symbolic marriage to, and absorption into, its primary images, Helen and the lily.

"Sueño de gloria" should, properly, be taken as a representation of elements from the "museum" preceding, as a refashioning not only of its symbolical units but also of its lexical and syntactical units. Compare, for example, the poetic line that introduces Helen ("Bajo el dosel de verdinegro olivo") to the opening line of the **"Prometeo"** sonnet ("Bajo el dosel de gigantesca roca"). Thus, Casal's own dream vision becomes a refashioning of the image, that is, of the "museum" as a totality of ideal forms. But the post-reading experience must deny a mode of perception that yields a vision of a succession of parts, in the same way that the individual sonnet must lend itself to perfect perception only at the moment of its final words or image. The sensation of totality achieved upon completion of the twelve poems is due to a number of factors, two of which are the poems' basic structural unit (museum) and the deific vision (the figurative representation of Poulet's romantic timelessness) of **"Sueño de gloria."**

The antithetical elements of intellectual effort and form, which by literary custom denied intellectual effort, are reconciled figuratively in the **"Sueño,"** where Casal is symbolizing Moreau's conquest over death by so incorporating the painter into his own subject matter that the painter, too, is concretized as image. In **"Sueño de gloria,"** Casal merges figures from the pagan classical world (Helen) and the present (Moreau) with biblical theme in a denial of temporal and spatial limitation. Casal achieves, without using the Parnassians' "perpetuating" sonnet form, an illusion of changelessness, through the thematic representation of a totality of time and space. And the "expanded consciousness" of the poet is represented by the expanded poetic form. In contrast to the restrictively directive (through the single point of view of the painter, figuratively speaking) entrance in **"Vestíbulo"** into the realms of Moreau's subjects from the Bible and classical myth, we have a symbolical exit in the form of ascent from death up to godhood. The direction is outward, rather than inward. The beginning and final poems of **"Mi museo ideal"** create a "minimum image" (Gombrich) by which Casal substitutes his collection of poems for Moreau's own museum. The idea of a temple for art, Gombrich might have said, is substitutionally operative once the **"Museo"** acquires an architectural aspect.

Notes

1. One notable exception is the recent study by Marie Josèphe Faurie, *Le Modernisme hispano-américain et ses sources françaises* (Paris, 1966), pp. 171-199. José Lezama Lima (*Analecta del reloj* [Havana, 1953], pp. 62-97) is primarily concerned with critical approach in his comparative treatment of Casal and Baudelaire. On the other hand, studies of "Mi museo ideal" are usually carried no further than a gleaning of the poems' subject matter. Bernardo Gicovate (*Conceptos fundamentales de literatura comparada: Iniciación de la poesía modernista* [San Juan, Puerto Rico, 1962], p. 112) says of the collection: "no nos queda más remedio que aceptar el juicio de la posterioridad y admitir un mero valor de documento histórico para esta parte de la obra de Casal." Esperanza Figueroa ("Julián del Casal y Rubén Darío," *Revista bimestre cubana,* L, No. 2 [1942], 191-208; "Julián del Casal y el modernismo," *Revista iberoamericana,* XXXI, No. 59 [1965], 47-69) and José María Monner Sans (*Julián del Casal y el modernismo hispanoamericano* [Mexico D. F., 1952]) have treated the poet's place in the Latin American "Modernista" movement. Gustavo Duplessis ("Julián del Casal," *Revista bimestre cubana,* LIV, Nos. 1, 2, 3 [1944] 31-75, 140-170, 241-286) published a thesis on the poet, valuable mostly for its documentary material. See also Rita Geada de Prulletti, "Bibliografía de y sobre Julián del Casal (1863-1893)," *Revista iberoamericana,* XXXIII, No. 63 [1967], 133-139.

2. Figueroa ("Casal y Darío," p. 206) mentions among Casal's readings Musset, Baudelaire, Gautier, Mendès, Maupassant, Verlaine, and Huysmans. Faurie (*Modernisme,* p. 195) states that "de tous les auteurs français Baudelaire est celui qui eut sur Casal la plus grande influence." We know, too, that Casal was highly regarded by certain of France's important literary figures and that, among these, Verlaine, Huysmans, and Moreau wrote in praise of Casal, and that Judith Gautier corresponded with him (see Duplessis, "Casal," p. 69; Faurie, *Modernisme,* p. 198). Gicovate states that "desde sus deudas para con Gautier y Huysmans hasta sus lecturas de Banville, Leconte de Lisle y sus traducciones e imitaciones de Hérédia y aun de Louis Bouilhet, todas las imitaciones directas de los parnasianos y los ecos que salpican aquí y allá una obra titubeante han sido señalados ya" (*Conceptes,* p. 110), and he goes on to say that "no queda por hacer sino el inventario de esta influencia parnasiana, preguntarse si algo quedó, si aprendió algo el poeta en esta larga esclavitud." As for the frequent mention of the Cuban-born José Maria de Hérédia in discussions of Casal, this is due mostly to points of similarity between the sonnet collection *Les Trophées* and a part of the work of Casal. The collected *Trophées* were published with a dedication to Leconte in 1893, one year after "Mi museo ideal" although some of the sonnets of the collection had appeared much earlier (in 1866, *Parnasse contemporain,* for example), and Casal had known them by way of various reviews (see Faurie, *Modernisme,* p. 181; also, Manuel de la Cruz's three-part article "José María Heredia," in the periodical to which Casal made frequent contributions of poems, *El fígaro,* VIII, Nos. 38, 39, 40 [6, 13, 20 November 1892], 2-3, 3, 6-7).

3. Still, Casal may very well have had paintings by Moreau in mind when he wrote the first and twelfth poems of "Mi museo ideal" e.g., the 1850 *Autoportrait* and the *Fleur mystique.*

4. Some of the poems were originally published separately. This is true, for example, of the final poem, "Sueño de gloria" (published in *La Habana literaria,* 30 December 1891), and Duplessis ("Casal," p. 156) cites the publication of "Gustavo Moreau" in *El fígaro,* 15 January 1892. Figueroa ("Casal y modernismo," p. 57) claims 1890 as the date for "Salomé." The subtitle for "Mi museo ideal" is "Diez cuadros de Gustavo Moreau." The published collection in *Nieve* (Havana: "La moderna" de Aurelio Miranda, 1892) and in subsequent editions includes the first and twelfth poems, whose full titles, placement within the collection, and various points of coincidence with the ten "cuadros" indicate that they were intended

as integral parts of the "Museo." (See one of the earliest announcements of the first publication of *Nieve* in the Havana literary periodical, *El fígaro,* VIII, No. 14 [24 April 1892], 9.) Throughout the present study, quotations from the Casal poems are from *Poesías,* Edición del Centenario (Havana, 1963).

5. The structural similarity of "Mi museo ideal" to Modest Moussorgsky's *Pictures from an Exhibition* is worth noting. *Pictures* was inspired by ten pictures and designs by Hartmann, a friend of the composer and an architect and painter by profession, and the suite was written after the 1874 exhibition of Hartmann's work in Saint Petersburg. The composition has as a principal motif a "Promenade," which evokes Moussorgsky entering and walking from piece to piece on exhibit, all the while recalling his artist-friend (see M. D. Calvocoressi, *Modest Mussorgsky: His Life and Works* [London, 1956], p. 182). No immediate connection with Casal is insisted upon here, but the suite is mentioned in conjunction with the collection of poems for its striking structural resemblance to the latter. We might consider, too, the contemporaneity of the two works.

6. E. H. Gombrich, *Meditations on a Hobby Horse and Other Essays on the Theory of Art,* 2d ed. (London, 1965), pp. 7-8. "Surrounded as we are by posters and newspapers carrying illustrations of commodities or events, we find it difficult to rid ourselves of the prejudice that all images should be 'read' as referring to some imaginary or actual reality. Only the historian knows how hard it is to look at Pygmalion's work without comparing it with nature. But recently we have been made aware how thoroughly we misunderstand primitive or Egyptian art whenever we make the assumption that the artist 'distorts' his motif or that he even wants us to see in his work the record of any specific experience" (p. 3).

7. Gustave Kahn, symbolist promoter of *vers libre,* wrote: "Qu'est-ce qu'un vers?—C'est un arrêt simultané de la pensée et de la forme de la pensée.—Qu'est-ce qu'une strophe? C'est le développement par une phrase en vers d'un point complet de l'idée.—Qu'est-ce qu'un poème? C'est la mise en situation par ses facettes prismatiques, qui sont les strophes, de l'idée tout entière qu'on a voulu évoquer" (cited by Jules Huret, *Enquête sur l'évolution littéraire* [Paris, 1891], p. 395. For Kahn, then, idea and form were inseparable in space and time; they were elaborations upon each other, and the total poem was equivalent to the whole idea or total form of that idea. Mallarmé said derisively that "les Parnassiens, eux, prennent la chose entièrement et la montrent." His com-

plaint was against the a priori perception of form and the necessary submission of the poet to it, thus depriving the poem of its self-generating nature and consequent "mystère." The Parnassians, for him, "manquent de mystère; ils retirent aux esprits cette joie délicieuse de croire qu'ils créent. *Nommer* un objet, c'est supprimer les trois quarts de la jouissance du poème qui est faite du bonheur de deviner peu à peu le *suggérer,* voilà le rêve" (cited by Huret, *Enquête,* p. 60).

8. Aaron Schaffer, *Parnassus in France: Currents and Cross-Currents in Nineteenth-Century French Lyric Poetry* (Austin, Texas, 1929), p. 32.

9. Théophile Gautier, *Portraits et souvenirs littéraires* (Paris, 1885), pp. 234-235.

10. Jean Ducros, *Le Retour de la poésie française à l'antiquité grecque au milieu de XIXe siècle* (Paris, 1918), pp. 96, 98.

11. Roman Jakobson, "On Linguistic Aspects of Translation," in *On Translation* (Cambridge, Mass., 1959), p. 238.

12. Karl D. Uitti, *The Concept of Self in the Symbolist Novel* (The Hague, 1961), p. 55. Uitti also points out, significantly: "It can be argued that all poets and novelists 'deform' language, that every work of literature conforms in one way or another to the distortion of vision of its author. Yet this truth, as we understand it today, was just making its impact felt on the literary consciousness of Lorrain's [Jean Lorrain, pseud. of Paul Duval, a symbolist] generation. These writers tried *systematically* to discover and impose a highly personal way of seeing things."

13. Schaffer, *Parnassus,* p. 36. This corresponds to a claim by Leconte de Lisle (*Revue européenne,* December 1861): "Nous ignorons, il est vrai, que les idées, en étymologie exacte et en strict bon sens, ne peuvent être que des formes et que les formes sont l'unique manifestation de la pensée" (Charles Marie Leconte de Lisle, *Oeuvres de . . .* [Paris: Alphonse Lemerre, n.d.], p. 282).

14. Fernand Calmettes, *Leconte de Lisle et ses amis* (Paris, n.d.), pp. 215-216.

15. Charles Marie Leconte de Lisle, the Avant-propos to "Les Poètes contemporains," *Oeuvres,* p. 241. Leconte de Lisle himself, "withdrawing into the study of the history and mythology of the peoples of the East, . . . espoused the stoical, pantheistic philosophy of the Buddhists" (Schaffer, *Parnassus,* p. 91).

16. Leconte de Lisle, *Oeuvres,* pp. 279-280.

17. José Maria Hérédia, cited by Gustave Kahn, *Symbolistes et décadents* (Paris, 1902), p. 370.

18. Charles Asselineau (*Histoire du sonnet,* 2d ed. [Alençon, 1856], p. 35) continued the Colletet tradition with his brief *Histoire*; he found the sonnet form symptomatic of "époques de forte poésie où l'imagination des poètes s'inquiète également du sentiment et de la forme, de l'art et de la pensée." Théophile Gautier, who referred his readers far back in time to Colletet's treatise on the sonnet (see *Les Grotesques* [Paris, 1882], pp. 235-236), struck a polemical reaction from Sainte-Beuve: "Je suis de ceux qui ont toujours reculé devant cette poésie Louis XIII, et je n'ai jamais pu m'en inoculer le goût. . . . C'est en somme une très-mauvaise compagnie" (Charles Augustin Sainte-Beuve, "Théophile Gautier," *Portraits contemporains,* V [Paris, 1871], 121-122). See also the explication of Banville's *Petit Traité de poésie française* (1872) by Max Fuchs (*Théodore de Banville* [Paris, 1912], pp. 421-442).

19. Hérédia, cited by Kahn, *Symbolistes,* p. 369. Because of the tradition in which we find Casal the length of a poem merits more discussion than we might offhand suspect. Jules Lemaître's reference to Hérédia's "sonnets si pleins qu'ils 'valent vraiment de longs poèmes'" (in his *Les Contemporains,* 2d ser. [Paris, 1891], p. 55) was accessible to Casal's literary circle, at least shortly after the publication of *Nieve,* that is, at least by 6 November 1892, the date of the first issue of Cruz's three-part article in *El fígaro*. It is recognized by most critics of Casal that one of the earliest of his French "teachers" was Baudelaire, a transmitter of the aesthetics of Poe. Turning to Poe's "Philosophy of Composition," we find, in effect, that length was his very first consideration in the composition of "The Raven," the poem he used to demonstrate what Baudelaire called "le choix des moyens" (Pierre Charles Baudelaire, *Critique littéraire et musicale,* ed. Claude Pichois [Paris, 1961], p. 206). It is not unlikely that Casal had introduced himself, through Baudelaire, to the principles stated by Poe. Northrup Frye *(Anatomy of Criticism* [New York, 1966], p. 278) calls Poe's essay an anticipation of the critical techniques of a new mode; for Frye, Poe's very conscious application of the medium restricted to some degree his lyrical initiative. Frye sees, also, "how far removed the lyrical initiative really is from whatever a *cri de coeur* is supposed to be," a fact indicated by the elaborateness of conventional forms like the sonnet. We might replace once and for all the ugly terminology ("sterile contemplation") used in so many discussions of the Parnassian sonnet tradition, and think instead in terms of a relative absence of lyrical initiative for this form. In this way, Casal's poetic form is a functional artistic choice, rather than an unhappy accident.

20. Pierre Charles Baudelaire, "Salon de 1846," *Curiosités esthétiques, L'Art romantique et autres oeuvres critiques,* ed. Henri Lemaître (Paris, 1962), p. 101.

21. Pierre Martino, *Parnasse et symbolisme: 1850-1900* (Paris, 1947), p. 85. "In all of its aspects form affirms its abhorrence of destruction. In W. R. D. Fairbairn's phrase, form seeks to safeguard 'the integrity of the object,' presenting everything in a way which emphasizes its wholeness and intactness . . . it seeks to protect from death itself both the material and the object it commemorates" (Simon O. Lesser, *Fiction and the Unconscious* [New York, 1962], p. 130).

22. Catulle Mendès, cited by Huret, *Enquête,* p. 289.

23. Dore Ashton, "Gustave Moreau," in *Odilon Redon, Gustave Moreau, Rodolphe Bresdin* (New York, 1961), p. 114. And Proust used a metaphor like Martino's when he wrote: "Sans doute cet homme [Moreau] en reste dans une certaine mesure sanctifié. Il est une espèce de prêtre dont la vie est vouée à servir cette divinité, à nourrir les animaux sacrés qui lui plaisent et à répandre les parfums qui facilitent ses apparitions. Sa maison est à moitié église, à moitié maison du prêtre. Maintenant l'homme est mort, il ne reste plus que ce qui a pu se dégager du divin qui était en lui. Par une brusque métamorphose, la maison est devenue un musée avant même d'être ainsi aménagée (Marcel Proust, "Gustave Moreau," *Nouveaux Mélanges,* ed. Bernard de Fallois [Paris, 1954], p. 392). My thanks to J. Theodore Johnson, Jr., for the Proust reference.

24. Théophile Gautier, "Le Musée ancien," *Tableaux à la plume* (Paris, 1880), pp. 3-5; appeared in *La Presse* (10 February 1849). It is curious to recall that Gautier considered art historians and treatisers deficient teachers compared with the museum, while he himself wrote endless pages on painters and paintings. See, for example, his *Guide de l'amateur au musée du Louvre,* a prose "promenade" through the Louvre, divided into different sections on individual painters and schools of painting.

25. See Leo Spitzer's criticism of Karl Shapiro's "A Farewell to Criticism," in the essay "Three Poems on Ecstasy," in *Essays on English and American Literature,* ed. Anna Hatcher (Princeton, N.J., 1962). Also, Frances A. Yates, in the interesting critical work "The Emblematic Conceit in Giordano Bruno's *De gli eroici furori* and in the Elizabethan Sonnet Sequences" (*Journal of the Warburg and Courtauld Institutes,* VI [1943], 101-121), has pointed out how a whole tradition of poetry and poetic forms may be explicated by a

discussion of "the sonnet language itself as an artistic phenomenon." Yates notes that most of the poems of *Eroici furori*—a work comprised of prose descriptions of emblems or devices that would be plates in an illustrated emblem book; poems in which visual forms appearing in the emblems occur as poetic conceits; and expositions of philosophical meanings latent in the imagery of both the emblems and the poems—are in sonnet form.

26. Frye, *Anatomy,* p. 301. See also Spitzer's essay "The 'Ode on a Grecian Urn,' or Content vs. Metagrammar," in *Essays.* Spitzer comments on the "circularity" of the poem, in inward and outward form, which reproduces symbolically the form of the art object, whether real or imaginary.

27. R. Blanco-Fombona (*El modernismo y los poetas modernistas* [Madrid, 1929], p. 89) says: "También son de pura descripción pictórica los sonetos inspirados en los cuadros de Gustavo Moreau, aunque jamás pudo [Casal] apreciarlos sino por grabados y descripciones." The consensus is that Casal had never seen an actual painting by Moreau. Roberto Meza Fuentes (*De Díaz Mirón a Rubén Darío* [Santiago, Chile, 1940], p. 99) remarks: "Entonces el poeta . . . sueña . . . en los personajes de Huysmans y en los cuadros de Moreau, que no llega a conocer nunca sino a través de fotografías. Y, sobre motivos de esos cuadros, teje en sonetos la filigrana de su "Museo Ideal." ¡Pobre poeta! ¡Ha edificado todo un castillo de ensueño sobre un mundo de fotografía!" Faurie (*Modernisme*) pays special attention to Casal's poetic translation of Huysmans' prose description of Moreau's works. Meza Fuentes and Blanco-Fombona, in implying the lack of validity of the photograph or the prose description as a source for a workable *ekphrasis,* have disregarded Casal's subjectivization of Moreau's works.

28. Frye, *Anatomy,* p. 274. An obvious example of the exploitation of the pictorial in the lyric is Appollinaire's "Il pleut," where the meaning of the subject is suggested by the shape of the poem.

29. In "Retrato de Gustavo Moreau," the opening "Vestíbulo" sonnet, Casal chose to depict Moreau with "frente austera / aureolada de larga cabellera, / donde al mirto se enlazan los laureles." Although self-portraits of Moreau do not depict him with this "encadrement," Casal has chosen to imitate the fashion of intricate frame—reminiscent of the way in which Moreau designed his own museumhouse—in order to emblematize his subject. With respect to Moreau's own elaborate framing of his pictures, Faurie (*Modernisme,* p. 177) comments that "*La Péri,* avec son large encadrement floral, semble l'œuvre d'un calligraphe pour la decoration d'un manuscrit."

30. "The primary illusion of virtual space comes at the first stroke of brush or pencil that concentrates the mind entirely on the picture plane and neutralizes the actual limits of vision. That explains why Redon felt driven, at the sight of a blank paper on his easel, to scrawl on it as quickly as possible with anything that would make a mark. Just establish one line in virtual space, and at once we are in the realm of symbolic forms. The mental shift is as definite as that which we make from hearing a sound of tapping, squeaking, or buzzing to hearing speech, when suddenly in the midst of the little noises surrounding us we make out a single word. The whole character of our hearing is transformed. The medley of physical sound disappears, the ear receives language, perhaps indistinct by reason of interfering noises, but struggling through them like a living thing. Exactly the same sort of reorientation is effected for sight by the creation of any purely visual space. The image, be it a representation or a mere design, stands before us in its expressiveness: significant form" (Susanne K. Langer, *Feeling and Form: A Theory of Art* [New York, 1953], p. 84). The point is important for our understanding of how Casal uses the sonnet's structure for the purpose of *ekstasis.*

31. "The purpose of all plastic art is to articulate visual form, and to present that form . . . as the sole, or at least paramount, object of perception" (Langer, *Feeling,* p. 71). Leo Spitzer ("Lope de Vega's 'Al triunfo de Judit,'" *Modern Language Notes,* LXIX, No. 1 [1954], 1-11) discusses spatial arrangement within the sonnet and its relationship to the pictorial form.

32. "The poem of the quiet mind, if it has a subject beyond recommending itself, attempts to communicate to the reader a private and secret possession, which brings us to the next cardinal point, the riddle. The idea of the riddle is descriptive containment: the subject is not described but circumscribed, a circle of words drawn around it. In simple riddles, the central subject is an image, and the reader feels impelled to guess, that is, to equate the poem to the name or sign-symbol of its image" (Frye, *Anatomy,* pp. 299-300).

33. Frank Kermode, *Romantic Image* (New York, 1964), p. 2.

34. Static drama is often represented in the works of Moreau: "The two mythical figures gaze at each other transfixed. This is characteristic of Moreau who again and again suggests an ambiguous mirror-image, two aspects, two abstract entities that confront each other and recognize each other

all too well" (Ashton, "Moreau," p. 115, commenting on Moreau's representation of Oedipus and the Sphinx).

35. Benedetto Croce, cited by Mario Praz, *The Romantic Agony,* trans. Angus Davidson, 2d ed. (Cleveland, 1967), p. xv.

36. It will not do merely to name a mood; critical understanding can be achieved here only by a discussion of sensorial perception, for "La aparición" itself explicitly names that mood "deleite." "The most integral and involving time sense imaginable is that expressed in the Chinese and Japanese cultures. Until the coming of the missionaries in the seventeenth century, and the introduction of the mechanical clocks, the Chinese and Japanese had for thousands of years measured time by graduations of incense. Not only the hours and days, but the seasons and zodiacal signs were simultaneously indicated by a succession of carefully ordered scents. The sense of smell, long considered the root of memory and the unifying basis of individuality, has come to the fore again in the experiments of Wilder Penfield. During brain surgery electric probing of brain tissue revived many memories of the patients. These evocations were dominated and unified by unique scents and odors that structured these past experiences. The sense of smell is not only the most subtle and delicate of the human senses; it is, also, the most iconic in that it involves the entire human sensorium more fully than any other sense" (Marshall McLuhan, *Understanding Media: The Extensions of Man* [New York, 1964], p. 136). See, for example, Baudelaire's "Correspondances," "Parfum Exotique," or "La Chevelure," where sense of smell is the means to immediate transport.

37. Georges Poulet, "Timelessness and Romanticism," *Journal of the History of Ideas,* XV, No. 1 (1954), 3-22; Wylie Sypher, *Rococo to Cubism in Art and Literature* (New York, 1960), p. 98.

38. Kermode, *Image,* p. 70. See also n. 27 above. Joris Karl Huysmans, in the fifth chapter of his novel of 1884, *A rebours,* has his protagonist, Des Esseintes, acquire Moreau's *Salomé* and *L'Apparition.* Casal knew *A rebours* and also wrote an article on Huysmans for *La Habana literaria* (15 March 1892), most recently published in Casal's *Prosas,* I, Edición del Centenario (Havana, 1963), 173-178. Moreau, too, repeatedly correlated the harmonious with the pathological: "The favorite theme of Moreau, which he never tires of treating in his pictures, is that of Fatality, of Evil and Death incarnate in female beauty" (Praz, *Agony,* p. 295).

39. Let us establish once and for all that the dancer-into-flower progression that Casal used had great significance in the nineteenth century's artistic tradition: "The Tree is in a sense necessary to the Dancer, since it so powerfully reinforces the idea of integrity—'root, shoot, blossom'—in the Image, and provides a traditional analogy in support of the Image's independent life" (Kermode, *Image,* p. 102). See also Oscar Wilde's "The Decay of Lying" (*Selections from the Works of . . . ,* ed. Graham Hough [New York, 1960], p. 267), where the *first* doctrine of "the new aesthetics" is stated: "Art never expresses anything but itself. It has an independent life, just as Thought has, and develops purely on its own lines." Kermode (*Image,* pp. 43-44) points out that for the tradition behind Casal's work, "fundamentally the unanimity of the witnesses is impressive. The work of art itself is symbol, 'aesthetic monad'; utterly original and not in the old sense 'imitated'; 'concrete,' yet fluid and suggestive; a means to truth, a truth unrelated to, and more exalted than, that of positivist science, or any observation depending upon the discursive reason; out of the flux of life, and therefore, under one aspect, dead; yet uniquely alive because of its participation in a higher order of existence, and because it is analogous not to a machine but to an organism; coextensive in matter and form; resistant to explication; largely independent of intention, and of any form of ethical utility; and itself emblematised in certain images, of which . . . the Dancer is the most perfect." Today, "it must be remembered, of course, that a work of art is not an actual organism, but presents only the appearance of life, growth, and functional unity" (Langer, *Feeling,* p. 373).

40. Faurie, *Modernisme,* p. 177.

41. Moreau knew that as he was arranging his paintings in his home, he was "sculpting his own tomb," as Mallarmé would have phrased it ("le cas d'un poète, en cette société qui ne lui permet pas de vivre, c'est le cas d'un homme qui s'isole pour sculpter son propre tombeau"; cited by Huret, *Enquête,* p. 61). And Edmond de Goncourt takes us on a promenade through *La Maison d'un artiste,* endlessly cataloging the art in each room there. After mentioning in his Préambule "l'éducation de l'œil des gens du XIXᵉ siècle, et encore un sentiment tout nouveau, la tendresse presque humaine pour les *choses,*" he confesses himself to be "le plus passionné de tous les collectionneurs" (I [Paris, 1898], 3). The degree to which the poet is artist, then, is in part determined by the *quantity* of beauty contained in the external world that he has occasion and capacity to perceive and tirelessly remake. Casal hung his Moreau reproductions on his walls (see Duplessis, "Casal," p. 59), as did Des Esseintes, who had be-

come the model "Décadent" for so many of Casal's generation (see Monner Sans, *Casal,* p. 97).

42. Cited by Duplessis, "Casal," pp. 66-67; more recently published in Casal's *Prosas,* III, 84-87. See Francisco Chacón ("Casal," in *El fígaro,* VIII, No. 14 [24 April 1892], 2) for confirmation of this attitude and Casal's use of the "Museo ideal" poems as a means of evading worldly preoccupation. Wen Gálvez, in his unsympathetic review of *Nieve* (in *El fígaro,* VIII, No. 20 [12 June 1892], 6) could correctly describe the life-style in question, but he could not admit the ethic it represented.

43. Ralph Freedman, *The Lyrical Novel* (Princeton, N.J., 1966), p. 36. The maligning criticism of Wen Gálvez stresses the image of the young Casal as a retiring "visionista"; according to Gálvez, Casal accepted this description (the review of *Nieve* in *El fígaro,* VIII, No. 20, 6).

44. "Moreau's two guiding principles, according to Renan, who claimed he heard Moreau discourse on them frequently, were the principles of *la belle inertie* and *la richesse nécessaire*" (Ashton, "Moreau" [n. 23 above], p. 118). "Moreau advocated [these] two principles, in opposition to the emotional qualities which he held to be an infiltration of literature into painting" (Praz, *Agony* [n. 35 above], p. 289). An *ekphrasis* by *ekstasis,* then, minimizing the empathetic response of the reader, is precisely what Moreau would have advocated for a "transposition" of his paintings into Casal's medium.

45. Irving Putter ("Leconte de Lisle and His Contemporaries," *University of California Publications in Modern Philology,* XXXV, No. 2 [1951], 69) tells how Leconte de Lisle "disoriented readers and met with a chorus of disapproval or condemnation" when he tried out a new system of orthography on both proper and, even, common nouns, attempting to approximate Greek pronunciation. Doubtless Leconte produced a visual effect with this device equivalent to the effect of Moreau's "richesse nécessaire." Those who opposed Leconte de Lisle's poetic method and endlessly compared his work "to the Great Pyramid, which is composed of innumerable small, dirty stones, all alike, whose mass effect is *overwhelming*" (italics mine; Putter, p. 86) did show a partial—though scarcely sympathetic!—comprehension of the aesthetics in question.

46. Ashton, "Moreau," p. 114.

47. Kermode, *Image,* p. 30. Casal's withdrawal from an antiaesthetic world is further indicated by the dedication of "Mi museo ideal" to Eduardo Rosell y Malpica, who fought for Cuban independence and recorded his impressions during the military movement (see *Diario del Teniente Coronel Eduardo Rosell y Malpica: 1895-1897,* II, ed. Benigno Souza [Havana, 1950]). Casal's choice of subject for his dedication, in other words, points to the poet's subjective, aesthetic withdrawal into isolation, away from "a world built for action."

48. Frye, *Anatomy,* p. 301.

Robert Jay Glickman (essay date 1972-73)

SOURCE: Glickman, Robert Jay. "Julián Del Casal: Letters to Gustave Moreau." *Revista Hispanica Moderna* 37, nos. 1-2, (1972-73): 101-35.

[*In the following essay, Glickman assesses the significance of Casal's correspondence with painter Gustave Moreau, noting that the letters served to battle the loneliness and despair of Casal's everyday life.*]

Julián del Casal was one of the most sensitive and emotionally vulnerable of the Spanish American Modernists. Disagreeing with the values of contemporary society, opposing authority-figures whom he considered unjust, and moving farther and farther away from the Church despite his desperate need for religious faith, Casal constantly tried to discover ways of protecting himself from the pain that life inflicted on him. He sought escape from daily miseries through dream and through art. He replaced nature with an artificial world of his own making; he cultivated the exotic; he investigated the macabre. And possessed of a boundless need to love and be loved, but incapable of forming close emotional ties with women, he used his artistic interests as a vehicle for establishing platonic relationships that would help him conquer loneliness.

It is in the latter respect, primarily, that Casal's epistolary activities are important. He corresponded with compatriots such as Cirilo Villaverde, Esteban and Juana Borrero, Aurelia Castillo de González, América Du-Bouchet, and Edouard Cornelius Price, as well as with distinguished non-Cubans such as Rubén Darío, Manuel Gutiérrez Nájera, Luis G. Urbina, Francisco A. de Icaza, Enrique Gómez Carrillo, José María Bustillos, Emilia Pardo Bazán, Pedro II of Brazil, Judith Gautier, Paul Verlaine, Count Robert de Montesquiou-Fézensac, Joris-Karl Huysmans, and Gustave Moreau. Whenever a friend or colleague visited his modest quarters, Casal would joyously display the letters he had received. These papers, he would say, are "los compañeros de mi vida."[1] So great an impression did this ritual make on Rubén Darío that he continued to recall it vividly many years after Casal's demise.[2]

Realizing how valuable Casal's epistolary treasures were, Aniceto Valdivia expected that Carmen del Casal would collect them and preserve them after her brother's death.[3] If Carmen did collect these documents, she guarded them so jealously that they eventually became inaccessible to the scholarly community. Another serious loss resulted when Dulce María Borrero died before she could publish the letters that Casal and her sister Juana had exchanged.[4]

In spite of the factors that have militated against their survival, a few of the letters that Casal wrote to his contemporaries have come down to us. A facsimile of the poet's first letter to Luis G. Urbina was published in the April 1909 issue of the *Revista Moderna de México.* Five brief notes were collected by José Antonio Fernández de Castro and were printed in the March 1923 issue of *Social.* Three letters were found by Gustavo Duplessis and were incorporated into his doctoral dissertation, which was published in 1944 by the *Revista Bimestre Cubana.* In the following decade, four new letters by Casal came to the attention of José María Chacón y Calvo; these were printed together with some already-known material in the Fall 1958 issue of the *Boletín de la Academia Cubana de la Lengua.* Two additional notes came out in 1963, when Cuba's Consejo Nacional de Cultura published its Centenary Edition of Casal's works.[5] And so it goes: every once in a while, some part of Casal's correspondence turns up and is placed at the disposition of scholars.

Now, twelve letters that Casal sent to Gustave Moreau have become available for study. These letters span the period 11 August 1891-1 January 1893. Eleven of them were written in the poet's imperfect but highly expressive French, and one was composed in Spanish. In order to facilitate research on this material, the complete collection is designated as *C* (i.e., *Cartas*), each letter within the collection is tagged with a number that represents its position in the series (C1, C2, etc.), and each line within a letter is assigned a sequence number. According to this system, the designation "C5/8-14" refers the reader to "letter 5, lines 8 through 14."

The significance of these letters becomes apparent at once. To begin with, they provide information about Casal's level of proficiency in French. But more important, they shed light on an aspect of his life that has been shrouded in mystery for some eighty years: his relations with his most venerated source of inspiration in the world of art, Gustave Moreau.[6]

. . . . .

Born in Paris on 6 April 1826, Gustave Moreau came to be one of Europe's most outstanding symbolist painters. The dominant theme in Moreau's art is the perpetual conflict between the forces of Good and the forces of Evil. These opponents are symbolically represented through the eternal war between the sexes. In Moreau's opinion, all the major virtues are inherent in Man, while all the major vices are inherent in Woman. In his paintings, therefore, qualities such as altruism, courage, and justice are generally embodied in handsome young men like Prometheus or Hercules, while covetousness, corruption, and cruelty appear in the form of women like Helen of Troy and Salomé. Indifferent to the suffering she causes, Woman is particularly dangerous because of the irresistible attraction which her sensuous beauty exerts on the targets of her destructive instincts. As far as style is concerned, critics have repeatedly used two terms to describe the essential characteristics of Moreau's art: "la belle inertie" and "la richesse nécessaire." The former alludes to the almost enchanted stillness of the figures in his compositions; the latter refers to the immense number of decorative elements which the artist believed necessary to convey his ideas to the observer.

In spite of the fact that Moreau received numerous honors, awards, and commendations during his lifetime,[7] it should be emphasized that he was not especially well known to the general public and that his creations elicited sharp criticism as well as extravagant praise. For example, while an admirer such as Ary Renan felt that the work of Moreau was a monument of pure art, Degas severely criticized Moreau for indulging in excessive ornamentation: the artist, Degas sarcastically quipped, would like us to believe that the gods wore watch chains. Be that as it may, the fact is that Moreau was in great favor with some of the most outstanding writers of his time—among them, Théophile Gautier and Joris-Karl Huysmans. What these men admired most in his works were his expression of an ultra-refined aestheticism, his expert handling of detail, and his mastery of symbolism.

Although it is impossible to determine when Casal first became familiar with the art of Gustave Moreau, it seems that his initial exposure came about through the medium of Joris-Karl Huysmans in the spring of 1890.[8] In any case, it could not have been later than 21 September 1890, for on that date, in *La Habana Elegante,* he published **"Salomé,"** the first of the ten *cuadros* that ultimately appeared in the **"Mi museo ideal"** section of *Nieve.* Casal's enthusiasm led him to write to a contact in Paris—most likely Huysmans himself—at some time between the summer of 1890 and the summer of 1891, in order to find out how he could obtain reproductions of Moreau's paintings. Before the beginning of August 1891, he received prints of *Hélène sur les murs de Troie* and *Galatée.* The first of these inspired him to compose **"Elena"**; the second, **"Galatea."** Casal published these sonnets in *La Habana Elegante* on 2 August and 9 August 1891, respectively. Then, on the 11th of the month, he wrote his first letter to Moreau; with it he enclosed copies of the three sonnets he had already written under the inspiration of Moreau's work.[9] Since he did not know the address of his "Très-adorè maître,"[10] however, he sent the letter by registered mail to Huysmans, with a request that it be forwarded to Moreau.[11]

Three days after mailing this letter, Casal received a shipment of pictures from the Photographie des Beaux-Arts, 8 rue Bonaparte, Paris. A catalogue number was written on the back of each item, but none of the photos had a title. The only works that Casal identified positively were *L'Apparition, Hercule et l'Hydre de Lerne,* and *Prometheus.* Of the eleven remaining pictures, he thought he could recognize the subject of eight (C2/25-40),[12] but had no idea of what the others represented. Casal's failure to identify three of the pictures was a disappointment of only minor importance, however, since the works that he did succeed in recognizing more than lived up to his expectations about the quality of Moreau's art (C2/59-79).

In the days that followed, while waiting for Moreau to identify the doubtful items and to tell him where he could purchase additional photographs,[13] Casal wrote seven new sonnets: **"Prometeo," "La aparición," "Hércules ante la Hidra," "Venus Anadyomena," "Una peri," "Júpiter y Europa,"** and **"Hércules y las Estinfálides."** Then, on 30 August 1891, he published all ten Moreau-inspired sonnets in *La Habana Elegante.* The poems were grouped under the generic title **"Mi museo ideal"** and had as their subtitle the rubric "(Cuadros de Gustavo Moreau)." Beneath the subtitle was a four-line quotation from Joséphin Soulary.[14] This, in turn, was followed by a dedication to Casal's friend Eduardo Rosell.

On 16 September 1891, after receiving his first letter from Moreau, Casal sent the painter a copy of the *La Habana Elegante* version of **"Mi museo ideal"** plus a photograph of himself. This picture was made by Ignacio Misa from a portrait that Armando Menocal had done a short time before. On the reverse side was the following inscription:

> A
> Gustave Moreau,
> au
> maitre venerable et impeccable,
> en temoignage de profond admi-
> ration et de reconnaissance infinie,
> cet portrait est respectueusement
> dediè, par son fervent et obscur
> admirateur
>
>   Julián del Casal

Evidence suggests that Casal sent these gifts to Moreau for three reasons: first, because he wanted to give Moreau tangible proof of his great devotion; second, because he was ill and did not know whether he would live long enough to present himself in person to Moreau; and third, because he hoped that his gesture would induce Moreau to send a photograph of himself, in return.

On 15 December 1891, as an additional sign of esteem, Casal sent Moreau two still unpublished compositions, **"Sueño de gloria"** and **"Vestíbulo."** The former, he insisted, was not a masterpiece by any stretch of the imagination, but it did represent a sincere expression of his feelings. The latter was a verbal portrait of Moreau. If it contained some inexactitudes, Casal explained, these were due to the fact that he had never seen a picture of the great master. After giving Moreau this exclusive preview of the poems, Casal published them in Cuba: **"Sueño de gloria"** came out in *La Habana Literaria* on 30 December 1891 and **"Vestíbulo,"** presented under the title **"Gustave Moreau,"** appeared in *El Figaro* on 15 January 1892 and in *El Pais* on 21 January of the same year.

Initially, Casal told Moreau that he would publish *Nieve* in the winter of 1891-1892 and that **"Mi museo ideal"** would be the third section in the book (C1/23-27). For reasons that are still not clear, *Nieve* was published in the spring of 1892 and **"Mi museo ideal"** was moved up to second place in the volume. Furthermore, the subtitle that Casal had used for the Moreau poems in August 1891 was replaced in *Nieve* by "(Diez cuadros de Gustavo Moreau)," the epigraph of the original version was suppressed, and Casal's most recent compositions, **"Vestíbulo"** and **"Sueño de gloria,"** were added to the series.[15]

Apparently flattered by these attentions, Moreau suggested that José María de Heredia might translate one of Casal's poems into French. With sincere modesty, Casal protested that he was unworthy of such an honor. Heredia was one of the gods in his literary pantheon: not only had Casal translated "Chanson de Torero" into Spanish (see **"La canción del torero"** in *Hojas al viento*—), but he had also tried to imitate the style of Heredia's sonnets in **"Mi museo ideal"** (C6/99-129). For a relatively unknown writer like himself, to do this was right and proper; but to think that a person of Heredia's stature might want to translate *his* poetry seemed rather presumptuous to Casal.[16]

This tone of extreme humility is evident throughout Casal's correspondence with Moreau. The young Cuban honestly felt that he was "un rêveur malade sans valeur" (C5/21-22) and when he wrote to persons of eminence such as Moreau, he sounded like an adolescent addressing a stage idol or a popular hero. But this was something which he could not avoid, for he was unable to love halfway (C3/66), and love for him was a *sine qua non* of existence: as he put it, "Je vis d'adorations, comme d'autres de méprises" (C6/114-116). His love was most intense, however, when it was directed to someone far away. In order to nurture his dreams, which were his most important possession, he needed to have a master in some distant land. That person had to be guided by the highest of values and had also to be a victim of life's incomprehension and cruelty. In Casal's view, such a person would be characterized by an uncompromising devotion to the ideal of *art for art's sake* and by a steadfast resistance to the enticements of Fame. In Casal's estimation, Moreau exemplified these traits better than anyone else on the continent of Europe (C6/ 38-69).

After glorifying his beloved master in **"Mi museo ideal,"** Casal composed five *ballades* and several *odelettes* under the inspiration of Moreau's work (C8/ 17-26, C10/37-39). Unfortunately, none of these poems has ever been found. An even greater loss to scholars, however, is the disappearance of preliminary notes that Casal had taken for a monograph he proposed to write on the life and works of Gustave Moreau. As background for his study, Casal planned to read everything that had been written about the painter (C6/79-91). Then, he would travel to Paris in order to meet Moreau and work on the book. According to his estimate, he would be able to stay in Paris for about two months. After completing the monograph, he would ask the artist for his frank opinion of it—and if Moreau did not understand Spanish well enough, Casal would get a bilingual friend, possibly Cornelius Price, to translate it into French (C12/38-62).

As had happened so often in the past, however, the poet did not have the good fortune to realize his dream. Although direct evidence on the subject has never come to light, it appears that the deteriorating state of his health was a major cause of this new disappointment. By the spring of 1892, Casal was already plagued by fevers, fainting spells, loss of vision, and paralysis; and, at times, he suffered pain so intense that he could not even hold a pen (C8/49-53). These were unmistakable signs of the seriousness of his illness—a disease, incidentally, which for a while he thought was heart trouble (C3/50-54). As the pernicious malady spread through Casal's body, it lessened his ability to endure the physical hardships involved in a trip from Havana to Paris. But it raised other barriers to the fulfilment of his dream, as well. First of all, it considerably reduced his economic potential. Casal had always been in precarious financial straits, but by mid-1891 the worsening condition of his health made it increasingly difficult for him to carry a normal work load. Besides limiting his ability to meet his material needs, Casal's life-sapping illness affected his emotional equilibrium. On the one hand, it increased the frequency with which he turned to his private world of glowing fantasy and away from the somber reality of common men. On the other, it decreased his ability to maintain his composure when reality intruded on the dreams that he had so laboriously fashioned. This im-

balance is evident in his relationship with Moreau. In his letters, Casal expressed a degree of emotional involvement that went beyond the range of normalcy. And, as he perceived Moreau's reluctance to respond with similar fervor, he adopted the plaintive tone of a suitor whose beloved fails to satisfy his longings for a sign of true affection. What hurt him most deeply, however, was Moreau's refusal to grant his request for a photograph.

The matter of the photograph may seem trivial to us, but it was not to Casal. There is ample evidence to show that the poet was in the habit of sending his picture to persons whom he admired, and that he was accustomed to ask them to reciprocate. His success in the latter regard is verified by Manuel Márquez Sterling, who affirms that the walls of Casal's room were covered by a "nube de retratos."[17] Casal's attempts to obtain a photograph from Moreau began in September 1891. The months passed, but Moreau sent no photograph. This led the poet to exclaim: "¿N'avez pas vous recu une lettre a moi, en vous demandant votre portrait? Son envoi vous couterais si peu et me rendrerai heureux, si heureux!" (C10/57-61). Moreau's answer was that he had received the letter, but preferred not to send Casal a picture of himself.

Moreau's refusal was not designed to slight Casal personally but was dictated by his sincere belief that, while an artist's work should be freely accessible to the public, the artist himself should disappear from view. So strong, in fact, was his feeling about this matter, that he instructed future executors of his estate not to sanction the inclusion of his portrait in any book that might be written about him after his death.[18]

Although Casal understood Moreau's reasons for denying his request, he let over four months go by without answering his beloved master. One obvious cause of his silence was disappointment at Moreau's unwillingness to make an exception in his case—an exception which, in view of the importance that Moreau gave to the rule, would have provided excellent proof of his affection for Casal. Another cause of the long silence was Casal's fear that he might weary Moreau if he persisted in lavishing attentions upon him. The 1st of January 1893, however, provided Casal with an excuse for writing once again. Reaffirming his constancy, he sent Moreau greetings for the New Year and expressed the hope that he would ultimately be able to visit him in Paris. From all appearances, Moreau did not answer this letter and Casal did not attempt to write to him again. In spite of this, there is nothing to suggest that Casal ever gave up being Moreau's "très fidèle, très loyal et très passionnè admirateur . . ." (C12/66-67).

Notes

1. Manuel Márquez Sterling, "Julián del Casal," *Revista Azul*, II, 21 (24 March 1895), 329.

2. See "Films habaneros," *El Fígaro* (Havana), 30 October 1910. The entire article is quoted by José María Monner Sans in *Julián del Casal y el modernismo hispano-americano* (Mexico: El Colegio de México, 1952), pp. 254-257, and an excerpt from it is presented in the *Edición del Centenario* of Casal's work (Havana: Consejo Nacional de Cultura, 1963), III, 129-132.

3. Aniceto Valdivia, "Julián del Casal" (*La Lucha*, 23 October 1893; *La Habana Elegante*, 29 October 1893); reproduced in *Ed. del Cent.*, "Poesías," pp. 295-300.

4. Monner Sans, p. 266.

5. See José Antonio Fernández de Castro, "Fragmentos de una correspondencia de Julián del Casal," *Social*, VIII, 3 (March 1923), 13; Gustavo Duplessis, "Julián del Casal," *Revista Bimestre Cubana*, LIV, 1 (July-August 1944), 65-67; José María Chacón y Calvo, "En torno a un epistolario de Julián del Casal," *Boletín de la Academia Cubana de la Lengua*, VII, 3-4 (July-December 1958), 346-373; and Casal, *Edición del Centenario*, III, 81-90.

6. I take this opportunity to express my thanks to Jean Paladilhe, Curator of the Musée Gustave Moreau, and to Pierre-Louis Mathieu, whose splendid cooperation was an invaluable asset to me in my research on the relationship between Casal and Moreau.

7. In addition to winning awards for paintings exhibited at the Salon, he was named to the Légion d'honneur (1875), he was elected to membership in the Académie des Beaux-Arts (1888), and he was chosen to succeed Élie Delaunay as professor of painting at the Académie (1892). Casal refers to the latter appointment in C9/76-78.

8. In C2/5-7, Casal tells Moreau that he is indebted to Huysmans for "la inmensa dicha de conoceros. . . ." It appears that Casal had discovered Moreau by reading Huysmans' novel *À rebours*, which was published in 1884. Casal's earliest allusions to Huysmans are found in "Semana Santa" and "Verdad y poesía," which he published in *La Discusión* on 5 April and 26 April 1890, respectively (see *Ed. del Cent.*, II, 99, 115), and antedate all known references to Moreau.

9. The fact that "Salomé" came out almost a full year before the other sonnets raises a question for which there is still no positive answer: namely, despite what he said in C1 and C2, did Casal really wait until he obtained a photograph of *Salomé* before composing the sonnet, or did he use Huysmans' detailed description in *À rebours* as his immediate source of inspiration? An examination of that selection will show that if Casal read the Huysmans passage, he would obtain at least as much information about Moreau's *Salomé* as he would by studying a simple black and white photograph of the painting, for, as Casal himself indicated, "La pluma de Huysmans rivaliza con el pincel de cualquier pintor" ("Joris-Karl Huysmans," *La Habana Literaria*, II [15 March 1892], 110). For opinions on the genesis of "Salomé," see also, John Kenneth Leslie, "Casal's *Salomé*: The Mystery of the Missing Prophet," *Modern Language Notes*, LXII, 6 (June 1947), 402-404, and Arturo Torres Rioseco, "*À Rebours* and Two Sonnets of Julián del Casal," *Hispanic Review*, XXIII, 4 (October 1955), 295-297.

10. Casal's spelling of French and Spanish is reproduced exactly in all instances in the present article.

11. In a letter addressed to Huysmans on 4 October 1891, Moreau wrote the following postscript: "Je ne dois pas oublier, Monsieur, que je suis chargé par Mr. Julian del Casal de la Havane, un de vos fervents admirateurs, de vous bien remercier de l'obligeance si gracieuse que vous avez mise à être un trait d'union entre lui et moi."

12. Among the works that Casal believed he had identified was *La Péri*. However, in *Le Modernisme hispano-américain et ses sources françaises* (Paris: Centre de recherches de l'Institut d'études hispaniques, 1966), Marie-Josèphe Faurie correctly observes that *La Péri* "n'offre aucune ressemblance avec le sonnet de Casal. . . . Nous avouons ignorer quelle Œuvre de Moreau servit de modèle au poète pour composer son sonnet" (p. 177, n. 24). A possible solution to the problem was offered to me by Pierre-Louis Mathieu, who, in a letter dated 30 December 1970, suggested that Casal had probably mistaken *Sapho se précipitant dans la mer* for *La Péri*. Comparison of Casal's "Una peri" with Moreau's *Sapho* tends to corroborate Mathieu's impression.

13. In particular, Casal wanted copies of *Phaeton, David,* and *Le Jeune Homme et la Mort* (C2/53-58). As far as we know, none of these works became the source of inspiration for a poem, but the last one mentioned did serve as the basis for a very interesting prose image in Casal's article on José Arburu: see *Bustos y rimas* (Havana: Imprenta La Moderna, 1893), p. 120; *Ed. del Cent.*, I, 280.

14. Casal considered Soulary (b. Lyon, 23 February 1815; d. Lyon, 28 March 1891) to be one of the best poets in Europe (see *Ed. del Cent.*, II, 144-145). The epigraph which Casal chose for "Mi museo ideal" was the second stanza of the "Pro-

logue," dated 18 December 1880, that introduced Soulary's *Les Jeux divins*: "Pour nous, fils de l'Art, rien ne vaut / Le mythe et sa légende rose; / Nous mourons de la vie en prose / Où le merveilleux fait défaut."

15. Evidence suggests that Casal wrote "Sueño de gloria" before "Vestíbulo" and intended to use it as the opening poem of "Mi museo ideal," but that he moved it to the end of the section while *Nieve* was being typeset (see Robert Jay Glickman, "The Poetry of Julián del Casal: A Critical Edition," unpublished manuscript, Part II, N18).

16. Among the holdings of the Musée Gustave Moreau is a copy of *Nieve* which Moreau was supposed to pass on to Heredia (see C9/10-25). The dedication in that volume reads as follows:

> A José Maria de Heredia,
> en testimonio de ardiente
> simpatía y de profunda ad-
> miración,
>
> Julián del Casal 20 Abril 1892

A provocative insight into the influence of Heredia and other Parnassians on the poems of "Mi museo ideal" is provided by Lee Fontanella in "Parnassian Precept and a New Way of Seeing Casal's *Museo ideal*," *Comparative Literature Studies,* VII, 4 (December 1970), 450-479.

17. Márquez Sterling, p. 328.

18. See Henri Rupp's introduction to *Catalogue sommaire des Peintures, Dessins, Cartons et Aquarelles exposés dans les galeries du Musée Gustave Moreau* (Paris, 1926). Rupp was the executor of Moreau's estate.

Ivan A. Schulman (essay date 1976)

SOURCE: Schulman, Ivan A. "Casal's Cuban Counterpoint of Art and Reality." *Latin American Research Review* 6, no. 2 (1976): 113-28.

[*In the following essay, Schulman presents a comparative analysis of Casal and José Martí's philosophy of art.*]

It has been traditional to treat the life and art of Julián del Casal and José Martí as antithetical statements.

> Si Martí encarna entre nosotros las nupcias del espíritu con la realidad, con la naturaleza y con la tierra misma, Julián del Casal (1863-93) significa todo lo contrario. Su incapacidad radical para asumir la realidad, que unas veces interpreta como signo de "idealismo," de pureza y anhelo inconciliables con lo mezquino de la

circunstancia, y otras, las más, como fatal "impotencia" de su ser, se resuelve en un estado de ánimo dominante: el hastío.[1]

These two central figures of Cuban Modernism were born only ten years apart, inherited a common legacy of romantic idealism, but cultivated a literature and life style whose diversity is not unrelated to the nature and substance of their separate concepts of man, history, and Cuban colonial society. Martí's aspirations for perfection and beauty are inseparable from the revolutionary struggle for a free Cuba whose redemption his painful exile and his fervent Americanism permitted him to perceive with a clarity that his uninterrupted residence in the colony might have denied him. Casal, on the other hand, lacking Martí's capacity for sacrifice, irrevocably tied—physically—to the spectacle of "nuestros desastres políticos, . . . nuestras tristezas incurables y nuestra decadencia material,"[2] fell victim to the contradictions of the colony and sought brief, fitful periods of reprieve in what might be regarded as the *internal* equivalent of the *dynamic motif* embodied in Martí's exile: A scanning of infinite and frigid horizons in search of the meaning of man, his destiny, and the divine spirit. This process, which we should prefer to characterize as one of *internal displacement,* has resulted in Casal's identification as a dreamer, an escapist, a victim of neuroses and aberrations in the style of the French decadents, or, at best, a *poseur par excellence* closer to Victor Hugo, Alfred de Musset, Gustave Moreau, or Baudelaire than to his native Cuba.

Many of Casal's values with respect to art and reality are shared by his generation of the early Modernist period (1875-1918). His exotic fantasies, his yearning for delicate, aesthetic art forms, his reverence for French models are undeniably related to a social and cultural crisis whose Europeanized writers often preferred imagined to real landscapes or the vagaries of historical and mythic experiences to the exigencies of the domestic scene. Casal's own acid comments easily lead—and perhaps mislead us—in this very direction: "Que no vean ya mis ojos / la horrible Realidad que me contrista" (**"Tras una enfermedad"**); "Cualquiera [leyenda], por vulgar que sea, es preferible a la realidad" (***Prosas,*** 2:101); "sólo guardo en lo interior del alma / la nostalgia infinita de otro mundo" (**"Esquivez"**). This doleful rejection of reality alternates with a fin-de-siècle tedium whose motifs may be Baudelairian, but whose roots, we feel, are Cuban: "En mi alma desolada siento, / el hastío glacial de la existencia / y el horror infinito de la muerte" (**"Paisaje espiritual"**).

But, between the poles of a repugnant, material reality and an unattainable visionary idealism lies not only Casal's state of resolved *hastío,* which Vitier so cogently identifies as a middle ground, but an even more significant search for infinity and distance whose temporal and spatial dimensions suggest the philosophic agonizing of his age.

A TELESCOPIC STRUCTURE

Concepts of reality, irreality, escapism, and oneirism lie at the center of the motivational forces of Casal's art. These should be understood not in their most literal or obvious sense, but in the context of the conflicts of the individual artist with his milieu. Casal's revulsion for Cuban society "no lo sitúa necesariamente entre los frustrados y evadidos. . . . Todo su exotismo es desde luego un modo de ocultarse, . . . pero ocultarse no es huir, sino replantear la batalla en otro terreno."[3]

Even a superficial reading of Casal's works, particularly his verse, reveals an attraction for counterposed or oppositional imagistic structures whose two conflicting spatial levels constitute a metaphorical statement, devoid of allegorical implications,[4] on the nature of reality. These antithetical structures are based upon a nucleus of negative and positive signs. At the negative pole are such images as *pantano, abismo, miasma, cieno, lodazal, fango.* These are contrasted with elevational or ideal images such as *cima, mariposa, perfume, lirio,* or *rosa,* which suggest a second, superior reality. The two worlds may be juxtaposed in successive lines:

> Así mi ensueño, pájaro canoro
> de níveas plumas y rosado pico,
> al querer en el mundo hallar cabida,
> encontró de lo real los muros de oro
> y deshecho, cual frágil abanico,
> cayó entre el fango inmundo.

> ("**Mi ensueño**")

Or, they may be arranged strophically with a contrasting enumerative technique as in **"Cuerpo y alma."** Only occasionally does Casal attempt a union of the two strata of reality either as an indication of conflict resolution or as a harmonious synthesis in the style of the prevailing revival of Pythagorean philosophy. Equally lacking are the moral overtones of transformational structures in which movement from lower to higher spheres goes beyond Neoplatonic overviews and suggests a dynamic restructuring of the universe of the variety Martí embodied in similar metaphorical constructs.

In view of the strain of literary Romanticism which permeates Casal's work, we might simply attempt to relate these antithetical structures to the Romantics' dualistic vision of the forces of the universe, but only as a "conciencia *dramáticamente* alienada del mundo, y, por ende, una búsqueda de principios reconfortantes, ya sean individuales o colectivos, que bloqueen la pungente y conturbadora realidad social, económica, cultural, ideológica."[5] Or, guided by Monner Sans's remarks, we might simply consider them a reflection of Baudelaire's aesthetics,[6] particularly of the forces of heaven and hell: "Il y a dans tout homme, à toute heure, deux postulations simultanées, l'une vers Dieu, l'autre vers Satan. L'invocation à Dieu, ou spiritualité, est un désir de monter en grade; celle de Satan, ou animalité, est un joie de descendre."[7] Finally, these polar forms might be associated with universal concepts of realism and idealism.[8]

While all of these alternatives seem valid, the specific nature of Casal's polar structures, that is, their non-transformational, nonsynthetic substance suggests implications that we feel lead to a reconsideration of Casal as the Cuban[9] antithesis of Martí's dynamic, social vision.

If, as has been so often indicated, Casal were merely a dreamer or escapist, how do we explain his predilection for dual realities with contrapuntally arranged motifs. Instead of a single, fancied, escapist structure, Casal's polarities embody what Mario Praz has termed a *telescopic structure,* one in which the realities of the more immediate world as well as those of another more perfect sphere are combined in the same canvas or poem. In contrast with the telescopic structure, Praz speaks of one characterized by an "exoticism which represents to itself as actually present the land of the heart's desire."[10] The fact that Casal chose the telescopic or dualistic perspective is, in our view, a stylistic signal indicative of an overwhelming attachment to the irritating, ever-present realities of a moribund culture in whose grip he languished.

Our conviction that the spatial dynamics of the telescopic structures are tied to a particular view of social, political, and cultural realities is supported by discursive statements and their associated signs, especially in the abundant prose now available in the centenary edition.[11] In his collected prose, Casal's counterpoint of art and reality is presented in numerous contexts, exemplified by the following sharp antithetical impression:

> Al salir del estudio [del pintor Collazos], para entrar de nuevo en el mundo, el ánimo se siente dolorosamente impresionado por la realidad. Tal parece que hemos descendido, desde un palacio italiano, poblado de maravillas artísticas, hasta un subterráneo, lóbrego y húmedo, donde resuenan lamentaciones, de esos que se contemplan en las aguas fuertes de Paranése [sic]. Pero el ánimo pronto se consuela, con el recuerdo de lo que ha visto y de lo que ha admirado, porque el arte proporciona todos los goces . . . ¡hasta el de olvidar!

> (*Prosas,* 1:153)

Two spatial levels point to two realities, while the opiating function of art as recalled experience serves to compensate for a lower stratum (material reality) and moves us to a higher realm (artistic reality). The imagery of shade, cavern, and humidity has a specificity not always apparent in the verse.[12] And, the summoning of Piranesi-like visions to describe Cuba's social malaise acquires an imagistic fixity in this and other antithetically structured passages.

Even Parnassian aesthetics can reveal social significance. Its objects of luxury (*seda, oropeles*), which in Casal's verse so often signify ideal beauty, in the passage that follows is a veneer incapable of screening abject misery (*hedor purulento, llagas*). A double reality is thus symbolically represented by contrasted paired images: *Rincón azul de Paraíso* x *lóbrego Infierno*: "Y es que la miseria ha penetrado en el seno de los hogares cubanos, sin que se la pueda expulsar de ellos. Aunque se la oculte, bajo manto de seda, recamado de oropeles, en el último rincón de la casa, se perciben el eco de sus gemidos y el hedor purulento de sus llagas. . . . No vemos siquiera un rincón azul de Paraíso, desde el lóbrego Infierno en que vivimos sepultados" (*Prosas,* 2:27). Casal's anguish, like Bonifacio Byrne's, was a triple martyrdom "de su destino, de su aspiraciones y de su medio social" (*Prosas,* 1:274).

AN ESTHETE'S VIEW OF SOCIETY[13]

The poet's attachment to his environment is evident not only in his preference for a dualistic rather than an oneiric vision, but, on a discursive level, in his "hovering" or morose descriptions of Cuban society. And these, in turn, constitute the substance that generates the creative structures and images mistakenly identified, on an absolute basis, with the artist as dreamer or escapist.

Casal's social analyses admittedly fall short of the profundity of Martí's; they lack a grasp of the roots of political problems. It is precisely because he is caught and limited by a colonial dependence that Casal's vision is shallow and riddled with oversights and inconsistencies. He rejected the Spanish presence in Cuba and was openly anti-yanqui: "Por más que el espectáculo [de los payasos norteamericanos] me aburrió, me repugnó y casi me enfermó como aburre, repugna y enferma a los que tienen un poco de gusto artístico todo lo que procede del pueblo norte-americano, de ese pueblo que dejó morir a Edgard Poe, en la miseria, que compra las obras de los grandes artistas, no para venerarlas, sino para especular con ellas" (*Prosas,* 2:60). But it is not the problem of a double colonial dependence created by the growing American influence within the older Spanish colonial system[14] that disturbs Casal. He sees its effects without being concerned about its full implications. Thus, his distrust of the United States is based on its cultural pharisaism. His grasp of the fundamental meaning of the Modernist crisis is not more incisive. And yet, the general nature of the crisis and his individual anguish with respect to it are not absent. But, again, it is the vision of the artist that prevails; Casal speaks not of capitalist or neocolonial structures, but

rather of a mercantilist spirit, "el mercantilismo, que se dilata como lepra asquerosa por nuestro cuerpo social" (*Prosas,* 1:151). A broadening of his critique brings him not to the specifics of political or economic problems but to an ideological quandary whose nature he presents by means of a dualistic structuring:

> En ningún final de siglo más que en el nuestro se han visto tantas cosas contradictorias e inesperadas. De ahí ha nacido en los espíritus una incertidumbre que cada día reviste caracteres más alarmantes. El análisis nos ha hecho comprender que, después de tantos siglos, no es posible determinar a punto fijo el progreso de la humanidad. Más bien se puede afirmar que ha retrocedido, porque ha amado muchas cosas que hoy sólo puede odiar. Tanto desespera ese estado de ánimo que muchos de los seres que lo experimentan se despeñan por los riscos de la extravagancia, no por el afán de llamar la atención, sino por olvidarse de que no pueden creer en nada, pues la verdad de hoy es la mentira de mañana, y porque sienten al mismo tiempo la necesidad imperiosa de albergar en su alma alguna creencia.
>
> Sabiendo que ese estado no se puede prolongar, porque nos hace la vida insorportable, se cree vagamente que el remedio será descubierto en la década que resta de [sic] siglo; pero como se teme también que las muchedumbres hambrientas promuevan un gran cataclismo social, la incertidumbre de que he hablado, o sea la *tristeza fin de siglo,* se va introduciendo, como los microbios de una epidemia, en todos los espíritus, no sólo de Europa, sino de todos los países civilizados.

> (*Prosas,* 3:18)

In spite of his limited capacity for social analysis, Casal is aware of a rising popular rebellion in European industrialized states and its conceivable reverberations in Cuba. And it is obvious he is also cognizant of the vertiginous changes of his times that have left man without firm ideological or spiritual supports, or, in fact, a standard by which to measure the direction of his progress. Ideological confusion leads to exacerbated materialism. The evil is both social and moral; Cuba is passing through what in Casal's view is a "noche moral": "A pesar del profundo escepticismo, de las numerosas aberraciones y de la falta de sentido moral que vienen minando, como *llagas purulentas,* el seno lacerado de nuestra sociedad; todavía se encuentran, en la Habana, almas privilegiadas que han logrado preservarse del contagio y conservar su pureza virginal" (*Prosas,* 2:40-41). The dual levels of reality perceived by this nineteenth-century moralist expose his social roots. His specifically moral perspective is elucidated in the antithetical imagery identified with his hovering over and contemplating a corrupt environment:

> Son semejantes [estas almas privilegiadas] a estas *plantas verdes, coronadas de flores blancas,* que se levantan en las superficies de los *pantanos,* sin que una gota de *fango* ennegrezca el verde de sus hojas o el armiño de sus pétalos. Mientras todo se corrompe a su alrededor esparcen el *perfume* delicado de su seno, purifi-

cando la atmósfera de los gérmenes mortales que contiene diseminados . . . Desde la altura de su posición social, algunas saben descender, como los ángeles legendarios, a los antros oscuros de la vida, donde la miseria habita, el vicio acecha y ruge la desesperación.

(Prosas, 2:41; emphasis mine)

A similar spatial dichotomy lends support to the theory we wish to advance in explanation of the fundamental social sense of Casal's metaphors as an embodiment not only of ideological concepts—realism as opposed to idealism—but, in addition, as a reflection of his lingering preoccupation with a society he detests but whose odious presence he fails to place out of mind and sight. In writing of Esteban Borrero Echevarría's traits of intelligence he observes: "No podían [los frutos de su inteligencia] ser avalorados, por deficiencias del medio, en el mercado intelectual"; "su temperamento lo arrastraba al ensueño y la realidad lo conduzo a la acción." This conflict is represented on the one hand by an aspirational, elevational structure—*ascender en pos de las águilas hacia el sol*—followed by a resigned movement of descent—*marchar tras los reptiles hacia el lodazal* *(Prosas,* 1:261-62). Crass reality thus prevails over visions of art and idealism.

Where are the solutions to these social ills? The conventional Romantic refuge in the past has but a momentary triumph over the compelling forces of the social scene: "Tal parece que, olvidada [nuestra población] de su cruenta miseria y despierta de su mortal letargo, surgía rejuvenecida ante los ojos, mostrando el entusiasmo juvenil y la estruendosa animación de pasados días" *(Prosas,* 2:14). There is also the notion of physical displacement as a source of solace, a solution entertained by Arsenio in **"La última ilusión."** The present is irreconcilable with Arsenio's character, aesthetic inclinations and education. In canvassing alternatives he describes the corrupt, inept and decadent society of his time. Paris is the obvious antidote to Havana. But even Paris offers two cultures: The one he detests is rich, robust, bourgeois, and universal; the other, his ideal, is rare, exotic, delicate, sensitive, and artificial. But just as Arsenio—Casal's alter ego—is incapable of taking his life, so is he also incapable of the dynamic act of rerooting his existence: "Porque si me fuera," he confesses, "yo estoy seguro que mi ensueño se desvanecería como el aroma de una flor cogida en la mano, hasta quedar despojado de todos sus encantos." To this Arsenio adds the disjunctive which bears directly upon Casal's worldview, his relationship to his environment, and, finally, the ties of his milieu to his art: "Mientras que viéndolo [su ensueño] de lejos, yo creo todavía que hay algo, en el mundo, que endulce el mal de la vida, algo que constituye mi última ilusión, la que se encuentra siempre, como perla fina en cofre empolvado, dentro de los corazones más tristes, aquella ilusión que nunca se pierde, quizás" *(Prosas,* 1:226-29). Nonrealization,

nonfulfillment, in short, nonmovement, are thus transformed, via suspension, into preserved illusions. Immobility acquires qualities of an ideal as the artist is incapacitated by the conflicts and contradictions of the colony and the cultural crisis of his age.

THE STRUGGLE FOR LIFE

The process by which inaction is idealized and fashioned into aesthetic motifs reveals attempts at dynamic change, thus providing psychological insights into the relationship of the individual artist to his social medium. While Casal was undoubtedly impotent as far as social action was concerned, he nevertheless understood something of its substance, and even its significance for Cuba. Of Antonio San Miguel's paper *La Lucha* he wrote:

Su diario ha llegado a ser, en corto espacio de tiempo, el órgano de la opinión pública, la cual está por encima de todos los poderes. Ocupándose minuciosamente de lo sucedido, diciéndolo todo sin ambages ni rodeos, interpretando los sentimientos populares, pidiendo el cumplimiento de reformas prometidas y anunciando las que reclama el porvenir; ha hecho temerse, no sólo de los que desempeñan los primeros cargos públicos, sino de todos los parásitos que pululan alrededor de éstos. No se comete un solo acto de ilegalidad, sin que al instante sea denunciado por el diario democrático.

(Prosas, 1:148)

These comments on *La Lucha* broaden our vision of a picturesque Casal enclosed in a miniscule room decorated with *japonerías.*

The tensions of his desperate irresolution created a morbid fascination for the theme of action. Of Juana Borrero he wrote: "Dentro de poco tiempo, toda vez que una artista de tan brillantes facultades no puede permanecer en la sombra, ya porque una mano poderosa la arrastre a la arena del combate, ya porque se lance ella misma a cumplir fatalmente su destino" *(Prosas,* 1:271). But of himself he noted his desire to take refuge "en ese lugar paradisíaco [Vento] y de no retornar al combate de la vida, donde hay que permanecer en el puesto señalado hasta quemar el último cartucho, hasta exhalar el último suspiro" *(Prosas,* 2:42); or "Perdió mi corazón el entusiasmo / al penetrar en la mundana liza" (**"Paisaje espiritual"**). Like the gladiator of his **"Bajo-Relieve,"** though encouraged and cajoled, he succumbed time and time again.

A letter dated 1890 substantiates Casal's realization that he was drawn to dynamic figures: "Sólo he encontrado en estos días una persona que me ha sido simpática. ¿Quién se figura usted sea? Maceo, que es un hombre bello, de complexión robusta, inteligencia clarísima, y voluntad de hierro." To which he adds: "No sé si esa simpatía que siento por nuestro General es efecto de la neurosis que padezco y que me hace admirar los seres de condiciones y cualidades opuestas a las mías" (***Prosas,*** 3:82). This reverence, while it raises unresolved psychological speculations, also serves to point up the force of Casal's Cuba as an artistic motif in his work. Under the influence of this social presence, the final lines of "A un héroe," written in celebration of Maceo's brief visit to Havana in 1892, convey the impression of a depraved, materialistic ruling class presiding over a hopelessly weakened enslaved population: "Hallas sólo que *luchan sin decoro* / espíritus famélicos de oro / imperando entre míseros *esclavos*" (emphasis mine). In contrast with these lines are those of **"Oración"** where antipodal images (*sombra, luminosos haces*) embody Casal's hope for an end to the untenable state of his personal inaction, with its concomitant motifs of tedium, distance or coldness:

> ¡Oh, Señor!, si la sombra no deshaces
> y en mi alma arrojas luminosos haces,
> como un sol en oscuro firmamento,
>
> haz que sienta en mi espíritu moroso
> primero la tormenta que el reposo,
> primero que el hastío . . . ¡el sufrimiento!

DISTANCE

By distance we mean not simply perspective but a structural motif by means of which the poet, in his function of *voyeur,* moves his vision to the outer and upper levels of a *telescopic structure* as a reaction or alternative to his hostile environment. Arsenio's previously cited comments on Paris are an embodiment of this concept: "*Viéndolo de lejos,* yo creo todavía que hay algo que endulce el mal de la vida" (emphasis mine). Or, when Casal elucidates his ideas on Maceo he concludes: "Ya se ha marchado y no sé si volverá. Después de todo me alegro, porque las personas aparecen mejor a nuestros ojos *vistas de lejos*" (***Prosas,*** 3:82; emphasis mine).

Distance, in an aesthetic and ideological context, constitutes both an expansion of the telescopic structure and a counterstatement to frustrated attempts at harmonious social integration. As a counterstatement it represents a search for transcendency at the heights of human experience. In **"Bohemios,"** for example, Casal explains his admiration for the women "de mirada abrasadora":

> Yo os amo porque os lleva el devaneo
> donde el peligro vuestra vida afronte,
> y en vuestros ojos soñadores leo
> ansias de traspasar el horizonte

Traspasar el horizonte here is a metaphorical embodiment reminiscent of Praz's ideas on "interiority," an indication of a voyeuristic rather than a visionary quest for the hidden sense of what lies most immediately be-

yond us.[15] In terms of Casal's worldview, the conflicts of his inadaptability to his real world and his rejection of its values create his indecisive suspension—the "hovering" to which we have referred—in which there is a contemplation of the frontiers of a subjectivized perspective (distance) of infinities and coldness. In **"Bohemios"** *glacial* and *ilusión* are counterposed; the women Casal admires have eluded "el soplo glacial del desengaño" by pursuing "la sed insaciable de lo extraño." Their illusions constitute a dynamic motif, a fiery trail (contrasted with Casal's sombre, frigid inaction)—*ígneo rastro/que os traza en lo infinito vuestro ensueño*—a metaphor suggesting the dynamic of perennial search for transcendence (distance: *Ver el* [sitio] *que más lejos se levanta*) as an alternative to reduction. Through structured distance the poet comes to terms with the limitations of his conflictive existence without abandoning unrealized ideals nor the realities of life, however imperfect or repugnant they may be. Hence the significance of the concept of distance as an enlargement of one of the two perspectives of a telescopic structure. In the style of his "hombre de las muletas de níquel," whose illusions insulated him against society's materialism, Casal chose a life of intense interiority, and, like his fictional creation, strained his vision, "sus miradas, rígidas y glaciales, hacia lo lejos, hacia lo más lejos que podían alcanzar" (***Prosas,*** 1:233).

BRUMAS, SOMBRA, FRÍO

While the images of the lower spheres of a spatially conceived construct constitute the objectionable substance of material reality—*lodo, pantano, fango,* etc.— the pursuit of alternatives viable for Casal brings him to the fringes of a composite reality. From the mire of repugnant reality the poet rises and extends his vision toward a horizon that he desperately trusts will be illuminated both for himself and for Cuba. The components of such a system of values are apparent in the following brief passage in which Casal's enthusiasm approaches the equivalent of dynamic action resulting in the idealized displacement or *replanteamiento* to which Cintio Vitier has referred:[16] "[La legión heroica de los conquistadores del ideal] se ha impuesto la gloriosa tarea de *elevar* hasta los últimos *confines* de nuestra patria la antorcha luminosa de la civilización, cuyos brillantes fulgores disiparán las *sombras* que ennegrecen el *horizonte,* e iluminarán el camino que hemos de atravesar" (***Prosas,*** 2:28; emphasis mine). The juxtaposition of *elevar, confines, horizonte* in this conventionally phrased description is scarcely fortuitous. Implicit in the imagistic grouping is the process of "scanning the horizons" as anguish seeks relief in an uncertain future: "La sombra tenebrosa de las inquietudes del porvenir" (***Prosas,*** 1:157); or solace from the weight of the past: "La bruma de los recuerdos" (***Prosas,*** 1:157). While Casal speaks of "la tristeza del recuerdo" (***Prosas,*** 1:163), suggesting his generally melancholy temporal concepts, by contrast, he refers to "el esplendor de la distancia" (**Prosas,** 1:163).

In **"Sueño de gloria"** (dedicated to Moreau), the poet, in his voyage toward the ideal via an apotheosis of the painter, announces "de la Tierra en los *confines,* / el juicio universal de los humanos" and summons the Creator from behind "brumas opalinas." The poem contains a universal construct with its valley and firmament, its light and shade. From the "sombra glacial" in the first line we reach the "fulgores siderales," the "ambiente lumínico" of the last.

In the light of these and other contexts, it seems reasonable to generalize and identify horizons with an ascensional movement toward spiritual values or artistic ideals, difficult though these may be to attain. Their elusiveness, however, explains the poet's iteration of *frío, hielo, glacial* as the embodiment of a middle ground. When Casal characterized Huysman's life he spoke of his languishing (*languidece*) between two poles, an alternate view of our previous allusions to the state of suspended animation of the Cuban's psyche. "Fuera de esos dos polos," writes Casal, "es decir del extremo entusiasmo o de la extrema repugnancia, su alma languidece sobre le monotonía de la vida, como la sombra de un ahorcado sobre un abismo de hielo, asfixiada de hastío, humedecida de lágrimas, enervada de asco, adolorida de desencantos" (**Prosas,** 1:174). Casal's *hastío* is conceptually related to *frío,* but with the latter image suggesting not a final solution but a middle term, the psychological impassivity of the superior being who needs to and has been obliged to rise above the *abismo de hielo.* The qualities of indifference and concentration implicit in *frío* provide, at the same time, for a potential spiritual fulfillment through passionate identification. Thus, Elena, deified and united with Moreau in **"Sueño de gloria"** is first portrayed in the sonnet as impassive: "Indiferente a lo que en torno pasa, / mira Elena hacia el lívido horizonte / irguiendo un lirio en la rosada mano." Her frigid scrutiny is modified by an idealized passion in the presence of Moreau: "Colorean su tez matices rojos, intensa conmoción su seno agita" (**"Sueño de gloria"**).

Passion points to spiritual realization. But the distance and difficulties between the latter and material reality are such that the poet slips into an entranced state of suspension: "Yo hubiera querido permanecer, por tiempo infinito, en ese estado de calma inalterable, de olvido profundo y de perfecta beatitud, estado en que hunde el espíritu . . . siempre que el cuerpo se encuentra mecido, arrullado y entumecido por las ondas" (**Prosas,** 2:71). *Frío* and *calma* are associated with immobility or balance. The cessation of external movement is the lot of the artist: "Aunque trate de luchar, en los primeros tiempos, su energía se gasta, su inteligen-

cia se atrofia . . . [se explica que] se detengan repentinamente sin atreverse a avanzar, como viajeros sorprendidos, en mitad del camino, por inesperado abismo, donde la sombra ondea, el frío impera y fermentan las impurezas" (**Prosas,** 2:71).

There is a further shade of distinction between *frío* and *hastío.* The latter, in a sense, represents a descent, a falling away from struggle, whereas *frío,* though tied to *abismo,* is an abstraction, a transitory but painful incapacitation, but with the potential of piercing the *brumas, sombras,* and *neblina* of the horizon.

In the elaboration of these images Casal undoubtedly was influenced by Gustave Moreau's spatial structuring. The painter's inspiration is evident, for example, in the *inertia* x *movement* antitheses of the sonnets from **"Mi Museo ideal."** The Cuban poet, like the French painter, was attracted to physical immobility, a fascination that Moreau analyzed in connection with his canvases:

> Une chose domine en moi, l'entraînement et l'ardeur la plus grande vers l'abstraction. L'expression des sentiments humains, des passions de l'homme m'intéresse sans doute vivement, mais je suis moins porté à exprimer ces mouvements de l'âme et de l'esprit qu'à rendre pour ainsi dire visibles les éclairs intérieurs qu'on ne sait à quoi rattacher, qui ont quelque chose de divin dans leur apparente insignifiance et qui, traduits par les merveilleux effets de la pure plastique, ouvrent des horizons magiques, je dirai même divins.[17]

And, as José Pierre comments, "prôner 'la belle inertie' en plein coeur du XIXe siècle, n'est-ce-pas d'ailleurs aller sciemment à retours de l'éloge de l'energie."[18] Frigidity and fixity are thus not merely signs of an incapacity for full integration of the individual and his milieu but also an inverse reaction, at bottom, a protest against the energy and momentum of a "mercantilist" society whose values repulsed both the French painter and his Cuban admirer. For Cintio Vitier these values are directly related to the Cuban malaise: "Ese escalofrío de Casal, por ejemplo, siempre hemos sospechado que está dando testimonio del *frío interior* que hay en nuestro país. . . . Casal, que no tuvo la pasión política, que arrebató nuestro carácter durante casi un siglo, empezó a sentir, en sí mismo y en los otros, en el fenómeno de lo cubano como mundo existencial cerrado, ese fondo frío que ya desde los años 20, más o menos, constituye el visible y escalofriante *substratum* de nuestra vida nacional. . . . Casal nos produce el efecto de que ya sabe que pertenece a un pueblo *sin destino.*"[19]

Two Static Structures

Tied to the concept of coldness is the first of two structures whose syntactic arrangement suggests overwhelming tedium and debilitation: *La enumeración inerte.*[20] Locked into place with the alternative of an impassive searching of the horizons for spiritual alternatives, Casal dwelled on what lay before him (in keeping with his telescopic structuring) with an almost hypnotic fascination: "Todas las noches, en la Habana, son iguales. Siempre vemos el mismo cielo, tachonado de los mismos astros; aspiramos el mismo ambiente, impregnado de los mismos olores; recorremos las mismas calles, alumbradas por los mismos mecheros de gas; penetramos en los mismos cafés, invadidos por las mismas gentes" (***Prosas,*** 2:27).

In the telescopic structure the sense of hovering is balanced by the dualities of its perspective. In the pluralities of the enumeración inerte there is a senseless accumulation of a single variety of details:

> Fétido como el vientre de los grajos
> al salir del inmundo estercolero
> donde, bajo mortíferas miasmas,
> amarillean los roídos huesos
> de leprosos cadáveres; viscoso
> como la baba que en sus antros negros
> destilan los coléricos reptiles
> al retorcer sus convulsivos cuerpos
> entre guijarros húmedos
>
> **("Cuerpo y alma")**

The same pattern—adjective plus *al* plus a connective—is employed in the remaining lines of the first section of the poem, and, with variations, in the second.[21]

A correlative structure[22] of the enumeración inerte is also pluralistic, of the variety described by Dámaso Alonso in his study "Sintagmas no progresivos y pluralidades: tres calillas en la prosa castellana." Such expressions, needless to say, are a constant of Hispanic prose, and the nonprogressive tagmemes (*sintagmas no progresivos*) which are of special significance in Casal's prose are those in which "todas las voces . . . tienen una misma función sintáctica."[23] Each age, each writer, responds to the circumstances and stimuli of his environment fashioning distinct pluralistic patterns. Casal's formulations in this regard reveal a fascinating consistency: "Rubén Darío, que, *por su fantasía, por su estilo* y *por sus lucubraciones* más que un escritor nicaragüense, parece un artista parisiense" (***Prosas,*** 1:170); "qué gustos *tan nobles, tan puros, tan elevados*" (***Prosas,*** 1:175); "lo que seduce a Huysmans, *bajo cualquiera forma, en cualquiera época* y *por cualquiera causa,* es el sufrimiento" (***Prosas,*** 1:176); "estas novelas *no pertenecen a ninguna escuela, no tienen hermanas en ninguna literatura, no pueden compararse* más que *a si mismas*" (***Prosas,*** 1:178); "dentro de la casa todo revela *orden, pobreza* y *pulcritud*" (***Prosas,*** 1:204). These triadic, almost classic, formulations are not unconscious structures. And if they were, the substance of our contention would not be significantly altered. However, the following example of two successive triads leaves little room to doubt the existence of a

fully conscious technique: "Fruto de sus primeros amores, *lo colma de agasajos, lo cubre de besos* y *lo estrecha entre sus brazos* temblorosos. Ella siente por el *lo que la concha por su primera perla, lo que el árbol por su primer fruto, lo que la planta por su primera flor*" (***Prosas,*** 1:205).

Balance, symmetry, and measured structuring—stylistic hallmarks in an age of imbalance and rapid metamorphosis, in a troubled society repugnant to the writer—can only suggest, once again, an implied protest, an abstraction, a state of suspension, and, finally an ironic contrast with the constancy of injustice amidst Cuba's crying need for change.

Frío, brumas, infinito, hastío, enumeración interte, sintagmas no progresivos, are images, motifs and structures whose function within Casal's prose and poetry reflects the Cuban's personal psychological reactions to the iniquities of colonial society. Casal's descriptions of "La sociedad de la Habana" hardly admit speculation regarding his critical view of Cuba. Even though his point of view was elitist, his social preoccupations those of an esthete, his social chronicles lay bare the open wounds of the colony. His social action was nil, and attempts at flight frequent. It would be futile to deny his escapism, for numerous are the expressions which echo the lines of "Pax animae":

> Tan sólo llega a percibir mi oído
> algo extraño y confuso y misterioso
> que me arrastra muy lejos de este mundo.

But, more significant than his yearning for distance, either as physical displacement or as a metaphor of spiritual attainment, is the appreciation of the stamp of Colonial Cuba that he himself undertook to analyze—albeit in his limited fashion—and that obviously occupied his thoughts, molded his style, but thus far has been neglected in the scant body of imaginative Casal criticism.

Notes

[This article was] [s]upported as part of the project "Literature and Society: Aspects of Conformity and Disconformity in Mexico, Argentina and the Spanish Antilles (1830-1940)" by the Joint Committee on Latin American Studies of the Social Science Research Council and the American Council of Learned Societies.

1. Cintio Vitier, *Lo cubano en la poesía* (La Habana: Instituto del Libro, 1970), p. 285.

2. Julián del Casal, *Prosas* (La Habana: Consejo Nacional de Cultura, 1963), 2:54. In preparing this study we have used the three volumes of prose of the Centenary Edition published by the Consejo Nacional de Cultura, 1963-64. References to this

edition will be made within the text in abbreviated form: *Prosas,* 2:54. For the poetry we have used the Mario Cabrera Saqui edition: *Poesías completas* (La Habana: Dirección de Cultura, 1945). References to the poetry will be made within the text by title only.

3. Vitier, *Lo cubano,* p. 297.

4. "La perla" constitutes a rare example of allegorical embodiment.

5. Eduardo López Morales in his "Prólogo" to Jorge Isaacs' *María* (La Habana: Casa de las Américas, 1970), p. ix.

6. José María Monner Sans, *Julián del Casal y el modernismo hispanoamericano* (México: El Colegio de México, 1952), p. 73.

7. Charles Baudelaire, *Oeuvres* (Paris: La Pleiade, 1932), 2:647.

8. See our study, "Las estructuras, polares en la obra de José Martí y Julián del Casal" in *Génesis del modernismo* (México: El Colegio de México, 1966), pp. 153-87.

9. We are using this adjective in the sense of Monner Sans's characterization of Casal as "el primer lírico de *formacion cubana.*" *Julian del Casal,* p. 118.

10. Mario Praz, *Mnemosyne, the Parallel between Literature and the Visual Arts* (Princeton: Princeton University Press, 1970), p. 163.

11. See note 2.

12. Compare:

> Porque al oír tu voz, amante y tierna,
> la tristeza del alma, se evapora,
> cual la sombra de lóbrega caverna
> al resplandor resodado de la aurora.
>
> ("Versos azules")

13. Needless to say we cannot present a full study of Casal's analysis of Cuban society here. Instead, we have chosen those aspects that have a direct bearing on the explication of the stylistic elements of his work singled out for study in a social context. Among the significant essays not studied systematically are the articles entitled "La sociedad de la Habana" (*Prosas,* 1:131-57) and Casal's specific comments on General Salamanca (*Prosas,* 1:154-55).

14. See Tulio Halperin Donghi, *Historia contemporánea de América Latina* (Madrid: Alianza Editorial, 1970), pp. 278-79.

15. Praz, *Mnemosyne,* p. 164.

16. See note 3.

17. Quoted by Jean Paladilhe, *Gustave Moreau* (Paris: Fernand Hazan, 1971), p. 32.

18. José Pierre, "Gustave Moreau au regard changeant des générations," in Paladilhe, *Gustave Moreau,* p. 80.

19. Vitier, *Lo cubano,* pp. 309-10. These lines were originally written in prerevolutionary Cuba.

20. Vitier, *Lo cubano,* pp. 291-92, n.3.

21. The enumeration of section 2 is based on terms of purity. But Casal's preoccupation with its antithesis is evident in the last three lines which precede the *Envío:*

> Tal es, oh, Dios!, el alma que tú has hecho
> vivir en la inmundicia de mi carne,
> como vive una flor espesa en el cieno.

22. In verse, an interesting parallel might be drawn with Casal's use of the monorrimo in "En el campo."

23. Dámaso Alonso, with Carlos Bousoño, *Seis calas en la expresión literaria española* (Madrid: Gredos, 1951), p. 25.

Luis Felipe Clay Méndez (essay date 1979)

SOURCE: Méndez, Luis Felipe Clay. "Julián del Casal and the Cult of Artificiality: Roots and Functions." In *Waiting for Pegasus: Studies of the Presence of Symbolism and Decadence in Hispanic Letters,* edited by Roland Grass and William R. Risley, pp. 155-68. Macomb, Ill.: Western Illinois University, 1979.

[*In the following essay, Méndez examines the cult of artificiality in Casal's prose, tracing its literary and contextual antecedents.*]

> haz, ¡oh, Dios!, que no vean ya mis ojos
> la horrible Realidad que me contrista.
>
> —Julián del Casal[1]
>
> [*Grant, oh, Lord!, that my eyes no longer see
> the horrible Reality that afflicts me.*]

Despite traditional interpretations that persisted in stressing an innate deficiency that determined Julián del Casal's character, a new and more accurate consideration of the social, political, and cultural pressures that weighed upon him is being brought to bear.[2] It is no longer valid, therefore, to simplify his artistic pose under the mistaken assumption that his production was conceived exclusively within, and related only to, an alienated point of view. Partly accountable for this sophism was the fact that it stemmed basically from an analysis of Casal's poetry. The prose, much more copious and revealing, still awaits being properly incorporated into the Cuban artist's overall production. This study will have as its main objective the itemization of the antecedents—literary and environmental—that motivated, shaped, and maintained the cult of artificiality as expressed primarily in Casal's prose.

Julián del Casal approached literature as a way to release both his talents and his anxiety. In doing so, he manifested a tendency to depersonalize himself in order to better achieve cohesion with other writers who advocated similar emotional aberration, disenchanted with the oppressive environment and firmly committed to changing it.[3] After a considerable amount of eclectic reading by Casal, French poetic schools became the most propitious source from which he could draw sound inspiration as well as a mode of expression. Of these the one that provided the best and most accessible means of change and escape was French Symbolism. The powerful capabilities inherent in the cult of artificiality, which was a pervasive element in that movement, became Casal's overriding premise, broken down to its essential components. From the symbolists Casal inherited a priority of purpose that could be synthesized by the dictum that "the first duty in life is to be as artificial as possible."[4] Eagerly adopting this dictum as an intellectual obsession in the manner of Joris-Karl Huysmans, Casal then developed the principles of what Gustavo Duplessis calls "la estética de lo artificial"[5] [the esthetic of the artificial], which guides and limits the scope of his most recurrent themes.

WITHDRAWAL FROM SOCIETY

One evident cause of Casal's devotion to artificiality was an intense desire to withdraw from the social and political constituents of the world around him, perpetrated by the stagnant form of government that imperial Spain imposed on Cuba, with its archaic regulations and ill-fated goals. The resulting social climate was one of deprivation and overt materialism, which contrasted sharply with the refined and exquisite creed espoused by Casal.[6] Unable, therefore, to negotiate the patulous "abyss" that separated him from his fellow men, Casal opted for total separation by isolating himself in a virtually impenetrable and artificial world of his own. By means of evasion, which resulted from his convictions and not from instinctive impulses, Casal attempted to minimize the impure influences of his milieu while simultaneously devoting his efforts to more dependable reinforcements. In this artificial realm of alienation Casal was able to delve into his own self, a process that Ricardo Gullón calls "confinamiento en el yo"[7] [confinement in the self], which is the center of artistic creation. The writer, as Casal himself points out, "acude a sí mismo, única fuente de consuelo, para adormecer sus penas con la cadencia de las estrofas que arranca de lo más profundo de su corazón"[8] [resorts to himself, the only source of consolation, in order to appease his sorrows with the cadence of the stanzas that he tears out of the depths of his heart].

Solitude provides both shelter and a mood conducive to meditation and illumination. Casal infers this transition when he recalls his farewell to a bookstore owner who had told him the story of a young man who lived much like Casal himself: "sin decir una palabra, estreché su mano, cogí el sombrero y me refugié en mi soledad, donde he pensado mucho y donde pienso todavía en aquel extraño joven que, para conjurar su spleen, ha hecho del sufrimiento una voluptuosidad" (*I*, 237) [without saying a word, I shook his hand, took my hat and sought refuge in my solitude, where I have thought a lot and where I still think about that strange young man who, in order to exorcise his despondency, has turned suffering into voluptuousness]. The apparent solidarity—suggested by "I shook his hand" and "I still think"—transcends to a level of spiritual perversion with "my solitude" serving as a catalyst. Worthy of mention in this regard is the deliberate use of the possessive adjective ("mi soledad"), normally omitted in Spanish, employed here to underline the personal nature of solitude. But Casal's awareness that others also had an affinity for solitude led to a further awareness that there exists a brotherhood of marginal entities who share a common purpose in suffering and shattered aspirations. Since they are in an alien environment, however, they are unable to sustain their creed and are equally unable to share those alien values. "Whatever the beginning of his solitude," Ralph Harper has written, "an outsider knows he is not like most men; and the knowledge of his difference hurts. The nineteenth and twentieth centuries in art and real life have left a frieze of outsiders of all kinds, ranging from epic and tragic heroes to orphans and refugees. They are all brothers of communion of displacement and loneliness."[9]

As an "outsider," Casal eventually makes solitude an ideal that presupposes "vivir obscurecido, solo, arrinconado e invisible para todos" (*III,* 85) [living in obscurity, alone, set aside and invisible to everyone]. Nevertheless, there is suffering associated with this flight, stemming from the confrontation—as Rodríguez-Fernández puts it—of the self and the alien world.[10] Casal himself clearly outlines the causal relationship: "aquel hombre ha vivido un día entre sus semejantes y, desencantado de ellos, se ha retirado a la soledad, sin dignarse mostrar su desprecio a los demás" (*III,* 27) [that man has lived one day among his fellow men and, disenchanted with them, has withdrawn to solitude, without condescending to show his scorn toward others].

Eventually, Casal recognizes that his "lúgubre aislamiento" (p. 46) [gloomy isolation] has become obsessive since, as he admits, "en cualquier lugar he de encontrarme solo" (p. 51) [I will feel alone anywhere]. This is when the anguished writer begins to consider death as the ultimate solitude:

> Procuraré irme a vivir en un barrio lejano, cerca del mar, para aguardar allí la muerte, que no tardará muchos años en venir. Mientras llegue, viviré entre libros y cuadros, trabajando todo lo que pueda literariamente, sin pretender alcanzar nada con mis trabajos, como no sea matar el tiempo.
>
> (*III*, 85)

> [I will try to go and live in a faraway neighborhood, near the sea, to await death there, which will not take many years to come. While it is arriving, I will live among books and paintings, working literarily as much as I can, without pretending to attain anything with my work other than killing time.]

Casal has tried to arrange his remaining years so that they will be as artificial as possible, surrounding himself with works of art and adopting nihilistic aspirations that will isolate him from the outside world. It is by no means accidental that his final location is distant from everything and near the sea, a powerful symbol of escape and hope frequently utilized by French Symbolists.[11]

The sea provides an extension of self-confinement and a way to alter the physical circumstances by linking them with an artificial environment where the bemused spirit might find solace and inspiration. Again, we must establish a direct relationship between the impoverished state of Casal's homeland and the respite inherent in travel; accordingly, Casal then summoned three components of artificiality and "built for himself a secluded world of oriental art, of sensory perceptions, of imaginary wanderings"[12] that was diametrically opposed to the real world. Casal favors this avenue of escape because he can carefully reconstruct his visions to conform to a particular need at any given moment. His vacillating moods account for paradoxical expectations in the "bello país desconocido" (p. 217) [beautiful unknown country]. In a poem entitled **"Nostalgias"** (p. 135), Casal lets his mind wander like Rimbaud's "drunken boat"[13] and whimsically changes the make-up of his imaginary landscape: "soplo helado del viento" [frozen breath of the wind], "campos olorosos" [odorous fields], "llanura africana" [African plain], "bambú corpulento" [strong bamboo tree], "flor de loto" [lotus flower], or "taitiano archipiélago" [Tahitian archipelago]. Behind all the confusion there is a unifying desire to flee, with no specific heading, to "otro cielo, otro monte, / otra playa, otro horizonte, / otro mar, / otros pueblos, otras gentes / de maneras diferentes / de pensar" [another sky, another hill, / another beach, another horizon, / another sea, / other towns, other people / with a different way / of thinking].

Casal realizes that he cannot make his dreamland too definite, lest it become perilously like a natural place, physically accessible. It is precisely for this reason that, after having dreamed of Paris and made plans to visit it, when he found himself in Europe he categorically refused to fulfill his dream. He explains this incident in terms of not wishing to see his visions turn into a disappointing reality:

> Porque si me fuera, yo estoy seguro que mi ensueño se desvanecería, como el aroma de una flor cogida en la mano, hasta quedar despojado de todos sus encantos; mientras que viéndolo de lejos, yo creo todavía que hay algo en el mundo, que endulce el mal de la vida, algo que constituye mi última ilusión.
>
> (*I*, 229)

> [Because if I left, I am sure that my reverie would vanish, like the aroma of a flower taken in the hand, until becoming stripped of all its charms; while seeing it from afar, I still believe that there is something in the world that may sweeten life's evil, something that constitutes my last illusion.]

This vital stance is representative of Julián del Casal's devotion to artificiality and his preference of illusion over a reality that could prove to be disappointing and even more deceiving than make-believe. Since distance was necessary to the development of his vision, Casal always maintained as an ultimate goal the enticingly exotic land where "todo es bello, rico y tranquilo, donde la fantasía ha construido y decorado una China occidental, donde la vida es dulce de respirar, donde la dicha está casada con el silencio. Allá es preciso que vayamos a vivir, allá es preciso que vayamos a morir" (*II*, 151) [everything is beautiful, rich, and tranquil, where fantasy has constructed and decorated an occidental China, where life is sweet to breathe, where happiness is married to silence. There we must go to live, there we must go to die].

AGAINST NATURAL LAW

Similar to the way that social, economic, and political conventions promote self-confinement and an obsessive desire for exotic climes, the physical environment—both primary nature and the man-made metropolis—triggers in devoted advocates of artificiality an immediate and uncompromising tendency to rejection. Despite the intrinsic antithesis of the two alternatives, the artist is unable to cope with either one since, in a materialistic environment, he is denied an atmosphere in which he can survive esthetically. Nature represents a competitive creative force that overwhelms the artist with its inflexible manner, justifying the symbolists' aversion to natural law, which Paul Verlaine (to cite but one example of many that are available) delineates in his poem "L'Angoisse" ["Anguish"]: "Nature, rien de toi ne m'émeut, ni les champs / Nourriciers, ni l'écho vermeil des pastorales / Siciliennes, ni les pompes aurorales, /

Ni la solennité dolente des couchants" ["Nature, nothing in you moves me, not the fruitful / Fields, not the roseate echo of the pastorales / Of Sicily, not the grandeur of the dawns, / Not the solemn ruefulness of sunsets"].[14] The negative aspect of these lines complements the attitude shared by other nineteenth-century writers, who viewed nature as an entity that had little to offer the tired senses: its omniscient powers are wasted and reduced to a cyclical pattern of monotony.

This finitude renders nature inferior to the boundless powers of artifice, which is capable of ridding objects of "sus defectos naturales" (**II**, 81) [their natural defects]. Artists envision the day when the triumph will be absolute, when synesthetic combinations will be achieved that are not possible in the realm of natural law: "Si las piedras preciosas tuvieran aromas, como los tendrán algún día, porque el Arte se encargará de curarlas de esa imperfección natural." (**III**, 46) [If only precious stones had aromas, as they will have some day, because Art will be responsible for curing them of that natural imperfection]. Casal looks forward to this day and also to a certain country that will attest to this victory: "Es un país singular, superior a los otros, como el Arte lo es a la Naturaleza, donde ésta está reforzada por el ensueño, donde está corregida, embellecida, refundida" (**II**, 152) [It is a singular country, superior to others, as Art is superior to Nature, where the latter is reshaped by reverie, where it is corrected, beautiful, recast].

Further evidence of nature's shortcomings is the corruptibility of its accomplishments. Charles Baudelaire, an ardent exponent of the enmity between artist and nature, often captures it through images of putrefaction in his poetry, as in "une Charogne" ["A Carcass"]: "Le soleil rayonnait sur cette pourriture, / Comme afin de la cuire à point, / Et de rendre au centuple à la grande Nature / Tout ce qu'ensemble elle avait joint" ["The sun shone hotly on all this rottenness / As if it were in some sense boiling, / As when Nature in her absolute nothingness / Cares nothing for her creature's spoiling"].[15] The poem epitomizes nature's impassiveness and obvious lack of interest in man's debased and putrid existence. Emulating this champion of the perverse and macabre, Casal also takes morbid pleasure in describing the putrefying process within himself:

De me cráneo, que un globo formaba
erizado de rojos cabellos,
descendían al rostro deforme,
saboreando el licor purulento,
largas sierpes de piel solferina
que llegaban al borde del pecho,
donde un cuervo de pico acerado
implacable roíame el sexo.

(p. 150)[16]

[From my skull, shaped like a globe
bristling with red hairs,

descended, to the deformed face,
savoring the purulent liquor,
long serpents of purplish skin
that arrived at the edge of my chest,
where a raven with a steel beak
implacably gnawed at my sex.]

Since nature has been exposed both for its imperfections and for its perishability, in Casal's view, mankind no longer "acude a refugiarse en los brazos de la naturaleza, porque sabe que no tiene alma" (**I**, 168) [seeks refuge in the arms of nature, knowing that it has no soul]. Hence, it follows, if one reasons as Baudelaire did, that, since nature is heartless, "everything natural in man is bad and whatever is good is artificial and acquired—from virtue to face-paint."[17] Nature is therefore diametrically opposed to the essential components of the artist's ethical and esthetic make-up. Casal expressed this through an antipathy even for those artists—such as gifted singers—who had God-given talents and did not have to endure the agony of concentration, study, and hard work before succeeding, as writers did: "Yo los odio, como odio todo aquello en que predomina la obra de la naturaleza y en que apenas se reconocen las huellas del estudio, de la paciencia y de la propia personalidad" (**III**, 57) [I hate them, as I hate everything in which the work of nature predominates and in which traces of study, patience, and even the personality itself are barely recognized].

Casal himself was living proof of nature's inadequacy since he was sporadically plagued by the ominous signs that foreshadow an early death and that forced him to withdraw to more healthful places. His infirmity, consequently, can be taken to account for the value inversion that chooses instead of "el olor de un bosque de caoba, / el ambiente enfermizo de una alcoba" (p. 190) [the odor of a mahogany forest, / the sickly atmosphere of a bedroom]. These preventive measures suggest the special care required by a delicate being because of "la pobreza de su organismo, que lo obligaría a vivir, como una planta de invernadero, tras las vidrieras de la casa paterna, buscando la sombra y huyendo de la luz de sol" (**I**, 230) [the weakness of his organism, that would force him to live, like a nursery plant, behind the windows of his paternal home, seeking the shade and fleeing from the sunlight]. Sunlight, being a product of nature, is destructive and threatens to "exterminate" the "freshness" of any feeble vegetable (p. 62). The ability to survive in the shade heralds another type of triumph—however perverted—over the devastating effects of nature.

Casal's embittered resentment of natural law appears at a very early stage of his thematic development, when the poet chastises nature for instilling a sense of boredom:

¡Qué insípidos tus dones conocidos!
¡Cómo al verte el hastío me consume!

Muere al fin, creadora ya agotada,
o brinda algo de nuevo a los sentidos . . .
¡Ya un color, ya un sonido, ya un perfume!

(p. 119)

[How insipid are your known talents!
How tedium consumes me when I see you!
Die once and for all, creator already spent,
or offer something new to the senses . . .
Either a color, or a sound, or a perfume!]

It is precisely the inalterable quality of the Cuban landscape that prevents Casal from finding any redeeming value in it, as we can see in a letter written shortly after his return from a convalescing excursion to the country, where he felt "el hastío más insoportable a la vista de un cielo siempre azul, encima de un campo siempre verde. La unión eterna de estos dos colores produce la impresión más antiestética que se puede sentir" (*I,* 241) [the most unbearable tedium at the sight of an ever-blue sky above an ever-green field. The union of these two colors produces the most antiesthetic impression that one can feel]. Incapable of tolerating the unchanging exuberance of his countryside, Casal professes "el impuro amor de las ciudades" (p. 190) [the impure love of the cities], where there exists a pervasive artificiality more attuned to his aberrant psyche. Nevertheless, subjected as he was to sporadic changes of mood brought about by a sudden aggravation of his pathological symptoms, Casal also admits that he is unable to maintain emotional stability in a synthetic world of human beings whom he finds terribly irritating: "creo que mi neurosis, o como se llame mi enfermedad, depende en gran parte de vivir en la ciudad, es decir, rodeado de paredes altas, de calles adoquinadas, oyendo incesantemente estrépito de coches, ómnibus y carretones" (*III,* 85) [I believe that my neurosis, or whatever my illness might be called, stems in part from living in the city, that is to say, surrounded by high walls, cobblestone streets, incessantly hearing the deafening noise of coaches, omnibuses, and carts]. His alienated spirit and refined tastes clashed in the city with the daily reminders of another type of existence that was extremely active, mechanized, and chaotic. Moreover, urban life can ultimately lead to a rhythm that denotes the same despised invariability as that encountered in the countryside.[18] As George Ridge has pointed out, the decadent hero "detests the great city, his megalopolis, which holds him captive through the fatal appeal of its artificiality."[19] On the one hand, the city contains every conceivable perversion and symbolizes man's victory over nature; on the other hand, its environment is comprised of multitudes that augment "la sensación más triste que se puede experimentar: la del aislamiento entre la multitud" (*II,* 99) [the saddest sensation that can be experienced: that of isolation within a crowd].

Since the urban setting is incapable of fulfilling his insatiable appetite for artificiality, Casal must create a synthetic reality within the immediate reality. For this purpose he resorts to various ploys, from dressing like a monk and living an ascetic existence to surrounding himself with oriental objects that created an ambiance of exotic preciousness. He clung to this world by refusing to recognize the signs that threatened to dissolve his illusive reality: "Los globos de luz eléctrica, colgados entre las columnas rojas, eran lo único que desvanecía a ratos mi ilusión. Pero yo procuraba no mirarlos jamás" (*III,* 57) [The electric light bulbs, hung among the red columns, were the only things that at times made my illusion vanish. But I tried not ever to look at them]. This state of mind, however, was not tenable for long. Consequently, realizing the precarious and ephemeral function of this kind of self-deceit, Casal also tried to produce artificiality through the use of drugs, a means of escape utilized by Baudelaire in his journeys to "the real land of Cockaigne."[20]

Casal's relationship to drugs was more esthetic than practical and his hallucinatory experiences were normally related to literary trances or the commitment to modify reality: "Durante la lectura, mi pensamiento se sumerge, desde la primera página, en una especie de letargo cataléptico, del que no quisiera nunca salir. Cada párrafo me produce el efecto de una bocanada de éter" (*I,* 207-08) [while reading, my thoughts are submerged, from the first page, in a kind of cataleptic lethargy which I would never want to leave. Each paragraph produces in me the effect of a whiff of ether]. Literature, like ether, becomes a cathartic agent and has an effect similar to the one outlined in **"La canción de la morfina"** [**The Song of Morphine**], in which the drug is animated for the purpose of enticing the reader with its powers:

Amantes de la quimera,
yo calmaré vuestro mal:
soy la dicha artificial,
que es la dicha verdadera.

(p. 69)

[Lovers of the chimera,
I will calm your sickness:
I am artificial happiness,
which is true happiness.]

This assertion of a perverted truth by the morphine is one of the chief justifications for using hallucinatory agents. Through drugs the artist is able to confuse the delicate balance that separates reality from artificiality. Furthermore, while he is under the influence of drugs, he can expand the sensorial boundaries that stimulate creation by unleashing the limitless dimensions of synesthesia:

doy al cuerpo sensaciones;
presto al espíritu alas.
Percibe el cuerpo dormido

por mi mágico sopor,
sonidos en el color,
colores en el sonido.

(p. 70)

[to the body I give sensations;
to the spirit I lend wings.
The body that lies asleep
under my magic stupor
perceives sounds in color
and colors in a sound.]

Precisely because of this esthetic inducement, Casal, like many other artists of his time, fell prey to the drug habit. As Guerard has stated: "few believers in Art for Art's sake are free from the *À Rebours* taint, the willful quest of the abnormal."[21] All symbolist-decadent perversion had its roots either in the rejection of the prevailing circumstances or in some sort of sordid experimentation purported to broaden the scope of artistic creativity. The latter, in the case of Casal, will compensate for the cultural myopia of colonial Cuba.

THE POWER OF ART

Although Julián del Casal remains somewhat aloof and confessional in his poetry, his prose provides his readers with an objective and accurate account of the cultural stagnation of his time, which should be considered among his most recurrent and significant themes. The overall picture is one of deprivation, beginning with "la indiferencia glacial, la falta de estímulo y la poca estimación que acompañan a los que viven aquí dedicados a los trabajos intelectuales" (*II*, 28) [the glacial indifference, the lack of stimulation, and the little esteem that accompany those who live here dedicated to intellectual work]. These factors, among innumerable others are responsible for Casal's defeatist question: "¿Puedo aspirar a algo, en nuestro medio social, que esté en consonancia con mi carácter, con mi educación o con mis aspiraciones?" (*I*, 228) [Can I aspire to anything, in our social medium, that is in consonance with my character, my education, or my aspirations?]

In such a demoralizing milieu the artist may succumb, for his "inteligencia se atrofia, y su carácter se agria, cayendo en la más negra misantropía" (*II*, 71) [his intelligence is atrophied, and his character becomes bitter, falling into the blackest kind of misanthropy]. Only artists who can pursue and maintain a commitment to esthetic ideals may overcome the cultural circumstances, and Enrique José Varona is—like Casal himself—one of them:

un gran escritor en un medio propicio para realizar toda clase de empresas, menos para las intelectuales, lo cual demuestra que poseía una vocación más sólida que ningún otro escritor cubano y que es un hombre que ama verdaderamente su Ideal, amor que no se ha visto justipreciado por su pueblo, porque no teniendo éste

más que el de la vida material, difícil le sería comprender que un individuo pueda perseguir otro más noble, más elevado, más inmaterial.

(*I*, 251-52)

[a great writer in an environment conducive to the accomplishment of all kinds of plans, except intellectual ones, which shows that he possessed a more solid vocation than any other Cuban writer and that he is a man who truly loves his Ideal, a love that his people have not appreciated because they, having love only for a material life, could hardly understand how an individual could pursue a nobler one, more elevated, less materialistic.]

Casal establishes an antithesis between literary dedication and the prevailing values, underscoring the merit of artists who survive under such adverse conditions. This contraposition becomes a prevalent stylistic element in Casal's production, employed whenever the young writer addressed an intrinsic duality: "Su pensamiento anhelaba ascender en pos de las águilas hacia el sol y tuvo que marchar tras los reptiles hacia el lodazal" (*I*, 262) [His thoughts longed to ascend after the eagles toward the sun and had to march behind the reptiles toward the swamp].

Devotion to art establishes the polar, elevated world seen above, where the follower of this cult can develop it, nourishing what Guerard calls "a perversity inherent in the artistic temperament, a shrinking from the bustle of the market place, a nostalgia for the solitude of the Ivory Tower, a timidity which half-reveals the haunting secret of self-diffidence."[22] In this stance there is a resulting "estado de alta espiritualidad"[23] [state of high spirituality] derived from the willful acceptance of "la penitencia purificante de la vida" (*I*, 37) [the purifying penitence of life] that either protects the artist from denigrating stains or cleanses him afterward. The esthete may then consider himself a martyr who "ha sacrificado su existencia en aras de su ideal" (*III*, 62) [has sacrificed his existence on the altar of his ideal].

In addition to affording a mystical purification of life, the devotion to art can indeed supply protection to "el confiado cominante que pasa por el sendero de la vida, aspirando el olor de las flores abiertas y bebiendo la lumbre de los astros" (*III*, 35) [the confident traveler who goes along the path of life, inhaling the aroma of open flowers and drinking the brightness of the stars]. Anyone who identifies with refined and dignifying things is worthy of "la mirada consoladora de las estrellas" (*I*, 213) [the consoling glance of the stars] since artistic devotion is a powerful ally, providing "el talismán que conjura al maleficio, el ácido que aniquila al microbio, la fuerza que arranca la pistola al suicida, la moneda de oro en el fango del arroyo, la tea fulgurante que deshace el pavor de las tinieblas" (*I*, 258) [the talisman that conjures the spell, the acid that annihilates the microbe, the force that tears the pistol away from the would-be suicide, the gold coin in the mud of the stream, the bright torch that dispels the fear of the darkness]. The deliverance is immediate:

> Cuando tu cuerpo, acribillado de heridas, caiga sangrando sobre las piedras del camino; cuando tus labios, cerrados para siempre, exhalen el último suspiro; ceñiré a tu frente el lauro de los inmortales y te abriré las puertas de mi templo. ¿Quieres seguirme? Piensa en que me aborrecen las muchedumbres, porque soy *El Arte*.
>
> (*II*, 83)

> [When your body, riddled with wounds, falls bleeding on the rocks of the road; when your lips, closed forever, exhale the last sigh; I will place on your forehead the wreath of the immortals and open for you the doors of my temple. Do you want to follow me? Remember that the multitudes abhor me, because I am *Art*.]

The symbolism here is overwhelming; the dual options represent the multiple vicissitudes of life ("wounds," "rocks," "the sigh," and "the multitudes"), counterpoised by the withdrawal that is inherent in artificiality, the "temple."

Casal readily accepts this invitation, hoping that artistic devotion will succor him and alleviate his suffering:

> Para olvidar entonces las tristezas
> que, como nubes de voraces pájaros
> al fruto de oro entre las verdes ramas,
> dejan mi corazón despedazado,
> refúgiome del Arte en los misterios.
>
> (p. 16)

> [To forget then the sadnesses
> that, like clouds of voracious birds
> on the golden fruit among the green branches,
> leave my heart in pieces,
> I take refuge in the mysteries of Art.]

This confidence in art has an immediate advantage: the conscientious esthete can eventually disregard the "voracious birds" that threaten him with the new realization that "el verdadero artista no se debe ocupar del prestigio que le concede el público, sino perfeccionarse en su arte y nada más" (*III*, 85) [the true artist should not concern himself with the prestige that the public bestows on him, but with the perfection of his art and nothing else]. Such a striving for perfection is the basis of what Auerbach has called in the French Symbolists "the Idolatry of art."[24] Casal's self-imposed and rigid standards were extremely difficult to attain; and, unwilling to acquiesce to prevailing norms, he was rarely satisfied with his own work. What Casal wrote about José Arburu could have been said of Casal himself: "nunca quedaba satisfecho con sus obras, porque había colocado muy alto su ideal" (*I*, 282) [he was never satisfied with his works because he had set his ideal very high]. Casal's epitaph attests to his overriding and pri-

mary esthetic drive: "Amó solamente la Belleza / Que ahora encuentre la Verdad su alma" (p. 55) [He loved only Beauty / Let his soul now find Truth].

In his never-ending quest for an innovative expression and for intellectual and sensory stimulation, Julián del Casal promoted an extension of literature. Through a diffusion of techniques he attempted to establish a continuity between the written word and the plastic arts. His collection **"Mi museo ideal"** [**"My Ideal Museum"**] consists of ten sonnets that correspond to an equal number of paintings by the French symbolist artist Gustave Moreau. Each of the poems is a verbal painting that approximates the chromatic richness of a particular canvas while simultaneously probing its meaning; the poems reveal the palette of a painter who has a keen sense of color, an artist who feels through his senses.[25]

The apprenticeship of Julián del Casal was a long, steady, and conscientious one, beginning with the appreciation and emulation of compatible approaches by other artists, like Joris-Karl Huysmans who, according to Casal, "traspasa las fronteras literarias, refundiendo los procedimientos más refinados de las otras artes, especialmente los de la orfebrería, el mosaico y la pintura" (*I*, 177) [goes beyond literary boundaries, recasting the most refined procedures of other arts, especially those related to gold or silver work, mosaic, and painting]. It is quite fitting that Casal used the French writer to illustrate the extensive scope of literature. Huysmans created a character—Des Esseintes—with whom the bemused Casal might be identified, a refined spirit who also had "unrealizable ideals and was beginning to outline his experiments in colour."[26] Undoubtedly, Casal himself began to manipulate color when he first lamented "que nuestra pluma no tenga, en estos momentos, la fineza de un pincel" (*II*, 25) [that our pen does not have, in these moments, the fineness of an artist's brush]. Eventually he developed this technique, and his profound admiration for plastic expression provided the incentive: "Habiendo sentido siempre un gran amor por la pintura, yo había tratado de hacer, en aquella composición, dos cuadros poéticos, uno en el estilo de Perugino y otro en el estilo de Rembrandt" (*I*, 267) [Having always felt a great love for painting, I tried to make, in that composition, two poetic paintings, one in the style of Perugino and another in the style of Rembrandt].

Bearing in mind that the underlying intention is to form an artificial realm as discordant with the environment as possible, it should come as no surprise that Casal avails himself of the illusive capabilities of the plastic arts. Once he has achieved his purpose, the painter can reap its benefits:

> la hora de arrinconar la tela esbozada, pasar la espátula sobre la paleta y aprisionar el color en sus frascos, dejando que su espíritu, como halcón desencantado, se

aleje de la tierra y se remonte a los espacios azules de
la fantasía, donde las quimeras, como mariposas de oro
en torno de una estrella, revolotean sin cesar.

(I, 265)

[the time for laying aside the sketched canvas, for passing the knife over the palette and closing the colors in
their tubes, allowing his spirit, like a disenchanted fal-
con, to withdraw from the earth and to flee to the blue
spaces of fantasy, where chimeras, like golden butterflies around a star, flutter incessantly.]

By means of a powerful symbol of elevation and freedom, the writer has achieved the levitation of a deserving spirit to an artificial and ethereal region of recognition and dreams. Supplementary images—"blues,"
"butterflies," and "a star"—enhance the dignifying nature of this realm. Since both literary and plastic arts
espouse no other objective than "el de satisfacer una
necesidad espiritual" (**II**, 177) [the satisfaction of a
spiritual necessity], they can share the attainment of
this level of fulfillment and reward, where "el Arte se
conserve, en las más puras cimas" (**I**, 177) [Art may be
kept on the purest summits].

Access to this artificial world in which dreams, aspirations, hopes and recompense amalgamate harmoniously,
was possible only for superior beings whose entire lives
were an exemplary devotion to esteticism of one sort
or another, and who possessed a spirit that was "impa-
ciente por abrir las alas" (**III**, 64) [impatient to spread
its wings]. In Casal's view, Rafael Díaz Albertini and
Gaspar Villate were such spirits: "Albertini transportaba
las llamas desconocidas, en las notas de oro de su vio-
lín, al paraíso azul del Ideal y Villate, por medio de sus
creaciones, iba ascendiendo a la Cumbre Sagrada, donde
la Gloria aguarda a sus elegidos" (**III**, 60) [Albertini
transported the unknown flames, in the golden notes of
his violin, to the blue paradise of the Ideal; and Villate,
by means of his creations, was climbing to the Holy
Summit, where Glory awaits the chosen ones]. Again
we must notice the ascending motion imparted by the
use of appropriate images. Casal himself fervently
strove to reach this world of artificiality and consequent
spirituality. As a poet, he was cognizant of the potential
innate in his literary production:

Aves mis versos son, que se detienen
en las páginas blancas de tu libro,
pidiéndote, con voz arrulladora,
que les dejes hacer en tu alma un nido.

(p. 212)

[My verses are birds that stop
on the white pages of your book,
asking you, in a lulling voice,
to let them build a nest in your soul.]

Unfortunately, a prolonged stay in this artificial region
is untenable. Despite the unquestionable protection it

offered to the aberrant spirit, there is always the inexorable return to the real world, expressed by Casal in
terms of a descending motion:

Así mi ensueño, pájaro canoro
de níveas plumas y rosado pico,
al querer en el mundo hallar cabida,

encontró de lo real los muros de oro
y deshecho, cual frágil abanico,
cayó entre el fango inmundo de la vida.

(p. 143)

[Thus my reverie, a song bird
of snowy feathers and rosy beak,
wanting to find a place in this world,

found the golden walls of reality
and, in pieces, like a fragile fan,
fell into the filthy mud of life.]

Casal's artificial creation crumbles due to the constant
pressures of his materialistic milieu; and, however hard
he tries to sustain his visions, he is constantly haunted
by overwhelming signs that herald his fall. Literature,
art, dreams, and any other means of artificiality are sup-
portive only to a certain degree, inasmuch as "Al salir
del magnífico establecimiento, mi espíritu se sintió do-
lorosamente impresionado por el espectáculo de las
calles. Me parecía haber descendido desde la altura de
un antiguo palacio italiano, poblado de maravillas artís-
ticas, hasta el fondo de inmundos subterráneos, intermi-
nables y angostos, llenos de quejas, gritos y blasfemias"
(**II**, 77) [Upon leaving the magnificent establishment,
my spirit felt itself painfully impressed by the spectacle
of the streets. It seemed as if I had descended from the
heights of an ancient Italian palace, filled with artistic
marvels, to the depths of filthy tunnels, endless and narrow, filled with grumblings, screams, and blasphemies].
This is a Dantesque descent to the infernal atmosphere
of the surroundings that, through brutal contrast, clari-
fies the need for these evocations.

Even though Julián del Casal was unable to find constant security in artificiality, he was able to sustain it
long enough to provide himself with respite from a reality that he strongly abhorred. To these moments of
solitude and tranquility we owe a unique and personal
blending of literary and esthetic influences and the expression of an anxiety that was genuine. Casal's message will have enduring relevance as long as there are
beings who cannot cope with their immediate circumstances and who seek ways to evade them.

Notes

1. "Tras una enfermedad," in *Poesías* (Havana: Consejo Nacional de Cultura, 1963), p. 123. Throughout this paper references to the poetry of Julián
del Casal—page numbers only, given parentheti-

cally in the text—will be to this edition. The translations are mine.

2. For an example of the traditional interpretation consult Rufino Blanco Fombona, *El modernismo y los poetas modernistas* (Madrid: Mundo Latino, 1929), p. 29. The new interpretation was spearheaded by Ivan A. Schulman in *Génesis del modernismo* (Mexico City: El Colegio de México, 1968), pp. 16-17.

3. Juan J. Geada y Fernández says in "Introducción a la Selección de Poesías de Julián del Casal," *Colección Libros Cubanos*, 23 (1931), xxxviii: "Por el gran número de autores que leía, podemos llegar a la conclusión de que fue tal la influencia por ellos ejercida, que la personalidad real de Casal fue sustituyéndose por una personalidad puramente artística. Desde entonces no se ajustaba a la realidad del vivir de los demás. Vivía en su propio ambiente, hijo de sus lecturas en amoroso consorcio con la fantasía" [Because of the great number of authors that he read, we can reach the conclusion that their influence was such that the real personality of Casal was replaced by a purely artistic personality. From then on the could not adjust to the reality of other people's lives. He lived in his own environment, offspring of his readings in amorous consortium with fantasy].

4. Roland N. Stromberg, *Realism, Naturalism, and Symbolism: Modes of Thought and Expression in Europe, 1848-1914* (New York: Harper, 1968), p. 238.

5. Gustavo Duplessis, "Julián del Casal," *Revista Bimestre Cubana*, No 3 (1945), p. 268.

6. Schulman states that Casal lived "en medio de fuerzas contradictorias, polares, condenado a comparar con dolor el profundo e intransitable abismo entre sus gustos refinados y exquisitos y los valores materialistas y positivistas que lo circundaban" (p. 17) [in the midst of contradictory, polar forces, condemned to compare with sorrow the deep and unbreachable abyss between his refined and exquisite tastes and the materialistic and positivistic values that surrounded him].

7. Ricardo Gullón, *Direcciones del modernismo* (Madrid: Gredos, 1963), p. 96.

8. Julián del Casal, *Prosas*, 3 vols. (Havana: Consejo Nacional de Cultura, 1963-1964), I, 168. Henceforth, all prose quotations will be indicated in the text by volume number and page number. The translations are mine.

9. Ralph Harper, *The Seventh Solitude: Metaphysical Homelessness in Kirkegaard, Dostoevsky and Nietzsche* (Baltimore: Johns Hopkins Press, 1965), p. 5.

10. Mario Rodríguez-Fernández, *El modernismo en Chile y en Hispanoamérica* (Santiago de Chile: Editorial Universitaria, 1967), p. 47.

11. See, e.g., Stéphane Mallarmé, "Sea Breeze," in *An Anthology of French Poetry from Nerval to Valéry in English Translation with French Originals,* ed. Angel Flores (New York: Doubleday, 1958), p. 147 (cited hereafter as Flores), and Arthur Rimbaud, "Delirium (II)," in *Baudelaire, Rimbaud, Verlaine: Selected Verse and Prose Poems,* ed. Joseph M. Bernstein (New York: Citadel, 1947), p. 186 (cited hereafter as Bernstein).

12. John E. Englekirk, Irving A. Leonard, John T. Reid, and John A. Crow, *An Anthology of Spanish American Literature,* 2nd ed. (New York: Appleton, 1968), II, 394.

13. See Flores, p. 109.

14. Flores, pp. 85 and 338.

15. Bernstein, p. 30.

16. Casal's "Horridum Somnium" bears a remarkable resemblance to Baudelaire's "Un Voyage à Cythère" ["A Voyage to Cythera"]: "Les yeux étaient deux trous, et du ventre effondré / Les intestins pesants lui coulaient sur les cuisses, / Et ses bourreaux, gorgés de hideuses délices, / L'avaient à coups de bec absolument châtré" ["The eyes were holes, and from the ruined gut / Across the thighs the heavy bowels poured out, / And crammed with hideous pleasures, peck by peck, / His butchers had quite stripped him of his sex"] (Flores, pp. 43 and 314).

17. A. E. Carter, "The Cult of Artificiality," *University of Toronto Quarterly,* 25 (1956), 455.

18. "Todas las noches, en La Habana, son iguales. Siempre vemos el mismo cielo, tachonado de los mismos astros; aspiramos el mismo ambiente impregnado de los mismos olores; recorremos las mismas calles, alumbradas por los mismos mecheros de gas; penetramos en los mismos cafés, invadidos por las mismas gentes. . . . Vivimos condenados a girar perpetuamente, en el mismo círculo, sin poder escaparnos de él. Así la vida nos parece abominable, y brota incesantemente de nuestros labios impíos la súplica diabólica de Raudelaire:

O Satan! aie pitié de ma longue misère" (II, 27).

[All the nights in Havana are alike. We always see the same sky, spattered with the same stars; we breathe in the same atmosphere, impregnated by the same smells; we walk the same streets, illuminated by the same gas lights; we enter the same cafés, invaded by the same people. . . . We live to gyrate perpetually, in the same circle, without being able to escape from it. Thus, life appears abominable to us, and from our impious lips incessantly comes Baudelaire's diabolical supplication:

> Oh, Satan, have pity on my long misery!]

19. George Ross Ridge, *The Hero in French Decadent Literature* (Athens: Univ. of Georgia Press, 1961), p. viii.

20. Bernstein, p. 120.

21. Albert L. Guerard. *Art for Art's Sake* (New York: Schocken, 1936), p. 292.

22. Ibid., p. 337.

23. Rafael Ferreres, *Los límites del modernismo* (Madrid: Editorial Torres, 1964), p. 68.

24. Erich Auerbach, "The Aesthetic Dignity of the *Fleurs du mal,*" in *Baudelaire: A Collection of Critical Essays,* ed. Henri Peyre (Englewood Cliffs, N.J.: Prentice-Hall, 1962), p. 168.

25. Cf. Duplessis (see n. 4, above), p. 255.

26. Joris-Karl Huysmans, *Against Nature,* trans. Robert Baldick (Suffolk: The Chaucer Press, 1976), p. 211.

Priscilla Pearsall (essay date 1980)

SOURCE: Pearsall, Priscilla. "Julián del Casal's Portraits of Women." In *The Analysis of Literary Texts: Current Trends in Methodology,* edited by Randolph D. Pope, pp. 78-88. Ypsilanti, Mich.: Bilingual Press/ Editorial Bilingüe, 1980.

[*In the following essay, Pearsall analyses Casal's representations of women in his prose and poetry, remarking that his powerful images of women represented one of the major culminations of his poetic vision.*]

Julián del Casal's portraits of women in prose and poetry were central to the development of his aesthetic world. There is a need to examine the way in which Casal's deeply ambiguous and fragmented attitude toward women evolved through his poetry and how it continued to develop in his prose.[1] It was in large part through the portraits of women that Casal developed the powerful, independent imagery that represents one of the culminations of his poetic vision.

Casal portrayed creative women like the French actress Jeanne Samary, the Cuban novelist Aurelia Castillo de González, and the young Cuban painter Juana Borrero. Cultivated intellectual women living in Havana interested him, women who seem the heiresses of the eigh-

teenth century and who were a catalyst for others' creativity. Casal drew from a variety of subjects outside middle-class life, including, often, the courtesan and the prostitute. From the beginning we find a tendency to see the female as an aesthetic object rather than in terms of a more direct experience of her. It was easier for him to relate to a portrait—whether it was created through oils, photography, poetry, or prose—than to a *mujer de carne y hueso.*

The works to be examined in this paper are from 1890-91, the period in which Casal was publishing the poems of *Nieve,* his second book of poetry. These were years in which the aesthetic and confessional strands of Casal's poetry were developing rapidly; he wrote about portraiture at this time. One of the most revealing statements appeared in an article published March 3, 1890, in which he explains that the portrait exists not only at an aesthetic level, but on a psychological plane as well:

> Para hacer un buen retrato el artista digno de este nombre debe reproducir, no sólo la figura que tiene ante los ojos, sino el espíritu que la anima . . . Hay que mirar el modelo, decía el gran David y leer en él.[2]

Casal initially sought in his ethereal, idealized image of the woman the child's highly fantasized vision of the mother. Casal's own mother died when he was four years old, and this trauma left him obsessed with an unrealistic idea of her. In **"A mi madre"** in *Nieve* he writes that her image rises from the depths of his remote past;[3] he tended to project this vision on the women he portrayed. Accordingly, like much of his art world, Casal's *retratos de mujeres* must be understood in terms of the creation and destruction of illusion. They belong to a group of poems and articles in which Casal deals with the theme of the impossibility of love. In the early poem **"La urna"** he had written about his loss of enchantment with women. In *Nieve* the process is complete; in **"A la castidad"** Casal states flatly, "Yo no amo la mujer . . ." (*Poesías,* 120), for he feels that she is incapable of enduring love. Yet Casal sought in poem after poem to recapture the illusory vision of the woman that belonged to a lost infantile dream.

The ambiguity of the portraits is paralleled by a simultaneous loss of artistic idealism. In one of his earliest poems, **"El poeta y la sirena,"** published when he was seventeen, Casal had assigned a transcendent role to the poet; he represented "la luz de la verdad," as his voice resounded in eternity (*Poesías,* 205). By the time Casal wrote *Rimas,* his artistic aspirations had run aground within the mist of his own mind:

> Como encalla entre rocas un navío
> que se lanza del oro a la conquista,
> así ha encallado el Ideal de artista
> entre las nieblas del cerebro mío . . .

> (*Poesías,* 188).

The portraits of women reflect the gradual disintegration of Casal's artistic and affective idealism, his increasing inability to believe that either love or art has any meaning. They are characterized, moreover, by his attempt to recreate, through aesthetic vision, the fantasies about both women and art which in truth he knew were lost forever.

We see how strong the element of illusion is in an early poem, **"Ante el retrato de Juana Samary,"**[4] published October 18, 1890. The poem represents the contemplation of a painting of Jeanne Samary,[5] the celebrated actress of the Comédie Française. Robert Jay Glickman, in his article "Letters to Gustave Moreau," has studied the way in which Casal's love was most intense when it was directed to someone far away.[6] In an article on Samary, published October 18, 1890, Casal discussed the way in which illusive, inaccessible women like the Samary of the painting stimulated his fantasies and were more desirable than any *amada existente* could ever be:

> Todo hombre, por muy poco desarrollada que tenga la facultad de soñar, tiene sus amadas ideales, por las que suspira, en horas de abatimiento, con todo su corazón. Esas mujeres, ya estén en el mundo, ya reposen en brazos de la muerte, llegan a adquirir mayor importancia que las amadas existentes, porque nunca se han conocido y la fantasía se complace en revistirlas de atributos inmortales.[7]

Casal writes that among the women he has loved without ever meeting, Jeanne Samary "figura en primera línea" (*Prosas, III,* 13). This is evident in the line with which he begins the poem, "Nunca te conocí, mas yo te he amado . . ." (*Poesías,* 127). Casal wrote the poem in front of the painting after receiving news of her death; the element of death and the remoteness of the woman link her with Casal's infantile image of the mother. Casal idealizes the painting calling it an "imagen ideal" (*Poesías,* 127), and he emphasizes Samary's ethereal, transcendent role when he calls her flight in death "el raudo vuelo hacia el bello país desconocido" (*Poesías,* 127). In addition, he underlines the dreamlike quality of the entire collection, of which this is the first poem, by entitling it **"La gruta del ensueño."** The desire to assign a transcendent role to woman in his art, yet its impossibility, was a conflict Casal never resolved. In his last poem, **"Cuerpo y alma,"** published posthumously, Casal still desires this vision of woman, as he captures it for the last time in Poe's incorporeal heroines who inhabit the golden mists of dream and show the way to the elusive "palacio de la Dicha."[8]

Casal emphasizes first the surface happiness and beauty of the portrait, and then the contradictory emotional reality which it hides. Underneath the image he senses the woman's sadness and terror of death. Casal's poem is revealing not for what we learn about the French actress, but because of what it reveals about both Casal's aesthetic world and his psychology. The Poet can identify with his subject; he writes, "en ti hallaba un alma hermana, / alegre en lo exterior y dentro triste" (*Poesías,* 127). The tension between the apparent gaiety and the interior sadness are characteristic of Casal's whole art world in *Nieve* at that time, for there is a constant contradiction between the beauty and luxuriance of his aestheticism and the developing melancholy of his confessional poetry.

Ultimately the vision of the woman is so ephemeral that it hardly exists; the poetry is shifted into an affective plane as he muses

> si tú nunca sabrás que yo te he amado
> tal vez yo ignore siempre quién me ama
>
> (*Poesías,* 128).

At the end of the poem Casal destroys the image he has created; the compelling reality is the poet's underlying sense of the inevitable failure of love.

In another poem from *Nieve,* **"Blanco y negro,"**[9] published November 1, 1890, two weeks after "Ante el retrato de Juana Samary," the attempt to seek a vision of transcendence through plasticity is more evident than in the previous poem. In **"Blanco y negro"** the woman is approached as a source of sculptural values through which the illusion of the infinite can be created. Ethereal images are heaped one upon the other; they emerge from the depths of the poet's unconscious into his awareness, associated through a stream of consciousness:

> Sonrisas de las vírgenes difuntas
> en ataúd de blanco terciopelo
> recamado de oro; manos juntas
> que os eleváis hacia el azul del cielo
> como lirios de carne; tocas blancas
> de pálidas novicias absorbidas
> por ensueños celestiales . . .
>
> (*Poesías,* 129).

The female images of **"Blanco y negro"** are surrounded by an ambience created through a series of related images which are ethereal and at the same time extremely sensuous. Some of them evoke delicate tactile qualities: ". . . los finos celajes errabundos / por las ondas de éter . . ." (*Poesías,* 129). There are joyous auditory values: ". . . francas / risas de niños rubios . . ." (*Poesías,* 129); and, especially, shimmering visual qualities: "tornasoles / que ostentan en sus alas las palomas / al volar hacia el Sol . . ." (*Poesías,* 129). This world of sensation heaped upon sensation is the means of seeking a metaphysical realm.[10] Casal beseeches the profusion of imagery, which spirals upward with accelerating speed, to carry him to transcendent heights; he writes mysteriously that that which he has loved will probably be in this infinite region.

In the second part of the poem there is another series of three-dimensional values, each more violently destructive than the other. They represent an opposing downward spiral; the images here, too, are female

> hidra de Lerna armada de cabezas . . .
> . . . hachas
> que segasteis los cuellos sonrosados
> de las princesas inocentes . . .

> > (*Poesías,* 130).

The plasticity of the second part exists in a world as filled with sensation as that of the previous one. Now there are violently wracking impressions, including visual, ". . . relámpago del cielo / que amenazas la vida del proscrito / en medio de la mar . . ." (*Poesías,* 130); tactile, ". . . rachas / de vientos tempestuosos . . ." (*Poesías,* 130); and entirely interiorized emotion, ". . . pesadillas / que pobláis el espíritu de espanto . . ." (*Poesías,* 130). The downward spiral, just as the ascending thrust, carries the poet to a nihilistic region where he searches for an elusive *lo que yo he amado.*

The world of sensation of the first part of the poem is destroyed by the second; it bore the seeds of its own destruction, for Casal's world of female imagery is as filled with the pathologically destructive as it is with the sublimely ethereal. They both lead only to "el seno de la nada."[11] As the illusion created through female imagery collapses, its extreme luxuriance contrasts with the nihilism which underlies it, for it represents a vain attempt to pursue something elusive, beyond, which even Casal does not understand, cannot define. The underlying preoccupation of the poem, just as in **"Ante el retrato de Juana Samary,"** is the frustration of love, here of love lost and not clearly remembered. As in the earlier poem, an artistic realm that had been created as a means of seeking transcendence is in the end the way to a vision of nihilism and pathology.

There are other female images in *Nieve* in which we see the same combination of ethereal and destructive values that we find in **"Ante el retrato de Juana Samary"** and **"Blanco y negro."** One of them is the portrait of Casal's muse whom he describes in the poem **"La reina de la sombra,"**[12] published May 10, 1891. He portrays her as an incorporeal being existing in a voluptuously supernal ambiance:

> Tras el velo de gasa azulada
> en que un astro de plata se abre
> y con fúlgidos rayos alumbra
> el camino del triste viandante,
> en su hamaca de nubes se mece
> una diosa de formas fugaces
> que dirige a la tierra sombría
> su mirada de brillos astrales

> > (*Poesías,* 138).

Yet she also has a bizarre aspect; Casal shows in her *retrato* the juxtaposition of the sublime and the pathological so characteristic of his art[13]

> Ora muestra su rostro de virgen
> o su torso de extraña becante . . .

> > (*Poesías,* 140).

She is above all the muse of his confessional poetry:

> Esa diosa es mi musa adorada,
> la que inspira mis cantos fugaces,
> donde sangran mis viejas heridas
> y sollozan mis nuevos pesares

> > (*Poesías,* 140).

It is this pathological element—not the ethereal—that Casal will increasingly emphasize in the portraits of women.

The failure to sustain the illusion of the ethereal qualities associated with woman takes its final toll in the poem **"Kakemono,"**[14] published March 22, 1891, three weeks before **"La reina de la sombra."** The poem can be related to the earlier **"Ante el retrato de Juana Samary,"** for Casal also wrote **"Kakemono"** before a portrait of a woman. In this poem, however, the poet reproduces the Oscar Held photograph of María Cay so that the poem, instead of being the contemplation of a painting, represents the transposition of a photograph into poetry. María, the sister of a friend of Casal, had dressed for the photographer in the Japanese costume she had worn to a masked ball given a short time earlier.[15]

The title **"Kakemono"** means Japanese hanging scroll, and the poem is in fact envisioned as an Oriental screen. Casal uses the same technique of heaping imagery upon imagery that we saw in **"Blanco y negro."** We are drawn into his art world; sensation is heaped upon sensation in the creation of an extraordinarily sensually-charged poetic vision. The auditory, the olfactory, the visual, and the tactile all come into play as we become lost in Casal's artifice. Esperanza Figueroa Amaral has studied the way in which art form is piled upon art form as was never done in Europe.[16] The poem's rhythm, too, is typical of Casal. He breaks his hendecasyllables irregularly; this contributes auditorially to a sense of incantation to dazzle us further with his aestheticism. Yet the portrait is haunting for its absence of human emotion. Casal is interested in its artistic properties only; the woman he portrays interests him little as a person. In fact, her identity is changed as she is transformed into a Japanese woman.

In the poem we see the collapse of Casal's attempt to create illusion through the sensuous portrait of a woman; the ethereal, idealized vision glimpsed in **"Ante**

el retrato de Juana Samary" is no longer accessible to Casal. The portrait is paradoxical because, although it is made as light and diaphanous as an Oriental screen by such technical elements as the use of light and the airy landscape images on the gown, it becomes entrapped in its own delirium of aestheticism. Its extreme sensuousness leads nowhere beyond itself.

In recreating the portrait of María as she looked on the night of the masked ball, Casal attempts to evoke, in an almost Proustian sense, the youthful illusions which he had felt then. Yet he reveals that his experience has been the opposite; although he can recreate the image of María, he is incapable of recapturing the memories and emotions of that night. The woman's image remains at the end of the poem as a hollow shell, weighed down by its own dazzling artistry, and stripped of the emotions of joy which originally gave it meaning. The theme of the poem becomes the failure of all illusion because plasticity has become incapable of reaching beyond itself to glimpse a metaphysical realm, and joyous, youthful illusion is revealed to be as evanescent as aesthetic vision. The emptiness of the image is all that remains; it evokes the artist's *glacial tristeza,* the feeling of interior coldness which was to become a hallmark of Casal's poetry.

The vision of the woman as image or aesthetic object and a sense of the failure of illusion pervade Casal's prose articles on women. On June 3, 1890, he published two portraits which are important to the development of the imagery of his later poetry. In one of these, entitled **"La derrochadora,"**[17] Casal portrays a Parisian *demi-mondaine,* a high-class prostitute; the figure of the courtesan was one that intrigued Casal, and he wrote numerous articles about her. She became for him a symbol of his aesthetic world, for her artificial beauty and elegance were as transitory yet compelling as those of his own artistic vision.

In this article we find that with the failure to create transcendent illusion through his aesthetic world, Casal's portraiture of women has lost its ethereally diaphanous quality. Now it is becoming increasingly hard and jewel-like. The *demi-mondaine* lives surrounded by objects; she reminds one of Manet's *Olympia* as we see her at her morning ritual of bathing and being perfumed by her maid among glitteringly polished mirrors, jewels, and jasper. Their hard surfaces are accentuated by the contrast with the soft texture of the courtesan's robe and skin. The maid transforms her into an aesthetic object and a sex object. In this world of *cosas,* in which she is herself another one, the woman spends her days buying art objects

> . . . en cada tienda, halla algo nuevo que comprar. Ya es un brazalete de oro, cuajado de pedrería digno de una Leonor de Este; ya un abanico ínfimo, con paisaje

grotesco, todo hecho con tintas de relumbrón; ya una estatua de mármol, obra maestra de un artista desconocido, pero que firmaría un Falgiere; ya un cromo americano . . .

(*Prosas,* I, 238).

The aestheticism, in spite of its hard, object quality, is now very evanescent; her search for these art objects is frenzied and compulsive. What she buys one day is discarded almost immediately to make room for the next day's purchases—as the prostitute herself is interchangeable with many others who are objects bought and used for a short time.[18]

The one emotional quality which Casal emphasizes in this woman is her lack of attachment to any other person; the *demi-mondaine* by definition has an ambivalent relationship to the bourgeois society which exploits her and off which she lives. The prose portrait is related to the *retratos* in poetry in their conflictual attitude toward love. Here the woman's attitude is entirely cynical; Casal writes that when anyone mentions love to her, her response is an ironic, "¡Desdichados! ¿Todavía créeis en eso?" (*Prosas,* I, 238).

Ultimately the portrait reveals much about Casal's aesthetic world for he was becoming as detached from reality as the woman he portrays.[19] He would write two years later in the *busto* of the young Cuban artist Juana Borrero that artists construct in their fantasy an ideal quarantine where they live "con sus ensueños."[20] Casal's portraits of women seem increasingly to belong to this family of imaginary beings created within his own fantasy.

As Casal felt that aesthetic illusion and reality were slipping from his grasp, he attempted to concretize that illusion—and eventually all experience—in compensation for its extreme tenuousness. In *Nieve* his art became one where, at times, everything was seen in sculptural terms. Although the concrete, dazzling aestheticism of the portraits of women becomes increasingly frenetic, its coldness only reflects the underlying emotional sterility of the writer who created it.[21] Three days after he published this portrait of the French courtesan, Casal would write in a review of Aurelia Castillo de González's *Pompeya* that modern art is essentially the expression of ennui and pathology: "el malestar permanente, el escepticismo profundo, la amargura intensa, las aspiraciones indefinidas y el pesimismo sombrío . . ."[22] There is no better metaphor for Casal's own *glacial tristeza,* his sadness expressed in icily sculptural form, than the Parisian *demi-mondaine* as she is seen dwelling in a nightmare vision of life experienced entirely in terms of objects by a psyche devoid of emotion.

The vision of pathology with which Casal's portraits of women are so closely associated is given deeper expression in another prose portrait, **"Croquis fe-**

menino,"[23] published the same day as **"La derro-chadora."** The woman of this sketch, like the prostitute, remains unnamed, but she represents another type of woman Casal admired. She is one of the wealthy, cultivated Cuban women who lived apart from the *haute-bourgeoisie* of Havana, and whose houses were meeting places for writers and artists. Like the French courtesan, she lives in an environment dominated by objects. Casal gives an exhaustive inventory of her salón:

> Espejos venecianos, con marcos de bronce, ornados con ligeros amorcillos; pieles de tigres arrojados al pie de olorosos divanes; tibores japoneses, guarnecidos de dragones y quimeras; mesas de laca incrustadas de nácar, cubiertas de un pueblo de estatuitas; óleos admirables, firmados por reputados pintores, todo se encuentra en aquel salón . . .

> *(Prosas,* II, 141).

Just one month earlier, on April 26, 1890, Casal had written an article **"Verdad y poesía"**[24] rejecting Zola. Yet in these sketches Casal evidences a Zola-like preoccupation with exterior reality.

It is not, however, only exterior reality that is seen in terms of plasticity in this article; the objects which fill the world of the prose portraits are becoming interiorized. When Casal expresses the woman's psychology, he turns to the plastic qualities of the fairy tale to create an interior vision. He writes that this nameless woman is one of the people of his time who

> . . . viven siempre inclinados sobre sí mismos, mirándose por dentro, como si llevaran allí, a semejanza de la heroína de los cuentos de hadas, una gruta formada de piedras preciosas, donde ven una ninfa encantadora que se adormece entre los cantos de pájaros maravillosos y los aromas de flores desconocidas

> *(Prosas,* II, 140).

We see that even the woman's introversion is expressed in terms of glittering, gem-like preciosity, for the grotto, where she dwells within this fantastically sculptured psychological world, is formed of jewels.

Casal emphasizes that she, like the prostitute of **"La derrochadora,"** is detached from reality and incapable of feeling emotion for the people around her. Her writes ironically that she is so pathologically linked with the objects in her environment that she has fallen in love with one of them, a portrait of Murat which hangs in a corner of her living room:

> En uno de los ángulos de su salón, hay un cuadro al óleo, puesto sobre un caballete de madera negra incrustada de bronce, que representa a Murat, con su traje de seda color de rosa, guarnecido de encajes; con su casco de terciopelo negro, coronado de plumas blancas; y con su espada brillante, de puño de oro, esmaltado de pedrerías, suspendida en el aire, en actitud de marchar al frente de invisibles granaderos

> *(Prosas,* II, 141).

The art object is now so interiorized that it is becoming the imagery of the woman's mind. She fills the void of her soul with three-dimensional values in an attempt to give form to the nihilism within. Casal writes that as she drives through the streets of Havana she resembles a legendary queen in exile, trying to forget her lost kingdom,

> . . . una Semíramis moderna derribada de su trono . . . que ha venido a olvidar entre los esplendores naturales del nuevo mundo, la imagen torturadora de su Asiria perdida

> *(Prosas,* II, 140).

The woman is herself an image tormented by an image in this *Through-the-Looking-Glass* delirium of highly fantasized plasticity.

In this *croquis femenino* the future development of Casal's aesthetic vision can be perceived, for Casal was becoming as haunted by imagery as the woman he portrays. At the end of another prose portrait written two and one-half years later, Casal would confess that the image of the person depicted has become an obsession that tortured him, and that its expression was a pathological necessity:

> . . . su imagen me obsede de tal manera que, cansado de tenerla conmigo, ya en mis días risueños, ya en mis noches de insomnio, yo he decidido arrojarla hoy de mi cerebro al papel, del mismo modo que un árbol arroja, en vigoroso estremecimiento, sobre el polvo del camino, al pájaro errante que, posado en su copa, entona allí una canción vaga, extraña, dolorosa y cruel.[25]

Casal's attitude toward the image is as ambiguous as his view of other aspects of his art world. The poet's desire to free himself of the pain and cruelty with which it haunts him constitutes in part a rejection of the image; yet it is something he sought incessantly.

As the plasticity of his artistic vision evolved, Casal became less and less dependent upon pictorial devices like portraiture and landscape for its development. At the same time that he was writing about his portraiture in the passage quoted above, Casal was publishing the poem **"Dolorosa,"**[26] in which we see the emergence of the powerful, independent image of the dagger. It emerges from the depths of the poet's psyche and evokes the conflict between the forces of life and death within. In **"Dolorosa"** the imagery, which evokes sexual mystery and violence, exists in a much more abstract, psychological world than that of the portraits. The *retratos de mujeres,* however, had already begun to evoke the artist's inner conflicts—his anguished attitude toward love, and the meaning of aestheticism—for Casal in the early portraits, especially, seems undecided about whether his artistic world is the means of searching for transcendence or a route to a vision of pathology. It is only in the later portraits that it becomes understood as the means to a vision of nihilism and pathology.

Three months after he published **"La derrochadora"** and **"Croquis femenino,"** Casal published, on September 3, 1890, an article in which he dealt with the problem which was central to Baudelaire's essays on the Salon of 1859, that of the distinction between historical and photographic reality and the deeper interior reality of the novel.[27] Baudelaire had dealt with the question of reality specifically in relation to the portrait; he had said that portraiture meant capturing the drama of a life.[28] When we study the images of women created at the time Casal wrote on Baudelaire's theories and made his own earlier statements concerning portraiture, we see that the *retratos de mujeres* evoke not so much the lives of the women he portrays, as they reveal the unfolding drama of Casal's own aesthetic and emotional development. They are central to his poetic world, beginning with a gradual sense of the failure of aesthetic and psychological illusion, through the increasing plasticizing of experience, to the eventual interiorization of the art object until it becomes the imagery of a landscape of the mind. Casal's portraits of women necessarily fail as portraits for they are essentially narcissistic—highly polished mirrors of the evolution of an art world. Although their subject is other human beings, they remain as Casal's statement of the impossibility of communication and love. In their final pathological vision of hard, cold aestheticism in an emotional void, they evoke above all Casal's own *glacial tristeza,* the coldness at the center of the artist's soul.

Notes

1. There have been several studies dealing with Casal's attitude toward women. Carmen Poncet sees Casal's dualistic vision of women as one more aspect of polarity in a work where everything tends to be seen in dualistic terms, the fragmented vision of an author hopelessly divided against himself. See Carmen Poncet, "Dualidad de Casal," *Revista Bimestre Cubana,* 53 (1944), 193-212. In the same year Gustavo Duplessis studied the ambiguity of Casal's attitude toward women. Gustavo Duplessis, "Julián del Casal," *Revista Bimestre Cubana,* 54 (1944), 31-75, 140-70, 243-86. Monner Sans discusses the mystery that surrounds Casal's relationships with women both in his life and in his art. José María Monner Sans, *Julián del Casal y el modernismo hispanoamericano* (México: Colegio de México, 1952). More recently Robert Jay Glickman has noted Casal's compulsive need to give and receive affection, yet his inability to establish relationships with women. Robert Jay Glickman, "Letters to Gustave Moreau," *Revista Hispánica Moderna,* 37 (1972-73), 101-35. Carlos Blanco Aguinaga has studied Casal's poem "Neurosis" in which the woman is one more meaningless object in a decadent turn-of-the-century society. Carlos Blanco Aguinaga, "Crítica marxista y poesía: Lectura de

un poema de Julián del Casal," in *Analysis of Hispanic Texts: Current Trends in Methodology,* ed. Mary Ann Beck and others (New York: Bilingual Press, 1976), pp. 191-205.

2. Julián del Casal, "Armando Menocal: Nuevos retratos," in *Prosas* (La Habana: Consejo Nacional de Cultura, 1963), II, 63. Further notes in the text of this paper refer to Casal, *Prosas* (La Habana: Consejo Nacional de Cultura, 1963-64), I, II, III and Casal, *Poesías* (La Habana: Consejo Nacional de Cultura, 1963). All dates of publication for Casal's poetry and prose are from Esperanza Figueroa Amaral's chronological bibliography. Esperanza Figueroa Amaral, "Bibliografía cronológica de la obra de Julián del Casal," *Revista Iberoamericana,* 35 (1969), 385-99.

3. Casal, *Poesías,* p. 117.

4. Casal, "Ante el retrato de Juana Samary," in *Poesías,* p. 127.

5. The portrait which is the subject of Casal's poem is generally identified as the Renoir painting of the actress. In the "Crónica semanal" published the day after the poem, however, Casal himself identifies the artist as the French portrait painter Jacques-Fernand Humbert. See Casal, "Crónica semanal," in *Prosas,* III, 13.

6. Glickman, p. 106.

7. Casal, "Crónica semanal," in *Prosas,* III, 12.

8. Casal, "Cuerpo y alma," *Poesías,* p. 196. In "Cuerpo y alma," Casal's fragmented vision of women is especially apparent. Although he exalts Poe's incorporeal women and relates them to what he perceives to be the spiritual side of his nature, he equates the physical aspect of his being with frenetic, emotionless sex with a prostitute.

9. Casal, *Poesías,* p. 129.

10. The previous spring, Casal had translated an excerpt from Maupassant's *La Vie errante* which deals with one of the ideas most central to nineteenth-century thought, that the senses are the means to transcending the limits of the material. See "Casal's Translations of Baudelaire and Maupassant: The Failure of Transcendent Vision," in *Essays in Honor of Jorge Guillén on the Occasion of his Eighty-Fifth Year* (Cambridge, Mass.: Abedul Press, 1977), pp. 64-73.

11. Casal had written only slightly more than one month earlier, on September 27, 1890, in his portrait of the Cuban poet José Fornaris, that the modern poet is a nihilist like Leconte de Lisle or Leopardi who want only to "disolverse en el seno de la nada." Casal, "José Fornaris," in *Prosas,* I, 278.

12. Casal, "La reina de la sombra," *Poesías,* p. 138.

13. In the same year, on December 30, 1891, Casal would publish his poem "Sueño de gloria: Apotesois de Gustavo Moreau" (*Poesías,* 104); there a woman, Helen of Troy, symbolizes the decadent beauty Casal sought through his art. The image of Helen fuses the ethereal and the pathological, values which were becoming central to Casal's aesthetic. Casal admired Gustave Moreau's paintings of Helen and Salomé and transposed both of them into the poetry of "Mi museo ideal," of which "Sueño de gloria" is the final poem. Moreau and Huysmans, both of whom had a decisive influence upon the poetry of "Mi museo ideal," combined aesthetic and pathological elements in their portraits of women. See Mario Praz, *The Romantic Agony,* trans. Angus Davidson, 2nd ed (1933; rpt London: Oxford University Press, 1970); Frank Kermode, *Romantic Image* (New York: Macmillan, 1957), p. 70; and Lee Fontanella, "Parnassian Precept and a New Way of Seeing Casal's *Museo ideal,*" *Comparative Literature Studies,* 7 (1970), 466.

14. Casal, "Kakemono," *Poesías,* p. 132.

15. Casal had discussed the Oscar Held photograph of María in "Album de la ciudad: Retratos femeninos" (*Prosas,* II, 95), published April 1, 1890, one year before "Kakemono" appeared. María Cay is the "cubana japonesa" of Darío's poetry. See Esperanza Figueroa Amaral, "El cisne modernista," in *Estudios críticos sobre el modernismo,* ed. Homero Castillo (Madrid: Editorial Gredos, 1968), p. 313. María Cay's family had lived in the Orient because her father had been the Cuban consul in Japan.

16. Figueroa, "El cisne modernista," p. 313.

17. Casal, "Croquis femenino: Derrochadora," in *Prosas,* II, 147.

18. In this productive period during the final three years of his life, Casal would turn increasingly to Huysmans in the development of his aesthetic. In an article he wrote in 1892, Casal discussed the manner in which, for Huysmans, art was an unending search for sensuous stimulation; this sense of the artistic is apparent in these two prose portraits of women. See Casal, "Jorís Karl Huysmans," *Prosas,* I, 173.

19. In the following year, on March 19, 1891, Casal wrote a letter to his friend Esteban Borrero Echeverría that he believed that the ideal life for him was now to live alone, in obscurity, "solo, arrinconado e invisible a todos, exceptos para usted y dos o tres personas." Casal, "Cartas a Esteban Borrero Echeverría," in *Prosas,* III, 85. Frank Ker-

mode sees the isolation of the artist as essential to the pursuit of imagery. See Kermode, *Romantic Image,* p. 2.

20. Casal, "Juan Borrero," in *Prosas,* I, 267.

21. In an article of art criticism published July 11, 1890, one month after this portrait appeared, Casal wrote that in the final period of an artist's development his work reflects the coldness of his soul. Casal, "Academia de Pintura: Dos cuadros," in *Prosas,* II, 177,

22. Casal, "Libros nuevos: I *Pompeya* por Aurelia Castillo de Gonzáles," ibid., p. 145.

23. Casal, "Croquis femenino," ibid., p. 140.

24. Casal, "Verdad y poesía," ibid., p. 115.

25. Casal, "El hombre de las muletas de níquel," in *Prosas,* I, 233.

26. Casal, "Dolorosa," *Poesías,* p. 178.

27. Casal, "En el cafetal," in *Prosas,* I, 222.

28. Charles Baudelaire, "Le Portrait," in *Salon de 1859,* in *Oeuvres complètes,* ed. Y.-G Le Dantec (Paris: Editions Gallimard, 1961), p. 1072. Casal's portraits of men are more perceptively written in that they capture the conflicts central to the lives of their subjects—as his portraits of women never do.

Priscilla Pearsall (essay date 1984)

SOURCE: Pearsall, Priscilla. "Julián Del Casal: Modernity and the Art of the Urban Interior." In *An Art Alienated from Itself: Studies in Spanish American Modernism,* pp. 11-39. University, Miss.: Romance Monographs, Inc., 1984.

[*In the following essay, Pearsall explains Casal's concept of modernity, tracing the influence of other poets, such as Baudelaire, on his work.*]

Of all of the Modernist writers, none was more concerned with the problem of literary modernity than Julián del Casal. He wrote one of Modernism's most thoughtful definitions of modern art when he examined, in his review of Aurelia Castillo de González's long poem *Pompeya,* the European authors of his time whom he admired, and defined them as modern because

> en sus obras se reflejan, como en bruñido espejo, el malestar permanente, el escepticismo profundo, la amargura intensa, las aspiraciones indefinidas y el pesimismo sombrío, frutos amargos y ponzoñosos extraídos del fondo de sus almas, a fuerza de sufrimientos, de estudio, de análisis y de investigaciones que envenenan

la atmósfera y les inoculan el asco de la vida, haciendo volver el pensamiento a esos seres morfinizados de ideal hacia los espacios siderales del ensueño o hacia los campos remotos de las edades grandiosas, lejanas y desaparecidas.[1]

These poets, among whom he includes Baudelaire, Théophile Gautier, and Verlaine, are modern because their works reflect interior psychological values—a *fin de siglo* sensibility which in turn causes them to seek evasion through time and space. Casal, in his emphasis upon the centrality of *hastío* to contemporary literature, accepts Théophile Gautier's affirmation that the decadent spirit represents the essence of modernity because it reflects the crisis of contemporary culture.[2] In his review article, furthermore, Casal specifically mentions the French author's famous essay on decadence, i.e., Gautier's introduction to *Les Fleurs du mal*,[3] when Casal writes of the Italian poet Stecchetti: "Olindo Guerrini, conocido por el pseudónimo de Lorenzo Stécchetti [*sic*], . . . siguiendo el consejo de Gauthier [*sic*] para ser original en este tiempo, sólo escucha las confidencias de la neurosis, las revelaciones de la pasión apagada que se deprava y las alucinaciones extrañas de las ideas fijas que arrastran a la locura."[4]

It is quite possible that Casal also based his concept of modernity upon Baudelaire's discussions of modern art in the essays on the Salon of 1846, for Baudelaire served as a model of the modern for Casal as well as for Gautier. In an article published in *El País* in October, 1890, four and one-half months after the publication of his review of *Pompeya,* Casal specifically linked modernity as a reflection of the affective with Baudelaire when he identified Baudelaire and Mallarmé as "los poetas contemporáneos que reflejan en sus composiciones los matices más imperceptibles del alma moderna" (*Prosas,* III, 17). There are numerous similarities between Casal's Castillo de González review and Baudelaire's essays on the Salon of 1846. Casal and Baudelaire both link modernity with classical antiquity, and they compare the modern and classical conceptions of certain themes.[5] Especially striking are the two poet's discussions of others' misunderstanding of modernity as the "official" *topoi* of contemporary society, for in "De l'Héroïsme de la vie moderne," his concluding essay on the Salon of 1846, Baudelaire had written, "la plupart des artistes qui ont abordé les sujets modernes se sont contentés des sujets publics et oficiels, de nos victoires et de notre héroïsme politique . . . Cependant il y a des sujets privés qui sont bien autrement héroïques."[6] Casal's opening to his review of Castillo de González's *Pompeya* parallels the passage from "De l'Héroïsme de la vie moderne," for he writes that many people believe that the poet should treat only the large, historical topics of his time: "las luchas, las glorias, y los ideales de su tiempo" (*Prosas,* II, 143). He attacks Núñez de Arce for having given wide circu-

lation to this attitude.[7] Casal, like Baudelaire, believed that this concept of poetry revealed a lack of comprehension that the greatness of modern art lies not in its treatment of exterior, public themes, but in its reflection of the artist's psychology.

In "Qu'est-ce que le Romantisme?" from the *Salon de 1846,* Baudelaire defined modern art as a *manière de sentir,* derived from Romanticism's interiorization; his definition also included Romanticism's search for transcendence:

> Le romantisme n'est précisément ni dans le choix des sujets ni dans la vérité exacte, mais dans la manière de sentir.
>
> Ils l'ont cherché en dehors, et c'est en dedans qu'il était seulement possible de le trouver.
>
> Pour moi, le romantisme est l'expression la plus récente, la plus actuelle du beau.
>
> . . . . .
>
> Qui dit romantisme dit art moderne,—c'est-à-dire intimité, spiritualité, couleur, aspiration vers l'infini, exprimées par tout les moyens que contiennent les arts.[8]

Baudelaire's esthetic of modernity is profoundly ambivalent, for there is a deep, unresolved conflict in defining the modern as on the one hand interiorization (a *manière de sentir*) and, on the other, search for transcendence *(aspiration vers l'infini).* There is also a serious ambivalence in equating modern art, with its emphasis upon immediacy of feeling *(l'expression la plus récente, la plus actuelle du beau),* with Romanticism, a temporal concept rooted in the past.[9]

The strength of Casal's definition of modernity, which from all indications he based on Baudelaire's concept, and Gautier's study of Baudelaire, lies in the Cuban's overcoming the ambivalence present in Baudelaire. By emphasizing the emotional and cultural crises essential to modern art, Casal shatters the Romantic myth of temporal and spatial transcendence through art by placing it upon a purely psychological basis ("haciendo volver el pensamiento a esos seres morfinizados de ideal hacia los espacios siderales del ensueño o hacia los campos remotos de las edades grandiosas, lejanas y desaparecidas") (*Prosas,* II, 145); i.e., by considering it to be a fiction of the mind.

In Casal's writings, everything would be consumed by the interiorizing, narcissistic aim of his art, by his obsession with making poetry into a mirror of the self. Nowhere is this phenomenon more evident than in his transformation of the art objects of the urban interior into metaphors which reveal interior emotional states. In his definition, modern art exists on two levels: first, on an esthetic plane, as a *bruñido espejo*; and then at a psychological level, as a reflection of a modern *manière de sentir.* In order to create his glittering esthetic mirror,

Casal used the turn-of-the century urban interior filled with art objects. An article, **"Album de la ciudad. El Fénix,"** written for the March 13, 1890, issue of *La Discusión,* described one of the elegant stores of Havana, which sold art objects and jewels destined to fill the homes of the city:

> Hay tibores japoneses, alrededor de los cuales vuelan monstruos, pájaros y flores; lámparas de metal, con su pantalla de seda, guarnecida de encajes; relojes de mesa, encerrados en urnas de cristal; vasos de Sèvres, de distintos tamaños; búcaros de barro húngaro y barro italiano, traídos de la exposición de París. También se encuentran, tanto en las vidrieras como en el interior, abanicos de carey, con países de plumas; álbumes elegantes, con broches caprichosos; figuras en relieve, encuadradas en marcos elegantes; devocionarios de marfil, esmaltados de cifras de metal; rosarios de nácar, engarzados en oro; y un número infinito de *bibelots,* minúsculos fragmentos de obras de arte que, como observa Bourget,[10] han transformado la decoración de todos los interiores y les han dado una fisonomía arcaica tan continuamente curiosa y tan dócilmente sometida que nuestro siglo, a fuerza de recopilar y comprobar todos los estilos, se ha olvidado de hacerse el suyo.

> (*Prosas,* II, 76-77)

The chaotic profusion of art objects in Casal's writings reflects the break-down in literary and artistic values at the end of Romanticism. He would take advantage of this cultural vacuum to transform the surfeit of *objets d'art* of the urban interior from a relatively anarchic style into a hard, glittering reflection of his own icy despair.

The urban interior and the art objects which fill it are explicitly a refuge from the streets of Havana, and the vitality and movement of the city. Although it has been a commonplace in Spanish American Modernist criticism to study Casal as a writer isolated from middle-class Havana, his art is, in fact, deeply conditioned by the life of the urban *haute bourgeoisie.* With the rise of industrialism and mercantilism in the nineteenth century, the newly-affluent upper middle class retreated into the interiors of their homes, which they filled with art objects from all over the globe, making their drawing rooms into a kind of international theater. This realm dominated by objects provided an escape from the deteriorating quality of modern city life, with its combination of pressures and dullness.[11] Casal wrote during the period immediately preceding the development of *art nouveau,* before a unified vision of the urban interior had developed.[12] He notes the lack of style in the late nineteenth-century dwelling when he writes that the art objects, eclectically gathered, "han transformado la decoración de todos los interiores y les han dado una fisonomía arcaica tan continuamente curiosa y tan dócilmente sometida que nuestro siglo, a fuerza de recopilar y comprobar todos los estilos, se ha olvidado de hacerse el suyo" (*Prosas,* II, 77). From the cultural void

which tended to suck in everything at the end of Romanticism, there emerges an obsession with form, for it provided the possibility of stability in a shifting, uncertain world.

Many of Casal's writings on art which appeared during the spring and summer of 1890, just before he began to publish the poetry of *Nieve,* reveal that he sought the principles governing the transformation of exterior reality into the artist's deeply personalized vision. Although he rejected Zola's novelistic style, in his parody of the latter's *La Bête humaine,*[13] because of the French novelist's preoccupation with the objects of his environment, no other passion informs Casal's esthetic so much as the frenzied pursuit of form. He wrote, in an article on the Cuban poet Armando Menocal, that poets and artists should not just observe objects, but "escuchar esa voz ideal que canta alrededor de las cosas, esparciendo sobre ellas, como benéfico rocío, sus gracias y sus encantos" (*Prosas,* II, 63).

The search for an understanding of the uses of plasticity led to the Cuban's interest in Baudelaire, the greatest poet of the urban interior, who fantasized a world of form to displace the decay he saw all around him in Paris. Casal very early translated Baudelaire repeatedly, above all, the latter's prose poems dealing with plasticity. Casal especially chose to translate Baudelaire's writings in which objects were a means to a vision beyond themselves; the French author's works deeply influenced the development of his imagery.

On October 16, 1887, Casal had published **"La moral del juguete,"**[14] a translation of Baudelaire's "La Moral du joujou," which has as its theme one of Baudelaire's now best-known theories, that the roots of artistic sensitivity lie in childhood. In returning to infancy to find the earliest contact with art, Baudelaire observed that the child wants to find the "soul" of the toy. Because of the child's failure, it becomes the work of the artist to continue to search for the essence of form. In April and May of 1890, Casal published translations of several of Baudelaire's prose poems. In **"El loco y la Venus,"** a translation of "Le Fou et la Vénus," Casal returned to the theme of **"La moral del juguete,"** that objects exist with great intensity, that they have a silent, ecstatic being. Baudelaire—and Casal in his translation—heightens the sensuous intensity of the three-dimensional scene he portrays: "Parece que una luz siempre creciente hace brillar cada vez más los objetos; que las flores excitadas arden en deseos de rivalizar con el azul del cielo por la energía de los colores y que el calor, haciendo visibles los perfumes, los hace subir hacia el astro como si fueran humo" (*Prosas,* III, 120).

Casal had translated an excerpt from Maupassant's *La Vie errante* which dealt with the Neoplatonic belief that sensuous perception was a means to a vision beyond itself. John Locke had written in the seventeenth century that nothing is in the mind that was not first in the senses; the nineteenth century further denigrated rational intelligence. Maupassant now finds this exaltation of sensual awareness essential to modern art at the end of Romanticism: "La inteligencia tiene cinco barreras entreabiertas y encadenadas que se llaman los cinco sentidos y los hombres enamorados del arte nuevo sacuden hoy, con todas sus fuerzas, esas cinco barreras" (*Prosas*, III, 113).

On April 27, 1890, Casal published **"Un hemisferio en una cabellera,"**[15] his translation of Baudelaire's "Un Hémisphère dans une chevelure." The woman's hair contains a reverie; it holds entire seas whose winds carry the poet to faraway lands, where the sky is bluer and deeper, where the air is perfumed by fruits, by leaves, and by human flesh. The previous day, on April 28, 1890, Casal had published his translation of Baudelaire's "Le *Confiteor* de l'artiste," in which the artist becomes one with the objects which surround him; he can no longer distinguish his own thought from theirs: "todas esas cosas piensan por mí o pienso por ellas (porque en la grandeza del ensueño, el *yo* se pierde pronto) . . ." (*Prosas*, III, 117). Casal's awareness that objects, in their appeal to the senses, can be used to evoke a new reality, and his sensation of fusion with the material world surrounding him, combined dramatically in an "imitation" of Baudelaire's prose poem "La double Chambre," which he published shortly before the poetry of *Nieve*. The physical existence of the room in which the poet dwells is transformed, through the intensification of sensation, into "una cámara semejante a una fantasía" (*Prosas*, II, 155). The artist is in touch with the mysterious life of the objects around him: "Las cortinas hablan una lengua muda, como las flores, como los cielos, como los soles ponientes. . . . Los muebles tienen formas prolongadas, dolientes, abatidas. Parece que sueñan . . ." (*Prosas*, II, 155). The transformation of a material world into pure impression is essential to the vision he seeks. In his flight from city life into the highly sculptural poetic reality of the urban interior, Casal, like Baudelaire, would return to the original idea of art, for he would enter a place identified as a sanctuary to seek the mystery held within the forms depicted.

In his interest in the artist's complex relationship with the physical realm surrounding him, Casal turned to Baudelaire's discussion, in the essays on the Salon of 1859, of the distinction among various levels of reality,[16] which Marcel Ruff considers one of the French author's most original contributions to modern art.[17] Baudelaire distinguished between photographic and historical reality, and the psychological truth of the novel. Casal, like Baudelaire, rejects photographic realism; the truth of any work—even the realist novel—is beyond the photographic for it reaches a level more profound and more universal than photographic exactitude. Casal

also rejects historical accuracy as Baudelaire never had, for Baudelaire felt that the paintings of Ingres and David were excellent examples of historical vision in painting. What emerges is Casal's insistence, beyond that of Baudelaire, upon the detachment of the image from exterior reality, and its association with an interior psychological realm.

One of Casal's earliest works dealing with the interiorization of the image was **"Amor en el claustro,"** published on August 1, 1887. The anecdotal substance of the poem is simple; a young nun prays in the chapel of her convent late at night. As she looks at the crucifix it dissolves before her eyes, and in its place she sees the face of her dead lover. Already, for Casal, the decisive image is the interiorized one. The deeply assimilated vision of the *amado* is more powerful than the form of the crucifix which has not been appropriated by the self, and which, therefore, does not ultimately reveal the self.

Casal would reveal six years later, as he was writing his last book of poetry, that the image of the person portrayed had become as interiorized and obsessive for him as the face of her lover was for the young nun. In one of his portraits in the series *Seres enigmáticos*, entitled **"El hombre de las muletas de níquel,"** Casal confesses that the vision of the once elegant, crippled man haunts him and that its expression has become a pathological necessity.[18]

Among the nineteenth-century writers whom Casal admired most was Flaubert, for in Flaubert's works, as in much nineteenth-century fiction, art is considered to be a mirror of reality. Casal, as we have seen, sought to make his own poetry into a reflection of the artist's psychology. He noted, however, a narcissistic quality in Flaubert when he wrote that, although the French novelist is considered the most impersonal of authors, *Bouvard et Pécuchet* is in many ways a portrait of Flaubert himself.[19] The metaphor used by Flaubert, of art as a mirror of reality, is in fact ambiguous. What we discover in much nineteenth-century writing is indeed a mirror, but it is displaced: instead of the artist's work having become a reflection of the world, it is the world which the artist has transformed into a mirror.[20] This transformation of exterior reality into a portrait of the artist is nowhere more evident than in Casal's art of the urban interior.

The woman was one of the major art objects of the Cuban writer's urban interiors. During the spring of 1890, the same period immediately preceding publication of the poems of *Nieve*, in which he was publishing the translations of Baudelaire and his writings on esthetics, Casal published, on June 3, a word portrait of a Parisian *demi-mondaine*, entitled **"La derrochadora."**[21] The figure of the courtesan, a woman of the turn-of-the-century *salons,* intrigued Casal, and he wrote numerous articles about her. She became for him a symbol of his esthetic world, for her artificial beauty and elegance were as compelling yet transitory as those of his own artistic vision. In **"La derrochadora"** the *demi-mondaine* lives surrounded by objects; she reminds one of Manet's *Olympia* as she is portrayed at her morning ritual of bathing and being perfumed by her maid among glitteringly polished mirrors, jewels, and jasper. The hard surfaces of these objects are accentuated by the contrast with the soft texture of the courtesan's robe and skin. Her maid transforms her into an esthetic object and a sex object, and in this world of *cosas,* in which she herself is another one, the woman spends her days buying art objects: "En cada tienda, halla algo nuevo que comprar. Ya es un brazalete de oro, cuajado de pedrería digno de una Leonor de Este; ya un abanico ínfimo, con paisaje grotesco, todo hecho con tintas de relumbrón; ya una estatua de mármol, obra maestra de un artista desconocido, pero que firmaría un Falguière; ya un cromo americano . . ." (*Prosas,* I, 238). Her search for art objects is frenzied and compulsive; what she buys one day is discarded almost immediately to make room for the next day's purchases—as the prostitute herself is interchangeable with many others, objects bought and used for a short time. The one emotional quality which Casal emphasizes in the woman is her lack of attachment to any other person; the *demi-mondaine* by definition has an ambivalent relationship to the bourgeois society which exploits her and off which she lives. Like many of Casal's writings on women, the portrait of the elegant prostitute is characterized by a conflictual attitude toward love; he writes that when anyone mentions love to her, the woman's response is a cynical "¡Desdichados! ¿Todavía creéis en eso?" (*Prosas,* I, 238).

The portrait of the elegant prostitute was published only three days before Casal's definition of modern art as a reflection of the artist's ennui and pathology: "el malestar permanente, el escepticismo profundo, la amargura intensa, las aspiraciones indefinidas y el pesimismo sombrío. . . ." There is no better reflection of Casal's own *glacial tristeza,* his depression expressed in icily sculptural form, than the Parisian *demi-mondaine* as she is seen dwelling in a nightmarish vision of life experienced entirely in terms of objects by a psyche devoid of emotion. Casal's portraits of women, however, ultimately fail as portraits, for they are a deeply narcissistic—highly polished mirror of the artist—proof of his own existence.

That the art object was becoming increasingly interiorized in Casal's writings is apparent in another portrait of a woman, entitled simply **"Croquis femenino,"** published the same day as **"La derrochadora."** The subject of this sketch, like the prostitute, remains unnamed, but she represents another type of woman Casal ad-

mired. She is one of the wealthy, cultivated Cuban women who lived apart from the *haute bourgeoisie* of Havana, and whose houses were meeting places for writers and artists. Like the French courtesan, she lives in an environment dominated by objects. Casal presents an exhaustive inventory of her salon: "Espejos venecianos, con marcos de bronce, ornados con ligeros amorcillos; pieles de tigres arrojados al pie de olorosos divanes; tibores japoneses, guarnecidos de dragones y quimeras; mesas de laca incrustadas de nácar, cubiertas de un pueblo de estatuitas; óleos admirables, firmados por reputados pintores, todo se encuentra en aquel salón" (*Prosas,* II, 141). When Casal describes the woman's psychology, he turns to the plasticity of the fairy tale to create an interior vision. He writes that she is one of the people of his time who "viven siempre inclinados sobre sí mismos, mirándose por dentro, como si llevaran allí, a semejanza de la heroína de los cuentos de hadas, una gruta formada de piedras preciosas, donde ven una ninfa encantadora que se adormece entre los cantos de pájaros maravillosos y los aromas de flores desconocidas" (*Prosas,* II, 140). Even the woman's introversion is expressed in terms of glittering, gem-like preciosity, for the grotto, where she dwells within this fantastically sculptured psychological world, is formed of jewels.

Casal emphasizes that she, like the prostitute of **"La derrochadora,"** is detached from reality and incapable of feeling emotion for the people around her. He notes ironically that she is so pathologically linked with the objects in her environment that she has fallen in love with one of them, a portrait of Murat which hangs in the corner of her living room. The art object is now so interiorized that it is becoming the imagery of the woman's mind. Casal writes that, as she drives through the streets of Havana, she resembles a legendary queen in exile "que ha venido a olvidar entre los esplendores naturales del nuevo mundo, la imagen torturadora de su Asiria perdida" (*Prosas,* II, 140). The woman is, herself, an image tormented by an image in this *Through-the-Looking-Glass* delirium of highly-fantasized plasticity.

The imagery of Casal's **"Museo ideal"** reveals the same interiorized, often narcissistic function that one observes in the writings published immediately before *Nieve.* Our examination of the **"Museo ideal"** will concentrate on two of Casal's best-known works, the Salome poems entitled **"Salomé"** and **"La aparición,"** which are based on two of Gustave Moreau's masterpieces, the oil painting *Salomé* (in the Mante Collection) and the watercolor *L'Apparition* (now in the Luxembourg Museum). No other group of works by Casal has received more attention from critics than the **"Museo ideal."** More than a quarter of a century ago Arturo Torres Ríoseco contended that the poems of the collection were transpositions into poetry of Huysmans' prose descriptions of Moreau's paintings in *À rebours.*[22] The recent scholarship of Robert Jay Glickman, however, shows that Casal was in contact with Moreau himself through correspondence between August 11, 1891, and January 1, 1893.[23] In a letter of August 15, 1891, Casal wrote to Moreau that he had been introduced to the French artist's paintings by Joris-Karl Huysmans.[24] Glickman notes, "We may assume that Casal meant that he had discovered Moreau by reading Huysmans' novel *À rebours,* which was published in 1884,"[25] for the paintings by Moreau which appear in Casal's **"Museo ideal"** are those which Des Esseintes, the protagonist of Huysmans' novel, chooses to decorate the interior of the house in Paris into which he retreats from the life of the city. It seems natural that Casal's art of the urban interior would lead him to *À rebours,* the novel which was fast becoming a kind of decadent manifesto.

After Casal had written all of the poems of the **"Museo ideal,"** he published, in *La Habana Literaria,* on March 15, 1892, an article on Huysmans, in which he stated that in *À rebours* Huysmans had established "el proceso artístico de nuestro tiempo" (**Prosas,** I, 178). Casal's evaluation of the French novelist's place within the literary currents of the time is noteworthy: "Hasta hace pocos años, Huysmans ha militado en la escuela naturalista, de la que se alejó más tarde . . ." (**Prosas,** I, 177), for Huysmans remained much closer to Zola than Casal liked to believe. If there is one problem in Casal's understanding of Huysmans, it is his failure to comprehend the ironic nature of Des Esseintes' retreat into his house filled with art objects. Huysmans, through his protagonist, attempted to show the impossibility of withdrawing entirely from one's environment, i.e., of breaking completely with Naturalism. The writers like Casal, and they were legion, who saw in *À rebours* the essence of decadent art, did not understand that Huysmans never entirely escaped the early influence of Zola; nor did they perceive that Zola was a much greater visionary than Huysmans, who was not an exceptionally original writer.

It remains unclear whether or not Casal had seen a photograph of Moreau's *Salomé* before he published his sonnet of the same title, although Casal wrote to Moreau on August 11, 1891, that the poems **"Salomé," "Elena"** and **"Galatea"** were based on photocopies of Moreau's paintings.[26] Four days later, in another letter to the French painter on August 15, he stated that these three sonnets were "escritos por mí ante copias de vuestras divinas y sugestivas figuras de *Elena, Salomé y Galatea.*"[27] In spite of Casal's repeated assertion of Moreau's painting as his source, other evidence suggests that Huysmans' prose description may have in fact been Casal's model, for **"Salomé"** was published on September 21, 1890, almost one year before **"Elena"** and **"Galatea"** appeared on August 2 and August 9, 1891, respectively. Casal's earliest references to Huysmans, futhermore, antedate all references to Moreau.[28]

Casal's correspondence suggests that **"La aparición,"** the second of the poems of the **"Museo ideal,"** was based at least partially upon a photocopy of Moreau's *L'Apparition,* and not entirely upon Huysmans' prose description. A reproduction of Moreau's painting reached Havana on or about August 13, 1891.[29] Casal's poem was published somewhat later, on August 30, 1891, in *La Habana Elegante,* when Casal first published as a group the works which would form the body or gallery of his **"Museo ideal,"** i.e., the entire collection minus **"Vestíbulo: Retrato de Gustavo Moreau"** and **"Sueño de gloria: Apoteosis de Gustavo Moreau."** The group bore the title **"Mi museo ideal"** (*Cuadros de Gustavo Moreau*).

The versions of the two Salome poems which appeared in *La Habana Elegante* on August 30, 1891, were very close to the versions which would appear in **Nieve.** Since holograph copies of only four of Casal's poems are extant, it is impossible to trace the evolution of his poetry from its inception. In the case of **"Salomé"** and **"La aparición"** one cannot determine with absolute certainty the dates when the poems were actually written, and then compare them with the dates on or by which Casal had in his possession copies of Moreau's paintings.

Casal and Moreau faced many of the same problems in their work, because they both sought an art which would be simultaneously sculptural and evocative. Just as Casal had begun to write under the influence of the Parnassian poets, Moreau had started his career as an academic painter. Moreau, however, had too eccentric a vision of life to be a very successful academic painter. He had prepared for the Salon of 1869, but had failed to win a prize; one of the paintings which had taken an award was a *Salomé.* With his lack of success, Moreau, in the decade before he showed most of the works which Casal would include in his **"Museo ideal,"** had withdrawn from exhibiting in order to develop a style more suited to his temperament.[30] During this time he reinforced both the sculptural and evocative qualities of his painting. For the first time, he began to work in sculpture; the resulting plasticity is apparent in both *Salomé* and *L'Apparition.* It should also be noted that Moreau's maquettes indicate that he drew his sketches of Salome from living models.[31] Ironically, Moreau and Casal, both of whom exalted the artificial and denigrated everything natural, portrayed nature very sensitively.[32] For the first time, too, Moreau experimented with the use of large spaces to evoke psychological depth in his paintings. The lamp hanging in the darkened chamber in *Salomé* appears to have been copied from a Rembrandt which he owned.[33] He evidently admired and was influenced by the Dutch painter's evocation of emotional profundity through the use of light and shadow.

Conflict and ambiguity are the psychological qualities which dominate Moreau's Salome paintings. Throughout his other works also, this ambivalence focuses on the woman, who is perceived to be both compelling and destructive; Moreau believed that the great *femme fatale,* Salome, like Helen of Troy, conveyed the threateningly powerful nature of the woman. In his word portrait of another *femme fatale,* Emma Crouch, the celebrated courtesan of the court of Napoleon III, Casal wrote that she was a "female don Juan."[34] The Romantic myth had become inverted in these figures admired by the *fin de siglo,* for the woman was now the vortex which drew men to her, only to destroy them. Mario Praz has noted the sexually ambivalent quality of Moreau's paintings;[35] his Venuses have, for example, the faces of men, and Hercules has the face of a young woman. The lotus which Salome holds is conflictual in its symbolism, for it evokes both spirituality and sexuality.[36] The ambiguity and destruction present in the images of the **"Museo ideal"** would find their culmination in the mysteriously violent, sexual symbolism of **"Dolorosa."**

As an artist, Casal was much closer in temperament and interests to Moreau than he was to Huysmans. The latter tended to distort reality by projecting upon it a vision of physical pathology; his frequent references to syphilis are an example.[37] Casal was much more interested in certain psychological and esthetic properties of Moreau's paintings. It is useless, however, to talk about true *ekfrasis*—transposition from painting into poetry—in Casal's works, even in the cases like **"La aparición"** in which it is known that he had seen a photocopy of the Moreau painting before the publication of his poem.[38] It is apparent that Casal's understanding of Moreau was not exceptionally thorough or deep, for Glickman has shown that Casal did not identify some of Moreau's works properly. **"Una peri"** was likely written describing Moreau's *Sapho se précipitant dans la men,*[39] and **"Venus Anadeomena"** describes *La Naissance de Vénus* and another unidentified painting.[40] Moreau, one of the great teachers of his time, with whom both Matisse and Rouault studied, researched his paintings in a thorough and painstaking manner. In order to understand Moreau's works, they must be approached in the same scholarly manner in which the artist undertook them, for he combined fantasy with a great deal of historical accuracy. These historical details, however, were much less important to Casal than to Moreau, for it should be remembered that in discussing Baudelaire's study of the levels of artistic reality, Casal had rejected historical reality as an important criterion of art.

During the same period (September, 1890, until April, 1892), in which he was publishing the poem-paintings of the **"Museo ideal,"** Casal was also writing the confessional poetry which would be included in the section of *Nieve* entitled **"Marfiles viejos."** The **"Museo ideal"** has not been studied sufficiently in light of its being more or less contemporary with the **"Marfiles viejos,"** for many of the psychological properties present in the latter collection are mirrored in the **"Museo ideal."** The extreme anxiety which surrounded erotic fantasy for Casal, expressed in the violence and destruction seen in the Salome poems, is also present in the sonnet **"A la castidad"** from **"Marfiles viejos"**:

> Yo no amo la mujer, porque en su seno
> dura el amor lo que en la rama el fruto,
> y mi alma vistió de eterno luto
> y en mi cuerpo infiltró mortal veneno.
>
> Ni con voz de ángel o lenguaje obsceno
> logra en mí enardecer al torpe bruto
> que si le rinde varonil tributo
> agoniza al instante de odio lleno.
>
> ¡Oh blanca castidad! Sé el ígneo faro
> que guíe el paso de mi planta inquieta
> a través del erial de jas pasiones
>
> y otórgame, en mi horrendo desamparo,
> con los dulces ensueños del poeta
> la calma de los puros corazones.[41]

The icy pathology of the portraits of Salome reflects the poet's emptiness and self-alienation, two of the most powerful motifs of the **"Marfiles viejos." "Tristissima nox,"** the opening work of the collection, and the first poem to be written, introduces the theme, "el vacío profundo de mi alma." This stoic disillusion is echoed repeatedly in the poetry; in his tribute to Leopardi, for example, which follows **"Tristissima nox,"** Casal, in characterizing the Italian poet as "águila que vivió preso en el lodo," refers to the modern poet for whom all the old illusions have died, leaving nothing to replace them. Casal's disenchantment with the art to which he had been deeply committed is explicit in **"Paisaje espiritual"**: "no endulcen mi infernal tormento / ni la Pasión, ni el Arte, ni la Ciencia . . ." (*Poetry,* I, 143). The self-alienation of **"Pax animae"** parallels his earlier discussion of modern art, for he had written that their suffering led modern writers to escape "hacia los espacios siderales del ensueño." The emotional mechanism underlying Casal's mysticism is apparent:

> No me habléis más de dichas terrenales
> que no ansío gustar. Está ya muerto
> mi corazón y en su recinto abierto
> sólo entrarán los cuervos sepulcrales.
>
> Del pasado no llevo las señales
> y a veces de que existo no estoy cierto,
> porque es la vida para mí un desierto

poblado de figuras espectrales.

No veo más que un astro obscurecido
por brumas de crepúsculo lluvioso,
y, entre el silencio de sopor profundo,

tan sólo llega a percibir mi oído
algo extraño y confuso y misterioso
que me arrastra muy lejos de este mundo.

(*Poetry,* I, 140)

The desire for flight into a world of illusion expressed here is echoed in the final lines of "A un crítico": "tranquilo iré a dormir con los pequeños / si veo fulgurar ante mis ojos, / hasta el instante mismo de la muerte, / las visiones doradas de mis sueños" (*Poetry,* I, 145). The repeated insistence upon fantasy and transcendent vision is convincing only as a wish for evasion; his mysticism compensates for and is severely undermined by his nihilism.

The experience of emotional disintegration voiced in the confessional poetry of the **"Marfiles viejos"** is captured in the glittering images of the **"Museo ideal."** When we compare Casal's **"La aparición"** with Moreau's painting of the same name, which he had seen before he published his poem, it is evident that the poet's plasticity is more luminous and fluid than Moreau's relatively static composition. As Salome screams at the vision of the decapitated John the Baptist, esthetic break-down reflects the psychological disintegration as the image dissolves into a shower of crimson drops of blood on the marble pavement:

Nube fragante y cálida tamiza
el fulgor del palacio de granito,
ónix, pórfido y nácar. Infinito
deleite invade a Herodes. La rojiza

espada fulgurante inmoviliza
hierático el verdugo, y hondo grito
arroja Salomé frente al maldito
espectro que sus miembros paraliza.

Despójase del traje de brocado
y, quedando vestida en un momento,
de oro y perlas, zafiros y rubíes,
    huye del Precursor decapitado
que esparce en el marmóreo pavimento
lluvia de sangre en gotas carmesíes.

(*Poetry,* I, 115)

Casal's art has become so profoundly a mirror of his affective world, that it is engulfed and finally shattered by the very emotional properties it was designed to reflect. The psychological and esthetic disintegration in his works, however, was ultimately so overwhelmingly threatening to Casal that he attempted, in the **"Museo ideal,"** to transform his fluid, unstructured poetic world into a highly-structured series of rigidly framed images juxtaposed between a fixed beginning and ending.

A study of the changes in sequence of the poems of the **"Museo ideal"** in the course of their various dates of publication reveals that the poems were not always written for the places ultimately assigned to them in *Nieve.* When Casal first published the poems of his **"Museo ideal"** as a group on August 30, 1891, several of the poems did not appear in the order in which they were written and originally published, for **"Salomé,"** **"Elena,"** and **"Galatea"** had been previously published separately.[42] The final arrangement of the collection seems to have been reached as a result of trial and error over a period of time, with no overall scheme; a possible exception is the use of **"Salomé"** and **"La aparición"** as the first poem-paintings within the gallery, for this opening sequence of the August 30, 1891, publication of his "Museum" in *La Habana Elegante* was repeated in *Nieve.*

Nor did Casal settle immediately upon a beginning for his collection. He first used as epigraph for the **"Museo ideal"** the second stanza of Joséphin Soulary's 1880 "Prologue" to *Les Jeux divins* espousing myth and the marvellous in art: "Pour nous, fils de l'art, rien ne vaut / Le mythe et sa légende rose; / Nous mourons de la vie en prose / Où le merveilleux fait défaut."[43] These lines were followed by a dedication to his friend Eduardo Rosell, which was maintained in *Nieve.* The epigraph from Soulary's "Prologue" was later suppressed in favor of Casal's own poem, **"Vestíbulo. Retrato de Gustavo Moreau,"** which served to give a physical sense of an entry hall into his museum.

Because the holograph copy of **"Vestíbulo. Retrato de Gustavo Moreau"** which Casal sent to Moreau is extant, we know that Casal conceived of the poem almost from the beginning as the entrance to his **"Museo ideal,"** for the term *vestíbulo* was very early incorporated into the title. The holograph copy is dated December 12, 1891; Casal first mentioned the poem in a letter to Moreau on December 15, 1891, when he indicated that **"Vestíbulo"** was going to have an important role in his book because it would function as the gateway to the series he planned to entitle **"Mi museo ideal."**[44] The poem appeared in *Nieve* with the same title that it had borne in the holograph version, i.e., **"Vestíbulo. Retrato de Gustavo Moreau,"** although it had twice been published under the title **"Gustavo Moreau."**

Casal did not conceive so quickly of **"Sueño de gloria. Apoteosis de Gustavo Moreau"** as the conclusion to his **"Museo ideal."** In the holograph version the apotheosis of Moreau is placed before **"Vestíbulo."** This copy of the poems suggests that **"Sueño de gloria,"** dated December 8, 1891, was written earlier than the vestibule-portrait poem, which is dated December 12, 1891. Casal's correspondence with Moreau, too, suggests that the apotheosis poem was conceived earlier than the portrait poem, for Casal included what Glickman characterizes as a "detailed outline" of **"Sueño de gloria"** in a letter to Moreau dated November 1, 1891.[45] He did not mention **"Vestíbulo"** until his December 15, 1891, letter. Publication dates are further evidence that **"Sueño de gloria"** is the earlier work, for it was published in *La Habana Literaria* on December 30, 1891. **"Vestíbulo"** first appeared, under the title **"Gustavo Moreau,"** in *El Fígaro,* more than two weeks later on January 15, 1892.

As late as after the typesetting of *Nieve* had begun, Casal appears to have still planned to place **"Sueño de gloria"** at the beginning of the **"Museo ideal,"** either before or immediately after **"Vestíbulo."** In the 1892 edition of *Nieve* a centered rule was printed beneath the title **"Sueño de gloria. Retrato de Gustavo Moreau."** The only other poems which have this mark beneath the title are the first seven poems of *Nieve,* i.e., the **"Introducción,"** the five works which form the **"Bocetos antiguos"** (the collection which precedes the **"Museo ideal"**), and **"Vestíbulo. Retrato de Gustavo Moreau."** **"Sueño de gloria"** was evidently to have been included in this sequence since the printer included it in the group whose titles were underlined with the centered rule. Casal evidently decided to move the poem—decisions made concerning poem sequence are generally the author's—after the typesetting of *Nieve* had already begun.[46]

The fact that Casal placed his images within rigidly juxtaposed frames and between a beginning (**"Vestíbulo. Retrato de Gustavo Moreau"**) and an ending (**"Sueño de gloria. Apoteosis de Gustavo Moreau"**) cannot obscure entirely the lack of underlying structure, or the emotional disintegration, of the **"Museo ideal."** This unstructured, tenuous art world, moreover, both explains the need for and is severely weakened by the imposition of a rigid form upon it. In **"Sueño de gloria. Apoteosis de Gustavo Moreau,"** the final poem of the collection, Casal further undermines his own unstructured, disintegrating poetic vision by returning to the outmoded Romantic myth of transcendence through art, already discredited in his own Modernist esthetic. His allegorical depiction of art in this poem as the union of Genius—the "divine" Moreau—with Beauty—a decadent Helen of Troy—is so trite that it weakens the radical sense of modernity of the **"Museo ideal,"** the moments in which the poem-paintings fulfill Casal's definition of modern art as a reflection of the poet's psychology.

The poem **"Dolorosa"** from *Rimas* represents the culmination of Casal's poetry of the urban interior. In the rich effects of the artificial lighting upon the luxuriant surfaces ("Tendía la lamparilla / en el verde cortinaje, / franjas de seda amarilla / con transparencias de encaje," *Poetry,* I, 234), the play of light and shadow dissolves the concrete objects into an abstract psychological

world, from which emerges the image of the dagger which dominates each of the three sections of the poem. As the imagery shimmers evanescently it seems to have acquired the quality of the *bruñido espejo* which Casal believed essential to modern poetry:

> Brilló el puñal en la sombra
> como una lengua de plata,
> y bañó al que nadie nombra
> onda de sangre escarlata.
>
> (*Poetry,* I, 234)

The metaphors are tinged with violence and mysterious sexuality, as the most powerful of Casal's imagery often is. They evoke the poet's self-alienation, his psyche turned against itself. Casal portrays, in frenetic plasticity, the self-destructive force within:

> ¡Cómo en la sombra glacial
> tus ojos fosforecían,
> y de palidez mortal
> tus mejillas se cubrían!
>
> ¡Cómo tus manos heladas
> asíanse de mi cuello,
> o esparcían levantadas
> las ondas de tu cabello!
>
> Arrojándote a mis pies,
> con la voz de los que gimen,
> me confesaste después
> todo el horror de tu crimen.
>
> (*Poetry,* I, 235-36)

In **"Dolorosa,"** as in the **"Museo ideal,"** Casal's definition of modern art is fulfilled in the poetry of the urban interior; we see both the highly polished mirror of his esthetic world and the dark reverse side of the self which it reveals. The icy materialism of Casal's interiors, moreover, formed one of his closest links with the values of turn-of-the-century middle-class Havana. As the art objects were transformed into a deeper psychological reality, furthermore, this sanctuary increasingly dissolved into a reflection of the poet's frozen solitude and psychic disintegration. The exaltation of the urban interior in Casal's works is, as a result, its destruction, for it failed to provide the artist with a refuge either from himself or the bourgeois society which surrounded him.

As his poetic world, with its frenetic emphasis upon form and sensation, developed, it ultimately ended in the denial of form and sensation. One of the least understood aspects of synesthesia is that, although it represents a heightening of awareness of the things of this world, its end result is the negation of objects and the senses. Impressionism is based on the idea that impressions of objects are important, not the *cosas* themselves. In the literary generation which follows Casal's, the increasingly complex function of the perception of exterior reality can be observed in the works of authors like Proust and Azorín. Proust, by means of impressions, transformed visual and other sensory elements taken from Combray, Balbec, and Paris, into metaphors which became mirrors of interior emotional states. The first stages of this process are apparent in Casal's transformation of the art objects of the urban interior into the *bruñido espejo* of a psychological world—the ultimate destruction of the sensuous art object.

Casal's desire to impose a rigid form upon the **"Museo ideal"** is paralleled in his attempt to structure the equally unstructured *Rimas,* his final volume of poetry. Although the manuscript of the work is no longer extant, it is unlikely that the author would have left the poems in the order in which they now appear, which is the sequence in which they were left at his death. When he originally published the poems separately he assigned to a number of them subheadings similar to those used in *Nieve*; these would probably have been used as subtitles for groups of poems.[47]

The epigraph which appears in the posthumous, and subsequent, editions of *Rimas* are the lines from Baudelaire's "Bénédiction" dealing with suffering as the preparation for the transcendent *paradis révélé*: "Soyez béni, mon Dieu, qui donnez la souffrance / Comme un divin remède à nos impuretés / Et comme la meilleure et la plus pure essence / Qui prépare les forts aux saintes voluptés!"[48] Casal returns to the long-discredited (in his own works) Romantic myth of epiphany through art when he quotes one of Baudelaire's most uninteresting and least original poems.

It is uncertain that Casal actually intended to use the lines from "Bénédiction" as the epigraph to *Rimas*. In **"Mi museo ideal,"** as we have seen, although he had originally included the "Prologue" to the French poet Joséphin Soulary's *Les Jeux divins* as an epigraph, he replaced it with a poem of his own, **"Vestíbulo. Retrato de Gustavo Moreau,"** in the final version for inclusion in *Nieve*. It seems especially likely that he would have done the same in *Rimas* since he had used his own poems as the introductory statements for his previous two books of poetry. However, even if the epigraph which the work has always borne had been replaced, the obsessive insistence upon the discredited metaphysical theme would have remained. The book's cover, which Casal designed and which it seems unlikely that he would have changed,[49] shows the seated figure of Poetry and bears the inscription "Ars Religio Nostra." **"A la Belleza,"** the first poem of *Rimas* to be written, and the poem which, up to his death, Casal left as the introductory work of the volume, also echoes the Baudelairean desire for apocalyptic vision.

Because the lines from "Bénédiction" have remained as the epigraph to *Rimas,* Casal's Neoplatonism is more easily traced than that of many other Modernist writers.

Casal wrote in **"A la Belleza"** that he had glimpsed a vision of absolute beauty in the poetry of only one poet. In all likelihood, this poet is Baudelaire,[50] since **"A la Belleza"** is placed immediately after the Baudelairean stanza dealing with the preparation for the *paradis révélé*. The roots of Casal's quest for metaphysical experience in art lie, through the French author, deep in a nineteenth-century Neo-platonic tradition. In commenting on Edgar Allan Poe's *Poetic Principle,* Baudelaire presented his theory of correspondences, in which the material objects of earth are like parts of a puzzle which give us an intuition of a spiritual realm beyond: "C'est cet admirable, cet immortel instinct du beau qui nous fait considérer la terre et ses spectacles comme un aperçu, comme une correspondance du ciel."[51] This theory of art was deeply influenced by Poe. For example, in a reference to the "wild effort" that poets expend to reach Beauty, Poe stated that, "Inspired by an ecstatic prescience of the glories beyond the grave, we struggle, by multiform combinations among the things and thoughts of Time, to attain a portion of that Loveliness whose very elements, perhaps, appertain to eternity alone."[52] Indeed, it was Poe's struggle toward an all but undefinable ideal that most strongly attracted Baudelaire to him.[53]

The theories of Poe upon which Baudelaire relied so heavily in the development of his own writings on art were in turn highly derivative. Poe and Baudelaire had read the essays of Emerson, and were familiar with Swedenborg's doctrine of correspondence, both of which were influenced by Plato. There was a basic ambiguity in Emerson's thought that was never resolved. He states the underlying assumption of transcendental symbolism when he writes in his essay "Nature": "It is not words only that are emblematic; it is things which are emblematic. Every natural fact is a symbol of some spiritual fact."[54] Emerson, however, never confronted the question of where this world beyond the components of nature lay. He continues, in "Nature," saying that this spiritual realm "is less a transcendent divinity revealed through nature from beyond than a transcendent state of mind projected onto nature from within."[55] And in his essay "The Poet," Emerson wrote that the universe was "the externalization of the soul."[56]

From the time of Emerson, then, transcendence was a contradiction in terms; it held a tragic ambiguity, for it never really affirmed that there is any ultimate reality beyond the individual. Although, as we have seen, Casal had earlier avoided Baudelaire's esthetic ambiguity, he later incorporated, in his poetic vision of *Rimas,* the basic ambivalence in Baudelaire's thought without resolving it. The resulting conflict sprung from the failure of either poet to relinquish an idealistic sense of art in the face of his belief that modern poetry could only be the expression of a psychological world.

The uncertainty of Casal's transcendent concept of art, by the time he wrote **Rimas,** is evident in **"A la Belleza."** Although he describes his quest for metaphysical beauty, the poem is strangely confused. He severely weakens the artistic mysticism he seeks to perpetuate when he concedes that the epiphany sought through art perhaps belongs only to an interior psychological realm: "Quizás como te sueña mi deseo / estés en mí reinando, / mientras voy persiguiendo por el mundo / las huellas de tu paso" (**Poetry,** I, 198).

"Cuerpo y alma," the final poem of **Rimas,** is dominated by two major themes of the work: pathology[57] and the desire for cosmic vision. The last poem of the collection to be written,[58] and the only one published posthumously (October 29, 1893, eight days after Casal's death on October 21), its function appears to have been to give a sense of an ending to **Rimas.** The initial sections of **"Cuerpo y alma,"** a chain of downward-spiralling images evoking illness, and a corresponding series of ethereal images evoking transcendence, symbolize the irreconcilable struggle between the poet's sick body and the purity of his soul. The conflict between the two is resolved in the closing *envío*'s promise of fulfillment, through death, of the long-frustrated desire for the infinite. The synthesis of major themes of **Rimas** found in this final poem, and the attitude of acceptance of death, gave finality, and the suggestion of unity and form, to a collection left unfinished and unstructured by the poet's own premature death.

The similarity of theme between the *envío* of **"Cuerpo y alma"** and the ending of *Les Fleurs du mal* merits consideration, for Casal appears to have found the model for his conclusion to **Rimas** in the ending of the French work. After referring to Baudelaire as "el más grande poeta de nuestros tiempos" in his posthumous *busto* "El doctor Francisco Zayas," published in *La Habana Elegante* on October 22, 1893, Casal quoted the final lines from "Le Voyage," the closing poem of *Les Fleurs du mal*:

O Mort, vieux capitaine, il est temps! Levons l'ancre!
Ce pays nous ennuie, ô Mort! Appareillons!
Si le ciel et la mer sont noirs comme de l'encre,
Nos cœurs que tu connais sont remplis de rayons!
Verse-nous ton poison pour qu'il nous réconforte!
Nous voulons, tant ce feu nous brûle le cerveau,
Plonger au fond du gouffre, Enfer ou Ciel, qu'importe?
Au fond de l'Inconnu pour trouver du *nouveau*![59]

Although Baudelaire insisted that his book "n'est pas un pur album, et qu'il a un commencement et une fin,"[60] Marcel Ruff, in his study of the structure of *Les Fleurs du mal,* contends that the individual poems were not always written for the places ultimately assigned to them.[61] This is especially true of the use of "Le Voyage" as a general conclusion to the collection, for at the time he wrote the poem, Baudelaire planned to conclude his

work with an epilogue addressed to the city of Paris, which would have shifted the perspective of the book away from the introspection and destiny of the artist onto a spiritual drama played across the entire city. Although it was an afterthought, the position of "Le Voyage" at the end of *Les Fleurs du mal* is justifiable, for like **"Cuerpo y alma,"** it unifies major themes of the work it concludes.[62] The ending of Baudelaire's poem especially, quoted during the final days of Casal's life when he was writing **"Cuerpo y alma,"** must have provided the young Cuban with a model, for Baudelaire had used the closing theme of acceptance of death, as Casal would in his *envío,* to give a sense of finality and unity to a profoundly unstructured and psychically disrupted work.

Notes

1. Julián del Casal, *Prosas, Edición del Centenario,* II (Havana: Consejo Nacional de Cultura, 1963), 145. References to the Centennial Edition of Casal's prose will be cited in the notes and within the text of this study as *Prosas,* followed by volume and page number.

2. Renato Poggioli, *The Theory of the Avant-Garde,* trans. Gerald Fitzgerald (Cambridge: Harvard University Press, 1968), p. 75. For a detailed discussion of decadence as a crisis of consciousness see Matei Calinescu, *Faces of Modernity* (Bloomington: University of Indiana Press, 1977), pp. 149-221.

3. Théophile Gautier, Introd., *Les Fleurs du mal,* by Charles Baudelaire, 2nd ed. (Paris: Lévy Frères, 1869), p. 17. Calinescu observes that the first "entirely approbative and widely influential view of decadence as a *style* occurs in the preface that Théophile Gautier wrote in 1868" for *Les Fleurs du mal.* See Calinescu, p. 164.

4. Casal, *Prosas,* II, 144. Casal quotes almost *verbatim* Gautier's phrase "écoutant pour les traduire les confidences subtiles de la névrose, les aveux de la passion vieillissante qui se déprave et les hallucinations bizarres de l'idée fixe tournant à la folie." See Gautier, p. 17.

5. Baudelaire contrasts modern and classical treatment of various themes in "De l'Héroïsme de la vie moderne," the concluding essay on the Salon of 1846. See Baudelaire, "De l'Héroïsme de la vie moderne," in *Salon de 1846,* in *Œuvres complètes,* ed. Claude Pichois (Paris: Gallimard, 1976), II, 493-96.

6. Baudelaire, "De l'Héroïsme de la vie moderne," p. 495.

7. Casal, *Prosas,* II, 144.

8. Baudelaire, pp. 420-21.

9. For Paul de Man, Baudelaire's writings reveal the ambivalence inherent in modernity. In his famous essay on the French artist Constantin Guys, "Le Peintre de la vie moderne," Baudelaire's conception of modernity is very close to that of Nietzsche in his second *Unzeitgemässe Betrachtung.* In Baudelaire's essay we find an acute sense of the present as essential to all esthetic experience: "Le plaisir que nous retirons de la représentation du présent tient non seulement à la beauté dont il peut être revêtu, mais aussi à sa qualité essentielle de présent." De Man observes, "The paradox of the problem is potentially contained in the formula *'représentation du présent'* which combines a repetitive with an instantaneous pattern without apparent awareness of the incompatibility. Yet this latent tension governs the development of the entire essay." Paul de Man, "Literary History and Literary Modernity," in *In Search of Literary Theory,* ed. Morton W. Bloomfield (Ithaca: Cornell University Press, 1972), p. 256.

10. In his theory of decadence found in his article on Baudelaire, published in the *Nouvelle revue* of November 15, 1881, and reprinted in *Essais de psychologie contemporaine* (1883), Paul Bourget had defined decadent societies as those in which cultural elements were no longer subordinated to an "organic" whole.

11. Walter Benjamin, *Charles Baudelaire: A Lyric Poet in the Era of High Capitalism,* trans. Harry Zohn (London: NLB, 1973), pp. 167-68.

12. I tend to disagree with Esperanza Figueroa, who relates Casal's style to *art nouveau.* Casal does not subordinate all artistic elements to a central design, as *art nouveau* demands. See Esperanza Figueroa, "El cisne modernista," in *Estudios críticos sobre el modernismo,* ed. Homero Castillo (Madrid: Editorial Gredos, 1968), pp. 311-14.

13. Casal, "Verdad y poesía", in *Prosas,* II, 115-17.

14. Casal, "La moral del juguete," in *Prosas,* III, 96-100.

15. Casal, "Un hemisferio en una cabellera," in *Prosas,* III, 119.

16. Casal, *"En el cafetal,"* in *Prosas,* I, 222. Malpica, the writer whose novel Casal reviews, had translated Baudelaire into Spanish.

17. Marcel Ruff, *Baudelaire, L'Homme et l'œuvre* (Paris: Hatier-Boivin, 1955), p. 58.

18. Casal, "El hombre de las muletas de níquel," in *Prosas,* I, 233.

19. Casal, "Esteban Borrero Echeverría," in *Prosas,* I, 263.

20. Leo Bersani, *Baudelaire and Freud* (Berkeley: University of California Press, 1977), p. 110.

21. Casal, "Croquis femenino: Derrochadora," in *Prosas,* II, 147-48.

22. See Arturo Torres Ríoseco, "*À Rebours* and Two Sonnets of Julián del Casal," *Hispanic Review,* 23 (1955), 295-97.

23. See Robert Jay Glickman, "Julián del Casal: Letters to Gustave Moreau," *Revista Hispánica Moderna,* 37 (1972-1973), 101-35; and Glickman, *The Poetry of Julián del Casal, A Critical Edition,* II (Gainesville: University Presses of Florida, 1978), 180-87.

24. Glickman, *The Poetry of Julián del Casal,* II, 180.

25. Glickman, *The Poetry of Julián del Casal,* II, 187.

26. Glickman, *The Poetry of Julián del Casal,* II, 192.

27. Glickman, *The Poetry of Julián del Casal,* II, 192.

28. Glickman, *The Poetry of Julián del Casal,* II, 206.

29. Glickman, *The Poetry of Julián del Casal,* II, 207.

30. Julius Kaplan, *Gustave Moreau* (Los Angeles: Los Angeles County Museum of Art and New York Graphic Society, 1974), p. 34.

31. Kaplan, p. 95.

32. In his poem "En el campo," for example, at the same time that he rejects the natural, Casal portrays it with sensitivity.

33. Kaplan, p. 34.

34. Casal, *Prosas, Edición del Centenario,* III, 189.

35. Mario Praz, *The Romantic Agony,* trans. Angus Davidson, 2nd ed. (New York: Oxford University Press, 1970), p. 304.

36. In *À rebours* Des Esseintes broods upon the multiple symbolism of the lotus as a phallic symbol, an allegory of fertility, a symbol of "la danseuse, la femme mortelle, le Vase souillé, cause de tous les péchés et de tous les crimes." He also relates it to the embalming custom of ancient Egypt, in which lotus petals were inserted in the sexual organs of the corpses for the purpose of purification. Gladys Zaldívar accepts Juan Eduardo Cirlot's identification of the lotus as a "centro místico," which has the same evocations as the rose in Western culture, in the sense that Mary is called the Mystic Rose, an archetype of innocence and chastity. See Gladys Zaldívar, "Dos temas de la búsqueda metafísica," in *Julián del Casal: Estudios críticos sobre su obra* (Miami: Ediciones Universal, 1974), p. 144; and Juan Eduardo Cirlot,

Diccionario de símbolos tradicionales (Barcelona: Miracles, 1958), p. 270.

37. Zaldívar, p. 144.

38. Lee Fontanella has studied the absence of Parnassian *ekfrasis* in Casal's deeply personal interpretations of Moreau's paintings; see Lee Fontanella, "Parnassian Precept and a New Way of Seeing Casal's *Museo ideal*," *Comparative Literature Studies,* 7 (1970), 450-79.

39. Glickman, *The Poetry of Julián del Casal,* II, 212-13.

40. Ibid., pp. 211-12.

41. Glickman, *The Poetry of Julián del Casal: A Critical Edition,* I (Gainesville: The University Presses of Florida, 1976), 146. References to this volume of Glickman's three-volume critical edition will be cited as *Poetry,* I, within the body of this study. In "A la Belleza," in order to demobilize the threatening fantasies of the woman, Casal insists upon the non-sexual nature of Beauty: "Yo sé que eres más blanca que los cisnes, / más pura que los astros, / fría como las vírgenes y amarga / cual corrosivos ácidos."

42. "Salomé" was first published on September 21, 1890, in *La Habana Elegante.* "Elena" and "Galatea" were published in *La Habana Elegante* on August 2 and 9, 1891, respectively.

43. Reproduced in Glickman, *The Poetry of Julián del Casal,* II, 182.

44. Ibid., pp. 190-91.

45. Ibid., p. 190.

46. Ibid., p. 215.

47. Ibid., p. 288.

48. "Bénédiction" is the first poem in the collection *Spleen et idéal* at the beginning of *Les Fleurs du mal.*

49. Glickman, *The Poetry of Julián del Casal,* II, 288.

50. Cintio Vitier presumes that this poet is Baudelaire, "de cuyo ideario y sensibilidad . . . estaba tan penetrado Casal." See Cintio Vitier, "Casal como antítesis de Martí. Hastío, forma, belleza, asimilación y originalidad. Nuevos rasgos de lo cubano. 'El frío' y 'lo otro,'" in *Prosas, Edición del Centenario,* I, by Casal, p. 94.

51. Charles Baudelaire, "Notes nouvelles sur Edgar Poe," in *Nouvelles Histoires extraordinaires par Edgar Poe,* ed. M. Jacques Crépet (Paris: Louis Conard, 1933), p. xx.

52. Edgar Allan Poe, *Selected Works of Edgar Allan Poe,* ed. E. H. Davidson (Boston: Houghton Mifflin, 1956), p. 470.

53. Robert Mitchell Torrance, "Ideal and Spleen: The Failure of Transcendent Vision in Romantic, Symbolist and Modern Poetry," Diss. Harvard 1969, p. 112.

54. Ralph Waldo Emerson, "Nature," in *Selections from Ralph Waldo Emerson,* ed. Stephen E. Whicher (Boston: Houghton Mifflin, 1957), p. 32.

55. Emerson, "Nature," p. 32.

56. Emerson, "The Poet," in *Selections from Ralph Waldo Emerson,* p. 227.

57. The poems of *Rimas* were written while Casal was dying from the illness which would kill him before publication of the work could be completed. Not surprisingly, therefore, his personal suffering is reflected in the themes of illness, pain, and death which are repeated throughout the poetry. Esperanza Figueroa identifies Casal's illness as tuberculosis. See Esperanza Figueroa, "Comentario bibliográfico y rectificaciones," in *Julián del Casal: Estudios críticos sobre su obra,* pp. 18-21.

58. See Esperanza Figueroa, "Bibliografía cronológica de la obra de Julián del Casal," *Revista Iberoamericana,* 35 (1969), 398.

59. Casal, *Prosas,* I, 254. Corrections to the text have been based on the Antoine Adam edition of *Les Fleurs du mal* (Paris: Editions Garnier Frères, 1961), pp. 68-9.

60. Letter to Alfred De Vigny, in *Correspondance générale de Charles Baudelaire,* ed. Jacques Crépet, IV (Paris: Louis Conard, 1948), 9.

61. Ruff, p. 108. For additional discussions of the structure of *Les Fleurs du mal* see L. F. Benedetto, "L'Architecture des 'Fleurs de mal'," *Zeitschrift für französische Sprache und Literatur,* 39 (1912), 18-70; and Albert Feuillerat, "L'Architecture des *Fleurs du mal*," in *Studies by Members of the French Department of Yale University* (New Haven: Yale University Press, 1941), pp. 221-330.

62. Ruff, p. 121.

Oscar Montero (essay date 1995)

SOURCE: Montero, Oscar. "Julián del Casal and the Queers of Havana." In *¿Entiendes?*, edited by Emilie L. Bergmann and Paul Julian Smith, pp. 92-112. Durham: Duke University Press, 1995.

[In the following essay, Montero places some of the erotic images in Casal's writings within the context of the homosexual subculture of Cuba.]

By the end of the nineteenth century, the gentle re-proaches of cultural patriarch Andrés Bello about the "melindrosa y femenil ternura," [affected, feminine tenderness] and the "arrebatos eróticos," [erotic raptures] of certain writers had paradoxically hardened into the ambiguous aesthetic of *Modernismo,* nurtured on the one hand by the decadent, and often implicitly homo-erotic literatures of Europe and North America, and fueled on the other by the none too subtle homophobia of various discourses of national affirmation.[1] In the context of such discourses, founded and developed during the second half of the nineteenth century, the life and works of Cuban *modernista* Julián del Casal constitute a peculiar case. Casal's literary novelty and his position among the first *modernistas* are familiar; what is less clear, although it is a recurring topic among his readers, is Casal's role in the deviant side of a foundational erotics of politics, as Doris Sommer has aptly called it. The pages that follow review some of the more suggestive aspects of Casal's eroticism and tentatively frame it with the explicit evidence of a homosexual subculture flourishing in fin de siècle Havana.

Evidence of such a culture is found in two treatises dealing with prostitution and homosexuality in Havana around 1890. The first, *La prostitución en La Habana,* is a sociomedical treatise published by Dr. Benjamín Céspedes in 1888. The second treatise, an attack on Céspedes and his work, was published a year later by Pedro Giralt with the odd title of *El amor y la prostitución. Réplica a un libro del Dr. Céspedes* [*Love and Prostitution. Reply to a Book by Dr. Céspedes*]. The two treatises, a pseudo-scientific study and its moralizing response, very likely provoked a *crónica* published by Casal in *La Discusión* on 28 December 1889.[2] Casal's *crónica,* **"A través de la ciudad. El centro de dependientes"** [**"Throughout the City. The Center for Store Clerks"**] describes a visit to a residence for store clerks, one of the places of homosexual activity discussed in the treatises. The treatises in question outline a portrait of queer Havana that frames Casal's *crónica* and that may enrich, or even taint, a literary persona long frozen in aesthetic isolation.[3]

Questions concerning Casal's sexuality rose almost as soon as he began publishing, and comments about the peculiar eroticism of his work became a commonplace of literary histories; yet the relationship between the two has remained obscure, or at best oblique. Obscurity and obliqueness are not necessarily undesirable, though repeated references to the mystery surrounding Casal's sexuality have gone hand in hand with a canonization of his text as a brilliant, though marginal and unique parcel of *Modernismo*'s cultural monument. A tentative, perhaps controversial, and certainly provisional turn from that monument is in order. Suppose that the monument occupies Havana's main promenade around 1889; and in the evening, when the music plays, out come the queers, "*maricones*" and their "clients," marginal types who seem to circle the monolithic monument.

Any mention or allusion to Casal's sexuality has always carried the implication that it was not only aberrant in some way or other but radically unique. Whatever Casal was, he was the only one; it follows, or so the argument suggests, that Casal's work is at once brilliant and anomalous. Casal's secret is his alone. The founding gesture of homosexual panic, evident in the critical writings about Casal, is not really intolerance (Casal is admired for his poetic gifts etc.), but isolation: Casal is different, unique, as a poet and as an individual. The sexuality of Casal's body not only does not have a name but it is reduced to the category of the anomalous and the isolated. The psychological vocabulary used in a great deal of criticism (repression, sense of guilt, abnormality), has contributed to that isolation. Yet, independent of Casal, removed from the complex metaphoric web where illness, sexual preference, and literary production shift vertiginously to produce various readings, what was it like to be queer in Havana around 1890? If it is impossible, and perhaps unnecessary or undesirable, to out Casal (the hard evidence is certainly missing), it does seem pertinent to people the dreary isolation of his sexuality with other bodies, with some background noise as it were, provided by so-called hustlers, drag queens, pretty boys, and their bourgeois clients.

The frequent comments about the peculiarities of Casal's textual eroticism, and the sexuality that seems to nurture it, have gone hand in hand with a characteristic flight into what may be called the more readable, and more palatable, side of his "nature" and his writing, that is to say, his **"Nihilismo"** and his **"Neurosis,"** the titles of two of his best-known poems, which have been read as a rather narrow aesthetic credo, or more radically still, as the definitive expression of a vital ideology.[4] Along these same lines, Casal's tropical *mal de siècle* is somehow justified by his early death from an illness seemingly willed by the poet, a fitting ending for a morbid trinity of "isms": exoticism, eroticism, pessimism.

Whether well-intentioned or apologetic, Casal's first readers reveal a peculiar version of homosexual panic.[5] One of the most explicit versions of this panic, though not the only one, may be found in the portrait written by a contemporary of Casal, writer and polemist Manuel de la Cruz (1861-96). In the portrait written by De la Cruz for his *Cromitos cubanos* [*Cuban Sketches*], the contrast between a desired virility and Casal's ambiguous interior, the place of culture but also of abnormality and neurosis, is explicit.[6] Casal's often quoted definition of the modern writer as a "neurótico sublime, o un nihilista, o un blasfemo, o un desesperado" [a sublime neurotic, or a nihilist, or a blasphemer, or a desperado] deliberately and forcefully inverts the terms of national virility spelled out by De la Cruz.[7] Casal's rather militant swerving from a virile national discourse is backed by European models yet remains no less nationalistic, however peculiarly so. Nevertheless, the charges of De la Cruz and others have stuck; Casal's self-sublimation of neurosis has remained isolated and anomalous and for that reason perfectly coherent with *Modernismo*'s parceling of the aesthetic and correlative professionalization of the writer.[8]

Yet such parceling, however historically justified, seems to dampen the impact of Casal's neurotic sublime version of the writer, aesthetic in the etymological sense of the word, still touching the emotions and the senses, certainly mine at any rate. In a visit to one of the Centers for Clerks, accused of sheltering explicit homosexual practices, Casal, the neurotic sublime of his own definition of the artist, brushes what was on the streets of Havana at the time he wrote, c. 1890: that is, a full-blown queer culture, violently pushed to the edge by the scientific and moralizing discourses of professionals and pamphleteers, some of whom also doubled as readers of Casal and arbiters of culture in the emerging republic. Before taking it to the streets, so to speak, a brief aside on queer theory is in order.

Max Nordau, the popularizer of a homophobic version of decadence, wanted artistic representations to come into the "bright focal circle of consciousness" (61). By contrast, queer theory, because it flees, like Blanche at the bowling alley, from the merciless glare of such a cruel metaphor, may produce hazy results. Queer theory is "fuzzily defined, undercoded, or discursively dependent on more established forms" (Lauretis iii). Paradoxically, richly so one must add, Spanish American *modernismo* partakes of a double coincidence: on the one hand, it coincides with the development of nationalistic cultures, "ostensibly grounded in 'natural' heterosexual love" and marriage (Sommer 6); on the other hand, *Modernismo* may be said to be the founding moment of Spanish American literary queerness, inasmuch as an "against the grain," often willful marginality comes to be a part, if not the central part, of the new aesthetic, rejected by the likes of Manuel de la Cruz and embraced by Casal. The queer "revels in the discourse of the loathsome, the outcast, the idiomatically proscribed position of same-sex desire," the queer "attacks the dominant notion of the natural, is the taboo-breaker, the monstrous, the uncanny" (Case 3). At one point or another, so were most *modernistas,* but when the winds of homophobia blew their way, they lay their cards on the table and beat a hasty retreat; hence the other side of *Modernismo,* the cure, the antidote, the healing of the wound of European decadence, one of whose secrets was a newly named "perversion": homosexuality.

Casal was born in Havana in 1863, the son of a well-to-do Spanish immigrant and a Cuban woman of Irish and Spanish descent. By the time he was ten, whatever remained of what according to his biographers must have been a rather pleasant childhood was wiped out. 1868, the same year Casal's mother died, also marks the beginning of the first war for Cuban independence, ten years of battles and skirmishes that devastated the Cuban countryside; before the war ended, the father's business, and Casal's patrimony, lay in ruins. These biographical misfortunes form an anecdotal core used by generations of readers to anchor the recurring themes of physical decadence and moral defeat. Thus physical and spiritual exhaustion becomes the referent of what may be called the weariness of representation, the other side of creative desire, a commonplace of artistic modernity and certainly one of the salient characteristics of *Modernismo.*[9] The representation of the *mal de siècle* in *modernista* texts is frequently associated with the erotic, remarkably so in the work of Casal, whose erotic drift is backed by a vaguely defined sexual deviance, ambiguously though insistently named, and by illness. The pairing of sexual deviance and illness is of course common in the medicolegal systems worked out during the second half of the nineteenth century. Casal's case exemplifies the homophobic slant of discourses about sexuality and nationalism adapted to the Cuban situation: illness triumphs as a referent (Casal dies before his thirtieth birthday), while sexual deviance or uncertainty are eclipsed, though never silenced, becoming Casal's open secret.[10]

It is true that Casal's death was as dramatic as it was premature, seemingly staged like so many things about him, his room, his impoverished dandyism, the settings of his poems, and of course his elegant writing style. Having recovered from an almost deadly bout of high fevers, the result of a vaguely diagnosed lung ailment, Casal attended a soiree at a friend's house. Between puffs of his cigarette, a telling prop for a man in cigar-smoking Cuba, certainly so in 1893, he laughed at a joke, and the laughter turned into a vomit of blood that stained the white shirt front: a kind friend removed the still burning cigarette from Casal's fingers. The pose of the laughing smoker, vaguely erotic like everything about Casal, wedded to a horrible death, has become part of his literary legend: Eros meets Thanatos in the tropical night. Yet in the hands of his first critics, the force of Thanatos won out as if Casal had been meant to die, and somehow his death justified all of his poetry; he was "enamored of Thanatos," wrote Darío.[11] Whatever his sexual orientation, Casal's famous illness eclipses and in a sense excuses whatever deviance might have lurked in the lurid images of his writing. The reading of Casal's death as a predetermined aesthetic consequence of his writing is commonplace. There is no question that illness and imminent death are sources of imagery for Casal's poetry and prose, but the creative energy to bring this about must not be slighted. However, in the hands of friends and critics, the so-called morbid aspect of Casal's literary persona has been bound in the straitjacket of biographical causality, succeeding all too well in setting Casal and his work in a barren field, however exotic and attractive it might be.

Subsequent generations of critics would refer to the mystery of Casal's sexuality, ever veiled and ever suggestive of death. The tortured yet dazzling eroticism of Julián del Casal's writing is inevitably associated by an entrenched critical tradition with the mystery of that sexuality, repressed, death-driven, certainly neurotic. The evident culture-building aspect of his erotic literary representations is thus masked, and such a mask, or rather pall, enshrines Casal among the *modernistas* and at the same time robs him, and us, of an empowering legacy. A hundred years after Casal's death, the devastating reality of AIDS is made more bearable, and culturally more fruitful, when that legacy is appropriated, when its queer aspects are allowed to mirror, however speculatively, our own predicament. The web of lies generated by AIDS is countered by a rereading of Casal that would deliberately blur the traditional image of Casal as a rather marginal, however significant, *modernista*. This cultural speculation is what queer theory and, as far as I am concerned, what queer identity are about: to be permitted a cultural presence, to be subjects, however illusory that position might be, of culture rather than the objects of various attempts, old as the word "homosexuality" itself and as recent as the latest weekly rag, to find the causes of our so-called deviance.

In spite of the secret character of Casal's sexuality, references to it are plentiful; yet they are also repetitive, oscillating between the writer's biography and his work, both of which feed on and feed the secret of Casal's sexual identity, or more properly perhaps, his sexual orientation, either homosexuality or a quasi-masochistic asceticism. Max Nordau's famous definition of "degeneration" lurks in many of the comments made by Casal's early critics, not necessarily because they had read Nordau's treatise, which was published in 1892, but because they share the same sources, that is the naming and parceling of sexuality that is one of the strongest branches of scientific positivism.[12] In his biography of Casal, Emilio de Armas gives a summary of the question of sexuality in the legend about Casal. Referring to Casal's secret, Emilio de Armas writes, "sus amigos solían hablar de él en el tono de quienes comparten un secreto de iniciados" [his friends would speak about him in the hushed tones of those who share the secret of the initiates].[13] Casal's secret is "la extraña cosa / que te deje el alma helada" [the strange thing that will chill your soul] of his poem "Rondeles" [*Rondeaux*] which begins thus: "De mi vida misteriosa, / tétrica y desencantada, / oirás contar una cosa / que te deje el alma helada" [About my life, disenchanted, mys-

terious, and somber, you will hear something that may chill your soul].[14]

Another Casal critic, Mario Cabrera Saqui, writes apologetically that the poet was "un supertímido por la exagerada diferenciación de su instinto varonil, un tímido superior de la categoría de Amiel" (273) [a supertimid because of the exaggerated differentiation of his masculine instinct, a superior timid on the order of Amiel]. According to Carmen Poncet, Casal was "un tipo sicológicamente intersexual" [a psychologically intersexual type], one of those individuals possessing "un mecanismo sexual perfecto; pero que frecuentemente se inhiben por la falsa conciencia que experimentan de su capacidad" (35-40) [a perfect sexual mechanism, but who are inhibited by the false awareness they have of their abilities]. In other words, Casal had the right equipment but was afraid to use it, that is, afraid to use it as a heterosexual. It is certainly remarkable that Professor Poncet was able to assess the perfection of Casal's "sexual mechanism" nearly fifty years after his death. According to Argentine scholar José María Monner Sans, the issue should be closed; it is too complicated, he writes somberly, full of anecdotes and episodes. The stage is thus set for a safe, and not altogether unhasty, return to the text, to the representations of sexuality, enlightened or obscured as the case might be, by the secret in question. Thus any reading that mentions or skirts, as is often the case, the question of sexuality in Casal, or more properly the question of its textual representations, is predetermined by the ambiguous character of Casal's open secret. Certainly, its very ambiguity is one of the strands in Casal's work that still crackles and sears with the peculiar energy that went into its making. In Casal's case, temporarily turning from the text will hardly lead to the solving of a back fence riddle but rather will enrich an inexorable and desired return. So a detour is in order, a cruise around the square: it's 1889 and what's doing in Havana?

As it emerges in the writing of the day, treatises, newspaper stories, and literary texts, Havana was a busy, somewhat ragged, colonial capital, as cosmopolitan perhaps as much larger Latin American cities, but certainly limited in the geographical as well as the cultural sense of the word; it must have been, and still is, a hard city to get totally lost in. I know that Casal went by those same squares and sidewalks where men and women cruised. I cannot affirm, or deny, whether he rejected that marginal space or if he simply crossed the street, but in order to deal with what Lezama Lima called "el quitasol de un inmenso Eros" [the umbrella of a huge Eros] in his "Ode to Julián del Casal," in order to share the verses that say "Nuestro escandaloso cariño te persigue" [Our scandalous love pursues you], that transform the secret and the punishment woven around

Casal's sexuality into erotic sympathy, the presence of those others must be mentioned, those who cruised the periphery of Havana's squares.

The "problem" of homosexuality in the city is discussed in a chapter on male prostitution in Benjamín Céspedes's *La prostitución en La Habana*; Pedro Giralt deals with the topic throughout his irate reply, *El amor y la prostitución*. A useful aspect of the two works is their explicit vocabulary. At the same time, a series of complex metaphoric twists run from the body and its "sexually transmitted diseases" to the city and the national question, the question of the day among Cuban intellectuals. By contrast, in Casal's *crónica,* while vaguely but almost certainly alluding to one of the treatises, the relationship among the young clerks is described exclusively in terms of friendship and fraternity not of course in sexual terms. The rather elaborate description of the main room of the residence takes up almost half of the brief article. Casal's version shows the nature of the censorship in the press where he published much of his works or perhaps the limits that the writer imposed on himself. It also shows that the sublimation at work in the *crónica,* rather than merely repressive, is also fruitfully subjective: in other words, self-sublimation is also self-representation, a cultural practice that is subtly yet powerfully opposed to the insistent objectivity of the scientific and political treatises that deal with the clerks' deviant sexuality.

If Dr. Céspedes discusses sexuality from the point of view of a physician and sociologist, Giralt replies by condemning the moral implication of such an analysis. Both consider the body of the homosexual as the grotesque referent of a number of maladies. In his prologue to the Céspedes book, Enrique José Varona, an early Casal critic and one of the most prominent literary and political figures of the day, praises it because "nos invita a acercarnos a una mesa de disección, a contemplar al desnudo úlceras cancerosas, a descubrir los tejidos atacados por el virus" (xi) [it invites us to approach a dissecting table, to gaze at the exposed cancerous sores, to discover the tissues attacked by the virus]. Varona prefaces the doctor's sociomedical treatise by deploying the prestigious metaphor of social disorder as illness; he moves seamlessly from the tissues on the doctor's table to the city: in both cases dissection is not only useful but necessary because pointing out the locus of disease somehow marks the beginning of the healing process.

The distancing maneuvers are significant, and Dr. Céspedes uses a common device: he did not himself examine the young pederast; he is merely reporting on the examination conducted by an anonymous learned colleague. In a chapter titled "La prostitución masculina" [Male Prostitution], there is a detailed description of the city's queer underworld. The following paragraph pre-

sents a fundamental definition of homosexuality, an "aberration" that is repeatedly compared to prostitution, in other words, not the aberration of an individual or a group of individuals, but a highly socialized phenomenon that threatens the rest of the populace:

> Y aquí en la Habana, desgraciadamente, subsisten con más extensión de lo creíble y con mayor impunidad que en lugar alguno, tamañas degradaciones de la naturaleza humana; tipos de hombres que han invertido su sexo para traficar con estos gustos bestiales, abortos de la infamia que pululan libremente, asqueando a una sociedad que se pregunta indignada, ante la invasión creciente de la plaga asquerosa; si abundando tanto pederasta, habrán también aumentado los clientes de tan horrendos vicios.
>
> (190)

> [And unfortunately here in Havana, there subsist, more extensively than one may believe and with greater impunity than anywhere else, enormous degradations of human nature; types of men who have inverted their sex in order to traffic in bestial desires, abortions of infamy teeming freely among us, revolting our society, which facing the growing invasion of such a disgusting plague, asks with outrage if the abundance of so many pederasts does not also signal an increase in the number of clients for such horrible vices.]

Dr. Céspedes comments on the relationship between homosexuals and prostitutes, but much more disturbing is the presence of the so-called clients, suggesting the sort of exchange that has transformed the capital "en una de esas ciudades sodomíticas [into one of those sodomitic cities] an insular version of decadent Rome. The doctor divides pederasts into three groups: "el negro, el mulato y el blanco" [negroes, mulattos, and whites]. Classifying is of course a way to insist on scientific objectivity and to distance the observer from a supposedly marginal group that nevertheless appears to be spread throughout the entire city: "repartidos en todos los barrios de la Habana" [spread throughout all the neighborhoods of Havana]. Like prostitutes or vampires, "por la noche se estacionan en los puntos más retirados del Parque y sus alrededores más solitarios" [at night they stake out the periphery of the Square and its more isolated surroundings]. There follows a description of the "effeminate pederast," also archetypal. It could apply to decadent Rome or to the New York of tomorrow:

> Durante las noches de retreta circulan libremente confundidos con el público, llamando la atención, no de la policía, sino de los concurrentes indignados, las actitudes grotescamente afeminadas de estos tipos que van señalando cínicamente las posaderas erguidas, arqueados y ceñidos los talles, y que al andar con menudos pasos de arrastre, se balancean con contoneos de mujer coqueta. Llevan flequillos en la frente, carmín en el rostro y polvos de arroz en el semblante, ignoble y fatigado de los más y agraciado en algunos. El pederasta responde a un nombre de mujer en la jerga del oficio.
>
> (191)

[When the band plays in the evening, they walk about freely, mingling with the populace; the grotesquely effeminate gestures of these types call the attention, not of the police, but of the outraged gathering; they walk cynically showing off their prominent buttocks, their waist arched and cinched, walking with small, mincing steps, swaying this way and that like a flirtatious woman. They wear bangs on their foreheads, rouge and rice powder on their face, ignoble and worn for the most part yet charming among some others. In the slang of their trade, pederasts go by a woman's name.]

The repulsion that one is asked to feel before the archetypical stereotype of the effeminate homosexual is undermined by the mention of the charming faces among them. Dr. Céspedes goes on to say that some of them have a favorite lover and that they celebrate parties among themselves, where they "mimic" (*fingen*) births and baptisms. From the point of view of the doctor, this mimicking of heterosexuality at its most "natural," birth, and its most sacred, baptism, is particularly repellent.[15] Following the lead of nineteenth-century sociology, particularly echoing Lombroso's physiognomically typed offenders, the doctor links homosexual behavior with criminality and disease; yet because of his scientific objectivity, he avoids making an explicit moral judgment, adding that "no siempre son pasivos en sus relaciones sexuales" [they are not always passive in their sexual relations] and sometimes "se prestan a ser activos" [lend themselves to an active role]. Dr. Céspedes's description proves that the practice of homosexual acts, at least among men in late-nineteenth-century Havana, was a relatively public, fully socialized affair. The fact that such practices are never mentioned, never explicitly so at any rate, by Casal, or any of the writers grouped around the journal *La Habana Elegante,* only confirms the transgressive character of such practices and the need to keep them secret, that is to say unwritten about except in sociomedical treatises. It is important to point out that the dominant strategy of suppression is to keep homosexuality out of written texts not classified as legal or medical, which is to say to keep it out of literature. By contrast, as will be seen in the comments on Giralt's response to Dr. Céspedes, homosexuality, particularly as it affected the relationship between the urban elite and the working classes, was the talk of the town.

The "vice" described by Dr. Céspedes has another privileged location, the communal residences of young apprentices and clerks, many of them recent arrivals from Spain. The chapter on male prostitution concludes with the report of an interview with a young clerk, approximately fifteen years of age, who visits the doctor because he says he may be "dañado por dentro" [hurt inside]. The doctor tells him he has a "chancro infectante sifilítico," an [infectious, syphilitic sore] and then goes on to describe the boy: "noté lo afeminado de su rostro, tan agraciado como el de cualquier mujer, y lo redondo y mórbido de sus formas de adolescente" [I noticed his effeminate face, as charming as that of any woman, and the morbid roundness of his adolescent body], "morbid" of course in the double sense of "soft and delicate" and "diseased or causing disease." The word is one of the key adjectives of the various discourses on decadence and signals illness as well as "erotomania" and "egomania," Nordau's double-headed *bête noire.*

The interview with the boy reveals another aspect of the queer life of the period. In the residence for clerks where he lives, some of the men caress him and "hacían conmigo ciertos manejos" [they did certain things with me]. "Con casi todos" [with most of them], he admits. The boy then says that they hit him ("me pegaban") and goes on to say that the men "me besaban y me cogían de la mano y yo tenía que hacerles" [they kissed me and they took my hand and I had to do it with them or to them]. Among the faceless "all of them," there is a remarkable exception. The boy says that "Habían [*sic*] dos que dormían juntos, pero a esos se les miraba con más respeto" [There were two who slept together, and they were looked upon with more respect]. The gay boy is abused by men whose sexual identity is not in question because their sexually active role simultaneously ratifies their heterosexuality and masks the evident homosexuality of their acts. In this violent setting, the boy's mention of two men who slept together, and were thus respected as a couple, is remarkably moving. Faced with what must have been the daunting authority of the doctor, this nameless boy manages to point to a homosexual role model, as if to add its worth to the doctor's scientific diagnosis. In other words, in the interview with the doctor, quoted verbatim by Dr. Céspedes and probably conducted by him in the first place, the references to the grotesque and the sick are countered by the respect of a group of men for a gay couple who slept together. As for the person in charge of the residence, he is as indifferent as the police and "con tal de no aflojar dinero, en lo demás no se mete en esas cosas feas" (194) [as long as he didn't have to shell out any money, he didn't get mixed up in those ugly things], which suggests the relative tolerance toward the sexual practices in the residence.

Though referring only to "pederasty," Dr. Céspedes reproduces the two fundamental aspects of the original definition of homosexuality:[16] on the one hand, it is a disease with identifiable symptoms, especially when the body, as in the case of the boy in the interview, is marked by "sores" etc.; on the other hand, as the corporal metaphor broadens its scope, it is a social disease that "infects" the rest of the healthy political body, the same metaphoric slippage harrowingly at work in current AIDS phobia. The somatic metaphors have an evident source in the boy's body; but even before the interview, such anthropomorphic metaphors are applied to the city, in the same way that they are applied to the decadent aspects of Casal's work. In the description of queer life in Havana, the metaphoric web deployed by the doctor, and by Varona in his prologue, is at one with the epistemology of the period. It is in fact the common denominator of discourses dealing with illness and homosexuality, as well as with various symbolic practices, specifically literature, which is decadent when it favors "external adornment," Nordau's expression, in short when it does not signify clearly. Nordau repeatedly refers to the decadents' failure to grasp "the phenomenon of the universe" (266) and to their obsession with form and ornament, which are supposedly devoid of meaning. This is the crux of Varona's founding, extremely influential, criticism of Casal's work: too precious for its own good and certainly not good for the republic, neither the culturally sound Cuban republic of letters nor the yet-to-be-founded political republic.

Dr. Céspedes locates homosexuality between disease and symbolic practice. Pederasts are depraved beings, marked by the symptoms of disease. They also mimic the social behavior that defined "woman" at the time, particularly woman as prostitute: they wear makeup and sway as they walk.[17] The setting described by Dr. Céspedes is absolutely marginal. Homosexuals live in dens, and although they cruise the heart of the city, they confine themselves to the periphery of its square and to the late evening hours. Dr. Céspedes's pederasts are marginal not only because of their sexual preference but because of their social class, which he hastens to define by lumping together career criminals, "dirty alcoholics," and hairdressers and "maids" of prostitutes. The clerks of the guild residences are foreigners for the most part and dangerously close to the class in question; besides, the doctor asserts, their living conditions tend to foster aberrant same-sex practices. Except in the passing, though alarmed, mention of the clients, the class of intellectuals and professionals, such as the doctor himself, is beyond the reach of the marginal group, thus reified in the name of science and presented as an object of study, a monstrosity in a natural history museum. The nature of the solution finally offered by the doctor is neither moral nor psychological, but social: "mancebos célibes" [celibate young men] should not be lodged in phalansteries, where the absence of women must lead them to "incontinencia bestial entre hombres" (195) [bestial incontinence among men].

Dr. Céspedes's *La prostitución en La Habana* had an almost immediate answer. They year after the study's publication Pedro Giralt y Alemán published *El amor y la prostitución. Réplica a un libro del Dr. Céspedes* [*Love and Prostitution. Reply to a Book by Dr. Céspedes*]. Giralt defends the virility of the clerks and accuses Dr. Céspedes of being an anti-European charlatan. Giralt's book unwittingly broadens the scope of homosexuality in the colonial capital. He rants about the "vices" of the bourgeoisie and the professional classes, specifically the *criollo* class. According to Giralt, the doctor is "hombre vulgarísimo y completamente inepto para especular seriamente en los altos y sublimes principios de la Ciencia [a most vulgar man, totally inept for the serious study of the lofty, sublime principles of Science]. He goes on to say that the doctor has blamed an entire social group for the isolated defects of one individual, namely the young boy interviewed by the doctor (83). In his angry pamphlet, Giralt attacks the "fanaticism of *criollismo*," because he believes that the doctor has suggested that prostitution and homosexuality are European vices that have contaminated the island's national aspirations. In other words, barely five years before the second war of independence, Cuban nationalists or *criollistas* wrongly blame Europe, specifically a hated Spain, for the queering of the capital, so goes Giralt's argument. Giralt's name-calling defense merely turns the table: you Cubans, especially bourgeois professionals, are the queers, not the poor immigrant boys trying to survive in their new home, even if such survival means an occasional sexual transaction with one of the hated clients, the real villains in Giralt's diatribe.[18]

Giralt's argument has no rhyme or reason, but his vigorous mudslinging is enlightening. He drags the doctor's scientific study into the debate about nationalism that was the order of the day. Giralt turns his ire not on the pederasts but on their clients, who are not clerks but *criollo* members of the urban elite:

> ¿Cómo calificaremos, pues, a estos pederastas activos y *paganos* que van o iban a solicitar a los *maricones* para *ocuparlos* pagándoles con dinero? No obstante estos, más culpables que los *pasivos,* no han sido deportados, y se están paseando por las calles de la Habana. ¿Serán dependientes? ¡Ah, si se pudiera decir ciertas cosas que la vergüenza pública prohibe revelar; si fuera lícito contar con nombres y apellidos ciertas historias íntimas y secretas cuyos detalles se cuentan *sotto voce* por los corrillos; las confidencias de algunas mujeres a sus comadres y de éstas a sus íntimos, aparecerían a la luz del sol con toda su repugnante fealdad más de cuatro entes, al parecer bien educados, que llevan levita y ocupan señalados puestos.

> (emphasis in the original, 83-85)

[How should we label these active, pagan pederasts who pursue these queers in order to pay them for their services? They are more to blame than the *passive* ones, yet they have not been deported, and they walk the streets of Havana with impunity. Are they clerks? Oh, if only one could say certain things that public decency forbids us to reveal, if it were lawful to name certain names, and certain intimate, secret stories whose details are told *sotto voce* here and there, what women whisper to their friends (*comadres*), and what these in turn whisper to others, the repugnant ugliness of more than one apparently well-educated so-and-so, who wears coat and tie and goes to a respectable job, would be forced into the light of day.]

Giralt is up on the latest back-fence gossip in colonial Havana, and he wants nothing less than to out the professional *criollos,* whose vice is that much more repugnant because they practice it out of choice not out of need, as do some of the poor boys described by the doctor. As opposed to Dr. Céspedes's attempts to sound scientific, Giralt is refreshingly explicit in his pamphleteering: the people in question are queers, "*maricones.*" His comments reveal that homosexuality was not at all marginal; what makes a homosexual marginal is his class, not his sexual preference. The less fortunate ones, those from the working classes, are deported to the Isle of Pines, but their clients stroll about freely because their good name, their education, in short their social class, the class of those who "wear a frock coat and occupy distinguished posts," protect them. Giralt's defense of "the honest, suffering class of store clerks" suggests the breadth and complexity of homosexual and homosocial practices in the Havana of 1889.[19] Moreover, if Giralt's challenge to Céspedes's scientific authority is chaotic and illogical, it also rejects the body of the boy examined by the doctor as the source of an ambiguous metaphoric web and transforms the question of homosexuality into a sociopolitical contrast between classes: on the one hand, the working classes, in this case made up for the most part of recently arrived Spanish immigrants; on the other, the local professional bourgeoisie, which controlled the local press and, as did Casal, often directed more or less veiled attacks at the colonial authorities.

Casal's *crónica,* "A través de la ciudad, El Centro de Dependientes" ["Throughout the City. The Center for Store Clerks"]

was published under the pseudonym of Hernani on 28 December 1889; it was written after a visit to the Center, located on the top floors of the building that housed the Albizu theater. The Center was one of many *centros, liceos* and *colonias,* social and residential guilds that spread throughout the island for the purpose of housing the newly arrived work force and in many cases teaching various skills to its members. Casal describes the conditions that drove the young men to abandon their homeland, the effort of their toil and the way in which many of them are integrated into Cuban society. The Center's secretary guides the visitor through the various rooms, which compose a true phalanstery with reading halls and classrooms, where the members have free access to the curriculum of a business school.

Céspedes's book was published in 1888, and Giralt's the following year. Casal returned from a brief stay in Madrid, his only travel outside of Cuba, during January 1889. It is highly improbable that he did not know of the two books, one of them with a prologue by the prominent Enrique José Varona, who was to write reviews of Casal's own books.[20] More than likely, Casal was given the assignment of writing a *crónica* for *La*

Discusión in order to smooth over the debate between *criollos* and *peninsulares,* that is between pro-independence nationalists and supporters of Spanish rule. Giralt's attack on Dr. Céspedes had dragged the thorny issue of sexual deviance into the debate, and Casal's *crónica* must also gloss over the allegations about the clerks' sexual practices.

Casal writes that he is driven by curiosity; he wants to gather "los datos que reclamaba nuestra insaciable curiosidad" (2:18) [the facts required by our insatiable curiosity]. It is unlikely that a mere residence for clerks would have provoked much curiosity, certainly not an "insatiable curiosity." The gossip about the two pamphlets and the sexual doings of the clerks and their so-called clients must have been the topic of conversation in what is still a rather chatty, extroverted city. Significantly however, Casal's curiosity for the facts leads to silence. Unlike other *crónicas* where the subjective reaction of the writer is almost immediately present, the *crónica* about the Center reads more like a reporter's account of the scene of a crime. The Center is absolutely empty, except for the neutral presence of its secretary, a hazily outlined third party.

In order to show that the lurid details mentioned by the boy interviewed in *La prostitución en La Habana* are not the norm, Giralt refers to the "strict discipline" maintained at the Centers and to the fact that "está prohibido hablar de política" [it is forbidden to talk about politics]. Casal almost quotes Giralt when he writes that at the Center "está permitido hablar de todo menos de política" [one may speak about anything except politics], and he goes on to describe the love among the young men in terms of sympathy and friendship:

> ¿No es más agradable comunicarse sus ensueños de riqueza y sus proyectos para lo porvenir? ¿No es más bello recordar la patria lejana, donde se ha pasado la infancia y donde hay seres queridos que nos aguardan? De este modo ¿no se obtiene más pronto el fin apetecido, que es el de estrechar cada día más los lazos de cariño, simpatía y amistad entre los dependientes?
>
> (2:19)

> [Is it not more agreeable for them to share their dreams of wealth and their projects for the future? Is it not more beautiful to remember the distant homeland, the place of their childhood, where there are loved ones awaiting us? This way, is not the cherished goal more quickly obtained, that is, to bind more strongly the ties of love, sympathy and friendship among the clerks?]

If the doctor pointed to the sores in the boy's ass, a clear sign of the activities at the Centro, Casal sentimentalizes the relationships among the men who live there. On the one hand, one may recall the respect for the couple who slept together, mentioned by the boy, and the possibility of sentimentalizing such a relationship, in other words, of placing it beyond the doctor's scientific hold; on the other hand, one should point to the strong current of sentimentality in *Modernismo,* a version of the tradition of sensibility rooted in the eighteenth century and later exemplified by Spanish poet Gustavo Adolfo Bécquer and French poet François Coppée, both admired by the *modernistas.*

Modernismo's tradition of sentimentalism retreated before its ultimately triumphant formalism, the good side of *Modernismo,* bequeathed to the various avant-gardes. Yet in the homophobic setting of fin de siècle Havana, sentimentalism, rather than just quaintly maudlin, may be a strategy of survival; oblique, sentimental appeals to the reader defer self-representation and the representation of others, and this deferral is both our loss and our gain. On the one hand, Casal's unwillingness or inability to deal frontally with his sexuality and that of the clerks robs us, queers of today, of a potentially empowering legacy; on the other, the sentimentalism and deliberate pathos that at times characterize his style must be considered in the context of other representational strategies that have fared better in the critical tradition, namely, his unquestionable formal mastery. As queer readers, our task may be to superimpose loss and gain, to find our identity not only in the affirmative proclamation of same-sex desire but also in its various disguises: in the sentimental appeals to the reader as well as in the fabulously masked, exotically draped, richly embossed *modernista* image brilliantly created by Casal, the Helen of his **"Museo"** to linger briefly on just one: "Envuelta en veste de opalina gasa, / recamada de oro . . . indiferente a lo que en torno pasa, / mira Elena hacia el lívido horizonte, / irguiendo un lirio en la rosada mano" (*1*:118) [Wrapped in a vestment of opalescent gauze, / embroidered in gold . . . indifferent to what is happening around her, / Helen looks toward the livid horizon, / raising a lily in her rosy hand].

If in the poetry, the image of the draped, ambiguously sexed body triumphs, in Casal's *crónica* about the store clerks, the body of the boy in the doctor's interview, with its sores, but also with its "morbid" shape and attractive face, disappears. Yet Casal's other *crónicas,* as well as his poetry and fiction, teem with bodies, arabesque of sores at the doctor's office, flying bodies at the circus, the lapidary flesh of the heroes in the museum. At the circus, the body of an acrobat becomes a "símbolo viviente," a "living symbol" in a remarkable slippage between choreography and writing. In Casal's **"Museo"** an ever-present erotic gaze seems to convulse the rigid statuary: Prometheus, "marmóreo, indiferente y solitario, / sin que brote el gemido de su boca" (*1*:116) [marmoreal, indifferent and solitary, / never a moan issuing from his mouth]; and Polyphemus, "mirando aquella piel color de rosa, / incendia la lujuria su ojo verde" (*1*:117) [gazing at that rosy skin, / lechery his green eye sets aflame]. By contrast, in the *crónica* about the Center, the emptiness of the place is remarkable.

The clerks are lost in an abstract, bodiless plural as if the love, sympathy and friendship among them depended on their very absence, somehow compensated by an abundance of signifiers describing in detail the decorations of the interior, rather an interior within an interior, for the great hall contains "un teatrito precioso, alegre como una pajarera y reluciente como una caja de juguetes" (*2*:19) [a precious little theater, happy as a bird cage and shining like a toy box]. The aesthetic reduction of the large hall is breathless, almost violent, as if to close itself off from the possible entrance of a body. In the broadest sense, such a reduction glosses over the bodies that were there. The eye is fixed on the ornamentation of the walls, decorated with *panneaux,* which in turn contain Venetian mirrors, draped and tasseled. In the middle of the great hall, perhaps peopled by the very young men who are the subjects of the two pamphlets, the roving eye and the subjectivity that it signals seem to seek refuge in that "precious little theater," in turn reduced first to a "bird cage" then to a "toy box." What cannot be named in the *crónica* is not only homosexuality or pederasty; it is the erotic body, which must be aesthetically transformed, which must be moved to another register. In other words, it must be represented in a different way, in other places, by its very absence in "a precious little theater," or by its contortions at the circus, frozen in the statuary of the **"Museo"** deformed by disease, transformed into a vision of terrible beauty set in privileged, distant, aesthetic places, that is, represented as symbolic sublimation, where any reading must inexorably return.[21]

That return to the text, however, is now tainted by the echo of those queers, drag queens, and clients of fin de siècle Havana, transformed into objects of study and scorn by the sociologist-doctor and the moralizing pamphleteer. The morbidness of a boy's body, radically distanced by the doctor, now echoes the morbidness of Casal's style, radically distanced by a critical tradition, always thought to possess a masterful upper hand and certainly the last word when it comes to Casal. Little matter whether he so much as exchanged a greeting with the queers in Havana's main square. They inhabited his city and will lend their choral presence to any subsequent reading. Thus, though never fully open, the door to Casal's interior, to the transgressive nature of his eroticism, aesthetically distanced, deliberately veiled by the signifiers of draping and adornment, ever suggestive in its homoerotic imagery, is invitingly ajar.

Notes

1. Bello, "Juicio sobre las obras poéticas de Don Nicasio Alvarez de Cienfuegos," *Obras completas* 9:210.

2. *Prosas* 2:17-20. All subsequent references to Casal's *Prosas* will be given parenthetically. Unless otherwise noted, all translations are mine. I

thank Emilie Bergmann, whose comments were so helpful during the revision and rewriting of this paper. Part of my research on Casal has been funded by a grant from the Professional Staff Congress of the City University of New York, whom I also thank.

3. Some critics, notably Cintio Vitier and Emilio de Armas, have sought to counteract the aesthetic marginality imposed on Casal: Vitier by affirming Casal's sincerity and the power of that very isolation; de Armas by reading Casal in the context of Cuba's oppressive political and cultural climate. Both approaches are illuminating, but they don't challenge the premise of isolation imposed on Casal's aestheticism, grounded on the commonplace that states that the "superficial" aspects of Casal's work and of *modernismo* inexorably lead to an aesthetic, and implicitly a moral, impasse.

4. "Read 'Nihilismo' and you will see how sincere was the poet's desire for death," writes Anderson Imbert in his influential *Historia de la literatura hispanoamericana* 206.

5. The term has been fruitfully reactivated by Sedgwick; Marjorie Garber points out that it was coined by Dr. Edward Kempf in 1920 "to describe the fear fostered by same-sex contiguity in army camps, prisons, monasteries, boarding schools" (137); and Centers for Clerks in fin de siècle Havana, one might add.

6. The contrast between Manuel de la Cruz's "virile," patriotic exterior and Casal's problematic, and implicitly deviant, interior is discussed by Agnes Lugo-Ortiz, "Patologizar el interior" 162-166. I thank Agnes for sending me a copy of her manuscript. The *modernista* interior as the autotelic place of luxury and pleasure is contrasted to the museum as the imposition of order over nature by Aníbal González 33ff.

7. Casal's definition is from his *busto* of José Fornaris (1827-90), *Prosas* 1:275-80; significantly, Fornaris was one of the founders of *Siboneísmo*, the poetry of national affirmation, thrown in the face of colonial oppression. See Vitier's "Fifth Lesson," *Lo cubano en la poesía* 131-79.

8. On the parceling of the aesthetic in *Modernismo*, see Angel Rama, *La ciudad letrada* 164-71, and "El poeta frente a la modernidad," *Literatura y clase social* 78-143.

9. Akin to what Terry Eagleton calls Schopenhauer's "death of desire."

10. On the open secret in the context of the binary oppositions of the second half of the nineteenth century, see Sedgwick 67-90.

11. From Darío's prologue to the poems of Manuel Pichardo, quoted by Monner Sans 257-58.

12. If for Bataille eroticism is always transgressive, for Foucault it operates inexorably within the "machinery of power." As Casal's case suggests, however, it is perhaps less a question of a radical polarization between transgression and the powers that defuse it than a drift, Wilde's "to drift with every passion," taken from the early Pater. See Richard Ellman's introduction to *The Artist as Critic* ix-xviii.

13. The comments by De Armas summarize most of the critical references to a "conflict [in Casal] whose origin is sexual," although Casal's erotic life remains "draped in total darkness." See 32-41 of the sensitive, well-documented biography by De Armas.

14. *Rimas, The Poetry of Julián del Casal* 1:209. All subsequent references to this edition of Casal's poetry will be given parenthetically.

15. The role of such theatrics in the building of gay and lesbian culture is discussed by Judith Butler and Marjorie Garber, respectively.

16. On the development of the term "homosexuality," see Chauncey.

17. In the *Crónica Médico-Quirúrgica de la Habana* 16 (1890): 79-81, in a section titled "Pederasty in Havana," a Dr. Montané notes, as does Dr. Céspedes, that "pederasts" wear makeup and otherwise adorn themselves; he also mentions "their strange taste for perfumes and bright objects, their monomania for photographs, in which they appear [*en las que se hacen representar*] in theatrical costumes or in women's dresses." The doctor circulated "among the members of the Congress" he is addressing "some samples he was able to procure," seemingly of photographs, perhaps still kept in some archive in Havana. I am grateful to George Chauncey for the gift of a photocopy of the pages cited. For discussion of similar photographs in Argentina, see Jorge Salessi in this volume.

18. On active-passive roles in Mexico and Latin America, see Almaguer, and Murray and Dynes. Significantly, the ubiquitous and persistent active-passive pairing seems to be threatened by Dr. Céspedes's objectivity—not all were passive who seemed so, he says. Giralt, however, insists on it, though he damns the "active" ones more than their "victims."

19. The political implications of class divisions in the gay population of 1889 Havana are no less significant today and are particularly pertinent in a Latin American and Latino context. For a suggestive discussion of homosexuality and class among Chicano men and in contemporary Mexico, see Almaguer and Blanco, respectively.

20. Varona wrote a review of Casal's first book of poems, *Hojas al viento,* for *Revista Cubana* (May 1890), and a review of his second book, *Nieve,* for the same publication (August 1892). The first is included in *Prosas,* and both are included in *The Poetry of Julián del Casal.* Casal in turn dedicated one of his "*bustos*" to the formidable *homme de lettres,* who wrote a moving eulogy after Casal's death, also in *The Poetry of Julián del Casal.*

21. On Casal's "museo ideal" and on his visit to the circus, see my *Erotismo y representación en Julián del Casal* (Amsterdam: Editions Rodopi, 1993).

Works Cited

Almaguer, Tomás. "Chicano Men: A Cartography of Homosexual Identity and Behavior." *Differences* 3.2 (1991): 75-100.

Anderson Imbert, Enrique. *Historia de la literatura hispanoamericana.* 1st ed. México: Fondo de Cultura Económica, 1954.

Armas, Emilio de. *Casal.* La Habana: Letras Cubanas, 1981.

Bataille, Marcel. *Erotism: Death and Sensuality.* Trans. Mary Dalwood. 1957; San Francisco: City Lights Books, 1986.

Bello, Andrés. "Juicio sobre las obras poéticas de Don Nicasio Alvarez de Cienfuegos." *La Biblioteca Americana* I (London, 1823): 35-50. In *Obras completas.* 22 vols. Caracas: Ministerio de Educación, 1951-1969. 1956; 9:197-213.

Blanco, José Joaquín. "Ojos que da pánico soñar." *Función de medianoche.* México: Era, 1981. 183-90.

Butler, Judith. *Gender Trouble: Feminism and the Subversion of Identity.* New York: Routledge, 1990.

Cabrera Saqui, Mario. "Julián del Casal." *Poesías.* By Julián del Casal. Edición del Centenario. La Habana: Consejo Nacional de Cultura, 1963. 265-87.

Casal, Julián del. *The Poetry of Julián del Casal.* Ed. Robert J. Glickman. 3 vols. Gainesville: University of Florida Press, 1978.

———. *Prosas.* Edición del Centenario. 4 vols. La Habana: Consejo Nacional de Cultura, 1963.

Case, Sue-Ellen. "Tracking the Vampire." *Differences* 3.2 (1991): 1-20.

Céspedes, Benjamín. *La prostitución en La Habana.* La Habana: Tipografía O'Reilly, 1888.

Chauncey, George. "From Sexual Inversion to Homosexuality." *Salmagundi* 58-59 (1982-83): 114-46.

Cruz, Manuel de la. "Julián del Casal." *Cromitos cubanos.* 1892; Madrid: Calleja, 1926. 229-43.

Eagleton, Terry. *The Ideology of the Aesthetic.* Oxford: Basil Blackwell, 1990.

Foucault, Michel. *The History of Sexuality. Volume I: An Introduction.* Trans. Robert Hurley. New York: Vintage, 1980.

Garber, Marjorie. *Vested Interests. Cross-dressing and Cultural Anxiety.* New York: Routledge, 1992.

Giralt, Pedro. *El amor y la prostitución. Réplica a un libro del Dr. Céspedes.* La Habana: La Universal, 1889.

González, Aníbal. *La crónica modernista hispanoamericana.* Madrid: José Porrúa Turranzas, 1983.

Lauretis, Teresa de. "Queer Theory: Lesbian and Gay Sexualities: An Introduction." *Differences* 3.2 (1991): iii-xviii.

Lezama Lima, José. *Poesía completa.* La Habana: Instituto del Libro, 1970.

Lugo-Ortiz, Agnes I. *Identidades imaginadas: biografía y nacionalidad en Cuba 1860-1898.* Diss. Princeton University, 1990.

Monner Sans, José María. *Julián del Casal y el modernismo hispanoamericano.* México: El Colegio de México, 1952.

Montané, Dr. (?). "La pederastia en La Habana." *Crónica Médico-Quirúrgica de la Habana* 16 (1890): 79-81.

Murray, Stephen O., and Wayne Dynes. "Hispanic Homosexuals: Spanish Lexicon." *Male Homosexuality in Central and South America.* Ed. Stephen O. Murray. Gai Saber Monograph. San Francisco: Instituto Obregón, 1987.

Nordau, Max. *Degeneration.* 1892; New York: Appleton, 1895.

Poncet, Carmen. "Dualidad de Casal." *Revista Bimestre Cubana* 53 (1944): 193-212.

Rama, Angel. *La ciudad letrada.* Hanover, N.H.: Ediciones del Norte, 1984.

———. *Literatura y clase social.* Mexico: Folios Ediciones, 1983.

Sedgwick, Eve Kosofsky. *Epistemology of the Closet.* Berkeley: University of California Press, 1990.

Sommer, Doris. *Foundational Fictions: The National Romances of Latin America.* Berkeley: University of California Press, 1991.

Varona, Enrique José. "*Hojas al viento*: Primeras poesías. Por Julián del Casal," *La Habana Elegante,* 1 June 1890. In *The Poetry of Julián del Casal* 2:421-23; and in Casal, *Prosas* 1:26-29.

———. "*Nieve.* Por Julián del Casal. Habana 1892." *Revista Cubana* 16 (August 1892): 142-46. In *The Poetry of Julián del Casal* 2:436-39.

———. "Julián del Casal." *Revista Cubana* 18 (October 1893): 340-41. In *The Poetry of Julián del Casal* 2:413.

Vitier, Cintio. *Crítica sucesiva*. La Habana: Contemporáneos, 1971.

———. *Lo cubano en la poesía*. La Habana: Instituto del Libro, 1970.

Wilde, Oscar. *The Artist as Critic: Critical Writings of Oscar Wilde*. Ed. Richard Ellman. New York: Random House, 1968.

FURTHER READING

Criticism

Aching, Gerard. "On the Creation of Unsung National Heroes: Barnet's Esteban Montejo and Armas's Julian Del Casal." *Latin American Literary Review* 22, no. 43 (January-June 1994): 31-50.

> Examines biographies of Montejo and Casal for insight into Cuban nationalist thought.

Beebee, Tom. "Orientalism, Absence, and the Poéme en Prose." *Rackham Journal of the Arts and Humanities* 2, no. 1 (fall 1980): 48-71.

> Focuses on the use of the Orient in the prose poems of Casal and Baudelaire.

Berger, Margaret Robinson. "The Influence of Baudelaire on the Poetry of Julián del Casal." *Romantic Review* 37, no. 2 (April 1946): 177-87.

> Discusses Baudelaire's influence on Casal's writing, specifically with respect to the themes of melancholy and despair.

Glickman, Robert Jay. *The Poetry of Julian del Casal: A Critical Edition*. 3 vols. Gainesville: University Presses of Florida, 1976-78.

> Provides an in-depth critical overview of Casal's poetry collections, focusing on the contemporary reception they received.

Kirkpatrick, Gwen. "Technology and Violence: Casal, Darío, Lugones." *Modern Language Notes* 102, no. 2 (March 1987): 347-57.

> Theorizes that the developing cities of the nineteenth century, as well as the burgeoning technology of the time, affected the poetic rhythms of many modernist poets, including Casal.

Leslie, John Kenneth. "Casal's 'Salomé': The Mystery of the Missing Prophet." *Modern Language Notes* 62, no. 6 (June 1947): 402-04.

> Provides an analysis of Casal's sonnet, "Salomé," one of a group of poems inspired by the paintings of Moreau.

Pearsall, Priscilla. "Casal's Translations of Baudelaire and Maupassant: The Failure of Transcendent Vision." In *Essays in Honor of Jorge Guillen on the Occasion of His 85ᵗʰ Year,* pp. 64-73. Cambridge, Mass.: Abedul Press, 1977.

> Notes that Casal's translations of authors such as Baudelaire and Maupassant were partly inspired by his efforts to explore themes and artistic elements that were important to his own writing.

———. "A New Look at Duality in Julián Del Casal." *Chasqui: Revista de Literatura Latinoamericana* 8, no. 3 (May 1979): 44-53.

> Explores the relationship between Casal's sense of art and his feelings of alienation and loneliness.

———. "Julian Del Casal's *Rimas*: An Unfinished Work." *Critica Hispanica* 2, no. 2 (1980): 143-47.

> Provides a brief overview of Casal's *Rimas*.

———. "Neoplatonism and Modernity in Julián del Casal." *Revista Canadiense de Estudios Hispanicos* 5, no. 1 (autumn 1980): 106-09.

> Discusses Casal's poetry within the context of Neoplatonism.

Torres-Rioseco, Arturo. "*A Rebours* and Two Sonnets of Julian Del Casal." *Hispanic Review* 23, no. 4 (October 1955): 295-97.

> Theorizes that it was Huysmans's work that inspired Casal to write his famous sonnets, and not Moreau's paintings, as is widely believed.

Mihai Eminescu
1850-1889

(Also Mihail Eminescu; born Mihail Imin or Emin; surname changed to Iminovici or Eminovici) Romanian poet, dramatist, short story writer, essayist, and journalist.

The following entry provides criticism on Eminescu's works from 1972 through 1998. For additional information on Eminescu's life and career, see *NCLC,* Volume 33.

INTRODUCTION

Eminescu is one of the most important figures in Romanian poetry. Considered a quintessential Romantic poet, his experiments with language and literary genre have resulted in his being credited with anticipating some of the most important and defining aspects of modern poetry.

BIOGRAPHICAL INFORMATION

The seventh child of Gheorghe Eminovici, a well-off tax collector and farmer, and his wife Raluca, Eminescu was born January 15, 1850, in Botoşani but lived part of his childhood in Ipoteşti in northern Moldavia. He entered the Ober Gymnasyum in Cernăuti after three years of attending the local primary school. At seventeen, he was hired as an actor and prompter with a theater group. Two years later, he began formal studies in philosophy, history, law, political economy, and philology at the University of Philosophy in Vienna. He later pursued further studies in Berlin, this time partly funded by a literary society, Junimea, which published his early poetry in its journal *Convorbiri literare.* In Berlin, Eminescu encountered German Romantic literature and the philosophy of Arthur Schopenhauer, two significant influences on his later work. After leaving Berlin (and a paid position there at the Romanian consulate), he became the director of the Central Library in Iasi, Romania, and two years later, in 1876, worked as a proofreader and editor of the newspaper *Curierul de Iasi.* The following year, in a move that sealed his abiding reputation not only as poet but as journalist, he took a position as editor at the distinguished journal *Timpul.* For the next six years, Eminescu was exceptionally productive, writing frequently for *Timpul* and seeing his poetry published in some of Romania's most highly ac-

claimed journals. At the end of this period, however, he suffered the first of four hospitalizations, a consequence of mental and physical illness associated with inherited syphilis. After 1883 he produced little and died in an asylum in Bucharest in 1889.

MAJOR WORKS

Junimea's journal *Convorbiri literare* published many of Eminescu's love poems from the early 1870s, introducing him to the Romanian reading public. Among his more famous poems are some of his earliest, including "Inger si demon" ("Angel and Demon") and "Imparat si poletar" ("Emperor and Proletarian"), works that reflect his interest in Romanian national identity and sympathy for the victims of oppression who typified that identity for Eminescu. Later poems, such as the much extolled "Călin," reflect his increasing disillusionment over the capacity of the socially and politically oppressed to overcome their condition, along with a consequent idealization of the peasantry. In Eminescu's poetry nature is offered as an idyllic refuge, and the peasant as a paradigm of virtue. Poetry from Eminescu's final and most productive period—including "Rugăciumea unui Dac" ("A Dacian's Prayer"), the "Scrisoarea" ("Epistle") poems, and, most notably, "Luceafărul" ("The Evening Star")—delves increasingly into philosophical concerns, the difficulties inherent in the human condition, and the nature of genius.

CRITICAL RECEPTION

Eminescu's enduring interest in his country's identity, along with the fact that he wrote in the Romanian language, made his work relatively inaccessible outside of his homeland and may have denied him some of the celebrity of his contemporaries among European poets. However, the twentieth century has seen his work translated into other languages with marked frequency. Roy MacGregor-Hastie notes that Eminescu has been translated into English, German, Italian, French, Hungarian, Russian, Spanish, Yiddish, Albanian, and Arabic and is now recognized as one of the world's geniuses of lyric poetry. For Constantin Ciopraga, Eminescu was "the conscience of the nation" of Romania, and Ilie Badescu observes in Eminescu's journalism an early articulation of sociological studies in that country. Mircea Scarlat concludes that in Eminescu's journalism the reader can find "qualities in full consonance with the poet's genius," while Amita Bhose considers him "the last of the European Romantics of universal standing," comparable in importance to such earlier Romantic poets and John Keats and William Wordsworth. Considered by many Romanians as their national poet to this day, Eminescu occupies a place in the history of Romanian culture that in some ways parallels Shakespeare's importance to the cultural history of England. For some critics, Eminescu not only aspired to attain a Shakespearean level of genius, but in fact achieved it.

PRINCIPAL WORKS

Poesii (poetry) 1884
Opere Complecte [*Complete Works*]. 13 vols. (poetry, short stories, drama, criticism, essays, journalism, and letters) 1964-93
Poems (poetry) 1980
Poems and Prose of Mihail Eminescu (poetry and prose) 2000

CRITICISM

Grigore Tănăsescu (essay date 1972)

SOURCE: Tănăsescu, Grigore. "Ovid and Mihai Eminescu—Two Points of Confluence of Two Poetics." *Romanian Review* 26, no. 2 (1972): 50-4.

[*In the following essay, Tănăsescu establishes Ovid as a source of erotic themes in Eminescu's poetry.*]

Mihai Eminescu's first acquaintance with Ovid might have been occasioned by G. Reinbeck's book *Mythologie für Nichtstudierende,* which he thoroughly studied in his school days at Cernăuţi. Such mythological names as Atlas, Hercules, Nessus, Venus and Adonis, Diana, Aurora, Narcissus, Echo, Phaëthon, a.s.o. found in Ovid's work and quite frequently referred to by the author of the above-mentioned mythology penetrated into Eminescu's symbolism as early as his first poems. Later on, the mythological temptation was to develop, reaching fabulous proportions in the representations of the Romanian poet. For Eminescu, Ovid meant not only the creator of *The Metamorphoses,* of mythological fabulation, but also the poet of love, with which these very *Metamorphoses* are imbued. In a manuscript note dat-

ing from the period when he was elaborating the poem **"The Love of a Marble"** (1868) the Romanian poet—"one of the great martyrs of Eros" (Perpessicius)—mentioned the Latin bard among those "mad out of love: Şincai—Horia—Ovid" and then in the posthumous poem **"The Icon in its Frame"** he characterized himself, after Ovid's fashion, "What am I? A weak soul joined to a weak mind." (See Ovid *Molle Cupideis nec inexpugnabile telis / Cot mihi . . . fuit. The Tristia,* IV, 10, v. 65-66.)

Eminescu's interest in the work and personality of the poet relegated at Tomi can also be seen in another note in which, concerned—since the epoch before his student years, therefore before Vasile Alescandri—with introducing the classical tragedy into Romanian culture, in the spirit of Corneille and Racine, the Romanian poet postulated: "The so-called classical tragedy could be introduced by such plays as *Ovid* (in Dacia), *character and ideas in his works* (G. Călinescu, Mihai Eminescu's Work, Literature Publishing House, Bucharest, 1969, p. 70, see p. 329). This note referring to Ovid's ideas as well as to his character shows that Eminescu had read the latter's work (at least partially).

In Eminescu's artistic evolution the myths he might have come across in Ovid's poetry go beyond the usual significance, marking a transition to symbolic meanings. The echo—present both with Ovid and Virgil—assumes artistic shape with our poet as a "light" murmur, "thirsty of love" (**"Undine"**). In the poem **"The Ghosts"** Arald is embodied as a romantic Orpheus in search of his lost beloved. Orpheus' mythic image, is alongside Apollo's, one of Eminescu's most meaningful symbols of mythological type. We come across the same image as a sublimated image of the "song," of poetry, in the *Greek* episode of **"Memento Mori"** as well as in **"The Morning Star"**: "And will you have me sing that song / Whose tuneful melody / Will move the wooded mountains and / The islands of the sea?"

Orpheus' image overlapping that of Apollo—whence Hyperion's representation derives—symbolizes, both with Eminescu very much as with the ancients, the royalty of poetry, the bard being invested with the attributes of *poeta vates,* urged on by the choir of the muses, the "sweet sisters" who give "wings to his thoughts" and fill his inspired song with "pride." Both the "fair" Phoebus Apollo (*flavus Apollo* with Ovid) embodying the sun's brightness—that is the "serenity" of poetic inspiration—and his godlike sister, Diana, with her selenic attribute, her "silvery" shade (Ovid also calls her *Phoebe*—that is the feminine "pale," selenic reflection of the solar principle of *Phoebus*; she also appears as the infernal *Hecate*) are to be found quite often in the verses of the classicizing romanticist Eminescu.

In the poems **"First Epistle," "The Dacian's Prayer"** and in the posthumous poem **"The Twins,"** the cosmogonic vision, made up especially of elements of Indian philosophy, also renders something of the texture of the exordium of the Latin poet's *Metamorphoses*—in its ample rhythm as well as in some of its moments.

Because of the Alexandrine nature of his creation, Ovid used and abused of the term *ars* in its multiple meanings. Eminescu grasped the Ovidian meaning of "craftsmanship," using it in the verses of the **"Gloss"**: "If they cry and if they quarrel / You, alone, keep by yourself / And can gather from their moral / What is wrong and what is right / ," or in the dramatic fresco **"Mureşanu"**: "And should your hand be holding the book of history / *Arts* most majestic volume in it you're sure to see." Besides this transfer into the social historical domain where the term has the Latin etymological meaning, Ovid's *art* functions with Eminescu in a courteous erotic sense as well, embodied in the woman with her sweet "cunning," with her "shrewd" pleasures: "And with a skill I've never experienced before / The last string of my being you could but too well strike" (**"You So Much Tortured Me with Words of Love"**). In the work of Ovid and of other Latin elegiac poets, as well as in Eminescu's work, one comes across *tener* as an attribute of gentleness, of purity, opposed to *art* in the above-mentioned sense. But Ovid's "candour" is interpreted by Quintilian from another angle, with another nuance, characterizing the Latin poet as "too deeply enamoured of his own genius" (*nimium amator ingenii sui),* which might explain the voluptuousness with which Narcissus' myth is rendered in *The Metamorphoses* as also in Eminescu's poems.

A characteristic of the classicizing temptation in the creation of the romantic poet Eminescu is the obsessive frequency of graphical, visual images, the eye perceives. The eye in the conception of the ancients is the organ of the most refined of senses, of graphical representations directly connected with the tangible, concrete reality, translated—on the erotic plane—into concupiscence and aphrodisiac voluptuousness. In his third *Roman Elegy,* Goethe, a fervent disciple and admirer of the ancients, revives under our eyes, as if he were transcribing passages from *The Metamorphoses* "the heroic times when gods and goddesses fell in love, when one glance alone gave birth to irresistible lusts followed by unspeakable delights." In the work of Eminescu, an apprentice both of Goethe and of the ancients, the erotic mood is made up of the same primary, demonic attributes: "Our painful love of yore / Chimeric was and heathen / A languorous child that darkness bore / A self-consuming demon" (**"Our Love Is Gone"**—a variant). Or, in another poem, the self-devouring "thirst" of eternal, Platonic "shapes" is expressed by and smelt as it were with the eyes: "It is of forms that I am thirsty / And with my burning eyes behold / Your treacherous dress that without mercy / Their beauty gracefully unfolds" (**"The Wish"**).

In the spiritual family of a Shakespeare, Goethe, Leopardi, Hölderlin—all drawing their inspiration from the Ancients—Eminescu showed a strong, palinodic, Proteic propensity, marked by a cyclic treatment of themes, recurrence of motifs, oscillations and—on the plane of artistic composition—by insertions, recompositions, repetitions of images, and even of key poetic sentences. The history of European literature preeminently records the palinodic character of Ovid's creation. *Ars Amandi* has its palinode entitled *Remedia Amoris. The Festae* and *The Metamorphoses* are each other's palinodes. The erotic attraction and repulsion—Catullus's *odi et amo*—in Eminescu's work, too, is repulsion interwoven with voluptuous attraction (**"Venus and Madonna"**). At the level of the poetic discourse, inclusions and detachments of fragments are the proof of Eminescu's palinodic genius so akin to Ovid's. **"A Dacian's Prayer"** is but a fragment of the posthumous poem **"The Twins"** included in then detached from it. The posthumous poems **"Darkness and the Poet," "In a World of Darkness,"** and **"Undine"** are palinodes of the dramatic poem **"Mureşanu"** which, as already pointed out, took shape in the same thematic atmosphere as **"Demonism"** and **"The Story of the Star-Travelling Magus."** "In its turn," underlined George Călinescu, "the poem *Emperor and Proletarian* should be considered as a continuation of and derivation from the **"Panorama"** in keeping with which and under whose principle it develops . . ."

Candid, confident in his friends—whom he judged by himself, as Ovid did—in moments of bitter disillusionment and in order to comfort himself, Eminescu translated the famous Ovidian distich in an original metre: "As long as you are happy by thousands you may count your friends / As soon as times grow dark you are left utterly alone" (Ovid, *Tristia,* l. 9, 5-6: *Donec eris felix . . .)*

The Romanian poet's artistic creed coincides with the Ancients' way of considering creation, with the principle of the *serenity* of the poetic act proclaimed by Ovid even in the bitter years of his exile at Tomi: "*Carmina proveniunt animo deducta sereno*" (*Tristia,* 39) and rendered by Eminescu in lines such as "it's only in the soul's serenity and peace profound / that you will find the true and unique beauty (**"Odyn and the Poet"**). Like the Ancients, the Romanian poet is eager to get the "wreath of laurels" he deserves for the tune of his "antique harp." His call is that of a genuine *poeta vates*—he calls on people to listen only to "the voice of serene truth" and to express it in the "mild murmur of poetry."

In his work, Eminescu often develops the myth of Philemon and Baucis, rendered famous by Ovid's pen (*The Metamorphoses,* VIII): in the poem **"The Girl in the Golden Garden,"** which lies at the basis of **"The**

Morning Star," in **"The Legend of the Morning Star"** and in other manuscript notes where we come across the names of the venerable pair: "Oh, where is love / Where is Philemon, the tender and peaceful idyl?" George Călinescu has pointed out that Eminescu knew at least parts of Ovid's *Metamorphoses*; the scholar also drew attention to the sentence of the Latin poet quoted by Eminescu: "Video meliora proboque, deteriora sequor." It is not altogether impossible that Eminescu should have represented the myth of Philemon and Baucis after having read Faust (II, 5). Anyhow, one of Eminescu's distichs, an elegiac couplet written in Ovid's favourite metre and alluding to the myth (manuscript 2283, 111) leads us rather to the Ovidian source as primary.

The mythological character of Cupid—strikingly Ovidian—fills many of Eminescu's pages. Starting from "erotic gambolling" up to the image of "retinal love" spreading its enticing charms over whatever breathes in the universe, and up to "blind love" thirsty of victims, the ensemble of Eminescu's erotic symbols takes us to the realm of love, sung by Ovid more beautifully than by anybody else. Tentacular, insidious love, retinal love, is graphically represented in Latin lyricism—quite often in Ovid's—through the image of a hunter who lays his traps in order to capture his victim. In **"The Morning Star"** we read, to the same effect, the incantatory stanza where the maid (*puella*) is initiated (*docta*), in love's arcana: "Just as the hunter lay his net / For birdies in the thicket / When I my left arm offer you / Just offer yours and take it."[1]

With Eminescu, Cupid is one and the same with *Kama, Kamadeva*, the "Indian god," shrewd "like a child," cruel (*saevus puer*, with Ovid) "fair-haired" (*vitta, flavus*, with the Roman elegiac poets) invoked to steal into the beloved's bower: "Cupid, playful page, is going the lamp's violet light to screen / With his hand, my darling lady, graceful mistress of my dreams" (**"The Fourth Epistle"**; see *The Diamond of the North—Capriccio*). These lines make us also think of the final part of Goethe's *Tenth Roman Elegy* where he too is tributary to Ovid. Eminescu's erotic imagery therefore reveals a *gallant* moment of both romantic and Ovidian nature in representing *Cupid* who is depicted by the Roman poet too as wearing "ribbons and trinkets," thus lending a special flavour to Eminescu's eroticism.

Note

1. D. Caracostea, *Eminescu's Craftsmanship*, Bucharest' 1958, p. 354 sqq, where the author, inter alia, analyzing *The Morning Star*, refers to Ovid's *Ars Amandi* without making an adequate parallel text analysis.

Constantin Ciopraga (essay date 1979)

SOURCE: Ciopraga, Constantin. "History and Myth." *Romanian Review* 33, no. 12 (1979): 121-31.

[*In the following essay, Ciopraga presents Eminescu as the voice of the Romanian conscience.*]

In a broad sense it is History that spoke through Eminescu. Not a history *in abstracto,* but a pathetically human one, animated by questions about destiny, a history—to be more precise—seen as a succession of existential realities, within the frame of which the whole governs the parts. Moment and eternity become terms with polar functions marking the state of existence, underlining transition in particular, "the eternal flight" under the sign of repetition. The idea of circular movement—from non-being to life and hence to death—asserted in a poem of 1874 (**"Emperor and Proletarian"**) had previously emerged in his Viennese academic period: *Forever the same longings draped in another dress, / The same men, everlasting, in the unchanged mankind.*" Or this even more pregnant emphasis upon blind mechanics: *While ever human history its age-old course will ply / as on time's heavy anvil blind hammers heedless fate.* As eternity and transitoriness perpetually and never unrelentingly clash, as the world is a sequence of transparencies and mysteries, the feeling of universal relativism invades conscience, whence the never ending show of flux and reflux. Seen as a spectacle (mention should be made of *Vanity Panorama* as subtitle of the poem **"Memento Mori"**), the world invoked by the poet runs aground in anonymities. It struggles between *to be* and *to seem.* A posthumous line imbued with sadness reiterates the idea: *History is life that written is on water* . . . (**"Woman . . . Apple of Discord"**). Such generalizing statements become incorporated with the philosophy of history alluding to a *spectaculum mundi.* The thinker who speaks is outraped by the limitations of human condition and contradicted in his romantic aspirations after perfection. It seems certain that such considerations have something in common with Vico's theses put forth in *Scienza nuova* (1725); Croce regarded the illustrious Neapolitan as "a philosopher primarily since, by concerning himself with eternal history, the latter, for the very fact that it is eternal, is not history but philosophy itself . . ."

From among the principles enunciated by Vico, the founder of the philosophy of history, the ones set forth in books IV-V, concerning the so-called *corsi* and *ricorsi*, are to be found again with Eminescu. The philosopher knew how to work out a scheme from facts, a pattern for "an ideal eternal history according to which the histories of all nations develop . . ." The poet of **"Memento Mori"** in his turn witnesses: *How nations born do live and fall, / Same virtue, vice, repeated misery in all* . . ." Circular movement! It is exactly the *course* described by Vico; its very *recourse* which Eminescu renders by repetition at the end of his poem. Being "reiterated in advance", world history offers no more surprises: *The future if you want to read, be mindful of the past.* Less probable are the affinities with Herder in *Ideen zur Philosophie der Geschichte der Menschheit* (1784-1791), the work of a divided philosophic mind oscillating between Enlightenment and theological ideals, basically believing in the cyclic progress of humanity. As to the historical series referred to by A. D. Xenopol (*The Fundamental Principles of History*), demonstrating that the causally determined series of facts do not repeat themselves because identical conditions are not possible—these theses were put forth after the poet's death.

The Junimea society frequented by Eminescu was a good audience for Schopenhauer, "the desperate recluse", as Nietzsche was to call him. We learn about the way he viewed history from *The World as Will and Idea*: "History is knowledge only, not science. For nowhere does it study individuality by means of generality, it must examine individual objects with their peculiarities and still somehow creep in the dust of experience (. . .) Being systems of concepts, sciences always talk about genres: history about individuals. It would, therefore, be a science of individuals, which is a contradiction (. . .); the essence of human life, as well as of nature, exists everywhere, in any present, in all its entity, and to be thoroughly known, therefore, it only asks for depth of perception. History, however, hopes to replace depth by length and width, because any present is but a fragment that must be made complete by the past the length of which is nevertheless infinite, a fragment to which an infinite future is then chained. Hence steams the antagonism between philosophic and historical heads: the former wanting to investigate thoroughly, the latter to count up into the end . . . History seen as a means of cognition of mankind, is inferior to poetry . . ., it is not a science proper (. . .); the attempt to build it up as a body with beginnings, middle and end, and with rational connexion, is vain and founded upon false comprehension . . ." However impregnated with Schopenhauer the poet might have been, however compact his idea about an oppressive determinism under the pressure of which human condition remains inevitably tragical, Eminescu is in fact an explorer of human essence in light. Disappointed but not nihilistic. The examination to the point, undertaken with subtlety by Liviu Rusu (*Eminescu and Schopenhauer,* 1966) makes the correction, inviting to a real perspective.

* * *

The differences between considerations of this kind pertaining to the philosophy of history and Eminescu's reflexions on national history are evident, making fact (construction) come into view as an ethic imperative.

The fundamental argument: "Should a generation have a merit, it is that of being a true agent of history, of bearing the tasks inevitably imposed on it by the place it holds in the concatenation of time . . ." We read further, in the ***Political Work***: "Those are not disinherited who carry in their soul that treasure of memories which makes the solitary man also feel a part, a result of his country's history . . ." Morally invigorated and strengthened by turning towards the deeds of the ancestors, the romantic poet systematically withdraws to a homeland of the soul, where eroticism becomes the mark of an active philosophy. From the level of Decebal or that of a heroic thousand four hundred he decrypts and intercepts voices demonstrating that a soul of the nation travels from century to century. This makes history constitute itself as an antidote to subsequent irregularity and decadence. Considering its therapeutic, energetic support, a sentence such as *the past has always fascinated me,* from a Jassy letter (November 8, 1874), must be read as expressing the poet's aspiration for archetypes. The more remote, the more eagerly do primary dimensions ally themselves to myth which has become the echo of truth. Mythopoetical ideas in wide circulation today, such as the ones set forth by Mihail Sadoveanu in his novel *The Golden Bough* or by Lucian Blaga (e.g. the play *Zamolxe* or the poem "Magic Sunrise"), are anticipated by Eminescu with whom the history based upon "for ever concrete" facts, open to the "means of experience and analysis" requires mythic completion: "We must never lose sight of the fact that history is the development of one and the same human spirit, that we must often abandon ourselves to historical phantasy where experience is not sufficient . . ." The romantic resurrection of old times claims the conversion of real to unreal by breaking up current topic—the former change from fabulous to real. The logic of the heart moves to the foreground, as is also argued in a play (***Mira***); "I often take from history, from its sad guardian of the past, his gold keys, and I open up the gates of my heart . . ."

Within the context of these dominant directions, the appeal to gigantic models which violate thought spurring on endless changes combines with dream—an instrument opening on to miracle. Forgotten is the Schopenhauer *evil* about which the philosopher says it "makes history." The nostalgia for depth does not only once lead to the Dacian pantheon made real by sacred figures invested with Homeric powers. Eminescu's inspiration finds an exceptional source in the imposing *hereditas dacica,* so that it is not at all surprising if, indignant at Rössler's false theories (*Dazien und Romänen,* 1868; *Romanische Studien,* 1871) and at those of his followers, the poet holds up Dacianism as a primary form of Romanian ethnology. As opposed to Vico, with whom former ages have nothing idyllic about them, the myth of the golden age comes to play an important part. A visionary lyricism joins mythic thinking; the ideas which now systematically bear Eminescu's mark are conveyed by images either completely magical, as in **"Miradoniz,"** or striking a solemn note, painful even, as in **"Sarmis"** and **"The Twins."** As consubstantial realities, translating the need of certainty and reverie, history and poetic myth are initiatory forms oscillating between concrete and transcendental. The eye leaves details behind, the past becoming, as later on with Blaga, a pretext for mythosophy. The genius in **"Hyperion,"** the expression of the incandescent spirit, is counterbalanced on the mythohistorical plane by the Titan, the symbolization of action, both projected in colossal dimensions with the hallucination of time and space. The projection of the lyrical into the epic, characteristic of Eminescu, agrees with a certain type of cognition, history being both *rememorizing* and *integration*; myth, on the other hand, is deciphering and ciphering, an opening up to a certain level and closing, the assault of mystery and its desertion. The return to archetypes implies a general fluidity of proportions, the beginnings of our history developing in rocky spaces set with diamonds, silver and gold. Flowers, big as trees, golden miraculous birds, gigantic butterflies, golden stars, an "unprecedented fairy play"—this is the realm of fay *Miradoniz* once more invoked in the Dacian passage from **"Memento Mori."**

It is noteworthy that out of the one thousand three hundred and two lines of the ample **"Memento Mori"** almost half (642) recall the Dacian world, not in a sad perspective, but as a force defying Roman imperialism: *"Sturdy arms and soul upright, strong-built backs and shoulders broad, / Granite helmets black on their foreheads wrought, / Long black locks fall down their necks of demigods . . ."*

Of interest is the analogy between Decebal's retort (*"Woe to you most potent Romans! To darkners, dust and scum / Your great splendour will crumble"*) and that of prince Mircea the Old addressed to the Ottoman invader in the **"Third Epistle"**: *"Armies have we none, however, your great fame will not appall / Our devotion to the homeland, for it is a sturdy wall."* Within the metaphorical system, the mountains (rock, granite, basalt respectively) have a polarizing function symbolizing not force only, but an exceptional spiritual Alpinism at the same time. The ascensional line is obvious, "Dacia's heaven", "the kingdom of the gods" being a *topos* emitting grandiosity, a close antecedent of dream. The architectural representation virtually rests upon three elements, *the Mountain, the Dome, the Forest,* all three of them obsessively repeated, contributing towards making the whole sacred. The idea of certain theoreticians of myths (Mircea Eliade, *Le Sacré et le profane*) about the mountain as symbolization of the world centre is thus verified. The sun, the moon, the stars centre their existence in accordance with a Dacian mountain, *"half rising here, half in infinity"*. Natural sumptuosity passes

into fabulosity: *"Golden groves with starry glades rise there, / Silver forests stir their branches lit into the air, / Woods of coppered red there echo sweet, / / Mountains tower, vales descend and rivers glitter in the sun, / In their maiden beds white magic islands onward run, / Giant plots of ground with trees in blown they look . . . / There Dochia's palace stands on rock of dapple-grey, / A wood its roof which mountains pillars stay, / There trees do quiver in the clouds' sequester'd nook . . ."*

Across a world which must have "thought in fairy-tales" spans the celestial vault: the *dome*—a hemisphere with Greek and Latin resonances. A cloud *"Is born to freeze, then turn into a whole wide dome / Shadows of columns all around."* Night "enters the dome"; the "pious" stars *"enter the foggy night of silvery, multicoloured domes . . ."* Dacian remoteness, in short, does not so much maintain the myth of a paradisiac state, but a certain quietude necessary to the one who, as an observer of his time, made use of the pamphlet.

By the agency of Bogdan Petriceicu Hasdeu (in *The Dacians, Have they Perished?* 1860), the poet had, more than from chronicles, the revelation of the Dacian phenomenon; in point of its mystery, this subsequently became a resplendent obsession. As part of his project of Romanian mythology, the poems **"Sarmis,"** **"The Twins,"** **"Miradoniz"** are unfinished columns. Not only do his peregrinations take him to a non-historical, fairytale-like Dacia; the romantic poet composes his own myth of Zamolxe preferring the rustle of legend wings, the watchful dream, to demythologized history. Imaginarily, he feels history from within, in all its permanences, reconstructing it from folk suggestions, discovering it crude in nature, or, more clearly even, in people's spiritual structure. In old, immemorial layers he searches for the cause of some subsequent phenomenon that manifested itself in the Middle Ages or later. Accompanied by our pathetic guide, we penetrate into an eternal present of the Romanian people, an age of miracle as it were. Noteworthy is a fabulosity in the manner of Hugo, fluctuating between decorative and jovial, not lacking in solemnity. The white hair of the gods "shines", *"their beards flow into their lap"*, *"merrily they laugh to hear their glasses clink."* *"Playing the doina on a leaf"*, the moon commands the sublime: *"Wisents of perennial woods, their ashen mane she fondles, / Parts their mane and softly beats their neck, / Kisses on their head bestows to seal them all with diamond scars, / Thence she climbs the mountains black on streams of myriad stars, / Soft she glides and slow she travels on the bright celestial trek."*

The magic of remoteness in time intervenes, so that crisp scenes lose their intensity, the scenery making room for light and retrospective quietude. The air, therefore, is of "diamond", "gold pomegranates" grow in the grove, flowers "seem to be melted stars", "clear light" pours in across "clear lakes", across the gardens of "clear" dawns. In lunar projection or solar light, the scenery is exceptionally picturesque, close to the fairytale. The vegetal aspect, powerfully suggestive in point of colour, arrests attention: "*From boughs up high the drooping vine / The slate-blue hoary grapes, its white and golden fruit lets shine, / And busy bees the lustruous honey suck.*"

As far as visionary evocation goes, Eminescu disposes of prodigious resources. On a different plane, with a different imagination, Sadoveanu is, subsequently, a follower of Eminescu, in his subtext, acting convergently in the same direction. Lucian Blaga, himself up to a certain extent concerned as a playwright with the myth of *Zamolxe,* or as a philosopher referring to "the revolt of our non-Latin soul" (in other words: supporting the idea of the resistance of the Dacian heritage to the Latin spirit), comes to join them. Eminescu and Sadoveanu could have a subscribed to the formula set forth by Blaga, personal in expression but not in content. Mircea Eliade's learned research in *De Zamolxis à Gengis-Khan,* which brings out the persistence of the Dacian archetypes as against the myths of others, supplies facts where others proposed intuition. When mythologizing, Eminescu is sooner a *voyant,* an *Orphic,* a creator of decorative-musical manner, static (reflective sometimes) rather than dynamic, in constant pursuit of the lyrical thrill and unconstrained hypostasis. The Romans were eminently lucid constructors, hostile (E. R. Curtius considers) to metaphysical divagations, whence the precariousness of myth in their literature. The Greek, the Orientals in general, but likewise the Germans, are prone to the metaphysical dimension. They are all concomitantly creators of myths. It seems Dacian spirituality was, as well as the Gothic (rich in austere embodiments), particularly sensitive to the sylvan mystery, whence, probably Eminescu's bent for Valhalla's gods.

The death of the Dacian king Sarmis urges to meditation on the imperfections of existence, myth discreetly blending with ethical allusions. As interpreter of the universal evil, invoking utmost pain (a condition for posthumous peace with the Dacians), the poet must have had the feeling of liberation from his own torture out into the abstract. **"The Twins"** are both myth and fable at the same time. "The gods of ancient Dacia", led by Zamolxe, have come as guests to Brigbel's (Sarmis' brother) unlawful wedding, a character bearing demonic stigmata, who has become king and master of former queen Tomiris. A primitive "Scythian bagpipe" spurs on "the heavy dance", young lads strike their "hatchets dancing" while "*Young maidens with them dance, they bustle all around. / They turn, they sway, their palms give forth such gentle sound.*" Just like in fairytales "*dismal Brigbel sits on his throne / With hair long-locked and black*" next to "golden Tomiris". If

bards did not declaim happenings from Egypt and Hellas (a pretext and escape into fabulosity) to everyone's delight we should think ourselves in the proximity of a Shakespeare. The ghost of the dead king intervenes uncannily, the "dead one" holding up against the nuptial pomp the punishing voice of destiny. Of outstanding force, but little known, Sarmis' curse is of the same kind as the famous imprecations in Corneille's *Horatii* or those of Agrippina against Nero in Racine's *Britannicus.* Through Sarmis' words, yet differently motivated than Arghezi's future curses, breaks out the Dacian moral content whose distinctive feature is vigour: "*Ye can now tear to tags our, soiled banner, / The wisent to which flocked same kind and manner. / Henceforth your king forever shall entomb / His sway o'er land and sea together doom. / And now, to thee my brother, I shall turn / To see thy face look pale, thy soul within thee burn (. . .) / In every man shalt find an enemy of thine, / And may thy soul grow stranger to itself in time. / In dread of thine own power, rebel thou shalt be, / And sleep, the officer of life, will cease to claim his fee . . .*"

The fantastical Sarmis, like Eminescu, praises the forest, the wood becoming a meditative doublet of the Poet, uttering words just like him. We cannot imagine the visions in **"The Twins"** other than part of the large organic scale of Eminesu's poetry.

In a study of 1872 (*Forest Life in Dacia*) Bogdan Petriceicu Haşdeu referred to the mountain, the forest implicitly as decisive elements in the psychology of the natives. We find them again, unseparated, in a literary form, with Eminescu, at times in nebulous, tragic passages—echoing Tieck probably—or, more clearly in Mihail Sadoveanu. Kesarion Breb in the letter's novel *The Golden Bough,* a priest of Zamolxe, is nothing but "the old mage" from Eminescu's poem **"The Ghosts,"** keeping watch from his "throne of stone", pale, blind and hieratic. In Eminescu, and subsequently in Sadoveanu, the forest, associated with the mountain, outlines a mythology in which light coexists with mystery in a chiaroscuro of an intense lyrical voluptuousness. In Blaga, mountain, plain, light and mystery will he part of the same mythic dimension.

* * *

At the age of seventeen, a *poeta vagans* then, accompanying a group of actors, Eminescu thinks of a national stage repertoire. After a short time, the Vienna and Berlin of the decisive "*Lehrhjare*" strengthen his intention of writing for the theatre; he sketches some fragments. Out of the project of a dramatic dodecameron (undated) concerning the history of Moldavia in some of its crucial moments, he brought no play to an end; a **Bogdan-Dragoş** of around 1876-1878, however, is conclusive though abandoned at the beginning of the third act. The play betrays his method of work. Other titles among which *Alexander the Kind, Stephen the Great, Bogdan the Blind, Petru Rareş, Alexandru Lăpuşneanu, Despot Vodă,* outline a set universe. Similar paths of re-memorization were followed by old Asachi in whose *Dragoş* history, legend and fairy-tale merge together. At historical level, Heliade and Negruzzi, in their turn, will stimulate Eminescu's imagination at the time of his grand projects. Basically lyrical, inclined to fable freely, the author evoking Bogdan Dragoş gives way to subjective mythologies; the play (posthumously published by Iuliu Dragomirescu in 1906) fits organically into romantic patterns. The poet needed a character to unite history and myth and this is the protagonist of his dramatic poem. If "every mythology conquers and models the forces of nature in and by imagination"—as Marx observes—we can read this poem about the beginnings of the Land as an Apollo myth: the oscillations of the leading character between the incipient eros and the awareness of a historical mission are constantly kept within the scope of serene options.

Here are some elements in order to form an idea about the "dramatic" content. The personages are grouped into noble characters and their opponents: against Dragul, the Prince of Maramureş, reflective and hermetic, rises secretly his cousin Sas. Bogdana, the ambitious wife of Sas, tries to do away with Bogdan Dragoş, the Prince's son, but siding with him are hetam Bodei and Ana, boyard Toader Lupăşteanu's daughter from the Bistriţa valley. It is not only the poison furtively squeezed into his cup by his dissembling cousin and Bogdana that works upon him, but also the enmities with Prince Ludovic or the Pope, set up by the same Bogdana and her accomplice; the disappearance of the Prince of Arieş seems inevitable. Concomitantly, on the other side, we witness a miraculous bright resurrection, Bogdan Dragoş and Ana, their dismounting in Moldavia symbolizing a new perspective. Founder of the Land, Bogdan Dragoş, a seductive character combining purity and charm, is a mediaeval *chanson de geste*-like appearance. Characters are trenchantly differentiated. There is cunning Sas, on the one hand, manoeuvring "like a spider" from behind in order to seize the throne, assisted by Bogdana, a monstrous figure—"*a witch that makes the blood clog and the sun grow pale*", on the other hand, a childish Bogdan Dragoş and a shy Ana afraid of incubuses, and between them a sad Prince of Maramureş, a stern conscience of "cold pride", comparable to Al. Davila's Vlaicu-Vodă. Beset by anxieties, "wounded to death and stripped by thieves", Dragul meditates in a Shakespearian manner upon an adverse destiny (Shakespeare is in fact the supreme model): "*With dread we see how slow our days do / Creep away—each one a year (. . .). / Boyars! A burden like a mountain is our crown, / Our robes feel heavy, our limbs aweary, / And readily Our Person would rid itself of both / To flee the vast of life . . .*"

At other times the mask of the defeated suddenly changes its aspect either in the dialogues with Sas who is reproached with treason ("you are planning an ill-deed") or with Bodei (the equivalent of the devoted Romanian Gruie in *Vlaicu-Vodă*) who ably complains of his own stupidity: "Forgive me for speaking thus, my word, I am a quach too stupid . . ." The words have hidden meanings and traps in the face of which, found guilty, Sas remains disconcerted. "I have put on this lambish mask enough . . . So, down with it," he concludes. If Sas, undetermined hesitates, Bogdana is a demonic Lady Macbeth, without problems, luring to evil "the way a cold serpent's eye does". Noteworthy are in the character-drawing the discreet echoes from "the divine Brit" as for example in the confrontation between Dragul and Bodei when, alarmed by the prince's apparent resignation, the latter bursts out: "*Well? What do I care? What dost thou want old man? / Husks in your skull instead of brain . . . Thou art / not fit to be a Prince, as I am not made to be a pope . . . / Thy child thou hast deprived of bread, / Dogs hast thou fed . . . and Sas is a mere dog . . .*"

Machinations, poisonings, political feuds, confrontations with the Catholic dogma, these are characteristics which imply similarities to the above-mentioned *Vlaicu-Vodă*, which, however, being performed in 1902, before the publication of Eminescu's play, cannot be suspected of influences. The analogies are telling, nevertheless. The dismounting in Moldavia in Eminescu's play, as well as the fight for safeguarding the independence of Wallachia in Davila's play, belong to the same ethic and sentimental register asserting a patriotism of Romanian nature. Victor Eftimiu's play *Ringala* ties close to them; also worth mentioning is the more recent *Star of the Wisent* by Valeriu Anania. Leading Eminescu-type characters such as Bogdan Dragos accompanied by pages of western fashion, or evoking, like hetman Bodei churches "with organ sound", are abandoned to archaic recollections. The phantom of Decebal, a remote ancestor, borders on myth. Mircea and Anca in Davila's play bear analogies to Bogdan and Ana in Eminescu's play which is more imbued with (his) specific poetry. Allegorically speaking Moldavia and Ana, compensatory realities, are both values generating the sublime, whence their tonic function, and the necessity for the momentary sacrifice of eros in favour of patriotic duty. Through young Bogdan who tells the prince about a fairytale-like realm inhabited by people "speaking the same language" speaks an Eminescu rhapsode, the one who concomitantly panegyrized Dacian grandiosity.

Bogdan's symbolic coronation by the Prince of Maramureş is part of a series of other symbols. It is worth remembering that the protagonist of the play is an Adonis, a Theseus and a Prince Handsome at the same time, whence the mythic element superposed on the historical truth. In order to suggest erotic fervour all of Eminescu's poetic devices are called upon in some sequences of intense chromatic and melodic voluptuousness, so that the second act of the play seems a display of miracles. When he declares his love Bogdan is an *alter ego* of the poet who wrote **"Longing"** or **"The Forest Pool,"** living a *story*. There is no documentary inconvenience in the description of the setting. A lonely castle in the fir wood, the "ruddy" glow of the moon, the swans gliding through the reeds, the balcony where the "guitar" can be heard, make up an adequate setting for the sublime, in which the "for ever worshipped one" is of an angelic candour: *"pure she is like a white way candle"*; "sweet darkness" flows from her "soft" eyes; blossoms from the lime-tree *"full of scent fall onto her yellow hair."*

Unseen, Lermontov's demon addressing Tamara, seems to prompt Bogdan's prayer to Ana: *"What would I? Nay, what would I not? / I would I held the wide world's sway / With humankind my word subserviently obey, / Palaces I would I had, gardens, riches, many a town, / Of shining gold a royal throne of great renown (. . .) / The beauty of the day on whom depends the earth, / A sun amongst all kings, the river's immortal birth, / I would the crown upon my head became a spring of beams, / Thus (he kneels down) to thee I could bow—an icon as beseems. / When all the undreamt of wealth thou'dst see / I would I said: Take all, take me . . ."*

The phantom of the incubus from "fairy-tales" merges with "the sweet sound of the horn" coming from the forest in moonlight, as a consequence of which Ana, "an angel of gentleness", experiences a frenzy between dream and reality. In the young girl's confession—addressed to the moon—we recognize in a first variant melodies from a future memorable poem: *"O'er the woods the moon's afloat, / Leaves move softly in the breeze, / Midst the branching alder trees / Sounds the horn its plaintive note."*

Such formulae as "killing sweet", "sweet pain," "the sweet look", horn sounds blended with the feeling of disappearance, belong to Eminescu's typical language. The foundation of the land that is being born is basically presided over by light, youth and love, which explains the ample place allotted to young people in this poem. In a similar setting Ionut Jder from Sadoveanu's historical epos *The Jderi Brothers* is a counterpart of Bogdan, both in point of psychology and charm. We can only regret that Eminescu's play, so much organically linked to his work as a whole, was left an unfinished symphony.

The fascination exercised by the Romanian Middle Ages upon the end and the beginning of another period is basically linked to the prestige of certain monumental figures (Mircea the Old, Stephen the Great,) but also to the spectacle of a nature meant for legend. As for Ro-

manians *historical existence* was synonymous with the idea of resistance, to oppose the social imperfections of around 1880 with the memory of the Wallachian victory over the Ottoman invader becomes the support of a masterpiece. No other evocation we know of comes near to the tension of Eminescu's language.

The repartees addressed to Bajazet convey the **"Third Epistle"** exceptional resonances: *"Do you pride yourself on having put to flight a myriad / Of imperial and knightly soldiers, brave and armour-clad? / You aver you have been challenged by resistance of the West? / What has been the West's main purpose? Why were they to battle pressed? / Every knight had done his utmost to despoil you of the bays / On your iron brow, to shatter your faith's victory and praise. / I? I just defend my poorness, and my troubles, and my folk . . . / So, what stirs here in this country, be it river, breeze or oak, / Is a staunch friend to me only and to you a deadly foe, / And despite your unawareness everything but hate will show. / Armies have we none, however, your great fame will not appall / Our devotion to the homeland, for it is a sturdy wall!"*

A young lad "breastplate on and cap of sheepskin black" hunts with the bow in the woods of Upper Moldavia. It is Stephen, the prince in the prime of his youth. A stately empress with hair "touching her heel" welcomes him symbolically in the shade of the oak trees, "boys with hawks on their shoulders and many young girls" their shoulders "laden with wooden pails, big and small" surround him. The decorative pageantry is part of a ceremonious synthesis with allegorical undertone: the whole country hails the young Muşatin.

* * *

For an exact outlining of Eminescu's profile we must tell ourselves that the idea of independence implies a day by day affirmation, a *continuum*,—not a heritage coming exclusively from the past. Shortly before the War of Independence (1877), in the *Curierul de Iaşi*, Eminescu pronounced on the imperative necessity to fight: "If for a moment the existence of Romania did not seem to need cannons and bayonettes", this was an "optical illusion" maintained by great powers who profited by the position of the Romanians. "Whichever the causes that have up to now prevented the great powers from clearly guaranteeing the neutrality of the Romanian territory, be it weakness, ill-will, or the mental reservations of the different cabinets, it seems to us they are no longer of interest to us. Since, should anything be done to our advantage, our good look will certainly not be the cause of such an event, and should, on the other hand, something be done to our disadvantage, we shall defend what we have as best we can . . ." It is the conscience of the nation that spoke through Eminescu—a nation accustomed to respecting others on condition that its own being be respected.

Amita Bhose (essay date 1979)

SOURCE: Bhose, Amita. "A Fundamental Motif in Eminescu's Poetry." *Romanian Review* 33, no. 12 (1979): 131-40.

[*In the following essay, Bhose examines death as a motif in Eminescu's poetry.*]

The literary début of Mihai Eminescu was occasioned by the death of Aron Pumnul, his professor at Cernăuţi High School. There was a strong affectionate bondage between the two, and the death of the teacher deeply affected the young student. Thanks to T. V. Ştefanelli, a classmate of the future poet, description of that important day in Eminescu's life has remained a memorable page in the history of Romanian literature.

It was for the first time that Ştefanelli saw Eminescu weeping. Later on, in the evening, he was surprised to see his friend composing verses dedicated to the dead man. The poem was published in the brochure *Tears of the Students of Cernăuţi High School at the Death of their Most Beloved Professor Aron Pumnul* on the day of burial, 12/24 January, 1866 (T. V. Ştefanelli, *Recollections about Eminescu,* p. 43).

It is significant that Eminescu discovered his poetic talent at his first contact with death and that poetry served him as a means to unburden his soul. Since then, the motif of death remained for ever attached to his thought and creation. From the funeral ode **"At the Grave of Aron Pumnul"** to his own poetic epitaph, **"The Boon which I Last Crave,"** death appeared in Eminescu's poems in different forms. Images of death in his poems are always new, one different from another.

At he age of sixteen, in the poem of début, Eminescu sees death donned in garments of mythology. He looks upon death as a gateway towards the other world. In conformity with Christian Mythology, he imagines that the soul of the great son of Bucovina is awaited by a choir of angels in paradise; it will pass from one glory to another, a greater one than earth could offer. The pang of separation is theirs who lost him. Death thus means a continuation of life in another level, and there seems to be no contradiction between the two. The poem is born of sadness, but its tone is almost happy. The happiness is an outcome of mythological precepts and not of philosophical concepts.

In Spring that year Eminescu leaves the Bucovinian town and sets out on a journey through Transylvania, where he goes once again in 1868. For three years he lives a wayfarer's life, sometimes as a porter in the port of Galaţi, sometimes as a prompter in the National Theatre of Bucharest, and often as a simple traveller on the paths of the country. He works hard, knows poverty, learns to suffer hunger, becomes acquainted with the misery of peasant life and witnesses the dance of death in the Transylvanian revolution of 1868, which he describes in the novel *Barren Genius.*

The cruelty of death and the harshness of life that he comes to know in these days are reflected in **"To the Friend F. I.,"** a poem published three years after that of the début. Now life is synonymous with "past dreams" and "withered flowers". At the threshold of youth the poet feels that he drags his fate "as a vulture drags its wounded wings." Nor does death show any tenderness. He hears the song of death in winter blizzards, "death laughs at him from all corners." Eminescu has already heard the deafening laughter of death in the revolution of 1868.

At this phase, Eminescu is confronted with the ruthless faces of both life and death, of which that of death appears less severe. Death seems to be a way of escape from the difficulties of life. It raises a hope for recompensation in the other world. There is an aspiration after posthumous glory as well.

> "If the thought of my days is put off in the mind of God
> and if my soul finds its recluse only in the stars and not in this world, I would like you to put a wreath on my forehead and a lyre near my head on the day when His
> angels will take my pale shadow to the white mountains."

Death haunts him even in moments of love. In **"Would I Die or Should You Die"** (1869), the poet is overwhelmed with the fear of death, which might separate him from his beloved. The presentiment of the young lover comes true in **"Mortua est!"** (1871). At the beginning of the poem Eminescu sees death through the prism of mythology.

> "Like silver-lit shadows to me you appear—
> Their wings now preparing a skyward career;
> Pale soul, you're ascending on scaffolds of clouds
> Through showers of raylets and star-studded crowds.
> (. . .)
> But maybe you find there fine palaces built,
> With star-spangled archways resplendently gilt,
> With silver-made bridges and rivers of fire,
> And myrrh-scented meadows which strike up a choir."
>
> (Trs. Andrei Bantaş)

The idea of the superiority of death over life is more prominent than in any earlier poem. The antithesis between life and death has assumed a well-defined shape.

> "Oh, death is but chaos, a star-sea it seems,
> While life is a fenland of riotous dreams;
> Oh, death is like eras flowered with suns,
> While bleak is life's story—it wastefully runs."
>
> (Trs. as above)

The metaphors surprise us with their strangeness. While the death of an individual is associated here with the motive of light, in another stanza that follows "eternal death", the end of the world, is associated with darkness, with "black sky" and sift "universe." Nowhere in Eminescu's poetry is the play of life and shade so surprising, so mysterious.

Did the Romanian poet come across the verses of *Shvetashvatara Upanishad* of India as early as that: "I have known the great man bright as the Sun standing beyond darkness; only by knowing him one can surpass death, there is no other way to overcome it."

Taken as a whole, the poem does not manifest any knowledge of Indian philosophy. Though some philosophical nuances twinkle here and there like flittering fireflies, contradictory ideas betray the fact that a proper philosophical concept was not crystallized in the poet's mind till then. In one of the drafts, death is described as the return of the soul "to its eternal source" (M. Eminescu, **Works,** edited by Perpessicius, Vol. I, p. 301). If he would have borrowed the idea from the *Upanishads,* or at least were conscious of the philosophical value of the expression, perhaps he would not have left it out. The approach to the *Upanishads* thus seems to be caused by way of intuition. It is nothing more than a happy coincidence.

Lack of a clear vision about death and immortality results in the weakness of the structure of the poem. At the beginning, the idea of the other world is glorified by all means, but the conception that death of the body makes it possible for the soul to enter a happier world cannot console the poet till the end. The last verses turn down all preconceived notions, contradict all that has been said before and declare an open challenge against the so-called destiny.

> "But wherefore? . . . Are not all things *sheer madness indeed?*
> *Why was, my sweet angel, your death so decreed?*
> *Where lies the world's* meaning? *So smiling and gay,*
> *Did you, dear, live only to die in this way?*
> *If this has some meaning, it's godless and odd:*
> *Upon your wan forehead one cannot read 'God'!"*

(Trs. as above)

The God of mythology does not satisfy Eminescu any more. He sets out on another road to search for the truth about life and death.

The demon who revolted against the open sky calms down for a moment in **"Angel and Demon"** (1873). The demon-hero dies in a church, and just before death sees the angel-heroine praying for him. At the moment of death, love comes as reconciliation. Death is the Saviour that relieves the hero of the pains of life. Instead of promising any recompensation in the other world, it brings him the supreme reward, love, in earth itself. In Eminescu's vision death has already discarded its robe of mythology. Now he looks for the meaning of life and death in religion.

Yet, Eminescu's mind was too advanced to be limited to a dogma, to any particular religion. He was a poet of philosophy, not of religion. So, in **"Emperor and Proletarian"** (1874) he denounces religion and shatters all mythological concepts about death that influenced him till now.

> *"Religion? They've invented this hurdy-gurdy burden*
> *That by its magic power you may be kept laid low:*
> *If in your inmost nature there were no hope of guerdon,*
> *When you have toiled a lifetime and borne the beggar's burden,*
> *Could you endure the trials of oxen at the plough?*
> *With unsubstantial shadows they have bedimmed your sight*
> *And made of you believers in ransoms from on high.*
> *No! death of life has smothered all possible delight—*
> *For he who here has only known pain, and grief, and plight*
> *Has nought in the hereafter, for* dead *are those that die."*

(Trs. Leon Leviţchi)

The concept of death is no longer linked with mythology, nor with religion. Death is no more a continuation of life. The antithesis between life and death is clear, devoid of any ambiguities.

In **"The Ghosts"** (1876) Eminescu returns to the Dacian myth and makes a daring step in the domain of Thanatos. Arald, the hero who had turned the earth upside down like the one in **"Angel and Demon,"** marries his dead lover. Dead himself as well, both are engaged by Death. Just as in the old Romanian ballad *Miorița,* the nuptial combines with the funereal. The atmosphere of the supernatural poem is dominated by the unseen presence of Zalmoxis, the Dacian god. Death is once again the continuation of life, not in the afterworld, but on earth itself. The heroes *live* their lives after death along with living beings.

Now we are in the year 1876, when after his return from Berlin the poet is absorbed in an ardent activity of creation. Till now he acquired a thorough knowledge of different systems of philosophy. He has learnt the teachings of Buddhism, which according to him is "the most poetic, most beautiful and the most profound religion of the world" (T. V. Ştefanelli, *op. cit.,* p. 72). His concept of life and death has started to crystallize. The terror of death has gone. Now Death appears to be a well-wisher, a bestower of peace. Sentimental proximity to death brings Eminescu nearer to life, to Nature. Nature is all the more linked with love in this period. Even the thorns of disappointment are not so pointed.

In **"The Lake"** (1876) the poet sobs and suffers in vain on the bank of a blue lake, the heroine does not come to him. But love meets its fulfilment in **"The Desire"** (1876), the poem that succeeds it immediately. Here life is a happy dream harmonised with Nature. In **"The Story of the Forest"** (1878), forest, "the gracious emperor", plays host to the lovers. They meet in the land of imagination, as it happens in most love poems of Eminescu. The dream is not shattered as in **"The Lake,"** nor does the fright of death darkens the poet's mind, as it did in poems of adolescence.

Sadness comes back in **"Away from You"** (1878). At twenty-eight the poet feels old and it seems to him that his beloved is dead long ago. The longing for communion with Nature goes on increasing in urban surroundings, which finds its expression in the nostalgic question, "Where are you, o childhood, with your forest and all?" in **"Oh, Stay On"** (1879). There was such a strong heart-to-heart relation between Eminescu and Nature that the separation from her meant sheer exile to him. In city life he feels like a banished person, a misfit; world, life, love everything loses its charms.

Disappointment reappears in the poems **"In the Same Old Lane,"** **"Whenever I Remember"** and some others written in 1879. The beloved is frequently lost in "the horizon of the eternal morning." Bitterness in life leads the poet to conclusions like "the world is divided between the fool and the crafty" (**"The Twins,"** published posthumously) and "behold the beautiful reward: a shroud and four planks" (ibidem).

In **"The Twins,"** perhaps the most shocking poem of Eminescu, death changes its gentle appearance. Distinctly different from **"The Ghosts,"** death in this poem disintegrates life and love. After the death of king Sarmis, priests try to bring him back to life by invocations, but the dead does not respond immediately. Then they arrange the coronation of his twin brother Brigbelu, who will at the same time, marry Sarmis's fiancée. When everything is ready, Sarmis enters the festive hall unexpectedly, reproaches Zalmoxis, who came to preside over the coronation and the marriage, then curses his brother and kills him.

The seamy side of life and death is once again prominent in **"The Twins."** Love is nothing but an illusion that can never be realized in life, because "there is no room for so much mercy and so much luck in this world of misery and tears." Woman is deception embodied; only Zalmoxis is capable of, observes Sarmis satirically, "combining so much charm with so much infidelity." Death is not the same compassionate spirit which married Arald with his dead lover. It is again a terror, as is evident from Sarmis's curse to his brother Brigbelu, "Let the terror of death enter every bone of yours."

The motive of black is abundant. Boats are black, black branches of lime shake off flowers towards the dark sea and the Sun blackens "the course of centuries", time. The latter two images appear constantly as refrains. The poet's world is plunged in darkness.

Death destroys the life of Brigbelu, and Sarmis's return to life is a greater catastrophe.

"A Dacian's Prayer," written in the period 1876-1879, is created from a manuscript, of which **"The Twins"** form a part. The name of Zalmoxis is not spelled out, but it is understood from some fragments related to the poem that he is the god to whom the poet bows and it is his glory that is sung in the opening stanzas, which happen to be an adaptation of a hymn from the Indian *Rigveda*. Apart from assimilating *The Hymn to an Unknown God (Rigveda,* X, 121), Eminescu uses some terms belonging to Indian philosophy, for example, "eternal rest" and "extinction for ever."

It was discussed if the following verses were not inspired from the idea of self-torture of Indian yogins (C. Papacostea, *Ancient Philosophy in Eminescu's Works,* p. 29).

> *"To curse all those who pity will show for me, to bless*
> *All those who make me suffer and ruthlessly oppress*
> *. . .*
> *And if, by all accursèd, I die a stranger, they*
> *Upon the street my body to dogs shall throw away,*
> *And him who sets them on me, that they may tear my*
> *   heart,*
> *O him, my gracious Father, the highest crown impart,*
> *And him who stones will on me with hatred throw, o*
> *   give*
> *My Lord, that he in glory eternally may live!"*

> (Trs. P. Grimm)

In Yoga, an ascetic submits his body to different trials so that the spirit is liberated from the bondage of sense organs. The respective practices are but steps towards attaining spiritual equilibrium, the very factor totally lacking in this poem. The hero separates and isolates himself from humanity, even curses his mother and manifests a state of utmost agitation, which tears him to pieces. The reason of his fury cannot be understood from the contents of the poem. One can only guess it with reference to its prototype, **"The Twins."**

The poem has textual similarities with the Vedic cosmogony and some Buddhist ideas, but the feelings expressed in it are foreign to Indian systems of thought. The poet's aspiration after the eternal extinction does not originate from the extinction of passions, an essential condition of the Buddhist *nirvana*. On the other hand, the hero is not at all indifferent to the fate of his body after death. This is not in conformity with the philosophy of the *Upanishads* or of the *Bhagavad Gita*. According to these, the soul cannot be cut with arms, not can it be burnt with fire. You can kill one's body, but not his soul. As a man throws his old garments away and takes new ones, the immortal soul passes from one body to another after physical death (*Bhagavad Gita,* II, 22-23). So it matters little for the spirit liberated from the body if the body is thrown on a street or is embalmed with myrrh. The hero of **"A Dacian's Prayer"** has not attained such indifference to his body.

The last part of the poem offers a sharp contrast to the first one. It is therefore difficult to decipher the message of the poem, to understand the poet's attitude towards life and death. We have noted a similar state of confusion in **"Mortua est!"** To our minds, Eminescu passed through another phase of spiritual transition in these days.

Till now he has come to know two important systems of Indian philosophy, namely the philosophy of the *Upanishads* and the Buddhist philosophy. They serve him as some sources of inspiration, but are not yet amalgamated with his own system of thought. He has found the road which would lead him to the truth about life and death, but has not attained the goal. The end of the way is far off. His mind is not yet prepared for the eternal rest. Perhaps the poet himself was conscious of the fact, and this might have been the reason that made him abandon the title, *Nirvana,* extinction of passions, which he gave to one of the variations of the poem.

The year 1879, in which **"A Dacian's Prayer"** was published, was a year full of journalistic and literary activities for Eminescu. During this year he used to write at least a page a day of the newspaper *The Time,* of which he was the Editor. At the same time he worked at the finalisation of the *Epistles* group of poems, which were published one by one in 1881.

In Spring of 1880 he writes to his sister Harieta, "Autumn of the year comes only once, and it is followed by Spring. You never know when and from where the Autumn of life comes . . . You only find that everything has passed and that it will never come back. And then you feel old, very old and you would like to die" (M. Eminescu, *Works,* edition quoted, II, p. 169). The regret that his days are passing away for ever has already started.

Almost in the same time he publishes **"O, Mother,"** a poem dedicated to his mother, whom he lost in 1876. His mother's death is remembered in **"Lost for Me, You Move Smilingly in the World"** (1876).

> "I did not love my poor mother so much / as I love you. /
> Yet, when they covered her with earth, it seemed that the world turned black and that my heart would crack.
> I
> would have liked to be put in the same grave with her.

When the bell rang and its copper cried, my wandering
mind shouted, 'Where are you, mother?' I looked at the
bottom of the grave, and tears flowed down like rivers from my unworthy eyes on her black coffin. I did not know what happened to me, nor how I could live in this
world all by myself, like a stranger. My heart shrank and my life stayed in the throat."

The poem was not published during the life time of the poet. It would have been quite unnatural for Eminescu to publish his tearful sobs. He needed four years to suppress the cry of the orphan and helpless child, to write about his mother with self-control.

The years 1879 and 1880 bring maturity to Eminescu's thought. His mother's death makes him conscious of the fact that death is more than a mere idea; it is a concrete reality. Now he has the presentiment of the end of his life. He waits for death, not as an inevitable evil, but a desired end. At this stage death means to him a deep, undisturbed sleep. The sinister laugh of death does no more ring in winter blizzards. To the contrary, he hears his mother's voice in the rustling of acacia leaves over her grave. He no longer desires the death of an Orpheus, does not pine for posthumous glory, does not want to have wreaths and lyre on his grave. Only a branch of the holy lime and a few drops of tears of his beloved are all that he wants. In the poem **"To the Friend F. I."** he wanted to be buried on the mountains; now he wants his grave on the bank of a river. The flowing water, symbol of eternal life, is linked with the thought of death, as it was seen in his short story **"Cezara"** (1876). Feelings of purity and solitude are intensified. Interiorization of mind is reflected in the simplicity of language. The homage to his mother is a forerunner to his own epitaph, **"The Boon Which I Last Crave."**

Eminescu's philosophical vision is fully developed in the **"First Epistle"** (1881). The antithesis between life and death has totally disappeared. The image of the individual's death is integrated in the panorama of the end of the world. The concepts of the infinite and the eternity have crystallized. Microcosm has met macrocosm. *Atman,* the individual soul, has found its way to *Brahman,* the universal soul. The greatness of death has assumed proportions bigger than ever. The moon has become a symbol of death's genius. Like an Indian *kavi,* poet-philosopher, Eminescu has arrived at the conclusion that life and death are but two aspects of eternal life.

After the *Epistles,* **"Hyperion"** is published (1883)—Eminescu's masterpiece, with an altogether new idea of death. The astral hero and the earthly heroine can never unite. She will not leave the earth and he cannot leave the sky. She is subjected to the laws of death, and he is chained to the order of immortality. The Evening Star requests Demiurge to take back his halo of immortality, for He is "the fountain of life and the giver of death". But the Demiurge does not set him free from cosmic orders, an idea which corresponds to the conception of *rita* in the *Rigveda.* The laws of creation separates the loving souls coming from two different worlds, the heaven and the earth.

Usually death is conceived as a way of escape from the sufferings of life. In this poem Eminescu conceives it as a possible exit from the sufferings of immortality. The tragedy of the genius rests in the fact that the boon of death is denied to him; he will have to carry his burden of solitariness for ever. The mortals will attain uninterrupted peace at death; but the "thirst for eternal peace" of the immortal will never be quenched. By such an interpretation of the tragedy of the Evening Star, Eminescu makes death more desirable than immortality, and throws a new light on the myth of paradise.

The synthesis of life and death is more developed in **"The Gloss"** (1883) mainly inspired from Buddhist philosophy. Quite different from the hero of **"A Dacian's Prayer,"** who isolated himself from the world and challenged the creator with hate and curse, the poet of **"The Gloss"** stays in the midst of humanity, but does not hate anybody, nor is he attached to anything.

It is said in the Buddhist code of morals, *Dhammapada,* "Let us live among men who hate each other, and let us not hate anybody. Let us live in the midst of agitation and let us be calm and live happily" (*Dhammapada,* XV, 1-3). A similar spirit of detachment is observed in **"The Gloss."**

> "Give their touch a wide, wide berth;
> Hold your tongue if they blaspheme;
> Since you know what they are worth,
> What could your advice redeem?
> Let all say whate'er they like:
> Never mind whom they surpass;
> Lest you should endear some tyke,
> Keep as cool as ice or glass."

(Trs. Andrei Bantaş)

Seated at the "cool balance of thought", Eminescu arrives at the control of passions. Now he is equally indifferent to the pleasant and the unpleasant. The disciple of the Buddha has come near *nirvana.* The spirit of **"The Gloss"** is also in conformity with that of the *Bhagavad Gita,* which maintains that one who is not moved by either happiness or sorrow, gain or loss, who remains the same in victory and defeat, and who is free from fear, anger and bitterness can verily be called wise" (*Bhagavad Gita,* II, 38, 56).

"The Gloss" is immediately followed by **"Ode in Sapphic Metre"** (1883), permeated with an acute longing for death. To Eminescu's mind, death no longer signi-

fies the exit from sufferings. The teachings of the Buddha guides him not to look for salvation through death. He calls the "sad indifference" to make him pass over the humdrums of daily life. The poet believes that at last he has learnt to die.

The year 1883 is the last year of Eminescu's creative life. He loses his mental lucidity this year and dies in 1889. Now he feels steps of death within himself, and waits for it with the quietness of a philosopher. The love of life increases at the same time, but it is not mixed with any lust for living. Death and life attract him equally, but there is no conflict, no dichotomy between the two.

> "My mind tries hard to lead me along oft-trodden roads
> For Life and Death to liken, my soul it lures and goads;
> But my thought's scales and balance to change are ever loath
> Because the tongue is lying unmoved between them both."

('*Tis Midnight Struck.* Trs. Andrei Bantaş)

The time has come for death to put him to sleep. After the intense restlessness of a dramatic life, Eminescu is left with one single desire, the last desire, to die at the border of the sea. No rich coffins are wanted, no banners, no tears. He wants to be one with the earth in a bed woven with tender twigs, to have the blessings of the holy lime and to be assimilated in Nature:

> "As I shall cease at last
>   To wade in the world's muddle,
> Dear moments of the past
>   Will to my tombstone huddle.
> The stars, my friends that peep
>   Through shady firs, of yore,
>   Will smile and evermore
> Will watch and guard my sleep.
>   Torn by her passions rude,
> The sea will sing and cry,
> While I am dust and lie
>   In perfect solitude."

(*The Boon Which I Last Crave.* Trs. Leon Leviţchi)

Death will link him to life for ever.

The Romanian poet searched for the sense of death in mythology, in religion and in philosophies of the world over. In the last days of his life he discovered it in "the mioritic space", in the fundamental idea of *Miorita,* the ballad of his native land.

And, he left us his epitaph and his testament, **"The Boon Which I Last Crave,"** the poetry and the philosophy of his immortal life.

Elizabeth Close (essay date 1980)

SOURCE: Close, Elizabeth. "Eminescu's 'Călin': From Folktale to Poem of Love." *Southeastern Europe/ L'Europe du Sud-Est* 7, no. 1 (1980): 32-49.

[*In the following essay, Close describes Eminescu's rendering of a Romanian folktale in his poem "Călin".*]

Between about 1871 and 1875, Eminescu composed verse forms of three Romanian folktales: **"Călin Nebunul"** (**"Călin the Madcap"**), **"Fata în grădina de aur"** (**"The Girl in the Golden Garden"**) and **"Miron şi frumoasa fără corp"** (**"Miron and the Beautiful Girl without a Body"**). The original versions of the latter two tales are known only through the German translations of Richard Kunisch,[1] but for **"Călin Nebunul"** we have the original prose tale collected by Eminescu[2] and preserved among his manuscripts, his poeticised version of it,[3] and a very personal poem of love created from some of the material in this poeticised version. The personal poem of love, **"Călin—file din poveste"** (**"Călin—Leaves from a Folktale"**) was published in 1876.[4] Through a study of the content and structure of these three texts one can trace the stages by which Eminescu worked on the raw material of the unsophisticated folktale until he transformed it into a vehicle for his own obsessions.

It is not proposed in the present article to make an analysis of individual words or constructions, as one of the most illuminating aspects of Eminescu's language has already been studied in great detail by L. Gáldi: the modification of adjectives and adjectival phrases between the three versions.[5] Gáldi found, surprisingly perhaps, that Eminescu uses the same types of learned epithets in both the poeticised version of the folktale and the personal poem, even though the latter has given many critics a general impression of being more sophisticated in language and style.[6]

In his poeticised version of the folktale, Eminescu modified the way the story is told, but not the story itself. Later, he selected certain incidents from his poem and used them as the basis of a love poem which succeeds in recalling some of the magical atmosphere of the folktale at the same time as it expresses a passionate and very personal desire for a perfect and exalted yet homely love, a desire which is found in a number of Eminescu's poems of the period 1875-77. This final poem, which cannot be regarded as a version of the folktale, is the only part of the Calin material to have been published by Eminescu.

The prose tale, **"Călin Nebunul"** (**"Călin the Madcap"**) seems to be an amalgamation of two folktales belonging to the category called "the dragonslayer,"[7] though it is further removed from the type than most versions. Călin, who is generally considered in his village to be rather odd, is the youngest of three brothers who set out to rescue the three daughters of a king, abducted by three mysterious young men, ogres in disguise. Călin's exploits during the quest soon set him apart from his brothers, who achieve little or nothing. One night, while seeking embers for the fire he has allowed to go out, he is captured by twelve ogres, who offer to spare his life if he will help them abduct the Red King's daughter from her father's palace. Călin agrees, and as they set off he sees a young man, resembling him, tied to a tree. The young man struggles to free himself, and in so doing tears off his arms before fleeing. At the palace, Călin cuts off each ogre's head as he helps him over the palace wall. He then goes to the girl's bedroom, where he simply kisses her, takes her ring, and departs. On his way out of the palace, he cuts off the ogres' tongues and takes them with him. Now the story returns to the original quest. Călin goes back to his brothers, who are still asleep because he had magically lengthened the night by tying up Dusk, Midnight and Dawn, then untying them as he returned from the Red King's palace.

The three brothers go as far as the Golden Wood, which Călin alone can enter. There, he finds the king's eldest daughter, preparing food for her ogre-husband. When the ogre returns, Călin, who has eaten all of his food, fights and kills him. Leaving the girl to wait while he rescues her sisters, he goes to the Silver and Brass Woods, where he rescues the middle and youngest sisters. The only differences in treatment are that he falls in love with the middle sister, and has a much harder fight, won by supernatural means, with the last ogre. Taking the sisters back to his brothers, Călin claims the middle one as his bride, then lies down to sleep. His brothers promptly cut off his legs, and take all three sisters away.

The tale then returns to the theme of the Red King's daughter. Călin meets up with the young man who lost his arms, and together they have their limbs miraculously restored, and arrive at the Red King's palace in time to prevent his daughter's marriage to a cook who had falsely claimed to have killed the ogres. Călin declines the girl's hand, but his suggestion that she marry his companion is accepted by all parties.

After the wedding, Călin returns home, to find that his brothers have married the eldest and youngest of the King's daughters and banished Călin's sweetheart, now the mother of his son, to a humble cottage. Călin kills his brothers by hurling an iron ball in the air, declaring that it will fall on the guilty one(s). The tale ends with the marriage of Călin and his sweetheart.

The story of **"Călin Nebunul"** has all the simplicity of outline combined with attention to ritual details which one expects of a supernatural folktale. In his poeticised version,[8] Eminescu remains remarkably faithful to the content, but only partly to the form and atmosphere. The only factual changes in the poem are the omission or modification of insignificant details, and the minor tidying-up of loose ends. Nevertheless, a number of incidents are expanded by the addition of subjective material characteristic of Eminescu's poetic inspiration, material which tends to be descriptive and emotive, and which changes the tenor of the poem.

The first such incident occurs at the beginning of the tale. In the prose version, the account of the reception of the three mysterious suitors is very short and simple:

> Acu-ntro-o sară a venit trei tineri și le-o cerut, da'el
> n-o vrut să le dea[9]

Eminescu describes the youths in vaguely menacing terms, and regrets that they asked the king for his daughters. Their evil act is thus foreshadowed in the poetry:

> Da-ntr-o sară-n drum de țară cine dealul mi-l coboară?
> Trei feciori voinici de frunte ca trei șoimi voinici de
>   munte,
> Vin în zale îmbrăcați, pe cai negri-ncălicați,
> Spițelați, ușori ca vîntul, de-o frumseță-ntunecoasă,
> Au venit să-i ceară, Doamne, fetele cele frumoase.
> Dar mai bine-ar fi să-i ceară tot bielșugul de pe țară!
> Și ce nu se pun de-i cer trei luceferi de pe cer!
> De-ar puté, de n-ar putea, trei luceferi el li-ar da,
> Dară fetele lui ba.[10]

The subject matter has not been changed, the suitors in the poem are identical to those in the prose tale; but the atmosphere of the poetic version allows us to anticipate the unhappy fate of the sisters.

The second expanded incident is a purely descriptive one, an evocation of a clear, moonlit night against which the Red King's castle looms majestically:

> Luna iese dintre codri, noaptea toată stă s-o vadă.
>
>   . . . . .
>
> Înrădăcinată-n munte, cu trunchi lung de neagră stîncă,
> Repezită mult în aer din prăpastia adîncă,
> A-mpăratului cel Roșu stă măreața cetățuie,
> Poalele-i în văi de codri, fruntea-n ceruri i se suie.[11]

This description, a late and pale reflection of the fantastic palaces in some of Eminescu's earlier works,[12] leads into the incident which later proves to be one of the most personal and deeply-felt in the entire poem: Călin's visit to the bedroom of the Red King's daughter. It is briefly sketched in the prose tale: "Da' era lună ș-o mîndreață afară, și luna bătea în casă unde dormea fata. Da' fata era așa de frumoasă de cît de nepovestit. Călin Nebunul a sărutat-o și i-o luat inelul de pe mînă și s-o dus."[13]

Eminescu takes up the reference to moonlight and to the girl's beauty, and makes his Călin perform the same actions; but whereas the prose tale is flat and factual, the poet's words suggest an idealised eroticism which he was unable to develop in this poem—for Călin must not fall in love with the Red King's daughter—but which haunted him so much that he made it the keystone of his second poem. Even in his **"Călin Nebunul,"** however, he lingers over the description of the room: the gentle moonlight, the soft carpets, the flower-strewn bed, the emerald spider in a web sparkling like diamonds; and gazing through the web he contemplates the sleeping girl:

> Și prin mreaj-asta vrăjită vedeai patul ei de flori,
> Ea cu umeri de zăpadă și cu părul lucitor
> Și mai goală este-n somnu-i, numai bolta naltă, sură
> A ferestei este rece și simțirea nu o fură,
> Dar de pînz-acoperită-i cu un colb de piatră scumpă.
> S-apropie-ncet voinicul și cu mîna va s-o rumpă,
> Apoi lin o dă-ntr-o parte, peste fată se înclină,
> Pune gura lui fierbinte pe-a ei buze ce suspină[14]

The emotions underlying this description are clarified only in **"Călin—file din poveste."** In **"Călin Nebunul"** it remains a fairy-tale interlude in the main story.

Ritual repetitions of various sorts are one of the most obvious characteristics of oral tales, and one which occurs with particular frequency is the series of similar incidents described in exactly similar terms. In **"Călin Nebunul"** the release of Călin's nighttime prisoners and then of the three sisters are typical examples of the formula. Eminescu's treatment of both episodes is significant. The first he reduces to two lines: an unimportant incident in the story is thus scaled down to something like the position it merits, whereas in the oral version each release is described separately, with the same details each time.

The second series, the release of the king's daughters from the ogres, is in the folktale another simple narrative with stylised repetitions. The formula is varied only in the reaction of the middle sister to Călin, and in the climax to the third fight. This series is indeed absolutely typical of the oral style, giving us that reassuring familiarity with the unfolding story that we expect from the folktale.

Eminescu remains faithful to the technique of ritual repetition, but he makes some interesting modifications to both content and form.[15] He adds a description of each wood in a lyrical passage in which he indulges his Romantic weakness for moonlit scenes of fantastic splendor. The most magnificent is the Silver Wood, where he is to find the girl with whom he falls in love:

> În pădurea argintoasă iarba pare de omăt,
> Flori albastre tremur ude în văzduhul tămîiet,

Pare că şi trunchii mîndri poartă suflete sub coajă,
Ce suspină pintre ramuri cu a glasului lor vrajă,
Crengile sunt ca vioare pintre care vîntul trece,
Frunze sunt ca clopoţeii, trezind ceasul doisprezece.[16]

Then follows a description of the girls in the wood, each in turn shown as being very different from her sisters. The most developed portrait is that of the girl in the Silver Wood, with whom Călin falls in love at first sight. While the oral version says simply that he fell in love with her as soon as he saw her, and she with him, Eminescu has as well a poetic description of her, culminating in a lovely image:

Şi cu poalele ei albe şterge stelele-i senine,
Lacrimi lungi ce curg pe faţa-i ca şi fire diamantine[17]

—and followed by an internal monologue in which Călin takes up this image and meditates on the beauty of a few tears, the tragedy of unleashing them all:

Stea ce cade taie lumea ca o lacrimă de-argint,
Pe seninul cer albastru frumos lacrimile-l prind,
Şi din cînd în cind vărsate frumos lacrime te prind
Dar de seci întreg izvorul, vai de ochiul tău cel blînd[18]

This highly poetic evocation of Călin's love, and its presentation in Romantic terminology, contrasts with the naturalness of the girl's reaction to the same emotion. And while Călin provides his own commentary, the girl's feelings are analysed by Eminescu as narrator, with simplicity and a touch of humor:

"Dar ce vînt te bate-ncoace şi ce rău te-aduce-aice?"
Zise ea zîmbind—de multă vreme zîmbi-ntîia dată,
Căci şi ei îi cade drag el, deşi n-ar vré s-o arate—
Ştie ea de ce îi place, ca să n-o prindă de veste,
Ce frumos îl află dînsa, cum îi stă, ce drag îi este?[19]

When Călin finds the sisters, they are singing, not preparing food as in the prose tale. The songs,[20] traditional laments of the bride who has been separated from her parents, give the supernatural story an element of unaffected intimacy which brings it into the orbit of ordinary Romanian country life.

Other vivid pictorial touches are provided by the brief but apt descriptions of the three irate ogres, and by the epic style of the account of the final battle:

Vine zmeul, vine iute, mişcînd codrii cei de aur,
Cu cap mare ca cuptorul şi cu aripi de balaur.

. . . . .

După ce mai odihniră, zise zmeul:—Măi Căline,
Nu s-alege-ntre noi lupta, ci-ostenim aşa, vezi bine,
Da' m-oi face-o pară roşă şi te-i face-o pară verde
Ş-om lupta pîn' din noi unul se va stinge şi s-a pierde.

. . . . .

Ei jucau pin crengi înalte, pintre trestie, pe baltă,
Balta tremură adîncă, somnoros şi lin sclipeşte,

Azvîrlind întunecată cîte-o muscă, cîte-un peşte
Către flamele-ostenite. . . . Peste ei deodată zboară
Ca o pată de cerneală-n noaptea aurită-o cioară.
Zice zmeul:—Moaie, cioară, aripa-ţi în apă, stinge
Flacăra cea verde, care nu-s în stare a o-nvinge.
—Împărate pré nălţate, moaie-ţi aripa în apă,
Zice-atunci Călin, şi stinge flacăra roşă—mă scapă.
Iară cioara, cumu-i coiară, cum aude că o urcă,
Nici una, nici două, iute se coboară, nu se-ncurcă
Şi lăsînd din bot să-i cadă două picături de apă,
Potoleşte para roşă, ce tresare, fuge, crapă,
Şi cu botul o ciupeşte, curge sînge ca fier roş,
Încît lacul cel albastru e-ncruşit ca vinul roş.
Zmeul a murit. . . .[21]

The folktale's unadorned style of swift factual narration has thus given way in the episode of the three woods to a colorful portrayal of the ogres and the battles, a sensitive appreciation of the idyllic forests, a sympathetic understanding of the plight of the sisters, and above all a tender evocation of the nascent love between Călin and the middle sister.

In the folktale the next episode, Călin's return to his brothers with the three girls, crucial though it is, is passed over more swiftly than the content demands, even in the oral style: for this is after all the night when Călin's son is conceived. All we have is:

. . . s-o pornit ş-o ajuns la fraţii lui.
Ş-o zis aşa:
    —Fraţilor, pe aste două le-ţi lua voi,
dar ast' mijlocie e-a mea; şi s-o culcat să
doarmă.[22]

In the poem, this incident is developed in two ways. First, Eminescu shows us a happy, carefree, intimate camp, similar in atmosphere to the tranquil, loving cottage interiors which he described in various other poems:[23]

La o ploscă de vin negru stînd de vorbă bucuroşi,
Parcă-i zugrăveşte focul cu răsfrîngerile-i roşi.

. . . . .

Iar Călin, lungit pe burtă şi cu mîinile pe coate,
Cam cu chef le povesteşte întîmplările lui toate.[24]

Second, he describes the simplicity and naturalness of the love between Călin and the middle sister:

El o simte-n a lui braţe tînără, rotundă, tare
Şi ea tremură ca varga de oţel de-a lui strînsoare.
Îşi ascunde faţa roşă de iubire şi sfială,
Ochii-n lacrimi îi ascunde-n părul moale de peteală..
Şi adorm.[25]

He does not emphasize the sexual aspect: there is no need to do so, for the whole passage is shot through with discreet eroticism.

In a similar vein, Călin's return home after years of wandering is portrayed as a return to his only love. In the prose tale, the girl is mentioned only when the child tells Călin "Mama-mi spune că-s a lui Călin Nebunul, cine-a mai fi acela,"[26] and subsequently as his wife; but for Eminescu the focus of this final episode is Călin's entry into her cottage, whither she has been banished by the jealous brothers. The detailed, loving description sounds as if it were a cherished memory—or a dream—for the poet himself:

> Hîrîie-n colţ colbăită noduros rîşniţa veche,
> În cotlon toarce motanul, pieptănîndu-şi o ureche;
> Sub icoana afumată unui sfînt cu comănac
> Arde-n candelă-o lumină cît un sîmbure de mac.
>
> . . . . .
>
> Cofa-i albă cu flori negre şi a brad miroase apa,
> De lut plină, rezimată, stă pe coada ei o sapă.[27]

The reunion of the lovers is tender, too emotional for words to pass between them, and gently erotic. A union of soul and body, such as Eminescu often dreams of in his poetry:[28]

> Pleacă gura la ureche-i, blînd pe nume el o cheamă,
> Ea deschide somnoroasă lunge gene de aramă
> Şi adînc la el se iută, i se pare că visează.
> Ar zîmbi şi nu se-ncrede, ar striga şi nu cutează.
> Ş-apoi îi suceşte părul 'n-a ei degete subţire
> Şi-şi ascunde faţa roşă pe-al lui piept duios de mire.
> El ştergarul i-l desprinde şi-l împinge lin la vale,
> Drept în creştet o sărută pe-al ei păr de aur moale.[29]

Eminescu was to return to this last episode of **"Călin Nebunul,"** as to the portrait of the Red King's daughter asleep in her marvellous room, in **"Călin—file din poveste,"** to create from them two of the finest passages in which personal experience and private dreams are fused with the material provided initially by the folktale.

Although the genesis of **"Călin—file din poveste"** in **"Călin Nebunul"** is quite clear (and although stylistically they would seem from Gáldi's masterly analysis to be particularly close to each other), the intention behind the later poem is quite different. There are also some curious elements in it, which have been regarded as ill-assimilated.[30] However, as Eminescu chose to publish the poem, after experimenting with a number of versions,[31] it is worth making a serious attempt to appreciate it as a finished work of art.

The poem[32] is divided into eight sections of very unequal length, preceded by a fourteen-line dedicatory *gazel*[33] addressed to a beloved woman and linked thematically to section three of the poem.

In the first section, a hero visits a sleeping princess in her moonlit room in a castle, kisses her and takes her ring. This section has its origins in Călin's visit to the daughter of the Red King. The second section, only four lines long, describes the girl's thoughts on waking next morning, and the third continues the same theme

with an extended comparison of the girl's thoughts and dreams with those of Narcissus. Her reveries, it seems, enable her to conjure up her mysterious lover; and section four describes their nightly meetings, idyllic love-scenes in which Eminescu expresses his perpetual longing for perfect love. In section five, the poet addresses the girl, abandoned by her lover and weeping at her window, and pleads with her not to cry. He then turns to the girl's father, "a foolish old king" and upbraids him, in section six, for banishing his daughter to bear her child in obscurity. The physical description of the father is based on that of the king in **"Călin Nebunul"** after the loss of his daughters. Section seven describes the return of the lover, now named for the first time as Călin. His return is virtually identical to the return home of the hero in **"Călin Nebunul."** The eighth and last section, describing the magnificent wedding of the young couple with the sun and moon as witnesses, opens with a description of a forest very similar to the Silver Wood in **"Călin Nebunul,"** and ends with a humorous wedding in miniature, that of a butterfly and a violet, celebrated alongside the wedding of Călin and his sweetheart.

Guillermou sees **"Călin—file din poveste"** as a new poem with a different meaning from the previous **"Călin."**[34] In this he is perfectly correct; but it is not so certain that he is right to reduce the "essential" themes to only two: the romantic fantasy of Călin's visit to the girl's room, and the butterfly's wedding.[35] He is, however, undoubtedly correct in his assessment of these themes: the former is a reflection of Eminescu's obsession with a particular woman (as are also the dedicatory lines and the third section);[36] and the latter completes the portrait of Călin's wedding by making it part of the infinite series of unions of which Nature is composed, from the greatest to the smallest.[37]

It is, however, a mistake to stay too close to the surface details of this poem. Guillermou tends to do this, even describing some themes as "secondary," others as "accidental."[38] As our analysis will show, **"Călin—file din poveste"** has an essential unity in diversity, an impressive singleness of purpose drawing the threads together as the central fire of a diamond concentrates the light from all its facets.

The principal strands to the inspiration which gave us this poem seem to be three: the supernatural hero who exchanges his immortality for a human idyll; the experience, or dream, of perfect and mutual love; and opposition to a society which condemns a love prohibited by its conventional moral code.

The theme of the unearthly lover, here a "zburător cu negre plete,"[39] who seduces a human girl and abandons her to the reproaches of society only to return to her finally and take her as his bride, is of course taken from the earlier **"Călin"** and the folktale, but for its meaning in the present poem we must look forward to **"Luceafărul."** In this poem, perhaps Eminescu's masterpiece, a heavenly being, Hyperion, who adopts the form of the Evening Star, is called down to Earth by an emperor's daughter who has fallen in love with him. Reluctantly, on her refusal to follow him out of space, time and mortality, he agrees to renounce his immortality and marry her on Earth. But the girl is unfaithful, and the poem ends with Hyperion's sorrowful yet proud withdrawal to the universe of the immortals. In **"Călin—file din poveste"** the girl does not seek to hold her lover in her mortal world, nor is she unfaithful to him, and she is ultimately rewarded by his voluntary return.

The other themes in **"Călin—file din poveste"** arise from this central one. Thus the flawless love of hero and heroine is the love which Eminescu was prepared to offer only if he could receive it too: he suggests that he would be willing to give up his aspirations to artistic immortality for a woman who loved him without reservations. And that woman was without doubt the great love of the years he spent in Iaşi (1874-77): Veronica Micle.[40]

The third theme, castigation of a society which cannot tolerate a love which transgresses the accepted moral code may, because of Veronica's marital situation, be a personal outburst directed against her enemies or her lover's.

In **"Călin—file din poveste,"** love triumphs over both art and conventional morality, and so should be read as a supreme appeal to Veronica to put her faith in love. The following analysis attempts to show how Eminescu grafted his own obsessions and experience onto existing material—his own and the folktale's—and transformed it into a personal, almost secret affirmation of the supremacy of love.

The nighttime visit of the hero to the girl's bedroom, with which the poem opens, contains a description of the room which has the same atmosphere as the parallel passage in **"Călin Nebunul"**: in both rooms, decked with flowers and lit by the moon, the sleeping girl is covered by a fantastic spider's web glittering with precious stones. But it is only in **"Călin-file din poveste"** that the poet describes the girl herself—for in **"Călin Nebunul"** he was not destined to fall in love with her:

> Răsfiratul păr de aur peste perini se-mprăştie,
> Tîmpla bate liniştită ca o umbră viorie,
> Şi sprîncenele arcate fruntea albă i-o încheie,
> Cu o singură trăsură măiestrit le încondeie;
> Sub pleoapele închise globii ochilor se bat,
> Braţul ei atîrnă leneş peste marginea de pat.[41]

The kiss itself is described in similar terms to the kiss in **"Călin Nebunul,"** but now the hero, moved by the girl's beauty, takes her in his arms:

> A frumseţii haruri goale ce simţirile-i adapă,
> Încăperile gîndirii nu mai pot să le încapă.
> El în braţe prinde fata, peste faţă i se-nclină,
> Pune gura lui fierbinte pe-a ei buze ce suspină.[42]

Only the last line and a half of this quotation are found in **"Călin Nebunul."** There is thus in the present poem an erotic note which was barely suggested in the earlier one. This note is reinforced by the girl's reaction when she wakes next morning:

> Ea a doua zi se miră cum de firele sunt rupte,
> Şi-n oglind-ale ei buze vede vinete şi supte—
> Ea zîmbind şi trist se uită, şopoteşte blînd din gură:
> —Zburător cu negre plete, vin' la noapte de mă fură.[43]

The lover is thus established as a supernatural figure, a being set apart from the rest of the world who bewitches his mistress and transports her to an idyllic dreamworld where the rules of conventional society have no power.[44]

The third section develops the ideas in section two: the girl continues to gaze at her own reflection—Dar ea seamănă celora îndrăgiţi de singuri ei-şi—and she whispers to herself:

> "Vis frumos avut-am noaptea. A venit un zburător
> Şi strîngîndu-l tare-n braţe, era mai ca să-l omor. . . .
> Şi de-aceea cînd mă caut în păretele de oglinzi,
> Singurică-n cămăruţă braţe albe eu întinz
> Şi mă-mbrac în părul galben, ca în strai uşor ţesut,
> Şi zărind rotundu-mi umăr mai că-mi vine să-l sărut.
> Şi atunci de sfiiciune mi-iese sîngele-n obraz—
> Cum nu vine zburătorul ca la pieptul lui să caz?"[45]

Guillermou may well be right to suggest that this passage, like the dedicatory *gazel,* is an oblique reference to Veronica Micle's self-centred attitude.[46] At the same time, it is a sensitive insight into the feelings of a girl touched by love or passion for the first time, half convinced that she can bring her lover to her by the intensity of her longing. She gives her lover the total, unquestioning adoration which Eminescu longed to receive from a woman, she is the poet's ideal mistress at this moment.

The next section leads naturally out of this passionate monologue. The opening line—Astfel vine-n toată noaptea zburător la al ei pat[47]—suggests that she succeeds in bringing him to her by the power of her longing for him. Then follows an idyllic love scene full of natural, unforced happiness, painted by the lover in simple terms. Again Eminescu returns to his need for total, unquestioning love:

> Al vieţii vis de aur ca un fulger, ca o clipă-i,
> Şi-l visez, cînd cu-a mea mînă al tău braţ rotund îl pipăi,
> Cînd pui capul tu pe pieptu-mi şi bătăile îi numeri,
> Cînd sărut cu-mpătimire ai tăi albi şi netezi umeri
> Şi cînd sorb al tău răsuflet în suflarea vieţii mele
> Şi cînd inima ne creşte de *un* dor, de-o dulce jele.[48]

The next two sections of the poem (five and six) seem odd at first sight, because the poet ceases to identify himself completely with the lover, to become the poet, watching first the girl weeping at her window, then her remorseful father. Both passages are written by a first-person narrator, which permits the poet to address the girl and her father directly. There are two advantages to this technique at this point in the poem: it allows the reader a more direct involvement with very deeply-felt emotions, and it permits the poet to adopt a role which is often that of narrator and lover simultaneously.

Addressing the weeping girl, Eminescu warns her of the danger of shedding all her tears, in nearly the same terms as the earlier Călin in his internal monologue, when he sees and falls in love with the weeping girl in the Silver Wood; but now the image likening tears to stars, and eyes which have no tears left to a starless night sky is taken further, and the meaning of this curious image becomes clearer:

> Noaptea stelelor, a lunei, a oglinzilor de rîu
> Nu-i ca noaptea cea mocnită şi pustie din sicriu;
> Şi din cînd în cînd vărsate, mîndru lacrimile-ţi şed,
> Dar de seci întreg izvorul, atunci cum să te văd?"[49]

In his analysis of these lines, which have no exact equivalent in "Călin Nebunul,"[50] Guillermou argues persuasively that in this passage the eyes are the person, and if the eyes no longer express feeling, then the person is lost.[51]

Whatever the precise meaning of the image, the general significance of the passage is clear: Eminescu as poet and as lover tries to comfort the desolate girl. It does not seem out of place here to compare Veronica Micle's position with the girl's, for if Călin's mistress, abandoned by her supernatural lover and shunned by the world for her sin deserves pity and compassion, then so does Veronica, a married woman in love with another man (and whether or not she genuinely loved him, Eminescu surely thought that she did).

The poet's tender concern for the unhappy girl leads naturally to castigation of her father for sending her away to bear her child in a lonely hovel. Although the physical description of the distraught king owes much to the description of the king in **"Călin Nebunul,"** the atmosphere is quite different, for this father is suffering a just punishment. Indeed, Eminescu sounds as if he were condemning all straitlaced members of society for their attitude towards lovers who dare flout the conventions:

> O, tu crai cu barba-n noduri ca şi cîlţii cînd nu-i perii,
> Tu în cap nu ai grăunţe, numai pleavă şi puzderii.
> Bine-ţi pare să fii singur, crai bătrîn fără de minţi,
> Să oftezi dup-a ta fată, cu ciubucul între dinţi?[52]

The hero's return after seven years is in all but insignificant details a repetition of the account in **"Călin Nebunul,"** and is even more apposite here, coming as it does at the climax of a poem which has been stripped of folkloric incident to become the story of a moving love affair. The naturalness of the lovers' reunion has an air of magical inevitability akin to that of the original union in the girl's fairy-tale bedroom: the circumstances may be very different—the wonderful room has become a peasant's cottage—but again the world stands still for the lovers. The hero returns to his chosen mistress, and is accepted by her without hesitation. This is how Eminescu would have liked to be accepted by *his* mistress.

The last section of the poem, describing the splendid wedding of the young couple, is largely new, but the opening description of the forest is almost identical to the Silver Wood, though the last four lines are taken from the Golden Wood in **"Călin Nebunul."** The wedding itself brings together Eminescu's personal preoccupations at this time as poet and lover, the magical world of folk literature, and the homely world of the village:

> Acum iată că din codru şi Călin mirele iese,
> Care ţine-n a lui mînă mîna gingaşei mirese.
> Îi foşnea uscat pe frunze poala lung-a albei rochii,
> Faţa-i roşie ca mărul, de noroc i-s umezi ochii;
> La pămînt mai că ajunge al ei păr de aur moale,
> Care-i cade peste braţe, peste umerele goale.
> Astfel vine mlădioasă, trupul ei frumos îl poartă,
> Flori albastre are-n păru-i şi o stea în frunte poartă.
> 　　Socrul roagă-n capul mesei să poftească să se pună
> Nunul mare, mîndrul soare, şi pe nună, mîndra lună.
> Şi s-aşează toţi la masă, cum li-s anii, cum li-i rangul,
> Lin vioarele răsună, iară cobza ţine hangul.[53]

Although Eminescu says nothing direct, the special significance of the *zburător*'s return to the mortal world, and his marriage to his mortal mistress, is suggested by the blue flowers worn in her hair by the bride. In a poem called **"Floare albastră"** (**"Blue Flower"**), published in 1873, Eminescu recalls a beloved sweetheart who had urged him to abandon his intellectual preoccupations for a life of love and tranquillity in the forest. He was never able to make the choice, however, because she died, leaving him alone in the world. In the last, sorrowful verses, Eminescu addresses his dead sweetheart as "blue flower":[54]

> Înc-o gură—şi dispare . . .
> Ca un stîlp eu stam în lună!
> Ce frumoasă, ce nebună
> E albastra-mi, dulce floare!
>
> 　　. . . . .
>
> Şi te-ai dus, dulce minune,
> Ş-a murit iubirea noastră—
> Floare-albastră! floare-albastră! . . .
> Totuşi este trist în lume![55]

Now, in **"Călin—file din poveste,"** the *zburător* makes the decision which a part of Eminescu regrets not having been able to make: he gives up his supernatural existence to live out a human idyll.

The presence of the sun and moon at the wedding serves to indicate the acceptance by the natural world of the marriage.[56] This integration of the natural and the human worlds, which is a traditional theme of Romanian folk literature, makes an ideal transition to the butterfly's wedding, at once supernatural and comically realistic, an unexpected but delightfully happy conclusion to a magnificent hymn to the power of love:

> Iată vine nunta-ntreagă—vornicel e-un grierel,
> Îi sar purici înainte cu potcoave de oțel;
> În veșmînt de-catifele, un bondar rotund în pîntec
> Somnoros pe nas ca popii glăsuiește-ncet un cîntec;
> O cojiță de alună trag locuste, podu-l scutur,
> Cu musteața răsucită șede-n ea un mire flutur;
> Fluturi mulți de multe neamuri, vin în urma lui un lanț,
> Toți cu inime ușoare, toți șagalnici și berbanți.
> Vin țînțarii lăutarii, gîndăceii, cărăbușii,
> Iar mireasa viorică i-așteapta-ndărătul ușii.
>   Și pe masa-mpărătească sare-un greier, crainic sprinten
> Ridicat în două labe, s-a-nchinat bătînd din pinten;
> El tușește, își încheie haina plină de șireturi:
> —Să iertați, boieri, ca nunta s-o pornim și noi alături.[57]

Notes

1. R. Kunisch, *Bukarest und Stambul, Skizzen aus Ungarn, Rumänien und der Türkei* (Berlin: Publisher?, 1861).

2. Probably collected in Moldavia in 1869 (Perpessicius, *M. Eminescu Opere alese,* 2nd ed., 3 vols. [București: Minerva, 1973], III, 475, 519).

3. The final version was probably written in Iași in 1875 (*ibid.,* p. 475).

4. In *Convorbiri literare,* 1 Nov. 1876.

5. L. Gáldi, *Stilul poetic al lui Mihai Eminescu* (București: Minerva, 1964), pp. 142-56.

6. More detailed research into technique, of the type carried out so admirably by Gáldi, is needed. I. Rotaru, for example, has the impression that there is a marked contrast between the two poems, that in "Călin Nebunul" Eminescu made as few modifications as possible to the best parts of the tale, but that "Călin—file din poveste," at the other extreme, has only the occasional phrase to recall the original (I. Rotaru, *Eminescu și poezia populară* [București: Minerva, 1965], pp. 146-48, 160). G. Călinescu, too, regarded "Călin Nebunul" as a masterpiece in the peasant style, "Călin—file din poveste" as an oversentimental and cloyingly Ro-

mantic poem (G. Călinescu, *Opere,* 13 vols. [București: Editura Pentru Literatura, 1964-70], XIII, 524). A Guillermou describes "Calin Nebunul" as even more popular in style than the prose tale (A. Guillermou, *La Genèse intérieure des poésies d'Eminescu* [Paris: Didier, 1963], pp. 126-27). One might wish that these critics had provided as many detailed examples in support of their contentions as Gáldi did in support of his findings.

7. Aarne-Thompson classification Type 300, in Antti Aarne and Stith Thompson, *The Types of the Folktale* (Helsinki: Suomalainen Tiedeakatemia, 1961), p. 88. I give only the outline of the tale, omitting a few incidents which are not material to Eminescu's treatment and which will not figure in the discussion. The tale as it exists in Eminescu's notes is published in Perpessicius, III, 337-47.

8. The edition used for this article is *ibid.,* pp. 9-28.

9. "One evening three young suitors came to woo the princesses but the King would not give them his daughters." The English translation is by Ioana Sturdza, and is published in *Fairy Tales and Legends from Romania* (Bucharest: Meridiane, 1971), pp. 51-63.

10. "But one evening, who was seen coming down the pathway from the hills? Three young men as wonderfully strong as three strong mountain hawks, clad in suits of mail and riding black horses, slender, as light as the wind, with a sombre beauty. They came to seek his three beautiful daughters in marriage. It would have been better had they asked for all the wealth of his country! Or why did they not ask for three stars from the sky! Whether he could do it or not, he would have managed to give them three stars sooner than his daughters." All the translations from Eminescu's poetry are my own.

11. "The moon glided out from between the trees, and the night stood still to watch her. . . . Rooted in the depths of the mountain side, its body a tall black rock rising high in the sky above the yawning chasm, stood the magnificent fortress of the Red King, its foot hidden in wooded valleys, its forehead reaching up to the very heavens."

12. The reworked folktale *Făt-Frumos din Lacrimă* (*Prince Charming of the Tear*), the novella *Sărmanul Dionis* (*Poor Dionis*), and the unpublished poems "Miradoniz" and "Memento Mori" (all 1870-72).

13. "The moon was shining and the girl was too beautiful for words. Călin the Madcap kissed her, and taking her ring from her finger, left on tiptoe."

14. "And through this enchanted net you could see her flowery bed: and she herself, with snow-white

shoulders and shining hair, was almost naked in her sleep. Only the lofty grey arch of the window was cold, and touched by no feeling. Precious stones lay scattered like dust over the web which covered her. The hero approached her quietly, and stretched out his hand to tear the web, then gently moved it aside, bent over the girl, and laid his burning mouth on her trembling lips."

15. He even adds to the symmetry of the story by leaving the second sister as well as the first in her wood to await his return. And he changes the order of the woods from Gold—Silver—Brass to Brass—Silver—Gold, thus making a more satisfactory climax.

16. "In the Silver Wood the grass was like snow, blue flowers trembled dew-bedecked in the perfumed air; even the proud trees seemed to hide a soul beneath their bark, sighing with enchanted voice among the boughs; the branches were like violins played by the soughing breeze, the leaves like tinkling bells announcing the mid-day hour."

17. "And with her white robe she wiped away her tranquil tears, stars flowing down her face like sparkling diamonds."

18. "A falling star cuts through the air like a silver tear, beautiful tears are scattered over the clear blue sky, and tears shed from time to time make you beautiful too; but if you dry up the source, your gentle eyes will live no more."

19. "'But what wind blows you this way, what evil brings you here?' she said with a smile—she had been smiling for some time, because she was attracted to him too, although she didn't want to show it. Did she know why she liked him, did she want him to guess how handsome she thought him, how much she loved him?"

20. The three songs are *doine,* collected by Eminescu and modified to some extent to fit the context of "Călin Nebunul" (Rotaru, p. 152).

21. "The ogre came, came swiftly, thrusting aside the golden trees, an ogre with a head as big as an oven and with dragon's wings. . . . After they had rested a while, the ogre said: 'Călin, we shan't be able to decide between us by fighting, we shall just wear ourselves out. So while I turn myself into a red flame, you turn yourself into a green flame, and we'll fight until one of us is extinguished. . . .' They flickered among the lofty boughs, in the reeds and on the lake; and the depths of the lake trembled, its smooth surface gleamed somnolently, throwing now a fly, now a fish up to the tired flames. . . . Suddenly there flew above them, like a patch of ink in the golden night, a crow. Said the ogre: 'Crow, dip your wing

in the water and put out that green flame which I cannot conquer.' Then said Călin: 'O lofty emperor, dip your wing in the water and put out that red flame—you'll save me.' The crow, being a crow, on hearing himself thus dignified, didn't hesitate, but flew down swiftly, and letting two drops of water fall from his beak, damped down the red flame, which shuddered, fled and died, and with his beak the crow snatched it up: blood flowed like red-hot iron, so that the blue lake seemed to have rivers of red wine criss-crossing it. The ogre was dead."

22. "Then they set out to rejoin his brothers, and Călin said to them: 'Brothers, you may marry these two girls but the second is mine.' Whereupon he lay down to rest."

23. For example, "Cînd crivățul cu iarna . . ." ("When the winter wind . . . ," ca. 1870) and "Afară-i toamnă" ("It's autumn outside," 1878).

24. "They talked joyfully round the fire, their faces lit up by the glowing firelight, and passed around a gourd of red wine. . . . And Călin, lying on his stomach, propped up on his elbows, gaily recounted all his deeds."

25. "He could feel her young, rounded, firm body in his arms, and she trembled like a shaft of steel when he embraced her. She hid her face, blushing with shy love, and hid her tear-filled eyes beneath her soft golden hair; and they fell asleep."

26. "Mummy tells me I'm the son of Călin the Madcap, whoever he may be."

27. "An old, dusty food-mill was wheezing in one corner, in another a tom-cat was purring, preening his ear; under the smoke-stained icon of a saint dressed as a priest, a tiny light, as small as a poppy seed, was burning. . . . The wooden pail was white with black flowers, the water was scented with fir, and a mud-caked spade leaned against the wall."

28. For example, "Noaptea" ("Night," 1871), "Dorința" ("Longing," 1876), "Povestea codrului" ("The tale of the forest," 1878), "Povestea teiului" ("The tale of the limetree," 1878).

29. "He put his mouth against her ear, and gently spoke her name. She sleepily raised her long copper eye-lashes and looked deeply at him, thinking that she was dreaming. She wanted to smile, but couldn't trust herself, she wanted to cry out but didn't dare. Then she entwined his hair in her slender fingers and hid her blushing face against her bridegroom's loving heart. He untied her kerchief and gently pushed it away, and kissed the top of her soft golden hair."

30. Thus Guillermou (p. 131) on the changes from third-person narrative to direct speech and back again: "These changes . . . make 'Călin' seem oddly heterogeneous" (my translation).

31. Perpessicius (I, 298), describes three groups of mss, very varied in content and form.

32. The edition used for this article is *ibid.*, pp. 83-91.

33. A *gazel* is a poem in which the second line of each couplet after the first rhymes with both lines of the first couplet.

34. Guillermou, p. 127.

35. *Ibid.*, pp. 133-37.

36. *Ibid.*, pp. 129-31.

37. *Ibid.*, p. 137. Rosa del Conte (*Mihai Eminescu o dell'assoluto* [Modena: Società Tip. Editrice Modenese, 1962], p. 224) on the contrary, sees this episode as incongruous: "a popular fairy-tale pantheism, phantasmagoric certainly, but which fails to achieve mystical resonances and seems to be in discord with the refined atmosphere and platonic climate built up by the poet" (my translation).

38. For example, the girl's Narcissism and her tears, and other "inessential" themes which occur in mss but not in the final version (Guillermou, pp. 128-33).

39. The *zburător* is traditionally an evil, winged spirit who torments women and girls, but the word has come to mean also an idealised lover. It is best left ambiguous here.

40. There is little solid information, much unsubstantiated legend about Eminescu's affair with Veronica Micle, a married woman with two children. Although a certain degree of discretion seems to have been maintained by them and their friends, at least in writing, until her husband's death in 1879, circumstantial and later evidence points to their having had a passionate relationship in Iaşi, punctuated by quarrels or, at the least, misunderstandings (G. Munteanu, *Hyperion I: Viaţa lui Eminescu* [Bucureşti: Minerva, 1973], p. 176; A. Z. N. Pop, *Mărturii . . . Eminescu—Veronica Micle* [Bucureşti: Editura Tineretului, 1967], pp. 41-66). It should be noted too that 1874-77 marks the composition of some of Eminescu's most intense love-poems, of which "Călin—file din poveste" must be ranked among the greatest.

41. "Her golden mass of hair lay spread over the pillow, her temple throbbed gently like a mauve shadow, and arched eyebrows, painted with a single masterly stroke, bordered her white forehead. Her eyes fluttered beneath the closed lids, and her arm hung relaxed over the edge of the bed."

42. "He was no longer content merely to gaze upon the feast of naked beauty presented to his senses. He took the girl in his arms, and bending over her face he laid his burning mouth on her trembling lips."

43. "Next morning, she wondered why the covers were torn, and saw in the mirror how pale and drawn her lips were. Smiling sadly she looked at herself and whispered softly, 'Heavenly black-haired lover, come by night and steal me away.'"

44. As Guillermou perceptively observes (p. 128): "a good deal of the mystery of 'Călin' is founded on the delicate interplay of dream and reality" (my translation).

45. "She is like a person in love with herself. . . . 'I had a beautiful dream last night. A heavenly lover came to me, and holding him close in my arms, I almost thought to kill him. . . . And so now, when I look at myself in the mirror, alone in my room I stretch out my white arms and cover myself with my blond hair, as if it were a finely woven dress, and catching sight of my rounded shoulder I almost kiss it. And then for shame the blood rushes to my cheeks—Why doesn't my heavenly lover come so that I can lie against his chest?"

46. Guillermou, p. 130. The last three lines of the *gazel* show the lover holding a mirror for his mistress so that she can watch herself "dreaming and smiling."

47. "And so the heavenly lover comes to her bed every night."

48. "A golden dream of life is like a flash of lightning, gone in an instant; and I have that dream when my hand caresses your rounded arm, when you put your head on my breast and count my heart-beats, when I passionately kiss your smooth white shoulders, when I breathe in your breath and when our hearts swell with one single longing, one sweet sorrow."

49. "The night known to the stars, the moon and the glassy rivers is nothing like the gloomy, lonely night of the coffin; and the tears shed from time to time make you wondrously beautiful. But if you dry up the source, how shall I see you?"

50. The first couplet does not occur, the second has the form: Şi din cînd în cînd vărsate frumos lacrime te prind / Dar de seci întreg izvorul, vai de ochiul tău cel blînd (For translation, see above, note 18).

51. Guillermou, pp. 132-33.

52. "You, o King, with your matted beard like un-combed tow, you haven't any seeds of wisdom in your head, only chaff and husks. Are you happy to be alone, foolish old king, sighing for your daughter, with your hookah hanging out of your mouth?"

53. "And then came Călin the bridegroom, forth from the forest, leading his dainty bride by the hand. The dry leaves rustled beneath her long white dress, her cheeks were as red as an apple, her eyes wet with happiness; her soft golden hair, flowing over her arms, over her bare shoulders, nearly reached the ground. And so she advanced, beautiful and graceful, wearing blue flowers in her hair and a star on her forehead.

The bride's father invited the witnesses, the magnificent sun and moon, to sit at the head of the table. All the guests sat down too, according to their age and rank, and the violins played softly, accompanied by a *cobza*."

54. Similarities with Novalis's "blaue Blume" are biographical (Guillermou, p. 92) and superficial (the phrase itself—Al. Philippide, "Ceva despre 'Floarea albastră'," in *Caietele Mihai Eminescu*, 2 [1974], 12-18).

55. Perpessicius, I, 60-62. "One more kiss—and she disappears . . . I was left standing in the moonlight like a wooden post! How beautiful, how simple is my sweet blue flower! . . . And yet, the world is a sad place."

56. Guillermou, p. 137, and cf. above, note 37. This is not the only occasion on which Eminescu visualised the natural world blessing a lovers' union. In 'Dorinţa', published in 1876 but previously sent to Veronica Micle (*ibid.*, pp. 120-21) he pleads with his mistress to join him in the forest and accept a love sanctified by the concordance of the natural world (Perpessicius, I, 81-82). A similar plea is made in "Povestea codrului," published in 1878, but considered to belong to the love-poems of Eminescu's Iaşi period (*ibid.*, pp. 103-05).

57. "And then appeared the whole wedding party: the best man was a cricket, preceded by leaping fleas shod with steel. Clad in a velvet robe, a round-bellied bumble-bee slowly intoned a hymn in a sleepy nasal tone just like a priest's. The spider's-web bridge shook as locusts drew across it a hazel-nut shell bearing an elegantly-moustached butterfly—the bridegroom. A vast number of butterflies from many tribes were strung out behind him, all light of heart, all full of jokes, all ladies' men. Then came the musicians—mosquitos, and beetles and cockchafers, while the bride, a violet, waited behind the door.

On to the king's table jumped a cricket, a jaunty master of ceremonies. He stood on his back feet, bowed with a clicking of spurs, coughed, did up his elaborate coat: 'Excuse us, my lords, we'd like to have our wedding along-side yours.'"

Alexandru Opera (essay date 1980)

SOURCE: Opera, Alexandru. "The Journalist's Physiognomy." *Romanian Review* 40, no. 1 (1986): 10-23.

[*In the following essay, originally published in 1980, Opera pronounces Eminescu the exemplar of a Romanian journalist.*]

By the brilliance of its example, Eminescu's journalism has definitively justified the concept of the committed writer as a sensitive seismograph and spokesman of his nation's sorrows and aspirations.

True, at the time when the great poet had become "managing editor" of *Curierul de Iaşi,* Romanian journalism—a redoubtable weapon of great topicality—had already been launched on its specific path. Versatile authors, headed by Ion Eliade Rădulescu, had made a decisive contribution by their many flourishing publications, all tending to evince some peculiar feature. C. A. Rosetti—the poet's future victim—had produced in his *Românul,* the first modern-type Romanian daily.

As in poetry, the value of Eminescu lies not simply in the "introduction" of literary genres or formulae, but in sanctioning them, the effort being aimed at synthesis, as the incandescent retort of his talent fused and sublimated "discoveries" of his forerunners.

An interesting study could be made of his relationships to writer-journalists of the 1848 period. Eminescu compared himself to Cezar Bolliac, mainly on account of some similitudes of stance—the fact that the author of *The Bondmen* was the only one to devote so much of his writing, and so passionately, to the fate of the Romanian peasantry. When dealing at closer range with Bolliac's journalism, he would, however, point our specific expressive features too, praising *Buciumul* and *Trompeta Carpaţilor* for being "written in the living tongue of the people, with that common sense and that richness of tropes and those phrases which make for the purity and for the national character of our language" (*Timpul,* VI, 1881, No. 45, 27 February, p. 1).

G. Călinescu's opinion, that "Without any obvious verbal resemblance, Bolliac is substantially the forerunning poet closest related to the Eminescu mode," seems to apply even better to Eminescu's political journalism. The same investigation into the sources of the poet's "culture" enables the critic to find a term of comparison in the work of Eliade Rădulescu too. G. Călinescu found similarities and ideas in the sense of a moderate evolutionism condemning the indiscriminate borrowing of new "forms." There are also some points of resemblance in terms of the pamphleteer's skill, both stressing the Dantesque side—a vindictive furor tempting them to send their contemporaries into the bolgias of an imaginary Hell.

Eminescu's journalism strikes us by its forcefulness in blending—into an original alloy—features of the romantic-generous phase of the beginnings with the current, traditional habitudes of the modern journalist. For, as is known, for many writers of the 1848 generation journalism was only an occasional act, somehow subordinate to a kind of programmatic immediacy, sometimes characterized—with some exceptions, of course—by a certain amateurism, a superficial fervour to do a little of everything. Eminescu's contributions are notable, however, for their high professionalism, the poet doing journalism as a veritable métier, with all its prerogatives. It should be added that, capable of coping with the humdrum toil of everyday journalism, he never gave in to routine and convention, and raised the printed page to the height of conscience problems, keeping unaltered the old sacerdotal role of the written word.

The study of Eminescu's model is the more illuminating as this model emerged at a time when confusion among the genres had come to an end, when each domain strove to strictly impose its own specific status, resisting all inroads from outside. If this holds true in a general statement, the more so it is in the case of the opposition—exaggerated by many—between poetry and journalism.

One may recall, in this respect, the symbol used by Titu Maiorescu—the marble statue looking down with a smile, from the august height of eternal art, upon the bustle of men engaged in politics, that is in the ephemeral. Yet Eminescu, while in no way untrue to the eternal laws of poetic creation, at the same time lives incandescently amid the most "prosaic" problems of his day, problems of major significance, in actual fact, to his country's destiny. We know the explanation: his espousal of the position held by the peasantry, the basic class of the nation. This spiritual platform helps him to avoid being a captive within his strictly poetic horizon.

The situation is not, indeed, simple. In the previous historical periods, relations between authors and the public at large were, for the most part, spontaneous. But from the moment labour division imposed a sharp specialization—with autonomous tendencies—among the various forms of activity, the social basis of creation became problematical, raising obstacles to the restoration of spiritual completeness, to identification with the community, and generating phenomena of moral alienation. Eminescu was perfectly conscious of these truths. The

forerunners believed what they asserted, and quite naturally felt themselves to be members of the community, whereas "most of our modern authors leave one the impression that they are not for the public, nor the public for them." The poet is far from passing a superficial judgment, he understands that in the modern age a writer can no longer benefit by "sincere, unconscious naïveté, for he has eaten of the forbidden fruit: "We the newer ones know our own condition, we feel the spirit of the century, and that is why he have so much cause for discouragement." This is confirmed by his poetical works, which often enough let us glimpse the black waters of darkness. But while expressing, with dramatic sincerity, the *mal du siècle,* Eminescu's thinking never became a slave to it, never mythicized it—as do so many writers of yesterday and today—but found in itself the necessary strength to tend towards a global, balanced, harmonious outlook on life capable of supporting his spiritual links with his people's being. It goes without saying that the mainspring of moral vitality and the means by which Eminescu discovers the *terra firma* of his certainties are related to his journalistic capacity. A critic like Pompiliu Constantinescu wrote, perhaps a little too trenchantly: "It is surprising to see how the same sensibility experiences the categorical idea of nothingness in poetry, while (in journalism) it breathes out a vitalism raised to the value of an entity of the idea of nation, identified with the peasant and the voivodes."

One should also note, in the same connection, the way in which Eminescu receives Schopenhauer's influences. This aspect has been examined at length by almost all specialists, and a unanimous conclusion has been reached on the wide gulf separating the two in the field of ethics, since Eminescu could not accept, in his own self, the state of ataraxy resulting from the mortification of life and of any vital urge. As for the philosophical impact, recent studies have cogently proved that Schopenhauer may also have attracted the young poet by his large-scale demythicizing campaign against artificial optimism and shallow meliorism. It has been pointed out, none the less—that in Eminescu's meditations the perception of the evil sides of life developed not towards absolutizing the ontological plane—as in the German thinker's metaphysics—but towards discovering the many interferences with the historical determinations of phenomena. And that was a gradual evolution, in the course of time. Quite illuminating in this regard is a note by Eminescu, from 1888, in which the poet admits that an exaggeration of pessimistic exercises can result in "a joy to live and a desire to fight."

G. Călinescu, dealing in one of his "Chronicles of an Optimist" with Eminescu and his contemporaries, attacks Titu Maiorescu's "Schopenhauerian-escapist philosophy," pointing out that "while starting off from the same Schopenhauer, Eminescu was actually a fighter."

The distinction was true, with the well-known correction that, despite some theories he professed, Titu Maiorescu too, in his own way, suited to his own nature, had been a fighter and had set in motion what was styled as "the Junimea criticism," characteristic of an entire period.

From this general angle, one cannot overlook certain real points of contact between the physiognomy and spirit of Eminescu's criticism and Schopenhauer's criticism. It is true that in his articles the poet does not engage exclusively or preferentially in speculative-philosophical discourses, but strikes out into other territories as well, such as history (in the first place) and political economy. One should note, though, the fervour of his general ideas, his journalistic interventions, no matter how closely linked to the immediate reality, revealing clear theoretical opinions (even if not presented at length, in a series of doctrinal essays). This manner of theorizing may have been to the taste of the Junimea society, led by Titu Maiorescu, of which the poet was a member. On the other hand, Eminescu—whose journalism lacks the characteristics of the written style, while retaining, no matter how specious at times, all the savour of oral expression—may have been sensitive to the charms of the Junimea spirit, with its conversationalism and oratorical demonstrations.

We hasten to recall the "science" of Eminescu's polemics, his close, implacable manner of demonstration, which used the whole arsenal of the principles of formal logic to bring out the truth, and which might betray some influences of Maiorescu's campaigns. (The unbridled "1848-type" fervour passes, no doubt, through a filter of clarification and subservience to the ideas.) But in trying to find the similarities we come across even more differences. For, as shown by Pompiliu Constantinescu, "Maiorescu moved in the colder sphere of reason, while Eminescu addressed himself to a vital instinct, to obscure ancestral forces." Or: "Eminescu's political prose creates a spiritual value, it is more the expression of feeling than the result of cold reflection."

I have mentioned the oratorical model. The Junimea members loved the agreeable role of barristers bent on showing off with their striking phraseology and with their art of the gesture, while the poet did not care about outward brilliance and took an austere, monastic attitude; the role to his liking, in a law-court, would have been that of prosecutor. An old-time prosecutor—a mixture of people's tribune and biblical prophet. The latter comparison is, in fact, widespread in Romanian criticism. To N. Iorga, Eminescu is "a fighter, a prophet, but one like the prophets of ancient Judaea, lashing and branding on the one hand, revealing on the other, in the name of the same God of wisdom."

The metaphor is warranted by the fervour with which he feels and imparts his convictions: veritable tongues of flame illumine his writings. He seeks absolute identification with his ideas and rejects any other approach to them than the grave, solemn one, as in the case of things sacred, which could never be taken lightly. One can imagine what a striking figure could Eminescu have cut in the Junimea circle inclined towards light banter, and scathing irony, where all and everything was mocked at, in short, where nothing was held to be sacred. G. Panu, the Junimea memoirist, tells us that the poet did not make much of his company because of his manner of laughing up his sleeve: "Eminescu too was, when in good humour, witty and talkative, though always with a tinge of melancholy, but he never tolerated jesting about his beliefs and convictions."

This portrait is quite true to life, and it agrees with the moral principles openly stated by the poet in his articles. Thus, in **"Our Dramatic Repertoire"** he writes: "We too take pleasure in a sharper joke, but it needs must be moral, and not at the expense of what is proper." In his first contribution, **"A Critical Letter,"** we must see not only a stricture on anhistoricism but also one on the polemic manner of the Junimea members, who gratuitously mocked at principles defectively expressed but staunchly followed, by Transylvanian publicists in their struggle for the nation's interests. We recall his objection: "Attack it (the defective form—A. O.) with the rigour and seriousness of conviction, but not with ridiculous, worthless squibs." At the time he even found a label for such criticism: "feminine." The formula was to be revived years later, with more serious moral implications, involving the inconstancy of opinions, the cant phraseology, the stealthy, perfidious, cowardly insincere manner of waging the "journalistic duel." In *Timpul* he thus slashed at the journalists of *Românul*: "We wonder, then, if they are men or sybarites? If they are men, then let them speak up and look us straight in the eyes, let them be worthy of talking with us rather than choose to sneak on hidden paths where we could never follow them."

To conclude the comparison, we shall note that Eminescu displays a "rural" and the Junimea an urban type of sensibility.

Let us try to examine the way in which, endowed with such a spiritual structure coupled with an unswerving ethical conception, the poet moves in the domain of journalism. To start with, we shall take our examples from *Curierul de Iaşi*. The picture of Eminescu's work in those years has so far been usually reduced to a few contributions of a more or less cultural character. We do not refer only to the quantitative aspect, although one wonders at the "editor's" appetite for writing in spite of the crammed space of the periodical which once more refutes the idea of him working unwillingly like a modest wage-earner. Quite remarkable is the mark of talent that Eminescu has left on that small publication—a mere bulletin, after all—, seen in such preeminently modern attributes of journalism as diversity, the various subjects alternating with great liveliness and sense of the topical.

To characterize this journalistic panorama one could borrow the poet's own formula, used in his review of A. Odobescu's *Pseudokynegeticos*: a "mosaic," with the appended explanation: "that kind of picture which attempts to imitate the colours of nature by using small pieces of marble, coloured stone, glass, or fired clay."

Undoubtedly, by this mosaic-like structure "Curierul de Iaşi" somehow reminds us of the first Romanian periodicals, which were almanacs of a more or less encyclopaedic character. It would be wrong, however, to ignore the fact that, compared with the purely informative, eclectic descriptivism of those magazines meant for "family" audiences, Eminescu—in keeping with the modern spirit mentioned above—cultivates a journalism of attitude, involving public opinion in discussing the major problems of the day. Just as, in the realm of ancient myths, Midas was cursed to turn into gold everything he touched, one could say that every topic dealt with by the poet assumed grave inflections and a profound meaning, and became the pretext for stating a credo. (Obviously, literary talent also plays a part here: a mere administrative note that, owing to the rain, the streets were impassable, is ennobled by the expressiveness of the form, the poet evoking the archaic times of the lake-dwellings.)

Take, for instance, the notes on the "summer theatre" shows given in the gardens of the Iaşi town-hall. The purely local aspects of this initiative do not stop him from analysing the specific laws of drama, presenting "nature" as the absolute "teacher" and voicing his preference for Molière, whom he opposes to Corneille and Racine ("these illustrious forerunners on stilts"). From the views on dramaturgy—which should observe the laws of "truth and nature," and Eminescu condemns "all the intellectual paraphernalia of the lucid drama"—he passes on to the acting, criticizing the poor articulation due to failure to grasp the differences between the ethical or logical (or intentional) stress of speech and the purely grammatical.

No wonder, then, that the most trivial news story bears the imprint of competent judgement, if we remember that, already in one of his first press contributions, **"Our Dramatic Repertoire"** (*Familia,* 18/30 January 1870), the young Eminescu clearly showed that he had formed a sure conception (evidently, using his own experiences in the theatre as well). What strikes one, even at that early date, is the total character of his outlook, as he dealt with both the ethical and the aesthetic values of the repertoire, even though, in those early conditions, he suggested that "the plays may not be of great aes-

thetic worth, but the ethical should be absolute," with the actors' art—the repertoire is the soul; the actors: the body—and with the problem of the public, as the performances were designed "to raise the public to their level and, none the less, to be understood by it."

Although in dealing with such interest and consistency of the theatre, Eminescu referred, implicitly, to a certain area of literature (for his aesthetic view were generally valid), one will readily share the surprise of G. Ibrăileanu: "Curiously enough, our greatest poet spoke little about literature." The explanation lies perhaps in the fact that the literary movement of those years did not reveal such major sore points as to give rise to heated controversy. It is not a matter of evading the question, as some works were, indeed, reviewed, and the portrait of Constantin Bălăcescu, **"The Monument to I. Heliade Rădulescu"** or **"Literature from Botoşani"** illustrate his abilities as a literary critic, with a keen sense of value hierarchies. Even more significant is the fact that, throughout his publicistic career, Eminescu promoted the trend of popular realism. Since the opinion can still be heard that the poet merely "adhered" to Titu Maiorescu's views on this question, we shall quote Tudor Vianu, who, in the spirit of truth, writes: "To French comedy he prefers the Russian comedy of Gogol (*The Government Inspector*), belonging to the trend of popular realism, which—before Maiorescu—he noticed in the works of the German Fritz Reuter, the American Bret Harte, the Hungarian Petöfi, and also of the Romanians Anton Pann and I. Slavici, to whom he added I. Creangă."

While Eminescu was, indeed, more reserved in passing judgments on the literary phenomenon, the same is not true with other realms of culture, which he analysed in detail with characteristic keenness. We shall dwell, *exempli gratia,* on education. Illuminating comparisons could be made between the Romanian poet and, say, Lev Tolstoy as to both these problems were not only theoretical questions but also matters of lifelong interest involving personal experiences of their own (Eminescu as a school inspector and, occasionally, as a substitute teacher; the Russian author running a school at Yasnaya Polyana or writing textbooks). They opposed mechanical study in schools—what Eminescu called "routine learning" or simply "dressage"—and favoured intuitive learning, with due emphasis on the children's mental abilities, thereby adhering to the new, modern trends in education. They share the same position when stressing the role of manual training, of learning a trade, and the Romanian poet published several articles on these subjects in *Curierul de Iaşi.*

Lastly, the two men shared a passionate insistence on resting all instructing on the principles of moral education. Tolstoy espoused Rousseau's principle of "negative education," favouring a "free school" that could ensure unlimited freedom to the children. Eminescu was more restrictive, possibly fearing the idea of anarchy. And, just as in the natural state he assigns the central role to the monarch as "matrix" of the community, in education he inclines to overemphasize the role of the teacher (who should substitute for the bad textbooks that, in certain subjects, "should simply be thrown away"). There are, however, disagreement in establishing the priority of certain subjects. Tolstoy, for instance, thought highly of classical culture, though more as a writer than as an educator and, at any rate, did not go as far as Eminescu went. For reasons easy to understand, the Romanian poet saw in "the Latin spirit" a "constant regulator of mind and character, and the source of the historical sense."

If there is an essential resemblance between the two great writers, it lies, no doubt, in their common love of the peasant, the most diverse problems of education being reduced, in the last analysis, to the way in which they are reflected in the human condition of the class embodying the spiritual entity of the people. The poet impassionately writes: "The cause of poor attendance is not our people's aversion to schooling but simply poverty", a fact proved by the good attendance found "where a trace of economic independence has remained, namely in the freeholder villages."

We shall forgo discussing other aspects and shall pass on from the "interval" review to the characteristics of the "external." We do this also because so far, this facet of Eminescu's activity has been largely overlooked. The reason is easy to see: many investigators think that what appeared in this section consisted of clippings from articles and news reports published elsewhere. And this was not very far from the truth: in many of his notes Eminescu merely translated or summarized news stories from the foreign press. The question is whether we can underrate the fact that the translation and "processing" were the poet's, who, no doubt, left his own stylistic mark on them and who, when least expected, did not refrain from personal observations. The injustice is patent, however, when one ignores the original comments, which give Eminescu the merit of being among the first in Romanian journalism to introduce the foreign news report and commentary, as they were to be cultivated in the years to come.

The events that aroused the poet's interest and soon assumed an engrossing quality were related to the so-called "Eastern war" of the time, i.e. the armed conflicts between the oppressed Balkan peoples and the Porte. Eminescu, as we know him now, commits himself entirely, regretting that in a magazine like *Curierul de Iaşi* he could only have one page at his disposal, doing veritable layout acrobatics to put the major news into relief, opening a special column "From the Battlefield," and so on.

As in other fields, with characteristic care for detail, he strives to form a clear outlook and a suitable methodology. The first principle put forward by him is that of critically processing information. He is aware that the Vienna *Neue Freie Presse* was "hostile to the Slavic movements" in the Balkans and Turcophile (he calls it "the odalisque rag") and consequently quotes it sparingly, noting that he reproduced the stories "with all the reserve possible. Nor does he accept uncritically what comes from Serbian sources—although emotionally siding with it. Thus he notes somewhere that "the reader, accustomed to the victory bulletins from this theatre of war, turning the page and reading in reverse will find the exact opposite of what the Serbs maintain."

Eminescu regards as another essential principle of a foreign editor the amalgamation of the news into a kind of "organic unity" into a general picture of the strategic and tactical plans of the warring parties. It is highly rewarding reading to follow his reconstructions of the war theatre—as if he had a map on which he traces the troops movements in great detail—, his military advice, his rebukes to General Chernayev for the latter's "mania for adorning with strategy every one of his tactical moves, implementing it with the greatest complication possible and with division of forces." Elsewhere the Serbs are praised for having applied the tactics once used by the Moldavians against the Turks. And this is not the only occasion for Eminescu to bring references to our people into the foreign section.

The range of subjects—beyond the consistency of interest—may be varied, as may the range of his journalistic techniques. Prince Nicholas of Montenegro is honoured with a portrait in the brightest of colours. Actually, Eminescu resorts the technique of poetic idealization, styling him. "The Voivode of the Black Mountains" and enwrapping him in the halo of legendary heroes: "Born into the valiant family of Nyegos ruling over a race of poor freeholders of great personal courage, Prince Nicholas resembles the brave young man of the tales, who went into the wide world to learn what fear was and could not find it anywhere." To account for his fame among the Slavic peoples of the Balkans, whose "spiritual food" was found in "the folk songs," the poet projects him into the world of ancient epics, Nicholas joining poetry to sword, is a man of simple habits, talking and behaving like any other man of his people, and playing the part of Achilles in that assembly of elders which is the Senate of Montenegro and where one can no doubt see many hoary-bearded, honey-tongued Nestors."

On the other hand, to portray Sultan Abdul Hamid the poet resorts to biting irony. The satirical formula is one of false eulogy: "People say that Abdul Hamid is a spendthrift who likes to read novels, but people are liars; on the contrary, he may be said to be a regular pennypincher of very simple habits, for besides his legitimate wife he has only one concubine and utterly ignores the other odalisques in his harem." Then, pushing his description into the grotesque, Eminescu notes the Sultan's preferences for "all manner of domestic animals" and, particularly, for birds: "thus he has a cockatoo, with which he spends hours on end." "Not of little interest to him are various stuffed animals: snakes, lizards, monkeys, and of late he has turned his collecting zeal to beetles . . ."

Anyone reading Eminescu's journalistic work of these years will find that, unlike the last period, when the frowning-polemic attitude would prevail, the poet now indulged in a certain satirical delight, diversifying and brightening his tone, and occasionally not refraining from a racy, rustic-type joke. One could say that his articles are *feuilleton* pieces rather than squibs, even though he never rose to the refinement of subtle raillery or parlour irony, as his fighting nature, with prompt reactions, would soon get the better of him.

Although when employing the weapons of joyfulness the poet shows a certain awkwardness, no one can say that, in the evolution of his journalistic writing, Eminescu failed to make felicitous use of the vivid resources to found in folk humour.

Thus, from the series *Icons Old and New* published in *Timpul,* we select the portrait of Stephen the Great, drawn with Moldavian wit and verve in what amounts to a light parody of the chroniclers' style: "Poor Prince Stephen! He could crush the Turks, Poles and Magyars, knew a little Slavonic, had had several wives, drank heavily old Cotnari wine and, from time to time, cut off the head of some boyar or the nose of some Tartar chief. Then he would dismount in towns along the rivers, allot to his soldiers good places for the grazing of Moldavian horses, sheep and cattle, and build churches and monasteries, then again beat the Turks, again dismounted in towns and again got married, until, he passed away in the fortress at Suceava and was buried with full honours at Putna Monastery."

Eminescu's capacity as thinker is another addition to his journalistic physiognomy, often reduced to the figure of a vindictive lampoonist. We have already noted his taste for general ideas. Eminescu's articles have two sides, one embracing the concrete fact, the other dealing with the abstraction and demonstrating a principle. This ambivalence may, of course, take on various forms, depending on the subject. There are cases when Eminescu feels the need for some programmatic clarifications, as in *Icons Old and New.* More often than not, though, he presents the concrete aspect of the arguments, with but a glimpse of the deeper dimension, as in the well-known iceberg metaphor. What we will stress here is the fact that in his most direct polemic

thrusts we discover a remote plane of ideas. Eminescu himself, after all, pointed out that there are two ways of engaging in a "serious, honest discussion": one *ad rem,* which "proves the truth of the thesis as such", the other *ad hominem,* showing that "the opponent himself has advocated or done the very thing he is now decrying." With great bitterness the poet notes that his "adversaries" will very seldom provide opportunities for arguments *ad rem:* "Carried by the wish not to waste the years and strength of our life, we would like to find men willing to discuss with us the principles that we advance." In view of these very principles, this is how Eminescu describes his activity with *Timpul,* stating his adherence to a journalism of ideas: "The columns of *Timpul* may not be exactly a treasure-house of great ideas, but even our opponents must admit that they are a valuable source for the historian who will some day start studying the life of ideas in our time."

N. Iorga was right when, from the comparison with the old prophets of Judaea, he also singled out the side of violent invective as well as that of sagacity. The publicist's reflective nature enabled him to state, with aphoristic force, various ideas—some of which have been included in special collections. We will resist all temptation to exemplify and merely point out that, in order to lend more strength to his moralizing conclusions, Eminescu frequently resorts to the graphicalness of proverbs. In his time he was, no doubt, next to Creangă, the author who, both theoretically and practically, made the best use of this side of Romanian folklore.

Drawing the poet's portrait as it appears from his journalistic work, D. Murăraşu admires his skill in blending thought and passion, logical argumentation and mural indignation, stressing his "great ability in composition" and noting that, especially in his early articles, Eminescu "does not disregard the laborious art of composition," for, later on, "the ideas and feelings will emerge tumultuously, just like the soul of this impassioned castigator of social evils and iniquities." The remark is by and large, well-founded.

Eminescu's later contributions show a greater emphasis on the scientific style, visible in the effort to find Romanian equivalents of some nebulous terms from German philosophy and economic doctrines, this being an adjunct to the poet's ambition to practise an "objective" criticism. Thus, after a passionate apostrophe, he stops the course of his demonstration because "we are afraid we might lose the patience to treat that matter with equanimity."

In other words, the arguments *ad rem* prevail. The poet seeks not so much to stir the consciences as to convince. In the last part of his journalistic work—and after losing some of his social illusions and sinking even deeper into the "vanity fair"—the figure of an austere, vindictive moralist comes to the fore. Are these articles poorer writing? Not at all, but they observe different rules, of a definitely subjective character. In short, Eminescu becomes more lyrical. To say that the poet's ideas and feelings are mixed and fused in a red-hot crucible is to verge on tautology. He never quite manages to be an impassible observer, and there is no article by him that should not reveal the presence of a warm, sensitive soul. Now there is more to all this, a kind of excessive sensibility. The scenes of misery and pain, the hideous triumph of evil in life is reflected in the moralist's mind with a violence that bursts out in invective, sarcasm and scathing satire. His laughter has turned to gnashing. He demands "fiery colours", and to those who complain of his polemic excesses he answers: "Do not pretend to take offence at what we say, you had better get angry about what is happening, about reality itself . . . However cruel the form in which we voice our opinions, this reality is still crueller, still more repulsive." And again elsewhere: "To be able to exaggerate what is happening in this country, in its parliament and administration, in the economic and moral life of most of our nation, one should have to borrow the dark colours of Dante's *Inferno*." And did not Eminescu do like Dante, sending his contemporaries into an avenging Inferno?

Much has been said about the vehemence of his style. And with good reason. Eminescu has contributed in the largest measure, by the force of his talent, towards introducing direct invective into the current language and manners of journalism. The use of veiled irony, of a euphemistic style does not satisfy him, since they cannot help him to explosively discharge the holy wrath boiling in his soul. The poet himself is conscious of this trait of his, and justifies it by saying that to remove the evils "one cannot employ the edulcorating ointment of euphemism but has to take up the surgeon's scalpel", and consequently "we cut deep into the rottenness of our national sore and want the national protoplasm to fill up the gaps made by our cuts . . ." This directness of Eminescu's satire, devoid of all stylistic ornament, aspiring for the nudity of red-hot iron (and, it must be admitted, proving here the full measure of his talent) was strikingly and suggestively defined by G. Călinescu: "Eminescu is possessed by a sublime fury, of straightforward anger, and only a genius of his stature could seize the redhot iron with the naked hands."

But, quite surprisingly, although his articles have direct targets, being aimed at the politicians of the time, and, as such, constitute attacks *ad personam,* no distinct portrait of any of his victims has emerged from them. The cause should be sought in the essential quality of his satire, in its destructive force acting so absolutely and annihilating all constructive elements, altering the real features and expanding them grotesquely till they assume nightmarish proportions. The Liberal politicians are pictured as apocalyptic monsters, "black Lucifers"; to discredit them irredeemably, he portrays them as degenerates of "obvious physical decrepitude," "goitrous morons lacking all mental abilities", and so on, and so forth. C. A. Rosetti, the "repulsive monster," becomes, under a heap of grossly exaggerated negative attributes, an image of Antichrist himself.

It is certain that the value of Eminescu's satire lies in this demoniacal power to distort, in a personal vision that shifts the accents from the individual to the universal, depicting contemporary life not so much with the colours of Dante's *Inferno* as with those of the Apocalypse. Eminescu makes explicit use of this device, mentioning a legend to the effect that the Antichrist, "the enemy of the world, will be born near the mouth of the Danube." He is already born: "Here, where patent traitors to their country pass for great patriots, here in Babel, where the words have lost their original meaning, and those so unfortunate as to live here will envy those resting in their graves." Eventually the poet will make war on the fantastic projections of his own imagination. One can understand, then, why C. A. Rosetti—as Iacob Negruzzi relates—could find amusement in the "enemy's" articles, admiring in him a virtuoso of passionate outbursts. The pathos of Eminescu's outlook, restricted to black and white, and separating into good and evil whatever happened in the nation's past and present, somehow reminds us of the simplicity and poetic ingenuity found in the chroniclers' satire. The poet amply uses apocalyptic colours to describe the present, and paradisiac to recall the past. More examples of this sort would be superfluous. The "Moldavian Paradise," the "most blooming land" is glorified in hymns reminiscent of *The Song* of *Songs.*

Eminescu's articles are run through by an incandescent thread that uplifts them and broadens their literary scope. It would be wrong to regard them as mere sentimental outbursts without any interior organization. Eminescu lays down his own stylistic laws and, lending artistic expression to the tumult of his passions, can so forcefully act upon his readers. The torrent of his prose acquires a specific rhythm and, thus illumined, they rise to the summits of lyricism. The best example is found in his evocation of Bukovina's rape by the Habsburg Empire. The poet's feelings of grief and revolt are emphasized by the image of never-healing spiritual wounds. The cadence reminds us of the biblical verses. At the end we find the folk legend that in 1777 the votive lamps on Stephen the Great's tomb at Putna Monastery went out. The last words turn into a veritable cry of despair, raising the lyrical tension to its peak: "Will the lamps on the tomb ever light up again? Will the old portrait ever shine again?"

This image can be found in several of Eminescu's articles. The same holds true of other symbol-metaphors which, by repetition, take on the force of poetic obsessions. Some have been tempted to inventory the suggestive formulae created by Eminescu in the stormy progress of his journalistic activity. And, indeed, one could have found sufficient causes for satisfaction, as the poet naturally collaborates with the fighter, clothing his ideas in the imperial purple of metaphor—we mention, among many others, a comparing of the country's independence to a prince sleeping with the crown and sceptre by his side. Such statistical operations can always prove useful, though not very conclusive. For the fascination of Eminescu's journalism lies not in this or that technique but in their blending by some arcane method that will take one—as does the charm of his verse—into the realm of ineffability (. . .).

Eminescu's journalistic writing meets one with a mosaic of "genres" and formulae: essays, squibs, *feuilleton* pieces, doctrinal articles, etc. The next stage was, in Romanian journalism, one of diversification and specialization, each genre seeking to build its own status in terms of expressive specificity. The articles are no longer strictly functional, they now express not only one's outlook on life but also—programmatically—one's aesthetic attitude.

That is what happened in the case of the squib, which, as handled by Tudor Arghezi, took on the attributes of a literary genre. Some similarities to Eminescu's squibs cannot be denied, even if we considered only one characteristic: the diatribe of the *Timpul* editor, overshooting the strictly polemic target, conjuring up nightmarish visions, heaping monstrous physical and moral deformities and reconstructing the atmosphere of the Apocalypse—all these being features that Arghezi develops, methodically, beyond the possible limits through "his genius for mockery raised to metaphysical heights" (M. Ralea). The press experience of our national poet has become a common asset of our journalism, and its echoes have been inextricably fused into the alloy of original syntheses. Advancing a model of what is known as an all-round journalist, some authors will, quite naturally, point to these or those qualities of Eminescu's, but such qualities will increasingly become points of reference to be used in clarifying one's own interests. Certainly, the impact of Eminescu's journalistic writing is still far from being exhausted. Yet, with the passage of time there naturally occurs a process of sublimation, with serious moral and civic implications. The essential teaching to be drawn from Eminescu's example could be reduced to the idea of *responsibility to one's nation.* For writers and journalists will always look back with emotion to the crucial period sacred by his name, a time when journalism, without renouncing any of its prerogatives, was also apostolate and sacerdocy. They will constantly return to his model as to an *alma mater* embodying the supreme example of complete involvement, with all one's resources of talent and inner combustion, in the service of civic commandments.

This, we think, is the means by which Eminescu's journalism will always irradiate the field of our letters like "a column of light" (to us the poet's own phrase). Beyond the matters of skill and expression are involved problems of conscience concerning the very titles of honour of the Romanian writer-journalist.

Elizabeth Close (essay date May 1985)

SOURCE: Close, Elizabeth. "From the Familiar to the Unfamiliar: A Rumanian Contribution to European Fantasy: 'Sŭrmanul Dionis' by Mihai Eminescu." *AUMLA: Journal of the Australasian Universities Language and Literature Association* 63 (May 1985): 43-52.

[*In the following essay, Close argues for the inclusion of Eminescu's "Poor Dionis" among Europe's most successful fantastic tales.*]

There appears to be no generally-agreed definition of fantasy, but one of the essential criteria to which a would-be fantastic tale must conform is surely that of having its starting-point in the familiar world, so that the reader is led gently into an unfamiliar world, without ceasing to believe in the plausibility of the tale. The best description of the process remains Hoffmann's, in *Die Serapionsbrüder*:

> die Basis der Himmelsleiter, auf der man hinaufsteigen will in höhere Regionen, befestigt sein müsse im Leben, so dass jeder nachzusteigen vermag . . .[1]

Tzvetan Todorov, in his important study *Introduction à la littérature fantastique,* emphasises this criterion most clearly when he contrasts Kafka's with the traditional fantastic tale. In *Die Verwandlung,* he says:

> L'événement étrange n'apparaît pas à la suite d'une série d'indications indirectes, comme le sommet d'une gradation: il est contenu dans la toute première phrase. Le récit fantastique partait d'une situation parfaitement naturelle pour aboutir au surnaturel, *La Métamorphose* part de l'événement surnaturel pour lui donner, en cours de récit, un air de plus en plus naturel.[2]

It is the aim of the present study to show that a little-known Rumanian fantastic tale, Mihai Eminescu's **"Sŭrmanul Dionis"** (**"Poor Dionis"**; 1872) deserves to be added to the rather small number of European fantastic tales which succeed in keeping the reader's confidence as the author leads him into the world of fantasy.

"Poor Dionis" has even in Rumania been overshadowed by the author's magnificent poetry, and has received only a fraction of the critical attention devoted to the latter. An early critic did indeed suggest that it was a fantastic tale of real status in European literature, but no-one else has taken up his perceptive comment:

"Poor Dionis" is worthy to stand beside the tales of Hoffmann and all the most interesting fantasies of Romantic literature of all ages, especially because of Eminescu's simple yet suggestive techniques, free of all mannerisms and needless complexities.[3]

It should be noted that "Poor Dionis" is not only a fantastic tale, but also a clever and plausible attempt to demonstrate the validity of Schopenhauer's tenet that only the Will exists. Indeed, the way in which the tale is presented suggests strongly that Eminescu's primary aim was to show that Schopenhauer's hypothesis could be the explanation of the mystery of man's place in the universe. But for the reader of today, "Poor Dionis" stands or falls as a fantastic tale, not as an essay in philosophical inquiry.

The coherence of the story within its own terms of reference, the vividness of the character-portrayals, the rich yet precise language contribute to the success of "Poor Dionis" but would hardly be sufficient to make the reader accept its strange universe. The essential reason why it achieves this suspension of disbelief on the part of the reader lies in the author's skilful manipulation of two familiar phenomena: the dream and the shadow.

As the tale is not easily accessible in English, it is necessary to preface a study of the roles of dreams and shadows in "Poor Dionis" with a brief synopsis of the story.[4]

To demonstrate the validity of the hypothesis that each of us has an eternal, unchanging soul which goes through countless incarnations over vast periods of time and huge physical distance (time and space being, for Eminescu as for Schopenhauer, purely human creations) Eminescu imagines a nineteenth-century student, Dionis, who dreams himself into a former existence, that of a fifteenth-century monk, Dan. As Dan, he is freed from his temporary body to soar up to the Moon, whence he returns as both Dan and Dionis. It is important to note that the personalities of the two men are essentially the same, for they are but different physical manifestations of the same soul. By means of skilful transitions from one man to the other, and the clever siting of the soul in the human's shadow, Eminescu finally achieves a fusion of student and monk, so that in the epilogue he can ask the reader:

> To which man did these things really happen: Dan or Dionis? . . . Are we not perhaps like actors in a crowd scene who cross the stage again and again to give the impression of a huge army? . . . Is it not true that the actors remain the same though the plays change?[5]

He does not give any answers to this question, but it is clear that he prefers to believe in metempsychosis.

The devices of the dream and the shadow are equally important in winning the reader's compliance with the author's definition of the universe, in the first place because both of them are familiar yet mysterious companions of all of us throughout our lives. The role played by Dan's shadow seems to be original to Eminescu; the use of the dream-world to present phenomena which do not fit into the framework of so-called 'normal' life is not so.

The world of dreams fascinated the Romantic writers of Germany and France,[6] who regularly interpreted it as the spiritual and infinitely superior counterpart to our waking life, as a return of the soul to the golden age when the cosmos was perfectly unified and coherent, without distinction between phenomena which are now regarded as opposites: waking and sleeping, life and death, male and female. Dreams permit this return to the primeval unity of all things because, unbounded by time and space, they bring the sleeper into contact with the universal life which knows nothing of the constraints of chronology or place. They may therefore reveal events in past or future phases of the dreamer's existence.

The freedom of the dream-world enables Eminescu to demonstrate the existence of an eternal soul of which each successive life reveals only a part. He differs from such profoundly Romantic writers as Hoffmann and Nerval in that he does not regard the dream-world as superior to the day-time world but, like Schopenhauer, sees both worlds as different pages in the same book.[7]

This use of the dream-device in "Poor Dionis" adds not a little to the suspension of disbelief and even to the acceptability of the philosophical hypothesis being tested by Eminescu, because we all know that dreams really are outside the confines of time and space, that they do permit the mind to make fantastic journeys, that they can seem strangely prophetic, that they do sometimes give the dreamer the sensation of being himself and yet a different person.

The simplest way to demonstrate Eminescu's artistry in the manipulation of this motif is to quote some of the passages in which one man dreams himself into the body and life of the other.

At the beginning of the tale, Dionis sits with a book before him, his mind wandering in a strange dream-world. Suddenly he wakes from his reverie and asks himself why one can travel from one place to another but not from one era to another. Then he touches a mystical pattern like a red cobweb in his book, and is gradually transported back through time:

> 'Yes,' he murmured, returning to the idea which obsessed him, 'the world, that vast wasteland, exists in our minds; but why only space, why not time, why not the past?' He looked again at the red cobweb, and its strands began to move. He placed his finger in the centre of the web, and was overwhelmed with a spiritual

ecstasy. He thought he could hear the low voices of the old men who when he was a child had held him on their knees on winter nights and told him fantastic tales of fairies dressed in gold and light who led lives of innocence and purity in crystal palaces; and it seemed only yesterday that he had twined his fingers in their white beards and listened to their soft, sagacious voices recounting the wisdom of the past, the knowledge of our forebears. He could no longer doubt it . . . an unseen hand was drawing him into the past. He saw princes arise, dressed in sable and gold—he listened to them speaking from their high thrones in ancient castles, he saw a council of old men, he saw an eager, Christian people flowing like the waves of the sea through the princely court—but all was still confused.

And now the lines of the astrological sign moved horribly, like snakes of live coals. The spider grew larger and larger. 'Where shall we stop?' said a voice from the burning centre of the book. 'The reign of Alexander the Good,' he managed to whisper with a firm voice, for joy and wonder were overwhelming his soul and . . . slowly, so slowly, the red web grew bigger and more filmy, until it had become a glowing sunset sky. He was lying on a new-mown field, surrounded by the perfume of haycocks, beneath a high, clear, blue evening sky across which hosts of fiery golden-red clouds were sweeping. The hills were shrouded in purple, birds hung in the air, the rivers mirrored the flaming sky, the tremulous voice of a church bell filled the evening, calling everyone to Vespers, and he—he— what strange clothes! A rough woollen cassock and the black hat of a monk . . . in his hand, the book about astrology. And everything seemed familiar to him! He was no longer himself. It seemed so natural to him that he should have awakened in this world. He knew for certain that he had come into the field to read, and had fallen asleep over his book. That darkened room, the life of a man called Dionis, how strange . . . he had been dreaming! 'Of course,' he thought, 'it's the fault of my book, because I dreamed such a lot of extraordinary things after I'd been reading it. What an odd world, what odd people, and their language, like ours, but foreign too, different . . . How strange!' The monk Dan had dreamed that he was a layman called Dionis . . . and he had the impression that he had been in another age, among other people! A strange feeling!

The transition from one age and one person to another is extremely skilful: the reader, as so rarely in supernatural literature, is carried along with Dionis and feels it to be quite natural that the person who wakes up should not be Dionis, but Dan, a fifteenth-century monk. Dan remembers dreaming that he was living five hundred years after his time, and without hesitation accepts his fantastic dream as a vision of the truth:

> 'And now I, a monk, understand how the soul travels from one age to another. It is the same soul; but death makes it forget that it has lived before. . . . How many people are there within a single person? As many as there are stars in a single drop of dew beneath the clear night sky.'

As the story progresses, the transitions between the two men—the one falling asleep to wake as the other, the

recognition by one of people met by the other—culminate in the fusion of the two in the reader's mind, so that it becomes impossible to say that either has priority or is dreaming the other into existence.

It is difficult to select an example from the latter part of the story which will make sense out of context, but perhaps this one will give an idea of the skilful merging of the two men:

> 'You've gone and you've sold me to the tormentor of souls,' whispered Dan with bitter resignation, falling back on his pillows. 'He has a fever . . . he's delirious,' said the bald man in a sombre voice.
>
> * * *
>
> Night-time . . . A gentle refreshing breeze comes in through the open windows, and Dionis, lying on his bed, trembles with fever, his lips dry, his forehead pearled with sweat, his head heavy.

Eminescu's achievement lies in the extraordinary skill with which he uses a familiar motif to make a daring hypothesis seem plausible.

The other great artistic device in **"Poor Dionis,"** the identification of Dan's shadow with his immortal soul, appears to be new in literature. The concept is put forward by Dan's teacher, Ruben, from whom Dan seeks an explanation of his dream.

Ruben confirms that each soul has a series of physical lives, and explains that the difference between God and Man is that a man knows only one of his lives at a time, whereas God is Time itself, containing within Him all the peoples who have been, are or will be. He answers Dan's doubts as to the possibility of a man's leaving his present body to inhabit an earlier or a later one by explaining that one's shadow is nothing more nor less than one's eternal soul, which moves, its essence unchanged, from one incarnation to the next:

> 'You have seen that in each man there is an unending line of men. Let one of those men in you take your place for as long as you will be away. He will not be a complete man, because if he were he would negate your existence. But the eternal man, from whom comes that line of ephemeral men, is beside each one of us, all the time. You can see him, though you cannot take hold of him—he is your shadow. For a time you can exchange beings: if you give your shadow your present, ephemeral existence, your shadow will give you his eternal existence, and as a shadow endowed with eternity you will even acquire a little of God's omnipotence, for your wishes will be fulfilled even as you form them . . .'

Ruben explains that Dan will be able to pass into a time and space of his own deliberate creation, by opening his book—the very book which Dionis was reading—at any place and then reading every seventh page: thus will God's secret formula for travel through time and space be revealed to him.

At home, Dan turns the pages as instructed, until his shadow, looming fantastically over him, begins to speak. It explains that it is his eternal being, 'Dan' merely one of many ephemeral envelopes, as Zoroaster had once been:

> 'Your soul, although you cannot remember it, was once in the bosom of Zoroaster, he who made the stars move by the profundity of his words and the complex logic of his mathematics. His book, which contains all the secrets of his knowledge, lies open in front of you. Men through the ages have tried to unravel it but no-one has succeeded completely. Only I can do so, because I spoke to Zoroaster from the wall beside him, just as I am speaking to you today.'

The shadow then says that if it and Dan change places, the shadow becoming the mortal body and Dan taking on the form of a luminous shadow, Dan will be able to travel through time and space just as if he were the shadow for whom they are no barrier:

> 'Leave me to live your life, with your sweetheart's shadow made flesh, with your friends; condemn me to forget my omniscient being while you and your beloved journey to whatever part of the universe you choose . . . to the moon, for example. There, you will live a century and it will seem to you but a day.'

The shadow makes it clear that the time and space which Dan will create will have an objective existence, by pointing out that he will be able, if he wishes, to reduce the Earth to the size of a pearl, without the inhabitants realising it:

> 'You can even take the Earth with you, without any trouble at all. Change it into a pearl pendant and hang it on your sweetheart's necklace: and believe me, although everything on Earth will be thousands of times smaller, the proportions will be unchanged and the inhabitants will think they are just as big as they are now. Their time-scale? An hour of your life will be a century for them.'

The exchange is effected, and Dan, leaving the shadow sleeping in his bed in his physical form, to live out Dan's life and write his memoirs, goes to the home of his sweetheart, Maria.[8] He transforms her just as he has been transformed, and they soar to the Moon together. Dan reduces the Earth to a pearl, and places it in Maria's necklace.

Dan's shadow thus plays an important role in the mechanics of the story, by concretising the soul and bringing home to the reader the meaning of the theory of reincarnation: '"I spoke to Zoroaster just as I am speaking to you."' We are familiar with our shadow, that mirror image, sometimes faithful, sometimes bizarrely distorted, of our outline, whose greyness veils it in mystery: it is so tempting to believe it is part of us that Eminescu's siting of the soul in it actually increases the plausibility of the story.

While, as has been shown, Eminescu's treatment of the world of dreams is a simple modification of a popular motif, the notion of placing in one's shadow an eternal soul which is reincarnated countless times is so different from the roles attributed to the shadow by earlier writers that it would seem to be a genuinely novel way of pursuing the Romantic theme of the multiplicity of the human personality.

I have attempted, with the help of the foremost expert on the shadow theme in European literature, Dr. Gero von Wilpert, to discover precedents for Eminescu's particular motif, but so far without success.

The shadow, as is well known, is regarded as the soul of the individual person in many folk-beliefs and mythologies, but Eminescu's interpretation of its role as the unchanging site of an unchanging, frequently reincarnated soul, does not seem to occur in any known mythology. Frazer's *Golden Bough* and Bächtold-Stäubli's *Handwörterbuch des deutschen Aberglaubens*[9] were consulted fruitlessly for folk-motifs. Dr. von Wilpert kindly gave me his considered opinion on the matter in a personal communication:

> During my investigation of the motif, I have not come across any treatment of the motif that might even slightly resemble Eminescu's treatment of it, but though I feel tempted to regard it as original, there might be some similar aspects in folklore and mythology like the realm of the shadows in Hades in Greek mythology.

I have so far been unable to find any such similar aspects.

Literary precedents are as hard to come by as folkloric ones. Chamisso's *Peter Schlemihl* is normally quoted by critics as being Eminescu's source, but there is no similarity between the motifs of the two authors. Von Wilpert, in his book on the lost shadow, considers that Oscar Wilde's story *The Fisherman and his Soul* (1891) was the first to use the motif to postulate the existence of two different worlds within the human personality:

> Solche Ausweitung des Motivs von der Persönlichkeits-spaltung bis zur Deklarierung zweier verschiedener Welten mit zwei verschiedenen Wertssystemen bringt erst Oscar Wildes Kunstmärchen.[10]

It would seem that Eminescu should replace Wilde as the first known writer to use the motif; but it must be acknowledged that the characteristics of the double worlds inhabited by the two heroes are completely different, as are the purposes of their creators.

The nearest parallel found so far is in the writings of Schopenhauer, to whom Eminescu was indebted for much of his philosophical thought. On several occasions in *The World as Will and Representation,* Schopenhauer uses an image in which he equates the body with the will, the shadow with the phenomenon, which is the opposite of Eminescu's interpretation but could perhaps have suggested the idea to him. For example:

> As the will is the thing-in-itself, the inner content, the essence of the world, but life, the visible world, the phenomenon, is only the mirror of the will, this world will accompany the will as inseparably as a body is accompanied by its shadow.[11]

At present, then, it would seem reasonable to suppose that the shadow-motif as developed in **"Poor Dionis"** is original to Eminescu.

In conclusion, I would argue that thanks to Eminescu's skill in leading his reader slowly into an unfamiliar universe, **"Poor Dionis"** is worthy to stand beside the very best European fantastic tales of the nineteenth century. Indeed, it deserves to be compared with such masterpieces as Hoffmann's *Der goldene Topf,* Villiers de l'Isle Adam's *Véra* and Maupassant's *Le Horla.*

Notes

1. Quoted by Rosemary Lloyd, *Baudelaire et Hoffmann: affinités et influences,* (Cambridge Univ. Press, 1979), p. 244.

2. (Paris, Du Seuil, 1970), p. 179.

3. Sanielevici, Henric, '*Sărmanul Dionis*', an article originally published in his *Cercetări critice si filozofice,* (Bucharest, 1915), republished in 1968 in an anthology of Sanielevici's work, bearing the same title as the 1915 volume and selected by Z. Ornea, edited by C. Botez, pp. 48-84. Quotation from p. 77 of the 1968 edition. The translation is my own.

4. The only English translation was made by Sylvia Pankhurst (n.d.), and has been published only in a journal: *Romanian Review,* 33 no. 12 (1979), pp. 36-69. I consulted this translation when making my own translation of the quotations from *Poor Dionis* used in this paper.

5. One is tempted to see here the influence of the transformed actors in E. T. A. Hoffmann's *Prinzessin Brambilla* (see Charles E. Passage's introduction to his translation, in *Three Märchen of E. T. A. Hoffmann,* Carolina, Univ. of South Carolina Press, 1971, pp. xviii-xxii) but it should be noted that Eminescu was very interested in the theatre and had spent some time in 1867 and 1868 in touring companies (see George Călinescu, *Viata*

lui Mihai Eminescu, Bucharest, Editura Eminescu, 1973, pp. 99-116).

6. Béguin, Albert, *Les Romantiques et le rêve,* 2 vols. (Marseille, Cahiers du sud, 1937), I *passim,* but especially pp. 269-271.

7. Schopenhauer, Arthur, *The World as Will and Representation,* translated by E. F. J. Payne, 2 vols, (1958; New York, Dover, 1966), I, 8: "Life and dreams are leaves of one and the same book. The systematic reading is real life, but when the actual reading hour (the day) has come to an end, and we have the period of recreation, we often continue idly to thumb over the leaves, and turn to a page here and there without method or connection. We sometimes turn up a page we have already read, at others one still new to us, but always from the same book."

8. Eminescu suggests that Dan leads a double life as a studious monk by day and a romantic youth by night; but this unconventional situation is not exploited in *Poor Dionis.*

9. Frazer, J. G., *The Golden Bough: a study in magic and religion,* 12 vols, (London, Macmillan, 1936-38), III, 78-79; Bächtold-Stäubli, H., *Handwörterbuch des deutschen Aberglaubens,* 10 vols, (Berlin and Leipzig, W. de Gruyter, 1927-41), IX, cols, 126-142, *s. v. Schatte*[*n*].

10. von Wilpert, Gero, *Die verlorenen Schatten: Varianten eines literarischen Motivs* (Stuttgart, Kröner, 1978), p. 120.

11. Schopenhauer, *op.cit.,* I, 275.

Ilie Badescu (essay date 1986)

SOURCE: Badescu, Ilie. "Sociological Horizon." *Romanian Review* 40, no. 1 (1986): 23-31.

[In the following essay, Badescu asserts that Eminescu qualifies both as Romania's greatest poet and the founder of that country's "positive sociology."]

Reading the recently published volumes of journalism in the standard edition of Mihai Eminescu's **Works** one comes to the conclusion that the greatest Romanian poet is also the founder of "positive sociology" (as contrasted with the speculative sociological theories on society) in Romanian culture. The epistemological programme of the new science belongs in the great family of European scientific spirit. "We are not such as [. . .] to rely in our argumentation on the dogmas of divine right, on historical figments, on the imagined shadow of previous states of things," wrote Eminescu. Sons of the nineteenth century, we are only aiming in our researches at two things: to cite precise facts and to include them in a general formula."[1]

The three aspects of the traditional, anti-positive, un-scientific spirit, which, as we have seen, the poet rejects, had been imputed to him by some of his critics. Long exercised in the spirit of the new theoretical value, Eminescu succeeded in supplying one of the simplest and most accurate definitions of positive sociology, pointing out its specific character. "To cite precise facts and to include them in a general formula"—this is, no doubt, the essential feature of positive sociology. It appears as a theoretical value opposed to speculative sociology, which draws its essence from the speculative constructivism of our minds. Eminescu thinks that sociology can build its system on the unity of facts, discovering their "general formula." This general formula is actually the law of social facts. "The great social phenomena will occur, we believe, in a causal order as necessary as the elemental events [. . .]. It is not hatred that we can feel towards such an elemental event as the mass immigration of some ethnic element that has developed certain economic practices that we do not like [. . .][2] Hence, in studying the phenomena and finding their "general formula" (their law) one must not be influenced by idiosyncratic, affective, moralizing, but ineffective states of mind; it is none the less necessary to reveal, in the framework of a critical sociology, the negative tendencies, and to advance modes of action. At the basis of the programme for action put forward by Eminescu, with a view to ensuring the country's progress (the organization of agricultural work, the establishment and growth of a national industry, the introduction of new, compensatory relations between the "superposed classes" and the producer classes), lies positive sociology, in the spirit of which he examines the phenomena of parasitic exploitation, surplus-product drain, negative selection, predominance of the extrovert classes, etc. Investigation of these phenomena enabled Eminescu to detect the "general formula", the law underlying them. Did he manage to provide the most general formula of the social facts in Romania's modern age, capable of revealing to us the structure of the Romanian social conditions and their deepest meaning. Did he point out the type of society that was being built in Romania in his time, and what distinguished it from other types? We think he did, and in the following we shall try to examine this side of his outlook.

As far as we can realize, Eminescu made equal use of the two approaches peculiar to nineteenth-century positive sociology: the comparative-historical analysis and the direct statistico-economic investigation of the contemporary situation. In Eminescu's sociological studies, historical and synchronic research were blended, using the whole range of techniques (professional monographs, reports, sociological monographs—such as A.

V. Millo's *The Peasant*—demographic and economic statistics, time and income budgets, directly or indirectly recorded conversations, direct and indirect systematic observation, psychological diagnoses and descriptions, etc.).

Many of Eminescu's critics saw in the poet's comparative historical approach a proof of "love for the past." For instance, conclusions alien to the spirit of Eminescu's sociology were forcibly drawn from an idea like this: "But this is the hotel [the country—I. B.] of professional patriots and of foreigners. The true country, the country of Matei Basarab, is poor and neglected."[3] To Eminescu, "the time of Prince Matei Basarab [the mid-seventeenth century—I. B.] is the time of a Romanian civilization and of a national society."[4] The population was growing, and there emerged a "standard language common to the entire Romanian nation [. . .]," "a unity, ideal at least, of the outspread Romanian people . . ." favoured a return to the past. This is what the poet himself wrote: ". . . I have so often repeated that reaction in the true sense of the word, reaction as an attempted historical reconstruction of the pre-Phanariot age, is no longer possible in Romania, and we are not so Utopian as to ask for what God Himself could not do."[5]

When Eminescu mentions the time of Matei Basarab's reign, he does this to point out the moment of rupture: with the Phanariot period, which practically covers the whole eighteenth century, the people was pushed into the Ottoman suburbia ("the morass of the Ottoman homestead"). There followed a second stage: the historic homeland was pushed into the condition of a "European suburbia." As Eminescu sees them, these stages are, compared with the Matei Basarab moment, a very long step backwards. But he does not suggest a return to that moment; on the contrary, he theoretically calls, as "a child of the nineteenth century", for citing precise facts and for including them in a general formula. While practically he proposes a "relation of compensation" between the "superposed classes" and the "positive class", the producers of wealth. Contrasted with the time of Matei Basarab, when—as Eminescu thought—the Romanian people made its own history, acting as one agent in an organic social complex, the Phanariot period paved the way for an era of history controlled, through the "superposed class", by the magnates of Western capitalism.

Eminescu sees in the voivode times a kind of pattern, a historic model of organic evolution. In his opinion, the events of 1848 were truly a change in our history, though not for an organic evolution but for the "Atlantic revolution", i.e. a revolution made to fulfil the needs of the urban classes, of a Western-type bourgeoisie poorly represented in the Romanian Lands. This favoured the infiltration of a usurious, commercial bourgeoisie that later on pushed our society in an artificial direction of non-organic evolution.

In Eminescu's opinion, a proper, positively oriented reform programme should be placed in the "horizon" of the historical period when the Romanians made their own history. That was the voivodes' period, and its use as a model for historically building a modern society was the essence of the concept of "adoptive era."

Let us explain the terms. Developing Lucian Blaga's theory of "adoptive topics," I. Em. Petrescu reveals the mechanism by which the spiritual model of an age, social group or even nation can push its roots into an "adoptive model," which may be "in complete disagreement with the established model [. . .] of the time."[6] Thus the *adoptive model* becomes a mode of approaching and "resolving" the problem facing the personality or the social group situated in the horizon of that model. In advancing the concept of "adoptive era" we are developing the thesis of Lucian Blaga, through the interpretation of I. Em. Petrescu, considering that Eminescu was fully aware of the possibility of placing the acts of cultural creation (including the political) in a deliberately chosen cultural horizon. This is the sense to be inferred from Eminescu's manner of orienting the political and cultural options of his time in the spirit and traditions of Matei Basarab's period. We think that Eminescu envisaged the possibility of fully crystallizing the general orientations of the "collective imaginary" (of the class having the power to impose reforms) in line with and in the direction required by values with a "modelling role" evolved in another period. This process of relating creative activities of the present to values evolved in another historical period is, essentially the mechanism which we have termed "adoptive age" and which is one of the factors acting in the tradition-innovation relationship.

Eminescu introduces in Romanian sociology the positive study of negative processes. He advances the term "semi-barbarism" to suggest that in the modern age the peoples of southeastern Europe had been pushed back into the dark past, into their condition of "exploited classes." In this geographic area the social regimes build "socio-political" complexes for "draining" the surplus product, and articulated "economic modes": above—the administration, turned into an economic mode of spoliation; below—agriculture, turned into an economic mode of enslavement, in the form of agricultural journeywork. Mihai Eminescu clearly notes the distinction—to be further investigated by his mind—between civilization and "semi-barbarism", the two historical "species of society" arisen on the European scene. This distinction, drawn in the heat of a polemic with the Socialistically-minded brothers Nădejde, is the result of a great deal of historical and empirical research work. It shows that between the "rationalist (i.e.

"artificial", imposed from outside) organization" and the "more natural organization" resulting from an objective causality in the historical becoming of a society there is a significant. difference The latter type of organization seems to be peculiar to "civilization", i.e. to the Western societies, whereas the former is characteristic of the Eastern societies. Eminescu rejects the idea (shared by the brothers Nădejde) that in itself "an organization based on capital" is "the cause of misery." Capital begets exploitation, though not necessarily misery, in the form of a whole range of social degradation processes, all stemming from economic decay. In the West the organization based on capital did not result in economic decay. On the contrary, and then, says Eminescu, one must look for the real specific cause, that which generates first economic decay and later on in, close relation to it, moral, religious, cultural decay, and even biological degeneracy. "We think that the real cause of misery lies in quite another place [than in the organization based on capital and property, as the brothers Nădejde point out in their pamphlet—I. B.]; that it is inherent in the whole of liberal development started in the last century, that originates from the rationalist organization instead of the earlier, more natural, organization [. . .]. There are here thousands upon thousands of people who in no way make good the work of the society supporting them, who [. . .] draw from the nation, in virtue of their organization into an exploiting society, large sums of money as annual payments. The aristocratic needs of the ignorant plebs, of the liberal pleby—intellectually barren and morally decayed—this is what oppresses the people. This pressure could not be exerted by the inherited capital, nor by the capital earned by one's work, which, on the contrary, is constantly at the workers' disposal, or else would remain unproductive. If the Romanian socialists chose to look into the many budgetary forms—at the commune, country or national level—of squandering the very last penny, earned by the common man through his work, in order to feed the class of office-seekers and ordinary sycophants living on the general misery, with no compensation to their fellow man, then they would see for themselves that with us the evil is of a totally different nature. With us misery is produced artificially by introducing alien structures and laws, unsuited to the country's stage of economic development—a structure which is too expensive and produces nothing."[7]

Therefore, by "organic evolution" Eminescu means that evolution which is based on the organic link between the people and the upper classes, i.e. on a relation of compensation, in which the people produce the wealth and the "upper" class produces the form of organization, the intelligence and culture required by a positive economic relation in which the profits exceed the costs. In Eminescu's view, the capital relation makes such a mode of social organization possible. But in South-Eastern Europe one has a negative "rational organization" based on a relation of "superposition" in which consumption exceeds output and the upper class promotes an "exploitation society" without any organic links to the real society and, hence, without a positive, compensatory economic relation. That is the reason why the analytic model for the "suburbia" must differ from the one peculiar to the metropolitan areas.

Yet regardless of the area, Eminescu firmly places civilizations and cultures in a relation of dependence on the economy. He writes: "Economists have noticed [. . .] that the religious systems too, no matter how old and how deeply rooted in man's moral nature, will be altered, or even die out and be replaced by others after a moment of great economic decline, which is always accompanied or followed by great moral decline. We are far from praising the inferior condition of the peasant under the *Réglement Organique* [the basic law of the Danubian Principalities in 1830-1859—I. B.], far from wishing that the old state of things should return with its disadvantages. But as regards the normal, natural development of our nation, as regards the tolerable proportion between the hardships it endured and the welfare resulting as a benefit from those hardships, we should be blind, and unjust to our parents, if we did not see that that condition was far, far better for the lower classes than the present one. Far from us the intention of being *laudatori temporis acti*. The chief defect of the old organization lay in the fact that it did not take sufficient account of the middle class; but the peasant and the big landowner were both well-off [. . .], being in perpetual contact [. . .]. One could say that the old boyar was peasant-like, and the old peasant had a kind of boyar-like pride. But with the emigration abroad, with the introduction of foreign, expensive habits, with the absenteeism equally favoured by all our leading classes [. . .], the old relation became altered (. . .). There is no longer any other distinction between people than that established by money, no matter how it is acquired . . ."[8]

It is obvious, we think, that with Eminescu this is not a reactionary nostalgia for the past, but a certain view of the types of society: the "natural" (organic) and the "artificial" (limiting). In the natural societies a basic law is at work, namely the "law of the dynamic proportional" (which to Eminescu is a universal law). The essential defect of the old society was its failure "to take sufficient account of the middle class," which prevented the effects of the law of the dynamic proportional from becoming fully realized. Another expression of this law is the positive economic relation between the "productive" and the "upper" classes, which necessarily entails "a tolerable proportion between the hardships endured by the people and the welfare resulting as a benefit from these hardships." This would be a sign of progress in terms of material and moral civilization, for in Eminescu's opinion "economic decline is always accompanied or followed by a great moral decline."

Using the comparative-historical method, Eminescu proves that immediately after the reign of Matei Basarab there began in the Romanian Lands an artificial-society era in which the action of the law of the dynamic proportional was blocked by the emergence of a negative economic ratio between the basic classes and the Phanariot "upper" class. The results of this were seen in a historical series of negative-sign processes. Eminescu's major contribution lies, however, in the positive examination of the second stage in the negative historical series, viz. the stage in which the Romanian nation was pushed into the surburbia of the West. His fundamental thesis is that, with the modern age, our gravitation axis was changed and we were pushed into the Western suburbia. The agent which effected this shift was, in Eminescu's opinion, the liberal system. It gave rise to a lumpenbourgeois oligarchy and enslaved the country to the Western capitalists (the Austrian included). In this context he deals with the question of railway building and of the Western and Central European notably Austrian influences. Eminescu's analysis is a contribution *avant la lettre* to a world accumulation theory with the definition of the place and role of the periphery, and he was the first to advance the theory of the "peripheral" space, the theory of the difference between the developed capitalist society and the "artificial" ones found on the outskirts of the West. Eminescu proves that the real cause of the decline was not capital but the superposed class with its system of negative relations with the people.

The capital relation makes it possible to have an organic relation between the classes, and also a positive economic relation based on the dynamic "proportional" production-welfare. The modern theories of world capital accumulation and the theory of unequal exchanges between the national economies support Eminescu rather than the brothers Nădejde. Actually, the metropolises have a direct proportion between the growth of the productive forces and the wage rate. This situation was analysed in depth by Karl Marx, and it lies at the basis of the law of the tendential decrease of the profit rate, (i. e., an inverse proportion between the growth of the productive forces and the profit rate), which once again shows that a progressive historical amount of profit was oriented towards internal development, towards growth and progress, rather than towards consumption. On the outskirts, however, as pointed out by Samir Amin,[9] this law is ineffective; actually, between the growth of the productive forces (capital accumulation) and the wage rate there is an inversely proportional relation. Hence the organic link was broken under the systematic impact of a complex of factors. Eminescu works out the "artificial society" theory, revealing the negative historical relation established in such a society between the upper classes and the producing people, the latter being, to use a term from the theoreticians of "peripheral capitalism," marginalized", i. e., increasingly pushed out of civilization and exposed to the direct action of nature's laws—a higher death-rate, a shorter life-span, physical and mental degeneracy (hence, a deculturative process). The field reports used by Eminescu are highly illustrative in this respect. Above a certain limit, this law becomes destructive even to the system's reproduction as a minimal system. Thus, along with the decline of the population Eminescu finds a regression in the economic-productive potential, hence in the amount of society's productive forces. Therefore another aspect of the operation of the negative economic ratio, i.e., of the deviation from the metropolitan law of capital, is the fact that the "periphery" shows a tendency of progressive capital decrease, i.e., a progressive decapitalization, along with—paradoxically—a relative increase in the profit rate in favour of the "superposed class." This is accounted for by the great exploitation of the people, by the lowering of their income level (hence a decrease in the "wage scale") and the turning of the internal economy into a grain-exporting economy.

This process is tantamount to the shift of the country from the Ottoman suburbia into the Central European (German, Austrian, British and French capital). Thus Eminescu also places the cultural influences in their true light: they are not so much a rise in civilization as a mechanism for achieving negative historical relations.

Eminescu points out that the profits of the superposed class are due to the international economic mechanism, i. e., to the system of negative economic relations between the Central European and the national economies, the southeast European economies generally—a system into which Romania was being pushed by the play of purely political relationships.

Eminescu grasps the true face of political relations in the European-suburb system (an instrument of "dependent accumulation", i. e., of enrichment of the extrovert superposed class and of draining the surplus product towards the metropolitan economies). Using the methods of positive sociology, he reveals the results of his own investigations, highly conclusive for the theory of the specifically Eastern cause of the people being pushed into a state of "semi-barbarism": "I have known patriots [. . .] who collected taxes on poultry from the peasants, taxes computed in money and translated into labour. I have known liberals who demanded the produce from four ewes for an ewe's grazing. Economically absurd, but such absurd pretensions took the form of money demands calculated on the basis of ridiculous prices (. . .). Thus the uneducated—though healthy and very intelligent—people became a prey to all those who could jot two words on paper and apply to them the

provisions of a formal law copied from the civilized nations and suited to different needs, different people and different economic conditions."[10]

In Central Europe (the case of Austria-Hungary and Germany) and in Western Europe (Britain, France), or in other historical societies (the Venetian Republic, the Roman Empire, etc.) there had emerged natural societies in which organic relations were established between the people and the upper classes, positive economic relations of compensation, and the principle of the "dynamic proportional" acted as a "natural" law of human history. In contrast to these global societal types, the South-East European society was "artificial", with a superposed class, "orbital" (cosmopolitan) in its culture, non-historical in its forms (empty forms), negative in terms of its economic and moral civilization, etc. He describes, also comparatively, the organic, compensatory peasant-boyar relation, based on their cultural and national identity, as a type of social relation opposed, *also strictly comparatively,* to the type of artificial relation in which the two classes—the upper and the lower—are merely agglutinated, with no cultural, social, politico-juridical or any other contact. Decidedly, the contrast between the two forms of historical societies evolved on Romanian soil, the natural (in Matei Basarab's time) and the artificial (in Eminescu's own time) has a strictly comparative meaning.

Eminescu never rejects modern civilization out of hand; on the contrary, he acknowledges its presence as a historical civilization (and, hence, organic, based on a positive economy) in Central and North-Western Europe. He rejects, sociologically, not the society built on the civilization of capital (which he duly appreciates) but the type of artificial society built on super-exploitation of labour with no compensation in the structure and amount of capital. In the same sense he rejects, any theoretical attempt to apply to the Romanian Lands a "cosmopolitan and nihilistic pattern" where "the sentiments of country and nationality are trifles." Eminescu's theory is one of "artificial societies" built on a "negative economy" and thrown into the suburbs of European history by extroverted superposed classes that push the nations into superexploitation with the aim of superconsumption and of enabling the surplus product to be drained by foreign companies. Eminescu points out that the condition of historical suburbia into which South-Eastern Europe was being pushed was determined by the tendency of equalizing the levels, and structure of *consumption* among the various economies, though not the levels and structure of output. Whereas in some geographic areas the levels of output and consumption rose simultaneously, in the Romanian Lands the superposed class equalized its consumption with that of the Western upper classes by reducing capital and pushing the people into misery, and by bringing the nation into a state of "dependence on foreign countries."

Has there ever existed, in our area, a type of natural society capable of creating historical civilization? Yes, there has, says Eminescu: the historical society of the Romanians up to the Phanariot period. With the latter began the series of "negative history." Only such societies can create civilization that rest on positive economic relations and obtain a "benefit" from the production-consumption relation. To make this possible, it is necessary to have a compensation relation between the classes, so that neither can consume something without supplying something else in return.

Notes

1. Article published by daily *Timpul,* May 20, 1881; cf. M. Eminescu, *Opere* (*Works*), Vol. 12, Publishing House of the Academy of the Socialist Republic of Romania, Bucharest, 1985, p. 179

2. Article published by daily *Timpul,* December 17, 1881; cf. *loc. cit.,* p. 443

3. Article published by daily *Timpul,* May 20, 1881; *loc. cit.,* p. 179

4. M. Eminescu, *Opere* (*Works*), Vol. 4, Ion Creţu edition, Cultura Românească Publishing House, Bucharest, 1938-1939, p. 188

5. *Idem,* p. 110

6. I. Em. Petrescu, *Modele cosmologice şi viziunea poetică* (*Cosmologic Patterns and Poetic Vision*), Minerva Publishing House, Bucharest, 1978, p. 14

7. M. Eminescu, *Opere* (*Works*), Vol. 12, Publishing House of the Academy of the Socialist Republic of Romania, Bucharest, 1985, p. 212

8. Articled published by daily *Timpul,* July 10, 1881; cf. M. Eminescu, *Opere* (*Works*), Vol. 12, Publishing House of the Academy of the Socialist Republic of Romania, Bucharest, 1985, p. 237

9. A. G. Franck, Samir Amin, *L'accumulation dépendente,* Editions Anthropos, Paris, 1975, pp. 181-185

10. Article published by daily *Timpul,* July 10, 1881; cf. M. Eminescu, *Opere* (*Works*), Vol. 12, Publishing House of the Academy of the Socialist Republic of Romania, Bucharest, 1985, p. 238

Mircea Scarlat (essay date 1986)

SOURCE: Scarlat, Mircea. "Aesthetic Interest." *Romanian Review* 40, no. 1 (1986): 31-6.

[*In the following essay, Scarlat investigates Eminescu's significance as a journalist.*]

One of the great Romanian publishing events of late has, undoubtedly been the publication of bulky volumes comprising Mihail Eminescu's journalism. The interest awaken by these volumes (9th-12th of the monumental edition launched by Perspessicius and continued now by a research team at the Museum of Romanian Literature) exceeds by far the specialists' circle, and motivates our attempt at finding it an explanation. Since the writer is first known as a poet (among the greatest 19th c. European poets), the standard edition volumes containing his poetry have met with natural interest. As it happens, the edition (for the first time in its complete form) of journalism has met with widely popular success, reaching its heyday.

Journalism was not a mere complementary activity to Eminescu's literary achievements. In a letter sent in early 1878, he presented himself as "an occasional writer," hence hinting that he was a professional journalist (in 1877-1833 period, he was an editor of Bucharest Conservative newspaper *Timpul,* often editing almost the whole issue). In all likelihood, this explains (besides the extraordinary artistic self-exigency) the small number of poems he published in his lifetime. Few of the writer's contemporaries realized the value of his poetry; he was better known, in his lifetime for his journalistic activity, *Timpul* being one the mostly read Romanian newspapers of the time. The articles published in that newspaper are the acme of Mihai Eminescu's journalistic activity; it was preceded by his contribution to *Federaţiunea,* a newspaper issued in Pest (in 1870) and his editing activity at *the Curierul de Iaşi,* in 1876-1877.

Eminescu's journalistic activity has been eulogized by all literary critics. We shall quote now only the most important Romanian literary historian—G. Călinescu—and an European authority in the field, Professor Klaus Heitmann, head of the seminar of Romance studies at the Heidelberg University. G. Călinescu viewed Eminescu's journalism as "the paragon in the Romanian writing history and yet unrivalled by others," and Klaus Heitmann stated in an in-depth study—*Eminescu, a Political Thinker,* that "Romania's national poet was, likewise, one of the most prominent journalists of his country."

Nowadays, not only literary critics and historians are, none the less, interested in the articles Eminescu had published in the press of his time, but also the public at large. Quite uncommon, since journalism means ephemeral. In other cases (and this makes up the overwhelming majority), the newspaper article vanishes once the event it has commented upon sinks into oblivion. The fact that, after more than a century since the publication of the articles in *Timpul,* their reading is aesthetically rewarding, tellingly prove that they have intrinsic artistic value, corroborated with the documentary aspects.

Speaking of the latter, we spotlight the fact that Eminescu's journalism runs over a short but extremely important time span in the history of the Romanian people. Hence, the articles evince a major ideational and informational interest, any study in Romania's modern history could not do away with. We are not going to tackle these aspects now, but we shall focus on the *literary* interest in Eminescu's journalism.

Naturally, the extraordinary success of the volumes—comprising the great poet's newspaper articles—is motivated not only by the author's towering prestige but also by the recent interest in documentary literature. Artistic literature itself has tended to become "lesser literature," consequently shaping the taste of the receptor of literature as well. Gaëtan Picon noted in *Panorama de la littérature française* that most 20th century writers, "the literature that ambitions to be *literary* is doomed to vanish, the future belongs to 'non-literary' literature."

In this sense, one can notice an ever marked tendency of Romanian literary criticism to analyzing the artistic implications of nonfictional texts, wherein artistic intentionality has not stood in the foreground of the authors' concerns. For example: the old chronicles (written by Grigore Ureche, Miron Costin, Ion Neculce a.s.o.), rhetoric writings (Antim Ivireanul), 19th-century memoirs (Ion Ghica in the main, scientific and journalistic writings. Important critics have attentively analyzed, previously often ignored, works, hence, they have met public taste.

The interest in nonfictional literature is symptomatic for modern intelligentsia to the same extent to which the 19th century chroniclers delved in folk traditions. Nowadays, the document ever more seriously contends fictional literature. Literary latencies are being objectivized despite the lack of artistic intentionality, mainly in the case of a great poet like Mihai Eminescu. Of an artistic intentionality in the literal meaning of the word one cannot speak in his journalism; nonetheless, his care for using the proper word is certain, the yearning after stylistic mastership being not exclusively related, naturally, to fictional literature.

No matter how engrossed in politics Eminescu-the-journalist was (he was on the editorial staff of a press organ of a leading party of the time), certain artistic means in his fictional poetry and prose are detectable also in his journalism, and the critics of the writer's literary work have often referred, in their commentaries, to the articles published in *Timpul.*

Eminescu's basic criterion in judging the value of a literary writing was linguistic accuracy. In one of his articles, he drew the hierarchy of modern Romanian writers on the way they handled the language. Referring to Ion Heliade Rădulescu, he wrote that his "main merit" lies in his linguistic achievements: "He wrote in everyday language, oral speech was his master of style. He unfettered language of its conventional Middle-Age and prayer-book spelling rules, which became a safe tool for expressing any modern idea. From this vantage, Eliade was the first modern writer of the Romanians and the father of the literary language we are speaking nowadays." In the same article (**"Ioan Eliad"**, *Timpul,* November 21, 1881) he said that the revolution achieved by Heliade was the *naturalness* of his expression.

Previously, Eminescu had highlighted Titu Maiorescu's merit (a critic and aesthetician, the mentor of the "Junimea" cultural society to have contributed to "cleaning" and purifying language, **"The Debate over the Election of Mr. Maiorescu,"** *Timpul,* February 8, 1878). A classical language had been one of Eminescu's desiderata since his studies at the University in Vienna (1869-1872). In his views, the maturity of a people is closely related to the stage of the development of the national language. Therefore, "each national language is the crux of national feeling, focusing all dimensions of spiritual life, it indicates the level of spiritual public life. "The poet grounded his opinion on the conviction that "language, power of selection and expression in oral or written form is an essential element, even a criterion of culture." (Unpublished notes).

Moreover, Eminescu indissolubly related the maturation of language to its writing. "The consistency of a language begins with its writing," the poet noted, underlining that writing is the force that lends the necessary stability to subsequent refinement. Hence, the role devolving, in his outlook, on writers who were likely to influence the evolution of the language, and turn it stable and pure.

Likewise, the models of style had to be sought in the vernacular (he thought it to be the most precious thesaurus of a nation) and in old language. This explains his admiration for authors such as: Ion Creangă and Petre Ispirescu in **"Bibliographical Notes,"** *Timpul,* 6, 7, 8, May, 1880, and the frequent references to old writings. For example, in his study **"The Austrian Influence on the Romanians in the Principalities,"** published in Convorbiri literare, August 1, 1876, he praised "the beautiful and rich language of the chroniclers"; he tackled the same topic in his article **"Grigore Ghica-voevod,"** *Curierul de Iaşi,* October 1 and 3, 1876. He valued the old chronicles not only for the richness of historical information but also for the conciseness, accuracy and picturesqueness of images.

Eminescu's journalism abounds in the above-mentioned qualities. In the article **"The Old and the Young,"** published on December 14, 1877, *Timpul,* as the third serial of the cycle **"Old Icons and New Icons,"** Eminescu evinced that the portrait of the Prince Stephen the Great made by chronicler Grigore Ureche was a rewarding reading after more than two centuries since the chronicle had been written. Eminescu's articles have now a similar impact: owing to the writer's out-of-ordinary talent they arouse a constant interest beyond the questions they generated; it has occurred, we think, a shift of accent, in reading them, toward an admiration of the style, the dominant becoming, throughout time, the aesthetic pleasure of reading these texts.

Literary excellence is profusive all through Eminescu's pieces of journalism; unfortunately, only by reading them in the original one can grasp the subtle stylistic effects otherwise inevitably lost by translation. He who reads in Romanian these articles will "relish" the energetic, sure cut of the sentence. Likewise, the stages of the stylistic evolution of Eminescu's nonfictional prose can be traced out. The rhetorics of his youth (whose plenary expression we find out in the articles published in 1870 in the *Federaţiunea* newspaper, of Pest, under the pseudonym "Varro") has gradually vanished, the language turning classic throughout his editorial activity at *Timpul.*

Let's take an example to point out the interest we are speaking about. A history of the Romanian pamphlet will undoubtedly devote one of its most important chapters to Eminescu. And worth mentioning is that the great poet continued in fact a tradition. This literary species was excellently illustrated since the 17th century, when masterpieces of religious pamphlet had been produced (Barlaam, "The Answer against Calvinistic Catechism") and of lay pamphlet (Miron Costin, "Of the Moldavians' Kin"). Pamphlet-like pages are to be found also in the 18th-century works of Dimitrie Cantemir, Ion Neculce, Ion Budai-Deleanu and in certain 18th-century anonymous chronicles in verse. In the 19th century, the pamphlet was cultivated by the generation preceding Eminescu (the writers of the revolutionary movement of 1848) and also by the poet's own generation, as for instance, Titu Maiorescu).

Eminescu had a real vocation for pamphlet writing, obvious chiefly during his activity at *Timpul.* Eminescu elevated pamphlet writing to a *polemical strategy* status opposing years in a stretch the ideas propagated by *Românul,* the Liberal Party press organ, a newspaper backing up C. A. Rosetti's views, against whom Eminescu directed most of his attacks.

The artistic means Eminescu conveyed in his pamphlets are exceptionally diverse, from the hardly perceptible irony to a lashing merciless language. Always polemicizing, the journalist wrote so incisive articles as he almost called for a reply. His long polemics can be read as real novels *in nuce,* whereas ignoring, in fact, the political struggles they were generated by.

The adversary is sometimes ridiculed by suggesting the rudimentary topic he tackled. For example, we shall excerpt now the opening paragraph of his article **"Polemica cu România liberă" ("The Polemics with the România liberă"):** "We are not content that we are pushed into a debate over the rudimentary theories of state life, since discussions of these matters always prove the political non-maturity of those that bring them up for consideration." (*Timpul,* September 2, 1878). That premise discredited, from the onset, the adversary. A similar method is used in the article **"Dezvoltarea istorică a României" ("Romania's Historical Development"),** *Timpul,* May 6, 1881, wherein the comical effect is enhanced: "Shall we discuss with (the newspaper) *Timpul* matters elementary for any man knowing history, to read it the primer of the State's historiography and physiology? It would be a twofold ungrateful mission, first since the people we a talking to, as clever as they might be, will not find in the reminiscences of the four elementary forms and a course for violoncello enough elements to grasp us, and second, because, although we could level down to their intellectual power and turn a puerile mind, let's say, on a par with them, they would not, nonetheless, understand us, because they have no interest to.

A predilect device in Eminescu's polemic journalism is the caricaturing of certain persons (the preferred culprit: the Liberals' leader C. A. Rossetti) or of some entire groups. If the great historian and revolutionary leader Nicolae Bălcescu would by [some] miracle [rise] from the dead, wrote Eminescu, "he would come upon parliaments of stupid puppets, universities where some professors do not know how to write a sentence correctly, journalists having four elementary forms, in a word, people that, realizing their void of ideas, concoct empty words, damaging the good old structure of the Romanian tongue, making as if they have something to say, simulating a culture they do not have and an understanding mother nature refused to endow them with" (**"Bălcescu and His Followers,"** *Timpul,* November 24, 1877). Sometimes the sarcasm of the pamphlet writer is let loose and actually his adversaries extremely painfully bear the violent words. Eminescu himself was aware of the excessive vehemence of certain texts and he motivated it by the manner the fierce political struggles used to be waged between adversary parties (**"Should We Temper Our Words?",** *Timpul,* March 23, 1883). We shall not infer that Eminescu's articles present interest resides, exclusively, in their pamphlet-like test; we have dealt with this aspect because it is, perhaps, the most representative one. Modern readers can be amazed by many other aspects, finding out aphorisms, sentences that can be read as verses, memorable portraits, extraordinarily zestful evocations. This brief notation cannot contain an in-depth study of so vast a subject matter. Hence, we have attempted mainly to bring to the fore the real interest it has for any reader nowadays, Eminescu's journalism, which only now, in the standard edition of his works, reveals its many-sided artistic qualities, in full consonance with the poet's genius.

Valentin F. Mihaescu (essay date 1986)

SOURCE: Mihaescu, Valentin F. "The Sap of Ideas." *Romanian Review* 40, no. 1 (1986): 36-41.

[*In the following essay, Mihaescu studies the relationship between Eminescu's poetry and his journalism.*]

After the death of Mihai Eminescu, about whom Titu Maiorescu, with all his reticence in using superlatives, wrote in 1886 that "he had brought Romanian poetry to a peak of perfection," his work became a real object of worship for the younger generations. A wave of epigones, among whom noteworthy are Alexandru Vlahuţă (1858-1919) and Panait Cerna (1881-1913), imitated his style punctiliously, and Eminescu's poetry, especially the anthumous poems, steadily penetrated deeper and deeper in the readers' conscience, thanks to the proliferation of editions from his poems and biographical novels. If before 1884, (the date when Titu Maiorescu put together the first edition of poems, with a preface by himself), Eminescu's fame did not get beyond the circle of "Junimea", for two decades beginning with 1892 (when Vlahuţă gave a conference on "The Eminescu Trend" at the Romanian Atheneum) the poet's fame rose to an apogee and his name became synonymous with the idea of national poet. When there were fewer imitators, the new generations appropriated another dimension of Eminescu's genius. His journalistic activity at *Timpul* gains ground in the conscience of the public and soon Eminescu's political doctrine became an inalienable landmark in the ideology of the time. "His conservative doctrine," Şerban Cioculescu noted in a 1939 article, "proves its efficacy through a row of generations, carried his theses further in time by adhering to them (. . .) The poet, whose literary domination was exhausted before the war, continued to exercise an influence through the unusual persuasion in his political articles. In this sense 'Eminescianism' lasted, although sometimes abusively identified with a nationalist orientation."

As against these two unilateral stages in the reception of Eminescu's work to which one might add another—the dispute on the priority in value of his anthumous poetry as against his posthumous poetry or the reverse—the present suggest a radical change of angle. As the standard edition of his works is now nearing completion one can speak about an integral reception, which casts light on the parts in order to make the whole visible. Eminescu's work is thus perceived as a harmonious body, full of the same generous substance of ideas. This is the sense of philosopher Constantin Noica's definition of Eminescu as "the accomplished man of Romanian culture." From this angle, and considering outdated the prejudice according to which Eminescu had to accept to work as a journalist to the detriment of poetic creation in order to make a living, his journalistic activity and poetry appear as two complementary undertakings, two illustrations of one and the same set of ideas. Tackling this aspect with regard to the level of expression Şerban Cioculescu discovered a number of syntagms that pass from poetry into the newspaper article and the other way round. The initial direction of this movement is impossible to detect, since Eminescu only accidentally kept the drafts of his articles, while the manuscripts were thrown into the wastepaper basket, in contempt of the subsequent literary history. At the same time an approximate dating of the poems in manuscript, for the purpose of comparison with articles published in the press appears equally devoid of efficiency, because it took sometimes years for a poem to cover all phases from a rough sketch to the definitive form.

Nevertheless, how can the presence of figures of speech in exactly the same form in poetry and in journalism be explained? In our opinion the phenomenon is due to Eminescu's extraordinary memory, a gift he acknowledges without pride or reticence, "I know what it is from the trouble I had with mathematics in my childhood because of the wrong approach I was given, although I was one of the cleverest boys. At 20 I had not yet managed to know the Pythagorean table and this because it does not appeal to one's judgement but rather to one's memory. *And although my memory was phenomenal . . .*" It is his phenomenal memory that explains the similarities of expression. At a deeper level, however, the identity of views and ideas, which will be tackled in the following, shows a perfect consistency of Eminescu's personality throughout his work. His is an indivisible system of ideas, obviously expressed by specific means in poetry and in journalism, but essentially the same.

In a romantic spirit but with positivist arguments Eminescu praises in his articles the past of the country, the values of patriarchal civilization, the spans of stability during the glorious rules of Mircea the Old, Stephen the Great, Matei Basarab, Alexander the Kind. Those are moments in history when all political factors converge towards the preservation of national independence and the rulers give priority to the defence of the country, beyond personal or family interests. "The wonder," Eminescu noted in an article dated January 22, 1881, "consists in the fact that at a time when Europe was in disarray we were lucky to have Mircea in Wallachia and then Stephen the Great in Moldavia. The latter was Mircea's adoptive child; he spent his childhood at

Curtea de Argeş and Tîrgovişte and he had the same tendency to unite Christendom against the Ottoman Porte; in one word his ideas exceeded his individuality." In heavy battles or through highly efficient diplomacy given the conditions Mircea and Stephen managed to preserve the country's sovereignty. In his writings Eminescu keeps dwelling on these glorious eras, setting models of patriotism, dignity and wisdom for the present. In 1880, for instance he blended pathetic discourse with historical argument in a study that contains his main economic, social and political theses." How really brilliant and how matchlessly great these past representatives of the independence of the Romanian principalities were as compared to the present! Mircea, during a 38-year long rule and Stephen the Great for 46 years had no other concern than the country's independence. Mircea the First—this luminous prototype of warfare and diplomatic arts with the Romanians—had no other goal all his life than to maintain the country's independence. In 1394 he defeated Bajazet Ilderym in the memorable battle at Rovine, which remained in the memory of the entire Balkan peninsula; in 1395 he concluded an alliance treaty with Hungary; in 1396 he took part in the battle of Nicopolis; in 1398 he beat Bajazet all alone near the Danube; in 1406 he stretched his arm into Asia to dig out Musa as pretender against Suleiman I, gave him money and made him an emperor; in 1412 he supported another pretender Mustafa, against Muhammad I, and in the very year of his death, 1418, he gave money and weapons to a sectory of the time, by name Mahmud Bedreddin, hoping to reap political successes from religious splits among the Turks. A similar policy of skillful balance between the Christian powers, and of direct battles with the Turks was promoted by Stephen the Great. The attitude of these two princes explains how our principalities were able to bow to the Turkish power and in the process to preserve their entire inside and outside sovereignty, how the submission treaties contained the interdiction for Muslims to settle in the country, how a glimpse of the old independence was reflected even on the shabby Phanariot rulers, as they too dared to call themselves princes *by the grace of God,* even though they were appointed and dismissed by firman, although *Dei Gratia* is appended only to sovereigns. (. . .) Were our two greatest rulers right or wrong when preferring a nominal Turkish supremacy to a real Christian supremacy? Reality showed that it was what they could do best. Absolutely all Danubian countries had became pashalics; the great kingdom of Hungary also was turned into a pashalic for 100 years. Poland was divided and divided it is today, while our old treaties, written in big, stiff letters on calf's skin had been until recently the spring of our real independence, the source from which the successive acts of emancipation from under the Turkish rule derived. Tudor invoked them when he asked the Porte to reintroduce native rulers,

while the ad-hoc Divans found no other, stronger, arms before the conclave of Europe than those." (**"Studies on the Situation,"** II, *Timpul,* February 19, 1880).

Similar ideas flow from under the poet's quill. As poetry is not a listing of historical arguments but their sublimation, Eminescu chose moments of maximum tension in order to enhance the emotional impact upon the reader. In his **"Satire III,"** published in 1881, after the first part, obviously symbolical, which describes the growth of the Ottoman Empire as far as the Danube, under Bajazet Ilderim, follows the confrontation scene between the sultan and Mircea the Old. In his portrait of the Romanian prince, Eminescu stresses his popular origin. This is not accidental. In a reply published also in 1881 to the newspaper *Românul,* organ of the Liberal Party, then in power, Eminescu wrote, *"The constitutive cell of the old Romanian states is the peasant republic,* such as it was preserved for a long time at Cîmpulung (in Bucovina) and in Vrancea, a mostly aristocratic republic. To liken that world, *where the glory of one was the glory of the entire commune, where ownership was referred to the nation, with its history and traditions, rather than to the individual,* to the present times, in which the basis for inequality is neither *intelligence* nor *valour* nor *character* but money, international money, made by whatever means, to use money as a measure for the past is a sacrilege vis-à-vis our national history." In other words the individual cannot stand out from the community by anything else than intelligence, valour and character. That is why Mircea is a simple old man. During the face-to-face encounter with Bajazet and then during the battle ("Mircea himself led on his men midst storm of battle dust") he becomes *different,* he *stands out* through his representative traits. In a first phase of his dialogue with Bajazet, when the stands are not yet sharply taken, Mircea tries to avoid military confrontation diplomatically, by a show of modesty as against the greatness of his opponent, "'Isn't Mircea?' / 'Yes your Highness!' / 'Take heed, for caution warns, / Lest you your crown exchange against a wreath of thorns. / That you have come, great emperor, no heed be your aim, / While still at peace I hail you, our greetings that you came! / But, as to your good council, o may the Lord forgive, / If you dream to win this land by force imperative; / Had you not better return home with calm and peaceful mind / And show in you imperial strength that you are just and kind . . .'" When, however, Bajazet's intentions appear in the open, Mircea forgets about any diplomatic formulas and states his creed plainly on behalf of his community, "I?, I defend the poverty and the needs of a struggling land / And therefore all the rocks and streams and hills that guardian stand / And all that grows and moves and breathes to me is ally true, / We have small hosts, yet love of soil had every power to rid / This flowering land of all its foes. Prepare then Bayazid!'" As can be seen Mircea in the **"Satire III"** is one and the same person with the prince in Eminescu's articles. What wins over is a higher idea than his individuality—the country. The unity of action of the entire people, which Mircea never doubts, is not a piece of rhetoric meant to intimidate his enemy. It springs from the same "love for the country," and later on sanctions a type of relations between state and individual which Eminescu was well aware of: "Whether good or bad, the old regime had an undeniable quality, a quality that made it justifiable in the eyes of all, namely it did not cost anything or nearly anything. The traditional ducat that every family had to pay for the treasury did not leave any peasant poor; it did not have any influence on his diet—actually it was the price of a sheep and that was all there was to it. This traditional ducat paid for the school (which was better than it is today), the administration undoubtedly bad but less corrupt and greedy than today), the judges (less foreign than today) and a few good-for-nothing (less demanding and more modest than today). The peasant was not the target of outrage from the subprefect, mayor, notary, tax collector—all of them townspeople, all of them scum of the lanes, all of them his direct or indirect exploiters. The chief, and the old men of the village collected the taxes in keeping with everybody's income and the money was taken to the treasury and it was really very seldom that the state money was ever touched by these so simple, so just, so righteous and so honest people."

Models from the past put forward by Eminescu's poetry and newspaper articles have a *therapeutic purpose*. They are replies addressed to the corrupt present, and meant to heal the socio-political body. Eminescu does not reject the new liberal institutions for the sake of conservatism. He only requests the new forms to be filled with a content that should justify them and make them really operate. Even the most enthusiastic mottoes are regarded with utmost mistrust as long as they are just words in the rhetoric of the politicians: "Public morality, public spirit in this country have taken a very dangerous turn and the party that has been ruling for the last four years contributed substantially in altering them. From a governing principle the principle of equality in front of the law has become a weapon in the war among classes; all social conditions seem to have collapsed and melted into a kind of promiscuity; the country's traditions have been completely forgotten; a new ruling class has risen to power without traditions and without authority and so the country at large—the foundation and basis of our nation—cannot find the conscience of political relationships with the rulers; political rights are no longer the reward for the service rendered, according to tradition but rather an instrument of ambition, of fulfilment of private interests (. . .) The moral is tolerance for all vulgar interests, and this distinguishes our political life. It is true that we do not

shun from invoking the name of the homeland and the name of freedom, but this as just one more hypocrisy meant to facilitate the fulfilment of private interests (. . .) What is difficult, however, is in any human undertaking, it to found and build solid institutions, to form the national character. The national character, however, cannot be based on public morality that admits greed as a principle, nor can the institutions be founded on empty talks about equality and freedom", "Pathology of Our Society," 4 January 1881). Similar vehemence is met with in the poem *Emperor and Proletarian* (1874). The urge to revolt in the proletarian's speech actually means rejection of "empty talk" and a propensity to lend meaning to the words through solidary action, *"Hurl to the earth their scheme founded on greed and wrong / This system that divides, making us rich and poor! / Since there will be no prize in death awaited long, / Demand the rights today that do to you belong, / And let us live in equal brotherhood secure!"*

The poor are the peasants, craftsmen and workers, or the "positive classes", to use Eminescu's newspaper language. While paying homage to them he violently attacks the upper strata, enriched by exploiting the work of others, strata made up of political clients, parasites in the administration and profiteers of all sorts, "As for the shapeless substance that makes up a state within a state, placed above the institutions and above the people, there is little else to say. Living on politics and through politics and not having any other kind of material resources or possibilities to make a living they are capable to pervert anything, including electoral lists, elections, parliamentary forms, economic ideas, science and literature. No wonder therefore that we can see this incompetent and ambitious protean being taking on all possible forms: ministers, financiers, entrepreneurs of public works (with a capital of empty words), MP's, administrators, mayors, soldiers (who had taken the redoubt of Grivița with their lips), actors, everything (. . .) Therefore, this is a new dominant class in Romania, which distinguishes itself through its absolute lack of productiveness. ("Studies on the Situation," February 1880).

As in a hall of mirrors his poetry records a similar image. The last part in the *Satire III* is a pamphlet of unique virulence in Romanian poetry. Eminescu's words inquire and punish, lash the demagogue out of his empty talk and expose him to infamy, suffocating him under an avalanche of invectives, only to pass this capital sentence in the end, *"Rise once more o Țepeș! Take and divide these men / As lunatics and rogues in two big tribes, and then / In mighty, twin infirmaries by force both tribes intern, / And with a single faggot prison and madhouse burn."*[1]

Most of the socio-political ideas in Eminescu's newspaper articles are recurrent in his social poetry. It is natural to be so, because the discourse of that type of poetry allows for a logical construction, in which ideology appears at the level of expression without causing disturbance. This structural compatibility, operational just for a limited area of poetic creation, produces an area of significant blending of journalism and poetry, in which idea and image enhance each other by mutual reflection.

Note

1. Quotations from *Satire III* and *Emperor and Proletarian* are excerpted from Mihai Eminescu, *Poems*, English version by Corneliu M. Popescu, Eminescu Publishing House, Bucharest, 1978, pp. 161 and 98

Valentin F. Mihaescu (essay date 1987)

SOURCE: Mihaescu, Valentin F. "Aspects of the Love Discourse." *Romanian Review* 41, no. 1 (1987): 62-7.

[In the following essay, Mihaescu discusses love and eroticism in Eminescu's poetry.]

In Mihai Eminescu's poetry, very much as in the work of all the great poets of the world, the erotic theme holds an essential place both by its frequency and especially by the profoundness of its treatment. His typically romantic temperamental structure presupposing tremendous interior combustions, and certain biographical conjunctures that seemed to foster the poet's restless and perpetually dissatisfied spirit imparted to the erotic relationship in his poetry a dramatic dimension with tragic accents of grief. An analysis of the love discourse in the poems published during Mihai Eminescu's lifetime offers the complex picture of an exceptional sensitivity coupled with a rare reflexive capacity. Eminescu's lyric hero is "love-sick" and he turns this suffering and the memory of it into a singular mood, different from both the Werther model and the post-Romantic Baudelairean spleen, not so much through the intensity of his emotions as through his greater metaphysical bitterness.

In his early poems, such as **"If I Had"** and **"A Horse Ride at Dawn,"** when Eminescu tries his hand at writing in the bucolic manner of his predecessor Vasile Alecsandri, love is a desired, liberating state, largely equated with the joy of living. The poems are conventionally Romantic outdoors walks, in which the image of the woman is made up of diminutives—"floricică" (from flower), "tinerică" (from young woman), "copiliţă" (from child), "mîndruliţă" (from sweetheart), "drăguţă" (from beloved) which reflect the taste of the time but also transcribe the will and desire for protection of a serene spirit for whom Eros is just a conven-

tionally communicated presentiment. Only the "mournful song" mentioned in **"A Horse Ride at Dawn"** seems to presage the future suffering. The harmony of the couple and a certain joviality of the erotic discourse are—we could say—the dominant notes of the opening pages of Eminescu's love "story". But another poem written in the same period (c. 1866) presents us a different manifestation of the lyric hero, calling our attention to the contradictions of the Romantic soul. The beloved woman in **"If I Had"** and **"A Horse Ride at Dawn"** is submissive, she listens to and accepts in delight her lover's discourse, her reactions being extensions or suave complements of the man's desires. The latter, in his turn, experiences a state of beatitude similar to happiness. The couple seems indestructible, and it is so indeed, but on an imaginary level, accredited as such by the paradisiac vision of the consensus of all elements. In the poem **"In Love with a Marble"** the lover, getting down from daydreaming to the sphere of experience, is desperate, his "soul in ruins", "broken", for "the icon he loved" (the projection in ideality of his wishes) has proved impassive like marble. The images of despair are grandiloquent, the hero creates an exceptional status for himself, in order to emphasize the discrepancy between his ideal and reality." "I have no one to tell my terrible sorrow, / I have no one to tell how madly I'm in love / For I alone am blessed with the bitter comfort / Of adoring a stone / Hope for the dying man, revenge for fury / The prophet has the curse, for faith there is God, / A shadow drives away the suicide's despair, / Nothing at all for me." *Beatitude* and *despair* are the extremes between which Eminescu's love discourse oscillates from the very beginning, revealing through images that are not entirely original as yet the fundamental antithesis of the Romantic soul and prefiguring the later drama of the genius. Until then, despondency becomes conscious suffering in a number of poems among which **"Venus and Madonna"** marks a significant moment in the evolution of Eminescu's amatory poetry. After the "Edenic stage", the awareness of the two partners' incompatibility in **"Love with a Marble"** is now detailed, argued and demonstrated up to a certain point. The gap between the two gets wider as the woman is vested with infernal attributes, while the man is the Poet, the Artist, superior to her even though, or precisely because, he fails to modify fictionally the woman's image: "And thus I, who in the night of a life of poetry lonely dwell, / Espied you, o barren woman, without soul and without fire / And of you have made an angel, sweet as secret magic spell, / When across a desert world luck and longing do conspire / (. . .) I gave to you the radiance that lights with sparkling fairy / The sacred mien of praying nun, of pious child celestial: / Out of a demon made a saint, out of discord harmony, / And lit within your heart impure a virgin brilliance matinal. / (. . .) As Raphael on canvas bare did the Madonna's portrait paint / With gleaming diadem of stars and eyes lit with a virgin smile, / So I a pallid mortal girl transformed into a deathless saint, / A girl with barren empty soul and body soiled, depraved and vile."

However, to remain at this resolution of the dramatic tension through the lampoon would mean to suspend the very essence of Romantic "dialectics". Love cannot be cured by discourse, it is a datum, a fatality, a damnation which the Romantic lover assumes with the voluptuousness of pain. He himself contains, as fundamental dimensions of his split personality, *angelism* and *demonism*. That is why the woman's infernal nature is accepted as "amor fati". It is not the beloved woman's tears that earn her forgiveness but the consciousness of the sovereignty of this sentimental dialectics, specific to the Romantic spirit. Threatened by the classic radicalness of the conscience, the love discourse is saved by the Romantic sentimental mobility. Sisyphus can resume his eternal climb up the hill: "You weep, dear child? But don't you know that in your will the power lies / With but a single pleading glance my yearning heart again to bind. / I kneel down humbly at your feet and seek for pardon in your eyes / I kiss your hands again, again and beg that I forgiveness find. / No, dry your eyes, dear one, don't weep, my accusations do not heed / For they were naught but empty lies, unfounded, wicked and unfair. / Why, were you demon, so much love would make you holy then indeed, / And I adore this demon saint with big blue eyes and golden hair." Although Eminescu's misogyny, as an effect of the beloved woman's evolution on a phenomenal level, grows according as his poetry acquires ample philosophical significances, his belief in love's liberating power does not dissipate. It is only transferred into the ideal plane in which the woman, who is a demon—even though adored—in the phenomenal world, becomes an angel as a projection of the man's hope: "Good child, are you demon that just at one glance / Of our eyes through their lashes thrown softly askance / My angel and friend left his long vigilance? / . . . But no, let your long lashes fall, / That your pale lovely features again I recall, / For you . . . you are he" (**"Guardian Angel"**). As a result of this objective impossibility of decision, Eminescu's lyric hero lives with equal intensity the phenomenal and the noumenal state of things, aspiring after—but unable to attain, at least erotically—the *coincidentia oppositorum*: the love discourse dramatically oscillates between rejection and attraction, trying to explain, in the presence or in the absence of the love object (especially in its absence) that Eros could have been a superior form of self-knowledge. The poet regards love as an aspiration after happiness, and woman as a symbol ("blue flower") of this aspiration. However, this type of erotic relation proves illusory (possible only in the oneiric or imaginary realm), the beloved woman's incapacity to understand the deep meaning of the

love discourse being the cause of the couple's split. "She will fail to see it is not you who wants her . . . that in you / There abides a demon thirsting for her light, the sweet, the true, / That he weeps or laughs, unable his own deep laments to hear, / That he wants her . . . thereby hoping for a sight of Self more clear" (**"Fifth Epistle"**).

More often than not, Eminescu's love poems are monologues. This, like everything else in Eminescu's poetry, is not an accidental trait. There are numerous explanations for the predominantly monologic form of the love discourse, and all of them detail the erotic drama. One of the apparently simplest explanations which, after all, includes all the others is that the dialogue partner is missing. *Why? And how?* The answers to these questions can comprehensively define Eminescu's Eros. For instance, in **"If I Had"** we saw that love is a desirable state. It has not come yet, but it could possibly come, and in anticipation of it the adolescent builds a conventional portrait of the ideal lover, which promises the happiness of the potential couple. It is, as we said, the "Edenic stage" of Eros, unreal, but regarded as possible. That is why the monologue is serene, free from the presentiment of the future drama: In **"In Love with a Marble,"** the monologue becomes passionate, desperate (though excessively affected), for the beloved woman is absent. Her absence in this case is not resented physically but rather in the sense of impassiveness and inaccessibility. At this stage, the loved woman is an ideal which the young supplicant cannot approach. Communication is denied to the man in love and all that is left to him is to protest his unhappiness. His drama is that of distressing waiting, without far-reaching resonance as yet.

In **"Mortua est!,"** the monologue is called for by the beloved woman's death. But here the lover's death remains only the occasion (pretext) for some quasi-philosophical interrogations on the meaning of existence. "Where lies the world's meaning?" the young man wonders, certainly grieved by his sweetheart's death, only to find out later that love could give meaning to the world! With **"Venus and Madonna,"** the love drama generated by the opposition between the subjective aspiration after meaning (that particular meaning!) and the objective impossibility to reach it acquires greater depth. The verse quoted from the **"Fifth Epistle"** quintessentially express this drama. The erotic failure is a failure of self-knowledge and, consequently, of knowing the world. From now on, the beloved woman can be physically present or not, for she is absent anyway, being inapt for the proposed dialogue. Even when it is she who utters the love discourse, as in the poem **"Blue Flower!"** The communication (meaning) fails to be established, as the woman's invitation only concerns the erotic game ("As rosy as an apple's rind / Will be my cheeks burnt by the sun, / And my long golden hair undone / Around your neck in coils you'll wind"), while the man dreams of the ideal love, the "blue flower". The reunion of the original couple (**"If I Had"**) is impossible: "Day by day, I'm farther, beloved one, from you, / And slowly, cold and darkness do take me for their prey . . . / While you fly on for ever, midst time's eternal day." (**"How Many a Time, Beloved . . ."**). The only thing that remains is the sad waiting, the hopeless hope cried in the wilderness of the soul and reverberated by the refrain-question of an endless monologue: "Why don't you come, why don't you come?"

Yet, there is one instance (in **"Călin, Pages from a Fairy Tale"**) when the love discourse takes on the dialogic form (a sort of dialogue also occurs in the great poem **"Hyperion,"** whose significances we shall reveal further on), seemingly contradicting our entire demonstration so far. The words of love whispered by Călin and the king's daughter do not seem to be the expression of that "vain instinct, common impulse, that e'en birds feel twice a year" in the **"Fourth Epistle."** They will not be forgotten even after a temporary separation, the end of the poem offering the bracing picture of the apotheosis of fulfilled love. In other words, in **"Călin"** love does not mean suffering, it leads to the harmony of the couple, to the suspension of the struggle of contraries, to happiness. The ideal envisaged in **"If I had"** has become reality, essence and appearance have merged into a new essence: love. "Where lies the world's meaning?" **"Călin"** provides the answer. But, alas, for one moment we have forgotten that this is a fairy tale, in which anything can happen. Even happiness is possible here. On the contrary, as the sceptic voice in the **"Second Epistle"** affirms, "In a world of vulgar strivings do not dream! For if you cherish / Fond illusions, there is danger to be made fun of and perish." Viewed from a certain angle, any lover is ridiculous, for he behaves in a "suspect" manner, he departs from the accepted standards, he contradicts them. All the more "ridiculous" is the immortal Hyperion, the celestial character in the poem **"Lucifer,"** symbol of the genius, in love with the "wondrous" Cătălina. Wondrous, but mortal. Hyperion, consumed by his burning passion, thinks that love can efface this structural incompatibility, addresses Cătălina [with] fiery amorous calls and draws her luring pictures of their future happiness together. In her turn, Cătălina loves Hyperion, desires him and calls him. It looks like a dialogue conducive to the making of an original couple. But it is a false dialogue, denounced as such by Cătălina: "I hate big words, nor do I know / How to begin my plea; And although thy discourse is clear / I don't understand thee." The drama of the genius is contained in Cătălina's statement. His messages do not reach the mortals, they *cannot* reach them, for the language of his messages is inaccessible to them. But the messages sent by such a one as Cătălin, who is willing

to show the girl "and piecemeal, too, / What is love" do reach their target. Hyperion (Lucifer) understands that his revolt against the heavenly order (his decision to renounce immortality) is a useless gesture as long as his communication with the woman he loves remains an impossibility considering their essentially belonging to different, even opposed worlds (phenomenal/ideal). His value judgement at the end of the poem has an axiomatic character: "You live in your sphere's narrowness / And luck rules over you— / But in my steady world I feel / Eternal, cold and true!" The final word in Hyperion's reply also marks the end of the love discourse. The genius has severed his ties with the world and, shutting himself up in his own loneliness, resumes, like a sad memory, the naive song he used to sing in the beginning: "If I had a lovey-dovey / With a young girl's milky face . . ."

Roxana Sorescu (essay date 1987)

SOURCE: Sorescu, Roxana. "Eminescu and Poe." *Romanian Review* 41, no. 11 (1987): 62-8.

[*In the following essay, Sorescu inspects motifs common to Eminescu and Edgar Allan Poe.*]

Let us start a literary discussion by assuming the condition of any discussion about literature: that of perpetrating an impiety. Let us put side by side two summaries, the reduced, skeletonized, rationalized models of two masterpieces, Mihail Eminescu's poem **"Melancholy"** and Edgar Allan Poe's tale "The Fall of the House of Usher." Not without recalling the challenge issued— with that mixture of frankness, lucidity, insolence and desire to startle that characterize his theoretical writings—by Poe himself in "The Philosophy of Composition": "of all melancholy topics, what, according to the *universal* understanding of mankind, is the *most* melancholy?" Death—was the obvious reply "And when", I said, "is this most melancholy of topics most poetical"? From what I have already explained at some length, the answer, here also, is obvious—"When it most closely allies itself to *Beauty*: the death, then, of a beautiful woman is, unquestionably, the most poetical topic in the world—and equally is it beyond doubt that the lips best smiled for such topic are those of a bereaved lover"[1]. We do not know whether it is more poetic, but another, closely related subject is certainly more terrifying: one's own death, glimpsed as strange spectacle by a man recording his agony, actor and spectator alike. Eminescu and Poe have both approached the theme, with a similarity of motifs and of symbolic senses that prompts us to place the Romanian poet in a different spiritual family than the one currently accepted hitherto. It should be stated, from the very start, that this is not a matter of influences in the sense of expressions, themes or collections transferred from one work to the other, but one of analogies involving not only the upper layers of consciousness. Eminescu knew Poe's work, at least the tales translated by Baudelaire—possibly also the poems—for he translated "Morella" with Veronica Micle (or merely brushed up her translation). In fact, Poe was appreciated in the *Junimea* circle, where Maiorescu enjoyed reading from his work, while Caragiale took a close look at his devices in building the fantastic. But such circumstances could have been absent without altering the profound coincidences between the two poets' literary thinking.

An admirable analysis of the state of dissatisfaction, anxiety, weariness and lack of confidence in the virtues of reason and passion in world and Romanian literature has been undertaken by Zoe Dumitrescu-Buşulenga in the "Melancholy Motif."[2] Dürer and Shakespeare, Milton and Keats, Gérard de Nerval, Eminescu and Blaga are examined in the subtle nuances assumed by the expression of the despondency, apathy, indecision and despair of man when confronted with the spectacle of the world.

Melancholy, cultivated as the other side of the medal, especially in the periods that exalted individuality and confirmed Titanism, in the Renaissance in the Romantic age notably, can be defined only with difficulty. And Eminescu's particularly. The poet gave this title to a poem that he lyrically assumed, after he ascribed it, in his dramatic attempt *Mira,* to Prince Stefăniţă, dissatisfied with all and self-disdaining, torn between an impulse to murder and deepest apathy, cultivating only a chimerical love for a strange, hard-hearted being—the daughter of old Arbore—who gives her name to the play without ever being seen other than through the eyes of those fascinated by her. The lyric monologue takes shape, in the characteristic Eminescu manner (constantly detected in the structure of the *Letters*), as a landscape description, a scene selected by a beholding eye in relation to a certain psychic state, followed by direct expression of the feeling that determined the selection and description. The eye looking downwards, from the astral worlds to the terrestrial, records, under the deathly light of the pale moon, the ruins of a windbeaten church, deserted by the images of faith and by faith itself. (Faith in the sense of trust in an ideal of perfection and purity, which is nothing but the projection of inward security into the power to create spiritmoved worlds.) There follows an identification of the lyric self with the church ruins, accompanied by the anguish of self-estrangement, of the painful awareness of a dual personality, culminating in the domination of an autoscopic vision. Beginning and ending under the sign of overruling Death ("the Queen of Night, now dead;" "I seem to be long dead"), the poem includes some essential motifs of Eminescu's poetic imagination: the moon—a dead queen, the church that degradation of

the marks of faith has turned into a mere sign of the inevitable disappearance of forms, the introduction into this deserted place of small noises by indifferent creatures (The priest, a small grasshopper, spins a dim, slender thought, / The canter is a beetle under the age-old wall"[3]; the split personality, identified with the ruinous landscape on the side shown to the beholder and with an indifferent, ironical demon of the beholding side.

"The Fall of the House of Usher" is a narrative told in the first person by a friend of Roderick Usher, whom this has called to keep him company in the difficult moments of his twin sister's agony and death. The narrator approaches the House of Usher "as the shades of the evening drew on": "I know not how it was—but, with the first glimpse of the building, a sense of insufferable gloom pervaded by spirit (. . .). I looked upon the scene before me—upon the mere house, and the simple landscape features of the domain—upon the black walls— upon the vacant eye-like windows—upon a few rank sedges—and upon a few white trunks of decayed trees—with an utter depression of soul which I can compare with no earthly sensation more properly than to the after-dream of the reveller upon opium—the bitter lapse into everyday life—the hideous dropping off of the veil. There was an iciness, a sinking, a sickening of the heart—an unredeemed dreariness of thought which no goading of the imagination could torture into aught of the sublime."[4] (In Eminescu: "And through the broken windows I hear the wind awhistling;" "I vainly my world seek in my exhausted brain, / A cricket hoarsely chirps a sad, autumnal song / And vainly now I press my hand on my desolate heart."). To the narrator, as to anybody else, the man inhabiting the house blends with it to the degree of actually becoming one. With a cadaverous complexion, Roderick Usher takes his guest into the depth of his terror—the illness and agony of his sister, the Lady Madeline: "a settled apathy, a gradual wasting away of the person, and frequent although transient affection of a partially cataleptical character." (Mira, as seen by Ştefăniţă: "Her gaze is vacant like a mad girl's. / I often sought to tell her of my love / But her harsh eye, also her godless smile / My heart would always crush . . ."). When the death of his sister seems a reality, Roderick places her corpse in a vault within a main wall of the building. An obscure guilt keeps him in a constant state of tension and watchfulness until, one evening, the two men's reading together is broken by the spectral appearance of the Lady Madeline who, out of the vault where she had been buried alive, "with a low moaning cry, fell heavily inward upon the person of her brother, and in her violent and now final death-agonies, bore him to the floor a corpse, and a victim of the terrors he had anticipated. The narrator flees aghast from the accursed mansion, which he sees bursting and collapsing behind him, in the unreal radiance of the "full, setting, and blood-red noon."

"Melancholy" and "The Fall of the House of Usher" confront us not with accidental descriptive coincidences but with a constellation of motifs essential to the two authors, having very similar symbolic values and being used for the same expressive purpose. In both texts the ego is identified with a ruined building, the ruins are placed in a deathly lunar light (while, pale in Eminescu, blood-red in Poe), the ego is split into an anxiously contemplative and a death-oriented side (Roderick-Madeline) and "Who's the one to tell the tale now by heart . . . I seem to be long dead."

Psychoanalysis has recorded the role of the shelter in the configuration of the deep ego, the feminine semantics of the house, which is assimilated with the maternal womb: "Tell me what your imaginary house looks like, and I'll tell you who you are . . . The home is a double, a super-determination of the resident's personality."[5] To imagine two buildings in a strikingly similar condition may be regarded as the sign of an almost identical state of mind. It should be noted from the start that all the common symbolic elements used by Eminescu and Poe are placed under the sign of the double: the church or house—personality's double, the moon—an element prefiguring androgyny, the ego split into Animus and Anima, male and female, through distinct characters in Poe, through an autoscopic vision in Eminescu. And one split part is always under the sign of Death: the outward projection is a ruin, the Lady Madeline dies, "On my desolate heart I vainly my hand press / It beats, a death-watch beetle, in a coffin's soft wood."

The symbolism of the moon and of the lunar deities has been decoded, by the frequency of apparitions, as being subject to the idea of androgyny: "the philosophy underlying every lunar theme is a rhythmical view of the world—a rhythm achieved by the succession of contraries, by an alternation of antithetic modalities: life and death, form and latency, being and non-being, wound and consolation (. . .). Still, the moon is not a mere model of mystic confusion but a dramatic scansion of time. The lunar hermaphrodite itself retains the distinct traits of its double sexuality.[6] In Eminescu, the lunar androgyny is marked by changing the gender of the nouns designating the heavenly body: "the Queen of Night" and "You, sweet and adored king of our nights." It may also happen that the alterations dictated by exterior elements, as the rhyme, depend on the deep structures. There is, however, in both the texts a specific mark: the moon absolutely represents Death alone, losing the ambiguity implicit in the possibility of renewal. The landscape dominated by the dead monarch transforms, in Eminescu, the world into a vast temple dedicated to extinction. With far less emphasis on the lunar motif but expanding to the degree of hallucination the symbolism of the house turned into a tomb, Poe's text suggests its meanings by reducing the cosmos to the shelter of the split being.

With Eminescu the moon correlates also with the other essential element of the poet's psychic structure, namely with rhythm. The grass hopper and the beetle with their small noises almost invariably fill the need of "musicalizing" the universe. In "Melancholy" their rhythm, usually gentle and monotonous, is amplified by apocalyptic signals coming from the decaying church: "The steeple is a-creaking, the pillars are a-beating." That the grasshopper, the dead-watch beetle, or, elsewhere, the mice "with their patter" come most probably from the poet's everyday experience seems obvious, but their significance may indeed transcend that of mere daily occurrences, Eminescu having selected from reality mostly such elements as his cultural memory could enrich with mythical senses. In the *Phaedrus,* Plato tells the story of how grasshoppers were born: "A lover of music like yourself ought surely to have heard the story of the grasshoppers, who are said to have been human beings in an age before the Muses. And when the Muses came and song appeared they were ravished with delight; and singing always, never thought of eating and drinking, until at last in their forgetfulness they died. And now they live again in the grasshoppers; and this is the return which the Muses make to them—they neither hunger, nor thirst, but from the hour of their birth are always singing, and never eating or drinking; and when they die they do and inform the Muses in heaven who honours them on earth."[7] The grasshopper offers the poet not only a rhythm but also a double of himself, both natural and legendary.

In Poe's tale, the rhythm governing the outward projection of the ego is replaced by a pictorial symbolism, by a kind of emblematizing through a lyric and a legendary text: the picture painted by Roderick (representing a room without any outlet, a vault ghastly illuminated from an invisible source), the poem about "The Haunted Palace" and the tale of the dragon's killing. As forms of exorcising terrors, of introducing order into chaos, all these elements play a role similar to that which, in Eminescu, is played by the rhythms of harmless creatures.

The motif of the double takes on multiple aspects in Eminescu, all being found in Poe as well: a shadow cast by the body upon the world, a primary physical form, dark and without consistency, a realm of night; a face reflected (in a clear water, in mirrors), which Eminescu particularly sees as a manifestation of feminine split personality, a projection of human narcissism; the twin motif—identical but antagonistic brothers, one angelic, the other demonic, Sarmis-Brighelu, the two William Willsons, Roderick-Madeline, a metamorphosis of the Narcis complex into the Cain-Abel complex; the motif of succession, of the appearance at different times, in different forms, of the same psychic entity, the motif of avatar and metempsychosis ("Poor Dionis," "The Avatars of the Pharaoh Tlà," and "Morella"—the tale of a mother who transfers her spirit into her daughter, which Eminescu selected for translation—all belong to the same family); the motif of a hermaphrodite split into a couple that seek to restore the primary unity through Eros; and lastly, in close association with the preceding, the motif of psychic splitting into two identical units, one watching the death of the other. Related to the motif of the couple rejoined through Eros, the motif of the deceased double turns into the motif of love for a dead being, the motif of Animus recognizing and searching for his lifeless Anima. The way in which these two last motifs are rejoined assumes, profound similarities in Eminescu's and Poe's texts. **"The Ghosts"** and **"Lenore"** are poetical constructions born of the same psychic complex split in search of unity, as are **"Melancholy"** and **"The Fall of the House of Usher."**

Of primary interest to us is the presence of common motifs in Eminescu and Poe. The general meanings of the symbolic elements used by the two poets come from the ancestral fund of humanity, are "anthropological structures of the imaginary," where the reader is supposed to be almost as competent as the writer in order to understand him, but we are most concerned with the fact that such motifs are interconnected in the works of both Eminescu and Poe into repetitive *networks* and that these constellations, these networks are very similar. In other words, we can regard them as "obsessive metaphors" tending to become a "personal myth," the same personal myth in Eminescu and Poe, the myth of projecting a basically schizoid myth into a contemplative and a death-oriented phase, linked together by an unspeakable terror and an irresistible attraction.

The attempt to find out the personal myth common to **"Melancholy"** and **"The Fall of the House of Usher"** raises two points of method worth discussing. The first relates to the right, boldness and ability of comparative analysis to extend its scope beyond the usual recording of loans, transfers and influences, nay, beyond the structural homologies of works deriving from mentality homologies of the societies in which the authors live. The second, refers to the relation that can be established between the lyric and epic elements, since a text that we empirically regard as lyric can be identical in its deep structures with another that we usually consider epic.

The comparative method, when based on the semiotic of anthropological symbols, can undoubtedly bring the revelation of unknown or only vaguely suspected spiritual families, but it contains, like any other duality, the vice of its own virtues, the risk such a decoding of the symbols as the interpreter can give ("We may be on the right path. And yet this could be merely a series of coincidences. We must find a correspondence rule." "Where can we find it?" "In our heads. Let us invent it, and then see whether it is the true one." Umberto Eco, *The Name of the Rose).* Starting in the analysis of lit-

erature from the concept of "archetypal pattern," a concept that offers the advantage of associating the reader, "implicitly" or not, with the author, we come rapidly enough to "the anthropological structures of the imaginary," which corrects the subjectivism of interpreting through records of meaning frequencies in dictionaries of symbols, some with comments, others organized according to the psychic distribution of the symbolic constellations (like Durand's work). Such dictionaries thus tend to become, from repertories of symbols, repertories of allegories. ("But then", I made bold to comment, "you are very far from solving the problem." "I am very close," said Guglielmo, "but they are very sure of their mistakes." "And you," I asked with a childish imprudence, "You never make mistakes?" "Quite often," he said. "But instead of conceiving one, I invent several, and so I am never enslaved to any one." *Ibidem).*

In other words, having found the common genotext of different phenotexts (J. Kristeva), we have somehow reduced the lyric and the epic to the same denominator. And this common denominator is the symbolic, more exactly the existence of networks of common symbols in a state of mutual tensions, latent in a lyric text and objectivized in the epic. The archetypal pattern (Maud Baudkin), the personal myth (Charles Mauron) the symbolic senses of the imaginary (Jung, Bachelard, Durand,) the architext (Genette) and the genotext (Kristeva) prove that the critical languages, beyond their approximating capacity, lead us, along the path of logical reductionism, towards the idea that grouping the writers according to the deep elements of their works can yield results which are as suggestive as those yielded by grouping them by outward similarities (biographical coincidences such as the year of birth, thematic coincidences, etc.). But the fact that, whichever route we take, we do not go very far from one another, is no doubt encouraging. Other voices, the same gamut.

Notes

1. "The Philosophy of Composition," in *Poe's Poems and Essays,* Everyman's Library, Dent-Dutton, London-New York 1964, p. 170

2. cf. *Eminescu, Culture and Creation,* Eminescu Publishing House, 1976, pp. 107-127

3. All quotations from Eminescu's poetry are from *Poems,* ed. D. Murăraşu, vols. I-III, Minerva Publishing House, 1970-72

4. *The Fall of the House of Usher,* in *Tales of Mystery and Imagination,* Collins Clear-Type Press, n.d., p. 119

5. Gilbert Durand, *The Antropological Structures of the Imaginary,* Univers Publishing House, 1977, pp. 301 ff

6. *Ibidem,* pp. 365, 365, 366.

7. *The Works of Plato,* The Jowelt Translation, The Modern Library, New York, 1956, p. 302

Corina Popescu (essay date 1988)

SOURCE: Popescu, Corina. "Eminescu and Leopardi: The Revelation of the Infinite." *Romanian Review* 42, no. 11 (1988): 85-94.

[*In the following essay, Popescu suggests how and why Eminescu affected Romania's reception of the work of Giacomo Leopardi.*]

The reception of Giacomo Leopardi's work in Romania is directly linked to the way the poetry of Mihai Eminescu (1850-1889) broadened the readers' horizon.

The kinship between the lyrical formulas employed by the two poets was for the first time pointed out by the high critical authority of professor Titu Maiorescu (1840-1917). In his study devoted to European echoes of translations from Romanian literature published in the monthly *Convorbiri literare* on 1 January 1882, entitled "Romanian Literature and the Foreign Countries," Maiorescu reproduced from a German publication a reference made to the "spiritual kinship" of the two poets. In a new study of 1886, "Poets and Critics" he gave a brilliant award in the dispute between the admirers of the poet Vasile Alecsandri (1821-1890) and the enthusiasm of "Eminescianism": to measure by one criterion alone the first great poets of 19th century Romanian literature is as little possible as to establish whether Leopardi is a greater poet than Victor Hugo. (". . . The impossibility to find an answer only attests to the lack of clarity of the question. If it were a matter of lyrical poetry alone and even within lyrical poetry only of the finest expression of deep melancholy, in the midst of the aspiration after the ideal and at the same time of the bitterest satire, Leopardi is unattainable and rises above Victor Hugo. But could this alone be the matter? Victor Hugo is the embodiment of the French genius of his time, in its most poetical aspirations . . .")

In 1889—the year of Eminescu's death—Titu Maiorescu published the study "Eminescu and His Poems" in which he asserted that 20th century Romanian literature would start under the sign of this creation. In order to define Eminescu's poetical personality, the critic again resorted to an evocation of Leopardi: "The terms of happy and unhappy love cannot apply to Eminescu in their everyday acceptation (. . .) Like Leopardi in his 'Aspasia' he only saw the woman he loved as the imperfect copy of an unachievable prototype."

The name of the Italian poet was to revert often enough in the correspondence Titu Maiorescu kept up with the younger prosewriter and poet Duiliu Zamfirescu (1858-1922). Fascinated by Leopardi, with whose writings he had become acquainted during his stay in Italy and from whom he began translating in 1889, Duiliu Zamfirescu "read" the latter's poetry as an "Eminescian," as a writer trained at the school of Eminescu's language; for instance here is how Zamfirescu commented upon the suggestiveness of a verse by Leopardi: "*Torna dinanzi al mio pensier talora / Il tuo sembiante, Aspasia.* Suddenly you penetrate the melancholy of the soul addressing you. *Torna talora il tuo sembiante*: your image sometimes returns . . . It is as if a star rose from the darkness of times. It is a sonorous value with indescribable evocative power."

As a matter of fact Duiliu Zamfirescu was the first to remark a number of stylistic affinities between the two poets, mentioning "the incomparable simplicity," the "subjectiveness," the "pessimism" and yet—with highly modern intuition—the suggestiveness of the word (he called "comprehensiveness of words.")

Two decades later, in 1909, in an academic speech entitled "The Metaphysics of Words and Literary Aesthetics" the same Duiliu Zamfirescu analysed the relationships between Leopardi and Eminescu in point of "the influence of metaphysics upon poetic elocution," on that occasion remarking that the two poets "reach the vast expanses of the human soul" thanks to "the spiritual power of ponderation, of nonmaterial things;" the unique note struck by these poets does not occur out of the sumptuous lexis ("it is not words that sparkle like gems, but the inner power of their relativity. Leopardi's words seem to be detached from the lead of the ore") but out of the power to capture and to transmit a loftier sense with which each word is invested.

Subsequently, the parallel between Eminescu and Leopardi was examined from various angles by literary critics and historians upholding the most diverse formulas, from George Călinescu to Dimitrie Caracostea, Pompiliu Constantinescu and Tudor Vianu.

As regards the destiny of the two poets, similarities were remarked, among others, by Mircea Eliade. Talking about the isolation of Eminescu among his mediocre contemporaries, M. Eliade wrote in 1939: "He was perhaps as lonely as the invalid Leopardi. Yet Leopardi at least had the chance of not running into clever people every day. Eminescu on the other hand was fated to struggle in intellectual circles. And while ignorance and naivety are appeasing for a genius, aggressive and boastful mediocrity sometimes become a curse. His loneliness was aggravated by the mediocrity of those who claimed to be Romania's cultural élite. Faced with the incomprehension of the multitude, a genius only preserves the forgiving smile of Messiah driven away with stones. Yet in front of the opaqueness of the would-be élites, the smile becomes bitter and scorn is paired with disgust."

More recently various aspects and contexts of the relationship Eminescu-Leopardi were also investigated by the well-known Italian scholars in Romania, Nina Façon and Alexandru Balaci. In 1983 Eleonora Cărcăleanu wrote a Ph.D. thesis on Leopardi in Romania. We owe a more complex treatment of the theme to Iosif Cheia-Pantea, who dedicated to the many facets of this rapprochement a book around the concept of elective affinities: *Eminescu and Leopardi,* published in 1980.

But, in the perspective of modern reception, Leopardi and Eminescu appear to us related not only through those features of romantic psychology evidenced by this century's criticism, but also through the anticipatory force of their creation, as pioneers of building the structures of modern European lyricism.

Nobody has ever denied the importance of Eminescu's writings for the whole subsequent evolution of Romanian literature; still, a global approach to the relationship between 20th century Romanian poetry and Eminescu has not yet been undertaken. Leopardi on the other hand was from the very beginning claimed as one of the guardian angels of tutelary spirits of Italian literature after the first world war, while the representatives of hermeticism, headed by Ungaretti, imposed the recognition of some "modern heritage of his poetry, appreciating the contribution of Leopardi's lyrical poetry to the emergence of that kind of modern poetry which replaces the ephemeral reality by a new, nonmimetic reality, and suggesting that Mallarmé would appear to us in an entirely different light if Leopardi's experience could continue."

It has been remarked with good justification that Leopardi's creative evolution itself is exemplary and, we could say, emblematic of the trends of modern poetry: withdrawing poetry from its public role in lyricism to the space and time of the individual experience, from discursiveness and imagery into the complex musical expression of "song," therefore the dissolution of the rigid framework of the traditional species and the birth of new structures, based on a new type of coherence, all of them are visible in the very chronological succession of Leopardi's writings.

Moreover, the arrangement of poems in the volume of *Canti* testifies to a modern acceptation of poetry, for, even before Baudelaire Leopardi detached himself from the tradition of romantic selections of verse and built his representative volume on the idea of a general sense.

A century ago, the similarity between the two poets was based on what seemed to be a thematic novelty en vogue in the epoch of the impressive success with the public of Schopenhauer's writings: the pessimistic profession of faith. When we re-read them today, Eminescu and Leopardi appear to us twinned not only through that tragic feeling of existence, unanimously grasped—whether it be called disappointment, despair, anxiety, but also through their very work born out of that sentiment, a work whose substance included the heroic protest to man's isolation in the world, to the world's ever worse and irremediable degradation and, at the same time, the aspiration to recuperate poetry—considered as the only way to save the human element—in a hostile environment.

Through the assertion of a poetical ego that functions as the centre of the universe, through the attempt to build a kind of poetry that should no longer enounce a problematic truth, but should be the truth itself, the two poets are integrated into a lyrical formula which surpasses romanticism and expresses contemporary seekings.

Out of the manifold aspects of the affinities between Leopardi's verse and 20th century poetry, prolonging typically romantic attitudes, there emerges what one may term the poetics of distance.

The *near-far* dichotomy deeply marks Leopardi's poetical seekings following the writing of the famous *Discorso di un Italiano intorno alla poesia romantica* (1818), generating the fundamental antithesis between the *here,* whose imperfection is painfully felt and a *somewhere else* better suiting the human wish for the absolute, the prefiguration of the Baudelairian *anywhere out of this world.*

The romantic "thirst for the absolute" acquires a similar configuration with Leopardi and Eminescu, and the consciousness that man is exiled into imperfection is accompanied by the attempt to come out of this exile, opposing the vacuum of existence to the poetical discourse itself.

Leopardi's aspiration after what is *remoto* in time and space, the tendency to expand the poetical ego find correspondents in Eminescu's placing man within cosmic horizons, which justifies the formula of "titanism of distance."

Even a cursory glance immediately reveals to us the bipolarity *near-far* as typical of all of Leopardi's lyrical verse: the poet always depicts himself as attracted by the mirage of some distance—more than once imaginary—: "*mirando il ciel ed ascoltando il canto / della rana rimota;*" remote landscapes (*quel lontano mar, quei monti azzurri*) inspire *pensieri immensi* to the man who contemplates them from here (*che di qua scopro*).

In Eminescu's poetry, distance is not merely opposed to nearness, and the cosmic landscape does not serve as a mere background for human gestures, but are interpenetrated, integrated into one and the same structure, in which the suggestions of the whole can be found again in details, while the miniature is complementary to the grandiose. Thus, the thrill of erotic approach is tantamount to the maximum distance of cosmic mysteries: "You don't know that the closeness of your eyes / Is balsam for my heart as soothing, mild, / As stars which in evening quiet rise."

Love itself is thus projected with Leopardi into a distance which purifies it of earthly implications: it has taken flight from immediate, ardent living (*lungi volasti*); the adored woman inspires love "from a distance" (*amore lunge m'inspiri*); quiet can be attained through the contemplation of distances by the man who is nailed to the *here* where he finds himself exiled (Qui *neghittoso immobile giacendo / Il mar la terra e il ciel miro e sorrido*). Even Silvia, the personification of hope indicates by a desperate gesture the grave—the limit of mortals' life—*di lontano*. As a matter of fact the poet was conscious of this particular preference for the remoteness of the adored object: in one of his "annotations" to the 1827 edition, he defined himself as the only lover who accepted to have "*il telescopio*" interposed between him and his beloved.

Let us note that this remoteness is as often as not due to the fact that love episodes are projected into the past, contemplated, though not lived through the senses. The only typically romantic moment of suffering, "*pien di travaglio e di lamento*", the one in "*Il primo amore*" is also distilled in memory.

Being dominated by the nostalgia for nearness, imbued with images of plastic sensuality, Eminescu's love poetry nevertheless began and ended elegiacally, while its essential direction was the return to the past. Very much as with Leopardi, with Eminescu love is not so much lived as re-lived. What prevents its sensorial living is the awareness of time's flight, the dominant fear of losing the moment in the time's flow.

Nor is it difficult to realize that with both Leopardi and Eminescu, we have to do with a genuine obsession of time. The aspect is obvious first of all at the thematic and discursive level and most investigators of the Eminescu-Leopardi parallel have studied comparatively the antithesis between the illustrious tradition and the degenerate present, following the treatment of this theme in Leopardi's *Canzoni* and in Eminescu's **"Epigones" "Third Epistle"**, etc. With Leopardi the historical present is characterized exclusively in negative terms, in sharp contrast with an idealized past, the break between the past and the present corresponding to a marked decay of values. (*In peggio precipitano i tempi*). It is however to be noted that for Leopardi, the illustrious past *is no historical time* but rather an absolute value, the standard for all civic and moral values. Models are actually sought in a mythical time, in an original state of prehistoric childhood of humanity: let

us confine our suggestions to the *Inno ai Patriarchi*". "People who would think in legends—all a world who spoke in verse" as evoked by Eminescu do not belong to temporality proper: this past has disappeared and nevertheless it is recurrent in the childhood of each individual. Thus transfigured into mythical dimensions, the historic past becomes the golden age, the lost paradise: both Eminescu and Leopardi oppose to the negative present not the dimension of a remote historical time, but that of the myth—therefore a non-time.

In the system of Leopardi's *Canzoni,* one distinguishes a permanent tension between *tempo storico* and *tempo privato,* and the author's final option—evasion from the historical time institutionalized in the experience of individual grief and passion—results in the birth of a kind of poetry which is to a great extent *construction* opposed to vacuum, *invention* of an immobile time.

Eminescu's poetical universe has been described by the Italian professor Rosa Del Conte as being centred around cosmic imagination and around the obsession of the evasion from time; still, the problems of philosophy and gnosis raised by this kind of poetry give rise to a finite, perishable ideological model and it is not in this area that one ought to seek its current values.

Let us follow the obsession of time not in the so-called "philosophical poetry" as in Eminescu's love poems and in Leopardi's idylls.

The drama of perceiving the duration of whatever is human is perfectly representative of the permanent unrest of the romantic soul. The present time is seen by Eminescu as a permanent flow, as "eternal passage," yet the outlook is not Heraclitian: it is singularized by the fact that this ceaseless movement tends towards an end, towards extinction, towards death. In Eminescu's lyrical poems, stars "perish" in the distance, longing and yearning "are extinguished" in the "night" of oblivion, dreams "fly and fade on the horizon, like the light birds of the ocean" the aim of the uninterrupted flow is the territory of total extinction—Nirvana.

In Leopardi's poetry, the specifically romantic intuition of the evolution of world's realities and the awareness of the fragility of moments acquire pathetical accents, more than once in memorable wordings: "*Come fuggiste, o belle ore serene!*" or "*Umana cosa piccol' tempo dura.*" The lapse of time ravishes the joys of dreamy childhood ("*Ogni più lieto / Giorno di nostra età prima s'invola / Sottentra il morbo, e la vecchiezza, e l'ombra / Della gelida morte*") darken the most serene moments ("*E fieramente mi si stringe il core / A pensar como tutto al mondo passa / E quasi orma non lascia*"). The restlessness engendered by the irreparable flight of time proves an overwhelmed fright, which prevents the poet from experiencing the deep feeling of love at the same time as living it through the senses. That is why, the retrospective becomes the major modality of living time, in which two other possible romantic attitudes are dissolved: the aspiration after an indiscernible future and spleen—the feeling of sterile time. "*Il piacere può essere solo passato o futuro*" Leopardi noted in his "Zibaldone", indicating as the only way to penetrate the essences of sentiment *remoteness,* the distance from the immediate manifestation, i.e. "*il rimembrar delle passate cose.*"

With Eminescu, regressive lapse into the past occurs in two distinct ways: either under the empire of nostalgia which presupposes the return to a certain moment of existence already outlived, or under that of melancholy, not oriented towards a specific object. A fundamental feature of the romantic spiritual structure, melancholy begins as an abrupt perception of the transience of the moment and ends by meaning "a longing for the current moment itself," taking possession of the present as a remembrance.

Among Eminescu's posthumous poems, there is a variant included in the laboratory of creation for **"So Fresh and Frail"** which illustrates this desire to wish the miraculous present as a remembrance, in order to save it from sliding into nothingness. The thrill of losing love brings about on the one hand "sweet suffering" which is by far more intense than the exulting living, and on the other hand out of the "gloomy heap" of past times, the "adored face" can be slowly brought back, revived, up to the reiteration of the supremely intense moment of the loss which stamps upon the soul "the sweet sorrow" of death.

In this mechanics of rememoration the Romanian poet discovers the modality infinitely to renew emotional living which, however intense, would otherwise have been limited to one moment of the fluid present. In its essence, rememoration is a movement for slowly bringing close an image from another space: "If branches tap my window-pane / And aspens quiver sear, / ' tis to remember you again / And slowly bring you near."

Very much as in Leopardi's case, an *amarissima ricordanza* may become the source for *lunga doglia,* thus prolonging the intense sensorial experience; thanks to it one may recover the sometime fervour (*vive quel foco ancor, vive l'affetto*), while the adored image is restored to its life (*spira nel pensier mio la bella imago*).

The signs of the outer world favour this movement of drawing near a spatialized time which is rememoration, yet does not univocally determine it: the re-spatialization generating painful delight is a voluntary operation. Nor does Leopardi act differently in "Aspasia" ("... *E mai non sento / Mover profumo di fiorita piaggia / né di fiori olezzar vie cittadine / ch'io non ti vegga ancor*

qual eri") as well as in "Le Ricordanze" ("... *e fia compagnia / Dogni mio vago immaginar, di tutti / I miei teneri sensi, i tristi e cari / Moti del cor, la rimembranza acerba.*") Perhaps we ought to see here not a mere manifestation of what we usually call affective memory, but rather an aesthetic attitude to the erotic feelings, projected into a distance from which it can be contemplated and relished.

The transfer into the past is tantamount to the full possession of the object of adoration: the past is an area over which "the worm of times" (*il tarlo della morte*) no longer has power. The beloved "lost for ever" becomes "for ever adored," while the human feeling acquires an infinite perspective.

The recuperation of the past through memory, in fact through a reverie in which memory and dream are united—and whose prototype we find in Petrarch's lyricism—, illustrates what the Romanian professor Edgar Papu (b. 1908) called the "dynamics of a vegetal type" of the romantic mind, a gesticulating kind of dynamics though not ambulatory of élans alternating with ebbing movements. In "A Silvia", for instance, the enthusiastic evocation is followed by the resigned meditation upon universal vanity; an upswing is followed by a retractile movement: the imaginative élan which mobilizes the soul of the lyrical hero does not wrest the latter from his form anchoring into the terrestrial element, not just fortuitously vegetal—"*sull'erba*" (Leopardi), "near the host of yellow lilies / on the brink of that blue lake" (Eminescu).

Memory holds a central place in the universe of Leopardi's poetry: sorrowful at all times, it is nevertheless a source of delight ("*e pur mi gioia La ricordanza, e il noverar l'etate del mio dolore*"). Love re-lived in remembrance is a source of infinite torment ("*cagion diletta d'infiniti affanni / meco sarmi per morte a un tempo spento*") as well as of celestial joy ("*gioia celeste*"). The fascination of remembrance is similar to that exerted upon the poet by indefinite space, by indistinct sounds. With Leopardi, the function of remembrance is twofold: of an analgesic—which enables one to put up with the inferno of reality ("*Quasi incredibil parmi / Che la vita in felice e il mondo sciocco / Cià per gran tempo assai / Senza te sopporta*") or of a stimulant which gives birth to an artificial paradise, where the depth of feeling may reach its limits. The paradise to which it raises the remembrance of the beloved being is synonymous with the abolition of earthly time: "*Che mondo mai, che nova / "Immensità che paradiso è que lo / Là dove spesso il tuo stupendo incanto / Parmi innalzari dov'io / Sott'altra luce che l'usata arrando / Il mio terreno stato / E tutto quanto il ver pongo in obblio.*" Regression in time carries the poet towards an Edenic state, towards immersion into a restoring mythical time: "*Come da' nudi sassi / Dello scabro Apennino*

/ A un campo verde che lontan sorrida / Volge gli occhi bramoso il pellegrino; / Tal io dal secco ed aspro / Mondano conversar vogliosamente. / Quasi in lieto giardino a te ritorno / E ristora i miei senzi il tuo soggiorno". The visions elicited by the retrospective reliving of love are similar to the dreams of gods (*"i sogni de l'immortali"*) truer than the primary truth of everyday life: they are a delusion (*"inganno"*) of divine origin, *"che incontro al ver tenacemente dura / e spesso al ver'sadegua".*

Submitting of his own accord to the penalty of remembrance ("To reach your gentle shadow I stretch my arms in vain / out of the waves of time, now, I can't raise you again") erotic Eminescu too in hours of ecstasy invoked the face of his beloved "out of the waves of time": acquiring the consistency of a dream apparition, this will again turn into the aim of despondent adoration and the poet almost simultaneously experienced both the sadness and the joy of meeting again in remembrance: "Is there a chance to wrest you out of your misty ocean? / To lift you to my bosom, dear angel of devotion (. . .) Alas, you are not real, if you can pass like this / And lose your very shadow in some dark cold abyss / To leave myself down hearted, once more, bereft and lonely, / To love the dream of rapture in sad remembrance only . . ."

Throughout Eminescu's verse, recollections acquire almost material coherence: "Above them all / Memories like grigs are chirping / In some cracked and darkened wall; / or fall heavily through soothing / Crushing sadly on my hood / Like the tapers slowly dripping / At the effect of Jesus' Road."

The memory of the infatuated man is prolonged infinitely through the ancestral memory of the species: "I love you much, with heathen eyes / In which but suff'ring gathers / Bequeathed by people old and wise / By fathers and grand-fathers." With Eminescu, very much as with Leopardi, behind all things, as well as in the depth of the soul, we permanently encounter the mysterious presence of Eternity which, as in Baudelaire's poetry later on, brings about the need to outgrow ones own life through the immense prolongation of ancestral memory and of previous lives.

The voice of the forest in **"Oh, Stay with Me"**, evokes the complementarity specific to Eminescu of distance along various axes in the image of the moon which sets fire to the lakes (not *the lake,* the plural evoking infinite distances, broadening the horizon). No less essential is the dilatation of time in memory, a privileged space of erotic ecstasy in which time is immobilized: "As you gaze at moonlit water / Shimmering like fiery tears / All your life seems but a moment / And sweet moments seem long years."

Rememoration, rebuilding the flow of life out of discrete elements, is a kind of exorcism directed against the nightmare of Time. For the modern poet, life itself becomes coherent, to the extent to which its duration is no longer unfolded but composed. The detachment from the space of passionate-romantic living, remoteness from immediate sensations, is the condition necessary for purifying the erotic feelings and for raising them to a higher stage of reality. The counterpoise of time is space, and the total function of poetry—in Rilke's wording—is the adaptation of things subject to time to the quieter world of the pure space, which is just another face of nature.

The preference for night and the moon, for the respective atmosphere, is justified by this aspiration after wresting love from the empire of time. The attraction exerted by night upon a poet of Eminescu's kind is that of a space for recollection and meditation upon life, of dreams and of memories, extracted from the solar space of action. The effect of immersion in this area, an area in which living is suspended in favour of dreams or of meditative watchfulness, is obviously the distancing from immediate sensations and the possibility to re-live the impulses of diurnal existence with enhanced intensity.

Exiling love into memory, its contemplation from afar, as in the verse of Leopardi and Eminescu, gradually detaches feelings from any topicality, lending them an infinite perspective and freeing them from the dominion of time.

The feminine figures that populate Leopardi's poetry—Silvia, Nerina, Aspasia—appear in the space of memory, liberated from time, being reincarnated into apparitions with a human face out of the distilled essences of memory and dream. The highest point of this transposition outside human time is embodied in the canzone "Alla sua donna", a hymn devoted to the woman who does not exist (*"Alla donna che non si trova"*) present in the atemporal dimension of sleep, in stellar spaces, in the proto-historical age of gold, as a cosmic emblem of the feminine principle.

A poem that begins and ends in the shadow of death such as one of Leopardi's most amazing productions "A Silvia" manages to revive though "singing" the very experience of destruction, restoring the delight of *being* in the very description of universal ruin and vanity. It is also Eminescu's modality of rendering *the negative positive*—a process which 20th-century poetry was going to carry to the most dramatic summits. Leopardi had theorized that miraculous effect which he had ascribed to art generally: even when he offers a representation of life's zero value, *le opere di genio* bring a certain solace to the sensitive leader, *"e non trattando nè rappresentando altro che la morte, le rendono almeno momentaneamente quella vita che aveva perduta."*

For a poet like Eminescu, human creation begins through a refusal of his own temporal limits, with a voluntary detachment from immediate living and with recuperation of life through remembrance. Imagination manages to overcome the boundaries of limited human perception; by begetting visions and by imposing human truth on the world through words, man recovers / regains his own dignity: "As Nature only has its bounds / There is boundlessness in man."

Eugen Todoran (essay date 1989)

SOURCE: Todoran, Eugen. "The Sacred Mountain and the Abysmal Phenomenon." *Cahiers Roumains d'Etudes Litteraires,* no. 2 (1989): 12-25.

[*In the following essay, Todoran compares Eminescu to two later Romanian poets, Tudor Arghezi and Lucien Blaga.*]

"To speak about the poet is as if you shouted in a large cave. . . . Your words cannot reach him without disturbing his silence. The language of strings only could retell his delicate, lonely glory, by lulling it on a harp . . . You must only whisper respectfully, in an undertone . . . In a way, Eminescu is the all-immaculate saint of Romanian verse . . . His dimensions are by far greater than even our surrendering piety imagines . . . The mountain begins all around us and has no paths whatever . . . As you can't climb it, you just look at it and are contented with a few elf-like images . . . How could one possibly ever render the portrait of a shadow and of the endless time?"[1] These are the first words of Tudor Arghezi's evocation of Mihai Eminescu, fifty years after the latter's death; he views the poet projected against the background of eternity, as a perpetually gravitating constellation, never reached by mortals, for whom it gleams however, in a blue votive light, placed at a crossroads.

This vision of the "sacred mountain"—the "all-immaculate saint of Romanian verse"—identified by Arghezi with Eminescu, is opposed to the personality of Lucian Blaga, placed in a perspective which results from that particular construction of the philosophy of culture, which the latter poet applies to the Romanian phenomenon. Such a theory was put forth by the poet and philosopher Lucian Blaga in his *Ewe-Lamb Space,* in connection with the catalytic and moulding influences exerted upon Romanian culture in order to assimilate it to the intricate network of European decisive factors, as a specific phenomenon of "intellectuality" rendered manifest by very complex means[2]. Hypothetically imagined as a spiritual substratum of the anonymous creations of Romanian culture, the "ewe-lamb space" is a "matrix space" which integrates the landscape in a certain way of regarding man's thought as related to the outer world; the "abysmal" is therefore a constant value of the soul, as if the cultural phenomenon, "stylistically" determined, found its true dimension only within itself. According to Blaga, the main feature of Romanian matrix space is the "descending transcendent", the tendency towards the "organic", as manifested in all the forms of folk culture and art; as an "abysmal phenomenon", this feature was revealed in Eminescu's works, too. Namely, using the philosopher's own words: "a deep process, an organically Romanian one, burst out of 'the nether world', due first of all, to the poet's spiritual substance, but equally due to no lesser extent, to various foreign influences, which, in the last analysis, meant also in actual fact, a firm appeal to his own self . . . There is an 'idea Eminescu', and this idea conceived under Romanian stars."[3]

If we compare the two appreciations of Eminescu's works namely T. Arghezi's and L. Blaga's, it is quite obvious that the two perspectives stand for two opposed directions taken by the fundamental relation between *idea* and *image* in the poet's thought. A research concerning the "idea Eminescu"—filtered through the "reverberating" features of the fundamental strata in his work within a generic "portrait" of Romanian culture (i.e. not a historically and culturally determined portrait, but an abysmal-structural one), as a modality of understanding the poetic "heights" by analysing its very "depths"—should motivate such a relation by deeply investigating Eminescu's poetry, actually the source of the two other poets, different though they are from one another.

In any modern poetic work, sense can be explored in relation to an "axis mundi", provided such a work allows a complex exploration of its meaning; its constant values are then *height* and *depth,* the former being placed *above,* belonging to the "sky" while the latter is always placed *beneath,* as it belongs to "earth", in the poet's thought (in *any* poet's thought), this axis is always represented by the two functions of the poetic, namely the *idea* and the *image,* as well as in various possible relations, which bear various labels in historical treatises of poetic, e.g. *idea* and *figure,* as the Antiquity used to call them, *idea* and *form,* as they appear in modern aesthetics, *significans* and *signified,* as the methods of the "new criticism" dub them. It is from such a twofold perspective that we are to define the main lines of Eminescu's poetic thought within Romanian literature, starting, of course, with the two other poets, already quoted.

T. Arghezi considered that Eminescu's "perfections", like all perfection, are based on simplicity, therefore on the "idea"; still he viewed it not as a spontaneous, easily perceived idea, a void "concept", but as an elaborate, geometrical one, since with Eminescu "the word is always matched with the idea". As to Lucian Blaga, he speaks of the "unique atmosphere" in the poet's world, of his "imponderable elements of poetic magic, hardly perceived, vaguely seen, unexpected". However, in Arghezi's appreciation, we ought perhaps to recognize his classical conception about poetry, in which the "image", by substituting the poetic language for the standard one, is a "deviation" from the "idea", so that, by a transfer of meaning, in the act of poetic thinking, any "image" can be reduced to an "idea". Or, as Arghezi himself would have said, when commenting upon the simplicity of the poet's *idea* in spite of the diversity of the poetic *images*: "I've snatched a few lines from the Eminescian space, in order to convey the immersion of a different atmosphere in each and every line and the different shadow left by every image, in close dependence on the different sun beholding it. Within the poet's space, from its upper vault, the light floods divergently, in all directions. The Chaos is crowned by a round dance of moon-like stars". On the other hand, Blaga has a modern concept about poetry as he says that: "Eminescu's poetry is built on various staves. It is pervaded with intricate complexes of highly personal underlying structures and it is by such original aspects that Eminescu is revealed to us".

From Blaga's first motivation, from his idea of the "inner style" of culture, we infer that the "Idea Eminescu", conceived from the "abysmal phenomenon", from the "Fore-Mothers Stratum", is equivalent with what Arghezi called "the Mountain", viewed however from the inverted perspective of its invisible depths, i.e. of the "earth", the "sacred mountain" of Romanian poetry; on its heights, the voice of the harp strings is surrounded by "silences", for, as Blaga puts it, this vibration originates in a "matrix", in a "depth" of its integration into, of its assimilation with, creative stylistic possibilities—born under Romanian stars—of the "Idea Eminescu". The decisive elements of the matrix space of the "Idea Eminescu" should be revealed by the analysis of the poet's work, but even at this moment we can notice that the "Idea", measured on the height of the "mountain", is not an abstraction, but a "reality"; therefore the poet who appears "under the Romanian signs of the zodiac" is not, historically speaking, an unaccountable and unforeseen phenomenon within the space of Romanian culture; on the contrary, he brings with him exactly what belongs to the traditional background to the "Fore-Mothers Stratum", moulded in his own work by a personal original form, closely depending on the genius of his creation.

But the considerations we've made so far concerning the poetic mood of the "Eminescian spirit" have only aimed to motivate the two parallel appreciations made by T. Arghezi and L. Blaga, because, for each one of them, as part of Eminescu's posterity, the fundamental aspects already noticed are not in harmony with their views as regards their own poetry; here, the perspectives are inverted. With Arghezi, the sense of the "real"

intrudes between Silence and the word, it is the sense of the *ugly* which takes over the functions discharged by the *beautiful*; in the section of the central poetic stratum, the ugly is the *lower* level of the impetus towards the heights of the sublime, it illustrates the poetic vision of the *sacred ugliness*. With Blaga, on the other hand, the Word and the silence are always separated by a vibration revealing—"within" the real things—a *transcendence* of their own, due to their "ideal" nature from "beyond": it is the *upper* level of their epiphanic mystery[4].

In search of an immediate cultural influence, as far as Arghezi's poetry is concerned, we refer to Baudelaire's poetry, namely to the "descent" towards the abysses. The poet of the *Fleurs du Mal* founded his poetic art on a novel vision of the unity of the world, which, beyond the breaches of the "spiritual" and of the "animal", of the desire to "ascent" and of the joy of the "descent", leads to the being's reconstruction by the confrontation of two simultaneous attitudes: towards God and towards Satan, in a space of the "differance", a means of sense revelation, in the poetic act, which by fostering the conflicts between the Same and the "other", transforms the alterity into a consciousness of his own finite nature, viewed by the poet as a ceaseless search of passage[5]. And, along the same line, the transcendence towards mystery, viewed as Blaga's own attitude towards his poetry, can be referred to the "new-style", entrusting the poet with the mission to penetrate into the core of things, rendered "present" to the spirit, which maintains the cognition function of poetry by inviting the agents to doubt about hopes by destroying the equilibrium between the inner and the outer world, always in favour of the former, since the latter is the recipient of spirit, the place of visible and tangible symbols, of all analogies, as Baudelaire used to think; such a poetry boasts metaphysical ambitions, by moulding the clear ideas of the mind into the forms of a complex mythology, the test of a mysterious capacity passing beyond the conscientious thought and even beyond the superior forms of emotional life[6].

But, while thus referring the two poets to Baudelaire, a question arises in close connection to the "paradox" of the possible *inversions* occurring within poetry, namely as far as Arghezi is concerned: How is the *immanent,* from the *idea* to the *image*—while plunging us into the central poetic stratum—equally represented into the *transcendent,* in order to be able to speak about the *descent* as an act transferring to the *transcendent* the meaning of *things,* the "enchanting" meaning of words, while revealing the idea as a poetic image, so that the meaning which *things* transfer upon the transcendent is a perpetual "search" of the *idea* in the poetic image, and, with Blaga: How can the *transcendent,* from the *image* to the *idea* by ascending to the central poetic space, be represented at the level of the *immanent*; or, to put it differently, how can we refer to *ascendence* as an act which confers meaning to things from within themselves, a meaning always *revealing* the poetic *image,* opposed to the *revelation* as a poetic *idea.*

This question concerning Arghezi and Blaga, put in order to come back to Eminescu, arises from the "paradox" of modern poetry, namely from the *reversion* of contrary terms—the idea and the image, actually a reduplication of the double—, in order to outline the meaning which underlies poetic thought. In the rhetorical treaties of the Antiquity, the lineage of which, passing through the tradition of Classicism, can be still traced in the 19th century, classical poetry, which has resisted all the innovations brought about by Romanticism, was conceived as an example of perfect concord between the *idea* and the *image,* the latter being, in effect, a mere "deviation" from the former, a figure of expression within poetic language, as compared to the direct expression of the standard language. In modern poetry, the "deviation" becomes a substitution, never censored by reason, by a conception of the *image* as *idea.* Modern poetics views the terms of the opposition not as *replaceable,* but as *recessive*; one term is "represented" by the other, in such a way that the "primary", dominant, term always brings about the second "recessive" one, which, though subordinate, confers *significance* to the former.

By thus relating two opposed terms—the *idea* and the *image*—of the poetic thinking, we can motivate their *inversion* in the "paradoxical" vision of modern poetry, namely with Arghezi and with Blaga. With Arghezi, a poet of the senses and of the material, the first, dominant, term is that of the "image", it is a "visualisation" of the *real,* whereas the latter, secondary term, the recessive one, is the "ideal", "divine" one, which conveys its significance to the former "by raising it towards a non-existent transcendent, in a search "without an object". With Blaga, a poet of the metaphysical and of the mystery, the first, dominant, term is the "spiritual" term of the "idea", while the secondary, recessive, one is a "real", "earthly" term, which confers its significance to the former by making it "descend" towards a "transfigured" immanent, in a search of the absolute in the transcendence of the "mystery".

Therefore, both in Arghezi's and in Blaga's case, the modern poetic vision is that of the Unity of the world, a fall from the Primordial, which poetry tends to remake through ceaselessly searching a "passage"; it is an originary reintegration of the outer world within the inner one. Such a vision was foretold by Baudelaire's poetry, who, by his comments upon those aspects of Romantic poetry, put forth a theory of the *search* as the basic meaning of the poetic; this way he was able to consider Romantic poetry as an embryo of a new form of poetic thinking, in actual fact, the very essence of modern poetry.

In the Romantic poems which view the world as a whole, irrespective of its particular aspects, the image is more important than the idea: poetry becomes a world by means of *the word,* from a primary idea, the latter becomes an image. In modern poetry, whatever is "beyond the word" is a "remake" of the wholeness of the world through the idea which, once included in the "image", transforms the latter into an "idea"; consequently, "beyond the word" means "within the word"; the poem is a world *within the word.*

By thus turning back from modernism to Romanticism, in order to find in the latter trend the embryo of the former, we come again, as far as Romanian poetry is concerned, to the Eminescu moment, as he was a forerunner of Arghezi and Blaga, of the two philosophical directions of their poetry, one of them—a vision of the *immanent,* the other—of the *transcendent,* in a poetic language which, by the two opposite meanings of the "otherness" existing within the feeling of the "unity" of the world, renders the relation between the "idea" and the "image" by a perpetual alternation between the "descent" and the "ascent", within the space of poetic thinking, by preserving the "paradoxical" coincidence of both contraries and *unity,* in one and the same *world,* namely the world of *poetry.*

Eminescu's poetic language discharges this double function: *by means of the word* it conveys an "idea" in a "different way", always a philosophical meditation about the world, and also it conveys a "different" idea by the "image" of the world; in its turn, the latter is equally a meditation about the world, also made *by means of the word.*

To illustrate the distinction between the "idea" and the "image" in the "ewe-lamb-space" of poetry, let us quote from Eminescu's lines this metaphor of the "poetic", for the sense of its building, within poetic thinking, at the surface level of the communication of the "idea" from the deep level of its "image" structure; the sample belongs to **"The Panorama of Vanities"**:

> "My herd of dreams I take to pasture as a herd of
>   golden sheep
>
>   . . . . .
>
> One thing is the world of phantasms, spread with
>   lovely golden flowers,
> Quite another, were you trying life to forge like a
>   goldsmith
> Who tries hard metal to mould by the matrix of cold
>   thought"[7]

"The herd of golden sheep", "taken to pasture" by the poet[8] as he identifies them with the "herd" of his dreams, or the "golden flowers" of his fantasy are the deviations or the "figures" of his language, "images" which, in the process of directly communicating his "ideas" are moulded by "cold", uninvolved thinking (in compliance with the classical conception of poetry); nevertheless, during Romanticism, poetry becomes a means of cognition of the "intelligible", as, beyond the word, now viewed as a means of making them equivalent, the image tells more than the idea, since the word is substituted by the "imaginary"; in its turn, the latter is a signal of reality, "transfigured" into an "ideal" by poetic thinking. But, at the meeting point of Romanticism and modernism, the imaginary (which belongs to the deep level of the image manifests a *world* at the surface level of the idea, by poetically matching the elements of this world, by moulding them in a sense-revealing matrix; this way the idea tells more than the image, for, even by replacing the abstract idea, it remains still intact, it is still an image, this way making poetry an instrument of re-creating the world, into an *image-idea* or into the symbol of poetic thinking.

In several of Eminescu's poems, the *poet's* philosophy is a meditation of the *philosopher* about the unity of the world in time and space, viewed as a self-consistent *universe* within the boundaries of its existence, whereas some other poems represent a poetic reorganization of the world by means of a language revealing metaphysical meanings. But it can also be the case that two different modalities of poetic thinking intermingle in one and the same poem. According to the first modality, in some lines of the former version of the **"First Epistle"**—preserved among the manuscript of the translation of the *Critique of Pure Reasoning,* the "aged teacher" pondering about the "borders" of existence in space and time is called Kant, which is, of course, a direct reference to the philosopher; in the next versions he became the "sage" teacher; taken back by thinking to what no human mind could comprehend to have existed, beyond whatever is perceived to exist:

> "Over there an aged teacher, with his elbows jutting out
> Through the threadbare jacket reckons and the sums cause him to pout.
>
> . . . . .
>
> Skinny as he is and hunch-backed, a most wretched ne'er-do-well,
> He has in his little finger all the world, heaven and hell;
> For behind his brow are looming both the future and the past,
> And eternity's thick darkness he'll unravel at long last,
> As, of old mythical Atlas propped the skies upon his shoulder,
> He props universe and Chronos in a number—which is bolder . . ."[9]

The phrase "for behind his brow are looming both the future and the past" implies the *subjective nature* of time and space, according to Kant's philosophy viewed

as a theory of the a priori forms of cognition of the objective world, incognizable in itself, beyond the surface of its subjective forms, whenever the thinker ponders upon its unity. This also explains the philosophical meaning of the old teacher's reflection upon the unity of the world, an *object* which—as it can be viewed almost as an "existence"—is offered to cognition in two ways: either as an *appearance,* perishable in time and changeable in space, or as an *eternal* reality, beyond these *transcendental* forms, as they are related to the *transcendental* as such, to the "thing as such", unknowable since, once comprehended, it ranks among the forms of subjectivity and thus becomes *appearance.*

This is an old distinction in the history of philosophy. The relation between thinking and existence implies the distinction between *to be* within the *thing* and *to be* within the *idea*; Kant took it over from Plato as a distinction between the *intelligible world* of the "ideas" and the *sensible world* of the "images". As a matter of fact, Plato himself was merely attempting to devise an interpretation of the two aspects of *unity,* namely the intelligible *general* and the sensible *particular,* as a possible reply to the fundamental questions lying at the basis of what Pythagora was the first to call "philosophy", namely the "effort towards wisdom", regarding the *world* as a unity of its constituents, i.e. a *cosmos.* The philosopher's questions and answers were as follows: "Which is the wisest entity? The number. Which is the most beautiful? The harmony."

But these questions lead us to the philosopher's meditation about the philosophy of poetry. When, in Eminescu's poetry, the "old teacher"'s thinking "props universe and Cosmos in a number", he is much "older" than Kant himself, he is the *philosopher* in the primary sense of the word. He ponders about the "borders" of existence in the relation between the *comprehensible* and the *sensible,* in compliance with the Pythagorean idea of the correspondence of the qualitative phenomena and of the quantitative process within a given order. A profound and unforeseen unity is perceived along the diversity; it is the fundamental principle which, according to the Pythagorean doctrine—based, in its turn, on the Orphic cosmogonies—is the *cosmic* unity, in which *things are numbers.* The unity of *countable* things in the *world* is a secret *harmony,* revealed only to those who, being initiated in the "mysteries", can hear the "music of spheres", as Eminescu puts it, in a Pythagorean vision of the *cosmos.*

However, we do not know too much about the originary form of the Orphism, as it was very early confounded with other mysteries and with Pythagoreanism, originated in a cult of nature, in Dionysiac rituals, which viewed nature as a cycle of oppositions as an "eternal return". Beyond the religious doctrine of the initiation, Pythagoreanism equally implied a particular cosmogony; it was based on the opposition between the Sky and the Earth, translated by the proselytes in numerical relations, not without implying a dualist doctrine, of a Babylonian origin, based, in its turn, on Oriental philosophy, Pythagoreanism stipulated a coincidence of contraries to lie at the basis of the Universe. The Unity or the Monad comprises two fundamental oppositions: the Unlimited and the Limited, mixed by Harmony. "The Doctrine of Monads" could be inferred by Pythagora's disciples from the previous philosophy of the Ionians, from Anaximandros' hypothesis regarding the origin of the world in the mixture between air and fire around various condensing points; this hypothesis could lead to the idea of an infinite primordial substance, the matrix of things, conceived as a fire generating the matter as such by condensing it around a group of points or centers, forming a solid core, i.e. the Monad; the rarefied air which surrounded it also separates it from other, similar, masses[10].

According to the Pythagorean doctrine, harmony was at the basis of all numbers; the latter are the essence of all things, therefore the world itself, namely the Limited and the Unlimited. This primary opposition generated a few others: the odd numbers correspond to the Limited, the even ones—to the Unlimited. Such is also the case of various other dualities, e.g. unity and plurality, rest and movement, masculine and feminine, straight and curve, light and darkness, good and bad. In Eminescu's cosmogony, which we've been used to interpret through the grill of other sources, namely the Rig-Veda Hymns and the Kant-Laplace theory, there are nevertheless various elements of the orphic cosmogonies. If the "old teacher" props "Cronos in a number", the hypothesis of a pythagoreic vision cannot be excluded; in its turn the latter includes Anaximandros' cosmogonic hypothesis expressed by poetic images:

> "Thinking takes him back through thousands upon thousands of hoar ages
> To the very first, when being and non-being were nought still,
>
> . . . . .
>
> There was no estate of wisdom, nor a mind to comprehend.
> For the darkness was as solid as is still the shadows' ocean,
> And no eyes, had there been any, could have formed of it a notion.
> Of the unmade things the shadows had not yet begun to gleam
> And, with its own self-contented, peace eternal reigned supreme
> Suddenly, a dot starts moving—the primeval lonely Other . . .
> It becomes the father potent, of the void it makes the mother.
> Weaker than a drop of water, this small dot that moves and bounds

> Is the unrestricted ruler of the world's unbounded bounds."[11]

In the tables made by the Pythagorean philosophers, analogies are based on the signification function, therefore the first column comprises the terms: limited, odd, one, rest, man, light, good—, whereas the second column contains the terms: unlimited, even, more, movement, woman, darkness, bad. These very oppositions also appear in Eminescu's cosmogony, ranged in an isotopic correspondence, viz. first column: light, movement, father, borders; second column: darkness, rest, mother, unbounded.

Leaving aside all other meanings implied by the poet's cosmogony, the pattern of the Pythagorean monads is quite obvious, and the more so is the possibility to consider Anaximandros' cosmogonical hypothesis as a source of Eminescu's cosmic image. We've been used to consider the old teacher's meditation to refer only to the "beginning" of the world, and not at all to its "ending"; the "end of the world" is the second term of Anaximandros' cosmogonical hypothesis. It is a revolution of the planets in the infinite primary substance, in compliance with the Pythagorean idea, transformed by the poet in a sombre vision, confirming the nothingness of the human world against the background of the cosmic infinite:

> "Nowadays a thinker's judgement is restricted by no tether,
> He projects it in a moment over centuries together.
> To his eye the sun all-glorious is a red orb wrapt in shrouds,
> Closing like a bleeding ulcer among all-darkening clouds,
> He sees how the heavenly bodies in vast spaces freeze and run
> Rebels that have torn the fetters of the dazzling light and sun
> And, behold, the world's foundation is now blackened to the core,
> And the stars, like leaves in autumn, flicker out and are no more
> Lifeless time distends his body and becomes endless duration,
> Because nothing ever happens in the boundless desolation.
> In the night of non-existence all is crumbled, all are slain,
> And, in keeping with its nature, peace eternal reigns again."[12]

This "end of the world" vision, symmetrical to that of the "genesis", besides its philosophical sources, confirms Schopenhauer's metaphysics of the "eternal present"; the existence of man is characterized by the completely useless "perishable" nature of all human elements, in sharp contrast with the "eternal" universe. This is a philosophical attitude of the thinker's irony; he looks down on the world, from the "height" of his reasoning, but, besides the ethics of renunciation, the Pythagorean model is equally present within the Schoppenhauerian pattern by the metaphysical considerations regarding the sense of the human values, always in a relation of opposition; these elements belong to a doctrine taken over by Pythagora's disciples from the Orphic philosophy.

Schopenhauer's metaphysics took over the renunciation ethics from the wisdom of the *Upanishads,* while, in its turn, in the Ancient Indian philosophy, the latter explain the Vedic meanings, as lesson about Unity. Eminescu's cosmogony, due to the influence of his native background, as an abysmal phenomenon in the surface stratum of the poetic idea, is given in **"A Dacian's Prayer,"** also a structurally abysmal motivation of the poetic vision, based on the matrix of the anonymous creations—beliefs and myths—belonging to an archaic structure of Romanian structure, by including the poetic symbols within an Orphic space, as a phenomenon of "spirituality"; this way a *Romanian myth* is created, where the cosmogony is actually a theogony of the Geto-Dacians, the ancestors of the Romanian people.

The cosmogony of the Rig-Vedic Hymns, used by Eminescu in the first version of **"A Dacian's Prayer"** was actually a theogony, the question about the "genesis" being the question about the name of that god who was there alone, before the creation of the world:

> "Which God alone stood there before the Gods existed—
> I wonder who the god is to whom we burn our embers?"[13]

The next versions are much closer to the poem **"The Twins,"** where the Dacian curses Zalmoxis, denying his almightiness, and celebrates the void, in the final version of the poem.

> "When death did not exist, nor yet eternity,
> Before the seed of life had first set living free,
> When yesterday was nothing, and time *had not begun,*
> And one included all things, and *all* was less than one.
> When sun and moon and sky, the stars, the spinning earth
> Were still part of the things that had not come to birth,
> And You quite lonely stood . . . I ask myself with awe,
> Who is this mighty God we bow ourselves before".[14]

It is along the folklore tradition that the poet explains the representation of the ancient Dacian city, as a city of rocks and forests, mythologically personified by Fairy Dockya. Her way towards the time of the genesis appears even more grand, as it is amplified by the "golden flowers" of the imagination, projected against a mythical background:

> "A big mountain arises all along the East horizon—
> It is twice as height as any look uplifted to the sky can reach—
> Rock piled on rock for ever, step by step endlessly seem
> To the infinite to mount, and its top, wrapped in the heights,
> Mere edges shows to humans in the darkness coloured blue:
> It's mountain belonging half to our world of humans, half to godly infinite."[15]

This description of Dockya's way—especially the main idea expressed in the last line—indicates the passage towards the source of historical time, which has unlimited dimensions and, for this very reason, return to the "beginnings" is mediated by a cosmogonic thought. A big "gate" appears in the core of the mountain:

> "It's there that the Sun's charriot passes by his fiery horses driven;
> It's there that at night rises the blonde Moon of silver shine
> And the millions of stars spring in ever brighter flights
> Spreading on the sky they people like saint flowers of gold."[16]

Dockya's way, symbolically described as genesis witnessing the birth of gods, could have no other end in this fable of the "saint flowers" than the dwelling of the Dacian gods:

> "Dacia's gods were living there—behind this solar gate—
> And towards the world of mortals rocky stairs had to descend.
> In the green darkness of forests Dacia's gods were gathering."[17]

Zalmoxis, a god for the Getae, a man who had become a god, for the Greeks, a disciple of Pythagora, according to the information supplied to the latter by Herodotus—although the historian, who doubts its accuracy, specifies that Zalmoxis must have lived long before—, had retired, according to the same source, from among his worshipers and lived in a cave on the Kogaionon mountain, reappearing only three years afterwards only to show them that the secret of death is a gate towards immortality. In Eminescu's poetic myth, the mountain "belonging half to our world of humans, half to godly infinite" is the "Idea", the initiation place, an Orphic space of the "descent", enabling man to "ascend" towards the God's immortality.

Whether Zalmoxis' was a God of the Sky or a God of the Earth, philosophers can tell much more accurately than historians, because the "gate in the mountain", from which the light emanates reaching "the world of mortals" is a "border", marking the "coincidence" of opposites, according to the Orphic tables of Pythagora's disciples; this opposition enabled Plato to distinguish between the *intelligible world* and the *sensible world.*

The latter world is an image of the former, in a "partici-pation" relation that the philosopher explained by re-sorting to a "myth of the cave"; its inhabitants are un-able to see the light directly, it is only its shade that reaches them and, whenever the philosopher descends in the sensible world, he is astonished by the darkness hiding the clarity of the Idea. Consequently, if perfec-tion is identified to the Idea, the sensible world is only a "beautiful image" of the intelligible one.

A "beautiful image" therefore, since the Beautiful is only a sensible replica of the Intelligible. The ancient philosopher's enunciations allows us however to "reha-bilitate" the poet, but the poet himself, starting from the very Antiquity, has acquired a right to be rehabilitated by his "beautiful" art. By the Orphic background of its mysteries, Pythagoreanism preserved the sense of man's spiritual liberation, according to the archetypal model of Dionysos-Zagreus, torn out by the Titans and revived as a divine spark in the soul of man; this theory was expressed by the Pythagorean doctrine in terms of an opposition, by ranging all things in a duality or polarity of their own, based on the coincidence of contraries, all deriving from the fundamental distinction between the *intelligible idea* and the *sensible image.* This coinci-dence is the source of the mist, which, according to Plato, another philosopher initiated in the Pythagorean doctrine, is to permeate the sparkling theory of the Ideas; the mist spread its obscurity over the future speculative attempts of Pythagora's disciples; the influ-ence of this doctrine was to be felt; the same like Or-phism (in its different versions) and like Neo-Platonicism, until the modern times: In the Renaissance, it was a discovery of man's real being, during the Age of Reasoning it took the form of religion and of as-tronomy, whereas the Romanticism expressed it as the harmonies and symbols of the invisible, as well as by the vision of darkness—a necessary step in the initia-tion of the "clairvoyant", in all its hypostases, i.e. de-mon, titan, prophet, sage.

With Eminescu, such a vision becomes characteristic of Romanian poetic space, too; it is a poetic structure of the relation between the "idea" from the *upper* level of the "participation" and the "image" from its *lower* level. From Eminescu's very first lines, called *Darkness and the Poet,* a vision of the "darkness" which revives the "spirit" the poet defined the axis of his poetic thinking along the Orphic column of the two Dawns' palace, namely the *Music* and the *Drama,* that is to say *Poetry* and *History,* one of them being the "muse", the "music from the stars above us", the cosmic harmony pervad-ing Orpheus enticing tune, whereas the other is the real life of mankind, revived by the poet's "song" in their "spirit", i.e. "psyché", namely the inner side of the hu-man being, a demon that man is "doomed" to search

within himself; according to the archaic tradition, this demon is related to the revolution of stars on the sky, to the "music of the spheres", as the poet would have put it.

In an "abysmal" foundation of what has been called the "Idea Eminescu", conceived within the "matrix space" of Romanian culture, the "sacred mountain" of poetic cosmogonies is the "mountain" of the magnus "as old as the world", from the **"Ghosts,"** a historical episode added to the dowry of the Fairy Dockya. In his way to-wards his dwelling hidden in the mountains, the magus appears as a master of wilderness and a spirit of life, and he is the one searched, in the epoch of the gradual constitution of the Romanian people, by the conqueror from the North, who begs of them the resurrection of his sweetheart, "the Danube Queen":

> "Reaching at last the forest that clothes the rising hills,
> Where does a sweet spring murmur, well out from 'neath a stone,
> Where grey with scattered ashes an old hearth stands alone,
> Where far off in the forest the earth-hound sounds his tone
> And with his distant barking the midnight silence fills."[18]

The Magus is seen like a force of cosmic love, there-fore, within the inner being of man, he represents the Sources of Life, towards which all Romantic poets aimed; thus these Sources are equivalent to the feeling of the unity of the world, to the feeling of the Absolute.

The Magus of the **"Ghosts"** is also the one appearing in **"The Emperor's Son without a Star,"** a Romanian folklore tale, equally based on Dockya's myths, as a matrix stratum to which anyone aiming to understand the life secret is doomed to come back:

> "From that source of the foamy rivers falling down
> In the dark shadow left by endless woods of beech,
> On the huge mountain whose forehead among the clouds steals out
> Aiming to reach the Sun, an old Magus lives
>
>   . . . . .
>
> Whatever mortal wants the secret of life to penetrate,
> Is doomed this sacred mountain slowly to clamber up."[19]

After this way towards the old Magus' wisdom, in the dream of the mortal who turns towards his inner self, by means of his own replica, a distinction is revealed, namely man comes to discern between sensitivity and reasoning:

> "You think . . . By cold rays thought penetrates,
> Striking the sweet elf-image that fantasy created.
> And this elf-image then becomes as pale as ghost

So that no longer seen, it vanishes, confounded
With its source: the clouds or the unstable wave."[20]

The elf-image created by fantasy and struck by the cold rays of thought which transforms it into a ghost is deprived by the sensible "reality", whereas its return to the source, namely to the clouds and the unstable wave, is a clear reference to the genesis. In the relation between the "idea" and the "image" within the space of the imaginary, this elf-image is a generator of the poetic thinking between the "upper" level of reasoning and the "lower" level of imagination.

From this space placed between reasoning and imagination, the "mountain belonging half to the world of mortals and half to infinite" will open towards the "infinite" in **"Hyperion"**'s cosmogony-where the immortal being's "descent" in the real world triggers the "ascent" of the mortal to the Ideal equally comprising the "Idea" and the "image"; this way both the sky and the earth have a *recessive* nature, as they engender the imaginary, a generator of "fantasy" moulding the poet's reasoning. The "Star" of the **"Magus Wandering among the Stars"** (the title of another of Eminescu's poems), deprived of its primitive, magical significance during the elaboration of the poetic symbol, reaches the inner being of the genius, his immortal consciousness. The genius reaches this condition by being confronted to the "mortal", in order to reveal an "immortal" meaning to the "mortals" by means of the Ideal dominating both "idea" and the "image", i.e. the "double" aspect of man: mortality and immortality.

As a self-consciousness of the man of genius in the matrix space of Romanian culture, this is the "Idea Eminescu".

Notes

1. T. Arghezi, *Eminescu,* "Vremea", 1943, pp. 7-13.

2. L. Blaga, *Spaţiul mioritic,* 2nd edition, 1936, pp. 213-226.

3. E. Todoran, *Secţiuniliterare,* 1973, p. 293.

4. Id. *ibid.,* p. 263.

5. Jean Burgos, *Pentru o poetică a imaginarului,* Univers, 1989, p. 239.

6. M. Raymond, *De la Baudelaire la suprarealism,* Univers, pp. 384-385.

7. Translation of the lines Mariana Neţ.

8. F. Enriques et G. de Santullans, *Pythagoricens et Eleates,* Hermann, 1936, p. 17.

9. Translation of the lines by Leon Leviţchi

10. Th. Gomperz, *Les penseurs de la Grèce,* I, Payot, 1928, p. 141.

11. Translation of the lines by Leon Leviţchi.

12. Translation of the lines by Leon Leviţchi

13. Translation of the lines by Corneliu M. Popescu.

14. Translation of the lines by Corneliu M. Popescu.

15. Translation of the lines by Mariana Neţ.

16. Translation of the lines by Mariana Neţ.

17. Translation of the lines by Mariana Neţ.

18. Translation of the lines by Corneliu M. Popescu.

19. Translation of the lines by Corneliu M. Popescu.

20. Translation of the lines by Mariana Neţ.

Domnica Radulescu (essay date spring 1991)

SOURCE: Radulescu, Domnica. "Eminescu and the Romantic Interpretation of *Don Quijote.*" *Cervantes: Bulletin of the Cervantes Society of America* 11, no. 1 (spring 1991): 125-33.

[*In the following essay, Radulescu probes Eminescu's interpretation of* Don Quijote de la Mancha.]

The first translation of *Don Quijote de la Mancha* in Romanian appeared in 1840 from the French version of Jean Pierre Florian. Ten years later, in a small village in the valleys of northern Romania, one of the last Romantics of the world was born: Mihai Eminescu. In one of his lesser known poems, he recreated the story and character of the last knight-errant in the light of the symbolism and atmosphere of late Romanticism. The poem appeared in 1877. Its first title **"Viziunea lui Don Quijote" ("The Vision of Don Quixote")** was later changed to **"Diamantul Nordului" ("The Diamond of the North")**. The poem was neglected by critics in Romania as well as everywhere else, and it has never yet been considered and analyzed as a Romantic interpretation and adaptation of the story and character of the Spanish hero. The purpose of this study is to undertake such an analysis.

Eminescu merged his knowledge of the greatest philosophies and literatures of the world and the colorful wisdom and beauty of the folklore of his country. His readings ranged from the Rig Veda, Horace and Homer to Dante and Shakespeare, from Confucius to Schopenhauer, Goethe, Schiller and Novalis. His first encounter with the hero of La Mancha must have been through the Romanian translation; but since he pursued a good portion of his studies in Austrian and German universities, and spent much of his youth reading German philosophy and literature, it is also probable that he read a German translation of *Don Quijote.* He was likely influenced as well by the Romantic view of the hero through the writings of Tieck, Jean Paul Richter and the Schlegel brothers.

In his book *Cervantes et le romantisme allemand*, J.-J. A. Bertrand noted that Richter saw in *Don Quijote* "le tableau de la lutte entre le réalisme et l'idéalisme,"[1] A. W. Schlegel saw in the book "la peinture de l'antagonisme entre la réalité prosaique et le rêve de l'imagination,"[2] while Tieck considered it "une union du sublime et spirituel avec le monde bas et misérable."[3] Throughout Eminescu's life, his work oscillated between the highest spheres of idealism and the most bitter disillusionment.

Beyond the typical German Romantic view of Don Quijote as the embodiment of the desire of the absolute, and of the duality between ideal and reality, Eminescu also saw in Don Quijote a symbol of his own personal drama and that of his nation. A crossroad in the middle of the Balkans, a prey to invaders from all sides, a country whose language was little used outside its borders, Romania was home to intellectuals who had to struggle to make their voices heard. As a late Romantic, Eminescu tried to soar, through his poetry, in the purest realms of the spirit, pleading with the world to return to Romantic ideals and to listen to the voice of his nation. But, like Cervantes, he also contemplated the harshness and prosaic nature of reality and of his time and smiled ironically at his own idealism.

The poem he wrote about Don Quijote has sixty 4-line strophes, and it traces the imaginary travels and adventures of a knight in search of a magic stone hidden at the bottom of the *Northern Sea*. Once in possession of the stone he would, supposedly, lift the spell that had been cast on his mistress and thus gain her love. After battles with giants and monsters, after wandering through deserts and mountains and facing the unleashed forces of a hostile nature, he finally retrieves the magic stone from the bottom of the sea and brings it to his beautiful Iñez. She tells him she loved him anyway and had only wanted to test his love. At that very moment he opens his eyes only to realize it had all been a dream and his cruel beloved, whom he had serenaded earlier, had not even opened her window.

The adaptations of the Cervantine themes to Romantic motifs and symbols are clear. Don Quijote's travels in search of adventure, of occasions that would call on his courage and faith and would allow him to prove his endless love for Dulcinea del Toboso, are transformed by Eminescu into a search for a magic stone. Also called "piatra luminei"[4] (the stone of light), the diamond at the bottom of the sea suggests the Romantic search for the absolute, the quest for the ideal love, or to use Bertrand's words referring to the symbolism of the love for Dulcinea, the journey towards the priceless diamond also suggests "la poursuite métaphysique de la connaissance."[5]

In the serenade that Altisidora sings to Don Quijote (II.44)[6], there is an allusion to "La Sola," the peerless jewel of the crown that had been fished up in the *Southern Sea* and then lost forever when the palace in Madrid burned. Altisidora mentions the priceless stone when trying to woo Don Quijote; she tells him in her serenade that her love for him is so powerful that she would bring him the most precious gifts and stones in the world, were he to share her love. In Eminescu's poem, Iñez tells the knight who has serenaded her that she is under a spell that prevents her from giving him her love, until he brings her the priceless stone. The Romanian poet seems to have reversed the Cervantine motifs or rather, to have created their counterpart: in the poem, it is the knight who serenades his beloved, and the priceless jewel is found at the bottom of the *Northern Sea*.

If the first German Romantics were enchanted mostly by "la côte méditerranéenne,"[7] by the Spain "si curieusement orientale,"[8] and "romanesque,"[9] depicted by Cervantes, the Romantics such as Novalis or Hölderlin shifted their interest towards "la poésie de rêve, à la fantaisie exaspérée et insatiable."[10] As a late Romantic and the only outstanding Romantic of his land, Eminescu covered both periods in his lifetime: the poetry of Novalis had a certain impact on his writing, especially with respect to the boreal atmosphere and motifs. And, since his own country had aspects of the meridional, oriental and "romanesque" atmosphere of Spain, he turned toward the icy, crystalline and remote beauty of the North as a symbol of the purest and unreachable realms of the spirit.

In Eminescu's poem, Don Quijote becomes the alter ego of the poet who is always torn by insatiable longings, and by unquenchable desires for perfection; the serenade of the knight is both a way of alluring the indifferent maid and of transcending his longings through poetry. In both Cervantes' novel and Eminescu's poem, most of the action takes place at the imaginary level: Altisidora is not really in love with Don Quijote but is playing a trick on him, the radiantly beautiful Dulcinea to whom he dedicates most of his travels and adventures is only a creation of his mind, while the peasant woman he takes for Dulcinea is truly a peasant woman laughing at his foolishness. In Eminescu's poem the beautiful woman is not really under a spell, and she sends him in search of the priceless stone only to test the power of his love. Most ironic of all, when he thinks he has Iñez's love forever, he realizes it has all been a dream and that she has never even responded to his serenade.

Don Quijote becomes the symbol of the Romantic hero who, always disillusioned in reality, finds the fulfillment of his desires only in dreams. Yet the irony and humor are revealed at the end of the poem when the knight, embarrassed by the foolishness of his own dreams, hides in the bushes for fear someone would see him while Iñez's indifferent laughter drifts from the balcony. He gives Quijote the Romantic aura of the singular virtuous hero always in search of the purest essence of love and existence. Then he brings his hero back to earth and awakens him to the tangible, often cruel colors and sounds of reality.

Eminescu's attitude towards his hero is thus parallel to that of Cervantes towards Don Quijote. If Cervantes ironically smiled through his hero at the books of chivalry of the time and at the foolishness of falling under their spell, Eminescu might also ironically smile through his poem at Romanticism itself and at the very spell it cast on him.

The nature and atmosphere in Eminescu's poem elicits a sense of awe. The poet has transformed both the actual places crossed by Don Quijote in his travels and those existing only in his imagination into one natural realm in which the fantastic and the real are totally immersed in one another. Typical of Romanticism and of Eminescu in particular, nature becomes the immense extension of the hero's existence and imagination. The descriptions of the natural landscapes contain elements that clearly remind one of the story and atmosphere of *Don Quijote*: the castle, the giants, the dark rocks, the meadows and groves which stir with the mysterious life of summer nights, and the forests full of threatening shadows and voices.

The castle in the poem could be either an echo of the inn which becomes, in Quijote's imagination, "un castillo con sus cuatro torres y chapiteles de luciente plata," (I.2) or an echo of the castle of the duke and duchess who play a whole series of tricks on Don Quijote in order to bring him to his senses. The first glimpse that the reader has of the castle in Eminescu's poem is through its reflected image in the mirror of a lake. In both the story of Don Quijote and Eminescu's ballad, the world in the mind of the hero is projected on the outside world. But while in Cervantes' novel the clash between the two worlds is an obvious and important element of the story and a continuous source of humor, in Eminescu's poem the two worlds are intertwined, the borderline between them is vague and diluted, creating an oneiric atmosphere. Reflection and reflected object become one; reality and dream merge into one another.

The giants and dragons whose embodiments Don Quijote sees in windmills or wineskins, find in Eminescu's poem a parallel in the form of hyperbolic images

of nature. The hills and rocks that surround the castle are compared to giants guarding a golden treasure, that is, the rising moon. Hyperbole and personification are the main devices through which Don Quijote's mind grasps reality: windmills and wineskins are to him vicious giants; a homely peasant is to him the beautiful maid of his dreams, under a wicked spell. In Eminescu's poem, the entire landscape is the result of the hyperbolic transformation of such familiar Romantic motifs as the full moon, the crystalline lake, the ominous mountains.

There are, in Cervantes' narrative itself, motifs which lend themselves to a Romantic adaptation and, moreover, to an adaptation by Eminescu, something of a Don Quijote himself, pining for an ideal love among the majestic hills and mountains of his country. The rocks and mountains described in the poem could very well be taken as a Romanian analogue of the rocks of Sierra Morena on which Quijote sings to the indifferent cosmos a hymn of love dedicated to his Dulcinea. At the same time, the enchanting atmosphere "al pie de una alta montaña" (I.25) finds striking echoes in the descriptions of the "umbroase cărări"[11] (shady paths) and of the whispering meadows through which Eminescu's knight is wandering and serenading his beloved. In *Don Quijote* the beauty of the meadow inspires the knight to perform penance for the sake of his love:

> Corría por su falda un manso arroyuelo, y hacíase por todo su redondez un prado tan verde y vicioso, que daba contento a los ojos que le miraban. Habia por allí muchos arboles silvestres y algunas plantas y flores, que hacían el lugar apacible. Este sitio escogió el Caballero de la Triste Figura para hacer su penitencia.

> (I.25)

In Eminescu's poem, "Dumbrava şopteşte, izvoarele sună,"[12] (the meadow is whispering, the streams are singing), the summer air, the blooming flowers and the crickets singing in the luscious grass are all unified in the pulsing life of the universe and inspire the knight to touch the strings of his guitar and serenade the beautiful maid.

The charms and freshness of nature are, in *Don Quijote*, part of the reality which the knight distorts and absorbs into his imagination, thus creating a comic effect. The details of the natural landscape offer a pretext for the knight to give vent to his delirious pathos in words such as these:

> ¡O vosotros, quienquiera que seáis, rústicos dioses, que en este inhabitable lugar tenéis vuestra morada, oíd las quejas deste desdichado amante!

> (I.25)

Reality and dream are clearly separated by the down-to-earth voice of Cervantes: Quijote "comenzó a decir en voz alta, como si estuviera sin juicio." (I.25) Eminescu amplifies the beauty of the natural details and creates a dream-like universe in which the passionate words of the amorous cavalier are harmoniously integrated, apparently without a trace of irony on the author's part. The sound of the guitar and the words of the lover seem to be miraculously woven into the magic beauty of the night:

> Prin vinăta umbră, prin rumăna sară,
> In farmecul firei rasună ghitara.
> (Through the bluish shadows, through the ripe evening,
> In the charmed air guitar sounds are rising.)[13]

The words of the serenade express the ecstatic adoration for the angelic beauty of the cruel maid. If Don Quijote expresses his admiration for the unparalleled beauty of Dulcinea in an elevated chivalrous manner, full of hyperbolic images devoid of concrete allusions to her physical charms, Eminescu's knight sings of the maid's beauty in sensual images that reflect both the romantic ideal of feminine beauty and the sensuality and worldliness of the folklore of his country. The comic and dramatic genius of Cervantes has his character disclose his passion for an ideal in exalted tones that inspire both laughter and tears: "¡Oh Dulcinea del Toboso, día de mi noche, gloria de mi pena, norte de mis caminos, estrella de mi ventura . . . !" (I.25). The tormented, idealistic, yet sensual nature of Eminescu's genius shines through the mesmerizing beauty of the words of his hero, with whom he partly identifies. The shadow of his beloved is "-n lumină-nmuietă"[14] (soaked in light), her blue eyes are "mari lacrimi a mării"[15] (huge tears of the sea), her blond hair shines through the night which is "ninsă de-a lunei zăpadă"[16] (covered by the snow of the moon). Eminescu has taken one of the verbal sources of humor in Cervantes' novel, and turned it into poetic beauty.

The universe that Eminescu's knight crosses in his search for the magic stone is in many ways comparable to the universe crossed by Don Quijote either in his mind or in reality, as he seeks out adventures and ways of disenchanting Dulcinea. Dark forests, gloomy deserts, awesome mountains and chasms loom and vanish and loom again on the path of Eminescu's knight with all the speed and fluidity of dreams. Cervantes' hero on the other hand, spends many a night in forests and groves,

> pensando en su señora Dulcinea, por acomodarse a lo que había leído en sus libros, cuando los caballeros pasaban sin dormir muchas noches en las florestas y despoblados, entretenidos con las memorias de sus señoras.
>
> (I.8)

Eminescu's descriptions of the places covered by his hero seem to actualize, with their trance-like colours and shapes, the very fantasies that populate Quijote's mind. On his way, Eminescu's knight also encounters an old man with "barbargintoasa"[17] (silver beard) and long white hair coming out of a stately palace, who shows him the way to the magic stone. This episode reminds one of Don Quijote's descent into "la profunda cueva de Montesinos" (II.23) and of the dream he has about the encounter with the old Montesinos. The "venerable anciano" (II.23) is himself under a spell that can be lifted only with the help of a valiant knight. In Eminescu's poem, the old man is, on the contrary, the one who helps the knight in his search. The "venerable" but tearful figure in Don Quijote's dream finds its Romantic echo in the awesome god-like figure that appears along the way of the knight. Don Quijote's dream is but another instance of his illusory identity and of the way in which chivalric literature affected both his conscious and subconscious mind. The encounter of Eminescu's knight with the demiurgic figure of the old man points to the Romantic aspiration for absolute knowledge of and communication with the universe and with the transcendent forces that govern it.

The tempting and wooing of Don Quijote by Altisidora seems also to have found an echo in Eminescu's poem. Along his way, the hero suddenly crosses from the ominous lands of his travels into a paradisiacal meadow where he encounters a strikingly beautiful woman riding a horse and trying to allure him with her charms. The exact opposite of Iñez, she has dark hair in which "lucesc amorțite / Flori roşi de jăratec frumos incilcite"[18] (red flowers of embers entangled, are shining, unmoved), her blue eyes are of "bogat intuneric"[19] (rich darkness) like "basme pagine"[20] (pagan tales). Her beauty makes the forests and the waters shiver, while from the clouds "un colb de diamante"[21] (a dust of diamonds) is raining. Demon and angel: the dark-haired temptress and the golden-haired indifferent maid represent the two extremes between which the Romantic genius of Eminescu oscillates in his endless search for the ideal love. But in the same way as Don Quijote overcomes his temptations and remains faithful to his Dulcinea, Eminescu's knight resists the charms of the beautiful temptress and continues his travels until he finally finds the magic stone. But the moment in which Iñez assures him of her eternal love for him is also the moment of his awakening to reality and of the painful recognition of the illusory nature of his adventures.

The Romanian poet created through his hero a combination of the idealistic, dreamy figure of Don Quijote whose view of the world is a huge projection of his fantasies, and a down-to-earth figure who sparkles with popular humor and who mocks his alter ego trying to awaken him to reality. The abrupt ironic ending of the poem, in which the hero wakes up with his clothes all wet from the dew and tiptoes through the bushes for fear of being seen or heard, the mocking voice of the poet who asks rhetorically: "Si ce-i mai ramine sa facă săracul?"²² (and what else could the poor man do?) make it even more obvious that Eminescu saw in Quijote both an embodiment of the idealism and aspirations of Romanticism and an expression of the failure of Romanticism to grasp reality. If Cervantes turned the dreams and failures of his hero into an aesthetic victory of captivating narrative and humor, Eminescu turned the dreams and failures of his hero into an aesthetic victory of mesmerizing lyricism and subtle irony.

From among the valleys of his native country, one of the last Romantic poets identified with the last knight-errant and, just like him, awoke from his dreams only to realize that Romanticism, like knight-errantry, had already become part of the irrecoverable past. And, as with Cervantes, Eminescu's humor and irony towards his hero reflect a compassionate view of the dreams and failures of the great idealists of the world.

Notes

1. J.-J. A. Bertrand, *Cervantes et le romantisme allemand,* (Paris: Librairie Félix Alcan, 1914), p. 337.

2. *Ibid.,* p. 407.

3. *Ibid.,* p. 546.

4. Mihai Eminescu, *Poezii,* (Bucuresti: Editura Pentru Literatura, 1969), p. 417.

5. Bertrand, *op.cit.,* p. 208.

6. I quote from the edition of *Don Quijote de la Mancha,* published by Ediciones Zeus, Barcelona in 1968.

7. Bertrand, *op.cit.* p. 204.

8. *Ibid.,* p. 204.

9. *Ibid.,* p. 204.

10. *Ibid.,* p. 223.

11. Eminescu, *op.cit.,* p. 416.

12. Eminescu, *op.cit.,* p. 416.

13. Eminescu, *op.cit.,* p. 416.

14. Eminescu, *op.cit.,* p. 416.

15. *Ibid.,* p. 416.

16. *Ibid.,* p. 416.

17. Eminescu, *op.cit.,* p. 418.

18. Eminescu, *op.cit.,* p. 420.

19. *Ibid.,* p. 420.

20. *Ibid.,* p. 420.

21. *Ibid.,* p. 421.

22. *Ibid,* p. 423.

Ioan Saizu (essay date spring 1993)

SOURCE: Saizu, Ioan. "The Idea of Economic Progress in the Writings of Eminescu." *Romanian Civilization* 2, no. 1 (spring 1993): 75-93.

[*In the following essay, Saizu pursues Eminescu's "idea of economic progress" as it unfolds in his journalism.*]

> "The progress of mankind doesn't often lie in the numbers of its geniuses—nations with many and bright geniuses are often unhappy, but in those mute personages of history who are working tirelessly without any other reward than the consciousness that progress lies in all, not in one or in some."

When Eminescu began his brilliant activity as a publisher, human society was passing through an acute process of economic, social, political, and cultural changes. Likewise, the Romanians were certain, around 1877, but especially after gaining national independence, that they had considerably widened their possibilities to aspire to the acceleration of progress.¹ The period covered by Eminescian journalism was part of an interval outlined by the living rhythm of development, even by dynamism in some components, although the political context, due to the consequences of the commercial conventions, especially with Austria-Hungary was unfavorable. This fact allowed observers to consider Romania as a "Belgium of Orient" or "Japan of the European continent."²

The historian Gheorghe Platon rightly noticed that, starting with the modern period, the progress of Romanian society has been organized and accelerated in all fields after 1878, this does not mean that this was the starting point, for Al. I. Cuza had also tried after 1859, not always with complete success, to confer on it "a unitary and harmonious basis." The gaining of independence, during which the poet developed his journalistic career, had already found Romanian society deeply involved in modernizing structures, in a process of integration in a certain cycle of development through synchronizing, in trying to solve imperious economical problems.³ Furthermore, the context had become appropriate for organizing certain manifestations with a national character aimed at the development of the production process, circulation, exchange, and consumption, according to modern frameworks and the emancipation from under foreign economic domination, a thing that led to a movement which, in that epoch bore the name of an "economic crusade," "economic revolution" or "economic uprising."⁴

The respective process of modernization was subjected⁵ to at least three sources that generated tensions and inadaptabilities: the perpetuance of some old structures at the foundation of the social edifice, the tendency towards superficiality, and improvisation in the action of joining with the capitalist economy of the west and with the model of western civilization. Because the transformation produced on all social levels and in all spheres was heterogenous (more rapid rhythms on the political-administrative plane and slower ones, lacking the necessary scope in the economic-social field, especially in agriculture, the main production branch and the main source of income) the process of modern reorganization of society was not organic.

In order to understand correctly the becoming of mankind and the place of Romanians in the world community[6] the concept of progress in history for a long time captivated the thoughts of Eminescu. Watching it through the prism of social dynamics, he noticed that in the complex process of fulfilling progress, society manifested a double mechanism: one of respecting all that is vicious for the social organism so that the effort may not be useless; one of assimilation of any activity which ensures advances in civilization. In his belief, the young nations, for hastening the rhythm of development, are regarding as a "provision already earned," the intellectual results of the more advanced peoples. Seen through the prism of the mankind's progress, the dowry received takes on the significance of succession through a complex and irreversible mechanism. The energy spent by advanced peoples and which is reflected in intellectual results is transmitted to those young ones, constituting for their civilization "only the starting point."

As such, the new nations receive a new life sometimes with unpredictable effects because an idea born in an old state can provoke in this one a drowsy mood or at best little interest, but in a young nation it has the capacity to make a revolution, to turn wish into reality. In their turn, in the infinite of time, the young nation may add to the inherited dowry with their own energy which they historically spend on a cultural plane and after that, getting older, they fade away, passing the results to those peoples that are being formed. Out of this succession, Eminescu drew the conclusion that, while "the progress of nation is limited, the progress of mankind is infinite."[7] With the same value, his judgment can be brought in the field of understanding progress in one and the same people, as a succession among generations.

On the other hand, the poet tenaciously proved that the progress of mankind doesn't lie in the number of geniuses, for nations with many exceptional individuals are often unhappy, but "in those mute personages of history who are tirelessly working without any other reward than the consciousness that progress lies in all, not in one or in some."[8] In other words, progress should have been the result or the vector of the planetary community's efforts. Being sure that the earth is poorer in geniuses than the universe is in fixed stars, and that it is easier for a new solar system to be born in the unmea-

sured valleys of chaos than a genius on the earth, the poet has seen in the dozens of exceptions to this rule (Homer, Shakespeare, Raphael, Newton, Galileo, Kant, Darwin, and others) those kings of thought who "set us to work for generations ahead."[9] Henceforth, his exemplary theory on the one side that it is more useful for society to practice some trade than to manifest a pseudo-talent in literature, and on the other hand that each inhabitant of the Earth should have the right to the benefit of his time's progress. Making such an assessment, Eminescu hasn't forgotten for one instant that there is not a general civilization, accessible to each nation in the same degree and in the same way, that in the planetary collectivity each people has "its own civilization although in it there enters a multitude of elements common to other peoples as well."[10]

On this scheme Eminescu has built his whole demonstration of progress in Romania, as the succession of a dowry in perpetual but organic growth from one generation to another and the necessity that the access to its benefits be extended to all Romanians, and not to represent an exclusive caste's appendage. This for the sound reason that the "any real progress operates not outwards, but inwards and . . . the greater the unjustified appearances of progress are, the more difficult real progress is to be attained."[11] This is the reason why he so strongly defended the idea that it "was no longer possible for Romanians to live in this framework, more or less continuous up to now,"[12] and that for internal and external reasons, the concept of progress should have been admitted as "a gradual and continuous development of physical an intellectual work."[13] Exactly as other exponents of Romanian writing after 1877,[14] the poet made the observation that, in it's secular fight for independence, Romania, preoccupied in the great idea of national emancipation, had neither the time, nor the necessary peace to create for itself an organized system resulting from "the profound and conscientious study of our local needs and which suit our intellectual power and the means of wealth of our population."[15]

That is why, together with the entry in the European concert, the state should have imperatively begun the phase of the optimal solving of problems necessary to achieve progress, in which the poet had included as the main problems the raising of the intellectual level of the population, the development of activities on every level, including the reevaluation of the distribution of wealth.

Eminescu had perfectly realized that, as an independent state, Romania had to ensure for itself, with a view to achieving real progress, a proper international context, through wise policies, and this since the Romanians are located "on an edge of separation between two different worlds,"[16] an "edge of the world at this crossroads of peoples which consider us only as a sort of fence over which they quarrel."[17] To the same purpose, two other

Eminescian reflections must be remembered even if in a brief form: on the one hand a warning that without valuing economic worth, political prestige becomes illusory, even null, resulting in the inducement that progress should become an instrument and a defensive reflex against economic pressures and, as such, politics came from outside; on the other hand, that a people, following their chances, enlarged by the achievement of national independence, should not seek isolation because communication with cultured and civilized Europe has been and should remain a necessity without which progress itself was not possible.

In such an external context, Eminescu, dealing for a long time with the theoretical dispute over answering the question "what is the direction for our evolution" (a debate continued, in fact, until after the creating of the national unitary state in 1918),[18] has made, before uttering his own opinion, an analysis of the ideological currents that were confronted. He had noticed first that in the common arena of the fight for the nation's progress, each modern doctrine defined itself as the main force meant to assure the prosperity of society: the Liberals, considering themselves descendants of the "forty-eighters" claimed to want Romania to develop rapidly, bringing in harmony the institutionalization of the state with the French civilizing pattern, the way it resulted from the revolution in 1789, something that, by copying the forms without substance, led, in Eminescu's terminology to a "pseudo-civilization," while the conservatives, as partners of "the government rotary," also considering themselves as forty-eighters, stressed the ancestral traditions, of slow continuous process, without thresholds or great leaps, like the British prototype, which maintains a civilization by preserving the old historical forms permanently renewed by modern spirit and work.

Second, he made a critical analysis of the state of things in the epoch in which he lived, over which there had already been made pertinent demonstrations.[19] His analytical approach was well-founded as the respective epoch showed that the society's structures, although superior to those of previous times, were not spared countless shortcomings. That is why he made frequent critical references to the system, showing that the bad things that haunted society had nothing in common with the Liberal's principles nor with the Conservative's ones, but were incorporated in the social organism, in the tendencies and ideas that dominated it. Preoccupied with assuring the advances of modern civilization for the entire Romanian people, not only for one party or another, not only for one class or another, Eminescu contested the existence of progress even during the years when the state had been led by the Conservatives. Nevertheless, the attack was aimed especially at the essence of the Liberal regime which was far from the seductive democratic principles of 1848.

The Eminescian criticism is detaching itself also from the way he criticized a society which had contracted modern needs, without creating the corresponding possibilities on the intellectual and economic planes, knowing full well that "the introducing of the forms of a foreign civilization without existing its economic basis is simply useless."[20]

Going deeper in his analysis, the poet demonstrated that we lack the means of progress as shown by our supporting a much too expensive government for the level of instruction, of education, and of a modern organization of the people's work, that the needs of the superior classes were much too many for it to satisfy, that the people, being agricultural, had no capacity to cover the ultramodern needs (typical of an industrial state) of a totally unproductive aristocracy.

In order to persuade his contemporaries, Eminescu stressed the demonstration that an organism is the result of two opposing forces: that of heredity, as a conservative principle, through which there are preserved and transmitted to the heirs the qualities that were necessary in the struggle for existence, and that of adaptability, a progressive principle, through which there are gained the aptitudes necessary to conform to a changing environment. In order that adaptability should bring about new characteristics it needed time, the economic and social environment a people lives in could not be changed all of a sudden, but had to be done slowly for a people to have the time to accommodate to new conditions. Consequently, as a supporter of the principle of progressive adaptability, the poet stressed on the gradual, unhastened quality of modern aptitudes, without "throwing into the water any tradition," since the qualities in the past become insufficient for supporting the exigencies of the present and the sum of the wasted forces overtake the sum of these instead, and there follows deficits translated into morbidity and misery.[21] Fighting against "leaps in progress," the Titan has started from the biological truth that even the nervous system is an advancing instrument, but slowly and gradually because "to artificially make old a child, to transplant plants without roots in order to have the garden ready within two hours, doesn't mean progress, but devastation."[22]

Hence, the permanent pleading that any true progress "cannot be but historical, in connection with the past"[23] on the basis of personal, cultural, and historical values, both having to interact and to amplify each other through a partial return to the past, to its good and healthy elements proper for development, in which to build further, otherwise one doesn't do anything but go backwards.[24] Advancement—as Eminescu stated—should be made slowly and only by preserving unaltered the Romanian character, taking as a basis for development "its historical traditions, the way they settled in the flow of times,"[25] by introducing "an ever new spirit" into old frameworks, by continuously refreshing the content and preserving the forms, something that explained, up to that time, also the great mystery of our existence.

Real progress—wrote Eminescu in an article[26]—"is not accepted by us except in the gradual and continuous development of physical and intellectual work. Because who ever desires "progress" cannot realize it but together with its natural laws, with its gradual continuity." Real progress is "a natural link between the past and the future."[27]

In the opposition with his poetic creation, dominated by pessimism, lowered sometimes to negation, the poet fervently believed in progress, in the struggle to accomplish it. As proof, among others, he also concluded that "just as any moment of growth is a conservation of those earned in the past and an adding of the elements conquered again, so true progress cannot be hoped for but by preserving, on the one hand, and adding on the other," something that means, "a lively connection between present and future and not a series of irregular leaps."[28] This implied that a real program, as a natural connection between past and future, must be inspired by traditions, avoiding "improvised innovations and hazardous adventures."[29] In other words, the natural relation between the two times—past and future—determined that real progress should represent an organic growth, to correspond to the stage of a state's development, to identify itself with the very form of moving of the social organism achieved by the masses and not only by exceptional individuals, rejecting the education of progress, on account of natural laws, the establishment of forms without content.

Out of these ideas, and through what he himself engaged to undertake as one of the "agents of a future world," that is to let himself be led by the thought and the needs of the people, not by those "intercepted from foreigners,"[30] Eminescu embodied—as Nicolae Iorga once said—"the thing that the national tradition had most original and that which could useful for foreign civilizations in developing this historical and traditional meaning."[31] This is the proof that the poet didn't cling to the rational arguments, encountered with those from "Junimea," which underlined the specific and which in no way hindered progress and modernization, but offered the concept of traditionalism as a strong effective substance, while leaning its construction on former historical patterns, and also on the adaptability to modernism, especially on the economic plane.

This is the reason why he asked for the creating of a social climate of solidarity and harmony in the absence of which progress was to be merely superficial. That is why he validated as true only laws that modified "an old or wrong pattern" in order that the moving of thought and of the public will be directed only towards two series of essential ideas: the organization of agriculture, and the creation and the defense of industrial activity, both "of equal value" which were meant to ensure the national existence and that of the state against political dangers and that of foreign economic domination. Only these were, in the poet's view, the ideas worthy "to move the Romanians, but also worthy to unify them, for the search of the most practical and patriotic solution."[32] Such a conduct was also imposed by the international statute of Romania, the state having to avoid all manifestations which could irritate the great empires, equally strong and dangerous. "If we had a good location like Spain or England—he wrote on 11 December 1877—we could fight, yet still the old Romanian habits would rise up as oil over the water. But being surrounded by these peoples, out of quarrels only the enemy wins."[33]

The concept of progress also stressed the necessity of assuring the preeminence of the Romanian nation, without being an exclusivist, being led by "too strong a feeling of justice and equity."[34] Eminescu asked for a politics in conformity with which all economic and juridical provisions would come forth from the supreme law of "preserving the nationality of the country by all means, no matter how,"[35] that the national element to seal its own seal on all that constituted social or cultural activity where the specific was due to be synchronized with the Romanians' own mission in world history.

As for progress, Eminescu reserved a main place for the material factor. In a general view the education of making goods implied—according to him—three terms applied to work: production, consumption, and reproduction, on which depended the level of progress in the society. If the first two elements were equal one could notice an economic standstill proved by the fact that all was consumed that was produced; if the consumption overwhelmed the production one could watch a regression. Analyzing the relation among these three factors, the poet reached—economically speaking—the conclusion, formulated on 23 February 1880, that progress appears only in the conditions in which production overwhelms consumption, the difference entering in the process of reproduction.[36] Over more than two years, that is on 22 July 1882, Eminescu was going to stress the third hypostasis, considering that it couldn't be named real production but the act from which results a product which is superior to all kinds of services absorbed by the operation,"[37] and on 17 August in the same year, after he found out about the convoking of the first Economics Congress in Romania[38] to demonstrate—in a close relation with the necessity of achieving material progress by superior production to the consumption—that the sum of those enclosed in the productive activity should be, for its benefit and the benefit of the entire society, "infinitely greater than the number of the merchants of words and even of merchandise."[39]

In order to understand the meaning of economic progress in the poet's view, we must first notice[40] that in the universe of Eminescian ideas there is to be found a specific duality; the solidarity with traditional values, with things that came out of a superior organized past; the beneficiary being a man of modern times, of new forms of economic activity, rightly considering that the reaching of new parameters of national production implied the intensifying of work, including industrialization and the rejection of the pattern of unilateral activity, that is to say agriculture. Furthermore, seeing that the national economy represented the "science of a lively process, that the domination over nature constituted true civilization, that which a people owns "lies on the shoulders of the past," that the present is but a part of the history of all social work's branches, he showed that the notion of a national economy itself "is undoubtedly woven in history's forecourt."[41] The critical spirit of national economy was meant to lead to "the developing of liberty through industrial possession," and this while the gaining of liberty through the laws of national economy constituted—in his view—"the true and deep core of history."[42] And let us not omit[43] that Eminescu supported the necessity of the development of industry as a means of establishing the material basis of society as a necessity of civilization, not as the political option of the Liberals who, in fact, had not yet definitely turned to promoting and encouraging industry.

That is why the poet used numerous arguments in behalf of the progress of national economy in general, through phrases such as "true liberty and economic independence are two identical terms,"[44] the organizing of work was meant to assure the national existence,[45] but also special proof in industry's favor is the conviction that "we should not remain an agricultural people, but we must also become an industrial nation, at least for our own needs,"[46] that industrial progress was working every day towards the gradual modifying of work's hierarchy and was determining the improving of the structure of society; physical power was replaced by a cheaper and more powerful mechanical forces. "In the industries it transforms—said Eminescu—progress follows and human work successively changes its nature; from wholly physical in the beginning, especially in inferior functions, it becomes more and more intellectual."[47] In other words, economic progress made certain, unlike in the past, that modern industry should need less the intervention of the muscular power of man and in exchange a greater degree of using mental and moral faculties.

Eminescu had also put in balance other advantages of industrialization. "The quality of industrial work—he synthetically wrote—is economically superior," adding that "never could a nation that produces wheat afford itself the luxury of the developed industrial nations,"[48] that in a country with only agricultural exports, only the peasant is the one that "works for all, alone and incontestably,"[49] that by the multiplication of the intermediaries that manipulate the merchandise between the producer and the consumer, the agricultural nation will always loose, that the difference among values is huge (out of 500 wagons of wheat you could get half a wagon of luxury articles), that, finally, the agricultural nation exposed itself to the exploitation of its industrialized neighbors and proletarianize its manufacturers by failing to oppose the rivalry of foreign objects. That is why he more than once accused the lack of dynamism in the economy and the progressive outrun of useless expenses according to profits.

The poet has also pointed out another unfavorable consequence derived from the delimitation of economic life to agriculture, that is a people that is only working the land "reaches suddenly a point in which all progress stops where it ends" because "the persistence over the possession of land gives way to a limitation of history and unliberty of people."[50] In other words, the structure of the economic and social life could by no means be indifferent to the state and society on their way to modernization.

It is not at all astonishing that the most conclusive and dense arguments in connection with the necessity of economic progress were brought into debate by Eminescu as soon as the social forces, willing to inoculate dynamism to the aims in the society after gaining national independence, had announced the convocation in Iaşi between 10 and 14 October 1882 of the first Economics Congress in Romania, a congress that released a huge enthusiasm, and was considered as the only means of salvation.[51] Indeed, there took part directly or indirectly the economists A. D. Xenopol, Mina Minovici, and P. S. Aurelian, the literary men I. Creangă, B. P. Haşdeu and V. Alecsandri, the doctors S. Konya and N. Garoflide, even the pupils Artur Gorovei and Gr. Trancu, among numerous officials of the national or local press, including many from Transylvania.[52]

In this framework the poet could develop his meditations concerning the economic progress, building his motivations on the one side on the establishment extracted from analysis of the consequences of the commercial convention with Austro-Hungary that "the economic dependence of old times is changing unfortunately in our era in the economic extermination of those whose working place or whose level of culture doesn't provide the same advantages as those of his happier neighbor . . . , that things can be more frightening for the weak economist, for the uncultivated one, when the competition is entirely free" and on the other hand the belief that "the condition of a state's civilization is the economic civilization."[53]

That is why, exactly as A. D. Xenopol who, overwhelmed by the abnormal situation, asked for urgent measures[54] in order to change from the "false and expensive" civilization the society was used to,[55] Eminescu strongly struck by the same truth contested the reality of progress in Romania, where there wasn't valuable production in industry, where the local working force was used only in raw activities and where, despite all this, society contracted needs, typical of a modern industrialized state. The contesting of progress was also made for the unmanaged main branch of the national economy, so that Eminescu could notice not only this truth, but also the fact that if the exploitation of the agricultural fields had been made rationally they could, for a long time, serve as an example for the whole country, and could raise the intellectual level of the cultivators, could regenerate and improve the cattle breeds, could set free the working classes from under the slavery of an old system and of a heavy culture."[56]

This is the reason why, after the convocation of the Congress was made public, following the appeal launched on 6 August 1882 by the "Concordia Society,"[57] the poet increased his implication in theorizing the necessity of developing a modern economy. Thus, on 18 August 1882, noticing that for a couple of years we manifest "an obvious tendency for creating a national industry," he expressed his appreciation that especially the "Concordia Society" has known how to gather in its bosom several men, of different social conditions who, "deploring the ruin of almost all branches of national activity, felt the urge to awake to a new life the work which was paralyzed by foreign rivalry and by the lack of an agricultural education."[58] It was rendered through the poet's words the idea of the appeal signed by D. C. Butculescu, the vice-president of "Concordia Society," and also in other documents of the epoch.

Furthermore, Eminescu had much appreciated that, although it wasn't splendid, the exhibition organized a while ago by the "Concordia Society" proved the Romanian's capacity to practice whatever hard trades, and that only the lack of opportunity prevented him from developing his aptitudes. This thing made him conclude that economic activity could not develop without close study and the development of skills, and that one needed "to encourage this work, to diversify it, to create something where nothing existed before, to give the national aptitudes the liberty of fitting different branches of production, to wisely lead, through combined measures, an up to now agricultural people to the division of labor, to give them the opportunity to use it's spare time productively."[59]

The understanding of his option for the concept of real progress is also clearly shown by the observation that a people being at a low stage of civilization has modest needs but it wasn't right that these should remain stationary—something that would prove the lack of impulse and of progressive principle towards a superior activity. Hence the observation for being worse the multiplication of needs while "among people penetrates labor division, the multilateral ability to satisfy one's own needs by one's activity."[60] Trying to turn to principles and to appeal to the conscience of his contemporaries, Eminescu underlined the necessity of a radical change in individual mental qualities that conditions the exemplary fulfillment of labor, being certain that the majority of Romanians "couldn't be outside their country, otherwise than strengthening it, otherwise than developing its aptitudes."[61]

In other words, progress started from needs, from the modern, even ultramodern multiplying of state's and society's needs, hence the imperative that "when a society like ours contracts new needs, it also has to contract—wrote the poet on 12 October 1882 in the very time of the first Economics Congress—new attitudes,"[62] that a multiplying of needs without the existence of a growth in production[63] had the consequence of introducing a pseudo-civilization. Therefore, the growth of needs had to be in correspondence with the growth of production and with the number of laborers, being known that the "level of civilization of a people is not counted by the number of polished boots, of French phrases, or of newspapers, but by its aptitude to submit to men's purpose the blind forces of nature," that "the more man masters the wind, the water, and steam, turning them to laboring slaves, the higher the resulting civilization is."[64]

Shortly before the opening of the Congress, Eminescu had mainly stressed that the asphyxiating environment industry started to develop in, including the "Concordia Society," was due to the unfavorable social framework, to the lack of capital, determined by spending on useless luxury staff and unproductively the income achieved by agriculture, as well as to the lack of instruction concerning the most effective use of these aptitudes.

The poet's enthusiasm following the convoking of the Economics Congress must also be considered from two other points of view as important as the former. First, pleading on behalf of industry, he underlined the necessity of industrial education. Second, reviving on a superior plane a former idea, he maintained, on the one hand, that economic civilization is "the mother of the political one"[65] and on the other that," since the beginning of the world nobody has seen a people being politically strong and economically weak, both states of being finding themselves in close connection."[66] If we also consider his reflection that against permanent misery "there aren't to be found other remedies than labor and culture"[67] we shall better understand what the poet expected the economic reunion in Iaşi to be; he hoped that out of a policy of protection and cultivation the physical and intellectual features should result in a division of labor, as "the main factor against misery," that the division itself couldn't occur while the trades were paralyzed by the rivalry of foreign products, that finally, "our industrial education is the one that demands sacrifice and deserves it more than that sterile education which produces tens of thousands of aspirants to bureaucratic functions."[68]

During the work of the Congress, relating the event to the economic state of the society, Eminescu condemned the liberalism that facilitated the introduction of a false civilization without realizing any progress for the latest 30 years. Although he had access only at the summary of some reports and brief accounts, he concluded that, in Iaşi, the Congress "had no praiseworthy words for the economic development of Romania and neither could it have."[69] The daily regress of trade and handicraft in Romania, the substitution of indigenous elements, the corrupt administration, the inhumanity of the regime the peasant lived under, and so on; ideas that constitute in fact the essence of the five reports presented at the Congress, formed the chief themes that preoccupied the participants as well. From this point of view the poet was sure that the success of the Congress' debates "greatly depended on a good state administration," that, in order to promote economic development, it was necessary for "the administrative mechanism to be stronger, more free from political fluctuations than it was."[70]

The contesting of progress was not entirely justified if we consider, even briefly, that the railways had been nationalized, something imposed for financial-tariff reasons, the Romanian National Bank had been founded—the most important credit institution, an act of great importance for national development, that the Values Exchange had been opened, being of a huge interest for internal and external financial transactions (this institution in Bucharest being closely linked with similar ones in London, Paris, and Brussels, and shortly becoming a representative institution for the entire zone of the Lower Danube) that there had been elaborated a series of laws according to which there had been founded great industrial enterprises.

In the same period, Eminescu had denied any progress during the last three decades in the field of culture, a fact perfectly true for physics, mechanics, chemistry, mechanical engineering, and military techniques, but not so for other fields.[71]

Praiseworthy is the fact that on 12 October 1882, that is during the Economics Congress, the poet stressed the possibility for the people, while assimilating other's skill and knowledge, "to equal the production of advanced peoples, but also directed hard criticism towards those who wanted to use the advantages of foreign civilization without "introducing in the country the conditions of culture under which such results can produce themselves" and "without a parallel increase of economic and intellectual aptitudes."[72] Otherwise, the consumption was not an indicator of the degree of civilization. This showed that, without an increase of production, the sum of the past features became insufficient to support "the exigencies of the present, the sum of the dispersed powers always exceeding the ones put back instead; the organism concludes its daily counts with deficits to be translated into morbidness and misery."[73] At the end of the Economics Congress, Eminescu renewed the above observations, subordinating them this time to the idea that, although the needs have changed, the development of Romania didn't create "a new class of producers, nor the raising of the worker to a higher level of culture and better existence, but a new class of masters, a new aristocracy made up of people less cultivated but full of importance, with a lot of teasing spirit and with shameful little character."[74]

The announcement made by A. D. Xenopol that, at the end of the Congress all materials presented in Iaşi would be published in order to remain for history a proof of the enthusiasm for directing energy toward the economic field, fully satisfied Eminescu who was ready to deal with them again as soon as they would be gathered in an authentic edition. The reports and the works of October, 1882 were never published, a fact that prevented Eminescu from developing his demonstrations. But even the things mentioned in this article to support his concept of economic progress are enough to show that in few distinct articles containing arguments of an economic character, the Titan has given not only a remarkable proof of his involvement in the modern solving of material production's problems, as he had also shown engaging in the political polemic with the Liberals willing to give a new content to the forms of progress, but he has recommended solutions of high scientific authority.

The resolutions given in Iaşi were far from political, as Eminescu feared. The Congress, as an ideological prime manifestation, in a period illustrated by political and economic deeds decisive for the future development of the Romanian state, struck aims as it centered its debates on the consultation and general fixing of the participants' behavior in connection with their dealing with the major matters of that historical epoch. After two years reconfirming the idea, the next Congress (held in Iaşi from 6-8 January 1884) had as a result the unanimous adoption of the program and statuary documents, and the determination of possibilities to accomplish these foresights. Especially the program of economic protection has been praised as "the creed of the whole country."[75]

The most conclusive proof was given on 6 March 1885 when, in the headquarters of the Romanian "Concordia Society," the members of the Central Committee gathered in order to debate the draft law concerning "General Measures for Aiding National Industry," a project initiated by Emil Constantinescu, and resulting in the law adopted on 12 May 1887.[76] There were present then, in 1885, as a proof that the solving of the economic problems was the preoccupation of all kinds of political men, also the conservatives, Al. Marghiloman and Tache Ionescu,[77] in order to express their support for the Liberal project of Emil Constantinescu.

In creating economic progress, Eminescu pointed out the necessity to increase the competence of specialists, rightly believing that it was bad economists who obliged his nation "to import everything from abroad so that it remains forever inapt and incapable of producing for itself, in a manly way, what it needs," instead of adapting it to "the different kinds of productive work that exists in the world."[78] Hence, his discontent that although during the application of the convention with Austro-Hungary, based, as is known, on free trade principles, there was an obvious protectionist current and the desire to build a national industry, but it failed to notice that there took place neither the close analysis of economical phenomena, nor the study of the circumstances under which that very industry could be built.

That is why, already on 4 July 1876, the poet had correctly noticed that in order to lead the national economy one needed, besides the assimilation of information written in foreign books and encyclopedias, a healthy judgement to afford "the knowledge of the right proportion between the means and the aimed purpose," knowing well that no matter the purposes "they are wrong and useless if they do not equal the sacrifices made for their fulfillment."[79] For the same reason he asked[80] that they who dealt with the administration of the counties should have special knowledge of the national economy, of finances and statistics, besides the knowledge of the country's laws, in order to rightly decide what was secondary or of absolute need in the area they administrated. This was the expression of the Eminescian effort to remove the economic and social dilettantism that pushed the people towards "agricultural slavery" and towards the copying without a real basis of foreign forms, being certain that introducing "the most perfect and beautiful laws in a country they don't fit, you ruin the society no matter how clean your thought or kind your heart,"[81] that in the so-called educated circles "there has spread the habit of not thinking anything on one's own and of blindly clinging to foreign books" which,

especially in the continuously changing field of economy, "have but a relative value, being written out of the reflection over some states of things much different than ours,"[82] that what could be good on the banks of the Seine, are not necessarily as good on the banks of the Dâmboviţa's or Târnava.[83]

That is why, as a genuine economic theorist, he proved and asked the science be laid at the foundation of each activity of material production; instead of activities undertaken without a true professional knowledge, there was needed "intellectual labors, the serious study of the country's needs, the harmonizing of great agricultural interests, the creation of industrial work."[84]

Yet, this was not enough, especially as Eminescu was sure—as we have shown—that progress often depends on "those mute personages of history who are tirelessly working. . . ."[85] Damian Hurezeanu rightly noticed[86] that of all economic categories Eminescu discussed, labor especially preoccupied him and this was so in order to validate its importance as a means of wealth, as a factor generating values, as the only steady and prosperous pledge of a society haunted by evil, which had nothing in common, neither with the Conservative nor with the Liberal principles, and for the avoiding of which "no dialectics or oratory is needed, but labor, equity and truth."[87] In fact, the severe criticism towards the social-political estates of his time[88] aimed to determine the responsible factors to imply themselves in finding the solutions necessary for progress. The poet himself obsessed in his judgement by the truth that labor is "the law of the modern world, in which there is no room for the lazy," set the first example through his superhuman effort.[89] Besides, he indicated the most brilliant proofs, already from the beginning of his journalistic career. So, on 22 December 1878 he demonstrated in *Curierul de Iaşi* that economic progress could not be assured but through labor, and this because neither the academies nor other similar organizations had the capacity to replace labor, and a state of things that does not find itself on it is a phantom that lasts more or less, but turns into smoke at the blow of cold reality."[90]

Combatting the introduction of foreign forms in a totally unfit background, Eminescu has shown in many articles that the foundation of a state and the wealth of a people lies in labor (18 December 1877) that regular and certain progress is obtained "only through labor" (10 October 1878) that progress is conditioned by the continuous development of physical and intellectual work (17 February 1880). There is but a single remedy against evils—he wrote somewhere else—but that must be applied "in all rigor, with all exclusivism, labor—this mechanic correlation of the truth; the truth, this intellectual correlation of labor."[91] In terms of equity it was all about "the social theory of compensation" as the poet named it in *Timpul* (20 October 1881), a theory that stated that only through physical and intellectual work an individual of any social class compensated for what they received from society. The law of social compensation had the quality, for Eminescu, of equity and even ethics, while he has underlined that every good a man enjoys is greatly the deed of others and, consequently "his possession should be compensated through an equivalent of work."[92] On the respective mathematic equivalent, the poet has fixed the duty of the leading classes to "gather as much culture as possible in order to make easier the work of the lower classes, in order to illuminate them and lead them towards moral and material welfare."[93] Hence the imperative that everybody should carry out labor of use for progress and only in this case they should earn the right to enjoy life in the state. As Damian Hurezeanu has noticed,[94] the effect should be double: on the one side the removal of all categories of speculators interposed on the path from producer to consumer, of the parasitic strata from among the politicians, of the useless bureaucracy, and, on the other hand, full rights and complete support from the central authorities for the problems of the working class of laborers and peasants. Only by enthroning the principle of equality one could move manpower towards production, turning matter into utile forms and narrowing the sphere of the merchants of words and the area of vices.

Eminescu has pointed also the ideal connection between concept and labor, between theory and practice, between effort and social merit. Everything started from the belief that there was no greater danger for the conscience of the people than "the sight of corruption and of rewarded nullity, than the praising of the unworthy," a sight that was taking away from the people "the confidence in the value of labor and in the certainty of promoting through merit,"[95] that, by virtue of the social theory of compensation, everybody was obliged to carry out an effective and useful work, and only that could guarantee rights in the state. That is why, he concluded that "there exists neither liberty, nor culture without labor," that anyone who believed that "by uttering a series of phrases he replaced labor, that is liberty and culture, is to be counted among the parasites of human society,"[96] and that "always there should exist the possibility for a man to climb, through labor and merit, the social hierarchy that shouldn't be but a hierarchy of labor."[97] By considering equally labor and culture, Eminescu has pointed the directions that should be implanted in society so that progress should be obvious.

As much labor as possible, not at random, but through the scientific coordination of efforts by education, something that should be translated—in the poet's words—"in a constant habitation to save force and then use it for objects worthy to be acquired."[98] Due to this statement we have to consider him among the predecessors that pleaded for the necessity of the scientific organiza-

tion of physical labor. This problem has been also set for intellectual activities, obvious in the statement that the directions and the domains of labor were so vast that the youth returning from his studies had enough room to manifest their preoccupations. The reality shows that, by misunderstanding the needs of the country, speaking jargon instead of the Romanian language, and not knowing that history and society's laws should be the foundation of development, the youth returning from studies in the west "entirely lacked a sense of history."[99]

From this angle it is not at all accidental for Eminescu to see the attributes of man in society in three hypostasis: of intelligence—the antithesis between culture and science; of practical activity—the antithesis between culture and morality; of aesthetics—the link between culture and the sense of beauty. In connection with these, but with the purpose to turn manual work into aptitude,[100] the most favorable situation could result only by giving the laborer the possibility to choose freely an occupation suited to his aptitudes in which "to have a maximum of interest to work well."[101]

Consequently, a pattern of efficiency by coordinating the work to fit the aptitudes, something that allowed a diversification of occupations and economic activities, saving the whole people from practicing "a single kind of work which to make it unilateral and inept in all fields except one."[102] In other words, a division of work in which the process of professional education fully contributes, by establishing schools with various profiles, even polytechnical schools.

If progress was to be obtained by fully engaging labor, then the object of public attention was due to be reserved to the man, not to what he would achieve, hence the Eminescian observation that the aim of progress was identified with the very need to assure a real civilization in the historical space of the Romanian people, under the conditions in which the national principle was gaining intensity and extension and with the duty to guarantee the capacity of defense against external dangers. For this very reason he has asked that our little country, in which there is to be found "every possibility of development just as in any other place, no matter how large," must be enlarged through "the fruits of our labor and through the greatness of our merits.[103] A duty as tied as possible to the pacifist vocation of the people. Furthermore, the poet held the belief—essential in its essence and aspiration—that by achieving progress on multiple planes, Romania could obtain the function to play an important civilizing role among the peoples of the European Orient and, at the same time, could obtain the ability to free itself from under the influence of the great powers, all equally dangerous. Consequently, only by means of progress, culture and civilization, expressed by deeds of great value and long lasting, the Romanians could ensure their survival, unity and national independence, annihilating any aggressive or monopolizing politics.

Eminescu has pointed not only the aim of progress, but also the direction of it. Relating to the truth that the peasantry constituted more than 80% of the whole active population, being, in fact, the element fundamentally productive in the national economy and which embodied and conserved all that the nation had most genuine (language, tradition, feeling, and thought), he directed especially the idea of economic progress towards the village world and this as much as the sources of income that covered the needs of that pseudo-civilization showed that out of the small surplus of the private producer's farm lived "the foreign structure of ideas, of institutions, and of forms, lacking content," having "nothing of what is genuinely Romanian, or national culture, in the proper meaning of the word,"[104] as all achieved progress, sterile both on the economic and intellectual plane, "turned into a terrible fiscal and administrative burden for the peasant."[105] Furthermore, while the artificial needs imported from abroad grew, multiplying the peasant's obligations, he went on working, exactly like in olden times, for the upper class, too much subordinated to Western civilization, without finding the most proper way to integrate the respective influence into the national culture. Henceforth the poet's great admiration for the peasantry, "the best class of all, the most conservative in language, costume, tradition, the bearer of the people's history, the nation in the truest meaning of the word."[106]

Making a survey of humankind's evolution, Eminescu has formulated the conclusion that, although in the monarchic states progress has been gradual, without leaps, but sure and steady,"[107] many misfortunes still marked the existence of these peoples. Towards the end of the 1880's, on 4 December 1888, he wrote in the article **"Fântâna Blanduziei"** (**"Blanduzia's Fountain"**) that, although new discoveries in the field of industry increased living conditions, and though teaching and civilization has spread in almost all European and trans-Atlantic states, "mankind is unhappier than ever."[108] Such a statement was explained on 25 December 1888 by the fact that "in all continents, people are worried by a stormy future,"[109] and also in the article with the suggestive title **"Ziua de mâine"** (**"The Day of Tomorrow"**) which for Eminescu was to come loaded with tragedy, that "nations go on working today as they used to yesterday, waiting for better circumstances and conditions of living to occur,"[110] that among the various peoples numbered very many supporters of the thesis that the social-political organization is *neither consonant with the percepts of normal reason, nor with the results given by experimental, physical and natural laws, and that such a situation could not be steadily and consistently continued in the direction chosen.*"[111]

In the Romanian space, Eminescu had included in the balance, an increase in mortality over the birth rate, the hasty admittance of unsuitable forms from Western civilization, without a basis for these, as well as the impoverishing of the people through the "waste of labor," everything being far from "representing a proper compensation for the sacrifices."[112] The general way of a real progress identified a few years earlier[113] took place mainly on a political level. As for the rest, "mere mockery, empty forms of foreign culture with no content at all, soap bubbles which, breaking, disappear and nobody misses them, except maybe the budget eaters; this is wrote the poet somewhere else—the progress we have made!"[114] This fact determined him, while sensing that the structures and superstructures of the things the society of his time accomplished were taking part in the category of the improper ones, because they didn't manage to determine progress and welfare for the whole nation (the peasant's uprisings of those years have proved it), to try and give the concept itself a content suited to the specific of the nation and of the international statute of Romania. His pleading for starting and sustaining progress on both grounds had at its starting point his belief about the irreversible character of the sense of history in an epoch of economic and moral upheaval among peoples.

Notes

1. M. Muşat, I. Ardeleanu, *De la statul geto-dac la statul român unitar,* Bucureşti, 1983, p. 298.

2. St. Zeletin, Burghezia română, *Origina şi rolul ei istoric,* Bucureşti, 1925, p. 99; Amintiri despre jubileul de 40 ani de domnie a M. S. Regelui Carol I, 1866-1906, Bucureşti, 1906, p. 151, 185; C. I. Brătianu, *Câteva amintiri din rostul nostru social în timpul celor din urmă 40 de ani. 1866-1907,* Bucureşti, 1908, pp. 11-15, 17-25.

3. Gh. Platon, *România la sfîrşitul secolului al XIX-lea. Observaţii privind specificul dezvoltării, în Stat, societate, naţiune. Interpretări istorice,* Cluj-Napoca, 1982, p. 129; I. Bulei, *Lumea românească la 1900,* Bucureşti, 1984, p. 38; Anastasie Iordache, *Pe urmele lui Dumitru Brătianu,* Bucureşti, 1984, p. 315.

4. C. Botez, I. Saizu, *Acţiuni ale României după războiul de independenţă.* "De la Plevna politică la Plevna economică", Iaşi 1988, p. 15.

5. Damian Hurezeanu, *Analist al civilizaţiei române moderne, în Eminescu: sens, timp şi devenire istorică,* Eds. Gh. Buzatu, Şt. Lemny, I. Saizu, Iaşi, 1988, p. 660.

6. I. Saizu, Gh. Buzatu, *Rostul românilor în istoria universală,* in idem, pp. 683-707.

7. M. Eminescu, *Fragmentarium,* Ed. Magdalena D. Vatamaniuc, Bucureşti, 1981, p. 52.

8. Ibidem; *Opere,* IX, Bucureşti, 1980, p. 459.

9. Idem, *Fragmentarium . . .* , p. 178.

10. Idem, *Opere,* XII, Bucureşti, 1985, p. 379.

11. Idem, *Opere,* XIII, Bucureşti, 1985, p. 130.

12. Idem, *Opere,* 3, Ed. I. Creţu, Bucureşti, 1938-1939, p. 204.

13. Idem, *Opere,* IX, Bucureşti, 1984, pp. 17-18.

14. C. Botez, I. Saizu, op.cit., p. 55ff.

15. M. Eminescu, *Opere,* XII, p. 431.

16. Idem, *Opere,* IX, p. 242.

17. Idem, *Opere,* 2, Ed. I. Creţu, Bucureşti, 1938-1939, p. 158.

18. Z. Ornea, *Tradiţionalism şi modernitate în deceniul al treilea,* Bucureşti, 1980, p. 301ff.

19. Damian Hurezeanu, op.cit., passim.

20. M. Eminescu, *Opere,* 2, p. 203.

21. Idem, *Opere,* XIII, p. 201.

22. Idem, *Opere,* XI, p. 18.

23. Idem, *Opere,* XII, p. 18.

24. Idem, *Opere,* IX, p. 184.

25. Idem, *Opere,* 3, p. 211.

26. Damian Hurezeanu, op.cit., p. 671.

27. M. Eminescu, *Opere,* XI, pp. 17-18.

28. Ibidem, p. 18.

29. Ibidem.

30. Idem, *Opere,* IX, p. 99.

31. N. Iorga, *Eminescu,* Ed. N. Liu, Iaşi, 1981, p. 289.

32. M. Eminescu, *Opere,* XIII, p. 33.

33. Idem, *Opere,* 2, p. 160.

34. Damian Hurezeanu, op.cit., p. 664.

35. M. Eminescu, *Opere,* 3, p. 69.

36. Idem, *Opere,* XI, p. 41.

37. Idem, *Opere,* XIII, pp. 145-48. Mihaela Carp, I. Saizu, *Eminescu despre primul Congres Economic din România. Opinii şi soluţii, in "Anuarul Centrului de Ştiinţe Sociale,"* Iaşi, 1989, passim.

39. M. Eminescu, *Opere,* XIII, p. 172.

40. Damian Hurezeanu, op.cit., p. 668.

41. M. Eminescu, *Fragmentarium,* p. 154.

42. Ibidem, p. 158.

43. Damian Hurezeanu, op.cit., p. 668.

44. M. Eminescu, *Economia Naţională,* Ed. Vasile C. Nechita, Iaşi, 1983, p. 137.

45. Idem, *Opere,* XIII, p. 33.

46. Idem, *Economia naţională,* p. 263.

47. Idem, *Fragmentarium,* p. 174.

48. Idem, *Icoane vechi şi icoane nouă,* Vălenii de Munte, 1909, p. 15.

49. Idem, *Opere,* IX, p. 173.

50. Idem, *Fragmentarium,* p. 155

51. D. Cantemir, *Congresul Economic din Iaşi in "Asachi,"* III, 1884, 5, p. 109.

52. C. Botez, I. Saizu, op.cit., pp. 66-67.

53. M. Eminescu, *Opere,* 2, p. 203.

54. Mihaela Crap, I. Saizu, A. D. Xenopol şi primul Congres Economic din România (Iaşi, 10-14 octombrie 1882), in "Anuarul Institutului de Istorie şi Arheologie 'A. D. Xenopol' Iaşi," XXVI, 1989, 1, p. 8.

55. "România liberă," 15 octombrie 1882, p. 2; "Naţiunea," 15 octombrie 1882, p. 2.

56. M. Eminescu, *Opere,* XIII, p. 152.

57. Arh. St. Bucureşti, Fond D. C. Butculescu, dosar II/140, f. 1.

58. M. Eminescu, *Opere,* XIII, p. 173.

59. Ibidem.

60. Ibidem, p. 205.

61. Ibidem, p. 356. Ibidem, p. 201

63. Ibidem, p. 202.

64. Ibidem, p. 130.

65. Ibidem, p. 182.

66. Ibidem.

67. Ibidem, p. 189.

68. Ibidem, p. 178.

69. Ibidem, p. 206.

70. Ibidem, pp. 206-207.

71. I. Saizu, Gh. Buzatu, *Sintagma eminesciană "strat de cultură" ca necesitate istorică permanentă, in Eminescu: sens, timp şi devenire istorică,* II, Iaşi, 1990, pp. 205-207.

72. M. Eminescu, *Opere,* XIII, p. 202.

73. Ibidem, p. 201.

74. Ibidem, p. 206.

75. Romulus Scriban, *Istoria economiei politice, a comerciului şi a navigaţiunei României,* Galaţi, 1885, p. 148.

76. "Cooperatorul român," 10 martie 1885, pp. 1-2; C. Hamangiu, *Codul general al României,* II, Bucureşti, 1900, pp. 265-267.

77. "Cooperatorul român," 10 martie 1885, pp. 1-2.

78. M. Eminescu, *Fragmentarium,* p. 233.

79. Idem, *Opere,* IX, p. 146.

80. Ibidem, p. 297.

81. Idem, *Opere,* 2, p. 180.

82. Idem, *Opere,* 3, p. 142.

83. Idem, *Opere,* XII, p. 237.

84. Idem, *Opere,* XIII, p. 33.

85. Idem, *Fragmentarium,* p. 52; *Opere,* IX, p. 459.

86. Damian Hurezeanu, op.cit., pp. 661-662.

87. M. Eminescu, *Opere,* XIII, p. 238.

88. Damian Hurezeanu, op.cit., passim.

89. "Flacăra Iaşului," 27 aprilie 1989, p. 1.

90. M. Eminescu, *Opere,* IX, p. 292.

91. Idem, *Opere,* XIII, p. 292.

92. Idem, *Opere,* XII, p. 135.

93. Ibidem.

94. Damian Hurezeanu, op.cit., pp. 657-658.

95. M. Eminescu, *Opere,* XIII, p. 124.

96. Idem, *Opere,* XI, p. 19.

97. Idem, *Opere,* XIII, p. 172.

98. Idem, *Fragmentarium,* p. 233.

99. Ibidem, p. 74.

100. Ibidem, p. 176.

101. Idem, *Opere,* XIII, p. 87.

102. Ibidem.

103. Idem, *Opere,* 3, pp. 206-207.

104. Idem, *Icoane vechi,* p. 40.

105. Idem, *Opere,* XIII, p. 187.

106. Idem, *Opere,* IX, p. 173.

107. Ibidem, p. 218.

108. Idem, *Opere,* XIII, p. 328.

109. Ibidem, p. 333.

110. Ibidem.

111. Ibidem, p. 328.

112. Ibidem, p. 331.

113. Idem, *Opere,* XI, p. 18.

114. Idem, *Opere,* XII, p. 179.

Alexandru Husar (essay date spring 1998)

SOURCE: Husar, Alexandru. "The Meaning of Civilization in Eminescu's Thinking." *Romanian Civilization* 7, no. 1 (spring 1998): 77-92.

[*In the following essay, Husar elucidates Eminescu's concept of civilization.*]

Regarded as "a lucid man, an intellectual with an acute understanding of political life, a thinker concerned with outlining a social-political system, with clear opinions on foreign policy, a man active in the sphere of public life,"[1] Eminescu compels recognition through his practical way of thinking—quite an original one for a journalist in the political climate between 1876 and 1883.

Eminescu's entrance into journalism in 1873 marked the beginning of "a road taken only by him and which advanced only through his primary thinking and his public positions. It is the path of a philosophy of society; not an abstract society, but Romanian society in 1877 and in the following years—a period whose hallmark was the extraordinarily rapid evolution of social relations, a period of modern development concerning state organization, culture, and material civilization."[2]

We would not, at this point of our discussion, go back to this aspect of his contribution ("the first national contribution on an international level and the bedrock of modern Romanian culture"[3]) if we did not admit that "Eminescu's role in our culture does not have a universal meaning" (Constantin Noica) and, secondly, if we did not agree that "by defining the ideal of progress and civilization, Eminescu asserts very current ideas."[4]

First, what did Eminescu mean by civilization? How did he define civilization in general?

An ordinary term in our times, in its modern usage given by the eighteenth century rationalists, mainly by Voltaire and the French rationalists, a definition drawn on the antithesis between civilization and feudalism, between the Enlightenment and the previous Dark Ages, civilization—as opposed to barbarianism and pointing to a relatively advanced stage in the development of mankind—conveys, philosophically speaking, the active sense of culture and man's universal vocation. Thus, this first idea referred to the relation between man and civilization. In his view, civilization consisted mainly in the natural, organic development of one's powers and faculties. Furthermore, "there is no general human civilization accessible to all people in the same degree or in the same manner. Rather each people has its own civilization, although this involves many elements common to other people as well."[5]

By emphasizing the diversity of civilizations—an idea promoted more and more insistently by anthropological research[6]—Eminescu's thinking proved very accurate. The pragmatic obverse of this idea regarded, on the one hand, the relationship between culture and civilization, and, on the other hand, history, that is the evolution specific to each people. Eminescu took into account and developed both sides of this idea. According to him, culture implied the existence of fundamental works in the field of positive natural sciences; the second way of measuring a nation's degree of culture had in view "the people's skill in substituting natural agents with physical force, in creating and using machines."[7]

The correlative of culture, civilization became a result, a reality derived from it. From this perspective, the degree of civilization reached by a people was not measured, as Eminescu metaphorically put it, "in terms of the number of polished boots, French sentences, and the number of journals, but in terms of one's capacity to make the blind forces of nature submit to man's goals." For "the more powerful is man's sway over wind, water, and steam, so that he makes them his working slaves, the higher his degree of civilization is; the more man masters man, the greater his barbarism."[8]

Thus, civilization incorporates a more complex relation, including both an economic and a social aspect. The determining factor for the civilization of a state, Eminescu pointed out, was economic civilization. Real freedom and economic independence were identical notions in Eminescu's opinion. If a national economy was to subdue nature, it followed that the more rigorous the domination was, the more advanced were the people that exerted its power. The overall result of mankind's power over nature stood for real civilization. Each nation aimed at conquering nature, at reaching the highest degree of dominance."[9]

Hence the meaning ascribed to "the sanctity of work" as a condition for any civilization; the beneficial habit of regular work as a source or requisite of production and welfare, the economic dimension and fundamental factor of civilization. The substance of a nation's life is work. The purpose of work is good living, fortune—which are indeed essential things. But "the wealth of a state lies neither in laws, nor in money, but, again, in labor. By gathering a lot of money in a country where work is absent one will have to pay a napoleon for a day's work." For, as the poet explained, "where manpower is wanting or the quality of production is low, one can hardly speak of a wealthy country."[10]

On 22 December 1876, having just returned to Romania, Eminescu suggested in *Curierul de Iaşi* that work was what lent significance to civilization, or, as he put it, "the substance of civilization can be achieved only through work. Not even journals, laws, academies, or a form of organization similar to the most advanced ones, are able to replace work, and a state of affairs that is not grounded in work is a phantasmagoria which will last a longer or a shorter period, but it will turn into smoke when faced with cold reality."[11]

His arguments were based on a solid principle: "Work is the mainspring of political economics. Only the reality of work, when work is done under circumstances demanded by political economics, with its surplus of *production* over *consumption,* can resist all crises and commotions."[12] What was important was the equilibrium between consumption and production. It was bad when consumption exceeded production. The big secret concerning poverty was, in Eminescu's eyes, the increase in the number of consumers who do nothing to make up for the work of the producers who support them.[13]

Eminescu placed economic activity at the basis of social life, the physical and intellectual work performed by the productive classes; work, for Eminescu, meant, first and foremost, "the production of material goods." As far as the value of the productive classes was concerned, Eminescu, together with the physiocrats, and, to a certain extent with Adam Smith, stressed the importance of the peasant class as being the one which produced the essential material goods."[14]

Influenced by the physiocrats, he did not include commerce in the category of productive activities. Vehemently denouncing "parasitism," he deemed merchants as being parasites. Still, the poet introduced the thesis concerning the importance of productive labor in general, being remarkably aware of its economic implications—the diversification of industrial production, and the intensification of economic activity; in a broader sense, he admitted that "it is not their point of origin which accounts for a people's lasting existence, but rather their work, either physical or spiritual."[15]

Eminescu claimed, more than once, that "the fundamental evil of the country springs from the lack of social organization and consequently from the lack of labor diversification, its reduction to the one-sided exploitation of the land." Eminescu envisioned "a social reorganization meant to defend and to promote work, and to do away with the parasites and superfluous individuals in the domain of public life."[16] In his opinion, "any gain without benefit for the public good is immoral." The source of evil was identified with the phenomenon of regression to a lower social position, or as he put it, "over-multiplying the number of people who live off the labor of the same number of producers."

Eminescu acknowledged that "there is indeed, in a normal state which is decently governed, a compensation for the sacrifices made by people of the lower station"; but, "In other countries, the privileged classes make up for the physical work done by the lower classes through their intellectual activity."[17] Starting from this assumption, Eminescu noticed that "art and science are the offspring of luxury, but they also have a compensatory function. The technological inventions in all fields of modern life, in factories and manufacturing, require a thousand times more exertion than the hands of all those who perform manual labor."

Many critics have carefully focused on these economic aspects in Eminescu's work. Extensive writings, already mentioned, are representative of his economic thinking which sought the fulcrum that validated the importance of work as a source of wealth, as a factor generative of values and guarantee of the establishment of a durable and prosperous society.[18] This paper concerns itself with the sense of work in context, within the general framework of the poet's thinking, and regarding its theoretical implications.

In this respect, work became a determining factor of economic emancipation, the only lever of improvement, and the only means of healing a society; "there is"—the poet clamored—"only one remedy to this end: work. Work, rather than banqueting with the scum of French civilization; work, rather than pornography on the boulevard; work, rather than alms—this is how a nation can thrive."[19] According to Eminescu, "only a strict organization, which would weaken the people's capacity for work and production, an organization that would render social climbing more difficult when it came to public office, and would open, by establishing another economic regime, a market which would protect the manpower engaged in a real working process, could heal the evils society suffers from."[20]

This idea was later explored in all its amplitude and it was based on logic: "There is indeed a single remedy against these evils, but this remedy must be administered very rigorously and exclusively: work, this mechanic correlative of truth; truth, this intellectual correlative of work."[21] Thus, when it came to civilization and its logic, work was significantly important if—as Eminescu wrote in *Timpul* (13 October 1881)— "civilization proper consists in the sum of truths understood and applied by a people. As civilization reaches higher levels, the larger the sum of those truths is."[22]

On the other hand, work acquired a more complex meaning, both social and political, closely related to the very culture it determined: "There can be neither freedom, nor culture without work. One who thinks that by professing a few sentences he has replaced work, and consequently freedom and culture, unknowingly becomes one of the parasites of Romanian society."[23]

Admitting that "there is no real remedy against misery other than work and culture,"[24] Eminescu repeatedly asserted, that "It is work, and only work, that is the spring of freedom and happiness."[25] In many of his articles the poet emphasized the moral value that work had for any civilization; in his eyes, the lack of real culture was equated with the "lack of morality in a higher sense of the word" and, in consequence, he also emphasized the judicial value of labor: "Work is the only creative factor of all rights; finally, earnest work is the only justified thing on this earth."[26]

The relationship between work and culture became a criterion of civilization in Eminescu's analysis. In the modern age, work and culture represented and still represent the terms by which the civilization of a people is measured. Besides its economic basis, work constituted the judicial ground of civilization, and also its ethical underpinning. A close connection between truth, justice, and virtue—in his opinion justice was truth, virtue was truth (an absolute truth, not a relative one)—led to the conclusion that "truth, justice, virtue—all three are so closely interrelated that you might think them as one."[27] Hence, the corollary: "civilization means love of truth, virtue, and justice."[28] Civilization implied a stage in the moral and judicial, not only the economic evolution of a people.

II

Eminescu dealt with the issue of civilization in a more concrete way, and not in abstract, speculative terms. What he referred to "was not modern civilization" in itself, as opposed to past forms of civilization, but a certain hypostasis of modern civilization in a given society. Thus, his thinking had a precise, definite aim: "The phenomena that interested him were Romanian ones; it was these phenomena that captured the attention of the great journalist."[29]

During Eminescu's time, a serious process of internal organization was initiated on the basis and through the elements of civilization that emerged or took shape between 1840-1880. It was a period in which modern Romania was being formed, when modern civilization and culture penetrated the three Romanian provinces, when the question of the assimilation of foreign culture was urgent and topical. The fundamental problems that were raised had to do with the development of Romanian civilization struggling against this historical context—a context which also circumscribed Eminescu's thinking (or what has been called his "practical thinking") as revealed in his journalism, as it was written at a distinct moment in the movement of ideas in Romania. The poet's contribution lay in the fact that he was—as has been pointed out—"the first who saw in the events of the seventh and eighth decades of the last century the crystallization of a civilization, of a coherently articulated state of the society."[30]

Eminescu condemned this civilization which consisted, in his eyes, "in maintaining the external forms of the Western culture" and the incongruity of these forms with the organic development of the country. "The advanced forms of the superficial civilization which have been brought to our territory like an exotic plant are indeed inappropriate,"[31] Eminescu wrote. He thought that "the empty forms of foreign culture were a simulacrum, devoid of substance, nothing more than soap bubbles." He denounced this "French smattering, this infinitesimal civilization, misunderstood and borrowed from foreigners."[32]

His statements were based on two criteria: the first has in view the logic of the evolutionary process, the second, its rhythm. Eminescu asserted that: 1) By introducing forms borrowed from the more advanced civilizations of other nations, the thread of historical development was broken off; 2) The hasty attempt at reaching, without the support offered by culture and material prosperity, the advanced level of Western civilization resulted in a gap between real civilization and its appearances.

Distinguishing between appearance and essence, forms and substance, Eminescu noticed that, dazzled by Western civilization, the past generation thought that by introducing its external forms, its content would also be brought in."[33] Hence the utopian character of this civilization: "Not only one utopia"—as he put it—"but thousands of utopias filled the heads of the past generation, a generation which believed freedom was possible without work, culture without learning, modern organization without analogous economic development."[34]

Aware of both the economic and cultural complexity of this problem, Eminescu acknowledged that "to insert the forms of a foreign civilization where its economic correlative is missing is a futile endeavor."[35] This is because—as the poet explained—"in our country the former economic dependency is unfortunately turning into the economic extermination of that person to whom the place where he works or his level of culture do not offer the same advantages as to his happier neighbor; when competition is given free rein things turn out to be very threatening for the economically weak and for the uneducated."[36]

It was obvious to him that "There is no man of even shallow learning to question the fact that a relatively backward people, brought too soon into contact with a foreign civilization, is in danger of perishing." Eminescu anxiously wrote, explaining with the clear-sightedness of an economist the consequences of this state of things: "Once a Romanian has entered into contact with thousands of people with more energetic economic habits, more selfish, and more developed from a cultural point of view, it is clear that those people have become the hunters and he the prey . . ." Having been forewarned, Eminescu saw the confirmation of this fact abroad: "Each time we think of the development of Romanian economic life," he wrote on 21 October 1882, "we are reminded of an apparently paradoxical idea, yet even truer, asserted by an American economist: 'for a culturally backward country communication with the foreign countries is dangerous.'"[37]

On another occasion, the poet attacked the false belief that the establishment of the external forms of Western culture could supplement for the lack of a solid and substantial indigenous culture, for—Eminescu warned—"an uneducated nation can enjoy the pleasures of civilization, but at the price of degeneration."[38] Hence, a consistent principle of his practical thinking: "It is mathematically certain that whatever is done without a parallel preliminary development of culture is futile, that any real progress takes place not outside, but inside people."[39]

The poet's thinking was receptive to the premises of civilization, more exactly, its generative conditions, on Romanian territory. What Eminescu actually criticized was the fact that "nobody thinks about this. Everyone hopes to benefit from the advantages of foreign civilization, but no one thinks of introducing into the country those cultural conditions in which such results would be self-productive."[40] However, it was "not so much the actual introduction of forms of foreign (imported) civilization that bothered Eminescu, but the fact that, in the given circumstances, the other conditions that would assure an organic assimilation of these forms of civilization, if not of their content as well, were not also introduced.

Eminescu was convinced that "a people's real civilization consists not in the arbitrary enforcement of laws, forms, institutions, labels, clothes, etc., but in the natural development of its own powers, its own faculties." As far as the essence of civilization was concerned, one of the ideas that was frequently and consistently sustained by him concerned "the multidimensional development of people and nations, which represents the goal and the result of real civilization."[41] In Eminescu's opinion, real civilization was that whose supreme value was man, that which made it possible for "all physical and moral abilities to develop through intelligent and combined work. The idea is that all the abilities of a people should be cultivated and that a nation should not be condemned to a single type of work."[42]

Needless to say, such an idea, perhaps one of Eminescu's most valuable ones, had a primordial theoretical support which defined the logical meaning of civilization. On the other hand, the pragmatic obverse of this idea concerned the evolution of society in terms of its exigencies: "When a society such as ours develops new needs, it is also likely to contract new abilities"—Eminescu remarked in his firm, axiomatic style. Steadfast to this principle, he condemned the introduction of a pseudo-civilization through a multiplication of needs but without a parallel evolution of intellectual and economic abilities.[43] What he inevitably meant was the division of labor as a condition of civilization, both economic and social, as well as its direct premise on the cultural plane.

Eminescu obviously also had in mind industrial production. At a certain point, Eminescu saw the "lack of real culture" in the fact that, with the exception of few centers, the Romanian youth was no longer interested in any of the branches of industrial production.[44] The progress of industry implied successive changes in both societal and state responsibilities. The substitution of the physical force of workers with mechanical force, which made it more intellectual, involved a cultural process, but also a primordial economic approach. This approach included encouraging mechanical work, diversifying it, creating it where it was nonexistent, allowing national abilities to apply, each in its own way, to the diversity of productive branches, bringing the nation, agricultural as it still is, to the stage of the division of labor[45] through skillfully combined measures.

Despite the tendencies of estrangement manifested by Romanian industry, Eminescu undoubtedly had in mind the establishment of an indigenous national industry.[46] More than once Eminescu expressed his belief that "we must not remain agricultural, we must become an industrialized nation, to be able at least to meet our needs." "The columns of this paper," he wrote in *Timpul* in 1882, "have been in the past years witnesses to the fact that, within practical limits dictated by experience, I have supported the encouragement and protection of national industry."[47]

In his century, Eminescu was aware of what, in our century, might be necessary in organizing work at the national level. These necessities included: 1) the organization of agricultural labor; 2) the establishment and the protection of industrial work, each equally valued and necessary to protect the national existence of Romania against "the possible dangers from northeastern Europe, (the economic dominance which may come from the West)."[48] It was also true that "defense against the external danger is coupled with the need to assure a real civilization in the historical space of our people and with the principle of nationality which gains more and more ground."[49] Viewing civilization in the light of the

ideas embraced by the *Junimea* cultural society, Eminescu foresaw, in this spirit, first, the creation of the substance, and then of the forms of civilization, not vice versa. "A nation should be in the first place industrial and then have the laws and institutions of industrial nations."

III

The poet's doctrine concerning civilization could be derived from what has been already said. This doctrine is—as has been remarked—the expression of a profound conception about building civilization and culture in a national context. Eminescu emphasizes the importance of the creative capacity of each national community in the process of building a civilization.[50]

Convinced that a nation's real civilization rose out of "that nation's roots and depths and not out of the imitation of foreign habits, languages, and institutions,"[51] Eminescu frequently pointed out: "If there is ever going to be on this earth a real civilization it will be one that will have emerged from the elements of the old civilization." According to him, this implied a law of continuity which, had it been wanting in the development process, would have led to "fragmentarism."[52] It was in this sense that Eminescu severely criticized the hasty imitation of certain foreign "forms." In his opinion, national identity and continuity are assured, not through cultural leaps, but through the evolution of the very substance of civilization.

The idea of organic development (contrary to the so-called theory of "forms without substance"), of willful progress, did not imply stagnation, the elimination of change. The entry of Romanian society into a new evolutionary cycle was a necessity and could not be questioned. Isolation was not a solution in the poet's eyes, rather the cultural community of civilized Europe was "so absolutely necessary" for the Romanian people "that the attempt to weaken it would mean today the paralysis of any progress of our schools and, generally, of the Romanian state."[53]

Thus, while working at *Timpul,* Eminescu relentlessly developed and applied to the contingent reality his old political philosophy outlined at the Iaşi Conference, a philosophy akin to Maiorescu's ideas about the relationship between forms and substance. *Junimea*'s fundamental idea was, as G. Călinescu remarked, the creation of a natural political life, born out of a slow advancement toward progress, by contact with Western civilization,[54] and not by excluding it.

In the dialectical game of the relationship between form and substance it will be obvious for anyone intent on defining the great mystery of existence that this consists of the ongoing revitalization of substance and in the maintenance of the forms. As a particular example, Eminescu, agreeing with *Junimea,* had in mind England "which is the most civilized country in all respects" and which, the poet remarks, "still preserves the old historical forms, always refreshed by the modern spirit, by modern work."[55] This fact does not imply the immutability of forms, which can be always organically and naturally refreshed by the modern spirit and by modern work—without affecting the national identity or what Eminescu called "the nation's soul." On the contrary! Throughout his journalistic work, Eminescu emphasized the authentic modern spirit the way it existed in countries with traditions of modern development and the way he wished it also existed in Romania. What absorbed him were the fundamentals of the modern development processes which were, according to him, work, nation, the productive classes, tradition, etc. Being modern meant for Eminescu acknowledging the option of each national state of building a civilization originating from its own traditions. Real civilization was deeply rooted in national ground. The country's modern development was conceived by Eminescu in such a way that it was determined by conditions and factors specific to the Romanian nation.[56]

In view of this approach, the art of ruling was, in Eminescu's opinion, the art of harmonizing the interests of society because "everything that exists is a result of society: language, spirit, learning, wealth, civilization, and power. The main thing is that these should result from a society named *nation* and not the whole universe."[57] Consequently, it was the civilization which stimulated the shaping of a nation, that is, a people's abilities represented the most authentic civilization for Eminescu. "Besides this," Eminescu argued, "a people's civilization consists mainly in the development of those human pursuits common to all people, rich or poor, great or small; those guiding principles constitute the foundation of the entire life and of all human activity. The more developed these general principles and faculties are, the more civilized that nation is." For the poet concluded, "civilization is not represented only by the intellectual class, but it must encompass all social strata."[58]

Such an idea had with Eminescu a pronounced social implication, which nowadays is profoundly democratic and posed a fundamentally theoretic interest. Admitting that "an uneducated people that gradually but persistently strives to reach a level of civilization, that learns day by day how to assimilate other people's abilities and wisdom does succeed in equalizing the others," Eminescu also admitted a corollary, "the complete correspondence between territory and nation, between physical force and intelligence. Complete harmony: proportionality between the main power and the collateral ones," was in his eyes, "the climax of civilization."[59] Thus, civilization held a very deep meaning for Eminescu. Civilization was seen first as a phenomenon of real amplitude. It implied a relation between "territory" and "nation" and also a relationship between people and their abilities. Within the framework of society, civilization, in its modern sense, implied differences between people and classes in terms of their social role concerning the national potential or the competence of society, more exactly its work. Civilization thus became a total social phenomenon, as Mauss conceived of it, which excluded any one-sided limits, no matter whether this one-sidedness was economically or culturally determined.

Secondly, what was called the "national theoretical model," accounted, in Eminescu's opinion, for the shaping of modern civilization by asserting needs and ideals which stemmed from a national community's specific aspirations. The national theoretical model displays the pluralism of the means of modern development, a pluralism determined by cultural differences and by the existence of different systems of values. It also emphasizes the preeminence of the national and, at the same time, it acknowledges the interplay between "the national and the universal."[60] It thus was rightly assumed that "In spite of certain historical limits which are fully accountable, in many respects Eminescu promoted an amazingly new and correct understanding of civilization, of the relation between the national and the universal that were involved in its building, and of the relation between continuity and discontinuity that marked its evolution."[61]

More than that, "Eminescu is the first among Romanian analysts to perceive through the eyes of a sociologist the consequences of connecting backward societies to modern forms of civilization, of the interaction between areas of civilization." And, surprisingly, Eminescu tackled another side of the problem: what is the objective impact of drawing a backward society into the flux molded by modern Western civilization, and what are the costs implied by the multiplication of the articulations of the worldwide capitalist system? Although, "the poet did not insist on this matter, he only inferred it,"[62] he inferred it with his keen insight, with a vivid sense of evolution, with the premonition of actuality.

Issues concerning methods of development of certain countries desirous of an accelerated progress are much debated nowadays and, consequently, as the new exegetes suggest, Eminescu's approach with regard to development is very topical. Yet, "This does not mean that we artificially relate the Romanian thinker to contemporary ideological and theoretical trends."

Eminescu's doctrine is confirmed by the theory (about the "One-Sided Man") expounded by Herbert Marcuse, a member of the Frankfurt School, or in that of Arnold Toynbee, an English historian and sociologist, about "parallel civilizations." Thus, the thesis of the unity of civilization as being an error of opinion is refuted. Although, Toynbee remarks, "the states of the contemporary world are part of a unique political system, of occidental origin, still considering them as proof for the unity of civilization would be indeed superficial." Besides a few illusions generated by the worldwide success of occidental civilization, especially with respect to material wealth, the error in this conception of a "unity of history," endorsing the opinion that "there is only one civilizing trend, that is ours, and that the others are all subject to it or are lost in deserts of sand"[63] has to do with illusions and prejudices which are subtly signalled.

Studying the contacts between civilizations, both in space and in time, and including the consequences—both positive and negative—of the interplay between contemporary societies, the same profound thinker pointed out that "the insertion of occidental ideals and institutions in non-occidental societies often entails confusing results because 'one man's food is another man's poison.' The attempt at introducing an element of foreign culture by excluding the rest is doomed to fail . . ."[64]

The concept of nation, "a concept specific to European culture, which has spread it all over the world,"[65] represents nowadays "one of the most important and irrefutable issues of political science and of the contemporary historical process."[66] Eminescu's doctrine thus conveyed a fundamental necessity: the development of modern Romanian civilization starting from within the national community and then naturally expanding to other European cultural horizons. By conceiving of civilization in these terms, Eminescu proved that he had, in his time, an important message to convey, maybe not only to the Romanian nation of that time, but to our epoch as well.

Notes

1. M. Gafiţa, "Mihai Eminescu," in *Studii de istorie literară*, Bucureşti, 1979, p. 157.

2. *Ibidem*, p. 197.

3. P. Georgescu, "Eminescu şi contemporanii săi," in *Studii eminesciene*, Bucureşti, 1965, p. 591.

4. Th. Ghideanu, "Mihai Eminescu," in *Istoria filozofiei româneşti*, I, Bucureşti, 1985, p. 593.

5. *Timpul*, VI, 1881, no. 233, 25 October 1881, cf. Mihai Eminescu, "Despre culturš şi artă," Iaşi, 1970, pp. 15-16, edited by D. Irimia.

6. For more details see Clifford Geertz, *Savoir local, savoir global*, Paris, 1986, apud Constantin Schifirneţ, *Civilizaţie modernă şi naţiune*, Bucureşti, 1996, p. 91.

7. M. Eminescu, *Opera politică*, II, Bucureşti, 1941, p. 148.

8. *Antologia gândirii româneşti*, Bucureşti, 1973, p. 558.

9. M. Eminescu, *Fragmentarium*, 1981, p. 154 (manuscript 2257).

10. M. Eminescu, *Opera politică*, I, p. 140.

11. *Ibidem*, pp. 89-99.

12. *Op. cit.*, p. 62.

13. M. Eminescu, *Opere*, XI, Bucureşti, 1984, pp. 148-149.

14. M. Eminescu, *Opera politică*, II, p. 140.

15. M. Eminescu, *Opere*, XI, p. 157.

16. Idem, *Opera politică*, II, pp. 323-324.

17. Idem, *Opera politică*, II, p. 252.

18. D. Vatamaniuc retraces the itinerary of the poet's economic readings and follows the way in which he integrates the ideas of H. C. Cary, J. B. Say, Sismonde de Sismondi, Adam Smith, David Ricardo, Paul Leroy-Baulieu etc. in the laboratory of his own intellectual and journalistic activity (cf. D. Vatamaniuc, *Eminescu*, Bucureşti, 1988, chapter "Jurnal al formării intelectuale").

19. *Ibidem*, p. 52.

20. *Ibidem*, p. 466.

21. *Ibidem*, p. 475 sq and *Opere*, XIII, Bucureşti, 1985, p. 146.

22. *Opere*, XIII, p. 189.

23. *Timpul*, 17 February 1880.

24. *Opere*, XIII, p. 189.

25. Al. Tănase, *Introducere in filozofia culturii*, Bucureşti, 1968, p. 196.

26. *Opere*, XI, p. 290.

27. *Fragmentarium* (manuscript 2257), p. 1117.

28. *Ibidem*.

29. Damian Hurezeanu, "Analist al civilizaţiei române" in *Eminescu—sens, timp şi devenire istorică*, edited by Gh. Buzatu, Şt. Lemny, and I. Saizu, Iaşi, 1989, p. 673.

30. *Ibidem*, pp. 654-659.

31. *Opera politică*, II, p. 555.

32. *Opere*, IV, Bucureşti, 1938, p. 365.

33. *Opere*, IX, pp. 291-292.

34. *Opere*, XI, p. 18.

35. *Opere*, X, p. 187.

36. *Opera politică,* II, p. 203.

37. *Opere,* XIII, p. 193.

38. *Ibidem,* pp. 331-332, 201.

39. *Opera politică,* II, p. 498.

40. *Ibidem,* p. 497.

41. Al. Tănase, *op. cit.,* p. 195.

42. *Antologia gândirii româneşti,* p. 558.

43. *Opere,* XIII, pp. 201-202.

44. *Opere,* III, p. 403.

45. *Opere,* XIII, p. 173.

46. *Curierul de Iaşi,* nos. 64 and 65, 1876.

47. *Opere,* XII, p. 178.

48. *Opera politică,* p. 398.

49. I. Saizu, Gh. Buzatu, "Sintagma eminesciană «strat de cultură», ca necesitate istorică permanentă," in *Eminescu, sens, timp şi devenire istorică,* I, Iaşi, 1990, p. 202.

50. I. Constantin Schifrineţ, *op. cit.,* p. 70.

51. *Opere,* XII, p. 379.

52. *Fragmentarium,* manuscript 228f, f. 148.

53. *Opere,* XI, Bucureşti, 1985, p. 65.

54. G. Călinescu, *Viaţa lui M. Eminescu,* Bucureşti, 1938, pp. 354-355.

55. *Opera politică,* II, p. 247.

56. Constantin Schifrineţ, *op. cit.,* pp. 68-70.

57. *Fragmentarium,* manuscript 2262, Bucureşti, 1981, p. 232.

58. *Federaţiunea,* III, 1870, no. 38; *Opera politică,* I, 34.

59. *Fragmentarium,* manuscript 2255, p. 116.

60. Constantin Schifrineţ, *op. cit.,* p. 71.

61. Al. Tănase, *Introducere in filozofia culturi*i, p. 195.

62. Damian Hurezeanu, *op. cit.,* p. 675.

63. *Panorama des sciences humaines,* sous la direction de Denis Holler, Paris, 1973, p. 607.

64. Arnold J. Toynbee, *Estudio de la Historia,* 3, Compendio IX-XIII, Madrid, 1971, pp. 1368-375.

65. G. Petrillo, *Nazionalismo,* Milan, 1995 cf. E. Chabod, *L'idea di nazione,* Bari, 1972.

66. Guido Ravasi, "Réflexions sur le nationalisme: De la critique de «l'objectivisme aprioriste» à une nouvelle approche du nationalisme," in *Bulletin européen,* no. 10 (569) 1997, p. 14.

FURTHER READING

Criticism

Bantas, Andrei. "The Poetry of Mihai Eminescu: Challenges, Food for Thought." *Synthesis* 16 (1989): 17-24.
    Studies the formal and thematic qualities of Eminescu's poetry.

Bhose, Amita. "Cosmology of Mihail Eminescu." *Cahiers Roumains d'Etudes Litteraires,* no. 2 (1989): 76-85.
    Discusses Eminescu's "cosmology" in relation to the poet's writings.

Ciopraga, Constantin. "The Synthesis of the Romanian Genius." *Romanian Review* 29, no. 3 (1975): 104-07.
    Traces Eminescu's development as a poet and thinker.

Dominte, Constantin. "Mihai Eminescu's 'Of All the Ships': Textual Structure and Extratexual Hypotheses." *Cahiers Roumains d'Etudes Litteraires,* no. 4 (1984): 135-48.
    Provides a very technical formalist study of "Of All the Ships."

Moscaliuc, Mihaela. "On Translating an East European Romantic." *Romanian Civilization* 6, no. 3 (winter 1997-98): 67-72.
    Describes different approaches to translating Eminescu into English.

Niculescu, Alexandru. "Lyric Attitude and Pronominal Structure in the Poetry of Eminescu." In *Literary Style: A Symposium,* edited by Seymour Chatman, pp. 369-80. London and New York: Oxford University Press, 1971.
    Scrutinizes the personal pronoun and its linguistic significance in Eminescu's poetry.

Petrescu, Ioana Emanuela. "The Mystery of a Manuscript." *Romanian Review* 41, no. 1 (1987): 67-70.
    Expounds on the image of a "manuscript of signs" in Eminescu's story "Poor Dionis."

Prut, Constantin. "The Image of Genius." *Romanian Review* 33, no. 12 (1979): 141-46.
    Comments on Gheorghe Anghel's statue of Eminescu.

Serbanescu, Tia. "A Duty of Honour." *Romanian Review* 40, no. 1 (1986): 7-10.

> Documents a conversation with the editor of the thirteenth volume of the standard edition of Eminescu's *Works*.

Tohaneanu, G. I. "'The Desire'—A Possible Comment." *Cahiers Roumains d'Etudes Litteraires,* no. 2 (1989): 123-25.

> Offers a linguistic analysis of Eminescu's poem "The Desire."

Vrăjitaru, Liana. "Translation—A Cultural Bridge." *Romanian Civilization* 6, no. 2 (fall 1997): 91-94.

> Discusses the complexities of translating, particularly from Romanian.

Zancu, Liliana. "Burns, Eminescu, and Whitman: Romantic Nationalism or Xenophobia?" *History of European Ideas* 16, nos. 1-3 (January 1993): 351-57.

> Examines Eminescu, Robert Burns, and Walt Whitman as examples of Romantic poets whose works have enjoyed enduring popularity.

Additional coverage of Eminescu's life and career is contained in the following sources published by the Gale Group: *Literature Resource Center; Nineteenth-Century Literature Criticism,* **Vol. 33.**

How to Use This Index

CMW = St. James Guide to Crime & Mystery Writers
CN = Contemporary Novelists
CP = Contemporary Poets
CPW = Contemporary Popular Writers
CSW = Contemporary Southern Writers
CWD = Contemporary Women Dramatists
CWP = Contemporary Women Poets
CWRI = St. James Guide to Children's Writers
CWW = Contemporary World Writers
DA = DISCovering Authors
DA3 = DISCovering Authors 3.0
DAB = DISCovering Authors: British Edition
DAC = DISCovering Authors: Canadian Edition
DAM = DISCovering Authors: Modules
   DRAM: Dramatists Module; **MST:** Most-studied Authors Module;
   MULT: Multicultural Authors Module; **NOV:** Novelists Module;
   POET: Poets Module; **POP:** Popular Fiction and Genre Authors Module
DFS = Drama for Students
DLB = Dictionary of Literary Biography
DLBD = Dictionary of Literary Biography Documentary Series
DLBY = Dictionary of Literary Biography Yearbook
DNFS = Literature of Developing Nations for Students
EFS = Epics for Students
EXPN = Exploring Novels
EXPP = Exploring Poetry
EXPS = Exploring Short Stories
EW = European Writers
FANT = St. James Guide to Fantasy Writers
FW = Feminist Writers
GFL = Guide to French Literature, Beginnings to 1789, 1798 to the Present
GLL = Gay and Lesbian Literature
HGG = St. James Guide to Horror, Ghost & Gothic Writers
HW = Hispanic Writers
IDFW = International Dictionary of Films and Filmmakers: Writers and Production Artists
IDTP = International Dictionary of Theatre: Playwrights
LAIT = Literature and Its Times
LAW = Latin American Writers
JRDA = Junior DISCovering Authors
MAICYA = Major Authors and Illustrators for Children and Young Adults
MAICYAS = Major Authors and Illustrators for Children and Young Adults Supplement
MAWW = Modern American Women Writers
MJW = Modern Japanese Writers
MTCW = Major 20th-Century Writers
NCFS = Nonfiction Classics for Students
NFS = Novels for Students
PAB = Poets: American and British
PFS = Poetry for Students
RGAL = Reference Guide to American Literature
RGEL = Reference Guide to English Literature
RGSF = Reference Guide to Short Fiction
RGWL = Reference Guide to World Literature
RHW = Twentieth-Century Romance and Historical Writers
SAAS = Something about the Author Autobiography Series
SATA = Something about the Author
SFW = St. James Guide to Science Fiction Writers
SSFS = Short Stories for Students
TCWW = Twentieth-Century Western Writers
WLIT = World Literature and Its Times
WP = World Poets
YABC = Yesterday's Authors of Books for Children
YAW = St. James Guide to Young Adult Writers

Literary Criticism Series
Cumulative Author Index

Andrews, Elton V.
See Pohl, Frederik
Andreyev, Leonid (Nikolaevich)
1871-1919 .... **TCLC 3**
See Andreev, Leonid
See also CA 104; 185
Andric, Ivo 1892-1975 .... **CLC 8; SSC 36; TCLC 135**
See also CA 81-84; 57-60; CANR 43, 60; CDWLB 4; DLB 147; EW 11; EWL 3; MTCW 1; RGSF 2; RGWL 2, 3
Androvar
See Prado (Calvo), Pedro
Angelique, Pierre
See Bataille, Georges
Angell, Roger 1920- .... **CLC 26**
See also CA 57-60; CANR 13, 44, 70; DLB 171, 185
Angelou, Maya 1928- ... **BLC 1; CLC 12, 35, 64, 77, 155; PC 32; WLCS**
See also AAYA 7, 20; AMWS 4; BPFB 1; BW 2, 3; BYA 2; CA 65-68; CANR 19, 42, 65, 111; CDALBS; CLR 53; CP 7; CPW; CSW; CWP; DA; DA3; DAB; DAC; DAM MST, MULT, POET, POP; DLB 38; EWL 3; EXPN; EXPP; LAIT 4; MAICYA 2; MAICYAS 1; MAWW; MTCW 1, 2; NCFS 2; NFS 2; PFS 2, 3; RGAL 4; SATA 49, 136; WYA; YAW
Angouleme, Marguerite d'
See de Navarre, Marguerite
Anna Comnena 1083-1153 .... **CMLC 25**
Annensky, Innokenty (Fyodorovich)
1856-1909 .... **TCLC 14**
See also CA 110; 155; EWL 3
Annunzio, Gabriele d'
See D'Annunzio, Gabriele
Anodos
See Coleridge, Mary E(lizabeth)
Anon, Charles Robert
See Pessoa, Fernando (Antonio Nogueira)
Anouilh, Jean (Marie Lucien Pierre)
1910-1987 . **CLC 1, 3, 8, 13, 40, 50; DC 8, 21**
See also CA 17-20R; 123; CANR 32; DAM DRAM; DFS 9, 10; EW 13; EWL 3; GFL 1789 to the Present; MTCW 1, 2; RGWL 2, 3; TWA
Anthony, Florence
See Ai
Anthony, John
See Ciardi, John (Anthony)
Anthony, Peter
See Shaffer, Anthony (Joshua); Shaffer, Peter (Levin)
Anthony, Piers 1934- .... **CLC 35**
See also AAYA 11, 48; BYA 7; CA 21-24R; CAAE 200; CANR 28, 56, 73, 102; CPW; DAM POP; DLB 8; FANT; MAICYA 2; MAICYAS 1; MTCW 1, 2; SAAS 22; SATA 84; SATA-Essay 129; SFW 4; SUFW 1, 2; YAW
Anthony, Susan B(rownell)
1820-1906 .... **TCLC 84**
See also CA 211; FW
Antiphon c. 480B.C.-c. 411B.C. .... **CMLC 55**
Antoine, Marc
See Proust, (Valentin-Louis-George-Eugene) Marcel
Antoninus, Brother
See Everson, William (Oliver)
Antonioni, Michelangelo 1912- .... **CLC 20, 144**
See also CA 73-76; CANR 45, 77
Antschel, Paul 1920-1970
See Celan, Paul
See also CA 85-88; CANR 33, 61; MTCW 1

Anwar, Chairil 1922-1949 .... **TCLC 22**
See Chairil Anwar
See also CA 121; RGWL 3
Anzaldua, Gloria (Evanjelina)
1942- .... **HLCS 1**
See also CA 175; CSW; CWP; DLB 122; FW; RGAL 4
Apess, William 1798-1839(?) .... **NCLC 73; NNAL**
See also DAM MULT; DLB 175, 243
Apollinaire, Guillaume 1880-1918 .... **PC 7; TCLC 3, 8, 51**
See Kostrowitzki, Wilhelm Apollinaris de
See also CA 152; DAM POET; DLB 258; EW 9; EWL 3; GFL 1789 to the Present; MTCW 1; RGWL 2, 3; TWA; WP
Apollonius of Rhodes
See Apollonius Rhodius
See also AW 1; RGWL 2, 3
Apollonius Rhodius c. 300B.C.-c. 220B.C. .... **CMLC 28**
See Apollonius of Rhodes
See also DLB 176
Appelfeld, Aharon 1932- ... **CLC 23, 47; SSC 42**
See also CA 112; 133; CANR 86; CWW 2; EWL 3; RGSF 2
Apple, Max (Isaac) 1941- .... **CLC 9, 33; SSC 50**
See also CA 81-84; CANR 19, 54; DLB 130
Appleman, Philip (Dean) 1926- .... **CLC 51**
See also CA 13-16R; CAAS 18; CANR 6, 29, 56
Appleton, Lawrence
See Lovecraft, H(oward) P(hillips)
Apteryx
See Eliot, T(homas) S(tearns)
Apuleius, (Lucius Madaurensis)
125(?)-175(?) .... **CMLC 1**
See also AW 2; CDWLB 1; DLB 211; RGWL 2, 3; SUFW
Aquin, Hubert 1929-1977 .... **CLC 15**
See also CA 105; DLB 53; EWL 3
Aquinas, Thomas 1224(?)-1274 ..... **CMLC 33**
See also DLB 115; EW 1; TWA
Aragon, Louis 1897-1982 .... **CLC 3, 22; TCLC 123**
See also CA 69-72; 108; CANR 28, 71; DAM NOV, POET; DLB 72, 258; EW 11; EWL 3; GFL 1789 to the Present; GLL 2; LMFS 2; MTCW 1, 2; RGWL 2, 3
Arany, Janos 1817-1882 .... **NCLC 34**
Aranyos, Kakay 1847-1910
See Mikszath, Kalman
Arbuthnot, John 1667-1735 .... **LC 1**
See also DLB 101
Archer, Herbert Winslow
See Mencken, H(enry) L(ouis)
Archer, Jeffrey (Howard) 1940- .... **CLC 28**
See also AAYA 16; BEST 89:3; BPFB 1; CA 77-80; CANR 22, 52, 95; CPW; DA3; DAM POP; INT CANR-22
Archer, Jules 1915- .... **CLC 12**
See also CA 9-12R; CANR 6, 69; SAAS 5; SATA 4, 85
Archer, Lee
See Ellison, Harlan (Jay)
Archilochus c. 7th cent. B.C.- .... **CMLC 44**
See also DLB 176
Arden, John 1930- .... **CLC 6, 13, 15**
See also BRWS 2; CA 13-16R; CAAS 4; CANR 31, 65, 67; CBD; CD 5; DAM DRAM; DFS 9; DLB 13, 245; EWL 3; MTCW 1

Arenas, Reinaldo 1943-1990 .. **CLC 41; HLC 1**
See also CA 124; 128; 133; CANR 73, 106; DAM MULT; DLB 145; EWL 3; GLL 2; HW 1; LAW; LAWS 1; MTCW 1; RGSF 2; RGWL 3; WLIT 1
Arendt, Hannah 1906-1975 .... **CLC 66, 98**
See also CA 17-20R; 61-64; CANR 26, 60; DLB 242; MTCW 1, 2
Aretino, Pietro 1492-1556 .... **LC 12**
See also RGWL 2, 3
Arghezi, Tudor .... **CLC 80**
See Theodorescu, Ion N.
See also CA 167; CDWLB 4; DLB 220; EWL 3
Arguedas, Jose Maria 1911-1969 .... **CLC 10, 18; HLCS 1**
See also CA 89-92; CANR 73; DLB 113; EWL 3; HW 1; LAW; RGWL 2, 3; WLIT 1
Argueta, Manlio 1936- .... **CLC 31**
See also CA 131; CANR 73; CWW 2; DLB 145; EWL 3; HW 1; RGWL 3
Arias, Ron(ald Francis) 1941- .... **HLC 1**
See also CA 131; CANR 81; DAM MULT; DLB 82; HW 1, 2; MTCW 2
Ariosto, Ludovico 1474-1533 ... **LC 6, 87; PC 42**
See also EW 2; RGWL 2, 3
Aristides
See Epstein, Joseph
Aristophanes 450B.C.-385B.C. .... **CMLC 4, 51; DC 2; WLCS**
See also AW 1; CDWLB 1; DA; DA3; DAB; DAC; DAM DRAM, MST; DFS 10; DLB 176; LMFS 1; RGWL 2, 3; TWA
Aristotle 384B.C.-322B.C. .... **CMLC 31; WLCS**
See also AW 1; CDWLB 1; DA; DA3; DAB; DAC; DAM MST; DLB 176; RGWL 2, 3; TWA
Arlt, Roberto (Godofredo Christophersen)
1900-1942 .... **HLC 1; TCLC 29**
See also CA 123; 131; CANR 67; DAM MULT; EWL 3; HW 1, 2; LAW
Armah, Ayi Kwei 1939- . **BLC 1; CLC 5, 33, 136**
See also AFW; BW 1; CA 61-64; CANR 21, 64; CDWLB 3; CN 7; DAM MULT, POET; DLB 117; EWL 3; MTCW 1; WLIT 2
Armatrading, Joan 1950- .... **CLC 17**
See also CA 114; 186
Armitage, Frank
See Carpenter, John (Howard)
Armstrong, Jeannette (C.) 1948- .... **NNAL**
See also CA 149; CCA 1; CN 7; DAC; SATA 102
Arnette, Robert
See Silverberg, Robert
Arnim, Achim von (Ludwig Joachim von Arnim) 1781-1831 ..... **NCLC 5; SSC 29**
See also DLB 90
Arnim, Bettina von 1785-1859 ...... **NCLC 38, 123**
See also DLB 90; RGWL 2, 3
Arnold, Matthew 1822-1888 ..... **NCLC 6, 29, 89, 126; PC 5; WLC**
See also BRW 5; CDBLB 1832-1890; DA; DAB; DAC; DAM MST, POET; DLB 32, 57; EXPP; PAB; PFS 2; TEA; WP
Arnold, Thomas 1795-1842 .... **NCLC 18**
See also DLB 55
Arnow, Harriette (Louisa) Simpson
1908-1986 .... **CLC 2, 7, 18**
See also BPFB 1; CA 9-12R; 118; CANR 14; DLB 6; FW; MTCW 1, 2; RHW; SATA 42; SATA-Obit 47

Arouet, Francois-Marie
See Voltaire

Arp, Hans
See Arp, Jean

Arp, Jean 1887-1966 .... **CLC 5; TCLC 115**
See also CA 81-84; 25-28R; CANR 42, 77;
EW 10

Arrabal
See Arrabal, Fernando

Arrabal, Fernando 1932- ... **CLC 2, 9, 18, 58**
See also CA 9-12R; CANR 15; EWL 3;
LMFS 2

Arreola, Juan Jose 1918-2001 .... **CLC 147;**
HLC 1; SSC 38
See also CA 113; 131; 200; CANR 81;
DAM MULT; DLB 113; DNFS 2; EWL
3; HW 1, 2; LAW; RGSF 2

Arrian c. 89(?)-c. 155(?) .... **CMLC 43**
See also DLB 176

Arrick, Fran .... **CLC 30**
See Gaberman, Judie Angell
See also BYA 6

Arriey, Richmond
See Delany, Samuel R(ay), Jr.

Artaud, Antonin (Marie Joseph)
1896-1948 .... **DC 14; TCLC 3, 36**
See also CA 104; 149; DA3; DAM DRAM;
DLB 258; EW 11; EWL 3; GFL 1789 to
the Present; MTCW 1; RGWL 2, 3

Arthur, Ruth M(abel) 1905-1979 ..... **CLC 12**
See also CA 9-12R; 85-88; CANR 4; CWRI
5; SATA 7, 26

Artsybashev, Mikhail (Petrovich)
1878-1927 .... **TCLC 31**
See also CA 170

Arundel, Honor (Morfydd)
1919-1973 .... **CLC 17**
See also CA 21-22; 41-44R; CAP 2; CLR
35; CWRI 5; SATA 4; SATA-Obit 24

Arzner, Dorothy 1900-1979 .... **CLC 98**

Asch, Sholem 1880-1957 .... **TCLC 3**
See also CA 105; EWL 3; GLL 2

Ash, Shalom
See Asch, Sholem

Ashbery, John (Lawrence) 1927- .. **CLC 2, 3,**
4, 6, 9, 13, 15, 25, 41, 77, 125; PC 26
See Berry, Jonas
See also AMWS 3; CA 5-8R; CANR 9, 37,
66, 102; CP 7; DA3; DAM POET; DLB
5, 165; DLBY 1981; EWL 3; INT
CANR-9; MTCW 1, 2; PAB; PFS 11;
RGAL 4; WP

Ashdown, Clifford
See Freeman, R(ichard) Austin

Ashe, Gordon
See Creasey, John

Ashton-Warner, Sylvia (Constance)
1908-1984 .... **CLC 19**
See also CA 69-72; 112; CANR 29; MTCW
1, 2

Asimov, Isaac 1920-1992 ..... **CLC 1, 3, 9, 19,**
26, 76, 92
See also AAYA 13; BEST 90:2; BPFB 1;
BYA 4, 6, 7, 9; CA 1-4R; 137; CANR 2,
19, 36, 60; CLR 12, 79; CMW 4; CPW;
DA3; DAM POP; DLB 8; DLBY 1992;
INT CANR-19; JRDA; LAIT 5; LMFS 2;
MAICYA 1, 2; MTCW 1, 2; RGAL 4;
SATA 1, 26, 74; SCFW 2; SFW 4; SSFS
17; TUS; YAW

Askew, Anne 1521(?)-1546 .... **LC 81**
See also DLB 136

Assis, Joaquim Maria Machado de
See Machado de Assis, Joaquim Maria

Astell, Mary 1666-1731 .... **LC 68**
See also DLB 252; FW

Astley, Thea (Beatrice May) 1925- .. **CLC 41**
See also CA 65-68; CANR 11, 43, 78; CN
7; DLB 289; EWL 3

Astley, William 1855-1911
See Warung, Price

Aston, James
See White, T(erence) H(anbury)

Asturias, Miguel Angel 1899-1974 .... **CLC 3,**
8, 13; HLC 1
See also CA 25-28; 49-52; CANR 32; CAP
2; CDWLB 3; DA3; DAM MULT, NOV;
DLB 113; EWL 3; HW 1; LAW; LMFS
2; MTCW 1, 2; RGWL 2, 3; WLIT 1

Atares, Carlos Saura
See Saura (Atares), Carlos

Athanasius c. 295-c. 373 .... **CMLC 48**

Atheling, William
See Pound, Ezra (Weston Loomis)

Atheling, William, Jr.
See Blish, James (Benjamin)

Atherton, Gertrude (Franklin Horn)
1857-1948 .... **TCLC 2**
See also CA 104; 155; DLB 9, 78, 186;
HGG; RGAL 4; SUFW 1; TCWW 2

Atherton, Lucius
See Masters, Edgar Lee

Atkins, Jack
See Harris, Mark

Atkinson, Kate 1951- .... **CLC 99**
See also CA 166; CANR 101; DLB 267

Attaway, William (Alexander)
1911-1986 .... **BLC 1; CLC 92**
See also BW 2, 3; CA 143; CANR 82;
DAM MULT; DLB 76

Atticus
See Fleming, Ian (Lancaster); Wilson,
(Thomas) Woodrow

Atwood, Margaret (Eleanor) 1939- ... **CLC 2,**
3, 4, 8, 13, 15, 25, 44, 84, 135; PC 8;
SSC 2, 46; WLC
See also AAYA 12, 47; AMWS 13; BEST
89:2; BPFB 1; CA 49-52; CANR 3, 24,
33, 59, 95; CN 7; CP 7; CPW; CWP; DA;
DA3; DAB; DAC; DAM MST, NOV,
POET; DLB 53, 251; EWL 3; EXPN; FW;
INT CANR-24; LAIT 5; MTCW 1, 2;
NFS 4, 12, 13, 14; PFS 7; RGSF 2; SATA
50; SSFS 3, 13; TWA; YAW

Aubigny, Pierre d'
See Mencken, H(enry) L(ouis)

Aubin, Penelope 1685-1731(?) .... **LC 9**
See also DLB 39

Auchincloss, Louis (Stanton) 1917- .. **CLC 4,**
6, 9, 18, 45; SSC 22
See also AMWS 4; CA 1-4R; CANR 6, 29,
55, 87; CN 7; DAM NOV; DLB 2, 244;
DLBY 1980; EWL 3; INT CANR-29;
MTCW 1; RGAL 4

Auden, W(ystan) H(ugh) 1907-1973 . **CLC 1,**
2, 3, 4, 6, 9, 11, 14, 43, 123; PC 1;
WLC
See also AAYA 18; AMWS 2; BRW 7;
BRWR 1; CA 9-12R; 45-48; CANR 5, 61,
105; CDBLB 1914-1945; DA; DA3;
DAB; DAC; DAM DRAM, MST, POET;
DLB 10, 20; EWL 3; EXPP; MTCW 1, 2;
PAB; PFS 1, 3, 4, 10; TUS; WP

Audiberti, Jacques 1900-1965 .... **CLC 38**
See also CA 25-28R; DAM DRAM; EWL 3

Audubon, John James 1785-1851 . **NCLC 47**
See also ANW; DLB 248

Auel, Jean M(arie) 1936- .... **CLC 31, 107**
See also AAYA 7, 51; BEST 90:4; BPFB 1;
CA 103; CANR 21, 64, 115; CPW; DA3;
DAM POP; INT CANR-21; NFS 11;
RHW; SATA 91

Auerbach, Erich 1892-1957 .... **TCLC 43**
See also CA 118; 155; EWL 3

Augier, Emile 1820-1889 .... **NCLC 31**
See also DLB 192; GFL 1789 to the Present

August, John
See De Voto, Bernard (Augustine)

Augustine, St. 354-430 .... **CMLC 6; WLCS**
See also DA; DA3; DAB; DAC; DAM
MST; DLB 115; EW 1; RGWL 2, 3

Aunt Belinda
See Braddon, Mary Elizabeth

Aunt Weedy
See Alcott, Louisa May

Aurelius
See Bourne, Randolph S(illiman)

Aurelius, Marcus 121-180 .... **CMLC 45**
See Marcus Aurelius
See also RGWL 2, 3

Aurobindo, Sri
See Ghose, Aurabinda

Aurobindo Ghose
See Ghose, Aurabinda

Austen, Jane 1775-1817 ...... **NCLC 1, 13, 19,**
33, 51, 81, 95, 119; WLC
See also AAYA 19; BRW 4; BRWC 1;
BRWR 2; BYA 3; CDBLB 1789-1832;
DA; DA3; DAB; DAC; DAM MST, NOV;
DLB 116; EXPN; LAIT 2; LATS 1; LMFS
1; NFS 1, 14, 18; TEA; WLIT 3; WYAS
1

Auster, Paul 1947- .... **CLC 47, 131**
See also AMWS 12; CA 69-72; CANR 23,
52, 75; CMW 4; CN 7; DA3; DLB 227;
MTCW 1; SUFW 2

Austin, Frank
See Faust, Frederick (Schiller)
See also TCWW 2

Austin, Mary (Hunter) 1868-1934 . **TCLC 25**
See Stairs, Gordon
See also ANW; CA 109; 178; DLB 9, 78,
206, 221, 275; FW; TCWW 2

Averroes 1126-1198 .... **CMLC 7**
See also DLB 115

Avicenna 980-1037 .... **CMLC 16**
See also DLB 115

Avison, Margaret 1918- .... **CLC 2, 4, 97**
See also CA 17-20R; CP 7; DAC; DAM
POET; DLB 53; MTCW 1

Axton, David
See Koontz, Dean R(ay)

Ayckbourn, Alan 1939- ...... **CLC 5, 8, 18, 33,**
74; DC 13
See also BRWS 5; CA 21-24R; CANR 31,
59, 118; CBD; CD 5; DAB; DAM DRAM;
DFS 7; DLB 13, 245; EWL 3; MTCW 1,
2

Aydy, Catherine
See Tennant, Emma (Christina)

Ayme, Marcel (Andre) 1902-1967 ... **CLC 11;**
SSC 41
See also CA 89-92; CANR 67; CLR 25;
DLB 72; EW 12; EWL 3; GFL 1789 to
the Present; RGSF 2; RGWL 2, 3; SATA
91

Ayrton, Michael 1921-1975 .... **CLC 7**
See also CA 5-8R; 61-64; CANR 9, 21

Aytmatov, Chingiz
See Aitmatov, Chingiz (Torekulovich)
See also EWL 3

Azorin .... **CLC 11**
See Martinez Ruiz, Jose
See also EW 9; EWL 3

Azuela, Mariano 1873-1952 .. **HLC 1; TCLC**
3
See also CA 104; 131; CANR 81; DAM
MULT; EWL 3; HW 1, 2; LAW; MTCW
1, 2

Ba, Mariama 1929-1981 .... **BLCS**
See also AFW; BW 2; CA 141; CANR 87;
DNFS 2; WLIT 2

Baastad, Babbis Friis
See Friis-Baastad, Babbis Ellinor

Bab
See Gilbert, W(illiam) S(chwenck)

Babbis, Eleanor
See Friis-Baastad, Babbis Ellinor
Babel, Isaac
See Babel, Isaak (Emmanuilovich)
See also EW 11; SSFS 10
Babel, Isaak (Emmanuilovich)
1894-1941(?) .... **SSC 16; TCLC 2, 13**
See Babel, Isaac
See also CA 104; 155; CANR 113; DLB
272; EWL 3; MTCW 1; RGSF 2; RGWL
2, 3; TWA
Babits, Mihaly 1883-1941 .... **TCLC 14**
See also CA 114; CDWLB 4; DLB 215;
EWL 3
Babur 1483-1530 .... **LC 18**
Babylas 1898-1962
See Ghelderode, Michel de
Baca, Jimmy Santiago 1952- . **HLC 1; PC 41**
See also CA 131; CANR 81, 90; CP 7;
DAM MULT; DLB 122; HW 1, 2
Baca, Jose Santiago
See Baca, Jimmy Santiago
Bacchelli, Riccardo 1891-1985 .... **CLC 19**
See also CA 29-32R; 117; DLB 264; EWL
3
Bach, Richard (David) 1936- .... **CLC 14**
See also AITN 1; BEST 89:2; BPFB 1; BYA
5; CA 9-12R; CANR 18, 93; CPW; DAM
NOV, POP; FANT; MTCW 1; SATA 13
Bache, Benjamin Franklin
1769-1798 .... **LC 74**
See also DLB 43
Bachelard, Gaston 1884-1962 ...... **TCLC 128**
See also CA 97-100; 89-92; GFL 1789 to
the Present
Bachman, Richard
See King, Stephen (Edwin)
Bachmann, Ingeborg 1926-1973 .... **CLC 69**
See also CA 93-96; 45-48; CANR 69; DLB
85; EWL 3; RGWL 2, 3
Bacon, Francis 1561-1626 .... **LC 18, 32**
See also BRW 1; CDBLB Before 1660;
DLB 151, 236, 252; RGEL 2; TEA
Bacon, Roger 1214(?)-1294 .... **CMLC 14**
See also DLB 115
Bacovia, George 1881-1957 .... **TCLC 24**
See Vasiliu, Gheorghe
See also CDWLB 4; DLB 220; EWL 3
Badanes, Jerome 1937- .... **CLC 59**
Bagehot, Walter 1826-1877 .... **NCLC 10**
See also DLB 55
Bagnold, Enid 1889-1981 .... **CLC 25**
See also BYA 2; CA 5-8R; 103; CANR 5,
40; CBD; CWD; CWRI 5; DAM DRAM;
DLB 13, 160, 191, 245; FW; MAICYA 1,
2; RGEL 2; SATA 1, 25
Bagritsky, Eduard .... **TCLC 60**
See Dzyubin, Eduard Georgievich
Bagrjana, Elisaveta
See Belcheva, Elisaveta Lyubomirova
Bagryana, Elisaveta .... **CLC 10**
See Belcheva, Elisaveta Lyubomirova
See also CA 178; CDWLB 4; DLB 147;
EWL 3
Bailey, Paul 1937- .... **CLC 45**
See also CA 21-24R; CANR 16, 62; CN 7;
DLB 14, 271; GLL 2
Baillie, Joanna 1762-1851 .... **NCLC 71**
See also DLB 93; RGEL 2
Bainbridge, Beryl (Margaret) 1934- . **CLC 4,
5, 8, 10, 14, 18, 22, 62, 130**
See also BRWS 6; CA 21-24R; CANR 24,
55, 75, 88; CN 7; DAM NOV; DLB 14,
231; EWL 3; MTCW 1, 2
Baker, Carlos (Heard)
1909-1987 .... **TCLC 119**
See also CA 5-8R; 122; CANR 3, 63; DLB
103

Baker, Elliott 1922- .... **CLC 8**
See also CA 45-48; CANR 2, 63; CN 7
Baker, Jean H. .... **TCLC 3, 10**
See Russell, George William
Baker, Nicholson 1957- .... **CLC 61, 165**
See also AMWS 13; CA 135; CANR 63,
120; CN 7; CPW; DA3; DAM POP; DLB
227
Baker, Ray Stannard 1870-1946 .... **TCLC 47**
See also CA 118
Baker, Russell (Wayne) 1925- .... **CLC 31**
See also BEST 89:4; CA 57-60; CANR 11,
41, 59; MTCW 1, 2
Bakhtin, M.
See Bakhtin, Mikhail Mikhailovich
Bakhtin, M. M.
See Bakhtin, Mikhail Mikhailovich
Bakhtin, Mikhail
See Bakhtin, Mikhail Mikhailovich
Bakhtin, Mikhail Mikhailovich
1895-1975 .... **CLC 83**
See also CA 128; 113; DLB 242; EWL 3
Bakshi, Ralph 1938(?)- .... **CLC 26**
See also CA 112; 138; IDFW 3
Bakunin, Mikhail (Alexandrovich)
1814-1876 .... **NCLC 25, 58**
See also DLB 277
Baldwin, James (Arthur) 1924-1987 . **BLC 1;
CLC 1, 2, 3, 4, 5, 8, 13, 15, 17, 42, 50,
67, 90, 127; DC 1; SSC 10, 33; WLC**
See also AAYA 4, 34; AFAW 1, 2; AMWR
2; AMWS 1; BPFB 1; BW 1; CA 1-4R;
124; CABS 1; CAD; CANR 3, 24;
CDALB 1941-1968; CPW; DA; DA3;
DAB; DAC; DAM MST, MULT, NOV,
POP; DFS 11, 15; DLB 2, 7, 33, 249, 278;
DLBY 1987; EWL 3; EXPS; LAIT 5;
MTCW 1, 2; NCFS 4; NFS 4; RGAL 4;
RGSF 2; SATA 9; SATA-Obit 54; SSFS
2, 18; TUS
Bale, John 1495-1563 .... **LC 62**
See also DLB 132; RGEL 2; TEA
Ball, Hugo 1886-1927 .... **TCLC 104**
Ballard, J(ames) G(raham) 1930- . **CLC 3, 6,
14, 36, 137; SSC 1, 53**
See also AAYA 3, 52; BRWS 5; CA 5-8R;
CANR 15, 39, 65, 107; CN 7; DA3; DAM
NOV, POP; DLB 14, 207, 261; EWL 3;
HGG; MTCW 1, 2; NFS 8; RGEL 2;
RGSF 2; SATA 93; SFW 4
Balmont, Konstantin (Dmitriyevich)
1867-1943 .... **TCLC 11**
See also CA 109; 155; EWL 3
Baltausis, Vincas 1847-1910
See Mikszath, Kalman
Balzac, Honore de 1799-1850 ... **NCLC 5, 35,
53; SSC 5, 59; WLC**
See also DA; DA3; DAB; DAC; DAM
MST, NOV; DLB 119; EW 5; GFL 1789
to the Present; LMFS 1; RGSF 2; RGWL
2, 3; SSFS 10; SUFW; TWA
Bambara, Toni Cade 1939-1995 .... **BLC 1;
CLC 19, 88; SSC 35; TCLC 116;
WLCS**
See also AAYA 5, 49; AFAW 2; AMWS 11;
BW 2, 3; BYA 12, 14; CA 29-32R; 150;
CANR 24, 49, 81; CDALBS; DA; DA3;
DAC; DAM MST, MULT; DLB 38, 218;
EXPS; MTCW 1, 2; RGAL 4; RGSF 2;
SATA 112; SSFS 4, 7, 12
Bamdad, A.
See Shamlu, Ahmad
Bamdad, Alef
See Shamlu, Ahmad
Banat, D. R.
See Bradbury, Ray (Douglas)
Bancroft, Laura
See Baum, L(yman) Frank

Banim, John 1798-1842 .... **NCLC 13**
See also DLB 116, 158, 159; RGEL 2
Banim, Michael 1796-1874 .... **NCLC 13**
See also DLB 158, 159
Banjo, The
See Paterson, A(ndrew) B(arton)
Banks, Iain
See Banks, Iain M(enzies)
Banks, Iain M(enzies) 1954- .... **CLC 34**
See also CA 123; 128; CANR 61, 106; DLB
194, 261; EWL 3; HGG; INT 128; SFW 4
Banks, Lynne Reid .... **CLC 23**
See Reid Banks, Lynne
See also AAYA 6; BYA 7; CLR 86
Banks, Russell (Earl) 1940- ...... **CLC 37, 72;
SSC 42**
See also AAYA 45; AMWS 5; CA 65-68;
CAAS 15; CANR 19, 52, 73, 118; CN 7;
DLB 130, 278; EWL 3; NFS 13
Banville, John 1945- .... **CLC 46, 118**
See also CA 117; 128; CANR 104; CN 7;
DLB 14, 271; INT 128
Banville, Theodore (Faullain) de
1832-1891 .... **NCLC 9**
See also DLB 217; GFL 1789 to the Present
Baraka, Amiri 1934- .... **BLC 1; CLC 1, 2, 3,
5, 10, 14, 33, 115; DC 6; PC 4; WLCS**
See Jones, LeRoi
See also AFAW 1, 2; AMWS 2; BW 2, 3;
CA 21-24R; CABS 3; CAD; CANR 27,
38, 61; CD 5; CDALB 1941-1968; CP 7;
CPW; DA; DA3; DAC; DAM MST,
MULT, POET, POP; DFS 3, 11, 16; DLB
5, 7, 16, 38; DLBD 8; EWL 3; MTCW 1,
2; PFS 9; RGAL 4; TUS; WP
Baratynsky, Evgenii Abramovich
1800-1844 .... **NCLC 103**
See also DLB 205
Barbauld, Anna Laetitia
1743-1825 .... **NCLC 50**
See also DLB 107, 109, 142, 158; RGEL 2
Barbellion, W. N. P. .... **TCLC 24**
See Cummings, Bruce F(rederick)
Barber, Benjamin R. 1939- .... **CLC 141**
See also CA 29-32R; CANR 12, 32, 64, 119
Barbera, Jack (Vincent) 1945- .... **CLC 44**
See also CA 110; CANR 45
Barbey d'Aurevilly, Jules-Amedee
1808-1889 .... **NCLC 1; SSC 17**
See also DLB 119; GFL 1789 to the Present
Barbour, John c. 1316-1395 .... **CMLC 33**
See also DLB 146
Barbusse, Henri 1873-1935 .... **TCLC 5**
See also CA 105; 154; DLB 65; EWL 3;
RGWL 2, 3
Barclay, Bill
See Moorcock, Michael (John)
Barclay, William Ewert
See Moorcock, Michael (John)
Barea, Arturo 1897-1957 .... **TCLC 14**
See also CA 111; 201
Barfoot, Joan 1946- .... **CLC 18**
See also CA 105
Barham, Richard Harris
1788-1845 .... **NCLC 77**
See also DLB 159
Baring, Maurice 1874-1945 .... **TCLC 8**
See also CA 105; 168; DLB 34; HGG
Baring-Gould, Sabine 1834-1924 ... **TCLC 88**
See also DLB 156, 190
Barker, Clive 1952- .... **CLC 52; SSC 53**
See also AAYA 10; BEST 90:3; BPFB 1;
CA 121; 129; CANR 71, 111; CPW; DA3;
DAM POP; DLB 261; HGG; INT 129;
MTCW 1, 2; SUFW 2
Barker, George Granville
1913-1991 .... **CLC 8, 48**
See also CA 9-12R; 135; CANR 7, 38;
DAM POET; DLB 20; EWL 3; MTCW 1

Barker, Harley Granville
See Granville-Barker, Harley
See also DLB 10

Barker, Howard 1946- .... **CLC 37**
See also CA 102; CBD; CD 5; DLB 13, 233

Barker, Jane 1652-1732 .... **LC 42, 82**
See also DLB 39, 131

Barker, Pat(ricia) 1943- ...... **CLC 32, 94, 146**
See also BRWS 4; CA 117; 122; CANR 50, 101; CN 7; DLB 271; INT 122

Barlach, Ernst (Heinrich)
1870-1938 .... **TCLC 84**
See also CA 178; DLB 56, 118; EWL 3

Barlow, Joel 1754-1812 .... **NCLC 23**
See also AMWS 2; DLB 37; RGAL 4

Barnard, Mary (Ethel) 1909- .... **CLC 48**
See also CA 21-22; CAP 2

Barnes, Djuna 1892-1982 .... **CLC 3, 4, 8, 11, 29, 127; SSC 3**
See Steptoe, Lydia
See also AMWS 3; CA 9-12R; 107; CAD; CANR 16, 55; CWD; DLB 4, 9, 45; EWL 3; GLL 1; MTCW 1, 2; RGAL 4; TUS

Barnes, Jim 1933- .... **NNAL**
See also CA 108, 175; CAAE 175; CAAS 28; DLB 175

Barnes, Julian (Patrick) 1946- . **CLC 42, 141**
See also BRWS 4; CA 102; CANR 19, 54, 115; CN 7; DAB; DLB 194; DLBY 1993; EWL 3; MTCW 1

Barnes, Peter 1931- .... **CLC 5, 56**
See also CA 65-68; CAAS 12; CANR 33, 34, 64, 113; CBD; CD 5; DFS 6; DLB 13, 233; MTCW 1

Barnes, William 1801-1886 .... **NCLC 75**
See also DLB 32

Baroja (y Nessi), Pio 1872-1956 .... **HLC 1; TCLC 8**
See also CA 104; EW 9

Baron, David
See Pinter, Harold

Baron Corvo
See Rolfe, Frederick (William Serafino Austin Lewis Mary)

Barondess, Sue K(aufman)
1926-1977 .... **CLC 8**
See Kaufman, Sue
See also CA 1-4R; 69-72; CANR 1

Baron de Teive
See Pessoa, Fernando (Antonio Nogueira)

Baroness Von S.
See Zangwill, Israel

Barres, (Auguste-)Maurice
1862-1923 .... **TCLC 47**
See also CA 164; DLB 123; GFL 1789 to the Present

Barreto, Afonso Henrique de Lima
See Lima Barreto, Afonso Henrique de

Barrett, Andrea 1954- .... **CLC 150**
See also CA 156; CANR 92

Barrett, Michele .... **CLC 65**

Barrett, (Roger) Syd 1946- .... **CLC 35**

Barrett, William (Christopher)
1913-1992 .... **CLC 27**
See also CA 13-16R; 139; CANR 11, 67; INT CANR-11

Barrie, J(ames) M(atthew)
1860-1937 .... **TCLC 2**
See also BRWS 3; BYA 4, 5; CA 104; 136; CANR 77; CDBLB 1890-1914; CLR 16; CWRI 5; DA3; DAB; DAM DRAM; DFS 7; DLB 10, 141, 156; EWL 3; FANT; MAICYA 1, 2; MTCW 1; SATA 100; SUFW; WCH; WLIT 4; YABC 1

Barrington, Michael
See Moorcock, Michael (John)

Barrol, Grady
See Bograd, Larry

Barry, Mike
See Malzberg, Barry N(athaniel)

Barry, Philip 1896-1949 .... **TCLC 11**
See also CA 109; 199; DFS 9; DLB 7, 228; RGAL 4

Bart, Andre Schwarz
See Schwarz-Bart, Andre

Barth, John (Simmons) 1930- ... **CLC 1, 2, 3, 5, 7, 9, 10, 14, 27, 51, 89; SSC 10**
See also AITN 1, 2; AMW; BPFB 1; CA 1-4R; CABS 1; CANR 5, 23, 49, 64, 113; CN 7; DAM NOV; DLB 2, 227; EWL 3; FANT; MTCW 1; RGAL 4; RGSF 2; RHW; SSFS 6; TUS

Barthelme, Donald 1931-1989 ... **CLC 1, 2, 3, 5, 6, 8, 13, 23, 46, 59, 115; SSC 2, 55**
See also AMWS 4; BPFB 1; CA 21-24R; 129; CANR 20, 58; DA3; DAM NOV; DLB 2, 234; DLBY 1980, 1989; EWL 3; FANT; LMFS 2; MTCW 1, 2; RGAL 4; RGSF 2; SATA 7; SATA-Obit 62; SSFS 17

Barthelme, Frederick 1943- ...... **CLC 36, 117**
See also AMWS 11; CA 114; 122; CANR 77; CN 7; CSW; DLB 244; DLBY 1985; EWL 3; INT CA-122

Barthes, Roland (Gerard)
1915-1980 .... **CLC 24, 83; TCLC 135**
See also CA 130; 97-100; CANR 66; EW 13; EWL 3; GFL 1789 to the Present; MTCW 1, 2; TWA

Barzun, Jacques (Martin) 1907- ..... **CLC 51, 145**
See also CA 61-64; CANR 22, 95

Bashevis, Isaac
See Singer, Isaac Bashevis

Bashkirtseff, Marie 1859-1884 .... **NCLC 27**

Basho, Matsuo
See Matsuo Basho
See also PFS 18; RGWL 2, 3; WP

Basil of Caesaria c. 330-379 .... **CMLC 35**

Bass, Kingsley B., Jr.
See Bullins, Ed

Bass, Rick 1958- .... **CLC 79, 143; SSC 60**
See also ANW; CA 126; CANR 53, 93; CSW; DLB 212, 275

Bassani, Giorgio 1916-2000 .... **CLC 9**
See also CA 65-68; 190; CANR 33; CWW 2; DLB 128, 177; EWL 3; MTCW 1; RGWL 2, 3

Bastian, Ann .... **CLC 70**

Bastos, Augusto (Antonio) Roa
See Roa Bastos, Augusto (Antonio)

Bataille, Georges 1897-1962 .... **CLC 29**
See also CA 101; 89-92; EWL 3

Bates, H(erbert) E(rnest)
1905-1974 .... **CLC 46; SSC 10**
See also CA 93-96; 45-48; CANR 34; DA3; DAB; DAM POP; DLB 162, 191; EWL 3; EXPS; MTCW 1, 2; RGSF 2; SSFS 7

Bauchart
See Camus, Albert

Baudelaire, Charles 1821-1867 . **NCLC 6, 29, 55; PC 1; SSC 18; WLC**
See also DA; DA3; DAB; DAC; DAM MST, POET; DLB 217; EW 7; GFL 1789 to the Present; LMFS 2; RGWL 2, 3; TWA

Baudouin, Marcel
See Peguy, Charles (Pierre)

Baudouin, Pierre
See Peguy, Charles (Pierre)

Baudrillard, Jean 1929- .... **CLC 60**

Baum, L(yman) Frank 1856-1919 .. **TCLC 7, 132**
See also AAYA 46; BYA 16; CA 108; 133; CLR 15; CWRI 5; DLB 22; FANT; JRDA; MAICYA 1, 2; MTCW 1, 2; NFS 13; RGAL 4; SATA 18, 100; WCH

Baum, Louis F.
See Baum, L(yman) Frank

Baumbach, Jonathan 1933- .... **CLC 6, 23**
See also CA 13-16R; CAAS 5; CANR 12, 66; CN 7; DLBY 1980; INT CANR-12; MTCW 1

Bausch, Richard (Carl) 1945- .... **CLC 51**
See also AMWS 7; CA 101; CAAS 14; CANR 43, 61, 87; CSW; DLB 130

Baxter, Charles (Morley) 1947- . **CLC 45, 78**
See also CA 57-60; CANR 40, 64, 104; CPW; DAM POP; DLB 130; MTCW 2

Baxter, George Owen
See Faust, Frederick (Schiller)

Baxter, James K(eir) 1926-1972 .... **CLC 14**
See also CA 77-80; EWL 3

Baxter, John
See Hunt, E(verette) Howard, (Jr.)

Bayer, Sylvia
See Glassco, John

Baynton, Barbara 1857-1929 .... **TCLC 57**
See also DLB 230; RGSF 2

Beagle, Peter S(oyer) 1939- .... **CLC 7, 104**
See also AAYA 47; BPFB 1; BYA 9, 10, 16; CA 9-12R; CANR 4, 51, 73, 110; DA3; DLBY 1980; FANT; INT CANR-4; MTCW 1; SATA 60, 130; SUFW 1, 2; YAW

Bean, Normal
See Burroughs, Edgar Rice

Beard, Charles A(ustin)
1874-1948 .... **TCLC 15**
See also CA 115; 189; DLB 17; SATA 18

Beardsley, Aubrey 1872-1898 .... **NCLC 6**

Beattie, Ann 1947- ..... **CLC 8, 13, 18, 40, 63, 146; SSC 11**
See also AMWS 5; BEST 90:2; BPFB 1; CA 81-84; CANR 53, 73; CN 7; CPW; DA3; DAM NOV, POP; DLB 218, 278; DLBY 1982; EWL 3; MTCW 1, 2; RGAL 4; RGSF 2; SSFS 9; TUS

Beattie, James 1735-1803 .... **NCLC 25**
See also DLB 109

Beauchamp, Kathleen Mansfield 1888-1923
See Mansfield, Katherine
See also CA 104; 134; DA; DA3; DAC; DAM MST; MTCW 2; TEA

Beaumarchais, Pierre-Augustin Caron de
1732-1799 .... **DC 4; LC 61**
See also DAM DRAM; DFS 14, 16; EW 4; GFL Beginnings to 1789; RGWL 2, 3

Beaumont, Francis 1584(?)-1616 .. **DC 6; LC 33**
See also BRW 2; CDBLB Before 1660; DLB 58; TEA

Beauvoir, Simone (Lucie Ernestine Marie Bertrand) de 1908-1986 .... **CLC 1, 2, 4, 8, 14, 31, 44, 50, 71, 124; SSC 35; WLC**
See also BPFB 1; CA 9-12R; 118; CANR 28, 61; DA; DA3; DAB; DAC; DAM MST, NOV; DLB 72; DLBY 1986; EW 12; EWL 3; FW; GFL 1789 to the Present; LMFS 2; MTCW 1, 2; RGSF 2; RGWL 2, 3; TWA

Becker, Carl (Lotus) 1873-1945 ..... **TCLC 63**
See also CA 157; DLB 17

Becker, Jurek 1937-1997 .... **CLC 7, 19**
See also CA 85-88; 157; CANR 60, 117; CWW 2; DLB 75; EWL 3

Becker, Walter 1950- .... **CLC 26**

Beckett, Samuel (Barclay)
1906-1989 .. **CLC 1, 2, 3, 4, 6, 9, 10, 11, 14, 18, 29, 57, 59, 83; SSC 16; WLC**
See also BRWC 2; BRWR 1; BRWS 1; CA 5-8R; 130; CANR 33, 61; CBD; CDBLB 1945-1960; DA; DA3; DAB; DAC; DAM DRAM, MST, NOV; DFS 2, 7, 18; DLB

Benson, E(dward) F(rederic)
1867-1940 .... **TCLC 27**
See also CA 114; 157; DLB 135, 153;
HGG; SUFW 1

Benson, Jackson J. 1930- .... **CLC 34**
See also CA 25-28R; DLB 111

Benson, Sally 1900-1972 .... **CLC 17**
See also CA 19-20; 37-40R; CAP 1; SATA
1, 35; SATA-Obit 27

Benson, Stella 1892-1933 .... **TCLC 17**
See also CA 117; 154, 155; DLB 36, 162;
FANT; TEA

Bentham, Jeremy 1748-1832 .... **NCLC 38**
See also DLB 107, 158, 252

Bentley, E(dmund) C(lerihew)
1875-1956 .... **TCLC 12**
See also CA 108; DLB 70; MSW

Bentley, Eric (Russell) 1916- .... **CLC 24**
See also CA 5-8R; CAD; CANR 6, 67;
CBD; CD 5; INT CANR-6

ben Uzair, Salem
See Horne, Richard Henry Hengist

Beranger, Pierre Jean de
1780-1857 .... **NCLC 34**

Berdyaev, Nicolas
See Berdyaev, Nikolai (Aleksandrovich)

Berdyaev, Nikolai (Aleksandrovich)
1874-1948 .... **TCLC 67**
See also CA 120; 157

Berdyayev, Nikolai (Aleksandrovich)
See Berdyaev, Nikolai (Aleksandrovich)

Berendt, John (Lawrence) 1939- ...... **CLC 86**
See also CA 146; CANR 75, 93; DA3;
MTCW 1

Beresford, J(ohn) D(avys)
1873-1947 .... **TCLC 81**
See also CA 112; 155; DLB 162, 178, 197;
SFW 4; SUFW 1

Bergelson, David 1884-1952 .... **TCLC 81**
See Bergelson, Dovid

Bergelson, Dovid
See Bergelson, David
See also EWL 3

Berger, Colonel
See Malraux, (Georges-)Andre

Berger, John (Peter) 1926- .... **CLC 2, 19**
See also BRWS 4; CA 81-84; CANR 51,
78, 117; CN 7; DLB 14, 207

Berger, Melvin H. 1927- .... **CLC 12**
See also CA 5-8R; CANR 4; CLR 32;
SAAS 2; SATA 5, 88; SATA-Essay 124

Berger, Thomas (Louis) 1924- .. **CLC 3, 5, 8,**
11, 18, 38
See also BPFB 1; CA 1-4R; CANR 5, 28,
51; CN 7; DAM NOV; DLB 2; DLBY
1980; EWL 3; FANT; INT CANR-28;
MTCW 1, 2; RHW; TCWW 2

Bergman, (Ernst) Ingmar 1918- ...... **CLC 16,**
72
See also CA 81-84; CANR 33, 70; DLB
257; MTCW 2

Bergson, Henri(-Louis) 1859-1941 . **TCLC 32**
See also CA 164; EW 8; EWL 3; GFL 1789
to the Present

Bergstein, Eleanor 1938- .... **CLC 4**
See also CA 53-56; CANR 5

Berkeley, George 1685-1753 .... **LC 65**
See also DLB 31, 101, 252

Berkoff, Steven 1937- .... **CLC 56**
See also CA 104; CANR 72; CBD; CD 5

Berlin, Isaiah 1909-1997 .... **TCLC 105**
See also CA 85-88; 162

Bermant, Chaim (Icyk) 1929-1998 ... **CLC 40**
See also CA 57-60; CANR 6, 31, 57, 105;
CN 7

Bern, Victoria
See Fisher, M(ary) F(rances) K(ennedy)

Bernanos, (Paul Louis) Georges
1888-1948 .... **TCLC 3**
See also CA 104; 130; CANR 94; DLB 72;
EWL 3; GFL 1789 to the Present; RGWL
2, 3

Bernard, April 1956- .... **CLC 59**
See also CA 131

Berne, Victoria
See Fisher, M(ary) F(rances) K(ennedy)

Bernhard, Thomas 1931-1989 ..... **CLC 3, 32,**
61; DC 14
See also CA 85-88; 127; CANR 32, 57; CD-
WLB 2; DLB 85, 124; EWL 3; MTCW 1;
RGWL 2, 3

Bernhardt, Sarah (Henriette Rosine)
1844-1923 .... **TCLC 75**
See also CA 157

Bernstein, Charles 1950- .... **CLC 142,**
See also CA 129; CAAS 24; CANR 90; CP
7; DLB 169

Berriault, Gina 1926-1999 .... **CLC 54, 109;**
SSC 30
See also CA 116; 129; 185; CANR 66; DLB
130; SSFS 7,11

Berrigan, Daniel 1921- .... **CLC 4**
See also CA 33-36R; CAAE 187; CAAS 1;
CANR 11, 43, 78; CP 7; DLB 5

Berrigan, Edmund Joseph Michael, Jr.
1934-1983
See Berrigan, Ted
See also CA 61-64; 110; CANR 14, 102

Berrigan, Ted .... **CLC 37**
See Berrigan, Edmund Joseph Michael, Jr.
See also DLB 5, 169; WP

Berry, Charles Edward Anderson 1931-
See Berry, Chuck
See also CA 115

Berry, Chuck .... **CLC 17**
See Berry, Charles Edward Anderson

Berry, Jonas
See Ashbery, John (Lawrence)
See also GLL 1

Berry, Wendell (Erdman) 1934- ... **CLC 4, 6,**
8, 27, 46; PC 28
See also AITN 1; AMWS 10; ANW; CA
73-76; CANR 50, 73, 101; CP 7; CSW;
DAM POET; DLB 5, 6, 234, 275; MTCW
1

Berryman, John 1914-1972 ... **CLC 1, 2, 3, 4,**
6, 8, 10, 13, 25, 62
See also AMW; CA 13-16; 33-36R; CABS
2; CANR 35; CAP 1; CDALB 1941-1968;
DAM POET; DLB 48; EWL 3; MTCW 1,
2; PAB; RGAL 4; WP

Bertolucci, Bernardo 1940- ...... **CLC 16, 157**
See also CA 106

Berton, Pierre (Francis Demarigny)
1920- .... **CLC 104**
See also CA 1-4R; CANR 2, 56; CPW;
DLB 68; SATA 99

Bertrand, Aloysius 1807-1841 .... **NCLC 31**
See Bertrand, Louis oAloysiusc

Bertrand, Louis oAloysiusc
See Bertrand, Aloysius
See also DLB 217

Bertran de Born c. 1140-1215 .... **CMLC 5**

Besant, Annie (Wood) 1847-1933 ..... **TCLC 9**
See also CA 105; 185

Bessie, Alvah 1904-1985 .... **CLC 23**
See also CA 5-8R; 116; CANR 2, 80; DLB
26

Bestuzhev, Aleksandr Aleksandrovich
1797-1837 .... **NCLC 131**
See also DLB 198

Bethlen, T. D.
See Silverberg, Robert

Beti, Mongo .... **BLC 1; CLC 27**
See Biyidi, Alexandre
See also AFW; CANR 79; DAM MULT;
EWL 3; WLIT 2

Betjeman, John 1906-1984 ...... **CLC 2, 6, 10,**
34, 43
See also BRW 7; CA 9-12R; 112; CANR
33, 56; CDBLB 1945-1960; DA3; DAB;
DAM MST, POET; DLB 20; DLBY 1984;
EWL 3; MTCW 1, 2

Bettelheim, Bruno 1903-1990 .... **CLC 79**
See also CA 81-84; 131; CANR 23, 61;
DA3; MTCW 1, 2

Betti, Ugo 1892-1953 .... **TCLC 5**
See also CA 104; 155; EWL 3; RGWL 2, 3

Betts, Doris (Waugh) 1932- ..... **CLC 3, 6, 28;**
SSC 45
See also CA 13-16R; CANR 9, 66, 77; CN
7; CSW; DLB 218; DLBY 1982; INT
CANR-9; RGAL 4

Bevan, Alistair
See Roberts, Keith (John Kingston)

Bey, Pilaff
See Douglas, (George) Norman

Bialik, Chaim Nachman
1873-1934 .... **TCLC 25**
See also CA 170; EWL 3

Bickerstaff, Isaac
See Swift, Jonathan

Bidart, Frank 1939- .... **CLC 33**
See also CA 140; CANR 106; CP 7

Bienek, Horst 1930- .... **CLC 7, 11**
See also CA 73-76; DLB 75

Bierce, Ambrose (Gwinett)
1842-1914(?) ..... **SSC 9; TCLC 1, 7, 44;**
WLC
See also AMW; BYA 11; CA 104; 139;
CANR 78; CDALB 1865-1917; DA;
DA3; DAC; DAM MST; DLB 11, 12, 23,
71, 74, 186; EWL 3; EXPS; HGG; LAIT
2; RGAL 4; RGSF 2; SSFS 9; SUFW 1

Biggers, Earl Derr 1884-1933 .... **TCLC 65**
See also CA 108; 153

Billiken, Bud
See Motley, Willard (Francis)

Billings, Josh
See Shaw, Henry Wheeler

Billington, (Lady) Rachel (Mary)
1942- .... **CLC 43**
See also AITN 2; CA 33-36R; CANR 44;
CN 7

Binchy, Maeve 1940- .... **CLC 153**
See also BEST 90:1; BPFB 1; CA 127; 134;
CANR 50, 96; CN 7; CPW; DA3; DAM
POP; INT CA-134; MTCW 1; RHW

Binyon, T(imothy) J(ohn) 1936- .... **CLC 34**
See also CA 111; CANR 28

Bion 335B.C.-245B.C. .... **CMLC 39**

Bioy Casares, Adolfo 1914-1999 ... **CLC 4, 8,**
13, 88; HLC 1; SSC 17
See Casares, Adolfo Bioy; Miranda, Javier;
Sacastru, Martin
See also CA 29-32R; 177; CANR 19, 43,
66; DAM MULT; DLB 113; EWL 3; HW
1, 2; LAW; MTCW 1, 2

Birch, Allison .... **CLC 65**

Bird, Cordwainer
See Ellison, Harlan (Jay)

Bird, Robert Montgomery
1806-1854 .... **NCLC 1**
See also DLB 202; RGAL 4

Birkerts, Sven 1951- .... **CLC 116**
See also CA 128; 133, 176; CAAE 176;
CAAS 29; INT 133

Birney, (Alfred) Earle 1904-1 ',
6, 11; PC 52
See also CA 1-4R; CAN
DAC; DAM MST, P
MTCW 1; PFS 8; RGEI

Brooke, Rupert (Chawner)
1887-1915 ..... **PC 24; TCLC 2, 7; WLC**
See also BRWS 3; CA 104; 132; CANR 61;
CDBLB 1914-1945; DA; DAB; DAC;
DAM MST, POET; DLB 19, 216; EXPP;
GLL 2; MTCW 1, 2; PFS 7; TEA

Brooke-Haven, P.
See Wodehouse, P(elham) G(renville)

Brooke-Rose, Christine 1926(?)- ...... **CLC 40**
See also BRWS 4; CA 13-16R; CANR 58,
118; CN 7; DLB 14, 231; EWL 3; SFW 4

Brookner, Anita 1928- .. **CLC 32, 34, 51, 136**
See also BRWS 4; CA 114; 120; CANR 37,
56, 87; CN 7; CPW; DA3; DAB; DAM
POP; DLB 194; DLBY 1987; EWL 3;
MTCW 1, 2; TEA

Brooks, Cleanth 1906-1994 . **CLC 24, 86, 110**
See also CA 17-20R; 145; CANR 33, 35;
CSW; DLB 63; DLBY 1994; EWL 3; INT
CANR-35; MTCW 1, 2

Brooks, George
See Baum, L(yman) Frank

Brooks, Gwendolyn (Elizabeth)
1917-2000 ... **BLC 1; CLC 1, 2, 4, 5, 15,
49, 125; PC 7; WLC**
See also AAYA 20; AFAW 1, 2; AITN 1;
AMWS 3; BW 2, 3; CA 1-4R; 190; CANR
1, 27, 52, 75; CDALB 1941-1968; CLR
27; CP 7; CWP; DA; DA3; DAC; DAM
MST, MULT, POET; DLB 5, 76, 165;
EWL 3; EXPP; MAWW; MTCW 1, 2;
PFS 1, 2, 4, 6; RGAL 4; SATA 6; SATA-
Obit 123; TUS; WP

Brooks, Mel .... **CLC 12**
See Kaminsky, Melvin
See also AAYA 13, 48; DLB 26

Brooks, Peter (Preston) 1938- .... **CLC 34**
See also CA 45-48; CANR 1, 107

Brooks, Van Wyck 1886-1963 .... **CLC 29**
See also AMW; CA 1-4R; CANR 6; DLB
45, 63, 103; TUS

Brophy, Brigid (Antonia)
1929-1995 .... **CLC 6, 11, 29, 105**
See also CA 5-8R; 149; CAAS 4; CANR
25, 53; CBD; CN 7; CWD; DA3; DLB
14, 271; EWL 3; MTCW 1, 2

Brosman, Catharine Savage 1934- ..... **CLC 9**
See also CA 61-64; CANR 21, 46

Brossard, Nicole 1943- .... **CLC 115, 169**
See also CA 122; CAAS 16; CCA 1; CWP;
CWW 2; DLB 53; EWL 3; FW; GLL 2;
RGWL 3

Brother Antoninus
See Everson, William (Oliver)

The Brothers Quay
See Quay, Stephen; Quay, Timothy

Broughton, T(homas) Alan 1936- ..... **CLC 19**
See also CA 45-48; CANR 2, 23, 48, 111

Broumas, Olga 1949- .... **CLC 10, 73**
See also CA 85-88; CANR 20, 69, 110; CP
7; CWP; GLL 2

Broun, Heywood 1888-1939 .... **TCLC 104**
See also DLB 29, 171

Brown, Alan 1950- .... **CLC 99**
See also CA 156

Brown, Charles Brockden
1771-1810 .... **NCLC 22, 74, 122**
See also AMWS 1; CDALB 1640-1865;
DLB 37, 59, 73; FW; HGG; LMFS 1;
RGAL 4; TUS

Brown, Christy 1932-1981 .... **CLC 63**
See also BYA 13; CA 105; 104; CANR 72;
DLB 14

Brown, Claude 1937-2002 ... **BLC 1; CLC 30**
See also AAYA 7; BW 1, 3; CA 73-76; 205;
CANR 81; DAM MULT

Brown, Dee (Alexander)
1908-2002 .... **CLC 18, 47**
See also AAYA 30; CA 13-16R; 212; CAAS
6; CANR 11, 45, 60; CPW; CSW; DA3;
DAM POP; DLBY 1980; LAIT 2; MTCW
1, 2; NCFS 5; SATA 5, 110; SATA-Obit
141; TCWW 2

Brown, George
See Wertmueller, Lina

Brown, George Douglas
1869-1902 .... **TCLC 28**
See Douglas, George
See also CA 162

Brown, George Mackay 1921-1996 ... **CLC 5,
48, 100**
See also BRWS 6; CA 21-24R; 151; CAAS
6; CANR 12, 37, 67; CN 7; CP 7; DLB
14, 27, 139, 271; MTCW 1; RGSF 2;
SATA 35

Brown, (William) Larry 1951- .... **CLC 73**
See also CA 130; 134; CANR 117; CSW;
DLB 234; INT 133

Brown, Moses
See Barrett, William (Christopher)

Brown, Rita Mae 1944- .... **CLC 18, 43, 79**
See also BPFB 1; CA 45-48; CANR 2, 11,
35, 62, 95; CN 7; CPW; CSW; DA3;
DAM NOV, POP; FW; INT CANR-11;
MTCW 1, 2; NFS 9; RGAL 4; TUS

Brown, Roderick (Langmere) Haig-
See Haig-Brown, Roderick (Langmere)

Brown, Rosellen 1939- .... **CLC 32, 170**
See also CA 77-80; CAAS 10; CANR 14,
44, 98; CN 7

Brown, Sterling Allen 1901-1989 ...... **BLC 1;
CLC 1, 23, 59; HR 2**
See also AFAW 1, 2; BW 1, 3; CA 85-88;
127; CANR 26; DA3; DAM MULT,
POET; DLB 48, 51, 63; MTCW 1, 2;
RGAL 4; WP

Brown, Will
See Ainsworth, William Harrison

Brown, William Hill 1765-1793 .... **LC 93**
See also DLB 37

Brown, William Wells 1815-1884 ...... **BLC 1;
DC 1; NCLC 2, 89**
See also DAM MULT; DLB 3, 50, 183,
248; RGAL 4

Browne, (Clyde) Jackson 1948(?)- ... **CLC 21**
See also CA 120

Browning, Elizabeth Barrett
1806-1861 ... **NCLC 1, 16, 61, 66; PC 6;
WLC**
See also BRW 4; CDBLB 1832-1890; DA;
DA3; DAB; DAC; DAM MST, POET;
DLB 32, 199; EXPP; PAB; PFS 2, 16;
TEA; WLIT 4; WP

Browning, Robert 1812-1889 . **NCLC 19, 79;
PC 2; WLCS**
See also BRW 4; BRWC 2; BRWR 2; CD-
BLB 1832-1890; DA; DA3; DAB; DAC;
DAM MST, POET; DLB 32, 163; EXPP;
LATS 1; PAB; PFS 1, 15; RGEL 2; TEA;
WLIT 4; WP; YABC 1

Browning, Tod 1882-1962 .... **CLC 16**
See also CA 141; 117

Brownmiller, Susan 1935- .... **CLC 159**
See also CA 103; CANR 35, 75; DAM
NOV; FW; MTCW 1, 2

Brownson, Orestes Augustus
1803-1876 .... **NCLC 50**
See also DLB 1, 59, 73, 243

Bruccoli, Matthew J(oseph) 1931- ... **CLC 34**
See also CA 9-12R; CANR 7, 87; DLB 103

Bruce, Lenny .... **CLC 21**
See Schneider, Leonard Alfred

Bruchac, Joseph III 1942- .... **NNAL**
See also AAYA 19; CA 33-36R; CANR 13,
47, 75, 94; CLR 46; CWRI 5; DAM
MULT; JRDA; MAICYA 2; MAICYAS 1;
MTCW 1; SATA 42, 89, 131

Bruin, John
See Brutus, Dennis

Brulard, Henri
See Stendhal

Brulls, Christian
See Simenon, Georges (Jacques Christian)

Brunner, John (Kilian Houston)
1934-1995 .... **CLC 8, 10**
See also CA 1-4R; 149; CAAS 8; CANR 2,
37; CPW; DAM POP; DLB 261; MTCW
1, 2; SCFW 2; SFW 4

Bruno, Giordano 1548-1600 .... **LC 27**
See also RGWL 2, 3

Brutus, Dennis 1924- ... **BLC 1; CLC 43; PC
24**
See also AFW; BW 2, 3; CA 49-52; CAAS
14; CANR 2, 27, 42, 81; CDWLB 3; CP
7; DAM MULT, POET; DLB 117, 225;
EWL 3

Bryan, C(ourtlandt) D(ixon) B(arnes)
1936- .... **CLC 29**
See also CA 73-76; CANR 13, 68; DLB
185; INT CANR-13

Bryan, Michael
See Moore, Brian
See also CCA 1

Bryan, William Jennings
1860-1925 .... **TCLC 99**

Bryant, William Cullen 1794-1878 . **NCLC 6,
46; PC 20**
See also AMWS 1; CDALB 1640-1865;
DA; DAB; DAC; DAM MST, POET;
DLB 3, 43, 59, 189, 250; EXPP; PAB;
RGAL 4; TUS

Bryusov, Valery Yakovlevich
1873-1924 .... **TCLC 10**
See also CA 107; 155; EWL 3; SFW 4

Buchan, John 1875-1940 .... **TCLC 41**
See also CA 108; 145; CMW 4; DAB;
DAM POP; DLB 34, 70, 156; HGG;
MSW; MTCW 1; RGEL 2; RHW; YABC
2

Buchanan, George 1506-1582 .... **LC 4**
See also DLB 132

Buchanan, Robert 1841-1901 .... **TCLC 107**
See also CA 179; DLB 18, 35

Buchheim, Lothar-Guenther 1918- .... **CLC 6**
See also CA 85-88

Buchner, (Karl) Georg 1813-1837 . **NCLC 26**
See also CDWLB 2; DLB 133; EW 6;
RGSF 2; RGWL 2, 3; TWA

Buchwald, Art(hur) 1925- .... **CLC 33**
See also AITN 1; CA 5-8R; CANR 21, 67,
107; MTCW 1, 2; SATA 10

Buck, Pearl S(ydenstricker)
1892-1973 .... **CLC 7, 11, 18, 127**
See also AAYA 42; AITN 1; AMWS 2;
BPFB 1; CA 1-4R; 41-44R; CANR 1, 34;
CDALBS; DA; DA3; DAB; DAC; DAM
MST, NOV; DLB 9, 102; EWL 3; LAIT
3; MTCW 1, 2; RGAL 4; RHW; SATA 1,
25; TUS

Buckler, Ernest 1908-1984 .... **CLC 13**
See also CA 11-12; 114; CAP 1; CCA 1;
DAC; DAM MST; DLB 68; SATA 47

Buckley, Christopher (Taylor)
1952- .... **CLC 165**
See also CA 139; CANR 119

Buckley, Vincent (Thomas)
1925-1988 .... **CLC 57**
See also CA 101; DLB 289

Cabral de Melo Neto, Joao
1920-1999 .... **CLC 76**
See Melo Neto, Joao Cabral de
See also CA 151; DAM MULT; LAW;
LAWS 1

Cabrera Infante, G(uillermo) 1929- . **CLC 5,
25, 45, 120; HLC 1; SSC 39**
See also CA 85-88; CANR 29, 65, 110; CD-
WLB 3; DA3; DAM MULT; DLB 113;
EWL 3; HW 1, 2; LAW; LAWS 1; MTCW
1, 2; RGSF 2; WLIT 1

Cade, Toni
See Bambara, Toni Cade

Cadmus and Harmonia
See Buchan, John

Caedmon fl. 658-680 .... **CMLC 7**
See also DLB 146

Caeiro, Alberto
See Pessoa, Fernando (Antonio Nogueira)

Caesar, Julius .... **CMLC 47**
See Julius Caesar
See also AW 1; RGWL 2, 3

Cage, John (Milton, Jr.) 1912-1992 . **CLC 41**
See also CA 13-16R; 169; CANR 9, 78;
DLB 193; INT CANR-9

Cahan, Abraham 1860-1951 .... **TCLC 71**
See also CA 108; 154; DLB 9, 25, 28;
RGAL 4

Cain, G.
See Cabrera Infante, G(uillermo)

Cain, Guillermo
See Cabrera Infante, G(uillermo)

Cain, James M(allahan) 1892-1977 .. **CLC 3,
11, 28**
See also AITN 1; BPFB 1; CA 17-20R; 73-
76; CANR 8, 34, 61; CMW 4; DLB 226;
EWL 3; MSW; MTCW 1; RGAL 4

Caine, Hall 1853-1931 .... **TCLC 97**
See also RHW

Caine, Mark
See Raphael, Frederic (Michael)

Calasso, Roberto 1941- .... **CLC 81**
See also CA 143; CANR 89

Calderon de la Barca, Pedro
1600-1681 .... **DC 3; HLCS 1; LC 23**
See also EW 2; RGWL 2, 3; TWA

Caldwell, Erskine (Preston)
1903-1987 .... **CLC 1, 8, 14, 50, 60; SSC
19; TCLC 117**
See also AITN 1; AMW; BPFB 1; CA 1-4R;
121; CAAS 1; CANR 2, 33; DA3; DAM
NOV; DLB 9, 86; EWL 3; MTCW 1, 2;
RGAL 4; RGSF 2; TUS

Caldwell, (Janet Miriam) Taylor (Holland)
1900-1985 .... **CLC 2, 28, 39**
See also BPFB 1; CA 5-8R; 116; CANR 5;
DA3; DAM NOV, POP; DLBD 17; RHW

Calhoun, John Caldwell
1782-1850 .... **NCLC 15**
See also DLB 3, 248

Calisher, Hortense 1911- ..... **CLC 2, 4, 8, 38,
134; SSC 15**
See also CA 1-4R; CANR 1, 22, 117; CN
7; DA3; DAM NOV; DLB 2, 218; INT
CANR-22; MTCW 1, 2; RGAL 4; RGSF
2

Callaghan, Morley Edward
1903-1990 .... **CLC 3, 14, 41, 65**
See also CA 9-12R; 132; CANR 33, 73;
DAC; DAM MST; DLB 68; EWL 3;
MTCW 1, 2; RGEL 2; RGSF 2

Callimachus c. 305B.C.-c.
240B.C. .... **CMLC 18**
See also AW 1; DLB 176; RGWL 2, 3

Calvin, Jean
See Calvin, John
See also GFL Beginnings to 1789

Calvin, John 1509-1564 .... **LC 37**
See Calvin, Jean

Calvino, Italo 1923-1985 .... **CLC 5, 8, 11, 22,
33, 39, 73; SSC 3, 48**
See also CA 85-88; 116; CANR 23, 61;
DAM NOV; DLB 196; EW 13; EWL 3;
MTCW 1, 2; RGSF 2; RGWL 2, 3; SFW
4; SSFS 12

Camara Laye
See Laye, Camara
See also EWL 3

Camden, William 1551-1623 .... **LC 77**
See also DLB 172

Cameron, Carey 1952- .... **CLC 59**
See also CA 135

Cameron, Peter 1959- .... **CLC 44**
See also AMWS 12; CA 125; CANR 50,
117; DLB 234; GLL 2

Camoens, Luis Vaz de 1524(?)-1580
See Camoes, Luis de
See also EW 2

Camoes, Luis de 1524(?)-1580 . **HLCS 1; LC
62; PC 31**
See Camoens, Luis Vaz de
See also DLB 287; RGWL 2, 3

Campana, Dino 1885-1932 .... **TCLC 20**
See also CA 117; DLB 114; EWL 3

Campanella, Tommaso 1568-1639 .... **LC 32**
See also RGWL 2, 3

Campbell, John W(ood, Jr.)
1910-1971 .... **CLC 32**
See also CA 21-22; 29-32R; CANR 34;
CAP 2; DLB 8; MTCW 1; SCFW; SFW 4

Campbell, Joseph 1904-1987 .... **CLC 69;
TCLC 140**
See also AAYA 3; BEST 89:2; CA 1-4R;
124; CANR 3, 28, 61, 107; DA3; MTCW
1, 2

Campbell, Maria 1940- .... **CLC 85; NNAL**
See also CA 102; CANR 54; CCA 1; DAC

Campbell, (John) Ramsey 1946- ..... **CLC 42;
SSC 19**
See also AAYA 51; CA 57-60; CANR 7,
102; DLB 261; HGG; INT CANR-7;
SUFW 1, 2

Campbell, (Ignatius) Roy (Dunnachie)
1901-1957 .... **TCLC 5**
See also AFW; CA 104; 155; DLB 20, 225;
EWL 3; MTCW 2; RGEL 2

Campbell, Thomas 1777-1844 .... **NCLC 19**
See also DLB 93, 144; RGEL 2

Campbell, Wilfred .... **TCLC 9**
See Campbell, William

Campbell, William 1858(?)-1918
See Campbell, Wilfred
See also CA 106; DLB 92

Campion, Jane 1954- .... **CLC 95**
See also AAYA 33; CA 138; CANR 87

Campion, Thomas 1567-1620 .... **LC 78**
See also CDBLB Before 1660; DAM POET;
DLB 58, 172; RGEL 2

Camus, Albert 1913-1960 ...... **CLC 1, 2, 4, 9,
11, 14, 32, 63, 69, 124; DC 2; SSC 9;
WLC**
See also AAYA 36; AFW; BPFB 1; CA 89-
92; DA; DA3; DAB; DAC; DAM DRAM,
MST, NOV; DLB 72; EW 13; EWL 3;
EXPN; EXPS; GFL 1789 to the Present;
LATS 1; LMFS 2; MTCW 1, 2; NFS 6,
16; RGSF 2; RGWL 2, 3; SSFS 4; TWA

Canby, Vincent 1924-2000 .... **CLC 13**
See also CA 81-84; 191

Cancale
See Desnos, Robert

Canetti, Elias 1905-1994 .. **CLC 3, 14, 25, 75,
86**
See also CA 21-24R; 146; CANR 23, 61;
79; CDWLB 2; CWW 2; DA3; DLB 85,
124; EW 12; EWL 3; MTCW 1, 2; RGWL
2, 3; TWA

Canfield, Dorothea F.
See Fisher, Dorothy (Frances) Canfield

Canfield, Dorothea Frances
See Fisher, Dorothy (Frances) Canfield

Canfield, Dorothy
See Fisher, Dorothy (Frances) Canfield

Canin, Ethan 1960- .... **CLC 55**
See also CA 131; 135

Cankar, Ivan 1876-1918 .... **TCLC 105**
See also CDWLB 4; DLB 147; EWL 3

Cannon, Curt
See Hunter, Evan

Cao, Lan 1961- .... **CLC 109**
See also CA 165

Cape, Judith
See Page, P(atricia) K(athleen)
See also CCA 1

Capek, Karel 1890-1938 .... **DC 1; SSC 36;
TCLC 6, 37; WLC**
See also CA 104; 140; CDWLB 4; DA;
DA3; DAB; DAC; DAM DRAM, MST,
NOV; DFS 7, 11; DLB 215; EW 10; EWL
3; MTCW 1; RGSF 2; RGWL 2, 3; SCFW
2; SFW 4

Capote, Truman 1924-1984 . **CLC 1, 3, 8, 13,
19, 34, 38, 58; SSC 2, 47; WLC**
See also AMWS 3; BPFB 1; CA 5-8R; 113;
CANR 18, 62; CDALB 1941-1968; CPW;
DA; DA3; DAB; DAC; DAM MST, NOV,
POP; DLB 2, 185, 227; DLBY 1980,
1984; EWL 3; EXPS; GLL 1; LAIT 3;
MTCW 1, 2; NCFS 2; RGAL 4; RGSF 2;
SATA 91; SSFS 2; TUS

Capra, Frank 1897-1991 .... **CLC 16**
See also AAYA 52; CA 61-64; 135

Caputo, Philip 1941- .... **CLC 32**
See also CA 73-76; CANR 40; YAW

Caragiale, Ion Luca 1852-1912 ...... **TCLC 76**
See also CA 157

Card, Orson Scott 1951- .... **CLC 44, 47, 50**
See also AAYA 11, 42; BPFB 1; BYA 5, 8;
CA 102; CANR 27, 47, 73, 102, 106;
CPW; DA3; DAM POP; FANT; INT
CANR-27; MTCW 1, 2; NFS 5; SATA
83, 127; SCFW 2; SFW 4; SUFW 2; YAW

Cardenal, Ernesto 1925- .... **CLC 31, 161;
HLC 1; PC 22**
See also CA 49-52; CANR 2, 32, 66; CWW
2; DAM MULT, POET; EWL 3; HW 1, 2;
LAWS 1; MTCW 1, 2; RGWL 2, 3

Cardozo, Benjamin N(athan)
1870-1938 .... **TCLC 65**
See also CA 117; 164

Carducci, Giosue (Alessandro Giuseppe)
1835-1907 .... **PC 46; TCLC 32**
See also CA 163; EW 7; RGWL 2, 3

Carew, Thomas 1595(?)-1640 . **LC 13; PC 29**
See also BRW 2; DLB 126; PAB; RGEL 2

Carey, Ernestine Gilbreth 1908- ...... **CLC 17**
See also CA 5-8R; CANR 71; SATA 2

Carey, Peter 1943- .... **CLC 40, 55, 96**
See also CA 123; 127; CANR 53, 76, 117;
CN 7; DLB 289; EWL 3; INT CA-127;
MTCW 1, 2; RGSF 2; SATA 94

Carleton, William 1794-1869 .... **NCLC 3**
See also DLB 159; RGEL 2; RGSF 2

Carlisle, Henry (Coffin) 1926- .... **CLC 33**
See also CA 13-16R; CANR 15, 85

Carlsen, Chris
See Holdstock, Robert P.

Carlson, Ron(ald F.) 1947- .... **CLC 54**
See also CA 105; CAAE 189; CANR 27;
DLB 244

Carlyle, Thomas 1795-1881 ..... **NCLC 22, 70**
See also BRW 4; CDBLB 1789-1832; DA;
DAB; DAC; DAM MST; DLB 55, 144,
254; RGEL 2; TEA

Cela, Camilo Jose 1916-2002 .... **CLC 4, 13, 59, 122; HLC 1**
See also BEST 90:2; CA 21-24R; 206; CAAS 10; CANR 21, 32, 76; DAM MULT; DLBY 1989; EW 13; EWL 3; HW 1; MTCW 1, 2; RGSF 2; RGWL 2, 3

Celan, Paul .... **CLC 10, 19, 53, 82; PC 10**
See Antschel, Paul
See also CDWLB 2; DLB 69; EWL 3; RGWL 2, 3

Celine, Louis-Ferdinand .. **CLC 1, 3, 4, 7, 9, 15, 47, 124**
See Destouches, Louis-Ferdinand
See also DLB 72; EW 11; EWL 3; GFL 1789 to the Present; RGWL 2, 3

Cellini, Benvenuto 1500-1571 .... **LC 7**

Cendrars, Blaise .... **CLC 18, 106**
See Sauser-Hall, Frederic
See also DLB 258; EWL 3; GFL 1789 to the Present; RGWL 2, 3; WP

Centlivre, Susanna 1669(?)-1723 .... **LC 65**
See also DLB 84; RGEL 2

Cernuda (y Bidon), Luis 1902-1963 . **CLC 54**
See also CA 131; 89-92; DAM POET; DLB 134; EWL 3; GLL 1; HW 1; RGWL 2, 3

Cervantes, Lorna Dee 1954- ..... **HLCS 1; PC 35**
See also CA 131; CANR 80; CWP; DLB 82; EXPP; HW 1

Cervantes (Saavedra), Miguel de 1547-1616 .... **HLCS; LC 6, 23, 93; SSC 12; WLC**
See also BYA 1, 14; DA; DAB; DAC; DAM MST, NOV; EW 2; LAIT 1; LATS 1; LMFS 1; NFS 8; RGSF 2; RGWL 2, 3; TWA

Cesaire, Aime (Fernand) 1913- .... **BLC 1; CLC 19, 32, 112; PC 25**
See also BW 2, 3; CA 65-68; CANR 24, 43, 81; DA3; DAM MULT, POET; EWL 3; GFL 1789 to the Present; MTCW 1, 2; WP

Chabon, Michael 1963- ... **CLC 55, 149; SSC 59**
See also AAYA 45; AMWS 11; CA 139; CANR 57, 96; DLB 278

Chabrol, Claude 1930- .... **CLC 16**
See also CA 110

Chairil Anwar
See Anwar, Chairil
See also EWL 3

Challans, Mary 1905-1983
See Renault, Mary
See also CA 81-84; 111; CANR 74; DA3; MTCW 2; SATA 23; SATA-Obit 36; TEA

Challis, George
See Faust, Frederick (Schiller)
See also TCWW 2

Chambers, Aidan 1934- .... **CLC 35**
See also AAYA 27; CA 25-28R; CANR 12, 31, 58, 116; JRDA; MAICYA 1, 2; SAAS 12; SATA 1, 69, 108; WYA; YAW

Chambers, James 1948-
See Cliff, Jimmy
See also CA 124

Chambers, Jessie
See Lawrence, D(avid) H(erbert Richards)
See also GLL 1

Chambers, Robert W(illiam) 1865-1933 .... **TCLC 41**
See also CA 165; DLB 202; HGG; SATA 107; SUFW 1

Chambers, (David) Whittaker 1901-1961 .... **TCLC 129**
See also CA 89-92

Chamisso, Adelbert von 1781-1838 .... **NCLC 82**
See also DLB 90; RGWL 2, 3; SUFW 1

Chance, James T.
See Carpenter, John (Howard)

Chance, John T.
See Carpenter, John (Howard)

Chandler, Raymond (Thornton) 1888-1959 .... **SSC 23; TCLC 1, 7**
See also AAYA 25; AMWC 2; AMWS 4; BPFB 1; CA 104; 129; CANR 60, 107; CDALB 1929-1941; CMW 4; DA3; DLB 226, 253; DLBD 6; EWL 3; MSW; MTCW 1, 2; NFS 17; RGAL 4; TUS

Chang, Diana 1934- .... **AAL**
See also CWP; EXPP

Chang, Eileen 1921-1995 .... **AAL; SSC 28**
See Chang Ai-Ling
See also CA 166; CWW 2

Chang, Jung 1952- .... **CLC 71**
See also CA 142

Chang Ai-Ling
See Chang, Eileen
See also EWL 3

Channing, William Ellery 1780-1842 .... **NCLC 17**
See also DLB 1, 59, 235; RGAL 4

Chao, Patricia 1955- .... **CLC 119**
See also CA 163

Chaplin, Charles Spencer 1889-1977 .... **CLC 16**
See Chaplin, Charlie
See also CA 81-84; 73-76

Chaplin, Charlie
See Chaplin, Charles Spencer
See also DLB 44

Chapman, George 1559(?)-1634 . **DC 19; LC 22**
See also BRW 1; DAM DRAM; DLB 62, 121; LMFS 1; RGEL 2

Chapman, Graham 1941-1989 .... **CLC 21**
See Monty Python
See also CA 116; 129; CANR 35, 95

Chapman, John Jay 1862-1933 .... **TCLC 7**
See also CA 104; 191

Chapman, Lee
See Bradley, Marion Zimmer
See also GLL 1

Chapman, Walker
See Silverberg, Robert

Chappell, Fred (Davis) 1936- .... **CLC 40, 78, 162**
See also CA 5-8R; CAAE 198; CAAS 4; CANR 8, 33, 67, 110; CN 7; CP 7; CSW; DLB 6, 105; HGG

Char, Rene(-Emile) 1907-1988 .... **CLC 9, 11, 14, 55**
See also CA 13-16R; 124; CANR 32; DAM POET; DLB 258; EWL 3; GFL 1789 to the Present; MTCW 1, 2; RGWL 2, 3

Charby, Jay
See Ellison, Harlan (Jay)

Chardin, Pierre Teilhard de
See Teilhard de Chardin, (Marie Joseph) Pierre

Chariton fl. 1st cent. (?)- .... **CMLC 49**

Charlemagne 742-814 .... **CMLC 37**

Charles I 1600-1649 .... **LC 13**

Charriere, Isabelle de 1740-1805 .. **NCLC 66**

Chartier, Alain c. 1392-1430 .... **LC 94**
See also DLB 208

Chartier, Emile-Auguste
See Alain

Charyn, Jerome 1937- .... **CLC 5, 8, 18**
See also CA 5-8R; CAAS 1; CANR 7, 61, 101; CMW 4; CN 7; DLBY 1983; MTCW 1

Chase, Adam
See Marlowe, Stephen

Chase, Mary (Coyle) 1907-1981 .... **DC 1**
See also CA 77-80; 105; CAD; CWD; DFS 11; DLB 228; SATA 17; SATA-Obit 29

Chase, Mary Ellen 1887-1973 .... **CLC 2; TCLC 124**
See also CA 13-16; 41-44R; CAP 1; SATA 10

Chase, Nicholas
See Hyde, Anthony
See also CCA 1

Chateaubriand, Francois Rene de 1768-1848 .... **NCLC 3**
See also DLB 119; EW 5; GFL 1789 to the Present; RGWL 2, 3; TWA

Chatterje, Sarat Chandra 1876-1936(?)
See Chatterji, Saratchandra
See also CA 109

Chatterji, Bankim Chandra 1838-1894 .... **NCLC 19**

Chatterji, Saratchandra .... **TCLC 13**
See Chatterje, Sarat Chandra
See also CA 186; EWL 3

Chatterton, Thomas 1752-1770 .... **LC 3, 54**
See also DAM POET; DLB 109; RGEL 2

Chatwin, (Charles) Bruce 1940-1989 .... **CLC 28, 57, 59**
See also AAYA 4; BEST 90:1; BRWS 4; CA 85-88; 127; CPW; DAM POP; DLB 194, 204; EWL 3

Chaucer, Daniel
See Ford, Ford Madox
See also RHW

Chaucer, Geoffrey 1340(?)-1400 .. **LC 17, 56; PC 19; WLCS**
See also BRW 1; BRWC 1; BRWR 2; CD-BLB Before 1660; DA; DA3; DAB; DAC; DAM MST, POET; DLB 146; LAIT 1; PAB; PFS 14; RGEL 2; TEA; WLIT 3; WP

Chavez, Denise (Elia) 1948- .... **HLC 1**
See also CA 131; CANR 56, 81; DAM MULT; DLB 122; FW; HW 1, 2; MTCW 2

Chaviaras, Strates 1935-
See Haviaras, Stratis
See also CA 105

Chayefsky, Paddy .... **CLC 23**
See Chayefsky, Sidney
See also CAD; DLB 7, 44; DLBY 1981; RGAL 4

Chayefsky, Sidney 1923-1981
See Chayefsky, Paddy
See also CA 9-12R; 104; CANR 18; DAM DRAM

Chedid, Andree 1920- .... **CLC 47**
See also CA 145; CANR 95; EWL 3

Cheever, John 1912-1982 ..... **CLC 3, 7, 8, 11, 15, 25, 64; SSC 1, 38, 57; WLC**
See also AMWS 1; BPFB 1; CA 5-8R; 106; CABS 1; CANR 5, 27, 76; CDALB 1941-1968; CPW; DA; DA3; DAB; DAC; DAM MST, NOV, POP; DLB 2, 102, 227; DLBY 1980, 1982; EWL 3; EXPS; INT CANR-5; MTCW 1, 2; RGAL 4; RGSF 2; SSFS 2, 14; TUS

Cheever, Susan 1943- .... **CLC 18, 48**
See also CA 103; CANR 27, 51, 92; DLBY 1982; INT CANR-27

Chekhonte, Antosha
See Chekhov, Anton (Pavlovich)

Chekhov, Anton (Pavlovich) 1860-1904 ...... **DC 9; SSC 2, 28, 41, 51; TCLC 3, 10, 31, 55, 96; WLC**
See also BYA 14; CA 104; 124; DA; DA3; DAB; DAC; DAM DRAM, MST; DFS 1, 5, 10, 12; DLB 277; EW 7; EWL 3; EXPS; LAIT 3; LATS 1; RGSF 2; RGWL 2, 3; SATA 90; SSFS 5, 13, 14; TWA

Cheney, Lynne V. 1941- .... **CLC 70**
See also CA 89-92; CANR 58, 117

Chernyshevsky, Nikolai Gavrilovich
See Chernyshevsky, Nikolay Gavrilovich
See also DLB 238

Clarke, Austin C(hesterfield) 1934- .. **BLC 1;
CLC 8, 53; SSC 45**
See also BW 1; CA 25-28R; CAAS 16;
CANR 14, 32, 68; CN 7; DAC; DAM
MULT; DLB 53, 125; DNFS 2; RGSF 2

Clarke, Gillian 1937- .... **CLC 61**
See also CA 106; CP 7; CWP; DLB 40

Clarke, Marcus (Andrew Hislop)
1846-1881 .... **NCLC 19**
See also DLB 230; RGEL 2; RGSF 2

Clarke, Shirley 1925-1997 .... **CLC 16**
See also CA 189

Clash, The
See Headon, (Nicky) Topper; Jones, Mick;
Simonon, Paul; Strummer, Joe

Claudel, Paul (Louis Charles Marie)
1868-1955 .... **TCLC 2, 10**
See also CA 104; 165; DLB 192, 258; EW
8; EWL 3; GFL 1789 to the Present;
RGWL 2, 3; TWA

Claudian 370(?)-404(?) .... **CMLC 46**
See also RGWL 2, 3

Claudius, Matthias 1740-1815 .... **NCLC 75**
See also DLB 97

Clavell, James (duMaresq)
1925-1994 .... **CLC 6, 25, 87**
See also BPFB 1; CA 25-28R; 146; CANR
26, 48; CPW; DA3; DAM NOV, POP;
MTCW 1, 2; NFS 10; RHW

Clayman, Gregory .... **CLC 65**

Cleaver, (Leroy) Eldridge
1935-1998 .... **BLC 1; CLC 30, 119**
See also BW 1, 3; CA 21-24R; 167; CANR
16, 75; DA3; DAM MULT; MTCW 2;
YAW

Cleese, John (Marwood) 1939- .... **CLC 21**
See Monty Python
See also CA 112; 116; CANR 35; MTCW 1

Cleishbotham, Jebediah
See Scott, Sir Walter

Cleland, John 1710-1789 .... **LC 2, 48**
See also DLB 39; RGEL 2

Clemens, Samuel Langhorne 1835-1910
See Twain, Mark
See also CA 104; 135; CDALB 1865-1917;
DA; DA3; DAB; DAC; DAM MST, NOV;
DLB 12, 23, 64, 74, 186, 189; JRDA;
LMFS 1; MAICYA 1, 2; NCFS 4; SATA
100; SSFS 16; YABC 2

Clement of Alexandria
150(?)-215(?) .... **CMLC 41**

Cleophil
See Congreve, William

Clerihew, E.
See Bentley, E(dmund) C(lerihew)

Clerk, N. W.
See Lewis, C(live) S(taples)

Cliff, Jimmy .... **CLC 21**
See Chambers, James
See also CA 193

Cliff, Michelle 1946- .... **BLCS; CLC 120**
See also BW 2; CA 116; CANR 39, 72; CD-
WLB 3; DLB 157; FW; GLL 2

Clifford, Lady Anne 1590-1676 .... **LC 76**
See also DLB 151

Clifton, (Thelma) Lucille 1936- .... **BLC 1;
CLC 19, 66, 162; PC 17**
See also AFAW 2; BW 2, 3; CA 49-52;
CANR 2, 24, 42, 76, 97; CLR 5; CP 7;
CSW; CWP; CWRI 5; DA3; DAM MULT,
POET; DLB 5, 41; EXPP; MAICYA 1, 2;
MTCW 1, 2; PFS 1, 14; SATA 20, 69,
128; WP

Clinton, Dirk
See Silverberg, Robert

Clough, Arthur Hugh 1819-1861 ... **NCLC 27**
See also BRW 5; DLB 32; RGEL 2

Clutha, Janet Paterson Frame 1924-
See Frame, Janet
See also CA 1-4R; CANR 2, 36, 76; MTCW
1, 2; SATA 119

Clyne, Terence
See Blatty, William Peter

Cobalt, Martin
See Mayne, William (James Carter)

Cobb, Irvin S(hrewsbury)
1876-1944 .... **TCLC 77**
See also CA 175; DLB 11, 25, 86

Cobbett, William 1763-1835 .... **NCLC 49**
See also DLB 43, 107, 158; RGEL 2

Coburn, D(onald) L(ee) 1938- .... **CLC 10**
See also CA 89-92

Cocteau, Jean (Maurice Eugene Clement)
1889-1963 ...... **CLC 1, 8, 15, 16, 43; DC
17; TCLC 119; WLC**
See also CA 25-28; CANR 40; CAP 2; DA;
DA3; DAB; DAC; DAM DRAM, MST,
NOV; DLB 65, 258; EW 10; EWL 3; GFL
1789 to the Present; MTCW 1, 2; RGWL
2, 3; TWA

Codrescu, Andrei 1946- .... **CLC 46, 121**
See also CA 33-36R; CAAS 19; CANR 13,
34, 53, 76; DA3; DAM POET; MTCW 2

Coe, Max
See Bourne, Randolph S(illiman)

Coe, Tucker
See Westlake, Donald E(dwin)

Coen, Ethan 1958- .... **CLC 108**
See also CA 126; CANR 85

Coen, Joel 1955- .... **CLC 108**
See also CA 126; CANR 119

The Coen Brothers
See Coen, Ethan; Coen, Joel

Coetzee, J(ohn) M(axwell) 1940- ..... **CLC 23,
33, 66, 117, 161, 162**
See also AAYA 37; AFW; BRWS 6; CA 77-
80; CANR 41, 54, 74; CN 7; DA3;
DAM NOV; DLB 225; EWL 3; LMFS 2;
MTCW 1, 2; WLIT 2

Coffey, Brian
See Koontz, Dean R(ay)

Coffin, Robert P(eter) Tristram
1892-1955 .... **TCLC 95**
See also CA 123; 169; DLB 45

Cohan, George M(ichael)
1878-1942 .... **TCLC 60**
See also CA 157; DLB 249; RGAL 4

Cohen, Arthur A(llen) 1928-1986 ...... **CLC 7,
31**
See also CA 1-4R; 120; CANR 1, 17, 42;
DLB 28

Cohen, Leonard (Norman) 1934- ...... **CLC 3,
38**
See also CA 21-24R; CANR 14, 69; CN 7;
CP 7; DAC; DAM MST; DLB 53; EWL
3; MTCW 1

Cohen, Matt(hew) 1942-1999 .... **CLC 19**
See also CA 61-64; 187; CAAS 18; CANR
40; CN 7; DAC; DLB 53

Cohen-Solal, Annie 19(?)- .... **CLC 50**

Colegate, Isabel 1931- .... **CLC 36**
See also CA 17-20R; CANR 8, 22, 74; CN
7; DLB 14, 231; INT CANR-22; MTCW
1

Coleman, Emmett
See Reed, Ishmael

Coleridge, Hartley 1796-1849 .... **NCLC 90**
See also DLB 96

Coleridge, M. E.
See Coleridge, Mary E(lizabeth)

Coleridge, Mary E(lizabeth)
1861-1907 .... **TCLC 73**
See also CA 116; 166; DLB 19, 98

Coleridge, Samuel Taylor
1772-1834 ...... **NCLC 9, 54, 99, 111; PC
11, 39; WLC**
See also BRW 4; BRWR 2; BYA 4; CD-
BLB 1789-1832; DA; DA3; DAB; DAC;
DAM MST, POET; DLB 93, 107; EXPP;
LATS 1; LMFS 1; PAB; PFS 4, 5; RGEL
2; TEA; WLIT 3; WP

Coleridge, Sara 1802-1852 .... **NCLC 31**
See also DLB 199

Coles, Don 1928- .... **CLC 46**
See also CA 115; CANR 38; CP 7

Coles, Robert (Martin) 1929- .... **CLC 108**
See also CA 45-48; CANR 3, 32, 66, 70;
INT CANR-32; SATA 23

Colette, (Sidonie-Gabrielle)
1873-1954 .... **SSC 10; TCLC 1, 5, 16**
See Willy, Colette
See also CA 104; 131; DA3; DAM NOV;
DLB 65; EW 9; EWL 3; GFL 1789 to the
Present; MTCW 1, 2; RGWL 2, 3; TWA

Collett, (Jacobine) Camilla (Wergeland)
1813-1895 .... **NCLC 22**

Collier, Christopher 1930- .... **CLC 30**
See also AAYA 13; BYA 2; CA 33-36R;
CANR 13, 33, 102; JRDA; MAICYA 1,
2; SATA 16, 70; WYA; YAW 1

Collier, James Lincoln 1928- .... **CLC 30**
See also AAYA 13; BYA 2; CA 9-12R;
CANR 4, 33, 60, 102; CLR 3; DAM POP;
JRDA; MAICYA 1, 2; SAAS 21; SATA 8,
70; WYA; YAW 1

Collier, Jeremy 1650-1726 .... **LC 6**

Collier, John 1901-1980 . **SSC 19; TCLC 127**
See also CA 65-68; 97-100; CANR 10;
DLB 77, 255; FANT; SUFW 1

Collier, Mary 1690-1762 .... **LC 86**
See also DLB 95

Collingwood, R(obin) G(eorge)
1889(?)-1943 .... **TCLC 67**
See also CA 117; 155; DLB 262

Collins, Hunt
See Hunter, Evan

Collins, Linda 1931- .... **CLC 44**
See also CA 125

Collins, Tom
See Furphy, Joseph
See also RGEL 2

Collins, (William) Wilkie
1824-1889 .... **NCLC 1, 18, 93**
See also BRWS 6; CDBLB 1832-1890;
CMW 4; DLB 18, 70, 159; MSW; RGEL
2; RGSF 2; SUFW 1; WLIT 4

Collins, William 1721-1759 .... **LC 4, 40**
See also BRW 3; DAM POET; DLB 109;
RGEL 2

Collodi, Carlo .... **NCLC 54**
See Lorenzini, Carlo
See also CLR 5; WCH

Colman, George
See Glassco, John

Colonna, Vittoria 1492-1547 .... **LC 71**
See also RGWL 2, 3

Colt, Winchester Remington
See Hubbard, L(afayette) Ron(ald)

Colter, Cyrus J. 1910-2002 .... **CLC 58**
See also BW 1; CA 65-68; 205; CANR 10,
66; CN 7; DLB 33

Colton, James
See Hansen, Joseph
See also GLL 1

Colum, Padraic 1881-1972 .... **CLC 28**
See also BYA 4; CA 73-76; 33-36R; CANR
35; CLR 36; CWRI 5; DLB 19; MAICYA
1, 2; MTCW 1; RGEL 2; SATA 15; WCH

Colvin, James
See Moorcock, Michael (John)

Colwin, Laurie (E.) 1944-1992 .... **CLC 5, 13, 23, 84**
See also CA 89-92; 139; CANR 20, 46; DLB 218; DLBY 1980; MTCW 1

Comfort, Alex(ander) 1920-2000 .... **CLC 7**
See also CA 1-4R; 190; CANR 1, 45; CP 7; DAM POP; MTCW 1

Comfort, Montgomery
See Campbell, (John) Ramsey

Compton-Burnett, I(vy)
1892(?)-1969 ...... **CLC 1, 3, 10, 15, 34**
See also BRW 7; CA 1-4R; 25-28R; CANR 4; DAM NOV; DLB 36; EWL 3; MTCW 1; RGEL 2

Comstock, Anthony 1844-1915 ...... **TCLC 13**
See also CA 110; 169

Comte, Auguste 1798-1857 .... **NCLC 54**

Conan Doyle, Arthur
See Doyle, Sir Arthur Conan
See also BPFB 1; BYA 4, 5, 11

Conde (Abellan), Carmen
1901-1996 .... **HLCS 1**
See also CA 177; DLB 108; EWL 3; HW 2

Conde, Maryse 1937- ..... **BLCS; CLC 52, 92**
See also BW 2, 3; CA 110; CAAE 190; CANR 30, 53, 76; CWW 2; DAM MULT; EWL 3; MTCW 1

Condillac, Etienne Bonnot de
1714-1780 .... **LC 26**

Condon, Richard (Thomas)
1915-1996 .... **CLC 4, 6, 8, 10, 45, 100**
See also BEST 90:3; BPFB 1; CA 1-4R; 151; CAAS 1; CANR 2, 23; CMW 4; CN 7; DAM NOV; INT CANR-23; MTCW 1, 2

Confucius 551B.C.-479B.C. .... **CMLC 19; WLCS**
See also DA; DA3; DAB; DAC; DAM MST

Congreve, William 1670-1729 ... **DC 2; LC 5, 21; WLC**
See also BRW 2; CDBLB 1660-1789; DA; DAB; DAC; DAM DRAM, MST, POET; DFS 15; DLB 39, 84; RGEL 2; WLIT 3

Conley, Robert J(ackson) 1940- .... **NNAL**
See also CA 41-44R; CANR 15, 34, 45, 96; DAM MULT

Connell, Evan S(helby), Jr. 1924- . **CLC 4, 6, 45**
See also AAYA 7; CA 1-4R; CAAS 2; CANR 2, 39, 76, 97; CN 7; DAM NOV; DLB 2; DLBY 1981; MTCW 1, 2

Connelly, Marc(us Cook) 1890-1980 . **CLC 7**
See also CA 85-88; 102; CANR 30; DFS 12; DLB 7; DLBY 1980; RGAL 4; SATA-Obit 25

Connor, Ralph .... **TCLC 31**
See Gordon, Charles William
See also DLB 92; TCWW 2

Conrad, Joseph 1857-1924 . **SSC 9; TCLC 1, 6, 13, 25, 43, 57; WLC**
See also AAYA 26; BPFB 1; BRW 6; BRWC 1; BRWR 2; BYA 2; CA 104; 131; CANR 60; CDBLB 1890-1914; DA; DA3; DAB; DAC; DAM MST, NOV; DLB 10, 34, 98, 156; EWL 3; EXPN; EXPS; LAIT 2; LATS 1; LMFS 1; MTCW 1, 2; NFS 2, 16; RGEL 2; RGSF 2; SATA 27; SSFS 1, 12; TEA; WLIT 4

Conrad, Robert Arnold
See Hart, Moss

Conroy, (Donald) Pat(rick) 1945- ... **CLC 30, 74**
See also AAYA 8, 52; AITN 1; BPFB 1; CA 85-88; CANR 24, 53; CPW; CSW; DA3; DAM NOV, POP; DLB 6; LAIT 5; MTCW 1, 2

Constant (de Rebecque), (Henri) Benjamin
1767-1830 .... **NCLC 6**
See also DLB 119; EW 4; GFL 1789 to the Present

Conway, Jill K(er) 1934- .... **CLC 152**
See also CA 130; CANR 94

Conybeare, Charles Augustus
See Eliot, T(homas) S(tearns)

Cook, Michael 1933-1994 .... **CLC 58**
See also CA 93-96; CANR 68; DLB 53

Cook, Robin 1940- .... **CLC 14**
See also AAYA 32; BEST 90:2; BPFB 1; CA 108; 111; CANR 41, 90, 109; CPW; DA3; DAM POP; HGG; INT CA-111

Cook, Roy
See Silverberg, Robert

Cooke, Elizabeth 1948- .... **CLC 55**
See also CA 129

Cooke, John Esten 1830-1886 .... **NCLC 5**
See also DLB 3, 248; RGAL 4

Cooke, John Estes
See Baum, L(yman) Frank

Cooke, M. E.
See Creasey, John

Cooke, Margaret
See Creasey, John

Cooke, Rose Terry 1827-1892 ...... **NCLC 110**
See also DLB 12, 74

Cook-Lynn, Elizabeth 1930- .... **CLC 93; NNAL**
See also CA 133; DAM MULT; DLB 175

Cooney, Ray .... **CLC 62**
See also CBD

Cooper, Douglas 1960- .... **CLC 86**

Cooper, Henry St. John
See Creasey, John

Cooper, J(oan) California (?)- .... **CLC 56**
See also AAYA 12; BW 1; CA 125; CANR 55; DAM MULT; DLB 212

Cooper, James Fenimore
1789-1851 .... **NCLC 1, 27, 54**
See also AAYA 22; AMW; BPFB 1; CDALB 1640-1865; DA3; DLB 3, 183, 250, 254; LAIT 1; NFS 9; RGAL 4; SATA 19; TUS; WCH

Cooper, Susan Fenimore
1813-1894 .... **NCLC 129**
See also ANW; DLB 239, 254

Coover, Robert (Lowell) 1932- ...... **CLC 3, 7, 15, 32, 46, 87, 161; SSC 15**
See also AMWS 5; BPFB 1; CA 45-48; CANR 3, 37, 58, 115; CN 7; DAM NOV; DLB 2, 227; DLBY 1981; EWL 3; MTCW 1, 2; RGAL 4; RGSF 2

Copeland, Stewart (Armstrong)
1952- .... **CLC 26**

Copernicus, Nicolaus 1473-1543 .... **LC 45**

Coppard, A(lfred) E(dgar)
1878-1957 .... **SSC 21; TCLC 5**
See also BRWS 8; CA 114; 167; DLB 162; EWL 3; HGG; RGEL 2; RGSF 2; SUFW 1; YABC 1

Coppee, Francois 1842-1908 .... **TCLC 25**
See also CA 170; DLB 217

Coppola, Francis Ford 1939- ... **CLC 16, 126**
See also AAYA 39; CA 77-80; CANR 40, 78; DLB 44

Copway, George 1818-1869 .... **NNAL**
See also DAM MULT; DLB 175, 183

Corbiere, Tristan 1845-1875 .... **NCLC 43**
See also DLB 217; GFL 1789 to the Present

Corcoran, Barbara (Asenath)
1911- .... **CLC 17**
See also AAYA 14; CA 21-24R; CAAE 191; CAAS 1; CANR 11, 28, 48; CLR 50; DLB 52; JRDA; MAICYA 2; MAICYAS 1; RHW; SAAS 20; SATA 3, 77, 125

Cordelier, Maurice
See Giraudoux, Jean(-Hippolyte)

Corelli, Marie .... **TCLC 51**
See Mackay, Mary
See also DLB 34, 156; RGEL 2; SUFW 1

Corman, Cid .... **CLC 9**
See Corman, Sidney
See also CAAS 2; DLB 5, 193

Corman, Sidney 1924-
See Corman, Cid
See also CA 85-88; CANR 44; CP 7; DAM POET

Cormier, Robert (Edmund)
1925-2000 .... **CLC 12, 30**
See also AAYA 3, 19; BYA 1, 2, 6, 8, 9; CA 1-4R; CANR 5, 23, 76, 93; CDALB 1968-1988; CLR 12, 55; DA; DAB; DAC; DAM MST, NOV; DLB 52; EXPN; INT CANR-23; JRDA; LAIT 5; MAICYA 1, 2; MTCW 1, 2; NFS 2, 18; SATA 10, 45, 83; SATA-Obit 122; WYA; YAW

Corn, Alfred (DeWitt III) 1943- ...... **CLC 33**
See also CA 179; CAAE 179; CAAS 25; CANR 44; CP 7; CSW; DLB 120, 282; DLBY 1980

Corneille, Pierre 1606-1684 ... **DC 21; LC 28**
See also DAB; DAM MST; DLB 268; EW 3; GFL Beginnings to 1789; RGWL 2, 3; TWA

Cornwell, David (John Moore)
1931- .... **CLC 9, 15**
See le Carre, John
See also CA 5-8R; CANR 13, 33, 59, 107; DA3; DAM POP; MTCW 1, 2

Cornwell, Patricia (Daniels) 1956- . **CLC 155**
See also AAYA 16; BPFB 1; CA 134; CANR 53; CMW 4; CPW; CSW; DAM POP; MSW; MTCW 1

Corso, (Nunzio) Gregory 1930-2001 . **CLC 1, 11; PC 33**
See also AMWS 12; BG 2; CA 5-8R; 193; CANR 41, 76; CP 7; DA3; DLB 5, 16, 237; LMFS 2; MTCW 1, 2; WP

Cortazar, Julio 1914-1984 ... **CLC 2, 3, 5, 10, 13, 15, 33, 34, 92; HLC 1; SSC 7**
See also BPFB 1; CA 21-24R; CANR 12, 32, 81; CDWLB 3; DA3; DAM MULT, NOV; DLB 113; EWL 3; EXPS; HW 1, 2; LAW; MTCW 1, 2; RGSF 2; RGWL 2, 3; SSFS 3; TWA; WLIT 1

Cortes, Hernan 1485-1547 .... **LC 31**

Corvinus, Jakob
See Raabe, Wilhelm (Karl)

Corwin, Cecil
See Kornbluth, C(yril) M.

Cosic, Dobrica 1921- .... **CLC 14**
See also CA 122; 138; CDWLB 4; CWW 2; DLB 181; EWL 3

Costain, Thomas B(ertram)
1885-1965 .... **CLC 30**
See also BYA 3; CA 5-8R; 25-28R; DLB 9; RHW

Costantini, Humberto 1924(?)-1987 . **CLC 49**
See also CA 131; 122; EWL 3; HW 1

Costello, Elvis 1954- .... **CLC 21**
See also CA 204

Costenoble, Philostene
See Ghelderode, Michel de

Cotes, Cecil V.
See Duncan, Sara Jeannette

Cotter, Joseph Seamon Sr.
1861-1949 .... **BLC 1; TCLC 28**
See also BW 1; CA 124; DAM MULT; DLB 50

Couch, Arthur Thomas Quiller
See Quiller-Couch, Sir Arthur (Thomas)

Coulton, James
See Hansen, Joseph

Couperus, Louis (Marie Anne)
1863-1923 .... **TCLC 15**
See also CA 115; EWL 3; RGWL 2, 3

Coupland, Douglas 1961- .... **CLC 85, 133**
See also AAYA 34; CA 142; CANR 57, 90;
CCA 1; CPW; DAC; DAM POP
Court, Wesli
See Turco, Lewis (Putnam)
Courtenay, Bryce 1933- .... **CLC 59**
See also CA 138; CPW
Courtney, Robert
See Ellison, Harlan (Jay)
Cousteau, Jacques-Yves 1910-1997 .. **CLC 30**
See also CA 65-68; 159; CANR 15, 67;
MTCW 1; SATA 38, 98
Coventry, Francis 1725-1754 .... **LC 46**
Coverdale, Miles c. 1487-1569 .... **LC 77**
See also DLB 167
Cowan, Peter (Walkinshaw) 1914- .... **SSC 28**
See also CA 21-24R; CANR 9, 25, 50, 83;
CN 7; DLB 260; RGSF 2
Coward, Noel (Peirce) 1899-1973 . **CLC 1, 9,
29, 51**
See also AITN 1; BRWS 2; CA 17-18; 41-
44R; CANR 35; CAP 2; CDBLB 1914-
1945; DA3; DAM DRAM; DFS 3, 6;
DLB 10, 245; EWL 3; IDFW 3, 4; MTCW
1, 2; RGEL 2; TEA
Cowley, Abraham 1618-1667 .... **LC 43**
See also BRW 2; DLB 131, 151; PAB;
RGEL 2
Cowley, Malcolm 1898-1989 .... **CLC 39**
See also AMWS 2; CA 5-8R; 128; CANR
3, 55; DLB 4, 48; DLBY 1981, 1989;
EWL 3; MTCW 1, 2
Cowper, William 1731-1800 ..... **NCLC 8, 94;
PC 40**
See also BRW 3; DA3; DAM POET; DLB
104, 109; RGEL 2
Cox, William Trevor 1928-
See Trevor, William
See also CA 9-12R; CANR 4, 37, 55, 76,
102; DAM NOV; INT CANR-37; MTCW
1, 2; TEA
Coyne, P. J.
See Masters, Hilary
Cozzens, James Gould 1903-1978 . **CLC 1, 4,
11, 92**
See also AMW; BPFB 1; CA 9-12R; 81-84;
CANR 19; CDALB 1941-1968; DLB 9;
DLBD 2; DLBY 1984, 1997; EWL 3;
MTCW 1, 2; RGAL 4
Crabbe, George 1754-1832 .... **NCLC 26, 121**
See also BRW 3; DLB 93; RGEL 2
Crace, Jim 1946- .... **CLC 157; SSC 61**
See also CA 128; 135; CANR 55, 70, 123;
CN 7; DLB 231; INT CA-135
Craddock, Charles Egbert
See Murfree, Mary Noailles
Craig, A. A.
See Anderson, Poul (William)
Craik, Mrs.
See Craik, Dinah Maria (Mulock)
See also RGEL 2
Craik, Dinah Maria (Mulock)
1826-1887 .... **NCLC 38**
See Craik, Mrs.; Mulock, Dinah Maria
See also DLB 35, 163; MAICYA 1, 2;
SATA 34
Cram, Ralph Adams 1863-1942 ..... **TCLC 45**
See also CA 160
Cranch, Christopher Pearse
1813-1892 .... **NCLC 115**
See also DLB 1, 42, 243
Crane, (Harold) Hart 1899-1932 .... **PC 3;
TCLC 2, 5, 80; WLC**
See also AMW; AMWR 2; CA 104; 127;
CDALB 1917-1929; DA; DA3; DAB;
DAC; DAM MST, POET; DLB 4, 48;
EWL 3; MTCW 1, 2; RGAL 4; TUS

Crane, R(onald) S(almon)
1886-1967 .... **CLC 27**
See also CA 85-88; DLB 63
Crane, Stephen (Townley)
1871-1900 ...... **SSC 7, 56; TCLC 11, 17,
32; WLC**
See also AAYA 21; AMW; AMWC 1; BPFB
1; BYA 3; CA 109; 140; CANR 84;
CDALB 1865-1917; DA; DA3; DAB;
DAC; DAM MST, NOV, POET; DLB 12,
54, 78; EXPN; EXPS; LAIT 2; LMFS 2;
NFS 4; PFS 9; RGAL 4; RGSF 2; SSFS
4; TUS; WYA; YABC 2
Cranmer, Thomas 1489-1556 .... **LC 95**
See also DLB 132, 213
Cranshaw, Stanley
See Fisher, Dorothy (Frances) Canfield
Crase, Douglas 1944- .... **CLC 58**
See also CA 106
Crashaw, Richard 1612(?)-1649 .... **LC 24**
See also BRW 2; DLB 126; PAB; RGEL 2
Cratinus c. 519B.C.-c. 422B.C. ..... **CMLC 54**
See also LMFS 1
Craven, Margaret 1901-1980 .... **CLC 17**
See also BYA 2; CA 103; CCA 1; DAC;
LAIT 5
Crawford, F(rancis) Marion
1854-1909 .... **TCLC 10**
See also CA 107; 168; DLB 71; HGG;
RGAL 4; SUFW 1
Crawford, Isabella Valancy
1850-1887 .... **NCLC 12, 127**
See also DLB 92; RGEL 2
Crayon, Geoffrey
See Irving, Washington
Creasey, John 1908-1973 .... **CLC 11**
See Marric, J. J.
See also CA 5-8R; 41-44R; CANR 8, 59;
CMW 4; DLB 77; MTCW 1
Crebillon, Claude Prosper Jolyot de (fils)
1707-1777 .... **LC 1, 28**
See also GFL Beginnings to 1789
Credo
See Creasey, John
Credo, Alvaro J. de
See Prado (Calvo), Pedro
Creeley, Robert (White) 1926- .. **CLC 1, 2, 4,
8, 11, 15, 36, 78**
See also AMWS 4; CA 1-4R; CAAS 10;
CANR 23, 43, 89; CP 7; DA3; DAM
POET; DLB 5, 16, 169; DLBD 17; EWL
3; MTCW 1, 2; RGAL 4; WP
Crevecoeur, Hector St. John de
See Crevecoeur, Michel Guillaume Jean de
See also ANW
Crevecoeur, Michel Guillaume Jean de
1735-1813 .... **NCLC 105**
See Crevecoeur, Hector St. John de
See also AMWS 1; DLB 37
Crevel, Rene 1900-1935 .... **TCLC 112**
See also GLL 2
Crews, Harry (Eugene) 1935- ..... **CLC 6, 23,
49**
See also AITN 1; AMWS 11; BPFB 1; CA
25-28R; CANR 20, 57; CN 7; CSW; DA3;
DLB 6, 143, 185; MTCW 1, 2; RGAL 4
Crichton, (John) Michael 1942- .... **CLC 2, 6,
54, 90**
See also AAYA 10, 49; AITN 2; BPFB 1;
CA 25-28R; CANR 13, 40, 54, 76; CMW
4; CN 7; CPW; DA3; DAM NOV, POP;
DLBY 1981; INT CANR-13; JRDA;
MTCW 1, 2; SATA 9, 88; SFW 4; YAW
Crispin, Edmund .... **CLC 22**
See Montgomery, (Robert) Bruce
See also DLB 87; MSW
Cristofer, Michael 1945(?)- .... **CLC 28**
See also CA 110; 152; CAD; CD 5; DAM
DRAM; DFS 15; DLB 7

Criton
See Alain
Croce, Benedetto 1866-1952 .... **TCLC 37**
See also CA 120; 155; EW 8; EWL 3
Crockett, David 1786-1836 .... **NCLC 8**
See also DLB 3, 11, 183, 248
Crockett, Davy
See Crockett, David
Crofts, Freeman Wills 1879-1957 .. **TCLC 55**
See also CA 115; 195; CMW 4; DLB 77;
MSW
Croker, John Wilson 1780-1857 .... **NCLC 10**
See also DLB 110
Crommelynck, Fernand 1885-1970 .. **CLC 75**
See also CA 189; 89-92; EWL 3
Cromwell, Oliver 1599-1658 .... **LC 43**
Cronenberg, David 1943- .... **CLC 143**
See also CA 138; CCA 1
Cronin, A(rchibald) J(oseph)
1896-1981 .... **CLC 32**
See also BPFB 1; CA 1-4R; 102; CANR 5;
DLB 191; SATA 47; SATA-Obit 25
Cross, Amanda
See Heilbrun, Carolyn G(old)
See also BPFB 1; CMW; CPW; MSW
Crothers, Rachel 1878-1958 .... **TCLC 19**
See also CA 113; 194; CAD; CWD; DLB
7, 266; RGAL 4
Croves, Hal
See Traven, B.
Crow Dog, Mary (Ellen) (?)- .... **CLC 93**
See Brave Bird, Mary
See also CA 154
Crowfield, Christopher
See Stowe, Harriet (Elizabeth) Beecher
Crowley, Aleister .... **TCLC 7**
See Crowley, Edward Alexander
See also GLL 1
Crowley, Edward Alexander 1875-1947
See Crowley, Aleister
See also CA 104; HGG
Crowley, John 1942- .... **CLC 57**
See also BPFB 1; CA 61-64; CANR 43, 98;
DLBY 1982; SATA 65, 140; SFW 4;
SUFW 2
Crud
See Crumb, R(obert)
Crumarums
See Crumb, R(obert)
Crumb, R(obert) 1943- .... **CLC 17**
See also CA 106; CANR 107
Crumbum
See Crumb, R(obert)
Crumski
See Crumb, R(obert)
Crum the Bum
See Crumb, R(obert)
Crunk
See Crumb, R(obert)
Crustt
See Crumb, R(obert)
Crutchfield, Les
See Trumbo, Dalton
Cruz, Victor Hernandez 1949- ... **HLC 1; PC
37**
See also BW 2; CA 65-68; CAAS 17;
CANR 14, 32, 74; CP 7; DAM MULT,
POET; DLB 41; DNFS 1; EXPP; HW 1,
2; MTCW 1; PFS 16; WP
Cryer, Gretchen (Kiger) 1935- .... **CLC 21**
See also CA 114; 123
Csath, Geza 1887-1919 .... **TCLC 13**
See also CA 111
Cudlip, David R(ockwell) 1933- .... **CLC 34**
See also CA 177

Davies, Sir John 1569-1626 .... **LC 85**
See also DLB 172

Davies, Walter C.
See Kornbluth, C(yril) M.

Davies, William Henry 1871-1940 ... **TCLC 5**
See also CA 104; 179; DLB 19, 174; EWL
3; RGEL 2

Da Vinci, Leonardo 1452-1519 ..... **LC 12, 57, 60**
See also AAYA 40

Davis, Angela (Yvonne) 1944- .... **CLC 77**
See also BW 2, 3; CA 57-60; CANR 10, 81; CSW; DA3; DAM MULT; FW

Davis, B. Lynch
See Bioy Casares, Adolfo; Borges, Jorge
Luis

Davis, Frank Marshall 1905-1987 ...... **BLC 1**
See also BW 2, 3; CA 125; 123; CANR 42, 80; DAM MULT; DLB 51

Davis, Gordon
See Hunt, E(verette) Howard, (Jr.)

Davis, H(arold) L(enoir) 1896-1960 . **CLC 49**
See also ANW; CA 178; 89-92; DLB 9, 206; SATA 114

Davis, Rebecca (Blaine) Harding
1831-1910 .... **SSC 38; TCLC 6**
See also CA 104; 179; DLB 74, 239; FW;
NFS 14; RGAL 4; TUS

Davis, Richard Harding
1864-1916 .... **TCLC 24**
See also CA 114; 179; DLB 12, 23, 78, 79, 189; DLBD 13; RGAL 4

Davison, Frank Dalby 1893-1970 ..... **CLC 15**
See also CA 116; DLB 260

Davison, Lawrence H.
See Lawrence, D(avid) H(erbert Richards)

Davison, Peter (Hubert) 1928- .... **CLC 28**
See also CA 9-12R; CAAS 4; CANR 3, 43, 84; CP 7; DLB 5

Davys, Mary 1674-1732 .... **LC 1, 46**
See also DLB 39

Dawson, (Guy) Fielding (Lewis)
1930-2002 .... **CLC 6**
See also CA 85-88; 202; CANR 108; DLB
130; DLBY 2002

Dawson, Peter
See Faust, Frederick (Schiller)
See also TCWW 2, 2

Day, Clarence (Shepard, Jr.)
1874-1935 .... **TCLC 25**
See also CA 108; 199; DLB 11

Day, John 1574(?)-1640(?) .... **LC 70**
See also DLB 62, 170; RGEL 2

Day, Thomas 1748-1789 .... **LC 1**
See also DLB 39; YABC 1

Day Lewis, C(ecil) 1904-1972 . **CLC 1, 6, 10; PC 11**
See Blake, Nicholas
See also BRWS 3; CA 13-16; 33-36R;
CANR 34; CAP 1; CWRI 5; DAM POET;
DLB 15, 20; EWL 3; MTCW 1, 2; RGEL
2

Dazai Osamu .... **SSC 41; TCLC 11**
See Tsushima, Shuji
See also CA 164; DLB 182; EWL 3; MJW;
RGSF 2; RGWL 2, 3; TWA

de Andrade, Carlos Drummond
See Drummond de Andrade, Carlos

de Andrade, Mario 1892-1945
See Andrade, Mario de
See also CA 178; HW 2

Deane, Norman
See Creasey, John

Deane, Seamus (Francis) 1940- ...... **CLC 122**
See also CA 118; CANR 42

de Beauvoir, Simone (Lucie Ernestine Marie Bertrand)
See Beauvoir, Simone (Lucie Ernestine
Marie Bertrand) de

de Beer, P.
See Bosman, Herman Charles

de Brissac, Malcolm
See Dickinson, Peter (Malcolm)

de Campos, Alvaro
See Pessoa, Fernando (Antonio Nogueira)

de Chardin, Pierre Teilhard
See Teilhard de Chardin, (Marie Joseph)
Pierre

Dee, John 1527-1608 .... **LC 20**
See also DLB 136, 213

Deer, Sandra 1940- .... **CLC 45**
See also CA 186

De Ferrari, Gabriella 1941- .... **CLC 65**
See also CA 146

de Filippo, Eduardo 1900-1984 ... **TCLC 127**
See also CA 132; 114; EWL 3; MTCW 1;
RGWL 2, 3

Defoe, Daniel 1660(?)-1731 .. **LC 1, 42; WLC**
See also AAYA 27; BRW 3; BRWR 1; BYA
4; CDBLB 1660-1789; CLR 61; DA;
DA3; DAB; DAC; DAM MST, NOV;
DLB 39, 95, 101; JRDA; LAIT 1; LMFS
1; MAICYA 1, 2; NFS 9, 13; RGEL 2;
SATA 22; TEA; WCH; WLIT 3

de Gourmont, Remy(-Marie-Charles)
See Gourmont, Remy(-Marie-Charles) de

de Hartog, Jan 1914-2002 .... **CLC 19**
See also CA 1-4R; 210; CANR 1; DFS 12

de Hostos, E. M.
See Hostos (y Bonilla), Eugenio Maria de

de Hostos, Eugenio M.
See Hostos (y Bonilla), Eugenio Maria de

Deighton, Len .... **CLC 4, 7, 22, 46**
See Deighton, Leonard Cyril
See also AAYA 6; BEST 89:2; BPFB 1; CD-
BLB 1960 to Present; CMW 4; CN 7;
CPW; DLB 87

Deighton, Leonard Cyril 1929-
See Deighton, Len
See also CA 9-12R; CANR 19, 33, 68;
DA3; DAM NOV, POP; MTCW 1, 2

Dekker, Thomas 1572(?)-1632 ..... **DC 12; LC 22**
See also CDBLB Before 1660; DAM
DRAM; DLB 62, 172; LMFS 1; RGEL 2

de Laclos, Pierre Ambroise Franois
See Laclos, Pierre Ambroise Francois

Delafield, E. M. .... **TCLC 61**
See Dashwood, Edmee Elizabeth Monica
de la Pasture
See also DLB 34; RHW

de la Mare, Walter (John)
1873-1956 . **SSC 14; TCLC 4, 53; WLC**
See also CA 163; CDBLB 1914-1945; CLR
23; CWRI 5; DA3; DAB; DAC; DAM
MST, POET; DLB 19, 153, 162, 255, 284;
EWL 3; EXPP; HGG; MAICYA 1, 2;
MTCW 1; RGEL 2; RGSF 2; SATA 16;
SUFW 1; TEA; WCH

de Lamartine, Alphonse (Marie Louis Prat)
See Lamartine, Alphonse (Marie Louis Prat)
de

Delaney, Franey
See O'Hara, John (Henry)

Delaney, Shelagh 1939- .... **CLC 29**
See also CA 17-20R; CANR 30, 67; CBD;
CD 5; CDBLB 1960 to Present; CWD;
DAM DRAM; DFS 7; DLB 13; MTCW 1

Delany, Martin Robison
1812-1885 .... **NCLC 93**
See also DLB 50; RGAL 4

Delany, Mary (Granville Pendarves)
1700-1788 .... **LC 12**

Delany, Samuel R(ay), Jr. 1942- .... **BLC 1; CLC 8, 14, 38, 141**
See also AAYA 24; AFAW 2; BPFB 1; BW
2, 3; CA 81-84; CANR 27, 43, 115, 116;
CN 7; DAM MULT; DLB 8, 33; FANT;
MTCW 1, 2; RGAL 4; SATA 92; SCFW;
SFW 4; SUFW 2

De la Ramee, Marie Louise (Ouida)
1839-1908
See Ouida
See also CA 204; SATA 20

de la Roche, Mazo 1879-1961 .... **CLC 14**
See also CA 85-88; CANR 30; DLB 68;
RGEL 2; RHW; SATA 64

De La Salle, Innocent
See Hartmann, Sadakichi

de Laureamont, Comte
See Lautreamont

Delbanco, Nicholas (Franklin)
1942- .... **CLC 6, 13, 167**
See also CA 17-20R; CAAE 189; CAAS 2;
CANR 29, 55, 116; DLB 6, 234

del Castillo, Michel 1933- .... **CLC 38**
See also CA 109; CANR 77

Deledda, Grazia (Cosima)
1875(?)-1936 .... **TCLC 23**
See also CA 123; 205; DLB 264; EWL 3;
RGWL 2, 3

Deleuze, Gilles 1925-1995 .... **TCLC 116**

Delgado, Abelardo (Lalo) B(arrientos)
1930- .... **HLC 1**
See also CA 131; CAAS 15; CANR 90;
DAM MST, MULT; DLB 82; HW 1, 2

Delibes, Miguel .... **CLC 8, 18**
See Delibes Setien, Miguel
See also EWL 3

Delibes Setien, Miguel 1920-
See Delibes, Miguel
See also CA 45-48; CANR 1, 32; HW 1;
MTCW 1

DeLillo, Don 1936- ..... **CLC 8, 10, 13, 27, 39, 54, 76, 143**
See also AMWC 2; AMWS 6; BEST 89:1;
BPFB 1; CA 81-84; CANR 21, 76, 92;
CN 7; CPW; DA3; DAM NOV, POP;
DLB 6, 173; EWL 3; MTCW 1, 2; RGAL
4; TUS

de Lisser, H. G.
See De Lisser, H(erbert) G(eorge)
See also DLB 117

De Lisser, H(erbert) G(eorge)
1878-1944 .... **TCLC 12**
See de Lisser, H. G.
See also BW 2; CA 109; 152

Deloire, Pierre
See Peguy, Charles (Pierre)

Deloney, Thomas 1543(?)-1600 .... **LC 41**
See also DLB 167; RGEL 2

Deloria, Ella (Cara) 1889-1971(?) ..... **NNAL**
See also CA 152; DAM MULT; DLB 175

Deloria, Vine (Victor), Jr. 1933- ...... **CLC 21, 122; NNAL**
See also CA 53-56; CANR 5, 20, 48, 98;
DAM MULT; DLB 175; MTCW 1; SATA
21

del Valle-Inclan, Ramon (Maria)
See Valle-Inclan, Ramon (Maria) del

Del Vecchio, John M(ichael) 1947- .. **CLC 29**
See also CA 110; DLBD 9

de Man, Paul (Adolph Michel)
1919-1983 .... **CLC 55**
See also CA 128; 111; CANR 61; DLB 67;
MTCW 1, 2

DeMarinis, Rick 1934- .... **CLC 54**
See also CA 57-60, 184; CAAE 184; CAAS
24; CANR 9, 25, 50; DLB 218

de Maupassant, (Henri Rene Albert) Guy
See Maupassant, (Henri Rene Albert) Guy
de

Dembry, R. Emmet
    See Murfree, Mary Noailles
Demby, William 1922- .... **BLC 1; CLC 53**
    See also BW 1, 3; CA 81-84; CANR 81;
    DAM MULT; DLB 33
de Menton, Francisco
    See Chin, Frank (Chew, Jr.)
Demetrius of Phalerum c.
    307B.C.- .... **CMLC 34**
Demijohn, Thom
    See Disch, Thomas M(ichael)
De Mille, James 1833-1880 .... **NCLC 123**
    See also DLB 99, 251
Deming, Richard 1915-1983
    See Queen, Ellery
    See also CA 9-12R; CANR 3, 94; SATA 24
Democritus c. 460B.C.-c. 370B.C. . **CMLC 47**
de Montaigne, Michel (Eyquem)
    See Montaigne, Michel (Eyquem) de
de Montherlant, Henry (Milon)
    See Montherlant, Henry (Milon) de
Demosthenes 384B.C.-322B.C. ...... **CMLC 13**
    See also AW 1; DLB 176; RGWL 2, 3
de Musset, (Louis Charles) Alfred
    See Musset, (Louis Charles) Alfred de
de Natale, Francine
    See Malzberg, Barry N(athaniel)
de Navarre, Marguerite 1492-1549 ..... **LC 61**
    See Marguerite d'Angouleme; Marguerite
    de Navarre
Denby, Edwin (Orr) 1903-1983 .... **CLC 48**
    See also CA 138; 110
de Nerval, Gerard
    See Nerval, Gerard de
Denham, John 1615-1669 .... **LC 73**
    See also DLB 58, 126; RGEL 2
Denis, Julio
    See Cortazar, Julio
Denmark, Harrison
    See Zelazny, Roger (Joseph)
Dennis, John 1658-1734 .... **LC 11**
    See also DLB 101; RGEL 2
Dennis, Nigel (Forbes) 1912-1989 ...... **CLC 8**
    See also CA 25-28R; 129; DLB 13, 15, 233;
    EWL 3; MTCW 1
Dent, Lester 1904(?)-1959 .... **TCLC 72**
    See also CA 112; 161; CMW 4; SFW 4
De Palma, Brian (Russell) 1940- ...... **CLC 20**
    See also CA 109
De Quincey, Thomas 1785-1859 ..... **NCLC 4,
    87**
    See also BRW 4; CDBLB 1789-1832; DLB
    110, 144; RGEL 2
Deren, Eleanora 1908(?)-1961
    See Deren, Maya
    See also CA 192; 111
Deren, Maya .... **CLC 16, 102**
    See Deren, Eleanora
Derleth, August (William)
    1909-1971 .... **CLC 31**
    See also BPFB 1; BYA 9, 10; CA 1-4R; 29-
    32R; CANR 4; CMW 4; DLB 9; DLBD
    17; HGG; SATA 5; SUFW 1
Der Nister 1884-1950 .... **TCLC 56**
    See Nister, Der
de Routisie, Albert
    See Aragon, Louis
Derrida, Jacques 1930- .... **CLC 24, 87**
    See also CA 124; 127; CANR 76, 98; DLB
    242; EWL 3; LMFS 2; MTCW 1; TWA
Derry Down Derry
    See Lear, Edward
Dersonnes, Jacques
    See Simenon, Georges (Jacques Christian)

Desai, Anita 1937- .... **CLC 19, 37, 97, 175**
    See also BRWS 5; CA 81-84; CANR 33,
    53, 95; CN 7; CWRI 5; DA3; DAB; DAM
    NOV; DLB 271; DNFS 2; EWL 3; FW;
    MTCW 1, 2; SATA 63, 126
Desai, Kiran 1971- .... **CLC 119**
    See also BYA 16; CA 171
de Saint-Luc, Jean
    See Glassco, John
de Saint Roman, Arnaud
    See Aragon, Louis
Desbordes-Valmore, Marceline
    1786-1859 .... **NCLC 97**
    See also DLB 217
Descartes, Rene 1596-1650 .... **LC 20, 35**
    See also DLB 268; EW 3; GFL Beginnings
    to 1789
De Sica, Vittorio 1901(?)-1974 .... **CLC 20**
    See also CA 117
Desnos, Robert 1900-1945 .... **TCLC 22**
    See also CA 121; 151; CANR 107; DLB
    258; EWL 3; LMFS 2
Destouches, Louis-Ferdinand
    1894-1961 .... **CLC 9, 15**
    See Celine, Louis-Ferdinand
    See also CA 85-88; CANR 28; MTCW 1
de Tolignac, Gaston
    See Griffith, D(avid Lewelyn) W(ark)
Deutsch, Babette 1895-1982 .... **CLC 18**
    See also BYA 3; CA 1-4R; 108; CANR 4,
    79; DLB 45; SATA 1; SATA-Obit 33
Devenant, William 1606-1649 .... **LC 13**
Devkota, Laxmiprasad 1909-1959 . **TCLC 23**
    See also CA 123
De Voto, Bernard (Augustine)
    1897-1955 .... **TCLC 29**
    See also CA 113; 160; DLB 9, 256
De Vries, Peter 1910-1993 ..... **CLC 1, 2, 3, 7,
    10, 28, 46**
    See also CA 17-20R; 142; CANR 41; DAM
    NOV; DLB 6; DLBY 1982; MTCW 1, 2
Dewey, John 1859-1952 .... **TCLC 95**
    See also CA 114; 170; DLB 246, 270;
    RGAL 4
Dexter, John
    See Bradley, Marion Zimmer
    See also GLL 1
Dexter, Martin
    See Faust, Frederick (Schiller)
    See also TCWW 2
Dexter, Pete 1943- .... **CLC 34, 55**
    See also BEST 89:2; CA 127; 131; CPW;
    DAM POP; INT 131; MTCW 1
Diamano, Silmang
    See Senghor, Leopold Sedar
Diamond, Neil 1941- .... **CLC 30**
    See also CA 108
Diaz del Castillo, Bernal
    1496-1584 .... **HLCS 1; LC 31**
    See also LAW
di Bassetto, Corno
    See Shaw, George Bernard
Dick, Philip K(indred) 1928-1982 ... **CLC 10,
    30, 72; SSC 57**
    See also AAYA 24; BPFB 1; BYA 11; CA
    49-52; 106; CANR 2, 16; CPW; DA3;
    DAM NOV, POP; DLB 8; MTCW 1, 2;
    NFS 5; SCFW 1; SFW 4
Dickens, Charles (John Huffam)
    1812-1870 .... **NCLC 3, 8, 18, 26, 37, 50,
    86, 105, 113; SSC 17, 49; WLC**
    See also AAYA 23; BRW 5; BRWC 1, 2;
    BYA 1, 2, 3, 13, 14; CDBLB 1832-1890;
    CMW 4; DA; DA3; DAB; DAC; DAM
    MST, NOV; DLB 21, 55, 70, 159, 166;
    EXPN; HGG; JRDA; LAIT 1, 2; LATS 1;
    LMFS 1; MAICYA 1, 2; NFS 4, 5, 10,
    14; RGEL 2; RGSF 2; SATA 15; SUFW
    1; TEA; WCH; WLIT 4; WYA

Dickey, James (Lafayette)
    1923-1997 .... **CLC 1, 2, 4, 7, 10, 15, 47,
    109; PC 40**
    See also AAYA 50; AITN 1, 2; AMWS 4;
    BPFB 1; CA 9-12R; 156; CABS 2; CANR
    10, 48, 61, 105; CDALB 1968-1988; CP
    7; CPW; CSW; DA3; DAM NOV, POET,
    POP; DLB 5, 193; DLBD 7; DLBY 1982,
    1993, 1996, 1997, 1998; EWL 3; INT
    CANR-10; MTCW 1, 2; NFS 9; PFS 6,
    11; RGAL 4; TUS
Dickey, William 1928-1994 .... **CLC 3, 28**
    See also CA 9-12R; 145; CANR 24, 79;
    DLB 5
Dickinson, Charles 1951- .... **CLC 49**
    See also CA 128
Dickinson, Emily (Elizabeth)
    1830-1886 ... **NCLC 21, 77; PC 1; WLC**
    See also AAYA 22; AMW; AMWR 1;
    CDALB 1865-1917; DA; DA3; DAB;
    DAC; DAM MST, POET; DLB 1, 243;
    EXPP; MAWW; PAB; PFS 1, 2, 3, 4, 5,
    6, 8, 10, 11, 13, 16; RGAL 4; SATA 29;
    TUS; WP; WYA
Dickinson, Mrs. Herbert Ward
    See Phelps, Elizabeth Stuart
Dickinson, Peter (Malcolm) 1927- .. **CLC 12,
    35**
    See also AAYA 9, 49; BYA 5; CA 41-44R;
    CANR 31, 58, 88; CLR 29; CMW 4; DLB
    87, 161, 276; JRDA; MAICYA 1, 2;
    SATA 5, 62, 95; SFW 4; WYA; YAW
Dickson, Carr
    See Carr, John Dickson
Dickson, Carter
    See Carr, John Dickson
Diderot, Denis 1713-1784 .... **LC 26**
    See also EW 4; GFL Beginnings to 1789;
    LMFS 1; RGWL 2, 3
Didion, Joan 1934- . **CLC 1, 3, 8, 14, 32, 129**
    See also AITN 1; AMWS 4; CA 5-8R;
    CANR 14, 52, 76; CDALB 1968-1988;
    CN 7; DA3; DAM NOV; DLB 2, 173,
    185; DLBY 1981, 1986; EWL 3; MAWW;
    MTCW 1, 2; NFS 3; RGAL 4; TCWW 2;
    TUS
Dietrich, Robert
    See Hunt, E(verette) Howard, (Jr.)
Difusa, Pati
    See Almodovar, Pedro
Dillard, Annie 1945- .... **CLC 9, 60, 115**
    See also AAYA 6, 43; AMWS 6; ANW; CA
    49-52; CANR 3, 43, 62, 90; DA3; DAM
    NOV; DLB 275, 278; DLBY 1980; LAIT
    4, 5; MTCW 1, 2; NCFS 1; RGAL 4;
    SATA 10, 140; TUS
Dillard, R(ichard) H(enry) W(ilde)
    1937- .... **CLC 5**
    See also CA 21-24R; CAAS 7; CANR 10;
    CP 7; CSW; DLB 5, 244
Dillon, Eilis 1920-1994 .... **CLC 17**
    See also CA 9-12R, 182; 147; CAAE 182;
    CAAS 3; CANR 4, 38, 78; CLR 26; MAI-
    CYA 1, 2; MAICYAS 1; SATA 2, 74;
    SATA-Essay 105; SATA-Obit 83; YAW
Dimont, Penelope
    See Mortimer, Penelope (Ruth)
Dinesen, Isak .... **CLC 10, 29, 95; SSC 7**
    See Blixen, Karen (Christentze Dinesen)
    See also EW 10; EWL 3; EXPS; FW; HGG;
    LAIT 3; MTCW 1; NCFS 2; NFS 9;
    RGSF 2; RGWL 2, 3; SSFS 3, 6, 13;
    WLIT 2
Ding Ling .... **CLC 68**
    See Chiang, Pin-chin
    See also RGWL 3
Diphusa, Patty
    See Almodovar, Pedro

Disch, Thomas M(ichael) 1940- ... **CLC 7, 36**
    See Disch, Tom
    See also AAYA 17; BPFB 1; CA 21-24R;
    CAAS 4; CANR 17, 36, 54, 89; CLR 18;
    CP 7; DA3; DLB 8; HGG; MAICYA 1, 2;
    MTCW 1, 2; SAAS 15; SATA 92; SCFW;
    SFW 4; SUFW 2

Disch, Tom
    See Disch, Thomas M(ichael)
    See also DLB 282

d'Isly, Georges
    See Simenon, Georges (Jacques Christian)

Disraeli, Benjamin 1804-1881 ... **NCLC 2, 39, 79**
    See also BRW 4; DLB 21, 55; RGEL 2

Ditcum, Steve
    See Crumb, R(obert)

Dixon, Paige
    See Corcoran, Barbara (Asenath)

Dixon, Stephen 1936- .... **CLC 52; SSC 16**
    See also AMWS 12; CA 89-92; CANR 17,
    40, 54, 91; CN 7; DLB 130

Doak, Annie
    See Dillard, Annie

Dobell, Sydney Thompson
    1824-1874 .... **NCLC 43**
    See also DLB 32; RGEL 2

Doblin, Alfred .... **TCLC 13**
    See Doeblin, Alfred
    See also CDWLB 2; EWL 3; RGWL 2, 3

Dobroliubov, Nikolai Aleksandrovich
    See Dobrolyubov, Nikolai Alexandrovich
    See also DLB 277

Dobrolyubov, Nikolai Alexandrovich
    1836-1861 .... **NCLC 5**
    See Dobroliubov, Nikolai Aleksandrovich

Dobson, Austin 1840-1921 .... **TCLC 79**
    See also DLB 35, 144

Dobyns, Stephen 1941- .... **CLC 37**
    See also AMWS 13; CA 45-48; CANR 2,
    18, 99; CMW 4; CP 7

Doctorow, E(dgar) L(aurence)
    1931- .... **CLC 6, 11, 15, 18, 37, 44, 65, 113**
    See also AAYA 22; AITN 2; AMWS 4;
    BEST 89:3; BPFB 1; CA 45-48; CANR
    2, 33, 51, 76, 97; CDALB 1968-1988; CN
    7; CPW; DA3; DAM NOV, POP; DLB 2,
    28, 173; DLBY 1980; EWL 3; LAIT 3;
    MTCW 1, 2; NFS 6; RGAL 4; RHW;
    TUS

Dodgson, Charles L(utwidge) 1832-1898
    See Carroll, Lewis
    See also CLR 2; DA; DA3; DAB; DAC;
    DAM MST, NOV, POET; MAICYA 1, 2;
    SATA 100; YABC 2

Dodson, Owen (Vincent) 1914-1983 .. **BLC 1; CLC 79**
    See also BW 1; CA 65-68; 110; CANR 24;
    DAM MULT; DLB 76

Doeblin, Alfred 1878-1957 .... **TCLC 13**
    See Doblin, Alfred
    See also CA 110; 141; DLB 66

Doerr, Harriet 1910-2002 .... **CLC 34**
    See also CA 117; 122; 213; CANR 47; INT
    CA-122; LATS 1

Domecq, H(onorio Bustos)
    See Bioy Casares, Adolfo

Domecq, H(onorio) Bustos
    See Bioy Casares, Adolfo; Borges, Jorge
    Luis

Domini, Rey
    See Lorde, Audre (Geraldine)
    See also GLL 1

Dominique
    See Proust, (Valentin-Louis-George-Eugene)
    Marcel

Don, A
    See Stephen, Sir Leslie

Donaldson, Stephen R(eeder)
    1947- .... **CLC 46, 138**
    See also AAYA 36; BPFB 1; CA 89-92;
    CANR 13, 55, 99; CPW; DAM POP;
    FANT; INT CANR-13; SATA 121; SFW
    4; SUFW 1, 2

Donleavy, J(ames) P(atrick) 1926- .... **CLC 1, 4, 6, 10, 45**
    See also AITN 2; BPFB 1; CA 9-12R;
    CANR 24, 49, 62, 80; CBD; CD 5; CN 7;
    DLB 6, 173; INT CANR-24; MTCW 1,
    2; RGAL 4

Donnadieu, Marguerite
    See Duras, Marguerite
    See also CWW 2

Donne, John 1572-1631 ... **LC 10, 24, 91; PC 1, 43; WLC**
    See also BRW 1; BRWC 1; BRWR 2; CD-
    BLB Before 1660; DA; DAB; DAC;
    DAM MST, POET; DLB 121, 151; EXPP;
    PAB; PFS 2, 11; RGEL 2; TEA; WLIT 3;
    WP

Donnell, David 1939(?)- .... **CLC 34**
    See also CA 197

Donoghue, P. S.
    See Hunt, E(verette) Howard, (Jr.)

Donoso (Yanez), Jose 1924-1996 ...... **CLC 4, 8, 11, 32, 99; HLC 1; SSC 34; TCLC 133**
    See also CA 81-84; 155; CANR 32, 73; CD-
    WLB 3; DAM MULT; DLB 113; EWL 3;
    HW 1, 2; LAW; LAWS 1; MTCW 1, 2;
    RGSF 2; WLIT 1

Donovan, John 1928-1992 .... **CLC 35**
    See also AAYA 20; CA 97-100; 137; CLR
    3; MAICYA 1, 2; SATA 72; SATA-Brief
    29; YAW

Don Roberto
    See Cunninghame Graham, Robert
    (Gallnigad) Bontine

Doolittle, Hilda 1886-1961 . **CLC 3, 8, 14, 31, 34, 73; PC 5; WLC**
    See H. D.
    See also AMWS 1; CA 97-100; CANR 35;
    DA; DAC; DAM MST, POET; DLB 4,
    45; EWL 3; FW; GLL 1; LMFS 2;
    MAWW; MTCW 1, 2; PFS 6; RGAL 4

Doppo, Kunikida .... **TCLC 99**
    See Kunikida Doppo

Dorfman, Ariel 1942- .... **CLC 48, 77; HLC 1**
    See also CA 124; 130; CANR 67, 70; CWW
    2; DAM MULT; DFS 4; EWL 3; HW 1,
    2; INT CA-130; WLIT 1

Dorn, Edward (Merton)
    1929-1999 .... **CLC 10, 18**
    See also CA 93-96; 187; CANR 42, 79; CP
    7; DLB 5; INT 93-96; WP

Dor-Ner, Zvi .... **CLC 70**

Dorris, Michael (Anthony)
    1945-1997 .... **CLC 109; NNAL**
    See also AAYA 20; BEST 90:1; BYA 12;
    CA 102; 157; CANR 19, 46, 75; CLR 58;
    DA3; DAM MULT, NOV; DLB 175;
    LAIT 5; MTCW 2; NFS 3; RGAL 4;
    SATA 75; SATA-Obit 94; TCWW 2; YAW

Dorris, Michael A.
    See Dorris, Michael (Anthony)

Dorsan, Luc
    See Simenon, Georges (Jacques Christian)

Dorsange, Jean
    See Simenon, Georges (Jacques Christian)

Dos Passos, John (Roderigo)
    1896-1970 ... **CLC 1, 4, 8, 11, 15, 25, 34, 82; WLC**
    See also AMW; BPFB 1; CA 1-4R; 29-32R;
    CANR 3; CDALB 1929-1941; DA; DA3;
    DAB; DAC; DAM MST, NOV; DLB 4,
    9; DLBD 1, 15, 274; DLBY 1996; EWL
    3; MTCW 1, 2; NFS 14; RGAL 4; TUS

Dossage, Jean
    See Simenon, Georges (Jacques Christian)

Dostoevsky, Fedor Mikhailovich
    1821-1881 .. **NCLC 2, 7, 21, 33, 43, 119; SSC 2, 33, 44; WLC**
    See Dostoevsky, Fyodor
    See also AAYA 40; DA; DA3; DAB; DAC;
    DAM MST, NOV; EW 7; EXPN; NFS 3,
    8; RGSF 2; RGWL 2, 3; SSFS 8; TWA

Dostoevsky, Fyodor
    See Dostoevsky, Fedor Mikhailovich
    See also DLB 238; LATS 1; LMFS 1, 2

Doty, M. R.
    See Doty, Mark (Alan)

Doty, Mark
    See Doty, Mark (Alan)

Doty, Mark (Alan) 1953(?)- .... **CLC 176**
    See also AMWS 11; CA 161, 183; CAAE
    183; CANR 110

Doty, Mark A.
    See Doty, Mark (Alan)

Doughty, Charles M(ontagu)
    1843-1926 .... **TCLC 27**
    See also CA 115; 178; DLB 19, 57, 174

Douglas, Ellen .... **CLC 73**
    See Haxton, Josephine Ayres; Williamson,
    Ellen Douglas
    See also CN 7; CSW

Douglas, Gavin 1475(?)-1522 .... **LC 20**
    See also DLB 132; RGEL 2

Douglas, George
    See Brown, George Douglas
    See also RGEL 2

Douglas, Keith (Castellain)
    1920-1944 .... **TCLC 40**
    See also BRW 7; CA 160; DLB 27; EWL
    3; PAB; RGEL 2

Douglas, Leonard
    See Bradbury, Ray (Douglas)

Douglas, Michael
    See Crichton, (John) Michael

Douglas, (George) Norman
    1868-1952 .... **TCLC 68**
    See also BRW 6; CA 119; 157; DLB 34,
    195; RGEL 2

Douglas, William
    See Brown, George Douglas

Douglass, Frederick 1817(?)-1895 ..... **BLC 1; NCLC 7, 55; WLC**
    See also AAYA 48; AFAW 1, 2; AMWC 1;
    AMWS 3; CDALB 1640-1865; DA; DA3;
    DAC; DAM MST, MULT; DLB 1, 43, 50,
    79, 243; FW; LAIT 2; NCFS 2; RGAL 4;
    SATA 29

Dourado, (Waldomiro Freitas) Autran
    1926- .... **CLC 23, 60**
    See also CA 25-28R; 179; CANR 34, 81;
    DLB 145; HW 2

Dourado, Waldomiro Autran
    See Dourado, (Waldomiro Freitas) Autran
    See also CA 179

Dove, Rita (Frances) 1952- . **BLCS; CLC 50, 81; PC 6**
    See also AAYA 46; AMWS 4; BW 2; CA
    109; CAAS 19; CANR 27, 42, 68, 76, 97;
    CDALBS; CP 7; CSW; CWP; DLB 120;
    DAM MULT, POET; EWL 3; EXPP;
    MTCW 1; PFS 1, 15; RGAL 4

Doveglion
    See Villa, Jose Garcia

Dowell, Coleman 1925-1985 .... **CLC 60**
    See also CA 25-28R; 117; CANR 10; DLB
    130; GLL 2

Dowson, Ernest (Christopher)
    1867-1900 .... **TCLC 4**
    See also CA 105; 150; DLB 19, 135; RGEL
    2

Doyle, A. Conan
    See Doyle, Sir Arthur Conan

Faust, Frederick (Schiller)
1892-1944(?) .... **TCLC 49**
See Austin, Frank; Brand, Max; Challis,
George; Dawson, Peter; Dexter, Martin;
Evans, Evan; Frederick, John; Frost, Fred-
erick; Manning, David; Silver, Nicholas
See also CA 108; 152; DAM POP; DLB
256; TUS

Faust, Irvin 1924- .... **CLC 8**
See also CA 33-36R; CANR 28, 67; CN 7;
DLB 2, 28, 218, 278; DLBY 1980

Faustino, Domingo 1811-1888 ...... **NCLC 123**

Fawkes, Guy
See Benchley, Robert (Charles)

Fearing, Kenneth (Flexner)
1902-1961 .... **CLC 51**
See also CA 93-96; CANR 59; CMW 4;
DLB 9; RGAL 4

Fecamps, Elise
See Creasey, John

Federman, Raymond 1928- .... **CLC 6, 47**
See also CA 17-20R; CAAE 208; CAAS 8;
CANR 10, 43, 83, 108; CN 7; DLBY
1980

Federspiel, J(uerg) F. 1931- .... **CLC 42**
See also CA 146

Feiffer, Jules (Ralph) 1929- ...... **CLC 2, 8, 64**
See also AAYA 3; CA 17-20R; CAD; CANR
30, 59; CD 5; DAM DRAM; DLB 7, 44;
INT CANR-30; MTCW 1; SATA 8, 61,
111

Feige, Hermann Albert Otto Maximilian
See Traven, B.

Feinberg, David B. 1956-1994 .... **CLC 59**
See also CA 135; 147

Feinstein, Elaine 1930- .... **CLC 36**
See also CA 69-72; CAAS 1; CANR 31,
68, 121; CN 7; CP 7; CWP; DLB 14, 40;
MTCW 1

Feke, Gilbert David .... **CLC 65**

Feldman, Irving (Mordecai) 1928- ..... **CLC 7**
See also CA 1-4R; CANR 1; CP 7; DLB
169

Felix-Tchicaya, Gerald
See Tchicaya, Gerald Felix

Fellini, Federico 1920-1993 .... **CLC 16, 85**
See also CA 65-68; 143; CANR 33

Felltham, Owen 1602(?)-1668 .... **LC 92**
See also DLB 126, 151

Felsen, Henry Gregor 1916-1995 ..... **CLC 17**
See also CA 1-4R; 180; CANR 1; SAAS 2;
SATA 1

Felski, Rita .... **CLC 65**

Fenno, Jack
See Calisher, Hortense

Fenollosa, Ernest (Francisco)
1853-1908 .... **TCLC 91**

Fenton, James Martin 1949- .... **CLC 32**
See also CA 102; CANR 108; CP 7; DLB
40; PFS 11

Ferber, Edna 1887-1968 .... **CLC 18, 93**
See also AITN 1; CA 5-8R; 25-28R; CANR
68, 105; DLB 9, 28, 86, 266; MTCW 1,
2; RGAL 4; RHW; SATA 7; TCWW 2

Ferdowsi, Abu'l Qasem 940-1020 . **CMLC 43**
See also RGWL 2, 3

Ferguson, Helen
See Kavan, Anna

Ferguson, Niall 1964- .... **CLC 134**
See also CA 190

Ferguson, Samuel 1810-1886 .... **NCLC 33**
See also DLB 32; RGEL 2

Fergusson, Robert 1750-1774 .... **LC 29**
See also DLB 109; RGEL 2

Ferling, Lawrence
See Ferlinghetti, Lawrence (Monsanto)

Ferlinghetti, Lawrence (Monsanto)
1919(?)- ..... **CLC 2, 6, 10, 27, 111; PC 1**
See also CA 5-8R; CANR 3, 41, 73;
CDALB 1941-1968; CP 7; DA3; DAM
POET; DLB 5, 16; MTCW 1, 2; RGAL 4;
WP

Fern, Fanny
See Parton, Sara Payson Willis

Fernandez, Vicente Garcia Huidobro
See Huidobro Fernandez, Vicente Garcia

Fernandez-Armesto, Felipe .... **CLC 70**

Fernandez de Lizardi, Jose Joaquin
See Lizardi, Jose Joaquin Fernandez de

Ferre, Rosario 1938- ...... **CLC 139; HLCS 1;
SSC 36**
See also CA 131; CANR 55, 81; CWW 2;
DLB 145; EWL 3; HW 1, 2; LAWS 1;
MTCW 1; WLIT 1

Ferrer, Gabriel (Francisco Victor) Miro
See Miro (Ferrer), Gabriel (Francisco
Victor)

Ferrier, Susan (Edmonstone)
1782-1854 .... **NCLC 8**
See also DLB 116; RGEL 2

Ferrigno, Robert 1948(?)- .... **CLC 65**
See also CA 140

Ferron, Jacques 1921-1985 .... **CLC 94**
See also CA 117; 129; CCA 1; DAC; DLB
60; EWL 3

Feuchtwanger, Lion 1884-1958 .... **TCLC 3**
See also CA 104; 187; DLB 66; EWL 3

Feuillet, Octave 1821-1890 .... **NCLC 45**
See also DLB 192

Feydeau, Georges (Leon Jules Marie)
1862-1921 .... **TCLC 22**
See also CA 113; 152; CANR 84; DAM
DRAM; DLB 192; EWL 3; GFL 1789 to
the Present; RGWL 2, 3

Fichte, Johann Gottlieb
1762-1814 .... **NCLC 62**
See also DLB 90

Ficino, Marsilio 1433-1499 .... **LC 12**
See also LMFS 1

Fiedeler, Hans
See Doeblin, Alfred

Fiedler, Leslie A(aron) 1917-2003 ..... **CLC 4,
13, 24**
See also AMWS 13; CA 9-12R; 212; CANR
7, 63; CN 7; DLB 28, 67; EWL 3; MTCW
1, 2; RGAL 4; TUS

Field, Andrew 1938- .... **CLC 44**
See also CA 97-100; CANR 25

Field, Eugene 1850-1895 .... **NCLC 3**
See also DLB 23, 42, 140; DLBD 13; MAI-
CYA 1, 2; RGAL 4; SATA 16

Field, Gans T.
See Wellman, Manly Wade

Field, Michael 1915-1971 .... **TCLC 43**
See also CA 29-32R

Field, Peter
See Hobson, Laura Z(ametkin)
See also TCWW 2

Fielding, Helen 1959(?)- .... **CLC 146**
See also CA 172; DLB 231

Fielding, Henry 1707-1754 .... **LC 1, 46, 85;
WLC**
See also BRW 3; BRWR 1; CDBLB 1660-
1789; DA; DA3; DAB; DAC; DAM
DRAM, MST, NOV; DLB 39, 84, 101;
NFS 18; RGEL 2; TEA; WLIT 3

Fielding, Sarah 1710-1768 .... **LC 1, 44**
See also DLB 39; RGEL 2; TEA

Fields, W. C. 1880-1946 .... **TCLC 80**
See also DLB 44

Fierstein, Harvey (Forbes) 1954- ..... **CLC 33**
See also CA 123; 129; CAD; CD 5; CPW;
DA3; DAM DRAM, POP; DFS 6; DLB
266; GLL

Figes, Eva 1932- .... **CLC 31**
See also CA 53-56; CANR 4, 44, 83; CN 7;
DLB 14, 271; FW

Filippo, Eduardo de
See de Filippo, Eduardo

Finch, Anne 1661-1720 .... **LC 3; PC 21**
See also BRWS 9; DLB 95

Finch, Robert (Duer Claydon)
1900-1995 .... **CLC 18**
See also CA 57-60; CANR 9, 24, 49; CP 7;
DLB 88

Findley, Timothy (Irving Frederick)
1930-2002 .... **CLC 27, 102**
See also CA 25-28R; 206; CANR 12, 42,
69, 109; CCA 1; CN 7; DAC; DAM MST;
DLB 53; FANT; RHW

Fink, William
See Mencken, H(enry) L(ouis)

Firbank, Louis 1942-
See Reed, Lou
See also CA 117

Firbank, (Arthur Annesley) Ronald
1886-1926 .... **TCLC 1**
See also BRWS 2; CA 104; 177; DLB 36;
EWL 3; RGEL 2

Fish, Stanley
See Fish, Stanley Eugene

Fish, Stanley E.
See Fish, Stanley Eugene

Fish, Stanley Eugene 1938- .... **CLC 142**
See also CA 112; 132; CANR 90; DLB 67

Fisher, Dorothy (Frances) Canfield
1879-1958 .... **TCLC 87**
See also CA 114; 136; CANR 80; CLR 71,;
CWRI 5; DLB 9, 102, 284; MAICYA 1,
2; YABC 1

Fisher, M(ary) F(rances) K(ennedy)
1908-1992 .... **CLC 76, 87**
See also CA 77-80; 138; CANR 44; MTCW
1

Fisher, Roy 1930- .... **CLC 25**
See also CA 81-84; CAAS 10; CANR 16;
CP 7; DLB 40

Fisher, Rudolph 1897-1934 .... **BLC 2; HR 2;
SSC 25; TCLC 11**
See also BW 1, 3; CA 107; 124; CANR 80;
DAM MULT; DLB 51, 102

Fisher, Vardis (Alvero) 1895-1968 .... **CLC 7;
TCLC 140**
See also CA 5-8R; 25-28R; CANR 68; DLB
9, 206; RGAL 4; TCWW 2

Fiske, Tarleton
See Bloch, Robert (Albert)

Fitch, Clarke
See Sinclair, Upton (Beall)

Fitch, John IV
See Cormier, Robert (Edmund)

Fitzgerald, Captain Hugh
See Baum, L(yman) Frank

FitzGerald, Edward 1809-1883 .... **NCLC 9**
See also BRW 4; DLB 32; RGEL 2

Fitzgerald, F(rancis) Scott (Key)
1896-1940 ... **SSC 6, 31; TCLC 1, 6, 14,
28, 55; WLC**
See also AAYA 24; AITN 1; AMW; AMWC
2; AMWR 1; BPFB 1; CA 110; 123;
CDALB 1917-1929; DA; DA3; DAB;
DAC; DAM MST, NOV; DLB 4, 9, 86,
219; DLBD 1, 15, 16, 273; DLBY 1981,
1996; EWL 3; EXPN; EXPS; LAIT 3;
MTCW 1, 2; NFS 2; RGAL 4; RGSF 2;
SSFS 4, 15; TUS

Fitzgerald, Penelope 1916-2000 . **CLC 19, 51,
61, 143**
See also BRWS 5; CA 85-88; 190; CAAS
10; CANR 56, 86; CN 7; DLB 14, 194;
EWL 3; MTCW 2

Fitzgerald, Robert (Stuart)
 1910-1985 .... **CLC 39**
 See also CA 1-4R; 114; CANR 1; DLBY
 1980
FitzGerald, Robert D(avid)
 1902-1987 .... **CLC 19**
 See also CA 17-20R; DLB 260; RGEL 2
Fitzgerald, Zelda (Sayre)
 1900-1948 .... **TCLC 52**
 See also AMWS 9; CA 117; 126; DLBY
 1984
Flanagan, Thomas (James Bonner)
 1923-2002 .... **CLC 25, 52**
 See also CA 108; 206; CANR 55; CN 7;
 DLBY 1980; INT 108; MTCW 1; RHW
Flaubert, Gustave 1821-1880 .... **NCLC 2, 10,**
 19, 62, 66; SSC 11, 60; WLC
 See also DA; DA3; DAB; DAC; DAM
 MST, NOV; DLB 119; EW 7; EXPS; GFL
 1789 to the Present; LAIT 2; LMFS 1;
 NFS 14; RGSF 2; RGWL 2, 3; SSFS 6;
 TWA
Flavius Josephus
 See Josephus, Flavius
Flecker, Herman Elroy
 See Flecker, (Herman) James Elroy
Flecker, (Herman) James Elroy
 1884-1915 .... **TCLC 43**
 See also CA 109; 150; DLB 10, 19; RGEL
 2
Fleming, Ian (Lancaster) 1908-1964 . **CLC 3,**
 30
 See also AAYA 26; BPFB 1; CA 5-8R;
 CANR 59; CDBLB 1945-1960; CMW 4;
 CPW; DA3; DAM POP; DLB 87, 201;
 MSW; MTCW 1, 2; RGEL 2; SATA 9;
 TEA; YAW
Fleming, Thomas (James) 1927- ...... **CLC 37**
 See also CA 5-8R; CANR 10, 102; INT
 CANR-10; SATA 8
Fletcher, John 1579-1625 .... **DC 6; LC 33**
 See also BRW 2; CDBLB Before 1660;
 DLB 58; RGEL 2; TEA
Fletcher, John Gould 1886-1950 .... **TCLC 35**
 See also CA 107; 167; DLB 4, 45; LMFS
 2; RGAL 4
Fleur, Paul
 See Pohl, Frederik
Flooglebuckle, Al
 See Spiegelman, Art
Flora, Fletcher 1914-1969
 See Queen, Ellery
 See also CA 1-4R; CANR 3, 85
Flying Officer X
 See Bates, H(erbert) E(rnest)
Fo, Dario 1926- .... **CLC 32, 109; DC 10**
 See also CA 116; 128; CANR 68, 114;
 CWW 2; DA3; DAM DRAM; DLBY
 1997; EWL 3; MTCW 1, 2
Fogarty, Jonathan Titulescu Esq.
 See Farrell, James T(homas)
Follett, Ken(neth Martin) 1949- .... **CLC 18**
 See also AAYA 6, 50; BEST 89:4; BPFB 1;
 CA 81-84; CANR 13, 33, 54, 102; CMW
 4; CPW; DA3; DAM NOV, POP; DLB
 87; DLBY 1981; INT CANR-33; MTCW
 1
Fontane, Theodor 1819-1898 .... **NCLC 26**
 See also CDWLB 2; DLB 129; EW 6;
 RGWL 2, 3; TWA
Fontenot, Chester .... **CLC 65**
Fonvizin, Denis Ivanovich
 1744(?)-1792 .... **LC 81**
 See also DLB 150; RGWL 2, 3
Foote, Horton 1916- .... **CLC 51, 91**
 See also CA 73-76; CAD; CANR 34, 51,
 110; CD 5; CSW; DA3; DAM DRAM;
 DLB 26, 266; EWL 3; INT CANR-34

Foote, Mary Hallock 1847-1938 .. **TCLC 108**
 See also DLB 186, 188, 202, 221
Foote, Shelby 1916- .... **CLC 75**
 See also AAYA 40; CA 5-8R; CANR 3, 45,
 74; CN 7; CPW; CSW; DA3; DAM NOV,
 POP; DLB 2, 17; MTCW 2; RHW
Forbes, Cosmo
 See Lewton, Val
Forbes, Esther 1891-1967 .... **CLC 12**
 See also AAYA 17; BYA 2; CA 13-14; 25-
 28R; CAP 1; CLR 27; DLB 22; JRDA;
 MAICYA 1, 2; RHW; SATA 2, 100; YAW
Forche, Carolyn (Louise) 1950- .... **CLC 25,**
 83, 86; PC 10
 See also CA 109; 117; CANR 50, 74; CP 7;
 CWP; DA3; DAM POET; DLB 5, 193;
 INT CA-117; MTCW 1; PFS 18; RGAL 4
Ford, Elbur
 See Hibbert, Eleanor Alice Burford
Ford, Ford Madox 1873-1939 ... **TCLC 1, 15,**
 39, 57
 See Chaucer, Daniel
 See also BRW 6; CA 104; 132; CANR 74;
 CDBLB 1914-1945; DA3; DAM NOV;
 DLB 34, 98, 162; EWL 3; MTCW 1, 2;
 RGEL 2; TEA
Ford, Henry 1863-1947 .... **TCLC 73**
 See also CA 115; 148
Ford, Jack
 See Ford, John
Ford, John 1586-1639 .... **DC 8; LC 68**
 See also BRW 2; CDBLB Before 1660;
 DA3; DAM DRAM; DFS 7; DLB 58;
 IDTP; RGEL 2
Ford, John 1895-1973 .... **CLC 16**
 See also CA 187; 45-48
Ford, Richard 1944- .... **CLC 46, 99**
 See also AMWS 5; CA 69-72; CANR 11,
 47, 86; CN 7; CSW; DLB 227; EWL 3;
 MTCW 1; RGAL 4; RGSF 2
Ford, Webster
 See Masters, Edgar Lee
Foreman, Richard 1937- .... **CLC 50**
 See also CA 65-68; CAD; CANR 32, 63;
 CD 5
Forester, C(ecil) S(cott) 1899-1966 ... **CLC 35**
 See also CA 73-76; 25-28R; CANR 83;
 DLB 191; RGEL 2; RHW; SATA 13
Forez
 See Mauriac, Francois (Charles)
Forman, James
 See Forman, James D(ouglas)
Forman, James D(ouglas) 1932- .... **CLC 21**
 See also AAYA 17; CA 9-12R; CANR 4,
 19, 42; JRDA; MAICYA 1, 2; SATA 8,
 70; YAW
Forman, Milos 1932- .... **CLC 164**
 See also CA 109
Fornes, Maria Irene 1930- . **CLC 39, 61; DC**
 10; HLCS 1
 See also CA 25-28R; CAD; CANR 28, 81;
 CD 5; CWD; DLB 7; HW 1, 2; INT
 CANR-28; MTCW 1; RGAL 4
Forrest, Leon (Richard)
 1937-1997 .... **BLCS; CLC 4**
 See also AFAW 2; BW 2; CA 89-92; 162;
 CAAS 7; CANR 25, 52, 87; CN 7; DLB
 33
Forster, E(dward) M(organ)
 1879-1970 ...... **CLC 1, 2, 3, 4, 9, 10, 13,**
 15, 22, 45, 77; SSC 27; TCLC 125;
 WLC
 See also AAYA 2, 37; BRW 6; BRWR 2;
 CA 13-14; 25-28R; CANR 45; CAP 1;
 CDBLB 1914-1945; DA; DA3; DAB;
 DAC; DAM MST, NOV; DLB 34, 98,
 162, 178, 195; DLBD 10; EWL 3; EXPN;

 LAIT 3; LMFS 1; MTCW 1, 2; NCFS 1;
 NFS 3, 10, 11; RGEL 2; RGSF 2; SATA
 57; SUFW 1; TEA; WLIT 4
Forster, John 1812-1876 .... **NCLC 11**
 See also DLB 144, 184
Forster, Margaret 1938- .... **CLC 149**
 See also CA 133; CANR 62, 115; CN 7;
 DLB 155, 271
Forsyth, Frederick 1938- .... **CLC 2, 5, 36**
 See also BEST 89:4; CA 85-88; CANR 38,
 62, 115; CMW 4; CN 7; CPW; DAM
 NOV, POP; DLB 87; MTCW 1, 2
Forten, Charlotte L. 1837-1914 .... **BLC 2;**
 TCLC 16
 See Grimke, Charlotte L(ottie) Forten
 See also DLB 50, 239
Fortinbras
 See Grieg, (Johan) Nordahl (Brun)
Foscolo, Ugo 1778-1827 .... **NCLC 8, 97**
 See also EW 5
Fosse, Bob .... **CLC 20**
 See Fosse, Robert Louis
Fosse, Robert Louis 1927-1987
 See Fosse, Bob
 See also CA 110; 123
Foster, Hannah Webster
 1758-1840 .... **NCLC 99**
 See also DLB 37, 200; RGAL 4
Foster, Stephen Collins
 1826-1864 .... **NCLC 26**
 See also RGAL 4
Foucault, Michel 1926-1984 . **CLC 31, 34, 69**
 See also CA 105; 113; CANR 34; DLB 242;
 EW 13; EWL 3; GFL 1789 to the Present;
 GLL 1; LMFS 2; MTCW 1, 2; TWA
Fouque, Friedrich (Heinrich Karl) de la
 Motte 1777-1843 .... **NCLC 2**
 See also DLB 90; RGWL 2, 3; SUFW 1
Fourier, Charles 1772-1837 .... **NCLC 51**
Fournier, Henri-Alban 1886-1914
 See Alain-Fournier
 See also CA 104; 179
Fournier, Pierre 1916- .... **CLC 11**
 See Gascar, Pierre
 See also CA 89-92; CANR 16, 40
Fowles, John (Robert) 1926- . **CLC 1, 2, 3, 4,**
 6, 9, 10, 15, 33, 87; SSC 33
 See also BPFB 1; BRWS 1; CA 5-8R;
 CANR 25, 71, 103; CDBLB 1960 to
 Present; CN 7; DA3; DAB; DAC; DAM
 MST; DLB 14, 139, 207; EWL 3; HGG;
 MTCW 1, 2; RGEL 2; RHW; SATA 22;
 TEA; WLIT 4
Fox, Paula 1923- .... **CLC 2, 8, 121**
 See also AAYA 3, 37; BYA 3, 8; CA 73-76;
 CANR 20, 36, 62, 105; CLR 1, 44; DLB
 52; JRDA; MAICYA 1, 2; MTCW 1; NFS
 12; SATA 17, 60, 120; WYA; YAW
Fox, William Price (Jr.) 1926- .... **CLC 22**
 See also CA 17-20R; CAAS 19; CANR 11;
 CSW; DLB 2; DLBY 1981
Foxe, John 1517(?)-1587 .... **LC 14**
 See also DLB 132
Frame, Janet .. **CLC 2, 3, 6, 22, 66, 96; SSC**
 29
 See Clutha, Janet Paterson Frame
 See also CN 7; CWP; EWL 3; RGEL 2;
 RGSF 2; TWA
France, Anatole .... **TCLC 9**
 See Thibault, Jacques Anatole Francois
 See also DLB 123; EWL 3; GFL 1789 to
 the Present; MTCW 1; RGWL 2, 3;
 SUFW 1
Francis, Claude .... **CLC 50**
 See also CA 192

Francis, Dick 1920- .... **CLC 2, 22, 42, 102**
  See also AAYA 5, 21; BEST 89:3; BPFB 1;
  CA 5-8R; CANR 9, 42, 68, 100; CDBLB
  1960 to Present; CMW 4; CN 7; DA3;
  DAM POP; DLB 87; INT CANR-9;
  MSW; MTCW 1, 2

Francis, Robert (Churchill)
  1901-1987 .... **CLC 15; PC 34**
  See also AMWS 9; CA 1-4R; 123; CANR
  1; EXPP; PFS 12

Francis, Lord Jeffrey
  See Jeffrey, Francis
  See also DLB 107

Frank, Anne(lies Marie)
  1929-1945 .... **TCLC 17; WLC**
  See also AAYA 12; BYA 1; CA 113; 133;
  CANR 68; DA; DA3; DAB; DAC; DAM
  MST; LAIT 4; MAICYA 2; MAICYAS 1;
  MTCW 1, 2; NCFS 2; SATA 87; SATA-
  Brief 42; WYA; YAW

Frank, Bruno 1887-1945 .... **TCLC 81**
  See also CA 189; DLB 118; EWL 3

Frank, Elizabeth 1945- .... **CLC 39**
  See also CA 121; 126; CANR 78; INT 126

Frankl, Viktor E(mil) 1905-1997 ...... **CLC 93**
  See also CA 65-68; 161

Franklin, Benjamin
  See Hasek, Jaroslav (Matej Frantisek)

Franklin, Benjamin 1706-1790 .... **LC 25;**
  WLCS
  See also AMW; CDALB 1640-1865; DA;
  DA3; DAB; DAC; DAM MST; DLB 24,
  43, 73, 183; LAIT 1; RGAL 4; TUS

Franklin, (Stella Maria Sarah) Miles
  (Lampe) 1879-1954 .... **TCLC 7**
  See also CA 104; 164; DLB 230; FW;
  MTCW 2; RGEL 2; TWA

Fraser, Antonia (Pakenham) 1932- . **CLC 32,**
  107
  See also CA 85-88; CANR 44, 65, 119;
  CMW; DLB 276; MTCW 1, 2; SATA-
  Brief 32

Fraser, George MacDonald 1925- ...... **CLC 7**
  See also AAYA 48; CA 45-48, 180; CAAE
  180; CANR 2, 48, 74; MTCW 1; RHW

Fraser, Sylvia 1935- .... **CLC 64**
  See also CA 45-48; CANR 1, 16, 60; CCA
  1

Frayn, Michael 1933- . **CLC 3, 7, 31, 47, 176**
  See also BRWC 2; BRWS 7; CA 5-8R;
  CANR 30, 69, 114; CBD; CD 5; CN 7;
  DAM DRAM, NOV; DLB 13, 14, 194,
  245; FANT; MTCW 1, 2; SFW 4

Fraze, Candida (Merrill) 1945- .... **CLC 50**
  See also CA 126

Frazer, Andrew
  See Marlowe, Stephen

Frazer, J(ames) G(eorge)
  1854-1941 .... **TCLC 32**
  See also BRWS 3; CA 118; NCFS 5

Frazer, Robert Caine
  See Creasey, John

Frazer, Sir James George
  See Frazer, J(ames) G(eorge)

Frazier, Charles 1950- .... **CLC 109**
  See also AAYA 34; CA 161; CSW

Frazier, Ian 1951- .... **CLC 46**
  See also CA 130; CANR 54, 93

Frederic, Harold 1856-1898 .... **NCLC 10**
  See also AMW; DLB 12, 23; DLBD 13;
  RGAL 4

Frederick, John
  See Faust, Frederick (Schiller)
  See also TCWW 2

Frederick the Great 1712-1786 .... **LC 14**

Fredro, Aleksander 1793-1876 .... **NCLC 8**

Freeling, Nicolas 1927- .... **CLC 38**
  See also CA 49-52; CAAS 12; CANR 1,
  17, 50, 84; CMW 4; CN 7; DLB 87

Freeman, Douglas Southall
  1886-1953 .... **TCLC 11**
  See also CA 109; 195; DLB 17; DLBD 17

Freeman, Judith 1946- .... **CLC 55**
  See also CA 148; CANR 120; DLB 256

Freeman, Mary E(leanor) Wilkins
  1852-1930 .... **SSC 1, 47; TCLC 9**
  See also CA 106; 177; DLB 12, 78, 221;
  EXPS; FW; HGG; MAWW; RGAL 4;
  RGSF 2; SSFS 4, 8; SUFW 1; TUS

Freeman, R(ichard) Austin
  1862-1943 .... **TCLC 21**
  See also CA 113; CANR 84; CMW 4; DLB
  70

French, Albert 1943- .... **CLC 86**
  See also BW 3; CA 167

French, Antonia
  See Kureishi, Hanif

French, Marilyn 1929- .. **CLC 10, 18, 60, 177**
  See also BPFB 1; CA 69-72; CANR 3, 31;
  CN 7; CPW; DAM DRAM, NOV, POP;
  FW; INT CANR-31; MTCW 1, 2

French, Paul
  See Asimov, Isaac

Freneau, Philip Morin 1752-1832 .. **NCLC 1,**
  111
  See also AMWS 2; DLB 37, 43; RGAL 4

Freud, Sigmund 1856-1939 .... **TCLC 52**
  See also CA 115; 133; CANR 69; EW 8;
  EWL 3; LATS 1; MTCW 1, 2; NCFS 3;
  TWA

Freytag, Gustav 1816-1895 .... **NCLC 109**
  See also DLB 129

Friedan, Betty (Naomi) 1921- .... **CLC 74**
  See also CA 65-68; CANR 18, 45, 74; DLB
  246; FW; MTCW 1, 2; NCFS 5

Friedlander, Saul 1932- .... **CLC 90**
  See also CA 117; 130; CANR 72

Friedman, B(ernard) H(arper)
  1926- .... **CLC 7**
  See also CA 1-4R; CANR 3, 48

Friedman, Bruce Jay 1930- ...... **CLC 3, 5, 56**
  See also CA 9-12R; CAD; CANR 25, 52,
  101; CD 5; CN 7; DLB 2, 28, 244; INT
  CANR-25; SSFS 18

Friel, Brian 1929- .... **CLC 5, 42, 59, 115; DC**
  8
  See also BRWS 5; CA 21-24R; CANR 33,
  69; CBD; CD 5; DFS 11; DLB 13; EWL
  3; MTCW 1; RGEL 2; TEA

Friis-Baastad, Babbis Ellinor
  1921-1970 .... **CLC 12**
  See also CA 17-20R; 134; SATA 7

Frisch, Max (Rudolf) 1911-1991 ... **CLC 3, 9,**
  14, 18, 32, 44; TCLC 121
  See also CA 85-88; 134; CANR 32, 74; CD-
  WLB 2; DAM DRAM, NOV; DLB 69,
  124; EW 13; EWL 3; MTCW 1, 2; RGWL
  2, 3

Fromentin, Eugene (Samuel Auguste)
  1820-1876 .... **NCLC 10, 125**
  See also DLB 123; GFL 1789 to the Present

Frost, Frederick
  See Faust, Frederick (Schiller)
  See also TCWW 2

Frost, Robert (Lee) 1874-1963 .. **CLC 1, 3, 4,**
  9, 10, 13, 15, 26, 34, 44; PC 1, 39;
  WLC
  See also AAYA 21; AMW; AMWR 1; CA
  89-92; CANR 33; CDALB 1917-1929;
  CLR 67; DA; DA3; DAB; DAC; DAM
  MST, POET; DLB 54, 284; DLBD 7;
  EWL 3; EXPP; MTCW 1, 2; PAB; PFS 1,
  2, 3, 4, 5, 6, 7, 10, 13; RGAL 4; SATA
  14; TUS; WP; WYA

Froude, James Anthony
  1818-1894 .... **NCLC 43**
  See also DLB 18, 57, 144

Froy, Herald
  See Waterhouse, Keith (Spencer)

Fry, Christopher 1907- .... **CLC 2, 10, 14**
  See also BRWS 3; CA 17-20R; CAAS 23;
  CANR 9, 30, 74; CBD; CD 5; CP 7; DAM
  DRAM; DLB 13; EWL 3; MTCW 1, 2;
  RGEL 2; SATA 66; TEA

Frye, (Herman) Northrop
  1912-1991 .... **CLC 24, 70**
  See also CA 5-8R; 133; CANR 8, 37; DLB
  67, 68, 246; EWL 3; MTCW 1, 2; RGAL
  4; TWA

Fuchs, Daniel 1909-1993 .... **CLC 8, 22**
  See also CA 81-84; 142; CAAS 5; CANR
  40; DLB 9, 26, 28; DLBY 1993

Fuchs, Daniel 1934- .... **CLC 34**
  See also CA 37-40R; CANR 14, 48

Fuentes, Carlos 1928- .. **CLC 3, 8, 10, 13, 22,**
  41, 60, 113; HLC 1; SSC 24; WLC
  See also AAYA 4, 45; AITN 2; BPFB 1;
  CA 69-72; CANR 10, 32, 68, 104; CD-
  WLB 3; CWW 2; DA; DA3; DAB; DAC;
  DAM MST, MULT, NOV; DLB 113;
  DNFS 2; EWL 3; HW 1, 2; LAIT 3; LATS
  1; LAW; LAWS 1; LMFS 2; MTCW 1, 2;
  NFS 8; RGSF 2; RGWL 2, 3; TWA;
  WLIT 1

Fuentes, Gregorio Lopez y
  See Lopez y Fuentes, Gregorio

Fuertes, Gloria 1918-1998 .... **PC 27**
  See also CA 178, 180; DLB 108; HW 2;
  SATA 115

Fugard, (Harold) Athol 1932- . **CLC 5, 9, 14,**
  25, 40, 80; DC 3
  See also AAYA 17; AFW; CA 85-88; CANR
  32, 54, 118; CD 5; DAM DRAM; DFS 3,
  6, 10; DLB 225; DNFS 1, 2; EWL 3;
  LATS 1; MTCW 1; RGEL 2; WLIT 2

Fugard, Sheila 1932- .... **CLC 48**
  See also CA 125

Fukuyama, Francis 1952- .... **CLC 131**
  See also CA 140; CANR 72

Fuller, Charles (H.), (Jr.) 1939- .... **BLC 2;**
  CLC 25; DC 1
  See also BW 2; CA 108; 112; CAD; CANR
  87; CD 5; DAM DRAM, MULT; DFS 8;
  DLB 38, 266; EWL 3; INT CA-112;
  MTCW 1

Fuller, Henry Blake 1857-1929 .... **TCLC 103**
  See also CA 108; 177; DLB 12; RGAL 4

Fuller, John (Leopold) 1937- .... **CLC 62**
  See also CA 21-24R; CANR 9, 44; CP 7;
  DLB 40

Fuller, Margaret
  See Ossoli, Sarah Margaret (Fuller)
  See also AMWS 2; DLB 183, 223, 239

Fuller, Roy (Broadbent) 1912-1991 ... **CLC 4,**
  28
  See also BRWS 7; CA 5-8R; 135; CAAS
  10; CANR 53, 83; CWRI 5; DLB 15, 20;
  EWL 3; RGEL 2; SATA 87

Fuller, Sarah Margaret
  See Ossoli, Sarah Margaret (Fuller)

Fuller, Sarah Margaret
  See Ossoli, Sarah Margaret (Fuller)
  See also DLB 1, 59, 73

Fulton, Alice 1952- .... **CLC 52**
  See also CA 116; CANR 57, 88; CP 7;
  CWP; DLB 193

Furphy, Joseph 1843-1912 .... **TCLC 25**
  See Collins, Tom
  See also CA 163; DLB 230; EWL 3; RGEL
  2

Fuson, Robert H(enderson) 1927- .... **CLC 70**
  See also CA 89-92; CANR 103

Fussell, Paul 1924- .... **CLC 74**
  See also BEST 90:1; CA 17-20R; CANR 8,
  21, 35, 69; INT CANR-21; MTCW 1, 2

Futabatei, Shimei 1864-1909 .... **TCLC 44**
See Futabatei Shimei
See also CA 162; MJW
Futabatei Shimei
See Futabatei, Shimei
See also DLB 180; EWL 3
Futrelle, Jacques 1875-1912 .... **TCLC 19**
See also CA 113; 155; CMW 4
Gaboriau, Emile 1835-1873 .... **NCLC 14**
See also CMW 4; MSW
Gadda, Carlo Emilio 1893-1973 .... **CLC 11**
See also CA 89-92; DLB 177; EWL 3
Gaddis, William 1922-1998 ... **CLC 1, 3, 6, 8,
10, 19, 43, 86**
See also AMWS 4; BPFB 1; CA 17-20R;
172; CANR 21, 48; CN 7; DLB 2, 278;
EWL 3; MTCW 1, 2; RGAL 4
Gaelique, Moruen le
See Jacob, (Cyprien-)Max
Gage, Walter
See Inge, William (Motter)
Gaines, Ernest J(ames) 1933- .. **BLC 2; CLC
3, 11, 18, 86**
See also AAYA 18; AFAW 1, 2; AITN 1;
BPFB 2; BW 2, 3; BYA 6; CA 9-12R;
CANR 6, 24, 42, 75; CDALB 1968-1988;
CLR 62; CN 7; CSW; DA3; DAM MULT;
DLB 2, 33, 152; DLBY 1980; EWL 3;
EXPN; LAIT 5; LATS 1; MTCW 1, 2;
NFS 5, 7, 16; RGAL 4; RGSF 2; RHW;
SATA 86; SSFS 5; YAW
Gaitskill, Mary 1954- .... **CLC 69**
See also CA 128; CANR 61; DLB 244
Gaius Suetonius Tranquillus c. 70-c. 130
See Suetonius
Galdos, Benito Perez
See Perez Galdos, Benito
See also EW 7
Gale, Zona 1874-1938 .... **TCLC 7**
See also CA 105; 153; CANR 84; DAM
DRAM; DFS 17; DLB 9, 78, 228; RGAL
4
Galeano, Eduardo (Hughes) 1940- . **CLC 72;
HLCS 1**
See also CA 29-32R; CANR 13, 32, 100;
HW 1
Galiano, Juan Valera y Alcala
See Valera y Alcala-Galiano, Juan
Galilei, Galileo 1564-1642 .... **LC 45**
Gallagher, Tess 1943- .... **CLC 18, 63; PC 9**
See also CA 106; CP 7; CWP; DAM POET;
DLB 120, 212, 244; PFS 16
Gallant, Mavis 1922- ..... **CLC 7, 18, 38, 172;
SSC 5**
See also CA 69-72; CANR 29, 69, 117;
CCA 1; CN 7; DAC; DAM MST; DLB
53; EWL 3; MTCW 1, 2; RGEL 2; RGSF
2
Gallant, Roy A(rthur) 1924- .... **CLC 17**
See also CA 5-8R; CANR 4, 29, 54, 117;
CLR 30; MAICYA 1, 2; SATA 4, 68, 110
Gallico, Paul (William) 1897-1976 ..... **CLC 2**
See also AITN 1; CA 5-8R; 69-72; CANR
23; DLB 9, 171; FANT; MAICYA 1, 2;
SATA 13
Gallo, Max Louis 1932- .... **CLC 95**
See also CA 85-88
Gallois, Lucien
See Desnos, Robert
Gallup, Ralph
See Whitemore, Hugh (John)
Galsworthy, John 1867-1933 .... **SSC 22;
TCLC 1, 45; WLC**
See also BRW 6; CA 104; 141; CANR 75;
CDBLB 1890-1914; DA; DA3; DAB;
DAC; DAM DRAM, MST, NOV; DLB
10, 34, 98, 162; DLBD 16; EWL 3;
MTCW 1; RGEL 2; SSFS 3; TEA

Galt, John 1779-1839 .... **NCLC 1, 110**
See also DLB 99, 116, 159; RGEL 2; RGSF
2
Galvin, James 1951- .... **CLC 38**
See also CA 108; CANR 26
Gamboa, Federico 1864-1939 .... **TCLC 36**
See also CA 167; HW 2; LAW
Gandhi, M. K.
See Gandhi, Mohandas Karamchand
Gandhi, Mahatma
See Gandhi, Mohandas Karamchand
Gandhi, Mohandas Karamchand
1869-1948 .... **TCLC 59**
See also CA 121; 132; DA3; DAM MULT;
MTCW 1, 2
Gann, Ernest Kellogg 1910-1991 ..... **CLC 23**
See also AITN 1; BPFB 2; CA 1-4R; 136;
CANR 1, 83; RHW
Gao Xingjian 1940- .... **CLC 167**
See Xingjian, Gao
Garber, Eric 1943(?)-
See Holleran, Andrew
See also CANR 89
Garcia, Cristina 1958- .... **CLC 76**
See also AMWS 11; CA 141; CANR 73;
DNFS 1; EWL 3; HW 2
Garcia Lorca, Federico 1898-1936 ...... **DC 2;
HLC 2; PC 3; TCLC 1, 7, 49; WLC**
See Lorca, Federico Garcia
See also AAYA 46; CA 104; 131; CANR
81; DA; DA3; DAB; DAC; DAM DRAM,
MST, MULT, POET; DFS 4, 10; DLB
108; EWL 3; HW 1, 2; LATS 1; MTCW
1, 2; TWA
Garcia Marquez, Gabriel (Jose)
1928- .... **CLC 2, 3, 8, 10, 15, 27, 47, 55,
68, 170; HLC 1; SSC 8; WLC**
See also AAYA 3, 33; BEST 89:1, 90:4;
BPFB 2; BYA 12, 16; CA 33-36R; CANR
10, 28, 50, 75, 82; CDWLB 3; CPW; DA;
DA3; DAB; DAC; DAM MST, MULT,
NOV, POP; DLB 113; DNFS 1, 2; EWL
3; EXPN; EXPS; HW 1, 2; LAIT 2; LATS
1; LAW; LAWS 1; LMFS 2; MTCW 1, 2;
NCFS 3; NFS 1, 5, 10; RGSF 2; RGWL
2, 3; SSFS 1, 6, 16; TWA; WLIT 1
Garcilaso de la Vega, El Inca
1503-1536 .... **HLCS 1**
See also LAW
Gard, Janice
See Latham, Jean Lee
Gard, Roger Martin du
See Martin du Gard, Roger
Gardam, Jane (Mary) 1928- .... **CLC 43**
See also CA 49-52; CANR 2, 18, 33, 54,
106; CLR 12; DLB 14, 161, 231; MAI-
CYA 1, 2; MTCW 1; SAAS 9; SATA 39,
76, 130; SATA-Brief 28; YAW
Gardner, Herb(ert) 1934- .... **CLC 44**
See also CA 149; CAD; CANR 119; CD 5;
DFS 18
Gardner, John (Champlin), Jr.
1933-1982 ...... **CLC 2, 3, 5, 7, 8, 10, 18,
28, 34; SSC 7**
See also AAYA 45; AITN 1; AMWS 6;
BPFB 2; CA 65-68; 107; CANR 33, 73;
CDALBS; CPW; DA3; DAM NOV, POP;
DLB 2; DLBY 1982; EWL 3; FANT;
LATS 1; MTCW 1; NFS 3; RGAL 4;
RGSF 2; SATA 40; SATA-Obit 31; SSFS
8
Gardner, John (Edmund) 1926- .... **CLC 30**
See also CA 103; CANR 15, 69; CMW 4;
CPW; DAM POP; MTCW 1
Gardner, Miriam
See Bradley, Marion Zimmer
See also GLL 1
Gardner, Noel
See Kuttner, Henry

Gardons, S. S.
See Snodgrass, W(illiam) D(e Witt)
Garfield, Leon 1921-1996 .... **CLC 12**
See also AAYA 8; BYA 1, 3; CA 17-20R;
152; CANR 38, 41, 78; CLR 21; DLB
161; JRDA; MAICYA 1, 2; MAICYAS 1;
SATA 1, 32, 76; SATA-Obit 90; TEA;
WYA; YAW
Garland, (Hannibal) Hamlin
1860-1940 .... **SSC 18; TCLC 3**
See also CA 104; DLB 12, 71, 78, 186;
RGAL 4; RGSF 2; TCWW 2
Garneau, (Hector de) Saint-Denys
1912-1943 .... **TCLC 13**
See also CA 111; DLB 88
Garner, Alan 1934- .... **CLC 17**
See also AAYA 18; BYA 3, 5; CA 73-76,
178; CAAE 178; CANR 15, 64; CLR 20;
CPW; DAB; DAM POP; DLB 161, 261;
FANT; MAICYA 1, 2; MTCW 1, 2; SATA
18, 69; SATA-Essay 108; SUFW 1, 2;
YAW
Garner, Hugh 1913-1979 .... **CLC 13**
See Warwick, Jarvis
See also CA 69-72; CANR 31; CCA 1; DLB
68
Garnett, David 1892-1981 .... **CLC 3**
See also CA 5-8R; 103; CANR 17, 79; DLB
34; FANT; MTCW 2; RGEL 2; SFW 4;
SUFW 1
Garos, Stephanie
See Katz, Steve
Garrett, George (Palmer) 1929- .. **CLC 3, 11,
51; SSC 30**
See also AMWS 7; BPFB 2; CA 1-4R;
CAAE 202; CAAS 5; CANR 1, 42, 67,
109; CN 7; CP 7; CSW; DLB 2, 5, 130,
152; DLBY 1983
Garrick, David 1717-1779 .... **LC 15**
See also DAM DRAM; DLB 84, 213;
RGEL 2
Garrigue, Jean 1914-1972 .... **CLC 2, 8**
See also CA 5-8R; 37-40R; CANR 20
Garrison, Frederick
See Sinclair, Upton (Beall)
Garro, Elena 1920(?)-1998 .... **HLCS 1**
See also CA 131; 169; CWW 2; DLB 145;
EWL 3; HW 1; LAWS 1; WLIT 1
Garth, Will
See Hamilton, Edmond; Kuttner, Henry
Garvey, Marcus (Moziah, Jr.)
1887-1940 .... **BLC 2; HR 2; TCLC 41**
See also BW 1; CA 120; 124; CANR 79;
DAM MULT
Gary, Romain .... **CLC 25**
See Kacew, Romain
See also DLB 83
Gascar, Pierre .... **CLC 11**
See Fournier, Pierre
See also EWL 3
Gascoyne, David (Emery)
1916-2001 .... **CLC 45**
See also CA 65-68; 200; CANR 10, 28, 54;
CP 7; DLB 20; MTCW 1; RGEL 2
Gaskell, Elizabeth Cleghorn
1810-1865 .... **NCLC 5, 70, 97; SSC 25**
See also BRW 5; CDBLB 1832-1890; DAB;
DAM MST; DLB 21, 144, 159; RGEL 2;
RGSF 2; TEA
Gass, William H(oward) 1924- . **CLC 1, 2, 8,
11, 15, 39, 132; SSC 12**
See also AMWS 6; CA 17-20R; CANR 30,
71, 100; CN 7; DLB 2, 227; EWL 3;
MTCW 1, 2; RGAL 4
Gassendi, Pierre 1592-1655 .... **LC 54**
See also GFL Beginnings to 1789
Gasset, Jose Ortega y
See Ortega y Gasset, Jose

Greenberg, Ivan 1908-1973
  See Rahv, Philip
  See also CA 85-88
Greenberg, Joanne (Goldenberg)
  1932- .... **CLC 7, 30**
  See also AAYA 12; CA 5-8R; CANR 14,
  32, 69; CN 7; SATA 25; YAW
Greenberg, Richard 1959(?)- .... **CLC 57**
  See also CA 138; CAD; CD 5
Greenblatt, Stephen J(ay) 1943- ...... **CLC 70**
  See also CA 49-52; CANR 115
Greene, Bette 1934- .... **CLC 30**
  See also AAYA 7; BYA 3; CA 53-56; CANR
  4; CLR 2; CWRI 5; JRDA; LAIT 4; MAI-
  CYA 1, 2; NFS 10; SAAS 16; SATA 8,
  102; WYA; YAW
Greene, Gael .... **CLC 8**
  See also CA 13-16R; CANR 10
Greene, Graham (Henry)
  1904-1991 .... **CLC 1, 3, 6, 9, 14, 18, 27,**
    37, 70, 72, 125; SSC 29; WLC
  See also AITN 2; BPFB 2; BRWR 2; BRWS
  1; BYA 3; CA 13-16R; 133; CANR 35,
  61; CBD; CDBLB 1945-1960; CMW 4;
  DA; DA3; DAB; DAC; DAM MST, NOV;
  DLB 13, 15, 77, 100, 162, 201, 204;
  DLBY 1991; EWL 3; MSW; MTCW 1, 2;
  NFS 16; RGEL 2; SATA 20; SSFS 14;
  TEA; WLIT 4
Greene, Robert 1558-1592 .... **LC 41**
  See also BRWS 8; DLB 62, 167; IDTP;
  RGEL 2; TEA
Greer, Germaine 1939- .... **CLC 131**
  See also AITN 1; CA 81-84; CANR 33, 70,
  115; FW; MTCW 1, 2
Greer, Richard
  See Silverberg, Robert
Gregor, Arthur 1923- .... **CLC 9**
  See also CA 25-28R; CAAS 10; CANR 11;
  CP 7; SATA 36
Gregor, Lee
  See Pohl, Frederik
Gregory, Lady Isabella Augusta (Persse)
  1852-1932 .... **TCLC 1**
  See also BRW 6; CA 104; 184; DLB 10;
  IDTP; RGEL 2
Gregory, J. Dennis
  See Williams, John A(lfred)
Grekova, I. .... **CLC 59**
Grendon, Stephen
  See Derleth, August (William)
Grenville, Kate 1950- .... **CLC 61**
  See also CA 118; CANR 53, 93
Grenville, Pelham
  See Wodehouse, P(elham) G(renville)
Greve, Felix Paul (Berthold Friedrich)
  1879-1948
  See Grove, Frederick Philip
  See also CA 104; 141; 175; CANR 79;
  DAC; DAM MST
Greville, Fulke 1554-1628 .... **LC 79**
  See also DLB 62, 172; RGEL 2
Grey, Lady Jane 1537-1554 .... **LC 93**
  See also DLB 132
Grey, Zane 1872-1939 .... **TCLC 6**
  See also BPFB 2; CA 104; 132; DA3; DAM
  POP; DLB 9, 212; MTCW 1, 2; RGAL 4;
  TCWW 2; TUS
Griboedov, Aleksandr Sergeevich
  1795(?)-1829 .... **NCLC 129**
  See also DLB 205; RGWL 2, 3
Grieg, (Johan) Nordahl (Brun)
  1902-1943 .... **TCLC 10**
  See also CA 107; 189; EWL 3
Grieve, C(hristopher) M(urray)
  1892-1978 .... **CLC 11, 19**
  See MacDiarmid, Hugh; Pteleon
  See also CA 5-8R; 85-88; CANR 33, 107;
  DAM POET; MTCW 1; RGEL 2

Griffin, Gerald 1803-1840 .... **NCLC 7**
  See also DLB 159; RGEL 2
Griffin, John Howard 1920-1980 ..... **CLC 68**
  See also AITN 1; CA 1-4R; 101; CANR 2
Griffin, Peter 1942- .... **CLC 39**
  See also CA 136
Griffith, D(avid Lewelyn) W(ark)
  1875(?)-1948 .... **TCLC 68**
  See also CA 119; 150; CANR 80
Griffith, Lawrence
  See Griffith, D(avid Lewelyn) W(ark)
Griffiths, Trevor 1935- .... **CLC 13, 52**
  See also CA 97-100; CANR 45; CBD; CD
  5; DLB 13, 245
Griggs, Sutton (Elbert)
  1872-1930 .... **TCLC 77**
  See also CA 123; 186; DLB 50
Grigson, Geoffrey (Edward Harvey)
  1905-1985 .... **CLC 7, 39**
  See also CA 25-28R; 118; CANR 20, 33;
  DLB 27; MTCW 1, 2
Grile, Dod
  See Bierce, Ambrose (Gwinett)
Grillparzer, Franz 1791-1872 .... **DC 14;**
    NCLC 1, 102; SSC 37
  See also CDWLB 2; DLB 133; EW 5;
  RGWL 2, 3; TWA
Grimble, Reverend Charles James
  See Eliot, T(homas) S(tearns)
Grimke, Angelina (Emily) Weld
  1880-1958 .... **HR 2**
  See Weld, Angelina (Emily) Grimke
  See also BW 1; CA 124; DAM POET; DLB
  50, 54
Grimke, Charlotte L(ottie) Forten
  1837(?)-1914
  See Forten, Charlotte L.
  See also BW 1; CA 117; 124; DAM MULT,
  POET
Grimm, Jacob Ludwig Karl
  1785-1863 .... **NCLC 3, 77; SSC 36**
  See also DLB 90; MAICYA 1, 2; RGSF 2;
  RGWL 2, 3; SATA 22; WCH
Grimm, Wilhelm Karl 1786-1859 .. **NCLC 3,**
    77; SSC 36
  See also CDWLB 2; DLB 90; MAICYA 1,
  2; RGSF 2; RGWL 2, 3; SATA 22; WCH
Grimmelshausen, Hans Jakob Christoffel
  von
  See Grimmelshausen, Johann Jakob Christ-
  offel von
  See also RGWL 2, 3
Grimmelshausen, Johann Jakob Christoffel
  von 1621-1676 .... **LC 6**
  See Grimmelshausen, Hans Jakob Christof-
  fel von
  See also CDWLB 2; DLB 168
Grindel, Eugene 1895-1952
  See Eluard, Paul
  See also CA 104; 193; LMFS 2
Grisham, John 1955- .... **CLC 84**
  See also AAYA 14, 47; BPFB 2; CA 138;
  CANR 47, 69, 114; CMW 4; CN 7; CPW;
  CSW; DA3; DAM POP; MSW; MTCW 2
Grosseteste, Robert 1175(?)-1253 . **CMLC 62**
  See also DLB 115
Grossman, David 1954- .... **CLC 67**
  See also CA 138; CANR 114; CWW 2;
  EWL 3
Grossman, Vasilii Semenovich
  See Grossman, Vasily (Semenovich)
  See also DLB 272
Grossman, Vasily (Semenovich)
  1905-1964 .... **CLC 41**
  See Grossman, Vasilii Semenovich
  See also CA 124; 130; MTCW 1
Grove, Frederick Philip .... **TCLC 4**
  See Greve, Felix Paul (Berthold Friedrich)
  See also DLB 92; RGEL 2

Grubb
  See Crumb, R(obert)
Grumbach, Doris (Isaac) 1918- . **CLC 13, 22,**
  64
  See also CA 5-8R; CAAS 2; CANR 9, 42,
  70; CN 7; INT CANR-9; MTCW 2
Grundtvig, Nicolai Frederik Severin
  1783-1872 .... **NCLC 1**
Grunge
  See Crumb, R(obert)
Grunwald, Lisa 1959- .... **CLC 44**
  See also CA 120
Gryphius, Andreas 1616-1664 .... **LC 89**
  See also CDWLB 2; DLB 164; RGWL 2, 3
Guare, John 1938- .... **CLC 8, 14, 29, 67; DC**
  20
  See also CA 73-76; CAD; CANR 21, 69,
  118; CD 5; DAM DRAM; DFS 8, 13;
  DLB 7, 249; EWL 3; MTCW 1, 2; RGAL
  4
Gubar, Susan (David) 1944- .... **CLC 145**
  See also CA 108; CANR 45, 70; FW;
  MTCW 1; RGAL 4
Gudjonsson, Halldor Kiljan 1902-1998
  See Laxness, Halldor
  See also CA 103; 164; CWW 2
Guenter, Erich
  See Eich, Gunter
Guest, Barbara 1920- .... **CLC 34**
  See also BG 2; CA 25-28R; CANR 11, 44,
  84; CP 7; CWP; DLB 5, 193
Guest, Edgar A(lbert) 1881-1959 ... **TCLC 95**
  See also CA 112; 168
Guest, Judith (Ann) 1936- .... **CLC 8, 30**
  See also AAYA 7; CA 77-80; CANR 15,
  75; DA3; DAM NOV, POP; EXPN; INT
  CANR-15; LAIT 5; MTCW 1, 2; NFS 1
Guevara, Che .... **CLC 87; HLC 1**
  See Guevara (Serna), Ernesto
Guevara (Serna), Ernesto
  1928-1967 .... **CLC 87; HLC 1**
  See Guevara, Che
  See also CA 127; 111; CANR 56; DAM
  MULT; HW 1
Guicciardini, Francesco 1483-1540 ..... **LC 49**
Guild, Nicholas M. 1944- .... **CLC 33**
  See also CA 93-96
Guillemin, Jacques
  See Sartre, Jean-Paul
Guillen, Jorge 1893-1984 . **CLC 11; HLCS 1;**
  PC 35
  See also CA 89-92; 112; DAM MULT,
  POET; DLB 108; EWL 3; HW 1; RGWL
  2, 3
Guillen, Nicolas (Cristobal)
  1902-1989 .... **BLC 2; CLC 48, 79; HLC**
  1; PC 23
  See also BW 2; CA 116; 125; 129; CANR
  84; DAM MST, MULT, POET; DLB 283;
  EWL 3; HW 1; LAW; RGWL 2, 3; WP
Guillen y Alvarez, Jorge
  See Guillen, Jorge
Guillevic, (Eugene) 1907-1997 .... **CLC 33**
  See also CA 93-96; CWW 2
Guillois
  See Desnos, Robert
Guillois, Valentin
  See Desnos, Robert
Guimaraes Rosa, Joao 1908-1967 .... **HLCS 2**
  See also CA 175; LAW; RGSF 2; RGWL 2,
  3
Guiney, Louise Imogen
  1861-1920 .... **TCLC 41**
  See also CA 160; DLB 54; RGAL 4
Guinizelli, Guido c. 1230-1276 ...... **CMLC 49**
Guiraldes, Ricardo (Guillermo)
  1886-1927 .... **TCLC 39**
  See also CA 131; EWL 3; HW 1; LAW;
  MTCW 1

LAIT 5; MAICYA 1, 2; MAICYAS 1; MTCW 1, 2; SATA 4, 56, 79, 123; SATA-Obit 132; WYA; YAW

Hammett, (Samuel) Dashiell
1894-1961 .... **CLC 3, 5, 10, 19, 47; SSC 17**
See also AITN 1; AMWS 4; BPFB 2; CA 81-84; CANR 42; CDALB 1929-1941; CMW 4; DA3; DLB 226; DLBD 6; DLBY 1996; EWL 3; LAIT 3; MSW; MTCW 1, 2; RGAL 4; RGSF 2; TUS

Hammon, Jupiter 1720(?)-1800(?) .... **BLC 2; NCLC 5; PC 16**
See also DAM MULT, POET; DLB 31, 50

Hammond, Keith
See Kuttner, Henry

Hamner, Earl (Henry), Jr. 1923- ...... **CLC 12**
See also AITN 1; CA 73-76; DLB 6

Hampton, Christopher (James)
1946- .... **CLC 4**
See also CA 25-28R; CD 5; DLB 13; MTCW 1

Hamsun, Knut .... **TCLC 2, 14, 49**
See Pedersen, Knut
See also EW 8; EWL 3; RGWL 2, 3

Handke, Peter 1942- .... **CLC 5, 8, 10, 15, 38, 134; DC 17**
See also CA 77-80; CANR 33, 75, 104; CWW 2; DAM DRAM, NOV; DLB 85, 124; EWL 3; MTCW 1, 2; TWA

Handy, W(illiam) C(hristopher)
1873-1958 .... **TCLC 97**
See also BW 3; CA 121; 167

Hanley, James 1901-1985 ..... **CLC 3, 5, 8, 13**
See also CA 73-76; 117; CANR 36; CBD; DLB 191; EWL 3; MTCW 1; RGEL 2

Hannah, Barry 1942- .... **CLC 23, 38, 90**
See also BPFB 2; CA 108; 110; CANR 43, 68, 113; CN 7; CSW; DLB 6, 234; INT CA-110; MTCW 1; RGSF 2

Hannon, Ezra
See Hunter, Evan

Hansberry, Lorraine (Vivian)
1930-1965 ... **BLC 2; CLC 17, 62; DC 2**
See also AAYA 25; AFAW 1, 2; AMWS 4; BW 1, 3; CA 109; 25-28R; CABS 3; CAD; CANR 58; CDALB 1941-1968; CWD; DA; DA3; DAB; DAC; DAM DRAM, MST, MULT; DFS 2; DLB 7, 38; EWL 3; FW; LAIT 4; MTCW 1, 2; RGAL 4; TUS

Hansen, Joseph 1923- .... **CLC 38**
See Brock, Rose; Colton, James
See also BPFB 2; CA 29-32R; CAAS 17; CANR 16, 44, 66; CMW 4; DLB 226; GLL 1; INT CANR-16

Hansen, Martin A(lfred)
1909-1955 .... **TCLC 32**
See also CA 167; DLB 214; EWL 3

Hansen and Philipson eds. .... **CLC 65**

Hanson, Kenneth O(stlin) 1922- .... **CLC 13**
See also CA 53-56; CANR 7

Hardwick, Elizabeth (Bruce) 1916- . **CLC 13**
See also AMWS 3; CA 5-8R; CANR 3, 32, 70, 100; CN 7; CSW; DA3; DAM NOV; DLB 6; MAWW; MTCW 1, 2

Hardy, Thomas 1840-1928 .... **PC 8; SSC 2, 60; TCLC 4, 10, 18, 32, 48, 53, 72; WLC**
See also BRW 6; BRWC 1, 2; BRWR 1; CA 104; 123; CDBLB 1890-1914; DA; DA3; DAB; DAC; DAM MST, NOV, POET; DLB 18, 19, 135, 284; EWL 3; EXPN; EXPP; LAIT 2; MTCW 1, 2; NFS 3, 11, 15; PFS 3, 4, 18; RGEL 2; RGSF 2; TEA; WLIT 4

Hare, David 1947- .... **CLC 29, 58, 136**
See also BRWS 4; CA 97-100; CANR 39, 91; CBD; CD 5; DFS 4, 7, 16; DLB 13; MTCW 1; TEA

Harewood, John
See Van Druten, John (William)

Harford, Henry
See Hudson, W(illiam) H(enry)

Hargrave, Leonie
See Disch, Thomas M(ichael)

Hariri, Al- al-Qasim ibn 'Ali Abu Muhammad al-Basri
See al-Hariri, al-Qasim ibn 'Ali Abu Muhammad al-Basri

Harjo, Joy 1951- ..... **CLC 83; NNAL; PC 27**
See also AMWS 12; CA 114; CANR 35, 67, 91; CP 7; CWP; DAM MULT; DLB 120, 175; EWL 3; MTCW 2; PFS 15; RGAL 4

Harlan, Louis R(udolph) 1922- .... **CLC 34**
See also CA 21-24R; CANR 25, 55, 80

Harling, Robert 1951(?)- .... **CLC 53**
See also CA 147

Harmon, William (Ruth) 1938- .... **CLC 38**
See also CA 33-36R; CANR 14, 32, 35; SATA 65

Harper, F. E. W.
See Harper, Frances Ellen Watkins

Harper, Frances E. W.
See Harper, Frances Ellen Watkins

Harper, Frances E. Watkins
See Harper, Frances Ellen Watkins

Harper, Frances Ellen
See Harper, Frances Ellen Watkins

Harper, Frances Ellen Watkins
1825-1911 ..... **BLC 2; PC 21; TCLC 14**
See also AFAW 1, 2; BW 1, 3; CA 111; 125; CANR 79; DAM MULT, POET; DLB 50, 221; MAWW; RGAL 4

Harper, Michael S(teven) 1938- ... **CLC 7, 22**
See also AFAW 2; BW 1; CA 33-36R; CANR 24, 108; CP 7; DLB 41; RGAL 4

Harper, Mrs. F. E. W.
See Harper, Frances Ellen Watkins

Harpur, Charles 1813-1868 .... **NCLC 114**
See also DLB 230; RGEL 2

Harris, Christie 1907-
See Harris, Christie (Lucy) Irwin

Harris, Christie (Lucy) Irwin
1907-2002 .... **CLC 12**
See also CA 5-8R; CANR 6, 83; CLR 47; DLB 88; JRDA; MAICYA 1, 2; SAAS 10; SATA 6, 74; SATA-Essay 116

Harris, Frank 1856-1931 .... **TCLC 24**
See also CA 109; 150; CANR 80; DLB 156, 197; RGEL 2

Harris, George Washington
1814-1869 .... **NCLC 23**
See also DLB 3, 11, 248; RGAL 4

Harris, Joel Chandler 1848-1908 ..... **SSC 19; TCLC 2**
See also CA 104; 137; CANR 80; CLR 49; DLB 11, 23, 42, 78, 91; LAIT 2; MAICYA 1, 2; RGSF 2; SATA 100; WCH; YABC 1

Harris, John (Wyndham Parkes Lucas) Beynon 1903-1969
See Wyndham, John
See also CA 102; 89-92; CANR 84; SATA 118; SFW 4

Harris, MacDonald .... **CLC 9**
See Heiney, Donald (William)

Harris, Mark 1922- .... **CLC 19**
See also CA 5-8R; CAAS 3; CANR 2, 55, 83; CN 7; DLB 2; DLBY 1980

Harris, Norman .... **CLC 65**

Harris, (Theodore) Wilson 1921- .... **CLC 25, 159**
See also BRWS 5; BW 2, 3; CA 65-68; CAAS 16; CANR 11, 27, 69, 114; CDWLB 3; CN 7; CP 7; DLB 117; EWL 3; MTCW 1; RGEL 2

Harrison, Barbara Grizzuti
1934-2002 .... **CLC 144**
See also CA 77-80; 205; CANR 15, 48; INT CANR-15

Harrison, Elizabeth (Allen) Cavanna
1909-2001
See Cavanna, Betty
See also CA 9-12R; 200; CANR 6, 27, 85, 104, 121; MAICYA 2; SATA 142; YAW

Harrison, Harry (Max) 1925- .... **CLC 42**
See also CA 1-4R; CANR 5, 21, 84; DLB 8; SATA 4; SCFW 2; SFW 4

Harrison, James (Thomas) 1937- ...... **CLC 6, 14, 33, 66, 143; SSC 19**
See Harrison, Jim
See also CA 13-16R; CANR 8, 51, 79; CN 7; CP 7; DLBY 1982; INT CANR-8

Harrison, Jim
See Harrison, James (Thomas)
See also AMWS 8; RGAL 4; TCWW 2; TUS

Harrison, Kathryn 1961- .... **CLC 70, 151**
See also CA 144; CANR 68, 122

Harrison, Tony 1937- .... **CLC 43, 129**
See also BRWS 5; CA 65-68; CANR 44, 98; CBD; CD 5; CP 7; DLB 40, 245; MTCW 1; RGEL 2

Harriss, Will(ard Irvin) 1922- .... **CLC 34**
See also CA 111

Hart, Ellis
See Ellison, Harlan (Jay)

Hart, Josephine 1942(?)- .... **CLC 70**
See also CA 138; CANR 70; CPW; DAM POP

Hart, Moss 1904-1961 .... **CLC 66**
See also CA 109; 89-92; CANR 84; DAM DRAM; DFS 1; DLB 7, 266; RGAL 4

Harte, (Francis) Bret(t)
1836(?)-1902 ... **SSC 8, 59; TCLC 1, 25; WLC**
See also AMWS 2; CA 104; 140; CANR 80; CDALB 1865-1917; DA; DA3; DAC; DAM MST; DLB 12, 64, 74, 79, 186; EXPS; LAIT 2; RGAL 4; RGSF 2; SATA 26; SSFS 3; TUS

Hartley, L(eslie) P(oles) 1895-1972 ... **CLC 2, 22**
See also BRWS 7; CA 45-48; 37-40R; CANR 33; DLB 15, 139; EWL 3; HGG; MTCW 1, 2; RGEL 2; RGSF 2; SUFW 1

Hartman, Geoffrey H. 1929- .... **CLC 27**
See also CA 117; 125; CANR 79; DLB 67

Hartmann, Sadakichi 1869-1944 ... **TCLC 73**
See also CA 157; DLB 54

Hartmann von Aue c. 1170-c. 1210 .... **CMLC 15**
See also CDWLB 2; DLB 138; RGWL 2, 3

Hartog, Jan de
See de Hartog, Jan

Haruf, Kent 1943- .... **CLC 34**
See also AAYA 44; CA 149; CANR 91

Harvey, Gabriel 1550(?)-1631 .... **LC 88**
See also DLB 167, 213, 281

Harwood, Ronald 1934- .... **CLC 32**
See also CA 1-4R; CANR 4, 55; CBD; CD 5; DAM DRAM, MST; DLB 13

Hasegawa Tatsunosuke
See Futabatei, Shimei

Hasek, Jaroslav (Matej Frantisek)
1883-1923 .... **TCLC 4**
See also CA 104; 129; CDWLB 4; DLB 215; EW 9; EWL 3; MTCW 1, 2; RGSF 2; RGWL 2, 3

Hass, Robert 1941- ... **CLC 18, 39, 99; PC 16**
See also AMWS 6; CA 111; CANR 30, 50, 71; CP 7; DLB 105, 206; EWL 3; RGAL 4; SATA 94

Hastings, Hudson
See Kuttner, Henry

Hastings, Selina .... **CLC 44**
Hathorne, John 1641-1717 .... **LC 38**
Hatteras, Amelia
   See Mencken, H(enry) L(ouis)
Hatteras, Owen .... **TCLC 18**
   See Mencken, H(enry) L(ouis); Nathan, George Jean
Hauptmann, Gerhart (Johann Robert)
   1862-1946 .... **SSC 37; TCLC 4**
   See also CA 104; 153; CDWLB 2; DAM DRAM; DLB 66, 118; EW 8; EWL 3; RGSF 2; RGWL 2, 3; TWA
Havel, Vaclav 1936- ..... **CLC 25, 58, 65, 123; DC 6**
   See also CA 104; CANR 36, 63; CDWLB 4; CWW 2; DA3; DAM DRAM; DFS 10; DLB 232; EWL 3; LMFS 2; MTCW 1, 2; RGWL 3
Haviaras, Stratis .... **CLC 33**
   See Chaviaras, Strates
Hawes, Stephen 1475(?)-1529(?) .... **LC 17**
   See also DLB 132; RGEL 2
Hawkes, John (Clendennin Burne, Jr.)
   1925-1998 .. **CLC 1, 2, 3, 4, 7, 9, 14, 15, 27, 49**
   See also BPFB 2; CA 1-4R; 167; CANR 2, 47, 64; CN 7; DLB 2, 7, 227; DLBY 1980, 1998; EWL 3; MTCW 1, 2; RGAL 4
Hawking, S. W.
   See Hawking, Stephen W(illiam)
Hawking, Stephen W(illiam) 1942- . **CLC 63, 105**
   See also AAYA 13; BEST 89:1; CA 126; 129; CANR 48, 115; CPW; DA3; MTCW 2
Hawkins, Anthony Hope
   See Hope, Anthony
Hawthorne, Julian 1846-1934 .... **TCLC 25**
   See also CA 165; HGG
Hawthorne, Nathaniel 1804-1864 ... **NCLC 2, 10, 17, 23, 39, 79, 95; SSC 3, 29, 39; WLC**
   See also AAYA 18; AMW; AMWC 1; AMWR 1; BPFB 2; BYA 3; CDALB 1640-1865; DA; DA3; DAB; DAC; DAM MST, NOV; DLB 1, 74, 183, 223, 269; EXPN; EXPS; HGG; LAIT 1; NFS 1; RGAL 4; RGSF 2; SSFS 1, 7, 11, 15; SUFW 1; TUS; WCH; YABC 2
Haxton, Josephine Ayres 1921-
   See Douglas, Ellen
   See also CA 115; CANR 41, 83
Hayaseca y Eizaguirre, Jorge
   See Echegaray (y Eizaguirre), Jose (Maria Waldo)
Hayashi, Fumiko 1904-1951 .... **TCLC 27**
   See Hayashi Fumiko
   See also CA 161
Hayashi Fumiko
   See Hayashi, Fumiko
   See also DLB 180; EWL 3
Haycraft, Anna (Margaret) 1932-
   See Ellis, Alice Thomas
   See also CA 122; CANR 85, 90; MTCW 2
Hayden, Robert E(arl) 1913-1980 ..... **BLC 2; CLC 5, 9, 14, 37; PC 6**
   See also AFAW 1, 2; AMWS 2; BW 1, 3; CA 69-72; 97-100; CABS 2; CANR 24, 75, 82; CDALB 1941-1968; DA; DAC; DAM MST, MULT, POET; DLB 5, 76; EWL 3; EXPP; MTCW 1, 2; PFS 1; RGAL 4; SATA 19; SATA-Obit 26; WP
Hayek, F(riedrich) A(ugust von)
   1899-1992 .... **TCLC 109**
   See also CA 93-96; 137; CANR 20; MTCW 1, 2
Hayford, J(oseph) E(phraim) Casely
   See Casely-Hayford, J(oseph) E(phraim)

Hayman, Ronald 1932- .... **CLC 44**
   See also CA 25-28R; CANR 18, 50, 88; CD 5; DLB 155
Hayne, Paul Hamilton 1830-1886 . **NCLC 94**
   See also DLB 3, 64, 79, 248; RGAL 4
Hays, Mary 1760-1843 .... **NCLC 114**
   See also DLB 142, 158; RGEL 2
Haywood, Eliza (Fowler)
   1693(?)-1756 .... **LC 1, 44**
   See also DLB 39; RGEL 2
Hazlitt, William 1778-1830 ...... **NCLC 29, 82**
   See also BRW 4; DLB 110, 158; RGEL 2; TEA
Hazzard, Shirley 1931- .... **CLC 18**
   See also CA 9-12R; CANR 4, 70; CN 7; DLB 289; DLBY 1982; MTCW 1
Head, Bessie 1937-1986 ...... **BLC 2; CLC 25, 67; SSC 52**
   See also AFW; BW 2, 3; CA 29-32R; 119; CANR 25, 82; CDWLB 3; DA3; DAM MULT; DLB 117, 225; EWL 3; EXPS; FW; MTCW 1, 2; RGSF 2; SSFS 5, 13; WLIT 2
Headon, (Nicky) Topper 1956(?)- ..... **CLC 30**
Heaney, Seamus (Justin) 1939- ..... **CLC 5, 7, 14, 25, 37, 74, 91, 171; PC 18; WLCS**
   See also BRWR 1; BRWS 2; CA 85-88; CANR 25, 48, 75, 91; CDBLB 1960 to Present; CP 7; DA3; DAB; DAM POET; DLB 40; DLBY 1995; EWL 3; EXPP; MTCW 1, 2; PAB; PFS 2, 5, 8, 17; RGEL 2; TEA; WLIT 4
Hearn, (Patricio) Lafcadio (Tessima Carlos)
   1850-1904 .... **TCLC 9**
   See also CA 105; 166; DLB 12, 78, 189; HGG; RGAL 4
Hearne, Samuel 1745-1792 .... **LC 95**
   See also DLB 99
Hearne, Vicki 1946-2001 .... **CLC 56**
   See also CA 139; 201
Hearon, Shelby 1931- .... **CLC 63**
   See also AITN 2; AMWS 8; CA 25-28R; CANR 18, 48, 103; CSW
Heat-Moon, William Least .... **CLC 29**
   See Trogdon, William (Lewis)
   See also AAYA 9
Hebbel, Friedrich 1813-1863 . **DC 21; NCLC 43**
   See also CDWLB 2; DAM DRAM; DLB 129; EW 6; RGWL 2, 3
Hebert, Anne 1916-2000 .... **CLC 4, 13, 29**
   See also CA 85-88; 187; CANR 69; CCA 1; CWP; CWW 2; DA3; DAC; DAM MST, POET; DLB 68; EWL 3; GFL 1789 to the Present; MTCW 1, 2
Hecht, Anthony (Evan) 1923- ...... **CLC 8, 13, 19**
   See also AMWS 10; CA 9-12R; CANR 6, 108; CP 7; DAM POET; DLB 5, 169; EWL 3; PFS 6; WP
Hecht, Ben 1894-1964 ..... **CLC 8; TCLC 101**
   See also CA 85-88; DFS 9; DLB 7, 9, 25, 26, 28, 86; FANT; IDFW 3, 4; RGAL 4
Hedayat, Sadeq 1903-1951 .... **TCLC 21**
   See also CA 120; EWL 3; RGSF 2
Hegel, Georg Wilhelm Friedrich
   1770-1831 .... **NCLC 46**
   See also DLB 90; TWA
Heidegger, Martin 1889-1976 .... **CLC 24**
   See also CA 81-84; 65-68; CANR 34; MTCW 1, 2
Heidenstam, (Carl Gustaf) Verner von
   1859-1940 .... **TCLC 5**
   See also CA 104
Heidi Louise
   See Erdrich, Louise
Heifner, Jack 1946- .... **CLC 11**
   See also CA 105; CANR 47

Heijermans, Herman 1864-1924 .... **TCLC 24**
   See also CA 123; EWL 3
Heilbrun, Carolyn G(old)
   1926-2003 .... **CLC 25, 173**
   See Cross, Amanda
   See also CA 45-48; CANR 1, 28, 58, 94; FW
Hein, Christoph 1944- .... **CLC 154**
   See also CA 158; CANR 108; CDWLB 2; CWW 2; DLB 124
Heine, Heinrich 1797-1856 .... **NCLC 4, 54; PC 25**
   See also CDWLB 2; DLB 90; EW 5; RGWL 2, 3; TWA
Heinemann, Larry (Curtiss) 1944- .. **CLC 50**
   See also CA 110; CAAS 21; CANR 31, 81; DLBD 9; INT CANR-31
Heiney, Donald (William) 1921-1993
   See Harris, MacDonald
   See also CA 1-4R; 142; CANR 3, 58; FANT
Heinlein, Robert A(nson) 1907-1988 . **CLC 1, 3, 8, 14, 26, 55; SSC 55**
   See also AAYA 17; BPFB 2; BYA 4, 13; CA 1-4R; 125; CANR 1, 20, 53; CLR 75; CPW; DA3; DAM POP; DLB 8; EXPS; JRDA; LAIT 5; LMFS 2; MAICYA 1, 2; MTCW 1, 2; RGAL 4; SATA 9, 69; SATA-Obit 56; SCFW; SFW 4; SSFS 7; YAW
Helforth, John
   See Doolittle, Hilda
Heliodorus fl. 3rd cent. - .... **CMLC 52**
Hellenhofferu, Vojtech Kapristian z
   See Hasek, Jaroslav (Matej Frantisek)
Heller, Joseph 1923-1999 . **CLC 1, 3, 5, 8, 11, 36, 63; TCLC 131; WLC**
   See also AAYA 24; AITN 1; AMWS 4; BPFB 2; BYA 1; CA 5-8R; 187; CABS 1; CANR 8, 42, 66; CN 7; CPW; DA; DA3; DAB; DAC; DAM MST, NOV, POP; DLB 2, 28, 227; DLBY 1980, 2002; EWL 3; EXPN; INT CANR-8; LAIT 4; MTCW 1, 2; NFS 1; RGAL 4; TUS; YAW
Hellman, Lillian (Florence)
   1906-1984 .. **CLC 2, 4, 8, 14, 18, 34, 44, 52; DC 1; TCLC 119**
   See also AAYA 47; AITN 1, 2; AMWS 1; CA 13-16R; 112; CAD; CANR 33; CWD; DA3; DAM DRAM; DFS 1, 3, 14; DLB 7, 228; DLBY 1984; EWL 3; FW; LAIT 3; MAWW; MTCW 1, 2; RGAL 4; TUS
Helprin, Mark 1947- .... **CLC 7, 10, 22, 32**
   See also CA 81-84; CANR 47, 64; CDALBS; CPW; DA3; DAM NOV, POP; DLBY 1985; FANT; MTCW 1, 2; SUFW 2
Helvetius, Claude-Adrien 1715-1771 .. **LC 26**
Helyar, Jane Penelope Josephine 1933-
   See Poole, Josephine
   See also CA 21-24R; CANR 10, 26; CWRI 5; SATA 82; SATA-Essay 138
Hemans, Felicia 1793-1835 .... **NCLC 29, 71**
   See also DLB 96; RGEL 2
Hemingway, Ernest (Miller)
   1899-1961 .... **CLC 1, 3, 6, 8, 10, 13, 19, 30, 34, 39, 41, 44, 50, 61, 80; SSC 1, 25, 36, 40, 63; TCLC 115; WLC**
   See also AAYA 19; AMW; AMWC 1; AMWR 1; BPFB 2; BYA 2, 3, 13, 15; CA 77-80; CANR 34; CDALB 1917-1929; DA; DA3; DAB; DAC; DAM MST, NOV; DLB 4, 9, 102, 210; DLBD 1, 15, 16; DLBY 1981, 1987, 1996, 1998; EWL 3; EXPN; EXPS; LAIT 3, 4; LATS 1; MTCW 1, 2; NFS 1, 5, 6, 14; RGAL 4; RGSF 2; SSFS 17; TUS; WYA
Hempel, Amy 1951- .... **CLC 39**
   See also CA 118; 137; CANR 70; DA3; DLB 218; EXPS; MTCW 2; SSFS 2

Henderson, F. C.
See Mencken, H(enry) L(ouis)
Henderson, Sylvia
See Ashton-Warner, Sylvia (Constance)
Henderson, Zenna (Chlarson)
1917-1983 .... **SSC 29**
See also CA 1-4R; 133; CANR 1, 84; DLB
8; SATA 5; SFW 4
Henkin, Joshua .... **CLC 119**
See also CA 161
Henley, Beth .... **CLC 23; DC 6, 14**
See Henley, Elizabeth Becker
See also CABS 3; CAD; CD 5; CSW;
CWD; DFS 2; DLBY 1986; FW
Henley, Elizabeth Becker 1952-
See Henley, Beth
See also CA 107; CANR 32, 73; DA3;
DAM DRAM, MST; MTCW 1, 2
Henley, William Ernest 1849-1903 .. **TCLC 8**
See also CA 105; DLB 19; RGEL 2
Hennissart, Martha
See Lathen, Emma
See also CA 85-88; CANR 64
Henry VIII 1491-1547 .... **LC 10**
See also DLB 132
Henry, O. ..... **SSC 5, 49; TCLC 1, 19; WLC**
See Porter, William Sydney
See also AAYA 41; AMWS 2; EXPS; RGAL
4; RGSF 2; SSFS 2, 18
Henry, Patrick 1736-1799 .... **LC 25**
See also LAIT 1
Henryson, Robert 1430(?)-1506(?) ...... **LC 20**
See also BRWS 7; DLB 146; RGEL 2
Henschke, Alfred
See Klabund
Henson, Lance 1944- .... **NNAL**
See also CA 146; DLB 175
Hentoff, Nat(han Irving) 1925- .... **CLC 26**
See also AAYA 4, 42; BYA 6; CA 1-4R;
CAAS 6; CANR 5, 25, 77, 114; CLR 1,
52; INT CANR-25; JRDA; MAICYA 1,
2; SATA 42, 69, 133; SATA-Brief 27;
WYA; YAW
Heppenstall, (John) Rayner
1911-1981 .... **CLC 10**
See also CA 1-4R; 103; CANR 29; EWL 3
Heraclitus c. 540B.C.-c. 450B.C. ... **CMLC 22**
See also DLB 176
Herbert, Frank (Patrick)
1920-1986 .... **CLC 12, 23, 35, 44, 85**
See also AAYA 21; BPFB 2; BYA 4, 14;
CA 53-56; 118; CANR 5, 43; CDALBS;
CPW; DAM POP; DLB 8; INT CANR-5;
LAIT 5; MTCW 1, 2; NFS 17; SATA 9,
37; SATA-Obit 47; SCFW 2; SFW 4;
YAW
Herbert, George 1593-1633 ...... **LC 24; PC 4**
See also BRW 2; BRWR 2; CDBLB Before
1660; DAB; DAM POET; DLB 126;
EXPP; RGEL 2; TEA; WP
Herbert, Zbigniew 1924-1998 ..... **CLC 9, 43;
PC 50**
See also CA 89-92; 169; CANR 36, 74; CD-
WLB 4; CWW 2; DAM POET; DLB 232;
EWL 3; MTCW 1
Herbst, Josephine (Frey)
1897-1969 .... **CLC 34**
See also CA 5-8R; 25-28R; DLB 9
Herder, Johann Gottfried von
1744-1803 .... **NCLC 8**
See also DLB 97; EW 4; TWA
Heredia, Jose Maria 1803-1839 .... **HLCS 2**
See also LAW
Hergesheimer, Joseph 1880-1954 ... **TCLC 11**
See also CA 109; 194; DLB 102, 9; RGAL
4
Herlihy, James Leo 1927-1993 .... **CLC 6**
See also CA 1-4R; 143; CAD; CANR 2

Herman, William
See Bierce, Ambrose (Gwinett)
Hermogenes fl. c. 175- .... **CMLC 6**
Hernandez, Jose 1834-1886 .... **NCLC 17**
See also LAW; RGWL 2, 3; WLIT 1
Herodotus c. 484B.C.-c. 420B.C. .. **CMLC 17**
See also AW 1; CDWLB 1; DLB 176;
RGWL 2, 3; TWA
Herrick, Robert 1591-1674 .... **LC 13; PC 9**
See also BRW 2; BRWC 2; DA; DAB;
DAC; DAM MST, POP; DLB 126; EXPP;
PFS 13; RGAL 4; RGEL 2; TEA; WP
Herring, Guilles
See Somerville, Edith Oenone
Herriot, James 1916-1995 .... **CLC 12**
See Wight, James Alfred
See also AAYA 1; BPFB 2; CA 148; CANR
40; CLR 80; CPW; DAM POP; LAIT 3;
MAICYA 2; MAICYAS 1; MTCW 2;
SATA 86, 135; TEA; YAW
Herris, Violet
See Hunt, Violet
Herrmann, Dorothy 1941- .... **CLC 44**
See also CA 107
Herrmann, Taffy
See Herrmann, Dorothy
Hersey, John (Richard) 1914-1993 .... **CLC 1,
2, 7, 9, 40, 81, 97**
See also AAYA 29; BPFB 2; CA 17-20R;
140; CANR 33; CDALBS; CPW; DAM
POP; DLB 6, 185, 278; MTCW 1, 2;
SATA 25; SATA-Obit 76; TUS
Herzen, Aleksandr Ivanovich
1812-1870 .... **NCLC 10, 61**
See Herzen, Alexander
Herzen, Alexander
See Herzen, Aleksandr Ivanovich
See also DLB 277
Herzl, Theodor 1860-1904 .... **TCLC 36**
See also CA 168
Herzog, Werner 1942- .... **CLC 16**
See also CA 89-92
Hesiod c. 8th cent. B.C.- .... **CMLC 5**
See also AW 1; DLB 176; RGWL 2, 3
Hesse, Hermann 1877-1962 ... **CLC 1, 2, 3, 6,
11, 17, 25, 69; SSC 9, 49; WLC**
See also AAYA 43; BPFB 2; CA 17-18;
CAP 2; CDWLB 2; DA; DA3; DAB;
DAC; DAM MST, NOV; DLB 66; EW 9;
EWL 3; EXPN; LAIT 1; MTCW 1, 2;
NFS 6, 15; RGWL 2, 3; SATA 50; TWA
Hewes, Cady
See De Voto, Bernard (Augustine)
Heyen, William 1940- .... **CLC 13, 18**
See also CA 33-36R; CAAS 9; CANR 98;
CP 7; DLB 5
Heyerdahl, Thor 1914-2002 .... **CLC 26**
See also CA 5-8R; 207; CANR 5, 22, 66,
73; LAIT 4; MTCW 1, 2; SATA 2, 52
Heym, Georg (Theodor Franz Arthur)
1887-1912 .... **TCLC 9**
See also CA 106; 181
Heym, Stefan 1913-2001 .... **CLC 41**
See also CA 9-12R; 203; CANR 4; CWW
2; DLB 69; EWL 3
Heyse, Paul (Johann Ludwig von)
1830-1914 .... **TCLC 8**
See also CA 104; 209; DLB 129
Heyward, (Edwin) DuBose
1885-1940 .... **HR 2; TCLC 59**
See also CA 108; 157; DLB 7, 9, 45, 249;
SATA 21
Heywood, John 1497(?)-1580(?) .... **LC 65**
See also DLB 136; RGEL 2

Hibbert, Eleanor Alice Burford
1906-1993 .... **CLC 7**
See Holt, Victoria
See also BEST 90:4; CA 17-20R; 140;
CANR 9, 28, 59; CMW 4; CPW; DAM
POP; MTCW 2; RHW; SATA 2; SATA-
Obit 74
Hichens, Robert (Smythe)
1864-1950 .... **TCLC 64**
See also CA 162; DLB 153; HGG; RHW;
SUFW
Higgins, George V(incent)
1939-1999 .... **CLC 4, 7, 10, 18**
See also BPFB 2; CA 77-80; 186; CAAS 5;
CANR 17, 51, 89, 96; CMW 4; CN 7;
DLB 2; DLBY 1981, 1998; INT CANR-
17; MSW; MTCW 1
Higginson, Thomas Wentworth
1823-1911 .... **TCLC 36**
See also CA 162; DLB 1, 64, 243
Higgonet, Margaret ed. .... **CLC 65**
Highet, Helen
See MacInnes, Helen (Clark)
Highsmith, (Mary) Patricia
1921-1995 .... **CLC 2, 4, 14, 42, 102**
See Morgan, Claire
See also AAYA 48; BRWS 5; CA 1-4R; 147;
CANR 1, 20, 48, 62, 108; CMW 4; CPW;
DA3; DAM NOV, POP; MSW; MTCW 1,
2
Highwater, Jamake (Mamake)
1942(?)-2001 .... **CLC 12**
See also AAYA 7; BPFB 2; BYA 4; CA 65-
68; 199; CAAS 7; CANR 10, 34, 84; CLR
17; CWRI 5; DLB 52; DLBY 1985;
JRDA; MAICYA 1, 2; SATA 32, 69;
SATA-Brief 30
Highway, Tomson 1951- ...... **CLC 92; NNAL**
See also CA 151; CANR 75; CCA 1; CD 5;
DAC; DAM MULT; DFS 2; MTCW 2
Hijuelos, Oscar 1951- .... **CLC 65; HLC 1**
See also AAYA 25; AMWS 8; BEST 90:1;
CA 123; CANR 50, 75; CPW; DA3; DAM
MULT, POP; DLB 145; HW 1, 2; MTCW
2; NFS 17; RGAL 4; WLIT 1
Hikmet, Nazim 1902(?)-1963 .... **CLC 40**
See also CA 141; 93-96; EWL 3
Hildegard von Bingen 1098-1179 . **CMLC 20**
See also DLB 148
Hildesheimer, Wolfgang 1916-1991 .. **CLC 49**
See also CA 101; 135; DLB 69, 124; EWL
3
Hill, Geoffrey (William) 1932- ...... **CLC 5, 8,
18, 45**
See also BRWS 5; CA 81-84; CANR 21,
89; CDBLB 1960 to Present; CP 7; DAM
POET; DLB 40; EWL 3; MTCW 1; RGEL
2
Hill, George Roy 1921-2002 .... **CLC 26**
See also CA 110; 122; 213
Hill, John
See Koontz, Dean R(ay)
Hill, Susan (Elizabeth) 1942- ...... **CLC 4, 113**
See also CA 33-36R; CANR 29, 69; CN 7;
DAB; DAM MST, NOV; DLB 14, 139;
HGG; MTCW 1; RHW
Hillard, Asa G. III .... **CLC 70**
Hillerman, Tony 1925- .... **CLC 62, 170**
See also AAYA 40; BEST 89:1; BPFB 2;
CA 29-32R; CANR 21, 42, 65, 97; CMW
4; CPW; DA3; DAM POP; DLB 206;
MSW; RGAL 4; SATA 6; TCWW 2; YAW
Hillesum, Etty 1914-1943 .... **TCLC 49**
See also CA 137
Hilliard, Noel (Harvey) 1929-1996 ... **CLC 15**
See also CA 9-12R; CANR 7, 69; CN 7
Hillis, Rick 1956- .... **CLC 66**
See also CA 134

Jones, Robert F(rancis) 1934- .... **CLC 7**
See also CA 49-52; CANR 2, 61, 118
Jones, Rod 1953- .... **CLC 50**
See also CA 128
Jones, Terence Graham Parry
1942- .... **CLC 21**
See Jones, Terry; Monty Python
See also CA 112; 116; CANR 35, 93; INT
116; SATA 127
Jones, Terry
See Jones, Terence Graham Parry
See also SATA 67; SATA-Brief 51
Jones, Thom (Douglas) 1945(?)- ..... **CLC 81;
SSC 56**
See also CA 157; CANR 88; DLB 244
Jong, Erica 1942- .... **CLC 4, 6, 8, 18, 83**
See also AITN 1; AMWS 5; BEST 90:2;
BPFB 2; CA 73-76; CANR 26, 52, 75;
CN 7; CP 7; CPW; DA3; DAM NOV,
POP; DLB 2, 5, 28, 152; FW; INT CANR-
26; MTCW 1, 2
Jonson, Ben(jamin) 1572(?)-1637 . **DC 4; LC
6, 33; PC 17; WLC**
See also BRW 1; BRWC 1; BRWR 1; CD-
BLB Before 1660; DA; DAB; DAC;
DAM DRAM, MST, POET; DFS 4, 10;
DLB 62, 121; LMFS 1; RGEL 2; TEA;
WLIT 3
Jordan, June (Meyer)
1936-2002 .. **BLCS; CLC 5, 11, 23, 114;
PC 38**
See also AAYA 2; AFAW 1, 2; BW 2, 3;
CA 33-36R; 206; CANR 25, 70, 114; CLR
10; CP 7; CWP; DAM MULT, POET;
DLB 38; GLL 2; LAIT 5; MAICYA 1, 2;
MTCW 1; SATA 4, 136; YAW
Jordan, Neil (Patrick) 1950- .... **CLC 110**
See also CA 124; 130; CANR 54; CN 7;
GLL 2; INT 130
Jordan, Pat(rick M.) 1941- .... **CLC 37**
See also CA 33-36R; CANR 121
Jorgensen, Ivar
See Ellison, Harlan (Jay)
Jorgenson, Ivar
See Silverberg, Robert
Joseph, George Ghevarughese .... **CLC 70**
Josephson, Mary
See O'Doherty, Brian
Josephus, Flavius c. 37-100 .... **CMLC 13**
See also AW 2; DLB 176
Josiah Allen's Wife
See Holley, Marietta
Josipovici, Gabriel (David) 1940- ...... **CLC 6,
43, 153**
See also CA 37-40R; CAAS 8; CANR 47,
84; CN 7; DLB 14
Joubert, Joseph 1754-1824 .... **NCLC 9**
Jouve, Pierre Jean 1887-1976 .... **CLC 47**
See also CA 65-68; DLB 258; EWL 3
Jovine, Francesco 1902-1950 .... **TCLC 79**
See also DLB 264; EWL 3
Joyce, James (Augustine Aloysius)
1882-1941 .... **DC 16; PC 22; SSC 3, 26,
44, 64; TCLC 3, 8, 16, 35, 52; WLC**
See also AAYA 42; BRW 7; BRWC 1;
BRWR 1; BYA 11, 13; CA 104; 126; CD-
BLB 1914-1945; DA; DA3; DAB; DAC;
DAM MST, NOV, POET; DLB 10, 19,
36, 162, 247; EWL 3; EXPN; EXPS;
LAIT 3; LMFS 1, 2; MTCW 1, 2; NFS 7;
RGSF 2; SSFS 1; TEA; WLIT 4
Jozsef, Attila 1905-1937 .... **TCLC 22**
See also CA 116; CDWLB 4; DLB 215;
EWL 3
Juana Ines de la Cruz, Sor
1651(?)-1695 ...... **HLCS 1; LC 5; PC 24**
See also FW; LAW; RGWL 2, 3; WLIT 1
Juana Inez de La Cruz, Sor
See Juana Ines de la Cruz, Sor

Judd, Cyril
See Kornbluth, C(yril) M.; Pohl, Frederik
Juenger, Ernst 1895-1998 .... **CLC 125**
See Junger, Ernst
See also CA 101; 167; CANR 21, 47, 106;
DLB 56
Julian of Norwich 1342(?)-1416(?) . **LC 6, 52**
See also DLB 146; LMFS 1
Julius Caesar 100B.C.-44B.C.
See Caesar, Julius
See also CDWLB 1; DLB 211
Junger, Ernst
See Juenger, Ernst
See also CDWLB 2; EWL 3; RGWL 2, 3
Junger, Sebastian 1962- .... **CLC 109**
See also AAYA 28; CA 165
Juniper, Alex
See Hospital, Janette Turner
Junius
See Luxemburg, Rosa
Just, Ward (Swift) 1935- .... **CLC 4, 27**
See also CA 25-28R; CANR 32, 87; CN 7;
INT CANR-32
Justice, Donald (Rodney) 1925- .. **CLC 6, 19,
102**
See also AMWS 7; CA 5-8R; CANR 26,
54, 74, 121, 122; CP 7; CSW; DAM
POET; DLBY 1983; EWL 3; INT CANR-
26; MTCW 2; PFS 14
Juvenal c. 60-c. 130 .... **CMLC 8**
See also AW 2; CDWLB 1; DLB 211;
RGWL 2, 3
Juvenis
See Bourne, Randolph S(illiman)
K., Alice
See Knapp, Caroline
Kabakov, Sasha .... **CLC 59**
Kacew, Romain 1914-1980
See Gary, Romain
See also CA 108; 102
Kadare, Ismail 1936- .... **CLC 52**
See also CA 161; EWL 3; RGWL 3
Kadohata, Cynthia .... **CLC 59, 122**
See also CA 140
Kafka, Franz 1883-1924 ... **SSC 5, 29, 35, 60;
TCLC 2, 6, 13, 29, 47, 53, 112; WLC**
See also AAYA 31; BPFB 2; CA 105; 126;
CDWLB 2; DA; DA3; DAB; DAC; DAM
MST, NOV; DLB 81; EW 9; EWL 3;
EXPS; LATS 1; LMFS 2; MTCW 1, 2;
NFS 7; RGSF 2; RGWL 2, 3; SFW 4;
SSFS 3, 7, 12; TWA
Kahanovitsch, Pinkhes
See Der Nister
Kahn, Roger 1927- .... **CLC 30**
See also CA 25-28R; CANR 44, 69; DLB
171; SATA 37
Kain, Saul
See Sassoon, Siegfried (Lorraine)
Kaiser, Georg 1878-1945 .... **TCLC 9**
See also CA 106; 190; CDWLB 2; DLB
124; EWL 3; LMFS 2; RGWL 2, 3
Kaledin, Sergei .... **CLC 59**
Kaletski, Alexander 1946- .... **CLC 39**
See also CA 118; 143
Kalidasa fl. c. 400-455 .... **CMLC 9; PC 22**
See also RGWL 2, 3
Kallman, Chester (Simon)
1921-1975 .... **CLC 2**
See also CA 45-48; 53-56; CANR 3
Kaminsky, Melvin 1926-
See Brooks, Mel
See also CA 65-68; CANR 16
Kaminsky, Stuart M(elvin) 1934- ..... **CLC 59**
See also CA 73-76; CANR 29, 53, 89;
CMW 4
Kandinsky, Wassily 1866-1944 .... **TCLC 92**
See also CA 118; 155

Kane, Francis
See Robbins, Harold
Kane, Henry 1918-
See Queen, Ellery
See also CA 156; CMW 4
Kane, Paul
See Simon, Paul (Frederick)
Kanin, Garson 1912-1999 .... **CLC 22**
See also AITN 1; CA 5-8R; 177; CAD;
CANR 7, 78; DLB 7; IDFW 3, 4
Kaniuk, Yoram 1930- .... **CLC 19**
See also CA 134
Kant, Immanuel 1724-1804 ..... **NCLC 27, 67**
See also DLB 94
Kantor, MacKinlay 1904-1977 .... **CLC 7**
See also CA 61-64; 73-76; CANR 60, 63;
DLB 9, 102; MTCW 2; RHW; TCWW 2
Kanze Motokiyo
See Zeami
Kaplan, David Michael 1946- .... **CLC 50**
See also CA 187
Kaplan, James 1951- .... **CLC 59**
See also CA 135; CANR 121
Karadzic, Vuk Stefanovic
1787-1864 .... **NCLC 115**
See also CDWLB 4; DLB 147
Karageorge, Michael
See Anderson, Poul (William)
Karamzin, Nikolai Mikhailovich
1766-1826 .... **NCLC 3**
See also DLB 150; RGSF 2
Karapanou, Margarita 1946- .... **CLC 13**
See also CA 101
Karinthy, Frigyes 1887-1938 .... **TCLC 47**
See also CA 170; DLB 215; EWL 3
Karl, Frederick R(obert) 1927- .... **CLC 34**
See also CA 5-8R; CANR 3, 44
Kastel, Warren
See Silverberg, Robert
Kataev, Evgeny Petrovich 1903-1942
See Petrov, Evgeny
See also CA 120
Kataphusin
See Ruskin, John
Katz, Steve 1935- .... **CLC 47**
See also CA 25-28R; CAAS 14, 64; CANR
12; CN 7; DLBY 1983
Kauffman, Janet 1945- .... **CLC 42**
See also CA 117; CANR 43, 84; DLB 218;
DLBY 1986
Kaufman, Bob (Garnell) 1925-1986 . **CLC 49**
See also BG 3; BW 1; CA 41-44R; 118;
CANR 22; DLB 16, 41
Kaufman, George S. 1889-1961 ...... **CLC 38;
DC 17**
See also CA 108; 93-96; DAM DRAM;
DFS 1, 10; DLB 7; INT CA-108; MTCW
2; RGAL 4; TUS
Kaufman, Sue .... **CLC 3, 8**
See Barondess, Sue K(aufman)
Kavafis, Konstantinos Petrou 1863-1933
See Cavafy, C(onstantine) P(eter)
See also CA 104
Kavan, Anna 1901-1968 .... **CLC 5, 13, 82**
See also BRWS 7; CA 5-8R; CANR 6, 57;
DLB 255; MTCW 1; RGEL 2; SFW 4
Kavanagh, Dan
See Barnes, Julian (Patrick)
Kavanagh, Julie 1952- .... **CLC 119**
See also CA 163
Kavanagh, Patrick (Joseph)
1904-1967 .... **CLC 22; PC 33**
See also BRWS 7; CA 123; 25-28R; DLB
15, 20; EWL 3; MTCW 1; RGEL 2

Lacan, Jacques (Marie Emile)
  1901-1981 .... **CLC 75**
  See also CA 121; 104; EWL 3; TWA
Laclos, Pierre Ambroise Francois
  1741-1803 .... **NCLC 4, 87**
  See also EW 4; GFL Beginnings to 1789;
  RGWL 2, 3
Lacolere, Francois
  See Aragon, Louis
La Colere, Francois
  See Aragon, Louis
La Deshabilleuse
  See Simenon, Georges (Jacques Christian)
Lady Gregory
  See Gregory, Lady Isabella Augusta (Persse)
Lady of Quality, A
  See Bagnold, Enid
**La Fayette, Marie-(Madelaine Pioche de la
  Vergne)** 1634-1693 .... **LC 2**
  See Lafayette, Marie-Madeleine
  See also GFL Beginnings to 1789; RGWL
  2, 3
Lafayette, Marie-Madeleine
  See La Fayette, Marie-(Madelaine Pioche
  de la Vergne)
  See also DLB 268
Lafayette, Rene
  See Hubbard, L(afayette) Ron(ald)
La Flesche, Francis 1857(?)-1932 ...... **NNAL**
  See also CA 144; CANR 83; DLB 175
La Fontaine, Jean de 1621-1695 .... **LC 50**
  See also DLB 268; EW 3; GFL Beginnings
  to 1789; MAICYA 1, 2; RGWL 2, 3;
  SATA 18
Laforgue, Jules 1860-1887 . **NCLC 5, 53; PC
  14; SSC 20**
  See also DLB 217; EW 7; GFL 1789 to the
  Present; RGWL 2, 3
Layamon
  See Layamon
  See also DLB 146
Lagerkvist, Paer (Fabian)
  1891-1974 .... **CLC 7, 10, 13, 54**
  See Lagerkvist, Par
  See also CA 85-88; 49-52; DA3; DAM
  DRAM, NOV; MTCW 1, 2; TWA
Lagerkvist, Par .... **SSC 12**
  See Lagerkvist, Paer (Fabian)
  See also DLB 259; EW 10; EWL 3; MTCW
  2; RGSF 2; RGWL 2, 3
Lagerloef, Selma (Ottiliana Lovisa)
  1858-1940 .... **TCLC 4, 36**
  See Lagerlof, Selma (Ottiliana Lovisa)
  See also CA 108; MTCW 2; SATA 15
Lagerlof, Selma (Ottiliana Lovisa)
  See Lagerloef, Selma (Ottiliana Lovisa)
  See also CLR 7; SATA 15
La Guma, (Justin) Alex(ander)
  1925-1985 . **BLCS; CLC 19; TCLC 140**
  See also AFW; BW 1, 3; CA 49-52; 118;
  CANR 25, 81; CDWLB 3; DAM NOV;
  DLB 117, 225; EWL 3; MTCW 1, 2;
  WLIT 2
Laidlaw, A. K.
  See Grieve, C(hristopher) M(urray)
Lainez, Manuel Mujica
  See Mujica Lainez, Manuel
  See also HW 1
Laing, R(onald) D(avid) 1927-1989 . **CLC 95**
  See also CA 107; 129; CANR 34; MTCW 1
Lamartine, Alphonse (Marie Louis Prat) de
  1790-1869 .... **NCLC 11; PC 16**
  See also DAM POET; DLB 217; GFL 1789
  to the Present; RGWL 2, 3
Lamb, Charles 1775-1834 ..... **NCLC 10, 113;
  WLC**
  See also BRW 4; CDBLB 1789-1832; DA;
  DAB; DAC; DAM MST; DLB 93, 107,
  163; RGEL 2; SATA 17; TEA

Lamb, Lady Caroline 1785-1828 ... **NCLC 38**
  See also DLB 116
Lamb, Mary Ann 1764-1847 .... **NCLC 125**
  See also DLB 163; SATA 17
Lame Deer 1903(?)-1976 .... **NNAL**
  See also CA 69-72
Lamming, George (William) 1927- .. **BLC 2;
  CLC 2, 4, 66, 144**
  See also BW 2, 3; CA 85-88; CANR 26,
  76; CDWLB 3; CN 7; DAM MULT; DLB
  125; EWL 3; MTCW 1, 2; NFS 15; RGEL
  2
L'Amour, Louis (Dearborn)
  1908-1988 .... **CLC 25, 55**
  See Burns, Tex; Mayo, Jim
  See also AAYA 16; AITN 2; BEST 89:2;
  BPFB 2; CA 1-4R; 125; CANR 3, 25, 40;
  CPW; DA3; DAM NOV, POP; DLB 206;
  DLBY 1980; MTCW 1, 2; RGAL 4
Lampedusa, Giuseppe (Tomasi) di
  .... **TCLC 13**
  See Tomasi di Lampedusa, Giuseppe
  See also CA 164; EW 11; MTCW 2; RGWL
  2, 3
Lampman, Archibald 1861-1899 ... **NCLC 25**
  See also DLB 92; RGEL 2; TWA
Lancaster, Bruce 1896-1963 .... **CLC 36**
  See also CA 9-10; CANR 70; CAP 1; SATA
  9
Lanchester, John 1962- .... **CLC 99**
  See also CA 194; DLB 267
Landau, Mark Alexandrovich
  See Aldanov, Mark (Alexandrovich)
Landau-Aldanov, Mark Alexandrovich
  See Aldanov, Mark (Alexandrovich)
Landis, Jerry
  See Simon, Paul (Frederick)
Landis, John 1950- .... **CLC 26**
  See also CA 112; 122
Landolfi, Tommaso 1908-1979 .... **CLC 11, 49**
  See also CA 127; 117; DLB 177; EWL 3
Landon, Letitia Elizabeth
  1802-1838 .... **NCLC 15**
  See also DLB 96
Landor, Walter Savage
  1775-1864 .... **NCLC 14**
  See also BRW 4; DLB 93, 107; RGEL 2
Landwirth, Heinz 1927-
  See Lind, Jakov
  See also CA 9-12R; CANR 7
Lane, Patrick 1939- .... **CLC 25**
  See also CA 97-100; CANR 54; CP 7; DAM
  POET; DLB 53; INT 97-100
Lang, Andrew 1844-1912 .... **TCLC 16**
  See also CA 114; 137; CANR 85; DLB 98,
  141, 184; FANT; MAICYA 1, 2; RGEL 2;
  SATA 16; WCH
Lang, Fritz 1890-1976 .... **CLC 20, 103**
  See also CA 77-80; 69-72; CANR 30
Lange, John
  See Crichton, (John) Michael
Langer, Elinor 1939- .... **CLC 34**
  See also CA 121
Langland, William 1332(?)-1400(?) ..... **LC 19**
  See also BRW 1; DA; DAB; DAC; DAM
  MST, POET; DLB 146; RGEL 2; TEA;
  WLIT 3
Langstaff, Launcelot
  See Irving, Washington
Lanier, Sidney 1842-1881 . **NCLC 6, 118; PC
  50**
  See also AMWS 1; DAM POET; DLB 64;
  DLBD 13; EXPP; MAICYA 1; PFS 14;
  RGAL 4; SATA 18
Lanyer, Aemilia 1569-1645 ...... **LC 10, 30, 83**
  See also DLB 121
Lao-Tzu
  See Lao Tzu

Lao Tzu c. 6th cent. B.C.-3rd cent.
  B.C. .... **CMLC 7**
Lapine, James (Elliot) 1949- .... **CLC 39**
  See also CA 123; 130; CANR 54; INT 130
Larbaud, Valery (Nicolas)
  1881-1957 .... **TCLC 9**
  See also CA 106; 152; EWL 3; GFL 1789
  to the Present
Lardner, Ring
  See Lardner, Ring(gold) W(ilmer)
  See also BPFB 2; CDALB 1917-1929; DLB
  11, 25, 86, 171; DLBD 16; RGAL 4;
  RGSF 2
Lardner, Ring W., Jr.
  See Lardner, Ring(gold) W(ilmer)
Lardner, Ring(gold) W(ilmer)
  1885-1933 .... **SSC 32; TCLC 2, 14**
  See Lardner, Ring
  See also AMW; CA 104; 131; MTCW 1, 2;
  TUS
Laredo, Betty
  See Codrescu, Andrei
Larkin, Maia
  See Wojciechowska, Maia (Teresa)
Larkin, Philip (Arthur) 1922-1985 ... **CLC 3,
  5, 8, 9, 13, 18, 33, 39, 64; PC 21**
  See also BRWS 1; CA 5-8R; 117; CANR
  24, 62; CDBLB 1960 to Present; DA3;
  DAB; DAM MST, POET; DLB 27; EWL
  3; MTCW 1, 2; PFS 3, 4, 12; RGEL 2
La Roche, Sophie von
  1730-1807 .... **NCLC 121**
  See also DLB 94
**Larra (y Sanchez de Castro), Mariano Jose
  de** 1809-1837 .... **NCLC 17, 130**
Larsen, Eric 1941- .... **CLC 55**
  See also CA 132
Larsen, Nella 1893(?)-1963 .... **BLC 2; CLC
  37; HR 3**
  See also AFAW 1, 2; BW 1; CA 125; CANR
  83; DAM MULT; DLB 51; FW; LATS 1;
  LMFS 2
Larson, Charles R(aymond) 1938- ... **CLC 31**
  See also CA 53-56; CANR 4, 121
Larson, Jonathan 1961-1996 .... **CLC 99**
  See also AAYA 28; CA 156
Las Casas, Bartolome de
  1474-1566 .... **HLCS; LC 31**
  See Casas, Bartolome de las
  See also LAW
Lasch, Christopher 1932-1994 .... **CLC 102**
  See also CA 73-76; 144; CANR 25, 118;
  DLB 246; MTCW 1, 2
Lasker-Schueler, Else 1869-1945 ... **TCLC 57**
  See Lasker-Schuler, Else
  See also CA 183; DLB 66, 124
Lasker-Schuler, Else
  See Lasker-Schueler, Else
  See also EWL 3
Laski, Harold J(oseph) 1893-1950 . **TCLC 79**
  See also CA 188
Latham, Jean Lee 1902-1995 .... **CLC 12**
  See also AITN 1; BYA 1; CA 5-8R; CANR
  7, 84; CLR 50; MAICYA 1, 2; SATA 2,
  68; YAW
Latham, Mavis
  See Clark, Mavis Thorpe
Lathen, Emma .... **CLC 2**
  See Hennissart, Martha; Latsis, Mary J(ane)
  See also BPFB 2; CMW 4
Lathrop, Francis
  See Leiber, Fritz (Reuter, Jr.)
Latsis, Mary J(ane) 1927(?)-1997
  See Lathen, Emma
  See also CA 85-88; 162; CMW 4
Lattany, Kristin
  See Lattany, Kristin (Elaine Eggleston)
  Hunter

Leger, (Marie-Rene Auguste) Alexis Saint-Leger 1887-1975 .. **CLC 4, 11, 46; PC 23**
See Perse, Saint-John; Saint-John Perse
See also CA 13-16R; 61-64; CANR 43; DAM POET; MTCW 1

Leger, Saintleger
See Leger, (Marie-Rene Auguste) Alexis Saint-Leger

Le Guin, Ursula K(roeber) 1929- ..... **CLC 8, 13, 22, 45, 71, 136; SSC 12**
See also AAYA 9, 27; AITN 1; BPFB 2; BYA 5, 8, 11, 14; CA 21-24R; CANR 9, 32, 52, 74; CDALB 1968-1988; CLR 3, 28, 91; CN 7; CPW; DA3; DAB; DAC; DAM MST, POP; DLB 8, 52, 256, 275; EXPS; FANT; FW; INT CANR-32; JRDA; LAIT 5; MAICYA 1, 2; MTCW 1, 2; NFS 6, 9; SATA 4, 52, 99; SCFW; SFW 4; SSFS 2; SUFW 1, 2; WYA; YAW

Lehmann, Rosamond (Nina) 1901-1990 .... **CLC 5**
See also CA 77-80; 131; CANR 8, 73; DLB 15; MTCW 2; RGEL 2; RHW

Leiber, Fritz (Reuter, Jr.) 1910-1992 .... **CLC 25**
See also BPFB 2; CA 45-48; 139; CANR 2, 40, 86; DLB 8; FANT; HGG; MTCW 1, 2; SATA 45; SATA-Obit 73; SCFW 2; SFW 4; SUFW 1, 2

Leibniz, Gottfried Wilhelm von 1646-1716 .... **LC 35**
See also DLB 168

Leimbach, Martha 1963-
See Leimbach, Marti
See also CA 130

Leimbach, Marti .... **CLC 65**
See Leimbach, Martha

Leino, Eino .... **TCLC 24**
See Lonnbohm, Armas Eino Leopold
See also EWL 3

Leiris, Michel (Julien) 1901-1990 ..... **CLC 61**
See also CA 119; 128; 132; EWL 3; GFL 1789 to the Present

Leithauser, Brad 1953- .... **CLC 27**
See also CA 107; CANR 27, 81; CP 7; DLB 120, 282

Lelchuk, Alan 1938- .... **CLC 5**
See also CA 45-48; CAAS 20; CANR 1, 70; CN 7

Lem, Stanislaw 1921- ...... **CLC 8, 15, 40, 149**
See also CA 105; CAAS 1; CANR 32; CWW 2; MTCW 1; SCFW 2; SFW 4

Lemann, Nancy (Elise) 1956- .... **CLC 39**
See also CA 118; 136; CANR 121

Lemonnier, (Antoine Louis) Camille 1844-1913 .... **TCLC 22**
See also CA 121

Lenau, Nikolaus 1802-1850 .... **NCLC 16**

L'Engle, Madeleine (Camp Franklin) 1918- .... **CLC 12**
See also AAYA 28; AITN 2; BPFB 2; BYA 2, 4, 5, 7; CA 1-4R; CANR 3, 21, 39, 66, 107; CLR 1, 14, 57; CPW; CWRI 5; DA3; DAM POP; DLB 52; JRDA; MAICYA 1, 2; MTCW 1, 2; SAAS 15; SATA 1, 27, 75, 128; SFW 4; WYA; YAW

Lengyel, Jozsef 1896-1975 .... **CLC 7**
See also CA 85-88; 57-60; CANR 71; RGSF 2

Lenin 1870-1924
See Lenin, V. I.
See also CA 121; 168

Lenin, V. I. .... **TCLC 67**
See Lenin

Lennon, John (Ono) 1940-1980 .. **CLC 12, 35**
See also CA 102; SATA 114

Lennox, Charlotte Ramsay 1729(?)-1804 .... **NCLC 23**
See also DLB 39; RGEL 2

Lentricchia, Frank, (Jr.) 1940- .... **CLC 34**
See also CA 25-28R; CANR 19, 106; DLB 246

Lenz, Gunter .... **CLC 65**

Lenz, Siegfried 1926- .... **CLC 27; SSC 33**
See also CA 89-92; CANR 80; CWW 2; DLB 75; EWL 3; RGSF 2; RGWL 2, 3

Leon, David
See Jacob, (Cyprien-)Max

Leonard, Elmore (John, Jr.) 1925- . **CLC 28, 34, 71, 120**
See also AAYA 22; AITN 1; BEST 89:1, 90:4; BPFB 2; CA 81-84; CANR 12, 28, 53, 76, 96; CMW 4; CN 7; CPW; DA3; DAM POP; DLB 173, 226; INT CANR-28; MSW; MTCW 1, 2; RGAL 4; TCWW 2

Leonard, Hugh .... **CLC 19**
See Byrne, John Keyes
See also CBD; CD 5; DFS 13; DLB 13

Leonov, Leonid (Maximovich) 1899-1994 .... **CLC 92**
See Leonov, Leonid Maksimovich
See also CA 129; CANR 74, 76; DAM NOV; EWL 3; MTCW 1, 2

Leonov, Leonid Maksimovich
See Leonov, Leonid (Maximovich)
See also DLB 272

Leopardi, (Conte) Giacomo 1798-1837 .... **NCLC 22, 129; PC 37**
See also EW 5; RGWL 2, 3; WP

Le Reveler
See Artaud, Antonin (Marie Joseph)

Lerman, Eleanor 1952- .... **CLC 9**
See also CA 85-88; CANR 69

Lerman, Rhoda 1936- .... **CLC 56**
See also CA 49-52; CANR 70

Lermontov, Mikhail Iur'evich
See Lermontov, Mikhail Yuryevich
See also DLB 205

Lermontov, Mikhail Yuryevich 1814-1841 .... **NCLC 5, 47, 126; PC 18**
See Lermontov, Mikhail Iur'evich
See also EW 6; RGWL 2, 3; TWA

Leroux, Gaston 1868-1927 .... **TCLC 25**
See also CA 108; 136; CANR 69; CMW 4; SATA 65

Lesage, Alain-Rene 1668-1747 .... **LC 2, 28**
See also EW 3; GFL Beginnings to 1789; RGWL 2, 3

Leskov, N(ikolai) S(emenovich) 1831-1895
See Leskov, Nikolai (Semyonovich)

Leskov, Nikolai (Semyonovich) 1831-1895 .... **NCLC 25; SSC 34**
See Leskov, Nikolai Semenovich

Leskov, Nikolai Semenovich
See Leskov, Nikolai (Semyonovich)
See also DLB 238

Lesser, Milton
See Marlowe, Stephen

Lessing, Doris (May) 1919- ... **CLC 1, 2, 3, 6, 10, 15, 22, 40, 94, 170; SSC 6, 61; WLCS**
See also AFW; BRWS 1; CA 9-12R; CAAS 14; CANR 33, 54, 76, 122; CD 5; CD-BLB 1960 to Present; CN 7; DA; DA3; DAB; DAC; DAM MST, NOV; DLB 15, 139; DLBY 1985; EWL 3; EXPS; FW; LAIT 4; MTCW 1, 2; RGEL 2; RGSF 2; SFW 4; SSFS 1, 12; TEA; WLIT 2, 4

Lessing, Gotthold Ephraim 1729-1781 . **LC 8**
See also CDWLB 2; DLB 97; EW 4; RGWL 2, 3

Lester, Richard 1932- .... **CLC 20**

Levenson, Jay .... **CLC 70**

Lever, Charles (James) 1806-1872 .... **NCLC 23**
See also DLB 21; RGEL 2

Leverson, Ada Esther 1862(?)-1933(?) .... **TCLC 18**
See Elaine
See also CA 117; 202; DLB 153; RGEL 2

Levertov, Denise 1923-1997 .. **CLC 1, 2, 3, 5, 8, 15, 28, 66; PC 11**
See also AMWS 3; CA 1-4R, 178; 163; CAAE 178; CAAS 19; CANR 3, 29, 50, 108; CDALBS; CP 7; CWP; DAM POET; DLB 5, 165; EWL 3; EXPP; FW; INT CANR-29; MTCW 1, 2; PAB; PFS 7, 17; RGAL 4; TUS; WP

Levi, Carlo 1902-1975 .... **TCLC 125**
See also CA 65-68; 53-56; CANR 10; EWL 3; RGWL 2, 3

Levi, Jonathan .... **CLC 76**
See also CA 197

Levi, Peter (Chad Tigar) 1931-2000 .... **CLC 41**
See also CA 5-8R; 187; CANR 34, 80; CP 7; DLB 40

Levi, Primo 1919-1987 ...... **CLC 37, 50; SSC 12; TCLC 109**
See also CA 13-16R; 122; CANR 12, 33, 61, 70; DLB 177; EWL 3; MTCW 1, 2; RGWL 2, 3

Levin, Ira 1929- .... **CLC 3, 6**
See also CA 21-24R; CANR 17, 44, 74; CMW 4; CN 7; CPW; DA3; DAM POP; HGG; MTCW 1, 2; SATA 66; SFW 4

Levin, Meyer 1905-1981 .... **CLC 7**
See also AITN 1; CA 9-12R; 104; CANR 15; DAM POP; DLB 9, 28; DLBY 1981; SATA 21; SATA-Obit 27

Levine, Norman 1924- .... **CLC 54**
See also CA 73-76; CAAS 23; CANR 14, 70; DLB 88

Levine, Philip 1928- .. **CLC 2, 4, 5, 9, 14, 33, 118; PC 22**
See also AMWS 5; CA 9-12R; CANR 9, 37, 52, 116; CP 7; DAM POET; DLB 5; EWL 3; PFS 8

Levinson, Deirdre 1931- .... **CLC 49**
See also CA 73-76; CANR 70

Levi-Strauss, Claude 1908- .... **CLC 38**
See also CA 1-4R; CANR 6, 32, 57; DLB 242; EWL 3; GFL 1789 to the Present; MTCW 1, 2; TWA

Levitin, Sonia (Wolff) 1934- .... **CLC 17**
See also AAYA 13, 48; CA 29-32R; CANR 14, 32, 79; CLR 53; JRDA; MAICYA 1, 2; SAAS 2; SATA 4, 68, 119; SATA-Essay 131; YAW

Levon, O. U.
See Kesey, Ken (Elton)

Levy, Amy 1861-1889 .... **NCLC 59**
See also DLB 156, 240

Lewes, George Henry 1817-1878 ... **NCLC 25**
See also DLB 55, 144

Lewis, Alun 1915-1944 .... **SSC 40; TCLC 3**
See also BRW 7; CA 104; 188; DLB 20, 162; PAB; RGEL 2

Lewis, C. Day
See Day Lewis, C(ecil)

Lewis, C(live) S(taples) 1898-1963 .... **CLC 1, 3, 6, 14, 27, 124; WLC**
See also AAYA 3, 39; BPFB 2; BRWS 3; BYA 15, 16; CA 81-84; CANR 33, 71; CDBLB 1945-1960; CLR 3, 27; CWRI 5; DA; DA3; DAB; DAC; DAM MST, NOV, POP; DLB 15, 100, 160, 255; EWL 3; FANT; JRDA; LMFS 2; MAICYA 1, 2; MTCW 1, 2; RGEL 2; SATA 13, 100; SCFW; SFW 4; SUFW 1; TEA; WCH; WYA; YAW

Lewis, Cecil Day
See Day Lewis, C(ecil)

Lewis, Janet 1899-1998 .... **CLC 41**
See Winters, Janet Lewis
See also CA 9-12R; 172; CANR 29, 63;
CAP 1; CN 7; DLBY 1987; RHW;
TCWW 2

Lewis, Matthew Gregory
1775-1818 .... **NCLC 11, 62**
See also DLB 39, 158, 178; HGG; LMFS
1; RGEL 2; SUFW

Lewis, (Harry) Sinclair 1885-1951 . **TCLC 4,
13, 23, 39; WLC**
See also AMW; AMWC 1; BPFB 2; CA
104; 133; CDALB 1917-1929; DA; DA3;
DAB; DAC; DAM MST, NOV; DLB 9,
102, 284; DLBD 1; EWL 3; LAIT 3;
MTCW 1, 2; NFS 15; RGAL 4; TUS

Lewis, (Percy) Wyndham
1884(?)-1957 .. **SSC 34; TCLC 2, 9, 104**
See also BRW 7; CA 104; 157; DLB 15;
EWL 3; FANT; MTCW 2; RGEL 2

Lewisohn, Ludwig 1883-1955 .... **TCLC 19**
See also CA 107; 203; DLB 4, 9, 28, 102

Lewton, Val 1904-1951 .... **TCLC 76**
See also CA 199; IDFW 3, 4

Leyner, Mark 1956- .... **CLC 92**
See also CA 110; CANR 28, 53; DA3;
MTCW 2

Lezama Lima, Jose 1910-1976 .... **CLC 4, 10,
101; HLCS 2**
See also CA 77-80; CANR 71; DAM
MULT; DLB 113, 283; EWL 3; HW 1, 2;
LAW; RGWL 2, 3

L'Heureux, John (Clarke) 1934- ...... **CLC 52**
See also CA 13-16R; CANR 23, 45, 88;
DLB 244

Liddell, C. H.
See Kuttner, Henry

Lie, Jonas (Lauritz Idemil)
1833-1908(?) .... **TCLC 5**
See also CA 115

Lieber, Joel 1937-1971 .... **CLC 6**
See also CA 73-76; 29-32R

Lieber, Stanley Martin
See Lee, Stan

Lieberman, Laurence (James)
1935- .... **CLC 4, 36**
See also CA 17-20R; CANR 8, 36, 89; CP
7

Lieh Tzu fl. 7th cent. B.C.-5th cent.
B.C. .... **CMLC 27**

Lieksman, Anders
See Haavikko, Paavo Juhani

Li Fei-kan 1904-
See Pa Chin
See also CA 105; TWA

Lifton, Robert Jay 1926- .... **CLC 67**
See also CA 17-20R; CANR 27, 78; INT
CANR-27; SATA 66

Lightfoot, Gordon 1938- .... **CLC 26**
See also CA 109

Lightman, Alan P(aige) 1948- .... **CLC 81**
See also CA 141; CANR 63, 105

Ligotti, Thomas (Robert) 1953- ...... **CLC 44;
SSC 16**
See also CA 123; CANR 49; HGG; SUFW
2

Li Ho 791-817 .... **PC 13**

**Liliencron, (Friedrich Adolf Axel) Detlev
von** 1844-1909 .... **TCLC 18**
See also CA 117

Lille, Alain de
See Alain de Lille

Lilly, William 1602-1681 .... **LC 27**

Lima, Jose Lezama
See Lezama Lima, Jose

Lima Barreto, Afonso Henrique de
1881-1922 .... **TCLC 23**
See also CA 117; 181; LAW

Lima Barreto, Afonso Henriques de
See Lima Barreto, Afonso Henrique de

Limonov, Edward 1944- .... **CLC 67**
See also CA 137

Lin, Frank
See Atherton, Gertrude (Franklin Horn)

Lincoln, Abraham 1809-1865 .... **NCLC 18**
See also LAIT 2

Lind, Jakov .... **CLC 1, 2, 4, 27, 82**
See Landwirth, Heinz
See also CAAS 4; EWL 3

Lindbergh, Anne (Spencer) Morrow
1906-2001 .... **CLC 82**
See also BPFB 2; CA 17-20R; 193; CANR
16, 73; DAM NOV; MTCW 1, 2; SATA
33; SATA-Obit 125; TUS

Lindsay, David 1878(?)-1945 .... **TCLC 15**
See also CA 113; 187; DLB 255; FANT;
SFW 4; SUFW 1

Lindsay, (Nicholas) Vachel
1879-1931 .... **PC 23; TCLC 17; WLC**
See also AMWS 1; CA 114; 135; CANR
79; CDALB 1865-1917; DA; DA3; DAC;
DAM MST, POET; DLB 54; EWL 3;
EXPP; RGAL 4; SATA 40; WP

Linke-Poot
See Doeblin, Alfred

Linney, Romulus 1930- .... **CLC 51**
See also CA 1-4R; CAD; CANR 40, 44,
79; CD 5; CSW; RGAL 4

Linton, Eliza Lynn 1822-1898 .... **NCLC 41**
See also DLB 18

Li Po 701-763 .... **CMLC 2; PC 29**
See also WP

Lipsius, Justus 1547-1606 .... **LC 16**

Lipsyte, Robert (Michael) 1938- ...... **CLC 21**
See also AAYA 7, 45; CA 17-20R; CANR
8, 57; CLR 23, 76; DA; DAC; DAM
MST, NOV; JRDA; LAIT 5; MAICYA 1,
2; SATA 5, 68, 113; WYA; YAW

Lish, Gordon (Jay) 1934- ... **CLC 45; SSC 18**
See also CA 113; 117; CANR 79; DLB 130;
INT 117

Lispector, Clarice 1925(?)-1977 .... **CLC 43;
HLCS 2; SSC 34**
See also CA 139; 116; CANR 71; CDWLB
3; DLB 113; DNFS 1; EWL 3; FW; HW
2; LAW; RGSF 2; RGWL 2, 3; WLIT 1

Littell, Robert 1935(?)- .... **CLC 42**
See also CA 109; 112; CANR 64, 115;
CMW 4

Little, Malcolm 1925-1965
See Malcolm X
See also BW 1, 3; CA 125; 111; CANR 82;
DA; DA3; DAB; DAC; DAM MST,
MULT; MTCW 1, 2; NCFS 3

Littlewit, Humphrey Gent.
See Lovecraft, H(oward) P(hillips)

Litwos
See Sienkiewicz, Henryk (Adam Alexander
Pius)

Liu, E. 1857-1909 .... **TCLC 15**
See also CA 115; 190

Lively, Penelope (Margaret) 1933- .. **CLC 32,
50**
See also BPFB 2; CA 41-44R; CANR 29,
67, 79; CLR 7; CN 7; CWRI 5; DAM
NOV; DLB 14, 161, 207; FANT; JRDA;
MAICYA 1, 2; MTCW 1, 2; SATA 7, 60,
101; TEA

Livesay, Dorothy (Kathleen)
1909-1996 .... **CLC 4, 15, 79**
See also AITN 2; CA 25-28R; CAAS 8;
CANR 36, 67; DAC; DAM MST, POET;
DLB 68; FW; MTCW 1; RGEL 2; TWA

Livy c. 59B.C.-c. 12 .... **CMLC 11**
See also AW 2; CDWLB 1; DLB 211;
RGWL 2, 3

Lizardi, Jose Joaquin Fernandez de
1776-1827 .... **NCLC 30**
See also LAW

Llewellyn, Richard
See Llewellyn Lloyd, Richard Dafydd Vivian
See also DLB 15

Llewellyn Lloyd, Richard Dafydd Vivian
1906-1983 .... **CLC 7, 80**
See Llewellyn, Richard
See also CA 53-56; 111; CANR 7, 71;
SATA 11; SATA-Obit 37

Llosa, (Jorge) Mario (Pedro) Vargas
See Vargas Llosa, (Jorge) Mario (Pedro)
See also RGWL 3

Llosa, Mario Vargas
See Vargas Llosa, (Jorge) Mario (Pedro)

Lloyd, Manda
See Mander, (Mary) Jane

Lloyd Webber, Andrew 1948-
See Webber, Andrew Lloyd
See also AAYA 1, 38; CA 116; 149; DAM
DRAM; SATA 56

Llull, Ramon c. 1235-c. 1316 .... **CMLC 12**

Lobb, Ebenezer
See Upward, Allen

Locke, Alain (Le Roy)
1886-1954 .... **BLCS; HR 3; TCLC 43**
See also BW 1, 3; CA 106; 124; CANR 79;
DLB 51; LMFS 2; RGAL 4

Locke, John 1632-1704 .... **LC 7, 35**
See also DLB 31, 101, 213, 252; RGEL 2;
WLIT 3

Locke-Elliott, Sumner
See Elliott, Sumner Locke

Lockhart, John Gibson 1794-1854 .. **NCLC 6**
See also DLB 110, 116, 144

Lockridge, Ross (Franklin), Jr.
1914-1948 .... **TCLC 111**
See also CA 108; 145; CANR 79; DLB 143;
DLBY 1980; RGAL 4; RHW

Lockwood, Robert
See Johnson, Robert

Lodge, David (John) 1935- .... **CLC 36, 141**
See also BEST 90:1; BRWS 4; CA 17-20R;
CANR 19, 53, 92; CN 7; CPW; DAM
POP; DLB 14, 194; EWL 3; INT CANR-
19; MTCW 1, 2

Lodge, Thomas 1558-1625 .... **LC 41**
See also DLB 172; RGEL 2

Loewinsohn, Ron(ald William)
1937- .... **CLC 52**
See also CA 25-28R; CANR 71

Logan, Jake
See Smith, Martin Cruz

Logan, John (Burton) 1923-1987 .... **CLC 5**
See also CA 77-80; 124; CANR 45; DLB 5

Lo Kuan-chung 1330(?)-1400(?) .... **LC 12**

Lombard, Nap
See Johnson, Pamela Hansford

London, Jack 1876-1916 .. **SSC 4, 49; TCLC
9, 15, 39; WLC**
See London, John Griffith
See also AAYA 13; AITN 2; AMW; BPFB
2; BYA 4, 13; CDALB 1865-1917; DLB
8, 12, 78, 212; EWL 3; EXPS; LAIT 3;
NFS 8; RGAL 4; RGSF 2; SATA 18; SFW
4; SSFS 7; TCWW 2; TUS; WYA; YAW

London, John Griffith 1876-1916
See London, Jack
See also CA 110; 119; CANR 73; DA; DA3;
DAB; DAC; DAM MST, NOV; JRDA;
MAICYA 1, 2; MTCW 1, 2

Long, Emmett
See Leonard, Elmore (John, Jr.)

Longbaugh, Harry
See Goldman, William (W.)

Longfellow, Henry Wadsworth
1807-1882 .... **NCLC 2, 45, 101, 103; PC 30; WLCS**
See also AMW; AMWR 2; CDALB 1640-1865; DA; DA3; DAB; DAC; DAM MST, POET; DLB 1, 59, 235; EXPP; PAB; PFS 2, 7, 17; RGAL 4; SATA 19; TUS; WP

Longinus c. 1st cent. - .... **CMLC 27**
See also AW 2; DLB 176

Longley, Michael 1939- .... **CLC 29**
See also BRWS 8; CA 102; CP 7; DLB 40

Longus fl. c. 2nd cent. - .... **CMLC 7**

Longway, A. Hugh
See Lang, Andrew

Lonnbohm, Armas Eino Leopold 1878-1926
See Leino, Eino
See also CA 123

Lonnrot, Elias 1802-1884 .... **NCLC 53**
See also EFS 1

Lonsdale, Roger ed. .... **CLC 65**

Lopate, Phillip 1943- .... **CLC 29**
See also CA 97-100; CANR 88; DLBY 1980; INT 97-100

Lopez, Barry (Holstun) 1945- .... **CLC 70**
See also AAYA 9; ANW; CA 65-68; CANR 7, 23, 47, 68, 92; DLB 256, 275; INT CANR-7, -23; MTCW 1; RGAL 4; SATA 67

Lopez Portillo (y Pacheco), Jose
1920- .... **CLC 46**
See also CA 129; HW 1

Lopez y Fuentes, Gregorio
1897(?)-1966 .... **CLC 32**
See also CA 131; EWL 3; HW 1

Lorca, Federico Garcia
See Garcia Lorca, Federico
See also DFS 4; EW 11; RGWL 2, 3; WP

Lord, Audre
See Lorde, Audre (Geraldine)
See also EWL 3

Lord, Bette Bao 1938- .... **AAL; CLC 23**
See also BEST 90:3; BPFB 2; CA 107; CANR 41, 79; INT CA-107; SATA 58

Lord Auch
See Bataille, Georges

Lord Brooke
See Greville, Fulke

Lord Byron
See Byron, George Gordon (Noel)

Lorde, Audre (Geraldine)
1934-1992 .. **BLC 2; CLC 18, 71; PC 12**
See Domini, Rey; Lord, Audre
See also AFAW 1, 2; BW 1, 3; CA 25-28R; 142; CANR 16, 26, 46, 82; DA3; DAM MULT, POET; DLB 41; FW; MTCW 1, 2; PFS 16; RGAL 4

Lord Houghton
See Milnes, Richard Monckton

Lord Jeffrey
See Jeffrey, Francis

Loreaux, Nichol .... **CLC 65**

Lorenzini, Carlo 1826-1890
See Collodi, Carlo
See also MAICYA 1, 2; SATA 29, 100

Lorenzo, Heberto Padilla
See Padilla (Lorenzo), Heberto

Loris
See Hofmannsthal, Hugo von

Loti, Pierre .... **TCLC 11**
See Viaud, (Louis Marie) Julien
See also DLB 123; GFL 1789 to the Present

Lou, Henri
See Andreas-Salome, Lou

Louie, David Wong 1954- .... **CLC 70**
See also CA 139; CANR 120

Louis, Adrian C. .... **NNAL**

Louis, Father M.
See Merton, Thomas (James)

Louise, Heidi
See Erdrich, Louise

Lovecraft, H(oward) P(hillips)
1890-1937 .... **SSC 3, 52; TCLC 4, 22**
See also AAYA 14; BPFB 2; CA 104; 133; CANR 106; DA3; DAM POP; HGG; MTCW 1, 2; RGAL 4; SCFW; SFW 4; SUFW

Lovelace, Earl 1935- .... **CLC 51**
See also BW 2; CA 77-80; CANR 41, 72, 114; CD 5; CDWLB 3; CN 7; DLB 125; EWL 3; MTCW 1

Lovelace, Richard 1618-1657 .... **LC 24**
See also BRW 2; DLB 131; EXPP; PAB; RGEL 2

Lowe, Pardee 1904- .... **AAL**

Lowell, Amy 1874-1925 ... **PC 13; TCLC 1, 8**
See also AMW; CA 104; 151; DAM POET; DLB 54, 140; EWL 3; EXPP; LMFS 2; MAWW; MTCW 2; RGAL 4; TUS

Lowell, James Russell 1819-1891 ... **NCLC 2, 90**
See also AMWS 1; CDALB 1640-1865; DLB 1, 11, 64, 79, 189, 235; RGAL 4

Lowell, Robert (Traill Spence, Jr.)
1917-1977 .... **CLC 1, 2, 3, 4, 5, 8, 9, 11, 15, 37, 124; PC 3; WLC**
See also AMW; AMWC 2; AMWR 2; CA 9-12R; 73-76; CABS 2; CANR 26, 60; CDALBS; DA; DA3; DAB; DAC; DAM MST, NOV; DLB 5, 169; EWL 3; MTCW 1, 2; PAB; PFS 6, 7; RGAL 4; WP

Lowenthal, Michael (Francis)
1969- .... **CLC 119**
See also CA 150; CANR 115

Lowndes, Marie Adelaide (Belloc)
1868-1947 .... **TCLC 12**
See also CA 107; CMW 4; DLB 70; RHW

Lowry, (Clarence) Malcolm
1909-1957 .... **SSC 31; TCLC 6, 40**
See also BPFB 2; BRWS 3; CA 105; 131; CANR 62, 105; CDBLB 1945-1960; DLB 15; EWL 3; MTCW 1, 2; RGEL 2

Lowry, Mina Gertrude 1882-1966
See Loy, Mina
See also CA 113

Loxsmith, John
See Brunner, John (Kilian Houston)

Loy, Mina .... **CLC 28; PC 16**
See Lowry, Mina Gertrude
See also DAM POET; DLB 4, 54

Loyson-Bridet
See Schwob, Marcel (Mayer Andre)

Lucan 39-65 .... **CMLC 33**
See also AW 2; DLB 211; EFS 2; RGWL 2, 3

Lucas, Craig 1951- .... **CLC 64**
See also CA 137; CAD; CANR 71, 109; CD 5; GLL 2

Lucas, E(dward) V(errall)
1868-1938 .... **TCLC 73**
See also CA 176; DLB 98, 149, 153; SATA 20

Lucas, George 1944- .... **CLC 16**
See also AAYA 1, 23; CA 77-80; CANR 30; SATA 56

Lucas, Hans
See Godard, Jean-Luc

Lucas, Victoria
See Plath, Sylvia

Lucian c. 125-c. 180 .... **CMLC 32**
See also AW 2; DLB 176; RGWL 2, 3

Lucretius c. 94B.C.-c. 49B.C. .... **CMLC 48**
See also AW 2; CDWLB 1; DLB 211; EFS 2; RGWL 2, 3

Ludlam, Charles 1943-1987 .... **CLC 46, 50**
See also CA 85-88; 122; CAD; CANR 72, 86; DLB 266

Ludlum, Robert 1927-2001 .... **CLC 22, 43**
See also AAYA 10; BEST 89:1, 90:3; BPFB 2; CA 33-36R; 195; CANR 25, 41, 68, 105; CMW 4; CPW; DA3; DAM NOV, POP; DLBY 1982; MSW; MTCW 1, 2

Ludwig, Ken .... **CLC 60**
See also CA 195; CAD

Ludwig, Otto 1813-1865 .... **NCLC 4**
See also DLB 129

Lugones, Leopoldo 1874-1938 .... **HLCS 2; TCLC 15**
See also CA 116; 131; CANR 104; DLB 283; EWL 3; HW 1; LAW

Lu Hsun .... **SSC 20; TCLC 3**
See Shu-Jen, Chou
See also EWL 3

Lukacs, George .... **CLC 24**
See Lukacs, Gyorgy (Szegeny von)

Lukacs, Gyorgy (Szegeny von) 1885-1971
See Lukacs, George
See also CA 101; 29-32R; CANR 62; CD-WLB 4; DLB 215, 242; EW 10; EWL 3; MTCW 2

Luke, Peter (Ambrose Cyprian)
1919-1995 .... **CLC 38**
See also CA 81-84; 147; CANR 72; CBD; CD 5; DLB 13

Lunar, Dennis
See Mungo, Raymond

Lurie, Alison 1926- ..... **CLC 4, 5, 18, 39, 175**
See also BPFB 2; CA 1-4R; CANR 2, 17, 50, 88; CN 7; DLB 2; MTCW 1; SATA 46, 112

Lustig, Arnost 1926- .... **CLC 56**
See also AAYA 3; CA 69-72; CANR 47, 102; CWW 2; DLB 232; EWL 3; SATA 56

Luther, Martin 1483-1546 .... **LC 9, 37**
See also CDWLB 2; DLB 179; EW 2; RGWL 2, 3

Luxemburg, Rosa 1870(?)-1919 ..... **TCLC 63**
See also CA 118

Luzi, Mario 1914- .... **CLC 13**
See also CA 61-64; CANR 9, 70; CWW 2; DLB 128; EWL 3

L'vov, Arkady .... **CLC 59**

Lydgate, John c. 1370-1450(?) .... **LC 81**
See also BRW 1; DLB 146; RGEL 2

Lyly, John 1554(?)-1606 .... **DC 7; LC 41**
See also BRW 1; DAM DRAM; DLB 62, 167; RGEL 2

L'Ymagier
See Gourmont, Remy(-Marie-Charles) de

Lynch, B. Suarez
See Borges, Jorge Luis

Lynch, David (Keith) 1946- ...... **CLC 66, 162**
See also CA 124; 129; CANR 111

Lynch, James
See Andreyev, Leonid (Nikolaevich)

Lyndsay, Sir David 1485-1555 .... **LC 20**
See also RGEL 2

Lynn, Kenneth S(chuyler)
1923-2001 .... **CLC 50**
See also CA 1-4R; 196; CANR 3, 27, 65

Lynx
See West, Rebecca

Lyons, Marcus
See Blish, James (Benjamin)

Lyotard, Jean-Francois
1924-1998 .... **TCLC 103**
See also DLB 242; EWL 3

Lyre, Pinchbeck
See Sassoon, Siegfried (Lorraine)

Lytle, Andrew (Nelson) 1902-1995 ... **CLC 22**
See also CA 9-12R; 150; CANR 70; CN 7; CSW; DLB 6; DLBY 1995; RGAL 4; RHW

Lyttelton, George 1709-1773 .... **LC 10**
See also RGEL 2

Lytton of Knebworth, Baron
See Bulwer-Lytton, Edward (George Earle Lytton)

Maas, Peter 1929-2001 .... **CLC 29**
See also CA 93-96; 201; INT CA-93-96; MTCW 2

Macaulay, Catherine 1731-1791 .... **LC 64**
See also DLB 104

Macaulay, (Emilie) Rose
1881(?)-1958 .... **TCLC 7, 44**
See also CA 104; DLB 36; EWL 3; RGEL 2; RHW

Macaulay, Thomas Babington
1800-1859 .... **NCLC 42**
See also BRW 4; CDBLB 1832-1890; DLB 32, 55; RGEL 2

MacBeth, George (Mann)
1932-1992 .... **CLC 2, 5, 9**
See also CA 25-28R; 136; CANR 61, 66; DLB 40; MTCW 1; PFS 8; SATA 4; SATA-Obit 70

MacCaig, Norman (Alexander)
1910-1996 .... **CLC 36**
See also BRWS 6; CA 9-12R; CANR 3, 34; CP 7; DAB; DAM POET; DLB 27; EWL 3; RGEL 2

MacCarthy, Sir (Charles Otto) Desmond
1877-1952 .... **TCLC 36**
See also CA 167

MacDiarmid, Hugh .... **CLC 2, 4, 11, 19, 63; PC 9**
See Grieve, C(hristopher) M(urray)
See also CDBLB 1945-1960; DLB 20; EWL 3; RGEL 2

MacDonald, Anson
See Heinlein, Robert A(nson)

Macdonald, Cynthia 1928- .... **CLC 13, 19**
See also CA 49-52; CANR 4, 44; DLB 105

MacDonald, George 1824-1905 .... **TCLC 9, 113**
See also BYA 5; CA 106; 137; CANR 80; CLR 67; DLB 18, 163, 178; FANT; MAICYA 1, 2; RGEL 2; SATA 33, 100; SFW 4; SUFW; WCH

Macdonald, John
See Millar, Kenneth

MacDonald, John D(ann)
1916-1986 .... **CLC 3, 27, 44**
See also BPFB 2; CA 1-4R; 121; CANR 1, 19, 60; CMW 4; CPW; DAM NOV, POP; DLB 8; DLBY 1986; MSW; MTCW 1, 2; SFW 4

Macdonald, John Ross
See Millar, Kenneth

Macdonald, Ross ..... **CLC 1, 2, 3, 14, 34, 41**
See Millar, Kenneth
See also AMWS 4; BPFB 2; DLBD 6; MSW; RGAL 4

MacDougal, John
See Blish, James (Benjamin)

MacDougal, John
See Blish, James (Benjamin)

MacDowell, John
See Parks, Tim(othy Harold)

MacEwen, Gwendolyn (Margaret)
1941-1987 .... **CLC 13, 55**
See also CA 9-12R; 124; CANR 7, 22; DLB 53, 251; SATA 50; SATA-Obit 55

Macha, Karel Hynek 1810-1846 .... **NCLC 46**

Machado (y Ruiz), Antonio
1875-1939 .... **TCLC 3**
See also CA 104; 174; DLB 108; EW 9; EWL 3; HW 2; RGWL 2, 3

Machado de Assis, Joaquim Maria
1839-1908 .... **BLC 2; HLCS 2; SSC 24; TCLC 10**
See also CA 107; 153; CANR 91; LAW; RGSF 2; RGWL 2, 3; TWA; WLIT 1

Machen, Arthur .... **SSC 20; TCLC 4**
See Jones, Arthur Llewellyn
See also CA 179; DLB 156, 178; RGEL 2; SUFW 1

Machiavelli, Niccolo 1469-1527 ... **DC 16; LC 8, 36; WLCS**
See also DA; DAB; DAC; DAM MST; EW 2; LAIT 1; LMFS 1; NFS 9; RGWL 2, 3; TWA

MacInnes, Colin 1914-1976 .... **CLC 4, 23**
See also CA 69-72; 65-68; CANR 21; DLB 14; MTCW 1, 2; RGEL 2; RHW

MacInnes, Helen (Clark)
1907-1985 .... **CLC 27, 39**
See also BPFB 2; CA 1-4R; 117; CANR 1, 28, 58; CMW 4; CPW; DAM POP; DLB 87; MSW; MTCW 1, 2; SATA 22; SATA-Obit 44

Mackay, Mary 1855-1924
See Corelli, Marie
See also CA 118; 177; FANT; RHW

Mackenzie, Compton (Edward Montague)
1883-1972 .... **CLC 18; TCLC 116**
See also CA 21-22; 37-40R; CAP 2; DLB 34, 100; RGEL 2

Mackenzie, Henry 1745-1831 .... **NCLC 41**
See also DLB 39; RGEL 2

Mackey, Nathaniel (Ernest) 1947- .... **PC 49**
See also CA 153; CANR 114; CP 7; DLB 169

Mackintosh, Elizabeth 1896(?)-1952
See Tey, Josephine
See also CA 110; CMW 4

MacLaren, James
See Grieve, C(hristopher) M(urray)

Mac Laverty, Bernard 1942- .... **CLC 31**
See also CA 116; 118; CANR 43, 88; CN 7; DLB 267; INT CA-118; RGSF 2

MacLean, Alistair (Stuart)
1922(?)-1987 .... **CLC 3, 13, 50, 63**
See also CA 57-60; 121; CANR 28, 61; CMW 4; CPW; DAM POP; DLB 276; MTCW 1; SATA 23; SATA-Obit 50; TCWW 2

Maclean, Norman (Fitzroy)
1902-1990 .... **CLC 78; SSC 13**
See also CA 102; 132; CANR 49; CPW; DAM POP; DLB 206; TCWW 2

MacLeish, Archibald 1892-1982 ... **CLC 3, 8, 14, 68; PC 47**
See also AMW; CA 9-12R; 106; CAD; CANR 33, 63; CDALBS; DAM POET; DFS 15; DLB 4, 7, 45; DLBY 1982; EWL 3; EXPP; MTCW 1, 2; PAB; PFS 5; RGAL 4; TUS

MacLennan, (John) Hugh
1907-1990 .... **CLC 2, 14, 92**
See also CA 5-8R; 142; CANR 33; DAC; DAM MST; DLB 68; EWL 3; MTCW 1, 2; RGEL 2; TWA

MacLeod, Alistair 1936- .... **CLC 56, 165**
See also CA 123; CCA 1; DAC; DAM MST; DLB 60; MTCW 2; RGSF 2

Macleod, Fiona
See Sharp, William
See also RGEL 2; SUFW

MacNeice, (Frederick) Louis
1907-1963 .... **CLC 1, 4, 10, 53**
See also BRW 7; CA 85-88; CANR 61; DAB; DAM POET; DLB 10, 20; EWL 3; MTCW 1, 2; RGEL 2

MacNeill, Dand
See Fraser, George MacDonald

Macpherson, James 1736-1796 .... **LC 29**
See Ossian
See also BRWS 8; DLB 109; RGEL 2

Macpherson, (Jean) Jay 1931- .... **CLC 14**
See also CA 5-8R; CANR 90; CP 7; CWP; DLB 53

Macrobius fl. 430- .... **CMLC 48**

MacShane, Frank 1927-1999 .... **CLC 39**
See also CA 9-12R; 186; CANR 3, 33; DLB 111

Macumber, Mari
See Sandoz, Mari(e Susette)

Madach, Imre 1823-1864 .... **NCLC 19**

Madden, (Jerry) David 1933- ...... **CLC 5, 15**
See also CA 1-4R; CAAS 3; CANR 4, 45; CN 7; CSW; DLB 6; MTCW 1

Maddern, Al(an)
See Ellison, Harlan (Jay)

Madhubuti, Haki R. 1942- ... **BLC 2; CLC 6, 73; PC 5**
See Lee, Don L.
See also BW 2, 3; CA 73-76; CANR 24, 51, 73; CP 7; CSW; DAM MULT, POET; DLB 5, 41; DLBD 8; EWL 3; MTCW 2; RGAL 4

Madison, James 1751-1836 .... **NCLC 126**
See also DLB 37

Maepenn, Hugh
See Kuttner, Henry

Maepenn, K. H.
See Kuttner, Henry

Maeterlinck, Maurice 1862-1949 ..... **TCLC 3**
See also CA 104; 136; CANR 80; DAM DRAM; DLB 192; EW 8; EWL 3; GFL 1789 to the Present; LMFS 2; RGWL 2, 3; SATA 66; TWA

Maginn, William 1794-1842 .... **NCLC 8**
See also DLB 110, 159

Mahapatra, Jayanta 1928- .... **CLC 33**
See also CA 73-76; CAAS 9; CANR 15, 33, 66, 87; CP 7; DAM MULT

Mahfouz, Naguib (Abdel Aziz Al-Sabilgi)
1911(?)- .... **CLC 153**
See Mahfuz, Najib (Abdel Aziz al-Sabilgi)
See also AAYA 49; BEST 89:2; CA 128; CANR 55, 101; CWW 2; DA3; DAM NOV; MTCW 1, 2; RGWL 2, 3; SSFS 9

Mahfuz, Najib (Abdel Aziz al-Sabilgi)
.... **CLC 52, 55**
See Mahfouz, Naguib (Abdel Aziz Al-Sabilgi)
See also AFW; DLBY 1988; EWL 3; RGSF 2; WLIT 2

Mahon, Derek 1941- .... **CLC 27**
See also BRWS 6; CA 113; 128; CANR 88; CP 7; DLB 40; EWL 3

Maiakovskii, Vladimir
See Mayakovski, Vladimir (Vladimirovich)
See also IDTP; RGWL 2, 3

Mailer, Norman 1923- ... **CLC 1, 2, 3, 4, 5, 8, 11, 14, 28, 39, 74, 111**
See also AAYA 31; AITN 2; AMW; AMWC 2; AMWR 2; BPFB 2; CA 9-12R; CABS 1; CANR 28, 74, 77; CDALB 1968-1988; CN 7; CPW; DA; DA3; DAB; DAC; DAM MST, NOV, POP; DLB 2, 16, 28, 185, 278; DLBD 3; DLBY 1980, 1983; EWL 3; MTCW 1, 2; NFS 10; RGAL 4; TUS

Maillet, Antonine 1929- .... **CLC 54, 118**
See also CA 115; 120; CANR 46, 74, 77; CCA 1; CWW 2; DAC; DLB 60; INT 120; MTCW 2

Mais, Roger 1905-1955 .... **TCLC 8**
See also BW 1, 3; CA 105; 124; CANR 82; CDWLB 3; DLB 125; EWL 3; MTCW 1; RGEL 2

Maistre, Joseph 1753-1821 .... **NCLC 37**
See also GFL 1789 to the Present

Maitland, Frederic William
1850-1906 .... **TCLC 65**

Maitland, Sara (Louise) 1950- .... **CLC 49**
See also CA 69-72; CANR 13, 59; DLB 271; FW

Major, Clarence 1936- ... **BLC 2; CLC 3, 19, 48**
  See also AFAW 2; BW 2, 3; CA 21-24R; CAAS 6; CANR 13, 25, 53, 82; CN 7; CP 7; CSW; DAM MULT; DLB 33; EWL 3; MSW

Major, Kevin (Gerald) 1949- .... **CLC 26**
  See also AAYA 16; CA 97-100; CANR 21, 38, 112; CLR 11; DAC; DLB 60; INT CANR-21; JRDA; MAICYA 1, 2; MAIC-YAS 1; SATA 32, 82, 134; WYA; YAW

Maki, James
  See Ozu, Yasujiro

Malabaila, Damiano
  See Levi, Primo

Malamud, Bernard 1914-1986 .. **CLC 1, 2, 3, 5, 8, 9, 11, 18, 27, 44, 78, 85; SSC 15; TCLC 129; WLC**
  See also AAYA 16; AMWS 1; BPFB 2; BYA 15; CA 5-8R; 118; CABS 1; CANR 28, 62, 114; CDALB 1941-1968; CPW; DA; DA3; DAB; DAC; DAM MST, NOV, POP; DLB 2, 28, 152; DLBY 1980, 1986; EWL 3; EXPS; LAIT 4; LATS 1; MTCW 1, 2; NFS 4, 9; RGAL 4; RGSF 2; SSFS 8, 13, 16; TUS

Malan, Herman
  See Bosman, Herman Charles; Bosman, Herman Charles

Malaparte, Curzio 1898-1957 .... **TCLC 52**
  See also DLB 264

Malcolm, Dan
  See Silverberg, Robert

Malcolm X .... **BLC 2; CLC 82, 117; WLCS**
  See Little, Malcolm
  See also LAIT 5

Malherbe, François de 1555-1628 .... **LC 5**
  See also GFL Beginnings to 1789

Mallarme, Stephane 1842-1898 ...... **NCLC 4, 41; PC 4**
  See also DAM POET; DLB 217; EW 7; GFL 1789 to the Present; LMFS 2; RGWL 2, 3; TWA

Mallet-Joris, Françoise 1930- .... **CLC 11**
  See also CA 65-68; CANR 17; DLB 83; EWL 3; GFL 1789 to the Present

Malley, Ern
  See McAuley, James Phillip

Mallon, Thomas 1951- .... **CLC 172**
  See also CA 110; CANR 29, 57, 92

Mallowan, Agatha Christie
  See Christie, Agatha (Mary Clarissa)

Maloff, Saul 1922- .... **CLC 5**
  See also CA 33-36R

Malone, Louis
  See MacNeice, (Frederick) Louis

Malone, Michael (Christopher)
  1942- .... **CLC 43**
  See also CA 77-80; CANR 14, 32, 57, 114

Malory, Sir Thomas 1410(?)-1471(?) . **LC 11, 88; WLCS**
  See also BRW 1; BRWR 2; CDBLB Before 1660; DA; DAB; DAC; DAM MST; DLB 146; EFS 2; RGEL 2; SATA 59; SATA-Brief 33; TEA; WLIT 3

Malouf, (George Joseph) David
  1934- .... **CLC 28, 86**
  See also CA 124; CANR 50, 76; CN 7; CP 7; DLB 289; EWL 3; MTCW 2

Malraux, (Georges-)Andre
  1901-1976 .... **CLC 1, 4, 9, 13, 15, 57**
  See also BPFB 2; CA 21-22; 69-72; CANR 34, 58; CAP 2; DA3; DAM NOV; DLB 72; EW 12; EWL 3; GFL 1789 to the Present; MTCW 1, 2; RGWL 2, 3; TWA

Malzberg, Barry N(athaniel) 1939- ... **CLC 7**
  See also CA 61-64; CAAS 4; CANR 16; CMW 4; DLB 8; SFW 4

Mamet, David (Alan) 1947- .. **CLC 9, 15, 34, 46, 91, 166; DC 4**
  See also AAYA 3; CA 81-84; CABS 3; CANR 15, 41, 67, 72; CD 5; DA3; DAM DRAM; DFS 2, 3, 6, 12, 15; DLB 7; EWL 3; IDFW 4; MTCW 1, 2; RGAL 4

Mamoulian, Rouben (Zachary)
  1897-1987 .... **CLC 16**
  See also CA 25-28R; 124; CANR 85

Mandelshtam, Osip
  See Mandelstam, Osip (Emilievich)
  See also EW 10; EWL 3; RGWL 2, 3

Mandelstam, Osip (Emilievich)
  1891(?)-1943(?) .... **PC 14; TCLC 2, 6**
  See Mandelshtam, Osip
  See also CA 104; 150; MTCW 2; TWA

Mander, (Mary) Jane 1877-1949 ... **TCLC 31**
  See also CA 162

Mandeville, Bernard 1670-1733 .... **LC 82**
  See also DLB 101

Mandeville, Sir John fl. 1350- ...... **CMLC 19**
  See also DLB 146

Mandiargues, Andre Pieyre de .... **CLC 41**
  See Pieyre de Mandiargues, Andre
  See also DLB 83

Mandrake, Ethel Belle
  See Thurman, Wallace (Henry)

Mangan, James Clarence
  1803-1849 .... **NCLC 27**
  See also RGEL 2

Maniere, J.-E.
  See Giraudoux, Jean(-Hippolyte)

Mankiewicz, Herman (Jacob)
  1897-1953 .... **TCLC 85**
  See also CA 120; 169; DLB 26; IDFW 3, 4

Manley, (Mary) Delariviere
  1672(?)-1724 .... **LC 1, 42**
  See also DLB 39, 80; RGEL 2

Mann, Abel
  See Creasey, John

Mann, Emily 1952- .... **DC 7**
  See also CA 130; CAD; CANR 55; CD 5; CWD; DLB 266

Mann, (Luiz) Heinrich 1871-1950 ... **TCLC 9**
  See also CA 106; 164, 181; DLB 66, 118; EW 8; EWL 3; RGWL 2, 3

Mann, (Paul) Thomas 1875-1955 .... **SSC 5; TCLC 2, 8, 14, 21, 35, 44, 60; WLC**
  See also BPFB 2; CA 104; 128; CDWLB 2; DA; DA3; DAB; DAC; DAM MST, NOV; DLB 66; EW 9; EWL 3; GLL 1; LATS 1; LMFS 1; MTCW 1, 2; NFS 17; RGSF 2; RGWL 2, 3; SSFS 4, 9; TWA

Mannheim, Karl 1893-1947 .... **TCLC 65**
  See also CA 204

Manning, David
  See Faust, Frederick (Schiller)
  See also TCWW 2

Manning, Frederic 1882-1935 .... **TCLC 25**
  See also CA 124; 216; DLB 260

Manning, Olivia 1915-1980 .... **CLC 5, 19**
  See also CA 5-8R; 101; CANR 29; EWL 3; FW; MTCW 1; RGEL 2

Mano, D. Keith 1942- .... **CLC 2, 10**
  See also CA 25-28R; CAAS 6; CANR 26, 57; DLB 6

Mansfield, Katherine . **SSC 9, 23, 38; TCLC 2, 8, 39; WLC**
  See Beauchamp, Kathleen Mansfield
  See also BPFB 2; BRW 7; DAB; DLB 162; EWL 3; EXPS; FW; GLL 1; RGEL 2; RGSF 2; SSFS 2, 8, 10, 11

Manso, Peter 1940- .... **CLC 39**
  See also CA 29-32R; CANR 44

Mantecon, Juan Jimenez
  See Jimenez (Mantecon), Juan Ramon

Mantel, Hilary (Mary) 1952- .... **CLC 144**
  See also CA 125; CANR 54, 101; CN 7; DLB 271; RHW

Manton, Peter
  See Creasey, John

Man Without a Spleen, A
  See Chekhov, Anton (Pavlovich)

Manzoni, Alessandro 1785-1873 ... **NCLC 29, 98**
  See also EW 5; RGWL 2, 3; TWA

Map, Walter 1140-1209 .... **CMLC 32**

Mapu, Abraham (ben Jekutiel)
  1808-1867 .... **NCLC 18**

Mara, Sally
  See Queneau, Raymond

Maracle, Lee 1950- .... **NNAL**
  See also CA 149

Marat, Jean Paul 1743-1793 .... **LC 10**

Marcel, Gabriel Honore 1889-1973 . **CLC 15**
  See also CA 102; 45-48; EWL 3; MTCW 1, 2

March, William 1893-1954 .... **TCLC 96**
  See also CA 216

Marchbanks, Samuel
  See Davies, (William) Robertson
  See also CCA 1

Marchi, Giacomo
  See Bassani, Giorgio

Marcus Aurelius
  See Aurelius, Marcus
  See also AW 2

Marguerite
  See de Navarre, Marguerite

Marguerite d'Angouleme
  See de Navarre, Marguerite
  See also GFL Beginnings to 1789

Marguerite de Navarre
  See de Navarre, Marguerite
  See also RGWL 2, 3

Margulies, Donald 1954- .... **CLC 76**
  See also CA 200; DFS 13; DLB 228

Marie de France c. 12th cent. - ..... **CMLC 8; PC 22**
  See also DLB 208; FW; RGWL 2, 3

Marie de l'Incarnation 1599-1672 ...... **LC 10**

Marier, Captain Victor
  See Griffith, D(avid Lewelyn) W(ark)

Mariner, Scott
  See Pohl, Frederik

Marinetti, Filippo Tommaso
  1876-1944 .... **TCLC 10**
  See also CA 107; DLB 114, 264; EW 9; EWL 3

Marivaux, Pierre Carlet de Chamblain de
  1688-1763 .... **DC 7; LC 4**
  See also GFL Beginnings to 1789; RGWL 2, 3; TWA

Markandaya, Kamala .... **CLC 8, 38**
  See Taylor, Kamala (Purnaiya)
  See also BYA 13; CN 7; EWL 3

Markfield, Wallace 1926-2002 .... **CLC 8**
  See also CA 69-72; 208; CAAS 3; CN 7; DLB 2, 28; DLBY 2002

Markham, Edwin 1852-1940 .... **TCLC 47**
  See also CA 160; DLB 54, 186; RGAL 4

Markham, Robert
  See Amis, Kingsley (William)

Markoosie .... **NNAL**
  See Markoosie, Patsauq
  See also CLR 23; DAM MULT

Marks, J
  See Highwater, Jamake (Mamake)

Marks, J.
  See Highwater, Jamake (Mamake)

Marks-Highwater, J
  See Highwater, Jamake (Mamake)

Marks-Highwater, J.
  See Highwater, Jamake (Mamake)

Markson, David M(errill) 1927- .... **CLC 67**
  See also CA 49-52; CANR 1, 91; CN 7

Marlatt, Daphne (Buckle) 1942- .... **CLC 168**
See also CA 25-28R; CANR 17, 39; CN 7;
CP 7; CWP; DLB 60; FW

Marley, Bob .... **CLC 17**
See Marley, Robert Nesta

Marley, Robert Nesta 1945-1981
See Marley, Bob
See also CA 107; 103

Marlowe, Christopher 1564-1593 . **DC 1; LC 22, 47; WLC**
See also BRW 1; BRWR 1; CDBLB Before
1660; DA; DA3; DAB; DAC; DAM
DRAM, MST; DFS 1, 5, 13; DLB 62;
EXPP; LMFS 1; RGEL 2; TEA; WLIT 3

Marlowe, Stephen 1928- .... **CLC 70**
See Queen, Ellery
See also CA 13-16R; CANR 6, 55; CMW
4; SFW 4

Marmion, Shakerley 1603-1639 .... **LC 89**
See also DLB 58; RGEL 2

Marmontel, Jean-Francois 1723-1799 .. **LC 2**

Maron, Monika 1941- .... **CLC 165**
See also CA 201

Marquand, John P(hillips)
1893-1960 .... **CLC 2, 10**
See also AMW; BPFB 2; CA 85-88; CANR
73; CMW 4; DLB 9, 102; EWL 3; MTCW
2; RGAL 4

Marques, Rene 1919-1979 .. **CLC 96; HLC 2**
See also CA 97-100; 85-88; CANR 78;
DAM MULT; DLB 113; EWL 3; HW 1,
2; LAW; RGSF 2

Marquez, Gabriel (Jose) Garcia
See Garcia Marquez, Gabriel (Jose)

Marquis, Don(ald Robert Perry)
1878-1937 .... **TCLC 7**
See also CA 104; 166; DLB 11, 25; RGAL
4

Marquis de Sade
See Sade, Donatien Alphonse Francois

Marric, J. J.
See Creasey, John
See also MSW

Marryat, Frederick 1792-1848 .... **NCLC 3**
See also DLB 21, 163; RGEL 2; WCH

Marsden, James
See Creasey, John

Marsh, Edward 1872-1953 .... **TCLC 99**

Marsh, (Edith) Ngaio 1899-1982 .. **CLC 7, 53**
See also CA 9-12R; CANR 6, 58; CMW 4;
CPW; DAM POP; DLB 77; MSW;
MTCW 1, 2; RGEL 2; TEA

Marshall, Garry 1934- .... **CLC 17**
See also AAYA 3; CA 111; SATA 60

Marshall, Paule 1929- .. **BLC 3; CLC 27, 72; SSC 3**
See also AFAW 1, 2; AMWS 11; BPFB 2;
BW 2, 3; CA 77-80; CANR 25, 73; CN 7;
DA3; DAM MULT; DLB 33, 157, 227;
EWL 3; LATS 1; MTCW 1, 2; RGAL 4;
SSFS 15

Marshallik
See Zangwill, Israel

Marsten, Richard
See Hunter, Evan

Marston, John 1576-1634 .... **LC 33**
See also BRW 2; DAM DRAM; DLB 58,
172; RGEL 2

Martha, Henry
See Harris, Mark

Marti (y Perez), Jose (Julian)
1853-1895 .... **HLC 2; NCLC 63**
See also DAM MULT; HW 2; LAW; RGWL
2, 3; WLIT 1

Martial c. 40-c. 104 .... **CMLC 35; PC 10**
See also AW 2; CDWLB 1; DLB 211;
RGWL 2, 3

Martin, Ken
See Hubbard, L(afayette) Ron(ald)

Martin, Richard
See Creasey, John

Martin, Steve 1945- .... **CLC 30**
See also AAYA 53; CA 97-100; CANR 30,
100; MTCW 1

Martin, Valerie 1948- .... **CLC 89**
See also BEST 90:2; CA 85-88; CANR 49,
89

Martin, Violet Florence 1862-1915 .. **SSC 56; TCLC 51**

Martin, Webber
See Silverberg, Robert

Martindale, Patrick Victor
See White, Patrick (Victor Martindale)

Martin du Gard, Roger
1881-1958 .... **TCLC 24**
See also CA 118; CANR 94; DLB 65; EWL
3; GFL 1789 to the Present; RGWL 2, 3

Martineau, Harriet 1802-1876 .... **NCLC 26**
See also DLB 21, 55, 159, 163, 166, 190;
FW; RGEL 2; YABC 2

Martines, Julia
See O'Faolain, Julia

Martinez, Enrique Gonzalez
See Gonzalez Martinez, Enrique

Martinez, Jacinto Benavente y
See Benavente (y Martinez), Jacinto

Martinez de la Rosa, Francisco de Paula
1787-1862 .... **NCLC 102**
See also TWA

Martinez Ruiz, Jose 1873-1967
See Azorin; Ruiz, Jose Martinez
See also CA 93-96; HW 1

Martinez Sierra, Gregorio
1881-1947 .... **TCLC 6**
See also CA 115; EWL 3

Martinez Sierra, Maria (de la O'LeJarraga)
1874-1974 .... **TCLC 6**
See also CA 115; EWL 3

Martinsen, Martin
See Follett, Ken(neth Martin)

Martinson, Harry (Edmund)
1904-1978 .... **CLC 14**
See also CA 77-80; CANR 34; DLB 259;
EWL 3

Martyn, Edward 1859-1923 .... **TCLC 131**
See also CA 179; DLB 10; RGEL 2

Marut, Ret
See Traven, B.

Marut, Robert
See Traven, B.

Marvell, Andrew 1621-1678 .... **LC 4, 43; PC 10; WLC**
See also BRW 2; BRWR 2; CDBLB 1660-
1789; DA; DAB; DAC; DAM MST,
POET; DLB 131; EXPP; PFS 5; RGEL 2;
TEA; WP

Marx, Karl (Heinrich)
1818-1883 .... **NCLC 17, 114**
See also DLB 129; LATS 1; TWA

Masaoka, Shiki -1902 .... **TCLC 18**
See Masaoka, Tsunenori
See also RGWL 3

Masaoka, Tsunenori 1867-1902
See Masaoka, Shiki
See also CA 117; 191; TWA

Masefield, John (Edward)
1878-1967 .... **CLC 11, 47**
See also CA 19-20; 25-28R; CANR 33;
CAP 2; CDBLB 1890-1914; DAM POET;
DLB 10, 19, 153, 160; EWL 3; EXPP;
FANT; MTCW 1, 2; PFS 5; RGEL 2;
SATA 19

Maso, Carole 19(?)- .... **CLC 44**
See also CA 170; GLL 2; RGAL 4

Mason, Bobbie Ann 1940- ... **CLC 28, 43, 82, 154; SSC 4**
See also AAYA 5, 42; AMWS 8; BPFB 2;
CA 53-56; CANR 11, 31, 58, 83;
CDALBS; CN 7; CSW; DA3; DLB 173;
DLBY 1987; EWL 3; EXPS; INT CANR-
31; MTCW 1, 2; NFS 4; RGAL 4; RGSF
2; SSFS 3,8; YAW

Mason, Ernst
See Pohl, Frederik

Mason, Hunni B.
See Sternheim, (William Adolf) Carl

Mason, Lee W.
See Malzberg, Barry N(athaniel)

Mason, Nick 1945- .... **CLC 35**

Mason, Tally
See Derleth, August (William)

Mass, Anna .... **CLC 59**

Mass, William
See Gibson, William

Massinger, Philip 1583-1640 .... **LC 70**
See also DLB 58; RGEL 2

Master Lao
See Lao Tzu

Masters, Edgar Lee 1868-1950 ...... **PC 1, 36; TCLC 2, 25; WLCS**
See also AMWS 1; CA 104; 133; CDALB
1865-1917; DA; DAC; DAM MST,
POET; DLB 54; EWL 3; EXPP; MTCW
1, 2; RGAL 4; TUS; WP

Masters, Hilary 1928- .... **CLC 48**
See also CA 25-28R; CANR 13, 47, 97; CN
7; DLB 244

Mastrosimone, William 19(?)- .... **CLC 36**
See also CA 186; CAD; CD 5

Mathe, Albert
See Camus, Albert

Mather, Cotton 1663-1728 .... **LC 38**
See also AMWS 2; CDALB 1640-1865;
DLB 24, 30, 140; RGAL 4; TUS

Mather, Increase 1639-1723 .... **LC 38**
See also DLB 24

Matheson, Richard (Burton) 1926- .. **CLC 37**
See also AAYA 31; CA 97-100; CANR 88,
99; DLB 8, 44; HGG; INT 97-100; SCFW
2; SFW 4; SUFW 2

Mathews, Harry 1930- .... **CLC 6, 52**
See also CA 21-24R; CAAS 6; CANR 18,
40, 98; CN 7

Mathews, John Joseph 1894-1979 .. **CLC 84; NNAL**
See also CA 19-20; 142; CANR 45; CAP 2;
DAM MULT; DLB 175

Mathias, Roland (Glyn) 1915- .... **CLC 45**
See also CA 97-100; CANR 19, 41; CP 7;
DLB 27

Matsuo Basho 1644-1694 .... **LC 62; PC 3**
See Basho, Matsuo
See also DAM POET; PFS 2, 7

Mattheson, Rodney
See Creasey, John

Matthews, (James) Brander
1852-1929 .... **TCLC 95**
See also DLB 71, 78; DLBD 13

Matthews, Greg 1949- .... **CLC 45**
See also CA 135

Matthews, William (Procter III)
1942-1997 .... **CLC 40**
See also AMWS 9; CA 29-32R; 162; CAAS
18; CANR 12, 57; CP 7; DLB 5

Matthias, John (Edward) 1941- .... **CLC 9**
See also CA 33-36R; CANR 56; CP 7

Matthiessen, F(rancis) O(tto)
1902-1950 .... **TCLC 100**
See also CA 185; DLB 63

Meyer, Conrad Ferdinand
1825-1898 .... **NCLC 81**
See also DLB 129; EW; RGWL 2, 3
Meyer, Gustav 1868-1932
See Meyrink, Gustav
See also CA 117; 190
Meyer, June
See Jordan, June (Meyer)
Meyer, Lynn
See Slavitt, David R(ytman)
Meyers, Jeffrey 1939- .... **CLC 39**
See also CA 73-76; CAAE 186; CANR 54,
102; DLB 111
Meynell, Alice (Christina Gertrude
Thompson) 1847-1922 .... **TCLC 6**
See also CA 104; 177; DLB 19, 98; RGEL
2
Meyrink, Gustav .... **TCLC 21**
See Meyer, Gustav
See also DLB 81; EWL 3
Michaels, Leonard 1933-2003 ..... **CLC 6, 25;**
SSC 16
See also CA 61-64; 216; CANR 21, 62, 119;
CN 7; DLB 130; MTCW 1
Michaux, Henri 1899-1984 .... **CLC 8, 19**
See also CA 85-88; 114; DLB 258; EWL 3;
GFL 1789 to the Present; RGWL 2, 3
Micheaux, Oscar (Devereaux)
1884-1951 .... **TCLC 76**
See also BW 3; CA 174; DLB 50; TCWW
2
Michelangelo 1475-1564 .... **LC 12**
See also AAYA 43
Michelet, Jules 1798-1874 .... **NCLC 31**
See also EW 5; GFL 1789 to the Present
Michels, Robert 1876-1936 .... **TCLC 88**
See also CA 212
Michener, James A(lbert)
1907(?)-1997 .. **CLC 1, 5, 11, 29, 60, 109**
See also AAYA 27; AITN 1; BEST 90:1;
BPFB 2; CA 5-8R; 161; CANR 21, 45,
68; CN 7; CPW; DA3; DAM NOV, POP;
DLB 6; MTCW 1, 2; RHW
Mickiewicz, Adam 1798-1855 . **NCLC 3, 101;**
PC 38
See also EW 5; RGWL 2, 3
Middleton, (John) Christopher
1926- .... **CLC 13**
See also CA 13-16R; CANR 29, 54, 117;
CP 7; DLB 40
Middleton, Richard (Barham)
1882-1911 .... **TCLC 56**
See also CA 187; DLB 156; HGG
Middleton, Stanley 1919- .... **CLC 7, 38**
See also CA 25-28R; CAAS 23; CANR 21,
46, 81; CN 7; DLB 14
Middleton, Thomas 1580-1627 ...... **DC 5; LC**
33
See also BRW 2; DAM DRAM, MST; DFS
18; DLB 58; RGEL 2
Migueis, Jose Rodrigues 1901-1980 . **CLC 10**
See also DLB 287
Mikszath, Kalman 1847-1910 .... **TCLC 31**
See also CA 170
Miles, Jack .... **CLC 100**
See also CA 200
Miles, John Russiano
See Miles, Jack
Miles, Josephine (Louise)
1911-1985 .... **CLC 1, 2, 14, 34, 39**
See also CA 1-4R; 116; CANR 2, 55; DAM
POET; DLB 48
Militant
See Sandburg, Carl (August)
Mill, Harriet (Hardy) Taylor
1807-1858 .... **NCLC 102**
See also FW

Mill, John Stuart 1806-1873 .... **NCLC 11, 58**
See also CDBLB 1832-1890; DLB 55, 190,
262; FW 1; RGEL 2; TEA
Millar, Kenneth 1915-1983 .... **CLC 14**
See Macdonald, Ross
See also CA 9-12R; 110; CANR 16, 63,
107; CMW 4; CPW; DA3; DAM POP;
DLB 2, 226; DLBD 6; DLBY 1983;
MTCW 1, 2
Millay, E. Vincent
See Millay, Edna St. Vincent
Millay, Edna St. Vincent 1892-1950 .... **PC 6;**
TCLC 4, 49; WLCS
See Boyd, Nancy
See also AMW; CA 104; 130; CDALB
1917-1929; DA; DA3; DAB; DAC; DAM
MST, POET; DLB 45, 249; EWL 3;
EXPP; MAWW; MTCW 1, 2; PAB; PFS
3, 17; RGAL 4; TUS; WP
Miller, Arthur 1915- ...... **CLC 1, 2, 6, 10, 15,**
26, 47, 78, 179; DC 1; WLC
See also AAYA 15; AITN 1; AMW; AMWC
1; CA 1-4R; CABS 3; CAD; CANR 2,
30, 54, 76; CD 5; CDALB 1941-1968;
DA; DA3; DAB; DAC; DAM DRAM,
MST; DFS 1, 3, 8; DLB 7, 266; EWL 3;
LAIT 1, 4; LATS 1; MTCW 1, 2; RGAL
4; TUS; WYAS 1
Miller, Henry (Valentine)
1891-1980 .... **CLC 1, 2, 4, 9, 14, 43, 84;**
WLC
See also AMW; BPFB 2; CA 9-12R; 97-
100; CANR 33, 64; CDALB 1929-1941;
DA; DA3; DAB; DAC; DAM MST, NOV;
DLB 4, 9; DLBY 1980; EWL 3; MTCW
1, 2; RGAL 4; TUS
Miller, Jason 1939(?)-2001 .... **CLC 2**
See also AITN 1; CA 73-76; 197; CAD;
DFS 12; DLB 7
Miller, Sue 1943- .... **CLC 44**
See also AMWS 12; BEST 90:3; CA 139;
CANR 59, 91; DA3; DAM POP; DLB
143
Miller, Walter M(ichael, Jr.)
1923-1996 .... **CLC 4, 30**
See also BPFB 2; CA 85-88; CANR 108;
DLB 8; SCFW; SFW 4
Millett, Kate 1934- .... **CLC 67**
See also AITN 1; CA 73-76; CANR 32, 53,
76, 110; DA3; DLB 246; FW; GLL 1;
MTCW 1, 2
Millhauser, Steven (Lewis) 1943- .... **CLC 21,**
54, 109; SSC 57
See also CA 110; 111; CANR 63, 114; CN
7; DA3; DLB 2; FANT; INT CA-111;
MTCW 2
Millin, Sarah Gertrude 1889-1968 ... **CLC 49**
See also CA 102; 93-96; DLB 225; EWL 3
Milne, A(lan) A(lexander)
1882-1956 .... **TCLC 6, 88**
See also BRWS 5; CA 104; 133; CLR 1,
26; CMW 4; CWRI 5; DA3; DAB; DAC;
DAM MST; DLB 10, 77, 100, 160; FANT;
MAICYA 1, 2; MTCW 1, 2; RGEL 2;
SATA 100; WCH; YABC 1
Milner, Ron(ald) 1938- .... **BLC 3; CLC 56**
See also AITN 1; BW 1; CA 73-76; CAD;
CANR 24, 81; CD 5; DAM MULT; DLB
38; MTCW 1
Milnes, Richard Monckton
1809-1885 .... **NCLC 61**
See also DLB 32, 184
Milosz, Czeslaw 1911- ...... **CLC 5, 11, 22, 31,**
56, 82; PC 8; WLCS
See also CA 81-84; CANR 23, 51, 91; CD-
WLB 4; CWW 2; DA3; DAM MST,
POET; DLB 215; EW 13; EWL 3; MTCW
1, 2; PFS 16; RGWL 2, 3

Milton, John 1608-1674 ..... **LC 9, 43, 92; PC**
19, 29; WLC
See also BRW 2; BRWR 2; CDBLB 1660-
1789; DA; DA3; DAB; DAC; DAM MST,
POET; DLB 131, 151, 281; EFS 1; EXPP;
LAIT 1; PAB; PFS 3, 17; RGEL 2; TEA;
WLIT 3; WP
Min, Anchee 1957- .... **CLC 86**
See also CA 146; CANR 94
Minehaha, Cornelius
See Wedekind, (Benjamin) Frank(lin)
Miner, Valerie 1947- .... **CLC 40**
See also CA 97-100; CANR 59; FW; GLL
2
Minimo, Duca
See D'Annunzio, Gabriele
Minot, Susan 1956- .... **CLC 44, 159**
See also AMWS 6; CA 134; CANR 118;
CN 7
Minus, Ed 1938- .... **CLC 39**
See also CA 185
Mirabai 1498(?)-1550(?) .... **PC 48**
Miranda, Javier
See Bioy Casares, Adolfo
See also CWW 2
Mirbeau, Octave 1848-1917 .... **TCLC 55**
See also CA 216; DLB 123, 192; GFL 1789
to the Present
Mirikitani, Janice 1942- .... **AAL**
See also CA 211; RGAL 4
Miro (Ferrer), Gabriel (Francisco Victor)
1879-1930 .... **TCLC 5**
See also CA 104; 185; EWL 3
Misharin, Alexandr .... **CLC 59**
Mishima, Yukio ... **CLC 2, 4, 6, 9, 27; DC 1;**
SSC 4
See Hiraoka, Kimitake
See also AAYA 50; BPFB 2; GLL 1; MJW;
MTCW 2; RGSF 2; RGWL 2, 3; SSFS 5,
12
Mistral, Frederic 1830-1914 .... **TCLC 51**
See also CA 122; 213; GFL 1789 to the
Present
Mistral, Gabriela
See Godoy Alcayaga, Lucila
See also DLB 283; DNFS 1; EWL 3; LAW;
RGWL 2, 3; WP
Mistry, Rohinton 1952- .... **CLC 71**
See also CA 141; CANR 86, 114; CCA 1;
CN 7; DAC; SSFS 6
Mitchell, Clyde
See Ellison, Harlan (Jay)
Mitchell, Emerson Blackhorse Barney
1945- .... **NNAL**
See also CA 45-48
Mitchell, James Leslie 1901-1935
See Gibbon, Lewis Grassic
See also CA 104; 188; DLB 15
Mitchell, Joni 1943- .... **CLC 12**
See also CA 112; CCA 1
Mitchell, Joseph (Quincy)
1908-1996 .... **CLC 98**
See also CA 77-80; 152; CANR 69; CN 7;
CSW; DLB 185; DLBY 1996
Mitchell, Margaret (Munnerlyn)
1900-1949 .... **TCLC 11**
See also AAYA 23; BPFB 2; BYA 1; CA
109; 125; CANR 55, 94; CDALBS; DA3;
DAM NOV, POP; DLB 9; LAIT 2;
MTCW 1, 2; NFS 9; RGAL 4; RHW;
TUS; WYAS 1; YAW
Mitchell, Peggy
See Mitchell, Margaret (Munnerlyn)
Mitchell, S(ilas) Weir 1829-1914 .... **TCLC 36**
See also CA 165; DLB 202; RGAL 4
Mitchell, W(illiam) O(rmond)
1914-1998 .... **CLC 25**
See also CA 77-80; 165; CANR 15, 43; CN
7; DAC; DAM MST; DLB 88

Mitchell, William (Lendrum)
1879-1936 .... **TCLC 81**
See also CA 213
Mitford, Mary Russell 1787-1855 ... **NCLC 4**
See also DLB 110, 116; RGEL 2
Mitford, Nancy 1904-1973 .... **CLC 44**
See also CA 9-12R; DLB 191; RGEL 2
Miyamoto, (Chujo) Yuriko
1899-1951 .... **TCLC 37**
See Miyamoto Yuriko
See also CA 170, 174
Miyamoto Yuriko
See Miyamoto, (Chujo) Yuriko
See also DLB 180
Miyazawa, Kenji 1896-1933 .... **TCLC 76**
See Miyazawa Kenji
See also CA 157; RGWL 3
Miyazawa Kenji
See Miyazawa, Kenji
See also EWL 3
Mizoguchi, Kenji 1898-1956 .... **TCLC 72**
See also CA 167
Mo, Timothy (Peter) 1950(?)- ... **CLC 46, 134**
See also CA 117; CN 7; DLB 194; MTCW 1; WLIT 4
Modarressi, Taghi (M.) 1931-1997 ... **CLC 44**
See also CA 121; 134; INT 134
Modiano, Patrick (Jean) 1945- .... **CLC 18**
See also CA 85-88; CANR 17, 40, 115; CWW 2; DLB 83; EWL 3
Mofolo, Thomas (Mokopu)
1875(?)-1948 .... **BLC 3; TCLC 22**
See also AFW; CA 121; 153; CANR 83; DAM MULT; DLB 225; EWL 3; MTCW 2; WLIT 2
Mohr, Nicholasa 1938- .... **CLC 12; HLC 2**
See also AAYA 8, 46; CA 49-52; CANR 1, 32, 64; CLR 22; DAM MULT; DLB 145; HW 1, 2; JRDA; LAIT 5; MAICYA 2; MAICYAS 1; RGAL 4; SAAS 8; SATA 8, 97; SATA-Essay 113; WYA; YAW
Moi, Toril 1953- .... **CLC 172**
See also CA 154; CANR 102; FW
Mojtabai, A(nn) G(race) 1938- ..... **CLC 5, 9, 15, 29**
See also CA 85-88; CANR 88
Moliere 1622-1673 ..... **DC 13; LC 10, 28, 64; WLC**
See also DA; DA3; DAB; DAC; DAM DRAM, MST; DFS 13, 18; DLB 268; EW 3; GFL Beginnings to 1789; LATS 1; RGWL 2, 3; TWA
Molin, Charles
See Mayne, William (James Carter)
Molnar, Ferenc 1878-1952 .... **TCLC 20**
See also CA 109; 153; CANR 83; CDWLB 4; DAM DRAM; DLB 215; EWL 3; RGWL 2, 3
Momaday, N(avarre) Scott 1934- ...... **CLC 2, 19, 85, 95, 160; NNAL; PC 25; WLCS**
See also AAYA 11; AMWS 4; ANW; BPFB 2; CA 25-28R; CANR 14, 34, 68; CDALBS; CN 7; CPW; DA; DA3; DAB; DAC; DAM MST, MULT, NOV, POP; DLB 143, 175, 256; EWL 3; EXPP; INT CANR-14; LAIT 4; LATS 1; MTCW 1, 2; NFS 10; PFS 2, 11; RGAL 4; SATA 48; SATA-Brief 30; WP; YAW
Monette, Paul 1945-1995 .... **CLC 82**
See also AMWS 10; CA 139; 147; CN 7; GLL 1
Monroe, Harriet 1860-1936 .... **TCLC 12**
See also CA 109; 204; DLB 54, 91
Monroe, Lyle
See Heinlein, Robert A(nson)
Montagu, Elizabeth 1720-1800 .... **NCLC 7, 117**
See also FW

Montagu, Mary (Pierrepont) Wortley
1689-1762 .... **LC 9, 57; PC 16**
See also DLB 95, 101; RGEL 2
Montagu, W. H.
See Coleridge, Samuel Taylor
Montague, John (Patrick) 1929- ..... **CLC 13, 46**
See also CA 9-12R; CANR 9, 69, 121; CP 7; DLB 40; EWL 3; MTCW 1; PFS 12; RGEL 2
Montaigne, Michel (Eyquem) de
1533-1592 .... **LC 8; WLC**
See also DA; DAB; DAC; DAM MST; EW 2; GFL Beginnings to 1789; LMFS 1; RGWL 2, 3; TWA
Montale, Eugenio 1896-1981 ... **CLC 7, 9, 18; PC 13**
See also CA 17-20R; 104; CANR 30; DLB 114; EW 11; EWL 3; MTCW 1; RGWL 2, 3; TWA
Montesquieu, Charles-Louis de Secondat
1689-1755 .... **LC 7, 69**
See also EW 3; GFL Beginnings to 1789; TWA
Montessori, Maria 1870-1952 ...... **TCLC 103**
See also CA 115; 147
Montgomery, (Robert) Bruce 1921(?)-1978
See Crispin, Edmund
See also CA 179; 104; CMW 4
Montgomery, L(ucy) M(aud)
1874-1942 .... **TCLC 51, 140**
See also AAYA 12; BYA 1; CA 108; 137; CLR 8, 91; DA3; DAC; DAM MST; DLB 92; DLBD 14; JRDA; MAICYA 1, 2; MTCW 2; RGEL 2; SATA 100; TWA; WCH; WYA; YABC 1
Montgomery, Marion H., Jr. 1925- .... **CLC 7**
See also AITN 1; CA 1-4R; CANR 3, 48; CSW; DLB 6
Montgomery, Max
See Davenport, Guy (Mattison, Jr.)
Montherlant, Henry (Milon) de
1896-1972 .... **CLC 8, 19**
See also CA 85-88; 37-40R; DAM DRAM; DLB 72; EW 11; EWL 3; GFL 1789 to the Present; MTCW 1
Monty Python
See Chapman, Graham; Cleese, John (Marwood); Gilliam, Terry (Vance); Idle, Eric; Jones, Terence Graham Parry; Palin, Michael (Edward)
See also AAYA 7
Moodie, Susanna (Strickland)
1803-1885 .... **NCLC 14, 113**
See also DLB 99
Moody, Hiram (F. III) 1961-
See Moody, Rick
See also CA 138; CANR 64, 112
Moody, Minerva
See Alcott, Louisa May
Moody, Rick .... **CLC 147**
See Moody, Hiram (F. III)
Moody, William Vaughan
1869-1910 .... **TCLC 105**
See also CA 110; 178; DLB 7, 54; RGAL 4
Mooney, Edward 1951-
See Mooney, Ted
See also CA 130
Mooney, Ted .... **CLC 25**
See Mooney, Edward
Moorcock, Michael (John) 1939- ..... **CLC 5, 27, 58**
See Bradbury, Edward P.
See also AAYA 26; CA 45-48; CAAS 5; CANR 2, 17, 38, 64, 122; CN 7; DLB 14, 231, 261; FANT; MTCW 1, 2; SATA 93; SCFW 2; SFW 4; SUFW 1, 2

Moore, Brian 1921-1999 ... **CLC 1, 3, 5, 7, 8, 19, 32, 90**
See Bryan, Michael
See also BRWS 9; CA 1-4R; 174; CANR 1, 25, 42, 63; CCA 1; CN 7; DAB; DAC; DAM MST; DLB 251; EWL 3; FANT; MTCW 1, 2; RGEL 2
Moore, Edward
See Muir, Edwin
See also RGEL 2
Moore, G. E. 1873-1958 .... **TCLC 89**
See also DLB 262
Moore, George Augustus
1852-1933 .... **SSC 19; TCLC 7**
See also BRW 6; CA 104; 177; DLB 10, 18, 57, 135; EWL 3; RGEL 2; RGSF 2
Moore, Lorrie .... **CLC 39, 45, 68**
See Moore, Marie Lorena
See also AMWS 10; DLB 234
Moore, Marianne (Craig)
1887-1972 .... **CLC 1, 2, 4, 8, 10, 13, 19, 47; PC 4, 49; WLCS**
See also AMW; CA 1-4R; 33-36R; CANR 3, 61; CDALB 1929-1941; DA; DA3; DAB; DAC; DAM MST, POET; DLB 45; DLBD 7; EWL 3; EXPP; MAWW; MTCW 1, 2; PAB; PFS 14, 17; RGAL 4; SATA 20; TUS; WP
Moore, Marie Lorena 1957- .... **CLC 165**
See Moore, Lorrie
See also CA 116; CANR 39, 83; CN 7; DLB 234
Moore, Thomas 1779-1852 .... **NCLC 6, 110**
See also DLB 96, 144; RGEL 2
Moorhouse, Frank 1938- .... **SSC 40**
See also CA 118; CANR 92; CN 7; DLB 289; RGSF 2
Mora, Pat(ricia) 1942- .... **HLC 2**
See also AMWS 13; CA 129; CANR 57, 81, 112; CLR 58; DAM MULT; DLB 209; HW 1, 2; MAICYA 2; SATA 92, 134
Moraga, Cherrie 1952- .... **CLC 126**
See also CA 131; CANR 66; DAM MULT; DLB 82, 249; FW; GLL 1; HW 1, 2
Morand, Paul 1888-1976 .... **CLC 41; SSC 22**
See also CA 184; 69-72; DLB 65; EWL 3
Morante, Elsa 1918-1985 .... **CLC 8, 47**
See also CA 85-88; 117; CANR 35; DLB 177; EWL 3; MTCW 1, 2; RGWL 2, 3
Moravia, Alberto .... **CLC 2, 7, 11, 27, 46; SSC 26**
See Pincherle, Alberto
See also DLB 177; EW 12; EWL 3; MTCW 2; RGSF 2; RGWL 2, 3
More, Hannah 1745-1833 .... **NCLC 27**
See also DLB 107, 109, 116, 158; RGEL 2
More, Henry 1614-1687 .... **LC 9**
See also DLB 126, 252
More, Sir Thomas 1478(?)-1535 .... **LC 10, 32**
See also BRWC 1; BRWS 7; DLB 136, 281; LMFS 1; RGEL 2; TEA
Moreas, Jean .... **TCLC 18**
See Papadiamantopoulos, Johannes
See also GFL 1789 to the Present
Moreton, Andrew Esq.
See Defoe, Daniel
Morgan, Berry 1919-2002 .... **CLC 6**
See also CA 49-52; 208; DLB 6
Morgan, Claire
See Highsmith, (Mary) Patricia
See also GLL 1
Morgan, Edwin (George) 1920- .... **CLC 31**
See also BRWS 9; CA 5-8R; CANR 3, 43, 90; CP 7; DLB 27
Morgan, (George) Frederick 1922- .. **CLC 23**
See also CA 17-20R; CANR 21; CP 7
Morgan, Harriet
See Mencken, H(enry) L(ouis)

Morgan, Jane
See Cooper, James Fenimore
Morgan, Janet 1945- .... **CLC 39**
See also CA 65-68
Morgan, Lady 1776(?)-1859 .... **NCLC 29**
See also DLB 116, 158; RGEL 2
Morgan, Robin (Evonne) 1941- .... **CLC 2**
See also CA 69-72; CANR 29, 68; FW;
GLL 2; MTCW 1; SATA 80
Morgan, Scott
See Kuttner, Henry
Morgan, Seth 1949(?)-1990 .... **CLC 65**
See also CA 185; 132
**Morgenstern, Christian (Otto Josef
Wolfgang)** 1871-1914 .... **TCLC 8**
See also CA 105; 191; EWL 3
Morgenstern, S.
See Goldman, William (W.)
Mori, Rintaro
See Mori Ogai
See also CA 110
Moricz, Zsigmond 1879-1942 .... **TCLC 33**
See also CA 165; DLB 215; EWL 3
Morike, Eduard (Friedrich)
1804-1875 .... **NCLC 10**
See also DLB 133; RGWL 2, 3
Mori Ogai 1862-1922 .... **TCLC 14**
See Ogai
See also CA 164; DLB 180; EWL 3; RGWL
3; TWA
Moritz, Karl Philipp 1756-1793 .... **LC 2**
See also DLB 94
Morland, Peter Henry
See Faust, Frederick (Schiller)
Morley, Christopher (Darlington)
1890-1957 .... **TCLC 87**
See also CA 112; DLB 9; RGAL 4
Morren, Theophil
See Hofmannsthal, Hugo von
Morris, Bill 1952- .... **CLC 76**
Morris, Julian
See West, Morris L(anglo)
Morris, Steveland Judkins 1950(?)-
See Wonder, Stevie
See also CA 111
Morris, William 1834-1896 .... **NCLC 4**
See also BRW 5; CDBLB 1832-1890; DLB
18, 35, 57, 156, 178, 184; FANT; RGEL
2; SFW 4; SUFW
Morris, Wright 1910-1998 .. **CLC 1, 3, 7, 18,
37; TCLC 107**
See also AMW; CA 9-12R; 167; CANR 21,
81; CN 7; DLB 2, 206, 218; DLBY 1981;
EWL 3; MTCW 1, 2; RGAL 4; TCWW 2
Morrison, Arthur 1863-1945 .... **SSC 40;
TCLC 72**
See also CA 120; 157; CMW 4; DLB 70,
135, 197; RGEL 2
Morrison, James Douglas 1943-1971
See Morrison, Jim
See also CA 73-76; CANR 40
Morrison, Jim .... **CLC 17**
See Morrison, James Douglas
Morrison, Toni 1931- ..... **BLC 3; CLC 4, 10,
22, 55, 81, 87, 173**
See also AAYA 1, 22; AFAW 1, 2; AMWC
1; AMWS 3; BPFB 2; BW 2, 3; CA 29-
32R; CANR 27, 42, 67, 113; CDALB
1968-1988; CN 7; CPW; DA; DA3; DAB;
DAC; DAM MST, MULT, NOV, POP;
DLB 6, 33, 143; DLBY 1981; EWL 3;
EXPN; FW; LAIT 2, 4; LATS 1; LMFS
2; MAWW; MTCW 1, 2; NFS 1, 6, 8, 14;
RGAL 4; RHW; SATA 57, 144; SSFS 5;
TUS; YAW
Morrison, Van 1945- .... **CLC 21**
See also CA 116; 168
Morrissy, Mary 1957- .... **CLC 99**
See also CA 205; DLB 267

Mortimer, John (Clifford) 1923- ..... **CLC 28,
43**
See also CA 13-16R; CANR 21, 69, 109;
CD 5; CDBLB 1960 to Present; CMW 4;
CN 7; CPW; DA3; DAM DRAM, POP;
DLB 13, 245, 271; INT CANR-21; MSW;
MTCW 1, 2; RGEL 2
Mortimer, Penelope (Ruth)
1918-1999 .... **CLC 5**
See also CA 57-60; 187; CANR 45, 88; CN
7
Mortimer, Sir John
See Mortimer, John (Clifford)
Morton, Anthony
See Creasey, John
Morton, Thomas 1579(?)-1647(?) .... **LC 72**
See also DLB 24; RGEL 2
Mosca, Gaetano 1858-1941 .... **TCLC 75**
Moses, Daniel David 1952- .... **NNAL**
See also CA 186
Mosher, Howard Frank 1943- .... **CLC 62**
See also CA 139; CANR 65, 115
Mosley, Nicholas 1923- .... **CLC 43, 70**
See also CA 69-72; CANR 41, 60, 108; CN
7; DLB 14, 207
Mosley, Walter 1952- .... **BLCS; CLC 97**
See also AAYA 17; AMWS 13; BPFB 2;
BW 2; CA 142; CANR 57, 92; CMW 4;
CPW; DA3; DAM MULT, POP; MSW;
MTCW 2
Moss, Howard 1922-1987 . **CLC 7, 14, 45, 50**
See also CA 1-4R; 123; CANR 1, 44; DAM
POET; DLB 5
Mossgiel, Rab
See Burns, Robert
Motion, Andrew (Peter) 1952- .... **CLC 47**
See also BRWS 7; CA 146; CANR 90; CP
7; DLB 40
Motley, Willard (Francis)
1909-1965 .... **CLC 18**
See also BW 1; CA 117; 106; CANR 88;
DLB 76, 143
Motoori, Norinaga 1730-1801 .... **NCLC 45**
Mott, Michael (Charles Alston)
1930- .... **CLC 15, 34**
See also CA 5-8R; CAAS 7; CANR 7, 29
Mountain Wolf Woman 1884-1960 . **CLC 92;
NNAL**
See also CA 144; CANR 90
Moure, Erin 1955- .... **CLC 88**
See also CA 113; CP 7; CWP; DLB 60
Mourning Dove 1885(?)-1936 .... **NNAL**
See also CA 144; CANR 90; DAM MULT;
DLB 175, 221
Mowat, Farley (McGill) 1921- .... **CLC 26**
See also AAYA 1, 50; BYA 2; CA 1-4R;
CANR 4, 24, 42, 68, 108; CLR 20; CPW;
DAC; DAM MST; DLB 68; INT CANR-
24; JRDA; MAICYA 1, 2; MTCW 1, 2;
SATA 3, 55; YAW
Mowatt, Anna Cora 1819-1870 ..... **NCLC 74**
See also RGAL 4
Moyers, Bill 1934- .... **CLC 74**
See also AITN 2; CA 61-64; CANR 31, 52
Mphahlele, Es'kia
See Mphahlele, Ezekiel
See also AFW; CDWLB 3; DLB 125, 225;
RGSF 2; SSFS 11
Mphahlele, Ezekiel 1919- ... **BLC 3; CLC 25,
133**
See Mphahlele, Es'kia
See also BW 2, 3; CA 81-84; CANR 26,
76; CN 7; DA3; DAM MULT; EWL 3;
MTCW 2; SATA 119
Mqhayi, S(amuel) E(dward) K(rune Loliwe)
1875-1945 .... **BLC 3; TCLC 25**
See also CA 153; CANR 87; DAM MULT

Mrozek, Slawomir 1930- .... **CLC 3, 13**
See also CA 13-16R; CAAS 10; CANR 29;
CDWLB 4; CWW 2; DLB 232; EWL 3;
MTCW 1
Mrs. Belloc-Lowndes
See Lowndes, Marie Adelaide (Belloc)
Mrs. Fairstar
See Horne, Richard Henry Hengist
M'Taggart, John M'Taggart Ellis
See McTaggart, John McTaggart Ellis
Mtwa, Percy (?)- .... **CLC 47**
Mueller, Lisel 1924- .... **CLC 13, 51; PC 33**
See also CA 93-96; CP 7; DLB 105; PFS 9,
13
Muggeridge, Malcolm (Thomas)
1903-1990 .... **TCLC 120**
See also AITN 1; CA 101; CANR 33, 63;
MTCW 1, 2
Muhammad 570-632 .... **WLCS**
See also DA; DAB; DAC; DAM MST
Muir, Edwin 1887-1959 . **PC 49; TCLC 2, 87**
See Moore, Edward
See also BRWS 6; CA 104; 193; DLB 20,
100, 191; EWL 3; RGEL 2
Muir, John 1838-1914 .... **TCLC 28**
See also AMWS 9; ANW; CA 165; DLB
186, 275
Mujica Lainez, Manuel 1910-1984 ... **CLC 31**
See Lainez, Manuel Mujica
See also CA 81-84; 112; CANR 32; EWL
3; HW 1
Mukherjee, Bharati 1940- ..... **AAL; CLC 53,
115; SSC 38**
See also AAYA 46; BEST 89:2; CA 107;
CANR 45, 72; CN 7; DAM NOV; DLB
60, 218; DNFS 1, 2; EWL 3; FW; MTCW
1, 2; RGAL 4; RGSF 2; SSFS 7; TUS
Muldoon, Paul 1951- .... **CLC 32, 72, 166**
See also BRWS 4; CA 113; 129; CANR 52,
91; CP 7; DAM POET; DLB 40; INT 129;
PFS 7
Mulisch, Harry 1927- .... **CLC 42**
See also CA 9-12R; CANR 6, 26, 56, 110;
EWL 3
Mull, Martin 1943- .... **CLC 17**
See also CA 105
Muller, Wilhelm .... **NCLC 73**
Mulock, Dinah Maria
See Craik, Dinah Maria (Mulock)
See also RGEL 2
Munday, Anthony 1560-1633 .... **LC 87**
See also DLB 62, 172; RGEL 2
Munford, Robert 1737(?)-1783 .... **LC 5**
See also DLB 31
Mungo, Raymond 1946- .... **CLC 72**
See also CA 49-52; CANR 2
Munro, Alice 1931- .... **CLC 6, 10, 19, 50, 95;
SSC 3; WLCS**
See also AITN 2; BPFB 2; CA 33-36R;
CANR 33, 53, 75, 114; CCA 1; CN 7;
DA3; DAC; DAM MST, NOV; DLB 53;
EWL 3; MTCW 1, 2; RGEL 2; RGSF 2;
SATA 29; SSFS 5, 13
Munro, H(ector) H(ugh) 1870-1916 .... **WLC**
See Saki
See also AAYA 53; CA 104; 130; CANR
104; CDBLB 1890-1914; DA; DA3;
DAB; DAC; DAM MST, NOV; DLB 34,
162; EXPS; MTCW 1, 2; RGEL 2; SSFS
15
Murakami, Haruki 1949- .... **CLC 150**
See Murakami Haruki
See also CA 165; CANR 102; MJW; RGWL
3; SFW 4
Murakami Haruki
See Murakami, Haruki
See also DLB 182; EWL 3
Murasaki, Lady
See Murasaki Shikibu

Newton, (Sir) Isaac 1642-1727 ...... **LC 35, 53**
  See also DLB 252

Newton, Suzanne 1936- .... **CLC 35**
  See also BYA 7; CA 41-44R; CANR 14;
  JRDA; SATA 5, 77

New York Dept. of Ed. .... **CLC 70**

Nexo, Martin Andersen
  1869-1954 .... **TCLC 43**
  See also CA 202; DLB 214; EWL 3

Nezval, Vitezslav 1900-1958 .... **TCLC 44**
  See also CA 123; CDWLB 4; DLB 215;
  EWL 3

Ng, Fae Myenne 1957(?)- .... **CLC 81**
  See also CA 146

Ngema, Mbongeni 1955- .... **CLC 57**
  See also BW 2; CA 143; CANR 84; CD 5

Ngugi, James T(hiong'o) .... **CLC 3, 7, 13**
  See Ngugi wa Thiong'o

Ngugi wa Thiong'o
  See Ngugi wa Thiong'o
  See also DLB 125; EWL 3

Ngugi wa Thiong'o 1938- .... **BLC 3; CLC 36**
  See Ngugi, James T(hiong'o); Ngugi wa
  Thiong'o
  See also AFW; BRWS 8; BW 2; CA 81-84;
  CANR 27, 58; CDWLB 3; DAM MULT,
  NOV; DNFS 2; MTCW 1, 2; RGEL 2

Niatum, Duane 1938- .... **NNAL**
  See also CA 41-44R; CANR 21, 45, 83;
  DLB 175

Nichol, B(arrie) P(hillip) 1944-1988 . **CLC 18**
  See also CA 53-56; DLB 53; SATA 66

Nicholas of Cusa 1401-1464 .... **LC 80**
  See also DLB 115

Nichols, John (Treadwell) 1940- .... **CLC 38**
  See also AMWS 13; CA 9-12R; CAAE 190;
  CAAS 2; CANR 6, 70, 121; DLBY 1982;
  LATS 1; TCWW 2

Nichols, Leigh
  See Koontz, Dean R(ay)

Nichols, Peter (Richard) 1927- .... **CLC 5, 36, 65**
  See also CA 104; CANR 33, 86; CBD; CD
  5; DLB 13, 245; MTCW 1

Nicholson, Linda ed. .... **CLC 65**

Ni Chuilleanain, Eilean 1942- .... **PC 34**
  See also CA 126; CANR 53, 83; CP 7;
  CWP; DLB 40

Nicolas, F. R. E.
  See Freeling, Nicolas

Niedecker, Lorine 1903-1970 ..... **CLC 10, 42; PC 42**
  See also CA 25-28; CAP 2; DAM POET;
  DLB 48

Nietzsche, Friedrich (Wilhelm)
  1844-1900 .... **TCLC 10, 18, 55**
  See also CA 107; 121; CDWLB 2; DLB
  129; EW 7; RGWL 2, 3; TWA

Nievo, Ippolito 1831-1861 .... **NCLC 22**

Nightingale, Anne Redmon 1943-
  See Redmon, Anne
  See also CA 103

Nightingale, Florence 1820-1910 ... **TCLC 85**
  See also CA 188; DLB 166

Nijo Yoshimoto 1320-1388 .... **CMLC 49**
  See also DLB 203

Nik. T. O.
  See Annensky, Innokenty (Fyodorovich)

Nin, Anais 1903-1977 ..... **CLC 1, 4, 8, 11, 14, 60, 127; SSC 10**
  See also AITN 2; AMWS 10; BPFB 2; CA
  13-16R; 69-72; CANR 22, 53; DAM
  NOV, POP; DLB 2, 4, 152; EWL 3; GLL
  2; MAWW; MTCW 1, 2; RGAL 4; RGSF
  2

Nisbet, Robert A(lexander)
  1913-1996 .... **TCLC 117**
  See also CA 25-28R; 153; CANR 17; INT
  CANR-17

Nishida, Kitaro 1870-1945 .... **TCLC 83**

Nishiwaki, Junzaburo
  See Nishiwaki, Junzaburo
  See also CA 194

Nishiwaki, Junzaburo 1894-1982 .... **PC 15**
  See Nishiwaki, Junzaburo; Nishiwaki
  Junzaburo
  See also CA 194; 107; MJW; RGWL 3

Nishiwaki Junzaburo
  See Nishiwaki, Junzaburo
  See also EWL 3

Nissenson, Hugh 1933- .... **CLC 4, 9**
  See also CA 17-20R; CANR 27, 108; CN
  7; DLB 28

Nister, Der
  See Der Nister
  See also EWL 3

Niven, Larry .... **CLC 8**
  See Niven, Laurence Van Cott
  See also AAYA 27; BPFB 2; BYA 10;
  CAAE 207; DLB 8; SCFW 2

Niven, Laurence Van Cott 1938-
  See Niven, Larry
  See also CA 21-24R; CAAE 207; CAAS
  12; CANR 14, 44, 66, 113; CPW; DAM
  POP; MTCW 1, 2; SATA 95; SFW 4

Nixon, Agnes Eckhardt 1927- .... **CLC 21**
  See also CA 110

Nizan, Paul 1905-1940 .... **TCLC 40**
  See also CA 161; DLB 72; EWL 3; GFL
  1789 to the Present

Nkosi, Lewis 1936- .... **BLC 3; CLC 45**
  See also BW 1, 3; CA 65-68; CANR 27,
  81; CBD; CD 5; DAM MULT; DLB 157,
  225

Nodier, (Jean) Charles (Emmanuel)
  1780-1844 .... **NCLC 19**
  See also DLB 119; GFL 1789 to the Present

Noguchi, Yone 1875-1947 .... **TCLC 80**

Nolan, Christopher 1965- .... **CLC 58**
  See also CA 111; CANR 88

Noon, Jeff 1957- .... **CLC 91**
  See also CA 148; CANR 83; DLB 267;
  SFW 4

Norden, Charles
  See Durrell, Lawrence (George)

Nordhoff, Charles Bernard
  1887-1947 .... **TCLC 23**
  See also CA 108; 211; DLB 9; LAIT 1;
  RHW 1; SATA 23

Norfolk, Lawrence 1963- .... **CLC 76**
  See also CA 144; CANR 85; CN 7; DLB
  267

Norman, Marsha 1947- .... **CLC 28; DC 8**
  See also CA 105; CABS 3; CAD; CANR
  41; CD 5; CSW; CWD; DAM DRAM;
  DFS 2; DLB 266; DLBY 1984; FW

Normyx
  See Douglas, (George) Norman

Norris, (Benjamin) Frank(lin, Jr.)
  1870-1902 .... **SSC 28; TCLC 24**
  See also AMW; AMWC 2; BPFB 2; CA
  110; 160; CDALB 1865-1917; DLB 12,
  71, 186; LMFS 2; NFS 12; RGAL 4;
  TCWW 2; TUS

Norris, Leslie 1921- .... **CLC 14**
  See also CA 11-12; CANR 14, 117; CAP 1;
  CP 7; DLB 27, 256

North, Andrew
  See Norton, Andre

North, Anthony
  See Koontz, Dean R(ay)

North, Captain George
  See Stevenson, Robert Louis (Balfour)

North, Captain George
  See Stevenson, Robert Louis (Balfour)

North, Milou
  See Erdrich, Louise

Northrup, B. A.
  See Hubbard, L(afayette) Ron(ald)

North Staffs
  See Hulme, T(homas) E(rnest)

Northup, Solomon 1808-1863 ...... **NCLC 105**

Norton, Alice Mary
  See Norton, Andre
  See also MAICYA 1; SATA 1, 43

Norton, Andre 1912- .... **CLC 12**
  See Norton, Alice Mary
  See also AAYA 14; BPFB 2; BYA 4, 10,
  12; CA 1-4R; CANR 68; CLR 50; DLB
  8, 52; JRDA; MAICYA 2; MTCW 1;
  SATA 91; SUFW 1, 2; YAW

Norton, Caroline 1808-1877 .... **NCLC 47**
  See also DLB 21, 159, 199

Norway, Nevil Shute 1899-1960
  See Shute, Nevil
  See also CA 102; 93-96; CANR 85; MTCW
  2

Norwid, Cyprian Kamil
  1821-1883 .... **NCLC 17**
  See also RGWL 3

Nosille, Nabrah
  See Ellison, Harlan (Jay)

Nossack, Hans Erich 1901-1978 .... **CLC 6**
  See also CA 93-96; 85-88; DLB 69; EWL 3

Nostradamus 1503-1566 .... **LC 27**

Nosu, Chuji
  See Ozu, Yasujiro

Notenburg, Eleanora (Genrikhovna) von
  See Guro, Elena

Nova, Craig 1945- .... **CLC 7, 31**
  See also CA 45-48; CANR 2, 53

Novak, Joseph
  See Kosinski, Jerzy (Nikodem)

Novalis 1772-1801 .... **NCLC 13**
  See also CDWLB 2; DLB 90; EW 5; RGWL
  2, 3

Novick, Peter 1934- .... **CLC 164**
  See also CA 188

Novis, Emile
  See Weil, Simone (Adolphine)

Nowlan, Alden (Albert) 1933-1983 ... **CLC 15**
  See also CA 9-12R; CANR 5; DAC; DAM
  MST; DLB 53; PFS 12

Noyes, Alfred 1880-1958 ...... **PC 27; TCLC 7**
  See also CA 104; 188; DLB 20; EXPP;
  FANT; PFS 4; RGEL 2

Nugent, Richard Bruce 1906(?)-1987 ... **HR 3**
  See also BW 1; CA 125; DLB 51; GLL 2

Nunn, Kem .... **CLC 34**
  See also CA 159

Nwapa, Flora (Nwanzuruaha)
  1931-1993 .... **BLCS; CLC 133**
  See also BW 2; CA 143; CANR 83; CD-
  WLB 3; CWRI 5; DLB 125; EWL 3;
  WLIT 2

Nye, Robert 1939- .... **CLC 13, 42**
  See also CA 33-36R; CANR 29, 67, 107;
  CN 7; CP 7; CWRI 5; DAM NOV; DLB
  14, 271; FANT; HGG; MTCW 1; RHW;
  SATA 6

Nyro, Laura 1947-1997 .... **CLC 17**
  See also CA 194

Oates, Joyce Carol 1938- .. **CLC 1, 2, 3, 6, 9, 11, 15, 19, 33, 52, 108, 134; SSC 6; WLC**
  See also AAYA 15, 52; AITN 1; AMWS 2;
  BEST 89:2; BPFB 2; BYA 11; CA 5-8R;
  CANR 25, 45, 74, 113, 113; CDALB
  1968-1988; CN 7; CP 7; CPW; CWP; DA;
  DA3; DAB; DAC; DAM MST, NOV,
  POP; DLB 2, 5, 130; DLBY 1981; EWL
  3; EXPS; FW; HGG; INT CANR-25;
  LAIT 4; MAWW; MTCW 1, 2; NFS 8;
  RGAL 4; RGSF 2; SSFS 17; SUFW 2;
  TUS

Ophuls, Max 1902-1957 .... **TCLC 79**
See also CA 113

Opie, Amelia 1769-1853 .... **NCLC 65**
See also DLB 116, 159; RGEL 2

Oppen, George 1908-1984 ..... **CLC 7, 13, 34; PC 35; TCLC 107**
See also CA 13-16R; 113; CANR 8, 82; DLB 5, 165

Oppenheim, E(dward) Phillips 1866-1946 .... **TCLC 45**
See also CA 111; 202; CMW 4; DLB 70

Opuls, Max
See Ophuls, Max

Origen c. 185-c. 254 .... **CMLC 19**

Orlovitz, Gil 1918-1973 .... **CLC 22**
See also CA 77-80; 45-48; DLB 2, 5

Orris
See Ingelow, Jean

Ortega y Gasset, Jose 1883-1955 ...... **HLC 2; TCLC 9**
See also CA 106; 130; DAM MULT; EW 9; EWL 3; HW 1, 2; MTCW 1, 2

Ortese, Anna Maria 1914-1998 .... **CLC 89**
See also DLB 177; EWL 3

Ortiz, Simon J(oseph) 1941- .... **CLC 45; NNAL; PC 17**
See also AMWS 4; CA 134; CANR 69, 118; CP 7; DAM MULT, POET; DLB 120, 175, 256; EXPP; PFS 4, 16; RGAL 4

Orton, Joe .... **CLC 4, 13, 43; DC 3**
See Orton, John Kingsley
See also BRWS 5; CBD; CDBLB 1960 to Present; DFS 3, 6; DLB 13; GLL 1; MTCW 2; RGEL 2; TEA; WLIT 4

Orton, John Kingsley 1933-1967
See Orton, Joe
See also CA 85-88; CANR 35, 66; DAM DRAM; MTCW 1, 2

Orwell, George . **TCLC 2, 6, 15, 31, 51, 128, 129; WLC**
See Blair, Eric (Arthur)
See also BPFB 3; BRW 7; BYA 5; CDBLB 1945-1960; CLR 68; DAB; DLB 15, 98, 195, 255; EWL 3; EXPN; LAIT 4, 5; LATS 1; NFS 3, 7; RGEL 2; SCFW 2; SFW 4; SSFS 4; TEA; WLIT 4; YAW

Osborne, David
See Silverberg, Robert

Osborne, George
See Silverberg, Robert

Osborne, John (James) 1929-1994 .... **CLC 1, 2, 5, 11, 45; WLC**
See also BRWS 1; CA 13-16R; 147; CANR 21, 56; CDBLB 1945-1960; DA; DAB; DAC; DAM DRAM, MST; DFS 4; DLB 13; EWL 3; MTCW 1, 2; RGEL 2

Osborne, Lawrence 1958- .... **CLC 50**
See also CA 189

Osbourne, Lloyd 1868-1947 .... **TCLC 93**

Oshima, Nagisa 1932- .... **CLC 20**
See also CA 116; 121; CANR 78

Oskison, John Milton 1874-1947 .... **NNAL; TCLC 35**
See also CA 144; CANR 84; DAM MULT; DLB 175

Ossian c. 3rd cent. - .... **CMLC 28**
See Macpherson, James

Ossoli, Sarah Margaret (Fuller) 1810-1850 .... **NCLC 5, 50**
See Fuller, Margaret; Fuller, Sarah Margaret
See also CDALB 1640-1865; FW; LMFS 1; SATA 25

Ostriker, Alicia (Suskin) 1937- .... **CLC 132**
See also CA 25-28R; CAAS 24; CANR 10, 30, 62, 99; CWP; DLB 120; EXPP

Ostrovsky, Aleksandr Nikolaevich
See Ostrovsky, Alexander
See also DLB 277

Ostrovsky, Alexander 1823-1886 .. **NCLC 30, 57**
See Ostrovsky, Aleksandr Nikolaevich

Otero, Blas de 1916-1979 .... **CLC 11**
See also CA 89-92; DLB 134; EWL 3

O'Trigger, Sir Lucius
See Horne, Richard Henry Hengist

Otto, Rudolf 1869-1937 .... **TCLC 85**

Otto, Whitney 1955- .... **CLC 70**
See also CA 140; CANR 120

Ouida .... **TCLC 43**
See De la Ramee, Marie Louise (Ouida)
See also DLB 18, 156; RGEL 2

Ouologuem, Yambo 1940- .... **CLC 146**
See also CA 111; 176

Ousmane, Sembene 1923- ... **BLC 3; CLC 66**
See Sembene, Ousmane
See also BW 1, 3; CA 117; 125; CANR 81; CWW 2; MTCW 1

Ovid 43B.C.-17 .... **CMLC 7; PC 2**
See also AW 2; CDWLB 1; DA3; DAM POET; DLB 211; RGWL 2, 3; WP

Owen, Hugh
See Faust, Frederick (Schiller)

Owen, Wilfred (Edward Salter) 1893-1918 ... **PC 19; TCLC 5, 27; WLC**
See also BRW 6; CA 104; 141; CDBLB 1914-1945; DA; DAB; DAC; DAM MST, POET; DLB 20; EWL 3; EXPP; MTCW 2; PFS 10; RGEL 2; WLIT 4

Owens, Louis (Dean) 1948-2002 .... **NNAL**
See also CA 137; 179; 207; CAAE 179; CAAS 24; CANR 71

Owens, Rochelle 1936- .... **CLC 8**
See also CA 17-20R; CAAS 2; CAD; CANR 39; CD 5; CP 7; CWD; CWP

Oz, Amos 1939- .... **CLC 5, 8, 11, 27, 33, 54**
See also CA 53-56; CANR 27, 47, 65, 113; CWW 2; DAM NOV; EWL 3; MTCW 1, 2; RGSF 2; RGWL 3

Ozick, Cynthia 1928- .... **CLC 3, 7, 28, 62, 155; SSC 15, 60**
See also AMWS 5; BEST 90:1; CA 17-20R; CANR 23, 58, 116; CN 7; CPW; DA3; DAM NOV, POP; DLB 28, 152; DLBY 1982; EWL 3; EXPS; INT CANR-23; MTCW 1, 2; RGAL 4; RGSF 2; SSFS 3, 12

Ozu, Yasujiro 1903-1963 .... **CLC 16**
See also CA 112

Pabst, G. W. 1885-1967 .... **TCLC 127**

Pacheco, C.
See Pessoa, Fernando (Antonio Nogueira)

Pacheco, Jose Emilio 1939- .... **HLC 2**
See also CA 111; 131; CANR 65; DAM MULT; EWL 3; HW 1, 2; RGSF 2

Pa Chin .... **CLC 18**
See Li Fei-kan
See also EWL 3

Pack, Robert 1929- .... **CLC 13**
See also CA 1-4R; CANR 3, 44, 82; CP 7; DLB 5; SATA 118

Padgett, Lewis
See Kuttner, Henry

Padilla (Lorenzo), Heberto 1932-2000 .... **CLC 38**
See also AITN 1; CA 123; 131; 189; EWL 3; HW 1

Page, James Patrick 1944-
See Page, Jimmy
See also CA 204

Page, Jimmy 1944- .... **CLC 12**
See Page, James Patrick

Page, Louise 1955- .... **CLC 40**
See also CA 140; CANR 76; CBD; CD 5; CWD; DLB 233

Page, P(atricia) K(athleen) 1916- ...... **CLC 7, 18; PC 12**
See Cape, Judith
See also CA 53-56; CANR 4, 22, 65; CP 7; DAC; DAM MST; DLB 68; MTCW 1; RGEL 2

Page, Stanton
See Fuller, Henry Blake

Page, Stanton
See Fuller, Henry Blake

Page, Thomas Nelson 1853-1922 .... **SSC 23**
See also CA 118; 177; DLB 12, 78; DLBD 13; RGAL 4

Pagels, Elaine Hiesey 1943- .... **CLC 104**
See also CA 45-48; CANR 2, 24, 51; FW; NCFS 4

Paget, Violet 1856-1935
See Lee, Vernon
See also CA 104; 166; GLL 1; HGG

Paget-Lowe, Henry
See Lovecraft, H(oward) P(hillips)

Paglia, Camille (Anna) 1947- .... **CLC 68**
See also CA 140; CANR 72; CPW; FW; GLL 2; MTCW 2

Paige, Richard
See Koontz, Dean R(ay)

Paine, Thomas 1737-1809 .... **NCLC 62**
See also AMWS 1; CDALB 1640-1865; DLB 31, 43, 73, 158; LAIT 1; RGAL 4; RGEL 2; TUS

Pakenham, Antonia
See Fraser, Antonia (Pakenham)

Palamas, Costis
See Palamas, Kostes

Palamas, Kostes 1859-1943 .... **TCLC 5**
See Palamas, Kostis
See also CA 105; 190; RGWL 2, 3

Palamas, Kostis
See Palamas, Kostes
See also EWL 3

Palazzeschi, Aldo 1885-1974 .... **CLC 11**
See also CA 89-92; 53-56; DLB 114, 264; EWL 3

Pales Matos, Luis 1898-1959 .... **HLCS 2**
See Pales Matos, Luis
See also HW 1; LAW

Paley, Grace 1922- .. **CLC 4, 6, 37, 140; SSC 8**
See also AMWS 6; CA 25-28R; CANR 13, 46, 74, 118; CN 7; CPW; DA3; DAM POP; DLB 28, 218; EWL 3; EXPS; FW; INT CANR-13; MAWW; MTCW 1, 2; RGAL 4; RGSF 2; SSFS 3

Palin, Michael (Edward) 1943- .... **CLC 21**
See Monty Python
See also CA 107; CANR 35, 109; SATA 67

Palliser, Charles 1947- .... **CLC 65**
See also CA 136; CANR 76; CN 7

Palma, Ricardo 1833-1919 .... **TCLC 29**
See also CA 168; LAW

Pancake, Breece Dexter 1952-1979
See Pancake, Breece D'J
See also CA 123; 109

Pancake, Breece D'J .... **CLC 29; SSC 61**
See Pancake, Breece Dexter
See also DLB 130

Panchenko, Nikolai .... **CLC 59**

Pankhurst, Emmeline (Goulden) 1858-1928 .... **TCLC 100**
See also CA 116; FW

Panko, Rudy
See Gogol, Nikolai (Vasilyevich)

Papadiamantis, Alexandros 1851-1911 .... **TCLC 29**
See also CA 168; EWL 3

Papadiamantopoulos, Johannes 1856-1910
See Moreas, Jean
See also CA 117

Peirce, Charles Sanders
1839-1914 .... **TCLC 81**
See also CA 194; DLB 270

Pellicer, Carlos 1900(?)-1977 .... **HLCS 2**
See also CA 153; 69-72; EWL 3; HW 1

Pena, Ramon del Valle y
See Valle-Inclan, Ramon (Maria) del

Pendennis, Arthur Esquir
See Thackeray, William Makepeace

Penn, William 1644-1718 .... **LC 25**
See also DLB 24

PEPECE
See Prado (Calvo), Pedro

Pepys, Samuel 1633-1703 ... **LC 11, 58; WLC**
See also BRW 2; CDBLB 1660-1789; DA;
DA3; DAB; DAC; DAM MST; DLB 101,
213; NCFS 4; RGEL 2; TEA; WLIT 3

Percy, Thomas 1729-1811 .... **NCLC 95**
See also DLB 104

Percy, Walker 1916-1990 .... **CLC 2, 3, 6, 8,
14, 18, 47, 65**
See also AMWS 3; BPFB 3; CA 1-4R; 131;
CANR 1, 23, 64; CPW; CSW; DA3;
DAM NOV, POP; DLB 2; DLBY 1980,
1990; EWL 3; MTCW 1, 2; RGAL 4;
TUS

Percy, William Alexander
1885-1942 .... **TCLC 84**
See also CA 163; MTCW 2

Perec, Georges 1936-1982 .... **CLC 56, 116**
See also CA 141; DLB 83; EWL 3; GFL
1789 to the Present; RGWL 3

Pereda (y Sanchez de Porrua), Jose Maria
de 1833-1906 .... **TCLC 16**
See also CA 117

Pereda y Porrua, Jose Maria de
See Pereda (y Sanchez de Porrua), Jose
Maria de

Peregoy, George Weems
See Mencken, H(enry) L(ouis)

Perelman, S(idney) J(oseph)
1904-1979 .. **CLC 3, 5, 9, 15, 23, 44, 49;
SSC 32**
See also AITN 1, 2; BPFB 3; CA 73-76;
89-92; CANR 18; DAM DRAM; DLB 11,
44; MTCW 1, 2; RGAL 4

Peret, Benjamin 1899-1959 .... **PC 33; TCLC
20**
See also CA 117; 186; GFL 1789 to the
Present

Peretz, Isaac Leib 1851(?)-1915
See Peretz, Isaac Loeb
See also CA 201

Peretz, Isaac Loeb 1851(?)-1915 ...... **SSC 26;
TCLC 16**
See Peretz, Isaac Leib
See also CA 109

Peretz, Yitzkhok Leibush
See Peretz, Isaac Loeb

Perez Galdos, Benito 1843-1920 ..... **HLCS 2;
TCLC 27**
See Galdos, Benito Perez
See also CA 125; 153; EWL 3; HW 1;
RGWL 2, 3

Peri Rossi, Cristina 1941- .. **CLC 156; HLCS
2**
See also CA 131; CANR 59, 81; DLB 145;
EWL 3; HW 1, 2

Perlata
See Peret, Benjamin

Perloff, Marjorie G(abrielle)
1931- .... **CLC 137**
See also CA 57-60; CANR 7, 22, 49, 104

Perrault, Charles 1628-1703 ... **DC 12; LC 2,
56**
See also BYA 4; CLR 79; DLB 268; GFL
Beginnings to 1789; MAICYA 1, 2;
RGWL 2, 3; SATA 25; WCH

Perry, Anne 1938- .... **CLC 126**
See also CA 101; CANR 22, 50, 84; CMW
4; CN 7; CPW; DLB 276

Perry, Brighton
See Sherwood, Robert E(mmet)

Perse, St.-John
See Leger, (Marie-Rene Auguste) Alexis
Saint-Leger

Perse, Saint-John
See Leger, (Marie-Rene Auguste) Alexis
Saint-Leger
See also DLB 258; RGWL 3

Perutz, Leo(pold) 1882-1957 .... **TCLC 60**
See also CA 147; DLB 81

Peseenz, Tulio F.
See Lopez y Fuentes, Gregorio

Pesetsky, Bette 1932- .... **CLC 28**
See also CA 133; DLB 130

Peshkov, Alexei Maximovich 1868-1936
See Gorky, Maxim
See also CA 105; 141; CANR 83; DA;
DAC; DAM DRAM, MST, NOV; MTCW
2

Pessoa, Fernando (Antonio Nogueira)
1888-1935 ..... **HLC 2; PC 20; TCLC 27**
See also CA 125; 183; DAM MULT; DLB
287; EW 10; EWL 3; RGWL 2, 3; WP

Peterkin, Julia Mood 1880-1961 ...... **CLC 31**
See also CA 102; DLB 9

Peters, Joan K(aren) 1945- .... **CLC 39**
See also CA 158; CANR 109

Peters, Robert L(ouis) 1924- .... **CLC 7**
See also CA 13-16R; CAAS 8; CP 7; DLB
105

Petofi, Sandor 1823-1849 .... **NCLC 21**
See also RGWL 2, 3

Petrakis, Harry Mark 1923- .... **CLC 3**
See also CA 9-12R; CANR 4, 30, 85; CN 7

Petrarch 1304-1374 .... **CMLC 20; PC 8**
See also DA3; DAM POET; EW 2; LMFS
1; RGWL 2. 3

Petronius c. 20-66 .... **CMLC 34**
See also AW 2; CDWLB 1; DLB 211;
RGWL 2, 3

Petrov, Evgeny .... **TCLC 21**
See Kataev, Evgeny Petrovich

Petry, Ann (Lane) 1908-1997 .. **CLC 1, 7, 18;
TCLC 112**
See also AFAW 1, 2; BPFB 3; BW 1, 3;
BYA 2; CA 5-8R; 157; CAAS 6; CANR
4, 46; CLR 12; CN 7; DLB 76; EWL 3;
JRDA; LAIT 1; MAICYA 1, 2; MAIC-
YAS 1; MTCW 1; RGAL 4; SATA 5;
SATA-Obit 94; TUS

Petursson, Halligrimur 1614-1674 .... **LC 8**

Peychinovich
See Vazov, Ivan (Minchov)

Phaedrus c. 15B.C.-c. 50 .... **CMLC 25**
See also DLB 211

Phelps (Ward), Elizabeth Stuart
See Phelps, Elizabeth Stuart
See also FW

Phelps, Elizabeth Stuart
1844-1911 .... **TCLC 113**
See Phelps (Ward), Elizabeth Stuart
See also DLB 74

Philips, Katherine 1632-1664 . **LC 30; PC 40**
See also DLB 131; RGEL 2

Philipson, Morris H. 1926- .... **CLC 53**
See also CA 1-4R; CANR 4

Phillips, Caryl 1958- .... **BLCS; CLC 96**
See also BRWS 5; BW 2; CA 141; CANR
63, 104; CBD; CD 5; CN 7; DA3; DAM
MULT; DLB 157; EWL 3; MTCW 2;
WLIT 4

Phillips, David Graham
1867-1911 .... **TCLC 44**
See also CA 108; 176; DLB 9, 12; RGAL 4

Phillips, Jack
See Sandburg, Carl (August)

Phillips, Jayne Anne 1952- .... **CLC 15, 33,
139; SSC 16**
See also BPFB 3; CA 101; CANR 24, 50,
96; CN 7; CSW; DLBY 1980; INT
CANR-24; MTCW 1, 2; RGAL 4; RGSF
2; SSFS 4

Phillips, Richard
See Dick, Philip K(indred)

Phillips, Robert (Schaeffer) 1938- .... **CLC 28**
See also CA 17-20R; CAAS 13; CANR 8;
DLB 105

Phillips, Ward
See Lovecraft, H(oward) P(hillips)

Philostratus, Flavius c. 179-c.
244 .... **CMLC 62**

Piccolo, Lucio 1901-1969 .... **CLC 13**
See also CA 97-100; DLB 114; EWL 3

Pickthall, Marjorie L(owry) C(hristie)
1883-1922 .... **TCLC 21**
See also CA 107; DLB 92

Pico della Mirandola, Giovanni
1463-1494 .... **LC 15**
See also LMFS 1

Piercy, Marge 1936- .... **CLC 3, 6, 14, 18, 27,
62, 128; PC 29**
See also BPFB 3; CA 21-24R; CAAE 187;
CAAS 1; CANR 13, 43, 66, 111; CN 7;
CP 7; CWP; DLB 120, 227; EXPP; FW;
MTCW 1, 2; PFS 9; SFW 4

Piers, Robert
See Anthony, Piers

Pieyre de Mandiargues, Andre 1909-1991
See Mandiargues, Andre Pieyre de
See also CA 103; 136; CANR 22, 82; EWL
3; GFL 1789 to the Present

Pilnyak, Boris 1894-1938 . **SSC 48; TCLC 23**
See Vogau, Boris Andreyevich
See also EWL 3

Pinchback, Eugene
See Toomer, Jean

Pincherle, Alberto 1907-1990 ...... **CLC 11, 18**
See Moravia, Alberto
See also CA 25-28R; 132; CANR 33, 63;
DAM NOV; MTCW 1

Pinckney, Darryl 1953- .... **CLC 76**
See also BW 2, 3; CA 143; CANR 79

Pindar 518(?)B.C.-438(?)B.C. .... **CMLC 12;
PC 19**
See also AW 1; CDWLB 1; DLB 176;
RGWL 2

Pineda, Cecile 1942- .... **CLC 39**
See also CA 118; DLB 209

Pinero, Arthur Wing 1855-1934 .... **TCLC 32**
See also CA 110; 153; DAM DRAM; DLB
10; RGEL 2

Pinero, Miguel (Antonio Gomez)
1946-1988 .... **CLC 4, 55**
See also CA 61-64; 125; CAD; CANR 29,
90; DLB 266; HW 1

Pinget, Robert 1919-1997 .... **CLC 7, 13, 37**
See also CA 85-88; 160; CWW 2; DLB 83;
EWL 3; GFL 1789 to the Present

Pink Floyd
See Barrett, (Roger) Syd; Gilmour, David;
Mason, Nick; Waters, Roger; Wright, Rick

Pinkney, Edward 1802-1828 .... **NCLC 31**
See also DLB 248

Pinkwater, Daniel
See Pinkwater, Daniel Manus

Pinkwater, Daniel Manus 1941- .... **CLC 35**
See also AAYA 1, 46; BYA 9; CA 29-32R;
CANR 12, 38, 89; CLR 4; CSW; FANT;
JRDA; MAICYA 1, 2; SAAS 3; SATA 8,
46, 76, 114; SFW 4; YAW

Pinkwater, Manus
See Pinkwater, Daniel Manus

Pinsky, Robert 1940- .... **CLC 9, 19, 38, 94, 121; PC 27**
See also AMWS 6; CA 29-32R; CAAS 4; CANR 58, 97; CP 7; DA3; DAM POET; DLBY 1982, 1998; MTCW 2; PFS 18; RGAL 4

Pinta, Harold
See Pinter, Harold

Pinter, Harold 1930- .. **CLC 1, 3, 6, 9, 11, 15, 27, 58, 73; DC 15; WLC**
See also BRWR 1; BRWS 1; CA 5-8R; CANR 33, 65, 112; CBD; CD 5; CDBLB 1960 to Present; DA; DA3; DAB; DAC; DAM DRAM, MST; DFS 3, 5, 7, 14; DLB 13; EWL 3; IDFW 3, 4; LMFS 2; MTCW 1, 2; RGEL 2; TEA

Piozzi, Hester Lynch (Thrale) 1741-1821 .... **NCLC 57**
See also DLB 104, 142

Pirandello, Luigi 1867-1936 .. **DC 5; SSC 22; TCLC 4, 29; WLC**
See also CA 104; 153; CANR 103; DA; DA3; DAB; DAC; DAM DRAM, MST; DFS 4, 9; DLB 264; EW 8; EWL 3; MTCW 2; RGSF 2; RGWL 2, 3

Pirsig, Robert M(aynard) 1928- ... **CLC 4, 6, 73**
See also CA 53-56; CANR 42, 74; CPW 1; DA3; DAM POP; MTCW 1, 2; SATA 39

Pisarev, Dmitrii Ivanovich
See Pisarev, Dmitry Ivanovich
See also DLB 277

Pisarev, Dmitry Ivanovich 1840-1868 .... **NCLC 25**
See Pisarev, Dmitrii Ivanovich

Pix, Mary (Griffith) 1666-1709 .... **LC 8**
See also DLB 80

Pixerecourt, (Rene Charles) Guilbert de 1773-1844 .... **NCLC 39**
See also DLB 192; GFL 1789 to the Present

Plaatje, Sol(omon) T(shekisho) 1878-1932 .... **BLCS; TCLC 73**
See also BW 2, 3; CA 141; CANR 79; DLB 125, 225

Plaidy, Jean
See Hibbert, Eleanor Alice Burford

Planche, James Robinson 1796-1880 .... **NCLC 42**
See also RGEL 2

Plant, Robert 1948- .... **CLC 12**

Plante, David (Robert) 1940- . **CLC 7, 23, 38**
See also CA 37-40R; CANR 12, 36, 58, 82; CN 7; DAM NOV; DLBY 1983; INT CANR-12; MTCW 1

Plath, Sylvia 1932-1963 ..... **CLC 1, 2, 3, 5, 9, 11, 14, 17, 50, 51, 62, 111; PC 1, 37; WLC**
See also AAYA 13; AMWR 2; AMWS 1; BPFB 3; CA 19-20; CANR 34, 101; CAP 2; CDALB 1941-1968; DA; DA3; DAB; DAC; DAM MST, POET; DLB 5, 6, 152; EWL 3; EXPN; EXPP; FW; LAIT 4; MAWW; MTCW 1, 2; NFS 1; PAB; PFS 1, 15; RGAL 4; SATA 96; TUS; WP; YAW

Plato c. 428B.C.-347B.C. ... **CMLC 8; WLCS**
See also AW 1; CDWLB 1; DA; DA3; DAB; DAC; DAM MST; DLB 176; LAIT 1; LATS 1; RGWL 2, 3

Platonov, Andrei
See Klimentov, Andrei Platonovich

Platonov, Andrei Platonovich
See Klimentov, Andrei Platonovich
See also DLB 272

Platonov, Andrey Platonovich
See Klimentov, Andrei Platonovich
See also EWL 3

Platt, Kin 1911- .... **CLC 26**
See also AAYA 11; CA 17-20R; CANR 11; JRDA; SAAS 17; SATA 21, 86; WYA

Plautus c. 254B.C.-c. 184B.C. ...... **CMLC 24; DC 6**
See also AW 1; CDWLB 1; DLB 211; RGWL 2, 3

Plick et Plock
See Simenon, Georges (Jacques Christian)

Plieksans, Janis
See Rainis, Janis

Plimpton, George (Ames) 1927-2003 .... **CLC 36**
See also AITN 1; CA 21-24R; CANR 32, 70, 103; DLB 185, 241; MTCW 1, 2; SATA 10

Pliny the Elder c. 23-79 .... **CMLC 23**
See also DLB 211

Pliny the Younger c. 61-c. 112 ...... **CMLC 62**
See also AW 2; DLB 211

Plomer, William Charles Franklin 1903-1973 .... **CLC 4, 8**
See also AFW; CA 21-22; CANR 34; CAP 2; DLB 20, 162, 191, 225; EWL 3; MTCW 1; RGEL 2; RGSF 2; SATA 24

Plotinus 204-270 .... **CMLC 46**
See also CDWLB 1; DLB 176

Plowman, Piers
See Kavanagh, Patrick (Joseph)

Plum, J.
See Wodehouse, P(elham) G(renville)

Plumly, Stanley (Ross) 1939- .... **CLC 33**
See also CA 108; 110; CANR 97; CP 7; DLB 5, 193; INT 110

Plumpe, Friedrich Wilhelm 1888-1931 .... **TCLC 53**
See also CA 112

Plutarch c. 46-c. 120 .... **CMLC 60**
See also AW 2; CDWLB 1; DLB 176; RGWL 2, 3; TWA

Po Chu-i 772-846 .... **CMLC 24**

Poe, Edgar Allan 1809-1849 ..... **NCLC 1, 16, 55, 78, 94, 97, 117; PC 1; SSC 1, 22, 34, 35, 54; WLC**
See also AAYA 14; AMW; AMWC 1; AMWR 2; BPFB 3; BYA 5, 11; CDALB 1640-1865; CMW 4; DA; DA3; DAB; DAC; DAM MST, POET; DLB 3, 59, 73, 74, 248, 254; EXPP; EXPS; HGG; LAIT 2; LATS 1; LMFS 1; MSW; PAB; PFS 1, 3, 9; RGAL 4; RGSF 2; SATA 23; SCFW 2; SFW 4; SSFS 2, 4, 7, 8, 16; SUFW 2; TUS; WP; WYA

Poet of Titchfield Street, The
See Pound, Ezra (Weston Loomis)

Pohl, Frederik 1919- .... **CLC 18; SSC 25**
See also AAYA 24; CA 61-64; CAAE 188; CAAS 1; CANR 11, 37, 81; CN 7; DLB 8; INT CANR-11; MTCW 1, 2; SATA 24; SCFW 2; SFW 4

Poirier, Louis 1910-
See Gracq, Julien
See also CA 122; 126; CWW 2

Poitier, Sidney 1927- .... **CLC 26**
See also BW 1; CA 117; CANR 94

Pokagon, Simon 1830-1899 .... **NNAL**
See also DAM MULT

Polanski, Roman 1933- .... **CLC 16, 178**
See also CA 77-80

Poliakoff, Stephen 1952- .... **CLC 38**
See also CA 106; CANR 116; CBD; CD 5; DLB 13

Police, The
See Copeland, Stewart (Armstrong); Summers, Andrew James; Sumner, Gordon Matthew

Polidori, John William 1795-1821 . **NCLC 51**
See also DLB 116; HGG

Pollitt, Katha 1949- .... **CLC 28, 122**
See also CA 120; 122; CANR 66, 108; MTCW 1, 2

Pollock, (Mary) Sharon 1936- .... **CLC 50**
See also CA 141; CD 5; CWD; DAC; DAM DRAM, MST; DFS 3; DLB 60; FW

Pollock, Sharon 1936- .... **DC 20**

Polo, Marco 1254-1324 .... **CMLC 15**

Polonsky, Abraham (Lincoln) 1910-1999 .... **CLC 92**
See also CA 104; 187; DLB 26; INT 104

Polybius c. 200B.C.-c. 118B.C. ...... **CMLC 17**
See also AW 1; DLB 176; RGWL 2, 3

Pomerance, Bernard 1940- .... **CLC 13**
See also CA 101; CAD; CANR 49; CD 5; DAM DRAM; DFS 9; LAIT 2

Ponge, Francis 1899-1988 .... **CLC 6, 18**
See also CA 85-88; 126; CANR 40, 86; DAM POET; DLBY 2002; EWL 3; GFL 1789 to the Present; RGWL 2, 3

Poniatowska, Elena 1933- . **CLC 140; HLC 2**
See also CA 101; CANR 32, 66, 107; CDWLB 3; DAM MULT; DLB 113; EWL 3; HW 1, 2; LAWS 1; WLIT 1

Pontoppidan, Henrik 1857-1943 .... **TCLC 29**
See also CA 170

Poole, Josephine .... **CLC 17**
See Helyar, Jane Penelope Josephine
See also SAAS 2; SATA 5

Popa, Vasko 1922-1991 .... **CLC 19**
See also CA 112; 148; CDWLB 4; DLB 181; EWL 3; RGWL 2, 3

Pope, Alexander 1688-1744 ...... **LC 3, 58, 60, 64; PC 26; WLC**
See also BRW 3; BRWC 1; BRWR 1; CDBLB 1660-1789; DA; DA3; DAB; DAC; DAM MST, POET; DLB 95, 101, 213; EXPP; PAB; PFS 12; RGEL 2; WLIT 3; WP

Popov, Evgenii Anatol'evich
See Popov, Yevgeny
See also DLB 285

Popov, Yevgeny .... **CLC 59**
See Popov, Evgenii Anatol'evich

Poquelin, Jean-Baptiste
See Moliere

Porter, Connie (Rose) 1959(?)- .... **CLC 70**
See also BW 2, 3; CA 142; CANR 90, 109; SATA 81, 129

Porter, Gene(va Grace) Stratton .. **TCLC 21**
See Stratton-Porter, Gene(va Grace)
See also BPFB 3; CA 112; CWRI 5; RHW

Porter, Katherine Anne 1890-1980 ... **CLC 1, 3, 7, 10, 13, 15, 27, 101; SSC 4, 31, 43**
See also AAYA 42; AITN 2; AMW; BPFB 3; CA 1-4R; 101; CANR 1, 65; CDALBS; DA; DA3; DAB; DAC; DAM MST, NOV; DLB 4, 9, 102; DLBD 12; DLBY 1980; EWL 3; EXPS; LAIT 3; MAWW; MTCW 1, 2; NFS 14; RGAL 4; RGSF 2; SATA 39; SATA-Obit 23; SSFS 1, 8, 11, 16; TUS

Porter, Peter (Neville Frederick) 1929- .... **CLC 5, 13, 33**
See also CA 85-88; CP 7; DLB 40, 289

Porter, William Sydney 1862-1910
See Henry, O.
See also CA 104; 131; CDALB 1865-1917; DA; DA3; DAB; DAC; DAM MST; DLB 12, 78, 79; MTCW 1, 2; TUS; YABC 2

Portillo (y Pacheco), Jose Lopez
See Lopez Portillo (y Pacheco), Jose

Portillo Trambley, Estela 1927-1998 .. **HLC 2**
See Trambley, Estela Portillo
See also CANR 32; DAM MULT; DLB 209; HW 1

Posey, Alexander (Lawrence) 1873-1908 .... **NNAL**
See also CA 144; CANR 80; DAM MULT; DLB 175

Posse, Abel .... **CLC 70**

Post, Melville Davisson
    1869-1930 .... **TCLC 39**
    See also CA 110; 202; CMW 4
Potok, Chaim 1929-2002 ... **CLC 2, 7, 14, 26,**
    112
    See also AAYA 15, 50; AITN 1, 2; BPFB 3;
    BYA 1; CA 17-20R; 208; CANR 19, 35,
    64, 98; CLR 92; CN 7; DA3; DAM NOV;
    DLB 28, 152; EXPN; INT CANR-19;
    LAIT 4; MTCW 1, 2; NFS 4; SATA 33,
    106; SATA-Obit 134; TUS; YAW
Potok, Herbert Harold -2002
    See Potok, Chaim
Potok, Herman Harold
    See Potok, Chaim
Potter, Dennis (Christopher George)
    1935-1994 .... **CLC 58, 86, 123**
    See also CA 107; 145; CANR 33, 61; CBD;
    DLB 233; MTCW 1
Pound, Ezra (Weston Loomis)
    1885-1972 .. **CLC 1, 2, 3, 4, 5, 7, 10, 13,**
    18, 34, 48, 50, 112; PC 4; WLC
    See also AAYA 47; AMW; AMWR 1; CA
    5-8R; 37-40R; CANR 40; CDALB 1917-
    1929; DA; DA3; DAB; DAC; DAM MST,
    POET; DLB 4, 45, 63; DLBD 15; EFS 2;
    EWL 3; EXPP; LMFS 2; MTCW 1, 2;
    PAB; PFS 2, 8, 16; RGAL 4; TUS; WP
Povod, Reinaldo 1959-1994 .... **CLC 44**
    See also CA 136; 146; CANR 83
Powell, Adam Clayton, Jr.
    1908-1972 .... **BLC 3; CLC 89**
    See also BW 1, 3; CA 102; 33-36R; CANR
    86; DAM MULT
Powell, Anthony (Dymoke)
    1905-2000 .... **CLC 1, 3, 7, 9, 10, 31**
    See also BRW 7; CA 1-4R; 189; CANR 1,
    32, 62, 107; CDBLB 1945-1960; CN 7;
    DLB 15; EWL 3; MTCW 1, 2; RGEL 2;
    TEA
Powell, Dawn 1896(?)-1965 .... **CLC 66**
    See also CA 5-8R; CANR 121; DLBY 1997
Powell, Padgett 1952- .... **CLC 34**
    See also CA 126; CANR 63, 101; CSW;
    DLB 234; DLBY 01
Powell, (Oval) Talmage 1920-2000
    See Queen, Ellery
    See also CA 5-8R; CANR 2, 80
Power, Susan 1961- .... **CLC 91**
    See also BYA 14; CA 160; NFS 11
Powers, J(ames) F(arl) 1917-1999 ..... **CLC 1,**
    4, 8, 57; SSC 4
    See also CA 1-4R; 181; CANR 2, 61; CN
    7; DLB 130; MTCW 1; RGAL 4; RGSF
    2
Powers, John J(ames) 1945-
    See Powers, John R.
    See also CA 69-72
Powers, John R. .... **CLC 66**
    See Powers, John J(ames)
Powers, Richard (S.) 1957- .... **CLC 93**
    See also AMWS 9; BPFB 3; CA 148;
    CANR 80; CN 7
Pownall, David 1938- .... **CLC 10**
    See also CA 89-92, 180; CAAS 18; CANR
    49, 101; CBD; CD 5; CN 7; DLB 14
Powys, John Cowper 1872-1963 ... **CLC 7, 9,**
    15, 46, 125
    See also CA 85-88; CANR 106; DLB 15,
    255; EWL 3; FANT; MTCW 1, 2; RGEL
    2; SUFW
Powys, T(heodore) F(rancis)
    1875-1953 .... **TCLC 9**
    See also BRWS 8; CA 106; 189; DLB 36,
    162; EWL 3; FANT; RGEL 2; SUFW
Prado (Calvo), Pedro 1886-1952 ... **TCLC 75**
    See also CA 131; DLB 283; HW 1; LAW
Prager, Emily 1952- .... **CLC 56**
    See also CA 204

Pratolini, Vasco 1913-1991 .... **TCLC 124**
    See also CA 211; DLB 177; EWL 3; RGWL
    2, 3
Pratt, E(dwin) J(ohn) 1883(?)-1964 . **CLC 19**
    See also CA 141; 93-96; CANR 77; DAC;
    DAM POET; DLB 92; EWL 3; RGEL 2;
    TWA
Premchand .... **TCLC 21**
    See Srivastava, Dhanpat Rai
    See also EWL 3
Preseren, France 1800-1849 .... **NCLC 127**
    See also CDWLB 4; DLB 147
Preussler, Otfried 1923- .... **CLC 17**
    See also CA 77-80; SATA 24
Prevert, Jacques (Henri Marie)
    1900-1977 .... **CLC 15**
    See also CA 77-80; 69-72; CANR 29, 61;
    DLB 258; EWL 3; GFL 1789 to the
    Present; IDFW 3, 4; MTCW 1; RGWL 2,
    3; SATA-Obit 30
Prevost, (Antoine Francois)
    1697-1763 .... **LC 1**
    See also EW 4; GFL Beginnings to 1789;
    RGWL 2, 3
Price, (Edward) Reynolds 1933- ... **CLC 3, 6,**
    13, 43, 50, 63; SSC 22
    See also AMWS 6; CA 1-4R; CANR 1, 37,
    57, 87; CN 7; CSW; DAM NOV; DLB 2,
    218, 278; EWL 3; INT CANR-37; NFS
    18
Price, Richard 1949- .... **CLC 6, 12**
    See also CA 49-52; CANR 3; DLBY 1981
Prichard, Katharine Susannah
    1883-1969 .... **CLC 46**
    See also CA 11-12; CANR 33; CAP 1; DLB
    260; MTCW 1; RGEL 2; RGSF 2; SATA
    66
Priestley, J(ohn) B(oynton)
    1894-1984 .... **CLC 2, 5, 9, 34**
    See also BRW 7; CA 9-12R; 113; CANR
    33; CDBLB 1914-1945; DA3; DAM
    DRAM, NOV; DLB 10, 34, 77, 100, 139;
    DLBY 1984; EWL 3; MTCW 1, 2; RGEL
    2; SFW 4
Prince 1958- .... **CLC 35**
    See also CA 213
Prince, F(rank) T(empleton) 1912- .. **CLC 22**
    See also CA 101; CANR 43, 79; CP 7; DLB
    20
Prince Kropotkin
    See Kropotkin, Peter (Aleksieevich)
Prior, Matthew 1664-1721 .... **LC 4**
    See also DLB 95; RGEL 2
Prishvin, Mikhail 1873-1954 .... **TCLC 75**
    See Prishvin, Mikhail Mikhailovich
Prishvin, Mikhail Mikhailovich
    See Prishvin, Mikhail
    See also DLB 272; EWL 3
Pritchard, William H(arrison)
    1932- .... **CLC 34**
    See also CA 65-68; CANR 23, 95; DLB
    111
Pritchett, V(ictor) S(awdon)
    1900-1997 ... **CLC 5, 13, 15, 41; SSC 14**
    See also BPFB 3; BRWS 3; CA 61-64; 157;
    CANR 31, 63; CN 7; DA3; DAM NOV;
    DLB 15, 139; EWL 3; MTCW 1, 2;
    RGEL 2; RGSF 2; TEA
Private 19022
    See Manning, Frederic
Probst, Mark 1925- .... **CLC 59**
    See also CA 130
Prokosch, Frederic 1908-1989 ...... **CLC 4, 48**
    See also CA 73-76; 128; CANR 82; DLB
    48; MTCW 2
Propertius, Sextus c. 50B.C.-c.
    16B.C. .... **CMLC 32**
    See also AW 2; CDWLB 1; DLB 211;
    RGWL 2, 3

Prophet, The
    See Dreiser, Theodore (Herman Albert)
Prose, Francine 1947- .... **CLC 45**
    See also CA 109; 112; CANR 46, 95; DLB
    234; SATA 101
Proudhon
    See Cunha, Euclides (Rodrigues Pimenta)
    da
Proulx, Annie
    See Proulx, E(dna) Annie
Proulx, E(dna) Annie 1935- ...... **CLC 81, 158**
    See also AMWS 7; BPFB 3; CA 145;
    CANR 65, 110; CN 7; CPW 1; DA3;
    DAM POP; MTCW 2; SSFS 18
Proust, (Valentin-Louis-George-Eugene)
    Marcel 1871-1922 .... **TCLC 7, 13, 33;**
    WLC
    See also BPFB 3; CA 104; 120; CANR 110;
    DA; DA3; DAB; DAC; DAM MST, NOV;
    DLB 65; EW 8; EWL 3; GFL 1789 to the
    Present; MTCW 1, 2; RGWL 2, 3; TWA
Prowler, Harley
    See Masters, Edgar Lee
Prus, Boleslaw 1845-1912 .... **TCLC 48**
    See also RGWL 2, 3
Pryor, Richard (Franklin Lenox Thomas)
    1940- ....,...... **CLC 26**
    See also CA 122; 152
Przybyszewski, Stanislaw
    1868-1927 .... **TCLC 36**
    See also CA 160; DLB 66; EWL 3
Pteleon
    See Grieve, C(hristopher) M(urray)
    See also DAM POET
Puckett, Lute
    See Masters, Edgar Lee
Puig, Manuel 1932-1990 .... **CLC 3, 5, 10, 28,**
    65, 133; HLC 2
    See also BPFB 3; CA 45-48; CANR 2, 32,
    63; CDWLB 3; DA3; DAM MULT; DLB
    113; DNFS 1; EWL 3; GLL 1; HW 1, 2;
    LAW; MTCW 1, 2; RGWL 2, 3; TWA;
    WLIT 1
Pulitzer, Joseph 1847-1911 .... **TCLC 76**
    See also CA 114; DLB 23
Purchas, Samuel 1577(?)-1626 .... **LC 70**
    See also DLB 151
Purdy, A(lfred) W(ellington)
    1918-2000 .... **CLC 3, 6, 14, 50**
    See also CA 81-84; 189; CAAS 17; CANR
    42, 66; CP 7; DAC; DAM MST, POET;
    DLB 88; PFS 5; RGEL 2
Purdy, James (Amos) 1923- .... **CLC 2, 4, 10,**
    28, 52
    See also AMWS 7; CA 33-36R; CAAS 1;
    CANR 19, 51; CN 7; DLB 2, 218; EWL
    3; INT CANR-19; MTCW 1; RGAL 4
Pure, Simon
    See Swinnerton, Frank Arthur
Pushkin, Aleksandr Sergeevich
    See Pushkin, Alexander (Sergeyevich)
    See also DLB 205
Pushkin, Alexander (Sergeyevich)
    1799-1837 .... **NCLC 3, 27, 83; PC 10;**
    SSC 27, 55; WLC
    See Pushkin, Aleksandr Sergeevich
    See also DA; DA3; DAB; DAC; DAM
    DRAM, MST, POET; EW 5; EXPS; RGSF
    2; RGWL 2, 3; SATA 61; SSFS 9; TWA
P'u Sung-ling 1640-1715 .... **LC 49; SSC 31**
Putnam, Arthur Lee
    See Alger, Horatio, Jr.
Puzo, Mario 1920-1999 .... **CLC 1, 2, 6, 36,**
    107
    See also BPFB 3; CA 65-68; 185; CANR 4,
    42, 65, 99; CN 7; CPW; DA3; DAM
    NOV, POP; DLB 6; MTCW 1, 2; NFS 16;
    RGAL 4

Pygge, Edward
    See Barnes, Julian (Patrick)
Pyle, Ernest Taylor 1900-1945
    See Pyle, Ernie
    See also CA 115; 160
Pyle, Ernie .... **TCLC 75**
    See Pyle, Ernest Taylor
    See also DLB 29; MTCW 2
Pyle, Howard 1853-1911 .... **TCLC 81**
    See also BYA 2, 4; CA 109; 137; CLR 22;
    DLB 42, 188; DLBD 13; LAIT 1; MAI-
    CYA 1, 2; SATA 16, 100; WCH; YAW
Pym, Barbara (Mary Crampton)
    1913-1980 .... **CLC 13, 19, 37, 111**
    See also BPFB 3; BRWS 2; CA 13-14; 97-
    100; CANR 13, 34; CAP 1; DLB 14, 207;
    DLBY 1987; EWL 3; MTCW 1, 2; RGEL
    2; TEA
Pynchon, Thomas (Ruggles, Jr.)
    1937- ...... **CLC 2, 3, 6, 9, 11, 18, 33, 62,
    72, 123; SSC 14; WLC**
    See also AMWS 2; BEST 90:2; BPFB 3;
    CA 17-20R; CANR 22, 46, 73; CN 7;
    CPW 1; DA; DA3; DAB; DAC; DAM
    MST, NOV, POP; DLB 2, 173; EWL 3;
    MTCW 1, 2; RGAL 4; SFW 4; TUS
Pythagoras c. 582B.C.-c. 507B.C. . **CMLC 22**
    See also DLB 176

Q

    See Quiller-Couch, Sir Arthur (Thomas)
Qian, Chongzhu
    See Ch'ien, Chung-shu
Qian Zhongshu
    See Ch'ien, Chung-shu
Qroll
    See Dagerman, Stig (Halvard)
Quarrington, Paul (Lewis) 1953- ..... **CLC 65**
    See also CA 129; CANR 62, 95
Quasimodo, Salvatore 1901-1968 .... **CLC 10;
    PC 47**
    See also CA 13-16; 25-28R; CAP 1; DLB
    114; EW 12; EWL 3; MTCW 1; RGWL
    2, 3
Quatermass, Martin
    See Carpenter, John (Howard)
Quay, Stephen 1947- .... **CLC 95**
    See also CA 189
Quay, Timothy 1947- .... **CLC 95**
    See also CA 189
Queen, Ellery .... **CLC 3, 11**
    See Dannay, Frederic; Davidson, Avram
    (James); Deming, Richard; Fairman, Paul
    W.; Flora, Fletcher; Hoch, Edward
    D(entinger); Kane, Henry; Lee, Manfred
    B(ennington); Marlowe, Stephen; Powell,
    (Oval) Talmage; Sheldon, Walter J(ames);
    Sturgeon, Theodore (Hamilton); Tracy,
    Don(ald Fiske); Vance, John Holbrook
    See also BPFB 3; CMW 4; MSW; RGAL 4
Queen, Ellery, Jr.
    See Dannay, Frederic; Lee, Manfred
    B(ennington)
Queneau, Raymond 1903-1976 ..... **CLC 2, 5,
    10, 42**
    See also CA 77-80; 69-72; CANR 32; DLB
    72, 258; EW 12; EWL 3; GFL 1789 to
    the Present; MTCW 1, 2; RGWL 2, 3
Quevedo, Francisco de 1580-1645 .... **LC 23**
Quiller-Couch, Sir Arthur (Thomas)
    1863-1944 .... **TCLC 53**
    See also CA 118; 166; DLB 135, 153, 190;
    HGG; RGEL 2; SUFW 1
Quin, Ann (Marie) 1936-1973 .... **CLC 6**
    See also CA 9-12R; 45-48; DLB 14, 231
Quincey, Thomas de
    See De Quincey, Thomas
Quinn, Martin
    See Smith, Martin Cruz

Quinn, Peter 1947- .... **CLC 91**
    See also CA 197
Quinn, Simon
    See Smith, Martin Cruz
Quintana, Leroy V. 1944- ...... **HLC 2; PC 36**
    See also CA 131; CANR 65; DAM MULT;
    DLB 82; HW 1, 2
Quiroga, Horacio (Sylvestre)
    1878-1937 .... **HLC 2; TCLC 20**
    See also CA 117; 131; DAM MULT; EWL
    3; HW 1; LAW; MTCW 1; RGSF 2;
    WLIT 1
Quoirez, Francoise 1935- .... **CLC 9**
    See Sagan, Francoise
    See also CA 49-52; CANR 6, 39, 73; CWW
    2; MTCW 1, 2; TWA
Raabe, Wilhelm (Karl) 1831-1910 . **TCLC 45**
    See also CA 167; DLB 129
Rabe, David (William) 1940- .. **CLC 4, 8, 33;
    DC 16**
    See also CA 85-88; CABS 3; CAD; CANR
    59; CD 5; DAM DRAM; DFS 3, 8, 13;
    DLB 7, 228; EWL 3
Rabelais, Francois 1494-1553 .... **LC 5, 60;
    WLC**
    See also DA; DAB; DAC; DAM MST; EW
    2; GFL Beginnings to 1789; LMFS 1;
    RGWL 2, 3; TWA
Rabinovitch, Sholem 1859-1916
    See Aleichem, Sholom
    See also CA 104
Rabinyan, Dorit 1972- .... **CLC 119**
    See also CA 170
Rachilde
    See Vallette, Marguerite Eymery; Vallette,
    Marguerite Eymery
    See also EWL 3
Racine, Jean 1639-1699 .... **LC 28**
    See also DA3; DAB; DAM MST; DLB 268;
    EW 3; GFL Beginnings to 1789; LMFS
    1; RGWL 2, 3; TWA
Radcliffe, Ann (Ward) 1764-1823 ... **NCLC 6,
    55, 106**
    See also DLB 39, 178; HGG; LMFS 1;
    RGEL 2; SUFW 1; WLIT 3
Radclyffe-Hall, Marguerite
    See Hall, (Marguerite) Radclyffe
Radiguet, Raymond 1903-1923 ...... **TCLC 29**
    See also CA 162; DLB 65; EWL 3; GFL
    1789 to the Present; RGWL 2, 3
Radnoti, Miklos 1909-1944 .... **TCLC 16**
    See also CA 118; 212; CDWLB 4; DLB
    215; EWL 3; RGWL 2, 3
Rado, James 1939- .... **CLC 17**
    See also CA 105
Radvanyi, Netty 1900-1983
    See Seghers, Anna
    See also CA 85-88; 110; CANR 82
Rae, Ben
    See Griffiths, Trevor
Raeburn, John (Hay) 1941- .... **CLC 34**
    See also CA 57-60
Ragni, Gerome 1942-1991 .... **CLC 17**
    See also CA 105; 134
Rahv, Philip .... **CLC 24**
    See Greenberg, Ivan
    See also DLB 137
Raimund, Ferdinand Jakob
    1790-1836 .... **NCLC 69**
    See also DLB 90
Raine, Craig (Anthony) 1944- .. **CLC 32, 103**
    See also CA 108; CANR 29, 51, 103; CP 7;
    DLB 40; PFS 7
Raine, Kathleen (Jessie) 1908- ..... **CLC 7, 45**
    See also CA 85-88; CANR 46, 109; CP 7;
    DLB 20; EWL 3; MTCW 1; RGEL 2
Rainis, Janis 1865-1929 .... **TCLC 29**
    See also CA 170; CDWLB 4; DLB 220;
    EWL 3

Rakosi, Carl .... **CLC 47**
    See Rawley, Callman
    See also CAAS 5; CP 7; DLB 193
Ralegh, Sir Walter
    See Raleigh, Sir Walter
    See also BRW 1; RGEL 2; WP
Raleigh, Richard
    See Lovecraft, H(oward) P(hillips)
Raleigh, Sir Walter 1554(?)-1618 .... **LC 31,
    39; PC 31**
    See Ralegh, Sir Walter
    See also CDBLB Before 1660; DLB 172;
    EXPP; PFS 14; TEA
Rallentando, H. P.
    See Sayers, Dorothy L(eigh)
Ramal, Walter
    See de la Mare, Walter (John)
Ramana Maharshi 1879-1950 .... **TCLC 84**
Ramoacn y Cajal, Santiago
    1852-1934 .... **TCLC 93**
Ramon, Juan
    See Jimenez (Mantecon), Juan Ramon
Ramos, Graciliano 1892-1953 .... **TCLC 32**
    See also CA 167; EWL 3; HW 2; LAW;
    WLIT 1
Rampersad, Arnold 1941- .... **CLC 44**
    See also BW 2, 3; CA 127; 133; CANR 81;
    DLB 111; INT 133
Rampling, Anne
    See Rice, Anne
    See also GLL 2
Ramsay, Allan 1686(?)-1758 .... **LC 29**
    See also DLB 95; RGEL 2
Ramsay, Jay
    See Campbell, (John) Ramsey
Ramuz, Charles-Ferdinand
    1878-1947 .... **TCLC 33**
    See also CA 165; EWL 3
Rand, Ayn 1905-1982 ...... **CLC 3, 30, 44, 79;
    WLC**
    See also AAYA 10; AMWS 4; BPFB 3;
    BYA 12; CA 13-16R; 105; CANR 27, 73;
    CDALBS; CPW; DA; DA3; DAC; DAM
    MST, NOV, POP; DLB 227, 279; MTCW
    1, 2; NFS 10, 16; RGAL 4; SFW 4; TUS;
    YAW
Randall, Dudley (Felker) 1914-2000 . **BLC 3;
    CLC 1, 135**
    See also BW 1, 3; CA 25-28R; 189; CANR
    23, 82; DAM MULT; DLB 41; PFS 5
Randall, Robert
    See Silverberg, Robert
Ranger, Ken
    See Creasey, John
Rank, Otto 1884-1939 .... **TCLC 115**
Ransom, John Crowe 1888-1974 .. **CLC 2, 4,
    5, 11, 24**
    See also AMW; CA 5-8R; 49-52; CANR 6,
    34; CDALBS; DA3; DAM POET; DLB
    45, 63; EWL 3; EXPP; MTCW 1, 2;
    RGAL 4; TUS
Rao, Raja 1909- .... **CLC 25, 56**
    See also CA 73-76; CANR 51; CN 7; DAM
    NOV; EWL 3; MTCW 1, 2; RGEL 2;
    RGSF 2
Raphael, Frederic (Michael) 1931- ... **CLC 2,
    14**
    See also CA 1-4R; CANR 1, 86; CN 7;
    DLB 14
Ratcliffe, James P.
    See Mencken, H(enry) L(ouis)
Rathbone, Julian 1935- .... **CLC 41**
    See also CA 101; CANR 34, 73
Rattigan, Terence (Mervyn)
    1911-1977 .... **CLC 7; DC 18**
    See also BRWS 7; CA 85-88; 73-76; CBD;
    CDBLB 1945-1960; DAM DRAM; DFS
    8; DLB 13; IDFW 3, 4; MTCW 1, 2;
    RGEL 2

Ratushinskaya, Irina 1954- .... **CLC 54**
See also CA 129; CANR 68; CWW 2
Raven, Simon (Arthur Noel)
1927-2001 .... **CLC 14**
See also CA 81-84; 197; CANR 86; CN 7;
DLB 271
Ravenna, Michael
See Welty, Eudora (Alice)
Rawley, Callman 1903-
See (Rakosi), Carl
See also CA 21-24R; CANR 12, 32, 91
Rawlings, Marjorie Kinnan
1896-1953 .... **TCLC 4**
See also AAYA 20; AMWS 10; ANW;
BPFB 3; BYA 3; CA 104; 137; CANR 74;
CLR 63; DLB 9, 22, 102; DLBD 17;
JRDA; MAICYA 1, 2; MTCW 2; RGAL
4; SATA 100; WCH; YABC 1; YAW
Ray, Satyajit 1921-1992 .... **CLC 16, 76**
See also CA 114; 137; DAM MULT
Read, Herbert Edward 1893-1968 ..... **CLC 4**
See also BRW 6; CA 85-88; 25-28R; DLB
20, 149; EWL 3; PAB; RGEL 2
Read, Piers Paul 1941- .... **CLC 4, 10, 25**
See also CA 21-24R; CANR 38, 86; CN 7;
DLB 14; SATA 21
Reade, Charles 1814-1884 .... **NCLC 2, 74**
See also DLB 21; RGEL 2
Reade, Hamish
See Gray, Simon (James Holliday)
Reading, Peter 1946- .... **CLC 47**
See also BRWS 8; CA 103; CANR 46, 96;
CP 7; DLB 40
Reaney, James 1926- .... **CLC 13**
See also CA 41-44R; CAAS 15; CANR 42;
CD 5; CP 7; DAC; DAM MST; DLB 68;
RGEL 2; SATA 43
Rebreanu, Liviu 1885-1944 .... **TCLC 28**
See also CA 165; DLB 220; EWL 3
Rechy, John (Francisco) 1934- ...... **CLC 1, 7,
14, 18, 107; HLC 2**
See also CA 5-8R; CAAE 195; CAAS 4;
CANR 6, 32, 64; CN 7; DAM MULT;
DLB 122, 278; DLBY 1982; HW 1, 2;
INT CANR-6; RGAL 4
Redcam, Tom 1870-1933 .... **TCLC 25**
Reddin, Keith .... **CLC 67**
See also CAD
Redgrove, Peter (William) 1932- . **CLC 6, 41**
See also BRWS 6; CA 1-4R; CANR 3, 39,
77; CP 7; DLB 40
Redmon, Anne .... **CLC 22**
See Nightingale, Anne Redmon
See also DLBY 1986
Reed, Eliot
See Ambler, Eric
Reed, Ishmael 1938- ..... **BLC 3; CLC 2, 3, 5,
6, 13, 32, 60, 174**
See also AFAW 1, 2; AMWS 10; BPFB 3;
BW 2, 3; CA 21-24R; CANR 25, 48, 74;
CN 7; CP 7; CSW; DA3; DAM MULT;
DLB 2, 5, 33, 169, 227; DLBD 8; EWL
3; LMFS 2; MSW; MTCW 1, 2; PFS 6;
RGAL 4; TCWW 2
Reed, John (Silas) 1887-1920 .... **TCLC 9**
See also CA 106; 195; TUS
Reed, Lou .... **CLC 21**
See Firbank, Louis
Reese, Lizette Woodworth 1856-1935 . **PC 29**
See also CA 180; DLB 54
Reeve, Clara 1729-1807 .... **NCLC 19**
See also DLB 39; RGEL 2
Reich, Wilhelm 1897-1957 .... **TCLC 57**
See also CA 199
Reid, Christopher (John) 1949- .... **CLC 33**
See also CA 140; CANR 89; CP 7; DLB
40; EWL 3
Reid, Desmond
See Moorcock, Michael (John)

Reid Banks, Lynne 1929-
See Banks, Lynne Reid
See also AAYA 49; CA 1-4R; CANR 6, 22,
38, 87; CLR 24; CN 7; JRDA; MAICYA
1, 2; SATA 22, 75, 111; YAW
Reilly, William K.
See Creasey, John
Reiner, Max
See Caldwell, (Janet Miriam) Taylor
(Holland)
Reis, Ricardo
See Pessoa, Fernando (Antonio Nogueira)
Reizenstein, Elmer Leopold
See Rice, Elmer (Leopold)
See also EWL 3
Remarque, Erich Maria 1898-1970 . **CLC 21**
See also AAYA 27; BPFB 3; CA 77-80; 29-
32R; CDWLB 2; DA; DA3; DAB; DAC;
DAM MST, NOV; DLB 56; EWL 3;
EXPN; LAIT 3; MTCW 1, 2; NFS 4;
RGWL 2, 3
Remington, Frederic 1861-1909 ..... **TCLC 89**
See also CA 108; 169; DLB 12, 186, 188;
SATA 41
Remizov, A.
See Remizov, Aleksei (Mikhailovich)
Remizov, A. M.
See Remizov, Aleksei (Mikhailovich)
Remizov, Aleksei (Mikhailovich)
1877-1957 .... **TCLC 27**
See Remizov, Alexey Mikhaylovich
See also CA 125; 133
Remizov, Alexey Mikhaylovich
See Remizov, Aleksei (Mikhailovich)
See also EWL 3
Renan, Joseph Ernest 1823-1892 .. **NCLC 26**
See also GFL 1789 to the Present
Renard, Jules(-Pierre) 1864-1910 .. **TCLC 17**
See also CA 117; 202; GFL 1789 to the
Present
Renault, Mary .... **CLC 3, 11, 17**
See Challans, Mary
See also BPFB 3; BYA 2; DLBY 1983;
EWL 3; GLL 1; LAIT 1; MTCW 2; RGEL
2; RHW
Rendell, Ruth (Barbara) 1930- .. **CLC 28, 48**
See Vine, Barbara
See also BPFB 3; BRWS 9; CA 109; CANR
32, 52, 74; CN 7; CPW; DAM POP; DLB
87, 276; INT CANR-32; MSW; MTCW
1, 2
Renoir, Jean 1894-1979 .... **CLC 20**
See also CA 129; 85-88
Resnais, Alain 1922- .... **CLC 16**
Revard, Carter (Curtis) 1931- .... **NNAL**
See also CA 144; CANR 81; PFS 5
Reverdy, Pierre 1889-1960 .... **CLC 53**
See also CA 97-100; 89-92; DLB 258; EWL
3; GFL 1789 to the Present
Rexroth, Kenneth 1905-1982 .... **CLC 1, 2, 6,
11, 22, 49, 112; PC 20**
See also BG 3; CA 5-8R; 107; CANR 14,
34, 63; CDALB 1941-1968; DAM POET;
DLB 16, 48, 165, 212; DLBY 1982; EWL
3; INT CANR-14; MTCW 1, 2; RGAL 4
Reyes, Alfonso 1889-1959 .... **HLCS 2; TCLC
33**
See also CA 131; EWL 3; HW 1; LAW
Reyes y Basoalto, Ricardo Eliecer Neftali
See Neruda, Pablo
Reymont, Wladyslaw (Stanislaw)
1868(?)-1925 .... **TCLC 5**
See also CA 104; EWL 3
Reynolds, Jonathan 1942- .... **CLC 6, 38**
See also CA 65-68; CANR 28
Reynolds, Joshua 1723-1792 .... **LC 15**
See also DLB 104

Reynolds, Michael S(hane)
1937-2000 .... **CLC 44**
See also CA 65-68; 189; CANR 9, 89, 97
Reznikoff, Charles 1894-1976 .... **CLC 9**
See also CA 33-36; 61-64; CAP 2; DLB 28,
45; WP
Rezzori (d'Arezzo), Gregor von
1914-1998 .... **CLC 25**
See also CA 122; 136; 167
Rhine, Richard
See Silverstein, Alvin; Silverstein, Virginia
B(arbara Opshelor)
Rhodes, Eugene Manlove
1869-1934 .... **TCLC 53**
See also CA 198; DLB 256
R'hoone, Lord
See Balzac, Honore de
Rhys, Jean 1894(?)-1979 ...... **CLC 2, 4, 6, 14,
19, 51, 124; SSC 21**
See also BRWS 2; CA 25-28R; 85-88;
CANR 35, 62; CDBLB 1945-1960; CD-
WLB 3; DA3; DAM NOV; DLB 36, 117,
162; DNFS 2; EWL 3; LATS 1; MTCW
1, 2; RGEL 2; RGSF 2; RHW; TEA
Ribeiro, Darcy 1922-1997 .... **CLC 34**
See also CA 33-36R; 156; EWL 3
Ribeiro, Joao Ubaldo (Osorio Pimentel)
1941- .... **CLC 10, 67**
See also CA 81-84; EWL 3
Ribman, Ronald (Burt) 1932- .... **CLC 7**
See also CA 21-24R; CAD; CANR 46, 80;
CD 5
Ricci, Nino 1959- .... **CLC 70**
See also CA 137; CCA 1
Rice, Anne 1941- .... **CLC 41, 128**
See Rampling, Anne
See also AAYA 9, 53; AMWS 7; BEST
89:2; BPFB 3; CA 65-68; CANR 12, 36,
53, 74, 100; CN 7; CPW; CSW; DA3;
DAM POP; GLL 2; HGG; MTCW 2;
SUFW 2; YAW
Rice, Elmer (Leopold) 1892-1967 ...... **CLC 7,
49**
See Reizenstein, Elmer Leopold
See also CA 21-22; 25-28R; CAP 2; DAM
DRAM; DFS 12; DLB 4, 7; MTCW 1, 2;
RGAL 4
Rice, Tim(othy Miles Bindon)
1944- .... **CLC 21**
See also CA 103; CANR 46; DFS 7
Rich, Adrienne (Cecile) 1929- ... **CLC 3, 6, 7,
11, 18, 36, 73, 76, 125; PC 5**
See also AMWR 2; AMWS 1; CA 9-12R;
CANR 20, 53, 74; CDALBS; CP 7; CSW;
CWP; DA3; DAM POET; DLB 5, 67;
EWL 3; EXPP; FW; MAWW; MTCW 1,
2; PAB; PFS 15; RGAL 4; WP
Rich, Barbara
See Graves, Robert (von Ranke)
Rich, Robert
See Trumbo, Dalton
Richard, Keith .... **CLC 17**
See Richards, Keith
Richards, David Adams 1950- .... **CLC 59**
See also CA 93-96; CANR 60, 110; DAC;
DLB 53
Richards, I(vor) A(rmstrong)
1893-1979 .... **CLC 14, 24**
See also BRWS 2; CA 41-44R; 89-92;
CANR 34, 74; DLB 27; EWL 3; MTCW
2; RGEL 2
Richards, Keith 1943-
See Richard, Keith
See also CA 107; CANR 77
Richardson, Anne
See Roiphe, Anne (Richardson)

Rodriguez, Claudio 1934-1999 .... **CLC 10**
See also CA 188; DLB 134
Rodriguez, Richard 1944- .... **CLC 155; HLC 2**
See also CA 110; CANR 66, 116; DAM MULT; DLB 82, 256; HW 1, 2; LAIT 5; NCFS 3; WLIT 1
Roelvaag, O(le) E(dvart) 1876-1931
See Rolvaag, O(le) E(dvart)
See also CA 117; 171
Roethke, Theodore (Huebner)
1908-1963 .... **CLC 1, 3, 8, 11, 19, 46, 101; PC 15**
See also AMW; CA 81-84; CABS 2; CDALB 1941-1968; DA3; DAM POET; DLB 5, 206; EWL 3; EXPP; MTCW 1, 2; PAB; PFS 3; RGAL 4; WP
Rogers, Carl R(ansom)
1902-1987 .... **TCLC 125**
See also CA 1-4R; 121; CANR 1, 18; MTCW 1
Rogers, Samuel 1763-1855 .... **NCLC 69**
See also DLB 93; RGEL 2
Rogers, Thomas Hunton 1927- .... **CLC 57**
See also CA 89-92; INT 89-92
Rogers, Will(iam Penn Adair)
1879-1935 .... **NNAL; TCLC 8, 71**
See also CA 105; 144; DA3; DAM MULT; DLB 11; MTCW 2
Rogin, Gilbert 1929- .... **CLC 18**
See also CA 65-68; CANR 15
Rohan, Koda
See Koda Shigeyuki
Rohlfs, Anna Katharine Green
See Green, Anna Katharine
Rohmer, Eric .... **CLC 16**
See Scherer, Jean-Marie Maurice
Rohmer, Sax .... **TCLC 28**
See Ward, Arthur Henry Sarsfield
See also DLB 70; MSW; SUFW
Roiphe, Anne (Richardson) 1935- .. **CLC 3, 9**
See also CA 89-92; CANR 45, 73; DLBY 1980; INT 89-92
Rojas, Fernando de 1475-1541 ... **HLCS 1, 2; LC 23**
See also DLB 286; RGWL 2, 3
Rojas, Gonzalo 1917- .... **HLCS 2**
See also CA 178; HW 2; LAWS 1
Rolfe, Frederick (William Serafino Austin Lewis Mary) 1860-1913 .... **TCLC 12**
See Al Siddik
See also CA 107; 210; DLB 34, 156; RGEL 2
Rolland, Romain 1866-1944 .... **TCLC 23**
See also CA 118; 197; DLB 65, 284; EWL 3; GFL 1789 to the Present; RGWL 2, 3
Rolle, Richard c. 1300-c. 1349 .... **CMLC 21**
See also DLB 146; LMFS 1; RGEL 2
Rolvaag, O(le) E(dvart) .... **TCLC 17**
See Roelvaag, O(le) E(dvart)
See also DLB 9, 212; NFS 5; RGAL 4
Romain Arnaud, Saint
See Aragon, Louis
Romains, Jules 1885-1972 .... **CLC 7**
See also CA 85-88; CANR 34; DLB 65; EWL 3; GFL 1789 to the Present; MTCW 1
Romero, Jose Ruben 1890-1952 .... **TCLC 14**
See also CA 114; 131; EWL 3; HW 1; LAW
Ronsard, Pierre de 1524-1585 . **LC 6, 54; PC 11**
See also EW 2; GFL Beginnings to 1789; RGWL 2, 3; TWA
Rooke, Leon 1934- .... **CLC 25, 34**
See also CA 25-28R; CANR 23, 53; CCA 1; CPW; DAM POP
Roosevelt, Franklin Delano
1882-1945 .... **TCLC 93**
See also CA 116; 173; LAIT 3

Roosevelt, Theodore 1858-1919 ..... **TCLC 69**
See also CA 115; 170; DLB 47, 186, 275
Roper, William 1498-1578 .... **LC 10**
Roquelaure, A. N.
See Rice, Anne
Rosa, Joao Guimaraes 1908-1967 ... **CLC 23; HLCS 1**
See also CA 89-92; DLB 113; EWL 3; WLIT 1
Rose, Wendy 1948- . **CLC 85; NNAL; PC 13**
See also CA 53-56; CANR 5, 51; CWP; DAM MULT; DLB 175; PFS 13; RGAL 4; SATA 12
Rosen, R. D.
See Rosen, Richard (Dean)
Rosen, Richard (Dean) 1949- .... **CLC 39**
See also CA 77-80; CANR 62, 120; CMW 4; INT CANR-30
Rosenberg, Isaac 1890-1918 .... **TCLC 12**
See also BRW 6; CA 107; 188; DLB 20, 216; EWL 3; PAB; RGEL 2
Rosenblatt, Joe .... **CLC 15**
See Rosenblatt, Joseph
Rosenblatt, Joseph 1933-
See Rosenblatt, Joe
See also CA 89-92; CP 7; INT 89-92
Rosenfeld, Samuel
See Tzara, Tristan
Rosenstock, Sami
See Tzara, Tristan
Rosenstock, Samuel
See Tzara, Tristan
Rosenthal, M(acha) L(ouis)
1917-1996 .... **CLC 28**
See also CA 1-4R; 152; CAAS 6; CANR 4, 51; CP 7; DLB 5; SATA 59
Ross, Barnaby
See Dannay, Frederic
Ross, Bernard L.
See Follett, Ken(neth Martin)
Ross, J. H.
See Lawrence, T(homas) E(dward)
Ross, John Hume
See Lawrence, T(homas) E(dward)
Ross, Martin 1862-1915
See Martin, Violet Florence
See also DLB 135; GLL 2; RGEL 2; RGSF 2
Ross, (James) Sinclair 1908-1996 ... **CLC 13; SSC 24**
See also CA 73-76; CANR 81; CN 7; DAC; DAM MST; DLB 88; RGEL 2; RGSF 2; TCWW 2
Rossetti, Christina (Georgina)
1830-1894 .... **NCLC 2, 50, 66; PC 7; WLC**
See also AAYA 51; BRW 5; BYA 4; DA; DA3; DAB; DAC; DAM MST, POET; DLB 35, 163, 240; EXPP; LATS 1; MAICYA 1, 2; PFS 10, 14; RGEL 2; SATA 20; TEA; WCH
Rossetti, Dante Gabriel 1828-1882 . **NCLC 4, 77; PC 44; WLC**
See also AAYA 51; BRW 5; CDBLB 1832-1890; DA; DAB; DAC; DAM MST, POET; DLB 35; EXPP; RGEL 2; TEA
Rossi, Cristina Peri
See Peri Rossi, Cristina
Rossi, Jean-Baptiste 1931-2003
See Japrisot, Sebastien
See also CA 201; 215
Rossner, Judith (Perelman) 1935- . **CLC 6, 9, 29**
See also AITN 2; BEST 90:3; BPFB 3; CA 17-20R; CANR 18, 51, 73; CN 7; DLB 6; INT CANR-18; MTCW 1, 2

Rostand, Edmond (Eugene Alexis)
1868-1918 .... **DC 10; TCLC 6, 37**
See also CA 104; 126; DA; DA3; DAB; DAC; DAM DRAM, MST; DFS 1; DLB 192; LAIT 1; MTCW 1; RGWL 2, 3; TWA
Roth, Henry 1906-1995 ..... **CLC 2, 6, 11, 104**
See also AMWS 9; CA 11-12; 149; CANR 38, 63; CAP 1; CN 7; DA3; DLB 28; EWL 3; MTCW 1, 2; RGAL 4
Roth, (Moses) Joseph 1894-1939 ... **TCLC 33**
See also CA 160; DLB 85; EWL 3; RGWL 2, 3
Roth, Philip (Milton) 1933- ... **CLC 1, 2, 3, 4, 6, 9, 15, 22, 31, 47, 66, 86, 119; SSC 26; WLC**
See also AMWR 2; AMWS 3; BEST 90:3; BPFB 3; CA 1-4R; CANR 1, 22, 36, 55, 89; CDALB 1968-1988; CN 7; CPW 1; DA; DA3; DAB; DAC; DAM MST, NOV, POP; DLB 2, 28, 173; DLBY 1982; EWL 3; MTCW 1, 2; RGAL 4; RGSF 2; SSFS 12, 18; TUS
Rothenberg, Jerome 1931- .... **CLC 6, 57**
See also CA 45-48; CANR 1, 106; CP 7; DLB 5, 193
Rotter, Pat ed. .... **CLC 65**
Roumain, Jacques (Jean Baptiste)
1907-1944 .... **BLC 3; TCLC 19**
See also BW 1; CA 117; 125; DAM MULT; EWL 3
Rourke, Constance Mayfield
1885-1941 .... **TCLC 12**
See also CA 107; 200; YABC 1
Rousseau, Jean-Baptiste 1671-1741 ...... **LC 9**
Rousseau, Jean-Jacques 1712-1778 .... **LC 14, 36; WLC**
See also DA; DA3; DAB; DAC; DAM MST; EW 4; GFL Beginnings to 1789; LMFS 1; RGWL 2, 3; TWA
Roussel, Raymond 1877-1933 .... **TCLC 20**
See also CA 117; 201; EWL 3; GFL 1789 to the Present
Rovit, Earl (Herbert) 1927- .... **CLC 7**
See also CA 5-8R; CANR 12
Rowe, Elizabeth Singer 1674-1737 ..... **LC 44**
See also DLB 39, 95
Rowe, Nicholas 1674-1718 .... **LC 8**
See also DLB 84; RGEL 2
Rowlandson, Mary 1637(?)-1678 .... **LC 66**
See also DLB 24, 200; RGAL 4
Rowley, Ames Dorrance
See Lovecraft, H(oward) P(hillips)
Rowling, J(oanne) K(athleen)
1965- .... **CLC 137**
See also AAYA 34; BYA 13, 14; CA 173; CLR 66, 80; MAICYA 2; SATA 109; SUFW 2
Rowson, Susanna Haswell
1762(?)-1824 .... **NCLC 5, 69**
See also DLB 37, 200; RGAL 4
Roy, Arundhati 1960(?)- .... **CLC 109**
See also CA 163; CANR 90; DLBY 1997; EWL 3; LATS 1
Roy, Gabrielle 1909-1983 .... **CLC 10, 14**
See also CA 53-56; 110; CANR 5, 61; CCA 1; DAB; DAC; DAM MST; DLB 68; EWL 3; MTCW 1; RGWL 2, 3; SATA 104
Royko, Mike 1932-1997 .... **CLC 109**
See also CA 89-92; 157; CANR 26, 111; CPW
Rozanov, Vasily Vasilyevich
See Rozanov, Vassili
See also EWL 3
Rozanov, Vassili 1856-1919 .... **TCLC 104**
See Rozanov, Vasily Vasilyevich

POP; DLB 2, 102, 173; EWL 3; EXPN; LAIT 4; MAICYA 1, 2; MTCW 1, 2; NFS 1; RGAL 4; RGSF 2; SATA 67; SSFS 17; TUS; WYA; YAW

Salisbury, John
See Caute, (John) David

Salter, James 1925- .. **CLC 7, 52, 59; SSC 58**
See also AMWS 9; CA 73-76; CANR 107; DLB 130

Saltus, Edgar (Everton) 1855-1921 . **TCLC 8**
See also CA 105; DLB 202; RGAL 4

Saltykov, Mikhail Evgrafovich
1826-1889 .... **NCLC 16**
See also DLB 238:

Saltykov-Shchedrin, N.
See Saltykov, Mikhail Evgrafovich

Samarakis, Andonis
See Samarakis, Antonis
See also EWL 3

Samarakis, Antonis 1919- .... **CLC 5**
See Samarakis, Andonis
See also CA 25-28R; CAAS 16; CANR 36

Sanchez, Florencio 1875-1910 .... **TCLC 37**
See also CA 153; EWL 3; HW 1; LAW

Sanchez, Luis Rafael 1936- .... **CLC 23**
See also CA 128; DLB 145; EWL 3; HW 1; WLIT 1

Sanchez, Sonia 1934- .... **BLC 3; CLC 5, 116; PC 9**
See also BW 2, 3; CA 33-36R; CANR 24, 49, 74, 115; CLR 18; CP 7; CSW; CWP; DA3; DAM MULT; DLB 41; DLBD 8; EWL 3; MAICYA 1, 2; MTCW 1, 2; SATA 22, 136; WP

Sancho, Ignatius 1729-1780 .... **LC 84**

Sand, George 1804-1876 ..... **NCLC 2, 42, 57; WLC**
See also DA; DA3; DAB; DAC; DAM MST, NOV; DLB 119, 192; EW 6; FW; GFL 1789 to the Present; RGWL 2, 3; TWA

Sandburg, Carl (August) 1878-1967 . **CLC 1, 4, 10, 15, 35; PC 2, 41; WLC**
See also AAYA 24; AMW; BYA 1, 3; CA 5-8R; 25-28R; CANR 35; CDALB 1865-1917; CLR 67; DA; DA3; DAB; DAC; DAM MST, POET; DLB 17, 54, 284; EWL 3; EXPP; LAIT 2; MAICYA 1, 2; MTCW 1, 2; PAB; PFS 3, 6, 12; RGAL 4; SATA 8; TUS; WCH; WP; WYA

Sandburg, Charles
See Sandburg, Carl (August)

Sandburg, Charles A.
See Sandburg, Carl (August)

Sanders, (James) Ed(ward) 1939- .... **CLC 53**
See Sanders, Edward
See also BG 3; CA 13-16R; CAAS 21; CANR 13, 44, 78; CP 7; DAM POET; DLB 16, 244

Sanders, Edward
See Sanders, (James) Ed(ward)
See also DLB 244

Sanders, Lawrence 1920-1998 .... **CLC 41**
See also BEST 89:4; BPFB 3; CA 81-84; 165; CANR 33, 62; CMW 4; CPW; DA3; DAM POP; MTCW 1

Sanders, Noah
See Blount, Roy (Alton), Jr.

Sanders, Winston P.
See Anderson, Poul (William)

Sandoz, Mari(e Susette) 1900-1966 .. **CLC 28**
See also CA 1-4R; 25-28R; CANR 17, 64; DLB 9, 212; LAIT 2; MTCW 1, 2; SATA 5; TCWW 2

Sandys, George 1578-1644 .... **LC 80**
See also DLB 24, 121

Saner, Reg(inald Anthony) 1931- .... **CLC 9**
See also CA 65-68; CP 7

Sankara 788-820 .... **CMLC 32**

Sannazaro, Jacopo 1456(?)-1530 .... **LC 8**
See also RGWL 2, 3

Sansom, William 1912-1976 . **CLC 2, 6; SSC 21**
See also CA 5-8R; 65-68; CANR 42; DAM NOV; DLB 139; EWL 3; MTCW 1; RGEL 2; RGSF 2

Santayana, George 1863-1952 .... **TCLC 40**
See also AMW; CA 115; 194; DLB 54, 71, 246, 270; DLBD 13; EWL 3; RGAL 4; TUS

Santiago, Danny .... **CLC 33**
See James, Daniel (Lewis)
See also DLB 122

Santmyer, Helen Hooven
1895-1986 .... **CLC 33; TCLC 133**
See also CA 1-4R; 118; CANR 15, 33; DLBY 1984; MTCW 1; RHW

Santoka, Taneda 1882-1940 .... **TCLC 72**

Santos, Bienvenido N(uqui)
1911-1996 .... **AAL; CLC 22**
See also CA 101; 151; CANR 19, 46; DAM MULT; EWL; RGAL 4

Sapir, Edward 1884-1939 .... **TCLC 108**
See also CA 211; DLB 92

Sapper .... **TCLC 44**
See McNeile, Herman Cyril

Sapphire
See Sapphire, Brenda

Sapphire, Brenda 1950- .... **CLC 99**

Sappho fl. 6th cent. B.C.- ...... **CMLC 3; PC 5**
See also CDWLB 1; DA3; DAM POET; DLB 176; RGWL 2, 3; WP

Saramago, Jose 1922- ..... **CLC 119; HLCS 1**
See also CA 153; CANR 96; DLB 287; EWL 3; LATS 1

Sarduy, Severo 1937-1993 .... **CLC 6, 97; HLCS 2**
See also CA 89-92; 142; CANR 58, 81; CWW 2; DLB 113; EWL 3; HW 1, 2; LAW

Sargeson, Frank 1903-1982 .... **CLC 31**
See also CA 25-28R; 106; CANR 38, 79; EWL 3; GLL 2; RGEL 2; RGSF 2

Sarmiento, Domingo Faustino
1811-1888 .... **HLCS 2**
See also LAW; WLIT 1

Sarmiento, Felix Ruben Garcia
See Dario, Ruben

Saro-Wiwa, Ken(ule Beeson)
1941-1995 .... **CLC 114**
See also BW 2; CA 142; 150; CANR 60; DLB 157

Saroyan, William 1908-1981 ... **CLC 1, 8, 10, 29, 34, 56; SSC 21; TCLC 137; WLC**
See also CA 5-8R; 103; CAD; CANR 30; CDALBS; DA; DA3; DAB; DAC; DAM DRAM, MST, NOV; DFS 17; DLB 7, 9, 86; DLBY 1981; EWL 3; LAIT 4; MTCW 1, 2; RGAL 4; RGSF 2; SATA 23; SATA-Obit 24; SSFS 14; TUS

Sarraute, Nathalie 1900-1999 .... **CLC 1, 2, 4, 8, 10, 31, 80**
See also BPFB 3; CA 9-12R; 187; CANR 23, 66; CWW 2; DLB 83; EW 12; EWL 3; GFL 1789 to the Present; MTCW 1, 2; RGWL 2, 3

Sarton, (Eleanor) May 1912-1995 ..... **CLC 4, 14, 49, 91; PC 39; TCLC 120**
See also AMWS 8; CA 1-4R; 149; CANR 1, 34, 55, 116; CN 7; CP 7; DAM POET; DLB 48; DLBY 1981; EWL 3; FW; INT CANR-34; MTCW 1, 2; RGAL 4; SATA 36; SATA-Obit 86; TUS

Sartre, Jean-Paul 1905-1980 . **CLC 1, 4, 7, 9, 13, 18, 24, 44, 50, 52; DC 3; SSC 32; WLC**
See also CA 9-12R; 97-100; CANR 21; DA; DA3; DAB; DAC; DAM DRAM, MST,

NOV; DFS 5; DLB 72; EW 12; EWL 3; GFL 1789 to the Present; LMFS 2; MTCW 1, 2; RGSF 2; RGWL 2, 3; SSFS 9; TWA

Sassoon, Siegfried (Lorraine)
1886-1967 .... **CLC 36, 130; PC 12**
See also BRW 6; CA 104; 25-28R; CANR 36; DAB; DAM MST, NOV, POET; DLB 20, 191; DLBD 18; EWL 3; MTCW 1, 2; PAB; RGEL 2; TEA

Satterfield, Charles
See Pohl, Frederik

Satyremont
See Peret, Benjamin

Saul, John (W. III) 1942- .... **CLC 46**
See also AAYA 10; BEST 90:4; CA 81-84; CANR 16, 40, 81; CPW; DAM NOV, POP; HGG; SATA 98

Saunders, Caleb
See Heinlein, Robert A(nson)

Saura (Atares), Carlos 1932-1998 .... **CLC 20**
See also CA 114; 131; CANR 79; HW 1

Sauser, Frederic Louis
See Sauser-Hall, Frederic

Sauser-Hall, Frederic 1887-1961 ...... **CLC 18**
See Cendrars, Blaise
See also CA 102; 93-96; CANR 36, 62; MTCW 1

Saussure, Ferdinand de
1857-1913 .... **TCLC 49**
See also DLB 242

Savage, Catharine
See Brosman, Catharine Savage

Savage, Thomas 1915- .... **CLC 40**
See also CA 126; 132; CAAS 15; CN 7; INT CA-132; TCWW 2

Savan, Glenn (?)- .... **CLC 50**

Sax, Robert
See Johnson, Robert

Saxo Grammaticus c. 1150-c.
1222 .... **CMLC 58**

Saxton, Robert
See Johnson, Robert

Sayers, Dorothy L(eigh)
1893-1957 .... **TCLC 2, 15**
See also BPFB 3; BRWS 3; CA 104; 119; CANR 60; CDBLB 1914-1945; CMW 4; DAM POP; DLB 10, 36, 77, 100; MSW; MTCW 1, 2; RGEL 2; SSFS 12; TEA

Sayers, Valerie 1952- .... **CLC 50, 122**
See also CA 134; CANR 61; CSW

Sayles, John (Thomas) 1950- . **CLC 7, 10, 14**
See also CA 57-60; CANR 41, 84; DLB 44

Scammell, Michael 1935- .... **CLC 34**
See also CA 156

Scannell, Vernon 1922- .... **CLC 49**
See also CA 5-8R; CANR 8, 24, 57; CP 7; CWRI 5; DLB 27; SATA 59

Scarlett, Susan
See Streatfeild, (Mary) Noel

Scarron 1847-1910
See Mikszath, Kalman

Schaeffer, Susan Fromberg 1941- ..... **CLC 6, 11, 22**
See also CA 49-52; CANR 18, 65; CN 7; DLB 28; MTCW 1, 2; SATA 22

Schama, Simon (Michael) 1945- ..... **CLC 150**
See also BEST 89:4; CA 105; CANR 39, 91

Schary, Jill
See Robinson, Jill

Schell, Jonathan 1943- .... **CLC 35**
See also CA 73-76; CANR 12, 117

Schelling, Friedrich Wilhelm Joseph von
1775-1854 .... **NCLC 30**
See also DLB 90

Scherer, Jean-Marie Maurice 1920-
See Rohmer, Eric
See also CA 110

Selby, Hubert, Jr. 1928- .... **CLC 1, 2, 4, 8; SSC 20**
  See also CA 13-16R; CANR 33, 85; CN 7; DLB 2, 227
Selzer, Richard 1928- .... **CLC 74**
  See also CA 65-68; CANR 14, 106
Sembene, Ousmane
  See Ousmane, Sembene
  See also AFW; CWW 2; EWL 3; WLIT 2
Senancour, Etienne Pivert de
  1770-1846 .... **NCLC 16**
  See also DLB 119; GFL 1789 to the Present
Sender, Ramon (Jose) 1902-1982 ...... **CLC 8; HLC 2; TCLC 136**
  See also CA 5-8R; 105; CANR 8; DAM MULT; EWL 3; HW 1; MTCW 1; RGWL 2, 3
Seneca, Lucius Annaeus c. 4B.C.-c. 65 .... **CMLC 6; DC 5**
  See also AW 2; CDWLB 1; DAM DRAM; DLB 211; RGWL 2, 3; TWA
Senghor, Leopold Sedar 1906-2001 ... **BLC 3; CLC 54, 130; PC 25**
  See also AFW; BW 2; CA 116; 125; 203; CANR 47, 74; DAM MULT, POET; DNFS 2; EWL 3; GFL 1789 to the Present; MTCW 1, 2; TWA
Senna, Danzy 1970- .... **CLC 119**
  See also CA 169
Serling, (Edward) Rod(man)
  1924-1975 .... **CLC 30**
  See also AAYA 14; AITN 1; CA 162; 57-60; DLB 26; SFW 4
Serna, Ramon Gomez de la
  See Gomez de la Serna, Ramon
Serpieres
  See Guillevic, (Eugene)
Service, Robert
  See Service, Robert W(illiam)
  See also BYA 4; DAB; DLB 92
Service, Robert W(illiam)
  1874(?)-1958 .... **TCLC 15; WLC**
  See Service, Robert
  See also CA 115; 140; CANR 84; DA; DAC; DAM MST, POET; PFS 10; RGEL 2; SATA 20
Seth, Vikram 1952- .... **CLC 43, 90**
  See also CA 121; 127; CANR 50, 74; CN 7; CP 7; DA3; DAM MULT; DLB 120, 271, 282; EWL 3; INT CA-127; MTCW 2
Seton, Cynthia Propper 1926-1982 .. **CLC 27**
  See also CA 5-8R; 108; CANR 7
Seton, Ernest (Evan) Thompson
  1860-1946 .... **TCLC 31**
  See also ANW; BYA 3; CA 109; 204; CLR 59; DLB 92; DLBD 13; JRDA; SATA 18
Seton-Thompson, Ernest
  See Seton, Ernest (Evan) Thompson
Settle, Mary Lee 1918- .... **CLC 19, 61**
  See also BPFB 3; CA 89-92; CAAS 1; CANR 44, 87; CN 7; CSW; DLB 6; INT CA-89-92
Seuphor, Michel
  See Arp, Jean
Sevigne, Marie (de Rabutin-Chantal)
  1626-1696 .... **LC 11**
  See Sevigne, Marie de Rabutin Chantal
  See also GFL Beginnings to 1789; TWA
Sevigne, Marie de Rabutin Chantal
  See Sevigne, Marie (de Rabutin-Chantal)
  See also DLB 268
Sewall, Samuel 1652-1730 .... **LC 38**
  See also DLB 24; RGAL 4
Sexton, Anne (Harvey) 1928-1974 ..... **CLC 2, 4, 6, 8, 10, 15, 53, 123; PC 2; WLC**
  See also AMWS 2; CA 1-4R; 53-56; CABS 2; CANR 3, 36; CDALB 1941-1968; DA; DA3; DAB; DAC; DAM MST, POET;

DLB 5, 169; EWL 3; EXPP; FW; MAWW; MTCW 1, 2; PAB; PFS 4, 14; RGAL 4; SATA 10; TUS
Shaara, Jeff 1952- .... **CLC 119**
  See also CA 163; CANR 109
Shaara, Michael (Joseph, Jr.)
  1929-1988 .... **CLC 15**
  See also AITN 1; BPFB 3; CA 102; 125; CANR 52, 85; DAM POP; DLBY 1983
Shackleton, C. C.
  See Aldiss, Brian W(ilson)
Shacochis, Bob .... **CLC 39**
  See Shacochis, Robert G.
Shacochis, Robert G. 1951-
  See Shacochis, Bob
  See also CA 119; 124; CANR 100; INT CA-124
Shaffer, Anthony (Joshua)
  1926-2001 .... **CLC 19**
  See also CA 110; 116; 200; CBD; CD 5; DAM DRAM; DFS 13; DLB 13
Shaffer, Peter (Levin) 1926- .. **CLC 5, 14, 18, 37, 60; DC 7**
  See also BRWS 1; CA 25-28R; CANR 25, 47, 74, 118; CBD; CD 5; CDBLB 1960 to Present; DA3; DAB; DAM DRAM, MST; DFS 5, 13; DLB 13, 233; EWL 3; MTCW 1, 2; RGEL 2; TEA
Shakespeare, William 1564-1616 .... **WLC**
  See also AAYA 35; BRW 1; CDBLB Before 1660; DA; DA3; DAB; DAC; DAM DRAM, MST, POET; DLB 62, 172, 263; EXPP; LAIT 1; LATS 1; LMFS 1; PAB; PFS 1, 2, 3, 4, 5, 8, 9; RGEL 2; TEA; WLIT 3; WP; WS; WYA
Shakey, Bernard
  See Young, Neil
Shalamov, Varlam (Tikhonovich)
  1907(?)-1982 .... **CLC 18**
  See also CA 129; 105; RGSF 2
Shamloo, Ahmad
  See Shamlu, Ahmad
Shamlou, Ahmad
  See Shamlu, Ahmad
Shamlu, Ahmad 1925-2000 .... **CLC 10**
  See also CA 216; CWW 2
Shammas, Anton 1951- .... **CLC 55**
  See also CA 199
Shandling, Arline
  See Berriault, Gina
Shange, Ntozake 1948- ... **BLC 3; CLC 8, 25, 38, 74, 126; DC 3**
  See also AAYA 9; AFAW 1, 2; BW 2; CA 85-88; CABS 3; CAD; CANR 27, 48, 74; CD 5; CP 7; CWD; CWP; DA3; DAM DRAM, MST; DFS 2, 11; DLB 38, 249; FW; LAIT 5; MTCW 1, 2; NFS 11; RGAL 4; YAW
Shanley, John Patrick 1950- .... **CLC 75**
  See also CA 128; 133; CAD; CANR 83; CD 5
Shapcott, Thomas W(illiam) 1935- .. **CLC 38**
  See also CA 69-72; CANR 49, 83, 103; CP 7; DLB 289
Shapiro, Jane 1942- .... **CLC 76**
  See also CA 196
Shapiro, Karl (Jay) 1913-2000 ...... **CLC 4, 8, 15, 53; PC 25**
  See also AMWS 2; CA 1-4R; 188; CAAS 6; CANR 1, 36, 66; CP 7; DLB 48; EWL 3; EXPP; MTCW 1, 2; PFS 3; RGAL 4
Sharp, William 1855-1905 .... **TCLC 39**
  See Macleod, Fiona
  See also CA 160; DLB 156; RGEL 2
Sharpe, Thomas Ridley 1928-
  See Sharpe, Tom
  See also CA 114; 122; CANR 85; INT CA-122

Sharpe, Tom .... **CLC 36**
  See Sharpe, Thomas Ridley
  See also CN 7; DLB 14, 231
Shatrov, Mikhail .... **CLC 59**
Shaw, Bernard
  See Shaw, George Bernard
  See also DLB 190
Shaw, G. Bernard
  See Shaw, George Bernard
Shaw, George Bernard 1856-1950 .. **TCLC 3, 9, 21, 45; WLC**
  See Shaw, Bernard
  See also BRW 6; BRWC 1; BRWR 2; CA 104; 128; CDBLB 1914-1945; DA; DA3; DAB; DAC; DAM DRAM, MST; DFS 1, 3, 6, 11; DLB 10, 57; EWL 3; LAIT 3; LATS 1; MTCW 1, 2; RGEL 2; TEA; WLIT 4
Shaw, Henry Wheeler 1818-1885 .. **NCLC 15**
  See also DLB 11; RGAL 4
Shaw, Irwin 1913-1984 .... **CLC 7, 23, 34**
  See also AITN 1; BPFB 3; CA 13-16R; 112; CANR 21; CDALB 1941-1968; CPW; DAM DRAM, POP; DLB 6, 102; DLBY 1984; MTCW 1, 21
Shaw, Robert 1927-1978 .... **CLC 5**
  See also AITN 1; CA 1-4R; 81-84; CANR 4; DLB 13, 14
Shaw, T. E.
  See Lawrence, T(homas) E(dward)
Shawn, Wallace 1943- .... **CLC 41**
  See also CA 112; CAD; CD 5; DLB 266
Shchedrin, N.
  See Saltykov, Mikhail Evgrafovich
Shea, Lisa 1953- .... **CLC 86**
  See also CA 147
Sheed, Wilfrid (John Joseph) 1930- . **CLC 2, 4, 10, 53**
  See also CA 65-68; CANR 30, 66; CN 7; DLB 6; MTCW 1, 2
Sheehy, Gail 1937- .... **CLC 171**
  See also CA 49-52; CANR 1, 33, 55, 92; CPW; MTCW 1
Sheldon, Alice Hastings Bradley
  1915(?)-1987
  See Tiptree, James, Jr.
  See also CA 108; 122; CANR 34; INT CA-108; MTCW 1
Sheldon, John
  See Bloch, Robert (Albert)
Sheldon, Walter J(ames) 1917-1996
  See Queen, Ellery
  See also AITN 1; CA 25-28R; CANR 10
Shelley, Mary Wollstonecraft (Godwin)
  1797-1851 ...... **NCLC 14, 59, 103; WLC**
  See also AAYA 20; BPFB 3; BRW 3; BRWC 2; BRWS 3; BYA 5; CDBLB 1789-1832; DA; DA3; DAB; DAC; DAM MST, NOV; DLB 110, 116, 159, 178; EXPN; HGG; LAIT 1; LMFS 1, 2; NFS 1; RGEL 2; SATA 29; SCFW; SFW 4; TEA; WLIT 3
Shelley, Percy Bysshe 1792-1822 .. **NCLC 18, 93; PC 14; WLC**
  See also BRW 4; BRWR 1; CDBLB 1789-1832; DA; DA3; DAB; DAC; DAM MST, POET; DLB 96, 110, 158; EXPP; LMFS 1; PAB; PFS 2; RGEL 2; TEA; WLIT 3; WP
Shepard, Jim 1956- .... **CLC 36**
  See also CA 137; CANR 59, 104; SATA 90
Shepard, Lucius 1947- .... **CLC 34**
  See also CA 128; 141; CANR 81; HGG; SCFW 2; SFW 4; SUFW 2
Shepard, Sam 1943- .... **CLC 4, 6, 17, 34, 41, 44, 169; DC 5**
  See also AAYA 1; AMWS 3; CA 69-72; CABS 3; CAD; CANR 22, 120; CD 5; DA3; DAM DRAM; DFS 3, 6, 7, 14; DLB 7, 212; EWL 3; IDFW 3, 4; MTCW 1, 2; RGAL 4

Shepherd, Michael
See Ludlum, Robert
Sherburne, Zoa (Lillian Morin)
1912-1995 .... **CLC 30**
See also AAYA 13; CA 1-4R; 176; CANR
3, 37; MAICYA 1, 2; SAAS 18; SATA 3;
YAW
Sheridan, Frances 1724-1766 .... **LC 7**
See also DLB 39, 84
Sheridan, Richard Brinsley
1751-1816 .... **DC 1; NCLC 5, 91; WLC**
See also BRW 3; CDBLB 1660-1789; DA;
DAB; DAC; DAM DRAM, MST; DFS
15; DLB 89; WLIT 3
Sherman, Jonathan Marc .... **CLC 55**
Sherman, Martin 1941(?)- .... **CLC 19**
See also CA 116; 123; CAD; CANR 86;
CD 5; DLB 228; GLL 1; IDTP
Sherwin, Judith Johnson
See Johnson, Judith (Emlyn)
See also CANR 85; CP 7; CWP
Sherwood, Frances 1940- .... **CLC 81**
See also CA 146
Sherwood, Robert E(mmet)
1896-1955 .... **TCLC 3**
See also CA 104; 153; CANR 86; DAM
DRAM; DFS 11, 15, 17; DLB 7, 26, 249;
IDFW 3, 4; RGAL 4
Shestov, Lev 1866-1938 .... **TCLC 56**
Shevchenko, Taras 1814-1861 .... **NCLC 54**
Shiel, M(atthew) P(hipps)
1865-1947 .... **TCLC 8**
See Holmes, Gordon
See also CA 106; 160; DLB 153; HGG;
MTCW 2; SFW 4; SUFW
Shields, Carol 1935-2003 .... **CLC 91, 113**
See also AMWS 7; CA 81-84; CANR 51,
74, 98; CCA 1; CN 7; CPW; DA3; DAC;
MTCW 2
Shields, David 1956- .... **CLC 97**
See also CA 124; CANR 48, 99, 112
Shiga, Naoya 1883-1971 ..... **CLC 33; SSC 23**
See Shiga Naoya
See also CA 101; 33-36R; MJW; RGWL 3
Shiga Naoya
See Shiga, Naoya
See also DLB 180; EWL 3; RGWL 3
Shilts, Randy 1951-1994 .... **CLC 85**
See also AAYA 19; CA 115; 127; 144;
CANR 45; DA3; GLL 1; INT CA-127;
MTCW 2
Shimazaki, Haruki 1872-1943
See Shimazaki Toson
See also CA 105; 134; CANR 84; RGWL 3
Shimazaki Toson .... **TCLC 5**
See Shimazaki, Haruki
See also DLB 180; EWL 3
Sholokhov, Mikhail (Aleksandrovich)
1905-1984 .... **CLC 7, 15**
See also CA 101; 112; DLB 272; EWL 3;
MTCW 1, 2; RGWL 2, 3; SATA-Obit 36
Shone, Patric
See Hanley, James
Showalter, Elaine 1941- .... **CLC 169**
See also CA 57-60; CANR 58, 106; DLB
67; FW; GLL 2
Shreve, Susan Richards 1939- .... **CLC 23**
See also CA 49-52; CAAS 5; CANR 5, 38,
69, 100; MAICYA 1, 2; SATA 46, 95;
SATA-Brief 41
Shue, Larry 1946-1985 .... **CLC 52**
See also CA 145; 117; DAM DRAM; DFS
7
Shu-Jen, Chou 1881-1936
See Lu Hsun
See also CA 104
Shulman, Alix Kates 1932- .... **CLC 2, 10**
See also CA 29-32R; CANR 43; FW; SATA
7

Shusaku, Endo
See Endo, Shusaku
Shuster, Joe 1914-1992 .... **CLC 21**
See also AAYA 50
Shute, Nevil .... **CLC 30**
See Norway, Nevil Shute
See also BPFB 3; DLB 255; NFS 9; RHW;
SFW 4
Shuttle, Penelope (Diane) 1947- .... **CLC 7**
See also CA 93-96; CANR 39, 84, 92, 108;
CP 7; CWP; DLB 14, 40
Shvarts, Elena 1948- .... **PC 50**
See also CA 147
Sidhwa, Bapsy (N.) 1938- .... **CLC 168**
See also CA 108; CANR 25, 57; CN 7; FW
Sidney, Mary 1561-1621 .... **LC 19, 39**
See Sidney Herbert, Mary
Sidney, Sir Philip 1554-1586 . **LC 19, 39; PC 32**
See also BRW 1; BRWR 2; CDBLB Before
1660; DA; DA3; DAB; DAC; DAM MST,
POET; DLB 167; EXPP; PAB; RGEL 2;
TEA; WP
Sidney Herbert, Mary
See Sidney, Mary
See also DLB 167
Siegel, Jerome 1914-1996 .... **CLC 21**
See Siegel, Jerry
See also CA 116; 169; 151
Siegel, Jerry
See Siegel, Jerome
See also AAYA 50
Sienkiewicz, Henryk (Adam Alexander Pius)
1846-1916 .... **TCLC 3**
See also CA 104; 134; CANR 84; EWL 3;
RGSF 2; RGWL 2, 3
Sierra, Gregorio Martinez
See Martinez Sierra, Gregorio
Sierra, Maria (de la O'LeJarraga) Martinez
See Martinez Sierra, Maria (de la
O'LeJarraga)
Sigal, Clancy 1926- .... **CLC 7**
See also CA 1-4R; CANR 85; CN 7
Sigourney, Lydia H.
See Sigourney, Lydia Howard (Huntley)
See also DLB 73, 183
Sigourney, Lydia Howard (Huntley)
1791-1865 .... **NCLC 21, 87**
See Sigourney, Lydia H.; Sigourney, Lydia
Huntley
See also DLB 1
Sigourney, Lydia Huntley
See Sigourney, Lydia Howard (Huntley)
See also DLB 42, 239, 243
Siguenza y Gongora, Carlos de
1645-1700 .... **HLCS 2; LC 8**
See also LAW
Sigurjonsson, Johann 1880-1919 ... **TCLC 27**
See also CA 170; EWL 3
Sikelianos, Angelos 1884-1951 .... **PC 29; TCLC 39**
See also EWL 3; RGWL 2, 3
Silkin, Jon 1930-1997 .... **CLC 2, 6, 43**
See also CA 5-8R; CAAS 5; CANR 89; CP
7; DLB 27
Silko, Leslie (Marmon) 1948- .... **CLC 23, 74, 114; NNAL; SSC 37; WLCS**
See also AAYA 14; AMWS 4; ANW; BYA
12; CA 115; 122; CANR 45, 65, 118; CN
7; CP 7; CPW 1; CWP; DA; DA3; DAC;
DAM MST, MULT, POP; DLB 143, 175,
256, 275; EWL 3; EXPP; EXPS; LAIT 4;
MTCW 2; NFS 4; PFS 9, 16; RGAL 4;
RGSF 2; SSFS 4, 8, 10, 11
Sillanpaa, Frans Eemil 1888-1964 ... **CLC 19**
See also CA 129; 93-96; EWL 3; MTCW 1

Sillitoe, Alan 1928- .. **CLC 1, 3, 6, 10, 19, 57, 148**
See also AITN 1; BRWS 5; CA 9-12R;
CAAE 191; CAAS 2; CANR 8, 26, 55;
CDBLB 1960 to Present; CN 7; DLB 14,
139; EWL 3; MTCW 1, 2; RGEL 2;
RGSF 2; SATA 61
Silone, Ignazio 1900-1978 .... **CLC 4**
See also CA 25-28; 81-84; CANR 34; CAP
2; DLB 264; EW 12; EWL 3; MTCW 1;
RGSF 2; RGWL 2, 3
Silone, Ignazione
See Silone, Ignazio
Silver, Joan Micklin 1935- .... **CLC 20**
See also CA 114; 121; INT CA-121
Silver, Nicholas
See Faust, Frederick (Schiller)
See also TCWW 2
Silverberg, Robert 1935- .... **CLC 7, 140**
See also AAYA 24; BPFB 3; BYA 7, 9; CA
1-4R; 186; CAAE 186; CAAS 3; CANR
1, 20, 36, 85; CLR 59; CN 7; CPW; DAM
POP; DLB 8; INT CANR-20; MAICYA
1, 2; MTCW 1, 2; SATA 13, 91; SATA-
Essay 104; SCFW 2; SFW 4; SUFW 2
Silverstein, Alvin 1933- .... **CLC 17**
See also CA 49-52; CANR 2; CLR 25;
JRDA; MAICYA 1, 2; SATA 8, 69, 124
Silverstein, Shel(don Allan)
1932-1999 .... **PC 49**
See also AAYA 40; BW 3; CA 107; 179;
CANR 47, 74, 81; CLR 5; CWRI 5;
JRDA; MAICYA 1, 2; MTCW 2; SATA
33, 92; SATA-Brief 27; SATA-Obit 116
Silverstein, Virginia B(arbara Opshelor)
1937- .... **CLC 17**
See also CA 49-52; CANR 2; CLR 25;
JRDA; MAICYA 1, 2; SATA 8, 69, 124
Sim, Georges
See Simenon, Georges (Jacques Christian)
Simak, Clifford D(onald) 1904-1988 . **CLC 1, 55**
See also CA 1-4R; 125; CANR 1, 35; DLB
8; MTCW 1; SATA-Obit 56; SFW 4
Simenon, Georges (Jacques Christian)
1903-1989 .... **CLC 1, 2, 3, 8, 18, 47**
See also BPFB 3; CA 85-88; 129; CANR
35; CMW 4; DA3; DAM POP; DLB 72;
DLBY 1989; EW 12; EWL 3; GFL 1789
to the Present; MSW; MTCW 1, 2; RGWL
2, 3
Simic, Charles 1938- .... **CLC 6, 9, 22, 49, 68, 130**
See also AMWS 8; CA 29-32R; CAAS 4;
CANR 12, 33, 52, 61, 96; CP 7; DA3;
DAM POET; DLB 105; MTCW 2; PFS 7;
RGAL 4; WP
Simmel, Georg 1858-1918 .... **TCLC 64**
See also CA 157
Simmons, Charles (Paul) 1924- .... **CLC 57**
See also CA 89-92; INT CA-89-92
Simmons, Dan 1948- .... **CLC 44**
See also AAYA 16; CA 138; CANR 53, 81;
CPW; DAM POP; HGG; SUFW 2
Simmons, James (Stewart Alexander)
1933- .... **CLC 43**
See also CA 105; CAAS 21; CP 7; DLB 40
Simms, William Gilmore
1806-1870 .... **NCLC 3**
See also DLB 3, 30, 59, 73, 248, 254;
RGAL 4
Simon, Carly 1945- .... **CLC 26**
See also CA 105
Simon, Claude (Henri Eugene)
1913-1984 .... **CLC 4, 9, 15, 39**
See also CA 89-92; CANR 33, 117; DAM
NOV; DLB 83; EW 13; EWL 3; GFL
1789 to the Present; MTCW 1
Simon, Myles
See Follett, Ken(neth Martin)

Simon, (Marvin) Neil 1927- ... **CLC 6, 11, 31, 39, 70; DC 14**
See also AAYA 32; AITN 1; AMWS 4; CA 21-24R; CANR 26, 54, 87; CD 5; DA3; DAM DRAM; DFS 2, 6, 12, 18; DLB 7, 266; LAIT 4; MTCW 1, 2; RGAL 4; TUS

Simon, Paul (Frederick) 1941(?)- ..... **CLC 17**
See also CA 116; 153

Simonon, Paul 1956(?)- .... **CLC 30**

Simonson, Rick ed. .... **CLC 70**

Simpson, Harriette
See Arnow, Harriette (Louisa) Simpson

Simpson, Louis (Aston Marantz) 1923- .... **CLC 4, 7, 9, 32, 149**
See also AMWS 9; CA 1-4R; CAAS 4; CANR 1, 61; CP 7; DAM POET; DLB 5; MTCW 1, 2; PFS 7, 11, 14; RGAL 4

Simpson, Mona (Elizabeth) 1957- ... **CLC 44, 146**
See also CA 122; 135; CANR 68, 103; CN 7; EWL 3

Simpson, N(orman) F(rederick) 1919- .... **CLC 29**
See also CA 13-16R; CBD; DLB 13; RGEL 2

Sinclair, Andrew (Annandale) 1935- . **CLC 2, 14**
See also CA 9-12R; CAAS 5; CANR 14, 38, 91; CN 7; DLB 14; FANT; MTCW 1

Sinclair, Emil
See Hesse, Hermann

Sinclair, Iain 1943- .... **CLC 76**
See also CA 132; CANR 81; CP 7; HGG

Sinclair, Iain MacGregor
See Sinclair, Iain

Sinclair, Irene
See Griffith, D(avid Lewelyn) W(ark)

Sinclair, Mary Amelia St. Clair 1865(?)-1946
See Sinclair, May
See also CA 104; HGG; RHW

Sinclair, May .... **TCLC 3, 11**
See Sinclair, Mary Amelia St. Clair
See also CA 166; DLB 36, 135; EWL 3; RGEL 2; SUFW

Sinclair, Roy
See Griffith, D(avid Lewelyn) W(ark)

Sinclair, Upton (Beall) 1878-1968 ..... **CLC 1, 11, 15, 63; WLC**
See also AMWS 5; BPFB 3; BYA 2; CA 5-8R; 25-28R; CANR 7; CDALB 1929-1941; DA; DA3; DAB; DAC; DAM MST, NOV; DLB 9; EWL 3; INT CANR-7; LAIT 3; MTCW 1, 2; NFS 6; RGAL 4; SATA 9; TUS; YAW

Singe, (Edmund) J(ohn) M(illington) 1871-1909 .... **WLC**

Singer, Isaac
See Singer, Isaac Bashevis

Singer, Isaac Bashevis 1904-1991 .. **CLC 1, 3, 6, 9, 11, 15, 23, 38, 69, 111; SSC 3, 53; WLC**
See also AAYA 32; AITN 1, 2; AMW; AMWR 2; BPFB 3; BYA 1, 4; CA 1-4R; 134; CANR 1, 39, 106; CDALB 1941-1968; CLR 1; CWRI 5; DA; DA3; DAB; DAC; DAM MST, NOV; DLB 6, 28, 52, 278; DLBY 1991; EWL 3; EXPS; HGG; JRDA; LAIT 3; MAICYA 1, 2; MTCW 1, 2; RGAL 4; RGSF 2; SATA 3, 27; SATA-Obit 68; SSFS 2, 12, 16; TUS; TWA

Singer, Israel Joshua 1893-1944 .... **TCLC 33**
See also CA 169; EWL 3

Singh, Khushwant 1915- .... **CLC 11**
See also CA 9-12R; CAAS 9; CANR 6, 84; CN 7; EWL 3; RGEL 2

Singleton, Ann
See Benedict, Ruth (Fulton)

Singleton, John 1968(?)- .... **CLC 156**
See also AAYA 50; BW 2, 3; CA 138; CANR 67, 82; DAM MULT

Sinjohn, John
See Galsworthy, John

Sinyavsky, Andrei (Donatevich) 1925-1997 .... **CLC 8**
See Sinyavsky, Andrey Donatovich; Tertz, Abram
See also CA 85-88; 159

Sinyavsky, Andrey Donatovich
See Sinyavsky, Andrei (Donatevich)
See also EWL 3

Sirin, V.
See Nabokov, Vladimir (Vladimirovich)

Sissman, L(ouis) E(dward) 1928-1976 .... **CLC 9, 18**
See also CA 21-24R; 65-68; CANR 13; DLB 5

Sisson, C(harles) H(ubert) 1914-2003 .... **CLC 8**
See also CA 1-4R; CAAS 3; CANR 3, 48, 84; CP 7; DLB 27

Sitting Bull 1831(?)-1890 .... **NNAL**
See also DA3; DAM MULT

Sitwell, Dame Edith 1887-1964 ..... **CLC 2, 9, 67; PC 3**
See also BRW 7; CA 9-12R; CANR 35; CDBLB 1945-1960; DAM POET; DLB 20; EWL 3; MTCW 1, 2; RGEL 2; TEA

Siwaarmill, H. P.
See Sharp, William

Sjoewall, Maj 1935- .... **CLC 7**
See Sjowall, Maj
See also CA 65-68; CANR 73

Sjowall, Maj
See Sjoewall, Maj
See also BPFB 3; CMW 4; MSW

Skelton, John 1460(?)-1529 ..... **LC 71; PC 25**
See also BRW 1; DLB 136; RGEL 2

Skelton, Robin 1925-1997 .... **CLC 13**
See Zuk, Georges
See also AITN 2; CA 5-8R; 160; CAAS 5; CANR 28, 89; CCA 1; CP 7; DLB 27, 53

Skolimowski, Jerzy 1938- .... **CLC 20**
See also CA 128

Skram, Amalie (Bertha) 1847-1905 .... **TCLC 25**
See also CA 165

Skvorecky, Josef (Vaclav) 1924- ...... **CLC 15, 39, 69, 152**
See also CA 61-64; CAAS 1; CANR 10, 34, 63, 108; CDWLB 4; DA3; DAC; DAM NOV; DLB 232; EWL 3; MTCW 1, 2

Slade, Bernard .... **CLC 11, 46**
See Newbound, Bernard Slade
See also CAAS 9; CCA 1; DLB 53

Slaughter, Carolyn 1946- .... **CLC 56**
See also CA 85-88; CANR 85; CN 7

Slaughter, Frank G(ill) 1908-2001 ... **CLC 29**
See also AITN 2; CA 5-8R; 197; CANR 5, 85; INT CANR-5; RHW

Slavitt, David R(ytman) 1935- ..... **CLC 5, 14**
See also CA 21-24R; CAAS 3; CANR 41, 83; CP 7; DLB 5, 6

Slesinger, Tess 1905-1945 .... **TCLC 10**
See also CA 107; 199; DLB 102

Slessor, Kenneth 1901-1971 .... **CLC 14**
See also CA 102; 89-92; DLB 260; RGEL 2

Slowacki, Juliusz 1809-1849 .... **NCLC 15**
See also RGWL 3

Smart, Christopher 1722-1771 . **LC 3; PC 13**
See also DAM POET; DLB 109; RGEL 2

Smart, Elizabeth 1913-1986 .... **CLC 54**
See also CA 81-84; 118; DLB 88

Smiley, Jane (Graves) 1949- ...... **CLC 53, 76, 144**
See also AMWS 6; BPFB 3; CA 104; CANR 30, 50, 74, 96; CN 7; CPW 1; DA3; DAM POP; DLB 227, 234; EWL 3; INT CANR-30

Smith, A(rthur) J(ames) M(arshall) 1902-1980 .... **CLC 15**
See also CA 1-4R; 102; CANR 4; DAC; DLB 88; RGEL 2

Smith, Adam 1723(?)-1790 .... **LC 36**
See also DLB 104, 252; RGEL 2

Smith, Alexander 1829-1867 .... **NCLC 59**
See also DLB 32, 55

Smith, Anna Deavere 1950- .... **CLC 86**
See also CA 133; CANR 103; CD 5; DFS 2

Smith, Betty (Wehner) 1904-1972 .... **CLC 19**
See also BPFB 3; BYA 3; CA 5-8R; 33-36R; DLBY 1982; LAIT 3; RGAL 4; SATA 6

Smith, Charlotte (Turner) 1749-1806 .... **NCLC 23, 115**
See also DLB 39, 109; RGEL 2; TEA

Smith, Clark Ashton 1893-1961 .... **CLC 43**
See also CA 143; CANR 81; FANT; HGG; MTCW 2; SCFW 2; SFW 4; SUFW

Smith, Dave .... **CLC 22, 42**
See Smith, David (Jeddie)
See also CAAS 7; DLB 5

Smith, David (Jeddie) 1942-
See Smith, Dave
See also CA 49-52; CANR 1, 59, 120; CP 7; CSW; DAM POET

Smith, Florence Margaret 1902-1971
See Smith, Stevie
See also CA 17-18; 29-32R; CANR 35; CAP 2; DAM POET; MTCW 1, 2; TEA

Smith, Iain Crichton 1928-1998 .... **CLC 64**
See also BRWS 9; CA 21-24R; 171; CN 7; CP 7; DLB 40, 139; RGSF 2

Smith, John 1580(?)-1631 .... **LC 9**
See also DLB 24, 30; TUS

Smith, Johnston
See Crane, Stephen (Townley)

Smith, Joseph, Jr. 1805-1844 .... **NCLC 53**

Smith, Lee 1944- .... **CLC 25, 73**
See also CA 114; 119; CANR 46, 118; CSW; DLB 143; DLBY 1983; EWL 3; INT CA-119; RGAL 4

Smith, Martin
See Smith, Martin Cruz

Smith, Martin Cruz 1942- .. **CLC 25; NNAL**
See also BEST 89:4; BPFB 3; CA 85-88; CANR 6, 23, 43, 65, 119; CMW 4; CPW; DAM MULT, POP; HGG; INT CANR-23; MTCW 2; RGAL 4

Smith, Patti 1946- .... **CLC 12**
See also CA 93-96; CANR 63

Smith, Pauline (Urmson) 1882-1959 .... **TCLC 25**
See also DLB 225; EWL 3

Smith, Rosamond
See Oates, Joyce Carol

Smith, Sheila Kaye
See Kaye-Smith, Sheila

Smith, Stevie .... **CLC 3, 8, 25, 44; PC 12**
See Smith, Florence Margaret
See also BRWS 2; DLB 20; EWL 3; MTCW 2; PAB; PFS 3; RGEL 2

Smith, Wilbur (Addison) 1933- .... **CLC 33**
See also CA 13-16R; CANR 7, 46, 66; CPW; MTCW 1, 2

Smith, William Jay 1918- .... **CLC 6**
See also AMWS 13; CA 5-8R; CANR 44, 106; CP 7; CSW; CWRI 5; DLB 5; MAICYA 1, 2; SAAS 22; SATA 2, 68

Smith, Woodrow Wilson
See Kuttner, Henry

Spielberg, Steven 1947- .... **CLC 20**
   See also AAYA 8, 24; CA 77-80; CANR
   32; SATA 32
Spillane, Frank Morrison 1918-
   See Spillane, Mickey
   See also CA 25-28R; CANR 28, 63; DA3;
   MTCW 1, 2; SATA 66
Spillane, Mickey .... **CLC 3, 13**
   See Spillane, Frank Morrison
   See also BPFB 3; CMW 4; DLB 226;
   MSW; MTCW 2
Spinoza, Benedictus de 1632-1677 .. **LC 9, 58**
Spinrad, Norman (Richard) 1940- ... **CLC 46**
   See also BPFB 3; CA 37-40R; CAAS 19;
   CANR 20, 91; DLB 8; INT CANR-20;
   SFW 4
Spitteler, Carl (Friedrich Georg)
   1845-1924 .... **TCLC 12**
   See also CA 109; DLB 129; EWL 3
Spivack, Kathleen (Romola Drucker)
   1938- .... **CLC 6**
   See also CA 49-52
Spoto, Donald 1941- .... **CLC 39**
   See also CA 65-68; CANR 11, 57, 93
Springsteen, Bruce (F.) 1949- .... **CLC 17**
   See also CA 111
Spurling, Hilary 1940- .... **CLC 34**
   See also CA 104; CANR 25, 52, 94
Spyker, John Howland
   See Elman, Richard (Martin)
Squared, A.
   See Abbott, Edwin A.
Squires, (James) Radcliffe
   1917-1993 .... **CLC 51**
   See also CA 1-4R; 140; CANR 6, 21
Srivastava, Dhanpat Rai 1880(?)-1936
   See Premchand
   See also CA 118; 197
Stacy, Donald
   See Pohl, Frederik
Stael
   See Stael-Holstein, Anne Louise Germaine
   Necker
   See also EW 5; RGWL 2, 3
Stael, Germaine de
   See Stael-Holstein, Anne Louise Germaine
   Necker
   See also DLB 119, 192; FW; GFL 1789 to
   the Present; TWA
Stael-Holstein, Anne Louise Germaine
   Necker 1766-1817 .... **NCLC 3, 91**
   See also Stael; Stael, Germaine de
Stafford, Jean 1915-1979 .. **CLC 4, 7, 19, 68;**
   SSC 26
   See also CA 1-4R; 85-88; CANR 3, 65;
   DLB 2, 173; MTCW 1, 2; RGAL 4; RGSF
   2; SATA-Obit 22; TCWW 2; TUS
Stafford, William (Edgar)
   1914-1993 .... **CLC 4, 7, 29**
   See also AMWS 11; CA 5-8R; 142; CAAS
   3; CANR 5, 22; DAM POET; DLB 5,
   206; EXPP; INT CANR-22; PFS 2, 8, 16;
   RGAL 4; WP
Stagnelius, Eric Johan 1793-1823 . **NCLC 61**
Staines, Trevor
   See Brunner, John (Kilian Houston)
Stairs, Gordon
   See Austin, Mary (Hunter)
   See also TCWW 2
Stalin, Joseph 1879-1953 .... **TCLC 92**
Stampa, Gaspara c. 1524-1554 .... **PC 43**
   See also RGWL 2, 3
Stampflinger, K. A.
   See Benjamin, Walter
Stancykowna
   See Szymborska, Wislawa
Standing Bear, Luther
   1868(?)-1939(?) .... **NNAL**
   See also CA 113; 144; DAM MULT

Stannard, Martin 1947- .... **CLC 44**
   See also CA 142; DLB 155
Stanton, Elizabeth Cady
   1815-1902 .... **TCLC 73**
   See also CA 171; DLB 79; FW
Stanton, Maura 1946- .... **CLC 9**
   See also CA 89-92; CANR 15, 123; DLB
   120
Stanton, Schuyler
   See Baum, L(yman) Frank
Stapledon, (William) Olaf
   1886-1950 .... **TCLC 22**
   See also CA 111; 162; DLB 15, 255; SFW
   4
Starbuck, George (Edwin)
   1931-1996 .... **CLC 53**
   See also CA 21-24R; 153; CANR 23; DAM
   POET
Stark, Richard
   See Westlake, Donald E(dwin)
Staunton, Schuyler
   See Baum, L(yman) Frank
Stead, Christina (Ellen) 1902-1983 ... **CLC 2,**
   5, 8, 32, 80
   See also BRWS 4; CA 13-16R; 109; CANR
   33, 40; DLB 260; EWL 3; FW; MTCW 1,
   2; RGEL 2; RGSF 2
Stead, William Thomas
   1849-1912 .... **TCLC 48**
   See also CA 167
Stebnitsky, M.
   See Leskov, Nikolai (Semyonovich)
Steele, Sir Richard 1672-1729 .... **LC 18**
   See also BRW 3; CDBLB 1660-1789; DLB
   84, 101; RGEL 2; WLIT 3
Steele, Timothy (Reid) 1948- .... **CLC 45**
   See also CA 93-96; CANR 16, 50, 92; CP
   7; DLB 120, 282
Steffens, (Joseph) Lincoln
   1866-1936 .... **TCLC 20**
   See also CA 117; 198
Stegner, Wallace (Earle) 1909-1993 .. **CLC 9,**
   49, 81; SSC 27
   See also AITN 1; AMWS 4; ANW; BEST
   90:3; BPFB 3; CA 1-4R; 141; CAAS 9;
   CANR 1, 21, 46; DAM NOV; DLB 9,
   206, 275; DLBY 1993; EWL 3; MTCW
   1, 2; RGAL 4; TCWW 2; TUS
Stein, Gertrude 1874-1946 .... **DC 19; PC 18;**
   SSC 42; TCLC 1, 6, 28, 48; WLC
   See also AMW; AMWC 2; CA 104; 132;
   CANR 108; CDALB 1917-1929; DA;
   DA3; DAB; DAC; DAM MST, NOV,
   POET; DLB 4, 54, 86, 228; DLBD 15;
   EWL 3; EXPS; GLL 1; MAWW; MTCW
   1, 2; NCFS 4; RGAL 4; RGSF 2; SSFS 5;
   TUS; WP
Steinbeck, John (Ernst) 1902-1968 ... **CLC 1,**
   5, 9, 13, 21, 34, 45, 75, 124; SSC 11,
   37; TCLC 135; WLC
   See also AAYA 12; AMW; BPFB 3; BYA 2,
   3, 13; CA 1-4R; 25-28R; CANR 1, 35;
   CDALB 1929-1941; DA; DA3; DAB;
   DAC; DAM DRAM, MST, NOV; DLB 7,
   9, 212, 275; DLBD 2; EWL 3; EXPS;
   LAIT 3; MTCW 1, 2; NFS 1, 5, 7, 17;
   RGAL 4; RGSF 2; RHW; SATA 9; SSFS
   3, 6; TCWW 2; TUS; WYA; YAW
Steinem, Gloria 1934- .... **CLC 63**
   See also CA 53-56; CANR 28, 51; DLB
   246; FW; MTCW 1, 2
Steiner, George 1929- .... **CLC 24**
   See also CA 73-76; CANR 31, 67, 108;
   DAM NOV; DLB 67; EWL 3; MTCW 1,
   2; SATA 62
Steiner, K. Leslie
   See Delany, Samuel R(ay), Jr.
Steiner, Rudolf 1861-1925 .... **TCLC 13**
   See also CA 107

Stendhal 1783-1842 .. **NCLC 23, 46; SSC 27;**
   WLC
   See also DA; DA3; DAB; DAC; DAM
   MST, NOV; DLB 119; EW 5; GFL 1789
   to the Present; RGWL 2, 3; TWA
Stephen, Adeline Virginia
   See Woolf, (Adeline) Virginia
Stephen, Sir Leslie 1832-1904 .... **TCLC 23**
   See also BRW 5; CA 123; DLB 57, 144,
   190
Stephen, Sir Leslie
   See Stephen, Sir Leslie
Stephen, Virginia
   See Woolf, (Adeline) Virginia
Stephens, James 1882(?)-1950 .... **SSC 50;**
   TCLC 4
   See also CA 104; 192; DLB 19, 153, 162;
   EWL 3; FANT; RGEL 2; SUFW
Stephens, Reed
   See Donaldson, Stephen R(eeder)
Steptoe, Lydia
   See Barnes, Djuna
   See also GLL 1
Sterchi, Beat 1949- .... **CLC 65**
   See also CA 203
Sterling, Brett
   See Bradbury, Ray (Douglas); Hamilton,
   Edmond
Sterling, Bruce 1954- .... **CLC 72**
   See also CA 119; CANR 44; SCFW 2; SFW
   4
Sterling, George 1869-1926 .... **TCLC 20**
   See also CA 117; 165; DLB 54
Stern, Gerald 1925- .... **CLC 40, 100**
   See also AMWS 9; CA 81-84; CANR 28,
   94; CP 7; DLB 105; RGAL 4
Stern, Richard (Gustave) 1928- ... **CLC 4, 39**
   See also CA 1-4R; CANR 1, 25, 52, 120;
   CN 7; DLB 218; DLBY 1987; INT
   CANR-25
Sternberg, Josef von 1894-1969 .... **CLC 20**
   See also CA 81-84
Sterne, Laurence 1713-1768 .... **LC 2, 48;**
   WLC
   See also BRW 3; BRWC 1; CDBLB 1660-
   1789; DA; DAB; DAC; DAM MST, NOV;
   DLB 39; RGEL 2; TEA
Sternheim, (William Adolf) Carl
   1878-1942 .... **TCLC 8**
   See also CA 105; 193; DLB 56, 118; EWL
   3; RGWL 2, 3
Stevens, Mark 1951- .... **CLC 34**
   See also CA 122
Stevens, Wallace 1879-1955 . **PC 6; TCLC 3,**
   12, 45; WLC
   See also AMW; AMWR 1; CA 104; 124;
   CDALB 1929-1941; DA; DA3; DAB;
   DAC; DAM MST, POET; DLB 54; EWL
   3; EXPP; MTCW 1, 2; PAB; PFS 13, 16;
   RGAL 4; TUS; WP
Stevenson, Anne (Katharine) 1933- .. **CLC 7,**
   33
   See also BRWS 6; CA 17-20R; CAAS 9;
   CANR 9, 33, 123; CP 7; CWP; DLB 40;
   MTCW 1; RHW
Stevenson, Robert Louis (Balfour)
   1850-1894 ...... **NCLC 5, 14, 63; SSC 11,**
   51; WLC
   See also AAYA 24; BPFB 3; BRW 5;
   BRWC 1; BRWR 1; BYA 1, 2, 4, 13; CD-
   BLB 1890-1914; CLR 10, 11; DA; DA3;
   DAB; DAC; DAM MST, NOV; DLB 18,
   57, 141, 156, 174; DLBD 13; HGG;
   JRDA; LAIT 1, 3; MAICYA 1, 2; NFS
   11; RGEL 2; RGSF 2; SATA 100; SUFW;
   TEA; WCH; WLIT 4; WYA; YABC 2;
   YAW

Thoreau, Henry David 1817-1862 .. **NCLC 7, 21, 61; PC 30; WLC**
See also AAYA 42; AMW; ANW; BYA 3; CDALB 1640-1865; DA; DA3; DAB; DAC; DAM MST; DLB 1, 183, 223, 270; LAIT 2; LMFS 1; NCFS 3; RGAL 4; TUS

Thorndike, E. L.
See Thorndike, Edward L(ee)

Thorndike, Edward L(ee)
1874-1949 .... **TCLC 107**
See also CA 121

Thornton, Hall
See Silverberg, Robert

Thorpe, Adam 1956- .... **CLC 176**
See also CA 129; CANR 92; DLB 231

Thubron, Colin (Gerald Dryden)
1939- .... **CLC 163**
See also CA 25-28R; CANR 12, 29, 59, 95; CN 7; DLB 204, 231

Thucydides c. 455B.C.-c. 395B.C. . **CMLC 17**
See also AW 1; DLB 176; RGWL 2, 3

Thumboo, Edwin Nadason 1933- .... **PC 30**
See also CA 194

Thurber, James (Grover)
1894-1961 .. **CLC 5, 11, 25, 125; SSC 1, 47**
See also AMWS 1; BPFB 3; BYA 5; CA 73-76; CANR 17, 39; CDALB 1929-1941; CWRI 5; DA; DA3; DAB; DAC; DAM DRAM, MST, NOV; DLB 4, 11, 22, 102; EWL 3; EXPS; FANT; LAIT 3; MAICYA 1, 2; MTCW 1, 2; RGAL 4; RGSF 2; SATA 13; SSFS 1, 10; SUFW; TUS

Thurman, Wallace (Henry)
1902-1934 .... **BLC 3; HR 3; TCLC 6**
See also BW 1, 3; CA 104; 124; CANR 81; DAM MULT; DLB 51

Tibullus c. 54B.C.-c. 18B.C. .... **CMLC 36**
See also AW 2; DLB 211; RGWL 2, 3

Ticheburn, Cheviot
See Ainsworth, William Harrison

Tieck, (Johann) Ludwig
1773-1853 .... **NCLC 5, 46; SSC 31**
See also CDWLB 2; DLB 90; EW 5; IDTP; RGSF 2; RGWL 2, 3; SUFW

Tiger, Derry
See Ellison, Harlan (Jay)

Tilghman, Christopher 1948(?)- .... **CLC 65**
See also CA 159; CSW; DLB 244

Tillich, Paul (Johannes)
1886-1965 .... **CLC 131**
See also CA 5-8R; 25-28R; CANR 33; MTCW 1, 2

Tillinghast, Richard (Williford)
1940- .... **CLC 29**
See also CA 29-32R; CAAS 23; CANR 26, 51, 96; CP 7; CSW

Timrod, Henry 1828-1867 .... **NCLC 25**
See also DLB 3, 248; RGAL 4

Tindall, Gillian (Elizabeth) 1938- ...... **CLC 7**
See also CA 21-24R; CANR 11, 65, 107; CN 7

Tiptree, James, Jr. .... **CLC 48, 50**
See Sheldon, Alice Hastings Bradley
See also DLB 8; SCFW 2; SFW 4

Tirone Smith, Mary-Ann 1944- .... **CLC 39**
See also CA 118; 136; CANR 113; SATA 143

Tirso de Molina 1580(?)-1648 .... **DC 13; HLCS 2; LC 73**
See also RGWL 2, 3

Titmarsh, Michael Angelo
See Thackeray, William Makepeace

Tocqueville, Alexis (Charles Henri Maurice Clerel Comte) de 1805-1859 .. **NCLC 7, 63**
See also EW 6; GFL 1789 to the Present; TWA

Toffler, Alvin 1928- .... **CLC 168**
See also CA 13-16R; CANR 15, 46, 67; CPW; DAM POP; MTCW 1, 2

Toibin, Colm
See Toibin, Colm
See also DLB 271

Toibin, Colm 1955- .... **CLC 162**
See Toibin, Colm
See also CA 142; CANR 81

Tolkien, J(ohn) R(onald) R(euel)
1892-1973 .... **CLC 1, 2, 3, 8, 12, 38; TCLC 137; WLC**
See also AAYA 10; AITN 1; BPFB 3; BRWC 2; BRWS 2; CA 17-18; 45-48; CANR 36; CAP 2; CDBLB 1914-1945; CLR 56; CPW 1; CWRI 5; DA; DA3; DAB; DAC; DAM MST, NOV, POP; DLB 15, 160, 255; EFS 2; EWL 3; FANT; JRDA; LAIT 1; LATS 1; LMFS 2; MAICYA 1, 2; MTCW 1, 2; NFS 8; RGEL 2; SATA 2, 32, 100; SATA-Obit 24; SFW 4; SUFW; TEA; WCH; WYA; YAW

Toller, Ernst 1893-1939 .... **TCLC 10**
See also CA 107; 186; DLB 124; EWL 3; RGWL 2, 3

Tolson, M. B.
See Tolson, Melvin B(eaunorus)

Tolson, Melvin B(eaunorus)
1898(?)-1966 .... **BLC 3; CLC 36, 105**
See also AFAW 1, 2; BW 1, 3; CA 124; 89-92; CANR 80; DAM MULT, POET; DLB 48, 76; RGAL 4

Tolstoi, Aleksei Nikolaevich
See Tolstoy, Alexey Nikolaevich

Tolstoi, Lev
See Tolstoy, Leo (Nikolaevich)
See also RGSF 2; RGWL 2, 3

Tolstoy, Aleksei Nikolaevich
See Tolstoy, Alexey Nikolaevich
See also DLB 272

Tolstoy, Alexey Nikolaevich
1882-1945 .... **TCLC 18**
See also Tolstoy, Aleksei Nikolaevich
See also CA 107; 158; EWL 3; SFW 4

Tolstoy, Leo (Nikolaevich)
1828-1910 . **SSC 9, 30, 45, 54; TCLC 4, 11, 17, 28, 44, 79; WLC**
See Tolstoi, Lev
See also CA 104; 123; DA; DA3; DAB; DAC; DAM MST, NOV; DLB 238; EFS 2; EW 7; EXPS; IDTP; LAIT 2; LATS 1; LMFS 1; NFS 10; SATA 26; SSFS 5; TWA

Tolstoy, Count Leo
See Tolstoy, Leo (Nikolaevich)

Tomalin, Claire 1933- .... **CLC 166**
See also CA 89-92; CANR 52, 88; DLB 155

Tomasi di Lampedusa, Giuseppe 1896-1957
See Lampedusa, Giuseppe (Tomasi) di
See also CA 111; DLB 177; EWL 3

Tomlin, Lily .... **CLC 17**
See Tomlin, Mary Jean

Tomlin, Mary Jean 1939(?)-
See Tomlin, Lily
See also CA 117

Tomline, F. Latour
See Gilbert, W(illiam) S(chwenck)

Tomlinson, (Alfred) Charles 1927- .... **CLC 2, 4, 6, 13, 45; PC 17**
See also CA 5-8R; CANR 33; CP 7; DAM POET; DLB 40

Tomlinson, H(enry) M(ajor)
1873-1958 .... **TCLC 71**
See also CA 118; 161; DLB 36, 100, 195

Tonson, Jacob fl. 1655(?)-1736 .... **LC 86**
See also DLB 170

Toole, John Kennedy 1937-1969 ..... **CLC 19, 64**
See also BPFB 3; CA 104; DLBY 1981; MTCW 2

Toomer, Eugene
See Toomer, Jean

Toomer, Eugene Pinchback
See Toomer, Jean

Toomer, Jean 1894-1967 .. **BLC 3; CLC 1, 4, 13, 22; HR 3; PC 7; SSC 1, 45; WLCS**
See also AFAW 1, 2; AMWS 3, 9; BW 1; CA 85-88; CDALB 1917-1929; DA3; DAM MULT; DLB 45, 51; EWL 3; EXPP; EXPS; LMFS 2; MTCW 1, 2; NFS 11; RGAL 4; RGSF 2; SSFS 5

Toomer, Nathan Jean
See Toomer, Jean

Toomer, Nathan Pinchback
See Toomer, Jean

Torley, Luke
See Blish, James (Benjamin)

Tornimparte, Alessandra
See Ginzburg, Natalia

Torre, Raoul della
See Mencken, H(enry) L(ouis)

Torrence, Ridgely 1874-1950 .... **TCLC 97**
See also DLB 54, 249

Torrey, E(dwin) Fuller 1937- .... **CLC 34**
See also CA 119; CANR 71

Torsvan, Ben Traven
See Traven, B.

Torsvan, Benno Traven
See Traven, B.

Torsvan, Berick Traven
See Traven, B.

Torsvan, Berwick Traven
See Traven, B.

Torsvan, Bruno Traven
See Traven, B.

Torsvan, Traven
See Traven, B.

Tourneur, Cyril 1575(?)-1626 .... **LC 66**
See also BRW 2; DAM DRAM; DLB 58; RGEL 2

Tournier, Michel (Edouard) 1924- .... **CLC 6, 23, 36, 95**
See also CA 49-52; CANR 3, 36, 74; DLB 83; EWL 3; GFL 1789 to the Present; MTCW 1, 2; SATA 23

Tournimparte, Alessandra
See Ginzburg, Natalia

Towers, Ivar
See Kornbluth, C(yril) M.

Towne, Robert (Burton) 1936(?)- ..... **CLC 87**
See also CA 108; DLB 44; IDFW 3, 4

Townsend, Sue .... **CLC 61**
See Townsend, Susan Lilian
See also AAYA 28; CA 119; 127; CANR 65; CBD; CD 5; CPW; CWD; DAB; DAC; DAM MST; DLB 271; INT CA-127; SATA 55, 93; SATA-Brief 48; YAW

Townsend, Susan Lilian 1946-
See Townsend, Sue

Townshend, Pete
See Townshend, Peter (Dennis Blandford)

Townshend, Peter (Dennis Blandford)
1945- .... **CLC 17, 42**
See also CA 107

Tozzi, Federigo 1883-1920 .... **TCLC 31**
See also CA 160; CANR 110; DLB 264; EWL 3

Tracy, Don(ald Fiske) 1905-1970(?)
See Queen, Ellery
See also CA 1-4R; 176; CANR 2

Trafford, F. G.
See Riddell, Charlotte

Traill, Catharine Parr 1802-1899 .. **NCLC 31**
See also DLB 99

Wain, John (Barrington) 1925-1994 . **CLC 2, 11, 15, 46**
See also CA 5-8R; 145; CAAS 4; CANR 23, 54; CDBLB 1960 to Present; DLB 15, 27, 139, 155; EWL 3; MTCW 1, 2

Wajda, Andrzej 1926- .... **CLC 16**
See also CA 102

Wakefield, Dan 1932- .... **CLC 7**
See also CA 21-24R; CAAE 211; CAAS 7; CN 7

Wakefield, Herbert Russell
1888-1965 .... **TCLC 120**
See also CA 5-8R; CANR 77; HGG; SUFW

Wakoski, Diane 1937- ...... **CLC 2, 4, 7, 9, 11, 40; PC 15**
See also CA 13-16R; CAAE 216; CAAS 1; CANR 9, 60, 106; CP 7; CWP; DAM POET; DLB 5; INT CANR-9; MTCW 2

Wakoski-Sherbell, Diane
See Wakoski, Diane

Walcott, Derek (Alton) 1930- ... **BLC 3; CLC 2, 4, 9, 14, 25, 42, 67, 76, 160; DC 7; PC 46**
See also BW 2; CA 89-92; CANR 26, 47, 75, 80; CBD; CD 5; CDWLB 3; CP 7; DA3; DAB; DAC; DAM MST, MULT, POET; DLB 117; DLBY 1981; DNFS 1; EFS 1; EWL 3; LMFS 2; MTCW 1, 2; PFS 6; RGEL 2; TWA

Waldman, Anne (Lesley) 1945- .... **CLC 7**
See also BG 3; CA 37-40R; CAAS 17; CANR 34, 69, 116; CP 7; CWP; DLB 16

Waldo, E. Hunter
See Sturgeon, Theodore (Hamilton)

Waldo, Edward Hamilton
See Sturgeon, Theodore (Hamilton)

Walker, Alice (Malsenior) 1944- .... **BLC 3; CLC 5, 6, 9, 19, 27, 46, 58, 103, 167; PC 30; SSC 5; WLCS**
See also AAYA 3, 33; AFAW 1, 2; AMWS 3; BEST 89:4; BPFB 3; BW 2, 3; CA 37-40R; CANR 9, 27, 49, 66, 82; CDALB 1968-1988; CN 7; CPW; CSW; DA; DA3; DAB; DAC; DAM MST, MULT, NOV, POET, POP; DLB 6, 33, 143; EWL 3; EXPN; EXPS; FW; INT CANR-27; LAIT 3; MAWW; MTCW 1, 2; NFS 5; RGAL 4; RGSF 2; SATA 31; SSFS 2, 11; TUS; YAW

Walker, David Harry 1911-1992 ...... **CLC 14**
See also CA 1-4R; 137; CANR 1; CWRI 5; SATA 8; SATA-Obit 71

Walker, Edward Joseph 1934-
See Walker, Ted
See also CA 21-24R; CANR 12, 28, 53; CP 7

Walker, George F. 1947- .... **CLC 44, 61**
See also CA 103; CANR 21, 43, 59; CD 5; DAB; DAC; DAM MST; DLB 60

Walker, Joseph A. 1935- .... **CLC 19**
See also BW 1, 3; CA 89-92; CAD; CANR 26; CD 5; DAM DRAM, MST; DFS 12; DLB 38

Walker, Margaret (Abigail)
1915-1998 .... **BLC; CLC 1, 6; PC 20; TCLC 129**
See also AFAW 1, 2; BW 2, 3; CA 73-76; 172; CANR 26, 54, 76; CN 7; CP 7; CSW; DAM MULT; DLB 76, 152; EXPP; FW; MTCW 1, 2; RGAL 4; RHW

Walker, Ted .... **CLC 13**
See Walker, Edward Joseph
See also DLB 40

Wallace, David Foster 1962- ..... **CLC 50, 114**
See also AAYA 50; AMWS 10; CA 132; CANR 59; DA3; MTCW 2

Wallace, Dexter
See Masters, Edgar Lee

Wallace, (Richard Horatio) Edgar
1875-1932 .... **TCLC 57**
See also CA 115; CMW 4; DLB 70; MSW; RGEL 2

Wallace, Irving 1916-1990 .... **CLC 7, 13**
See also AITN 1; BPFB 3; CA 1-4R; 132; CAAS 1; CANR 1, 27; CPW; DAM NOV, POP; INT CANR-27; MTCW 1, 2

Wallant, Edward Lewis 1926-1962 ... **CLC 5, 10**
See also CA 1-4R; CANR 22; DLB 2, 28, 143; EWL 3; MTCW 1, 2; RGAL 4

Wallas, Graham 1858-1932 .... **TCLC 91**

Waller, Edmund 1606-1687 .... **LC 86**
See also BRW 2; DAM POET; DLB 126; PAB; RGEL 2

Walley, Byron
See Card, Orson Scott

Walpole, Horace 1717-1797 .... **LC 2, 49**
See also BRW 3; DLB 39, 104, 213; HGG; LMFS 1; RGEL 2; SUFW 1; TEA

Walpole, Hugh (Seymour)
1884-1941 .... **TCLC 5**
See also CA 104; 165; DLB 34; HGG; MTCW 2; RGEL 2; RHW

Walrond, Eric (Derwent) 1898-1966 .... **HR 3**
See also BW 1; CA 125; DLB 51

Walser, Martin 1927- .... **CLC 27**
See also CA 57-60; CANR 8, 46; CWW 2; DLB 75, 124; EWL 3

Walser, Robert 1878-1956 ..... **SSC 20; TCLC 18**
See also CA 118; 165; CANR 100; DLB 66; EWL 3

Walsh, Gillian Paton
See Paton Walsh, Gillian

Walsh, Jill Paton .... **CLC 35**
See Paton Walsh, Gillian
See also CLR 2, 65; WYA

Walter, Villiam Christian
See Andersen, Hans Christian

Walters, Anna L(ee) 1946- .... **NNAL**
See also CA 73-76

Walther von der Vogelweide c.
1170-1228 .... **CMLC 56**

Walton, Izaak 1593-1683 .... **LC 72**
See also BRW 2; CDBLB Before 1660; DLB 151, 213; RGEL 2

Wambaugh, Joseph (Aloysius), Jr.
1937- .... **CLC 3, 18**
See also AITN 1; BEST 89:3; BPFB 3; CA 33-36R; CANR 42, 65, 115; CMW 4; CPW 1; DA3; DAM NOV, POP; DLB 6; DLBY 1983; MSW; MTCW 1, 2

Wang Wei 699(?)-761(?) .... **PC 18**
See also TWA

Ward, Arthur Henry Sarsfield 1883-1959
See Rohmer, Sax
See also CA 108; 173; CMW 4; HGG

Ward, Douglas Turner 1930- .... **CLC 19**
See also BW 1; CA 81-84; CAD; CANR 27; CD 5; DLB 7, 38

Ward, E. D.
See Lucas, E(dward) V(errall)

Ward, Mrs. Humphry 1851-1920
See Ward, Mary Augusta
See also RGEL 2

Ward, Mary Augusta 1851-1920 ... **TCLC 55**
See Ward, Mrs. Humphry
See also DLB 18

Ward, Peter
See Faust, Frederick (Schiller)

Warhol, Andy 1928(?)-1987 .... **CLC 20**
See also AAYA 12; BEST 89:4; CA 89-92; 121; CANR 34

Warner, Francis (Robert le Plastrier)
1937- .... **CLC 14**
See also CA 53-56; CANR 11

Warner, Marina 1946- .... **CLC 59**
See also CA 65-68; CANR 21, 55, 118; CN 7; DLB 194

Warner, Rex (Ernest) 1905-1986 ...... **CLC 45**
See also CA 89-92; 119; DLB 15; RGEL 2; RHW

Warner, Susan (Bogert)
1819-1885 .... **NCLC 31**
See also DLB 3, 42, 239, 250, 254

Warner, Sylvia (Constance) Ashton
See Ashton-Warner, Sylvia (Constance)

Warner, Sylvia Townsend
1893-1978 .. **CLC 7, 19; SSC 23; TCLC 131**
See also BRWS 7; CA 61-64; 77-80; CANR 16, 60, 104; DLB 34, 139; EWL 3; FANT; FW; MTCW 1, 2; RGEL 2; RGSF 2; RHW

Warren, Mercy Otis 1728-1814 ..... **NCLC 13**
See also DLB 31, 200; RGAL 4; TUS

Warren, Robert Penn 1905-1989 .. **CLC 1, 4, 6, 8, 10, 13, 18, 39, 53, 59; PC 37; SSC 4, 58; WLC**
See also AITN 1; AMW; AMWC 2; BPFB 3; BYA 1; CA 13-16R; 129; CANR 10, 47; CDALB 1968-1988; DA; DA3; DAB; DAC; DAM MST, NOV, POET; DLB 2, 48, 152; DLBY 1980, 1989; EWL 3; INT CANR-10; MTCW 1, 2; NFS 13; RGAL 4; RGSF 2; RHW; SATA 46; SATA-Obit 63; SSFS 8; TUS

Warrigal, Jack
See Furphy, Joseph

Warshofsky, Isaac
See Singer, Isaac Bashevis

Warton, Joseph 1722-1800 .... **NCLC 118**
See also DLB 104, 109; RGEL 2

Warton, Thomas 1728-1790 .... **LC 15, 82**
See also DAM POET; DLB 104, 109; RGEL 2

Waruk, Kona
See Harris, (Theodore) Wilson

Warung, Price .... **TCLC 45**
See Astley, William
See also DLB 230; RGEL 2

Warwick, Jarvis
See Garner, Hugh
See also CCA 1

Washington, Alex
See Harris, Mark

Washington, Booker T(aliaferro)
1856-1915 .... **BLC 3; TCLC 10**
See also BW 1; CA 114; 125; DA3; DAM MULT; LAIT 2; RGAL 4; SATA 28

Washington, George 1732-1799 .... **LC 25**
See also DLB 31

Wassermann, (Karl) Jakob
1873-1934 .... **TCLC 6**
See also CA 104; 163; DLB 66; EWL 3

Wasserstein, Wendy 1950- .. **CLC 32, 59, 90; DC 4**
See also CA 121; 129; CABS 3; CAD; CANR 53, 75; CD 5; CWD; DA3; DAM DRAM; DFS 5, 17; DLB 228; EWL 3; FW; INT CA-129; MTCW 2; SATA 94

Waterhouse, Keith (Spencer) 1929- . **CLC 47**
See also CA 5-8R; CANR 38, 67, 109; CBD; CN 7; DLB 13, 15; MTCW 1, 2

Waters, Frank (Joseph) 1902-1995 .. **CLC 88**
See also CA 5-8R; 149; CAAS 13; CANR 3, 18, 63, 121; DLB 212; DLBY 1986; RGAL 4; TCWW 2

Waters, Mary C. .... **CLC 70**

Waters, Roger 1944- .... **CLC 35**

Watkins, Frances Ellen
See Harper, Frances Ellen Watkins

Watkins, Gerrold
See Malzberg, Barry N(athaniel)

Watkins, Gloria Jean 1952(?)- .... **CLC 94**
See also BW 2; CA 143; CANR 87; DLB 246; MTCW 2; SATA 115

Watkins, Paul 1964- .... **CLC 55**
See also CA 132; CANR 62, 98

Watkins, Vernon Phillips
1906-1967 .... **CLC 43**
See also CA 9-10; 25-28R; CAP 1; DLB 20; EWL 3; RGEL 2

Watson, Irving S.
See Mencken, H(enry) L(ouis)

Watson, John H.
See Farmer, Philip Jose

Watson, Richard F.
See Silverberg, Robert

Watts, Ephraim
See Horne, Richard Henry Hengist

Waugh, Auberon (Alexander)
1939-2001 .... **CLC 7**
See also CA 45-48; 192; CANR 6, 22, 92; DLB 14, 194

Waugh, Evelyn (Arthur St. John)
1903-1966 .. **CLC 1, 3, 8, 13, 19, 27, 44, 107; SSC 41; WLC**
See also BPFB 3; BRW 7; CA 85-88; 25-28R; CANR 22; CDBLB 1914-1945; DA; DA3; DAB; DAC; DAM MST, NOV, POP; DLB 15, 162, 195; EWL 3; MTCW 1, 2; NFS 13, 17; RGEL 2; RGSF 2; TEA; WLIT 4

Waugh, Harriet 1944- .... **CLC 6**
See also CA 85-88; CANR 22

Ways, C. R.
See Blount, Roy (Alton), Jr.

Waystaff, Simon
See Swift, Jonathan

Webb, Beatrice (Martha Potter)
1858-1943 .... **TCLC 22**
See also CA 117; 162; DLB 190; FW

Webb, Charles (Richard) 1939- ...... **CLC 7**
See also CA 25-28R; CANR 114

Webb, James H(enry), Jr. 1946- ...... **CLC 22**
See also CA 81-84

Webb, Mary Gladys (Meredith)
1881-1927 .... **TCLC 24**
See also CA 182; 123; DLB 34; FW

Webb, Mrs. Sidney
See Webb, Beatrice (Martha Potter)

Webb, Phyllis 1927- .... **CLC 18**
See also CA 104; CANR 23; CCA 1; CP 7; CWP; DLB 53

Webb, Sidney (James) 1859-1947 .. **TCLC 22**
See also CA 117; 163; DLB 190

Webber, Andrew Lloyd .... **CLC 21**
See Lloyd Webber, Andrew
See also DFS 7

Weber, Lenora Mattingly
1895-1971 .... **CLC 12**
See also CA 19-20; 29-32R; CAP 1; SATA 2; SATA-Obit 26

Weber, Max 1864-1920 .... **TCLC 69**
See also CA 109; 189

Webster, John 1580(?)-1634(?) ...... **DC 2; LC 33, 84; WLC**
See also BRW 2; CDBLB Before 1660; DA; DAB; DAC; DAM DRAM, MST; DFS 17; DLB 58; IDTP; RGEL 2; WLIT 3

Webster, Noah 1758-1843 .... **NCLC 30**
See also DLB 1, 37, 42, 43, 73, 243

Wedekind, (Benjamin) Frank(lin)
1864-1918 .... **TCLC 7**
See also CA 104; 153; CANR 121, 122; CDWLB 2; DAM DRAM; DLB 118; EW 8; EWL 3; LMFS 2; RGWL 2, 3

Wehr, Demaris .... **CLC 65**

Weidman, Jerome 1913-1998 .... **CLC 7**
See also AITN 2; CA 1-4R; 171; CAD; CANR 1; DLB 28

Weil, Simone (Adolphine)
1909-1943 .... **TCLC 23**
See also CA 117; 159; EW 12; EWL 3; FW; GFL 1789 to the Present; MTCW 2

Weininger, Otto 1880-1903 .... **TCLC 84**

Weinstein, Nathan
See West, Nathanael

Weinstein, Nathan von Wallenstein
See West, Nathanael

Weir, Peter (Lindsay) 1944- .... **CLC 20**
See also CA 113; 123

Weiss, Peter (Ulrich) 1916-1982 .. **CLC 3, 15, 51**
See also CA 45-48; 106; CANR 3; DAM DRAM; DFS 3; DLB 69, 124; EWL 3; RGWL 2, 3

Weiss, Theodore (Russell)
1916-2003 .... **CLC 3, 8, 14**
See also CA 9-12R; 216; CAAE 189; CAAS 2; CANR 46, 94; CP 7; DLB 5

Welch, (Maurice) Denton
1915-1948 .... **TCLC 22**
See also BRWS 8, 9; CA 121; 148; RGEL 2

Welch, James 1940- ... **CLC 6, 14, 52; NNAL**
See also CA 85-88; CANR 42, 66, 107; CN 7; CP 7; CPW; DAM MULT, POP; DLB 175, 256; LATS 1; RGAL 4; TCWW 2

Weldon, Fay 1931- . **CLC 6, 9, 11, 19, 36, 59, 122**
See also BRWS 4; CA 21-24R; CANR 16, 46, 63, 97; CDBLB 1960 to Present; CN 7; CPW; DAM POP; DLB 14, 194; EWL 3; FW; HGG; INT CANR-16; MTCW 1, 2; RGEL 2; RGSF 2

Wellek, Rene 1903-1995 .... **CLC 28**
See also CA 5-8R; 150; CAAS 7; CANR 8; DLB 63; EWL 3; INT CANR-8

Weller, Michael 1942- .... **CLC 10, 53**
See also CA 85-88; CAD; CD 5

Weller, Paul 1958- .... **CLC 26**

Wellershoff, Dieter 1925- .... **CLC 46**
See also CA 89-92; CANR 16, 37

Welles, (George) Orson 1915-1985 .. **CLC 20, 80**
See also AAYA 40; CA 93-96; 117

Wellman, John McDowell 1945-
See Wellman, Mac
See also CA 166; CD 5

Wellman, Mac .... **CLC 65**
See Wellman, John McDowell; Wellman, John McDowell
See also CAD; RGAL 4

Wellman, Manly Wade 1903-1986 ... **CLC 49**
See also CA 1-4R; 118; CANR 6, 16, 44; FANT; SATA 6; SATA-Obit 47; SFW 4; SUFW

Wells, Carolyn 1869(?)-1942 .... **TCLC 35**
See also CA 113; 185; CMW 4; DLB 11

Wells, H(erbert) G(eorge)
1866-1946 .... **SSC 6; TCLC 6, 12, 19, 133; WLC**
See also AAYA 18; BPFB 3; BRW 6; CA 110; 121; CDBLB 1914-1945; CLR 64; DA; DA3; DAB; DAC; DAM MST, NOV; DLB 34, 70, 156, 178; EWL 3; EXPS; HGG; LAIT 3; LMFS 2; MTCW 1, 2; NFS 17; RGEL 2; RGSF 2; SATA 20; SCFW; SFW 4; SSFS 3; SUFW; TEA; WCH; WLIT 4; YAW

Wells, Rosemary 1943- .... **CLC 12**
See also AAYA 13; BYA 7, 8; CA 85-88; CANR 48, 120; CLR 16, 69; CWRI 5; MAICYA 1, 2; SAAS 1; SATA 18, 69, 114; YAW

Wells-Barnett, Ida B(ell)
1862-1931 .... **TCLC 125**
See also CA 182; DLB 23, 221

Welsh, Irvine 1958- .... **CLC 144**
See also CA 173; DLB 271

Welty, Eudora (Alice) 1909-2001 .. **CLC 1, 2, 5, 14, 22, 33, 105; SSC 1, 27, 51; WLC**
See also AAYA 48; AMW; AMWR 1; BPFB 3; CA 9-12R; 199; CABS 1; CANR 32, 65; CDALB 1941-1968; CN 7; CSW; DA; DA3; DAB; DAC; DAM MST, NOV; DLB 2, 102, 143; DLBD 12; DLBY 1987, 2001; EWL 3; EXPS; HGG; LAIT 3; MAWW; MTCW 1, 2; NFS 13, 15; RGAL 4; RGSF 2; RHW; SSFS 2, 10; TUS

Wen I-to 1899-1946 .... **TCLC 28**
See also EWL 3

Wentworth, Robert
See Hamilton, Edmond

Werfel, Franz (Viktor) 1890-1945 ... **TCLC 8**
See also CA 104; 161; DLB 81, 124; EWL 3; RGWL 2, 3

Wergeland, Henrik Arnold
1808-1845 .... **NCLC 5**

Wersba, Barbara 1932- .... **CLC 30**
See also AAYA 2, 30; BYA 6, 12, 13; CA 29-32R, 182; CAAE 182; CANR 16, 38; CLR 3, 78; DLB 52; JRDA; MAICYA 1, 2; SAAS 2; SATA 1, 58; SATA-Essay 103; WYA; YAW

Wertmueller, Lina 1928- .... **CLC 16**
See also CA 97-100; CANR 39, 78

Wescott, Glenway 1901-1987 .. **CLC 13; SSC 35**
See also CA 13-16R; 121; CANR 23, 70; DLB 4, 9, 102; RGAL 4

Wesker, Arnold 1932- .... **CLC 3, 5, 42**
See also CA 1-4R; CAAS 7; CANR 1, 33; CBD; CD 5; CDBLB 1960 to Present; DAB; DAM DRAM; DLB 13; EWL 3; MTCW 1; RGEL 2; TEA

Wesley, John 1703-1791 .... **LC 88**
See also DLB 104

Wesley, Richard (Errol) 1945- .... **CLC 7**
See also BW 1; CA 57-60; CAD; CANR 27; CD 5; DLB 38

Wessel, Johan Herman 1742-1785 .... **LC 7**

West, Anthony (Panther)
1914-1987 .... **CLC 50**
See also CA 45-48; 124; CANR 3, 19; DLB 15

West, C. P.
See Wodehouse, P(elham) G(renville)

West, Cornel (Ronald) 1953- .... **BLCS; CLC 134**
See also CA 144; CANR 91; DLB 246

West, Delno C(loyde), Jr. 1936- .... **CLC 70**
See also CA 57-60

West, Dorothy 1907-1998 .. **HR 3; TCLC 108**
See also BW 2; CA 143; 169; DLB 76

West, (Mary) Jessamyn 1902-1984 ... **CLC 7, 17**
See also CA 9-12R; 112; CANR 27; DLB 6; DLBY 1984; MTCW 1, 2; RGAL 4; RHW; SATA-Obit 37; TCWW 2; TUS; YAW

West, Morris
See West, Morris L(anglo)
See also DLB 289

West, Morris L(anglo) 1916-1999 ..... **CLC 6, 33**
See West, Morris
See also BPFB 3; CA 5-8R; 187; CANR 24, 49, 64; CN 7; CPW; MTCW 1, 2

West, Nathanael 1903-1940 .. **SSC 16; TCLC 1, 14, 44**
See also AMW; AMWR 2; BPFB 3; CA 104; 125; CDALB 1929-1941; DA3; DLB 4, 9, 28; EWL 3; MTCW 1, 2; NFS 16; RGAL 4; TUS

West, Owen
See Koontz, Dean R(ay)

Literary Criticism Series
Cumulative Topic Index

This index lists all topic entries in Gale's *Classical and Medieval Literature Criticism* (CMLC), *Contemporary Literary Criticism* (CLC), *Drama Criticism* (DC), *Literature Criticism from 1400 to 1800* (LC), *Nineteenth-Century Literature Criticism* (NCLC), *Short Story Criticism* (SSC), and *Twentieth-Century Literary Criticism* (TCLC). The index also lists topic entries in the Gale Critical Companion Collection, which includes the following publications: *The Beat Generation* (BG), and *Harlem Renaissance* (HR).

Topic Index

NCLC Cumulative Nationality Index

Nationality Index

NCLC-131 Title Index

ISBN 0-7876-6919-9

9 780787 669195